Disclaimer: The systems, processes, and views described in this book reflect the judgments and interpretations of authors and editors, and do not necessarily represent the official policies or positions of the Department of the Army (DA), the Department of Defense (DOD), or the U.S. Government. The text is a synthesis and interpretation of existing and developing Army and Joint systems, processes, and procedures currently practiced, and is intended only for instructional purposes with the U.S. Army War College (USAWC) and Army Force Management School (AFMS), and as an informal desk reference for their graduates and other interested organizations and project officers.

DEPARTMENT OF THE ARMY
UNITED STATES ARMY WAR COLLEGE AND CARLISLE BARRACKS
CARLISLE, PENNSYLVANIA 17013-5210

REPLY TO
ATTENTION OF

July 15, 2013

Office of the Commandant

You need this handbook. If there was ever a time when leaders and staffs – military and civilian – needed a guide to understand our systems and process it is *right now*. Having been in a continuous state of conflict for the past 12 years and entering a history-impacting era of scarcity, you must use this reference to be an effective steward of our profession. This updated volume, the 29th Edition of *How the Army Runs; A Senior Leader Reference Handbook, 2013-2014*, is exceptionally relevant. Leaders who understand and can use the systems and processes documented and explained in this work will be able to keep the United States Army the best fighting force in the world, even in the face of uncertainty and declining resources.

Most of us were "raised" in this profession to find the best terrain – the key terrain – and then seize it or control it. Teammates and fellow leaders, this document, the intellectual understanding of how the Army runs, is key terrain for service at the senior leadership level. The worst thing you could do is put this on a shelf, bury the CD in a drawer, or ignore the vibrant and updated web site. Open up this handbook – see what is here – look for those areas that impact your current duties. Then, highlight and dog-ear and bookmark as you must: this should be a well-worn, frequently-consulted source of information close by your work station. Consider this your "how to fight" manual as you seek to manage momentous change and the impact of that change on our organizations, units and institution.

I am proud to tell you this text was prepared under the direction of the faculty of the Department of Command, Leadership, and Management, School of Strategic Landpower, United States Army War College. This edition is being released electronically on both fixed media (CD) and on the U.S. Army War College Internet site at: http://www.carlisle.army.mil/usawc/dclm/htar.cfm. It will also be published in hard copy. The CD includes the ability to link to our Internet site where changes will be posted between complete updates.

Every effort has been made to ensure that the text accurately describes the systems and processes as they are. Though originally intended for use in an academic environment and now also used as a reference for those who actually "run" the organizations, it is a reference for those who might desire to reform existing systems as well. In that context, for you practitioners, we look forward to your comments regarding the value of the text to you and to your organization.

Sincerely,

Anthony A. Cucolo III
Major General, U.S. Army
49th Commandant

Enclosure

PREFACE

This text is designed to explain and synthesize the functioning and relationships of numerous Defense, Joint, and Army organizations, systems, and processes involved in the development and sustainment of trained and ready forces for the Combatant Commanders.

It is designed to be used by the faculty and students at the U.S. Army War College (as well as other training and educational institutions) as they improve their knowledge and understanding of "How the Army Runs." We are proud of the value that senior commanders and staffs have placed in this text over the years and are pleased to continue to provide this reference.

The text is revised every two years as we strive to capture the most up-to-date information available. This involves the synthesis of a wide array of published and unpublished references from a variety of sources. Necessarily, there is a point in time at which updates must stop.

This volume contains our best description of the systems, processes, and organizations as of March 2013; however, we caution the reader that there may be some inaccuracies as the system or process may have evolved from the description in the text. We encourage all readers to contribute to its continued development and improvement. Please send your recommendations for changes, improvements, and additions to the Department of Command, Leadership, and Management, U.S. Army War College, Carlisle, Pennsylvania 17013-5240, ATTN: Editor, "How the Army Runs." To the maximum extent possible these changes will be posted to our Internet site pending the next complete update. The text can also be accessed over the Internet at http://www.carlisle.army.mil/usawc/dclm/htar.cfm.

Request the text contained on this web site not be quoted, extracted for publication, or otherwise copied or distributed without prior coordination with the Department of Command, Leadership, and Management of the U.S. Army War College. (You may contact us at commercial telephone number 717-245-4794.)

The U.S. Army War College also extends its appreciation to the staff and faculty of the Army Force Management School and other contributing organizations for their efforts in the publication of this text.

Harold W. Lord
Colonel, U.S. Army Retired
Editor, "How the Army Runs"

U.S. Army War College Faculty Editors

Chap #	Chap Title	Editor	Phone # 717-245- DSN 242-	EMail @mail.mil
1	Introduction	Dr. Richard Meinhart	4797	richard.m.meinhart.civ
2	Army Organizational Life Cycle	Prof. Ed Filiberti	3715	edward.j.filiberti.civ
3	Army Organizational Structure	Prof. Ed Filiberti	3715	edward.j.filiberti.civ
4	The Relationship of Joint and Army Planning	Dr. Richard Meinhart	4797	richard.m.meinhart.civ
5	Army Force Development	COL Fred Gellert	4785	frederick.j.gellert.mil
6	Planning for Mobilization and Deployment	Prof. Doug Waters	3821	douglas.e.waters.civ
7	Reserve Components	COL North Charles	4145	north.k.charles.mil
8	Force Readiness	COL Fred Gellert	4785	frederick.j.gellert.mil
9	Army Planning, Programming, Budgeting, and Execution Process	Prof. Harold Lord **(Volume Editor)**	4802	harold.w.lord.civ
10	Resource Management	Prof. Harold Lord	4802	harold.w.lord.civ
11	Material System Research, Development, and Acquisition Management	Prof. Lou Yuengert	4790	louis.g.yuengert.civ
12	Logistics	COL Dave Dworak	3561	david.d.dworak.mil
13	Military Human Resource Management	COL Patty O'Keefe	4793	patricia.l.okeefe.mil
14	Civilian Human Resource Management	Ms. Julie Manta	4872	julie.t.manta.civ
15	Army Training and Leader Development	Dr. George Woods	4741	george.g.woods6.civ
16	Army Knowledge Management	Dr. Jeff Groh	3587	jeffrey.l.groh.civ
17	Installation Management Community	Prof. Charles Allen	3460	charles.d.allen20.civ
18	Army Health System	COL Judy Robinson	4791	judith.d.robinson2
19	Civil Functions of the Department of the Army	COL Mike Chesney	4815	michael.s.chesney2.mil
20	Public Affairs	COL Thomas Galvin	3922	thomas.p.galvin.mil
21	Defense Support of Civil Authorities	COL Mike Chesney	4815	michael.s.chesney2.mil

Note: If you cannot contact a Chapter Editor, please contact the Volume Editor.

Army Force Management School, HQDA, and Army Agency Authors

Chap #	Chap Title	Author	Phone #	EMail @mail.mil
1	Introduction	LTC (Ret) Martha Granger, AFMS **(Volume Author)**	(703)805-5926	martha.g.granger.ctr
2	Army Organizational Life Cycle	LTC (Ret) Dave Retherford, AFMS		
3	Army Organizational Structure	LTC (Ret) Martha Granger, AFMS	(703)805-5926	martha.g.granger.ctr
4	The Relationship of Joint and Army Planning	COL (Ret) Doug DeLancey, AFMS		
5	Army Force Development	LTC (Ret) Dave Retherford, AFMS		
6	Planning for Mobilization and Deployment	COL (Ret) John Walsh, AFMS		
7	Reserve Components	COL (Ret) John Walsh, AFMS		
8	Force Readiness	COL Matthew Ferguson, DAMO-ODR	(703)697-5998	matthew.j.ferguson12.mil
9	Army Planning, Programming, Budgeting, and Execution Process	LTC (Ret) Colin Halvorson, AFMS	(703)805-4486	colin.o.halvorson.ctr
10	Resource Management	COL (Ret) John Walsh, AFMS		
11	Material System Research, Development, and Acquisition Management	LTC (Ret) Bob Keenan, AFMS		
12	Logistics	COL (Ret) Jerry Chastain, AFMS	(703)805-2122	jerry.s.chastain.ctr
13	Military Human Resource Management	LTC Robert Cavagna, G1	(703)693-3726	robert.r.cavagna.mil
14	Civilian Human Resource Management	Mrs. Doriot Mascarich, G1	(703)693-1468	doriot.a.mascarich.civ
15	Army Training and Leader Development	Mr. Douglas Mow, DAMO-TR	(703)614-9816	douglas.f.mow.ctr
16	Army Knowledge Management	MAJ (Ret) Joe Albert, AFMS		
17	Installation Management Community	LTC(Ret) Larissa Ginty, AFMS w/ ACSIM	(703)805-3507	larissa.a.ginty.ctr
18	Army Health System	Mr. Craig Dyer, OTSG	(210)295-8938	craig.d.dyer.civ
19	Civil Functions of the Department of the Army	Mr. Brian Sullivan, USACE	(202)761-1878	brian.j.sullivan @usace.army.mil
20	Public Affairs	Mr. Ed Spells, OCPA	(301)677-7374	edward.l.spells.civ
21	Defense Support of Civil Authorities	COL (Ret) Terry Melton, AFMS		

Note: If you cannot contact a Chapter Author, please contact the Volume Author.

TABLE OF CONTENTS

Table of Contents

Chapter 1—Introduction
Section I—Fulfilling the Intent of the Congress 1-1
Section II—Army Focus 1-3
Section III—Purpose, Scope, and Objectives of the Text 1-5
Section IV—Text Organization 1-6
Section V—Summary and References 1-7

Chapter 2—Army Organizational Life Cycle
Section I--Introduction 2-1
Section II—Force Management 2-4
Section III—Coordination of Force Integration Actions 2-7
Section IV--Changing How We Manage Change 2-9
Section V—Summary and References 2-11
Figures
Figure 2-1. The Army Organizational Life Cycle Model 2-2
Figure 2-2. Army Force Management Model .... (back of book fold-out)

Chapter 3—Army Organizational Structure
Section I—Introduction 3-1
Section II—The Production Subsystem 3-3
Section III—The Combat Subsystem 3-8
Section IV—The Integrating Subsystem 3-8
Section V—Strategy to Army Organizational Structure 3-12
Section VI—Summary and References 3-12
Figure
Figure 3-1. Headquarters, Department of the Army (HQDA) Organization 3-10

Chapter 4—The Relationship of Joint and Army Planning
Section I—Introduction 4-1
Section II—Joint Strategic Planning System 4-5
Section III—Planning and Resourcing 4-11
Section IV—Joint Operations Planning 4-12
Section V—Summary and References 4-14
Figures
Figure 4-1. Joint Strategic Planning System (JSPS) 4-3
Figure 4-2. Joint Requirements Oversight Council (JROC) 4-8
Figure 4-3. Joint Capabilities Board (JCB) 4-9
Figure 4-4. Functional Capabilities Board (FCB) 4-10
Figure 4-5. Unified Combatant Commands 4-13

Chapter 5—Army Force Development
Section I—Introduction 5-1
Section II—Phase I—Develop Capability Requirements 5-3
Section III—Phase II—Design Organizations 5-12
Section IV—Phase III—Develop Organizational Models 5-13
Section V—Phase IV—Determine Organizational Authorizations 5-16
Section VI—Phase V—Document Organizational Authorizations 5-23
Section VII—References 5-29
Figures
Figure 5-1. Force Development Process 5-2
Figure 5-2. Army Concept Framework (ACF) 5-5
Figure 5-3. Capabilities-Based Assessment (C-BA) Process 5-8
Figure 5-4. Solutions Documents 5-11
Figure 5-5. Force Design Update (FDU) 5-13
Figure 5-6. Modernization Over Time (Resource Driven) 5-15
Figure 5-7. Total Army Analysis "End-to-End" Process 5-18
Figure 5-8. Force Structure Components (COMPO) 5-23
Figure 5-9. Structure and Composition System (SACS) / Force Builder Process 5-27

i

HOW THE ARMY RUNS

Chapter 6—Planning for Mobilization and Deployment
Section I—Introduction 6-1
Section II—National Strategic Direction and Guidance, Joint Operations Planning, Joint Operations Planning Process . 6-2
Section III—Army Mobilization..6-15
Section IV—Industrial Preparedness...6-26
Section V—Summary and References..6-28
Figures
Figure 6-1. National Strategic Direction and Guidance 6-3
Figure 6-2. Joint Planning and Execution Community..6-4
Figure 6-3. Joint Operations Planning 6-6
Figure 6-4. Joint Operations Planning Process (JOPP) 6-8
Figure 6-5. Global Force Management (GFM) Bins 6-13
Figure 6-6. Army Mobilization Planning 6-15
Figure 6-7. Army Mobilization, Operations Planning and Execution System (AMOPES) Subsystems 6-18
Figure 6-8. Reserve Categories and Mobilization 6-22
Figure 6-9. Mobilization and Execution Process 6-25

Chapter 7—Reserve Components
Section I—Introduction 7-1
Section II—The Army National Guard 7-1
Section III—The Army Reserve 7-3
Section IV—Title 10, United States Code..7-4
Section V—Reserve Service 7-4
Section VI—Reserve Component Management...7-7
Section VII—Training...7-14
Section VIII—Equipment 7-15
Section IX—Readiness / Mobilization Assistance 7-16
Section X--Reserve Component Pay, Benefits, and Entitlements 7-19
Section XI—Reserve Component Transformation Campaign Plan 7-22
Section XII—Summary and References..7-21
Figures
Figure 7-1. Reserve Service Categories 7-5
Figure 7-2. National Guard Bureau (NGB) Management Structure..7-10
Figure 7-3. Army National Guard (ARNG) Directorate 7-11
Figure 7-4. Office of the Chief, Army Reserve (OCAR)..7-12

Chapter 8—Force Readiness
Section I—Introduction 8-1
Section II—Managing Army Readiness 8-1
Section III—Department of Defense Readiness Reporting System 8-3
Section IV—Department of Defense Readiness Reporting System Army...8-8
Section V—Summary and References..8-17
Figures & Tables
Figure 8-1. Chairman's Readiness System (CRS) 8-4
Figure 8-2. Joint Combat Capability Assessment (JCCA)..8-5
Figure 8-3. Chairman's Readiness System (CRS) Output 8-7
Figure 8-4. Strategic Readiness Concept Model..8-8
Figure 8-5. Department of Defense Readiness Reporting System Army (DRRS-A) Suite of Applications 8-10
Figure 8-6. Authoritative Data Inputs to Department of Defense Readiness Reporting System Army (DRRS-A)...........8-11
Figure 8-7. Commander's Unit Status Report (CUSR) Measured Areas 8-13
Figure 8-8. Readiness Reporting Channels 8-14
Figure 8-9. C-Levels..8-16
Figure 8-10. A-Levels..8-16
Table 8-1. Three-Tiered Readiness Metric 8-6
Table 8-2. Readiness Assessment Levels Definitions..8-6

Chapter 9—Army Planning, Programming, Budgeting, and Execution Process
Section I—Introduction 9-1
Section II—Department of Defense Planning, Programming, Budgeting, and Execution Process Description 9-3

TABLE OF CONTENTS

Section III—Army Planning, Programming, Budgeting, and Execution System Responsibilities 9-11
Section IV—Responsibilities for Planning, Programming, Budgeting, and Execution-Related Operational Tasks 9-15
Section V—Army Planning, Programming, Budgeting, and Execution 9-20
Section VI—Allocation of Resources... 9-22
Section VII—Army Planning, Programming, Budgeting, and Execution Deliberative Forums 9-26
Section VIII—Army Planning, Programming, Budgeting, and Execution Planning 9-30
Section IX—Operational Planning Link to the Department of Defense Planning, Programming, Budgeting, and Execution 9-33
Section X—Integrated Programming-Budgeting Phase 9-33
Section XI—Army Budget Execution Phase.. 9-40
Section XII—Program Performance and Review 9-44
Section XIII—Summary and References... 9-45

Figures & Tables
Figure 9-1. Department of Defense (DOD) Planning, Programming, Budgeting, and Execution (PPBE) Phases 9-4
Figure 9-2. Summary of Planning, Programming, Budgeting, and Execution (PPBE) Phases 9-4
Figure 9-3. Major Force Programs (MFP) 9-7
Figure 9-4. Future Year Defense Program (FYDP) 9-7
Figure 9-5. Department of Defense (DOD) Review / Decision-Making Bodies 9-10
Figure 9-6. Management Decision Package (MDEP)... 9-22
Figure 9-7. Management Decision Package (MDEP) Functions 9-23
Figure 9-8. Fiscal Year (FY) 14-18 Program Objective Memorandum (POM) Management Decision Package (MDEP)...... 9-24
Figure 9-9. Program Evaluation Groups (PEG)... 9-28
Figure 9-10. Program Evaluation Groups (PEG).. 9-29
Figure 9-11. Army Review / Decision-Making Bodies... 9-30
Figure 9-12. Fiscal Year (FY) 14-18 Army Resource Framework (ARF) 9-35
Figure 9-13. Program Objective Memorandum (POM) / Budget Estimate Submission (BES) 15-19 Timeline 9-36
Figure 9-14. Management Decision Packages (MDEP) 9-38
Figure 9-15. Planning, Programming, Budgeting, and Execution (PPBE) Timeline 9-39
Figure 9-16. Planning, Programming, Budgeting, and Execution (PPBE) Timeline 9-46
Table 9-1. Future Years Defense Program (FYDP) Programs and Subprograms with Army Proponents 9-6
Table 9-2. Program Evaluation Groups (PEG) 9-11
Table 9-3. Managers for Manpower and Force Structure Issues.. 9-12
Table 9-4. Program Indicators 9-18
Table 9-5. Composition of Army Planning, Programming, Budgeting, and Execution (PPBE) Deliberative Forums....... 9-26
Table 9-6. Topics Covered in Program Objective Memorandum / Budget Estimate Submission (POM / BES) 14-18 9-37
Table 9-7. Budget Activity (BA) Management Structure for Operation and Maintenance Appropriations................ 9-46
Table 9-8. Budget Activity (BA) Management Structure for Operation and Maintenance Appropriations- Army Manpower Only Activity Structure 9-49
Table 9-9. Budget Activity (BA) Management Structure for Operation and Maintenance Appropriation- Base Operations Support (BOS) 9-49
Table 9-10. Budget Activity (BA) Management Structure for Operation and Maintenance Appropriations- Sustainment, Restoration, and Modernization (SRM) 9-51
Table 9-11. Budget Activity (BA) Management Structure for Operation and Maintenance Appropriations- Army National Guard 9-52
Table 9-12. Budget Activity (BA) Management Structure for Operations and Maintenance Appropriations-U.S. Army Reserve... 9-53
Table 9-13. Army Appropriations-Managers for Functional Requirements and Program and Performance 9-53

Chapter 10—Resource Management
Section I—Introduction 10-1
Section II—Acquire Resources.. 10-6
Section III—Allocate Resources to the Field 10-7
Section IV—Account for the Use of Resources... 10-9
Section V—Analyze the Use of Resources 10-13
Section VI—Improving Management and Business Practices in the Army 10-14
Section VII—Non-Appropriated Funds 10-23
Section VIII—Summary and References... 10-25

HOW THE ARMY RUNS

Figures & Tables
Figure 10-1. Office of the Assistant Secretary of the Army (Financial Management and Comptroller) (ASA(FM&C)) **10-5**
Figure 10-2. Resource Management's "4-A's" **10-6**
Figure 10-3. Fund Distribution Process **10-7**
Figure 10-4. Cycle of Commitment and Review **10-21**
Figure 10-5. Cost Benefit Analysis (CBA) **10-23**
Table 10-1. Translating an Accounting Code **10-12**

Chapter 11—Material System Research, Development, and Acquisition Management
Section I—Introduction **11-1**
Section II—Capabilities Integration and Development **11-1**
Section III—Materiel Capabilities Documents **11-6**
Section IV—Traditional Materiel Requirements Validation **11-10**
Section V—Urgent Operational Need Validation **11-16**
Section VI—Traditional Materiel Systems Acquisition **11-21**
Section VII—Department of Defense Acquisition Organization and Management **11-24**
Section VIII—Army Acquisition Organization and Management **11-25**
Section IX—Traditional Acquisition Phases and Milestones **11-38**
Section X—Traditional Acquisition Oversight and Review **11-45**
Section XI—Traditional Acquisition Documentation **11-49**
Section XII—Testing and Evaluation **11-53**
Section XIII—Integrated Logistics Support **11-54**
Section XIV—Manpower and Personnel Integration Program **11-58**
Section XV—Training Development **11-60**
Section XVI—Agile Acquisition **11-62**
Section XVII—Acquisition Resource Management **11-65**
Section XVIII—Summary and References **11-70**

Figures & Tables
Figure 11-1. Technology Readiness Levels (TRL) **11-5**
Figure 11-2. Acquisition Categories (ACAT) **11-14**
Figure 11-3. Joint Urgent Operational Need (JUON) / Joint Emergent Operational Need (JEON) Validation Process **11-17**
Figure 11-4. Army Requirements and Resourcing Board (AR2B) Organization **11-20**
Figure 11-5. Defense Acquisition Management System (DAS) **11-22**
Figure 11-6. Army Acquisition Executive (AAE) **11-26**
Figure 11-7. Department of Defense (DOD) Acquisition Authority Chain **11-28**
Figure 11-8. Acquisition Strategy (AS) **11-50**
Figure 11-9. Total Package Fielding (TFP) Concept **11-57**
Figure 11-10. Army Agile Process **11-63**
Table 11-1. Prior Approval Threshold Reprogramming Levels* **11-67**

Chapter 12—Logistics
Section I—Introduction **12-1**
Section II—National Logistics Organization—Assistant Secretary of the Army (Acquisition, Logistics, and Technology), Army G-4, Army G-8, and Army Materiel Command **12-7**
Section III—National Logistics Organizations—Other **12-18**
Section IV—Summary and References **12-23**

Figures
Figure 12-1. Assistant Secretary of the Army (Acquisition, Logistics, and Technology) (ASA(ALT)) Organization **12-9**
Figure 12-2. Army G-4 Organization **12-10**
Figure 12-3. Army G-8 Organization **12-11**
Figure 12-4. Army Materiel Command (AMC) Organization **12-12**
Figure 12-5. Foreign Military Sales (FMS) Process **12-14**
Figure 12-6. Defense Logistics Agency (DLA) Organization **12-20**

Chapter 13—Military Human Resource Management
Section I—Introduction **13-1**
Section II—The Structure Function **13-4**
Section III—The Acquisition Function **13-7**
Section IV—The Compensation Function **13-10**

TABLE OF CONTENTS

Section V—The Distribution Function 13-12
Section VI—The Development Function 13-19
Section VII—The Sustainment Function 13-32
Section VIII—The Transition Function 13-33
Section IX—Summary and References 13-35

Figures & Tables
Figure 13-1. Manpower Strength Relationships 13-6
Figure 13-2. Enlisted Procurement 13-7
Figure 13-3. Manning Programs 13-11
Figure 13-4. Headquarters, Department of the Army (HQDA) Fiscal Year (FY) 13-15 Active Component (AC) Manning Guidance 13-13
Figure 13-5. Enlisted Automation Management System 13-14
Figure 13-6. Officer Distribution 13-18
Figure 13-7. Warrant Officer Training and Education 13-23
Figure 13-8. Warrant Officer Promotion Timeline 13-23
Figure 13-9. Functionally Aligned Officer Personnel Management System (OPMS) Design 13-26
Figure 13-10. Centralized Selection List (CSL) Categories 13-28
Table 13-1. Warrant Officer Promotion Goals 13-24
Table 13-2. Career Progression Pattern 13-30

Chapter 14—Civilian Human Resource Management
Section I—Introduction 14-1
Section II—Organization of Civilian Personnel Management 14-4
Section III—Civilian Human Resource Service Delivery 14-7
Section IV—Personnel Management at Installation / Activity Level 14-9
Section V—Equal Employment Opportunity in the Army 14-16
Section VI—Executive and Senior Professional Personnel 14-19
Section VII—Defense Civilian Intelligence Personnel System 14-21
Section VIII—Army Personnel Transformation 14-23
Section IX—Summary and References 14-23

Figures & Tables
Figure 14-1. Civilians Supporting the Army 14-2
Figure 14-2. Differences Between the Military and Civilian Systems 14-3
Figure 14-3. Annual Civilian Personnel Strength Review 14-13
Figure 14-4. Civilian Expeditionary Workforce (CEW) Model 14-22
Table 14-1. Executive Service Personnel 14-19
Table 14-2. Executives by Organization 14-20

Chapter 15—Army Training and Leader Development
Section I—Introduction 15-1
Section II—Army Training Overview 15-1
Section III—The Policy, Requirements, and Resourcing Process 15-7
Section IV—Training and Doctrine Command Organization and Training Development Systems 15-11
Section V—The Army School System 15-15
Section VI—Training in Units 15-23
Section VII—The Training Support System 15-31
Section VIII—Summary and References 15-33

Figures
Figure 15-1. Army Leader Development Model 15-3
Figure 15-2. Structure Manning Decision Review (SMDR) Overview 15-10
Figure 15-3. Basic Noncommissioned Officer (NCO) Leader Development Timeline 15-17
Figure 15-4. Officer Learning Continuum 15-18
Figure 15-5. Warrant Officer Learning Continuum 15-19
Figure 15-6. Civilian Education System (CES) 15-20

Chapter 16—Army Knowledge Management
Section I—Introduction 16-1
Section II—Chief Information Officer / G-6 Roles and Responsibilities 16-2
Section III—Army Enterprise Management 16-5

v

HOW THE ARMY RUNS

Section IV—Chief Information Officer / G-6 Organization 16-9
Section V—Other Strategic Partnerships with the Army Chief Information Officer / G-6.................16-12
Section VI—Summary and References..16-14

Chapter 17—Installation Management Community
Section I—Introduction 17-1
Section II—Roles and Missions..17-2
Section III—Initiatives and Programs 17-11
Section IV—Summary and References...17-14
Figures
Figure 7-1. Installation Management Hierarchy...17-2
Figure 17-2. Army Facility Strategy 2020 17-3

Chapter 18—Army Health System
Section I—Introduction 18-1
Section II—Army Medical Department Mission and Support to Commanders 18-3
Section III—The Army Health System 18-5
Section IV—Command and Management..18-7
Section V—Summary and References...18-13
Figure
Figure 18-1. Army Medical Command 18-7

Chapter 19—Civil Functions of the Department of the Army
Section I—Introduction 19-1
Section II—Civil Works Program 19-3
Section III—Support to Other Government Agencies 19-9
Section IV—Engineer Overseas Activities..19-11
Section V—Support to Unified Combatant Commanders...19-12
Section VI—Summary and References..19-13
Figures & Tables
Figure 19-1. U.S. Army Corps of Engineers (USACE) Organization..19-11
Table 19-1. Construction Support for Non-Department of Defense (DOD) Agencies..................19-10

Chapter 20—Public Affairs
Section I—Introduction 20-1
Section II—Army Public Affairs Organizations..20-5
Section III—Joint and Combined Public Affairs Organizations 20-7
Section IV—Information Mediums 20-8
Section V—Summary, Terms and References 20-10

Chapter 21—Defense Support of Civil Authorities
Section I—Introduction 21-1
Section II—Domestic Emergency Management Environment..21-4
Section III—Federal Role in the National Response Process 21-9
Section IV—Defense Support Process...21-14
Section V—Defense Support of Civil Authorities Mission Category—Disasters and Declared Emergencies 21-16
Section VI—Defense Support of Civil Authorities Mission Category—Restore Public Health and Services and Civil Order....................21-19
Section VII—Defense Support of Civil Authorities Mission Category—Special Events and Planned Periodic Support.......................21-22
Section VIII—Summary and References..21-23
Figures & Tables
Figure 21-1. Tiered Disaster / Emergency Response..21-5
Figure 21-2. National Response Plan (Stafford Act)..21-6
Figure 21-3. National Response Plan (Non-Stafford Act)...21-7
Figure 21-4. Initial Request for Department of Defense (DOD) Assistance 21-15
Figure 21-5. Civil Disturbance Support Mission Command..21-20
Table 21-1. Federal Response Plan Emergency Support Functions..21-11

Glossary G-1

INTRODUCTION

Chapter 1

Introduction

My intent is to sustain a high-quality All-Volunteer Army that remains the most decisive land force in the world; provides depth and versatility to the Joint Force; is agile, responsive, and effective for Combatant Commanders; and ensures flexibility for national security decision-makers in defense of the Nation at home and abroad.

General Raymond T. Odierno, Chief of Staff, U.S. Army (CSA)
"38th CSA Marching Orders: Waypoint #1," January 2013

In the spring of 1775, a group of militiamen cobbled together from various New England colonies to confront British troops near Boston, Massachusetts. Recognizing the need for a professional American force, our nation's leaders established the Continental Army on June 14, 1775, beginning our Army's rich heritage of successfully defending this great country and her citizens. George Washington received his appointment as commander-in-chief of the Continental Army the next day and formally took command at Boston on July 3, 1775. Throughout the last 237 years, the U.S. Army has remained the strength of our nation, ensuring her citizens and our national interests are protected. From the Civil War, to World War I and II, to Korea, Vietnam, and the Persian Gulf, our Army has defeated tyranny and advanced the cause of freedom. And following the attacks of September 11, 2001, the Army was decisively engaged in Iraq and continues to serve in Afghanistan to combat violent extremism and keep terrorism from our shores. The Army will always remain true to its enduring professional values, honoring the sacred trust bestowed by the Nation. As we look towards the next 10 years and beyond, the Army will remain vigilant, preparing for the challenges of an uncertain future, while always remembering to value the strength of our Soldiers and the support for their Family members, as it is the people who make our Army Strong.

It is the intent of Congress to provide an Army that is capable, in conjunction with the other Armed Forces, of preserving the peace and security, and providing for the defense of the United States; supporting the national policies; implementing the national objectives; and overcoming any nations responsible for aggressive acts that imperil the peace and security of the United States. ... [The Army] shall be organized, trained, and equipped primarily for prompt and sustained combat incident to operations on land. It is responsible for the preparation of land forces necessary for the effective prosecution of war except as otherwise assigned and, in accordance with integrated joint mobilization plans, for the expansion of the peacetime components of the Army to meet the needs of war.

Title 10, United States Code (USC), Section 3062 (a) and (b)

Section I
Fulfilling the Intent of the Congress

1-1. Changing How We Manage Change

Even after a decade of war, we must remain vigilant of new threats and capabilities. War is discovery—we must continue to out-think and out-adapt our adversaries. Only by remaining alert to the weak signals of change can we preserve the initiative and provide options for our civilian leaders. The men and women we send into harm's way merit the leadership and resources to succeed. We will adapt our structures and push capabilities "to the edge," and we will continue to send our best and brightest forward and sustain them until they all come home. The last casualty in our fights is no less a sacrifice than the first. In response to these challenges and others, we will lead, and we will enable others to lead. Moreover, we will do this—always—by coordinating military power with the diplomacy and development efforts of our government and those of our allies and partners.

General Martin E. Dempsey, Chairman of the Joint Chiefs of Staff (CJCS)

HOW THE ARMY RUNS

Chairman's Strategic Direction to the Joint Force (CSDJF), February 6, 2012

a. Fulfilling the intent of Congress, as well as National, Joint, and Army leadership, are formidable tasks. The Army is a dynamic organization that must constantly change to adapt to emerging threats and challenges to the Nation's security and the assignment of new missions. The Army must be capable of accomplishing a wide range of operations, including counterinsurgency, stability operations, regular and irregular warfare, counterterrorism, building partner capacity, and providing humanitarian assistance at home and abroad. This requires the continual adaptation and development across the Army's Doctrine, Organization, Training, Materiel, Leadership and Training, Personnel, Facilities, and Policy (DOTMLPF-P) domains.

b. Today, we find ourselves in an increasingly uncertain world, with threats ranging from terrorist and cyber attacks, to regional instability, to the proliferation of weapons of mass destruction. For our Army that means we will likely have to deal with near peer competitors in niche areas, and hybrid threats that mix regular, irregular and criminal activity—all while still facing the possibility of a conventional force-on-force conflict. The danger extends from the homeland to the theater where combat operations might occur. While conflict continues to occur across many domains, the Army will continue to be a critical part of the Joint Force because land power remains the politically decisive form of warfare and is essential to America's national security, defense, and military strategies. No major conflict has ever been won without "boots on the ground." By being tasked to seize, occupy and defend land areas, as well as to defeat enemy land forces, the Army is unique. The Army must not only deploy and defeat an adversary, but must also be prepared to remain in the region until the Nation's long-term strategic objectives are secured. Indeed, the insertion of ground troops is the most tangible and durable measure of America's commitment to defend our interests, protect our friends, and defeat our enemies.

c. Changing large organizations with well-developed cultures embedded in established bureaucracies can be incredibly difficult. Functioning complex organizational systems and embedded processes can tend to resist change or cause change to become more evolutionary in nature. The Army's systems and processes outlined in this text are no exception. The Army has the internal challenge to ensure these processes are both flexible and adaptable to facilitate and not impede change, while also inspiring creativity and rapidly incorporating technological, cognitive, and organizational innovations. By describing these systems within this text, the authors do not intend to advocate their continued use nor indirectly resist their modification or wholesale reform. Instead, this text is intended to be a reference for educating our leaders so that they may make informed decisions on how these organizations, systems, and processes work, and how they can be used or changed to better serve our Soldiers and our Nation. This text should provide a basis of understanding that empowers continued change in How the Army Runs (HTAR).

1-2. Managing The Army

The Army is globally responsive and regionally engaged; it is an indispensible partner and provider of a full range of capabilities to combatant commanders in a Joint, interagency, intergovernmental, and multinational environment. As part of the Joint Force and as America's Army, in all that we offer, we guarantee the agility, versatility and depth to Prevent, Shape, and Win.

Army Vision, 2013 Army Strategic Planning Guidance (ASPG)

a. The Army performs myriad functions within the framework of well-defined systems and processes to effect the changes that enable it to fulfill the vision of the Secretary of the Army (SECARMY) and CSA. Some of the many complex functions that the Army must address when managing change include the following: recruiting and accessing military and civilian manpower; providing individual and unit training and education; developing warfighting doctrine and requirements; designing and organizing units and activities; equipping and sustaining fielded units; mobilizing and demobilizing Reserve Component (RC) units; stationing and supporting units; and deploying and redeploying forces.

b. The Army's institutionalized systems and processes address those just described and many other functions. Systems such as the civilian and military personnel management systems, strategic planning, and the Army Health Services System, and processes such as Planning, Programming, Budgeting, and Execution (PPBE), combat development, force development, force integration, and materiel acquisition,

INTRODUCTION

are some examples of the systems and processes covered in the following chapters. The Army's capability to transform, fully execute its statutory obligations, and effectively accomplish the complex missions assigned to its activities and organizations depends upon how well the functions that are performed by any one of these systems or processes are integrated with the functions performed by each of the other systems and processes.

    c. Stated another way, the successful integration of new doctrine, organizations, and equipment into the Army and the subsequent sustainment of the force in a trained and ready posture requires the synchronization of many Army systems and processes. This needs to occur at many levels of leadership and management to perform the functions that are vital to enabling the Army to not only fully execute its current responsibilities, while also preparing for the future with significant challenges.

Section II
Army Focus

1-3. Background

    a. In response to the strategic environment briefly discussed above, the Army has faced tremendous challenges with continued success. The Army's focus is evident in this excerpt from the 2012 Army Posture Statement (APS) letter from the SECARMY and CSA: "We have been a Nation at war for the past 10 years, and America's Army has proven—on and off the battlefield—that we are the premier warfighting force in the world. Over the past year, we successfully concluded combat operations in Operation Iraqi Freedom/Operation New Dawn. In Afghanistan, more than 65,000 Soldiers continue to conduct combat operations and transfer security responsibilities to the Afghanistan National Security Forces. Today, over 192,000 American Soldiers remain committed to their missions while forward deployed in about 150 countries around the world. Our Army—Active, Guard, Reserve, and Civilian—has demonstrated its versatility by supporting homeland defense while conducting a wide range of operations, including counterinsurgency, stability operations, regular and irregular warfare, counterterrorism, building partner capacity, and providing humanitarian assistance at home and abroad. The 1.1 million Soldiers who deployed to combat during the past decade have demonstrated remarkable courage, mental and physical fortitude. In that time, U.S. Soldiers have earned 6 Medals of Honor, 24 Distinguished Service Crosses, more than 600 Silver Stars and nearly 14,000 other awards for valor. Our accomplishments in Iraq and Afghanistan have come with an enormous cost, as more than 4,500 Soldiers have rendered the ultimate sacrifice and almost 33,000 have returned as Wounded Warriors. Through all of this adversity, the courage and resilience of our Soldiers, Civilians, and Family members have demonstrated repeatedly that our Army remains the Strength of the Nation."

    b. The Army's challenge is in providing the right forces with the right capabilities to meet its many responsibilities. The Army recruits, organizes, trains, and equips Soldiers who operate as members of Joint, Interagency, Intergovernmental, and Multinational (JIIM) Teams in an integrated manner. The Army also provides logistics, communications, transportation, and other support to enable our Joint and Interagency partners to accomplish their missions, as well as support civil authorities in times of national emergencies. Responding to the strategic environment and the National Security, Defense, and Military Strategies that flow from these strategic documents, the Army continues to build and sustain an expeditionary and campaign quality force that is capable of deploying rapidly into any operational environment, conducting operations with modular forces anywhere in the world, and sustaining operations as long as necessary to accomplish the mission.

1-4. APS

    a. The SECARMY and CSA submit an annual Posture Statement of the United States Army to the Committees and Subcommittees of the United States Senate and House of Representatives. This is done in preparation for subsequent hearings on the Army budget. The annual APS is an unclassified summary of Army roles, missions, accomplishments, plans and programs. Designed to reinforce the SECARMY and CSA's posture and budget testimonies before Congress, the APS serves a broad audience as a basic reference on the state of the Army. As such, the APS should be read by Army Soldiers and civilians to appreciate both the current challenges and future direction that the systems and processes described in this text must address.

HOW THE ARMY RUNS

b. The February 17, 2012 APS, "Army Posture: The Nation's Force of Decisive Action," concludes with the following: "America's leaders face difficult choices as they chart the way ahead for our Nation. Familiar external threats persist and complex new challenges will emerge. Concurrently, fiscal limitations create internal challenges for our leaders. America's Army is prepared to fulfill its role in keeping the Nation secure. The Army will prevent conflict by remaining a credible force with sufficient capacity to dissuade adversaries from challenging American interests. The Army will shape the environment, building positive relationships and capabilities that enable nations to effectively protect and govern their citizenry. Finally, when called, the Army will fight for the Nation and win decisively. We understand these responsibilities and resolve not to reduce the size of the Army in a manner that does not permit us to reverse the process should demand for forces increase dramatically."

c. The 2012 APS also identifies these three focus areas: first, support to operations in Afghanistan; second, responsible stewardship, including institutional Army transformation, acquisition reform, and energy security; and third, a leaner Army with readiness and capability preserved. The four major areas for equipment modernization are the Network, Ground Combat Vehicle (GCV), Joint Light Tactical Vehicle (JLTV), and Soldier Systems. Finally, there are various subjects covered in the APS Addenda, including online information papers, important websites, the FY 13 President's Budget, RC Readiness, Army Force Generation, Transforming Business Practices, Army Energy Security Enterprise, cyberspace: Army Cyber Command and Cyberspace Operations, The Army Profession, Leader Development, Health Promotion & Risk Reduction (HP&RR) Transition, Comprehensive Soldier Fitness, Army Families, Equipment Modernization, and The Network.

1-5. The Army Plan (TAP)

a. TAP aligns Army planning documents with national guidance and its four main sections are organized as follows: Section I, ASPG, articulates vision and strategy; Section II, Army Planning Priorities Guidance (APPG), sets priorities and levels of effort; Section III, Army Program Guidance Memorandum (APGM), sets resource levels; and Section IV, Army Campaign Plan (ACP), synchronizes the details.

b. Section I of TAP, the 2013 ASPG, has the following purposes: articulates the SECARMY and CSA vision, direction, objectives and institutional strategy; serves as the foundation for strategic planning, priorities, and programming guidance to ensure Army resources are appropriately linked to strategy; describes the Army's Strategic Imperatives; and outlines the Army's objectives for each Strategic Imperative categorized by Near-Term (FYs 13-15); Mid-Term (FYs 16-20); and Long-Term (FY 21 and beyond). The four Strategic Imperatives of the 2013 ASPG are as follows: provide modernized and ready, tailored land force capabilities to meet Combatant Commanders' (CCDR) requirements across the range of military operations; develop leaders to meet the challenges of the 21st Century; adapt the Army to more effectively provide land power; and enhance the All-Volunteer Army. The Staff Lead for the ASPG is G-3/5/7, DAMO-SS.

c. Section II of TAP, the FY 11 APPG, translates the ASPG into operational guidance and priorities for programmers. The APPG focuses on FY 13-17 to establish the risk and risk framework, articulate Army requirements and the Quadrennial Defense Review (QDR) risk framework; and articulate risk guidance for operational (current operations); force management (properly structuring the Army for the future); future challenges (research/capabilities/system Support); institutional (transforming the generating force); and equipping (quantitative, qualitative, and industrial capacity). The Staff Lead for the ASPG is G-3/5/7, DAMO-CIR.

d. Section III of TAP, the APGM, provides general resourcing guidance as a start point for building the Army Program Objective Memorandum (POM). The APGM articulates the Army Resource Framework by organizing resourcing tasks based on people, readiness, materiel and services, and infrastructure enterprises (core enterprises/Military Decision Packages (MDEP)). Finally, the APGM provides programming guidelines for the six Program Evaluation Groups (PEG), which are as follows: Manning (MM); Training (TT); Equipping (EE); Organizing (OO); Sustaining (SS); and Installations (II).

e. Section IV of TAP, the ACP, is covered in detail in the Paragraph 1-6.

1-6. ACP

a. The ACP has been published since 2004 and is presented as Section IV of TAP. The ACP structure includes a main body (using a five-paragraph Operation Order (OPORD) format) with 26 annexes (ACP 2012). SECARMY and CSA guidance direct the entire document, most prominently in Paragraph 2,

INTRODUCTION

"Mission," and Paragraph 3a, "SECARMY/CSA Intent." ACP Operational Design depicts the coordinated and concurrent Lines of Effort (LOEs) to achieve the Army vision.

b. The 2012 ACP, published May 30, 2012, supports and guides the Army's end state—a versatile and agile mix of capabilities and formations that is rapidly deployable and sustainable in order to Prevent, Shape, and Win—using four LOEs: reform and restructure the institutional Army; prepare for tomorrow; win the current fight and sustain the force; and remain Army Strong.

c. The 2012 ACP Strategy Map assigns lead responsibilities for achieving objectives that support the four LOEs. There are nine Campaign Objectives as follows: man the Army and preserve the All-Volunteer Force; provide facilities, programs, and services to support the Army and Army Families; support global operations with ready land power; train the Army for 21st Century operations; equip the Army for 21st Century operations; sustain the force for 21st Century operations; shape the Army; achieve energy security and sustainability objectives; and sustain and enhance business operations. The ACP Campaign Objectives are interwoven throughout the ACP Operational Design, depicting their focus within and across the four LOEs.

d. Finally, the 2012 ACP offers more detail in annexes that cover operations, strategic guidance, force transformation, personnel, logistics, stationing, RC Campaign Plans, emerging programs and capabilities, and administrative references.

1-7. Transformation and "The Army in Transition"

Today the U.S. Army is the best-trained, best-equipped and best-led combat-tested force in the world. Today's Soldiers have achieved a level of professionalism, combat experience and civil and military expertise that is an invaluable national asset. Our warriors have accomplished every assigned task they have been given. But all we have accomplished in building this magnificent force can be squandered if we are not careful. We are an Army in transition, and we look to Congress to assist us in the difficult work to build the Army of 2020.

2012 Army Posture Statement

a. The concepts associated with transformation and transition have both impacted and influenced Army personnel, unit structure, and joint perspectives to meet national, defense, and military strategies. The past decade has seen the Army transform and transition in many ways. SECARMY White and CSA Shinseki provided an intellectual framework for transformation. SECARMY Harvey and CSA Schoomaker led the Operating Force transformation. SECARMY Geren and CSA Casey articulated the need to adapt institutions and restore balance. Now SECARMY McHugh and CSA Odierno address the subject in the opening letter of the 2012 APS: "During this decade of conflict, we have dramatically transformed our Army, and will continue to do so. We will emerge from the forthcoming budget reductions a leaner force, but one still fully capable of and committed to meeting our obligations to the Nation, the American people, and our Soldiers, Civilians and Family members. Although our Army will become smaller in the coming months and years, we will preserve the quality of the All-Volunteer Force. We must ensure our Army—as part of Joint Force 2020—is adaptive, innovative, flexible, agile, integrated, synchronized, lethal and discriminate."

b. "The Army in Transition" can be described by looking at recent events. The Army has concluded its mission in Iraq and begun a drawdown of surge forces in Afghanistan. Due to budget constraints, the Army is beginning reductions in end-strength, while also rebalancing force structure and making investment decisions to shape the Army of 2020. All of this is being done during a time of war. These transformational efforts are very significant. As the strategies of the President of the United States (POTUS) and Secretary of Defense (SECDEF) are implemented, the Army will continue its transition to a smaller, yet capable, force fully prepared to conduct a full range of operations worldwide. What enables the Army to achieve this transformation and transition is its ability to integrate a broad range of concepts, initiatives and institutional processes across the DOTMLPF-P domains. In doing so, the Army supports the broader defense effort and addresses the needs of the Joint Force, as well as the needs of the Army.

Section III
Purpose, Scope, and Objectives of the Text

HOW THE ARMY RUNS

1-8. Purpose

a. The purpose of this text is to provide a primer and ready reference to officers preparing to assume command, leadership, and management positions at the senior and strategic levels of leadership. It explains the relationships of the systems and processes that produce both future change and contribute to daily mission accomplishment. It is these systems and processes that will be taxed to their fullest capabilities and capacities during the execution of the ACP.

b. While a key use of this reference text is to support the Department of Command, Leadership, and Management's (DCLM) portion of the U.S. Army War College (USAWC) curriculum, there are additional objectives that serve broader purposes. These other objectives include its use in the following ways: by nonresident students in fulfilling the requirements of the USAWC's Distance Education Program; as a general reference for branch and service schools in the military education system; as a primary reference for force management specialists attending various courses at the Army Force Management School (AFMS) at Fort Belvoir, Virginia; and as a primer for all who seek to better understand the Army's organization and functions, along with its systems and processes.

c. The major focus of the text is on the United States Army as specified by its title. However, this text also addresses how the Army interfaces with the Office of the Department of Defense (DOD), other Services, the Joint Chiefs of Staff (JCS) and CCDRs to better achieve joint interdependence. Hence, it describes other systems and processes such as the Joint Strategic Planning System (JSPS) and the PPBE process.

1-9. Scope and Objectives

a. This text supports the DCLM portion of the USAWC curriculum, which focuses on strategic leadership, joint processes, defense management, and the development of landpower. Elihu Root founded the USAWC "not to promote war, but to preserve peace by intelligent and adequate preparation to repel aggression." He charged the faculty with directing "the instruction and intellectual exercise of the Army, to acquire information, devise the plans, and study the subjects indicated, and to advise the Commander-in-Chief of all questions of plans, armament, transportation, and military preparation and movement." That focus is addressed in the current USAWC mission statement: "The United States Army War College educates and develops leaders for service at the strategic level while advancing knowledge in the global application of landpower."

b. The DCLM presents that portion of the curriculum that promotes a better appreciation of the theory and practice of command, leadership, and management in the JIIM environment. This text is particularly used in the course entitled Defense Management, which includes methods of instruction with faculty presentations, lectures, and discussions with distinguished academics and prominent practitioners, seminar group discussions, case studies, independent reading, and practical exercises.

c. From 1977 to 1997, the primary reference text published by DCLM was entitled "Army Command, Management, and Leadership: Theory and Practice." Because of the growing volume of discussion and information in the category of theory, as well as the many changes that have occurred in Army organizations and systems since the end of the Cold War, the single theory and practice volume was replaced in 1997. The theory has been incorporated into a Course text that changes yearly. The current version of HTAR, which is published biannually, is an outgrowth of this division. This text addresses the operation and relationships of the systems and processes that enable the Army to fulfill its roles and accomplish its missions to meet the objectives articulated in National, Defense, and Military Strategies.

Section IV
Text Organization

1-10. Text Organization

a. This text is organized into 21 chapters, which cover Army structure, systems, and processes from broad as well as specific perspectives. For example, the Army structure is described from an organizational life cycle perspective before describing the various structural components. A separate chapter is devoted to the RC.

b. Broad systems and processes that impact the Army overall are first described, and when appropriate, they are covered from Defense, Joint, and Army perspectives to understand their interaction

INTRODUCTION

and synergy. This includes chapters that involve subjects such as: strategic planning; force development; mobilization and deployment; readiness; resources; and materiel system research, development and acquisition.

c. This text's later chapters focus more on Army functional organizations, systems, and processes. This includes chapters devoted to the following: logistics; military human resources; civilian personnel management; training; knowledge management; installations; health services; civil functions; and public affairs. Finally, the last chapter deals with the complex contributions made by DOD and the Army to the subject of Defense Support of Civil Authorities (DSCA).

Section V
Summary and References

1-11. Summary

There are some who have interpreted our new national strategy as questioning the relevance of Land Forces. There are others who would wish away a decade's worth of hard-won sacrifice and expertise with false assumptions about the future. To them I say: Our Army was created 237 years ago to defend this great nation and to secure the interests of the United States abroad. That imperative has not changed. As I have watched the strategic environment evolve over nearly four decades in uniform, I have seen many of the characteristics of conflict change. Technology has advanced, new threats have emerged, and connections between people have increased exponentially. But through it all, the nature of conflict has remained constant. From countering terrorism to irregular warfare, from stability operations to humanitarian disasters, when people are in trouble the United States responds. It is most frequently a U.S. Army Soldier that arrives on their doorstep. Why? Because preventing conflict demands presence, shaping the environment demands presence, restoring the peace demands presence, and more often than not, that presence proudly wears the uniform of an American Soldier.

General Raymond T. Odierno, CSA
Eisenhower Luncheon Speech, Association of the United States Army (AUSA), October 23, 2012

a. This text helps the reader understand how the Army operates within a strategic context and meets the critical challenges as addressed by National, Defense, Joint, and Army leaders and strategic documents. This text is about the systems and processes that will enable the Army to remain as effective in service to the Nation in the future as it has been in the past.

b. It is hoped that students and practitioners of the military art who use this text will more fully appreciate the truth in the words of General Harold K. Johnson, CSA 1964-1948: "The Army is like a funnel. At the top you pour in doctrine, resources concepts, equipment, and facilities. And out at the bottom comes one lone Soldier walking point." Understanding and applying the organizations, systems, and processes described in this text are part of the way leaders will continue the legacy of those who have come before us to keep the Army the most decisive land force in the world.

1-12. References
a. Army Strategic Planning Guidance, 2013
b. Army Posture Statement, 2012
c. 38th CSA Marching Orders: Waypoint #1, January 2013
d. Chairman's Strategic Direction to the Joint Force (CSDJF), February 6, 2012
e. Eisenhower Luncheon Speech, Association of the United States Army (AUSA), October 23, 2012
f. The Army Plan (TAP), 2012
g. Title 10, USC, http://uscodebeta.house.gov/

This page is intentionally left blank

ARMY ORGANIZATIONAL LIFE CYCLE

Chapter 2

Army Organizational Life Cycle

In his Biennial Report of the Chief of Staff of the United States Army to the Secretary of War for the period July 1, 1939, to June 30, 1941, General George C. Marshall described the stark situation in which he found the Army as the war in Europe erupted and threatened to involve a neutral United States. President Roosevelt's emergency proclamation of September 8, 1939 had given the authority for the Active Army to expand from 210,000 to 227,000 men and to reorganize from the World War I square divisions to the new triangular divisions. However, General Marshall's problems could not be solved by a manpower increase of less than 10% and division reorganization. He also had major training deficiencies to correct. There was such a shortage in motor transportation that divisional training was impracticable. A lack of corps headquarters and experienced commanders and obsolete doctrine and organizations further degraded capabilities. Over half the undermanned Active Army divisions were horse-mounted and the horse was still the primary means of mounted movement. At the same time Congress had reduced the Army Air Corps request for replacements to World War I aircraft to only 57 planes. It was even worse in the National Guard organizations. General Marshall's solution to these massive problems was to reconstruct the Army by resourcing, structuring, and integrating new equipment, personnel, and organizations while training. He also improved the youth and vitality of the Army by discharging elderly and substandard Soldiers. The U.S. Army's success in creating, deploying, and sustaining 89 divisions for the European Theater during World War II was largely due to General Marshall's genius and his skill at what, today, is known as force management.

Section I
Introduction

2-1. Chapter Content
 a. This chapter provides an overview of the systems and processes employed by the Army to manage change on a continuing basis. It reflects the fact, as General George C. Marshall understood, that, in complex organizations, every action or problem affects every other function of the organization. Army management systems and processes dictate the entire life cycle of the Army from the earliest stages of conceptual development to the final disposition of people, equipment, and facilities.

 b. The Army manages change by utilizing a myriad of institutional processes as it performs its legal function as specified in Title 10, United States Code (USC), Section 3062, to prepare forces "...organized, trained, and equipped primarily for prompt and sustained combat incident to operations on land. It is responsible for the preparation of land forces necessary for the effective prosecution of war except as otherwise assigned and, in accordance with integrated joint mobilization plans, for the expansion of the peacetime components of the Army to meet the needs of war."

 c. This chapter looks holistically at the interconnected systems and processes used to develop and manage the Army. The chapter is an overview of 'How the Army Runs' and addresses systems that are necessary to the overall leadership and management of the Army and that are integral to the force management processes. Subsequent chapters will expand upon the sub-elements presented here.

2-2. The Army Organizational Life Cycle Model (AOLCM)
 a. Managing change in any large, complex organization requires management of many interrelated processes. In the context of developing operational organizations with highly trained personnel, led by confident leaders, using technologically advanced equipment, and providing that capability when needed by the unified Combatant Commander (CCDR), the Army manages from an organizational life cycle view. The Army Organizational Life Cycle Model graphically captures the continuous cycle of developing, employing, maintaining, and eliminating organizations. The Army management approach recognizes the need to understand modernization and change as a complex adaptive system. The Army Plan and The Army Modernization Strategy (AMS) mandate the Army transformation and modernization efforts such as the Brigade Combat Team Modernization, modular force design, and Active/Reserve Component (AC/RC) rebalancing to produce relevant and ready landpower that is strategically agile and

HOW THE ARMY RUNS

expeditionary. The AOLCM provides a conceptual framework to both analyze and assess Army change efforts.

b. The AOLCM shown at Figure 2-1 reflects the stages that organizations and their personnel and equipment will experience at one time or another (and often concurrently) during their service in the Army. The functions performed in these stages develop, field, sustain, and modernize operational units and their supporting organizations; maintain their viability and effectiveness; and remove them or their assets (personnel and materiel) from the force as requirements change. Each individual asset (a Soldier or a civilian or materiel) required by a unit or activity will be managed at some stage of the model beginning with the establishment of the need and entry into the Army to ultimate separation or disposal. The model details the critical stages through which an organizational resource will move, at some point, during its life span. Generally, the model depicts the life cycle of Army organizations from their development and their progression (clockwise around Figure 2-1) to separation. The dynamic of the model, displayed by the interconnecting lines, illustrates that the Army leadership must resource and manage all of the functions simultaneously, since Army assets will be in each functional stage at any one time. Any change to a resource in a functional stage will affect resources in most, if not all, of the other functional stages. In other words, if you influence or change something in one functional node the response will impact the entire model affecting other nodes to some degree.

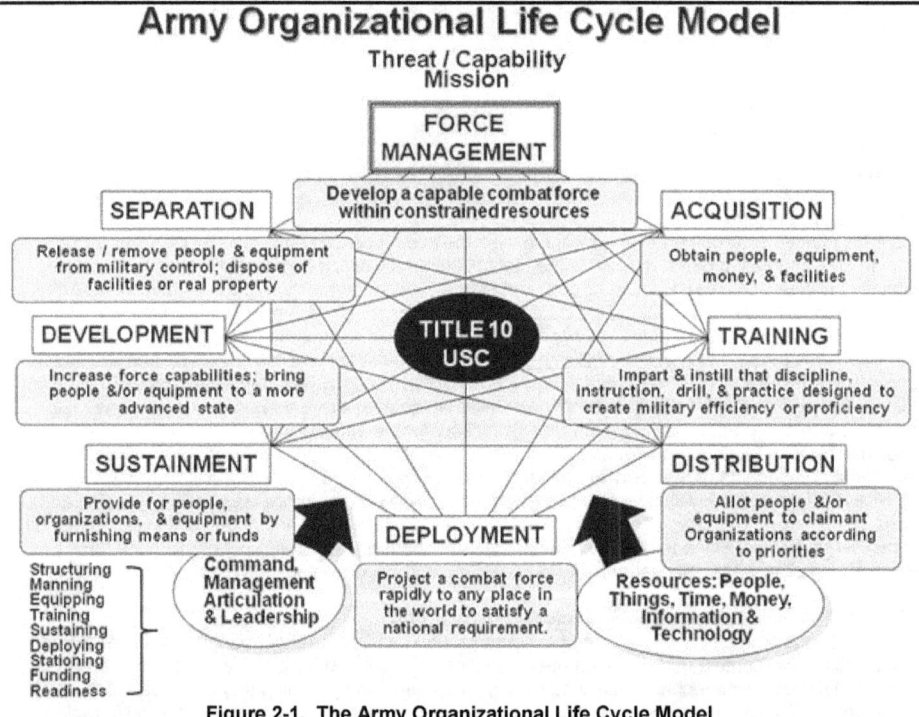

Figure 2-1. The Army Organizational Life Cycle Model

c. Life cycle functions are listed below.

(1) Force Management. As the first phase of the organizational life cycle model, force management becomes the key activity underlying all other functions. The process involves decision-making, and execution of activities encompassing conceptual development, capabilities requirements generation, force

ARMY ORGANIZATIONAL LIFE CYCLE

development, organizational development, force integration functions, and resourcing. Force management results in the development of a capable operational force within constrained resources.

(2) Acquisition. After the Congress authorizes, and the Department of Defense (DOD) provides, the budget and the End Strength (ES) (see para 13-7b) guidance, the Army must then acquire the people and materiel specified in the requirements and authorizations documents necessary to accomplish specified missions. From a materiel acquisition perspective, the acquisition function extends beyond the principal item being fielded and must consider other essential requirements such as the availability of Associated Support Items of Equipment and Personnel (ASIOEP), technical publications, repair parts, trained personnel, and facilities. From a human resource (HR) (see Chapters 13 and 14) acquisition perspective, the acquisition function must consider recruiting and accession missions in concert with the overall manpower management program and the influences of personnel life cycle functions.

(3) Training. The training function encompasses the processes for accomplishing the transition from civilian status to military service. In this context, the training function is somewhat different from what most Army leaders think of when discussing training. At this point in the life cycle, consider training from the aspect of initial entry training or the requirement to provide Soldiers with initial new equipment training or familiarization training on new or displaced equipment. In other words, this aspect of the training cycle imparts new skills to the Soldier or converts the civilian into a Soldier. It most often results in award of a Military Occupational Specialty (MOS) or Additional Skill Identifier (ASI). The training function also includes the transition of U.S. Military Academy (USMA), Reserve Officers Training Corps (ROTC), and Officer Candidate School (OCS) graduates into officers through the Basic Officer Leaders Course (BOLC). Traditional collective training and professional educational and leader development fall under the "development" phase of the Organizational Life Cycle Model.

(4) Distribution. Having produced or procured the resources necessary to form and sustain units they must be distributed according to established requirements, authorizations, and priorities. The distribution function includes the assignment of people from entry-level training to their initial unit and the delivery of new materiel from the wholesale level to the user. This activity is primarily managed and synchronized through the Army force generation process that focuses equipment and personnel distribution during the reset phase (see Para. 2-7b(3) below).

(5) Deployment. Once trained or prepared units, individuals, packages, or materiel become available to support worldwide operations. An individual Soldier, civilian, unit, or item of equipment may be subject to some, if not all, of the mobilization, deployment, redeployment, demobilization, and reconfiguration processes of this function. Deployment represents both a planning and operational function involving agencies on the Army Staff (ARSTAF), other levels of DOD, and the civilian transportation structure. Like many of other AOLCM activities, unit deployments are managed on a cyclical basis with Army force generation cycles.

(6) Sustainment. In peace or war the presence of people and materiel in units establishes a requirement for sustainment. People, skills, capability, and equipment must be maintained to the standard set for mission accomplishment by replacement, rotation, repair, and training operations. From a personnel perspective this function covers Soldier reassignments throughout a career or obligation period, quality of life and well-being programs, as well as other aspects of the personnel systems influencing retention. Repair parts and maintenance provide the sustainment process for materiel. Training in units covering the process of sustaining common Soldier skills that maintain unit or individual proficiency falls under this function as well. The manning priority level, the Dynamic Distribution System (DDS) (see para 13-19b), Dynamic Army Resourcing Priority List (DARPL), Basis of Issue Plan (BOIP), 10 classes of supply, the Authorized Stockage Lists (ASLs), and Prescribed Load Lists (PLLs) illustrate some of the systems or techniques used to manage authorizations and priorities within the sustainment function.

(7) Development. The Army must constantly develop and improve. We develop individuals through civilian, enlisted, and officer education programs that include character and leader development activities. Education and training programs range from individual self-development, including graduate-level degree programs, to the entire range of branch- and skill-related institutional training culminating at either the senior service college for officers and civilians or Sergeants Major Academy for enlisted Soldiers. Units develop through collective training processes that include individual training in units, home station training, and deployments for training. Examples are Collective Training Tasks (CTT), leader training, live fire and maneuver training, external evaluations such as those under the Army Training and Evaluation Program (ARTEP), deployment exercises, and training rotations to the Combat Training Centers (CTCs).

HOW THE ARMY RUNS

(8) Separation. Finally, there comes a time when people and equipment separate from military control. People may separate voluntarily by not extending following completion of an obligated service period or by retiring. Involuntary separation may occur due to Reduction in Force (RIF) actions or qualitative reasons. The Army normally separates materiel through the Defense Reutilization and Marketing Office (DRMO) process or through Foreign Military Sales (FMS) actions.

   d. There are two categories of external influences that affect the model.

     (1) The first category is the availability of resources. Resources include tangible objects in the form of funds, materiel, or personnel as well as intangible resources such as time, information, and technology.

     (2) The second category is the influence of command, management, and leadership in planning, organizing, directing, controlling, and monitoring the multitude of inputs, decisions, and actions to ensure that functions at each stage of the model execute effectively and at the appropriate time. These command and management activities are synchronized within the Army force generation process to ensure the timely allocation of scarce resources and to maximize the availability of trained and ready Army forces to meet CCDR Army force requirements.

Section II
Force Management

2-3. The U.S. Army War College (USAWC) Model

To aid in examining specific Force Management Systems (FMS) (see Chapter 5) and their interactions, the U.S. Army War College has adopted the force management model shown in Figure 2-2 (see the fold-out at the end of this book). This model reflects a system-of-systems approach (see Para. 11-9d), each of which provides an essential force management function, and, more importantly, how these functions relate to each other.

   a. In this network, strategic and senior leadership guidance, the processes for determining warfighting capabilities requirements, conducting Research and Development (R&D), and providing resources all provide input to the force development process. The resulting products of force development, in turn, provide the basis for the force integrating functions of acquiring and distributing materiel, as well as acquiring, training, and distributing personnel. This widely used model highlights key aspects and relationships of force management. The model shows the relationships of Army processes to each other and to the major DOD management processes. These processes drive and interact with Army processes. Each process displayed in the figure is examined in detail in other chapters of this text. The major DOD management processes are below.

     (1) Joint Strategic Planning System (JSPS) (see Chap. 4, Section II).

     (2) Joint Operations Planning and Execution System (JOPES) (see Chap. 4, Section IV).

     (3) Planning, Programming, Budgeting, and Execution (PPBE) Process (see Chap. 4, Section III and Chapter 9).

     (4) Materiel System Research, Development, and Acquisition Management process (see Chap. 11).

   b. The underlying basis for this model is that force management, in its simplest context, is the management of change using many interrelated and complex processes. Although the model depicts the flow of processes in a somewhat linear, sequential manner, the complexities of managing change mandate that at any one time an initiative may be simultaneously in several of these processes at some level of maturity. As organizations develop, these processes may run sequentially, be compressed, run in parallel, or even run in reverse depending on the urgency, risk, and senior leader guidance on the issue. History has shown, however, that eventually all of the steps must take place to produce a fully trained and equipped operational force at the right time and at the right place to support the Combatant Commander (CCMD).

2-4. Force Management Terms

This section will explore the terms commonly used when describing the force management process. Force management has two major sub-components: Force Development and Force Integration.

   a. Force Development. Force development determines Army Doctrine, Organization, Training, Materiel, Leadership and Education, Personnel, Facilities, and Policy (DOTMLPF-P) capabilities requirements and translates them into plans and programs, within allocated resources, to accomplish Army missions and functions. A capability provides the means to accomplish a mission or task decisively.

ARMY ORGANIZATIONAL LIFE CYCLE

Capability comes from organizations comprised of well-trained personnel with superior equipment, led by competent leaders employing sound doctrine. The following paragraphs offer a condensed explanation of the force development process. (For more detail see Chapter 5.)

(1) Generate Capabilities Requirements.

(a) The force development process has its roots in the process of developing operational concepts to meet the future functional needs of the Joint force. The Joint Capabilities Integration and Development System (JCIDS) (see Para. 5-3) identifies the required operational capability in terms of personnel, equipment, and unit structure. This process begins with national-level guidance such as: Quadrennial Defense Review (QDR); the National Security Strategy; the National Defense Strategy; the National Military Strategy; Defense Planning Guidance; guidance from the Army's senior leadership (The Army Plan (TAP)), which includes the Army Strategic Planning Guidance (ASPG), the Army Planning Priorities Guidance (APPG), the Army Programming Guidance Memorandum (APGM), and the Army Campaign Plan (ACP); and operational requirements of the geographic CCMDs. With this guidance, the military examines trends, patterns, and projections to forecast the future Joint Operating Environment (JOE). The military and the Army then develop a family of operational concepts expected to accomplish the strategic guidance and related operational objectives and prevail in the future environment. These include development of the Capstone Concept for Joint Operations (CCJO), supporting Joint Concepts, and the family of concepts in the Army Concept Framework (ACF). The ACF includes the Army Capstone Concept (ACC), Army Operating Concept (AOC), Army Functional Concepts (AFC), and leadership directed concepts. Existing Concept Capability Plans (CCP) will continue to be used but no new CCPs will be initiated. Additionally, Concept of Operations (CONOPS) and white papers may be developed to inform the ACF. The U.S. Army Training and Doctrine Command (TRADOC) assesses the future concepts through a series of analyses, tests, experiments, and studies to gain insights for solutions across DOTMLPF-P domains for emerging functional needs. Through this analysis key capability requirements are refined and documented.

(b) Army proponents (see Army Regulation (AR) 5-22) or TRADOC Integrated Capabilities Development Team (ICDT) pursue timely involvement of appropriate agencies/expertise to aggressively analyze and assess future operating capabilities requirements. Depending upon the capability, TRADOC may conduct a Capability Based Assessment (CBA) that includes Functional Area Analysis (FAA), Functional Needs Analysis (FNA), Functional Solution Analysis (FSA), and the preparation of capability documents. This assessment process leads to the identification by the Commanding General (CG) TRADOC to Headquarters, Department of the Army (HQDA) of DOTMLPF-P change recommendations (non-materiel solutions) or a materiel capability need. If the capability requires a change in doctrine, training, or leadership and education, TRADOC begins action to meet the requirement upon approval of HQDA Deputy Chief of Staff (DCS), G-3/5/7. For doctrinal changes, TRADOC prepares a Program Directive (PD) (normally approved by the CG, Combined Arms Center (CAC)) to define and document in detail the doctrinal requirement. PDs and other minor DOTMLPF-P Change Recommendation (DCR)-related doctrine changes become part of the Doctrine and Literature Master Plan (DLMP) periodic doctrinal updates and modifications. Should the analysis justify a training requirement, capability developers explore and identify potential training solutions that can result in changes to the Training Requirements Analysis System (TRAS), warfighter and unit training publications, training support packages, and training strategies. System training support requirements are developed and fielded by the Program Manager (PM) and are identified in Capability Development Documents (CDD) and Capability Production Documents (CPD) that are reviewed by the affected proponents' Capability Development Integration Directorates (CDID). The CDIDs then coordinate with the Army Capabilities Integration Center (ARCIC) to integrate these system training approaches into all associated training systems and strategies (see Chapters 11 and 15). Leadership and education requirements are managed by HQDA, G-3/57 (as the ARSTAF lead) and TRADOC as the lead for executing the Army Leader Development Program and for the integration of leadership and education requirements from a force modernization proponent perspective. If the analysis results in a need for change in Soldier occupational specialty structure, then the recommendation goes forward to U.S. Army Human Resources Command (HRC) for Army-wide coordination and approval (see Chapter 13). If the required capability needs a materiel solution, TRADOC conducts a more detailed Analysis of Materiel/Non-materiel Approaches (AMA) and, if appropriate, prepares an Initial Capabilities Document (ICD) and forwards it to HQDA DCS, G-3/5/7 for approval of the capability requirement through the Army Requirements Oversight Council (AROC) validation process. HQDA Deputy Chief of Staff (DCS), G-8 has responsibility for materiel

HOW THE ARMY RUNS

solutions and DOTMLPF-P integration throughout the program development/life cycle. (For more detail on fulfilling materiel capabilities requirements see Chapter 11.) If the solutions analysis determines a need for change in facilities, then the recommendation goes forward to the Assistant Chief of Staff for Installation Management (ACSIM) (see Para. 9-8b) for action (also see Chap. 17). If TRADOC determines the required capability needs an organizational solution, TRADOC prepares a Unit Reference Sheet (URS). TRADOC forwards the URS to HQDA for approval. All the above approved organizational-related solutions move to the next phase of force development.

(2) Design Organizations. As the conceptual change in organizational structure becomes recognized and codified, the organizational design process captures the organizational personnel and equipment requirements. The combat development community develops the proposed organization, as well as its mission and functions, to meet the required mission capabilities. Organizational solutions to capabilities requirements are captured in a URS in sufficient detail to support Army force design initiatives, and related studies and analyses. After the design has been developed, laid out, and analyzed by TRADOC, it moves forward to HQDA in the Force Design Update (FDU) process. The FDU process is used to gain consensus within the Army on new organizations and changes to existing organizations. Once approved, this design will be further refined into an organizational model known as a Table of Organization and Equipment (TOE) in the next phase (see Para. 5-9).

(3) Develop Organizational Models. Upon receipt of the URS from TRADOC during the FDU process, the U.S. Army Force Management Support Agency (USAFMSA) applies rules, standards, and related guidance to produce a doctrinally correct design representing a complete organizational model (TOE). The TOE is a requirements document that defines a fully resourced and mission-capable organization (i.e., assuming all personnel and equipment are available and resourced).

(4) Determine Organizational Authorizations. The HQDA approved TOE competes in the Total Army Analysis (TAA) process for resources. TAA develops requirements and authorizations defining the force structure the Army must build, raise, provision, sustain, maintain, train, and resource. Through TAA, the Army provides the GCCs with the proper force structure to execute assigned tasks. In the first phase, the TAA determines the demand for Army capabilities (number and type) of all approved TOEs. In the second phase, the TAA process resources the demands based upon Army leadership directives, written guidance, risk analyses, and the priorities of the Combatant Commanders. The second phase of the TAA ends with the approval of the changes by the Secretary of the Army and Chief of Staff of the Army. The resourcing and approval phase of TAA also accounts for the materiel requirements. TAA takes into account force guidance and resource availability to produce a balanced and affordable force structure (see Chap. 5, Section V).

(5) Document Organizational Authorizations.

(a) After approval of the resourced force structure by the Army leadership, USAFMSA manages the process of documenting the decision(s). This process results in organizational authorizations documented in the Modification Table of Organization and Equipment (MTOE) or Table of Distribution and Allowance (TDA) (see Chap. 5, Section VI). The force development process culminates with the HQDA approval and documentation of personnel and equipment authorizations as Army organizations in the force structure. The resource-constrained decisions on the allocation of authorizations are recorded in Army authorization documents and the Structure and Manpower Allocation System (SAMAS) (see Para. 5-23).

(b) The marriage of these two systems occurs in the Structure and Composition System (SACS). SACS produces the Army's time-phased demands for personnel and equipment over the current, budget, and program years and is extended for a total of a 10-year period. Additionally, SACS builds a fully modernized Objective TOE (OTOE) position for all units. In this way, SACS shows current levels of modernization, levels achieved at the end of the Program Objective Memorandum (POM) (see para 5-26a and 9-54) period, and a fully modernized Army (for planning purposes). SACS outputs combine information from BOIP, TOE, SAMAS, and known force structure constraints not included in the previous files. Key outputs are the Personnel SACS (PERSACS) and the Logistics SACS (LOGSACS) (see Chap. 5).

(c) SACS provides the data that drives the force integration processes to acquire, train, and distribute personnel and acquire and distribute materiel to the right place at the right time. Upon completion of force development, the management processes become integrating functions. These force integration functions take an approved force development program and incorporate it into the force.

b. Force Integration.

ARMY ORGANIZATIONAL LIFE CYCLE

(1) Effective force integration is a difficult and demanding process that involves coordinating many complex and unique procedures and data systems. Force integration is the synchronized, resource-constrained execution of approved force development plans and programs to achieve systematic management of change.

(a) The introduction, incorporation, and sustainment of doctrine, organizations, and equipment into the Army.

(b) Coordination and integration of operational and managerial systems collectively designed to improve the effectiveness and capability of the Army.

(c) Knowledge and consideration of the potential implications of decisions and actions taken within the execution process.

(2) The scope of force integration includes the functions of structuring organizations, manning, equipping, training, sustaining, deploying, stationing, and funding the force during the introduction and incorporation of approved organizational or force structure changes. It also includes the function of minimizing adverse impacts on force readiness during the introduction and incorporation of change. Force integration synchronizes these functional activities to produce combat ready organizations. Force integration is the enabling process of force management. Force integration focuses Army management actions toward organizations to ensure the orderly incorporation and sustainment of structure, equipment, and doctrine in the Army. The objective of the effort is to assess the combined impact of Army functional systems on units and ensure the appropriate mix of resources (structure, people, equipment, dollars, facilities, and information) result in fully operational units.

Section III
Coordination of Force Integration Actions

2-5. Information Exchange as a Key Element of Force Integration
Coordination of all aspects of force integration requires the constant exchange of information. In the Army's battle to achieve effective force integration, there have been and continue to be initiatives that focus on improving the information flow within and between the multiple systems and processes of force integration. Throughout this text, readers will find detailed descriptions of systems and processes that exchange information and help coordinate force integration actions.

2-6. The Team Approach to Force Integration
a. HQDA learned the value of Integrated Process Team (IPT) problem solving from the challenges of rapidly fielding the Stryker brigades, managing the modular conversions, and rebalancing the AC/RC. Correspondingly, teams of stakeholders meet to discuss and seek solutions to implementation challenges of force management initiatives. These cross-functional working groups have been able to work the complex issues faced by the accelerating pace of change in a manner superior to the linear and sequential methods used in the past. HQDA continues to use the team approach for force management. The three key staff officers that chair the major integrating working groups are the Requirements Staff Officer (RSO) assigned to the G-3/5/7, the Synchronization Staff Officer (SSO) assigned to the G-8, and the Department of the Army (DA) System Coordinator (DASC) assigned to the Assistant Secretary of the Army for Acquisition, Logistics and Technology (ASA(ALT)). They work with other team members including the G-3/5/7 Force Integrator (FI) (see para 2-6c), the G-3/5/7 Organizational Integrator (OI), the G-8 Program Analysis and Evaluation (PA&E) action officer, the Document Integrators (DIs) (see para 2-6c), the Personnel System Staff Officer (PERSSO) (see para 11-17f(1)), command managers, and Resource Integrators (RIs). As required, representatives from Army Commands (ACOMs), Army Service Component Commands (ASCCs), Direct Reporting Units (DRUs), Reserve Components, and other functional area and special interest representatives are included in this function and in staffing force management issues.

b. The integration team approach helps to ensure that every action is properly coordinated with representatives who have knowledge of the doctrine, design, structure, personnel, acquisition, equipping, resources, facilities, information management, and training activities that impact a unit. The G-3/5/7 RSO serves as the HQDA single point of contact and represents the HQDA position for DOTMLPF-P capabilities requirements. RSOs convene capabilities requirements teams to analyze, coordinate, refine, resolve critical comments and non-concurrences, and develop recommendations for the capability. The

HOW THE ARMY RUNS

SSO is the counterpart to the RSO for the G-8 and serves as the HQDA single point of contact for the integration and synchronization of approved capabilities requirements in order to achieve the Army Strategy, ACP priorities and modernization strategy. The DASC is the primary acquisition staff officer at DA. The DASCs are responsible for the day-to-day support of their assigned programs and serve as the PMs' representatives and primary points of contact within the Pentagon. These staff action officers are responsible for preparing, handling, and coordinating actions in their areas of expertise. For more detail on duties and responsibilities of these staff members (see Chapter 11).

c. Roles of other ARSTAF team members.

(1) FI. The FI assigned to G-3/5/7 represent the interests of functionally dissimilar force-level organizations (e.g., the entire force structure from Modular Brigade through Theater Army). They are horizontal force-level integrators and work with brigades, regiments, divisions, and corps and Theater Armies. Responsibilities of the FI are below.

(a) Assesses ability of functional systems to support major organizations.
(b) Recommends prioritization of resources.
(c) Assesses impacts of organizational change, at the appropriate force level, on readiness.
(d) Facilitates integration of units into major organizations.
(e) Evaluates and analyzes impact of incorporating personnel, facilities, equipment, doctrine, structure, and capability changes into major organizations.
(f) Ensures major units are represented in force integration and force planning processes (e.g., TAA, FDU, etc.).
(g) Assesses impacts of mid-range and long-range planning on major units including new doctrine, structure, manning, equipment, technology, facilities, stationing, strategic policy, and resource strategies.
(h) Links organization requirements to resource allocation.

(2) OI. The OIs are assigned to the G-3/5/7 Force Management Directorate and represent organizational interests of functionally similar organizations (e.g. Infantry, Armor, etc.). These individuals are organized into teams for Maneuver, Maneuver Support, and Maneuver Sustainment. The OI serves as the vertical integrator, in their area of specialization. Additionally, he or she provides subject matter expertise to the RSO regarding requirements documentation that deal with these functionally similar organizations. The duties of the OI include, but are not limited to, those listed below.

(a) Analyzing, coordinating, refining, and developing recommendations on requirements.
(b) Ensuring doctrinal linkage exists between organizational and current and emerging capabilities.
(c) Coordinating approval of TOEs and BOIPs.
(d) Participating in force management analysis reviews of all force management documentation.
(e) Developing and coordinating the HQDA position on proposed TAA process changes.

(3) Command Manager (CM). CMs (Force Structure) (CM(FS)) assigned to the G-3/5/7 represent the organizational interests of an ACOM/ASCC/DRU by managing its TDA units, and serves as the FI for the command's MTOEs. The second focus of the CM is managing program budget guidance by ensuring that the manpower allocation for each ACOM/ASCC/DRU is accurately reflected in the SAMAS in compliance with Army leadership decisions and within manpower controls established by Office of the Secretary of Defense (OSD). Duties include the following, listed below.

(a) Serving as point of contact for command plans and Concept Plans (CONPLANs).
(b) Maintaining the documentation audit trail on all additions, deletions, and other changes to unit MTOEs and TDAs.
(c) Producing manpower resource guidance for ACOM/ASCC/DRU Program and Budget Guidance (PBG).
(d) Managing command FSAs.
(e) Providing analysis and assessment of resource alternatives for organizational actions under consideration.
(f) Documenting current and programmed personnel strength, applicable Joint Research, Development and Acquisition (RDA) programs, and organization force structure.
(g) "Cross-walking" analysis of Army programming decisions with those of the DOD, Office of Management and Budget (OMB), and Congress.

(4) DI. The DIs are assigned to the USAFMSA, a DCS, G-3/5/7 Field Operating Agency (FOA). The DI produces organizational requirement and authorization documents that implement approved Army force programs. Their duties include the following, listed below.

ARMY ORGANIZATIONAL LIFE CYCLE

(a) Documenting the unit mission and required capabilities by applying equipment utilization policies, Manpower Requirements Criteria (MARC), standards of grade (SG), and BOIP to develop the proper mix of equipment and personnel for an efficient organizational structure.

(b) Developing MARC that serves as HQDA approved standards for determining the Minimum Mission Essential Wartime Requirement (MMEWR) for staffing to accomplish maneuver support and maneuver sustainment functions in TOE and MTOE documents.

(c) Reviewing proponent-proposed or approved authorization documents to ensure compliance with manpower, personnel, and equipment policies and directives.

(d) Centrally building ACOM/ASCC/DRU authorization documents based on HQDA guidance, Command Plan, and input from the ACOM/ASCC/DRU.

(5) ACOMs, ASCCs, and DRUs. Force management staffs at these echelons manage the planning and execution of the force integration mission.

(a) Document integration, including authorization document (MTOE and TDA) review, and database management.

(b) Systems integration, including requirements and authorization document review, the Materiel Fielding Plan (MFP) process, New Equipment Training Plan (NETP) review, and facilities support annex review.

(c) Organization integration, including the organizational assessment process, review of requirement and authorization documents, and doctrine review.

(d) Force structure management, including TDA manpower management and end-strength management.

(e) Force planning, including the TAA process, command plan process, force reduction planning and monitoring, and CONPLAN development.

(6) Corps, division, regiment, separate brigade, and installation. Force management staffs at these levels continue to manage force integration.

(a) Force structure management, including authorization document management, Commander's Unit Status Report (CUSR) (see para 8-17) monitoring, and force structure review and analysis.

(b) Systems integration, including action plan development, distribution plans reviews, and facilities review.

(c) Organization integration, including organizational assessments, force structure review and analysis, and authorization document review process.

Section IV
Changing How We Manage Change

2-7. Alterations to Force Management

a. The elements for managing change are themselves changing and this fundamentally alters force management. The processes that develop operational units often frustrate those who need the capabilities in the near term. Several factors contribute to this frustration. The pace of technological advances challenges our ability to envision future force capabilities and to properly plan for their development. The time required to change the primary long lead elements of the institution such as doctrine, materiel, and organizations can appear excessive. Materiel changes may require up to 15 years for developing and fielding, organizational change may require two to eight years, doctrine may require two to four years, and leader development and training follow changes in the other "drivers" by several years. For the future Army to benefit from the synergism of integrated doctrine, organizations, training, materiel, leader development, personnel, and facilities, it must continue to work to shorten development and fielding times and increase the ability to envision and conceive future warfighting capabilities. Because of these current operational exigencies and many more factors, the Army senior leadership continues to implement policies and procedures to streamline existing force management processes and improve their effectiveness. Today, the ARSTAF continues to evolve to meet the demanding requirements of force management. Initiatives for improving the ARSTAF enable HQDA to streamline the requirements approval process, replace and combine several legacy automated force management support systems, and field equipment to brigades as integrated sets.

b. Force Management Changes at HQDA.

HOW THE ARMY RUNS

(1) Support to Current Operations—Interim Policy on Capabilities Requests. In response to exigent capability requirements generated by current operations, HQDA instituted streamlined processes and staffing procedures to rapidly procure and distribute materiel solutions to identified operational deficiencies. Operational Needs Statements (ONS) and Authorized/Pre-validated request procedures were developed and implemented in order to support deployed or deploying units' accomplishment of their assigned missions. The Army Requirements and Resourcing Board (AR2B) process was developed for presenting critical operational needs to the Army's senior leadership for rapid decision making (accelerated fielding solutions). The response to an ONS is based on an ARSTAF validation supported by TRADOC, Army Materiel Command (AMC), and Materiel Developer (MATDEV) reviews. The AR2B determines validity of the need, availability of technology, and source of resources to fill the requirement. If the need is determined to be critical and can be resourced (at least for the present situation) a directed requirement may result. Additionally, the ARCIC has developed a process and supporting structure to accelerate capabilities development, such as those resulting from ONSs. Support to ongoing and emerging operational urgent requirements will likely continue to drive changes in force management organizations, systems, and processes (see Chap. 11).

(2) The Modular Conversion of Army Force Structure. To maximize force effectiveness, the Army is refining its modular, brigade-based force to create combat and support formations of common organizational designs that can be tailored to meet the varied demands of the GCCs–reducing joint planning and execution complexities. Additionally, the Army is redesigning organizations to perform as integral parts of the Joint Force, making them more effective across the range of military operations and enhancing their ability to contribute to joint, interagency, and multinational efforts. This modular conversion is a total Army effort affecting nearly every combat and support organization in the inventory. Most combat formations and headquarters have been completed; the current effort is mainly on converting and activating theater Army headquarters and Support Brigades. The restructuring of the force from Division-based to Brigade-based will likely impact many of the Army Force Management-specific organizations, systems and processes, and proponent and management relationships.

(3) Army Force Generation is a cyclic training and readiness process that synchronizes strategic planning, prioritization, and resourcing to generate trained and ready modular expeditionary forces tailored to Joint mission requirements. The currently proposed Future Force Generation Model is designed to provide the required capabilities for Army missions. U.S. Army Forces Command (FORSCOM) is the supported command for the Future Force Generation Model and it will ensure that every deploying unit is the best trained, led, and equipped force possible. It is a continuous and structured process for generating active Army and reserve component forces that provide increasing unit readiness over time. Force pools provide the framework for the structured progression of increased unit readiness. The Army uses these force pools in addition to mission requirements to prioritize resources over time and synchronize unit manning, equipping, resourcing, and training. Units transition through the force pools based on the unit commander's assessment or designated criteria, validated by the next-higher commander, and monitored by FORSCOM. The Army focuses units against future missions as early as possible and task organizes units in globally available force packages tailored to joint mission requirements. The currently proposed Mission Force Pool (MFP), Rotational Force Pool (RFP), and Operational Sustainment Force Pool (OSFP) provide a new framework for the structured progression of increasing readiness in Future Force Generation. Each force pool is defined by designated unit activities, capability levels, and the period of time allocated to each force pool. The Army uses the force pools in addition to mission requirements to prioritize resources over time, and to synchronize unit manning, equipping, resourcing, and training.

2-8. Basic Force Management Tools

Force integration carries a significant manpower bill across the HQDA staff. The required activities for detailed and interactive coordination contribute to and drive manpower requirements. Across the staff, it takes people to participate in the management, synchronization, and coordination activities and their collective knowledge to make force integration a viable function. These staff officers need access to the many different databases and models that provide information in order efficiently accomplish their functions and responsibilities. Correspondingly, steps are underway to apply technology to help reduce the manpower costs of this process. These automation and information technology improvements are continuous and on-going.

ARMY ORGANIZATIONAL LIFE CYCLE

a. The Army Equipping Enterprise System (AE2S), developed by the Army Strategic and Advanced Computing Center, is a decision support system designed to provide the ARSTAF with an integrated, quick turnaround planning tool to assess actual or notional force structures and/or policies across the Army's major functional areas (force structure, personnel, logistics, installations, and budget). Part of AE2S is the Army Flow Model (AFM), which supplements the legacy functional models. Many of these legacy functional models remain "stovepipe" systems and cannot easily conduct "What If" analyses in a timely manner. The AFM provides the capability to readily assess force structure or policy changes and examine the effects of these changes on unit fill levels and readiness both within and across functional areas. Users can access AE2S through Army Knowledge Online (AKO) (see para 16-18) or at https://afm.us.army.

b. USAFMSA has developed the FMS. This system replaces the four existing stovepipe automated support systems, Requirements Documentation System (RDS), SAMAS, and Force Builder. These legacy automated systems can only exchange data through manual file exchange. FMS is based upon a single integrated database providing access through an integrated set of user applications. The first phase of FMS (requirements documentation) is now operating with full implementation to take several years. No implementation timelines have been published (for more detail, see Chap. 5).

Section V
Summary and References

2-9. Summary

a. In modern, complex organizations there is a cause and effect relationship involving almost every process and system. An appreciation of these interrelationships and knowledge of the individual systems that contribute to force management will in turn lead to an understanding of how the Army runs.

b. Changes within the Army and the processes used to implement those changes require a holistic application of cross-functional factors. To be successful, future senior Army leaders and managers must understand the nature of the interrelations of the systems and subsystems, as well as the key players and functions. Senior leaders who understand how these processes work and where leadership can influence these processes will be more effective. Experience shows us that successful senior leaders understand how the Army develops and sustains its part of our nation's military capability and use this knowledge to make informed decision on how to use or change the processes to improve that capability. The overviews of the Army Functional Life Cycle Model and the USAWC Model introduced in this chapter provide a basis for subsequent and more detailed examinations of the Army management systems and processes in later chapters. Additional information can be found at the following web sites:

(1) http://www.carlisle.army.mil/
(2) http://www.afms1.belvoir.army.mil
(3) https://fmsweb.army.mil/

2-10. References

a. Public Law 99-433, DOD Reorganization Act of 1986
b. Public Law 103-62, Government Performance Results Act of 1993
c. Title 10, USC
d. HQDA, Army Campaign Plan 2012, 30 May 2012
e. General Orders Number 3 (GO 3), Assignment of Functions and Responsibilities Within Headquarters, Department of the Army
f. General Orders No. 2009-03 (GO 2009-03), Amendment to General Orders No. 2002-3, Assignment of Functions and Responsibilities within Headquarters, Department of the Army, 18 Mar 2009
g. See also: Army Force Management-A Selected Bibliography. Compiled by Virginia C. Shope. U.S. Army War College Library. Carlisle Barracks, PA: August 2002. Available from http://www.carlisle.army.mil/library/bibs/frcmgt02.htm
h. HQDA, Army Regulation 525-29, Army Force Generation, 14 March 2011
i. HQDA, Army Regulation 5-22, The Army Force Modernization Proponent System, Rapid Acquisition Review (RAR), 25 March 2011
j. Headquarters (HQ) TRADOC, TRADOC Regulation 71-20, Concept Development, Capabilities Determination, and Capabilities Integration, 23 Feb 2011

HOW THE ARMY RUNS

k. HQ TRADOC, TRADOC Regulation 25-36 C1, The TRADOC Doctrine Publication Program, 4 September 2012

ARMY ORGANIZATIONAL STRUCTURE

Chapter 3

Army Organizational Structure

The Army, as one of the three military departments (Army, Navy and Air Force) reporting to the Department of Defense (DOD), is composed of two distinct and equally important components: the active component; and the reserve component. The reserve component is comprised of the United States Army Reserve and Army National Guard. Regardless of component, the Army conducts both operational and institutional missions. The operational Army consists of numbered armies, corps, divisions, brigades, and battalions that conduct unified land operations around the world. Institutional organizations provide the infrastructure necessary to raise, train, equip, deploy, and ensure the readiness of all Army forces. The training base provides military skills and professional education to every Soldier—as well as members of sister services and allied forces. It also allows the Army to expand rapidly in time of war. The industrial base provides world-class equipment and logistics for the Army. Army installations provide the power-projection platforms required to deploy land forces promptly to support the Combatant Commander (CCDR). Once those forces are deployed, the institutional Army provides the logistics needed to support operations. Without the institutional Army, the operational Army cannot function. Without the operational Army, the institutional Army has no purpose.

Section I
Introduction

3-1. Chapter Content
   a. The United States Army is a strategic instrument of national policy that has served our country in peace and war for over two centuries. The Department of the Army (DA) is separately organized under the Secretary of the Army (SECARMY) (10 USC 3011). This chapter provides a discussion on how the Army is organized to perform its doctrinal tasks and how it responds to changes in its environment. The publications which provide the official description of Army organizations, as well as their roles, missions and functions include the following: DA Pamphlet (DA PAM) 10-1, Organization of the United States Army; DA General Orders (DAGO) 2012-01, Assignment of Functions and Responsibilities Within Headquarters, Department of the Army; Army Regulation (AR) 10-87, Army Commands, Army Service Component Commands, and Direct Reporting Units; and AR 10-88, Field Operating Agencies, Office of Chief of Staff, Army. The Army web site at http://www.army.mil/info/organization/ provides links to the home pages of the Army Headquarters (HQ) staff elements and the Army Commands (ACOM), Army Service Component Commands (ASCC), Direct Reporting Units (DRU), and Field Operating Agencies (FOA). These four types of managing headquarters and supporting activities, and their examples, are listed later in this chapter.
   b. How the Army operates as a system within an organizational, operational, and strategic environment to carry out its Title 10 functions provides insight into how the Army efficiently allocates resources and effectively manages change. Through these processes, the Army is able to provide trained and ready forces to the CCDR for prompt and sustained combat incident to operations on land. What follows is a discussion of the framework that describes the Army as an organization of headquarters, staffs, commands, and functional units.

3-2. The Army Organizational System
   a. The Army as an Open Organizational System.
   (1) In terms of management theory, the Army can be considered an open organizational system with three distinct components: the production subsystem; the combat subsystem; and the integrating subsystem. Each of these components includes tasks to be accomplished, operates in a given environment, and requires and acquires resources. Because of the size and complexity of the Army and its tasks, its corresponding organizational structure must provide as much flexibility as possible, given resources and mission requirements, while also maintaining the mission command necessary to accomplish the following: develop forces; marshal, deploy, and employ those forces; and sustain operations in support of a national strategy.

(2) The Army's organizational design has evolved over time and is continuously being adapted to ensure a goodness of fit between its overall structure and the conditions of the external environment. In essence, the Army exists as an open system and thus must be structured and restructured in such a way as to allow the system to adapt to external factors in the appropriate manner. To facilitate adaptation, the Army organizational system is composed of a combination of decentralized functionally-focused subordinate organizations empowered to adapt and make decisions to effectively and efficiency support or execute mission requirements. The Army system also has a centralized hierarchy designed to establish policies to effect coordination and cooperation between the sub-organizations and ensure cross-functional integration and differentiation.

b. Integration and Differentiation. Every complex and open organization that is functionally organized to allow for decentralized sub-optimization is also challenged with ensuring both the integration of its sub-organizational outputs and continued differentiation of those organizations as they adapt to the external environment. To manage integration and differentiation, organizations need to continuously scan their environment, both internally and externally, in order to best determine the following: the overall tasks and corresponding functional sub-tasks to be accomplished; the resource constraints placed on the organization; the extent of coordination that is needed within the organization in order to make effective and efficient decisions across all tasks and functional sub-tasks; whether accomplishment of new tasks or sub-tasks requires sufficiently unique skills, equipment, activities or management; whether the organization requires creation of a new sub-organization, or should or could be subsumed under an existing functional sub-organization; and the most effective and efficient overall organizational design needed to accomplish those tasks and, most importantly, to ensure the organization can rapidly adapt to future changes within and across the identified functional areas.

(1) Integration. The environments within which the Army competes require one primary output: mission-ready forces with a full range of operational capabilities. The Army is successful only to the extent that it produces such forces. The widely diverse operational environments also require a high degree of differentiation if the Army is to meet its full-spectrum requirements. These two environmental demands—output and high differentiation—must be reconciled, and the Army must integrate many elements to produce mission-ready forces. One should expect that the greater the degree of differentiation in an organization, the more difficult it is to get the necessary coordination and integration. Generally, there are three approaches to integrating diverse organizational activities ranging from the simple to the highly complex: standard rules and procedures; plans, directives, and orders; and active management and directed integration. The use of each of these devices depends on a wide range of situational factors. Each of these devices is operating in any Army organization to some extent, and effective and complex organizations facing dynamic and diverse environments will use all of these integrative processes simultaneously.

(a) The simplest devices that can be used to deal with more certain environments are standard rules and procedures. In these cases, integration is achieved through adherence by the sub-organizations to the specified rules and procedures and active management is normally not required.

(b) Somewhat more complex devices are plans, directives and orders. In these cases, integration is achieved through formulated guidance that specifies for the overall mission each organization's roles, responsibilities, and sub-tasks in time, space and purpose. Coordination and integration is achieved through the coherency of the planning concept and the sub-organization's compliance to both the letter and intent of the plan.

(c) The most complex device is the process of active management and directed integration leading to mutual adjustment in which iterative communication is required within the management hierarchy or chain of command, and which could also entail the formation and use of cross-functional teams or individual integrators. A good example of the last process is the battalion task force approach to integrating and maneuvering the combined arms team after contact with the enemy. A project management organization also exemplifies integration by mutual adjustment.

(2) Differentiation. Organizations should be tailored in design to meet specific mission requirements and avoid unnecessary redundancy. For example, to demonstrate a forward presence in an area of vital interest to U.S. security, such as Europe, and to enhance relations with our allies, the Army has organized U.S. Army, Europe (USAREUR). Conversely, the U. S. Army Recruiting Command (USAREC), which is a major subordinate command of Training and Doctrine Command (TRADOC), was established to deal with the Soldier acquisition task. To accommodate these different demands, the Army's systemic

ARMY ORGANIZATIONAL STRUCTURE

organizational response must be different. USAREUR would be as ineffective recruiting in the continental United States (CONUS) as USAREC would be in dealing with the Army's mission in Europe.

(a) Task or functional specialization is both a dimension and a requirement of the structure of Army organizations. Such functions as personnel management; resource management (e.g., funds and manpower); operations, intelligence and security; logistics; and research and development are found separately identified in both the management staffs and subordinate commands.

(b) A major result of task specialization is that organizations tend to be designed and structured to fit the requirements of their sub-environments. Depending on the demands of the environment, organizations in one functional specialty tend to be differentiated from organizations in other specialties in the following manner: unique functionally-related mission focus; orientation on time and results (e.g., short-term, mid-term, long-term); degree of formality of the structure of organizations (e.g., rules, job descriptions, chain of command, process or procedural adherence); interpersonal orientation and ways of dealing with people (e.g., mission-oriented vs. relationship-oriented).

Section II
The Production Subsystem

3-3. Statutory Requirements
The Army's mission is to fight and win our Nation's wars by providing prompt, sustained land dominance across the full range of military operations in support of the CCDR. We do this through the following processes: executing Title 10 and Title 32 United States Code (USC) directives, to include organizing, equipping, and training forces for the conduct of prompt and sustained combat operations on land; accomplishing missions assigned by the President of the United States (POTUS), Secretary of Defense (SECDEF) and CCDRs; and changing the force to meet current and future demands.

3-4. Production of Needed Resources
The production subsystem is the cornerstone of the process. This subsystem secures resources and raw materials for its many production efforts, to include the following: recruiting untrained personnel; searching for useable technology; and dealing with producers of outside goods and services. Its task, accomplished through its people and structure, is to convert the raw materials into the intermediate goods required by the combat system. To do this, the Army integrates Doctrine, Organizations, Training, Material, Leadership and Education, Personnel, Facilities, and Policy (DOTMLPF-P) to produce the desired end state. Training centers and schools transform untrained people into tank crewmen, infantrymen, and mechanics. Schools convert ideas and knowledge into doctrine, tactics, techniques, and training methods for the use of the combat subsystem. Laboratories, arsenals, and procurement and test organizations convert technology and contractor effort into weapons systems and equipment for the combat subsystem. Other parts of the production subsystem provide such sustaining support to the whole organizational system as health care, commissary support, and other services. The production subsystem serves primarily to meet the needs of the combat subsystem.

a. TRADOC.

(1) TRADOC is the first of two major components of the production subsystem. TRADOC's roles include: develop, educate and train Soldiers, civilians, and leaders; support unit training; and design, build and integrate a versatile mix of capabilities, formations, and equipment to strengthen the U.S. Army as America's force of decisive action. TRADOC is an ACOM consisting of HQ, TRADOC, and six major subordinate centers and commands. All TRADOC centers and schools are aligned under a major subordinate center or command, except the US Army War College (USAWC) and TRADOC Analysis Center (TRAC). The major subordinate centers and commands have direct authority over the centers and schools aligned under them, and are the linkage with non-TRADOC schools.

(2) TRADOC operates 32 Army schools organized under eight Centers of Excellence (CoE), each focused on a separate area of expertise within the Army (e.g., Maneuver, Signal, etc.). These centers train nearly 600,000 Soldiers and service members each year.

(3) The HQ TRADOC staff consists of a command group, personal staff, coordinating staff, and special staff.

(4) The HQ TRADOC staff provides staff management, facilitates external coordination, and assists the Deputy Commanding General/Chief of Staff (DCG/CofS) in the prioritization of resources. It ensures the

HOW THE ARMY RUNS

coordination and integration of DOTMLPF-P initiatives and functions between external commands and organizations and the TRADOC major subordinate centers and commands and special activities. The HQ TRADOC staff is the primary interface with external agencies (e.g., DOD, Headquarters, Department of the Army (HQDA), joint organizations, other services, and other external agencies and organizations) to provide TRADOC positions and receive taskings and requests for support.

(5) TRADOC's major subordinate centers and commands are also functionally aligned:

(a) Army Capabilities Integration Center (ARCIC). ARCIC's four lines of effort (LOE) include: develop concepts and capabilities; evaluate proposed Army modernization solutions; integrate these capabilities across DOTMLPF-P; and communicate with government, industry and Army stakeholders to ensure awareness and understanding of Army modernization priorities. These LOE align to support an agile and adaptive Army that meets current, future, and unexpected requirements of the joint force.

(b) Combined Arms Center (CAC). CAC provides leadership and supervision for leader development and professional military and civilian education; institutional and collective training; functional training; training support; mission command; doctrine; lessons learned; and activities in specified directed areas that serve as a catalyst for change and that support developing relevant and ready expeditionary land formations with campaign qualities in support of the joint force commander.

(c) Combined Arms Support Command (CASC). CASC develops logistics leaders, doctrine, organizations, training, and materiel solutions to sustain a campaign quality Army with joint and expeditionary capabilities in war and peace.

(d) Initial Military Training (IMT) COE. IMT COE conducts Basic Combat Training (BCT), Advanced Individual Training (AIT), One Station Unit Training (OSUT), Warrant Officer Basic Course (WOBC), and the Basic Officer Leader Course (BOLC) in order to transform civilian volunteers into Soldiers who can contribute to their first units of assignment.

(e) U.S. Army Cadet Command (USACC). USACC commissions officers to meet the Army's leadership requirements and provides a citizenship program that motivates young people to be strong leaders and better citizens.

(f) USAREC. USAREC is responsible for manning both the active Army and the U.S. Army Reserve (USAR), ensuring security and readiness for our Nation.

b. Army Materiel Command (AMC). The second major component of the production subsystem is AMC. AMC is the Army's premier provider of materiel readiness—technology, acquisition support, materiel development, logistics power projection, and sustainment—to the total force, across the full spectrum of military operations. If a Soldier shoots it, drives it, flies it, wears it, eats it or communicates with it, AMC provides it.

(1) AMC operates the following organizations: research, development and engineering centers; Army Research Laboratory (ARL); depots; arsenals; ammunition plants; and other facilities. AMC also maintains the Army Pre-Positioned Stocks (APS), both on land and afloat. The command is also the DOD Executive Agent for the chemical weapons stockpile and for conventional ammunition.

(2) To develop, buy and maintain materiel for the Army, AMC works closely with Program Executive Officers (PEO), the Army Acquisition Executive (AAE), industry and academia, the other services, and Other Government Agencies (OGA). AMC handles the majority of the Army's contracting including contracting services for deployed units and installation-level services, supplies and common-use information technology hardware and software.

(3) AMC's main effort is to achieve the development, support, and sustainment of the current and future force. AMC is the key to supporting, sustaining and resetting the current force. Its maintenance depots and arsenals restore weapon systems. The command's overhaul and modernization efforts enhance and upgrade major weapon systems—not just making them like new, but inserting technology to make them more operationally effective and reliable.

(4) AMC handles diverse missions that reach far beyond the Army. For example, AMC manages the multi-billion dollar business of selling Amy equipment and services to friends and allies of the U.S. and negotiates and implements agreement for co-production of U.S. weapons systems by foreign nations. AMC also provides numerous acquisition and logistics services to the other components of DOD and many OGA.

(5) Continuing support across the full spectrum of operations plays a large role in maintaining combat readiness. Perhaps no other organization is faced with such diversity and myriad cross-functional activities. Consequently, AMC is continuously adjusting its organizations to adapt to the changing operational and strategic environments, while ensuring both integration and differentiation of its

ARMY ORGANIZATIONAL STRUCTURE

subordinate organizations' roles, responsibilities and functions. AMC's Major Subordinate Commands (MSCs) include, but are not limited to the following:

(a) Research, Development, and Engineering Command (RDEC). RDEC is concerned with Research and Development (R&D) missions.

(b) Army Sustainment Command (ASC). ASC functions to accomplish the following: manage APS; administer the Logistics Civil Augmentation Program (LOGCAP) and Logistics Assistance Program (LAP), oversee the timely retrograde of war materiel from the theater to Army depots for reset; and support Army operations in strategic locations around the world through seven assigned deployable Army Field Support Brigades (AFSB).

(c) Joint Munitions Command (JMC). JMC provides the conventional ammunition life-cycle functions of logistics sustainment, readiness and acquisition support for all U.S. military services, OGA, and allied nations as directed.

(d) U.S. Army Security Assistance Command (USASAC). USASAC is concerned with security assistance programs to include Foreign Military Sales (FMS).

(e) Army Contracting Command (ACC). ACC provides worldwide contracting support to the war fighter by acquiring equipment, supplies and services vital to our Soldiers' mission and well-being.

(6) The AMC also coordinates directly with the Military Surface Deployment and Distribution Command (SDDC), concerned with ground transportation and port operations. The SDDC is under the Combatant Command (COCOM) of U.S. Transportation Command (USTRANSCOM) and serves as its ASCC. Concurrently, SDDC is also aligned as an MSC of AMC.

(7) AMC's four Life Cycle Management Commands (LCMC)—Aviation and Missile LCMC, Communications-Electronics Command (CECOM) LCMC, Joint Munitions and Lethality (JM&L) LCMC, and TACOM (not an acronym) LCMC—are commodity-oriented and perform life-cycle management over the initial and follow-on procurement and materiel readiness functions for items and weapon systems in support of the Army in the field (see Chap 12 for more detail on LCMCs). As an example, during Calendar Year (CY) 2012, personnel from AMC's LCMCs deployed in support of Operation Enduring Freedom (OEF) to achieve a total cost savings/avoidance valued at more than $393 million. In addition to the direct cost avoidance, money was saved by not having to send replacement parts or equipment to Afghanistan or equipment back to a source of repair in the U.S, thus reducing intra-theater equipment moves.

(8) AMC is headquartered at Redstone Arsenal, Alabama, and impacts or has a presence in all 50 states and 150 countries. Manning these organizations is a work force of more than 70,000 dedicated military and civilian employees, many with highly developed specialties in weapons development, manufacturing and logistics.

c. Installation Operations. Key to the production subsystem is the growing central role of Army installations. The subparagraphs below provide a general discussion and background for installations operations.

(1) The integration of installation organization and operations into the Army's overall organizational structure in the 1980s, both as a home station and training base, has proven to have a significant and positive effect on readiness. Installations are organized for and capable of training, mobilizing, deploying, sustaining, supporting, recovering, and reconstituting assigned and mobilized operating forces. Additionally, activities on the installation receive installation support in accomplishing their missions. Examples of these activities are schools, hospitals, Reserve Component (RC) elements, and tactical HQ and their subordinate units. However, the traditional boundary between tactical and sustaining base activities are disappearing as the installation power projection platforms assume an increasing role in the sustainment, support, and welfare of deploying operating forces. This is also occurring because Information Technology (IT), rapid transportation, and improved management techniques are enabling more consolidated installation activities and reach-back to the installations for deployed forces.

(2) On 24 October 2006, the Army reorganized its structure for managing installations with the activation of U.S. Army Installation Management Command (IMCOM). The Army established IMCOM to reduce bureaucracy, apply a uniform business structure to manage U.S. Army installations, sustain the environment, and enhance the well-being of the military community. IMCOM's mission is to synchronize, integrate, and deliver installation services and sustain facilities in support of senior commanders in order to enable a ready and resilient Army.

(3) IMCOM transformed the Army's installation management structure into an integrated command structure. As a DRU, IMCOM is accountable to the Assistant Chief of Staff for Installation Management

HOW THE ARMY RUNS

(ACSIM) for effective installation management in the following areas: construction; barracks and family housing; family care; food management; environmental programs; well-being; Soldier and family morale, welfare and recreation programs; logistics; public works; and installation funding. This evolution of the installation's role in the Army structure and its placement in the Army's organization has established it as a critical production subsystem of the Army.

d. Functional Commands.

(1) Not only is the installation operations task common to both the combat and production subsystems, but parts of the installation operations function have become recognizable specialty commands—and therefore part of the production subsystem—providing their goods and services usually to both the combat and production subsystems. For example, U. S. Army Medical Command (USMEDCOM) operates most Army medical activities in CONUS; and the U. S. Army Criminal Investigation Command (USACIDC) directs all criminal investigators.

(2) The principal reason for the establishment and continuation of functional commands is that the required degree of integration for their specialty activities differs substantially from those functions that are the responsibility of the installation commander. Each of the specialty functions is a goods or service provider that performs very different missions than those of the installation, whether it is force readiness or training. Mission performance does not require that telephone service, or commissary operations, or medical care delivery is totally integrated with facilities or maintenance so that unit readiness or training objectives can be met. The same is not true of functions like maintenance or personnel support, which more directly affect installation goal achievement.

(3) Further, the conceptual model would suggest that achieving greater performance on the delivery or performance of these functions could best be accomplished by improving the degree of corresponding organizational differentiation. The functional organizational model appears to do just that. The central control reinforces the commitment by the local agency to do the following: high quality, efficient telephone service and medical care; good commissary support; meeting recruiting objectives; and carrying out engineer construction projects. The process is successful because it emphasizes the uniqueness of the function and provides associated specialty career paths for employees.

e. HQDA Support Specialty Commands. Another secondary category of organizations within the producer subsystem is the group of service producing, special-purpose organizations reporting to HQDA. This category includes, among others, Human Resources Command (HRC). It has tasks that do not require field units to produce the service, and therefore does not fall into the functional command category. HRC's services are used by the producer and combat subsystems, as well as HQDA. Because of its specialty tasks, such agencies are directly linked to the HQDA staff, yet they are not classified as extensions to the staff because their functions are operational rather than policy. Most organizations operating in such manner are categorized as FOAs or DRUs. On the other hand, a Staff Support Agency (SSA) directly supports only an Army staff principal, usually with management information, analysis, or command and control support.

(1) A FOA is an agency with the primary mission of executing policy that is under the supervision of HQDA, but not an ACOM, ASCC or DRU. Listed below are the FOAs under the staff principal they support:

(a) Assistant Secretary of the Army (Financial Management and Comptroller) (ASA(FM&C))—U.S. Army Financial Management Command (USAFMCOM)
(b) Assistant Secretary of the Army (Manpower & Reserve Affairs) (ASA(M&RA)):
(i) U.S. Army Diversity and Leadership Office
(ii) U.S. Army Manpower Analysis Agency (USAMAA)
(iii) Army Review Boards Agency (ARBA)
(iv) Army Marketing & Research Group (AMRG)
(c) Office of the Army Auditor General—U.S. Army Audit Agency (USAAA)
(d) Office of the Chief of Public Affairs (OCPA)
(i) U.S. Army Public Affairs Center (APAC)
(ii) U.S Army Field Band
(e) Office of the Administrative Assistant (OAA) to the SECARMY:
(i) U.S. Army Resources and Programs Agency (RPA)
(ii) U.S. Army Headquarters Services (AHS)
(iii) U.S. Army Information Technology Agency (ITA)
(iv) U.S. Army Center of Military History (CMH)

ARMY ORGANIZATIONAL STRUCTURE

(f) Office of the Inspector General (OTIG)—U.S. Army Inspector General Agency (USAIGA)
(g) Office of the Director of the Army Staff (DAS)—U.S. Army Combat Readiness/Safety Center
(h) Office of the Army G-1:
(i) HRC
(ii) U.S. Army Civilian Human Resources Agency (CHRA)
(iii) U.S. Civilian Training Student Education Detachment
(i) Office of the Army G-3/5/7:
(i) U.S. Army Command and Control Support Agency (USACCSA)
(ii) U.S. Army Nuclear and Combating WMD Agency (USANCA)
(iii) U.S. Army Force Management Support Agency (USAFMSA)
(j) Office of the Army G-4—U.S. Army Logistics Innovation Agency (LIA)
(k) Office of the Army G-8—U.S. Center for Army Analysis (CAA)
(l) ACSIM—U.S. Army Installation Support Management Activity (USAISMA)
(m) Office of the Provost Marshal General (OPMG)—Army Corrections Command (ACC)
(n) Office of the Judge Advocate General (OTJAG):
(i) U.S. Army The Judge Advocate General's Legal Center and School (TJAGLCS)
(ii) U.S. Army Legal Services Agency (USALSA)

(2) A DRU is an Army organization comprised of one or more units with institutional or operational functions, designated by the SECARMY, providing broad general support to the Army in a normally, single, unique discipline not otherwise available elsewhere in the Army. DRUs report directly to a HQDA principal and/or ACOM and operate under the authorities established by the SECARMY. Listed below are the twelve HQDA DRUs:
(a) Reporting to Chief of Staff, U.S. Army (CSA):
(i) United States Military Academy (USMA)
(ii) U.S. Army Test and Evaluation Command (ATEC)
(iii) U.S. Army Military District of Washington (MDW)
(b) Reporting to the Executive Director Army National Military Cemetery—Arlington National Cemetery
(c) Reporting to the ASA(M&RA)—U.S. Army Accessions Support Brigade (USAASB)
(d) Reporting to Assistant Secretary of the Army (Acquisition, Logistics, and Technology) (ASA(ALT))—U.S. Army Acquisition Support Center (USAASC)
(e) Reporting to Chief Information Officer (CIO) (Secretariat and Army Staff)—U.S. Army Network Enterprise Technology Command
(f) Reporting to Deputy Chief of Staff, G-2—U.S. Army Intelligence and Security Command (INSCOM)
(g) Reporting to ACSIM—IMCOM
(h) Reporting to The Surgeon General (TSG)—USMEDCOM
(i) Reporting to the Chief of Engineers—U.S. Army Corps of Engineers (USACE)
(j) Reporting to the Provost Marshal General—USACIDC

(3) An example of an SSA is the U.S. Army Environmental Policy Institute (AEPI) that supports the Office of the Assistant Secretary of the Army for Installations, Energy and Environment (ASA(IE&E)).

(4) Comparison of DRUs and FOAs:
(a) DRUs:
(i) A DRU is established by DAGO signed by the SECARMY with its responsibilities contained therein.
(ii) A DRU is operationally oriented. It executes vice develops policy provided by its HQDA principal. It normally has a small headquarters and may lack a robust special staff inherent in an ACOM HQ (e.g., Inspector General (IG), Equal Employment Office (EEO), etc.)
(iii) A DRU may have subordinate units that perform purely operational tasks.
(iv) As stipulated in its DAGO, a DRU may be designated as an Operating Agency (OA) and exercise budget authority. Typically, a DRU submits resource/program requirements to its HQDA principal for programming/budget review and subsequently executes a program/budget approved by the HQDA principal.
(v) A DRU, in collaboration with its HQDA principal, develops appropriate input regarding the use of military and civilian manpower allocated directly by the Office of the ASA(FM&C), and performs its own internal personnel management functions (e.g., requisitions, civilian job classifications and announcements, officer and enlisted distribution plan management). A DRU's manpower and budget are not managed as a part of the HQDA OAA. Because a DRU may perform some functions categorically defined as Management Headquarters Account (MHA) functions in DOD Directive (DODD) 5100.73,

HOW THE ARMY RUNS

individual billets within the DRU headquarters may be classified as reportable Army MHA billets. A DRU is usually independent of OA 22, and therefore not under the management purview of the OAA.
   (b) FOAs:
   (i) A FOA is an agency under the supervision of DA and, like a DRU, has a primary mission of executing policy. However, a FOA has relatively limited scope and responsibilities and does not operate under the authorities established by the SECARMY.
   (ii) FOA manpower and budget are managed as a part of the HQDA OAA.
   (iii) The DAS is the final approving authority for all recommendations to establish, discontinue, increase or decrease FOAs.

Section III
The Combat Subsystem

3-5. Products of the Combat Subsystem
The combat subsystem's major task is to convert the Army's intermediate products, obtained from the production subsystem, into mission-ready forces of units and organizations. Each element of its structure welds together individual Soldiers, equipment, and procedures, and produces combat readiness. The combat subsystem engages in a process of continued interaction with its resource environment, primarily the production and the integrating subsystems. Its task environment includes the enemy threat, the Combatant Commands (CCMD), allied forces with whom it must deal, and, especially in peacetime, the Office of the Secretary of Defense (OSD) and Congress.

3-6. The Army in the Field
   a. This category of the Army's organizational structure consists of three ACOMs, including two of the commands previously addressed under the production subsystem and installation operations, and nine ASCCs.
   (1) An ACOM is an Army force, designated by the SECARMY, performing multiple Army Service Title 10 functions (3013b) across multiple disciplines. Command responsibilities are those established by the SECARMY. The three ACOMs are as follows:
      (a) U.S. Army Forces Command (FORSCOM)
      (b) TRADOC
      (c) AMC
   (2) An ASCC is an Army force designated by the SECARMY, comprised primarily of operational organizations serving as the Army component for a CCDR. If designated by the COCOM, it serves as a Joint Forces Land Component Command (JFLCC) or a Joint Task Force (JTF). Command responsibilities are those established by the SECARMY. The nine ASCCs are as follows:
      (a) U.S. Army Africa/Southern European Task Force (USARAF/SETAF)
      (b) U.S. Army Central (USARCENT)
      (c) U.S. Army North (USARNORTH)
      (d) U.S. Army South (USARSO)
      (e) USAREUR
      (f) U.S. Army Pacific (USARPAC)
      (g) U.S. Army Special Operations Command (USASOC)
      (h) SDDC
      (i) U.S. Army Space and Missile Defense Command/Army Strategic Command (USASMDC/ARSTRAT)
   b. In some respects, each command faces similar environments although they differ from each other in many ways. Several commands (e.g., FORSCOM, USAREUR, USARPAC, USASOC, and USARSO) have the principal task of providing mission-ready land forces—the primary output of the Army. As a result, each has developed an organizational structure reflecting its environment.

Section IV
The Integrating Subsystem

3-7. Tasks of the Integrating Subsystem

ARMY ORGANIZATIONAL STRUCTURE

a. The integrating subsystem ties all of the subordinate subsystems together for the Army as a whole. Its tasks are to decide what is to be produced or accomplished by the whole system, and to see to it that the system performs as expected. It also acts as the source of funds for the subsystems, obtaining them from DOD, Office of Management and Budget (OMB), and Congress.

b. In any large organization, the HQ has the major function to see to it that the overall mission and major tasks of the organization are accomplished. It is the most prominent integrating device in the organization. The challenge for the integrating subsystem is one of structuring the organization to accomplish the following tasks effectively:

(1) Determine the nature of current and future demands and requirements from the strategic and operational environments (e.g., from guidance from the Executive Branch and Congress, social trends, joint and other service developments, new or different external and domestic threats, technological opportunities, expanded or new domains (e.g., air, cyber, space, etc.), changes in the nature and form of war, increased resource constraints, etc.).

(2) Chart a course for the Army that can and will meet the projected demands/requirements.

(3) Secure the necessary resources (e.g., appropriations authority) for the Army.

(4) Allocate resources, responsibilities, objectives and performance requirements to the combat and production subsystems.

(5) Evaluate the performance of the subsystems' organizations against the requirements.

(6) Bring about change, whether evolutionary or revolutionary, in cases where performance does not meet present requirements, or the projected security needs of the nation require.

(7) Transform the Army to future force structure organizations in order to meet the National Security and Military Strategies.

3-8. Integration and Differentiation

The exercise of these functions calls for both cross-functional integration and a high degree of differentiation within the HQ. Each function must relate to a similar functional group in OSD, to some extent to interested committees in Congress, and to members of the same specialist community in the combat and production subsystems. Figure 3-1 reflects the current HQDA Organization.

HOW THE ARMY RUNS

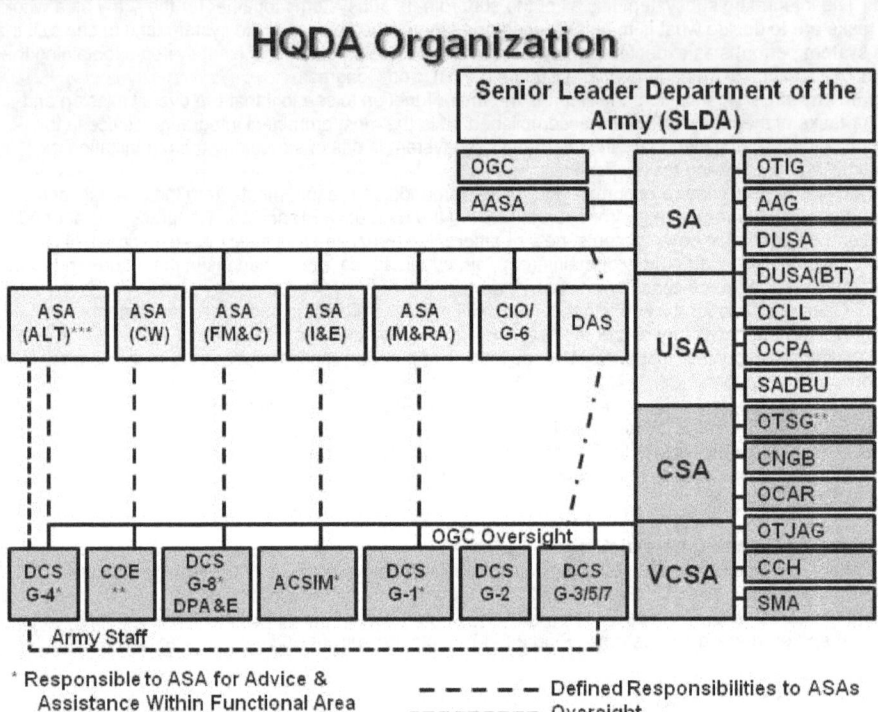

* Responsible to ASA for Advice & Assistance Within Functional Area
** Direct Reporting Unit (DRU) Commander
*** Army Acquisition Executive (AAE)

– – – – Defined Responsibilities to ASAs
– – – – – Oversight
– · – · – Director of the Army Staff (DAS)— Synchronize, Integrate

AASA: Administrative Assistant to the Secretary of the Army
AAG: Army Auditor General
ACSIM: Assistant Chief of Staff, Installation Management
ASA(ALT): Assistant Secretary of the Army for Acquisition, Logistics and Technology
ASA(CW): Assistant Secretary of the Army for Civil Works
ASA(FM&C): Assistant Secretary of the Army for Financial Management and Comptroller
ASA(I&E): Assistant Secretary of the Army for Installations and Environment
ASA(M&RA): Assistant Secretary of the Army for Manpower and Reserve Affairs
CCH: Chief of Chaplains
CIO/G-6: Chief Information Officer
COE: Chief of Engineers
CSA: Chief of Staff of the Army
CNGB: Chief, National Guard Bureau
DAS: Director of the Army Staff
DPAE: Director, Program Analysis & Evaluation
DRU: Direct Reporting Unit
DUSA(BT): Deputy Under Secretary of the Army for Business Transformation
OCAR: Chief, Army Reserve
OCLL: Chief, Legislative Liaison
OCPA: Chief, Public Affairs
OGC: General Counsel
OTIG: The Inspector General
OTJAG: The Judge Advocate General
OTSG: The Surgeon General
SA: Secretary of the Army
SADBU: Small and Disadvantaged Business Utilization Office
SMA: Sergeant Major of the Army
USA: Under Secretary of the Army
VCSA: Vice Chief of Staff of the Army

Figure 3-1. Headquarters, Department of the Army (HQDA) Organization

ARMY ORGANIZATIONAL STRUCTURE

a. Achieving Integration.

(1) Integration is achieved in a formal series of meetings at the senior staff level within the Army Secretariat (ARSEC) and the Army Staff (ARSTAF). The heads of the staff agencies, the deputy chiefs of staff themselves, have a principal integrating role, serving more as a corporate management committee than as simply representatives of their own staff agencies. There are also many task forces, working groups, and committees with membership drawn from throughout the ARSEC and ARSTAF that serve as important knowledge-based integrators.

(2) Integration is also the primary function of the Army's senior leadership, to include: the SECARMY; Under Secretary of the Army (USA); CSA; and VCSA. This group decides on management strategies for stability, modernization of equipment, allocation of scarce resources, and force structure issues. These strategies, enunciated in the annual Army Posture Statement (APS), are unifying, integrating statements of objectives that relate directly to the dominant overall issue—maintaining mission-ready forces.

(3) The annual APS, available through the U.S. Army Home Page at http://www.army.mil is an unclassified summary of Army roles, missions, accomplishments, plans, and programs. Designed to reinforce the SECARMY and CSA posture and budget testimony before Congress, the APS serves a broad audience as a basic reference on the state of the Army.

b. Achieving Differentiation.

(1) Differentiation is achieved through the assignment of functional responsibilities to the HQDA directorates and the HQDA special and personal staff sections. It is within the directorates that assigned tasks such as recruiting, planning, or budgeting are managed, goals are formulated, timing coordinated, and sub-organizational hierarchy and protocols established. The directorates possess knowledge and experience sufficient for most decisions that concern their task environments.

(2) It is important at HQDA that the requirements of the associated functional environments are communicated and analyzed. This includes both upward relationships—with OSD, OMB, and congressional committee staffers—and downward relationships with the subordinate organizations. The senior leadership of the Army has a large influence on goal-setting and performance evaluation for the whole functional or specialty community within the Army and a similar influence on getting the needed resources from OSD, OMB, and Congress.

c. Horizontal Differentiation in HQDA.

(1) Part of the past debate on HQDA reorganization was the belief that the structure of HQDA actually complicates the achievement of the required differentiation and performance. The criticism focused on the functional parts of the ARSEC and ARSTAF directorates which seemed to perform duplicate activities or have overlapping responsibilities. The *Goldwater-Nichols DOD Reorganization Act of 1986* required the integration of the two staffs into a single HQDA comprised of a Secretariat focused on managing the business of the Army and the CSA and deputy chiefs of staff responsible for planning, developing, executing, reviewing, and analyzing Army programs. The Army has continued to increase the integration of HQDA with the creation of the Executive Office of the HQDA, subsequently re-designated as Senior Leaders of the Department of the Army (SLDA), which increased administrative oversight by the DAS of both the ARSEC and ARSTAFF and required closer staff relationships.

(2) To achieve greater differentiation in acquisition management, Congress directed and placed into law that the service acquisition executive functions be placed within the service secretariats. Accordingly, the SECARMY appointed the ASA(ALT) as the AAE to centrally manage this function.

(3) As another example, the ACC's subordinate Expeditionary Contracting Command (ECC) now centralizes the Army's previously decentralized contracting outside CONUS. In FY2011 alone, the ECC executed more than 49,000 contract actions worth almost $1.9 billion through seven contracting support brigades, eight contingency contracting battalions, and 83 contingency contracting teams throughout the world.

(4) Similarly, the Army differentiates functions and tasks vertically. Efficiency and effectiveness demand that organizations eliminate any level that does not perform essential and unique tasks or perform critical integrating functions. The Army executes unique Title 10 functions and tasks and produces value-added outputs at the strategic, operational and tactical levels.

HOW THE ARMY RUNS

Section V
Strategy to Army Organizational Structure

3-9. Strategy
From the perspective of the Army Force Management Model (Figure 2-2), the start point for determining Army organizational design and structure is strategy.
   a. At the National level, strategy is directed by such documents as the National Security Strategy (NSS), Defense Strategic Guidance (DSG), and National Military Strategy (NMS).
   b. At the Army Level, the Army vision and strategy is depicted in the Army Strategic Planning Guidance (ASPG), which is part of The Army Plan (TAP). Also part of TAP is the Army Campaign Plan (ACP), which maps the Lines of Operation (LOO) the Army will pursue to manage change and achieve required future capabilities.

3-10. Concepts
   a. At the joint level, concepts are directed by such documents as the Capstone Concept for Joint Operations (CCJO), and further described by Joint Concepts (JC) and Joint Capability Areas (JCA), all of which provide direction for change.
   b. Finally, regarding Army concepts, the Army Capstone Concept (ACC), Army Operating Concept (AOC), and Army Functional Concepts (AFC) focus that direction for the Army. These concepts provide both a vision of the future operational environment and a cohesive description of how the Army intends to operate to prevail in that environment. By comparing current Army organizations and capabilities with those required by these future concepts, the Army can then develop plans and programs across the DOTMLPF-P domains to continuously modify its organizational structure to prevail in future wars.

Section VI
Summary and References

3-11. Summary
   a. This chapter presents a theoretical construct for the organizational design and structure of the Army by looking at the Army as an open organizational system composed of a production, combat, and integrating subsystem.
   b. This chapter presents the details of each subsystem's major components, organizations, roles, missions, and functions, to include the ACOMs, ASCCs, DRUs, and FOAs.
   c. Finally, this chapter examines the two defining characteristics of functional differentiation and integration.

3-12. References
   a. Army Regulation 10-5, HQDA
   b. Army Regulation 10-87, ACOMs, ASCCs, and DRUs
   c. Army Regulation 10-88, FOAs, Office of the Chief of Staff, Army
   d. Army Regulation 570-4, Manpower Management
   e. DAGO 2012-01, Assignment of Functions and Responsibilities Within HQDA
   f. DOD Reorganization Act of 1986 (Goldwater-Nichols)
   g. Joint Publication 1-02, DOD Dictionary of Military and Associated Terms

THE RELATIONSHIP OF JOINT AND ARMY PLANNING

Chapter 4

The Relationship of Joint and Army Planning

Joint matters, as identified in Public Law 99-433, Goldwater-Nichols Department of Defense Reorganization Act of 1986, are defined as "... matters relating to the integrated employment of land, sea, and air forces."

Section I
Introduction

4-1. Chapter Content
The 1986 Goldwater-Nichols Act profoundly changed the relationships among the Services and with the organizations of the Office of the Secretary of Defense (OSD), the Combatant Commands (CCMDs), and the Joint Chiefs of Staff (JCS). The Chairman of the Joint Chiefs of Staff (CJCS) and JCS were given additional responsibilities, the Combatant Commanders (CCDRs) were given greater authority and responsibilities to execute their missions, and Services and OSD realigned specific responsibilities and made organizational changes to include some that involved greater civilian oversight and control. This chapter addresses the processes used within the Department of Defense (DOD), the JCS, the CCMDs, and the Army to determine the joint capabilities and associated force levels required to meet the U.S. national security and military strategies and to fulfill CCMDs requirements. These processes also determine the capabilities that need to be resourced by Services' programs within the Planning, Programming, Budgeting, and Execution (PPBE) process and provide the basis for DOD's Future Years Defense Program (FYDP). While the emphasis of this entire text is on the Army management systems, it is first necessary to understand the relationships and processes of DOD, the JCS, and the CCMDs to the Army. Hence, this chapter provides more of a joint perspective to better appreciate and apply information in other chapters in this text. It is important to remember that the Army has significant input to the joint processes that support the development of requirements, programs, and budgets, as well as the CJCS's strategic planning system.

4-2. Secretary of Defense (SECDEF)
The SECDEF provides both formal and informal guidance to the Services, CCMDs, and Defense Agencies. The SECDEF's formal guidance is provided in two broad strategy documents called the National Defense Strategy (NDS) and the Quadrennial Defense Review (QDR). Additionally, in support of the President of the United States' (POTUS') strategic direction to DOD, the SECDEF released a new Defense Strategic Guidance (DSG) document in January 2012 called, Sustaining U.S. Leadership: Priorities for 21st Century Defense.

    a. The NDS, while not required under Title 10 United States Code (USC), was previously a capstone document for providing strategic guidance throughout DOD. Signed by the SECDEF, the document was designed to take the national goals and objectives delineated in the National Security Strategy (NSS) signed by the POTUS and turn them into DOD objectives and goals. The document was previously used to guide the formulation of the QDR required by Congress, other DOD strategy documents, and informed the development of the Chairman's National Military Strategy (NMS). The first NDS was published in 2005, and the second one was published in 2008. It provides a framework for other strategic guidance on campaign and contingency planning, force development, and intelligence, while addressing how the Armed Forces would fight and win the nation's wars and work with partner nations to enhance security and avert conflict. Most specifically, it identifies the defense objectives and ways to achieve those objectives, while identifying a risk framework. The QDR, mentioned above, has been used to either identify ways to implement the NDS or to identify a new defense strategy with its key components, as was done in the 2010 QDR. Specifically, the 2010 QDR identified new defense strategy objectives, main elements of the Services' force structure, as well as a series of enhancements and initiatives in specific capability areas. It appears that the NDS will not be published again, since the QDR and DSG accomplish the same purpose and in recent Pentagon briefings the NDS is not referenced.

HOW THE ARMY RUNS

b. The QDR, required under Title 10 USC, Section 118, occurs every four years. The QDR presents "ends" through defense objectives, "ways" through key missions, and "means" through force structure guidance. The QDR is conducted in consultation with the CJCS and constitutes a comprehensive examination of the strategic environment, defense objectives, force structure, force modernization, infrastructure, resource challenges, and other elements of the defense program. The QDR directly influences the defense program for the next decade as decisions are resourced. The QDR also defines the nature and magnitude of the political, strategic, and military risks associated with executing the missions called for under the defense strategy. The QDR is submitted to the Senate and House of Representatives Armed Services Committees within approximately a year after the QDR review process begins within OSD.

c. The DSG Sustaining U.S. Leadership: Priorities for 21st Century Defense was published in January 2012 and describes the projected security environment and those key military missions for which DOD will prepare for to achieve national interests. It identified the priorities that sustain U.S. global leadership in the 21st Century, and "it is intended as a blueprint for the Joint Force in 2020, providing a set of precepts that will help guide decisions regarding the size and shape of the force over future program and budget cycles." Additionally, the strategy highlights some of the strategic risks that could be associated with this transition, and states that the United States will, of necessity, rebalance to the Asia-Pacific region. The 2012 DSG identified 10 priority missions and major tenets, while stating that: "This country is at a strategic turning point after a decade of war and, therefore, we are shaping a Joint Force for the future that will be smaller and leaner but will be more agile, flexible, ready, and technologically advanced."

4-3. Other DOD Strategic Guidance

The DOD changed the format for its guiding documents by merging many strategic-level planning documents into two key documents: the Guidance for Employment of the Force (GEF) and the Defense Planning Guidance (DPG).

a. The GEF, which is considered both a POTUS and SECDEF document, meets the responsibilities for providing guidance for force employment identified in Title 10 USC, and is published every two years or as needed. The GEF is a classified document that translates national security objectives and high-level strategy in the NSS and QDR into DOD priorities and comprehensive planning direction. The GEF provides guidance that identifies how the military forces should be used, and it influences current operations and the current planning process. The GEF includes: strategic assumptions (theater or functional) for campaign planning; prioritized contingency planning scenarios and end states and global posture; security cooperation; and Global Force Management (GFM) guidance and priorities. The GEF also includes the Force Allocation Decision Model (FADM) and the Nuclear Weapons Planning Guidance. A companion document produced by the CJCS that uses guidance in the GEF to provide more specific advice to geographic and functional CCDRs is the Joint Strategic Capabilities Plan (JSCP).

b. The DPG meets the responsibilities for providing resource advice by the SECDEF identified under Title 10 USC and is currently published annually. This classified document, signed by the SECDEF, establishes the DOD resourcing priorities and consolidates and integrates DOD force development planning priorities. The DPG translates the defense strategy into specific planning, programming, and budgeting priorities for the FYDP, thus aligning capabilities with priorities and resources. The DPG provides planning and programming guidance by establishing DOD's priority missions, force sizing construct, force planning assumptions, and key capabilities to size and shape the Joint Force. The DPG also provides strategic guidance for internal audiences to achieve the goals and priorities established in the defense strategy.

4-4. CJCS

The CJCS, by Title 10 USC, is the principal military advisor to the POTUS, the SECDEF, the National Security Council (NSC), and the Homeland Security Council (HSC). The CJCS is required under the law to: assist the POTUS and SECDEF in providing strategic direction; conduct strategic planning; advise on preparedness of the Armed Forces; advise on requirements, programs, and budgets; and develop joint doctrine. The CJCS was required by Congress in 2004 to produce every even year a detailed report that reviewed the current NMS to include the strategic and military risks to execute that strategy, and during every odd year, the CJCS was to produce an assessment of the strategic and military risks associated with executing the current NMS.

THE RELATIONSHIP OF JOINT AND ARMY PLANNING

4-5. Joint Strategic Planning System (JSPS)
The JSPS was significantly revised in December 2008 to provide an integrated assessment, advice, and direction system to better enable the CJCS to assess the strategic environment, provide comprehensive military advice, and provide unified direction to the Armed Forces. The JSPS is the means by which the CJCS can, in the larger cycle of strategic planning by DOD, provide the assessments, advice, and direction to execute his responsibilities identified, both broadly and specifically, in Title 10 USC. Through the JSPS, the CJCS can conduct the comprehensive assessments needed to provide the statutory advice to the POTUS, SECDEF, NSC, HSC, and Congress. The JSPS provides the CJCS a formal planning system to assist the POTUS and the SECDEF with unified direction to the Armed Forces (see Figure 4.1).

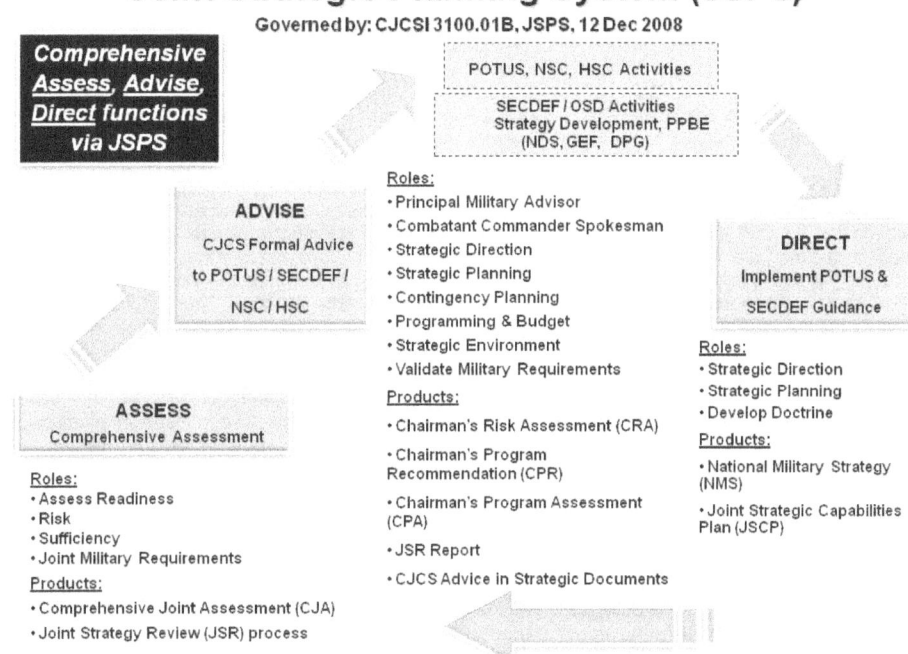

Figure 4-1. Joint Strategic Planning System (JSPS)

4-6. JSPS Overview
The three major components of the JSPS that address the CJCS's statutory responsibilities are: the CJCS's Assessment; the CJCS's Advice; and the CJCS's Direction. A way to envision these three major components is in Figure 4-1, which comes from the CJCS's 2008 instruction. While these three major components and the associated products are more fully discussed later, a brief summary of them provides broad context to appreciate this strategic planning system and its integrated nature.
 a. The CJCS's Assessment comes from both deliberate and continuous assessments to understand the security environment and its influence on the military in a variety of ways. These assessments focus on such topics as global trends, challenges, readiness, risk, sufficiency, and joint military requirements. The main formal products as a result of this assessment component are the Comprehensive Joint Assessment (CJA) and the Joint Strategy Review (JSR) process. Furthermore, there are various insights

HOW THE ARMY RUNS

associated from the CJCS's readiness system that are incorporated within these two formal products when appropriate.

b. The CJCS's Advice is a principal statutory requirement of the Chairman and is designed to provide independent military advice to the senior leadership to assist in their development of strategy, guidance, and policy. The key formal strategic planning products as a result of this advice component are the Chairman's Risk Assessment (CRA), Chairman's Program Recommendation (CPR), Chairman's Program Assessment (CPA), and JSR Report. While the NMS is not portrayed in Figure 4-1 as an advice document, as it is primary under the direct focus, it has an advice component associated with its assessment and implications of the strategic environment and ways the military can accomplish national security and defense strategy goals. The CJCS also provides advice in other strategic documents as needed to fulfill his statutory responsibilities.

c. The CJCS's Direction provides strategic direction on behalf of the POTUS and SECDEF to implement their guidance associated with the roles of strategic direction, strategic planning, and developing doctrine. The two formal products associated with these roles are the NMS and JSCP. The NMS provides broad direction and identifies objectives to the Armed Forces to support the National Security and Defense strategies. The JSCP provides guidance to CCDRs, Service Chiefs, Combat Support Agency Directors, Defense Agencies, and DOD Field Activity Directors to accomplish tasks and missions based on near-term capabilities. The JSCP implements planning guidance reflected in the GEF to provide specific direction as to the types of plans needed.

4-7. Army Participation in Joint Planning and Resourcing Processes

The Army participates fully in the strategic planning and resource processes. The Army Staff (ARSTAF) supports the SECDEF and Chief of Staff, U.S. Army (CSA) by participating in various ways in working groups associated with the QDR. The ARSTAF supports the CSA in his role as a member of the JCS by performing analyses and providing inputs to the JSPS. The ARSTAF supports the Vice Chief of Staff, U.S. Army (VCSA), in the role as a member of the Joint Requirements Oversight Council (JROC) and the Deputy's Management Action Group (DMAG), formerly known as the Deputies Advisory Working Group, by direct participation in the capabilities assessment process. The ARSTAF supports the SECDEF as a member of the Defense Resources Board (DRB) and DMAG by participating in JSPS, QDR, and JROC, and by performing additional analyses as required in support of the development of the DSG. In essence, the ARSTAF has developed parallel processes to provide the Army's perspective to these defense and joint systems and processes both at the working and general officer levels. Most of the outcomes of these efforts that affect the Army are then codified in The Army Plan (TAP), or more specifically in The Army Campaign Plan (ACP).

a. GFM is designed to integrate force apportionment, assignment, and allocation methodologies in support of the defense strategy and joint force availability requirements. It provides the comprehensive insights into the global availability of U.S. military forces and provides the senior decision makers a process to assess quickly and accurately the impact and risk of proposed changes in forces / capability assignment, apportionment, and allocation. GFM is designed to transform a reactive force management process into a more near-real-time, proactive process.

b. As specified in Title 10 USC and as identified in the Unified Command Plan (UCP) and the Forces For memorandum, forces are assigned to CCMDs. Forces are generally apportioned by the CJCS based on the GEF provided by the SECDEF and POTUS. Allocation of forces is the authority that resides with the SECDEF and POTUS. GFM integrates these two main responsibilities into a single overarching process. The two major elements are the Global Force Management Board (GFMB) and the Joint Force Providers (JFPs). The GFMB is chaired by the Director of the Joint Staff with advice from the other Joint Staff Directors and Services Operations Deputies. The GFMB provides overarching guidance for the process and reviews recommendations to be presented to the CJCS and SECDEF. The Army G-3, or a designated general officer from G3/5/7, represents the Army in making recommendations for final outcomes of this process that result in decisions by the SECDEF and the POTUS as to force assignment, allocation, and apportionment. The JFPs recommend solutions for Request for Forces (RFF) or Request for Capabilities (RFC) submitted by the CCDRs. The JFPs are responsible for recommending and developing risk assessments for conventional forces, special operating forces, mobility forces, and strategic and intelligence / surveillance / reconnaissance forces. The final outcome of GFM is the production of deployment orders and execution orders, which are primarily processed through the Joint Staff before being signed by the SECDEF.

THE RELATIONSHIP OF JOINT AND ARMY PLANNING

Section II
Joint Strategic Planning System

4-8. JSPS
   a. The CJCS is charged with preparing strategic plans and with assisting the POTUS and the SECDEF in providing strategic direction to the Armed Forces. The JSPS and the GFM Process, as prescribed by CJCS Instruction (CJCSI) 3100.01B and the SECDEF's Global Force Management Implementation Guidance (GFMIG), provide the framework for strategic planning and formulating strategic direction of the Armed Forces. Joint strategic planning informs the process to create the forces and associated capabilities that are then allocated to CCDRs for their planning. Since the capabilities integration and development process is essential to many of the formal strategic planning products and processes, CJCSI 3170.01E, which covers this Joint Capabilities Integration and Development System (JCIDS), helps to validate and prioritize joint warfighting requirements. JCIDS is also a key supporting process for DOD acquisition and PPBE processes. A primary objective of the JCIDS and associated processes is to ensure that the Joint Force receives the capabilities required to successfully execute the missions assigned to them. The Capstone Concept for Joint Operations (CCJO): Joint Force 2020, published in September 2012, describes potential operational concepts to guide joint force development to achieve those missions identified in the 2012 SECDEF's DSG.
   b. Within the Joint Staff, strategic planning is primarily the responsibility of the Strategic Plans and Policy Directorate, J-5, and capabilities and resources are primarily the focus of the Force Structure, Resources, and Assessment Directorate, J-8. They use input from the Joint Staff, OSD, other DOD and Defense Agencies, CCMDs, and the Services to assist in formulating policy, developing strategy, and providing force planning guidance. The Adaptive Planning Roadmap II and the review and approval of operations plans, reside with the Joint Force Development Directorate, J-7, and Operations Directorate, J-3. All of the above mentioned Joint Staff Directors are members of the GFMB. Furthermore, the J-1, J-4, and J-6 Directorates have responsibilities for providing direction to specific Functional Capabilities Boards (FCB). Hence, all elements of the Joint Staff work together to fully execute these processes in an integrated manner.
   c. The JSPS constitutes a continuing process in which formal products on a specific cycle such as the JSCP or other focused assessments or studies are produced as required to provide this formal direction. Some of these products provide specific direction, while others provide formal advice or shape the informal advice from the CJCS. For example, while not a formal strategic planning document identified in the CJCS's strategic planning instruction, the Chairman's Strategic Direction to the Joint Force (CSDJF) published in February 2012, provided broad advice to the four following areas: achieve our national objectives in current conflicts; develop Joint Force 2020; renew our commitment to the profession of Army; and keep faith with our military family. The CJCS uses this planning system to give him the formal ability to execute his Title 10 USC responsibilities to conduct continuous strategic assessments, assess risk, provide statutory and personal advice to the POTUS and SECDEF, develop strategic plans, and provide strategic direction to the Armed Forces.

4-9. CJCS's Assessments
The CJCS's Assessments are a major component of the JSPS. These assessments consist of obtaining and analyzing data concerning: the nature of the strategic environment; U.S. and allies' ability to operate and influence that environment; adversaries' and potential enemies' ability to operate and influence that environment; and the risk to the national strategies over the near-, mid- and far-term.
   a. The CJA is a deliberate process intended to reduce redundancy and facilitate integrated comprehensive CCMD, Service, and Joint Staff analysis. The CJA survey requests assessments from the Service Chiefs and CCMDs relating to statutory and UCP responsibilities in support of the NMS. The CJA primarily focuses on qualitative inputs. It also includes an assessment of the security environment, current operations, health of the force, near-term risk, and future-force implications. Further, the CJA draws on other assessments such as the Joint Combat Capability Assessment (JCCA), Defense Readiness Reporting System (DRRS), inputs related to Global Force Management process, and Service and CCDR Assessments. The CJCS uses these assessments to: formulate military advice to the POTUS and SECDEF on strategic direction for the Armed Forces; identify the most important military

issues; reconcile issues and requirements across Services and CCMDs; provide input to DOD processes; and provide information for Congressional reports.

　b. As CCMD Campaign Plans are developed and approved as directed by the JSCP and the GEF, assessments of those plans will become a part of the CJA. Until the plans are fully developed, Campaign Assessments will be incorporated in the CJA survey.

　c. The JSR process provides an analytical framework that looks in depth at a variety of CJCS's products to include strategic documents, directives, instructions, and memorandums. The JSR provides the synthesis of the CJA and the Joint Staff's functional estimates and processes. The components of the JSR process include: Joint Intelligence Estimate; Joint Strategic Assessment; JSR Report; Capability Gap Assessment; Joint Concept Development and Experimentation (CD&E); Joint Logistics Estimate; Joint Personnel Estimate/Health Force Metrics; CRA; and Operational Availability Studies.

4-10. CJCS's Advice
A major statutory responsibility of the CJCS is to provide military and strategic advice to the POTUS, SECDEF, NSC, and HSC. By providing formal advice, the CJCS enhances his ability to assist the nation's leadership in developing national security and defense strategies, as well as programs and budgets to execute those strategies.

　a. The CJCS's advice is developed using the information provided through the CJA and the analysis resulting from the JSR process, as well as the various ways readiness is assessed. The readiness component is covered in Chapter 8.

　b. The CJCS's formal advice provides National Security, Defense, and Agency staffs with a framework and military baseline for strategic policy and guidance, as well as provide direction for developing Joint Staff assessments and recommendations. More specifically, the CJCS's advice assists the POTUS, the SECDEF, and their staffs in the formulation of the NSS, DSG, Program Budget Review, GEF, DPG, QDR, and Service strategies.

　c. The CJCS's formal advice includes the following four documents: CPR; CPA; CRA; and JSR. As mentioned earlier, parts of the NMS also provide advice. Each of these five formal documents is briefly discussed below. Furthermore, the CJCS provides advice from various Chairman's briefings, Council Membership, and other formal correspondence and guidance statements.

　　(1) The CPR is initially developed under the leadership of the JROC using the FCB process to provide the CJCS's personal programmatic advice to the SECDEF. The CPR is also influenced by capability gap assessments, CCDR Integrated Priority Lists, and readiness reviews. Issues initially developed by the JROC for this advice are provided to CCDRs, Service Chiefs, and Joint Staff Directors as the CJCS considers these comments before finalizing his recommendations. This advice is designed to influence the SECDEF's DPG before it is published.

　　(2) The CPA is initially developed under the leadership of the JROC using the FCB process to shape the CJCS's personal advice and assessment of Service and Defense Agency Program Objective Memorandums (POMs) and Budget Estimate Submissions (BESs) to the SECDEF to influence the Program Budget Review (PBR). Again, after the initial development of this advice, the CJCS gains direct input from CCDRs, Joint Chiefs, and Joint Staff Directors before he finalizes it. This advice is used within various Pentagon meetings associated with translating the Services and Defense Agency POMs into the final DOD budget submission sent to Congress by the POTUS.

　　(3) The requirement for the CRA is contained in Title 10 USC in those sections requiring the CJCS to assess the nature and magnitude of the strategic and military risk to missions called for under the NMS and to confer with the CCDRs and Service Chiefs to provide that advice. This risk assessment is accomplished every year by the CJCS and is first transmitted to the SECDEF. The SECDEF is then required to transmit the report to Congress with the SECDEF's comments, and if that risk with executing the NMS is determined significant, the SECDEF shall include a plan for mitigating that risk.

　　(4) The JSR report, which is a classified document, is produced biennially or as required from the JSR review process described earlier in the assessment part of the strategic planning system. The report can be focused on particular subjects or on broad strategic environment assessment topics as determined by the CJCS.

　　(5) Primarily, the NMS provides strategic direction to the Armed Forces, but it also provides the CJCS's formal military advice on the global strategic environment. It identifies the military's best approach to accomplishing the interests and goals identified in the NSS and QDR. Using guidance from these two documents, the 2011 NMS identified the following four national military objectives: counter violent

THE RELATIONSHIP OF JOINT AND ARMY PLANNING

extremism; deter and defeat aggression; strengthen international and regional security; and shape the future force.

4-11. CJCS's Direction
The CJCS assists the POTUS and the SECDEF in providing unified strategic direction to the Armed Forces. He assists them with execution of their command function and performs directive functions, which Title 10 specifies, and includes planning, joint doctrine, education, and training. The CJCS's formal direction is executed through issuance of two primary documents, which are the NMS and the JSCP.

 a. Formal strategic direction is generally executed annually or biennially depending on the guidance, as the components of JSPS are sequenced to best support the formulation of key strategic documents and are integrated within SECDEF processes. However, formal strategic direction can occur as needed, as was previously discussed regarding the CSDJF published in 2012. The development of strategic direction begins with the issuance of CJCS's advice in key documents. The CJCS's advice informs the National Security and Defense Strategy developers and provides the military baseline for staff interaction and the development of critical work such as the NSS and QDR.

 b. The strategic direction by the CJCS comes from a collaborative effort requiring extensive coordination. The CJCS provides advice and recommendations to influence the NSS, NDS, DSG, DPG, GEF, UCP, Quadrennial Role and Missions Reviews (QRMs), and the QDR. While the CJCS issues many CJCS instructions and memorandums to provide strategic direction, the NMS and the JSCP are the two key formal direction documents signed by the CJCS and produced under the JSPS.

 (1) The NMS sets priorities and focuses the efforts of the Armed Forces, while providing the CJCS's advice on the security environment and necessary military capabilities to protect the nation's interests. Based on the NSS and QDR, the NMS provides the guidance that CCDRs use to employ the Joint Force to protect the nation's interest, and the Service Chiefs use to develop capabilities that support the Joint Force. The NMS provides military objectives to CCDRs and Service Chiefs, derived from the NSS and the QDR. The NMS provides the CJCS's advice on the strategic environment, the implications of that environment, and the best way to accomplish the objectives of the NSS and QDR. The NMS states the Joint Force's resolve to defend the American people and the nation's vital interests, while achieving the national and defense objectives. The NMS forms the basis for the advice in the CRA that is provided annually to the Congress.

 (2) The JSCP provides guidance to accomplish tasks and missions based on near-term military capabilities to CCDRs, Service Chiefs, Directors of the Combat Support Agencies, and applicable Defense Agency and DOD Field Activities Directors. The JSCP implements campaign, campaign support, contingency, and posture planning guidance from the GEF. The JSCP implements the objectives in the NSS and NDS through the resulting CCMD campaign and contingency plans. The JSCP provides a coherent framework for military planning advice from the POTUS and SECDEF and follows, implements, and augments POTUS and SECDEF guidance provided in the DSG, GEF, UCP, and the GFMIG. The JSCP provides the following: strategic planning direction; detailed planning guidance, force apportionment guidance, assumptions, and tasks; tasks for the CCDRs to prepare campaign, campaign support, contingency, and posture plans; and establishment of the synchronizing, supported, and supporting relationships.

4-12. JROC
Due to a recent change in Title 10 USC, the Vice CJCS (VCJCS) now chairs the JROC. Other formal members of the JROC are selected by the CJCS after consultation with the SECDEF, who are in the grade of General or Admiral that are recommended by their military departments. In addition, CCDRs now have a standing invitation to attend JROC sessions in an advisory role when matters related to their area of responsibility or functions are considered. Historically, the JROC has consisted of the VCJCS, the Vice Chiefs of Staff of the Army and Air Force, Vice Chief of Naval Operations, and the Assistant Commandant of the Marine Corps. In addition, the following DOD civilian officials now serve as advisors to the JROC on matters of their authority and expertise: the Under Secretary of Defense (Comptroller); the Under Secretary of Defense Acquisition, Technology, and Logistics (AT&L); the Director of Cost Assessment and Performance Evaluation (CAPE); the Under Secretary of Defense for Policy; and the Director of Operational Test and Evaluation. Other civilian officials within DOD can also advise the JROC as designated by the Secretry of Defense. Furthermore, FCB participating organizations have a standing invitation to attend JROC-related meetings in an advisory role to the JROC Chairman. The CJCSI that

HOW THE ARMY RUNS

covers this organization's functions and membership is 5123.01F. This instruction identifies those key Title 10 functions associated with the CJCS with which they assist, thus enabling him to execute these specific responsibilities as well as other duties in five broad areas (see Figure 4-2).

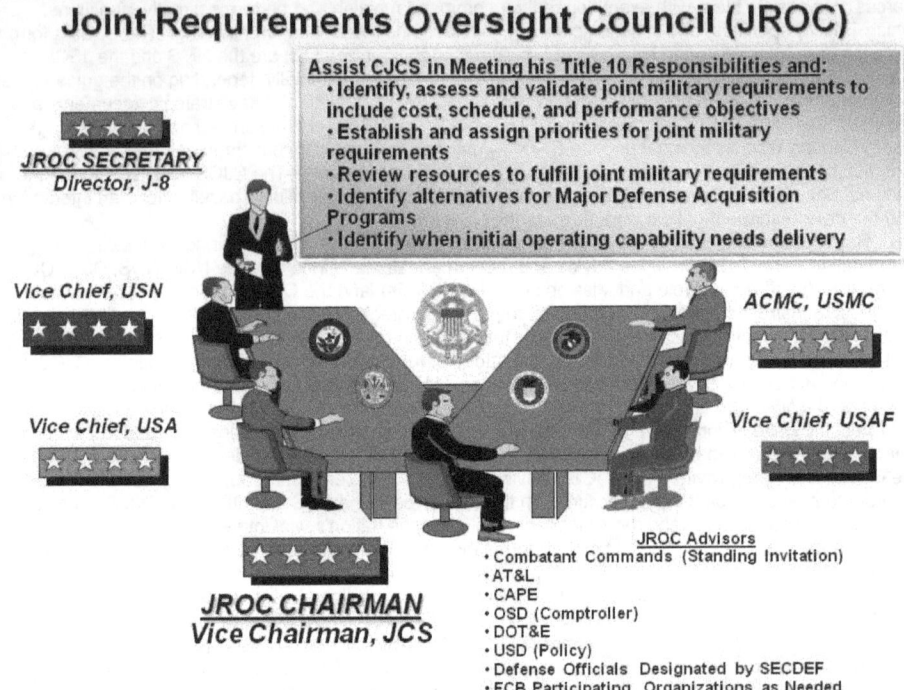

Figure 4-2. Joint Requirements Oversight Council (JROC)

a. The JROC has continued to broaden its strategic focus to include providing top down guidance in defining military capabilities from a joint perspective and integrating this advice within the planning, programming, and budgeting process. The JROC oversees the JCIDS and provides advice on acquisition programs as specified in CJCSI 3170.01H and DOD 5000.01. Additionally, the JROC has continued to focus on interacting with CCDRs on the full range of warfighting requirements and capabilities, as well as engaging DOD senior leaders who are now advisors to this council. Assessment teams that examine those requirements and capabilities or working groups are organized within the established FCBs. The domains of each of these FCBs include the following Joint Capability Areas (JCA): Battlespace Awareness; Force Application; Command, Control, Communications and Computers (C4)/Cyber; Protection; Logistics; and Force Support. Finally, the JROC continues to maintain its direct integration in the PPBE process. Significant effort is involved in the production of two JSPS documents that are signed by the CJCS: the CPR and the CPA that were discussed earlier in this chapter. By providing joint Capability-Based Assessments (C-BA) in the domains listed above, the JROC provides significant input into the development of the full range of the CJCS's programmatic advice required by Title 10.

b. The JROC chartered the Joint Capabilities Board (JCB) to serve as an executive-level advisory board to assist the JROC in fulfilling its many responsibilities. The JCB consists of the Director, J-8, as the CJCS, and appropriate Service and CCMDs designated general/flag officer or civilian equivalent

THE RELATIONSHIP OF JOINT AND ARMY PLANNING

representatives. The Chief, Joint Capabilities Division on the J-8 serves as the JCB Secretary. The JCB assists the JROC in overseeing the JCIDS process and the capabilities assessment process. The JCB reviews C-BA insights, findings, recommendations, and provides both guidance and direction. On issues that have a Joint Staff Designator of JCB interest, the JCB can make decisions and for others their recommendations are provided to the JROC for final review (see Figure 4-3).

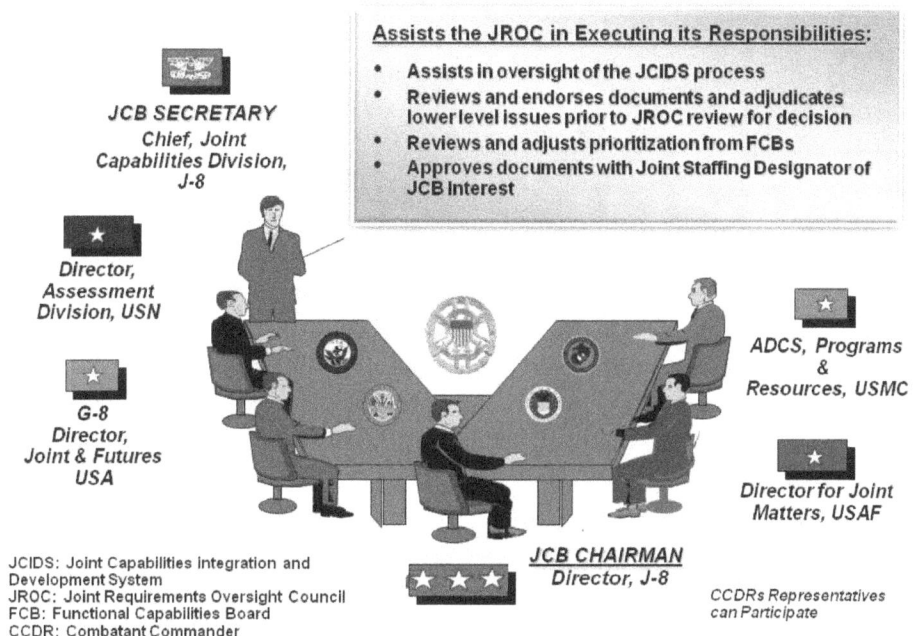

Figure 4-3. Joint Capabilities Board (JCB)

c. The FCBs serve as the points of entry for the JROC's actions related to the JCAs. Additionally, the FCBs, under the leadership of a Joint Staff or Functional CCMD flag officer or senior executive service civilian, serve as integrators of joint capability development and ensure that major programs are fully integrated into joint architectures from the outset. The JROC and its associated sub-organizations continue to evolve in order to remain focused on strategic issues and concepts. As an example of this strategic focus and desire to directly influence future systems and capabilities, each of the organizations within the JROC process has become more involved in developing operational concepts and operational architectures, as well as developing strategic guidance to influence capabilities. The overall intent is to provide more upfront guidance to ensure capabilities and systems are focused more on joint interdependency and resolve capability gaps while reducing redundancy (see Figure 4-4).

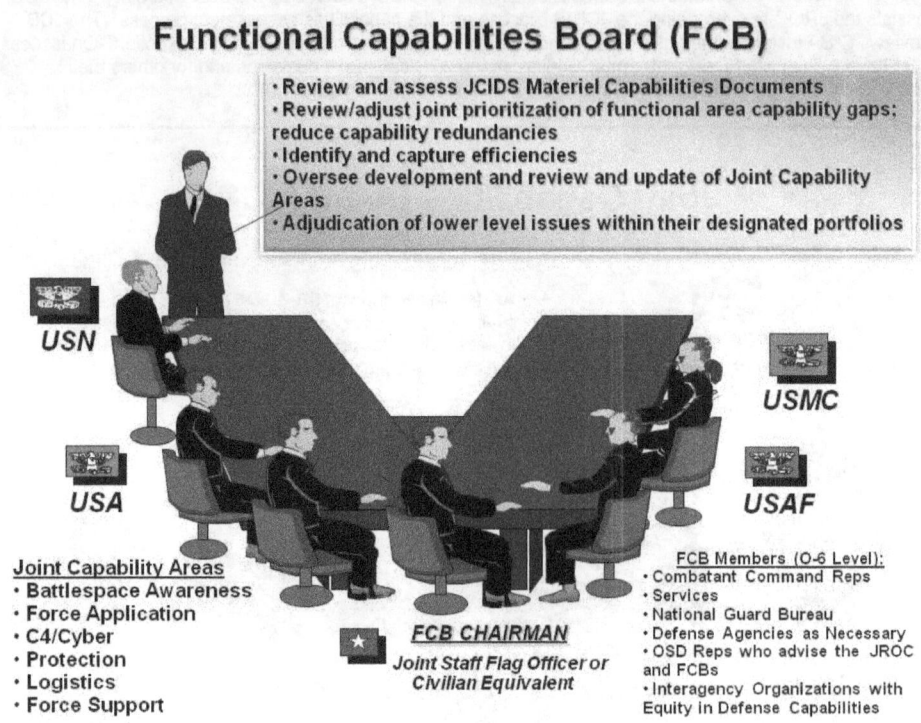

Figure 4-4. Functional Capabilities Board (FCB)

d. Along with the changes to the structures and establishment of these boards just discussed, advisory support to the JROC has also increased. For example, there are eight organizations within the OSD and Milestone Decision Authorities (MDA) such as Comptroller and Intelligence that now come to the capabilities meetings as part of the Functional Control Boards as well as provide advisory support the JROC. Further, there are certain defense and interagency organizations that have a standing invitation to attend and provide senior-level advisory participation at JROC-related meetings on specific subjects, such as the Defense Intelligence Agency (DIA), National Security Agency (NSA), Defense Logistics Agency (DLA), Defense Contract Management Agency (DCMA), Department of Homeland Security (DHS), and others. There are 19 defense and interagency organizations identified in the current JROC instruction that can provide this advice. This evolution allows for a broader vetting and input of issues and capabilities before they get to the most senior level for decision.

4-13. C-BAs

C-BA teams, under the supervision of a FCB, examine key relationships and interactions among JCAs and identify opportunities for improving warfighting effectiveness. Much of this work is focused on identifying and resolving capability gaps with an integrated and joint force perspective. The teams consist of warfighting and functional area experts from the Joint Staff, CCMDs, Services, OSD, DOD agencies, and others as deemed necessary. Assessment issues are presented to the FCB for initial issue review, to the JCB for further issue development, and then to the JROC for final recommendation to the CJCS depending on the issue. There is a gatekeeper within the J-8 that initially identifies at what level the issue

THE RELATIONSHIP OF JOINT AND ARMY PLANNING

will be examined. Through this process, the JROC is instrumental in helping the CJCS forge consensus and examine alternatives on the most important capabilities issues.

a. A series of documents provide guidance for the defense capabilities development process. Within this capabilities process, the CCJO is the overarching concept that guides the development of the joint concepts and JCAs (for more detail, see Chap. 11).

b. Guidance in the above documents is used by the C-BAs that are part of JCIDS, briefly described earlier. The CJCSI that describes this detailed process and the focus of documents produced by this process is 3170.01H. The documents produced by the JCIDS process that support the materiel and non-materiel solutions are as follows: Joint Capabilities Document (JCD); Initial Capabilities Document (ICD); Capabilities Development Document (CDD); Capability Production Document (CPD); and Joint Doctrine, Organization, Training, Materiel, Leadership and Education, Personnel, Facilities, and Policy (DOTMLPF-P) Change Recommendations (DCR).

Section III
Planning and Resourcing

4-14. DOD PPBE Process
The PPBE is a cyclical process containing the four interrelated phases of planning, programming, budgeting, and execution. The process provides for decision-making on future programs and permits prior decisions to be examined and analyzed from the viewpoint of the strategic environment and for the time period being addressed. Through the JSPS, the CJCS performs his statutory requirement to provide advice on requirements, programs, and budgets. Formal advice is provided broadly in the NMS on military objectives and more specifically in the CPR and CPA on capabilities and weapon platforms to achieve these objectives. These documents are designed to impact the planning, programming and budgeting phases of PPBE. Through JSPS, the Services, and CCMDs (by their input to the CJA process and other documents, and their input to the C-BA process, overseen by the JROC and lower level boards), assist the CJCS in providing formal advice to the PPBE process. The PPBE process is covered in detail in Chapter 9.

4-15. The Army Planning System
The Army planning system is designed to meet the demands of JSPS, JROC, GFM, Joint Operations Planning and Execution System (JOPES), and PPBE. Through its interfacing with the JSPS and the JROC's C-BA processes and its input as a member on the various councils and boards, the Army provides its input to joint assessments and strategic planning documents. Hence, the Army helps shape the advice and direction of the CJCS, in consultation with the other members of the JCS and the CCDRs, to the SECDEF and POTUS.

a. The Army PPBE initiates Army planning system. This planning system addresses the direction provided by defense policies and the military strategy for attainment of national security objectives and policies. It determines force requirements and objectives and establishes guidance for the allocation of resources for the execution of Army roles and functions in support of national objectives. It provides the forum within which the Army conducts its planning to integrate CJCS guidance and provide Service assistance. The Army's PPBE planning phase supports the DOD PPBE process and the JSPS. It also provides guidance for the subsequent phases of the Army PPBE. Planning is the continuing process by which the Army establishes and revises its goals or requirements and attainable objectives, chooses from alternative courses of action, and determines and allocates its resources to achieve the chosen course of action. The value of comprehensive planning comes from providing an integrated decision structure for an organization as a whole.

b. Planning requires considering the ways and means to achieve the goals identified to shape the future of an organization instead of adapting to a future that just unfolds. Planning is considering and assessing ideas that use the resources of an organization and address risk. It is designed to address and minimize risk by integrating as much data as possible upon which to make a decision, which includes the consideration and development of multiple options from varied perspectives.

c. The Army planning system includes strategic planning and force planning for both requirements and objectives. Strategic planning includes informing the development of national defense policy along with the ends, ways, and means associated with the various parts of the NMS. Strategic planning provides

HOW THE ARMY RUNS

direct support to the DOD's PPBE and the CJCS's JSPS in an integrated manner, while concurrently supporting the Army PPBE. These planning activities serve to guide the subsequent development of programs and budgets. Army planning includes the identification of the integrated and balanced military forces necessary to accomplish that strategy, and the provision of a framework for effective management of DOD resources toward successful mission accomplishment consistent with national resource limitations.

Section IV
Joint Operations Planning

4-16. JOPES
The joint operation planning process is a coordinated joint staff procedure used by commanders to determine the best methods of accomplishing tasks and to direct the actions necessary to accomplish those tasks. JOPES is used to conduct joint planning and facilitates the building and maintenance of Operations Plan (OPLAN) and concept plans. It aids in the development of effective options and operations orders through adaptation of OPLANs or creates plans in a no-plan scenario. JOPES provides policies and procedures to ensure effective management of planning operations across the spectrum of mobilization, deployment, employment, sustainment, and redeployment. As part of the Global Command and Control System (GCCS), JOPES supports the deployment and transportation aspects of joint operation planning and execution and contains five basic planning functions: threat identification and assessment; strategy determination; course of action development; detailed planning; and implementation.

    a. In 2008 the SECDEF initiated the Adaptive Planning and Execution (APEX) process to replace JOPES. The changes were to incorporate accelerating joint planning by integrating contingency planning, crises action planning, and execution processes and technology. This would enable plans to more quickly and transparently move to execution.

    b. In accordance with existing DOD guidance, the Military Departments will move to complete the conversion of the JOPES process to the APEX process by FY2015. However, there are ongoing technology challenges to fully implement APEX as designed. While the JOPES and APEX processes are currently being used, there is more frequent and iterative dialogue between the different DOD organizations and planners with in-progress review and associated meetings as needed. This continual review and assessment of assumptions enables the development of more viable options for the POTUS and SECDEF.

4-17. CCMDs
CCMDs provide for the integrated effectiveness of U.S. military forces in combat operations and for the projection of U.S. military power in support of U.S. national policies. They are established by the POTUS through the SECDEF, with the advice and assistance of the CJCS.

    a. UCP is the document approved by the POTUS that provides overall guidance to CCMDs. It establishes the responsibilities, missions, and force structure. For geographic CCMDs, it identifies the geographical area of responsibility and for functional CCMDs, it specifies their functional responsibilities.

    b. The chain of command extends from the POTUS to the SECDEF to the CCDRs. Forces are assigned under the authority of the SECDEF. A CCMD is assigned a broad continuing mission under a single commander and is composed of assigned components of two or more Services. CCMDs have full command of all forces assigned.

    c. There are two types of CCMDs: geographic, which have responsibility for specific areas; and functional, which have responsibility for executing certain functions. There are currently six geographic and three functional CCMDs (see Figure 4-5).

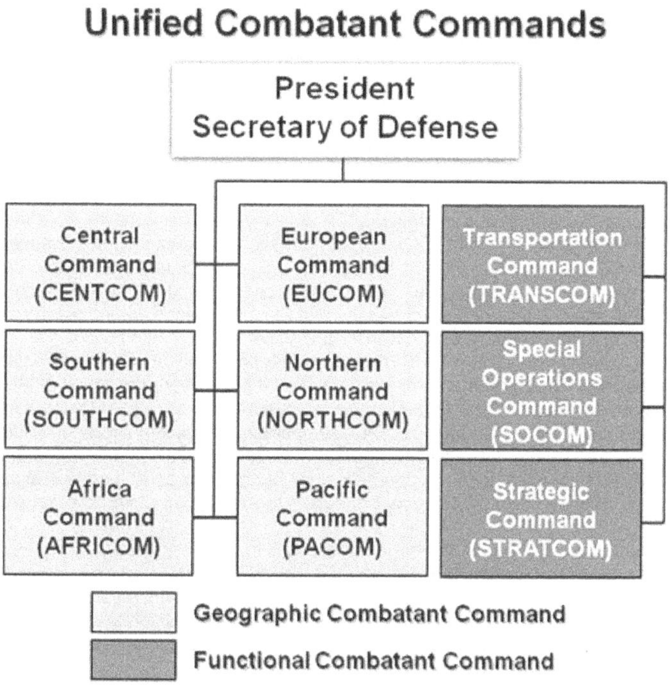

THE RELATIONSHIP OF JOINT AND ARMY PLANNING

Unified Combatant Commands

```
              President
         Secretary of Defense
```

- Central Command (CENTCOM)
- European Command (EUCOM)
- Transportation Command (TRANSCOM)
- Southern Command (SOUTHCOM)
- Northern Command (NORTHCOM)
- Special Operations Command (SOCOM)
- Africa Command (AFRICOM)
- Pacific Command (PACOM)
- Strategic Command (STRATCOM)

☐ Geographic Combatant Command
▨ Functional Combatant Command

Figure 4-5. Unified Combatant Commands

(1) U.S. Central Command's (USCENTCOM) area of responsibility includes 20 culturally and economically diverse nations located throughout the Horn of Africa, South and Central Asia, and Northern Red Sea regions, as well as the Arabian Peninsula. It includes the countries of Egypt, Iraq, Afghanistan, and Pakistan.

(2) U.S. European Command's (USEUCOM) area of responsibility includes 51 independent countries that comprise Europe, the region known as Caucuses and a small section of the Middle East that includes Israel. It is responsible for the U.S. contribution to North Atlantic Treaty Organization (NATO) and for commanding U.S. forces assigned to Europe. The Command USEUCOM is also Supreme Allied Commander, Europe (SACEUR), a major NATO commander, and as such is responsible for the defense of Allied Command Europe.

(3) U.S. Pacific Command's (USPACOM) area of responsibility includes the waters off the Pacific Ocean to the western border of India and from Antarctica to the North Pole. This area includes 36 nations that comprise the Asian Pacific region that are home to over 50% of the world's population and several of the world's largest armed forces. USPACOM has four Service component commands, which are headquartered in Hawaii, with forces stationed and deployed throughout the region.

(4) U.S. Special Operations Command (USSOCOM) is responsible to provide fully capable Special Operations Forces (SOF) to defend the United States and its interests. It synchronizes DOD plans against global terrorist networks, and, as directed, executes global operations. USSOCOM trains, organizes, equips, and deploys combat ready special operations forces to other CCMDs. It executes and exercises command authority of all Continental United States (CONUS)-based SOF. USSOCOM is

HOW THE ARMY RUNS

unique in that it is responsible for planning, programming, and budgeting for Major Force Program 11, so it can develop and buy special operations-peculiar equipment, supplies, or services.

(5) U.S. Southern Command's (USSOUTHCOM) area of responsibility includes the landmass of Latin America south of Mexico, the waters adjacent to Central and South America, and the Caribbean Sea. Its area of responsibility encompasses 31 countries and 15 areas of special sovereignty.

(6) U.S. Transportation Command (USTRANSCOM) is responsible for a global defense transportation system, which coordinates people and transportation assets to project and sustain forces whenever, wherever, and for as long as needed. Its three component commands are the Air Forces' Air Mobility Command (AMC), Army's Military Surface Deployment and Distribution Command (SDDC), and the Navy's Military Sealift Command (MSC). USTRANSCOM coordinates missions worldwide using both military and commercial transportation resources.

(7) U.S. Strategic Command (USSTRATCOM) is responsible to conduct global operations in coordination with other CCMDs, Services, and appropriate U.S. Government agencies to detect and deter strategic attacks against the U.S. and its allies, and is prepared to defend the nation as directed. Its major mission areas include: intelligence surveillance and reconnaissance; space control and surveillance; global strike; integrated missile defense; and cyber.

(8) U.S. Northern Command's (USNORTHCOM) area of responsibility includes the continental United States, Alaska, Canada, Mexico, and the surrounding water. It also includes the Gulf of Mexico and portions of the Caribbean region to include the Bahamas, Puerto Rico, and U.S. Virgin Islands. USNORTHCOM partners to conduct homeland defense operations, civil support, and security cooperation to defend and secure the United States and its interests. USNORTHCOM plans, organizes, and executes homeland defense and civil support missions but has few permanently assigned forces. The command will be assigned forces whenever necessary to execute missions as ordered by the POTUS and SECDEF.

(9) U.S. Africa Command (USAFRICOM) began operations in 2007 and was officially established in 2008. Its geographic area of operation is all islands and countries in the African continent and surrounding waters with the exception of Egypt, which is in USCENTCOM's area. In addition to interacting with African nations, USAFRICOM engages with the African Union and African regional security organizations to strengthen the defense of African states and regional areas.

4-18. Relationship of the CJCS to CCMD
The Title 10 USC specifies that the SECDEF may assign to the CJCS responsibility for assisting him with his command responsibilities. In further identifying that subject to the SECDEF, the CJCS can also serve as the spokesman for the CCMDs. In addition, the POTUS may direct that communications between the CCDRs and the POTUS or SECDEF be transmitted through the CJCS. This places the CJCS in a unique and pivotal position. However, this does not confer command authority on the CJCS and does not alter the responsibilities of the CCDRs. Subject to the direction of the POTUS, CCDRs perform duties under the authority, direction, and control of the POTUS and SECDEF, and respond directly to the POTUS and SECDEF for the preparedness of the command to carry out missions assigned to the command. These broad responsibilities of the CCMDs are also specified in Title 10 USC.

Section V
Summary and References

4-19. Summary
a. Joint strategic planning is conducted under the direction of the CJCS in consultation with the Services, CCMDs, and SECDEF. The formal JSPS integrates the CJCS's processes with those he coordinates with multiple products, processes, and boards to help enable him to meet his Title 10 responsibilities.

b. The JSPS is oriented toward identifying and evaluating the challenges facing the nation and assessing the ever changing strategic environment. It provides the basis for formulating the nation's military strategy and helps in defining resource needs in terms of capabilities, forces, and materiel. It accomplishes this with an overall integrated and comprehensive assess, advise, and direct framework that has specific documents and processes.

THE RELATIONSHIP OF JOINT AND ARMY PLANNING

   c. PPBE focuses on resource allocation, making it more dollar and manpower oriented. PPBE is concerned with the amount and direction of those resources necessary to provide the capabilities required to execute the planning guidance identified by the DPG, as well as the strategy guidance articulated in the QDR and other strategic direction guidance, while considering risk.

   d. The JROC, JCB, FCB, and C-BA boards and processes impact the PPBE starting with the planning phase by providing broad strategic advice contained in the NMS, more specific resource advice in the CPR, and again through the programming phase by assessing the Services and certain DOD Agency programs and budgets with the CPA.

   e. The JSPS, based on the GEF, directs the development of strategic plans through the JSCP. The JSCP requires that plans be completed to accomplish tasked missions within available resources. The COCOMs are the organizations that develop the various JSCP directed plans. The JSCP is the JSPS document that starts the deliberate planning process while being a formal link between JSPS and JOPES and the transition to APEX.

   f. The details of planning change constantly, to include some parts of the systems and processes just examined. However, the overall process includes the following: identifying the capabilities required; assessing various threats to include asymmetric and hybrid threats; developing a military strategy; structuring forces and determining capabilities to support the strategy; providing resources for priority requirements; and planning for the deployment of those forces to meet global military operations. These responsibilities are essentially a requirement from year to year, with a near-, mid-, and long-term focus depending on the operational and strategic challenges.

   g. Capabilities planning is not a precise activity, even though the resulting force levels to execute some of these capabilities are stated precisely in terms of brigades, air wings, carrier battle groups, and the like. There are many challenges involved in capabilities planning and the resultant analyses to determine force structure, as well as the risks inherent with a particular force level. All of this requires senior leader judgment integrating many different perspectives. Throughout all of these processes, the Army has developed internal processes and organizational structures, which will be covered in later chapters, to ensure the Army fully contributes to all these processes and the subsequent products.

4-20. References
   a. Adaptive Planning Road Map II 2008, March 2008
   b. Army Regulation 1-1, Planning, Programming, Budgeting, and Execution System
   c. Chairman's Strategic Direction to the Joint Force, February 2012
   d. CJCS Instruction 3100.01B, Joint Strategic Planning System, December 2008
   e. CJCS Instruction 3137.01D, The Functional Capabilities Board Process, January 2012
   f. CJCS Instruction 3170.01H, Joint Capabilities Integration and Development System
   g. CJCS Instruction 5123.01F, Charter of the Joint Requirements Oversight Council, January 2012
   h. CJCS Concept for Joint Operations: JF2020, Sep 2012
   i. Combatant Command's websites
   j. Global Force Management Guidance Implementation Guidance 2010-20, January 2010
   k. Joint Forces Staff College (JFSC) Pub 1, The Joint Staff Officer's Guide 2000
   l. Joint Publication 0-2, Unified Action Armed Forces (UNAAF)
   m. Joint Publication 5-0, Doctrine for Planning Joint Operations
   n. National Defense Strategy, June 2008
   o. National Military Strategy of the United States of America 2011, February 2011
   p. National Security Strategy of the United States of America 2010, May 2010
   q. Quadrennial Defense Review 2010, February 2010
   r. Sustaining U.S. Global Leadership: Priorities for the 21st Century Defense, January 2012

HOW THE ARMY RUNS

This page is intentionally left blank

ARMY FORCE DEVELOPMENT

Chapter 5

Army Force Development

Institutions, all institutions, just have a historical tendency to evolve slowly, if at all. That's especially true when you don't give them the construct and structure to make those changes.

> Hon. John McHugh, Secretary of the Army (SECARMY)
> Association of the United States Army (AUSA) Keynote Remarks, October 25, 2010

We'll have scalable and tailorable organizations that can provide options to our national security leaders in order to operate across the wide range of missions, from humanitarian support all the way to campaign quality conflicts, if necessary.

> GEN Raymond T. Odierno, Chief of Staff of the U.S. Army
> AUSA Annual Meeting and Exposition, October 22, 2012

Section I
Introduction

5-1. Force Development Overview

a. Force development starts with the operational capabilities desired of the Army as specified in national strategies and guidance such as the Quadrennial Defense Review (QDR), National Defense Strategy (NDS), Guidance for Employment of the Force (GEF), Defense Planning Guidance (DPG), the National Military Strategy (NMS), and the Army Strategy as well as the needs of the Combatant Commanders (CCDRs). Strategic guidance identifies the range of military operations that the national leaders expect its military forces to perform, the effects they must achieve, the attributes those forces must possess, where they must operate, and generally what kind and what size of force is expected to execute those operations. Strategic guidance informs the development of the Contemporary Operational Environment (COE) and future Joint Operating Environments (JOEs). These visualizations of the Operational Environment (OE) describe the composite of conditions, circumstances, and influences that affect commanders' decisions on the employment of military capabilities.

b. The JOE provides the framework for the development of more specific concepts that are intended to accomplish the strategic objectives and decisively prevail within the JOE. These concepts, in turn, provide a visualization of how joint and Army forces will operate 10-20 years in the future, describe the capabilities required to carry out the range of military operations against adversaries in the expected OE, and how a commander, using military art and science, might employ these capabilities to achieve desired effects and objectives. Concepts consist of future capability descriptions within a proposed projection of future military operations. Each concept describes the operational challenges, the components of potential solutions, and how those components work together to solve those challenges.

c. The force development process then determines Army Doctrinal, Organizational, Training, Materiel, Leadership and education, Personnel, Facilities, and Policy (DOTMLPF-P) capabilities-based requirements and produces plans and programs that, when executed through force integration activities, brings together people and equipment and forms them into operational organizations with the desired capabilities for the combatant commanders. Force development uses a phased process to develop operational and organizational plans, and then combines them with technologies, materiel, manpower, and constrained resources to eventually produce combat capability.

d. The force development process interfaces and interacts with the Joint Strategic Planning System (JSPS), the Defense Acquisition Management System (DAS), the Joint Operations Planning and Execution System (JOPES) (see Para. 6-3) and the Department of Defense (DOD) Planning, Programming, Budgeting, and Execution (PPBE) process.

HOW THE ARMY RUNS

5-2. Force Development Process Summary

a. This chapter explains the Army force development process (Figure 5-1). Force development initiates the organizational life cycle of the Army, and is the underlying basis for all other functions. It is a process that defines military capabilities, designs force structures to provide these capabilities, and produces plans and programs that, when executed through force integration activities, translate organizational concepts based on doctrine, technologies, materiel, manpower requirements, and limited resources into a trained and ready Army. The five-phased process includes:

(1) Develop capabilities.
(2) Design organizations.
(3) Develop organizational models.
(4) Determine organizational authorizations.
(5) Document organizational authorizations.

b. The Army Force Management Model (Figure 2-2) displays a schematic framework of the force development sub-processes as part of the force management process. The Army Force Management Model depicts how each process or system relates to others and contributes to the accomplishment of the overall process. The following sections will explain the phases of force development in detail.

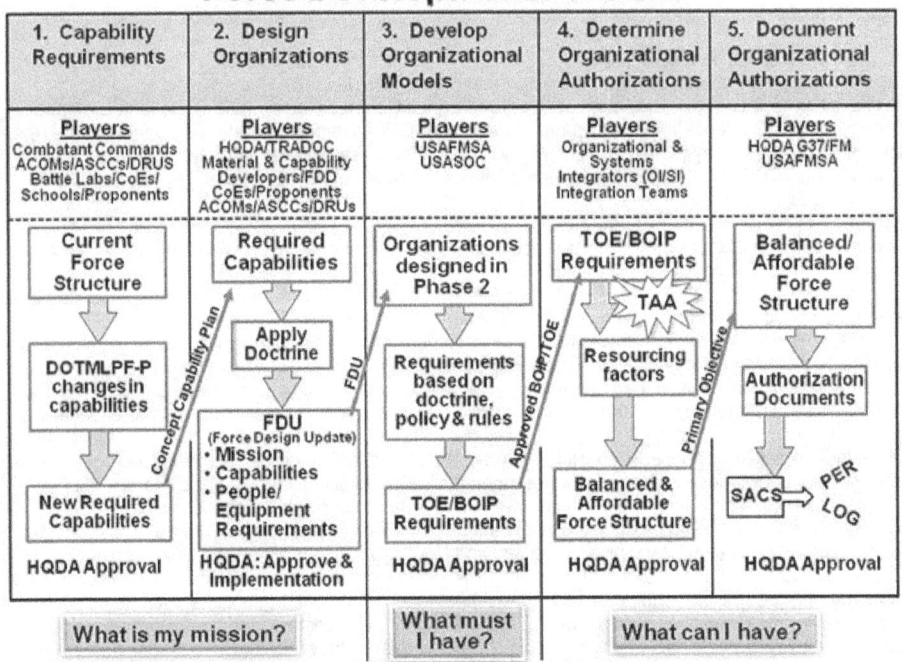

Figure 5-1. Force Development Process

ARMY FORCE DEVELOPMENT

Section II
Phase I—Develop Capability Requirements

5-3. Joint Capabilities Integration and Development System (JCIDS)
a. The JCIDS, the DAS, and the PPBE process form the DOD's three principal decision support processes for transforming the military forces to support the NDS. The procedures established in JCIDS support the Chairman of the Joint Chiefs of Staff (CJCS) and the Joint Requirements Oversight Council (JROC) in advising the Secretary of Defense (SECDEF) in identifying, assessing, and prioritizing joint military capabilities-based requirements (needs).

b. JCIDS is a need-driven, joint capabilities-based requirements generation process. The objective is to develop a balanced and synchronized (DOTMLPF-P) solution approach proposal that is affordable, militarily useful, supportable by outside agencies, and based on mature technology that is demonstrated in a relevant operational or laboratory environment. JCIDS implements an integrated, collaborative process, based on top-level strategic direction, to guide development of new capabilities through changes in DOTMLPF-P. Change recommendations are developed and evaluated in consideration of how to optimize the joint force's ability to operate as an integrated force. This integrated, collaborative approach requires a process that uses joint/services concepts and integrated architectures to identify prioritized high risk capability gaps and integrated joint DOTMLPF-P and policy approaches (materiel and non-materiel) to resolve those gaps (see Para. 5-6b below).

5-4. Army Implementation of JCIDS Overview
a. Capabilities-based requirements generation begins the Army force development process. Army JCIDS develops an integrated set of Army DOTMLPF-P requirements that support national strategic guidance, The Army Plan (TAP) and operational needs of the combatant commands. This process assesses future joint and Army warfighting concepts in the context of the future JOE to identify functional needs and solutions. The JOE describes the physical, demographic, political, economic, technological, and military conditions in which the Army will operate during the next two decades.

b. The Army begins the JCIDS process with the development of an Army Concept Framework (ACF), Army Capstone Concept (ACC), Army Operating Concept (AOC), Army Functional Concepts (AFCs), and concepts directed by CG, TRADOC. These concepts provide a conceptual foundation for conducting Capabilities-Based Assessment (C-BA) of the ability of our current force to meet the future operational challenges. Properly applied, Army JCIDS produces an integrated set of DOTMLPF-P solution approaches that collectively provide the Required Capabilities (RCs). As it is grounded in joint/Army concepts, the Army JCIDS provides traceability of all Army system and non-system solutions back to overarching national strategic guidance.

c. The C-BA identifies and documents capability gaps; determines the attributes of a capability or combination of capabilities that would resolve the gaps; and identifies non-materiel and/or materiel approaches for possible implementation. As a result, the concepts-centric Army JCIDS process is a robust analysis of warfighting capabilities required to prevail in the future operational environment. This process helps ensure the Army considers the most effective joint force capabilities and the integration of those capabilities early in the process. Appropriate component, cross-component, and interagency expertise; science & technology community initiatives; and wargaming and experimentation results are considered in the development of DOTMLPF-P solutions. See Para. 5-7.

d. Joint/Army JCIDS documentation - Initial Capabilities Document (ICD), Capability Development Document (CDD), Capability Production Document (CPD), and the DOTMLPF Change Recommendation (DCR) - provides the formal communication of DOTMLPF-P between the user and the acquisition, test and evaluation, and resource management communities. Capability documents are discussed in detail in chapter 11.

5-5. Standing Integrated Capabilities Development Teams (ICDT)
a. Standing ICDTs are a gathering of multi-disciplined personnel, formally chartered by the Director, TRADOC Army Capabilities Integration Center (ARCIC), to prioritize, integrate, and synchronize all DOTMLPF-P requirements within their assigned portfolio and those interdependent capabilities requiring integration across other TRADOC functional and/or organizational portfolios. A "portfolio" includes all solutions across the DOTMLPF-P within assigned Army Warfighting Functions (WFF) and organizations.

HOW THE ARMY RUNS

   b. The Director, ARCIC, chartered six Center of Excellence (CoE) standing ICDTs to conduct a complete warfighting functional portfolio review on a biennial basis to support the Army force generation process and products. Portfolio reviews include: conducting and/or updating the assigned WFF C-BA that addresses the RCs delineated in the assigned AFC (and any other applicable concepts); identification, risk assessment, and prioritization of gaps in all DOTMLPF-P domains; and proposing mitigating solutions across DOTMLPF-P for those gaps considered to have unacceptable risk. These reviews are Resource-Informed, Integration-Focused, and Outcome-Based (RIO) and address the full scope of assigned warfighting functions and solutions to include an assessment of all approved Programs of Record (PORs) and fielded systems. The assigned CoE will also be responsible for conducting DOTMLPF-P assessments, integration, and synchronization for their designated organizational structures (e.g., Fires Brigade).
   c. The ICDT membership and participants vary, depending on the specific product; however, core membership always includes representation across the DOTMLPF-P domains. The ICDT charter identifies the membership, the participating organizations, and the expected deliverables. While industry and academia are not members of the ICDT, their input is key to the process risks the Army may face and what it might cost.
   d. The six WfF standing ICDTs are:
   (1) Fires WfF—U. S. Army Fires CoE, Fort Sill, OK.
   (2) Intelligence WfF—U. S. Army Intelligence CoE, Fort Huachuca, AZ.
   (3) Mission Command WfF—U. S. Army Combined Arms Center, Mission Command CoE, Fort Leavenworth, KS.
   (4) Movement and Maneuver WfF—U. S. Army Maneuver CoE, Fort Benning, GA.
   (5) Protection WfF—U. S. Army Maneuver Support CoE, Fort Leonard Wood, MO.
   (6) Sustainment WfF—U. S. Army Combined Arms Support Command CoE, Fort Lee, VA.

5-6. Concept Development and Experimentation (CD&E)
CD&E is a campaign of learning supporting current and future force development through a two-path approach - concept development and prototyping. Concepts, developed and refined through wargames and experiments, are the basis for determining the capabilities required for the future force.
   a. Concepts. Concepts are the centerpiece of the CD&E process. An operational concept is a generalized visualization of operations. It describes a problem to be solved, the components of the solution to that problem, and the interaction of those components in solving the problem.
   (1) Concepts serve as the foundation for architecture development and for generating capabilities-based DOTMLPF-P solutions - doctrine (fundamental warfighting principles and Tactics, Techniques, and Procedures (TTPs)) development, organizational design changes, training initiatives, materiel solutions, leadership and education requirements, personnel solutions, facilities renovation/design, and policy - through an evolutionary development process that results in enhanced capabilities at the unit level.
   (2) Components of an operational concept include a description of the joint operating environment (JOE) and its associated range of operational challenges, a set of concepts that address the "how to" of countering and overcoming the challenges posed, and a corresponding set of RCs and initial force design principles needed to implement the concept.
   b. Joint/Army concept development. Fundamental ideas about future concepts of military operations and their associated capabilities are documented in operational concepts. The translation of concepts into capabilities is an iterative process. To maximize their future utility, concepts are broadly based and encompass both the art and science of future warfighting, continually refined through wargaming, experimentation, assessment, and analysis.
   (1) Joint concepts consists of a Capstone Concept for Joint Operations (CCJO), supporting Joint Concepts (JC) and Joint Capability Areas (JCA). These concepts address the period from just beyond the Future Years Defense Program (FYDP) out to 20 years. The National Security Strategy (NSS), Defense Strategic Guidance (DSG), NDS, Unified Command Plan (UCP), DPG, and QDR provide top-level strategic guidance for joint concept development and are the impetus for deriving capabilities needed to shape the joint force.
   (a) CCJO. The CCJO is the vision of the CJCS and the overarching joint concept that guides joint force development, bridges strategy and operational concepts/doctrine, and defines a "new way of war." The CCJO articulates a high-order vision of how the future force will operate, describes the future operating environment, advances new concepts for joint operations, and suggests attributes that will

ARMY FORCE DEVELOPMENT

define the future force. The CCJO aims to establish a bridge from strategic guidance to subordinate concepts, force development guidance, and follow-on doctrine. Service concepts and subordinate JCs and JCAs expand on the CCJO solution. The CCJO concludes by presenting risks and implications associated with the concept. The CCJO is approved by the CJCS. The current CCJO is "globally integrated operations" with the following key elements: mission command; regional focus with global agility; leverage partners to maximize mutual advantage; flexible options in establishing joint forces—Active Component/Reserve Component (AC/RC) mix; cross-domain synergy; use of flexible, low signature capabilities; and discrimination.

(b) JCs. JCs link strategic guidance to the development and employment of future joint force capabilities and serve as "engines for transformation" that may ultimately lead to DOTMLPF-P changes.

(c) JCAs. JCAs are collections of like (DOD) capabilities functionally grouped to support capability analysis, strategy development, investment decision making, capability portfolio management, and capabilities-based force development and operational planning. There are currently nine JCAs: Force Support; Battlespace Awareness; Force Application; Logistics; Command & Control; Net-Centric; Protection; Building Partnerships; and Corporate Management and Support.

(2) ACF. The Army documents its fundamental ideas about future joint operations in the ACF, promulgated in TRADOC 525-series pamphlets. The ACF family of concepts consists of a capstone concept, an AOC, AFCs, and concepts directed by CG, TRADOC. Concepts facilitate the visualization and communication of the Army's key ideas on future operations. The ACF is at Figure 5-2.

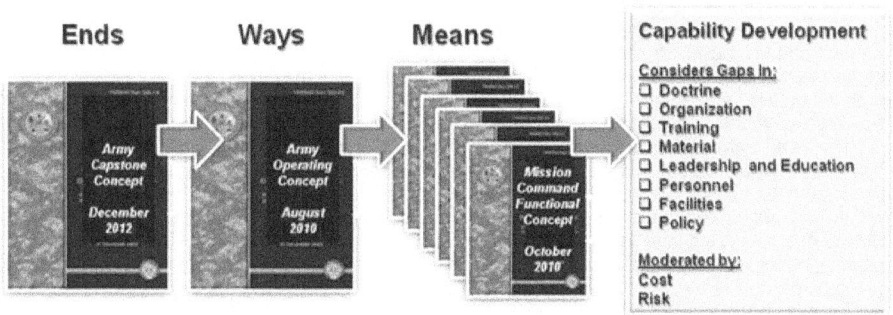

- The Army determines its required capabilities starting with concepts
- Current concept work is focused on 2020 and refreshed every two years
- The Army organizes its concepts through warfighting functions:
  - Mission Command
  - Intelligence
  - Movement and Maneuver
  - Fires
  - Protection
  - Sustainment
  - Shaping
- Additional concepts address Learning and Training, Building Partnership Capacity, and the Human Dimension

Figure 5-2. Army Concept Framework (ACF)

(a) As the lead document of the ACF, TRADOC Pam 525-3-0, The U.S. ACC describes our vision of the future operational environment, the role of the Army in the joint force, and the broad capabilities required by future Army forces. The ACC provides a guide to how the Army will apply available resources to overcome unpredictable and complex challenges and prevent, shape and win in support of recent strategic guidance. The ACC also serves as the foundation for a campaign of learning that will evaluate and refine its major ideas and required capabilities. Finally, the ACC provides a roadmap for development of a comprehensive investment strategy that will rebalance the Army's force structure, readiness, and modernization efforts in support of national strategy. The ACC establishes that the Army must maintain a credible capacity to win decisively and support combatant commanders across a wide range of military operations at home and abroad. Further, the ACC retains the idea of operational adaptability as the fundamental characteristic of the Army required to execute a wide variety of missions for both the institutional Army as well as the operating force. Within the ACF, this concept is the baseline of a campaign of experimentation and analysis which will test these ideas. The ACC is the unifying framework for developing the AOC, AFCs, and integrated architectures.

(b) The AOC, documented in TP 525-3-1, provides a generalized visualization of operations across the range of military operations. The AOC describes the Army's contribution to national security within the context of joint operations. It focuses on the operational and tactical levels of war and explains how the Army, 6-18 years in the future, employs combined arms maneuver and wide area security as part of unified land operations to accomplish military missions on land. By addressing these operations in a way that illustrates how the Army integrates its warfighting functions, the AOC provides a conceptual framework for the development of subordinate Army functional concepts. The functional concepts, in turn, contain more specific explanations of how Army forces operate within each warfighting function and outline their mutual dependencies. The AOC does not include the details required to initiate the JCIDS C-BA.

(c) The AFCs describe how the Army force will perform a particular military function across the full range of military operations 6-18 years in the future. AFCs support the capstone concept and the AOC, as well as joint concepts, and draw operational context from those documents. Organized along the lines of the classic functions of a military force, the 6 AFCs are Fires, Intelligence, Mission Command, Movement and Maneuver, Protection, and Sustainment. As an integrated suite of concepts, they describe the full range of land combat functions across the range of military operations. AFCs may include the details required to initiate the JCIDS C-BA.

(d) Three additional concepts devoted to learning, training, and the human dimension round out the ACF. The Army learning concept describes the learning model required by the future Army to develop adaptive, thinking Soldiers and leaders. The Army training concept outlines the requirements and capabilities of the future force to generate and sustain trained and capable units. TP 525-3-7 outlines how the Army will develop the cognitive, physical, and social components of every Soldier to operate within the Army in unified land operations. Collectively, the ACF defines the Army's vision of how it will operate in the future and provides the conceptual framework needed to determine the capabilities required across the Army to ensure future force effectiveness.

c. Concept of Operations (CONOPs). A CONOPS is a verbal or graphic statement, in broad outline, of a commander's assumptions or intent in regard to an operation or series of operations. It is designed to give an overall picture of the operation and provides a useful visualization of how a future operation would be conducted. It is frequently embodied in campaign and/or operational plans, particularly when the plans cover a series of connected operations to be carried out simultaneously or in succession. When used in concept development, it is a tool to help describe how a particular operation is conducted in the future.

(1) For joint concepts and ACF families of concepts, CONOPS provide the overall understanding of an operation and the broad flow of tasks assigned to subordinate/supporting entities. It presents the joint force or land component commander's plan that maps capabilities to effects to accomplish the mission for a specific scenario 8 to 20 years into the future. CONOPS focus on describing the end-to-end streams of activities and how the commander might organize and employ forces to accomplish those activities.

(2) The following two types of CONOPS may be used in the joint concepts and ACF families' concept development process:

(a) Illustrative vignettes provide operational context to describe how a joint force commander might organize and employ forces 8 to 20 years into the future. These vignettes are used to clarify and increase understanding of the concepts.

(b) Defense Planning Scenarios (DPS) and Army scenarios (based on DPS) are written 8 to 20 years into the future, in order to facilitate experimentation and C-BA under JCIDS. These scenarios have

ARMY FORCE DEVELOPMENT

classified CONOPS that provide a high level of specificity and defined parameters to aid in robust analysis of capabilities and a comparison of alternate solutions.

(3) For near-term requirements, CONOPS have a different use. They are written to describe how a joint force and/or Army commander may organize and employ forces now through 7 years into the future in order to solve a current or emerging military problem. These CONOPS provide the operational context needed to examine and validate current capabilities and examine new and/or proposed capabilities required to solve a current or emerging problem. There is no strict format for a CONOPS used to support capabilities development, but it should cover the following areas at a minimum: the problem being addressed; the mission; the commander's intent; an operational overview; functions or effects to be carried out/achieved; and the roles and responsibilities of affected organizations.

d. Force Operating Capabilities (FOCs).

(1) The TRADOC ARCIC establishes required FOCs as the foundation upon which to base the JCIDS C-BA process. These critical, force-level, measurable statements of operational RC frame how the Army will realize future force operations as stated in the approved capstone, operating and functional warfighting concepts. The FOCs help focus the Army's Science and Technology Master Plan (ASTMP) and warfighting CD&E efforts. All warfighting capabilities-based requirements must have direct linkage through an FOC to an approved Army concept (capstone, operating, and functional) and the TAP. FOCs are listed biannually in TRADOC Pamphlet 525-66.

(2) TRADOC Pamphlet 525-66 also guides Independent Research & Development (IR&D) efforts. By providing the private sector an unclassified, descriptive list of desired FOCs, the Army is able to tap into a wealth of information and new ideas on different means to achieve those capabilities. The Army encourages industry to share these ideas with the appropriate Capability Developer (CAPDEV) and Training Developer (TNGDEV) organizations.

e. Experimentation. Experimentation is the heart of JCIDS. Experimentation explores warfighting concepts to identify joint and Army DOTMLPF-P change recommendations and capabilities needs. It provides insight and understanding of the concepts and capabilities that are possible given the maturity of specific technologies and capabilities that need additional research and development emphasis. The results of joint/Army experimentation help define the art of the possible and support the identification of DOTMLPF-P solutions to provide new capabilities. Progressive and iterative mixes of high fidelity Live, Virtual, Constructive (LVC) and simulations using real Soldiers and units in relevant, tactically competitive scenarios provide joint/Army leaders with FOC insights. Warfighting experiments are conducted to gain an understanding about some aspect of future warfighting. Capability insights from warfighting experiments are "way points" used to plot the future course to the future force.

(1) The FY13 Joint Development Execution Plan is the Joint Staff, J-7's, directed plan supporting futures development. The plan provides a brief highlight of each experimentation project that will be executed during FY13, to include purpose, scope, end state, expected deliverables, and dates of completion.

(2) The FY13 Army Experimentation Plan is the Army's directed plan supporting futures development. It integrates Army CD&E in a coherent service/joint context to ensure the Army provides CCDRs) with sustained land capabilities that are an indispensable, decisive component of the joint force. The objective of the AEP is to validate Army concepts with the operational force prior to implementation, assess integration of significant, complex changes across the DOTMLPF-P spectrum, support the AOC central ideas; and through Army experimentation, provide Network Integrated Evaluations (NIE) with technology solutions ready for evaluation. Ultimately, the goal of CD&E is to reduce risk through learning, innovation, and pushing the limits of the possible. The AEP is a holistic effort that inductively and deductively examines the future, supporting both current and future force development. Simply put, the AEP is about what the Army must learn, when, and how. Army experimentation is hypothesis based - the overarching hypothesis is that the future force capabilities will provide the joint force commander a means to rapid decision-making by providing a much broader range of decisive capabilities. The AEP is about validating that hypothesis.

(3) The Army CD&E strategy spans two mutually supporting, yet distinct paths-prototyping and concept development:

(a) The prototype path satisfies critical operational needs and tests compelling technology to shape the future and spirals forward feasible future force capabilities. Prototype experiments address current force annually defined Capability Needs Analysis (CNA) capability gap areas. At any point in time, the Army has a mix of new and old capabilities. Prototyping also informs the future force and supports the Army

HOW THE ARMY RUNS

Brigade Combat Team Modernization Program (ABCTMP) by prototyping ABCTMP spinout capabilities. Spinout capabilities support development and validation of DOTMLPF-P products for ABCTMP spinout systems, and assist with System of Systems (SoS) and current force integration. "Spinout" is a term developed by OSD to describe the unique method in which the ABCTMP program provides mature ABCTMP capabilities/technologies to the current force while simultaneously maintaining focus on achieving threshold and objective capabilities for the Army's future force.

(b) The concept development path develops a concepts-based, coherently joint future force using LVC experimentation to provide actionable recommendations to reduce future force development risk. The concept development path is focused by approved foundational operational themes which contain the key ideas of Army warfighting concepts.

f. In summary, a robust CD&E program can optimize return on investment while acknowledging that there are elements of the future that cannot be planned. Conducting a deliberate and coordinated CD&E program enables transformation by ensuring some resources are allocated to prototyping emerging concepts and capabilities which, in turn, enable robust and adaptive transformation.

5-7. C-BA Process

The Army JCIDS C-BA is a structured, three-phased JCIDS process. The three major phases of the JCIDS directed C-BA are the Functional Area Analysis (FAA), the functional needs analysis (FNA), and the Functional Solution Analysis (FSA) of non-materiel and materiel approaches. The product of C-BA is a recommended DOTMLPF-P materiel or non-materiel solution approach. In the Army, the materiel approach is articulated in a functional area strategic framework delineating a modernization roadmap that satisfies the identified needs over the desired time-frame. These strategic frameworks produce timely input to the materiel acquisition (DAS) and resourcing (PPBE) processes. The results of the C-BA become the basis for the ICD and/or joint DCR (Figure 5-3). In this context, the C-BA results are merely a tool. Currently, the Joint Staff (JS) has streamlined the C-BA process and eliminated the terms FAA, FNA, and FSA, while retaining the C-BA methodology. The Army is retaining these terms.

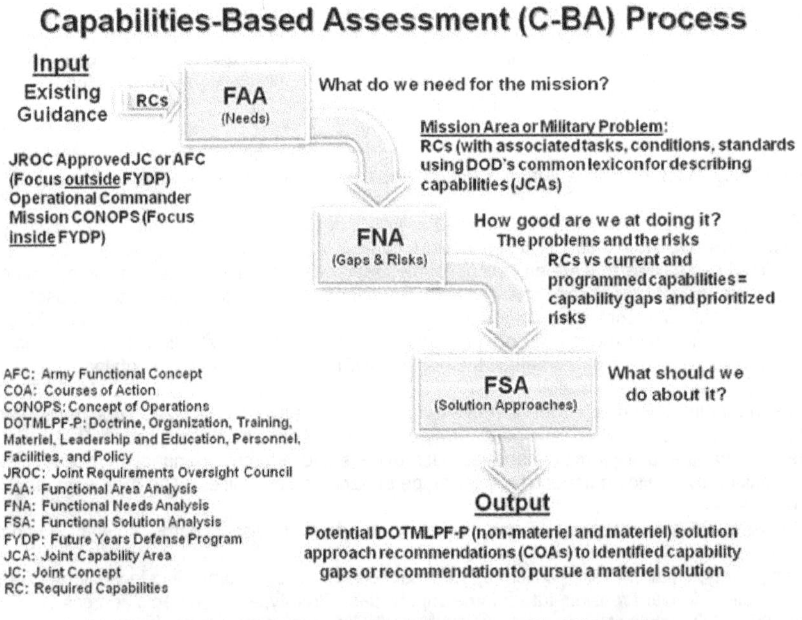

Capabilities-Based Assessment (C-BA) Process

Input
Existing Guidance — RCs → **FAA** (Needs)

What do we need for the mission?

Mission Area or Military Problem:
RCs (with associated tasks, conditions, standards using DOD's common lexicon for describing capabilities (JCAs)

JROC Approved JC or AFC (Focus outside FYDP)
Operational Commander Mission CONOPS (Focus inside FYDP)

FNA (Gaps & Risks)

How good are we at doing it?
The problems and the risks
RCs vs current and programmed capabilities = capability gaps and prioritized risks

AFC: Army Functional Concept
COA: Courses of Action
CONOPS: Concept of Operations
DOTMLPF-P: Doctrine, Organization, Training, Materiel, Leadership and Education, Personnel, Facilities, and Policy
JROC: Joint Requirements Oversight Council
FAA: Functional Area Analysis
FNA: Functional Needs Analysis
FSA: Functional Solution Analysis
FYDP: Future Years Defense Program
JCA: Joint Capability Area
JC: Joint Concept
RC: Required Capabilities

FSA (Solution Approaches)

What should we do about it?

Output
Potential DOTMLPF-P (non-materiel and materiel) solution approach recommendations (COAs) to identified capability gaps or recommendation to pursue a materiel solution

Figure 5-3. Capabilities-Based Assessment (C-BA) Process

ARMY FORCE DEVELOPMENT

a. JOE. The C-BA process begins with an analysis of the JOE. This analysis describes the physical, demographic, political, economic, technological, and military conditions in which the joint/Army force will operate during the next 25 years. The JOE results from an analysis of military and civilian documents, classified and unclassified, that describe future world conditions. Analyzed through the lens of Professional Military Judgment (PMJ), the JOE serves as a basis for shaping future FOCs, previously discussed. The JOE reflects the analysis and assimilation of dozens of futures studies conducted by DOD, other government agencies, academia and industry, considered in relation to the NSS, the NDS, and DPG. Joint experimentation and exercise wargames and the Army transformation process further supplement the development and definition of the JOE. Ultimately, these studies provide the basis for detailing the Army's future force, and for its subsequent preparation for combat.

b. FAA. The FAA is the first analytical phase of the JCIDS-directed C-BA. Strictly a capabilities-based task analysis, the FAA provides the framework to assess RCs in the follow-on FNA.

(1) The input to the FAA is an approved JCA, AFC, or CONOPS that describes how the force will operate, the timeframe and environment in which it must operate, its RCs (in terms of missions and effects), and its defining physical and operational characteristics. Any analysis begins with a problem statement, and the FAA must start with the military problem to be examined. From the examination of the problem statement, the FAA isolates the RCs documented in the concept, identifies those tasks that the force must perform, the conditions of task performance, and the required performance standards. The output is a list of RCs and associated tasks and attributes. Mapped to each RC, the tasks, conditions, and standards are developed to the level required for analysis against which current and programmed capabilities will be evaluated in the follow-on FNA. Not all warfighting concepts will necessarily generate an FAA.

(2) The FAA is based on professional military knowledge of established doctrine and standards that are modified to account for the projected concept for future operations and organizations. The FAA employs operational analysis that is primarily qualitative in nature. The analysis must identify the tasks that must be performed to accomplish the mission or achieve effects, and the specific conditions (e.g., weather, terrain, threat) in which the tasks must be performed. Many of these conditions are described in the Universal Joint Task List (UJTL), but they must be adapted based upon PMJ of related operational experiences and the forecasted influence of the future environmental factors. The performance standards developed for required tasks are found in the Army Universal Task List (AUTL), UJTL, approved concepts, or may also be based on operational experience.

c. FNA. The FNA is the second analytic phase in the C-BA. It assesses the ability of current and programmed Army capabilities to accomplish the tasks identified in the FAA, in the manner prescribed by the concept, under the full range of operating conditions, and to the prescribed standards. The FNA will identify any gaps and overlaps in capabilities and the risk posed by those gaps. The FNA determines which tasks identified in the FAA cannot be performed, performed to standard, performed in some conditions, or performed in the manner that the concept requires using the current or programmed force; and which of these gaps in capability pose sufficient operational risk to constitute needs that require a solution. Capability needs are defined as those capability gaps determined to present unacceptable risk. Following the FNA, the Director, ARCIC will direct the CoE standing ICDT chair or proponent to proceed with an FSA for those needs considered critical to executing operations IAW the concept.

(1) The tasks, conditions, and standards identified in the FAA and a list of current and programmed capabilities are the inputs to the FNA. The initial output of the FNA is a list of all gaps in the capabilities required to execute a concept to standard. When these gaps are subjected to risk analysis, the final output is a list of prioritized gaps (needs) – capabilities for which solutions must be found or developed. Not all capability gaps will be identified as needs.

(2) In its simplest form, the FNA is a comparison of RCs to existing and programmed capabilities and the identification of the corresponding gaps. It must accurately and fairly assess current and programmed solutions' ability to provide RCs when employed in the manner and conditions called for by the AFC/CONOPS. The FNA includes supportability as an inherent part of defining the capability needs. Emphasis will be placed on defining capabilities by functional domain, describing common attributes desired of subordinate systems, Family of Systems (FoS), or SoS and non-materiel solutions. Required capabilities must address joint and coalition warfare applications. The issue of determining whether the risk posed by specific capability gaps rises to the level of need, and to decide the relative priority of competing needs is a leadership decision. The FNA must provide the Army's leadership with an

HOW THE ARMY RUNS

understanding of the operational effect of each identified capability gap at levels ranging from the simplest functional or tactical task to tasks of potentially operational or strategic impact.

d. FSA. The FSA is the third analytic phase in the C-BA. It is an operationally based assessment of potential non-materiel doctrine, organization, training, leadership and education, personnel, facilities, and policy (DOTmLPF-P), and/or materiel approaches to solving (or mitigating) one or more of the capability needs determined from the FNA. The FSA describes the ability of each identified approach to satisfy the need. The FNA high-risk capability gaps are inputs to the FSA. The outputs of the FSA are the potential materiel and/or non-materiel approaches to resolve the capability needs. The FSA is composed of two sub steps: ideas for non-materiel approaches (DOTmLPF-P analysis); and ideas for materiel approaches.

(1) Approaches proposed by an FSA must meet three criteria: they are strategically responsive and deliver approaches when and where they are needed; they are feasible with respect to policy, sustainment, personnel limitations, and technological risk; and they are realizable—DOD could actually resource and implement the approaches within the timeframe required.

(2) Ideas for non-materiel approaches. Potential non-materiel solution approach recommendations are sometimes called DOTmLPF-P or DOT_LPF-P. The first sub step in the FSA identifies whether a non-materiel (DOTmLPF-P) or integrated DOTMLPF-P approach can address the capability gaps (needs) identified in the FNA. It first determines how the needed capability might be met by changes in DOTmLPF-P or existing materiel short of developing new systems. These include changes in quantity of existing materiel, improving existing materiel, adopting other services' materiel, or purchasing materiel from non U.S. sources. If the analysis determines that the capability can be partially or completely addressed by a purely DOTmLPF-P approach, a DCR is prepared and appropriate action is taken IAW the JCIDS Manual. If it is determined that DOTmLPF-P changes alone are inadequate and that product improvements to existing materiel, adoption of other service or interagency materiel, acquisition of foreign materiel, or a new materiel approach is required, the FSA process continues to sub step 2 below. Some capability proposals will involve combinations of DOTmLPF-P changes and materiel changes. Also, these proposals continue through the FSA process at sub step 2.

(3) Ideas for materiel approaches. In sub step 2, materiel approaches (courses of action) are identified to provide the RCs. The collaborative nature of this effort is meant to develop potential solutions that are truly "born joint"; in other words, solutions that involve all services. The process brainstorms possible materiel approaches and always includes existing and future materiel programs that can be modified to meet the capability need. The DOTLPF-P implications of a materiel solution must always be considered throughout the process.

e. C-BA recommendations. A C-BA offers actionable recommendations for both non-materiel and materiel solution approaches.

(1) Potential non-materiel solution approach recommendations include the following:
(a) Change policy
(b) Change doctrine
(c) Reorganize
(d) Train and educate DOD personnel differently
(e) Acquire commercial or non-developmental items
(f) Acquire more quantities of existing items or commodities to include increases in manpower operational tempo, spare parts, and fuel supplies
(g) Add or reassign personnel to mission areas
(h) Move or realign facilities to support new mission areas

(2) Materiel initiatives tend to fall into three broad categories (listed in terms of fielding uncertainty from low to high):
(a) Development and fielding of information systems (or similar technologies with high obsolescence rates) or evolution of the capabilities of existing information systems
(b) Evolution of existing systems with significant capability improvement (this may include replacing an existing system with a newer more capable system, or simple recapitalization)
(c) Breakout systems that differ significantly in form, function, operation, and capabilities from existing systems and offer significant improvement over current capabilities or transform how we accomplish the mission.

f. TRADOC ARCIC tasks a CoE standing ICDT or proponent to develop the initial DOTMLPF-P capabilities document(s) - ICD and/or joint DCR. When documented, TRADOC's ARCIC submits

ARMY FORCE DEVELOPMENT

DOTMLPF-P solution sets to HQDA G-3/5/7 for ARSTAF staffing and VCSA validation via the Army Requirements Oversight Council (AROC) validation process (discussed later in chapter 11). Figure 5-4 illustrates some documents that might initiate resourcing for DOTMLPF domains. This collection of possible solution approaches forms the strategic framework plan to reach the desired capability.

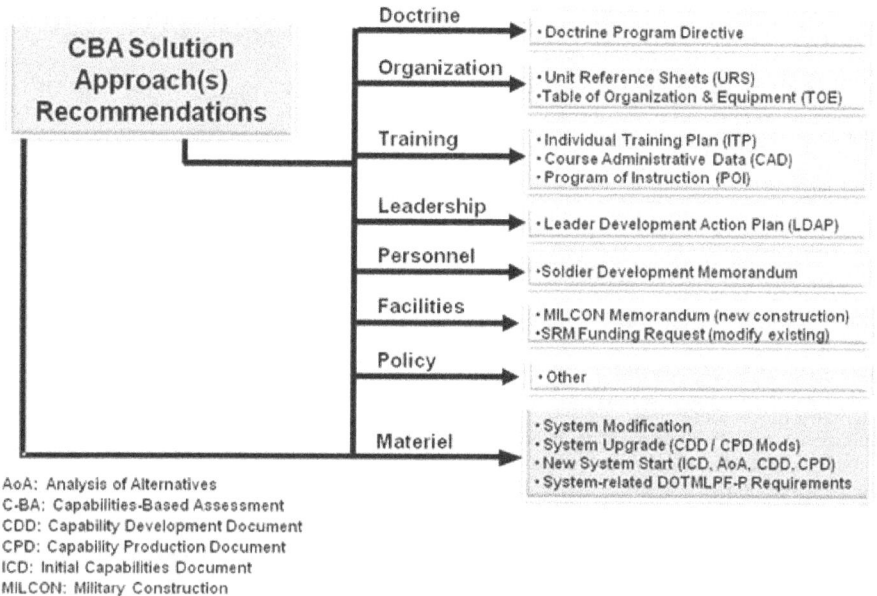

Figure 5-4. Solutions Documents

g. Processes that may substitute for the C-BA. DOD has several processes in place that can be used in lieu of a formal C-BA. They are listed below:

(1) Joint Capabilities Technology Demonstration (JCTD). The Military Utility Assessment (MUA), which is completed at the end of the JCTD, may be a suitable replacement for the required analysis used as the basis for ICD preparation. MUAs that do not contain the critical elements of information presented in the ICD (description of the capability gap(s); associated tasks, conditions and operational performance standards/metrics; and how the materiel and non-materiel approaches and analyses from the JCTD addressed these factors), will be augmented with a final demonstration report to qualify the results as equivalent to an ICD. The MUA/final demonstration report will be used to support the development and subsequent AROC and/or JROC validation of the CDD or CPD. A CDD or CPD, as appropriate, will be developed for the JCTD to transition into a DAS POR.

(2) Prototypes. Results of prototype projects and operationally validated quick reaction technology projects intended for direct transition to fielded capabilities may also be eligible for consideration as potential solution approaches. This consideration will be based on mission need validation and MUA processes as applied to JCTDs.

HOW THE ARMY RUNS

(3) Joint Improvised Explosive Devices Defeat Organization (JIEDDO) Initiative Transition. The JIEDDO Transition Packet, which is completed after JIEDDO validates an initiative, may be the appropriate replacement for the required analysis used as the basis for ICD preparation. The Transition Packet will be used as the CDD/CPD equivalent document for subsequent AROC and/or JROC validation and transition to a POR.

(4) Joint Urgent Operational Needs Statement (JUONS), Joint Emergent Operational Needs Statement (JEONS), or service's urgent needs processes. Capabilities developed and fielded to support the resolution of an operational commander's urgent need can be transitioned into the JCIDS process. An urgent need validated by the Joint Staff J-8, or the service as appropriate, may be used to enter the JCIDS process without an ICD. The sponsor can enter the JCIDS and DAS processes at milestone B or C by initiating development of a CDD or CPD as appropriate. Capabilities fielded to resolve an urgent need which will continue to be required and sustained for the duration of an on-going operation do not require additional JCIDS documentation.

h. Overall, the capabilities-based Army JCIDS process examines where we are, where we want to be, what risks we may face and what it might cost. The Army learned many lessons from the wars in Iraq and Afghanistan and accelerated (rapid fielding) processes used to develop the Stryker Brigade Combat Teams (SBCTs). These lessons have informed changes to how we generate current and future force structure requirements. Inserting an up-front and robust integrated analysis based on guidance from overarching joint and Army concepts, allows informed decisions earlier in the process, producing optimal DOTMLPF-P solution proposals and making it easier to synchronize development and fielding. In addition, this process allows requirements to be traced back to national strategies, concepts, and policies, thus helping to eliminate redundant capabilities within the Army and DOD.

Section III
Phase II—Design Organizations

5-8. Organizational Design
Organizational requirements flowing from the functional solution analysis determine whether a new or modified organization is required on tomorrow's battlefield. Once identified, organizational requirements are documented through a series of connected organizational development processes, to include: Unit Reference Sheet (URS) development; Force Design Update (FDU) process; Table of Organization and Equipment (TOE) development; Basis-Of-Issue Plan (BOIP) development, and Total Army Analysis (TAA). Every process may not always be required before organizational changes are made to the force structure and the processes may occur out of sequence. For instance, phase III, Development of Organizational Models, starts before the end of Phase II, Designing Organizations.

5-9. The Organizational Design Process
a. Organizations have their beginnings in warfighting concepts. They provide the conceptual basis for the proposed organization and address its mission, functions, and required capabilities. The Combat Developers (CBTDEV) at TRADOC Centers of Excellence and other force modernization proponents develop new organizational designs or correct deficiencies in existing organizations. The ARCIC Director integrates and validates concepts developed for future force capabilities. These concepts normally address:
   (1) Missions, functions, capabilities, and limitations
   (2) Mission command linkages
   (3) Individual, collective, and leader training requirements
   (4) Sustainment in field and garrison
   (5) Doctrinal impacts
   (6) Impacts on materiel programs

b. The FDU is used to develop consensus within the Army on new organizations and changes to existing organizations and to obtain approval and implementation decisions (Figure 5-5). On a semi-annual basis, the FDU process addresses organizational solutions to desired capabilities and improvements to existing designs in which other doctrine, training, materiel, leader development, personnel or facilities solutions were insufficient. The FDU serves as the link between the development of the URS and the development of the TOE. During the FDU, the URS is staffed throughout the Army to

ARMY FORCE DEVELOPMENT

include the Combatant Commanders and the Army's commands. HQDA then makes approval and implementation decisions. Force design issues will then go through a HQDA Force Integration Functional Analysis (FIFA). The FIFA reviews force structure issues and the impacts of force structure decisions on the total Army.

c. During the FIFA, the ARSTAF analyzes the force to assess affordability, supportability, and sustainability. At the macro level, within the limits of personnel and budgetary constraints, the FIFA determines the ability for the force to be manned, trained, equipped, sustained, and stationed. The FIFA may provide alternatives based on prior initiatives, unalterable decisions from the Army leadership or Program Budget Decisions (PBD). The FIFA can result in one of three recommendations:
  (1) HQDA can decide to implement the change and find resources
  (2) Or HQDA can return it to the ARCIC for further analysis
  (3) Or prioritize the issue for resourcing in the next TAA

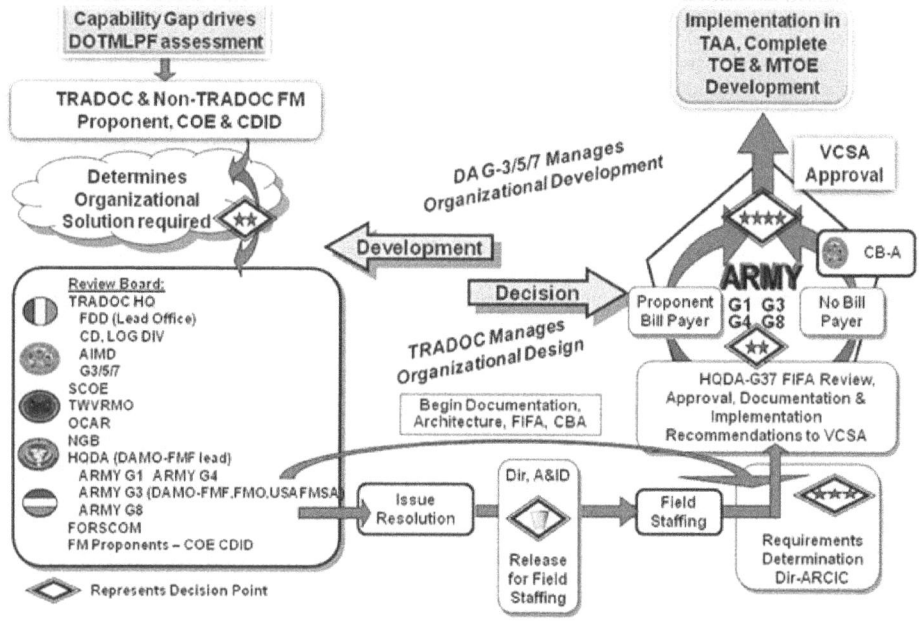

Figure 5-5. Force Design Update (FDU)

Section IV
Phase III—Develop Organizational Models

5-10. TOE and BOIP Development
a. Organizations in the process of being designed in the preceding phase become the start point for the next phase. Following the first level of approval of the URS during the FDU process, the design goes to U.S. Army Force Management Support Agency (USAFMSA) for documentation as a TOE. The

HOW THE ARMY RUNS

USAFMSA and the U.S. Army Special Operations Command (USASOC) develop TOEs and BOIPs codifying the input from the URS basic design.

b. TOEs and BOIPs are developed using an Army-wide development system and database called the Force Management System (FMS). FMS is currently being implemented and should reach full operational capability in the next few years. FMS will eventually feature a relational database for both requirement and authorization documentation and other information management systems as well.

c. Although the organization design phase and organizational model development phase are depicted as separate processes, they are closely related and frequently overlap. The proponent organization designers and the USAFMSA TOE developers work closely to ensure that the designs reflect requirements consistent with doctrine and policy and include all the elements necessary to provide an organization fully capable of accomplishing its doctrinal mission. The approved organization design should capture personnel and equipment requirements as accurately and completely as possible.

5-11. TOE Description

a. TOEs provide a standard method for documenting the organizational structure of the Army. A TOE prescribes the doctrinal mission, required structure, and mission essential wartime manpower and equipment requirements for several levels of organizational options for a particular type unit. These organizational options provide models for fielding a unit at full or reduced manpower authorizations if resource constraints so mandate. A TOE also specifies the capabilities (and limitations or dependencies) for the unit.

b. TOEs provide the basis for developing authorization documents and provide input for determining Army resource requirements for use by force managers. In addition, these unit models establish increments of capability for the Army to develop an effective, efficient, and combat-ready force structure.

c. The TOE is a collection of related records in the database. There are a variety of records to include narrative information, personnel requirements, equipment requirements, paragraph numbers and titles, and changes in the form of BOIP records to name a few. A TOE consists of Base TOE (BTOE) records and applicable BOIP records.

d. Document developers construct a TOE in levels of organization based on the manpower requirements necessary to achieve percentage levels such as level 1 (100%) Minimum Mission Essential Wartime Requirement (MMEWR), or an organization partially manned by personnel other than Soldiers (level B). As TOE level 1 is the wartime requirement, it is what is reflected in the "required" column of the authorization document (Modified Table of Organization and Equipment (MTOE)).

e. FDU decisions, branch proponent input, and Army commands' issues, along with force design guidance developed during capabilities analyses, provide TOE developers with recommended TOE additions/modifications. Policy and doctrine provide the missions and probable areas of employment of a unit. Policy includes guidance, procedures, and standards, in the form of regulations, on how to develop TOEs. Policy published in Human Resources Command's MOS Smartbook contains Standards of Grade (SG), duty titles, guidance for occupational identifiers (Area Of Concentration (AOC), MOS), skill identifier, Special Qualification Identifier (SQI), and ASIs used in the development of requirement documents and other organizational plans. Doctrine describes how each type of unit will perform its functions and details the mission and required capabilities.

f. TOE developers consider the unit mission and required capabilities when applying equipment utilization policies, Manpower Requirements Criteria (MARC), SG, and BOIPs to develop the proper mix of equipment and personnel for an efficient organizational structure. Resource guidance limits the development of draft TOEs, as they must use resources available in the inventory.

5-12. TOE System

The Army uses a TOE system with personnel and equipment modernization over time that reflects how the Army actually conducts its organizational and force modernization business. URSs form the basis for developing TOEs. The TOE system illustrates capability enhancements of an organizational model through the application of related doctrinally sound personnel and equipment changes in separately identifiable BOIPs. See Figure 5-6. A TOE begins with a doctrinally sound BTOE and through the application of BOIPs builds up to a fully modernized Objective TOE (OTOE). The TOE is a requirements document and is the basis for force programming. Upon HQDA approval of resources, specific unit designations, and Effective Date (EDATE) for the activation or reorganization of a unit, the TOE becomes an MTOE and becomes an authorization document. The MTOE is the authoritative source from which

ARMY FORCE DEVELOPMENT

personnel and equipment can be requested and is the document most often utilized by Soldiers and leaders in the field. The TOE system consists of the following components.

a. Base TOE. The BTOE is an organizational model design based on doctrine and equipment currently available. It is the least modernized version of a type of organization and identifies mission-essential wartime requirements for personnel and equipment.

b. Basis of issue plan. A BOIP is a doctrinally sound grouping of related personnel and equipment changes that is applied to a BTOE to provide an enhanced capability, increased productivity, or modernization.

c. OTOE. The OTOE is a fully modernized, doctrinally sound organizational model design achieved by applying all DA-approved BOIPs. The OTOE sets the goal for planning and programming of the Army's force structure and supporting acquisition systems.

d. A TOE in the revision, development, or staffing process and not yet DA approved is called a draft TOE (DTOE). DTOEs are reviewed by USAFMSA and coordinated with appropriate commands, agencies, and activities during an Area-Of-Interest (AOI) review. After AOI review, USAFMSA makes final changes before the responsible G-37 (FMO) OI staffs the TOE HQDA-wide and presents the DTOE to Director, Force Management for approval. Following approval, the DTOE status is changed to "DA approved" in the FMS.

e. A TOE becomes eligible for cyclic review every three years.

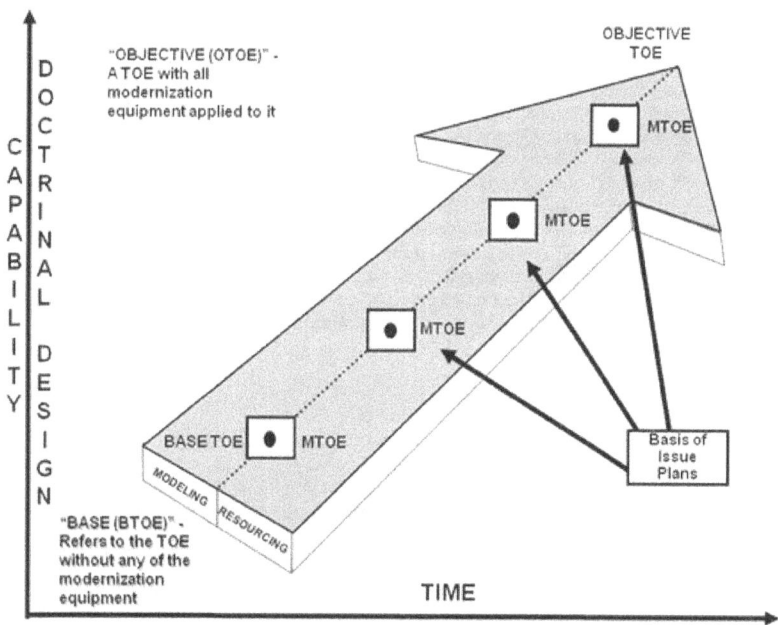

Figure 5-6. Modernization Over Time (Resource Driven)

5-13. BOIP

a. A BOIP specifies the planned placement of new or improved items of equipment and personnel in TOEs at 100 percent of wartime requirements. It reflects quantities of new equipment and Associated Support Items of Equipment and Personnel (ASIOEP), as well as changes to existing equipment and personnel requirements. In addition to its use for TOE development/revision, HQDA uses it for logistics support and distribution planning for new and improved items entering the Army supply system. Materiel Developers (MATDEV), Program Executive Officers (PEOs)/Program Managers (PMs), Army Materiel Command (AMC), and USASOC communities use it as input for concept studies, life cycle cost estimates, and trade-off analyses during the system development and demonstration phase of the system acquisition management process.

b. A BOIP provides personnel and equipment changes required to introduce a new or modified item into Army organizations. The development of a BOIP can play an integral part in TOE development. A BOIP provides the data to place a new or substantially changed materiel item into organizations along with associated equipment and personnel to maintain and operate it as specified in the materiel capability document and the Basis-Of-Issue Plan Feeder Data (BOIPFD).

c. BOIPFD, prepared by the MATDEV, contains a compilation of organizational, doctrinal, training, duty position, and personnel information that is incorporated into the BOIP. The information is used to determine the need to develop or revise military occupational specialties and to prepare plans for the personnel and training needed to operate and maintain the new or improved item. Human Resources Command (HRC) provides input to the BOIP through development of the Operator and Maintainer (O/M) decision. The BOIP process begins when the MATDEV receives an approved and resourced CDD. The project manager and/or MATDEV develop BOIPFD, and then obtain a Developmental Line Item Number (ZLIN) and Standard Study Number (SSN) from AMC.

d. The BOIPFD goes to USAFMSA via the Logistic Integrated Warehouse where the information is reviewed for accuracy, continuity, and completeness before the formal development of the BOIP. During staffing, the training impacts associated with the BOIP equipment and the associated personnel requirements are developed. If the O/M decision includes an occupational identifier, the personnel proponent must prepare a proposal per AR 611-1 for submission to HRC to revise the military occupational classification and structure. USAFMSA requests Table of Distribution and Allowances (TDA) requirements for new or modified items from the Army's commands and TDA requirements are entered into the BOIP at unit level. Note that BOIPs are not developed for TDA-only equipment. When the BOIP is complete, it goes to DA for approval. The G-37 (FMO) Organizational Integration officer, in coordination with the G-8 Synchronization Staff Officer is responsible for HQDA staffing and for presenting the BOIP to the HQDA, G-3/7, Director of Force Management (DFM) for approval.

e. There may be several iterations of the BOIP – an initial BOIP, developed during system development and demonstration, and amended BOIPs, which are based on updated information provided by the MATDEV as required. A BOIP may be amended at any time during system development and fielding, upon approval of HQDA, or when new or changed information becomes available.

Section V
Phase IV—Determine Organizational Authorizations

5-14. Determining Organizational Authorizations

a. The fourth force development phase, determining organizational authorizations, provides the proper mix of organizations, resulting in a balanced and affordable force structure. Force structuring is an integral part of the OSD management systems, PPBE and the JSPS. It is the resource-sensitive process portrayed in the "Determine Authorizations" section of the Army Force Management Model at Figure 2-2. It develops force structure in support of joint, strategic, and operational planning and Army planning, programming, and budgeting. Force structure development draws upon an understanding of the objectives, desired capabilities, and externally imposed constraints (e.g., dollars, total strength, roles, and missions).

b. The determination of the size and content of the Army force structure is an iterative, risk-benefit, trade-off analysis process, not all of which is exclusively within the purview of the Army. The national security strategies, NDS, NMS, QDR and DPG constitute the major JCS/DOD directives and constraints imposed upon Army force structure. Overall, TAP captures Army-specific strategic and programmatic

ARMY FORCE DEVELOPMENT

guidance. TAP articulates the SECARMY and CSA translation of the JCS/DOD guidance to all Services into specific direction to the ARSTAF and commands for the development of the Army POM, and the initiation of the TAA process. The TAP is the principal Army guidance for development of the Army POM submission.

c. TAA supports the evolving transition, providing the correct number and types of units over the POM period.

5-15. TAA

a. The TAA process identifies the capabilities necessary to achieve the Unified Land Operations missions expected of the Army as outlined in the TAP, national security documents, and Army operating concepts. It takes us from the Army of today to the Army of the future. It requires a doctrinal basis and analysis, flowing from strategic guidance and joint force capability requirements. TAA determines the best mix of forces for each program year. It has Army wide participation and culminates in a Senior Leaders of the Department of the Army (SLDA) decision and approval.

b. TAA builds a POM Force which serves as the basis for building the POM submission. TAA objectives are to:

(1) Develop, analyze, determine and justify a POM Force, aligned with the strategic guidance and TAP. The POM Force is projected to be raised, provisioned, sustained, and maintained within resources available during the FYDP.

(2) Provide analytical underpinnings for the POM Force for use in dialogue among Congress, OSD, Joint Staff, CCDRs, and the Army.

(3) Assess the impacts of planned and potential alternatives for materiel acquisition, the production base, and equipment distribution programs for the projected force structure.

(4) Assure continuity of demanded force structure within the PPBE process.

(5) Provide program basis for structuring organizational, materiel, and personnel requirements and projected authorizations.

c. The TAA principal products are the:

(1) Army's full range of demands for the capabilities necessary to achieve the Unified Land Operations expected of the Army (unconstrained and all uniformed military)

(2) Best mix of support forces (echelons above brigade support and sustainment) and identified risk

(3) Force resourced against requirements and budgetary constraints

(4) Army Structure (ARSTRUC) memorandum

(5) POM Force database

5-16. TAA Process

TAA determines the mix of organizations that comprise a balanced and affordable force structure. There are typically two phases associated with TAA: Capability Demand Analysis (force guidance and quantitative analysis) and Resourcing and Approval (qualitative analysis and leadership review).

a. TAA is the resource-informed process that integrates the decisions of the OSD, Joint, and Army Leadership into the PPBE process by building a force for the program years that can be used by programmers to build the Army budget.

b. TAA serves as the bridge between OSD/JS guidance and the Army's force structure planning and program building processes. It balances the Army's force structure demands (manpower, equipment, and dollars) against available and planned resources. TAA decisions shape the future composition of the Army and are made in the best interest of the Total Army. The Army's resourced force structure must support strategic guidance. Therefore, TAA develops a force that best meets guidance, within the defined scenarios, under the established resource constraints, and fulfills all the roles and missions within the parameters of congressional oversight and guidance.

c. Additionally, the TAA process is the means to transition force structure from the planning phase to the programming phase within the Army's PPBE process, assisting in determining, verifying and justifying Army capability demands, while assessing force capabilities. The process flows from internal Army actions, decisions and guidance (e.g., rules of allocation, resource assumptions, warfighting capabilities, and infrastructure priorities), and from external inputs from the President, SECDEF, CJCS, JS, OSD, and CCDR priorities (e.g., anticipated threats, scenarios, and assumptions). The Army develops the POM Force to achieve an affordable force capable of best supporting national objectives and CCDR Army warfighting needs. This force supports the joint strategic planning conducted by the JS, CCDRs and the

HOW THE ARMY RUNS

Services at the transition between planning and programming. The mix of capabilities that make up a balanced and affordable force structure must support Joint and Army planning, programming, and budgeting at the strategic, operational, and tactical levels within manageable levels of risk.

　d. The TAA process is focused on building an affordable balanced force for the program years. TAA is flexible and responsive to dynamic changes within those program years. Changes intended for the years preceding the program years can still be made using resources programmed in a previous TAA for the year of execution in question. The only limiting factor in the scope of pre-program year transformation is the availability and flexibility of resources in the year of execution budget.

　e. Figure 5-7 depicts the sequence of activities in the TAA process.

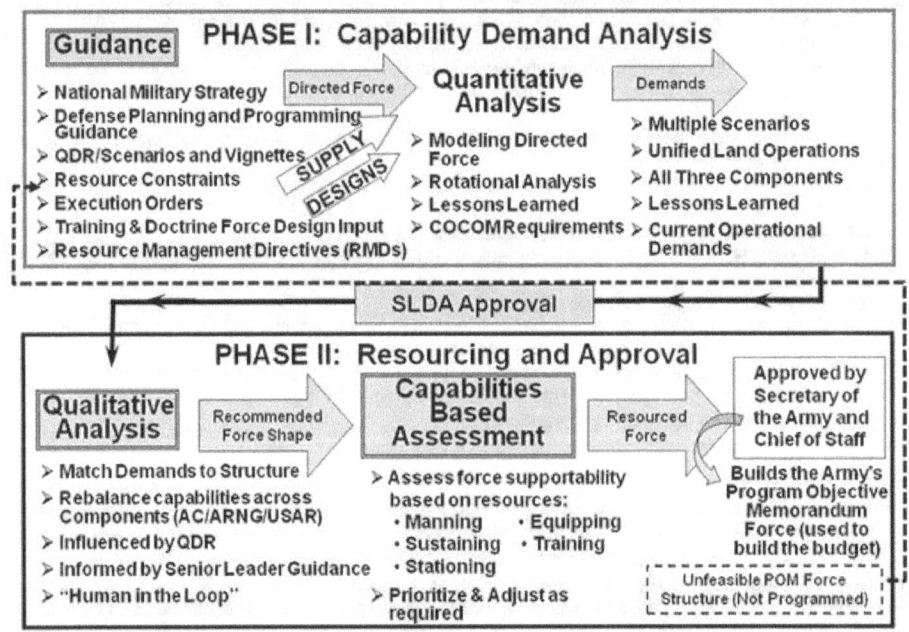

Figure 5-7. Total Army Analysis "End-to-End" Process

5-17. TAA Phase I—Capability Demand Analysis (CDA)

The Capability Demand Analysis Phase begins by leveraging OSD scenarios from Operational Availability (OA) series analytical work, the QDR and Integrated Security Campaigns to capture the Army's directed force (maneuver, fires and effects) Operating Force (OF) requirements. The scenarios are modeled and analyzed to develop the appropriate OF within the authorized end-strength necessary to accomplish the Unified Land Operations missions with "minimum risk." Accurate planning, consumption and workload factors, threat data, and allocation rules ensure accurate computer-modeled demands. This demand list, combined with previous TAA scenario demand lists, CCMDR War-plans and operational deployment data will be used to help determine the best mix of forces for the Army within authorized end strength. It is not intended to be used to determine the size of the Army. Because of the scenario size and complexity required to ensure every capability is fully exercised across the full Range Of Military Operations (ROMO), the range of demands on OF capabilities will likely far exceed the capabilities resident within the

ARMY FORCE DEVELOPMENT

authorized end-strength. During the Phase II, the Resourcing an Approval Phase, the determination must be made as to the level of acceptable "risk" to be taken for each capability. These capability demands are based on Army leadership directives, written guidance, risk analysis, the Army force generation and input from the Combatant Commander's Daily Operational Requirements (CCDOR). TAA builds a POM Force with which the PEGs can develop their portion of the Army's budget. The POM Force also will determine the OF enabler support force structure and define the Generating Force (GF) necessary to support and sustain the OF capabilities directed in strategic guidance. The determination of the composition of the Army force structure (shape) is an iterative, risk-benefit, trade-off analysis process. Capability Demand Analysis is made up of two separate events: force guidance and quantitative analysis.

   a. Force guidance. Force guidance consists of data inputs and guidance from various sources.

   (1) QDR. QDR is a permanent requirement (every four years). The principal purposes of the QDR are to: develop strategic guidance for the DOD; lay out an agenda for developing needed future capabilities; forecast defense requirements 20 years into the future; and satisfy statutory requirements. The 2010 QDR, along with the Ballistic Missile Defense Review (BMDR) and the Nuclear Posture Review (NPR) serve as the basis for the development of the DPG. 2014 QDR will be the basis for developing the force structure for the next four years.

   (2) DPG. The DPG establishes the DOD force development, resource and programming priorities, and consolidates and integrates DOD force development planning priorities. The DPG is a fiscally informed policy and strategy document.

   (3) TAP. The TAP is the principal Army guidance for development of the Army POM submission. The SECARMY and CSA translate the DOD guidance into specific direction to the ARSTAF and commands for the development of the Army POM. The TAP provides the senior leadership's vision, identifies strategic vision and intent, translates vision into prioritized capabilities, links vision with capabilities and resources, and provides the synchronized road map of "how" to implement the TAP through the Army Campaign Plan (ACP). The TAP provides the OF constituting the start point for force structuring activities (shaping). DAMO-SSW and DAMO-FMF determine the specific identification, size, and composition of the OF in accordance with TAP force structure guidance.

   b. Data and guidance inputs.

   (1) Homeland Defense (HD). NORTHCOM and PACOM have the responsibility to develop and identify the missions, threats, areas of responsibility and Army force structure demands to accomplish HD.

   (2) Analytic Agenda. OSD provides the directed scenarios, surge events (major campaigns) and vignettes within the Analytic Agenda.

   (a) Primarily focused on strategic analysis of future force capabilities (force effectiveness and sufficiency).

   (b) Integrated Security Campaigns (ISCs) - each ISC comprises multiple, simultaneous activities occurring over a multiyear timeframe to create one possible future; product includes Combatant Command foundational activities (from the vignettes and scenarios), concepts of operations, and associated data for each of the major activities.

   (c) Future force structure requirements will be generated through the current and future QDR influenced strategy, and updates to the National Security Strategy and National Defense Strategy.

   (d) OSD has executed several OA studies to determine mid-term warfighting scenarios or vignettes. They provide the OSD-approved scenarios.

   (3) Force sizing construct. Guidance from OSD in the DPG and dictates the force sizing guidance.

   (4) Foundational Activities.

   (a) Develop force requirements for COCOM activities to prevent and deter over time.

   (b) Other challenges - to develop force demands in support of a range of multiple, simultaneous operations at home & abroad (e.g., Stabilization, COIN, defeat regional aggressors(s), support to civil authorities in the U.S.) with the purpose of ensuring each capability is fully exercised across its full ROMO.

   (5) Parameters, planning and consumption factors, and assumptions.

   (a) HQDA DCS G-4, TRADOC, MEDCOM, U.S. Army Combined Arms Support Command (CASCOM), the theater commands and other elements of the HQDA staff (G-1, G-3/5/7, G-4, G-6 and G-8) provide specific guidance, accurate and detailed consumption factors, planning factors, doctrinal requirements, unit level rules of allocation, network requirements, weapons and munitions data, and deployment assumptions. The Center for Army Analysis (CAA) then conducts the series of Modeling and Simulation (M&S) iterations that are analyzed to develop and define the total capability demands for logistical

HOW THE ARMY RUNS

support necessary to sustain the combat force(s) in Homeland Defense, Army Support to Other Services (ASOS), Foundational Activities, each Major Combat Operation (MCO), and the GF.

(b) The parameters, factors, and assumptions contain theater-specific information concerning logistics and personnel planning, consumption and workload factors, host-nation support (HNS) offsets and other planning factors crucial to theater force development.

(6) Rules of Allocation. Another critical step during the force guidance development is the review and updating of support-force rules of allocation used by the CAA during the modeling process (quantitative analysis).

(a) These rules of allocation, developed by TRADOC and the functional area proponents, represent a quantitative statement of doctrine for each type of unit (maneuver, fires, effects, support and sustainment). They are adjusted as necessary to incorporate theater-specific planning factors. There are three basic types of rules:

(i) Direct input (manual) rules are stand-alone requirements for OF or GF units in a theater. These organizations are not doctrinally required in the warfight. They are required to support the warfight.

(ii) Existence rules tie a requirement for one unit to another. The allocation of units is based on the existence of other units, or a function of a theater's physical or organizational structure (e.g., for one large general purpose port—one each Harborcraft Company, requires one each Military Police Company, etc.)

(iii) Workload rules tie unit requirements to a measurable logistical workload or administrative services in proportion to the volume of those services (e.g., one each DS Maintenance Company per 375 daily man-hours of automotive maintenance or one each POL Supply Company per 2200 tons of bulk POL consumed per day).

(b) The rules of allocation need modification whenever unit TOEs, scenario assumptions, logistical support plans, or doctrinal employment concepts change.

(c) Council of Colonels (CoC) and General Officer (GO) level reviews ensure all rules of allocation are appropriate and approved for use in the current scenarios.

(7) CoC and GO-level review. These are decision forums where all the parameters, constraints, data inputs and guidance are identified and approved for inclusion in the current TAA cycle and CAA models.

(a) The term "GO-level" includes assigned Senior Executive Service (SES) personnel.

(b) The CoC reviews and recommends approval of all data inputs and required forces developed by CAA modeling.

(c) The GO-level review ensures all data input and guidance is appropriate and approved for use in the current scenario(s). It specifically addresses those unresolved issues from the CoC review.

c. Quantitative analysis. Warfighting capability demands are determined in this phase. CAA, through computer modeling and analysis, generates the scenario generated requirements (OF only) for types of units needed to ensure success of the BCTs, support brigades and headquarters commands directed in the different scenarios. CAA accomplishes the modeling through a series of analytical efforts and associated computer simulations. CAA uses the apportioned force provided in the OSD and Army guidance for employment in the MCO scenarios.

(1) OF. The OF is those forces whose primary missions are to participate in combat and the integral supporting elements thereof (JP 1-02):

(a) The TAP provides the number and type of BCTs.

(b) The CAA computer models and analysis generate resources (units or classes of supply) needed in each illustrative scenario. Based on the illustrative scenario, rules of allocation, and the capability demands generated for units or classes of supply, CAA modeling and analysis develops the unconstrained (minimum risk) demand for enablers to ensure success of the deployed BCTs in the warfight.

(2) GF. Army organizations whose primary mission is to generate and sustain the OF capabilities for employment by joint force commanders. As a consequence of its performance of functions specified, and implied by law, the GF also possesses operationally useful capabilities for employment by, or in direct support of, joint force commanders (FM 1-01). The GF determination is evolving through studies and inclusion of processes and procedures to link OF needs to GF size, configuration and design..

d. Review and approval. Phase I (Capability Demand Analysis) is complete after the CoC/GO-level reviews of the results of the range of demands produced for each capability (CAA modeling and analysis results, weighted and integrated with applicable TAA ISCs, CCDR Warplans and deployment data).

(1) The CoC/GO-level forums "review and approve" the warfighting capability as a fully structured and resourced force.

ARMY FORCE DEVELOPMENT

(2) Additionally, the CoC/GO-level forums review and reach agreement on the force structure demands supporting HD, Army Support to Other Services and Foundational Activities and the appropriate level of inclusion of contractor support, use of strategic partners, joint capabilities, and other risk mitigation variables to appropriately scope the capability demands within total strength ensuring a focus on shaping the Army and not on sizing the Army. The GO-level review recommends approval of the capability demands to the SLDA.

(3) The SLDA reviews and approves the capability demands. The SLDA review and approval is the transition to Phase II of TAA (Resourcing and Approval Phase).

5-18. TAA Phase II—Resourcing and Approval
Resource determination consists of two separate activities, qualitative analysis and leadership review. The qualitative analysis is the most emotional facet of the TAA process because the analysis results in the distribution of scarce resources, impacting every aspect of the Army. Therefore, this phase requires extensive preparation by participants to ensure all force structure tradeoffs are accurately assessed and the best warfighting force structure is developed.

a. Qualitative analysis. Qualitative analysis is conducted to develop the initial POM force, within total strength guidance, for use in the development of the POM. A series of resourcing forums, analyses, panel reviews, and CoC consider and validate the CDA analysis of those demands. The qualitative analysis begins in the CDA Phase as risk mitigation measures are applied but prior to the resourcing panels. The qualitative analysis will continue until the POM Force is approved by the SLDA.

b. The resourcing CoC is held in two separate sessions, Organizational Integrator (OI) Panels and Resourcing CoC.

(1) OI Panels.

(a) HQDA action officers and their counterparts enter an intense round of preparations for the resourcing panels. Since the quantitative analysis only determined capability demands for doctrinally correct, fully resourced maneuver, fires, effects, support and sustainment units, the determination of a need for additional units and the allocation of resourced units to Components (Active Army, Army Reserve (AR), Army National Guard (ARNG)) must all be accomplished during the OI Panels. HQDA bases force structuring options on an understanding of the objectives to be achieved, the desired capabilities and the constraints. The primary differences among various options are the extent to which risk, constraints and time are addressed. It is through the OI Panels that the "Art" of Force Management is applied to the "Science" introduced during the CDA Phase.

(b) The Resourcing CoC provides the opportunity for the ARSTAF, commands, proponent representatives and staff support agencies to provide input, propose changes, and to surface issues related to the OI Panel recommendations. The issues focus on COMPO and center on resolving risk mitigation issues, while balancing priorities. The AC/RC balance and total-strength concerns are key recommendation outputs of this CoC. It allows Army Service Component Commanders (ASCC) to verify theater specific capability demands are satisfied by Army force structure assigned/apportioned to their commands to meet current CCDR OPLAN/CONPLAN warfighting requirements and CCDOR. The Resourcing CoC is typically a multi-day event chaired by the DFM.

(c) The resourcing CoC focuses on identifying and developing potential solutions for the wide range of issues brought to TAA. The OI and Force Integrators (FIs) are key individuals in this forum. The OIs have the responsibility to pull together the sometimes diverse guidance and opinions, add insight from a branch perspective, and establish the best course of action. The OIs pull all the relevant information together for presentation to the CoC. During these presentations, the OI reviews the standard requirements codes (SRCs) of interest that fall under his/her area of responsibility, and presents recommendations on how to solve the various issues.

(d) The resourcing CoC integrates Generating Force issues and requirements, and reviews and resolves issues based upon sound military judgment and experience. The CoC forwards their recommendations and any unresolved issues to the resourcing General Officer Steering Committee (GOSC).

(2) Force Feasibility Review (FFR). The ARSTAF further analyzes the force, initially approved by the GO resourcing conferences, via the FFR. The FFR process uses the results of the TAA resourcing conference as input, conducting a review and adjusting the POM force to assure it is affordable and supportable. At the macro level, within the limits of personnel and budgetary constraints, the FFR determines if the POM force can be manned, trained, equipped, sustained, and stationed. The FFR

HOW THE ARMY RUNS

process identifies problems with the POM force and provides alternatives, based on prior TAA initiatives, unalterable decisions from the Army leadership, or PBD, to the GOSC for determining the most capable force within existing or projected constraints. The FFR process is the vehicle to analyze force structure options developed during the TAA process. Additionally, with the TAA/POM process on an annual schedule, the PEGs conduct the FFR each year while building the POM. Their feedback is injected back into the next OI Panel and Resourcing CoC.

(3) Resourcing GOSC. The qualitative phase culminates with the Resourcing GOSC. The GOSC reviews/approves the decisions of the Resourcing CoC and addresses remaining unresolved issues. The GOSC has evolved into a series of GO resourcing forums at the two- and three-star level. The GO forums review and approve the decisions of the resourcing CoC, and address remaining unresolved issues. The Resourcing GOSC approves the force that is forwarded to the SLDA for review and final approval.

(4) Leadership review. After the resourcing conference, sequential GO resourcing reviews meet to resolve any contentious or outstanding issues. The SECARMY, Undersecretary of the Army, CSA, and VCSA attend the SLDA meetings. The SECARMY reviews and approves the POM force.

5-19. ARSTRUC Memorandum

The ARSTRUC memorandum, produced by Army G-37 (Force Management), provides an authoritative record of Army's Senior Leadership final decisions made during the TAA process, as well as changes made as part of the out-of-cycle process since the last ARSTRUC. The ARSTRUC memorandum directs the commands to make appropriate adjustments to their force structure at the unit identification code (UIC) level of detail during the next command plan. Commands record changes during the Command Plan process in the Structure and Manpower Allocation System (SAMAS), the official database of record for the Army. SAMAS, along with the BOIP and TOE files, provides the basis for Army authorization documentations (MTOE and TDA).

5-20. The Product of TAA

a. The resourced TAA force (POM Force) represents the force structure for POM development, capturing all components (Active, Reserve, Host Nation [HN]) and type (MTOE, TDA) capability demands through the end of the POM years. The POM Force meets the projected mission requirements with appropriate risk within anticipated total strength and equipment level. The final output should result in an executable POM Force. The Army forwards the POM Force to OSD with a recommendation for approval. All approved units are entered into SAMAS to create the POM Force. TAA is the proven mechanism for explaining and defending Army force structure for budget submission.

b. The product of the TAA and POM processes is the approved force structure for the Army, which has been divided for resource management purposes into components: the Active Component (AC) (COMPO 1); the ARNG (COMPO 2); and the AR (COMPO 3). Three other components - direct host-nation support (COMPO 7), indirect host-nation support (COMPO 8), and logistics civil augmentation (COMPO 9) - comprise force structure offsets. Host-nation support agreements guarantee the COMPO 7 and 8 resources. COMPO 9 is an augmentation, not an offset and represents the contracts for additional support and services to be provided by domestic and foreign firms augmenting existing force structure (Figure 5-8). COMPO 4 is requirements to accomplish the Army's missions but not resourced.

ARMY FORCE DEVELOPMENT

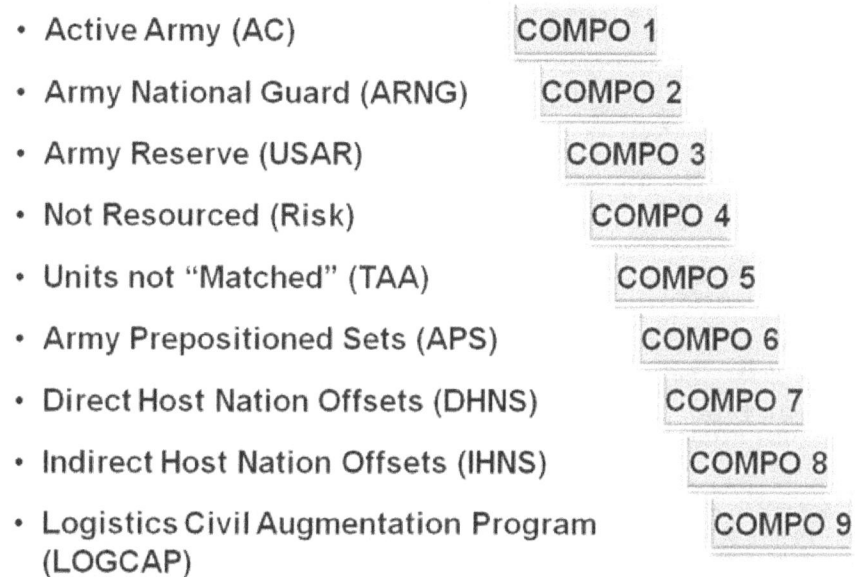

Figure 5-8. Force Structure Components (COMPO)

Section VI
Phase V—Document Organizational Authorizations

5-21. Documentation Components Overview
   a. The fifth and final phase of force development, the documenting of unit authorizations, can be viewed as the integration of organizational model development and organizational authorization determination. Battlefield requirements for specific military capabilities drive the development of organizational models. The results of this process are TOEs for organizations staffed and equipped to provide increments of the required capabilities. TOEs specify Army requirements. Determining organizational authorizations, on the other hand, is a force structure process that documents resources (people, equipment, dollars and facilities) for each unit in the Army.
   b. Because the Army is a complex array of people, each with one or more of a variety of skills, and many millions of items of equipment, there must be an organized system for documenting what is required and how much is authorized. More importantly, as the Army moves forward with transformation, modularity, equipment modernization, application of new doctrines, and the development of resulting organizations, the Army must have a way of keeping track of changes that are made so that they may be managed efficiently and with a minimum of turbulence. The following paragraphs will discuss the systems the Army utilizes to perform this function.
   c. Each unit in the Army has an authorization document, either an MTOE or a TDA, identifying its mission, structure, personnel and equipment requirements and authorizations. These documents are

HOW THE ARMY RUNS

essential at each level of command for the Army to function. A unit uses its authorization document as authority to requisition personnel and equipment and as a basis for readiness evaluation.

5-22. SAMAS

a. SAMAS is the force development automated database that records, maintains and distributes force structure information for all 7500+ units in the Army. SAMAS is the Army's "database of record" for all force structure actions. It maintains information for all COMPOs.

b. The primary inputs to SAMAS are the "operating" forces (BCTs, divisions, corps, ASCCs, ACRs and Special Forces groups and the forces required to support the combat structure) directed by the Army Leadership. "Generating" forces are derived during TAA and refined through the Force Management Review (FMR) and Command Plan processes.

c. SAMAS has two primary views. One is the Force Structure (FS) File (commonly referred to as the "force file"), which reflects the approved (programmed and documented) force structure position for each unit in the Army. The force file produces the Army's Master Force (MFORCE) which is the complete database of the entire Army's force structure. The second file is the Program and Budget Guidance (PBG) File (commonly referred to as the "budget file"). The budget file produces the manpower addendum to the PBG.

d. The force file is updated and maintained by the Force Structure Command Managers and Organizational Integrators at HQDA G-37/FM (DAMO-FM). The force file details the force structure for every UIC in the Army. There are approximately 46 total data items for each unit, displayed over time (previous, current and future programmed and approved actions). These data items include, for example, UIC, Troop Program Sequence Number (TPSN), unit number and regimental designation, unit description, SRC and EDATE. SAMAS supports the development of authorization documents, which contain the MTOEs and TDAs at paragraph, line, MOS and grade, Line Item Number (LIN), Equipment Readiness Code (ERC) and quantity level of detail.

e. The budget file is maintained by the PBG Command Managers, containing military and civilian manpower data and represents the manpower for which budget authority is available. The budget file also supports other HQDA data systems, most notably the HQDA Program Analysis and Evaluation (PA&E) Program Optimization and Budget Evaluation (PROBE) database, which captures the Army's POM and Budget submissions. It also provides civilian data to the Assistant SECARMY (Financial Management and Comptroller) (ASA(FM&C)) Civilian Manpower Integrated Costing System (CMICS) where civilian costing is performed for all PPBE process events. Primary inputs to the budget file come from the annual command plan submissions of the Army commands, concept plans, PBD, Budget Change Proposals, Program Change Proposals, and POM decisions. The primary output of the budget file is the manpower addendum to the PBG.

f. SAMAS is updated and "locked" annually, usually in the June timeframe, at the end of the documentation cycle. This locked position is called the Army's MFORCE and reflects the CSA-approved current, budgeted and programmed force structure of the Army. As such, it is the authoritative record of the total force over time.

5-23. Authorization Documents

a. Authorization documents. Every Army unit and Army components of other agencies must have an authorization document to reflect an organizational structure that can be supported in terms of manpower and equipment. Authorization documents detail a unit's approved structure and resources, and serve as the basis and authority for requisitioning of personnel and equipment. There are two types of authorization documents in the Army:

(1) MTOE. The MTOE is a modified version of a HQDA approved TOE prescribing the unit organization, personnel, and equipment necessary to perform a mission in a specific geographical or operational environment. It reflects the organizational option selected from the TOE as directed by the Army command and HQDA. It also reflects the level of modernization directed by the Army command and HQDA. At unit level, the MTOE is the base document for:
 (a) Requesting personnel and equipment
 (b) Distributing personnel and equipment resources
 (c) Unit status reporting
 (d) Reporting supply and maintenance status

ARMY FORCE DEVELOPMENT

(2) TDA. The TDA prescribes the organizational structure for a unit having a mission for which a TOE does not exist. TDAs are unique in that they are typically developed based on the type and level of workloads associated with the unit's mission. Units with similar missions, like U.S. Army garrisons, may be organized similarly but may have a substantially different mix and number of personnel and equipment authorizations due to differences in the population and composition of the post they support. All TDA documents are built at HQDA (USAFMSA). This allows for standardization of unit design for units with like-type missions provide the ability to conduct supportability analyses and compliance reviews, and enhance the capability to plan and evaluate changes. There are four specialized types of TDAs.

(a) Mobilization TDA (MOBTDA). The MOBTDA records the mission, organizational structure, and personnel and equipment requirements and authorizations for an Army unit to perform assigned missions upon mobilization. It reflects the unit's mobilization plan by identifying functions to be increased, decreased, established, or discontinued.

(b) Augmentation TDA (AUGTDA). The AUGTDA provides the functional support required for the MTOE unit to execute functions beyond the capabilities for which the MTOE was designed and are unique to that particular unit. AUGTDA may include military and/or civilian personnel and/or military or commercial equipment allowances required and authorized to augment or supplement an MTOE unit. An example is the augmentation of the 11th ACR at the National Training Center (NTC), Fort Irwin, CA with equipment authorizations for their "Visually Modified" (VISMOD) Opposing Forces (OPFOR) equipment.

(c) Full Time Support TDA (FTSTDA). The FTSTDA documents military (AC and AGR) and Federal Civil Service positions required and authorized to provide full-time support to RC MTOE and TDA units.

(d) Joint Table of Authorization/Joint Table of Distribution (JTA/JTD). JTAs and JTDs are documents that authorize equipment and personnel for joint activities supported by two or more services. Examples of this would be the Army component for the CCDR's staff or for the Joint Staff.

b. The development and documentation of authorization documents is supported by DA automated systems, e.g. SAMAS, Logistics Structure and Composition System (LOGSACS), and Personnel Structure and Composition System (PERSACS). Unit authorization documents and data are accessible through FMSWeb. This web site instructs users on how to obtain access to the FMSWeb tools.

c. Authorization document data includes organizational structure, personnel, and equipment requirements and authorizations. The basic procedures for documentation are the same for MTOE and TDA units; that is, all unit personnel and equipment requirements and authorizations are written in the same detail. However, the basis for developing the two documents differs.

(1) MTOEs are derived by adjusting/modifying TOEs to meet specific operational requirements at affordable modernization and manning levels. A unit will be organized under the proper level of its TOE to the greatest extent consistent with the mission and the availability of manpower spaces and equipment.

(a) Personnel authorizations are derived from SAMAS, FDUs, TOE design and leadership decisions.

(b) Equipment authorizations are derived from the Army Modernization Strategy (AMS), fielding time lines and distribution plans.

(2) TDAs are developed to attain essential manning, the most efficient use of personnel, and the most effective operational capability within the manpower spaces prescribed in the command force structure. Manpower surveys, manpower requirements models, TAA generating force directives and change requests through concept plans, are used to structure TDA manpower.

d. The HQDA annual Command Plan process reviews and approves all authorization documents (MTOEs and TDAs) to ensure compatibility among the unit's mission, capabilities, organization, Authorized Level of Organization (ALO), and the allocation of resources. Approved MTOEs and TDAs are documented in the SAMAS MFORCE.

5-24. The Force Documentation Process

a. The MTOE force structure authorization documentation process begins with documentation guidance released by HQDA G-37/FM at the start of the documentation cycle. The HQDA guidance establishes the focus ("target") of the documentation cycle and directs documentation of specific units and actions. USAFMSA builds draft MTOEs based on the documentation guidance and forwards these documents to HQDA and the Army commands for Subject Matter Expert (SME) and command review before being incorporated into the Command Plan process.

b. The TDA force structure authorization documentation process closely resembles the MTOE documentation process. USAFMSA initiates the process with the receipt of HQDA guidance and builds the appropriate draft TDAs to reflect current guidance. The TDAs will be staffed with the Army commands and appropriate ARSTAF office/agency SMEs before being incorporated into the Command Plan process.

c. Detailed integration and documentation of the force centers on the "Command Plan process," a yearlong process running from the approved June MFORCE until the next June's approved MFORCE. The Army uses this process to update and create MTOE and TDA documents up to two years out. These documents officially record decisions on missions, organizational structure, and requirements and authorizations for personnel and equipment. The command plan process also updates programmed decisions for the out years in SAMAS. The command plan is used to make adjustments between spaces programmed in SAMAS and the proposed draft authorization documents for that cycle. The command plan is also used by HQDA and the Army commands to comply with FMR directed force structure actions and to document approved concept plans and other HQDA directed actions.

d. The Reconciliation Process. At the close of each documentation window, Automatic Update Transaction System (AUTS) reconciles the forces programmed in SAMAS with the authorization documents submitted for approval at the UIC level of detail. Those authorization documents that match SAMAS programming at UIC, SRC, EDATE, MDEP, AMSCO, and requirements and authorizations strength level of detail (officer/warrant officer, enlisted, civilian), are approved and forwarded to the Army commands for distribution to the appropriate units. The approved SAMAS database and the approved authorization documents provide the basis for updating a number of other data bases and systems, including:

(1) The HQDA DCS, G-1/Army Human Resources Command (AHRC) Personnel Management Authorization Document (PMAD).

(2) The Structure and Composition System (SACS)-personnel and logistics.

(3) HQDA DCS, G-37/TR (Training) Battalion Level Training Model (BLTM) and the Training Resource Model (TRM) for developing Operating Tempo (OPTEMPO) funding.

(4) ASA (FM&C) Army Budget Office (ABO) for civilian costing through the CMICS model and budget estimate submission (BES) preparation.

(5) HQDA G-8 PA&E for POM preparation.

e. Organization Change Concept Plans.

(1) A Concept Plan is a detailed proposal by an Army command/Agency to create or change one or more units when the level of change reaches a specified threshold. The purpose of a Concept Plan is to ensure that appropriate resources are used to support Army objectives, priorities, and missions. AR 71-32 addresses Concept Plans, provides guidance, and formats for submission.

(2) To warrant creating a new organization or changing an existing one, Concept Plans must demonstrate a valid need for change, or demonstrate significant improvement to be realized, in order to warrant creating a new, or reorganizing an existing, organization.

(3) The HQDA approval process for Concept Plans includes an evaluation of the missions, functions, organization, workload data, and required operational capability of the organization affected and the proposed manpower and equipment requirements. The outcome of a successful submission and approval of a proposed concept plan is the establishment of the organizational/unit personnel and equipment requirements and positioning the organization/unit to compete for resourcing against the Army's priorities.

5-25. SACS

a. The SACS produces the Army's time-phased demands for personnel and equipment over the current, budget and program years. These demands are then extended for a total of a ten-year period. Additionally, SACS defaults to FY 2050 and builds a fully modernized OTOE position for all units. In this way, SACS shows current levels of modernization, levels achieved at the end of the POM, and a fully modernized Army (for planning purposes).

b. Operated and maintained by USAFMSA, SACS is produced by merging data from a number of management information systems and databases addressing force structure, personnel, manpower, and dollar resource constraints. Specifically, SACS combines information from BOIP, TOE, SAMAS, and resource constraints. SACS products are PERSACS and LOGSACS. Both PERSACS and LOGSACS are at the UIC/EDATE and MOS/Grade (GRD)/ LIN/ ERC/quantity (QTY) level of detail for requirements and authorization for MTOE and TDA units. The SACS process is shown in Figure 5-9.

(1) PERSACS combines data from the SAMAS, and TOE systems to tabulate military personnel requirements and authorizations by grade, branch, and MOS/AOC for each unit in the force for the 10

ARMY FORCE DEVELOPMENT

years of the SACS. This data supports planning for personnel recruiting, training, promoting, validating requisitions, and distribution. LOGSACS combines data from the SAMAS, TOE, BOIP, and EQ4 to tabulate equipment requirements and authorizations by LIN and ERC for each unit in the force for the current, budget, and POM years extended for a total of ten years.

(2) LOGSACS and PERSACS, while products of SACS, are themselves inputs to other processes. The Total Army Equipment Distribution Program (TAEDP), for example, uses equipment requirements and authorizations from LOGSACS to plan equipment distribution. The PMAD, used by DCS, G-1 and AHRC provides personnel requirements and authorizations.

c. USAFMSA typically produces SACS twice a year, once when the force locks (the MFORCE) or at a Force Review Point.

d. SACS output products (PERSACS and LOGSACS) are published after the AUTS process at the end of the command plan cycle. The reconciled MFORCE is the key force structure input to initiate the SACS cycle. See Figure 5-9.

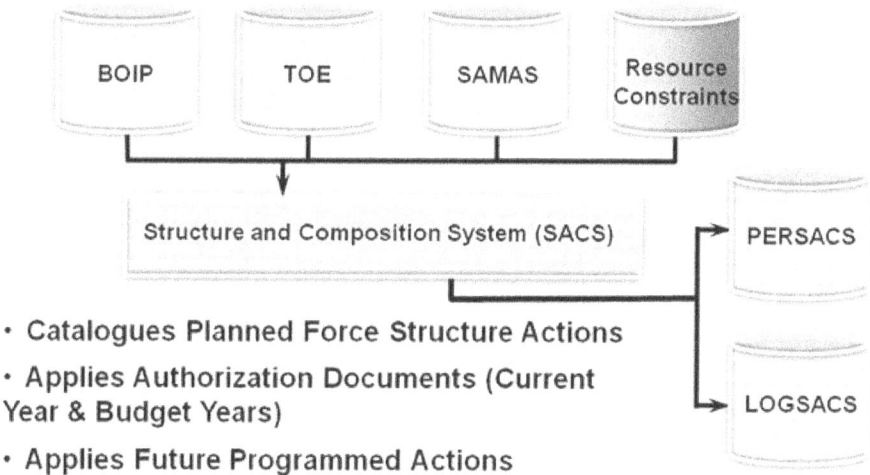

Figure 5-9. Structure and Composition System (SACS) / Force Builder Process

5-26. FMS

a. The increased complexity of the Army, together with the frequency and scope of changes, have made the task of coordinating the various systems and databases that direct, control or document the force increasingly difficult. To meet these challenges, HQDA G-37/FM, is developing the FMS under the management/oversight of PEO-Enterprise Information Systems (EIS). FMS will be an overarching automation system that will ultimately replace the existing systems for developing, documenting, accounting, and managing organizational requirements and authorizations. FMS will become the Army's single database for requirements and authorizations information. FMS will provide capability to plan

HOW THE ARMY RUNS

tactical unit conversions to new concepts and doctrine. It will also support databases in other Army organizations such as HQDA DCS G-1, G-4, G-8, and ASA-MRA with baseline and out-year force structure modernization authorization data. This integrated system will replace the four legacy systems, which evolved in the 1970s-80s. The FMS is critical to force management mission support including total Army force structure management and manpower allocation; development of organizational models (both operating and generating forces); providing analytical support in determining organization authorizations; and documenting organization authorizations across the Army both now and in support of future personnel and logistics planning efforts.

b. FMS is designed to effectively manage manpower, personnel, equipment, readiness, and force structure decisions and databases. Specifically, FMS has integrated the capabilities of SAMAS and the Requirements Documentation System (RDS).

c. The principal advantages FMS will bring to the Army's force management process include:

(1) A single, integrated, hierarchical unit structure across all Force Management processes with a single, common, integrated database system.

(2) An automated change management system utilizing integrated product dependencies enabling automatic pushing of approved changes to higher order products (NOFC, BOIP, Requirements, Authorizations, Structure).

(3) A single, integrated unit document combining TOE, MTOE, AUGTDA and other currently disparate document components.

(4) The ability to create TDA organizational templates, e.g. requirement documents, to enable the development of doctrinal standards for the Army Generating Force.

(5) A rule engine capable of storing and applying force management rules against new data condition sets in order to provide more consistent and efficient force management documentation processes.

(6) An Army Organizational Server to provide tailorable web services for FMS data consumers consistent with the GFM directives utilizing Enterprise Identifiers.

d. FMS brings to the Force Management community interactive tools, use of direct database access, web access technologies, supporting on-line transactions and on-line analysis. These capabilities will be available for daily use by all portions of the Force Management community. Initial operating capability of FMS was achieved in August 2006.

5-27. Global Force Management (GFM) Data Initiative (GFM DI)

a. Synopsis. GFM establishes a transparent and universal process to manage, assess, and display the worldwide disposition of U.S. Forces. This includes the availability, readiness, and capability information required to assess risks associated with proposed allocation, assignment, and apportionment options. The Army Organization Server (AOS) is the Army's Authoritative Data Source (ADS) for providing Army administrative default force structure prescribed by GFMDI. The FMS is the system of record the Army will use to maintain the AOS data.

b. Strategic Vision. The basic premise of GFM is that force structure is the common element between all systems within the DOD. Force structure acts as a common reference point that will allow computers to integrate and manipulate data. GFM is the foundation upon which force structure information will be captured, and used, to associate and aggregate information from the Soldier and business domains in order to form a coherent, integrated global picture.

(1) A key enabler for GFM is the GFM DI, which organizes force structure data in a hierarchal way for integration across DOD. The GFM DI defines how the Services electronically document organizational structures across the DOD enterprise and establishes a standard structure for the organization information needed. The GFM organization servers provide the means of implementing that plan through identification of force structure data sources by Component, creation and maintenance of that information in a standard format and, most important, a single ADS for the dissemination of that information across the DOD enterprise.

(2) The Army Organization Server is the Army's ADS for GFM data. This data is developed and maintained in the Army's FMS. Army G3 has oversight, with G3 FM-USAFMSA managing the completion of loading the organizational server with the force structure data. G3-FMP oversees the hierarchical interconnections and G3-SS managing the connectivity to downstream readiness, personnel, and equipment systems. The FMS consumes legacy force management systems and links to applicable funding, personnel, and equipment systems to ensure its validity as the Army's authoritative data source.

ARMY FORCE DEVELOPMENT

c. Mission. In support of the DOD GFM DI, the Army has developed net-centric web-based classified and unclassified organizational servers that are interoperable with the DOD organizational servers and that fulfill the requirements of the DOD GFM DI.

Section VII
References

5-28. References
   a. Army Regulation 71-32, Force Development and Documentation—Consolidated Policies, 3 March 1997
   b. CCJO, 10 September 2012
   c. CJCSI 3010.02C, JCD&E, 15 January 2012
   d. CJCSI 3170.01H, JCIDS, 10 January 2012 with supporting JCIDS Manual, 19 January 2012
   e. DODD 5000.71, Rapid Fulfillment of Combatant Commander Urgent Operational Needs, 24 August 2012
   f. General Orders #4, Redesignation of the United States Army Training and Doctrine Command Futures Center as the Army Capabilities Integration Center, 10 February 2006
   g. JCS J-8 Force Structure, Resources, and Assessments Directorate, C-BA Users Guide, Version 3, March 2009
   h. TRADOC ARCIC, Capabilities-Based Assessment Guide, Version 3.1, 10 May 2010
   i. TRADOC Pamphlet 71-20-3, TRADOC Concept Development Guide, 6 December 2011
   j. TRADOC Pamphlet 525-3-0, The U.S. ACC, 19 December 2012
   k. TRADOC Pamphlet 525-66 Force Operating Capabilities, 7 March 2008
   l. TRADOC Regulation 71-20, Concept Development, Experimentation, and Requirements Determination, 23 February 2011

PLANNING FOR MOBILIZATION AND DEPLOYMENT

Chapter 6

Planning for Mobilization and Deployment

"The Reserve components provide operational capabilities and strategic depth to meet the nation's defense requirements across the full spectrum of conflict. While these roles are not new, the degree to which the military services have relied upon the National Guard and Reserve to support operational missions has changed.... the Reserve components have been used in different ways and at unprecedented levels, most significantly after September 11, 2001, and the onset of the global war on terrorism. The demands of the persistent conflicts of the past seven years have been high--beyond the ability of the Active component to meet alone. The Reserve components have been relied on heavily to fill operational requirements--comprising close to 40 percent of forces in theater at the height of the mobilization. The role of the Reserves in the total force changed fundamentally. Today, the Department of Defense is asking much more of its Guard and Reserve members. Being in the Reserves is no longer about deploying once in a career, or maybe not at all. Today's reservist might deploy three or four times over the course of a career. This is a different type of commitment, based on different expectations--for members, their families, and employers. The military services are asking for more time from their reserve members--for more training and more frequent deployments."

Department of Defense White Paper "Managing the Reserve Components as an Operational Force," October 2008, Office of the Assistant Secretary of Defense for Reserve Affairs

Section I
Introduction

6-1. Chapter Content
As of December 11, 2012 the more than 864,000 Reserve Component Soldiers mobilized since September 11, 2001. Contingency Tracking System (CTS) Daily Processing Files produced by the Defense Manpower Data Center dramatically expresses today's mobilization and deployment requirements. Our Army is evaluating its ability to rapidly deploy decisive force throughout the world. In view of today's complex global environment, the Army must remain prepared, trained, and ready to deploy operationally. It must have the capability to expand rapidly through mobilization to meet its regional and territorial responsibilities. The Army force structure must be designed to allow force projection with maximum combat power and support units to sustain that power. The AC and RC must provide both capabilities without the lengthy preparation periods that have been characteristic of the past. The need for deploying a substantial number of RC units overseas in the initial stages of a conflict underscores the importance placed on the Army force structure. The deterrent value of mobilization resides not only in the AC and RC, but in the preparedness to convert civilian manpower and industrial production rapidly into military power, individual replacements, and supplies. The capability of the United States to expand the active force rapidly and efficiently through mobilization is essential to deter potential enemies. Such a capability assures our allies of U.S. resolve. Fundamental to achieving such a capability is the coordination of mobilization planning with the planned deployments for war that require mobilization.

6-2. Chapter Organization
This chapter covers mobilization and deployment planning systems. The initial focus is on joint planning systems, then shifts to how the Army mobilizes forces to respond to the requirements of the Combatant Commanders (CCDR). Also discussed are the DOD objectives for improving industrial preparedness in the United States and the Army industrial preparedness program.

HOW THE ARMY RUNS

Section II
National Strategic Direction and Guidance, Joint Operations Planning, Joint Operations Planning Process

6-3. Strategic Direction

a. Strategic Direction is the common thread that integrates and synchronizes the activities of the Joint Staff, Combatant Commands (CCMD), Services, and combat support agencies. As an overarching term, strategic direction encompasses the processes and products by which the President of the United States (POTUS), SECDEF, and CJCS provide strategic guidance. The function of national strategic guidance is to provide long-term and intermediate objectives.

(1) The POTUS provides strategic guidance through the National Security Strategy (NSS), Presidential Policy Directives (PPD), and other strategic documents, in conjunction with additional guidance from other members of the National Security Council (NSC). The National Security Council (NSC) System is the principal forum for coordinating executive departments and agencies to develop and implement national security policy. The NSC system advises the POTUS in integrating all aspects of national security policy. The NSC develops policy options, considers implications, coordinates operational problems that require interdepartmental consideration, develops recommendations for the POTUS, and monitors policy implementation. The most recent NSS was published in 2010.

(2) The SECDEF leads a Quadrennial Defense Review (QDR), which provides additional direction to the Department of Defense. The QDR, required by law to delineate a national defense strategy consistent with the most recent National Security Strategy, describes the strategic environment for the next 20 years and the direction DOD needs to go to be best prepared to meet the challenges of the environment. In essence, it provides continuity to DOD's efforts, and may provide the best source of long range planning guidance to DOD components. In previous years, the SECDEF has developed a separate National Defense Strategy (NDS), which establishes broad defense policy goals and priorities for the development, employment, and sustainment of U.S. military forces (again based on the NSS). The standalone NDS is not required by law and has not been published since 2008.

(3) The CJCS develops the National Military Strategy (NMS), which provides strategic direction for the Armed Forces of the United States to support the NSS, the most recent QDR, and any other national security or defense strategic guidance issued by the POTUS or the SECDEF. The last NMS was published in 2011.

PLANNING FOR MOBILIZATION AND DEPLOYMENT

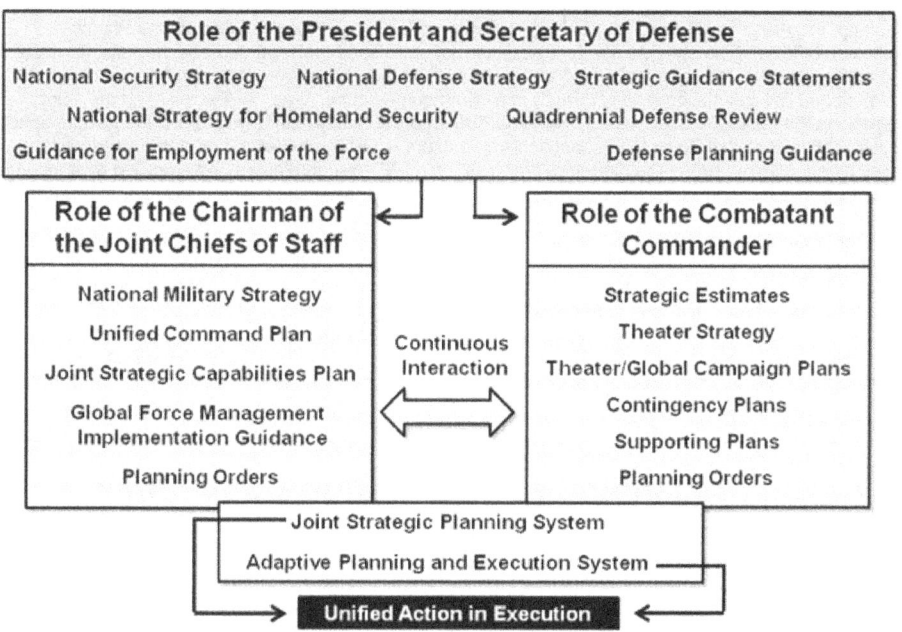

Figure 6-1. National Strategic Direction and Guidance

b. National Military Guidance.

(1) The Unified Command Plan (UCP), prepared by the CJCS for the POTUS to issue, sets forth basic guidance to all CCDRs. The UCP establishes CCMD missions and responsibilities, delineates geographic areas of responsibility for geographic CCDRs, and specifies responsibilities for functional CCDRs.

(2) The Guidance for Employment of the Force (GEF), prepared by SECDEF and approved by POTUS, transitions DOD's planning from a contingency-centric approach to a strategy-centric approach. It directs the CCDRs to create theater strategies expressed in single theater campaign plans to achieve strategic end states that are in accord with strategic direction from the national level. It also directs that certain contingencies be treated as branches to the theater's single campaign plan. The GEF is developed in parallel with the Joint Strategic Capabilities Plan (JSCP) to ensure complementary guidance from the SECDEF and CJCS. The Secretary of Defense (SECDEF) may issue a Strategic Guidance Statement to update the GEF. An SGS, issued only as needed, may be used to direct the Department to develop options or plans for an emerging crisis or to prevent a situation from becoming a crisis.

(3) The Joint Strategic Capabilities Plan (JSCP) provides specific guidance to the CCDRs by translating strategic policy end states from the GEF into military campaign and contingency plan guidance. Additionally, it apportions forces for planning based upon the knowledge of current and projected force deployments in support of ongoing operations.

6-4. Joint Operations Planning

Joint operations planning is the overarching process that guides CCDRs and/or JFCs to develop plans for the employment of military power within the context of national-strategic objectives and national military

HOW THE ARMY RUNS

strategy to shape events, meet contingencies, and respond to unforeseen crises. The continuous monitoring of global events may trigger the planning process to prepare military options.

a. Joint Operations Planning combines both art and science to develop plans and orders to enable the military to meet national strategic guidance. There are two major components of Joint Operations Planning: the Adaptive Planning and Execution System (APEX) and the Joint Operations Planning Process (JOPP). APEX consists of a formal system of automated tools, procedures, formats, templates, and databases to share military planning and execution information between all members of the Joint Planning and Execution Community (JPEC) in a common prescribed way. APEX replaced the Joint Operations Planning and Execution System (JOPES) in order to facilitate a way to provide flexible options for application of military force to national decision makers. JOPP provides a common procedure for developing a plan or order. The planning "products" of JOPP are coordinated and recorded by the Joint Planning and Execution Community (JPEC) through APEX. In this section we will discuss Joint Operations Planning and APEX. We will cover JOPP in more depth in section 6-5.

b. Joint Planning and Execution Community. The JPEC consists of the CJCS and the Joint Staff, the Military Services and their major commands, the geographic and functional CCMDs and their subordinate commands, and the combat support agencies. Though close coordination with interagency and coalition partners is encouraged, the formal procedures of joint strategic planning are limited to the JPEC. Note also that the Office of the SECDEF, though closely coordinated with the JPEC, is not part of the JPEC, but rather the key player in providing strategic guidance to the JPEC. The CJCS, in his Title 10 role as an adviser to the POTUS and SECDEF, provides the linkage between the JPEC and the national strategic level decision makers.

Figure 6-2. Joint Planning and Execution Community

PLANNING FOR MOBILIZATION AND DEPLOYMENT

c. Adaptive Planning and Execution System (APEX). APEX is a system of joint policies, processes, procedures, and reporting structures supported by communications and information technology that is used by the Joint Planning and Execution Community to monitor, plan, and execute mobilization, deployment, employment, sustainment, redeployment, and demobilization activities associated with joint operations. It occurs in a networked, collaborative environment, requires the regular involvement of senior leaders, and results in plans containing a range of viable options readily adaptable to defeat or deter an adversary and achieve national objectives.

(1) APEX is intended to coordinate integrated, flexible plans and fully integrated databases to enable rapid build of executable joint plans. This flexible planning system is intended to facilitate the adaptive planning principles:

(a) Clear strategic guidance and iterative dialogue
(b) Early integrated interagency and coalition planning
(c) Integrated intelligence planning
(d) Embedded options
(e) Living plans
(f) Parallel planning in a network-centric, collaborative environment

(2) Until republished as the APEX manuals later this year, the multi-volume set of Chairman of the Joint Chiefs of Staff Manuals (CJCSM 3122 series) prescribes the policies and procedures of JOPES. These CJCSMs will be re-titled APEX volumes and rewritten to complete the transition from the legacy system to APEX. APEX will evolve as the tools are developed to fully enable it to meet the intent described above. Portions of APEX are already in practice, such as the inclusion of In-Progress Reviews by CCDRs with the SECDEF during the plan development process. Joint doctrine is deleting references to JOPES and implementing APEX as the doctrine is rewritten and published.

(3) A key part of APEX is the plans review process to bring greater congruence between the CCMDs and the DOD civilian leadership. A series of four In-Progress Reviews (IPR) of the JSCP-directed plans is intended to achieve this end. Depending on the priority of the plan, it may go through all of the IPRs or only one or two. See Section 6-5 for more on SECDEF IPRs.

(a) IPR-A—Review strategic guidance. Result is an approved mission and assumptions.
(b) IPR-C—Review plan concept. Result is an approved concept for further development.
(c) IPR-F—Review the plan. Result is an approved plan.
(d) IPR-R—Assess the plan. Result is guidance for plan modification. Plans will be reviewed every 18 months, except for Theater Campaign Plans and Global Campaign Plans, which will be reviewed annually, unless the situation has changed significantly.

(4) Frequency of IPRs. The SECDEF may direct a plan IPR at any time, but the general scheme for IPRs is as follows (for an explanation of JSCP planning levels, see 4. a. below):

(a) Theater Campaign Plans and Global/Functional Campaign Plans will be reviewed at least annually, led by either the USD-Policy or the DASD-Plans, with SECDEF leading selected reviews. A paper review will be provided to the SECDEF;
(b) Major Contingency Plans (JSCP-directed Level 4 and Level 3T (with TPFDD)) will have three IPRs (IPR-A, IPR-C, and IPR-F) during the 2-year planning cycle, led by USD-P, DASD-P or SECDEF. A paper review may be provided to the SECDEF; and
(c) Lesser Contingency Plans (JSCP-directed Level 1, 2, and 3) will have one IPR during the planning cycle, led by USD-P or DASD-P, with a paper review to the SECDEF.

d. Types of Joint Operations Planning. Joint Operations Planning focuses on two types of planning: Deliberate Planning and Crisis Action Planning (CAP) (see Figure 6-3). With the further maturation of the Adaptive Planning and Execution System these two types will meld into one and CAP will mirror deliberate planning, but occur faster.

(1) Deliberate Planning occurs in non-crisis situations. Deliberate planning produces Theater and Global Campaign Plans (TCP/GCP) that are the basis for execution of theater strategy, Contingency Plans, which are branches to the TCP/GCP, and supporting plans of various types. All geographic CCDRs are required by the GEF and JSCP to develop and execute TCPs. Functional CCDRs and occasionally geographic CCDRs may be directed to lead the deliberate planning of specified GCPs. CCDRs must also develop Contingency Plans specified in the GEF and JSCP, but may also direct planning not specified in the GEF/JSCP to meet emerging requirements as they see fit for their theater.

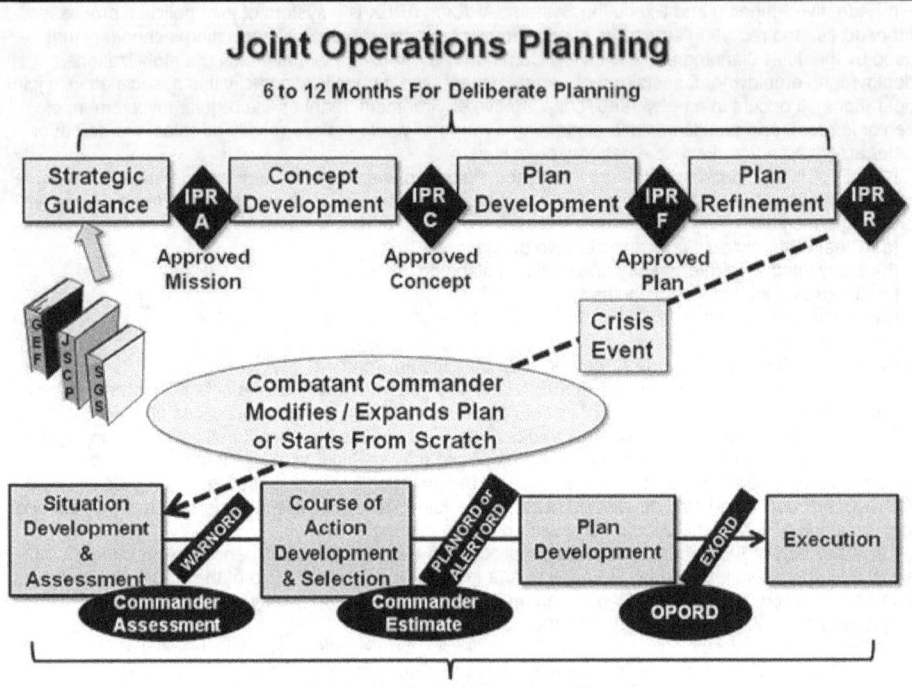

Figure 6-3. Joint Operations Planning

(a) Deliberate Planning is an iterative process and is adaptive to situational changes within the operational and planning environments. The process allows for changes in plan priorities, changes to the review and approval process, and contains the flexibility to adjust the specified development timeline to produce and refine plans. TCPs and GCPs are aimed at desired steady-state strategic conditions, and therefore must be inherently flexible to react to changing assumptions. Contingency plans, however, are based on specific assumptions; a review of critical assumptions is essential to ensure the continuing relevance of the contingency plan.

(b) The JSCP directs that CCDRs develop assigned contingency plans to a specified level. Similarly, the CCDR may direct preparation of internally-directed plans to a particular level of detail.

(i) Level 1 (Commander's Estimate). The CE provides a set of Courses of Action (COA), with a recommended COA, to address a contingency. The product may be a COA briefing or a command directive or memorandum. This level of detail provides the SECDEF with military COAs to meet a potential contingency.

(ii) Level 2 (BPlan). A Base Plan (BPLAN) describes a COA that is developed into an executable concept of operations (CONOPS) including key functional concepts and actions, required forces, and anticipated timelines for execution to complete the mission. A Level 2 plan normally does not include annexes or a TPFDD.

(iii) Level 3 (CONPLAN). A Concept Plan (CONPLAN) is an operational plan in abbreviated format that may require considerable expansion or alternation to convert it to an OPLAN or OPORD. It includes a base plan with selected annexes: (Task Org (A), Intel (B), Operations (C), Logistics (D), Command Relationships (J), Communications (K), Special Technical Operations (S), Interagency Coordination (V), Strategic Communication (Y), and Distribution (Z)). It may or may not include a troop list and TPFDD.

PLANNING FOR MOBILIZATION AND DEPLOYMENT

(iv) Level 4 (OPLAN). An Operations Plan (OPLAN) is a complete and detailed joint plan containing a full description of the campaign or major operation, all annexes, and a TPFDD. It identifies specific forces, functional support, and resources required to execute the plan, and provides closure estimates for the force flow into theater.

(2) Crisis Action Planning (CAP) occurs in crisis situations. A crisis is an incident or situation involving a threat to the US, its territories, citizens, military forces, possessions, or vital interests that develops rapidly and creates a condition of such diplomatic, economic, or military importance that commitment of military forces and resources is contemplated to achieve national objectives (JP 5-0). Such a crisis typically develops rapidly and creates a condition of such diplomatic, economic, political, or military importance that the POTUS or SECDEF considers commitment of US military forces and resources to achieve national objectives. There may be little or no warning, requiring accelerated decision making. Sometimes a single crisis may spawn another crisis elsewhere. The planning process for both contingency and crisis action planning is the same, though different products result. In a crisis, the CCDR has three options:

(a) Use an existing contingency plan that anticipated the crisis situation, with minor adaptations required.

(b) Use an existing contingency plan as a base but modify it significantly to meet the crisis situation.

(c) Build a new plan from scratch.

e. Joint Operations Activities. Joint operations planning encompasses the full range of activities required to conduct joint operations. These activities include the mobilization, deployment, employment, sustainment, redeployment, and demobilization of forces.

(1) Mobilization is the process by which all or selected parts of the Armed Forces of the United States are brought to the necessary state of readiness for potential military operations. Mobilization may include activating all or part of the Reserve Components (RC), and may include some industrial mobilization. Mobilization is primarily the responsibility of the Military Departments and Services in close cooperation with the supported CCDRs and their Service component commanders. (See JP 4-05, Joint Mobilization Planning).

(2) Deployment encompasses the movement of forces and their sustainment resources from their original locations to a specific destination to conduct joint operations. It includes movement of forces and their requisite, sustaining resources within the US, within theaters, and between theaters. Deployment is primarily the responsibility of the supported CCDRs and their Service component commanders, in close cooperation with the supporting CCDRs and USTRANSCOM. (See JP 3-35, Joint Deployment and Redeployment Operations).

(3) Sustainment is the provision of logistics and personnel services required to maintain and prolong operations until successful mission accomplishment. The focus of sustainment in joint operations is to provide the CCDR with the means to enable freedom of action and endurance and extend operational reach. Sustainment is primarily the responsibility of the supported CCDRs and their Service component commanders in close cooperation with the Services, combat support agencies, and supporting commands (see JP 4-0, Logistic Support).

(4) Employment encompasses the use of military forces and capabilities within an operational area. Employment planning provides the foundation for, determines the scope of, and is limited by mobilization, deployment, and sustainment planning. Employment is primarily the responsibility of the supported CCDRs and their subordinate and supporting commanders. (See JP 3-0, Joint Operations).

(5) Redeployment encompasses the movement of units, individuals, or supplies deployed in one area to another area, or to another location within the area for the purpose of further employment. Redeployment also includes the return of forces and resources to their original location and status. Redeployment is primarily the responsibility of supported CCDRs and their Service component commanders, in close cooperation with the supporting CCDRs and USTRANSCOM (see JP 3-35, Joint Deployment and Redeployment Operations).

(6) Demobilization is the transition of a mobilized military establishment and civilian economy to a normal configuration while maintaining national security and economic vitality. It includes the return of Reserve Component (RC) units, individuals, and materiel stocks to their former status. Demobilization is primarily the responsibility of the Military Departments and Services, in close cooperation with the supported CCDRs and their Service component commanders (see JP 4-05, Mobilization Planning).

f. Strategic Options. A major function of the CCDR is to assist the CJCS in his advisory role in informing the POTUS and SECDEF about military options to help them form national strategy and

HOW THE ARMY RUNS

guidance. This is a different requirement from developing plans that are directed in the GEF or directed during crisis, as those plans are dependent on the guidance provided, and generally focus on a single mission. Strategic options assist the senior leaders in the use of military force in the context of the instruments of national power paradigm, Diplomatic, Informational, Military, and Economic (DIME).

(1) There is a need for development of strategic options in both deliberate planning and crisis action planning. In deliberate planning, the best time to provide the options is during development of the Guidance for Employment of the Force, as the GEF provides the strategic objectives desired for the directed plans. CCDRs have a key role in the development of this document.

(2) In CAP, CCDRs engage early with the CJCS and SECDEF in providing analyzed military options to help shape the national strategy and guidance. Again, the various options presented by the CCDR will likely result in different missions for the CCMD.

(3) There is also a need to consider and communicate strategic options during execution. Commanders and staffs must acknowledge that the dynamic environment will likely require strategic reassessment and adaptation during execution. They therefore must be prepared to present options to adapt the strategy, and potentially the policy, to react to the changing environment.

6-5. Joint Operations Planning Process (JOPP)
JOPP provides a seven step structured process to formulate a mission, develop appropriate COAs to accomplish the mission, and coordinate and integrate the details of a plan to execute the selected COAs.

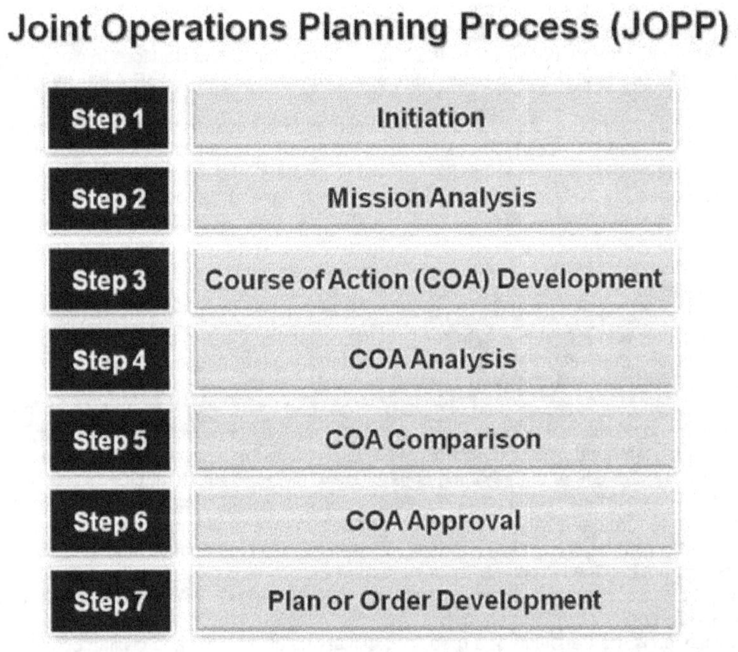

Joint Operations Planning Process (JOPP)

Step 1	Initiation
Step 2	Mission Analysis
Step 3	Course of Action (COA) Development
Step 4	COA Analysis
Step 5	COA Comparison
Step 6	COA Approval
Step 7	Plan or Order Development

Figure 6-4. Joint Operations Planning Process (JOPP)

a. Initiate Planning. Upon receiving strategic guidance from higher headquarters, or as directed by the commander, the staff begins the JOPP by initiating planning. The start point for the contingency plan is

PLANNING FOR MOBILIZATION AND DEPLOYMENT

the TCP. Likewise, the end state for the contingency plan should be to return to the desired conditions of the TCP. Some contingency plans, however, cause such a shift in the environment that a revised theater strategy is required.

 b. Conduct Mission Analysis. The staff analyzes the mission to provide a recommended mission statement to the commander, as well as detailed analysis to inform the commander's analysis of the environment and the problem. This helps him shape an operational approach. As the staff presents analysis on both the requirements and potential points of focus for the campaign, they enable the commander to further develop his vision to use synchronized, integrated military operations as a part of unified action. He can then provide detailed planning guidance to his staff and share his vision with his counterparts to enable unity of effort in application of all of the elements of power across the US government and our other partners.

 (1) In Progress Review—Assumptions (IPR-A). At the theater level, CCDRs conduct a series of in-progress reviews with the SECDEF (or his designated representative) to keep the orientation of the campaign planning in line with the thinking of the national leadership. If the CCMD does not identify the correct end state and corresponding objectives to orient the campaign, further planning is meaningless. Based on strategic direction, the supported CCDR will participate in this first of three IPRs to ensure the CCDR's views are in-synch with those of the SECDEF before further planning proceeds. The CCDR will normally present his initial analysis in the form of a briefing (8-10 slides max) that synopsizes his understanding of strategic guidance, the linkage of the theater/military end state to the national end state, the analysis of facts and assumptions, and proposed mission and intent for the upcoming campaign.

 (2) The SECDEF will approve the CCDR's mission statement and provide further guidance as required to guide continued design and planning. Following review and guidance by the SECDEF at IPR-A, the commander refines his vision for the campaign and provides further guidance to both staff and subordinate commands on how they should begin developing options for future, unified action.

 c. Develop COAs. The commander and staff will work together to refine and develop the commander's initial vision and intent for the campaign into a specific, well-developed concept to accomplish unified action. The staff supports the commander through in-depth analysis and presentation of a range of options for future military and non-military actions that will accomplish the strategic and military ends desired. One way staffs help commanders refine their visualization is to develop alternative COAs to execute the commander's envisioned operational approach and achieve the objectives. A COA is any force employment option in combination with other elements of power that, if adopted, could result in the accomplishment of the mission. For each COA, the staff must enable the commander to envision the employment of friendly forces and assets as a whole, taking into account externally-imposed limitations, the factual situation in the area of operations, and the conclusions from mission analysis. Equally important, the commander must envision how military force will work in conjunction with the other elements of national power to achieve military and strategic ends.

 d. Analyze COAs. Once the staff has completed COA development, each COA is analyzed in detail. The objective of this step is to analyze each COA critically, independently, and according to the commander's guidance, in an effort to determine the advantages and disadvantages associated with each COA. It is critical that the analysis first be a look at each COA independent from the other COAs. A comparison will come later.

 e. Compare COAs. After rigorous independent analysis of each COA to include wargaming, the COAs are compared using a common set of criteria. The purpose of the comparison is to determine which COA is the best fit for the commander's intent, with least cost and risk, and greatest chance of success. Using evaluation criteria (governing factors) derived mostly from the commander's intent and guidance, the staff analyzes and evaluates the COAs against the commander's standards--not against one another--in order to identify the one that best meets the commander's needs.

 f. Approve a COA. Results of the war gaming analysis and the COA comparison analysis are briefed to the commander to obtain a commander's decision on which COA to develop into the Concept of Operations (CONOPS) of the campaign. This enables the commander to refine his visualization of the campaign and provide further guidance to the staff on how to proceed with CONOPS development. It also prepares the commander for another In-Progress Review with the SECDEF (or his next higher command).

 (1) During the brief it is important that dissenting views be heard so that the commander can hear all aspects of the analysis. Staff officers should be encouraged to expound on issues in their functional areas if needed. Subordinate commands should be present, or linked via video-teleconference. Other

HOW THE ARMY RUNS

partners should also be invited to the brief, to include other government agencies and key multinational partners, to the extent possible or appropriate.

(2) Conduct In-Progress Review—Concept (IPR-C). During IPR-C, the SECDEF (or his representative) will consider the CCDR's analysis and approve (or modify) the CONOPS for further development. Based upon the SECDEF's decision and further strategic guidance, the CCDR will refine his CONOPS and reissue his intent and planning guidance to drive development of the plan during the next step of the process. For plans that are directed by the JSCP to be to Level 1 detail (Commander's Estimate), this is the last IPR. Oftentimes, IPRs A and C are combined into one briefing with the SECDEF, especially for the Theater Campaign Plan.

g. Develop the Plan. After the commander has approved a COA, and provided additional guidance to the staff for development of the CONOPS and the full plan (with updates as required after IPR-C for CCMDs), the staff develops the CONOPS into an Operations Plan or Operations Order. The CONOPS must be developed to provide the detail required for the staff to build the base plan and prepare supporting annexes and supporting and subordinate organizations to build supporting functional plans.

(1) Phase the Concept. The campaign should be phased. Each phase is designed to nest with the overall campaign intent and sequenced to achieve an end state that will provide conditions for commencement of the next phase. A phase generally represents a change in the commander's intent and/or the purpose of the campaign. Each phase must have a specified set of conditions to begin and a set of conditions that describe the intended end state for the phase. The type of phasing is dependent on the mission and the concept of operations of the campaign or operation. Most important to organizing phases is that there is a clear set of conditions that are met at the end of and beginning of each phase.

(a) Phase 0—Shape. The goal of Phase 0 is to assure success by shaping perceptions and influencing the behavior of both adversaries and allies, developing allied and friendly military capabilities for self-defense and coalition operations, improving information exchange and intelligence sharing, and providing US forces with peacetime and contingency access. Planning that supports most shaping requirements typically occurs in the context of day-to-day security cooperation, and CCDRs describe Phase 0 activities in the Theater Campaign Plan, with the Security Cooperation Plan as an annex. Some of the Phase 0 activities may take place routinely during steady-state operations, while others may be activated as a potential confrontation becomes more likely. Phase 0 may be viewed as the "gray area" between steady-state and implementation of a contingency plan.

(b) Phase I—Deter. The goal of Phase I is to deter undesirable adversary action by demonstrating the capabilities and resolve of the joint force. Though many actions in the deter phase build on security-cooperation activities from Phase 0, deterrence differs from the shape phase in that it is principally preparatory actions that support or facilitate the execution of subsequent phases of the operation/campaign. Once the crisis is defined, these actions may include mobilization, tailoring of forces and other pre-deployment activities, initial deployment into a theater, employment of ISR assets to provide real-time and near-real-time situational awareness, setting up of transfer operations at enroute locations to support aerial ports of debarkation, and development of mission-tailored C2, intelligence, force protection, transportation, and logistic requirements.

(c) Phase II—Seize the Initiative. JFCs seek to seize the initiative in combat and noncombat situations through the application of appropriate joint-force capabilities. In combat operations, execution of offensive operations at the earliest possible time is key to force the adversary to culmination and set the conditions for decisive operations.

(d) Phase III—Dominate. The dominate phase focuses on establishing control of the operational environment. When a campaign or operation focuses on conventional enemy forces, the dominate phase normally concludes with decisive offensive operations that drive an adversary to culmination and achieve the JFC's operational objectives. In an irregular conflict, decisive operations dominate and control the operational environment through a combination of offensive and defensive combat, security, engagement, and relief and reconstruction activities.

(e) Phase IV—Stabilize the Environment. The stabilize phase is required when there is no fully-functional, legitimate, civil-governing authority present. The joint force may have to perform limited local governance, integrating the efforts of other supporting/contributing multinational, international organizations, NGO, or USG agency participants until legitimate local entities are functioning. This assistance includes the provision of basic services to the population. The stabilize phase typically marks a change from sustained combat operations to stability operations. Stability operations are necessary to ensure that the threat, military and/or political, is reduced to a manageable level which the potential civil

PLANNING FOR MOBILIZATION AND DEPLOYMENT

authority can control or, in noncombat situations, to ensure that the situation leading to the original crisis does not reoccur. Redeployment operations may begin during this phase.

(f) Phase V—Enable Civil Authority. This phase consists predominantly of joint force support to legitimate civil governance in theater. Depending upon the level of indigenous capacity, joint force activities during Phase V may be at the behest of that authority or they may be under its direction. The goal is for the joint force to enable the viability of the civil authority and its provision of essential services to the largest number of people in the region.

(2) Expand the CONOPS into a Base Plan with Annexes. APEX provides specific guidance and procedures on the activities for organizations to prepare required plans and concepts. It directs the typical activities that other organizations will accomplish as they plan for joint operations. CJCSI 3122.01 contains these specific instructions. The staff and supporting commands focus on developing a cohesive and detailed plan for how to employ forces and capabilities throughout the campaign to realize the commander's vision. As the CONOPS develops into a fully-detailed plan, a number of activities coincide in a parallel, collaborative, and iterative fashion rather than in a sequential and time-consuming manner. Time is always a factor; conducting simultaneous, synchronized development activities at all levels will be critical to shorten the planning cycle and make best use of the limited time available.

(a) Force Planning. Force planning begins early during concept development but must be refined and finalized during detailed planning. There must be a balance between the flexibility provided by the plan and the requirements to identify forces, recalling that inclusion in a plan implies a level of preparation requirement for units. The commander determines force requirements, develops a letter of instruction for time phasing and force planning, and designs force modules to align and time-phase the forces in accordance with the concept under development. Major forces and elements initially come from those apportioned or allocated for planning by operational phase, mission, and mission priority.

(b) Support Planning. The purpose of support planning is to determine the sequence of the personnel, logistics, and other support required to provide distribution, maintenance, civil engineering, medical, and other sustainment in accordance with the concept of operation. Support planning is primarily the responsibility of the Service Component Commanders. Service Component Commanders identify and update support requirements in coordination with the Services, the Defense Logistics Agency, and USTRANSCOM. They initiate the procurement of critical and low-density inventory items, determine host-nation support (HNS) availability, develop plans for total asset visibility, and establish phased delivery plans for sustainment in line with the phases and priorities of the concept.

(c) Deployment and Redeployment Planning. The anticipated operational environment dictates the type of entry operations, deployment concept, mobility options, pre-deployment training, and force integration requirements. The CCDR is responsible for developing the deployment concept and identifying pre-deployment requirements. The CCMD is also responsible for movement planning, manifested through the Time-Phased Force Deployment Data (TPFDD) file, assisted by the force providers and TRANSCOM. In particular, TRANSCOM assists greatly with current analysis and assessment of movement C2 structures and systems, available organic, strategic and theater lift assets, transportation infrastructure, and competing demands and restrictions. The supported command is responsible for Joint Reception, Staging, Onward Movement, and Integration (JRSOI) planning. JRSOI planning ensures an integrated joint force arrives and becomes operational in the area of operations as required.

(d) Nuclear Strike Planning. Commanders must assess the military as well as political impact a nuclear strike would have on their operations. Nuclear-planning guidance issued at the combatant-commander level depends upon national-level political considerations and the military mission.

(e) Shortfall Identification. The supported commander continuously identifies limiting factors and capabilities shortfalls and associated risks as plan development progresses. Where possible, the supported commander resolves the shortfalls and implements required controls and countermeasures through planning adjustments and coordination with supporting and subordinate commanders.

(f) Feasibility Analysis. The focus in this activity is to ensure assigned mission accomplishment using available resources within the plan's contemplated time frame. The results of force planning, support planning, deployment planning, and shortfall identification will affect OPLAN or OPORD feasibility. The primary factors are whether the apportioned or allocated resources can deploy to the joint operational area (JOA) when required, be sustained throughout the operation, and be employed effectively, or whether the scope of the plan exceeds the apportioned resources and supporting capabilities.

HOW THE ARMY RUNS

(g) Synchronization Refinement. Planners frequently adjust the plan or order based on results of force planning, support planning, deployment planning, shortfall identification, revised JIPOE, changes to strategic guidance, or changes to the commander's guidance. Refinement continues even after execution begins with changes typically transmitted in the form of FRAGOs (Fragmentary Orders) rather than revised copies of the plan or order.

(3) Complete Coordination of the Plan. The planning requirements described above enable good coordination of the plan. The supported command's CONOPS drives the supporting concepts, but not until the supported command completes coordination of all of the annexes to the plan can the supporting commands and agencies ensure that they have addressed all of the requirements adequately.

(a) Planning for multinational operations is coordinated through various means. Individual treaty or alliance procedures set the stage for collective-security goals, strategies, and combined OPLANs, in accordance with US doctrine and procedures. Thus, much information and guidance for joint operations are conceptually applicable to alliance and coalition planning. The fundamental issues are much the same. Host-Nation Support and mutual support agreements facilitate combined operations.

(b) In a similar vein, coordination of the plan with interagency partners is conducted both informally and formally. CCDRs and JFCs should encourage and solicit maximum participation of appropriate interagency planners in the design of campaigns and operations. Their participation throughout planning is extremely beneficial to expand the perspectives and expertise provided in design and in achieving unity of purpose and then unity of effort in the campaign or operation. However, formal coordination of OPLANs is done at the Department level, once an OPLAN is approved by the SECDEF.

(4) Brief the Plan for Approval. Once completely coordinated, the plan should be briefed through to the Commander for his validation, as well as to prepare him to brief the plan to the national leadership.

(5) In Progress Review—Final (IPR-F). Once the plan is completed, the CCDR submits it with the associated TPFDD file to the JS for review. In conjunction with the CCDR's plan brief at IPR-F, the CJCS and USD (P) will also offer their military advice. This advice includes identification of national military strategic issues arising from, or resolved during, plan review, such as key strategic risks and national-level decision points. The result of IPR-F is SECDEF approval of the base plan and required annexes, the resolution of any remaining key issues, and approval to proceed with plan assessment, as applicable, with any amplifying guidance or direction. The JPEC reviews the plan for the following:

(a) Adequacy—does the plan satisfy the mission and comply with guidance provided
(b) Feasibility—are the required resources available in the timeframes anticipated
(c) Acceptability—are the anticipated operations proportional and worth the anticipated costs, is it politically supportable
(d) Completeness—does the plan include all required parts
(e) Compliance—does the plan comply with joint doctrine

(6) Issue the OPLAN or OPORD. The approved plan is distributed to all subordinate commands and supporting commands, agencies, and other appropriate organizations. The command will have a method of maintaining the plan, that is, distribute all changes to all actors, and solicit review of the plan.

6-6. Global Force Management (GFM)

GFM is the DOD process to align force assignment, apportionment, and allocation methodologies to support joint force availability requirements, enable comprehensive insight into global availability of US military forces, and provide senior decision makers a vehicle to accurately assess the impact and risk of proposed assignment, apportionment, and allocation changes.

a. GFM Implementation Guidance (GFMIG). The GFMIG lays out the process, roles, missions, and functions to support the sourcing of CCMD requests for capabilities and forces to support emerging or crisis-based requirements. This SECDEF document establishes the processes to implement the GFM framework. The SECDEF assigns forces to CCDRs to meet UCP missions and responsibilities, apportions forces to CCDRs for planning, and allocates forces to CCDRs to meet current operational requirements

(1) Apportionment for Planning. The GFMIG groups forces into one of three apportionment bins (Figure 6-5). The first bin contains forces apportioned for Homeland Defense planning. Bin "A" contains forces committed to ongoing operations. Bin "B" contains forces available for planning, both those that are readily available and those that are not readily available (units in a degraded readiness posture for a variety of reasons that will require time to attain a deployable status). If a CCMD's deliberate planning

PLANNING FOR MOBILIZATION AND DEPLOYMENT

determines it requires forces from Bin "A," the CCDR must address this unsourced requirement with the SECDEF through the GFM Board (GFMB) process.

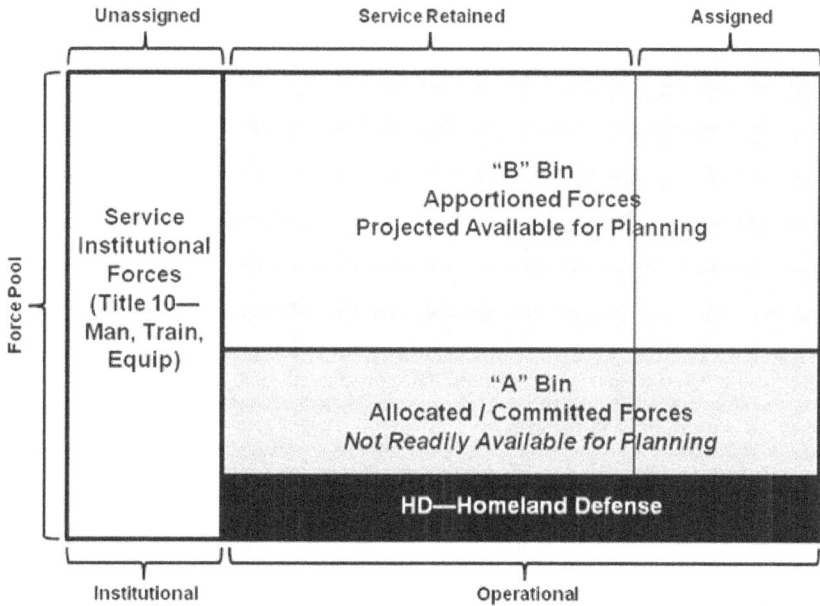

Figure 6-5. Global Force Management (GFM) Bins

(2) Allocation for Execution. Actual allocation of forces and capabilities occurs via the SECDEF allocation process. As a point of clarification, the GFMIG only provides guidelines, policy, and processes for force allocation.

b. GFMB. The Director, Joint Staff chairs the GFMB with membership by representatives from OSD, the Joint Staff, Services, and CCMDs. The GFMB assesses and prioritizes CCMD requests for rotational capabilities, provides a prioritized list of CCMD requests to the Joint Force Providers (JFPs) to use in identifying joint solutions for military capabilities among the Services, and frames any contentious issues for decision by the SECDEF.

c. JFPs. The JFPs working through their assigned Service components provide global sourcing recommendations via a Rotational Force Schedule (RFS) to fill GFMB-validated rotational force requirements.

(1) USSOCOM serves as the Special Operations Forces JFP.
(2) USTRANSCOM Command serves as the mobility JFP.
(3) The geographic CCMDs serve as JFP for the General Purpose Forces assigned to their commands.
(4) The Services serve as JFP for the General Purpose Forces not assigned to a CCMD (since the disestablishment of USJFCOM).
(5) DOD Agencies are JFPs for certain other capabilities not assigned to CCMDs or to the Services.
(6) USSTRATCOM serves as the JFM (Joint Force Manager) for ISR and missile defense to identify, develop, and recommend sourcing solutions for ISR and missile defense capabilities and associated

HOW THE ARMY RUNS

processing, exploitation, and dissemination capabilities. Once USSTRATCOM develops the sourcing solution, the JS J3 identifies the JFP which will provide the force.

　d. Global Force Management Process (GFMP). The GFMP is a nine-step process.

　　(1) Step 1. CCDRs develop a Request for Force or Capability (RFF/C) to support emerging operational requirements.

　　(2) Step 2. CCDR submits the RFF/RFC to the SECDEF via the CJCS with an information copy to the primary Joint Force Provider (JFP). The CJCS validates the RFF/C through the following actions.

　　　(a) Strategic risk assessment to prioritize the requirement in relation to other existing priorities e.g. ongoing operations and war plan response timelines pursuant to JSCP taskings.

　　　(b) Capability and/or force availability substitution guidance on alternate sourcing strategies to include coalition, civilian, or contracted sources.

　　　(c) Any required legal/policy review.

　　(3) Step 3. The Joint Staff validates the requirement by determining if the capability or force requested meets guidance and is prioritized among competing requests.

　　(4) Step 4. The JS J31 (after handoff of the validated RFF/C) directs the appropriate JFP to develop sourcing recommendations.

　　(5) Step 5. Designated JFPs develop sourcing COAs and recommended sourcing solution with the supporting CCDR or Federal agency in coordination as required with the Services and OSD. Using its assigned Service components, the JFP globally assesses available capabilities/forces and determines global sourcing options to include the reserve components that satisfy the Joint Staff-validated RFF/C. When required, the JFP will coordinate sourcing solutions directly with the CCMDs to attempt resolution of contentious sourcing issues. The role of the JFP in this step is to formally capture, through staffing, the assessed risks associated with a particular recommendation. The JFP addresses:

　　　(a) Operational or future challenges risk to the CCMD providing the force, submitted by the CCDR.

　　　(b) Force management, future challenges, or institutional risk to the Service providing the force, submitted by the Service providing the force.

　　　(c) Required mobilization actions to support its recommended sourcing solution.

　　(6) Step 6. The JFP provides its recommended global sourcing solution to the Joint Staff (J31). The JFP provides info copies to the other involved JFPs. The sourcing recommendation may include:

　　　(a) Global sourcing, identification of the recommended force(s), and the Service and/or CCMD furnishing the force to the supported commander.

　　　(b) Capability substitution recommendation(s) or action(s) taken.

　　　(c) Mobilization action(s) required that allow the Service or supporting CCDR to provide the requested forces.

　　　(d) Report of risk associated with global sourcing options based on benchmarks designated by the CJCS and the CCMDs or Services.

　　　(e) Sustainability assessment.

　　　(f) Force availability adjustments required to sustain an acceptable level of available capabilities and forces needed to satisfy validated CCMD requests for capabilities and forces.

　　(7) Step 7. The Joint Staff coordinates the Draft DEPORD with agencies and OSD. CCDRs and Service chiefs may communicate to the CJCS their assessment of risk or other issues associated with the JFP's recommended global sourcing solution. The Joint Staff coordinates with OSD, other agencies, Services, and CCMDs to articulate or adjudicate issues that would result in a non-concurrence or reclama. The Joint Staff will, as required, convene an off-cycle GFMB to address and attempt resolution of contentious sourcing solutions.

　　(8) Step 8. The Joint Staff forwards the recommended sourcing solution with the non-concurrence, if not adjudicated in the GFMB, to the SECDEF for decision.

　　(9) Step 9. Upon SECDEF approval, the JS forwards the DEPORD for force flow execution. JS publishes the decision in the GFMAP.

PLANNING FOR MOBILIZATION AND DEPLOYMENT

Section III
Army Mobilization

6-7. Framework for Mobilization Planning

a. Army participation in joint operations planning and Army planning for mobilization must be integrated. Joint Pub 4-05, Joint Mobilization Planning, facilitates integration of these processes by identifying the responsibilities of the JS, Services, CCMDs, transportation component commands, and other agencies engaged in mobilization planning. The mobilization annex of the JSCP guides the Army and CCMDs in preparing mobilization plans.

b. AR 500-5, Army Mobilization, incorporates DOD and CJCS mobilization planning guidance in a single Army publication. It recognizes the close relationship between operations planning and mobilization planning. It provides the means, within the Army, to accomplish both in a coordinated manner.

c. The mobilization plans of ACOMs, Army agencies, and Army components of CCMDs together with those of HQDA, constitute the Army Mobilization Plan (Figure 6-6). Army Mobilization, Operations Planning and Execution System (AMOPES) is the vehicle by which all components of the Army plan and execute actions to provide and expand Army forces and resources to meet the requirements of CCMDs. AMOPES serves as the Army supplement to the Adaptive Planning and Execution System (APEX). It provides the interface between the Army's plans to provide forces and resources and the CCDR's plans to deploy and use them. It also provides a standard set of guidelines for developing these plans and an integrated structure for the planning products.

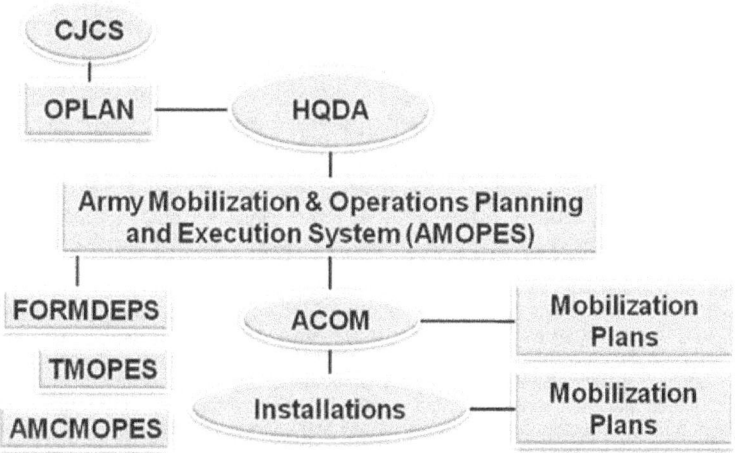

ACOM: Army Command
AMCMOPES: Army Materiel Command Mobilization and Operation Planning and Execution System
CJCS: Chairman of the Joint Chiefs of Staff
FORMDEPS: Forces Command Mobilization and Deployment Planning System
HQDA: Headquarters, Department of the Army
OPLAN: Operation Plan
TMOPES: Training and Doctrine Command Mobilization and Operation Planning and Execution System

Figure 6-6. Army Mobilization Planning

HOW THE ARMY RUNS

6-8. AMOPES Overview

a. AMOPES. AMOPES ensures that the Army plans and executes actions necessary to provide the forces and resources to meet requirements of the CCDR. It covers a wide range of general functions covering the full course of a military action, conflict, or war. These functions include training, exercises, mobilization, deployment, employment, and sustainment, expansion of forces beyond the approved force structure, redeployment, demobilization, and reconstruction of Army forces. The goal of AMOPES is to ensure that the Army can adequately support all future combat operations of the CCMD, as opposed to concentrating only on getting forces into the theater of operations. AMOPES is also adaptable for planning military operations in a peacetime or permissive environment. The system is not just a planning system, but also an execution system. The use of OPLAN format, with functional annexes and appendices, emphasizes the operational nature of the system.

b. Required mobilization plans. Each of the following commands/activities will prepare mobilization plans, to include deployment, redeployment, demobilization, and reconstitution actions when appropriate. Mobilization plans of ACOMs, Army components of CCMDs and other Army elements as indicated by the DCS G-3/5/7 HQDA are forwarded to HQDA for review prior to publication. Plans will be prepared in accordance with guidance contained in the AMOPES basic plan and the following annexes:

(1) ACOMs
(2) Army components of CCMDs
(3) Mobilization stations (Power Projection Platforms/Power Support Platforms) (PPP/PSP)
(4) Support installations (AR 5-9, Area Support Responsibilities)
(5) Staff support agencies and field operating agencies

c. Mobilization Files. Mobilization files in place of plans will be maintained as directed by Commander, FORSCOM or the Commanders of Eighth U.S. Army Europe (EUSA), U.S. Army, Europe (USAREUR), U.S. Army Special Operations Command (USASOC), and U.S. Army, Pacific (USARPAC). The latter commands will use FORSCOM guidance to develop mobilization files.

d. The Army Mobilization Plan. The Army mobilization plan is a collection of individually published mobilization plans of the ACOMs, Army components of CCMDs, and other designated Army elements. The Army mobilization plan currently consists of Volume I through Volume XIX. AR 500-5 further amplifies responsibility for each volume.

6-9. Mobilization Planning Responsibilities

a. Deputy Chief of Staff G-3/5/7. Army Staff organization responsible for developing Army mobilization and operations policy and guidance; developing priorities for mobilization of RC units; directing the call-up of RC units and preparing them for deployment; and establishing, publishing, and maintaining AMOPES. The AMOPES responsibilities include coordinating the structure and content of AMOPES with ARSTAF, ACOM, and other Army activities; tasking agencies and commands to prepare appropriate portions of AMOPES; reviewing agency and command mobilization plans; and ensuring AMOPES guidance, policies, and products satisfy applicable OSD and CJCS guidance and are updated biennially, as a minimum, but not later than 45 days after publication of the JSCP.

b. Principal DA Officials and Army Staff Agencies. Each agency is responsible for assisting the DCS G-3/5/7, HQDA, in developing and maintaining those portions of AMOPES pertaining to their respective areas of interest and for mobilization and operational planning activities within their respective functional areas. They disseminate additional guidance to staff support agencies and field operating agencies (FOA) on related matters in development of mobilization, deployment, redeployment, demobilization, reconstitution plans and other matters. They review and approve mobilization plans of their respective staff support agencies and FOA.

c. ACOMs. Each ACOM is responsible for assisting the DCS G-3/5/7, HQDA, in developing and maintaining those portions of the AMOPES pertaining to their respective mission areas. ACOMs are also responsible for mobilization and operations planning within their respective mission areas and for publishing a command mobilization plan as a volume of the Army Mobilization Plan. Such plans will be submitted to HQDA for review and approval prior to publication. ACOMs are also responsible for compliance with the guidance and procedures published in the AMOPES.

d. Specific Responsibilities.

(1) FORSCOM is the DA executing agent for CONUS unit mobilization, deployment, redeployment, demobilization, and reconstitution planning and execution. FORSCOM also develops the FORSCOM

PLANNING FOR MOBILIZATION AND DEPLOYMENT

Mobilization and Deployment Planning System (FORMDEPS) that standardizes policies and procedures for all Army mobilization efforts for CONUS based Army forces in support of approved military operations.

(2) USASOC and USARC are responsible for the alert notification of all RC special operations forces (RCSOF) units to include mobilization, validation, deployment, redeployment and demobilization for wartime or other assigned missions. USASOC provides follow-on personnel and equipment to sustain RCSOF units and individual replacements provided to the CCMDs.

(3) TRADOC acts as HQDA executive agent for CONUS Replacement Center (CRC) operations. TRADOC establishes and operates CRCs that receive and prepare individuals and replacement personnel for onward movement. TRADOC establishes procedures and ensures the training base infrastructure can be rapidly expanded to support contingency operations and that Individual Ready Reserve (IRR) Soldiers are properly assessed, trained and processed for onward movement in time of crisis. As part of the AMOPES, TRADOC develops and maintains the TRADOC Mobilization Operation Planning and Execution System (TMOPES).

(4) ACOMs and Army components of CCMDs support HQDA in developing and maintaining AMOPES, and assist FORSCOM units to ensure plans to mobilize, deploy, re-deploy, demobilize, and reconstitute are sound and workable. Memorandums of Understanding will be initiated with FORSCOM, where appropriate, for execution of Army Mobilization functions.

e. Mobilization Planning. Mobilization, under the concept of graduated mobilization response, is a tool provided to the POTUS and SECDEF to respond in varying degrees to crises as they occur. It is the act of preparing for war or other emergencies through assembling and organizing national resources. It is also the process by which the armed forces are brought to a state of readiness for war or other national emergency. It can include ordering the RC to active duty, extension of terms of service, and other actions necessary to transition to a wartime posture. This section provides an overview of the mobilization process within the framework of the AMOPES, the types of mobilization, and the interface with non-DOD agencies.

(1) AMOPES Major and Functional Subsystems. The primary objective of the Army mobilization process is to mobilize, deploy, and sustain the theater force. The major subsystems involved are theater force units, military manpower, and materiel. Supporting these subsystems are a number of interrelated CONUS-based functionally oriented subsystems; principally PPP/PSP, the training base, the logistics structure, the medical structure, and transportation support. These subsystems are interrelated as shown in Figure 6-7 and described in more detail below.

(2) Theater Force. The theater force consists of theater force units, military manpower (individuals), and materiel apportioned for deployment to the theater of operations. The objective of the theater force units subsystem is to ensure the orderly and timely availability of Army units at ports of embarkation (air and sea) for deployment as prescribed in war plans or as directed by the JS. It also may include new, or un-resourced, units that would be activated on order.

(a) Deployed or designated to support one or more OPLANs by the JSCP and Annex A of the AMOPES. When an emergency arises, the JS alerts CONUS-based active units through FORSCOM channels (through the PACOM CCDR channels for Hawaii and Alaska-based units). Active Army units do not require mobilization; they are either forward positioned or pre-position (PREPO) units which deploy by air to link up with pre- positioned equipment. Units with organic equipment load their equipment and move either to an air or seaport of embarkation. PREPO units turn in equipment that will remain behind, load equipment to accompany troops, load equipment not authorized pre-positioning (NAP) and items that may be short in PREPO, and move to a designated airport of embarkation. PREPO shortages may be shipped by air and/or sea as required by the TPFDD. Units may be deployed from an ongoing smaller contingency operation location to a higher priority large contingency operation at the direction of the POTUS or SECDEF.

(b) Army National Guard. During peacetime, the preparation of Army National Guard units for mobilization is the responsibility of the State Governor. Guidance is issued to the Governor by HQDA through the Chief, National Guard Bureau (CNGB) (see Para. 9-8l), and by FORSCOM and USARPAC to the adjutants general of the States within their area of operation. The State Governor commands ARNG units until they are federalized. Once federalized, ARNG units become AC units under the appropriate ACOM.

(c) Army Reserve. During peacetime, the preparation of Army Reserve units for mobilization is the responsibility of the CG, FORSCOM through the United States Army Reserve Command (USARC); the Commander, USARPAC; and Commander, USAREUR for assigned Army Reserve units. Army Reserve

HOW THE ARMY RUNS

units are usually apportioned to one or more OPLANs or designated to support the CONUS sustaining base. Selected later-deploying units may receive interim assignments to augment a particular element in the CONUS base. Human Resources Command, St. Louis (HRC St. Louis) is responsible for the management and continued training of the IRR and Retired Reserve. These groups provide the largest resource of pre-trained Soldiers. HRC St. Louis executes its peacetime mission through direction of the Office of the Chief Army Reserve (OCAR) and, on order of the Deputy Chief of Staff, G-1, orders selected numbers of individuals to active duty.

(d) Unresourced and New Units. FORSCOM prepares, in coordination with each supported CCMD, a proposed unit activation schedule for each major planning scenario identified in the JSCP. Changes emanating from the CCDR's response to biennial JSCP guidance (TPFDD shortfall), TAA determinations of which units in the required force structure will be un-resourced, and structure changes reflected in Program Objective Memorandum (POM) development will all be considered in the development of the proposed unit activation schedule (UAS). The prioritized activations include additional support units required to sustain the current force. In preparing this activation schedule, close attention is given to recognized equipment availability constraints, particularly major weapon systems. The composition of the proposed UAS and the recommended priorities will be reviewed and approved by HQDA.

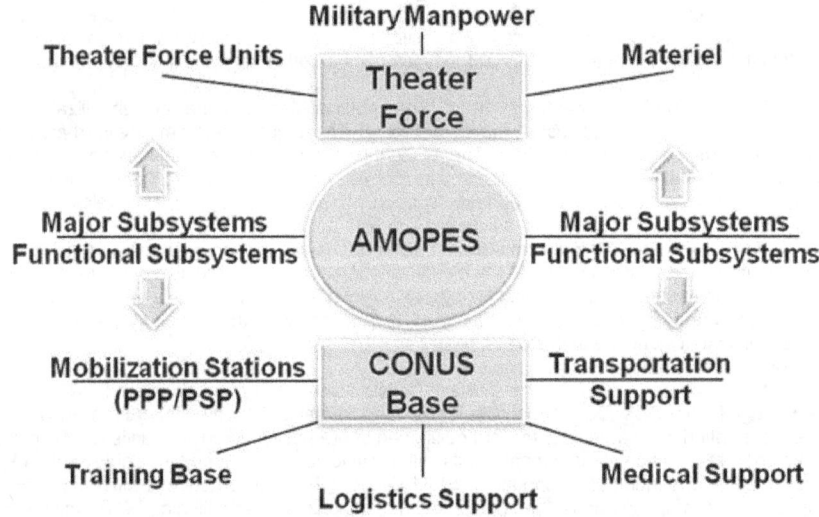

AMOPES: Army Mobilization and Operations Planning and Execution System
PPP: Power Projection Platforms
PSP: Power Support Platforms
CONUS: Continental United States

Figure 6-7. Army Mobilization, Operations Planning and Execution System (AMOPES) Subsystems

(e) Military Manpower. The objective of the military manpower subsystem is to ensure full and timely use of all available sources of individual military manpower to fill the requirements of theater force units for deployment, sustain the deployed force with trained replacements and provide mobilization augmentation for the CONUS sustaining base.

PLANNING FOR MOBILIZATION AND DEPLOYMENT

(i) Prior service personnel are grouped generally by their training status. Pre-trained individual manpower (PIM) is a generic term for the following manpower categories: Individual Ready Reserve (IRR), Inactive National Guard (ING), Individual Mobilization Augmentee (IMA), Standby Reserve (SBR), and the Retired Reserve. Qualified individuals in these categories are the primary source of manpower to reinforce AC and RC units during the early phases of mobilization. Unskilled individuals, principally IRR members whose skills have eroded or who were transferred to the IRR in lieu of discharge prior to the completion of initial entry training, will be ordered to an appropriate training center to complete training. Each of these PIM categories is explained further in Chapter 7.

(ii) Non-prior service personnel include Selective Service inductees, delayed entry enlistees, and volunteer enlistees who, by law, require a minimum of 12 weeks training prior to deployment.

(iii) Selective Service inductees constitute the largest single source of post-mobilization manpower. Delayed entry personnel are active and reserve enlistees who are high school graduates or students awaiting graduation, and reserve unit members who have completed basic training and are awaiting advanced training.

(iv) Replacement centers, which process and equip non-unit-related individual replacements, will be established by the Training and Doctrine Command (TRADOC) at sites normally collocated with Army Training Centers. These CONUS replacement centers (CRC) are close to Air Force Air Mobility Command (AFAMC) designated airfields with strategic lift capability. In addition to final preparation of replacements for overseas movement, Preparation for Overseas Replacement (POR) CRCs will issue individual clothing, equipment, and weapons.

(f) Materiel. The objective of the materiel subsystem is to ensure the full and timely availability of adequate military materiel to fill the requirements of theater force units for deployment and to sustain the deployed force in accordance with requirements and priorities.

(i) Sources of supplies and equipment include the organic equipment of deploying and non-deploying units, PREPO Unit Residual (left behind) Equipment (PURE) and that equipment scheduled for delivery through procurement and maintenance channels.

(ii) War reserve materiel stocks (WRMS) consist of military materiel acquired in peacetime to meet military requirements at the outbreak of war until the sustaining production base can be established. WRMS are acquired to meet the war reserve materiel requirement (WRMR) established in the Army guidance.

(g) Mobilization Stations or Power Projection Platforms/Power Support Platforms (PPP/PSP). The objective of the mobilization stations subsystem, now called (PPP/PSP), is to ensure the orderly expansion of Army posts, camps, and stations and their ability to receive, house, supply, train, and deploy theater force units in a timely manner.

(i) There are 15 designated PPP and 12 PSP. Mobilization stations develop mobilization TDAs (MOBTDAs) based on guidance provided by their parent ACOM to enable mobilization stations to meet surge population and operational requirements. Deleting non-mission-essential services; extending the workweek; executing option clauses in existing contracts; and contracting for personnel and services accomplish expansion of mobilization services.

(ii) When mobilized units arrive at their designated mobilization stations command passes to the mobilization station commander. The commander is then responsible for correcting readiness deficiencies that restrict the deployment readiness of the units. The mobilization station commander cross-levels personnel and equipment in accordance with established HQDA policies and priorities and FORSCOM/USARPAC instructions. The commander is responsible for unit training and deployment validation in accordance with HQDA policy as implemented by FORSCOM/USARPAC.

(h) Training Base. The objective of the training base subsystem is to ensure the orderly and timely availability of trained manpower to mobilize for CONUS base support and theater force requirements.

(i) TRADOC and HQDA are responsible for operating the component organizations that comprise the post-mobilization training base, induction centers, reception stations, training centers, and Service schools. HQDA (G-1) is the agent for DOD on all matters pertaining to the operation of the Military Entrance Processing Command (MEPCOM) and the military entrance processing stations (MEPS) (see Para. 13-13b(4)), also known as induction centers. MEPCOM, through the MEPS, is responsible for providing facilities for conducting physical and mental examinations and inducting qualified registrants into the armed forces.

(ii) The Army's capability to receive and process enlistees, inductees, and other accessions will be increased in the event of mobilization. The existing reception stations (all collocated with existing

HOW THE ARMY RUNS

TRADOC training centers) will be expanded. Army Reserve training divisions/brigades will be mobilized to increase the capacity of TRADOC training centers and establish new training centers at selected FORSCOM installations. This is important, especially during any large contingency operation; however it seldom happens or is very limited during smaller contingency operations.

(iii) The capacity and capability of the Army Service Schools will also be expanded. The existing TRADOC Service School structure will be expanded. Selected United States Army Reserve Forces (USARF) schools will be mobilized to expand the capability of designated TRADOC Service Schools and to augment the U.S. Army Training Centers.

(iv) AMC provides extensive refresher and skill sustainment training for both Army National Guard and Army Reserve units and individuals during peacetime and specialized post-mobilization training in accordance with existing agreements.

(i) Logistics Support System. The objective of the logistics support system is to provide logistical support to meet mobilization and deployment/employment requirements of the Army.

(i) Supply, maintenance, services, and facilities capabilities must be expanded to deploy and sustain the force. Storage policies will be relaxed to permit open storage on improved and unimproved sites, public warehouses, and contractor facilities. The waiving of formal advertising and competitive bidding will expedite the ability to procure goods and services. Suppliers will accelerate deliveries by going to multi-shift production operations. A major objective of the supply system will be to expedite the availability of needed materiel for entry into the transportation subsystem and responsive delivery to the recipient. The Army will call on the existing (wartime) authority to utilize the national industrial base for preplanned production and buy, lease, or contract for goods and services from any available commercial source.

(ii) Upon mobilization, the Army maintenance structure has several immediate goals. It absorbs RC combat service support units, executes emergency civilian hiring procedures in accordance with mobilization TDAs, and implements already negotiated maintenance contracts and inter-service and Federal agency support agreements. Mission-essential items receive the highest priority of maintenance effort. First priority is for equipment items for deployed and/or deploying theater force units. Second priority is for equipment in excess of mobilization needs left behind by deploying units. Third priority is specific items identified and managed by HQDA.

(iii) It will be necessary to expand troop service support (food services, laundry, dry cleaning, bath, and mortuary) to accommodate the expanded mobilization station population. Service facilities at newly activated mobilization stations will be renovated utilizing available materiel, funds, and manpower. As required, support units will be tasked to provide mobilization stations with unit facilities and equipment until general support force units can assume these functions.

(iv) The Army production base is comprised of Army-controlled industrial activities and contractor facilities. The Army will coordinate expanded production requirements with the DLA on common use items. Included in these industrial activities are active and inactive ammunition plants, arsenals and proving grounds, missile plants, and other miscellaneous plants. These facilities are to be activated or expanded to provide maximum wartime production levels of materiel.

(v) Expansion of the CONUS training and sustaining base facilities will be required at initial Presidential Reserve Call-Up (PRC) and will increase incrementally through partial and full mobilization as the mobilization surge passes through the mobilization stations and ports. Initially, expansion of capacity will be achieved from immediate cessation of nonessential activities; relaxation of space, environmental, and other constraining criteria; and the rehabilitation of facilities using available labor and the self-help effort of using units. New facilities construction will feature modern prefabrication technology to provide increased living, storage, and workspace needed early in the post-mobilization buildup period.

(j) Medical support. As dictated by crisis action, U.S. Army hospitals may initiate conversion to their planned mobilization configuration to accommodate the vastly increased military population and expected theater force casualties.

(i) Health care services (inpatient and outpatient) may be limited to active duty military personnel with the exception that outpatient occupational health services will continue for civil service employees. If so, all nonmilitary inpatients will be discharged or transferred to civilian or other Federal hospitals as expeditiously as possible. TRICARE service centers and the local military medical treatment facility will assist eligible beneficiaries in completing administrative requirements for procuring health care from civilian sources.

PLANNING FOR MOBILIZATION AND DEPLOYMENT

(ii) With the approval of the Commander, Medical Command (MEDCOM), and the Office of the Surgeon General (OTSG) (see Para. 18-8 and 18-10) HQDA, inpatient services may be continued beyond M-Day to D-Day for family members and retirees (if M-Day and D-Day do not coincide). Medical center (MEDCEN) (see Chapter 18)/medical department activity (MEDDAC) (see Chapter 18) commanders may continue outpatient services for family members and retirees as resources permit.

(k) Transportation Support. The objective of the transportation support subsystem is to move the entire force (units, individual replacements, and materiel) within CONUS, and to and from overseas commands. Overall responsibility for transportation support is vested in USTRANSCOM and its transportation component commands.

(i) The Surface Deployment and Distribution Command (SDDC) coordinates intra-CONUS movements of mobilizing units and materiel in cooperation with installation transportation officers and various state and local agencies. Strategic transportation to and from overseas theaters is the responsibility of the Military Sealift Command (MSC) and the AFAMC, the other two component commands.

(ii) Management of the surface lines of communication is split among SDDC, MSC, and the theater commanders. SDDC is responsible for CONUS line-haul and common-user terminal operations. MSC is charged with ship contracting and scheduling. The theater commander manages intra-theater surface movements. The schedule for cargo movement and port operations must interface with the schedule for ships. Port throughput capacity, both in CONUS and in a theater of operations, is a major consideration and is often a limiting factor. Finally, surface transportation planning procedures must be flexible enough to allow planners to adjust to exigencies such as ship or port losses.

(iii) AFAMC is responsible for airlift operations. To meet response times postulated by the JSCP, planners must be able to develop and maintain flow plans that can be executed rapidly. This capability requires detailed planning among the users of common-user airlift assets. In addition, AFAMC requires 3-4 days to achieve a full-surge airlift capability. This time is required to marshal Active Air Force elements and to mobilize and position essential Air National Guard and Air Reserve units. Therefore, to develop realistic flow plans, planners must carefully balance airlift requirements with capabilities until a full surge capability can be achieved and maintained. A limiting factor to U.S. airlift capability is the availability of Strategic Air Command (SAC) tanker resources, which are periodically tasked to support other national-level operations. Planners must consider the potential availability of tanker resources when developing flow plans and must closely coordinate with other claimants for refueling aircraft.

(iv) USTRANSCOM coordinates and monitors time-sensitive planning and execution of force and re-supply movements for deployment of CONUS-based Army and Air Force combat forces. It also coordinates deployment planning with Navy and Marine Corps forces. (These deployments should not be confused with the normal rotation of units, ships, squadrons, etc. in peacetime.) USTRANSCOM assists the JS in resolving transportation shortfalls with supported and supporting commanders, military transportation agencies, and the Services.

HOW THE ARMY RUNS

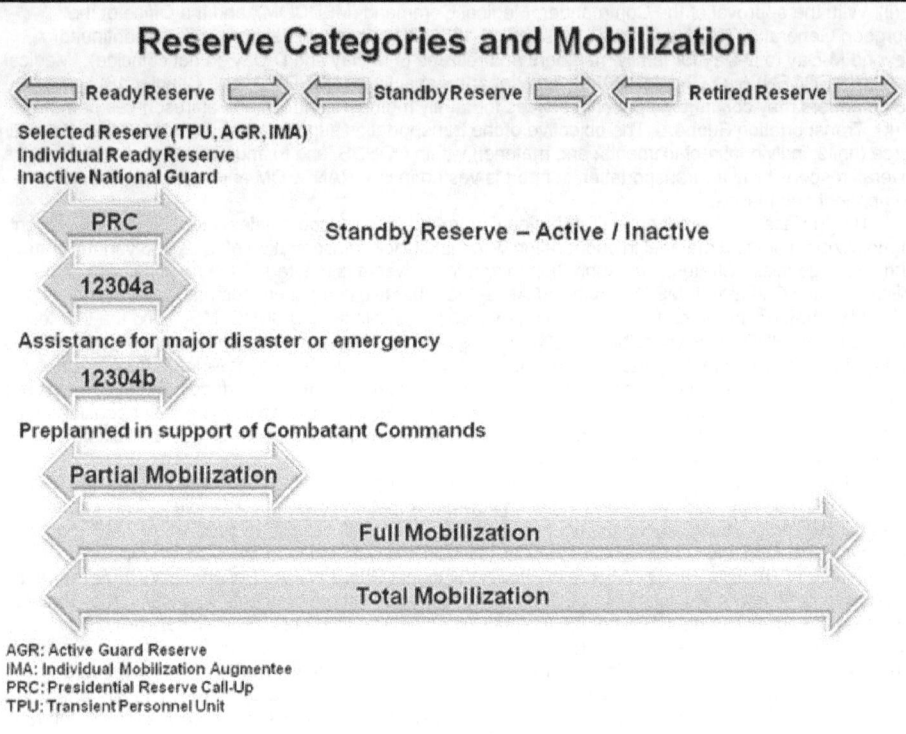

Figure 6-8. Reserve Categories and Mobilization

f. Types of Mobilization. Generally, the magnitude of the emergency governs the type of mobilization. As authorized by law or congressional resolution and when directed by the POTUS, DOD mobilizes all or part of the Reserve Components as shown in Figure 6-8. Concurrently, the DOD and other Federal agencies marshal national resources in order to sustain the mobilized force.

(1) Selective Mobilization. For "domestic emergencies," the POTUS may order expansion of the active armed forces by activation of RC units and/or individual Reservists to deal with a situation where the armed forces may be required to protect life, Federal property, or to prevent disruption of Federal activities. A selective mobilization would not be associated with a requirement for contingency plans involving external threats to the national security.

(2) Presidential Reserve Call-Up (PRC). The POTUS may augment the active forces by an involuntary call-up of units and individuals of the Selected Reserve or any member of the IRR designated as essential up to 200,000 persons from all Services for up to 365 days to meet an operational requirement. No more than 30,000 of the 200,000 may be members of the IRR. The POTUS must notify Congress whenever this authority to call up the RC is exercised.

(3) Partial Mobilization. In time of national emergency declared by the POTUS or when otherwise authorized by law, an authority designated by the Secretary concerned may, without the consent of the persons concerned, order any unit, and any member not assigned to a unit organized to serve as a unit, in the Ready Reserve under the jurisdiction of that Secretary to active duty for not more than 24 consecutive months. Not more than 1,000,000 members of the Ready Reserve may be on active duty, without their consent, under partial mobilization at any one time.

(4) Full Mobilization. In time of war or national emergency declared by the Congress, or when otherwise authorized by law, an authority designated by the Secretary concerned may, without the

PLANNING FOR MOBILIZATION AND DEPLOYMENT

consent of the persons affected, order any unit, and any member not assigned to a unit organized to serve as a unit, of a RC under the jurisdiction of that Secretary to active duty for the duration of the war or emergency and for six months thereafter.

(5) Total Mobilization. Total mobilization involves expansion of the active armed forces beyond the approved force structure by organizing and/or activating additional units to respond to requirements of the emergency. All national resources, to include production facilities, needed to sustain additional forces will also be mobilized. Congressional authorization is required for these actions.

(6) Two additional types of mobilization where added by the National Defense Authorization Act for Fiscal Year 2012. Title 10 United States Code (USC) was amended to add sections 12304a and 12304b. Section 12304a provides the SECDEF with the authority to order any unit, and any member not assigned to a unit organized to serve as a unit, of the Army Reserve, Navy Reserve, Marine Corps Reserve, and Air Force Reserve to active duty without their consent for a continuous period of not more than 120 days to respond to a Governor's request for Federal assistance regarding a major disaster or emergency. Section 12304b provides the Secretary of a Military Department the authority to order any unit of the Selected Reserve, without the consent of the members, to active duty for not more than 365 consecutive days when the Secretary determines that it is necessary to augment the active forces for a preplanned mission in support of a CCMD. To exercise this authority the manpower and associated costs of such active duty must be specifically included and identified in the defense budget materials for the fiscal year or years in which such units are anticipated to be ordered to active duty and the budget information on such costs must include a description of the mission for which such units are anticipated to be called to active duty and the anticipated length of time involuntarily on active duty. Not more than 60,000 members of the Reserve Component may be on active duty under this section at one time.

g. Mobilization Authority.

(1) The authority to order mobilization resides with the POTUS, Congress, SECDEF, and the Secretaries of the Military Departments as outlined in the types of mobilization above. The POTUS or Congress will declare a national emergency depending upon the type of mobilization invoked

(2) The National Emergencies Act passed in 1976 provides that when the POTUS declares a national emergency, the declaration or subsequent Executive order must specify the specific authorities being invoked. The POTUS's powers are limited to those invoked until the subsequent announcement of the invoking of additional specific authorities. Once the POTUS declares a national emergency for a specific purpose, the national emergency will remain in effect for one year, unless sooner rescinded or extended. Under the Federal Administrative Procedure Act of 1946, all Executive orders must be published in the Federal Register.

(3) The SECDEF, with the advice and recommendation of the CJCS and the Service Secretaries, recommends to the POTUS and the Congress the mobilization authority required to support a given contingency, OPLAN, or national emergency. The SECDEF directs mobilization of RC units and manpower through the military departments.

h. Peacetime Planning. The Army plans and prepares for mobilization in peacetime. It participates in war planning to establish Army forces and the requirements for their augmentation. It programs and budgets resources and acts to man, equip, and train the Army and to prepare for its employment during a war or other national emergency. Planning is accomplished in accordance with the provisions of the JOPES and AMOPES. This peacetime planning essentially consists of war planning intended to develop the OPLANs for the conduct of operations (addressed earlier in the chapter and in Chapter 4) and mobilization planning.

i. DOD Mobilization Planning Process. Mobilization planning, primarily a Service responsibility, is based on guidance from OSD and JCS. OSD guidance is included in the Defense Planning Guidance (DPG) and Guidance for Employment of the Force (GEF) (see Chapter 4). JS guidance is contained in the JSCP (see Chapter 4). In addition, Joint Pub 4-05, Joint Mobilization Planning, assigns general responsibilities and procedures for mobilization. The JS coordinates the mobilization plans of the Services and ensures the interface of these plans with deployment.

j. Mobilization planning in other Federal departments and agencies. In addition to DOD, approximately 50 Federal departments and agencies have emergency planning responsibilities. FEMA is the Federal government coordinator of these emergency management activities in both peace and war.

(1) FEMA's responsibilities include policy guidance and planning to ensure that government at all levels is able to cope with and recover from emergencies. FEMA assesses national civil mobilization capabilities and develops concepts, plans, and systems for management of national resources. It

HOW THE ARMY RUNS

identifies actual and potential shortages in natural, industrial, economic, and other resources; develops plans to mitigate their national security impacts; and fosters programs to reduce our national vulnerability to such resource shortages.

(2) FEMA is the principal respondent to military requirements for civilian sector resources during mobilization. It coordinates the response of the civil agencies to defense needs, always cognizant that without the might of the Nation's industrial production, transportation networks, work force, financial institutions, energy, and natural resources, there could be no national security. Likewise, without food, clothing, housing, health care, and education, there would be no civilian population to support the defense of our way of life and our constitutional government. FEMA must, therefore, see to it that national resources are used to meet both the military and the essential civilian needs of the nation.

k. Army Mobilization Planning. Army mobilization planning provides the resources required to support various OPLANs. This includes mobilizing the units, manpower, and materiel required for immediate implementation of an OPLAN as well as the resources required to sustain the operation. AMOPES incorporates the guidance of the DPG, GEF, JSCP, and Joint Pub 4-05 and specifies the planning process used to develop HQDA and ACOM mobilization plans. The FORSCOM Mobilization Plan, with its associated FORSCOM Mobilization and Deployment Planning System (FORMDEPS), details the time-phased flow of mobilizing RC units from home stations to their mobilization stations. The TRADOC Mobilization Operations Planning and Execution System (TMOPES) provides installations and training base augmentation units in the Army Reserve with guidance on training base expansion activities.

l. Relationships of War Planning and Mobilization Planning. AMOPES provides the linkage between war planning under JOPES and mobilization planning as directed by DOD and the JS. AMOPES establishes the "who, what, where, why and how" of mobilization. It further prescribes the Army Crisis Action System for managing the execution of mobilization and OPLANs. The principal products of AMOPES are prepared executable plans, supporting information, and databases prepared and maintained for use during national crises. Mobilization plans incorporate the specific actions and responsibilities that must be accomplished both in peacetime and upon the order to mobilize. HQDA and ACOM mobilization plans that constitute the Army Mobilization Plans are based on guidance contained in AMOPES and other documents. Most mobilization plans are oriented toward full mobilization. For selected contingencies, however, the Army has developed partial mobilization plans.

m. Peacetime Preparation. Preparation for mobilization proceeds concurrently with planning. The Army programs, budgets, and funds resources to overcome the shortfalls and limiting factors identified from a continuing analysis of the various operation plans. Concurrently, the Army trains units and individuals. Within its capabilities, it identifies and pre-assigns augmenting manpower and prepositions materiel to support those plans.

n. Alert, Mobilization, and Deployment (Figure 6-9).

(1) On receiving the order to mobilize, the Army begins a PRC, a partial mobilization or full mobilization, as directed by the SECDEF, of RC units, pre-trained manpower, and materiel. A portion or all of the mobilizing force may augment an established theater force such as Europe, or may augment a force deployed in a contingency operation. Under the general supervision of HQDA FORSCOM, USAREUR and USARPAC bring AC and RC units to combat-ready status and then deploy them by air and sea to the area(s) of operation according to the deployment plans.

(2) An initial pool of reserve materiel resources exists in war reserve stocks in CONUS and pre-positioned stocks in overseas areas. The initial resources sustain the deployed force until reinforcement and re-supply pipelines can be established or the emergency is resolved. AC units in place in the theater of operations are referred to as "forward-presence" units. Other AC units, most of them CONUS-based, are earmarked by FORSCOM war plans to support one or more requirements of the JSCP and AMOPES.

(3) When an emergency arises, units are alerted through FORSCOM, USAREUR, or USARPAC channels to deploy to the theater of operations in accordance with applicable OPLANs. RC units (ARNG and Army Reserve) are ordered to active duty by mobilization orders transmitted by HQDA through FORSCOM/ USARPAC command channels. Units may be apportioned to support one or more OPLANs or they may be apportioned to become part of the CONUS base.

o. FORSCOM Mobilization Planning.

(1) FORSCOM publishes the FORSCOM Mobilization and Deployment Planning System (FORMDEPS), FORSCOM Regulation 500-3, based on HQDA guidance contained in AMOPES. FORMDEPS contains planning directives and guidance to ACOM commanders, Continental U.S. Armies (CONUSA), major troop units, FORSCOM installation commanders, other ACOM installation

PLANNING FOR MOBILIZATION AND DEPLOYMENT

commanders, State adjutants general (in consonance with NGB), and the U.S. Army Reserve commands. FORMDEPS also contains annexes on the various functional aspects of mobilization and updates the GCCS-A Mobilization Planning Line based on OPLAN TPFDD.

(2) FORSCOM coordinates with USASOC, TRADOC, MEDCOM, TRANSCOM, Surface Deployment and Distribution Command (SDDC), AMC, and NGB in preparing data. The GCCS-A Mobilization Planning Line includes scenario dependent data for RC deploying and redeploying MTOE and TDA units in the Army Status of Resources and Training System (ASORTS). The Mobilization Planning Line includes the following data (as applicable) for these units:

(a) Unit description, component, and home station
(b) Power projection platform data
(c) Unit mobilization data (notional)
(d) Ready-to-load dates
(e) Deployment data for the applicable TPFDD(s)

p. Mobilization Flow. Mobilization execution is decentralized to commands. FORSCOM, USARPAC, and USAREUR are the principal commands that command mobilizing RC units. Other commands (USASOC, TRADOC, MEDCOM, AMC, and SDDC) assume command of designated non-deploying units. Upon receiving the order to mobilize, most RC units move to one of 15 PPPs and 12 PSPs within the First Army area and the USARPAC area to train before deploying or augmenting the CONUS base. Cross leveling of equipment and personnel assets, required to make units mission-capable, takes place primarily at PPPs. AMC provides wholesale management for materiel. Human Resources Command (HRC) serves in a similar management role for personnel. Medical Command expands medical support services and facilities. The U.S. Army Corps of Engineers (USACE) expands troop housing, training, industrial, and other facilities.

Mobilization and Execution Process

MOBLIZATION PHASE	PHASE I Pre-Mob	PHASE II Alert	PHASE III Home Station	PHASE IV Mobilization Station (MS)	PHASE V Alert
PRIMARY ACTIVITY LOCATION	Home Station (Armory or USAR Center)	Home Station (Armory or USAR Center)	Home Station (Armory or USAR Center)	MS	Air or Sea Port
ACTIVITY DURATION (DAYS)	As Time Permits	3 to 7 Days	3 Days	10 to 180 Days	1 to 2 Days
PRIMARY ACTIVITY	• Mobilization Planning • Training • SRP	• Unit Recall • Mobilization Order Prep • Personnel Screening • Equip & Records Check	• Continue SRP • Inventory Equipment • Cross-level Personnel & Equipment • Load for Movement • ADVON to MS	• Move to PPP • Complete SRP • Conduct Training • Complete Cross-level • Complete Validation • Load for Movement	• Move to POE • Load Transport • Deploy
OUTCOME	Planning	Notification	Preparation	Validation	Deployment

ADVON: Advance Party
USAR: United States Army Reserve
POE: Point of Embarkation
PPP: Power Projection Platforms
SRP: Soldier Readiness Processing

Figure 6-9. Mobilization and Execution Process

HOW THE ARMY RUNS

6-10. Department of the Army Mobilization Processing System (DAMPS)
Subsequent to the attacks of September 11, 2001, the Army Operations Center initiated development of an automated mobilization process resulting in DAMPS. DAMPS is the current system used to mobilize units and individuals. DAMPS electronically processes and tracks mobilization request packets through all necessary approval levels and stages enabling the rapid issuance of mobilization orders and improving the Army's ability to account for and track units and individuals throughout the mobilization process. DAMPS is an Army mobilization resource that is essential for the timely expansion and sustainment of military forces.

Section IV
Industrial Preparedness

6-11. The Need for Industrial Preparedness
In the post-Cold War era when global conflicts between nation states are unlikely, we must maintain a viable industrial base that can replenish expenditures of critical war materiel following regional conflicts or military operations in a peacetime or permissible environment in a timely manner. Most future conflicts will be "come as you are" actions. Although the industrial base may be called upon to sustain the deployed forces, more than likely it will be needed to expeditiously replace losses in order to be prepared for another contingency.

6-12. DOD Industrial Base Policy Objectives
 a. From the 2011 Annual Industrial Capabilities Report to Congress: "During the past decade the Department relied on market forces to create, shape, and sustain the industrial, manufacturing, and technological capabilities in the industrial base intervening only when absolutely necessary to sustain essential defense capabilities. As the wars in Iraq and Afghanistan continue to evolve, and our nation continues to recover from the worst economic recession since the Great Depression, the Department faces significantly greater constraints on resources. These constraints will have significant impacts on the defense industrial base. The Department must work closely with our partners in the defense industry to ensure that we are better stewards of the taxpayers' money in these fiscally austere times."
 b. There are seven guideposts set forth in DOD policy:
 (1) DOD will rely on normal market forces to make the most efficient adjustments to the defense industrial base. This is not only in accordance with good economic theory, but necessary to prevent the defense industry from becoming further distanced from the main currents of 21st century technology, creativity, and capital markets.
 (2) Competition is one of the key drivers of productivity and value in all sectors of the economy, including defense. Accordingly, DOD is not likely to support further consolidation of our principal weapons systems prime contractors. A number of initiatives are aimed at increasing competition among all our suppliers and throughout our procurement of goods and services.
 (3) DOD will be looking at our industry sector by sector – from shipbuilding to professional services, and from stealth to space – because the dynamics are different in each sector.
 (4) DOD's interest in the defense industrial base extends throughout its entire spectrum. The industrial base is not made up of only those who receive prime awards.
 (5) DOD will give heightened attention to the increasing importance of the "services" component of the "goods and services" the Department requires – again provided by firms not often considered "defense companies." These services are as essential as weapons systems to mission accomplishment, and we are taking a number of steps to better understand and manage this part of the Department's spend.
 (6) A key part of the DOD's defense industrial strategy is to encourage new entrants. They offer competition, renew and refresh the technology base, and ensure that defense is benefitting from the main currents of emerging technology.
 (7) Globalization is affecting security and commerce in profound ways, and this trend has implications for the defense industry. Globalization is not an option - it is a reality. DOD is committed to continue opening defense markets to leading firms around the world while at the same time striking the appropriate balance with security concerns.

PLANNING FOR MOBILIZATION AND DEPLOYMENT

c. DOD is conducting a sector-by-sector, tier-by-tier analysis of the defense industrial base. This analysis aims to locate early indicators of risks to defense programs, identify cross-program interdependencies throughout the supply chain, pinpoint areas of limited competition that may drive up costs, and find areas of overreliance on foreign sources that may exist. The sector-by-sector, tier-by-tier analysis will be conducted annually to ensure that the industrial base which the Department relies upon is healthy, vibrant, and flexible to meet the Department's needs today and well into the future. This analysis will be used to influence the Department's investment decisions.

6-13. DOD-Level Industrial Preparedness Management

a. It is DOD policy to maintain a state of industrial preparedness by working with private industry to produce, maintain, and repair materiel that meets mobilization requirements. Where it is determined that required mobilization items cannot be provided by the private sector, then government-owned facilities and equipment are acquired and maintained to produce them.

b. Overall responsibility for managing the Defense Industrial Base is vested in the Deputy Assistant Secretary of Defense for Manufacturing and Industrial Base Policy (DASD (MIBP)). The mission of the office of Manufacturing and Industrial Base Policy (MIBP) is to ensure robust, secure, resilient, and innovative industrial capabilities upon which the DOD can rely to fulfill Warfighter requirements.

c. MIBP supports the Office of the SECDEF and Service Acquisition Executives by providing detailed analyses and in-depth understanding of the increasingly global, commercial, and financially complex industrial supply chain essential to our national defense, and recommending or taking appropriate actions to maintain the health, integrity and technical superiority of that supply chain. MIBP is DOD's lead in all matters relating to mergers, acquisitions, and dissolutions of national security-related business.

d. MIBP addresses innovation within supply chain sectors and supports responsible investment to advance industrial productivity through a variety of authorities and programs, including the Defense Production Act and Manufacturing Technology (ManTech). The challenges of critical and fragile elements of the base are also analyzed to identify systemic and fundamental issues that can be resolved through engagement across the public and private sectors.

6-14. The Defense Priorities and Allocations System (DPAS)

a. This regulatory system (15 Code of Federal Regulations (CFR) 700), administered by the Department of Commerce (DOC), is used to ensure the timely availability of industrial resources to meet approved national defense and emergency preparedness program requirements and to provide an operating system to support rapid industrial response in a national emergency.

b. The authority for this regulatory system is found in Title I of the Defense Production Act (50 USC App. 2061, et seq.), which authorizes the POTUS to require:

(1) The priority performance of defense contracts and orders over all other contracts and orders.
(2) The allocation of materials, services, and facilities necessary and appropriate to promote the national defense.

c. The DPAS establishes two levels of contract priority: "DX" (highest national urgency); and "DO" (critical to national defense). DX priority rated contracts and orders take precedence over DO priority rated contracts and orders; and DO rated contracts and orders take precedence over un-rated / commercial contracts and orders. The DPAS requires that:

(1) Contractors and suppliers capable of their performance accept all priority rated contracts and orders
(2) Precedence is given to priority rated contracts and orders as necessary to achieve timely delivery
(3) Contractors extend the priority rating to contracts and orders placed with their vendors and suppliers

d. Although the DPAS is self-executing, in the event of a problem involving acceptance, scheduling, production, or any situation that would interfere with timely delivery of a priority rated contract or order, Special Priorities Assistance may be requested. DOC may take "official action" under the DPAS to resolve the problem

6-15. The National Defense Stockpile (NDS)

The Federal Government has maintained a supply of strategic and critical materials designed to decrease our nation's vulnerability to interruptions in the foreign supply of these materials in time of national emergency. Recently it was decided to dispose of the stockpile materials, retaining only a few of the most critical and essential to cover U.S. defense requirements for not less than three years of national

HOW THE ARMY RUNS

emergency. In April 2009, at the direction of Congress, DOD released a report on recommendations for the reconfiguration of the NDS. The report recommended a "reshaped NDS, the Strategic Materials Security Management System (SMSP), (which) would continuously monitor global markets, establish supply chain commitments with producers/suppliers; monitor performance to ensure timely availability of materials, and store only limited amounts and types of materials." The DOD through the Defense National Stockpile Center, a DLA organization, manages the stockpile.

6-16. DOD Key Facilities List (KFL)
KFL is a list of facilities of such importance that loss through sabotage, subversion, terrorism, or other hostile acts would seriously impair the national defense posture of the United States. FORSCOM uses the KFL in fulfilling its responsibility for CONUS land defense planning.

6-17. Army Industrial Preparedness Program
The DOD-level management philosophy applies to the Army's Industrial Preparedness Program as well. The Army depends on private industry as the foundation for production of military materiel. Therefore, when Army production facilities or depot-level maintenance do not exist, first consideration will be given to developing private industrial facilities that produce critically needed items. Management tools available include the following:

   a. Industrial Preparedness Planning (IPP). Conducted to ensure that an adequate industrial base is established, maintained, and retained to be responsive to military materiel requirements in the event of an emergency. It involves the assessment of the capability of the industrial base to support peacetime and emergency operations, and planning with industry to ensure adequate procurement, production, and maintenance capabilities to meet support requirements.

   b. DA Critical Items List (DACIL). Prepared by HQDA (Deputy Chief of Staff G-3/5/7), they provide biennially a priority list of items required to sustain war fighting for either an indefinite or surge contingency. They also provide stable mobilization requirements to support planning with industry. The DACIL are the basic documents from which IPP is conducted.

   c. Industrial Preparedness Planning List (IPPL). Prepared by AMC from the DACIL, the IPPL consists of critical items having long lead-time components. Many of these components require special manufacturing skills or present other production challenges requiring detailed planning.

   d. Production Base Analysis (PBA). PBA describes the status of the Army's industrial readiness. It shows the base required for production and depot-level maintenance of IPPL items. Contingency production requirements are matched against the capacity of the industrial base and actions needed to improve industrial base readiness are identified.

   e. Industrial Preparedness Measures (IPMs). These actions aid industry to overcome production deficiencies in the Army's industrial base. IPMs are designed to shorten production lead-time, increase production or repair capacity, and reduce inspection time. IPMs for accelerated production will only be used when they are cost-effective alternatives to stockpiling.

Section V
Summary and References

6-18. Summary
The utility of the Army to the Nation depends to a large extent on whether its forces can be rapidly and effectively mobilized, deployed, employed, and sustained. The process of planning for contingencies or for emergencies where Army forces are needed to accomplish specified tasks is a continuous, all-encompassing process. It incorporates all aspects of Army management including manpower procurement, training, materiel development, and fiscal assets and constraints. Central to the task of reinforcing active forces is the ability to mobilize RC assets and to deploy them with the least possible delay. Although the U.S. industrial base may be called upon to accelerate production to directly support the deployed forces, it will normally be utilized to repair and replace the damaged/destroyed equipment and munitions and other consumable expenditures following the conflict.

6-19. References
   a. Army Regulation 500-5, Army Mobilization, July 6, 1996

PLANNING FOR MOBILIZATION AND DEPLOYMENT

b. Army Regulation 700-90, Army Industrial Base Process, December 14, 2004

c. CJCS Manual 3122.01A, Joint Operation Planning and Execution System (JOPES), Volume I, (Planning Policies and Procedures), July 2, 2010

d. CJCS Manual 3122.03C, Joint Operation Planning and Execution System (JOPES), Volume II, (Planning Formats), August 17, 2007

e. CJCS Manual 3122.02C, Joint Operation Planning and Execution System (JOPES), Volume III, (Crisis Action Time-Phased Force and Deployment Data Development and Deployment Execution), April 16, 2008

f. CJCS Manual 3150.16D, Joint Operation Planning and Execution System Reporting Structure (JOPESREP), December 1, 2008

g. CJCS Manual, 3500.03C, Joint Training Manual for the Armed Forces of the United States, January 15, 2011

h. CJCSI 3100.01B Joint Strategic Planning System, December 12, 2008

i. CJCSI 5714.01D, Policy for the Release of Joint Information, April 18, 2012

j. DOD Directive 4400.01E, SUBJECT: Defense Production Act Programs, September 14, 2007

k. DOD Directive 1235.10 SUBJECT: Activation, Mobilization, and Demobilization of the Ready Reserve. November 26, 2008, Incorporating Change 1, September 21, 2011

l. FORSCOM Regulation 55-1, Unit Movement Planning, June 1, 2006

m. FORSCOM Regulation 500-3, FORSCOM Mobilization and Deployment Planning System (FORMDEPS), Vols. 1-5 (U), December 14, 2006

n. Joint Pub 1, Doctrine for the Armed Forces of the United States (Change 1), March 20 2009

o. Joint Publication 4-05, Joint Mobilization Planning, March 22, 2010

p. Joint Publication 5-0, Joint Operation Planning, August 11, 2011

q. Joint Publication 6-0, Joint Communications System, June 10, 2010

r. U.S. Army War College, Department of Military Strategy, Planning and Operations, Campaign Planning Handbook, 2013.

s. U.S. Department of Commerce, Defense Priorities and Allocations System (DPAS) Regulation (CFR, Title 15, Chapter VII, Part 700), 2009

t. U.S. DOD, DOD Annual Industrial Capabilities Report to Congress, August 2011

u. U.S. National Defense University, Joint Forces Staff College Publication 1, The Joint Staff Officer's Guide, 2000

This page is intentionally left blank

RESERVE COMPONENTS

Chapter 7

Reserve Components

Greater use of the Reserves...means higher resource requirements for time, for training, and for equipment. Effective management of the Guard and Reserve as an operational force requires changes in how Soldiers are recruited, trained, equipped, compensated, and resourced. Over the past decade and a half some changes in force management were made in support of the evolution of the Reserve components as an operational force. New management approaches evolved as the Department gained a better understanding of the demands of the new operational environment and the role played by the Guard and Army Reserve as part of an integrated total force. The Department is faced with a significant change in how the Reserve components are being used as part of the total force. This change is not temporary; it is not business as usual. Rather, it reflects a fundamental shift from the past. As such, a new approach to management is needed-one that also reflects a new way of doing business for the future. Incremental changes at the margin will no longer be enough.

Department of Defense (DOD) White Paper Managing the Reserve Components as an Operational Force, October 2008, Office of the Assistant Secretary of Defense for Reserve Affairs.

Section I
Introduction

7-1. Chapter Content
Traditionally, the Reserve Component (RC) provided the Army with the capacity to rapidly expand war fighting capability when the need arose. Over the last 20 years, the Army has relied more and more on the RC to meet demanding mission requirements in support of the National Military Strategy (NMS). In recent years, the Army has taken major steps to integrate the efforts of the Active Component (AC) and the RC, and today's power-projection force can only accomplish its missions through such integrated efforts. This chapter addresses the role, organization, structure, and contributions of the RC of the Army.

7-2. Reserve Components
The Reserve forces of the Army consist of two components: the Army National Guard (ARNG) and the United States Army Reserve (USAR). The ARNG represents Component 2 and USAR represents Component 3. The RCs–the ARNG and USAR–comprises nearly 50.5% of the Total Army's military force. The ARNG is currently structured with eight combat divisions and 28 Brigade Combat Teams (BCT). The ARNG has the only two RC Special Forces Groups which are part of U.S. Army Special Operations Command (USASOC). The USAR is largely structured with Combat Support (CS) and Combat Service Support (CSS) units. These support units are absolutely essential for the Army's operating force. For example, the USAR provides the lion's share of the Army's medical, civil affairs, and psychological operations force capability.

Section II
The Army National Guard

7-3. An American Tradition
Although inheriting the militia traditions of several European nations going back to the 1500s, the ARNG officially dates to 1636, when the Massachusetts Bay Colony organized its militia companies into regiments; these units are perpetuated today in the Massachusetts ARNG and are the United States Army's oldest units. Over two dozen ARNG units pre-date the United States itself. Militia units fought in every major conflict in North America during the colonial period, to include the French and Indian War, and some ARNG units trace their lineage back to militia organizations that fought on the side of the British during the French and Indian War and later against the British in the Revolutionary War. The term

HOW THE ARMY RUNS

National Guard was first used in connection with the militia to honor the Marquis de Lafayette upon a state visit to the United States. While visiting New York City in 1824, the 2nd Battalion, 11th New York Artillery, part of the honor guard receiving Lafayette, named itself the Battalion of National Guards in tribute to Lafayette's command of the la Garde nationale, the French militia established in 1789.

7-4. National Defense Act of 1916

With the National Defense Act of 1916 (NDA-1916), the term National Guard became the official name of the organized militia of the United States. The NDA-1916 also expanded the role of the National Guard in national defense. Though the Guard remained a state force, the act increased federal oversight and assistance for training and equipment. NDA-1916 also increased the number of times a National Guard unit was brought together for training, called drills. An annual training camp was increased from five to 15 days, and 48 four-hour drill periods were mandated (the origin of today's 48 Unit Training Assemblies (UTA) and 15-day Annual Training (AT) requirement). Additionally, NDA-1916 authorized National Guard units to perform 15 consecutive days of paid AT, pay for the drill periods, and increased overall federal funding. NDA-1916 also required National Guard units to be organized like regular Army units, established federal recognition processes for both units and commissioning officers in the National Guard, established the dual oath to support and defend state and federal constitutions, and gave the President of the United States (POTUS) authority to mobilize the National Guard in case of war or national emergency.

7-5. World War I

The National Guard has made significant contributions to the Army's combat power. The National Guard provided 17 of the 43 divisions for the American Expeditionary Force (AEF) in World War I. Soldiers of the 30th Division, from North Carolina, South Carolina, and Tennessee, received the highest number of Medals of Honor in the AEF. Following World War I, questions arose over the National Guard's status, which was ultimately resolved in the National Defense Act of 1933, also referred to as the National Guard Status Act. This act made the National Guard a permanent part of the Army during peacetime as well as wartime. The National Guard in active state service is referred to as the National Guard of the several states. The National Guard in active federal service is referred to as the National Guard of the United States. The National Guard of the United States is identical in personnel and units to the states' National Guard. This new component is part of the Army and can be ordered into federal service by the POTUS with or without a declaration of national emergency. At the same time, the National Guard provides the nation a force for disaster relief, maintaining public peace, and when in a state status, it provides the governors a force for utilization during state and local emergencies.

7-6. World War II

The entire National Guard was mobilized in 1940 during the period of National Emergency declared by President Roosevelt before the United States entered WWII. Several units, including New Mexico's 200th Coast Artillery and two multi-state tank battalions, were diverted from their training mission and were ordered to the Philippines as part of a peacetime reinforcement of the newly created U.S. Army Forces Far East. They soldiered on with their regular Army and Filipino counterparts as prisoners of war after U.S. forces surrendered on the Bataan Peninsula and Corregidor. Eighteen National Guard divisions fought in World War II, equally divided between the European and Pacific theaters. The first U.S. Army division to deploy overseas, the 34th Infantry Division, was a National Guard division. National Guard divisions were also an instrumental part of General MacArthur's island hopping campaign in the Pacific theater. In the European theater, National Guard divisions participated in all major campaigns from North Africa, to Sicily and Italy, to the Normandy Invasion and the subsequent breakout, the race across France, the Battle of the Bulge, and the final campaign to conquer Germany. Following World War II, the 29 pre-war observation squadrons of the National Guard were expanded into a force of 84 flying squadrons in what became a separate Air National Guard when the Air Force was established as a separate service in 1947.

7-7. Korean War

The Korean War caused a partial mobilization of the National Guard. A total of 138,600 ARNG Soldiers were mobilized, including eight infantry divisions and three regimental combat teams. Two of these divisions served as part of the Eighth Army in Korea, two divisions went to the Seventh Army in Europe,

RESERVE COMPONENTS

and four divisions remained in the U.S. to help constitute the Strategic Reserve. In addition, all ARNG Air Defense Artillery (ADA) units were mobilized for Continental United States (CONUS) air defense. Experience with this ARNG ADA mobilization contributed directly to the post-war ARNG ADA Gun Program and its successor the Nike-Ajax/Hercules missile defense program.

7-8. Vietnam War
During the Vietnam War, the National Guard played a much smaller role than in the past. This was primarily due to a political decision not to mobilize the country's RC forces. After the Tet Offensive of January 1968, a small number of RC units mobilized, including 34 Guard units. Most were support units.

7-9. Desert Shield / Desert Storm
During Operation Desert Shield / Desert Storm, RC units were on active duty within days after the invasion of Kuwait. The majority of the Army's CS and CSS units were in the RC. The first ARNG units mobilized were transportation, quartermaster, and military police. Later, two ARNG field artillery brigades deployed to southwest Asia, providing essential fire support capabilities. In total, 62,411 ARNG personnel were ordered to active federal service, of which 37,848 deployed to southwest Asia.

7-10. Post 9/11
In recent years, the role of the ARNG has expanded. Over the past decade, operations in Bosnia, Kosovo, and Sinai have become ARNG missions. ARNG units have been transformed as a result of continuing Active/Reserve Component (AC/RC) rebalancing initiatives. Since 11 September 2001, 371,055 ARNG Soldiers have been mobilized to support the war on terrorism. (Defense Manpower Data Center information as of 18 December 2012).

Section III
The Army Reserve

7-11. Evolution of the Army Reserve
Although the USAR has existed since 1908, the concept of non-state affiliated federal citizen-Soldiers serving this nation goes back much further, tracing back to the French and Indian War (1756-1763). During the War for Independence, General George Washington's Continental Line stood out as a non-state affiliated force that fought for the infant United States. Impressed by the citizen-Soldiers capabilities, General Washington, in 1783, was among the first to suggest that a well-regulated federal militia would eliminate the need for a large peacetime regular force, eventually leading to the formation of the USAR. On April 23, 1908, the USAR was founded as a permanent institution. In the beginning, only officers of the medical corps were included, and the organization was known as the Medical Reserve Corps. In 1912, the USAR expanded to include combat arms with the creation of the Officers Reserve Corps and the Enlisted Reserve Corps. They were later combined as the Organized Reserve. During World War II (1941-1945), the Army mobilized 26 Reserve (designated) infantry divisions and more than 200,000 USAR Soldiers. Approximately one-fourth of all Army officers who served during World War II were USAR Soldiers. The Korean War (1950-1953) saw more than 240,000 USAR Soldiers called to active duty. While the Korean Conflict was still underway, Congress made significant changes in the structure and role of the USAR, transforming the Officer Reserve Corps into the United States Army Reserve. This new organization was divided into a Ready Reserve, Standby Reserve, and Retired Reserve. In 1967, Congress established the Office of the Chief, Army Reserve (OCAR) on the Army Staff to give Army Reserve Soldiers an official spokesman at the Department of the Army level. In 1973, Congress established the Total Force Policy, which focused the Army Reserve's role as the Army's strategic force used primarily in the event of large-scale conventional war. In the 1990s, the USAR began its transition to an integral component of the Army's operational force and solidified its role as a critical provider of combat support and combat service support capabilities to the Total Army. After 11 September 2001, the USAR quickly evolved into a robust operational, expeditionary force replete with streamlined deployable headquarters and citizen-Soldiers who embodied an operational mindset and culture.

7-12. Current USAR

HOW THE ARMY RUNS

a. Without question, the USAR will continue to provide essential strategic depth for the Total Army. USAR units provide integral surge enablers within the Army force generation cycle. USAR generating forces, such as Initial Military Training (IMT) and Professional Military Education (PME) training divisions, greatly expand the training capacity of the Total Force. Additionally, the non-rotational Operational and Functional Commands (e.g., Engineer, Civil Affairs, and Theater Sustainment Commands) are available to provide the surge capability for contingencies.

b. Forces Available. Dedicated USAR Soldiers provide essential skills and capabilities supporting the functions and missions of the Total Army. The growing demand of force requirements necessary to address the complex security environment of the coming decade will ensure that the USAR is routinely called upon as the force of first choice for ready enablers. These USAR enabler packages will be drawn from two distinct sets of available forces:

(1) The Army Reserve Operating Force. The USAR is structured to provide Title 10 deployable enabler forces for Full-Spectrum Operations and steady-state Security Cooperation missions. The Operational Army Reserve will routinely provide forces in a cyclical manner to meet the nation's military demands. Many civil affairs, medical, transportation, and information operations (including Military Information Support Operations) capabilities reside exclusively, or predominately, within the USAR. Under ARMY FORCE GENERATION, our ability to mobilize trained USAR units quickly and responsively is essential to meeting the operational requirements for our nation's security.

(2) The Army Reserve Generating Force. USAR units support force generation, with units that provide IMT, PME, and mobilization support, as well as sustainment of Army units and personnel (all components) for unified land operations. Given its structure, geographic spread, and experience base, the USAR is well suited for future Generating Force activities and missions. This capacity to augment the training base, mobilization stations, and institutional or garrison activities is critical to the Army's ability to train, equip, and deliver combat forces worldwide. The Generating Force may also be used in an operational role to provide foreign military training abroad or assist with domestic disaster response.

Section IV
Title 10, United States Code

7-13. United States Code (USC)
Title 10 USC contains the general and permanent laws governing the Armed Forces. Various sections of Title 10 establish and govern the RC. Specific provisions of the Code pertaining to the Army and Air National Guard are contained in Title 32 USC.

7-14. Title 10 and Title 32
The role of the RC, as stated in section 10102, Title 10 USC, is to provide trained units and qualified persons available for active duty in time of war, national emergency, or when national security requires. Title 32 further states that ARNG units shall be ordered to federal active duty and retained as long as necessary whenever Congress determines they are needed. Policy statements further define these basic roles. The RC role clearly has expanded from one of a strategic reserve for wartime augmentation to being both an operational force as well as part of the strategic reserve. The RC is an integral part of the Total Force. The Army cannot prosecute a major contingency without all of its components. An integrated Total Army is no longer just a concept; it is a guiding principle.

Section V
Reserve Service

7-15. The Categories
There are three major categories of reserve service: the Ready Reserve, the Standby Reserve, and the Retired Reserve (Figure 7-1).

RESERVE COMPONENTS

Reserve Service Categories

Ready Reserve

- **Selected Reserve**
    - Troop Program Units (TPUs)
    - Active Guard/Reserve (AGR)
    - Individual Mobilization Augmentees (IMA) (AR only)
- **Individual Ready Reserve (IRR) (AR only)**
- **Inactive National Guard (ING) (ARNG only)**

Standby Reserve

Retired Reserve

AR: Army Reserve
ARNG: Army National Guard

Figure 7-1. Reserve Service Categories

7-16. The Ready Reserve
The Ready Reserve has three subcategories.
  a. The Selected Reserve.
  (1) The Selected Reserve consists of ARNG and USAR unit members, Active Guard Reserve (AGR) members, and Individual Mobilization Augmentees (IMA) (Army Reserve only). Normally, members of ARNG and USAR units attend 48 paid UTAs annually, each of which is a minimum of four hours in duration, and perform two weeks of AT each year (USAR: 14 days, ARNG: 15 days). Commanders may extend AT, with approval, up to 29 days. Members may also perform Additional Training Assemblies (ATA) as part of unit training. Inactive Duty Training (IDT) does not include work or study associated with correspondence courses. During AT, members are in an Active Duty for Training (ADT) status. ADT is a tour of active duty, which is used for training members of the RC to provide trained units and qualified persons to fill the needs of the Armed Forces in time of war or national emergency. The member is under orders that provide for his or her return to non-active status when the period of ADT is complete. In addition to AT, ADT includes special tours, school tours, and the Initial Entry Training performed by non-prior service enlistees.
  (2) Officers, Noncommissioned Officers (NCO), and members of high-priority units have increased AT and IDT requirements. RC units have conducted IDT in the form of Multiple Unit Training Assemblies (MUTA), what is referred to as Battle Assembly (USAR) and weekend drill (ARNG), since the 1960s (a two-day weekend consists of four, four-hour UTAs and is referred to as a MUTA-4). The minimum peacetime training objective is that each unit attains proficiency at platoon level in combat arms units and company level in CS/CSS units.

HOW THE ARMY RUNS

(3) Army Reserve Soldiers are acquired primarily through Army Reserve AGR recruiters working for the U.S. Army Recruiting Command (USAREC) and with RC career counselors who move Soldiers from the AC to RC at transition points. ARNG Soldiers are acquired primarily by ARNG AGR recruiters working for state ARNG recruiting organizations and, like USAR Soldiers, with the assistance of RC career counselors at transition points. Both ARNG and USAR units have Military Technicians (Mil-Tech) who serve as federal civil service employees during the week and as members of the unit during training assemblies or periods of active duty. RC personnel serving on active duty in an AGR status and members of the AC attached directly to RC units provide full-time support.

(4) The Human Resources Command (HRC) assigns officers from the Individual Ready Reserve (IRR) in coordination with the Regional Support Commands (RSC) and gaining Troop Program Units (TPU). The vast majority of officers are assigned to Army Reserve TPUs based on voluntary assignments.

(5) The allocation of Force Structure Allowance (FSA) above end strength created a situation where both the ARNG and USAR were over-structured. This caused authorized positions to go unfilled. To remedy this situation, the Army reduced the RC FSA below the authorized end strength thereby creating Trainee, Transient, Holdee, and Student (TTHS) accounts. TTHS accounts are also referred to as individuals accounts. (Note: The USAR has eliminated its over-structure and has had an established TTHS account since Fiscal Year (FY) 2005).

(6) The Selected Reserve also includes the Army Reserve IMA Program (USAR 140-145). These are positions documented on Army Mobilization Table of Distribution Allowances (MOBTDA) that are available for immediate support. All IMAs (except General Officers) are funded to support 48 MUTAs and 12 days of AT. IMAs are also assigned to DOD, Federal Emergency Management Agency (FEMA), Selective Service, and other positions as validated by the Headquarters, Department of the Army (HQDA) G-3.

  b. IRR (USAR Only).

(1) HRC exercises Command and Control (C2) over the IRR, the Standby Reserve, and the Retired Reserve. For strength accountability purposes, the IRR consists of pre-trained individual Soldiers assigned to various groups for control and administration. The IRR is available for mobilization in time of war or national emergency declared by Congress or the POTUS, and a portion of the IRR is available under Presidential Reserve Call-Up (PRC) Authority. The control group's AT consists of non-unit Ready Reserve members with a training obligation, who may receive a mandatory assignment to a unit by the HRC Commander. The control group's reinforcement consists of obligated members who do not have a mandatory training requirement and those non-obligated members interested in non-unit programs that provide retirement point credit. This includes USAR, ARNG, and discharged AC Soldiers that have met their training requirement but have not completed their eight-year service obligation.

(2) The Reserve Officer Personnel Management Act (ROPMA) replaced the Officer Personnel Management System–USAR (OPMS-AR) and defines the training requirements and opportunities for IRR and unit officers. The Enlisted Personnel Management System–USAR (EPMS-AR) focuses on training and management of IRR enlisted members. The USAR created the Individual Augmentation (IA) program, which serves as a single, unstructured holding account in the USAR for the assignment of individual Soldiers. Assigning individuals to one account precludes the need to break or reduce parent unit readiness and streamlines the mobilization process. Soldiers assigned to the IA program are volunteers (primarily USAR Soldiers) who are readily and immediately available to meet individual mobilization requirements and contingency operational needs. The IA program also allows qualified Soldiers to continue to serve, even though they do not reside near an USAR unit. As of 30 September 2008, approximately 4,000 USAR Soldiers were registered in the online volunteer database. Retention counselors assist in providing IA volunteers by advising qualified Soldiers who transfer from either the Active Army, USAR TPUs, or the ARNG to the IRR about the IA program.

(3) The IRR constitutes the largest category of the pre-trained individual manpower. These personnel provide the majority of filler personnel required to bring both the AC and Selected Reserve units to their wartime required personnel strength in the event of mobilization and initial casualty replacement/fillers in fighting theaters. Currently, IRR strength is approximately 214,674 as of 30 September 2010.

  c. Inactive National Guard (ING).

(1) The ING provides a means for individuals to continue in a military status in the ARNG who are otherwise unable to participate in an active status. While in the ING, individuals retain their federal recognition and Reserve of the Army status as members of ARNG units. Subject to immediate involuntary mobilization with their assigned units in time of federal or state emergency, personnel

RESERVE COMPONENTS

transferred to the ING normally are attached to their former ARNG units and are responsible to participate in an annual muster with their unit.

(2) Individuals assigned to the ING are included in the Ready Reserve strength of the Army. Each FY, ARNG units schedule an annual muster day assembly for their ING personnel that serves to:
 (a) Screen Soldiers for mobilization.
 (b) Inform Soldiers of unit training plans and objectives.
 (c) Conduct lay-down inspections of clothing and/or equipment.
 (d) Update personnel records.
 (e) Determine requirements for immunization and physical examination.
 (f) Discuss transfer back to active status (especially with those individuals who possess a critical skill).

7-17. Standby Reserve (USAR Only)

a. The Standby Reserve includes those Soldiers who have completed all active duty and reserve training requirements and have either requested reassignment to the Standby Reserve to maintain an affiliation with the military or who have been screened from RC unit or IRR roles for one of several cogent reasons. Key employees of the federal government–for example, members of Congress or the federal judiciary–who cannot vacate their positions during mobilization without seriously impairing their parent agency's capability to function effectively, are examples of Standby Reservists. Other reasons for a Standby Reserve assignment include graduate study, temporary (one year or less) medical disqualification, or temporary extreme hardship. Standby Reservists may not be ordered to active duty except during a declared national emergency.

b. The Standby Reserve is composed of an active list and an inactive list. Those assigned in an active status are authorized to participate in Ready Reserve training at no expense to the government. Such participation includes training to earn retirement points or to qualify for promotion. Individuals assigned in an inactive status are normally not authorized to participate in USAR training. As of 30 September 2010, the Standby Reserve consisted of 22,816 individuals.

7-18. Retired Reserve (USAR Only)

a. Individuals who are eligible for and have requested transfer to the Retired Reserve are in this third category of the Ready Reserve. The Retired Reserve includes those individuals who are entitled to retiree pay from the Armed Forces because of prior military service or who have completed 20 or more qualifying years of service in the RC (ARNG or USAR) and/or active service for which retirement benefits are not payable until age 60. In addition, ARNG/USAR officers and warrant officers who are drawing retired pay after completing 20 or more years of active federal service are, by statute, members of the Retired Reserve. Regular Army enlisted personnel retired after 20 but less than 30 years of active service are transferred to the Retired Reserve until they have completed 30 years of service.

b. Members of the Retired Reserve are not provided any form of training and are not available for military service except in time of war or a congressionally declared national emergency. However, Service Secretaries may recall retired personnel with 20 or more years of active service to active duty at any time in the interests of national defense.

Section VI
Reserve Component Management

7-19. Structure
All three Components of the Army are governed by Congress, and affected by recommendations of the Office of the Secretary of Defense (OSD) and Department of the Army (DA).

7-20. Congress
a. Committees. The House and Senate Armed Services Committees (HASC and SASC) establish end strength authorizations and other matters concerning the ARNG and USAR. Certain areas such as pay and allowances and officer promotions are closely controlled. Establishing and approving the annual paid end strength authorizations is the most significant congressional action. Each year, end-strength ceilings are authorized to support appropriations for reserve pay and allowances. The Defense Subcommittees of both the House and Senate Appropriations Committees prepare the appropriation acts that allow funding.

HOW THE ARMY RUNS

b. Uniform Services Employment and Reemployment Rights Act (USERRA). This congressional legislation is significant because it protects RC Soldiers' rights for employment and reemployment after military service or training. This act does not replace the Servicemembers Civil Relief Act (SCRA), but further codifies and clarifies 50 years of case law and court decisions. The USERRA entitles Reserve Soldiers to return to their civilian employment with the seniority, status, and pay they would have attained had they been continuously employed. Among other protections, it expands health care and employee benefit pension plan coverage.

7-21. OSD

a. Assistant Secretary of Defense (Reserve Affairs) (ASD(RA)). Overall responsibility for all RC issues at the OSD level is vested in the Office of the ASD(RA).

b. Reserve Forces Policy Board (RFPB). Also at the OSD level, the RFPB is, by statute, an independent adviser to the Secretary of Defense (SECDEF) to provide advice and recommendations to the secretary on strategies, policies, and practices designed to improve and enhance the capabilities, efficiency, and effectiveness of the reserve components (Title 10, USC § 10301). The RFPB consists of 20 members and includes a civilian chairman; two active or retired reserve officers or enlisted members from each of the three military departments (Army, Navy, and Air Force); one active or retired reserve officer or enlisted member of the Coast Guard; 10 United States citizens appointed or designated by the SECDEF that have significant knowledge of and experience in policy matters relevant to national security and reserve component matters; a general or flag reserve officer from the Army, Navy, Air Force, or Marine Corps to serve as military adviser to the chair, as military executive officer of the Board, and as supervisor of the operations and staff of the Board; and a senior enlisted member of a RC to serve as enlisted military adviser to the chair. The SECDEF is formally associated with the RC community through the RFPB. The SECDEF is required by statute to submit an annual report to the POTUS and Congress prepared by the RFPB on any RC matter that the RFPB considers appropriate to include in the report.

c. National Committee for Employer Support of the Guard and Reserve (ESGR). This OSD-level committee, in operation since 1972, is dedicated to improvement of relations between civilian employers and local ARNG and USAR units. The committee has successfully resolved many employer/employee misunderstandings arising from RC service. It operates on an informal basis with the goal of ensuring that individuals have the freedom to participate in training without employment obstacles or loss of earned vacations. In FY 1979, state chairmen were appointed to work with the national chairman. The use of state committees provides widespread support for the program.

7-22. Office of the Chairman of the Joint Chiefs of Staff (CJCS)

Section 901 of the National Defense Authorization Act for FY 1998 created two new two-star positions in the Office of the Joint Chiefs of Staff—the Assistant to the CJCS for National Guard Matters and the Assistant to the CJCS for Reserve Matters. They assist the CJCS in assuring that National Guard and Reserve Forces are fully integrated in the Joint arena and reach full potential in executing the NMS. Furthermore, Section 901 states that "The SECDEF, in consultation with the CJCS, shall develop appropriate policy guidance to ensure that, to the maximum extent practicable, the level of reserve component officer representation within the Joint Staff is commensurate with the significant role of the reserve components within the Total Force."

7-23. HQDA

The OCAR management structure is shown in Figure 7-4. Except for Outside of the Continental United States (OCONUS) units commanded by the U.S. Army in Europe (USAEUR) and U.S. Army, Pacific (USARPAC), almost all Army Reserve TPUs are commanded by the U.S. Army Reserve Command (USARC). State governors command their respective ARNG units unless they are in federal service.

a. Assistant Secretary of the Army (Manpower and Reserve Affairs) (ASA(M&RA)). Within HQDA, overall responsibility for RC is vested in the Office of the ASA(M&RA).

b. Reserve Component Coordination Council (RCCC). The RCCC, established in 1976, reviews progress on RC matters related to readiness improvement, examines problem areas and issues, coordinates the tasking of issues to the Army Staff (ARSTAF), and reviews staff efforts. The Council, chaired by the Vice, Chief of Staff, U.S. Army (VCSA), includes selected general officers from the ARSTAF, Chief of the Army Reserve, Director of the Army National Guard, the Forces Command (FORSCOM) Chief of Staff, and the Deputy ASA(M&RA).

RESERVE COMPONENTS

c. Army Reserve Forces Policy Committee (ARFPC). The ARFPC reviews and comments to the Secretary of the Army (SECARMY) and the Chief of Staff, U.S. Army (CSA) on major policy matters directly affecting the RC and the mobilization preparedness of the Army. Membership of the committee, which is appointed by the SECARMY, consists of five AC general officers on duty with the ARSTAF, five ARNG general officers, and five USAR general officers. There are also five alternate members appointed from the ARNG and five alternate members appointed from the USAR. RC principal members are appointed for a three-year term, RC alternate members are appointed for a one-year term, and AC members are appointed for the duration of their assignment to the ARSTAF. The ASA(M&RA), ARNG, OCAR, U.S. Army Training and Doctrine Command (TRADOC), and FORSCOM also provide liaison representatives. The Director of the ARSTAF serves as adviser to the committee. The committee chairman is selected from the RC members and serves a two-year term. The Goldwater-Nichols Department of Defense Reorganization Act of 1986 reassigned the committee from the Office of the CSA to the Office of the Secretary of the Army (OSA). The Chairman of the ARFPC now reports directly to the SECARMY. The act also modified the nomination procedures. The committee normally meets in March, June, September, and December.

7-24. The National Guard Bureau (NGB)

a. The NGB is a joint activity of the DOD and the legally designated channel of communication between the Departments of the Army and Air Force and the states, territories, and the District of Columbia as established by section 10501, Title 10 USC and DOD Directive 5105.77. The Chief, National Guard Bureau (CNGB) is a principal advisor to the SECDEF, through the CJCS, on matters involving non-federalized National Guard forces and on other matters as determined by the SECDEF and the principal advisor to the SECARMY and the CSA and to the Secretary of the Air Force and the Chief of Staff of the Air Force on matters relating to the National Guard, the ARNG, and the Air National Guard of the United States (Title 10 USC §10502 as amended by the National Defense Authorization Act of 2008). Additionally, the CNGB is a member of the Joint Chiefs of Staff (Title 10 USC §151(a) as amended by the National Defense Authorization Act of 2012).

b. The CNGB works directly with the State Adjutants General (TAG) (Figure 7-2). Although the CNGB has no command authority in these dealings, cooperation is facilitated through control and coordination of funds, end strength, equipment, force structure programs, and by authority to develop and publish regulations pertaining to the ARNG when not federally mobilized.

c. The CNGB is appointed to a four-year term by the POTUS, with the advice and consent of the Senate. Appointment is made from officers of the ARNG or the Air National Guard of the United States who:

(1) Are recommended for such appointment by their respective Governors or, in the case of the District of Columbia, the commanding general of the District of Columbia National Guard

(2) Are recommended for such appointment by the SECARMY or the Secretary of the Air Force

(3) Have had at least 10 years of federally recognized commissioned service in an active status in the National Guard

(4) Are in a grade above the grade of brigadier general

(5) Are determined by the CJCS, in accordance with criteria and as a result of a process established by the Chairman, to have significant joint duty experience

(6) Are determined by the SECDEF to have successfully completed such other assignments and experiences so as to possess a detailed understanding of the status and capabilities of National Guard forces and the missions of the NGB as set forth in section 10503 of Title 10 USC

(7) Have a level of operational experience in a position of significant responsibility, professional military education, and demonstrated expertise in national defense and homeland defense matters that are commensurate with the advisory role of CNGB

(8) Possess such other qualifications as the SECDEF shall prescribe for purposes of this section (Title 10 USC §10502 as amended by the National Guard Empowerment Act of 2007)

(a) An officer may be reappointed as CNGB. The grade authorized for this position is general.

(b) The functions of the NGB are delineated in Title 10 USC §10503 as amended by the National Guard Empowerment Act of 2007.

(c) The CNGB is the appropriation sponsor of six appropriations: three ARNG and three Air National Guard (pay and allowance, operations and maintenance, and construction). The CNGB delegates administration of the appropriations to the Directors of the Air National Guard and ARNG.

HOW THE ARMY RUNS

(d) The Director, ARNG (DARNG) is a federally recognized lieutenant general who directs resources to provide combat-ready units. In support of the federal mission, the DARNG formulates the ARNG long-range plan, program, and budget for input to the ARSTAF. The DARNG administers the resources for force structure, personnel, facilities, training, and equipment, and serves as the principal advisor to CNGB on Army matters. The ARNG Directorate assists the DARNG in these efforts.

(9) The Army National Guard Directorate serves as the primary channel of communications between DA and the states, territories, and the District of Columbia (Figure 7-2). The DARNG serves as the head of the Army National Guard Directorate which functions as part of the ARSTAF. Its mission is to acquire, manage, and distribute resources to meet the ARNG priorities and influence the development of policies in order to support the Combatant Commanders, Services, states, territories, and the District of Columbia. The ARNG Directorate is structured along the following functional areas:

(a) Personnel
(b) Operations, training, and readiness
(c) Force management
(d) Installations, logistics, and environment
(e) Aviation and safety
(f) Comptroller
(g) Information systems
(h) Missile Defense
(i) Operational support airlift

(10) Figure 7-3 shows the organization of the ARNG Directorate. The ARNG Directorate is both a staff agency interacting with the Army Staff (ARSTAF) and an operating agency that supports the ARNG of the 54 states, territories, and the District of Columbia. As part of the ARSTAF, the ARNG Directorate assists HQDA in identifying resource requirements and determining the allocation to ARNG units (including: funding, personnel, force structure, equipment, and supplies). To accomplish this, the ARNG Directorate coordinates with HQDA to ensure proposed policies are conducive and responsive to ARNG unique requirements. The ARNG Directorate assists the CNGB and Director, ARNG in the execution and implementation of ARNG policies and programs, prepares detailed instructions for the execution of approved plans, and supervises execution of plans and instructions.

Figure 7-2. National Guard Bureau (NGB) Management Structure

RESERVE COMPONENTS

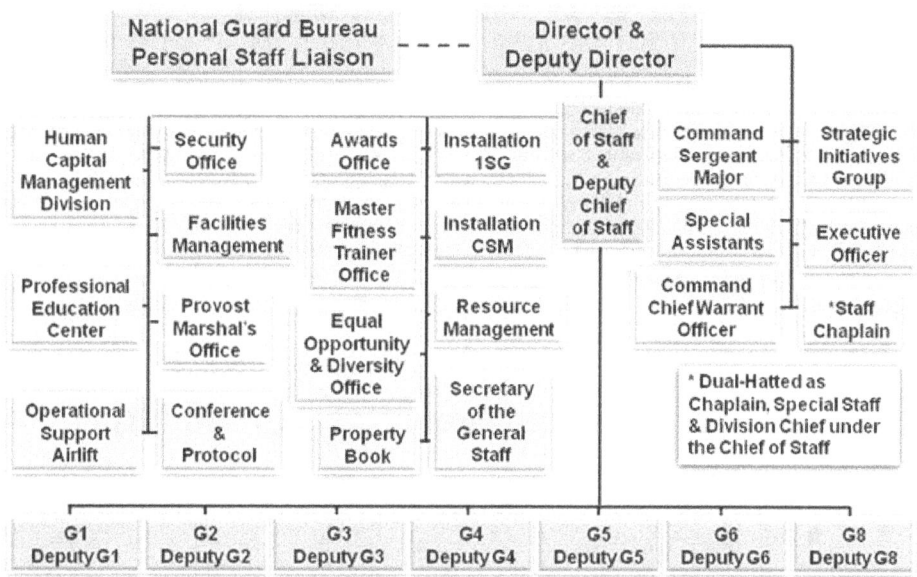

Figure 7-3. Army National Guard (ARNG) Directorate

7-25. OCAR
 a. The OCAR provides direction for USAR planning to accomplish the mission of providing trained units and individuals to support Army mobilization plans. The Chief, Army Reserve (CAR) is appointed by the POTUS with the advice and consent of the Senate and holds office for four years. The CAR may succeed himself one time and holds the rank of Lieutenant General, Army of the United States, for the duration of the appointment. The CAR also serves as Commanding General (CG), USARC. Figure 7-4 shows the organization of OCAR. The duties of the CAR are listed below.
 (1) Commander, USARC
 (2) Adviser to the CSA on USAR matters.
 (3) Directly responsible to the CSA for matters pertaining to the development, readiness, and maintenance of the USAR.
 (4) Responsible for implementation and execution of approved USAR plans and programs.
 (5) USAR representative in relations with governmental agencies and the public.
 (6) Adviser to ARSTAF agencies in formulating and developing DA policies affecting the USAR.
 (7) Assists in development of USAR mobilization policy and plans.
 (8) In coordination with other appropriate ARSTAF agencies, develops, recommends, establishes, and promulgates DA policy for USAR training.
 (9) Appropriation sponsor for three USAR appropriations (pay and allowances, operations and maintenance, and construction).
 (10) Member of DA and OSD committees as required.
 b. In 2003, the Army Reserve Personnel Center was reorganized and re-designated as the Human Resources Command-St. Louis (HRC-STL). In 2010, HRC-STL and HRC-Alexandria were consolidated

HOW THE ARMY RUNS

and simultaneously moved to Ft Knox, Kentucky and renamed HRC. HRC is a field operating agency of HQDA G-1. HRC has the mission of providing personnel life cycle management to all members of the Active, Inactive, and Retired Reserve. Critical responsibilities for HRC are listed below.

(1) Maintaining Official Military Personnel File using the Personnel Electronic Records Management System (PERMS).
(2) Conducting officer and enlisted selection boards required by law and policy.
(3) Managing officer and enlisted forces, including full-time support personnel (AGR Force).
(4) Managing life cycle personnel systems to optimize utilization of Human Resources (HR) assets.
(5) Synchronizing personnel activities across the USAR for peacetime, mobilization, and wartime.
(6) Administering the branch and functional area proponent and training requirements.
(7) Providing necessary services for maintaining individual morale and esprit de corps by administering to those individuals who are veterans or retirees. In this capacity, HRC provides information to various government agencies that is used as a basis for obtaining veteran/retiree entitlements or benefits. HRC corrects records, replaces essential documents, verifies status and service, and accomplishes many other functions involving the individual military personnel record. In addition, HRC provides administrative support for many DOD programs involving records in its custody, as well as records of discharged personnel in the custody of the National Archives and Records Administration.

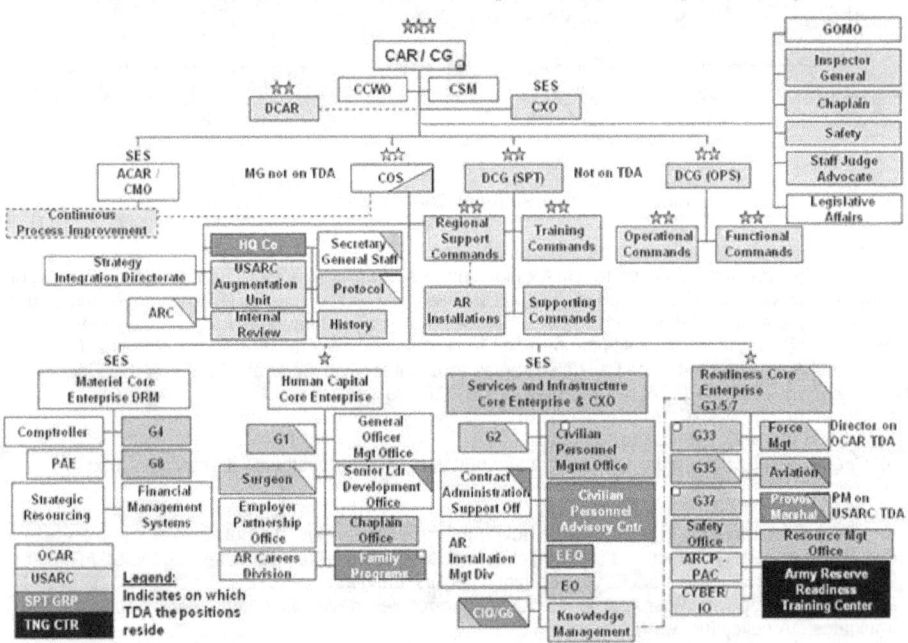

Figure 7-4. Office of the Chief, Army Reserve (OCAR)

RESERVE COMPONENTS

7-26. Army Commands (ACOM)

  a. U.S. Army FORSCOM.

  (1) The missions of the CG, FORSCOM, include command of all assigned USAR TPUs in CONUS and evaluation and support of training of the ARNG. The CG is responsible for organizing, equipping, stationing, training, and maintaining the combat readiness of assigned units. The CG, FORSCOM also manages the RC advisory structure and exercises command of the USAR units through the CG, USARC.

  (2) The USARC, established as a major subordinate command of FORSCOM on 18 October 1991, became fully operational on 1 October 1992. Subsequently the USARC became a Direct Reporting Unit (DRU) to the DA commanding and controlling all USAR TPUs assigned to FORSCOM. Today the USARC is once again a major subordinate command of FORSCOM and commands and controls assigned units through Operational and Functional Commands. Operational and Functional Commands are deployable elements that command units of the same or similar functional capabilities. For instance, USAR Medical Command (MEDCOM) commands all USAR medical units while the 11th Aviation Command commands all USAR aviation assets regardless of the unit's geographic location. Operational and Functional Commands are fully deployable as headquarters, individual units, or both. (See USAR web site at: http://www.armyreserve.army.mil/arweb/organization/commandstructure/usarc/operational/). RSCs provide base operations and administrative support to USAR units within their geographic region. In FYs 2008 and 2009, four Regional Readiness Commands transformed to become RSCs with larger geographic responsibilities. In addition, the 9th Regional Readiness Command transformed into the 9th Mission Support Command, the 7th Army Reserve Command (ARCOM) transformed into Civil Support Command Europe, and the 65th Regional Readiness Command transformed into the 1st Mission Support Command. Unlike the Regional Readiness Commands of the legacy USAR structure, RSCs do not have operational or C2 relationships with the units in their geographic areas. (See USAR web site at: http://www.armyreserve.army.mil/arweb/organization/commandstructure/usarc/support/default.htm).

  (3) The USARC also established four Mobilization Support Units (MSU) and reorganized port/terminal units, medical augmentation hospitals, movement control units, and replacement battalions/companies to provide the Army with a robust power-projection capability. These units, ready on the first day of any contingency, are essential to the successful deployment of AC brigade combat teams. The MSUs are also used to backfill AC base operations activities vacated by deploying AC units. In addition, the MSUs provide peacetime support to their respective AC counterparts.

  (4) USAR units include such diverse organizations as CS and CSS units; training divisions with a mission to provide tri-component individual and collective unit training, simulation training, special courses, and PME courses for AC, ARNG, and USAR Soldiers; and, Army garrison units with a mobilization mission of staffing an installation. The USAR, in addition to maintaining units, has individuals in non-unit control groups as described in the section on the IRR. In addition to the major USAR organizations, there are almost 2,000 company/detachment-sized units.

  b. TRADOC. TRADOC is responsible for the Initial Entry Training for RC members. All non-prior service enlistees under the Reserve Enlistment Program of 1963 (REP-63) perform Initial Active Duty for Training (IADT). This includes Basic Training (BT), Advanced Individual Training (AIT), and One Station Unit Training (OSUT) under AC auspices. An alternative method of conducting this training is the "split-option training" concept whereby an RC member may do BT during one year and AIT the following year.

7-27. State Adjutants General (National Guard)

  a. ARNG units are located in each of the 50 States, the District of Columbia, Guam, Puerto Rico, and the Virgin Islands. In addition, Guam and American Samoa signed a Memorandum of Agreement in 2010 whereby American Samoans are able to serve in the Guam ARNG. Command of the ARNG, when not in active federal service, is vested with the governors of the states and territories, who exercise command through TAG. The TAG is either an Army or Air National Guard officer who is appointed by the governor in all states and territories except for Vermont, South Carolina, and the District of Columbia. The Vermont TAG is elected by the state legislature; the South Carolina TAG is determined by popular election; and the POTUS appoints the CG of the District of Columbia. The TAG is also a state official whose authority is recognized by federal law. The authorized TAG grade is normally major general.

  b. TAGs and their management staffs (which include both state and federal employees) manage federal resources to build combat-ready units. Under the TAG, ARNG commanders lead their combat-ready units in training during peacetime.

HOW THE ARMY RUNS

c. A Joint Forces Headquarters-State (JFHQ-State) is organized within each state. The JFHQ-State is responsible for the manning, equipping, and training of ARNG units during pre-mobilization. As directed by FORSCOM and First Army and as coordinated by NGB, the JFHQ –State is responsible for providing increased levels of support to federalized units and moving federalized units to the mobilization station or port of embarkation. The JFHQ-State is also capable of providing some installation support, family support, and mobilization support to other RC units within the state upon declaration of a national emergency. The JFHQ-State continues to provide support to non-federalized ARNG units within the state. Upon mobilization, the gaining numbered Army or Combatant Command (COCOM) assumes C2 of federalized ARNG units. If the JFHQ-State is federalized for a domestic Homeland Defense mission, it will fall under the C2 of the respective geographic COCOM.

d. The U.S. Property and Fiscal Officer (USPFO) is an officer (Colonel) of the National Guard of the United States (Army or Air) ordered to active duty under the provisions of Title 10 USC and assigned to the NGB with duty in the state supporting the state TAG. The USPFO receives and accounts for all federal funds and property and provides financial and logistical resources for the maintenance of federal property provided to the state. The USPFO manages the federal logistics support systems (Army and Air Force) for the state and, upon mobilization of a supported unit, provides the support necessary for the unit to transition to active duty status. Additionally, the USPFO functions as a federal-contracting officer responsible for federal procurement activities within the state. The USPFO is also responsible for certifying the accuracy of federal payrolls.

e. Title 10 USC Chapter 1803 Facilities for Reserve Components, provides for federal support of construction of ARNG facilities. This law permits construction of facilities on sites furnished by states at no cost to the federal government or on federal property licensed to the state specifically for ARNG purposes. Funding for approved armory construction is normally 75% federal funds and 25% state funds with 100% federal support for other construction such as administrative, logistics support, and training facilities in direct support to sole federal functions. Operations and maintenance costs for these facilities are funded via cooperative agreements between the federal government and the state military departments. The federal government provides all funding for construction and maintenance of facilities for the USAR.

Section VII
Training

7-28. Goals
The training goals of the ARNG and the USAR are the same as the Regular Army. Plans to achieve objectives are accomplished during IDT, during UTAs, MUTAs, drills, or assembly periods and during an AT period. The same training standards apply to the RC that apply to the AC.

a. To meet current operational mission requirements, RC training is now based on the Army Future Force Generation Model, reducing post mobilization training requirements. To continue providing capabilities to support the Army in sustained joint and expeditionary operations and to provide predictability for Soldiers, families, and employers, the USAR implemented the Army Reserve Expeditionary Force (AREF). Beginning in 2005, 10 like-structured deployable organizations called Army Reserve Expeditionary Packages (AREP) were formed. Units in each AREP plan to mobilize for up to 12 months once every five years. Unit capabilities and readiness within an AREP are more formally validated as they approach the employment window. The USAR implemented the AREF in 10 phases. As the USAR transforms, early AREP rotations and their timelines were condensed. As the concept is implemented fully, the rotations and their phases become more distinct and sequential.

b. The USAR has sought innovative ways to continue contributing to the performance of training across the Army. To support combatant commanders, the USAR created the Foreign Army Training Assistance Command (FA-TRAC), which conducts foreign army training. In Operation Iraqi Freedom (OIF), the 98th Division deployed hundreds of USAR Soldiers to train the newly operational Iraqi National Army.

c. The mission of FA-TRAC is to provide foreign armed forces with advice, training, and organizational practices in leadership, Soldier skills, and unit tactics. USAR Soldiers assigned to FA-TRAC will deploy to the combatant command to live, train, and eat with the host-nation Soldiers. The FA-TRAC was built from the existing structure of a current USAR division (institutional training). FA-TRAC provides "plug and play" training teams to the combatant commander.

RESERVE COMPONENTS

7-29. Challenges
A key factor to understanding RC training challenges is comprehending the distinct differences between RC and AC training. Unlike AC units, which have Military Occupational Specialty (MOS)-qualified Soldiers assigned to them by HRC, RC units usually recruit Soldiers from the local area. Whether initial entry or prior service, these Soldiers are assigned to the unit and then must attend MOS qualification training. Qualification training, sustainment training, additional duty training, and professional development education are often conducted in lieu of scheduled UTAs and AT, and in some cases require more than a year to complete. Even though these RC Soldiers are counted against the unit's assigned strength (pending full implementation of the TTHS program), they are generally not available to participate in collective training. Another training challenge is that RC Soldiers and units must meet the same standards as AC units in a fraction of the time. Non-Directed Mission Essential Task List (DMETL) training, Non-Core Mission Essential Task List (CMETL) training, and other events, such as Army Physical Fitness Tests (APFT), weapons qualification, mandatory training, inventories, physicals, etc. have a greater impact because they take the same time as AC units within fewer available days.

7-30. Unit Training Assemblies
ARNG and USAR units, as elements of the Selected Reserve, are normally authorized 48 drill periods and a two-week (14-17 days) AT during the training year, which starts on 1 October and terminates on 30 September of the following year. The general trend is to consolidate UTAs during the year so that four UTAs (16 hours minimum) are accomplished during a single weekend. This MUTA-4 configuration provides continuity for individual and crew training, qualification firing, field training, and refresher training. Training for mobilization, i.e., completing Phase I and II actions identified in Functional Review (FR) 500-3-3, FORSCOM Mobilization and Deployment Planning System (FORMDEPS) Volume III Reserve Component Unit Commander's Handbook Annex E, Mobilization Checklist for Unit Commanders and Annex G, Required Documents Checklist, and the Soldier Readiness Program (SRP) checklist should be conducted during UTA.

7-31. Collective Tasks
AT is directed primarily toward collective pre-mobilization tasks. Individual training and weapons qualifications are typically performed during IDT. Soldiers and units train to established pre-mobilization levels of proficiency. Combat maneuver units generally train to individual/crew/platoon levels of proficiency. CS/CSS units are generally required to train to company level proficiency.

Section VIII
Equipment

7-32. Policy
The Army accepted risk over the years during the Cold War by not fully fielding force modernization equipment to authorized levels in its RCs. This risk seemed prudent at the time. The RCs were characterized as a strategic reserve and were not expected to immediately deploy in the event of a crisis. The global strategic environment has changed dramatically over the past two decades and, in order to meet the nation's national security demands today, the RCs function as both an operational force and a strategic reserve. In their operational role the RCs' deployment timeline has shortened considerably with the expectation that it will continue to move farther away from the Cold War paradigm of mobilize, train, deploy, and move closer and closer to the AC model of train deploy. As a result, DA policy today distributes equipment to units in first-to-fight/ first-to-support sequence. Later deploying units are provided the minimum-essential equipment required for training and to achieve acceptable readiness levels. The component to which a unit belongs (Active or Reserve), with the exception of specified programs (for example, National Guard and Reserve Equipment Appropriation (NGREA), formerly known as Dedicated Procurement Program (DPP)) is not a factor in equipment distribution. This policy ensures units employed first in time of crisis have the necessary equipment to accomplish the mission. Under this policy, the USAR and the ARNG have received substantial amounts of modern equipment in recent years and are programmed to receive even more in the near future.

HOW THE ARMY RUNS

7-33. NGREA
The NGREA is a special appropriation designated for the acquisition of equipment for the RC to improve readiness. Congress may further fence these funds for the purchase of specific items of equipment. NGREA funds complement the Service appropriations, which primarily fund force modernization, thereby improving training and readiness in the RC. Until the Army is able to support total Army modernization, the continued programming of NGREA funding will allow the USAR and the ARNG to procure critical modernization equipment in order to improve survivability and interoperability.

7-34. Withdrawal
Procedures are in place to ensure that new and/or serviceable equipment is not withdrawn from the RC without justification. Requests for withdrawal of NGREA appropriated equipment must be coordinated with the SECDEF. Waiver of this provision during a crisis allows the SECDEF to delegate that authority to the ASD(RA) after coordination with the CJCS. Requests for the delegation of authority for all withdrawals or diversions will be forwarded through the ASD(RA), who will coordinate with the Assistant Secretary of Defense (Special Operations and Low Intensity Conflict), for Ready Reserve units falling under his oversight, prior to submission to either the SECDEF or Deputy Secretary of Defense (DEPSECDEF). The Secretaries of the Military Departments will develop and submit projected replacement plans in accordance with published DOD directives, not later than 90 days from the date that the affected units are released from active duty under any provision of law. Replacement plans are also required within 90 days from the date of withdrawal, or diversion, for units not ordered to active duty, but from which equipment was withdrawn or diverted.

   a. DA has directed the USAR to leave equipment in theater known as Theater Provided Equipment (TPE). The continued use of USAR equipment as TPE to remain in theater to support other services and forces continues to degrade the ability of redeploying USAR units to reset and prepare for future deployments. Today almost 76% of on-hand USAR equipment is deployed, mobilized, demobilized, or assigned as TPE in theater. This equipment supports some 40% of the units assigned to the USARC.

   b. The USAR continues to support subsequent OIF/Operation Enduring Freedom (OEF) rotations and other requirements only through using the assets from its stateside-based institutional training structure. Much of the equipment returning from OIF/OEF has had its service life rapidly expended under combat conditions. This equipment will need to be replaced. The concept of a transformed, modular Army of "plug and play" units demands that all units, regardless of component, be equipped to the same levels and with compatible and interoperable systems. Current Army procurement planning in conjunction with congressionally directed procurement and the NGREA are keys to achieve this goal.

Section IX
Readiness / Mobilization Assistance

7-35. Background
In 1973, the Army leadership recognized the potential of many types of RC units for early deployment. Accordingly, the affiliation program was conceived to improve the mobilization and deployment readiness of selected RC units and provide added combat power earlier in the execution of contingency plans. As more structure and missions were added to the RC in the mid-to-late 1970s, the Army instituted several programs to facilitate achievement of higher training readiness levels for the RC. These included the AC/RC partnership program which aligned selected combat and Special Forces RC units with AC units, the counterpart program that aligned ARNG attack helicopter units with AC counterparts, and the Corps and Division Training Coordination Program (CORTRAIN) that associated AC/RC combat units with a CONUS corps for command post exercises. Together these programs provided resources and opportunities for RC unit leaders and Soldiers to work closely and share their experiences with their AC counterparts.

7-36. Training Support Organizations
In response to a lack of readiness and resources during ARNG deployments for the first Gulf War, Congress passed the ARNG Combat Readiness Reform Act of 1992 (Title XI of Public Law 102-484). The act as amended required the Army to assign not less than 5,000 active component personnel to RC units to provide training and readiness advice and support. The Army developed five USAR-flagged

RESERVE COMPONENTS

Training Support Divisions aligned with First and Fifth Armies composed of Active, Guard, and Reserve personnel to provide collective training support for RC units. Additionally, a portion of the 5,000 personnel were embedded in RC units as full-time support personnel. The Army Transformation Campaign Plan realigned the First and Fifth Armies into two different mission areas. Effective July 2006, Fifth Army became Army Forces North (ARNORTH), the Army Service Component Command (ASCC) providing support to United States Northern Command (NORTHCOM) for Homeland Defense and Civil Support missions. Effective October 2006, First Army assumed the mission for the entire continental United States of mobilizing, training, validating, and deploying RC units. First Army is organized with two divisions (First Army-East and First Army-West) which command Training Support Brigades (TSB), with associated ARNG and USAR elements that provide exercise support, pre-mobilization training, and post-mobilization validation capability for RC units to ensure Army standards and doctrinal mission capabilities are achieved prior to deployment. The USAR provides additional support through two Regional Support Groups (East and West) with assigned training support structure to provide a capability to conduct quality training and exercise events. In response to the Army's requirement to mobilize units more efficiently in order to maximize Boots on Ground (BOG) time the Army Reserve activated two (third programmed for FY 2010) Combat Support Training Centers (CSTC) to conduct pre-mobilization training. The objective is to provide 1st Army with USAR units that can be certified and deployed within 30 days of mobilization.

7-37. Force Management / Force Generation
Several transformational programs such as Global Force Basing, capabilities based versus threat based planning, the shift from Army of Excellence designs to modular Force designs and the shift from using the RC as strategic reserve to an operational force impact the way the Army manages its forces and prepares them for sustained as well as surge operations. The Army developed the Future Force Generation Model to manage these forces and develop increased readiness and mission capability through a cyclic process. Within Army force generation, the USAR employs a five-year cycle of not more than one-year deployed BOG and four years dwell. In the model, most USAR Modification Table of Organization and Equipment (MTOE) units are spread equally across the 10 AREPs within the five-year-group stacks. Some generating force units are held out of the rotational model: Table of Distribution and Allowances (TDA) Training Base Expansion (TBE) and CONUS Support Base (CSB) units, particularly. Theater aligned MTOE units, due to their unique capabilities and low density, are managed separately from the Army Future Force Generation Model. Individual's accounts, such as TTHS accounts and IMAs are also managed outside of the Army Future Force Generation Model.

   a. Through the use of this five-year rotation cycle, the AREF offers increased predictability to USAR Soldiers, their families, and employers. With this concept, the majority of USAR units are assigned to one of the 10 AREPs. While units at one end of the five-year spectrum are reconstituting after returning from a deployment, units at the other end of the spectrum are prepared, trained, and equipped to mobilize and deploy wherever needed.

   b. In conjunction with the new AREF strategy, the USAR is also implementing a new equipping strategy that is synchronized with the AREF. Resources are apportioned according to a unit's location in the cycle in order to obtain increasing levels of readiness and mission capability. As units progress through each year of the five-year cycle their state of readiness increases. Units ready to deploy are at the highest level of readiness. Units reconstituting from a deployment are at the lowest level. In the year prior to deployment, units receive full complements of modernized equipment compatible with AC equipment. This influx of equipment allows USAR units to train up on their go-to-war systems prior to mobilization and deployment. In this way, equipment is located where it is needed the most, with the units heading for deployment.

7-38. Overseas Deployment Training (ODT)
Although ODT has been severely curtailed because of overseas contingency operations, the program is still ongoing. The ODT program provides RC units the opportunity to exercise their skills in a realistic environment with the added benefits of reducing AC Operating Tempo (OPTEMPO) and providing needed operational support to Combatant Commanders. Within the Army force generation cycle, selected units from the Ready or Available pool may be designated to train in Joint Chiefs of Staff (JCS) exercises and in non-exercise mission training that enhances their awareness of mobilization/deployment processing. The ODT program has provided training opportunities to an increasing number of

HOW THE ARMY RUNS

companies/battalions. ODT reduces mobilization and deployment timelines, enhances readiness, and promotes unit cohesion.

7-39. Full Time Support (FTS)

a. The FTS program was directed by Congress to increase the readiness of ARNG and USAR units. The majority of FTS personnel work in ARNG and USAR units. The FTS staff performs all the day-to-day support functions for the unit to operate including personnel, administration, training, operations, maintenance, and supply which enables drilling reservists to use their limited training time (generally 39 days annually) to concentrate on their wartime tasks instead of sustainment functions.

b. The FTS program consists of AGR Soldiers, military technicians, DA civilians, and AC Soldiers. AGR Soldiers are traditional ARNG and USAR Soldiers who are on active duty. Military Technicians and DA civilians are full-time civilian employees; Military Technicians have the distinction of also being RC Soldiers who must maintain their reserve status as a condition of employment. The AC assigns Soldiers to support RC units and these Soldiers are considered part of the FTS program. ARNG and USAR technicians provide full-time, day-to-day assistance and support and act as the representative for their commanders during non-drill periods. Technicians ensure continuity in administration, supply, maintenance, and training and their services are critical to mobilization preparedness. Both ARNG and USAR technicians are federal civil service employees. The USAR technicians are governed by the provisions of the Civil Service System. ARNG technicians are governed by the same provisions except as modified by Public Law 90-486 (National Guard Technician Act of 1968) as well as Title 32 USC Section 709 and regulations prescribed by the NGB. As a provision of employment in the Military Technician Program (Civil Service) technicians must also be members of the ARNG or USAR. Many technicians are employed in the same unit to which they are assigned. AGR Soldiers serve on active duty in support of the RC. Title 10 USC AGR personnel are available for worldwide assignment whereas Title 32 USC AGR personnel receive assignments within their state, territory, or the District of Columbia.

7-40. The Army School System (TASS)

a. TASS ensures all Soldiers receive quality institutional training taught to a single standard throughout the Army. TASS is a composite school system made up of ARNG, Army Reserve (USAR), and Active Army institutional training systems.

b. The TASS mission statement is to "enhance Army readiness through an efficient, fully-integrated, educational system that guarantees Soldiers of all components are trained to a single standard." In order to meet this mission, TASS must complete and sustain the integration of training and develop future concepts.

c. TASS decentralizes training allowing AC and RC Soldiers to attend Noncommissioned Officer Education System (NCOES), Officer Education System (OES), or complete MOS reclassification close to their duty station, thus reducing unit temporary duty costs, improving Soldier quality of life (less family separation), and fostering retention.

d. TASS conducts initial entry military training, Military Occupational Specialty Training (MOS-T), officer, Warrant Officer (WO), and NCO training, as well as DA civilian education, functional training, and professional development training. Training is accomplished through both standard resident courses and distributed learning courses. TASS is the AC/RC integration vehicle for the Institutional Army which includes the TRADOC proponent schools, the United States Army Reserve Training Command, and the Army National Guard Regional Training Institutes.

e. The TASS initiative is a TRADOC program designed to leverage existing school resources. Army Reserve TASS units are functionally aligned and linked to appropriate training school proponents. Courseware and standards are the same throughout the system and students are chosen from all three components depending on the situation. During mobilization, the TASS school battalions have the mission to assist TRADOC in MOS-T training or refresher training for IRR Soldiers and recalled retiree personnel.

f. The Army Reserve 80th Training Command (TASS) provides MOS-T training and technical phases of NCOES for CS, CSS, and health services education. The 80th Training Command (TASS) has subordinate divisions and brigades responsible for these subject areas. USAR TASS Brigades are functionally aligned under respective Training Divisions with responsibility for aligned USAR TASS Battalions. The TASS training battalions and Regional Training Site Maintenance (RTSM) are proponent accredited schools responsible for functionally aligned instruction. RTSMs are functionally aligned with

RESERVE COMPONENTS

the Ordnance proponent Quality Assurance Office (QAO). High-tech RTSMs located in California and Pennsylvania are functionally aligned with the Signal proponent QAO.

g. The 84th Training Command (Leader Readiness) provides functional and leader development training for RC Soldiers and civilians. The 84th Training Command has subordinate Training Divisions, Training Brigades, and three Non-commissioned Officer Academies (NCOA) responsible for Intermediate Level Education (ILE) portions of the OES and the NCO Common Core and other NCO Training courses for the NCOES.

h. The USAR Training Command also coordinates and manages TASS training requirements with Multifunctional Training Brigades (MFTB). MFTBs are TASS training institutions located OCONUS. The MFTBs present unique situations because of their lack of proximity to other training facilities. They offer Officer and Non-commissioned Officer Professional Development Courses and MOS-T to all components of the Army. USAR MFTBs are located in Germany, Hawaii, and Puerto Rico.

i. The ARNG has faculty and support personnel executing the ARNG TASS mission in 54 states, territories, and the District of Columbia. The ARNG mission is to conduct leadership, combat arms, and selected CS/CSS training. There are seven Army National Guard Leadership Training Brigades and all have an officer candidate school and an NCOA. The Combat Arms Training Brigades conduct training in the Career Management Fields (CMF) of armor, field artillery, infantry, air defense artillery, and aviation. Additionally, in four of seven regions, the ARNG is responsible for the ordnance training battalion and provides assistance to the USAR in the remaining three regions.

Section X
Reserve Component Pay, Benefits, and Entitlements

7-41. Individual Status
In general, RC pay and allowances are determined on the basis of the individual reservist's status. During IDT periods, members of the Selected Reserve receive one day of basic pay (based upon years of service and grade) for each attended UTA. During ADT periods, members essentially receive the same compensation (basic pay, housing, and subsistence allowances) as their AC counterparts. Depending upon assignment, some reservists may be eligible for additional special pay, such as aviation duty, medical or dental service or hazardous duty pay, all on a pro rata basis.

7-42. Benefits
Eligibility for other service-associated benefits also depends upon the status of the service member. For example, members of the Army's RC, together with unaccompanied spouses with proper identification, are entitled to full use of the exchange and commissary systems. In addition, Reservists may use military clothing stores, official library services, and most clubs. Ready Reservists assigned or attached to units that schedule at least 12 drills yearly and ADT also are entitled to receive full-time Servicemen's Group Life Insurance and dental insurance. While on Active Duty for Operational Support (ADOS) or ADT, Reservists receive the same benefits and privileges as AC members. However, they generally do not receive TRICARE coverage or dental care unless the training period exceeds 30 days. Members of the Retired Reserve under age 60, known as Gray Area Retirees, are entitled to use the Post Exchange (PX), commissaries, military clothing stores, and official library services and receive a burial flag. Although retired AC enlisted Soldiers with less than 30 years of service are part of the Retired Reserve, their benefits differ. Upon reaching age 60, members of the Retired Reserve receive basically the same benefits as their retired AC counterparts except for military burial assistance and a military death gratuity.

7-43. Retirement
Members of the RC who accumulate 20 years of creditable service and reach age 60 are entitled to retired pay computed on the basis of accumulated retirement points. In general, a creditable year is one during which a Reservist accumulates 50 or more retirement points. Points are awarded on the basis of one point for each four-hour assembly, each day of active duty, and every three credits of completed correspondence courses. Additionally, 15 points are awarded for membership. However, no more than 90 points per year may be awarded for IDT activities. Retirement pay, for those with a Date Initially Entered Military Service (DIEMS) prior to 8 September 1980, is computed by totaling all accumulated retirement points and dividing by 360 to determine years of satisfactory service. The quotient is then

HOW THE ARMY RUNS

multiplied by 2.5%. The resulting percentage is then applied to the active duty basic pay of an individual with the same grade and number of years of service either at the time of separation for those who separate prior to age 60 or at age 60 for those who elect to transfer to the Retired Reserve until reaching age 60. For those with a DIEMS on or after 8 September 1980 retired pay is determined by multiplying the years of satisfactory service times 2.5% times the average of the highest 36 months of basic pay. The average of the highest 36 months of basic pay is determined at separation for those under age 60 who do not elect to transfer to the Retired Reserve and at age 60 for those who transfer to the Retired Reserve.

7-44. Uniform Code of Military Justice (UCMJ)
The UCMJ was extended to RC members as of 14 November 1986, when President Reagan signed into law the Military Justice Amendment of 1986 as part of the National Defense Authorization Act for Fiscal Year 1987. Under these changes, USAR Soldiers are subject to the UCMJ while in a drill (IDT) status. The military can now recall a Soldier to active duty for trial for crimes committed while performing ADT or IDT. The decision to activate a Soldier for trial must be approved through the USAR chain of command to the SECARMY if confinement is contemplated. In other cases, the Active Army General Court Martial Convening Authority (GCMCA) is the final decision authority. National Guard personnel are subject to UCMJ authority when in federal service; when in state service, they are subject to their state military code, which is generally patterned after the UCMJ.

Section XI
Reserve Component Transformation Campaign Plan

7-45. USAR Transformation
Army Transformation was a comprehensive undertaking that impacted all aspects of the Army from the Operational Army to the Institutional Army and across Army doctrine, organizations, training, materiel, leadership and education, personnel, and facilities. Implementation required an adaptive and flexible plan that incorporated changes over time. The Army Reserve Transformation Campaign Plan (ARTCP) integrated and synchronized the efforts of the USAR with those of the Army. The goal of the ARTCP was to develop a seamless plan for transformation with the Army while maintaining near-term capabilities and relevance. The ARTCP was designed to complement the Army's Transformation Campaign Plan while recognizing the unique skills, capabilities, and requirements of the USAR.

7-46. AREF
 a. As part of integrating the USAR with the Army's Transformation Campaign plan, the USAR built modular force packages to leverage the two-thirds of the structure that is already organized at battalion level and below. The move toward modularity provided a framework for more effectively identifying, defining, and organizing USAR capabilities relevant to today's battlefield. In FY 2005, the USAR implemented the AREF. AREF enables the USAR to use its resident capabilities to support the Army in sustained joint and expeditionary operations. The objective of AREF is to provide operationally ready units, give greater predictability in deployments to Soldiers and their families, and provide a force management process that incorporates readiness, mobilization, and deployments on a rotational basis. AREF adopted the model of train-alert-deploy versus the old model of alert-mobilize-train-deploy and represents a sea change for the RC culture.
 b. The AREF concept designates a number of pools called AREPs. Units assigned to the AREF maintain staggered states of readiness according to which package they are assigned. Under a steady state of Presidential Reserve Call-Up (PRC), each package is eligible for a nine- to 12-month mobilization one time in a five-year period. Operational requirements and AREP assignment determine which units in the package actually mobilize. Surges in OPTEMPO will require the Army to surge AREP to meet those needs. This may require partial mobilization and extension of the mobilization period. This force management process cycles units over time, and returning units "re-set" after each expeditionary mission. Each AREP contains capabilities whose readiness is formally validated prior to entering its employment window.

7-47. Multiple Component Units (MCU)

RESERVE COMPONENTS

An MCU combines personnel and/or equipment from more than one component on a single authorization document. The intent is to maximize integration of AC and RC resources. MCUs have unity of C2 similar to that of single-component units. MCU status does not change a unit's doctrinal requirement for personnel and equipment, force packaging, or tiered resourcing. No limit has been established for the number of MTOE units that may become MCU and the concept is available to both Active and Reserve Component units. MCU selection is based on mission requirements, unique component capabilities and limitations, readiness implications, efficiencies to be gained, and the ability and willingness of each component to contribute the necessary resources. Experience has shown that this initiative works best in CS and CSS organizations. Today, Army MCUs range from theater level headquarters (such as ASCC), Theater Support Commands, Signal Brigade HQs, and Military Police Brigade HQs) to engineer battalions and separate transportation companies. MCUs will not become seamless in the near term; however, the pursuit of that goal will influence the Army's institutional systems to become more integrated. MCUs have transitioned from experiment to experience. Adjustments past and present, although difficult, enabled the initiative to become a useful tool for organizing units in an austere environment.

Section XII
Summary and References

7-48. Summary
Over half of the Army's total deployable forces are in the ARNG and the USAR. The management of these forces is of paramount importance. The structure for RC management includes Congress, DOD, HQDA, Army Commands (ACOM), states, and units. Two key managers at HQDA are the NGB and OCAR. At the ACOM level, FORSCOM and its subordinate First Army and the USARC have a leading role in preparing RC forces for mobilization and deployment.

7-49. References
  a. Army Regulation 140-1, Army Reserve: Mission, Organization, and Training, 20 January 2004
  b. Army Regulation 140-10, Army Reserve: Assignments, Attachments, Details, and Transfers, 15 August 2005
  c. Army Regulation 140-145, Army Reserve Individual Mobilization Augmentation Program, 22 March 2007 with Rapid Action Revision (RAR), 17 July 2012
  d. DOD Directive 1200.17, Managing the Reserve Component as an Operational Force, 29 October 2008
  e. Title 10, USC
  f. Title 32, USC
  g. Public Law 90-486, The National Guard Technician Act of 1968 (as amended)
  h. Public Law 90-168, The Reserve Forces Bill of Rights and Revitalization Act, 1968

HOW THE ARMY RUNS

This page is intentionally left blank

FORCE READINESS

Chapter 8

Force Readiness

Force readiness is an integral function supporting the Army's strategic imperatives to: provide modernized and ready, tailored land force capabilities; develop leaders to meet the challenges of the 21st Century; adapt the Army to more effectively provide land power; and enhance the All-Volunteer Army. The Army's readiness reporting process supports requirements established by Congressional National Defense Authorization Act (NDAA), Office of the Secretary of Defense (OSD), Defense Readiness Reporting System (DRRS), Chairman's Readiness System (CRS) and the Army's current force generation process. This chapter provides details of the Defense and Joint level readiness systems that inform Army leaders on the higher processes and reporting requirements in which the Army processes operate. The key Army reporting components are then discussed as an overview as the details of Army readiness reporting are available in Army Regulation (AR) 220-1, Army Unit Status Reporting and Force Registration–Consolidated Policies.

Section I
Introduction

8-1. Maintaining Readiness
As the Army continues operating in the 21st century, it confronts the major challenge of maintaining readiness to meet current operational demands in a time of constrained resources. Maintaining readiness requires critical and often difficult decisions by the Army leadership, for they must strive for the proper balance between maintaining current readiness and resourcing future capability requirements.

8-2. Chapter Content
This chapter describes the updated and emerging changes to readiness and capabilities reporting systems throughout the Department of Defense (DOD). To make the decisions necessary for achieving and maintaining a quality Army with joint and expeditionary capabilities, the DOD, the Joint Chiefs of Staff (JCS), and the Department of the Army (DA) have developed reporting systems to assist the leadership at all levels in managing force readiness. This chapter discusses the methods used for measuring force readiness and the systems and procedures used to respond to force readiness issues. It provides insights regarding the processes qualitatively and quantitatively defining and describing force readiness. Further, it provides an executive overview of the CRS which establishes a common framework for assessing Unit readiness using force readiness reporting and strategic readiness utilizing the Joint Combat Capability Assessment (JCCA). The JCCA process is used to provide the CJCS a strategic readiness assessment of DOD's ability to meet the demands of the National Military Strategy (NMS). Finally, the readiness levels and capability assessments of Army organizations are reported in the DRRS. The Army component of this DOD system is DRRS-Army (DRRS-A).

Section II
Managing Army Readiness

8-3. Definitions of Readiness
Readiness as defined by AR 220-1 is the ability of U.S. military forces to fight and meet the demands of the NMS. Readiness is the synthesis of two distinct but interrelated levels: unit readiness and Joint readiness. Unit readiness is the ability to provide capabilities required by the Combatant Commanders (CCDR) to execute their assigned missions. This is derived from the ability of each unit to deliver the outputs for which it was designed. Joint readiness is the CCDR's ability to integrate and synchronize ready combat and support forces to execute their assigned missions. Continuing operational demands have required the Army to build and employ organizations capable of performing an assigned mission for which they may not have been specifically designed. This assigned mission may, in many cases, be just as important as the designed mission capability, and must be fully considered in the readiness reporting

processes. To that end, readiness reports consider a unit's ability to conduct its designed mission as well as its ability to perform an assigned mission. Force readiness is defined as the readiness of the Army within its established force structure, as measured by its ability to station, control, man, equip, replenish, modernize, and train its forces in peacetime, while concurrently planning to mobilize, deploy, employ, and sustain them in war to accomplish assigned missions. DOD defines military capability in relation to force readiness, sustainability, force structure, modernization, and infrastructure. This definition is directly linked to how the total force is planned, programmed, and budgeted.

8-4. Factors Affecting Force Readiness

a. Force readiness is affected by many quantitative and qualitative factors. For example, it is fairly easy to measure the status of personnel, equipment, or war reserves. It is not so easy to assign a value to morale or cohesion. Force readiness is dynamic, encompasses many functions, and is influenced by many factors. To illustrate its complexity, consider the following partial listing of factors that impact on the force readiness of the Army.
  (1) Unit status
  (2) Design of weapons systems
  (3) Construction of facilities
  (4) Availability of supplies
  (5) Relationship with allies
  (6) Strategic intelligence capability
  (7) Application of unit manning principles
  (8) Civilian personnel force planning
  (9) Quality of Soldier/family services
  (10) Availability of civilian and military transportation (e.g., land, air, sea)
  (11) Lines of communications
  (12) Availability of pre-stocked equipment
  (13) Mobilization capability
  (14) Recruitment of manpower for military and industry
  (15) Capability to receive, process, and transport forces in theaters
  (16) Senior leadership-quality of strategic planning and decision-making
  (17) Capability of the enemy
  (18) Quality and morale of personnel
  (19) Army values and doctrine
  (20) Army programs and processes

b. Estimating force readiness is difficult and highly situational. The American people and their elected representatives need to know how much capability is required and what it costs. Short of the military's performance in war or deterring war, a defined measure of return on the dollar that the Services can demonstrate is the level of force readiness to execute the NMS, as deduced from analytical tools and other indicators.

8-5. Cost of Force Readiness

a. Force readiness is expensive and must be balanced against other program needs. Within a finite amount of resources, the purchase of a balanced program that satisfies future investment needs, such as research and development and procurement, competes with current readiness needs such as spare parts, depot maintenance, and war reserves. The need for immediate response to a wide variety of requirements places great demands on the Army to maintain forces at a high state of mission capability.

b. Readiness costs increase sharply as higher levels of readiness are approached. At the unit level, maximum readiness is highly perishable. A unit can attain a very high level of readiness and a short time later, without continued intensive resource allocation, have the trained expertise and peak maintenance levels diminish. The availability of repair parts and supplies, length of time between training events, and personnel turbulence all have a tremendous influence on unit readiness.

FORCE READINESS

Section III
Department of Defense Readiness Reporting System

8-6. DOD Readiness Reporting System (DRRS) Overview

DRRS establishes a mission-focused, capabilities-based application that provides DOD users a collaborative environment to facilitate operational decision-making via readiness evaluation of U.S. Armed Forces in support of assigned missions. DRRS is a unique network of applications identifying the capabilities of military forces. The information in DRRS goes well beyond the standard resource accounting approach of traditional readiness reporting by providing assessments of each organization's ability to conduct assigned tasks either in the context of their core mission or other assigned operations. In addition, DRRS improves the efficiency of readiness reporting by merging previously unrelated stovepipe data into a single integrated, authoritative source. DRRS establishes a common language of tasks, conditions, and standards to describe capabilities essential to the completion of assigned missions. The valuable data within DRRS is used to provide timely, accurate readiness information including overall mission readiness and individual task readiness.

8-7. CRS

a. Purpose. The CRS was implemented at the end of 1994. While it was incrementally modified since then, it was significantly revised in 2002, 2004, 2007, and then most recently in November of 2010. The CRS provides a common framework for conducting commanders' readiness assessments, blending unit-level readiness indicators with Combatant Command (CCMD), Service, and Combat Support Agency (CSA) (collectively known as the C/S/As) subjective assessments of their ability to execute the NMS. Title 10 United States Code (USC) section 117d, requires the CJCS to conduct, on a quarterly basis, a joint review to measure the level of current military readiness based upon the reporting of the capability of the armed forces to carry out their wartime missions. The quarterly JCCA does this through the Joint Force Readiness Review (JFRR) which compiles the Services', CCMDs', and CSA's readiness assessments. Additionally, plans assessments, a readiness deficiency assessment and a quarterly readiness report to Congress are performed. The CRS, through JCCA, provides the means to meet the CJCS's statutory requirements while supporting a process that provides timely and accurate reporting to the DOD leadership.

b. Responsibilities. The CJCS is responsible for assessing the strategic level of readiness of the Armed Forces to fight and meet the demands of the full range of operations required by the military strategy. Readiness at this level is defined as the synthesis of readiness at the joint and unit levels. It also focuses on broad functional areas, such as intelligence and mobility, to meet worldwide demands. Joint readiness is the responsibility of the CCDRs. It is defined as the commander's ability to integrate and synchronize combat and support forces to execute assigned missions. Unit readiness is the primary responsibility of the Services and the United States Special Operations Command (USSOCOM). Unit readiness is defined as the ability to provide the capabilities required by CCDRs to execute their assigned missions. The CSAs are responsible for providing responsive support to the operating forces in the event of war or threat to national security. These definitions are considered key because they delineate the responsibilities of the CJCS, Service Chiefs, CCDRs, and CSA directors in maintaining and assessing readiness (Figure 8-1). The forum within the CRS for the assessment of joint, unit, and CSA readiness is the JFRR.

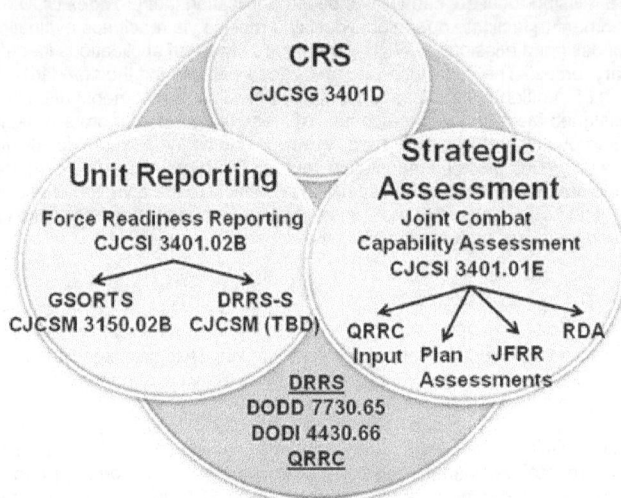

Figure 8-1. Chairman's Readiness System (CRS)

8-8. The Joint Combat Capability Assessment (JCCA) Process (Figure 8-2)

a. JCCA. The JCCA process implements the CRS. The JCCA inputs consists of a quarterly JFRR, an annual Readiness Deficiency Assessment (RDA), a Quarterly Readiness Report to Congress (QRRC), and a quarterly plans assessment.

b. Quarterly JFRR. The JFRR process evaluates the CCMDs', the Services', and the CSA's readiness to execute their portions of mission capabilities required by the NMS.

c. JFRR Required Data. Each quarterly review consists of the following data points.

(1) Overall Readiness Assessment. The JFRR provides a snapshot of current and current plus 12-month assessment of CCMDs, Services, and CSAs using the 4-Tiered Readiness Assessment (RA) metrics shown in Figure 8-3.

(2) Top Concerns. CCDRs, Service Chiefs, and Directors will identify their top two readiness concerns. The purpose is to inform the CJCS of their most important, near-term readiness issues.

(3) Yes/Qualified Yes/No (Y/Q/N) Assessments against Joint Mission Essential Tasks (JMET) and Joint Capability Areas (JCA). Commanders and Agency Directors will assess the ability of their organization to accomplish a task to standard under specified conditions in accordance with the Universal Joint Task List (UJTL). This assessment should be informed by observed performance, resource availability, military judgment and will be measured against the 3-Tiered, Y/Q/N, readiness metric. (See Figure 8-3).

(4) Y/Q/N Assessments against Core Missions and Plans. Service Chiefs will assess the ability of their Service to provide organized, trained, and equipped forces capable of executing their designed tasks and providing required capabilities to support assigned missions, reported against the JCAs at an appropriate level of aggregation (tier), measured using the Y/Q/N metric.

FORCE READINESS

(5) Deficiencies. CCMDs, Services, and CSAs are required to report readiness deficiencies every quarter as part of the JFRR so the Joint Chiefs of Staff and other senior leaders can maintain situational awareness on shortfalls impacting DOD's readiness to execute the NMS. Annually the J-3 will collect all readiness deficiencies reported over a fiscal year and forward them as part of the Readiness Deficiency Report to J-8 to inform the Annual Report on CCDR Requirements.

(6) Service/USSOCOM Readiness data from DRRS/Global Status of Resources and Training System (GSORTS). Service and USSOCOM readiness assessments will be reported in accordance with CJCS of the Joint Chiefs of Staff Instruction (CJCSI) 3401.02B, Force Readiness Reporting. The report will include current overall readiness for significant combat, combat support, and combat service support units using aggregated GSORTS data. This will include currently deployed, next to deploy (will deploy within the next 120 days) as well as non-deployed forces. Report will include deployed and next to deploy forces ability to perform assigned missions using the Percent Effective (PCTEF) readiness metric. The report also will address the ability of all remaining non-deployed forces to perform designed missions using the overall C-Level assessment. Note that Army units do not report PCTEF as that rating has been subsumed by the Army rating of Assigned Mission Level (A-Level).

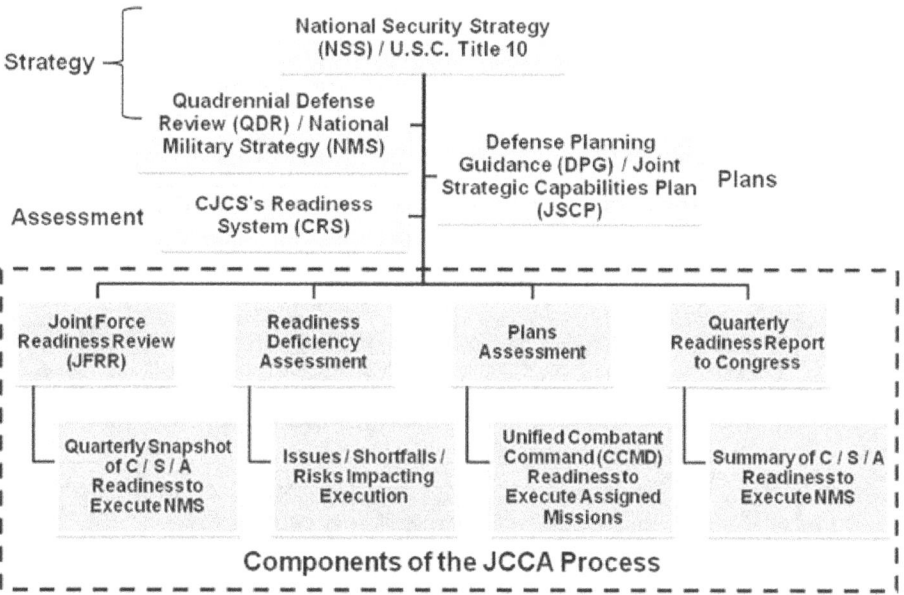

Figure 8-2. Joint Combat Capability Assessment (JCCA)

8-9. JFRR Metrics

JFRR Y/Q/N Criteria are defined in Table 8-1. The Services, CCMDs, and CSAs provide an overall Readiness Assessment of RA 1,2,3, or 4 and also assign a Y/Q/N assessment to each of the JMETs that apply to the execution of current missions, plus 12-month missions, and the required Mission Essential Tasks. The Services provide an overall Readiness Assessment of RA 1, 2, 3, or 4 and assign a Y/Q/N

HOW THE ARMY RUNS

assessment to each of the applicable JCAs. The CSAs assign a Y/Q/N assessment to each of the Agency Mission-Essential Tasks (AMET) that apply to the three assessment areas.

Table 8-1. Three-Tiered Readiness Metric

Metric	Definition
Yes (Y)	The organization can accomplish the task to standard under the specified conditions. A "Yes" assessment should reflect demonstrated performance in training or operations whenever possible.
Qualified Yes (Q)	The organization is expected to accomplish the task to standard, but this performance has not been observed or demonstrated in training or operations. Organizations assessing their task capability as a "Qualified Yes" may be employed for those tasks.
No (N)	The organization is unable to accomplish the MET to standard at this time.

8-10. JFRR Deficiencies
The Readiness Deficiency Assessment is a J-3 document that frames for senior leaders the cumulative impact of CCMD, Service, and CSA reported deficiencies on DOD's readiness to execute the NMS. Annually, the J-3 will collect readiness deficiencies reported over a fiscal year and identify readiness trends and highlight critical deficiencies, filtering all through the Defense Planning Guidance (DPG) in order to provide context and a relative value for each. A Joint Combat Capability Assessment Group (JCCAG) will review the results of the Readiness Deficiency Assessment and the Deputy J-3 will approve the assessment for release to inform J-8's Annual Report on CCMD Requirements (Figure 8-3).

8-11. JFRR RA Levels
In addition to reporting deficiencies in meeting requirements and linking them to degraded JMETs, AMETs, or JCAs, CCDRs, Services, and CSAs assign an overall RA-Level to their ability to execute current missions, plus 12-month missions, and the scenario. To determine the RA-Level, the reporting commands consider Joint Mission Essential Task List (JMETL)/Assigned Mission Essential Task List (AMETL)/JCA assessments, results of recent plan assessments, and readiness deficiencies. RA Levels are defined in Table 8-2.

Table 8-2. Readiness Assessment Levels Definitions

Readiness Assessment Level	Definitions
RA-1	Issues and/or shortfalls have negligible impact on readiness and ability to accomplish assigned missions.
RA-2	Issues and/or shortfalls have limited impact on readiness and ability to accomplish assigned missions
RA-3	Issues and/or shortfalls have significant impact on readiness and ability to accomplish missions.
RA-4	Issues and/or shortfalls preclude accomplishment of assigned mission

Note: 1. Overall Assessment uses RA-Levels to categorize risk to end state.

FORCE READINESS

8-12. CRS Outputs

a. The outputs of the CRS are synchronized to inform, through the Comprehensive Joint Assessment (CJA), other Joint Staff and OSD processes to include: J-5's CJCS's Risk Assessment (CRA); J-8's Annual Report on CCDR Requirements and OSD's Quarterly Readiness Report to Congress (refer to Figure 8-3 below). Through these informative relationships, the CRS does the following.

(1) Ensures senior leaders and staffs are operating off a common readiness picture.
(2) Supports the development of coordinated strategic documents.
(3) Is synchronized to facilitate timely senior leader decision making.
(4) Helps the Secretary of Defense (SECDEF) and CJCS fulfill their statutory requirements under Title 10 USC.

b. The strategic documents mentioned above and discussed in greater detail below help align ends, ways, means, and risks to accomplishing the NMS and enable the CJCS to provide the best military advice to the President of the United States (POTUS) and the SECDEF.

(1) CRA. In accordance with Title 10 USC Section 153 (b)(1), "the CJCS shall submit to the SECDEF a report providing the CJCS's assessment of the nature and magnitude of the strategic and military risks associated with executing the missions called for in the NMS." To help fulfill this statutory requirement, the JCCAG will forward to the J-5, annually, the Joint Combat Capability Assessment and the results of Plans Assessments to inform the CRA (Figure 8-3).

(2) Annual Report on CCDR Requirements. In accordance with Title 10 USC Section 153 (c)(1), "the CJCS shall submit to the congressional defense committees a report on the requirements of the CCMDs." In addition to consolidating the combatant command integrated priority lists, the report will "address each deficiency in readiness identified during the joint readiness review" (Title 10 USC Section 117 (d)(1)(a)). To help fulfill this statutory requirement, the JCCAG will forward to the J-8, annually, the Readiness Deficiency Assessment identifying the following.

(a) CCMD readiness deficiencies reported over the fiscal year.
(b) CCMD readiness deficiencies closed over the fiscal year.
(c) The status of CCMD readiness deficiencies not yet closed.

(3) Quarterly Readiness Report to Congress. Section 482 of Title 10 USC requires that within 45 days following the end of each calendar quarter a report be sent to Congress based on military readiness. The QRRC is reviewed and approved by the SECDEF and forwarded to Congress and fulfills this requirement.

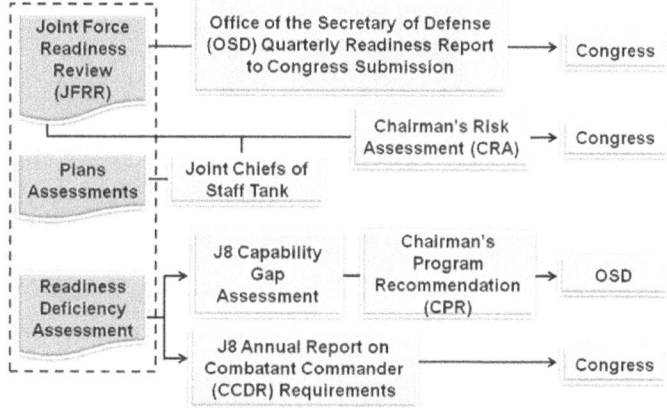

Figure 8-3. Chairman's Readiness System (CRS) Output

HOW THE ARMY RUNS

8-13. Strategic Readiness
Strategic Readiness is the assessment of the Army and its Army Commands (ACOM), Army Service Component Commands (ASCC) and Direct Reporting Units (DRU) ability to meet its current and future Title 10 responsibilities in support of the NMS. The current reporting system, codified by AR 220-1, focuses at the tactical and operational levels, and assesses individual units' personnel, materiel, and training status. Presently, Army Strategic Readiness does not exist in any regulation, doctrine, or codification in any form. In 2012, the Army began to develop the doctrine and concept aimed at providing a more holistic and predictive view of readiness. The forthcoming regulation, under development, establishes the Army's business rules for: assessing the holistic Army; 2 identifying the Army's strategic readiness deficiencies and leading indicators; and providing an ability to forecast future readiness to facilitate allocation of resources. The regulation establishes the quarterly Army Strategic Readiness Assessment process that provides the Army Strategic Readiness Assessment (ASRA) (Figure 8-4). In this process, Army organizations provide their respective top strategic measures and metrics (qualitative and quantitative) at the macro level in relation to the Strategic Readiness Tenets. Under this proposed construct, the proponents of the readiness tenets analyze and determine top strategic measures and metrics and participate in further analysis through the Strategic Readiness Assessment Group (SRAG). The SRAG is a Headquarters, DA (HQDA) integrated working group that convenes each Fiscal Year (FY) quarter at three levels: action officers; Council of Colonels; and General Officer Steering Committee (GOSC). Each quarter the SRAG GOSC will provide recommendations and the ASRA to Army senior leaders for final approval. The approved ASRA will inform other statutory requirements and outputs to include future readiness forecasting, JFRR, QRRC, and Deputy's Management Action Group (DMAG).

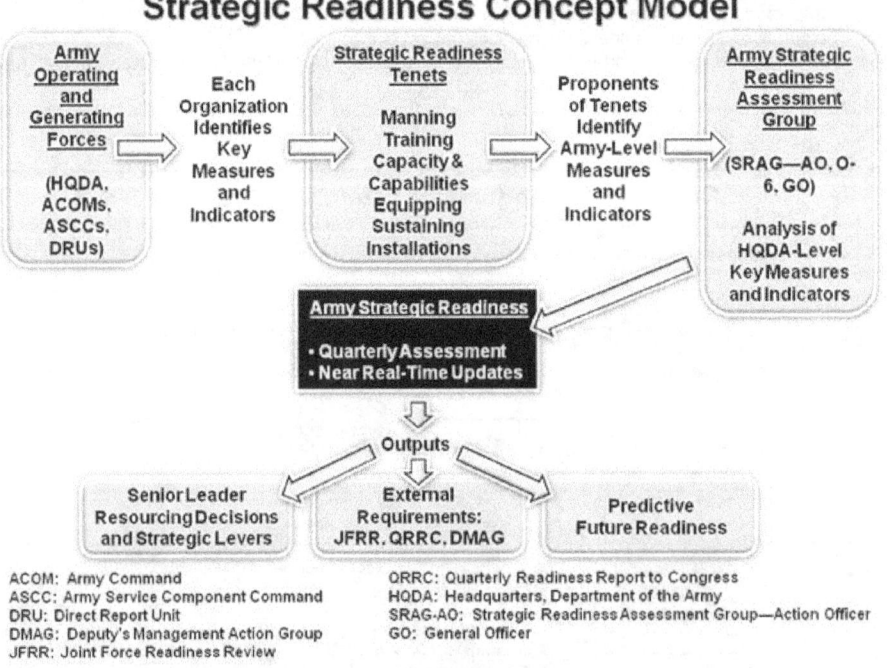

Figure 8-4. Strategic Readiness Concept Model

FORCE READINESS

Section IV
Department of Defense Readiness Reporting System Army

8-14. Department of Defense Readiness Reporting System Army (DRRS-A) Overview
DRRS-A is the Army-Specific Implementation of the DOD DRRS (see Para. 8-6 above).

  a. DRRS-A was developed by HQDA G-3/5/7 to accommodate the ongoing development and implementation of additional and/or revised readiness status reporting and force registration requirements by the SECDEF, the CJCS, and the Secretary of the Army (SECARMY)/Chief of Staff, U.S. Army (CSA) to meet their responsibilities under Title 10 USC. It is a family of related and supporting systems that includes: the DRRS-A database; the Net-Centric Unit Status Report (NetUSR) application; the Force Registration application; the Force Projection application; and the Army Readiness Management System (ARMS). DRRS-A also supports the evolution of Army force generation concepts and processes for manning, equipping, and training and the reporting of the progressive readiness of Army forces for unified land operations. The DRRS-A database is the Army's official readiness reporting database and the authoritative database of record and central registry for all currently existing and approved Army units, organizations, and installations. The DRRS-A database replaced the Army Status of Resources and Training System (ASORTS) database during FY 2008.

  b. DRRS-A Key Applications.

  (1) The NetUSR Application. A web-based readiness status data input tool that imports data from designated authoritative sources for reference to support required commander readiness status assessments. The NetUSR replaced the Personal Computer-Army Status of Resources and Training System (PC-ASORTS) application as the Army's official readiness status data input tool in October 2006.

  (2) The Force Registration Application. A web-based force management data input tool used by Army force registration officials and Unit Identification Code Information Officers (UICIO) to formally register currently existing and approved Army organizations and to update Basic Identity Data Elements (BIDE) in the DRRS-A database.

  (3) The Army Readiness Management System Application. The official DRRS-A business intelligence and output tool that provides visibility to selected Army readiness status and force registration data and information contained in the DRRS-A database and facilitates the detailed analysis of readiness status trends and force registration issues.

  (4) The Force Projection Application. This application provides execution information for the mobilization of Reserve Component forces in support of ongoing operations. Additionally, Force Projection provides mobilization and execution data to the Joint Operations Planning and Execution System (JOPES) in support of deployment operations to include validation requirements, strategic airlift schedules, and status of the deployment flow in conjunction with the Computerized Movement Planning and Status System (COMPASS).

  c. The Army developed the DRRS-A to accommodate the evolution of DRRS and to provide the readiness reporting flexibility necessary to support the current Army force generation process for manning, equipping, training, and readiness. The DRRS-A is a capabilities-based, adaptive, near-real-time readiness reporting system that ensures seamless coordination between the Army, OSD, and the CCDRs. It is linkage to the Army authoritative databases for personnel, medical, logistics, installations, training, and force management.

HOW THE ARMY RUNS

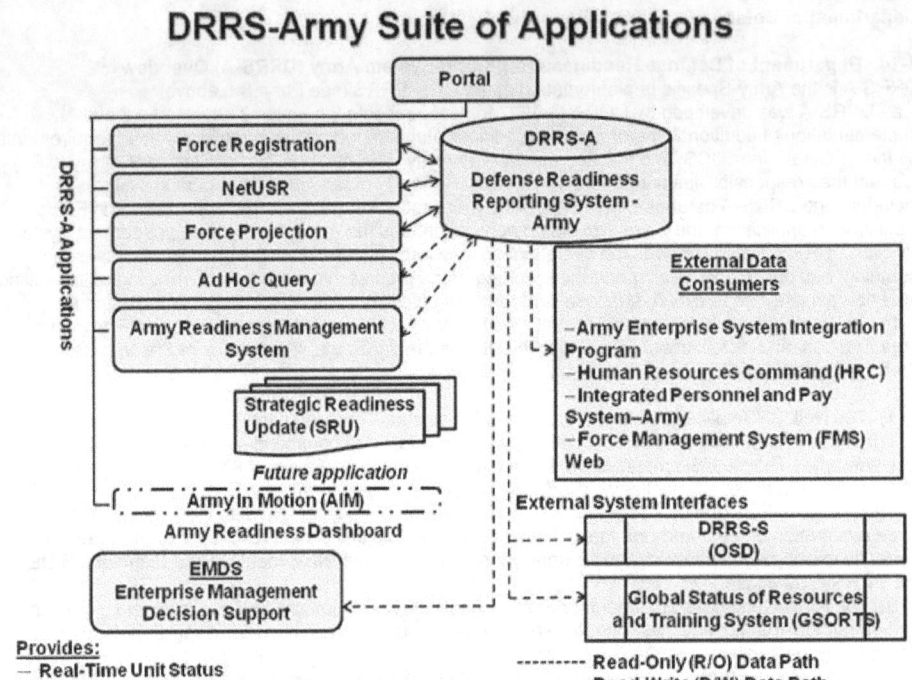

Figure 8-5. Department of Defense Readiness Reporting System Army (DRRS-A) Suite of Applications

FORCE READINESS

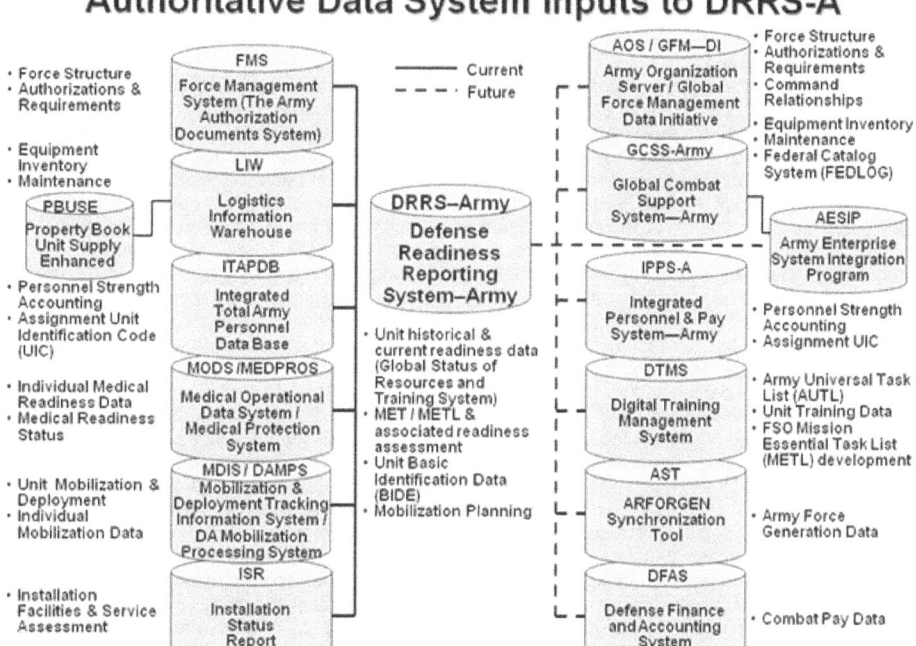

Figure 8-6. Authoritative Data Inputs to Department of Defense Readiness Reporting System Army (DRRS-A)

8-15. Unit Status Reporting Purpose

NetUSR is the software application used by commanders of Army units to provide readiness input to DRRS-A. The primary purpose of the reports prepared by commanders using NetUSR is to provide the POTUS, SECDEF, JCS, HQDA, and all levels of the Army's chain of command with the current status of U.S. Army units and necessary information for making operational decisions. The NetUSR application enables commanders to measure and report on the status of resources and training level in their units at a given point in time. The reports should not be used in isolation to assess overall unit readiness or the broader aspects of Army force readiness. The reports provide a timely single source document for assessing key elements of a unit's status. They do not provide all the information necessary to manage resources.

8-16. Army Unit Status Reporting (USR) Relationship to Joint Readiness

CJCSI 3401.01E and DOD Directive (DODD) 7730.65 establish policy and procedures for reporting and assessing the current readiness of the U.S. Armed Forces through the CRS. Units report their Mission Essential Tasks (MET) for their Core (designed) mission and for their Assigned Missions in addition to their status in the areas of personnel, equipment on hand, equipment readiness, and training to their Service or CCMDs for later incorporation to the JFRR. DRRS-A is established by Army Regulation 220-1 and provides the data required of Army organizations by the CJCSI and the DODD. The Army requires additional data that increases the value of the unit status report as a resource management and operations tool. The supplemental data required by the Army was selected by HQDA in coordination with

HOW THE ARMY RUNS

the ACOMs, ASCCs, and DRUs. This information passes through but is not retained by the joint staff (JS). The higher level of detail allows units to better express their status and all levels of command to use the report to analyze key status indicators.

8-17. USR Procedures

a. Commanders of all measured units are required to determine and report a C-Level that reflects their assessments of their units' ability to accomplish the core missions for which the units are designed (C-Level), an Assigned Mission Level (A-Level) that reflects their assessments of their units' ability to accomplish their primary directed missions, and also a Chemical-Biological Defense Readiness Training (CBDRT) Level indicating their units' readiness to perform their core mission under chemical or biological conditions. The C-Level, A-Level, and the CBDRT Level are overall levels that are described in Chapter 4 of AR 220-1. There are four measurements (personnel, equipment and supplies on-hand/available, equipment readiness/serviceability, and unit training level proficiency) that support the C-Level determination. Two measurements, Assigned Mission Manning (AMM) and Assigned Mission Equipment (AME), support the A-Level determination. Two measurements (Equipment and supplies and training) support the CBDRT Level determination. These resource and training status measurements are determined using the four tier rating scale. Analysis of these resource and training measurements provides insight into the measured unit's tactical-level capability (Figure 8-7).

b. Status levels are determined for each of these measured areas to support the overall assessments required. Measured area levels are determined by applying the specific resource or status criteria and/or metrics. Commanders cannot subjectively upgrade or downgrade the level of a measured area.

c. In general, measured units will measure and report readiness status against their currently effective Modification Table of Organization and Equipment (MTOE)/Table of Distribution and Allowances (TDA) document. However, in certain circumstances, units can report early against a future document. AR 220-1, Chapter 7 provides detailed instructions for determining the requirements document.

d. NetUSR data is transmitted through Administrative Control (ADCON) channels (Figure 8-8). Reporting units are required to submit a unit status report covering their specific resource and training status levels, their overall category levels (C-Levels), and their individual and overall MET assessments.

e. Overall Levels. The overall category level (C-1, C-2, C-3, C-4, C-5) indicates the degree to which a unit has achieved prescribed levels of fill for personnel and equipment, the training status of those personnel, and the maintenance status of the equipment. When assigned a current operational requirement, units also report an A-Level to indicate their readiness level for the current assigned mission. The four areas for which specific levels are calculated to support the C-Level determination are: personnel, equipment and supplies on-hand/available, equipment readiness/serviceability, and unit training level proficiency. These measured area levels reflect the status of the unit's resources and training measured against the resources and training required to undertake the wartime mission for which the unit is organized or designed. Category levels do not project a unit's combat ability once committed to action. The overall unit category level will be based only upon organic resources and training under the actual control of the reporting unit or its parent unit. The C-Level categories follow.

(1) C-1. The unit possesses the required resources and is trained to accomplish or provide the core functions and fundamental capabilities for which it was designed or to undertake the mission it is currently assigned. The status of resources and training in the unit does not limit flexibility in methods to accomplish core functions or assigned missions nor increase vulnerability of unit personnel and equipment. The unit does not require any compensation for deficiencies.

(2) C-2. The unit possesses the required resources and is trained to accomplish or provide most of the core functions and fundamental capabilities for which it was designed or to undertake most of the mission it is currently assigned. The status of resources and training in the unit may cause isolated decreases in the flexibility of choices to accomplish core functions or currently assigned missions. However, this status will not increase the vulnerability of the unit under most envisioned operational scenarios. The unit will require little, if any, compensation for deficiencies.

(3) C-3. The unit possesses the required resources and is trained to accomplish or provide many, but not all, of the core functions and fundamental capabilities for which it was designed or to undertake many, but not all, portions of the mission it is currently assigned. The status of resource and training in the unit will result in significant decreases in flexibility to accomplish the core functions or the assigned missions and will increase vulnerability of the unit under many, but not all, envisioned operational scenarios. The unit will require significant compensation for deficiencies.

FORCE READINESS

(4) C-4. The unit requires additional resources or training to accomplish or provide the core functions and fundamental capabilities for which it was designed or to undertake the mission currently assigned; however, the unit may be directed to undertake portions of the assigned mission with resources on hand (available).

(5) C-5. The unit is undergoing a HQDA-directed resource action and/or is part of a HQDA-directed program and is not prepared to accomplish or provide the core functions or fundamental capabilities for which it was designed. Units report C-5 in accordance with the policy and procedures established in paragraph 4–8. Level 5 is not applicable to A-Level reporting. C-5 units are restricted to the following.

(a) Units undergoing activation, inactivation, conversion, reset, or other HQDA directed resource action.

(b) Units that have their levels for authorized personnel and/or equipment established so that, even when filled to the authorized level, the established level does not allow the unit to achieve level 3 or higher.

(c) Units that are not manned or equipped but are required in the wartime structure.

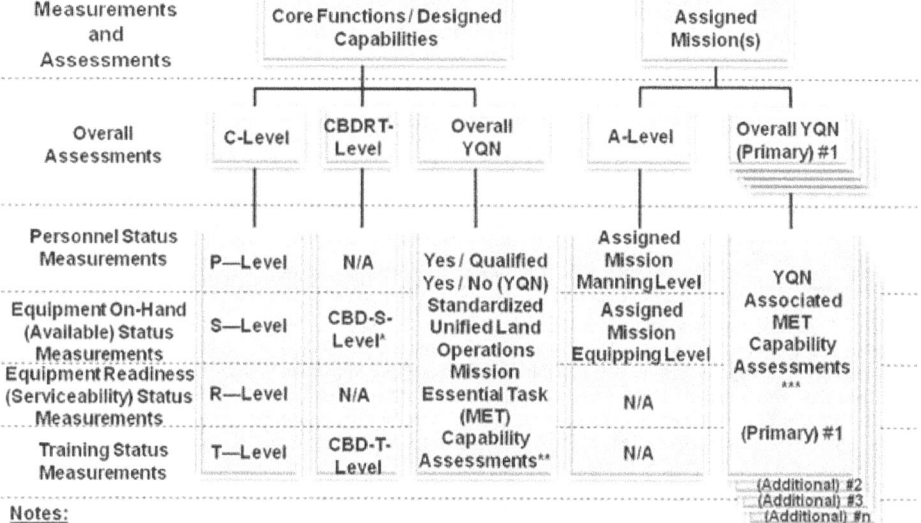

Figure 8-7. Commander's Unit Status Report (CUSR) Measured Areas

HOW THE ARMY RUNS

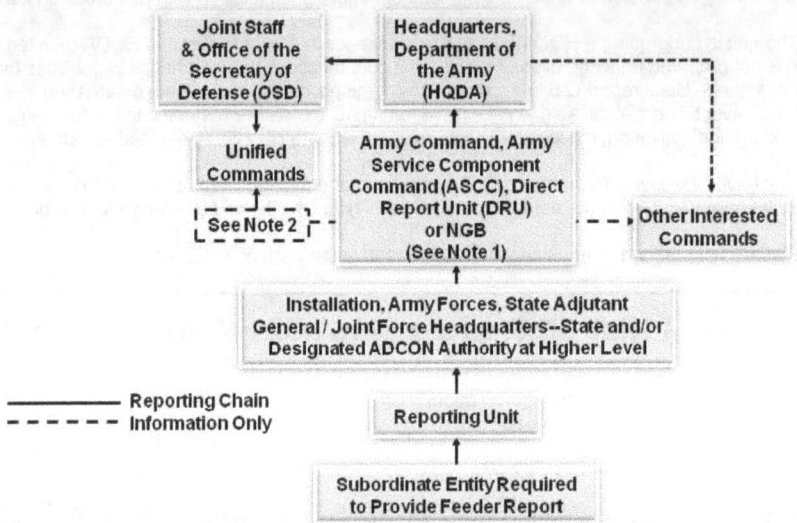

Figure 8-8. Readiness Reporting Channels

Notes:
1. Reports from the preponderance of Army National Guard units that are not on active duty are processed through National Guard Bureau (NGB) with information copies provided to Forces Command
2. Only designated Army Service Component Commands (ASCCs) are authorized to provide Commander's Unit Status Report data "for information" directly to Unified Commands

f. MET Assessments. The individual MET assessment (Y/Q/N) indicates the degree to which a unit has achieved proficiency in a mission-essential task within prescribed conditions and standards when resources and training constraints are considered. The metrics to assess task capability are below.

(1) Yes (Y). Organization can accomplish task to standard under specified conditions. Yes assessment should reflect demonstrated performance in training or operations whenever possible. Unit possesses the necessary resources, or those resources have been explicitly identified to the unit, to allow it to execute when so directed (e.g., "Fight tonight").

(2) Qualified yes (Q). Organization is expected to accomplish the task to standard, but this performance has not been observed or demonstrated in training or operations. Organizations assessing their task or mission as a "Qualified Yes" can be employed for those tasks. Unit possesses the necessary resources, or those resources have been explicitly identified to the unit, to allow it to execute when so directed (e.g., "Fight tonight").

(3) No (N). The organization is unable to accomplish the task to standard at this time.

g. Measured Area Levels.

(1) Personnel Level (P-Level). Army measured units will measure personnel readiness using three metrics for personnel fill percentages that are based on the unit's strength requirements for its core functions/designed capabilities: total available personnel strength divided by the required strength, available Military Occupational Specialty Qualified (MOSQ) strength by duty position divided by the required strength, and the available senior grade composite level determined by comparing the available and required strength in each of five senior grade categories. The applicable MTOE or TDA that reflects the unit's core functions/designed capabilities is the authoritative source for the unit's required strength. While Army measured units also are required to determine and report additional personnel data (for

FORCE READINESS

example the assigned strength percentage, turnover percentage, and so on), the personnel level is determined solely based on the results of these three P-Level metrics.

   (2) Equipment and Supplies On-Hand (S-Level). Army measured units determine and report an S-Level by determining by Line Item Number (LIN) the on hand/availability status of designated critical equipment items (pacing items) and the on–hand/availability status of the other mission essential equipment items (Equipment Readiness Code (ERC) A) that are listed on the unit's MTOE or TDA. Substitute items prescribed by HQDA via Sustainment Brigade (SB) 700–20 and In Lieu Of (ILO) substitutions directed by HQDA or determined by the commander are applied in accordance with the provisions of paragraph 9–3. Note that for this S-Level measurement, the on hand/availability status of equipment items is based solely on those equipment items currently in the unit's possession, under its control or, when applicable, available to it within 72 hours for mission execution. The S-Level measurement is not based solely on property accountability records, and it does not consider the operational readiness/serviceability of the equipment items. A discrete measurement is accomplished at the LIN Level of detail by comparing the equipment items currently in the unit's possession, under its control or available to it within 72 hours, to the equipment items required to accomplish its core functions/designed capabilities, and an S-Level rating is determined for each measurement. The applicable MTOE or TDA that reflects the unit's core functions/designed capabilities is the authoritative source for the unit's equipment requirements. The unit's S-Level rating is determined in accordance with a methodology that considers each of these by LIN S-Level measurements.

   (3) Equipment Readiness/Serviceability (R-Level). Army measured units will measure the operational readiness or serviceability of the critical equipment items that are in their possession, under their control or available to them within 72 hours, and that are designated by HQDA via the Maintenance Master Data File (MMDF) as reportable for maintenance. Separate measurements will be accomplished for each maintenance reportable pacing item and for all maintenance reportable equipment currently in the unit's possession (aggregate). An R-Level rating is determined for each measurement, and, subsequently, the unit's R-Level rating is determined in accordance with a methodology that considers each of these R-Level measurements.

   (4) Unit Training Level Proficiency (T-Level). Commanders of Army measured units will report the training status of their units based on the percentage of the unit's METs trained to standard. While Army measured units also are required to determine and report additional training data (for example, required training days, squad/crew/team manning, and qualification status, and so forth) the training level is determined solely based on the results of the MET proficiency assessments associated with the unit's core functions/designed capabilities.

   h. Determining the Unit's C-Level. To determine the overall C-Level, the commander reviews the status levels attained in the four measured resource areas. The overall unit C-Level will normally be the lowest level recorded in any of the unit's individually measured resource areas of personnel, equipment and supplies on-hand, equipment readiness/serviceability, and unit training level proficiency. There may be circumstances in which commanders may subjectively upgrade or downgrade a unit's C-Level based on mission evaluation, but the status level computed for each individually measured area must be reported without adjustment.

   i. Determining the Unit's A-Level. The A-Level is an overall readiness assessment that reflects the unit's ability to accomplish the assigned mission that it is preparing for, has been ordered to execute and / or is executing. Similar to the C-Level, the A-Level contains measured resource areas that indicate the availability status of resources (personnel and equipment) measured against the assigned mission requirements that have been established or conveyed by the Army Tasking Authority. If the core mission is directed for execution, then the A-Level and C-Level will coincide.

   j. C-Level and A-Level details are shown in Figures 8-9 and 8-10 below.

C—Levels

C1 — Unit is resourced & trained to undertake the full wartime mission for which it was designed or organized (no adverse impacts to flexibility or vulnerability)

C2 — Unit is resourced & trained to undertake most wartime missions for which it was designed or organized. The unit would require little, if any, compensation for deficiencies (isolated increases in flexibility but no increase in vulnerability under most operational scenarios)

C3 — Unit is resourced & trained to undertake many, but not all, portions of the wartime missions for which it was designed or organized. The unit would require significant compensation for deficiencies (significantly decreased flexibility and increased vulnerability under many, but not all, envisioned scenarios)

C4 — Unit requires <u>additional resources</u> or training to undertake its wartime missions, but may be directed to undertake some portions of its wartime mission with resources on hand

C5 — Unit is undergoing a <u>DA—directed</u> resource action and is not prepared to undertake the wartime mission for which it was organized or designed; however, the unit may be capable of performing non-traditional missions

<u>C—Level:</u> The Unit Commander's assessment of the level at which the unit possesses the required resources and is trained to undertake the full wartime (core) mission for which it is designed or organized

Figure 8-9. C-Levels

A—Levels

A1 — The unit possesses the required resources and is trained to undertake the full directed mission

A2 — The unit possesses the required resources and is trained to undertake most of the directed mission

A3 — The unit possesses the required resources and is trained to undertake many, but not all, portions of the directed mission

A4 — The unit requires additional resources or training to undertake the directed mission, but may be required to undertake portions of the directed mission with the resources on hand

<u>A—Level:</u> The Unit Commander's assessment of the unit's ability to execute the primary directed mission assigned

Figure 8-10. A-Levels

FORCE READINESS

8-18. Use of DRRS-A Data at HQDA

a. At HQDA, DRRS-A data is part of a larger readiness picture compiled from many functional reports and sources. It alerts senior leaders to unit readiness issues so that they can exercise the appropriate management actions and provide the required assistance. DA uses DRRS-A data in conjunction with other personnel and logistics reports to improve resource management of people, equipment, and the programming of facilities and training areas to increase the combat effectiveness of subordinate elements.

b. Unit commanders prepare their status reports using the NetUSR application and submit them through their major commands into the DRRS-A database. Subsequently, the Office of the Deputy Chief of Staff (ODCS), G-3/5/7 compiles the reports and provides them to GSORTS and the DOD DRRS. ODCS, G-3/5/7's ARMS allows all DA Staff elements and other ARMS users to access for analysis via Secure Internet Protocol Router Network (SIPRNet) all unit reports in the DRRS-A database.

c. The Vice Chief of Staff, U.S. Army (VCSA) receives a monthly Strategic Readiness Update (SRU) from the ODCS G3/5/7, with significant input and analysis from the ODCS G-1, ODCS G-4, ODCS G-8, and other Army Staff (ARSTAF) elements. The current readiness and capability status of major units is provided as well as trend analysis and projections

d. Each principal DA Staff element uses the information provided by the ODCS, G-3/5/7 to influence resource allocation. Aggregate data in DRRS-A also serves as a yardstick to measure how well the functional management system for personnel, logistics, and training are performing.

Section V
Summary and References

8-19. Summary

Readiness is a primary mission of military forces. Recognizing that readiness is highly situational and subjective, it is, nevertheless, a yardstick for programming and budgeting. The Army's readiness strategy entails maximizing readiness within available resources to meet the operational demands resulting from expeditionary requirements and contingency force requirements. The more accurately the Army captures and quantifies readiness, the better the Army can articulate resource needs to the DOD and the Congress.

8-20. References

a. Army Regulation 220-1, USR and Force Registration - Consolidated Policies
b. Army Regulation 700-138, Army Logistics Readiness and Sustainability
c. CJCS Guide 3401D, CJCS Guide to the CRS
d. CJCS Instruction 3401.01E, CRS
e. CJCS Instruction 3401.02B, Force Readiness Reporting
f. CJCS Manual 3150.02, Global Status of Resources and Training System
g. DOD Directive 5149.2, Senior Readiness Oversight Council (SROC)
h. DOD Directive 7730.65, DRRS
i. OSD Personnel and Readiness (P&R), DRRS Primer for Senior Leaders

HOW THE ARMY RUNS

This page is intentionally left blank

ARMY PLANNING, PROGRAMMING, BUDGETING, AND EXECUTION PROCESS

Chapter 9

Army Planning, Programming, Budgeting, and Execution Process

Before the era of Secretary of Defense (SECDEF) McNamara, each Service essentially established its own single-year budget and submitted it to Congress annually. SECDEF McNamara, however, applied a different approach founded on a study by the RAND Corporation. He required the Services to prepare a single document, the then Five-Year Defense Program, which detailed their resource requirements on a multi-year basis. He established himself as the sole authority for approving changes to the Five-Year Defense Program, including changes desired by the Services. That formed the rudimentary beginning of the Department of Defense (DOD) Planning, Programming, and Budgeting System, a continually evolving process that in 2003 under SECDEF Rumsfeld changed to the Planning, Programming, Budgeting, and Execution (PPBE) Process. On 9 April 2010, SECDEF Gates made significant changes to the annual planning and programming process.

Section I
Introduction

9-1. Chapter Content
This chapter describes how, at the beginning of CY 2013 the DOD PPBE process and the Army PPBE Process acquire, allocate, and manage resources for military functions. Prescribed by Army Regulation (AR) 1-1, the Army PPBE process is a component of the DOD PPBE process governed by DOD Directive (DODD) 7045.14 and DOD Instruction (DODI) 7045.14. This account describes the Army PPBE process in relation to its parent DOD PPBE process. It lays out the responsibilities of Army officials for overseeing Army PPBE, for managing the several phases of its process, and for performing PPBE-related operational tasks. Next, the chapter highlights principal forums and other key characteristics of the DOD PPBE process and then the Army PPBE process. After displaying a graphic representation of the process recurring events and organizational structure, the chapter concludes with a phase-by-phase discussion of the annual process.

9-2. PPBS—A Dynamic System Currently Renamed PPBE
First, however, consider the history of the former PPBS now approaching its 51st year. Significant events recorded by presidential administration show how the system has evolved, revealing a dynamic system.

   a. 1962—Kennedy/McNamara. The DOD PPBS began in 1962 as a management innovation of President Kennedy's SECDEF, Robert McNamara. Before McNamara, each Military Department had prepared its budget following individual Service interests with very little guidance. Previous SECDEF involvement was for the most part limited to dividing the budget ceiling of DOD between the Services. If the Services exceeded their "share of the pie," the SECDEF would reduce their budget, usually by a percentage cut across all appropriations. Introducing the PPBS changed all this. Based on a concept developed at the RAND Corporation in the 1950s, the PPBS inaugurated a multi-year programmatic focus. Annual ceiling reductions gave way to analysis centered on 10 major force and support programs over a 5-year program period.

   b. 1969—Nixon/Laird. The first major change in the PPBS occurred under President Nixon's SECDEF, Melvin Laird. The Laird management style stressed participatory management. The Office of the Secretary of Defense (OSD) no longer initiated detailed program proposals; it reviewed those put forward by the Services using specific budgetary ceilings.

   c. 1977—Carter/Brown. President Carter introduced zero-based budgeting to the Federal Budget. It achieved only limited success. The goal of zero-based budgeting was to identify marginal programs more clearly. Decision Packages arrayed resources at three different levels, giving OSD greater opportunity to alter Service program proposals. Each Service developed procedures to array the decision packages. As an aid in building and displaying its program, the Army installed a Program Development Increment Package (PDIP). Used internally and not reflected in programs and budgets forwarded by the Army, the PDIP has since evolved into a Management Decision Package (MDEP). In 1979, as a result of a RAND Corporation study (the Rice Study); SECDEF Brown formed the Defense Resources Board (DRB).

HOW THE ARMY RUNS

Designed to manage the PPBS more effectively, the DRB consisted of various OSD officials and the Chairman of the Joint Chiefs of Staff (CJCS).

d. 1981—Reagan/Weinberger. The Reagan Administration pledged to revitalize American military strength in the most effective and economical manner. This objective led to significant changes in the PPBS known as the Carlucci initiatives (Frank Carlucci was the Deputy Secretary of Defense (DEPSECDEF) and Chairman of the DRB). Initiatives included a greater emphasis on long-range planning, a greater decentralization of authority to the Services, closer attention to cost savings and efficiencies, a refocus of DRB Program Review to major issues only, and a general streamlining of the entire PPBS process. In addition, a restructured DRB added Service Secretaries as full members. The DRB would now review and approve policy and strategy in the planning phase, which produced defense guidance. Moreover, one initiative invited commanders of the Combatant Commands (CCMD) to participate in crucial DRB deliberations during the development of the defense guidance and the DRB Program Review.

e. 1984—Enhancement of the role of Combatant Commanders (CCDR) in the PPBS. DEPSECDEF Taft introduced procedures to allow CCDRs a greater voice in the process for developing Program Objective Memorandums (POM) and the DRB Program Review. The procedures included: submission by the commanders of prioritized requirements (via Integrated Priority Lists (IPL)); tracking their concerns during POM development and execution; visibility of CCMD requirements in the POMs; enhanced participation by commanders in DRB program review; and an enhanced role for the Joint Chiefs of Staff (JCS) in the review and coordination of commander concerns.

f. 1986—Conversion from annual to biennial PPBS cycle. In response to his Blue Ribbon Commission on Defense Management (Packard Commission) and the DOD Authorization Act of 1986 (Public Law 99-145), President Reagan issued National Security Decision Directive 219, directing that the Office of Management and Budget (OMB) and DOD produce a 2-year budget beginning with the FY 1988 and FY 1989 budget years. In response to this direction, OSD and the Military Departments implemented a biennial PPBS process. In practice, however, Congress still authorizes and appropriates annually, permitting an off cycle update of the five remaining POM years and the second budget year.

g. 1987—CCMD capabilities to participate effectively in the PPBS budget phase. Earlier decisions of the DRB gave CCDRs a role in the planning and programming phases of the PPBS. In October 1987, the DRB expanded the role of the commanders to include the budget review and execution phase.

h. 1989—Bush/Cheney. During the early stages of DOD downsizing, President Bush instituted a series of defense management review decisions. In another initiative, SECDEF Cheney modified the framework for PPBS decision-making, including in the structure a core group of DOD officials he used to help manage the Department.

i. 1993—Clinton/Aspin, Perry, Cohen. DOD downsizing continued under the Clinton Administration guided initially by SECDEF Les Aspin's Bottom Up Review and later by the results of the Defense Performance Review, Commission on Roles and Missions of the Armed Forces and the 1997 Quadrennial Defense Review (QDR). The Clinton administration continued the PPBS framework of the Bush Administration, using a core group of DOD managers and several review forums including a Program Review Group (PRG) expanded by the Administration.

j. 2001—Bush/Rumsfeld. Emphasis on Defense Transformation marked the early months of the Bush Presidency, a focus abruptly broadened by the events of September 11, 2001. U.S. Defense spending has since markedly increased-due not only to additional costs of the war on terror, but also to the end of the procurement holiday of the 1990s and the needs of Transformation. In a process change, DOD introduced closer program and budget correlation, requiring agencies to prepare a combined POM/Budget Estimate Submission (POM/BES) followed by an OSD concurrent program and budget review. Another initiative established a Senior Executive Council (SEC) to counsel the SECDEF in applying sound business practices. Chaired by the SECDEF, the council's membership comprises the DEPSECDEF, Under Secretary of Defense for Acquisition, Technology and Logistics, and the Secretaries of the Army, Navy, and Air Force.

k. 2003—Bush/Rumsfeld. On 22 May 2003, Management Initiative Decision 913 directed the elimination of the mini-POM and the amended budget estimate submission year and replaced them with Program Change Proposals (PCPs) and Budget Change Proposals (BCPs) respectively. On 31 October 2003, the SECDEF agreed with the recommendation of the Joint Defense Capabilities Study (Aldridge Committee) and directed the elimination of the Defense Planning Guidance, replacing it with the SECDEF Strategic Planning Guidance and the SECDEF Joint Programming Guidance (JPG). At the same time, the

ARMY PLANNING, PROGRAMMING, BUDGETING, AND EXECUTION PROCESS

SECDEF directed the establishment of the Enhanced Planning Process (EPP) as a joint capabilities-based forum to analyze SECDEF identified issues, develop alternative solutions to resolve the issues, and determine the joint implications associated with each alternative solution.

l. 2005—Bush/Rumsfeld. Process changes continue during this administration. Principally - they include strengthening the CCDR's role in the process by enhancing the IPL process and including the CCDRs in the decision process by expanding the Senior Leader Review Group to include them and calling the new body, The Strategic Planning Council.

m. 2006—Bush/Rumsfeld. Process changes implemented during this administration include changing the Program Change Proposals (PCP) and Budget Change Proposals (BCP) concepts to combine both into one process renamed as Change Proposals (CP). The ground rules for submitting change proposal effectively limited the ability of the Services to make changes to the next budget year being prepared to go to Congress.

n. 2008—Bush/Gates. New planning guidance documents for programming promulgated to replace the Strategic Planning Guidance. The SECDEF's strategic guidance is captured in the Guidance for the Development of Forces and the Guidance for Employment of Forces (GEF). The SECDEF also continued the publication of the National Defense Strategy (NDS) as guidance for the Services as they begin planning for the development of the POM.

o. 2010—Obama/Gates. Significant changes to the PPBE system were implemented on 9 April 2010 by SECDEF Gates. He established a single document, the Defense Planning and Programming Guidance as guidance for building the POM. He changed the POM planning years from six years to five years. He eliminated the two-year budgeting process and established single year budgeting. He also changed the concept of even-year and odd-year budgeting with only program and budget change proposals in the odd years and returned to building a POM and budget every year. He instituted the concept of Front End Analysis (FEA) to get early up-front decisions made in the programming process. The FEA process appears to be similar in nature to the Enhanced Planning Process as outlined in paragraph k above. In the 2009 Weapons System Acquisition Reform Act, the Congress established the position of Director Cost Assessment and Program Evaluation (CAPE) as a Presidential appointment requiring Senate confirmation and combined two organizations, The Cost Analysis Improvement Group (CAIG) and Program Analysis and Evaluation Directorate (PAE), were combined to form the CAPE Directorate. The Army retained its PAE position.

p. 2011—Obama/Panetta. In 2011, the Defense Planning and Programming Guidance was replaced with the Defense Planning Guidance (DPG).

Section II
Department of Defense Planning, Programming, Budgeting, and Execution Process Description

9-3. Purpose

a. The DOD PPBE process serves as the primary resource management system for the Department's military functions. Its purpose is to produce a plan, a program, and finally the defense budget. The system documents the program and budget as the FYDP.

b. Process and Structure. Beginning with the planning phase, sections III through XIII, which follow, present a phase-by-phase description of the DOD and Army PPBE process. First, however, a graphical overview of system process and structure sets the stage.

9-4. System Structure

HOW THE ARMY RUNS

DOD PPBE Phases

Planning
- National Security Strategy (NSS)—Annually with President's Budget (PB)—White House
- National Military Strategy (NMS)—Biennially—Chairman, Joint Chiefs of Staff (CJCS)
- Quadrennial Defense Review (QDR)—Quadrennial with PB—Office of the SECDEF (OSD)
- National Defense Strategy (NDS)—At discretion of SECDEF—OSD
- Defense Planning Guidance (DPG)—Annually—OSD
- The Army Plan (TAP)—Annually—Department of the Army (DA)—Consists of:
  - Army Strategic Planning Guidance (ASPG)—Annually Oct
  - Army Planning Priorities Guidance (APPG)—Annually Nov
  - Army Programming Guidance Memorandum (APGM)—Annually Dec
  - Army Campaign Plan (ACP)—annually Dec
- Research, Development, and Acquisition Plan (RDAP)—Annually March—DA
- Total Army Analysis (TAA)—Annually Dec—DA

Programming
- Chairman's Program Recommendation (CPR)—Annually—CJCS
- Technical Guidance Memorandum (TGM)—Annually—DA
- Fiscal Guidance (FG)—Annually—OSD
- Program Objective Memorandum (POM) / Budget Estimate Submission (BES)—Annually—DA
- Chairman's Program Assessment (CPA)—annually—CJCS
- Issue Papers—OSD

Budgeting
- Resource Management Decision (RMD)—Annually Sep to Nov—OSD
- Major Budget Issue (MBI)—Annually Dec—OSD
- Department of Defense Budget (DOD(B))—Annually Dec—OSD
- PB—Annually Jan / Feb—White House

Execution
- Authorization / Appropriation—DA—Sep 30th
- Execution—DA
- Assessment—DA
— Continuous

Figure 9-1. Department of Defense (DOD) Planning, Programming, Budgeting, and Execution (PPBE) Phases

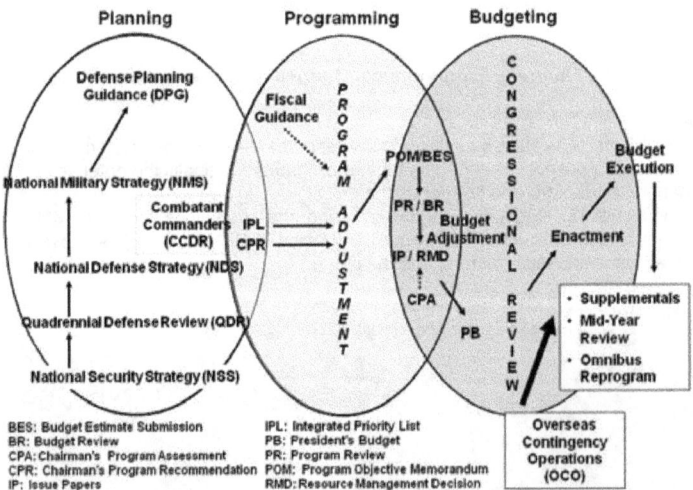

Figure 9-2. Summary of Planning, Programming, Budgeting, and Execution (PPBE) Phases

ARMY PLANNING, PROGRAMMING, BUDGETING, AND EXECUTION PROCESS

9-5. NSC Guidance
The National Security Strategy (NSS) set by the National Security Council (NSC) bears importantly on the PPBE process. The NSS outlines the major objectives for our nation. It addresses how we plan to deal with other nations and provides guidance to DOD related to the capabilities that are needed to implement the policies in the NSS.

9-6. Planning by OSD and the Joint Staff
PPBE planning is conducted by drawing on guidance from the National Security Council (NSC), OSD policy and resource planning and Joint Staff strategic planning. PPBE planning examines the military posture of the United States in comparison to national security objectives and resource limitations. It develops the national military strategy, and it identifies force levels to achieve the strategy. In addition, PPBE planning provides a framework of requirements, priorities, and risk. OSD uses the framework to give each CCDR the best mix of forces, equipment, and support attainable within defined fiscal constraints.

9-7. Joint Strategic Planning System (JSPS)
JSPS is used by the CJCS to provide advice to the President and SECDEF concerning the strategic direction of the armed forces and defense policy, programs and budgets. The system is described in detail in Chapter 4 of this text; however the two key documents produced by the system to inform the PPBE process are described here.

  a. Chairman's Program Recommendation (CPR). The CPR compares planning guidance and objectives with current and projected resource profiles from the most recent President's Budget (PB) and related FYDP. The CPR focuses on recommendations that will enhance joint readiness, promote joint doctrine and training, and better satisfy joint war fighting requirements. The CJCS solicits ideas from the CCDRs and the Services in preparation for writing his CPR.

  b. Chairman's Program Assessment (CPA). The CPA checks the balance and capabilities of composite force and support levels recommended by Service POMs. It compares recommended capabilities and levels with priorities established by the SECDEF. The document helps the SECDEF make decisions during OSD program and budget review reflected in RMDs. Both the CPA and previously mentioned CPR are considered personal CJCS recommendations to the SECDEF and are not widely distributed in their final forum.

9-8. OSD Planning Process Changes
In May of 2008 the SECDEF replaced the SECDEF's Strategic Planning Guidance with the Guidance for Development of Force (GDF) and the Guidance for Employment of the Force (GEF). In 2010 the SECDEF replaced the GDF and the Joint Programming Guidance (JPG) with the Defense Planning and Programming Guidance (renamed Defense Planning Guidance (DPG) in 2011).

  a. The DPG was designed as largely policy and strategy guidance with some programmatic direction on issues of paramount importance to the SECDEF concerning the development of the force during and beyond the POM period.

  b. The Guidance for Employment of Force (GEF) provides guidance for the use of the force in being. It outlines strategic objectives for campaign planning as well as strategic assumptions, objectives and priorities for contingency planning, security cooperation, global posture and global force management.

9-9. The Future Years Defense Program (FYDP)
  a. The FYDP officially summarizes forces and resources for programs developed within the DOD PPBE process and approved by the SECDEF. The FYDP specifies force levels and lists corresponding Total Obligation Authority (TOA) and manpower. For example, in addition to historical data, the FYDP for the FY 2014 budget would show projected costs through FY 2018.
  (1) Records totals for each resource group by:
  (a) Prior Fiscal Year (PY), in this case FY 2012.
  (b) Current Fiscal Year (CY), in this case FY 2013.
  (c) Budget Fiscal Year (BY), in this case FY 2014.
  (2) Extends TOA and manpower totals 4 years beyond the FY 2014 budget to FY 2018.
  (3) Extends force totals 7 years beyond the FY 2014 budget to FY 2021.

HOW THE ARMY RUNS

b. The FYDP comprises 11 major Defense programs. Table 9-2 lists the programs together with Army subprograms and Army proponent agencies. Each program consists of an aggregation of Program Elements (PE) that reflect a DOD force or support mission. PEs identifies specific activities, projects, or functions and contains the fiscal and manpower resources needed to achieve an objective or plan. PEs permit cross-Service analysis by OSD and congressional staff members.

c. HQDA submits the Army portion of the FYDP database to OSD at least twice each year.
(1) The first submission, forwarded in August, records the position of the combined Army POM/BES.
(2) The second submission, forwarded in late January or early February, records the position of the PB.

d. For each FYDP position, OSD publishes a Summary and PE Detail volume on a CD ROM.

e. As prescribed by 10 U.S.C 221(a), OSD provides the PB version of the FYDP to Congress each year at or about the time the PB is submitted to Congress.

f. OSD's Director of Cost Assessment and Program Evaluation (CAPE) manages the PE data structure and serves as the approval authority for any changes to that structure. Beginning with the FY 2002-2007 POM, OSD began gradually replacing the nearly 40-year old FYDP database format with a new Defense Programming Database (DPD). Transition to the DPD is complete and has standardized budget and program data while consolidating many of the FYDP's currently required supplemental reports and annexes.

Table 9-1. Future Years Defense Program (FYDP) Programs and Subprograms with Army Proponents

Nr	Major Defense program	Proponent [1]
1.	Strategic Forces	G-3/5/7
2.	General Purpose Forces	G-3/5/7
3.	Communications, Intelligence, and Space	
	Communications	CIO-/G-6
	Intelligence	G-2/G-3/5/7 [2]
	Space	SMDC [3]
4.	Mobility	G-3/5/7
5.	Guard and Reserve Forces	
	Army National Guard	DARNG
	Army Reserve	CAR
6.	Research and Development	ASA (FM&C)
7.	Central Supply and Maintenance	ASA (FM&C)
8.	Training, Health and Other Personnel Activities	
	Training	G-3/5/7
	Health	TSG [4]
9.	Administration	G-1
10.	Support of Other Nations	G-3/5/7
11.	Special Operations Forces	G-3/5/7

Note:
1. Within each applicable program, ACSIM serves as proponent for base operations and real property services and G-1 serves as proponent for management headquarters and manpower functions.
2. G-2 is the resource proponent for operational and strategic intelligence. G-3/5/7 is the resource proponent for tactical intelligence.
3. U.S. Army Space and Missile Defense Command.
4. The Surgeon General

ARMY PLANNING, PROGRAMMING, BUDGETING, AND EXECUTION PROCESS

Major Force Programs (MFP)

Numbered Major Force Programs
- Program 1—Strategic Forces
- Program 2—General Purpose Forces
- Program 3—Command, Control, Communications, Intelligence (C3I)
- Program 4—Mobility Forces
- Program 5—Guard and Reserve Forces
- Program 6—Research and Development
- Program 7—Central Supply & Maintenance
- Program 8—Training, Medical & Other General Personnel Activities
- Program 9—Administrative & Associated Activities
- Program 10—Support of Other Nations
- Program 11—Special Operations Forces

- DOD breaks the Future Years Defense Program (FYDP) into MFPs to identify forces and military capabilities
- MFPs cross service boundaries
- MFPs are dictated by Department of Defense (DOD), but they are also used by Congress
- Each MFP is comprised of a set of unique Office of the Secretary of Defense (OSD) Program Elements

Figure 9-3. Major Force Programs (MFP)

9-10. Resource Recording Structures.
FYDP. As mentioned, the FYDP accounts for the total of all resources programmed by the DOD. Using OSD PEs, DOD apportions decisions on dollars and manpower among the FYDP's 11 major force programs.

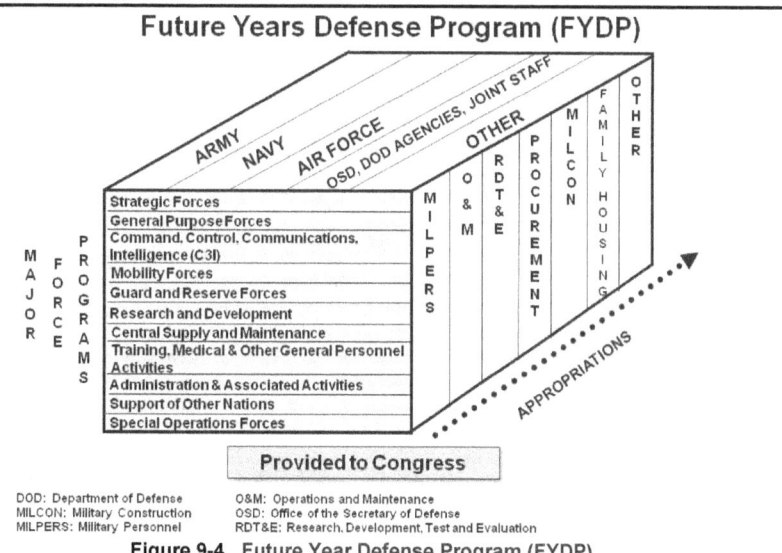

Figure 9-4. Future Year Defense Program (FYDP)

HOW THE ARMY RUNS

9-11. Key Participants
DOD officials, assisting the SECDEF as key participants in the PPBE process, include the following:

   a. The Deputy Secretary of Defense (DEPSECDEF). The DEPSECDEF assists the SECDEF in overall leadership of the Department. He exercises authority delegated by the SECDEF and conducts the day-to-day operation of DOD. The DEPSECDEF manages the PPBE process.

   b. CJCS. The CJCS serves as the principal military adviser to the President and SECDEF and helps them provide strategic direction to the armed forces. Shouldering responsibilities for planning, advising, and policy formulation, the CJCS participates in DOD's senior councils, where he speaks for the Joint Chiefs of Staff (JCS) and CCDRs.

   c. The Vice CJCS (VCJCS). The VCJCS, who is the second-ranking member of the Armed Forces, acts for the CJCS in his absence and chairs the Joint Requirements Oversight Council (JROC).

   d. The Service Secretaries. The Service Secretaries convey the Service perspective on Defense matters to the SECDEF and DEPSECDEF and, as key advisers, provide them with candid personal views.

   e. The Under Secretary of Defense for Acquisition, Technology, and Logistics (USD(AT&L)). The USD(AT&L) exercises responsibility for all matters relating to Defense acquisition, technology, and logistics and serves as the Defense Acquisition Executive (DAE).

   f. The Under Secretary of Defense for Policy (USD(P)). The USD(P) represents DOD on foreign relations and arms control matters and serves as the principal adviser to the DEPSECDEF for the PPBE planning phase.

   g. The Under Secretary of Defense (Comptroller) (USD(C)). The USD(C) exercises responsibility for all budgetary and fiscal matters.

   h. The Under Secretary of Defense (Personnel and Readiness) (USD(P&R)). The USD(P&R) exercises responsibility for all matters relating to Total Force Management as it concerns readiness, National Guard and Reserve Affairs, health affairs, training, and personnel requirements and management.

   i. The Director, Cost Assessment and Program Evaluation (CAPE). The Director, CAPE serves as the principal staff assistant to the SECDEF for cost assessment and program evaluation.

9-12. DOD Decision Bodies
The following groups have been organized to assist the SECDEF in making planning, programming, budgeting and execution resource decisions.

   a. The three bodies that counsel the SECDEF in applying sound business practices in the Military Departments, DOD agencies and other DOD components include the Secretary's Senior Leadership Council (SLC), the Senior Leader Review Group (SLRG) and the Deputy's Management Action Group (DMAG). When determined by the chair, heads of other DOD components participate as appropriate. For example, the chair may invite officials to participate from other Departments and agencies of the Executive Branch, including the Office of Management and Budget (OMB) and the National Security Council (NSC).

   b. The SLC, replacing the Defense Senior Leader Conference, is the senior information exchange body in the DOD resource management system. The SECDEF chairs the SLC. Membership includes the SLRG principals (enumerated in Para 9-12c below) and all CCDRs.

   c. The SLRG is the senior decision making body assisting the SECDEF and DEPSECDEF in making major program decisions. The SECDEF chairs the SLRG with the CJCS serving as vice chairman. The DEPSECDEF designates other OSD principals to participate in deliberations as necessary. SLRG members are as follows:

   (1) From OSD. The Deputy Secretary of Defense (DEPSECDEF); Under Secretary of Defense (Comptroller) and Under Secretaries of Defense for Policy (USD(P); Acquisition, Technology, and Logistics (USD(AT&L); Personnel and Readiness (USD(P&R); and Intelligence (USD(I); Director, CAPE; Assistant Secretaries of Defense for Legislative Affairs, Public Affairs and Networks and Information Integration, and CCDRs.

   (2) From the Joint Staff and Services. The CJCS, VCJCS, Director, Joint Staff and Secretaries of the Military Departments, who normally are accompanied by Chiefs of Services, Chief of the National Guard Bureau. Considering broad policy and developing guidance on high-priority objectives, the SLRG helps promote long-range planning and stability in the Defense program

   (3) Among other functions, the SLRG:

ARMY PLANNING, PROGRAMMING, BUDGETING, AND EXECUTION PROCESS

(a) Reviews guidance for planning and programming.
(b) Evaluates high-priority programs.
(c) Considers the effect of resource decisions on baseline cost, schedule, and performance of major acquisition programs and aligns the programs with the PPBE process.
(d) Helps tie the allocation of resources for specific programs and forces to national policies.
(e) Reviews the program and budget.
(f) Reviews execution of selected programs.
(g) Advises the SECDEF on policy, PPBE issues, and proposed decisions.
(4) When the SLRG meets to deliberate major issues on DOD-funded intelligence programs, it expands to include representatives of appropriate intelligence agencies. The DEPSECDEF and Director of Central Intelligence co-chair this Expanded SLRG (ESLRG).
(5) The Director, CAPE acts as Executive Secretary for both the SLRG and ESLRG. In this capacity, the Director manages the program review process and, with the chairs of the ESLRG, the intelligence program review. The Director of the CAPE also manages the preparation of Issue Papers (IP) to formulate Service level issues which challenge the Service program requests and the Intelligence RMDs (IRMDs) that reflect the SECDEF's program decisions.

d. The Deputy's Advisory Working Group (renamed the Deputies Management Action Group (DMAG) in 2011) was established to facilitate the development of the QDR 2006 and has continued to monitor its implementation as well as address other subjects as required. The DMAG participates in the program review process and comments on the IPs resulting from the review of the ODS IPs.
(1) The Deputy Secretary and VCJCS co-chair the DMAG. Membership is as follows:
(a) From OSD. The Undersecretaries of Defense; Acquisition, Technology, and Logistics; Comptroller, Personnel and Readiness; and Intelligence, Deputy Undersecretary for Policy, Assistant Secretary Defense Network Integration/CIO, Director and Principal Deputy, Program Analysis and Evaluation, Director Administration and Management, Assistant Secretary of Defense, Legislative Affairs and the General Counsel.
(b) From the Joint Staff and Services. Service Undersecretaries and Vice Chiefs, the Director Joint Staff, Director J-8 and Director J-5, Director National Guard Bureau and Deputy Commander USSOCOM. CCDRs or their Deputy Commanders are welcome when issues are being considered that impact their regional or functional responsibilities.
(2) The DMAG generally meets weekly to consider ongoing and cyclic issues including:
(a) Capability Portfolio development and management
(b) Defense Planning Scenarios and related analytical efforts
(c) Program and Budget Reviews
(d) IPs resulting from the Resource Decision Document process - directed studies
(e) Strategy and Policy Development including periodic reviews
(f) Regional and Functional Challenges
(g) Transformation

e. The OSD 3-star programmers group analyzes major issues and develops decision options during program review. It forwards issues sufficiently significant to warrant action by the SLRG to that body for consideration. Supporting the endeavor, OSD principal staff assistants conduct a series of Front End Assessments (FEA). As directed by the SLRG, assessments address topics or decisions that will influence the next POM and subsequent program review. Prepared in coordination with other OSD principal assistants, representatives of the CJCS, and Service chiefs, the assessments are briefed to the Three Star Group. As appropriate they are also briefed to the DEPSECDEF or SLRG. The Director, Cost Assessment and Program Review chairs the Three Star Group. Adding other OSD principals to participate in sessions as appropriate, the Three Star Group includes the following members:
(1) From OSD. Representatives from the Deputy Under Secretary of Defense (Comptroller, Policy, Intelligence, and Acquisition, Technology, and Logistics) and the Assistant Secretaries of Defense for Force Management Policy, Health Affairs, and Reserve Affairs, the Principal Deputy Assistant Secretary of Defense for Networks and Information Integration, the Director of Operational Test and Evaluation and Commander USSOCOM.
(2) From the Joint Staff. The Director for Force Structure, Resources, and Assessment (J-8).
(3) From the Services. The Army G-8, the Deputy Chief of Naval Operations (Resources, Warfare Requirements and Assessments), the Marine Corps Deputy Commandant (Programs and Resources), and the Air Force, Deputy Chief of Staff (Plans and Programs).

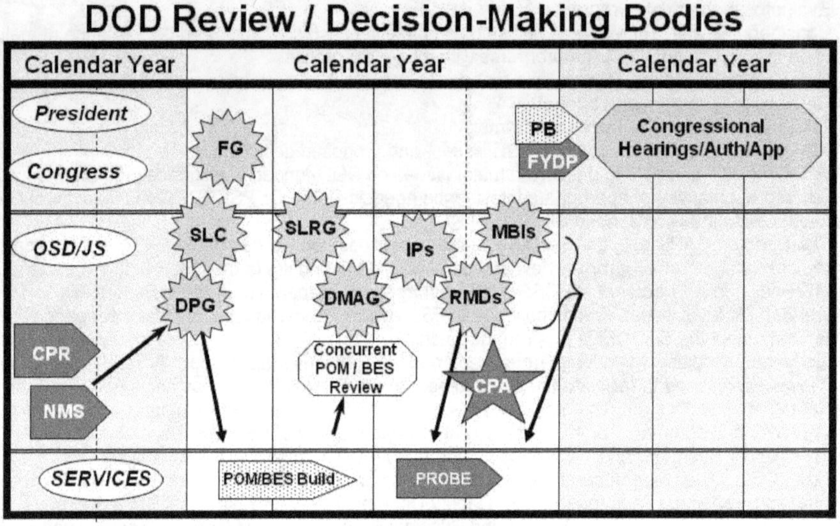

HOW THE ARMY RUNS

Figure 9-5. Department of Defense (DOD) Review / Decision-Making Bodies

BES: Budget Estimate Submission
CPA: Chairman's Program Assessment
CPR: Chairman's Program Recommendation
DMAG: Deputy's Management Action Group
DPG: Defense Planning Guidance
FG: Fiscal Guidance
FYDP: Future Years Defense Program
IP: Issue Paper
JS: Joint Staff
MBI: Major Budget Issue
NMS: National Military Strategy
OSD: Office of the Secretary of Defense
PB: President's Budget
POM: Program Objective Memorandum
PROBE: Program Objective & Budget Execution
RMD: Resource Management Decision
SLC: Secretary's Senior Leadership Council
SLRG: Senior Leader Review Group

9-13. Intelligence PRG

a. The Intelligence PRG (IPRG) identifies opportunities to advance the U.S. Government's Intelligence Strategy. It evaluates potential program changes from a mission perspective, considers tradeoffs, and forwards issue analyses to the Expanded SLRG (ESLRG) for consideration.

b. The Director, CAPE and the Executive Director for Intelligence Community Affairs co-chair the IPRG. Members include representatives of all Executive Branch organizations that manage or oversee intelligence capabilities.

9-14. Defense Acquisition Board and Joint Requirements Oversight Council

a. The Defense Acquisition Board (DAB) oversees Defense system acquisition, providing discipline through review of major programs. At each milestone in the system's life cycle, the DAB assures that programs have met established performance requirements, including program-specific exit criteria. As chairman and vice chairman, respectively, the USD (Acquisition, Technology, and Logistics) and VCJCS direct the efforts of the DAB.

b. The USD (Acquisition, Technology, and Logistics), with the DAB and JROC (below), helps link the acquisition process to planning, programming, and budgeting. Serving as a key adviser to the SECDEF and DEPSECDEF, the USD (Acquisition, Technology, and Logistics) participates in all resource decisions affecting the baselines of major acquisition programs, including costs, schedules, and performance.

c. The VCJCS chairs the JROC. Through the Functional Capabilities Boards (FCB) and Joint Requirements Board (JRB), the JROC explores new alternatives by assessing joint military war fighting capabilities and requirements posed by the CCDRs, Services, Joint Staff, and supported Defense agencies. The forum helps forge consensus underlying the CJCS's statutory advice to the SECDEF on

ARMY PLANNING, PROGRAMMING, BUDGETING, AND EXECUTION PROCESS

program and budget proposals. The JROC also helps the DAB and USD (Acquisition, Technology, and Logistics) articulate military needs and validate performance goals and program baselines at successive milestones of each DAB program.

Section III
Army Planning, Programming, Budgeting, and Execution System Responsibilities

9-15. Secretarial Oversight
a. PPBE oversight and Army wide policy development. The Assistant Secretary of the Army (Financial Management and Comptroller) (ASA(FM&C)):
 (1) Oversees the PPBE process and develops and issues Army-wide PPBE policy.
 (2) Serves as appropriation sponsor for all appropriations (funds) except ARNG and AR appropriations, whose sponsors are the Chief, National Guard Bureau and Chief, Army Reserve, respectively (see Para. 9-22d).
b. Functional Oversight. Principal officials of the Office of the Secretary of the Army (OSA) oversee operation of the PPBE process within assigned functional areas and provide related policy and direction.

9-16. System Management
ASA (FM&C) manages the PPBE process with the Deputy Chief of Staff, G-3/5/7, Deputy Chief of Staff, G-8, and Military Deputy for Budget and Execution acting as advisers. As provided in paragraphs 9-17, 9-18, and 9-19, below, the Assistant Deputy Chief of Staff (ADCS) G-3/5/7, the Director of Program Analysis and Evaluation (DPAE), and the Director of the Army Budget (DAB) manage functional phases of the process, each establishing and supervising policies and procedures necessary to carry out phase functions.

9-17. Planning Phase
a. Deputy Chief of Staff (DCS), G-3/5/7. Responsible for operations and planning functions, the Deputy Chief of Staff, G-3/5/7:
 (1) Through the Assistant G-3/5/7:
 (a) Manages the PPBE planning phase.
 (b) Co-chairs the Planning Program Budget Committee (PPBC) with the Director of Program Analysis and Evaluation (DPAE), and Director of the Army Budget (DAB).
 (c) Guides the work of Program Evaluation Groups (PEG) on planning and readiness matters to include requirements determination, prioritization, and the integration of security cooperation issues per the Army International Activities Plan (see Table 9-3 and Para. 9-37).
 (d) Assesses capabilities, deficiencies, and risks of the POM force at the end of the current POM.

Table 9-2. Program Evaluation Groups (PEG)

Title	Co-Chairs
Manning	ASA (M&RA)/G-1
Training	ASA (M&RA)/G-3/5/7
Organizing	ASA (M&RA)/AASA
Equipping	ASA (ALT)/G-8
Sustaining	ASA (ALT)/G-4
Installations	ASA (IE&E)/ACSIM

 (2) Serves as the principal adviser to the Chief of Staff, Army (CSA) on Joint matters, National Security Council (NSC) matters, and the politico-military aspects of international affairs.
 (a) Provides HQDA with strategic analysis pertaining to national security issues involving international and regional arms control treaties, agreements, and policies.
 (b) Plans for employment of Army forces to meet strategic requirements and shape Army forces for the future.

HOW THE ARMY RUNS

(3) Serves as overall integrator of Army transformation.

(a) Makes sure that military requirements reflect future Army Strategic Planning Guidance (ASPG), other planning guidance, and policy, and that the capability and applicability of total Army forces remain synchronized with the NSS, NDS and National Military Strategy (NMS).

(b) Provides the HQDA focal point for the organization, integration, and synchronization of decision making, as well as for requirements definition, force structuring, training developments, and prioritization.

(4) Prepares The Army Strategic Planning Guidance (ASPG), Army Planning Priorities Guidance (APPG), and Army Campaign Plan (ACP) as sections of The Army Plan (TAP); coordinates publication of the Army Programming Guidance Memorandum (APGM) as a section of TAP with Director, PAE; coordinates and publishes completed four sections of TAP.

(a) Defines Army planning assumptions.

(b) Sets requirements and priorities based on guidance from the SECDEF, Secretary of the Army (SECARMY), and CSA and priorities of the CCDRs.

(c) Sets objectives to meet requirements and overcome shortfalls.

(5) Monitors and reports on current operations.

(a) Develops and coordinates policy, programs, and initiatives to achieve directed levels of individual, leader, and unit training readiness for the Army.

(b) Oversees Army readiness reporting requirements and the reporting of Army readiness to provide an accurate picture for prioritization and resource allocation decisions within HQDA and externally.

(c) Assesses and coordinates support to US CCDRs and, through the Army Service Component Command (ASCC), provides the operational link between each CCMD, HQDA, and the Joint Staff.

(6) Performs all mobilization functions.

(7) Provides the HQDA focal point for executing military support to civil authorities.

(8) Executes the Continuity of Operations Program (COOP) for HQDA and OSD, the Army Infrastructure Assurance Program, and the Domestic Preparedness Program which provides support for special events.

(9) Provides support for special events.

(10) Provides the vision and strategy and manages the development of models and simulations.

(11) Develops policy and acts as the principal adviser to the CSA for information operations.

(12) Serves as proponent of the Training PEG (See Para. 9-37).

(13) Serves as proponent of programs within the FYDP. Programs include: 1-Strategic Forces, 2-General Purpose Forces, 4-Mobility, 10-Support of Other Nations, and 11-Special Operations Forces.

(14) Serves also as resource proponent for tactical intelligence, Army subprogram 3-Intelligence and proponent of Army subprogram 8-Training (see Para. 9-9)

(15) Manages force structure issues and manages functional requirements and program and performance for designated accounts of the Operation and Maintenance, Army appropriation (see Para 9-22 and Tables 9-8 through 9-14).

b. Deputy Chief of Staff, G-8. Responsible for the execution of approved materiel requirements, the Deputy Chief of Staff, G-8:

(1) Provides the HQDA focal point for program development, materiel integration, and assessments like the QDR.

(2) With the Assistant Secretary of the Army for Acquisition, Logistics, and Technology (ASA(ALT)), prepares the Research, Development, and Acquisition Plan (RDA Plan), which is represented by the database for the FYDP augmented for the Extended Planning Period (EPP).

(3) Prepares the Army Modernization Strategy and helps prepare Army input to OSD's Defense Program Projection.

(4) Serves as proponent of the PEG for Equipping (see Para. 9-37).

(5) Manages functional requirements for RDT&E and procurement appropriations (see Para. 9-22b and Table 9-11).

Table 9-3. Managers for Manpower and Force Structure Issues

Issue	Manager
Force structure/Unit Identification Code (UIC)/Resource Organization (Command) Code (ROC)	G-3/5/7
Military Manpower (Active)	G-1

ARMY PLANNING, PROGRAMMING, BUDGETING, AND EXECUTION PROCESS

Issue	Manager
Army National Guard Manpower	Director ARNG
U.S. Army Reserve Manpower	Chief AR
Civilian (End Strength and Full Time Equivalents)	G-1
Individuals Account	G-1
Army Management Headquarters Activities (AMHA)	G-1
Joint and Defense Accounts	G-1

The functional proponents outlined in Table 9-4 above and their supporting PEGs bear responsibility for setting the funding level of validated military requirements and validating and funding nonmilitary requirements generated by new equipment for unit set fielding, force modernization, or other new mission or doctrine.

9-18. Integrated Programming-Budgeting Phase
The Director Program Analysis and Evaluation (DPAE) and DAB jointly manage the integrated programming and budgeting phase to produce a combined POM and Budget Estimate Submission (BES).
 a. The Director of Program Analysis and Evaluation (DPAE). The Army DPAE takes the lead on programming matters and:
 (1) Provides the SECARMY and CSA with independent assessments of program alternatives and priorities.
 (2) Provides analytical and administrative support for PPBE forums.
 (3) Co-chairs the Planning Program Budget Committee (PPBC) with the Assistant Deputy Chief of Staff G-3/5/7 and the DAB.
 (4) Exercises overall responsibility at HQDA for Army program development in support of the POM and FYDP.
 (5) With the Assistant Deputy Chief of Staff G-3/5/7 and DAB, guides and integrates the work of PEGs throughout the PPBE process (see Para. 9-32)
 (6) With functional proponents:
 (a) Prepares Army responses to OSD programming guidance documents.
 (b) Structures the Army Program Guidance Memorandum (APGM) and Technical Guidance Memorandum (TGM) to articulate direction and guidance from the Defense Planning Guidance (DPG) and senior Army leadership.
 (c) Develops the Army program, including review of IPLs of the CCDRs and program submissions of the ACOMs, PEOs, and other operating agencies.
 (7) Codifies, and submits to OSD, the approved Army program in the POM.
 (8) Serves as HQDA point of contact for the POM and FYDP within HQDA and with OSD and the Joint Staff.
 (9) Manages the MDEP architecture.
 (10) Serves as host activity manager of the PPBE Enterprise System in coordination with ASA(FM&C), appropriation sponsors, manpower managers, the OSD Comptroller, OSD Director, CAPE, and Department of the Treasury.
 (a) Through the PPBC has established a PPBE Strategic Automation Committee (PSAC) to implement configuration management of the PPBE Enterprise System and oversee long-term plans for investing in Information Technology (IT) to improve the performance of PPBE functions.
 (b) Maintains the resource management architecture for automated support of PPBE processes and information systems and their integration into a common PPBE database. In particular:
 (i) Hosts the web services that provide coordination for the common data architecture, including PEs, Army PE (APE), resource organization (command) codes, the SSN-LIN Automated Management and Integrating System (SLAMIS) and, in coordination with the Defense Finance and Accounting Service (DFAS), the Army Management Structure (AMS).
 (ii) Maintains an integrated data dictionary of data elements in the PPBE data element structure and disciplines its use without re-keying by database users and component databases.
 (iii) Controls data entry and makes sure that PPBE data elements are consistent not only internally for programming, budgeting, and execution but, also externally with reporting requirements of the Standard

HOW THE ARMY RUNS

Data Collection System (SDCS), Service Support Manpower System (SSMS), and Comptroller Information System (CIS) or their successors.

(c) Maintains the official database position for Army Program and Budget Guidance (PBG) and through the SDCS, SSMS, and CIS or their successors updates OSD resource management databases with data that reflect the POM, BES, and the PB. Affected data include the Army BES for manpower, Army appropriations, and Army-managed Defense appropriations.

(d) Makes sure that the Army portion of FYDP submissions to OSD includes defense appropriations managed by the Army and that force structure and manpower information match positions in the force structure and accounting databases for the Active Army, Army National Guard (ARNG), U.S. Army Reserve (AR), and civilian work force.

(e) Issues the PBG after each PPBE phase.

(11) Provides feedback to each CCDR as to the resource status of the command's issues on forwarding the combined POM and Budget Estimate Submission (POM/BES) to OSD.

b. DAB. The DAB takes the lead on budgeting matters and:'

(1) Co-chairs the PPBC with the Assistant Deputy Chief of Staff G-3/5/7 and DPAE.
(2) Establishes budgeting policy and processes.
(3) Guides and integrates the work of the PEGs on budget matters. (See para 9-37)
(4) Reviews and consolidates the Army National Guard (ARNG) and U.S. Army Reserve (AR) budgets with the Active Army budget.
(5) Provides feedback to each CCDR on major budget issues affecting the command's resource requirements.
(6) Justifies the Army budget before OSD, Office of Management and Budget (OMB), and Congress.
(7) Maintains liaison and acts as point of contact with Congressional appropriations committees except for Civil Works issues.
(8) With the DPAE and data proponents, performs system and data management functions described in paragraph a (10), above.
(9) Serves as proponent of FYDP program 6-Research and Development and program 7-Central Supply and Maintenance. (See para 9-9)
(10) Manages functional requirements and program and performance for designated appropriation accounts. (See para 9-22 and tables 9-8 through 9-14)
(11) Manages the data architecture of Army PEs and Elements of Resource (EOR).
(12) Maintains and issues TOA controls for Army Appropriations for the BES and the President Budget cycles.
(13) Translates final budget decisions into program changes, posting PEs, Army PEs (APE), MDEPs, and command distributions, as required, updating the PPBE database to produce the PB position submitted to OSD and Congress.
(14) Manages the issue cycle to formulate IPs challenging the Service program requests and Major Budget Issue (MBI) processes. The IPs from the SECDEF challenge the Service program requests with suggested changes.
(a) Maintains coordination between the Under Secretary of Defense (Comptroller) and HQDA.
(b) Makes sure that adjustments to fiscal controls are correct on all records for each issue paper (verifying corresponding manpower controls, however, is a Deputy Chief of Staff, G-1 responsibility).
(15) Gives special attention to any issue paper under appeal since the DEPSECDEF may, on review, revise pending adjustments.
(16) When the SECDEF makes his final decision on change to the Service programs he issues Resource Management Decision (RMDs) which directs the Services to change their programs to comply with his resourcing decisions.

c. The Assistant Deputy Chief of Staff G-3/5/7. The ADCS G-3/5/7 ensures the optimal allocation of army resources by evaluating the integrated programming-budgeting phase for compliance with TAP and Army priorities.

ARMY PLANNING, PROGRAMMING, BUDGETING, AND EXECUTION PROCESS

9-19. Execution Phase

a. **Military Deputy for Budget and Execution.** For the Assistant Secretary of the Army (Financial Management and Comptroller) (ASA(FM&C)), the Military Deputy for Budget and Execution:

(1) Reviews program performance and, specifically, oversees Cost and Performance Measures designed to provide the senior Army leadership with a corporate view of business efficiencies and program accomplishment.

(2) Applies funds appropriated by Congress to carry out authorized programs.

(3) Through the DAB, manages the PPBE execution phase.

b. **DAB.** As provided in 9-19a(3) above, the DAB manages the PPBE Execution phase and, during financial execution:

(1) Establishes funding policy and processes.

(2) Supervises and directs financial execution of the congressionally approved budget.

(3) Allocates funds appropriated by Congress and monitors their execution

(4) Oversees accounting for and reporting on use of Army-managed funds to OSD and Congress by appropriation. As applicable to each appropriation, includes FYDP program, PEs, APEs, project number, Budget Line Item Number (BLIN), Standard Study Number (SSN), quantities, Budget Activity (BA), BA Group (BAG), Budget Sub-Activity (BSA), Element of Resource (EOR), and financing data. Also as applicable to an appropriation, accounts for and reports on the use of the manpower-by-manpower category

(5) With functional proponents and within stated restrictions and specified dollar thresholds, reprograms funds as required to meet unforeseen requirements or changes in operating conditions.

(6) With the Defense Finance and Accounting Service (DFAS):

(a) Oversees the development and maintenance of standard Army systems in support of financial accounting; and oversees implementation of the same standard Army systems in support of distribution, accounting, and reporting of funds.

(b) Makes sure that execution reports meet HQDA management information needs.

c. **Director of Program Analysis and Evaluation (DPAE).** During programmatic execution, the DPAE monitors how programmed resources are applied to achieve approved objectives to gain feedback for adjusting resource requirements.

d. **The Assistant Deputy Chief of Staff G-3/5/7.** The ADCS G-3/5/7 ensures the optimal allocation of army resources by evaluating the execution phase for compliance with TAP and Army priorities,

Section IV
Responsibilities for Planning, Programming, Budgeting, and Execution-Related Operational Tasks

9-20. HQDA Principal Officials

a. **The Assistant Secretary of the Army (Acquisition, Logistics, and Technology) (ASA (ALT)).**

(1) Exercises responsibility for, and oversees, all matters and policy related to acquisition, logistics, technology, procurement, the industrial base, and security cooperation (that is, security assistance and armaments cooperation).

(2) Serves as the designated Army Acquisition Executive (AAE).

(3) Represents the Army on the Defense Acquisition Board (DAB), the Nuclear Weapons Council Standing Committee, and the Conventional Systems Committee.

(4) Chairs the Army Systems Acquisition Review Council (ASARC).

(5) Integrates the development and acquisition of materiel into all phases of the PPBE process.

(6) With the Deputy Chief of Staff, G-8 helps prepare the Research, Development, and Acquisition Plan (RDA Plan).

(7) Manages functional requirements and program and performance for RDT&E and procurement appropriations, the Chemical Agents and Munitions Destruction, Army appropriation, and designated Miscellaneous accounts in Table 9-18, as well as the Contract Operations account of the Operation and Maintenance, Army appropriation, Tables 9-10 through 9-14 (see Para. 9-22).

b. **The Assistant Secretary of the Army (Installations, Energy and Environment) (ASA (IE&E)).** Exercises responsibility for, and oversees, all matters and policy related to installations, housing, installation-related-military construction, real estate and environment, safety, and occupational health.

c. **The Assistant Secretary of the Army (Manpower and Reserve Affairs) (ASA(M&RA)).**

HOW THE ARMY RUNS

(1) Promulgates Army wide policy for and oversees, all matters related to manpower, personnel, and Reserve affairs across all Army components (Active, Guard, Reserve, civilian, and contractor).

(2) Sets policy and:

(a) Oversees Army organization and force structure to include Army force management initiatives that affect the operating and generating forces (Active, Guard, and Reserve).

(b) Oversees Army manpower requirements determination and resource allocation for all Army components across all major Army Commands (ACOM) and separate agencies (Active, Guard, Reserve, Joint, and Defense).

(3) Reviews policies and programs pertaining to readiness, resource allocation, training, force structure, and professional and leader education and development.

d. The Administrative Assistant to the Secretary of the Army (AASA).

(1) Plans, programs, budgets, and accounts for the execution of resources for Headquarters, Department of the Army and its field operating and staff support agencies.

(2) Serves as proponent (provisional) of the Organizing PEG (see Para. 9-37).

e. The Chief Information Officer and Army G-6 (CIO/G-6).

(1) Exercises responsibility for Army information management functions per 10 USC 3014(c)(1)(d) and sets policy and determines objectives for, and oversees, all matters related to Army Mission Command Networks and Systems and IT functions.

(2) Provides CIO-validation of Army Mission Command Networks and Systems and IT requirements, and monitors the performance of IT programs for war fighting, base operations, administrative, and other mission-related processes associated with an Army Mission Command Networks and Systems and IT impact.

(3) Serves as Program Integrator for IT (see Table 9-5).

(4) Serves as proponent of the Army FYDP subprogram 3-Communications (see Table 9-2).

(5) Develops, maintains, and facilitates the IT architecture, that is, the Army Knowledge Enterprise Architecture (AKEA).

(6) Makes sure through advice and technical assistance that Army acquires IT and manages information resources in a manner that implements the policies, procedures, and goals of the Army Knowledge Management Strategic Plan.

f. The Deputy Chief of Staff, G-1.

(1) Develops, coordinates, and implements programs and policies directly associated with accession, development, distribution, and sustainment of military and civilian personnel readiness to include the personnel readiness of Army units and organizations.

(2) Develops human resource programs, budgets, and activities to execute life-cycle functions of manning, well-being, personnel technologies, Soldier-oriented R&D, and personnel transformation.

(3) Serves as proponent of the Manning PEG (see Para. 9-37).

(4) Serves as proponent of FYDP program 9-Administration (see Table 9-2).

(5) Serves as the Army proponent of Directed Military Over Strength (DMO) and military manpower requirements outside the DOD.

(6) Manages issues related to Army manpower accounts except for Army National Guard and Army Reserve manpower and manages functional requirements and program and performance for the Military Pay, Army appropriation and for designated personnel accounts and Manpower-Only accounts of the Operation and Maintenance, Army appropriation (see Para. 9-22 and Tables 9-8 through 9-14).

g. The Deputy Chief of Staff, G-2.

(1) In coordination with the DOD and National Intelligence Community, sets policy for Army intelligence and counterintelligence and security countermeasures.

(2) Prepares, justifies, and submits the program and budget for the Army portion of the National Foreign Intelligence Program (NFIP) per the policy, resource, and administrative guidance of the Director of Central Intelligence and DOD NFIP Program Managers. The Director of Central Intelligence is also responsible under statute and presidential order to do the following: develop, approve, and present to POTUS an annual budget for the NFIP for inclusion in the PB for transmittal to Congress pursuant to OMB guidance; and participate in the development by the SECDEF of the annual budgets for the Joint Military Intelligence Program (JMIP) and the Tactical Intelligence and Related Activities (TIARA).

(3) Serves as Army Staff lead for integrating intelligence, surveillance, and reconnaissance (ISR) matters into all phases of the PPBE process.

ARMY PLANNING, PROGRAMMING, BUDGETING, AND EXECUTION PROCESS

(4) Serves as the resource proponent for operational and strategic intelligence of Army FYDP subprogram 3-Intelligence (see Table 9-2).

(5) Manages functional requirements and program and performance for Security Programs of the Operation and Maintenance, Army appropriation (see Para. 9-22 and Tables 9-10 through 9-14).

h. The Deputy Chief of Staff, G-4.

(1) Develops and resources Army wide logistics operation programs for strategic mobility, supply, maintenance, war reserves and prepositioning, aviation, munitions, transportation, distribution, readiness, and integrated logistics support.

(2) Integrates and balances between acquisition and logistics the sustainment functions of readiness, supply, services, maintenance, transportation, aviation, munitions, security assistance, and related automated systems.

(3) Through the integration of logistics supportability, manages the readiness of new systems throughout the acquisition life cycle as well as current readiness of legacy systems.

(4) On behalf of the AAE:

(a) Develops policies for, and oversees, the PPBE of integrated logistics support.

(b) Makes sure that program executive offices have programmed and incorporated supportability requirements into the acquisition and fielding of new systems.

(5) Serves as proponent of the Sustaining PEG (see Para. 9-37).

(6) Manages functional requirements for the Procurement of Ammunition, Army appropriation and the Army Working Capital Fund and manages functional requirements and program and performance for Logistics Operations accounts of the Operation and Maintenance, Army appropriation, including those for Base Operations (see Para. 9-22 and Tables 9-10 through 9-14).

i. The Assistant Chief of Staff for Installation Management (ACSIM).

(1) Develops and directs planning, programming, and budgeting of installation management functions and the funding of installation-related military construction, housing, environmental protection, and facilities operation and sustainment.

(2) Provides ACSIM validation of requirements for managing and funding Army installations.

(3) Makes sure that installation management and environmental programs are integrated into all aspects of Army operations.

(4) Serves as proponent of the Installations PEG (see Para. 9-37).

(5) Manages functional requirements and program and performance for military construction appropriations and environmental restoration as well as Installation Management Operations and Maintenance appropriations (see Para. 9-22 and Tables 9-10 through 9-14).

j. The Chief of Engineers (COE).

(1) Supports and promotes resource requirements of the engineer regiment.

(2) Represents and promotes resource requirements of the U.S. Army Corps of Engineers (USACE).

(3) Acts for SECARMY in executing SECARMY Executive Agent responsibilities for military construction to include construction for the Air Force, Navy, National Aeronautics and Space Administration (NASA), and selected DOD activities and foreign nations.

(4) Manages functional requirements and program and performance for the Homeowners Assistance Fund, Defense (see Para. 9-22 and Table 9-14).

k. The Surgeon General (TSG).

(1) Exercises responsibility for development, policy direction, organization and management of an integrated Army wide health services system.

(2) Represents and promotes resource requirements of the U.S. Army Medical Department.

(3) Manages functional requirements and program and performance for reimbursable medical manpower of the Operation and Maintenance, Army appropriation (see Para. 9-22 Tables 9-10 through 9-14).

l. The Chief, National Guard Bureau (CNGB). Through the Director of the Army National Guard (DARNG):

(1) Plans and administers the budget of the Army National Guard (ARNG) and serves as appropriation sponsor for ARNG appropriations.

(2) Serves as proponent of the ARNG subprogram, FYDP program 5-Guard and Reserve Forces (see Table 9-2).

HOW THE ARMY RUNS

(3) Manages ARNG manpower issues and manages functional requirements and program and performance for ARNG appropriations and ARNG accounts of the Operation and Maintenance, Army National Guard appropriation (see Para. 9-22 and Tables 9-8 through 9-14).

(4) Serves as Program Integrator for the statutory, Defense, and Army requirements of the ARNG (see Figure 9-1).

m. The Chief, Army Reserve (CAR).

(1) Plans and administers the budget of the U.S. Army Reserve (AR) and serves as appropriation sponsor for AR appropriations.

(2) Serves as proponent of the AR subprogram, FYDP program 5-Guard and Reserve Forces (see Table 9-2).

(3) Manages AR manpower issues and manages functional requirements and program and performance for AR appropriations and AR accounts of the Operation and Maintenance, U.S. Army Reserve appropriation (see Para. 9-22 and Tables 9-8 through 9-14).

(4) Serves as Program Integrator for the statutory, Defense, and Army requirements of the AR.

Table 9-4. Program Indicators

Army National Guard (ARNG)	Infromation Technology (IT) – CIO/G-6
Provides techinal assistance to Title 10 PEGs and monitors actions to integrate into all phases of the PPBE processes the statutory, Defense, and Army requirements of the Army National Guard	Provides advice and technical assistance to Title 10 PEGs to make sure that the Army acquires IT and manages information resources ina manner that implements the policies, procedures, and goals of the Army Knowledge Management Strategic Plan.
Tracks ARNG program performance during budget execution	Validates IT requirements and monitors the performance of IT programs throughout all phases of the PPBE process. Develops. Maintains, and facilitates the IT architechture, that is, the Army Knowledge Enterprise Architectrure (AKEA), across the Army
U. S. Army Reserve (AR) Chief of Army Reserves	
Provides techinal assistance to Title 10 PEGs and monitors actions to integrate into all phases of the PPBE processes the statutory, Defense, and Army requirements of the U. S. Army Reserve.	
Tracks AR program performance during budget execution	

9-21. Army Commanders

a. Commanders of ACOMs and heads of other operating agencies. Commanders of ACOMs, Program Executive Officers (PEO), and heads of other operating agencies:

(1) Plan, program, and budget for assigned missions, responsibilities, and functions.

(2) Document manpower in their subordinate organizations per allocated manpower levels.

(3) Execute the approved ACOM or agency program within allocated resources, applying the inherent flexibility allowed by law and regulation.

(4) Assess ACOM or agency program performance and budget execution and:

(a) Account for and report on use of allocated funds by appropriation and MDEP. As applicable to each appropriation, include FYDP program, Army Management Structure Code (AMSCO), Army Program

ARMY PLANNING, PROGRAMMING, BUDGETING, AND EXECUTION PROCESS

Element (APE), project number, BLIN, SSN, BA, BAG, and EOR. Also account for and report on use of allocated manpower by unit identification code (UIC).

(b) Use manpower data and financial data from budget execution in developing future requirements.

(c) Make sure that below threshold reprogramming remains consistent with Army priorities.

b. Commanders of ACOMs serving as commanders of ASCC. ACOM commanders serving as commanders of ASCCs identify and integrate with their other missions and operational requirements the requirements of the CCMD.

c. Commander, Space and Missile Defense Command (SMDC). Serves as proponent of Army FYDP subprogram 3-Space (see Table 9-2).

9-22. Staff Managers and Sponsors for Congressional Appropriations

The Military Deputy for Budget and Execution, the Director of Army National Guard (DARNG), Chief, Army Reserve (CAR), and designated functional managers manage and control Army resources. One set of functional managers addresses manpower and force structure issues. Another set of functional managers assists appropriation sponsors. Tables 9-8 through 9-14 list assignments of appropriation sponsors and functional managers. Their general responsibilities are as follows:

a. Manager for manpower and force structure issues. The manager for manpower issues and the manager for force structure issues work together to maintain a continuous exchange of information and collaboration during each PPBE phase. As appropriate, they:

(1) Coordinate instructions to the field, and the processing of requests from the field, for manpower or force changes.

(2) Align and balance manpower and unit information among such PPBE database systems as the Structure and Manpower Allocation System (SAMAS), The Army Authorization Documents System (TAADS), the PPBE Enterprise System, and the FYDP.

(3) Provide lead support on manpower issues to PEG chairs.

(4) Verify manpower affordability.

b. Manager for functional requirements. The manager for functional requirements:

(1) Determines the scope, quantity, and qualitative nature of functional requirements for planning, programming, and budgeting.

(2) Checks how commands and agencies apply allocated manpower and dollars to make sure their use fulfills program requirements.

(3) Prioritizes unfunded programs submitted by ACOMs, PEOs, and other operating agencies.

(4) Using Army program and budget guidance and priorities, resolves conflicts involving unfunded requirements or decrements on which ACOMs, PEOs, and other operating agencies fail to reach agreement in developing the program or budget.

(5) Recommends to the PPBC (see Para. 9-30) the allocation of available resources, unfunded programs, and offsetting decrements.

(6) During program and budget reviews, and throughout the process, coordinates resource changes with agencies having responsibility for affected MDEPs and with the appropriate appropriation sponsor for relevant resources.

c. Manager for program and performance. The manager for program and performance:

(1) Represents the functional program and monitors its performance during each PPBE phase.

(2) As required, helps the appropriation sponsor perform the duties listed in d (2) and d (3), below.

(3) Translates budget decisions and approved manpower and funding into program changes and makes sure that data transactions update affected MDEPs and, in coordination with the appropriation sponsors, affected appropriations.

(4) Checks budget execution from the functional perspective.

(5) For investment appropriations:

(a) Operates and maintains databases in support of the PPBE Enterprise System.

(b) During budget formulation, determines how changes in fiscal guidance affect budget estimates and reviews and approves the documentation of budget justification.

(c) During review of the budget by OSD and OMB and by Congress, serves as appropriation advocate, helps prepare the Army response to OSD IPs which are the result of issue paper proposals, and prepares congressional appeals.

HOW THE ARMY RUNS

(d) During execution determines fund recipients, monitors execution, performs decrement reviews, plans reprogramming, and controls below threshold reprogramming. On RDT&E and procurement matters and otherwise as required, testifies before OSD and Congress.

d. Appropriation Sponsor. The appropriation sponsor:

(1) Controls the assigned appropriation or fund.

(2) Serves as Army spokesperson for appropriation resources.

(3) Helps resource claimants solve manpower and funding deficiencies.

(4) Issues budget policy, instructions, and fiscal guidance.

(5) During budget formulation:

(a) Bears responsibility for updating the PPBE database.

(b) Prepares and justify budget estimates, coordinating with functional and manpower representatives to make sure appropriate exhibits and database systems match.

(6) Testifies before Congress during budget justification.

(7) Manages financial execution of the appropriation and reprograms allocated manpower and funds to meet unforeseen contingencies during budget execution.

Section V
Army Planning, Programming, Budgeting, and Execution

9-23. Army's Primary Resource Management System

The PPBE process serves as the Army's primary resource management process. A major decision-making process, PPBE interfaces with joint strategic planning and with planning conducted by OSD. Linking directly to OSD programming and budgeting, the PPBE process develops and maintains the Army portion of the Defense program and budget. PPBE supports Army planning, program development, and budget preparation at all levels of command. Similarly supporting program and budget execution, it provides feedback to the planning, programming, and budgeting processes.

9-24. PPBE Concept

a. The PPBE process ties strategy, program, and budget all together. It helps build a comprehensive plan in which budgets flow from programs, programs from requirements, requirements from missions, and missions from national security objectives. The patterned flow from end purpose to resource cost defines requirements in progressively greater detail.

b. Long-range planning creates a vision of the Army 20 years into the future. In the 2- to 10-year midterm, long-range macro estimates give way to a specified size, composition, and quality of operational and support forces. Derived from joint strategic planning and intermediate objectives to achieve long-range goals, this operational and support force provides the planning foundation for program requirements.

c. In the midterm, guided by force requirements, the integrated program-budget process distributes projected resources. It seeks to support priorities and policies of the senior Army leadership while achieving balance among Army organizations, systems, and functions. For the 0- to 2-year near-term, the integrated process converts program requirements into budget requests for manpower and dollars. When enacted into appropriations and manpower authorizations, these resources become available to carry out approved programs.

d. By formally adding execution to the traditional emphasis on planning, programming, and budgeting, the Army emphasizes concern for how well program performance and financial execution apply allocated resources to meet the Army's requirements.

e. Documents produced within the PPBE process support Defense decision-making, and the review and discussion that attend their development help shape the outcome. For example:

(1) The Army helps prepare the SECDEF's Defense Planning Guidance (DPG) and planning documents produced by the Joint Strategic Planning System (JSPS). Army participation influences policy, strategy, and force objectives considered by the SECDEF and the CJCS, including policies for development, acquisition, and other resource-allocation issues.

(2) ACOM commanders, PEOs, and heads of other operating agencies similarly influence positions and decisions taken by the SECARMY and CSA. Commanders and heads of agencies develop and submit force structure, procurement, and construction requirements as well as assessments and data to

ARMY PLANNING, PROGRAMMING, BUDGETING, AND EXECUTION PROCESS

support program and budget development. Through periodic commanders' conferences held by the CSA, they also make their views known on the proposed plan, program, and budget.

(3) CCDRs influence Army positions and decisions through ACOM commanders serving as commanders of ASCCs, who integrate operational requirements of the CCMD into their program and budget submissions. CCDRs also highlight requirements in an IPL that receives close review during program development.

9-25. PPBE Objectives

The main objective of the PPBE process is to establish, justify, and acquire the fiscal and manpower resources needed to accomplish the Army's assigned missions in executing the National Military Strategy. Phase by phase objectives follow:

    a. Conduct planning, to size, structure, man, equip, train, and sustain the Army force to support the national military strategy.

    b. Analyze integrated programming and budgeting, to:

    (1) Distribute projected manpower, dollars, and materiel among competing requirements according to Army resource allocation policy and priorities, making sure that requirements get resourced at defensible, executable levels.

    (2) Convert resource allocation decisions into requests for congressional authorization and appropriations.

    c. Execute programs to apply resources to achieve approved program objectives, and adjust resource requirements based on execution feedback.

    d. Oversee budget execution, to manage and account for funds to carry out approved programs.

9-26. Control of Planning, Programming, and Budgeting Documents

    a. Papers and associated data sponsored by the DOD PPBE process give details of proposed programs and plans. The proposals often state candidate positions and competing options that remain undecided until final approval.

    b. Access to such tentative material by other than those directly involved in planning and allocating resources would frustrate the candor and privacy of leadership deliberations. Moreover, access by private firms seeking DOD contracts would imperil competition and pose serious ethical, even criminal, problems for those involved. For these reasons, DOD closely controls documents produced through the DOD PPBE process and its supporting databases. Thus, OSD restricts access to DOD and other governmental agencies directly involved in planning, programming, and budgeting Defense resources, primarily OMB.

    c. Exceptions to the limitations described require SECDEF approval. After coordination with the General Counsel, Army proponents may request an exception, but only for compelling need. Statutes and other procedures govern disclosure of information to Congress and the General Accountability Office (GAO).

    d. Guidance in DODD 7045.14 gives the Secretaries of the Military Departments, CJCS, the Under Secretaries and Assistant Secretaries of Defense, DCAPE, and the Director, Operational Test and Evaluation are designated as the approval authorities for disclosing PPBE documents and data outside the DOD and to other Government agencies directly involved in the defense planning and resource allocation process. This disclosure authority is restricted to PPBE documents and data generated by the offices and organizations they oversee,

    e. The list that follows cites some of the major PPBE and related PPBE documents and material requiring restricted access.

    (1) Planning Phase:
    (a) Defense Planning Guidance (DPG)
    (b) Guidance for Employment of Forces (GEF)
    (c) The Army Plan (TAP)
    (2) Programming Phase:
    (a) Fiscal Guidance.
    (b) POM.
    (c) FYDP documentation including FYDP annexes.
    (d) IPs (for example, major IPs, and cover briefs).

HOW THE ARMY RUNS

(e) Proposed Military Department program reductions (or program offsets).
(f) Tentative issues- in the form of draft IPs process at OSD.
(3) Budgeting Phase:
(a) FYDP documents for the Budget Estimate Submission (BES) and PB, including procurement, Research, Development, Test, and Evaluation (RDT&E), and construction annexes.
(b) Resource Management Decisions (RMD) which are implementing instructions from the SECDEF on his final decisions on programs.
(c) Automated Program and Financing Statements.
(d) Reports generated by the automated Comptroller Information System (CIS).
(e) DD Form 1414, Base for Reprogramming Actions.
(f) DD Form 1416, Report of Programs.
(g) Congressional data sheets.
(h) Management Initiative Decisions (MID).

Section VI
Allocation of Resources

9-27. Recording Resources

Figure 9-6. Management Decision Package (MDEP)

ARMY PLANNING, PROGRAMMING, BUDGETING, AND EXECUTION PROCESS

MDEP Functions

- What capability is resourced?
- How much is resourced?
- Why resource this capability?
- Who is responsible?
- When are resources available?

- Battlefield Observation 
- Capabilities (Survivability, Intelligence, etc.)
- DCS, G-3/5/7
- Year (Prior, Current, Budget, Program)?

The MDEP is an Army Programming Tool

Figure 9-7. Management Decision Package (MDEP) Functions

a. The Army MDEP serves as a key resource management tool. Collectively, MDEPs account for all Army resources. They describe the capabilities programmed over a 9-year period for the Active Army, Guard, Reserve, and civilian work force.

b. Recording the resources needed to gain an intended outcome, an individual MDEP describes a particular organization, program, or function and applies uniquely to one of the following areas for resource management:
  (1) Missions of Modified Tables of Organization and Equipment (MTOE) units.
  (2) Missions of Tables of Distribution and Allowances (TDA) units.
  (3) Acquisition, fielding, and sustainment of weapon and information systems (with linkage to organizations).
  (4) Special Visibility Programs (SVP).
  (5) Short-Term Projects (STP).

c. In short, the MDEP specifies the military and civilian manpower and dollars associated with a program undertaking; displays needed resources across relevant Army commands and relevant appropriations; and justifies the resource expenditure.

d. HQDA uses the MDEP to help develop programs to support the requirements, carry-out approved programs, and check program results.

e. HQDA uses the MDEP to link decisions by the SECARMY and CSA and their priorities to:
  (1) FYDP accounts that record Service positions in OSD.
  (2) Army Management Structure (AMS) accounts that record funding transactions in Army activities and installations.

f. HQDA uses the MDEP also to link key systems within the PPBE Enterprise System, for example:
  (1) The Structure and Manpower Allocation System (SAMAS) and The Army Authorization Document System (TAADS).

HOW THE ARMY RUNS

(2) The Army Training Requirements and Resources System (ATRRS) whose product, the Army Program for Individual Training (ARPRINT), shows valid training requirements and associated training programs.

(3) Depot maintenance programs.

g. For investment accounts, managers for construction, RDT&E, and procurement first allocate program and budget resources by Army Management Structure code (AMSCO), APE, project number, and BLIN. They then distribute the resources to MDEPs within the resource management areas, listed in Para 9-27b above.

9-28. Program and Budget Years Covered by the MDEP

a. The MDEP records manpower and TOA over the 9 fiscal years needed to display the program and budget. Which program year or which budget year each fiscal year addresses, depends on whether interest in the MDEP centers on the program or budget. Figure 9-8 shows the fiscal year structure of an MDEP applying to the President's FY 2014-2018 budget.

b. The MDEP shifts forward one year in the annual POM/BES submission. At the start of the cycle for the next annual POM/BES, the PPBE database drops the earliest year from the database and adds one new year. The first of the preceding years is the prior fiscal year (PY). It records resources spent in executing the budget the year before the current fiscal year (CY). The CY shows resources in the budget being executed. The last preceding year is called the budget year (BY). It lists resources requested in the PB being reviewed by Congress.

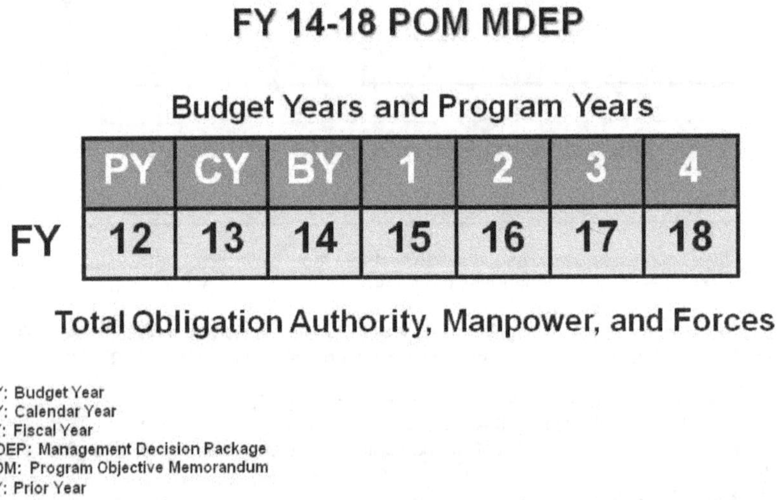

FY 14-18 POM MDEP

Budget Years and Program Years

	PY	CY	BY	1	2	3	4
FY	12	13	14	15	16	17	18

Total Obligation Authority, Manpower, and Forces

BY: Budget Year
CY: Calendar Year
FY: Fiscal Year
MDEP: Management Decision Package
POM: Program Objective Memorandum
PY: Prior Year

Figure 9-8. Fiscal Year (FY) 14-18 Program Objective Memorandum (POM) Management Decision Package (MDEP)

9-29. Extent that Manpower and Dollars can be Redistributed in the MDEP

a. The MDEP, as just described, has both budget-year and program-year increments. The two increments differ primarily by the flexibility the Army has with manpower and funds.

b. During the program or POM years, HQDA is constrained by Congress on total military end strength and by Fiscal Guidance. HQDA determines and approves civilian work year levels by balancing workload and available funding. Similarly, HQDA restricts program dollars only by TOA, not by individual appropriation. The distinctions allow redistributing previously programmed manpower and dollars to meet changing requirements. In later POM or budget submissions, for example, HQDA can, as needed, move program year resources between MDEPs, appropriations, and APEs.

ARMY PLANNING, PROGRAMMING, BUDGETING, AND EXECUTION PROCESS

c. Once HQDA sends the BES to OSD, OSD must approve any changes to manpower and dollars. Even tighter controls govern changes in manpower and funding in the budget years after the PB has gone to Congress.

(1) HQDA can redistribute previously budgeted manpower and dollars between MDEPs or commands and agencies, but must leave current budgeted dollars unchanged until current year appropriations become law.

(2) Some flexibility during execution permits financing unbudgeted requirements to meet unforeseen needs or changes in operating conditions. Even so, congressional rules and specified dollar thresholds severely restrict spending for purposes other than those originally justified and approved. In addition, during execution, HQDA can transfer military and civilian manpower within appropriations without a corresponding transfer of funds.

9-30. How Flexibility Affects the MDEP

a. Frequent change in MDEP resources. Competition at each stage of program development and budget formulation can produce frequent change in an MDEP's resource levels. Decisions resulting from OSD review of the POM/BES will further change amounts initially approved. Sometimes decisions may even affect requests in the PB already before Congress. Authorization and appropriation decisions by Congress often change amounts requested in the PB. Budget execution sometimes results in different rates and quantities of expenditure from those planned, and, at times, it results in different purposes.

b. Keeping MDEP resources current. Program and budget analysts continually update MDEPs through their respective feeder systems to reflect the position of the last program or budget event. The kinds of changes described require that resource managers continually weigh how the stream of program and budget actions affect the MDEP and how a change in the program year or budget year portion of the package may affect the out years. Managers continually ask, "In what ways do the changes: alter MDEP resource levels; shift resources between years; and affect resources in related MDEPs?"

c. Army Management Structure (AMS). The AMS serves as a second major resource recording structure. Based on congressional appropriations, the AMS relates program dollars and manpower to a standard classification of activities and functions per DFAS-IN Manual 37-100-**** (where **** stands for the Current Fiscal Year, e.g., 2013). Army Management Structure Codes (AMSCO) help record the data in the detail needed for budgeting, execution, and accounting.

9-31. Other Structures.

Other fiscal management structures include the 01 level BA structure for operation and maintenance appropriations shown in tables 9-8 through 9-14 (at the end of this chapter), SSN and BLIN for weapon systems, and project numbers for military construction automated support. The automated Army PPBE System supports Army PPBE functions and DOD PPBE data submissions to OSD, OMB, and Congress. Known simply as the PPBE database, it encompasses forces, funds, and manpower and serves as the database of record for Army resources.

a. PPBE Database. The PPBE database organizes and registers 9 years of dollar and manpower data used in the process, and 12 years of forces data. It gathers manpower and dollar data through keys tied to the MDEP, appropriation, PEs, APEs, and other identifiers including the command or resource organization code. HQDA uses the database to:

(1) Support user analysis.

(2) Build and record the combined POM/BES.

(3) Prepare the Army portion of the FYDP to reflect the POM/BES and later the PB.

(4) Report consistent Army resource positions to OSD through the Select and Native Programming (SNaP) Data Collection System, Standard Data Collection System (SDCS), Service Support Manpower System (SSMS), and Comptroller Information System (CIS).

(5) Issue Army commands Program and Budget Guidance (PBG) reflecting the FYDP resource position after each FYDP update.

(6) Provide MDEP execution and expenditure information.

b. Future System Enhancement. The Planning, Programming and Budgeting (PPB) Business Operating System (BOS) standardizes and better integrate the transactional automated information systems used in the Headquarters Department of Army level Programming and Budgeting processes. These systems are core to the PPBE business processes of the headquarters for gathering programmatic

HOW THE ARMY RUNS

requirements, balancing resources and delivering the Army's program budget to OSD. The Business Operating System streamlines programming and budgeting business processes and significantly improving strategic analysis capabilities. The BOS provides architecting, reengineering, streamlining and consolidating HQDA systems, feeder database systems, and streamlines the business processes associated with them. These improvements have improved capabilities, eliminated redundancies and reduced overall costs of operations.

Section VII
Army Planning, Programming, Budgeting, and Execution Deliberative Forums

9-32. Army Resources Board now called Senior Leaders of the Department of the Army (SLDA)
The Army Resources Board (ARB) is chaired by the SECARMY with the CSA as the vice chair. The current SECARMY changed the ARB to Senior Leaders of the Department of the Army (SLDA) and no longer uses the ARB structure. The SLDA serves as a senior Army leadership forum, through which the SECARMY and CSA review Army policy and resource allocation issues, particularly those emanating from the Army PPBE process. It sets policy and approves guidance and priorities. The SLDA approves the prioritization of Army programs and selects resource allocation alternatives. In addition, upon their completion, the SLDA approves TAP, and the POM/BES. Table 9-6 shows the composition of Army PPBE deliberative forums.

Table 9-5. Composition of Army Planning, Programming, Budgeting, and Execution (PPBE) Deliberative Forums

Forum	Chairs	OSA Members	Army Staff Members	Advisory and Support
SLDA	SECARMY-Chair CSA-Vice chair	USA ASA(ALT) ASA(FM&C) ASA(IE&E) ASA(M&RA) General Counsel CIO/G-6	VCSA G-3/5/7 G-8	Other participants as required Advisors ADCS G-3/5/7 DPAE DAB ARB Executive Secretary, ASA(FM&C)
SRG	USA-Co-chair VCSA-Co-chair	ASA(ALT) ASA(CW) ASA(FM&C) ASA(IE&E) ASA(M&RA) General Counsel CIO/G-6	G-1 G-2 G-3/5/7 G-4 G-8 ACSIM CAR DARNG	Other participants as required Advisors ADCS G-3/5/7 DPAE DAB SRG Executive Secretary, ASA(FM&C)
PPBC	Assistant G-3/5/7-Co-chair for Planning DPAE-Co-chair for Programming DAB-Co-chair for Budgeting and Execution	Representatives of- ASA(ALT) ASA(CW) ASA(IE&E) ASA(M&RA) AASA CIO/G-6	Representatives of- G-1 G-2 G-4 ACSIM TSG CAR DARNG	Other participants as required, including- Director of Operations and Support, ASA(FM&C) Director of Investment, ASA(FM&C)Director of Force Management, G-3/5/7 Director of Requirements, G-3/5/7 Director of Training, G-3/5/7 Director of Strategy, Plans, and Policy, G-3/5/7

ARMY PLANNING, PROGRAMMING, BUDGETING, AND EXECUTION PROCESS

Forum	Chairs	OSA Members	Army Staff Members	Advisory and Support
				Director of Force Development, G-8

9-33. Senior Review Group
 a. Co-chaired by the Under Secretary of the Army (USA) and Vice Chief of Staff, Army (VCSA) the Senior Review Group (SRG) serves as a senior level forum to resolve resource allocation and other issues but generally does not revisit decisions made at lower levels. The SRG monitors staff implementation of decisions of the SLDA and makes recommendations to the SLDA on-
 (1) The prioritization of programs.
 (2) Resource allocation alternatives.
 (3) Final TAP, and the POM/BES.
 (4) Other issues as determined by the Under Secretary of the Army (USA) and VCSA.
 b. See Table 9-6 for composition of the SRG.

9-34. Planning Program Budget Committee
 a. The Planning Program Budget Committee (PPBC) has three co-chairs, one of whom presides over the forum depending upon the subject matter under consideration - the ADCS G-3/5/7 for planning, the DPAE for programming, and the DAB for budgeting and execution.
 b. The PPBC serves the PPBE process in both a coordinating and executive-advisory role. It provides a continuing forum in which planning, program, and budget managers review, adjust, and recommend courses of action on relevant issues. The PPBC may return the results of committee deliberations to the Army Staff or Secretariat for action. It may pass them, in turn, to the SRG and ARB for review or approval. Among its responsibilities, the PPBC:
 (1) Maintains overall discipline of the PPBE process.
 (2) Oversees the PPBE schedule, with each chair controlling the chair's respective portion of the schedule.
 (3) Monitors force management and preparation of TAP, POM/BES, and PB.
 (4) Makes sure that Army policy remains internally consistent and that program adjustments remain consistent with Army policy and priorities.
 c. The PPBC maintains the PPBE Strategic Automation Committee to implement configuration management of the PPBE Enterprise process and to oversee long-term plans for investing in IT to improve the performance of PPBE functions (Para. 9-18a(10) above). As required, the PPBC may set up other standing committees or working groups to resolve issues that arise in managing the program or budget.
 d. See Table 9-6 for composition of the PPBC.

9-35. PPBC Council of Colonels
A group of colonels or civilian equivalents, who represent PPBC members, meet throughout the PPBE process in a forum known as the Council of Colonels. The Council is co-chaired by the Chief, Resource Analysis and Integration Office, G-3/5/7; Chief, Program Development Division, Program Analysis and Evaluation Directorate; and Deputy Director of Management and Control, ASA(FM&C). The group packages proposals, frames issues, and otherwise coordinates matters that come before the PPBC when it convenes.

9-36. Implementation of the Budget, Requirements and Program (BRP) Groups
The subsets of the three groups addressed in paragraphs 9-32 through 9-34 are more active in the process. These groups called the "Budget, Requirements and Program" (BRP or "burp") are composed of: the G-3, G-8 and MILDEP ASA(FM&C); ADCS, G3, Dir PAE and Dir ABO; and the Chief DAMO-CIR, Chief Program Development Division, PAE and Deputy Director Management and Control, ABO. These groups meet on a regular basis, and handle planning, programming, budgeting or resourcing decisions and issues appropriate to their level. The BRP can call meetings of the larger groups as needed to share information or gain wider perspective.

HOW THE ARMY RUNS

9-37. PEGs
HQDA uses six PEGs to support PPBE (Figure 9-5). Each is co-chaired by a representative of the Secretariat and a representative of the PEG's proponent, who provides the PEG with executive and administrative support. Permanent members include representatives of ASA(FM&C) appropriation sponsors, G-3/5/7 program prioritizers and requirements staff officers, and G-8-PAE program integrators.

   a. PEGs program and monitor resources to perform Army functions assigned by 10 USC, Subtitle B - Army and to support the CCMDs and OSD-assigned executive agencies. Each PEG administers a set of MDEPs within one of the following functional groupings: Manning, Training, Organizing, Equipping, Sustaining, and Installations.

   b. Each PEG, subject to existing program and budget guidance, sets the scope, quantity, priority, and qualitative nature of resource requirements that define its program. They monitor PEG resource transactions and, as required, make both administrative and substantive changes to assigned MDEPs. MDEP proponents, subject matter experts, and, as appropriate, representatives of commands and agencies participate in PEG deliberations.

   b. The DARNG, CAR, and CIO/G-6 serve as Program Integrators to the PEGs. Program Integrators provide technical assistance and monitor actions to integrate priorities and statutory, Defense, and Army requirements for the ARNG, AR and IT programs into the Army's overall program.

   d. PEGs, assisted by the Program Integrators, help HQDA functional proponents-
   (1) Build TAP and the Army program and help convert the program into budget-level detail.
   (2) Maintain program consistency, first during planning and later when preparing, analyzing, and defending the integrated program-budget.
   (3) Track program and budget performance during execution.
   (4) Keep abreast of policy changes during each phase of the PPBE process.

Program Evaluation Groups (PEG)

PEG Name	Proponent	Co-Chair for Policy Determination	Co-Chair for Requirements Determination	Appropriation Sponsor*	Program Integrator
Organizing	AASA (Provisional)	ASA (M&RA)	DCS G-3/5/7	ASA (FM&C)	G8 PA&E, G-3/5/7
Manning	DCS G-1	ASA (M&RA)	DCS G-1	ASA (FM&C)	G8 PA&E, G-3/5/7
Training	DCS G-3/5/7	ASA (M&RA)	DCS G-3/5/7	ASA (FM&C)	G8 PA&E, G-3/5/7
Equipping	DCS G-8	ASA (ALT)	DCS G-8	ASA (FM&C)	G8 PA&E, G-3/5/7
Sustaining	DCS G-4	ASA (ALT)	DCS G-4	ASA (FM&C)	G8 PA&E, G-3/5/7
Installations	ACSIM	ASA (IE&E)	ACSIM	ASA (FM&C)	G8 PA&E, G-3/5/7

AASA: Administrative Assistant to the Secretary of the Army
ACSIM: Assistant Chief of Staff for Installation Management
ASA(ALT): Assistant Secretary of the Army (Acquisition, Technology, and Logistics)
ASA (IE&E): Assistant Secretary of the Army (Installations, Energy, & Environment)
ASA(M&RA): Assistant Secretary of the Army (Manpower and Reserve Affairs)
PA&E: Program, Analysis, & Evaluation

* Includes CNGB & CAR

Figure 9-9. Program Evaluation Groups (PEG)

ARMY PLANNING, PROGRAMMING, BUDGETING, AND EXECUTION PROCESS

Program Evaluation Groups (PEG)

Manning (MM)
- Co-chaired by the ASA(M&RA) and G1
- Provides the Active Army, ARNG and USAR with authorized personnel by grade and skill
- Integrates the personnel authorizations for the ARNG and USAR

Training (TT)
- Co-chaired by ASA(M&RA) and G3/5/7
- Provides resources for Active Army, ARNG and USAR unit readiness (to include medical units) and unit collective training (Ground OPTEMP and the Flying Hour Program, fixed wing aircraft operation and maintenance, Combat Training Centers (CTC), mobilization, theater security cooperation activities and military contingency operations
- Provides for collective training, institutional training (initial entry training, leader development, professional development, functional training), and officer acquisition (USMA, ROTC, OCS). Supports multinational force compatibility through integrated training, military exercises, and command control exchanges with allies and coalition partners.
- Deals with programs, systems, and activities to satisfy intelligence requirements of POTUS and SECDEF as well as those of the senior leadership. These are requirements funded in the Army portion of the NFIP under Program 31 and intelligence support to national agencies under Program 9 (Equipping PEG manages most requirements for Tactical Intelligence and Related Activities (TIARA) managed by G8-FD under Program 2, and 4 through 10, as well as acquisitions to meet other Intelligence and Electronic Warfare (IEW) requirements.

Organizing (OO)
- Co-chaired by ASA(M&RA) and Admin Asst to the SECARMY
- Provides minimum essential Generating Forces for peacetime sustainment and training, and wartime mobilization and power projection capabilities for Operating Forces
- Supports Special programs that meet needs of the Army

Equipping (EE)
- Co-chaired by ASA(ALT) and G8
- Provides resources for the integration of new doctrine, training, organization, and equipment for developing and fielding warfighting capabilities for the Active Army, ARNG and USAR. Focuses mainly on materiel acquisition which comprises RDT&E and procurement of weapons and equipment
- Considers operating and support costs to field weapons and equipment, as well as the cost of combat development

Sustaining (SS)
- Co-chaired by ASA(ALT) and G4
- Provides resources to sustain operations of the Active Army, ARNG and USAR, stressing worldwide readiness. Scope embraces strategic mobility, reserve stocks, industrial preparedness, central supply, and internal operations of depots' materiel maintenance.
- Includes measures to assure the quality and timeliness of strategic logistics systems, manage weapons systems, provide security assistance, conduct logistical long-range planning, and reshape logistics.
- Addresses measures to streamline business operations, improve information management structure, further the integration, sharing, standardization, and interoperability of information systems

Installations (II)
- Co-chaired by the ASA(IE&E) and ACISM
- Provides resources to support Active Army, ARNG and USAR installations—the operational and service support centers where Soldiers, families and civilians work, live, and train.
- Plans and programs installation funding for base support, military construction, family housing, base realignment and closure, and environment restoration programs. Base support is provided in two parts:
  ✓ Base Operations Support (BOS) consisting of Base Operations (BASOPS), anti-terrorism, force protection, family programs, environment, and audio visual base communications
  ✓ Sustainment, Restoration and Modernization (SRM) providing for maintenance, demolition, improvement or replacement of facilities and infrastructure
- Provides for minimal essential workforce in support of installation management and continuously seeks to leverage current strength by converting non-core military to civilian employees for contract, where appropriate

Figure 9-10. Program Evaluation Groups (PEG)

HOW THE ARMY RUNS

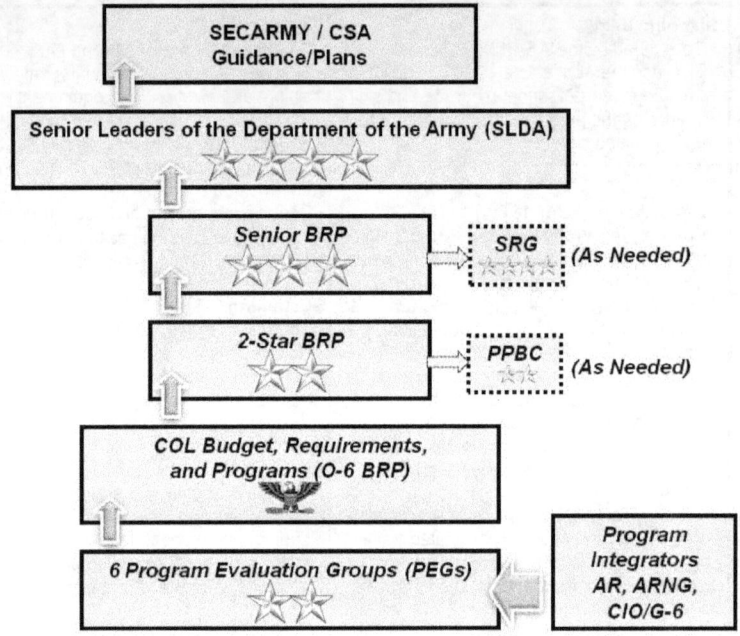

Figure 9-11. Army Review / Decision-Making Bodies

9-38. A Principal PPBE-Related Committee
Although not a PPBE forum, the ASARC helps integrate the development and acquisition of materiel into all PPBE phases. Chaired by the AAE, the ASARC serves as the Army's senior-level review body for Acquisition Category (ACAT) I and II programs. ACAT IC and ACAT IAC programs are Major Defense Acquisition Programs for which the AAE exercises Milestone Decision Authority (MDA). An ACAT II program is one that fails to qualify as an ACAT I program, but nevertheless meets the criteria for a major system.

Section VIII
Army Planning, Programming, Budgeting, and Execution Planning

9-39. Army Long Range Force Planning
In response to National, Defense and Joint strategy documents the Army Concept Strategy (ACS) documents lay out future Army War fighting concepts that will allow the Army to transform to meet the challenges of our changing national security environment. This family of concepts forms the analytical basis for determining the solutions for capability gaps that will, when approved through the Army Capability Integration and Development System, form the basis for resource allocation decisions. The ACS considers a period extending several decades.

9-40. The Army Plan (TAP)
a. Army planning responds to and complements OSD planning and joint strategic planning. In particular, Army planning:

ARMY PLANNING, PROGRAMMING, BUDGETING, AND EXECUTION PROCESS

   (1) Helps the senior Army leadership determine force requirements and objectives and set priorities.
   (2) Provides the basis for positions and comments supporting Army participation in OSD and joint processes.
   (3) Lays the planning basis for the Army program.
   b. The foundation of Army planning lies in The Army Plan (TAP), which provides strategic planning, priorities, programming, and execution guidance in four sequentially developed and substantively integrated sections:
   (1) The Army Strategic Planning Guidance (ASPG), which forms section I of the TAP-
   (a) Nests Army planning in National, OSD, and Joint strategic guidance.
   (b) Gives rationale for transforming The Army per the Army Vision.
   (c) Provides senior leader guidance.
   (d) Identifies joint demand for Army capabilities.
   (2) Army Planning Priorities Guidance (APPG), which is section II of TAP, links requirements to strategy and guides development of resource priorities for operational tasks.
   (3) The Army Program Guidance Memorandum (APGM), which exists as section III of TAP, relates operational tasks to resource tasks, thereby helping link operational tasks and their associated resources to Army Title 10 functions.
   (4) The Army Campaign Plan is Section IV of TAP. The nine campaign objectives of the ACP are as follows: support global operations; transform from the current to future force; optimize RC contribution; sustain the right all-volunteer force; adjust the global footprint; shape the future force; adapt the institutional Army; and develop a joint, interdependent logistics structure. These objectives incorporate Army transformation into the context of ongoing strategic commitments.

9-41. Army Strategic Planning Guidance (ASPG)
The G-3/5/7 Strategic Plans and Policy Directorate prepare the ASPG (TAP Section I). The ASPG is the Army's institutional strategy. It provides strategic guidance to translate requirements "to serve the Nation"-principally in terms of trained and ready forces capable of decisive action across the range of military operations and spectrum of conflict-into fielded capabilities. The AS provides a long-term general perspective (10-20 years) for planners through a common understanding of the Army's contribution to national security and the Joint Team. It also articulates the key Army concerns that must be addressed during the next POM period.

9-42. Army Planning Priorities Guidance (APPG)
The G-3/5/7 Resource Analysis and Integration Office prepares the APPG (TAP Section II). The APPG covers the mid-term period of the next 5-year POM plus 5-7 additional years. Adding substantial detail to Army Strategic Planning Guidance, the APPG identifies and prioritizes enduring operational capabilities needed now and in the future to maintain The Army's core competencies cited in Army Doctrine Publication 1. The APPG provides risk guidance as it relates to Army capabilities in accordance with the QDR Risk Framework.

9-43. Army Program Guidance Memorandum (APGM)
The G-8 Program Analysis and Evaluation Directorate prepares the APGM (TAP Section III), which links operational capabilities and programming. Providing direction to PEGs, the APGM conveys Army senior leader intent as well as broad, general guidance concerning acceptable levels of risk for the initial POM/BES build. Applying readiness and war fighting requirements derived from strategic and operational capabilities in TAP sections I and II to program development, it completes the succession of guidance from strategic planning to mid-term planning to programming. Guided by planning priorities, the APGM translates operational tasks known as core competencies to resource tasks to perform Army Title 10 functions. It then prescribes other, non-operational task requirements to assure carrying out the three interdependent components of the Army Vision-People, Current Readiness, and Future Forces. Through MDEPs, the APGM relates resource tasks to the Army's Title 10 functions, grouped under the PEG structure as Manning, Training, Organizing, Equipping, Sustaining, and Installations. A forwarding memorandum from the SECARMY and CSA provides HQDA agencies additional guidance.

HOW THE ARMY RUNS

9-44. Army Campaign Plan (ACP)
The G-3/5/7 Army Campaign Plan and Transformation Office prepares and maintains the ACP (TAP Section IV). The ACAP is an order that implements the ASPG, is informed by the CSA Vision and is integrated with the Army Imperatives. It provides campaign and other major objectives and integrates other major efforts of the department for Army force generation. It is as much a process as a product as there is an established battle rhythm that provides continuous monitoring of progress towards its goals.

9-45. Required Capability Determination
 a. The Army Concept Strategy (ACS) is the process that identifies needed future capabilities and potential solutions across the DOTMLPF domains. The process is designed to maintain consistency with both Defense and Joint capabilities guidance.

 b. The Army retains approval authority for validating military required capabilities at the level of the Chief of Staff, Army. Centralizing validation focuses efforts to develop clear value-added capabilities matched to both Joint and Army future goals. Toward this end, HQDA applies rigorous analysis of the contribution made by a required capability to overall operational objectives of the future Army force as well as to its joint interoperability and affordability.

  (1) HQDA procedure employs an Army Requirements Oversight Council (AROC) chaired by the VCSA. The AROC validates DOTMLPF requirements and recommends them for approval to the CSA through the Army Requirements Review Council (RRC). In discharging its function, the AROC aligns Army requirements closely to the Joint Capabilities Integration Development System and reviews Army and Joint requirements for validation within the Joint process.

  (2) HQDA uses G-3/5/7's Directorate of Requirements (DAMO-CI) as the Army's single point of entry for military requirements, whether emergency or routine. With representatives from selected commands and across the HQDA staff, the directorate shepherds each requirement through the validation and approval process. A major objective is to ensure that the Army program remains requirements based.

   (a) In furtherance of that aim, the directorate coordinates closely with the PEGs. Beginning in October and November, in the early stages of program development, requirements staff officer's work with PEGs to make sure that funded programs have a clearly definable and documented link to military requirements or leadership designated capabilities. Together, PEGs and their requirements staff representatives attempt to strengthen linkages of programs meeting this criterion and to terminate those failing to do so. From January, when formal preparation of the program gets under way through April, these efforts continue during deliberations to approve the individual MDEPs that make up each PEG program. Once again, the aim is to make sure the unfolding PEG program links to validated military requirements and leadership-designated capabilities.

   (b) If unresolved at the PEG level, a program earmarked for termination is forwarded through the ADCS G-3/5/7 to the PPBC for decision.

 c. More detailed information on this process can be found in Chapters 5 and 11 of this text.

9-46. Army Modernization Plan
 a. G-8 prepares the Army Modernization Plan (AMP). The AMP outlines the vision for modernizing the future force and a strategy for near- to mid-term force development and long-term evolution. Its modernization objectives reflect the vision and guidance of the senior Army leadership.

 b. The AMP describes required capabilities resourced through the PPBE process. It describes the relationship between desired future capabilities and the materiel solution.

 c. The AMP, the Army Science and Technology Master Plan (ASTMP), and the Weapons System Handbook present the total picture of the Army's RDA investment. The AMP also supports the review of the PB by congressional authorization and appropriation committees and their staffs.

9-47. Army Research, Development, and Acquisition Plan
The G-8 with the Assistant Secretary of the Army (Acquisition, Logistics, and Technology) (ASA (ALT)) prepares the Army Research, Development, and Acquisition (RDA) Plan. The RDA Plan analyses requirements for battlefield and infrastructure capabilities and ranks the requirements in priority order. It matches the requirements to materiel solutions, that is, to RDT&E and procurement programs. Developed by HQDA and the Training and Doctrine Command (TRADOC) and guided by the National

ARMY PLANNING, PROGRAMMING, BUDGETING, AND EXECUTION PROCESS

Military Strategy (NMS) and the materiel solutions provide an integrated RDA position. What follows describes the plan in greater detail.

   a. The RDA Plan is a 15-year plan for developing and producing technologies and materiel to advance Army modernization. Imposing mandatory TOA controls, the plan restricts modernization to those efforts that are both technically and fiscally achievable. The process truncates requirements developed through unconstrained planning into an RDA program that, within limited resources, maximizes war fighting capabilities and supporting infrastructure. See Chapter 11 for a more detailed discussion of the RDA plan.

   b. Represented by the G-8 RDA database, the plan presents the RDA program as a required set of MDEPs arrayed in 1-n order by G-8 and ASA(ALT). Each MDEP describes a program, function, or organization and the dollars and system quantities needed. It not only covers the 5-year FYDP but also the 9-year Extended Planning Period (EPP).

   c. A continuous process, the RDA Plan focuses on periodic revisions to the RDA database. Revisions typically occur during preparation of the Calendar year combined POM/BES (February to August) and the PB (September to January). During these periods, HQDA adjusts the FYDP years, or first 5 years of the RDA Plan. Then, the Army's RDA community adjusts the final 9 years making sure progression from POM/BES to the PB and Extended Planning Period (EPP) is not only affordable, but also executable.

   d. Each December, TRADOC provides HQDA its recommendations on materiel requirements, arriving at the recommendations through a Capability Needs Analysis (CNA). The process takes into account such guidance as the NMS and the TAP, the AMS, and IPLs of the CCDRs. The CNA compares future capabilities required by the total force against the fiscally constrained budgeted force. The comparison determines force modernization needs that TRADOC rank orders according to their contribution to mission accomplishment.

9-48. Force Development and Total Army Analysis
Force Development and its component Total Army Analysis are the systems and processes used by the Army to define military capabilities, design force structures to provide these capabilities, translate organizational concepts based on doctrine, technologies, materiel, manpower requirements, and limited resources into a trained and ready Army. These topics are addressed in detail in Chapter 5 of this text.

Section IX
Operational Planning Link to the Department of Defense Planning, Programming, Budgeting, and Execution

9-49. Operational Planning
Operational planning is addressed in detail in Chapter 6 of this text.

9-50. Missions and Tasks
The Joint Strategic Capabilities Plan (JSCP) carries out the NMS through Unified Command Operation Plans (OPLAN). Its accompanying intelligence estimate assesses potential threats and their impact on available U.S. Forces. Based on the assessment, the document assigns missions and planning tasks to CCDRs. It also apportions the combat forces expected to be available. Annexes amplify guidance, capabilities, and tasks in specified functional areas.

Section X
Integrated Programming-Budgeting Phase

9-51. Army Programming and Budgeting
An integrated decision process, Army programming-budgeting produces a combined POM and Budget Estimate Submission (POM/BES). In conjunction with OSD review, Army integrated programming and budgeting supports development of the PB. Once the PB goes to Congress, the Army presents and defends its portion of the budget in congressional hearings.

HOW THE ARMY RUNS

9-52. Guidance

a. The primary product of the OSD planning phase is, the Defense Planning Guidance (DPG) which provides key strategy, policy and limited programmatic guidance to the services and defense agencies.

b. APGM. The APGM provides direction to PEGs to prepare them for the POM/BES build. It outlines strategic guidance and issues programming guidelines. In addition, it defines resource tasks for PEG goals, relating each task to one or more MDEPs.

c. Technical Guidance Memorandum. G-8's Director of Program Analysis and Evaluation (DPAE) complement the APGM with a Technical Guidance Memorandum (TGM) outlining program intent with respect to allocating resources to attain the Army Vision. The TGM also provides coordinating instructions to guide PEGs during the POM/BES build. Additional, PEG-by-PEG, guidance lays out programming priorities for specific programs set by the SecArmy and CSA and, for some programs, specifies a particular level of funding.

d. Fiscal Guidance. Before completion of the POM/BES build, OSD issues Fiscal Guidance establishing the Army's TOA over the program years. DPAE then apportions the TOA to the PEGs for building their portion of the program. The guidance includes inflation factors and other administrative instructions.

e. Program and Budget Guidance. DPAE issues Program and Budget Guidance (PBG) typically twice each year, after forwarding the combined POM/BES to OSD for review and after the PB is forwarded to Congress. An enterprise product, the PBG is produced jointly by ASA(FM&C)'s Budget Formulation Division (SAFM-BUC-F) and the G-8's Program Budget Data Management Division (DAPR-DPI) in coordination with G-3/5/7's Force Accounting and Documentation Division (DAMO-FMP). The PBG provides resource guidance to major Army Commands (ACOM), Program Executive Offices (PEO), and other operating agencies. Narrative Guidance instructs commands and agencies, in addressing resource requirements, such as those related to flying hours, ground operating tempo (OPTEMPO), and rates for fuel, inflation, and foreign currency. A related automation file reflects the resource status of each command and agency. Commands and agencies use their PBG resource information to update their databases for the forthcoming PPBE cycle.

f. Integrated Program-Budget Data Call. HQDA publishes a multivolume Resource Formulation Guide (RFG) to facilitate the PPBE process. Issued in the fall, RFG volume 3 (Integrated Program-Budget Data Call) describes the data ACOMs, PEOs, and other operating agencies must submit to HQDA to prepare the POM and BES. Commands and agencies may propose changes to their resources over the program years. Volume 3, however, requires that changes remain zero-sum within the command or agency.

g. Programming Data Requirements. Before each POM submission, OSD updates a web-based manual entitled Programming Data Requirements (PDR). The PDR provides instructions for preparing and submitting data, requirements, and program justifications to support component POMs. Prescribing formats and exhibits, its instructions describe programming data requirements and some budgeting data, which components submit using OSD's Select and Native Programming (SNaP) Data Collection System.

h. POM Preparation Guidance. As required, HQDA issues RFG volume 4 augmenting OSD PDR with additional guidance for preparing the POM.

i. BES Preparation Guidance. Two OSD budget guidance documents affect content of the BES. Volume 2 of the DOD Financial Management Regulation prescribes various exhibits and displays to be used in presenting the budget. The Annual Budget Call Memorandum provides supplemental information such as current rate and pricing guidance. Complementing these documents, ASA(FM&C) also issues administrative instructions for preparing the Army's BES.

9-53. Army Resource Framework

The Army Resource Framework (Figure 9-12) is designed to organize the Army's resources in a consistent manner to facilitate resource decision making in all PPBE cycles. The major categories—People, Readiness, Materiel, and Service & Infrastructure—align with the emerging Army Enterprise Management structure.

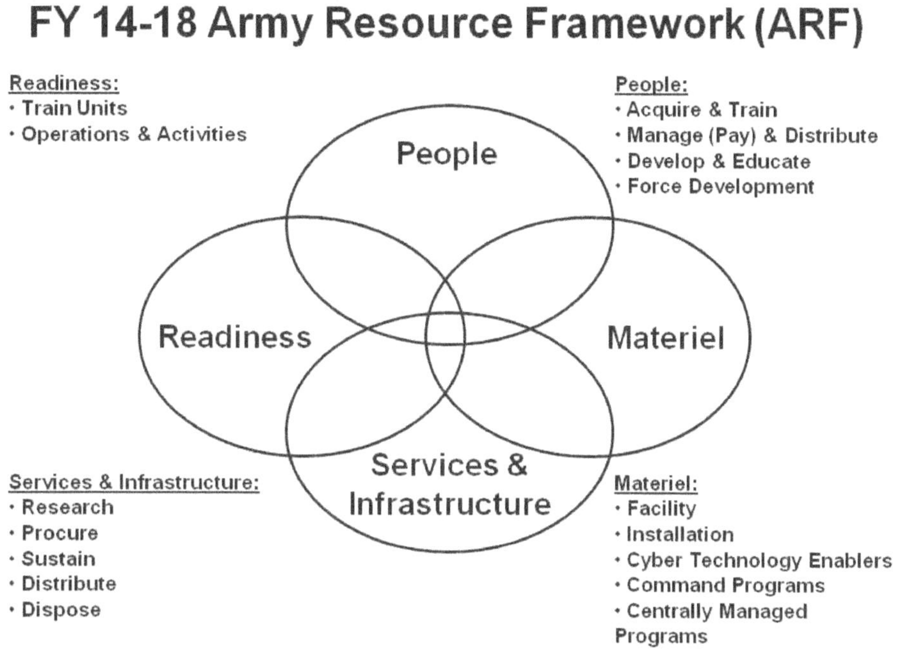

ARMY PLANNING, PROGRAMMING, BUDGETING, AND EXECUTION PROCESS

FY 14-18 Army Resource Framework (ARF)

Readiness:
- Train Units
- Operations & Activities

People:
- Acquire & Train
- Manage (Pay) & Distribute
- Develop & Educate
- Force Development

Services & Infrastructure:
- Research
- Procure
- Sustain
- Distribute
- Dispose

Materiel:
- Facility
- Installation
- Cyber Technology Enablers
- Command Programs
- Centrally Managed Programs

Figure 9-12. Fiscal Year (FY) 14-18 Army Resource Framework (ARF)

9-54. POM Preparation

a. Start Up. The annual integrated programming-budgeting phase of the process starts in October as OSD reviews the recently forwarded change proposals. In developing the Army program, programmers translate planning decisions, OSD programming guidance, and congressional guidance into a comprehensive allocation of forces, manpower, and funds. In doing this they integrate and balance centrally managed programs for manpower; operations; research, development, and acquisition; and stationing and construction. Concurrently, they incorporate requirements presented by ACOMs, PEOs, and other operating agencies for manpower, operation and maintenance, housing, and construction.

b. Initial Programmatic Review. From October through December, HQDA-
(1) Reviews the existing program to determine program deficiencies.
(2) Sorts existing MDEPs by PEGs.
(3) Establishes force structure and civilian manpower authorizations.
(4) Responds to changes recorded in and IPs generated by the OSD program and budget review (para 9-64, below).

c. Preparing the Database.
(1) Formal preparation of the POM/BES starts once the PB goes to Congress. This usually occurs after the first Monday in January but not later than the first Monday in February. As a start point, DPAE establishes a base file in the PPBE database that reflects the PB resource position. Afterwards, in a series of zero-sum adjustments that leave resource levels in the PB unchanged for the budget years, HQDA revises the database. The adjustments:
(a) Update earlier estimates with new information and revise them for inflation.
(b) Move resources between and among current Army Management Structure Codes (AMSCO) and MDEP structures.
(c) Consolidate or otherwise restructure individual programs through rolls and splits to make the overall Army program more manageable.

HOW THE ARMY RUNS

(d) Re-price existing programs as needed and, when required by modified resource levels, identify offsetting deductions as bill payers.

(2) Figure 9-16 shows timelines for updating the PPBE database and other significant events for the FY 2015-2019 POM/BES build.

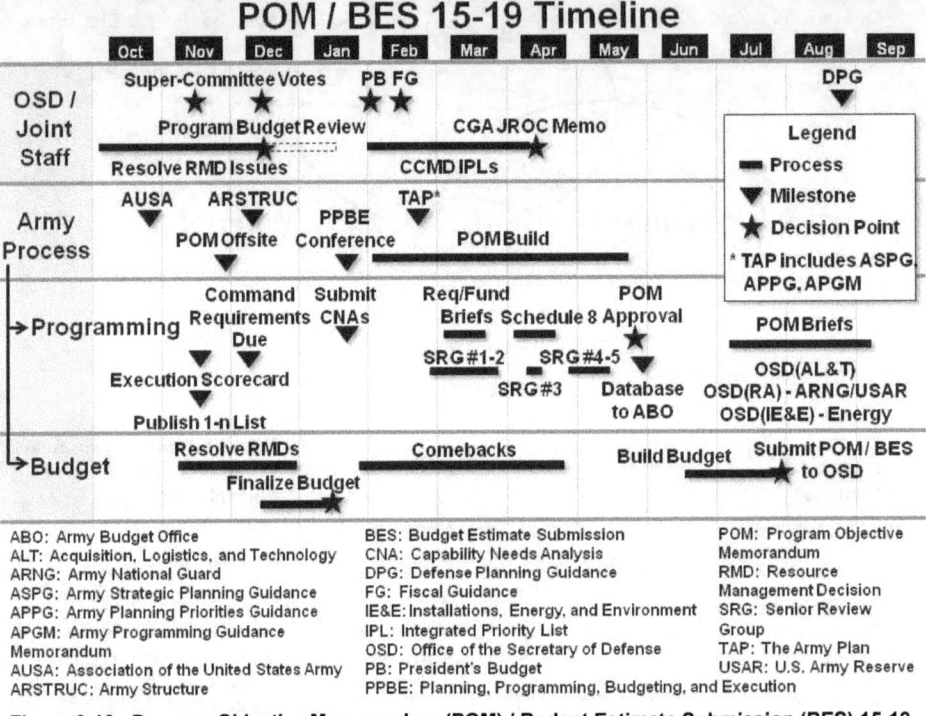

Figure 9-13. Program Objective Memorandum (POM) / Budget Estimate Submission (BES) 15-19 Timeline

d. Command participation. ACOMs participate in the PPBE process as do PEOs, which report through the Army Acquisition Support Center (ASC). These and other operating agencies make mission and operating requirements known through Commander's Narratives, Command-Requested Changes, and additional data submissions prescribed by RFG volume 3. ACOM commanders serving as commanders of ASCCs integrate operational requirements of the CCMD into their program and budget input. In addition, CCDRs highlight their pressing requirements in an IPL that receives close review during program development by HQDA, the Joint Staff, and OSD.

e. Use of PEGs.

(1) As mentioned, HQDA packages program requirements into MDEPs, each associated with one of six resource management areas (para 9-37, above). HQDA then assigns each MDEP to a PEG to help build and track the Army POM that forms the Army portion of the DOD FYDP.

(2) PEG POM-building activity begins in the fall and peaks March through May of the following year. Figure 9-10, outlines PEG areas of interest.

(3) PEGs administer assigned MDEPs. They set the scope, quantity, priority, and qualitative nature of resource requirements that define each PEG program. They monitor PEG resource transactions, making both administrative and substantive changes to their MDEPs as required. In the process, PEGs review assigned MDEPs in terms of TOA guidance. They review command and agency requested requirements

ARMY PLANNING, PROGRAMMING, BUDGETING, AND EXECUTION PROCESS

submitted via Schedule 1s and their POM. At the same time, PEGs review IPLs of the CCMDs as well as resource needs expressed by the supporting ASCC. PEGs relate these command operating requirements to HQDA guidance as well as to existing MDEPs and new initiatives.

(4) Meanwhile, serving as Program Integrators, the DARNG, CAR, and CIO/G-6 provide technical assistance to the PEGs and monitor actions to integrate priorities and statutory, Defense, and Army requirements for their respective programs.

(5) Based on review of military requirements related to their Title 10 area of responsibility, each PEG builds an executable program characterized by affordability, continuity, and balance. In the process, the PEG:

(a) Validates requested changes submitted by ACOMs, PEOs, and other operating agencies.

(b) Reconciles conflicts involving unfunded requirements or decrements on which commands fail to reach agreement.

(c) Recommends the allocation of available resources and offsetting decrements to support approved unfunded programs.

(d) Rank orders validated programs as PEG input to G-3/5/7's overall POM 1-n prioritized program list.

(e) Evaluates HQDA, command, and other agency zero-sum realignments that reallocate programmed resources to meet existing shortfalls and changed requirements.

(f) Coordinates resource changes with appropriate Service, DOD, and non-DOD agencies when required.

(g) Makes sure that proposed reallocations conform to legal restraints and Army policy and priorities, avoid imprudently high risk, and maintain the ability to execute mandatory programs and subprograms.

(h) Prices programmatic decisions that the Army can defend during review by OSD, OMB, and the Congress.

f. Internal Program Review. The Planning Program Budget Committee (PPBC) meets periodically throughout the POM/BES build to review and adjust the developing program, devising courses of action and recommendations on relevant issues as appropriate. Bearing on the PPBC review is the Army Commanders' Conference scheduled in February, which gives field commanders the chance to express their views on the prospective program. The Senior Review Group (SRG), in turn, convenes early in the process to approve guidance and, at key stages, to ratify PPBC decisions. The Senior Leaders of the Department of the Army (SLDA) Army Resources Board (ARB) convenes in one or more sessions in July to review and approve the completed ear program and associated budget estimate submission and the year developed program change proposals and budget change proposals.

g. POM. The annual POM, which documents the program decision of the SECARMY and CSA, presents the Army's proposal for a balanced and integrated allocation of its resources within specified OSD fiscal and manpower constraints. POM subject matter remains relatively constant from cycle to cycle, but varies as required to address special issues. Topics of the FY 2014-2018 POM appear in table 9-7.

Table 9-6. Topics Covered in Program Objective Memorandum / Budget Estimate Submission (POM / BES) 14-18

Introduction
Forces
Investment
Operations and Support
Infrastructure—Environmental
Infrastructure—Defense Agencies
Manpower and Personnel
Defense Working Capital Fund
CCDRs Integrated Priorities List (IPL)

9-55. Program and Budget Correlation

a. The POM defines what the Army intends to do over the 5-year program period. It uses the MDEP to package required resources by mission, function, and other program objectives. Throughout program development, however, both programmers and budgeters make sure that programmatic decisions receive proper costing and that Army resource decisions can be defended during budget reviews conducted by

HOW THE ARMY RUNS

OSD, OMB, and Congress. Working closely together, programmers and budgeters help the senior Army leadership consider all relevant information before the leaders make resource allocation decisions. The approach precludes the need, later in the integrated process, to revisit most issues. Moreover, it presents a near seamless transition from program to budget.

b. Figure 9-14 shows the complementary way that programmers and budgeters view resource requirements. The display shows from left to right the manpower and dollars needed to carry out missions and functions. From top to bottom, the display shows how these requirements are distributed among Army programs to form appropriation requests to Congress.

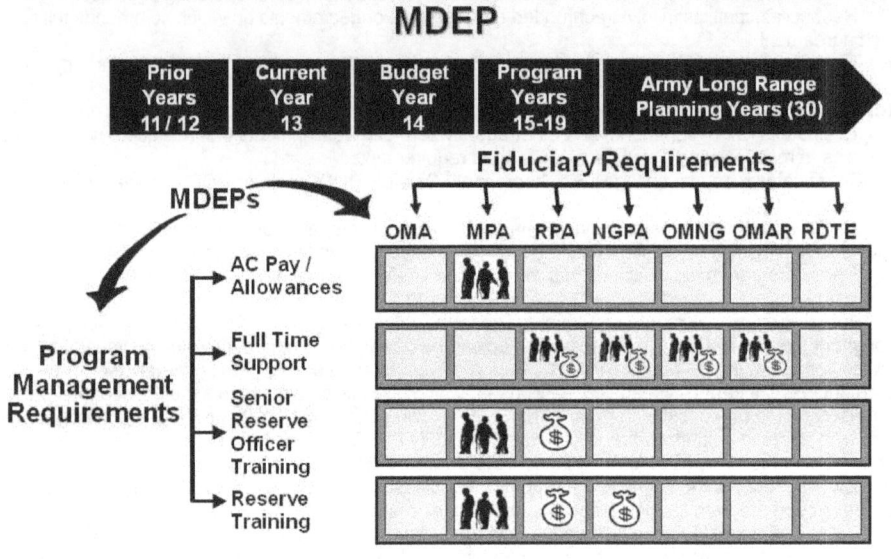

AC: Active Component
APE: Army Program Element
MDEP: Management Decision Package
MPA: Military Personnel Appropriations
NGPA: National Guard Pay Appropriations
OMA: Operations and Maintenance Appropriations
OMAR: Operations and Maintenance—U.S. Army Reserve
OMNG: Operations and Maintenance—National Guard
RDTE: Research, Development, Test, and Evaluation
RPA: Reserve Pay Appropriations

Figure 9-14. Management Decision Packages (MDEP)

9-56. BES Preparation

a. As mentioned, HQDA prepares the BES concurrently with the POM, submitting the combined POM/BES to OSD in August every year. The BES covers the first year of the program approved by the SECARMY and CSA.

b. In fact, however, one or more events may cause HQDA to re-address certain POM/BES decisions. For example, during program-budget preparation, Congress reviews the budget for the upcoming fiscal year. The review requires that the Army track resultant congressional actions and make appropriate adjustments in the BES. Also, after completing the POM, changes occur in rates and prices available during POM build. The later information often requires altering such rates and prices as those for the Army Working Capital Fund, pay, fuel, or inflation.

9-57. OSD Program and Budget Review

ARMY PLANNING, PROGRAMMING, BUDGETING, AND EXECUTION PROCESS

OSD begins review of the combined POM/BES soon after their submission in August. The program and budget review continues until late December. The review concludes when the Administration makes final Presidential Budget decisions. Figure 9-15 highlights events during review of POM/BES FY 14-18.

 a. Issues center on compliance with the Defense Planning Guidance, the overall balance of Service programs, and late-breaking significant issues.

 b. As issues arise, representatives of HQDA principal officials meet with their OSD counterparts. The Army representatives present the Army position and try to clarify the issue. If possible, the issue is resolved at this level.

 c. By late November, after review officials have debated and decided program issues, the DEPSECDEF issues one or more Resource Management Decisions (RMDs) directing specific changes to program positions of the submitted POM. Before completing the budget, if it is needed, the DEPSECDEF publishes a Summary RMD along with a memorandum describing the disposition of programmatic issues.

 d. Budget issues during the review are decided through draft IPs. Focusing on proper pricing, reasonableness, and program execution, An issue paper may be based on errors or on strength of justification. It may result from analytical disagreement or, it may be motivated by cost savings or changes in policy. After reviewing the issue paper responses the SECDEF issues RMDs which are final decisions directed by the SECDEF telling the services to change their program requests to align them with the SECDEF's decisions.

 e. After the DEPSECDEF or USD (Comptroller) has signed the RMDs, each Service selects as Major Budget Issues (MBI) certain adverse resource decisions. Army MBIs center on decrements to specific initiatives or broad issues that would significantly impair its ability to achieve its program intentions. An MBI addresses the adverse impact that would occur if the decrement were to prevail. At the end of the process, the Sec Army and CSA meet with the SECDEF and DEPSECDEF on Major Budget Issues. After the meeting, the SECDEF decides each issue, if necessary meeting with the Office of Management and Budget (OMB) or the President to request additional funds or recommend other action.

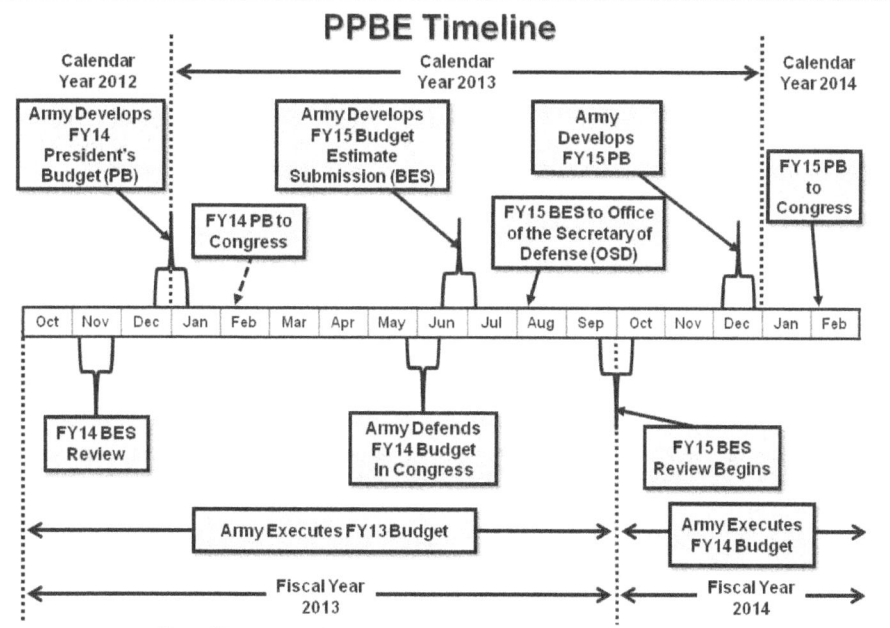

Note: Timeline and Other OSD Guidance Subject to Change Every Year

Figure 9-15. Planning, Programming, Budgeting, and Execution (PPBE) Timeline

9-58. PB

a. In December, OSD normally issues a final RMD or OSD memorandum incorporating any changes from deliberations on MBIs, thus completing the program and budget review process.

b. After implementing the final resource distribution at the BA and object class level, Army sends the information to OSD. OSD forwards the information as the Army's portion of the Defense budget to OMB and OMB incorporates the Defense budget into the PB. The PB covers prior year obligations and updated resource estimates for the current year. During the annual POM/BES cycle, the PB covers TOA estimates for the budget year.

9-59. Justification

a. Congressional Budget Hearings.

(1) During budget justification, the Army presents and defends its portion of the PB before Congress. The process proceeds formally and informally under the staff supervision of the Chief of Legislative Liaison and ASA(FM&C).

(2) After the President formally submits the budget, the Army provides detailed budget justification to the authorization and appropriations committees. First, however, appropriation sponsors will have prepared material in Army justification books to conform to decisions of the President and SECDEF and congressional requirements for formats and supporting information. Justification books undergo internal Army review by ASA(FM&C) and are then sent to OSD for final review.

(3) The Senate Armed Services Committee (SASC) and House Armed Services Committee (HASC) conduct authorization hearings for the various programs and appropriations. Concurrently, the Army's budget request goes before the House and Senate Appropriations Committees. In these hearings, the SECARMY and CSA normally testify first. Then with assistance from ASA (FM&C)'s Budget Liaison Office and the Office, Chief of Legislative Liaison, appropriation sponsors and functional proponents present and defend the details of the budget.

b. Legislative approval and enactment.

(1) When congressional committees complete their review, the Senate and House vote on the committee bills. Differences between the Senate and House versions are resolved via a joint conference.

(2) Budget justification ends when the President signs the authorization and appropriation bills for the coming fiscal year. Enacted into law, Army appropriations provide the legal authority to incur obligations and make payments.

c. Continuing Resolution Authority. When Congress fails to pass an appropriation by the end of September, it may pass a continuing resolution. Continuing Resolution Authority (CRA) derives from emergency legislation that authorizes the funding of Government operations in the absence of appropriations. A temporary measure, the CRA usually restricts funding to the prior year level and prohibits new initiatives. HQDA separately publishes specific policy on how the Army will operate under the CRA. Failure to pass either an appropriation or CRA could result in a temporary shutdown of government operations. Normally, however, until an appropriation or CRA is enacted, DOD would continue minimum essential operations based on national defense requirements.

Section XI
Army Budget Execution Phase

9-60. Management and Accounting

During execution, the Army manages and accounts for funds and manpower to carry out approved programs. Army checks how well HQDA, ACOMs, PEOs, and other operating agencies use allocated resources to carry out program objectives. Through the Army Joint Reconciliation Program, Army strengthens financial accounting and management to make sure financial reports accurately reflect the results of budget execution. The Army (and of even greater importance) OSD, OMB, and Congress apply execution feedback to adjust resource requirements during deliberation on the Army's budget.

ARMY PLANNING, PROGRAMMING, BUDGETING, AND EXECUTION PROCESS

9-61. Financial Management

The budget execution process applies funds appropriated by Congress to carry out authorized programs. This process first entails apportioning, allocating, and allotting funds. It then entails obligating and disbursing the funds and then reporting and reviewing the effectiveness of executing them. The procedure also involves performing in-progress evaluations and making necessary course corrections to reallocate resources to meet changing requirements that develop during execution. Known as reprogramming, making course corrections involves financing unbudgeted requirements that result from changed conditions unforeseen when submitting the budget and having higher priority than the requirements from which funds are diverted.

  a. Funds Control.

  (1) The Enterprise Funds Distribution system has standardized funding authorization documents (i. e. Obligation Authority (OA) letters, DD440 documents, DD460 documents and Annual Operating budget for Working Capital Funds appropriated funding. At the ODS level there is a system called the Enterprise Funds Distribution (EFD) which is a web-based system which combines Congressional tracking with funds distribution to the Army and contains specific instructions on funds control. The three ERP systems–GFEBS, the Logistics Modernization Program, and the Global Combat Support System-Army– provide the Army an integrated enterprise-wide system to provide decision-makers with data for better informed decision making and to comply with legal and mandatory reporting requirements. As "mixed systems," these three systems perform financial management functions to better support their primary missions and system functions.

  (2) The Army has developed a new system called General Fund Enterprise Business System (GFEBS) to distribute funds to the various commands. GFEBS capabilities will provide functionality in six core financial areas: general ledger management, payment management, receiving management, funds management, cost management, and reporting. GFEBS is a new way of doing business and tracking the execution of funds. The General Fund Enterprise Business System (GFEBS) is a Chief Financial Officers Council certified commercial off the shelf (COTS) Enterprise Resource Planning (ERP) system that will provide the Army and the DOD relevant, reliable, and timely financial information across the full spectrum of its operations. GFEBS is helping the Army standardize and streamline its financial business processes to provide continuous access to financial information, as well as contribute an important element in the development of an Army integrated enterprise-wide system.

  (3) GFEBS replaces existing information systems, to include: the Standard Army Finance System; the Defense Joint Accounting System; and the Standard Operation and Maintenance Army Research and Development System. GFEBS is a web-based system designed to integrate seamlessly into the Army's current IT environment. The project also includes significant business process reengineering, change management, and business case analysis support components.

  (4) GFEBS processes financial, real property, cost management, and performance data, and then integrates this data for decision support. GFEBS' primary objectives include improving performance; standardizing financial and business processes; ensuring capabilities exist to meet future needs; and complying with statutory and regulatory accounting requirements. Specifically, GFEBS' goals are as follows: provide decision support information to sustain Army capabilities; provide analytic data and tools to support institutional adaptation; reduce the cost of business operations; and improve accountability and stewardship.

  (5) Several events must occur before the Army can execute its programs for a new fiscal year under a new appropriations act:

  (a) OMB must apportion the appropriations, which provides obligation/budget authority. An apportionment distributes funds by making specific amounts available for obligation.

  (b) The Department of the Treasury must issue a Treasury Warrant providing cash.

  (c) The USD (Comptroller) must release program authority.

  b. Apportionment.

  (1) An apportionment requires a specific request. Using SF 132, Apportionment and Reapportionment Schedule, the ASA(FM&C) Funds Control Officer (SAFM-BUC-E) prepares the request within 5 days of the availability of an appropriations act or in response to approved reprogramming requests, supplementals, or rescissions. OSD approves or revises the apportionment requests and submits them to the Office of Management and Budget (OMB) for approval. OMB approves, changes, or disapproves the requests and returns apportionments through OSD to the Army for entry into PBAS. OMB apportions the following:

HOW THE ARMY RUNS

  (a) Operating Accounts-Operation & Maintenance (O&M), Military Personnel (MILPERS), and Army Family Housing, Operations (AFHO)-on a fiscal quarterly basis
  (b) Investment accounts-RDT&E, Procurement, Military Construction (MILCON), and Army Family Housing (Construction) (AFHC))-at the start of the fiscal year rather than on an incremental basis, funding the entire amount of the appropriation.
  (2) The apportionment determines the Budget Authority (BA) available in PBAS. For the operating accounts-even after releasing the entire program to the command-it is the cumulative amount of BA issued to commands and agencies by quarter that determines the execution level for the appropriation.
 c. Program Release.
  (1) For investment accounts, the Army releases program and budget authority in equal amounts. Actual expenditure, however, depends on OSD program controls wherein the USD (Comptroller) gives the Army specific program releases that further control expenditures.
   (a) For the RDT&E appropriation, the program is released at the PE level (SD Form 440, Research, Development, Test and Evaluation Program/Fund Authorization). These are the same levels as those authorized and appropriated by Congress and reported in the DD Form 1414, Base for Reprogramming Actions and DD Form 1416, Report of Programs, which are provided to Congress to show execution changes to appropriated amounts.
   (b) For the procurement appropriations (Aircraft, Missiles, Weapons & Tracked Combat Vehicles, Ammunition, and Other Procurement), the program is released at the budget line item (BLIN) level (SD Form 440).
   (c) Both the MILCON and the AFHC appropriations are released at the project level (OSD Format 460 for Military and Family Housing Construction accounts) as contained in the conference report accompanying the Military Construction Appropriations Act.
Program releases for the operating accounts (Operation and Maintenance (O&M) and Military Personnel (MILPERS) are contained in the obligation authority (OA) letter issued by the USD (Comptroller). OSD issues a separate OA letter for Army Family Housing (Operations) (AFHO).
 d. Allocation, Obligation, and Reconciliations. Guided by HQDA appropriation sponsors and using the PBAS, ASA (FM&C) allocates apportioned funds to commands and agencies. Then:
  (1) ACOMs and other operating agencies, in turn, make funds available to subordinate commands and installations by an allotment. Allotments authorize users to place orders and award contracts for products and services to carry out approved programs.
  (2) Installations obligate funds as orders are placed and contracts awarded. They authorize payments as materiel is delivered or as services are performed.
  (3) Installations, commands, and appropriation sponsors conduct joint reconciliations (see Para. 9-78, below). Reconciliations make sure financial statements and reports accurately represent the results of the apportionment, allocation, and allotment program. Reconciliations also make sure payments align properly with supporting obligations. The Deputy Assistant Secretary of the Army (Financial Operations) (SAFM-FO) manages the Army's Joint Reconciliation Program.
 e. Changes from the PB. After appropriations are enacted, appropriation sponsors and the Army Budget Office review the legislation to determine changes to the submitted budget. Changes include congressional adds, denial of programs, and changes to submitted funding levels. Changes also include identification of congressional special interest items, undistributed reductions, and any language relating to execution of the programs. Army applies such changes to amounts loaded into the PBAS. Appropriation sponsors must determine how to spread any undistributed reductions. In addition, they may also have to spread some unapplied reductions in the appropriations act, which are distributed to the Services (and appropriations) during the program review cycle using IPs that challenge the Service programming requests. For those reasons, the actual funding level for a particular project, Budget Line Item Mumber (BLIN), PEs, APEs, or BA may not be finally set until several months into the new fiscal year. This is so even if the appropriations act is passed before October 1, and the ultimate initial funding level for individual programs will almost certainly be less than shown in the joint conference reports.
 f. Funding Letters for O&M and AFHO. HQDA issues funding letters to commands and agencies for the Operation and Maintenance, Army (OMA) and Army Family Housing (Operations) (AFHO) appropriations. The Army National Guard (ARNG) and U.S. Army Reserve (AR) issue their own funding letters for their operation and maintenance appropriations. The letters indicate funded programs and give guidance on how the programs should be executed. The funding letters also provide an audit trail from the resource position in the PB to the revised, appropriated position. The OMA letter outlines the

ARMY PLANNING, PROGRAMMING, BUDGETING, AND EXECUTION PROCESS

funding posture and goals set by the senior Army leadership for command execution. Preparing and issuing the funding letter takes about 60 days after the appropriations act is passed.

9-62. Revised Approved Program for RDT&E
HQDA issues a Revised Approved Program (RAP) for the Research, Development, Test, and Evaluation (RDT&E) appropriation. The RAP shows congressional changes at both the PE and project level. In addition, the RAP spreads general reductions at the project level. It includes the amounts set aside for the Small Business Innovation Research Program (SBIR) and the Small Business Technology Transfer Pilot Program (STTR). The RAP also includes amounts withheld by the USD (Comptroller) and HQDA and provides language on congressional restrictions as well as congressional special interest items. Because of the level of detail and the extensive information included, the RAP does not become available until several months after the appropriations act is enacted.

9-63. Program Budget Accounting System
The Program Budget Accounting System (PBAS) is used to distribute classified programs and the Budget Authority (BA) to commands and agencies for all appropriations. Once appropriation sponsors determine the revised appropriated level for each appropriation, they adjust the amounts in PBAS. Each program and its Budget Authority (BA) are released in equal amounts for all appropriations except O&M, MILPERS, and AFHO. The Army uses the Program Budget Accounting System to distribute classified funds to their operating agencies. The primary role of the PBAS system is to distribute the funding authority to the operating agencies level. Before the Army agencies can execute their classified programs for the new fiscal year, it must load all these authorities into the Program Budget Accounting System. Additionally, PBAS must be loaded with execution restrictions in accordance with congressional language. Finally, appropriation sponsors must spread undistributed decrements in the appropriations act to the appropriate program. These accounts receive the total program for the fiscal year but receive Budget Authority (BA) quarterly throughout the year. Budget Authority (BA) controls the total amount of obligations a command or agency can execute through any given quarter but allows flexibility in its application against the program received.

   a. ASA(FM&C) controls the classified PBAS at the HQDA level. The appropriation sponsor may request release of the program and Budget Authority (BA) or below threshold reprogramming actions. ASA(FM&C)'s Funds Control Officer (SAFM-BUC-E) reviews requests for compliance with congressional language and guidance of the USD (Comptroller) before entering the action in PBAS. PBAS produces documents that display both Budget Authority (BA) and the classified program. The documents include a section for remarks for executing the program and footnotes that provide statutory restrictions according to provisions of 31 USC 1517.

   b. PBAS agrees with the program detail contained in DFAS-IN Manual 37-100-**** (The Army Management Structure (AMS)). Changes to PBAS appropriation structure can only be made at HQDA and must be approved as a change to DFAS-IN Manual 37-100-****. This manual initially agrees with the detail obtained in the PB request and is changed to incorporate congressional adds for classified programs. Any additional changes may be controlled by congressional language and vary from one appropriation to another.

9-64. Obligation and Outlay Plans
   a. During December and January, ASA(FM&C), in coordination with field activities and appropriation sponsors, develops obligation plans for each appropriation. Outlay plans are developed unilaterally at the ASA(FM&C) level. Obligation plans address unexpired funds. Outlay plans address unexpired, expired and no-year funds.

   b. ASA(FM&C) sends completed outlay plans to the USD (Comptroller). Although the USD (Comptroller) discontinued a requirement to submit obligation plans, the Army continues their use internally since OSD still reviews Army obligation rates and requests rationale for execution rates that fall outside normal parameters.

   c. The Transparency Process and the Secure Sheet process provide visible and auditable requirements, acquisition cycle and delivery of equipment to Congress. This system tracks the funding and procurement quantities from request through delivery to the unit. It also tracks the changes and capture the reasons and justifications for adds and/or decrements to component level allocations. It

HOW THE ARMY RUNS

tracks the changes to distributions to include the reasons and justifications for how the increases/decreases were applied to component level allocations.

d. Based on command estimates of annual obligations, both obligation and outlay plans tie to obligation and outlay controls in the PB. The importance of the outlay plan is that it relates directly to the projected amounts the Treasury must borrow to maintain proper balances to meet expected disbursements (outlays).

9-65. Financing Unbudgeted Requirements

a. Congress recognizes the need for flexibility during budget execution to meet unforeseen requirements or changes in operating conditions, including those to address minor, fact-of-life financial changes. Congress accepts that rigid adherence to program purposes and amounts originally budgeted and approved would jeopardize businesslike performance or mission performance. Thus, within stated restrictions and specified dollar thresholds, Congress allows federal agencies to reprogram existing funds to finance unfunded requirements. Typically, reprogramming diverts funds from undertakings whose requirements have lower priority than the new requirements being financed.

b. Congressional reprogramming language specifying budget authority limits, which varies by appropriation, controls the Army's ability to move budget authority within appropriations (below threshold reprogramming). Moving the program in excess of specified limits requires congressional approval via a formal reprogramming request (DD Form 1415, Reprogramming Action). Moving amounts between appropriations (transfer authority) always requires a formal reprogramming request.

c. Provided reprogramming authority is not required, another way to finance unfunded requirements is to apply obligation authority harvested from joint reconciliations. This means using unexpired funds originally obligated against a contract or order but identified as excess to the need and subsequently de-obligated. Reutilizing funds in this way gives allotment holders greater leverage in executing the budget and increases the buying power of the Army's financial resources.

d. Fiscal Year 1991 marked the first year of the Omnibus Reprogramming procedure, which except for construction accounts (that use a different process), consolidated all non-emergency DOD prior approval reprogramming actions into one very large reprogramming action. It identified all DOD reprogramming requirements at one time. This allowed the Congress and DOD to set priorities for limited funding and to make smarter decisions.

9-66. Oversight of Non-Appropriated Funds

Applying various methods, the ASA (FM&C) also oversees non-appropriated funds. One method is by participating on the Morale, Welfare, and Recreation (MWR) Board of Directors. The Deputy Assistant Secretary of the Army (Financial Operations) is a voting member of the MWR Executive Committee. In addition, the Principal Deputy Assistant Secretary of the Army (FM&C) chairs the Audit Committee, and the Chief Resource Analysis and Business Practices serves on the Investment Subcommittee. Through these positions the ASA(FM&C) influences virtually all aspects of MWR financial policy. As part of the responsibility of overseeing non-appropriated funds, the ASA(FM&C) presents non-appropriated funds issues to the SECARMY and CSA for decision.

Section XII
Program Performance and Review

9-67. Program Implementation

ACOMs, PEOs, and other operating agencies carry out the approved program within manpower and funds provided. They review budget execution and account for and report on the use of allocated funds by appropriation and MDEP. As applicable to each appropriation, they include FYDP program and subprogram, AMSCO, APE, Project Number, BLIN, SSN, BA, BAG, and EOR. They also account for use of allocated manpower by Unit Identification Code (UIC). The manpower and financial data obtained help commands and agencies develop future requirements.

ARMY PLANNING, PROGRAMMING, BUDGETING, AND EXECUTION PROCESS

9-68. Performance Assessment
a. ASA(FM&C) oversees the Cost & Performance Portal (CPP) which collects Army financial and performance data from disparate Army data systems, centralizes the data into a single data warehouse, and displays analytic information through various reports and graphical displays. The CPP is accessible to all Army users including resource managers, functional experts, and senior leaders through web-based interfaces with the ability to login via the Army Cost Accounting Codes (CAC).

b. The CPP provides real-time, relevant, accurate and transparent financial and performance information to senior leaders and HQDA staff to support decision-making.

9-69. Review of Selected Acquisition Systems
The means for checking system program performance include milestone reviews of designated acquisition programs conducted by ASA (ALT) using the ASARC and Major Automated Information Systems Review Council (MAISRC).

9-70. Joint Reconciliation Program
This program applies the skills of those responsible for various aspects of financial management. The skills include those of accountants, budget and program analysts, contracting professionals, logisticians, and internal review auditors. The program applies these combined skills to verify the validity of un-liquidated obligations, contractor work in progress, billing status, and the continued need for goods and services not yet delivered. The program achieves dollar savings by identifying and canceling obligations for goods and services no longer needed or duplicative. The program also reconciles current appropriations to verify the correctness of amounts obligated. In addition, the program assures the liquidation of appropriations to be canceled by the end of the fiscal year.

Section XIII
Summary and References

9-71. PPBE Concept
The PPBE process ties strategy, program, and budget all together. It helps build a comprehensive plan in which budgets flow from programs, programs from requirements, requirements from missions, and missions from national security objectives. The patterned flow-from end purpose to resource cost-defines requirements in progressively greater detail.

HOW THE ARMY RUNS

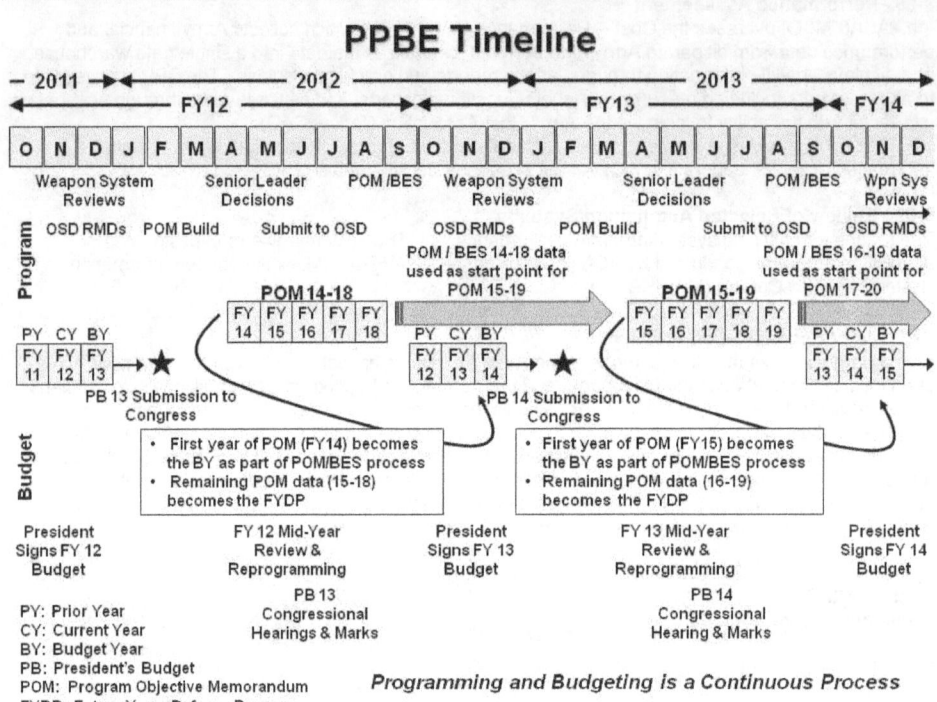

Figure 9-16. Planning, Programming, Budgeting, and Execution (PPBE) Timeline

9-72. System Products and Process
The PPBE process produces a departmental plan, program, and budget. Figure 9-16 lists typical events that occur during the process and shows the organizational framework within which the process operates.

Table 9-7. Budget Activity (BA) Management Structure for Operation and Maintenance Appropriations

Code	Description	Manager [1]
BA 1: Operating forces		
11	Land forces	G-3/5/7 Collective Training Division (DAMO-TRC)
111	Division	
112	Corps Combat Forces	
113	Corps Support Forces	
114	Echelon Above Corps (EAC)-Support Forces	
115	Land Forces Operations Support	
12	Land Forces Readiness	
121	Force Readiness Operations Support	G-3/5/7 Collective Training Division (DAMO-TRC)
122	Land Forces System Readiness	G-3/5/7 Training Simulations Division (DAMO-TRS)
123	Land forces depot maintenance	G-4 Directorate of Sustainment

ARMY PLANNING, PROGRAMMING, BUDGETING, AND EXECUTION PROCESS

Code	Description	Manager [1]
		(DALO-SM)
13	Land Forces Readiness Support	
131	Base Operations Support	ACSIM Resources Division (DAIM-ZR)
132	Sustainment, Restoration, and Modernization (Land Forces Readiness Support)	ACSIM Resources Division (DAIM-ZR)
133	Management and Operational Headquarters	G-1 Manpower Policy, Plans, and Program Division (DAPE-PRA)
134	Unified Commands	
135	Additional Activities	G-3/5/7 Resources and Programming Division (DAMO-TRP)
BA 2: Mobilization		
21	Mobility Operations	G-3/5/7 Collective Training Division (DAMO-TRC)
211	Strategic Mobility	G-3/5/7 Collective Training Division (DAMO-TRC) [2] G-4 Directorate for Force Projection/Distribution (DALO-FP) [3]
212	War Reserve	G-3/5/7 Collective Training Division (DAMO-TRC) [2] G-4 Directorate for Force Projection/Distribution (DALO-FP) [3]
213	Industrial Preparedness	G-4 Directorate for Force Projection/Distribution (DALO-FP) [3]
214	Prepositioned Materiel Configured to Unit Sets (POMCUS)	G-3/5/7 Collective Training Division (DAMO-TRC) [2] G-4 Directorate for Force Projection/Distribution (DALO-FP) [3]
BA3: Training and Recruiting		
31	Accession Training	
311	Officer Acquisition	G-3/5/7 Institutional Training Division (DAMO-TRI)
312	Recruit Training	G-3/5/7 Institutional Training Division (DAMO-TRI)
313	One Station Unit Training	G-3/5/7 Institutional Training Division (DAMO-TRI)
314	Senior Reserve Officers' Training Corps	G-3/6/7 Institutional Training Division (DAMO-TRI)
315	Service Academy Base Support	ACSIM Resource Division (DAIM-ZR)
316	Sustainment Restoration, and Modernization	ACSIM Resource Division (DAIM-ZR)
32	Basic Skill and Advance Training	
321	Specialized Skill Training	G-3/5/7 Institutional Training Division (DAMO-TRI)
322	Flight Training	G-3/5/7 Institutional Training Division (DAMO-TRI)
323	Professional Development Education	G-3/5/7 Institutional Training Division (DAMO-TRI)
324	Training Support	G-3/5/7 Institutional Training Division (DAMO-TRI)
325	Base Support	ACSIM Resource Division (DAIM-ZR)
326	Sustainment, Restoration, and Modernization	ACSIM Resource Division (DAIM-ZR)

HOW THE ARMY RUNS

Code	Description	Manager [1]
33	Recruiting, and Other Training and Education	
331	Recruiting and Advertising	G-1 Resource Division (DAPE-PRR)
332	Examining	G-1 Resource Division (DAPE-PRR)
333	Off Duty and Voluntary Education	G-1 Resource Division (DAPE-PRR)
334	Civilian Education and Training	G-1 Resource Division (DAPE-PRR)
335	Junior Reserve Officer Training Corps	G-1 Resource Division (DAPE-PRR)
336	Base Support-Recruiting and Examining	ACSIM Resource Division (DAIM-ZR)
BA 4: Administration and Service Wide Activities		
41	Security Programs	G-2 Directorate for Resource Integration (DAMI-RI)
411	Security Programs	
42	Logistics Operations	G-4 Directorate for Sustainment (DALO-SM) G-4 Directorate for Force Projection/Distribution (DALO-FP)
421	Service Wide Transportation	
422	Central Supply Activities	
423	Logistics Support Activities	
424	Ammunition Management	
43	Service Wide Support	
431	Administration	R/P-G-1 Manpower Policy, Plans, and Programs Division (DAPE-PRA)
432	Service Wide Communications	P-CIO/G-6 Program Execution Div (SAIS-ZR)
433	Manpower Management	G-1 Resource Division (DAPE-PRR)
434	Other Personnel Support	G-1 Resource Division (DAPE-PRR)
435	Other Service Support	Various
436	Army Claims and Administrative Support Activities	TJAG
437	Real Estate Management	ACSIM Resource Division (DAIM-ZR)
438	Base Support	ACSIM Resource Division (DAIM-ZR)
439	Defense Environmental Restoration Account (DERA) (FY 94-95)	None
44	Support of Other Nations	G-3/5/7 international Plans, Policy, Programs, and integration Division (DAMO-SSI)
441	International Military Headquarters	
442	Miscellaneous Support of Other Nations	
45	Closed Account	None
49	Defense Environmental Restoration Account (DERA) (FY96)	None

Legend
Army Manpower and TOA
n   BA
nn Activity Group (01 level)
nnn Budget Sub Activity
Records resources for Army Management Structure Code (AMSCO) nnn***, where nnn shows budget sub activity (see Chaps. AO-2020a-d, h, and j, DFAS-IN Manual 37-100-*** for further information)

Note:
5.   Manager for functional requirements and program and performance except as noted.

ARMY PLANNING, PROGRAMMING, BUDGETING, AND EXECUTION PROCESS

6. Manager for functional requirements

Table 9-8. Budget Activity (BA) Management Structure for Operation and Maintenance Appropriations-Army Manpower Only Activity Structure

Code	Description	Manager [1]
Category 8: Medical activities, manpower only-reimbursable labor		
84	Medical manpower-reimbursable	TSG Manpower and Programming Division (DASG-PAE-M) [2]
841	Examining activities	
846	Training medical spaces	
847	Care in Army medical centers	
849	Defense medical spaces	
Category 9: Other-manpower only		
91	Special operations forces manpower-reimbursable	G-1 Manpower Policy, and Program Division (DAPE-PRA) [3]
92	Defense agency manpower (military only)	
93	Outside DOD	
94	Transients, holdees, and operating strength deviation	

Legend
Manpower-only activity structure
The PPBE database generates categories 8 and 9 to meet manpower-reporting requirements. Category 8 records resources for AMSOC 84n*** where n-1, 6, or 7 shows the budget sub activity, category 9 records resources for AMSCO 9n****, where n=1, 2, 3, or 4 shows the 0-1 level structure.

Note:
7. Manager for functional requirement and program except as noted.
8. Manager for functional requirements.
9. Manager for program and performance.

Table 9-9. Budget Activity (BA) Management Structure for Operation and Maintenance Appropriation-Base Operations Support (BOS)

Code	Account	Manager [1]
	****19, ****20 Child develop services, family centers	ACSIM Resource Division (DAIM-ZR)
AMSCO		
AMSCO	****53, ****54, ****56 Environmental conservation, pollution prevention, environnemental compliance	ACSIM Resource Division (DAIM-ZR)
AMSCO	****75 Ant-terrorism/Force protection	ACSIM Resource Division (DAIM-ZR)
AMSCO .J0	****79 (Real Property Services) Operation of utilities	ACSIM Resource Division (DAIM-ZR)
*.M0	Municipal Services	ACSIM Resource Division (DAIM-ZR)

HOW THE ARMY RUNS

Code	Account	Manager [1]
.N0	Facilities engineering services	ACSIM Resource Division (DAIM-ZR)
.P0	Fire and emergency response services	ACSIM Resource Division (DAIM-ZR)
AMSCO	****90 Audio visual and visual information production, acquisition, and support	P-CIO/G-6 Program Execution Div (SAIS-ZR) [2] ACSIM Resource Division (DAIM-ZR) [3]
AMSCO	****95 Base communications	P-CIO/G-6 Program Execution Div (SAIS-ZR) [2] ACSIM Resource Division (DAIM-ZR) [3]
AMSCO	****96 (Base Operations Support) (BASOPS(-))	
.A0	Real estate leases	ACSIM Resource Division (DAIM-ZR)
.B0	Supply operations and management	G-4 Directorate for Sustainment (DALO-SM)
.C0	Materiel maintenance	G-4 Directorate for Sustainment (DALO-SM)
.D0	Transportation services	G-4 Directorate for Sustainment (DALO-SM)
.E0	Laundry and dry-cleaning services	G-4 Directorate for Sustainment (DALO-SM)
.F0	The Army food service program	G-4 Directorate for Sustainment (DALO-SM)
.K0	Civilian personnel management	R/P-G-1
.L0	Morale, welfare, and recreation	ACSIM Resource Division (DAIM-ZR)
.M0	Military personnel support	R/P-G-1
.Q0	Reserve component support	ACSIM Resource Division (DAIM-ZR)
.U0	Financial management	ASA (FM&C)
.V0	Management analysis	ASA(FM&C)
.W0	Contracting operations	ASA(ALT) Plans, Programs and Resources Directorate (SAAL-RI)
.X0	IT, management and planning	P-CIO/G-6 Program Execution Div (SAIS-ZR) [2] ACSIM Resource Division (DAIM-ZR) [3]
.Y0	Administrative services	P-CIO/G-6 Program Execution Div (SAIS-ZR) [2] ACSIM Resource Division (DAIM-ZR) [3]
.10	Provost Marshal	G-3 Security, Force Protection, and Law Enforcement (DAMO-ODL)
.20	Staff Judge Advocate	ACSIM Resource Division (DAIM-ZR)
.30	Chaplain	ACSIM Resource Division (DAIM-ZR)
.40	Public affairs	ACSIM Resource Division (DAIM-ZR)
.50	Inspector General	ACSIM Resource Division (DAIM-ZR)

ARMY PLANNING, PROGRAMMING, BUDGETING, AND EXECUTION PROCESS

Code	Account	Manager [1]
.60	Installation management	ACSIM Resource Division (DAIM-ZR)
.70	Operations	ACSIM Resource Division (DAIM-ZR)
.90	Unaccompanied personnel housing management	ACSIM Resource Division (DAIM-ZR)

Legend
Base Support
Base Operations Support (BOS) applies to sub activity groups 131, 315, 325, 336, and 438
Base support refers to the resources to operate and maintain Army installations (major, minor, stations, other). It comprises two sub activity groups: Base Operations Support (BOS) and Sustainment, Restoration, and Modernization (SRM). Resources are recorded in Army Management Structure Code (AMSCO) and nnn* yy, where nnn shows budget sub activity group (SAG) and yy designates specified subdivisions. Sometimes, resources are recorded as nnn*yy.z0, where .z0 refers to letter accounts, as below for BASOPS (-) and SRM. (See chap A9-BSSPT, DFAS-IN Manual 37-100-**** for further information.)

Note:
10. Manager for functional requirements and program and performance.
11. Manager for functional requirements.
12. Manager for program and performance.

Table 9-10. Budget Activity (BA) Management Structure for Operation and Maintenance Appropriations-Sustainment, Restoration, and Modernization (SRM)

Code	Account	Manager [1]
AMSCO	****76	
.L0	Minor construction	ACSIM Resource Division (DAIM-ZR)
AMSCO	****78 (Maintenance and Repair)	
.10	Surfaced areas (including bridges and other appurtenances)	ACSIM Resource Division (DAIM-ZR)
.20	Airfields, paved and unpaved (including bridges and other appurtenances)	ACSIM Resource Division (DAIM-ZR)
.40	Railroads (including bridges and other appurtenances)	ACSIM Resource Division (DAIM-ZR)
.50	Utility systems	ACSIM Resource Division (DAIM-ZR)
.A0	Maintenance and production facilities	ACSIM Resource Division (DAIM-ZR)
.B0	Training and operations facilities	ACSIM Resource Division (DAIM-ZR)
.C0	RDT&E facilities	ACSIM Resource Division (DAIM-ZR)
.D0	Supply and storage facilities	ACSIM Resource Division (DAIM-ZR)
.E0	Administrative facilities (including IT facilities)	ACSIM Resource Division (DAIM-ZR)
.F0	Unaccompanied personnel housing facilities	ACSIM Resource Division (DAIM-ZR)
.G0	Other unaccompanied personnel housing facilities	ACSIM Resource Division (DAIM-ZR)
.H0	Dining facilities	ACSIM Resource Division (DAIM-

HOW THE ARMY RUNS

Code	Account	Manager [1]
		ZR)
.Q0	Other facilities without facility category groups (FCG)	ACSIM Resource Division (DAIM-ZR)
.R0	Airfield facilities	ACSIM Resource Division (DAIM-ZR)
.S0	Training/instruction support facilities	ACSIM Resource Division (DAIM-ZR)
.T0	Ports	ACSIM Resource Division (DAIM-ZR)
.U0	Medical and hospital facilities	ACSIM Resource Division (DAIM-ZR)
.V0	Grounds	ACSIM Resource Division (DAIM-ZR)
.W0	Community support	ACSIM Resource Division (DAIM-ZR)
.X0	Family housing	ACSIM Resource Division (DAIM-ZR)
AMSCO	****93 Demolition of real property	ACSIM Resource Division (DAIM-ZR)

Note:
13. Manager for functional requirements and program and performance

Table 9-11. Budget Activity (BA) Management Structure for Operation and Maintenance Appropriations-Army National Guard

Code	Description	Manager [1]
	BA 1: Operating forces	DARNG [1]
11	Land Forces	
111	Division	
112	Corps combat forces	
113	Corps support forces	
114	Echelon above corps (EAC)-forces	
115	Land forces operations support	
12	Land forces readiness	
122	Land forces system readiness	
123	Land forces depot maintenance	
13	Land forces readiness support	
131	Base operations support (land forces readiness support)	
132	Sustainment, restoration, and Modernization	
133	Management and operational headquarters	
135	Weapons of mass destruction	
	BA 4: Administration and service wide activities	DARNG [1]
43	Service wide support	
431	Staff management	
432	Information management	
433	Readiness and personnel administration	
434	Recruiting and advertising	

ARMY PLANNING, PROGRAMMING, BUDGETING, AND EXECUTION PROCESS

Legend
Army National Guard
n BA
nn Activity Group (01 level)
nnn Budget Sub Activity

Note:
14. Budget Formulation Branch (NGB-ARC-BF): Manager for functional requirements and program and performance.
15. Budget Branch (DAAR-CFM): Manager for functional requirements and program and performance

Table 9-12. Budget Activity (BA) Management Structure for Operations and Maintenance Appropriations-U.S. Army Reserve

Code	Description	Manager[1]
	BA 1: Operating forces	CAR[2]
11	Land forces	
111	Divisions	
112	Corps combat forces	
113	Corps support forces	
114	Echelon above corps (EAC)-forces	
115	Land forces operations support	
12	Land forces readiness	
121	Force readiness operations support	
122	Land forces system readiness	
123	Depot maintenance	
13	Land forces readiness support	
131	Base operations support	
132	Sustainment, Restoration, and Modernization	
135	Additional activities	
	BA 4: Administration and service wide activities	CAR[2]
43	Service wide support	
431	Administration	
432	Service wide communications	
433	Personnel/financial administration	
434	Recruiting and advertising	

Legend
U.S. Army Reserve
n BA
nn Activity Group (01 level)
nnn Budget Sub Activity

Note:
16. Budget Formulation Branch (NGB-ARC-BF): Mangers for functional requirements and program and performance.
17. Budget Branch (DAAR-CFM): Manager for functional requirements and program and performance.

Table 9-13. Army Appropriations-Managers for Functional Requirements and Program and Performance

HOW THE ARMY RUNS

Resource Identification Code	Appropriation (Fund)[1]	Manager for Functional Requirements (R) Manager for Program and Performance (P)
	Investment	
RDT&E	Research, Development, Test, and Evaluation, Army	R-G-8 Programs and Priorities (DAPR-FDR) P-ASA(ALT) Plans, Programs and Resources Directorate (SAAL-RI)
ACFT (APA)	Aircraft Procurement, Army	R- G-8 Programs and Priorities (DAPR-FDR) P-ASA(ALT) Plans, Programs and Resources Directorate (SAAL-RI)
MSLS (MIPA)	Missile Procurement, Army	R- G-8 Programs and Priorities (DAPR-FDR) P-ASA(ALT) Plans, Programs and Resources Directorate (SAAL-RI)
WTCV	Procurement of Weapons and Tracked Combat Vehicles, Army	R- G-8 Programs and Priorities (DAPR-FDR) P-ASA(ALT) Plans, Programs and Resources Directorate (SAAL-RI)
AMMO (PAA)	Procurement of Ammunition, Army	R- G-8 Programs and Priorities (DAPR-FDR) R-G-4 Directorate for Sustainment (DALO-SM) P-ASA(ALT) Plans, Programs and Resources Directorate (SAAL-RI)
OPA	Other Procurement, Army	R- G-8 Programs and Priorities (DAPR-FDR) P-ASA(ALT) Plans, Programs and Resources Directorate (SAAL-RI)
	OPA 1	R- G-8 Programs and Priorities (DAPR-FDR) P-ASA(ALT) Plans, Programs and Resources Directorate (SAAL-RI)
	OPA 2	R- G-8 Programs and Priorities (DAPR-FDR) P-ASA(ALT) Plans, Programs and Resources Directorate (SAAL-RI) P-CIO/G-6 Program Execution Div (SAIS-ZR)
	OPA 3	R- G-8 Programs and Priorities (DAPR-FDR) P-ASA(ALT) Plans, Programs and Resources Directorate (SAAL-RI)
	OPA 4	R- G-8 Programs and Priorities (DAPR-FDR) P-ASA(ALT) Plans, Programs and Resources Directorate (SAAL-RI)
MCA	Military Construction, Army[2]	R-ACSIM Facilities Division (DAIM-FD) P-ACSIM Resources Division (DAIM-ZR)
MCNG	Military Construction, Army National Guard[2]	R-DARNG Engineering Directorate (NGB-AEN) P-ACSIM ACSIM Resources Division (DAIM-ZR)
MCAR	Military Construction, Army Reserve[2]	R-CAR Army Reserve Engineer Directorate (DAAR-EN) P- ACSIM Resources Division (DAIM-ZR)
CHEM	Chemical Agents and Munitions Destruction, Army	R- G-8 Programs and Priorities (DAPR-FDR) P-ASA(ALT) Plans, Programs and Resources Directorate (SAAL-RI)
AFHC	Family Housing, Army (Construction)	R/P- ACSIM Facilities Division (DAIM-FD)
	Operations	
ERA	Environmental Restoration, Army and Formerly Used Test Sites	R/P-ACSIM Environmental Division (DAIM-ED)
BRAC	Base Realignment and Closure	R/P-ACSIM BRAC Office (DAIM-BO)
AFHO	Family Housing, Army	R/P- ACSIM Facilities Division (DAIM-FD)

9-54

ARMY PLANNING, PROGRAMMING, BUDGETING, AND EXECUTION PROCESS

Resource Identification Code	Appropriation (Fund) [1]	Manager for Functional Requirements (R) Manager for Program and Performance (P)
	(Operations)	
OMA	Operation and Maintenance, Army	See Tables 9-8 through 9-11
OMNG	Operation and Maintenance, Army National Guard	See Table 9-12
OMAR	Operation and Maintenance, Army Reserve	See Table 9-13
MPA	Military Personnel, Army	R/P- G-1 Manpower Policy, Plans, and Program Division (DAPE-PRA)
NGPA	National Guard Personnel, Army	R/P-DARNG Budget Formulation Branch (NGB-ARC-BF)
RPA	Reserve Personnel, Army	R/P-CAR Budget Branch (DAAR-CFM)
HAF-D	Homeowners Assistance Fund Defense	R/P-COE

9-73. References

a. DODI 7045.14 Implementation of the Planning, Programming, and Budgeting System.
b. CJCS Instruction 3100.01B, Chairman's JSPS.
c. AR 1-1, PPBE Process.

HOW THE ARMY RUNS

This page is intentionally left blank

RESOURCE MANAGEMENT

Chapter 10

Resource Management

Today's global fiscal environment is driving defense budgets down for our partners and allies, as well as our Nation. Historically, defense spending has been cyclic with significant reductions following the end of major conflicts. The Army understands it cannot be immune to these fiscal realities and must be part of the solution. Our focus areas for the FY 13 budget demonstrate our concerted effort to establish clear priorities that give the Nation a ready and capable Army while being good stewards of all our resources.

2012 Army Posture Statement

As Army leaders we must be responsible stewards of the funds entrusted to our care. We must make the best possible use of our limited funds and ensure that no significant resource-related issue is decided without a thorough review of its costs, its projected benefits, and the tradeoffs that might be required to pay for it. In our decision making, we need to supplement professional experience and military judgment with solid data and sound analytical techniques.

Under Secretary of the Army and Vice Chief of Staff, Army Memorandum, SUBJECT: Cost-Benefit Analysis to Support Army Enterprise Decision Making, 30 December 2009

Section I
Introduction

10-1. The Need for Resource Management

a. The United States Army 2012 Posture Statement and the Cost Benefit Analysis (CBA) memorandum emphasize the need for effective resource management throughout the Army. Because the Army has a large and complex set of missions to execute and a limited set of resources with which to accomplish its missions and supporting tasks, the necessity to maximize the spending power of every dollar the Congress appropriates to the Army becomes paramount. Further, because the Army is vested with the public's trust and confidence for defending our Nation, all Army leaders have an incumbent responsibility to exercise effective and responsible stewardship for all the resources that have been entrusted to them. As such, responsible, effective, and efficient resource management is an integral part of all Army leaders' duties and functions and is essential for maintaining the Army's readiness to accomplish its assigned missions.

b. Resource management at the strategic level must address the issues of affordability, required force capabilities, and the entire supporting structure. Resource managers at this level must also deal with the larger questions of whether particular programs are needed, how they serve the specific missions assigned to the Army, and whether the strategies designed to accomplish the mission are correct and necessary. Programmatic and financial resource perspectives examine the efficiency with which funds are allocated and spent and how effectively particular programs are managed and integrated. At the program level this process encompasses the ways in which the Soldiers, civilians, facilities, equipment, information, time, and funds are integrated into the Army.

c. Implicit in this programmatic resource management perspective is the recognition that all of us participate in a resource decision stream that requires some of these decisions, once made, to remain unalterable. For example, placing a new facility at an installation typically requires a minimum of two or more years. The time to train instructors and then troops on a new piece of equipment varies with the complexity of the equipment. Ordering the secondary spares for new end items requires time. Integrating all three of these resource decisions requires that we consider them to be "irreversible," otherwise we could find new facilities constructed at one installation for a new piece of equipment and for Soldiers to be trained on that equipment, while we have actually placed the equipment and Soldiers on another installation.

d. More importantly, this "unalterable decision base" will have created "a receivables stream" such as aircraft, training packages, equipment shops, displaced equipment, and so forth of substantial proportion.

HOW THE ARMY RUNS

Reconfiguring these "receivables" into one's own conception without considering the previous decision rationale may well create resource management disconnects which tend to surface in OSD resource review forums and Congressional hearings.

10-2. Resource Management—A Definition
Resource management is the direction, guidance, and control of financial and other resources. It involves the application of programming, budgeting, accounting, reporting, analysis, and evaluation.

10-3. Resource Management Terms
Throughout this chapter, there are a number of unique terms associated with resource (specifically financial or fiscal) management that if understood enable you to more readily understand and use this chapter.

 a. Obligation. Any act that legally binds the United States Government to make a payment is an obligation. The concept of the "obligation" is central to resource management in the Government. From the central concept of "obligating the U.S. Government to make a payment" springs forth the foundation of our fiscal law and the legal parameters under which the Army must operate as a part of the U.S. Government. The obligation may be for a service rendered by a contractor, the acquisition of materiel items (for example, a tank), the construction or repair of a facility, salary for a Soldier or civilian, and so forth.

 b. Congressional Authorization. A law passed by the Congress and signed by the President that establishes or continues a federal program or agency, and sets forth guidelines to which it must adhere. Generally for every Fiscal Year (FY), he Congress passes a National Defense Authorization Act (for example, Public Law 111-383, Ike Skelton National Defense Authorization Act for Fiscal Year 2011), which directs by law what can be purchased, what manpower resource levels each Service can have, and how many weapon and other materiel systems can be bought. It also provides additions and changes to Title 10 of the United States Code (USC) that, among other laws, guides the management of the Army and the other activities of the Department of Defense (DOD). An authorization act however does not provide the Budget Authority (BA) to draw funds from the U.S. Treasury to pay an obligation.

 c. Congressional Appropriation. A law passed by the Congress and signed by the President that provides BA for the specific purpose(s) stated in the law. In the case of the annual DOD appropriations act (for example, Public Law 111-118, Department of Defense Appropriations Act, 2010) BA is provided for a number of appropriations (for example, Operations and Maintenance, Army (OMA); Military Personnel, Army (MPA); Research, Development, Test and Evaluation, Army (RDT&E,A); Military Construction (MILCON), Army (MCA), and so forth) for a specified period of time for the Army to incur legal obligations as it executes the programs authorized by Congress and other laws that guide Army operations.

 d. BA. BA is the authority to incur a legal obligation to pay a sum of money from the U.S. Treasury. BA is not "money." The U.S. Treasury actually disburses cash only after an agency (for example, Army Defense Finance and Accounting Service (DFAS) accounting office activity) issues a U.S. Treasury check withdrawing money from the Treasury and thus disburses the money to pay a previously incurred obligation.

 e. Disbursement. Payment of an obligation of the U.S. Government.

 f. FY. The FY is the Government's accounting period. For the federal government it begins on 1 October and ends on 30 September. The FY is designated by the calendar year in which it ends. For example, FY 2006 begins on 1 October 2005 and ends on 30 September 2006.

 g. Outlays. Outlays are the amount of money the Government actually disburses in a given FY.

 h. Asset leverage. The combination of government assets with private sector knowledge, expertise, equity and or financing in a venture (partnership) which results in long term benefit to the government.

10-4. Key Players in Army Resource Management
There are a number of different actors who play in the Army's resource management arena:

 a. Congress. Central to the function of obligating the Government to make a payment is the power invested by the U.S. Constitution in the Congress for the following: to raise revenue and borrow money (U.S. Constitution Article I, Section 8, Clause 1-2); to raise and support armies; and to provide and maintain a navy (U.S. Constitution Article I, Section 8, Clause 12-13), and no money shall be drawn from the Treasury but in consequence of appropriations made by law (U.S. Constitution Article I, Section 9,

RESOURCE MANAGEMENT

Clause 7). For Congress to meet these requirements they pass authorization and appropriation acts as described above.

b. Office of Management and Budget (OMB). OMB assists the President of the United States in overseeing the preparation of the federal budget and in supervising its administration in federal agencies. It evaluates, formulates, and coordinates management procedures and program objectives within and among federal departments and agencies. It also controls the administration of the federal budget, while routinely providing the President with recommendations regarding budget proposals and relevant legislative proposals. Additionally it plans, conducts, and promotes evaluation efforts that assist the President in assessing federal program objectives, performance, and efficiency. Finally, OMB also oversees and coordinates the Administration's procurement, financial management, information, and regulatory policies. Further details on the OMB organization and its functions can be viewed on-line at: "http://www.whitehouse.gov/omb/".

c. Under Secretary of Defense (Comptroller) (USD(C)). Within the OSD there is appointed an USD(C). The USD(C) advises and assists the Secretary of Defense (SECDEF) in exercising the SECDEF's budgetary and fiscal powers. As such the USD(C) supervises and directs the preparation of DOD budget estimates and establishes and supervises the execution of policies and procedures to be followed in connection with organizational and administrative matters relating to: preparation of budgets; fiscal, cost, operating, and capital property accounting; and progress and statistical reporting. Finally the USD(C) establishes and supervises the execution of policies and procedures relating to the expenditure and collection of funds administered by DOD and establishes uniform fiscal terminology, classifications and procedures used in the DOD's fiscal management. The USD(C) is the DOD Chief Financial Officer (CFO) (see Para. 10-28). Further details on the Office of the USD(C) organization and its functions can be viewed on-line at: "http://www.dtic.mil/comptroller/".

d. Secretary of the Army (SECARMY). Subject to the authority, direction, and control of the SECDEF and subject to the provisions of section 3013 of Title 10, USC, the SECARMY is responsible for, and has the authority necessary to conduct all affairs of the Department of the Army (DA), including the following functions:

(1) Recruiting
(2) Organizing
(3) Supplying
(4) Equipping (including research and development)
(5) Training
(6) Servicing
(7) Mobilizing
(8) Demobilizing
(9) Administering (including the morale and welfare of personnel)
(10) Maintaining
(11) The construction, outfitting, and repair of military equipment
(12) The construction, maintenance, and repair of buildings, structures, and utilities and the acquisition of real property and interests in real property necessary to carry out the responsibilities specified
(13) Further, subject to the authority, direction, and control of the SECDEF, the SECARMY is also responsible to the SECDEF for the following: the functioning and efficiency of the DA; the effective and timely implementation of policy, program, and budget decisions and instructions of the President or the SECDEF relating to functions of the DA; and the performance of the functions of the DA so as to fulfill the current and future operational requirements of the unified Combatant Commands. As such the SECARMY can be considered the Army's top resource manager because of the position's inherent decision-making authority over the affairs of the DA

e. Assistant Secretary of the Army (Financial Management & Comptroller) (ASA(FM&C)). Within the OSA there is appointed an ASA(FM&C). The ASA(FM&C) exercises the comptroller functions of the DA and advises the SECARMY on financial management as directed by 10 USC Sec. 3016. To execute this mission, the Office of the ASA(FM&C) is organized as follows (see Figure 10-1):

(1) Military Deputy for Budget. The Military Deputy for Budget is responsible for the Department of the Army's budget execution. The Director for Army Budget reports directly to the Military Deputy for Budget.

(2) Director of the Army Budget (DAB). The DAB is responsible for the Army's budget formulation, the presentation and defense of the budget through the congressional appropriation process, budget execution and analysis, reprogramming actions, and appropriation/fund control and distribution. The DAB

HOW THE ARMY RUNS

is a co-chairman of the Headquarters, Department of the Army (HQDA) Two Star Budget Requirements and Program (BRP) Board. To accomplish its missions and functions, the Office of the DAB is organized into four directorates (Operations and Support; Investments; Military Personnel and Facilities; and Management and Control).

(3) Deputy Assistant Secretary of the Army (Financial Operations) (DASA(FO)). The DASA(FO) is responsible for: policies, procedures, programs, and systems pertaining to finance and accounting activities and operations; Army financial management systems and data integration activities; Army programs for management control, internal review and audit compliance, the Government Travel Charge Card, and fraud, waste and abuse; and other management evaluation activities. To accomplish its missions and functions, the Office of the DASA(FO) is organized into three directorates (Accountability and Audit Readiness, Internal Review, and Finance and Accounting Oversight. Additionally, the U.S. Army Financial Management Command, a HQDA Field Operating Agency (FOA), is under the control of the DASA(FO).

(4) Deputy Assistant Secretary of the Army for Cost and Economics (DASA(C&E)). The Deputy is responsible for implementing the Army Cost and Economic Analysis Program through the development and promulgation of cost and economic analysis policy, cost estimating models, and cost databases for Army wide use. DASA(C&E) conducts component cost analysis for weapons and automated information systems (AIS) and manages the Army Cost Review Board and Army Cost Position (ACP) (see Para. 11-69f). DASA(C&E) is responsible for conducting force structure, operations and support (Operating Tempo (OPTEMPO)), personnel, and installation cost analyses. Other functions include implementation of the Army Activity Based Costing/Management Strategic Plan, management of the Army Cost Research Program, and review and approval of Cost Benefit Analyses.

(5) Director, Financial Information Management. The Director is responsible for advising, coordinating, and directing actions to achieve financial business transformation Army wide; capitalizing on on-going programs and projects; ensuring compatibility with and interoperability between Army financial systems and Defense systems; and incorporating advances in Army information technology, communications, and Government processes and systems. She serves the Army Financial Management community as Chief Architect and Chief Information Officer as well as the functional proponent for the General Fund Enterprise Business System (GFEBS). Further details on the Office of the Assistant Secretary of the Army for Financial Management and Comptroller (OASA(FM&C)) organization and its functions can be viewed on-line at: http://www.asafm.army.mil/.

f. Commanders of Army Commands (ACOM) & heads of other operating agencies. Commanders of Army commands and commanders and heads of operating agencies (e.g., Program Executive Officers (PEO), Program Managers (PM), and President, National Defense University) are responsible for developing, justifying, presenting, and defending programs supporting their assigned missions and responsibilities. Further, they are accountable for ensuring approved program budgets are properly executed and certified. This responsibility includes ensuring accounting and fund status reporting for appropriated and non-appropriated funds is accomplished in accordance with fiscal law and governing regulations and policies.

RESOURCE MANAGEMENT

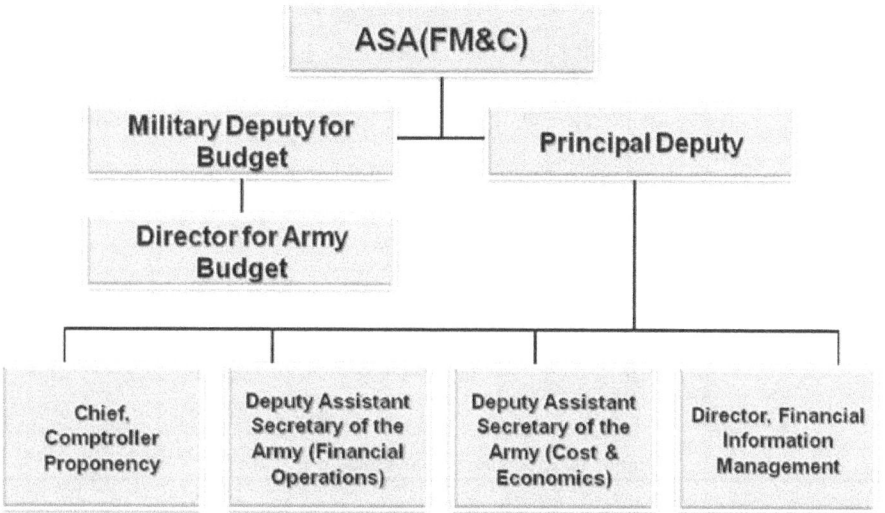

Figure 10-1. Office of the Assistant Secretary of the Army (Financial Management and Comptroller) (ASA(FM&C))

10-5. A Framework to Help Study Resource Management

a. For our study of the internal workings of the Army's Resource Management System and how it functions, it helps to use a model called the "Four A's":

(1) Acquire resources.

(2) Allocate those resources according to the priorities generally considered in terms of dollars and manpower.

(3) Account for those resources with a system that provides a decision support and tracking capability for the program and budget functions, and a system that performs accounting for fiscal compliance required by statutes.

(4) Analyze the execution of those resources and implement course corrections as required.

b. As illustrated in Figure 10-2, these functions are performed in a closed-loop process. Though it is recognized that there are other models that describe the elements of resource management, for our discussion the "4-A's" model meets our needs.

HOW THE ARMY RUNS

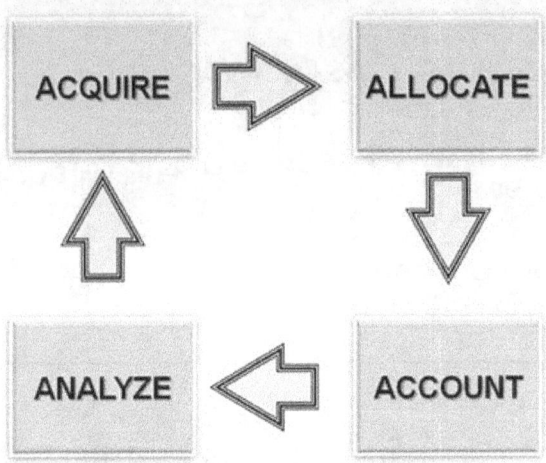

Figure 10-2. Resource Management's "4-A's"

Section II
Acquire Resources

10-6. Getting The Fiscal Resources For The Army To Use
Described in detail in Chapter 9, the Army's Planning, Programming, Budgeting, and Execution (PPBE) process provides the means by which the Army justifies and acquires its resources from Congress. After passage and signing into law of the authorization and appropriations acts, several interrelated functions are performed by OMB, the U.S. Treasury, the Office of the Under Secretary of Defense (Comptroller) (OUSD(C)) and OASA(FM&C) to acquire the Army's financial resources and distribute them to the field for execution. Figure 10-3 graphically portrays this process of getting resources to the Army.
   a. Apportionment requests. Apportionment is a process for the administrative control of appropriations and funds. It is also a distribution of a specified "amount of Obligation Authority (OA)" in an appropriation/fund that is available for specified time periods (for example, fiscal quarter), activities, projects or a combination thereof as approved by the OMB. The amounts so apportioned limit the obligations that may be incurred by the Army. After Congress passes an appropriation bill and the President signs it into law, the OASA(FM&C) submits an apportionment of funds request through OUSD(C) to OMB. OMB reviews the request, adjusts the amounts as may be necessary based on their analysis of prior Army spending patterns, approves the request, and transmits the approved request back down through OUSD(C) to the OASA(FM&C). Within OASA(FM&C), the HQDA Funds Control Officer loads the approved apportioned amounts into the Program-Budget Accounting System (PBAS). PBAS is the official funds control management system of the DOD and is used throughout the Army financial management community to control the fund distribution process. See Figure 10-3. Fund Distribution Process
   b. Program documents. In addition to the approved apportionment mentioned above, OUSD(C) may issue further restrictions on using the OA provided in the apportionment document by withholding amounts for specific programs. These restrictions come to HQDA via an OA letter (for Operations and Maintenance (O&M), Military Personnel (MILPERS), and Army Family Housing Operations (AFHO)

RESOURCE MANAGEMENT

appropriations), a DD Form 440 (for Procurement and Research, Development, Test, and Evaluation (RDT&E) appropriations), or a DD Form 460 (for the MILCON appropriations).

10-7. Treasury Warrants
After the President signs the appropriations bill(s), the U.S. Treasury issues appropriations warrants to establish "bank accounts" on the books of the U.S. Treasury for each appropriation. The Treasury Warrant is a financial controlling mechanism and gives the Army the authority to disburse funds ("cut a check to pay for an obligation") from those accounts. Without this authority, the Army cannot make any payments citing the non-warranted appropriation.

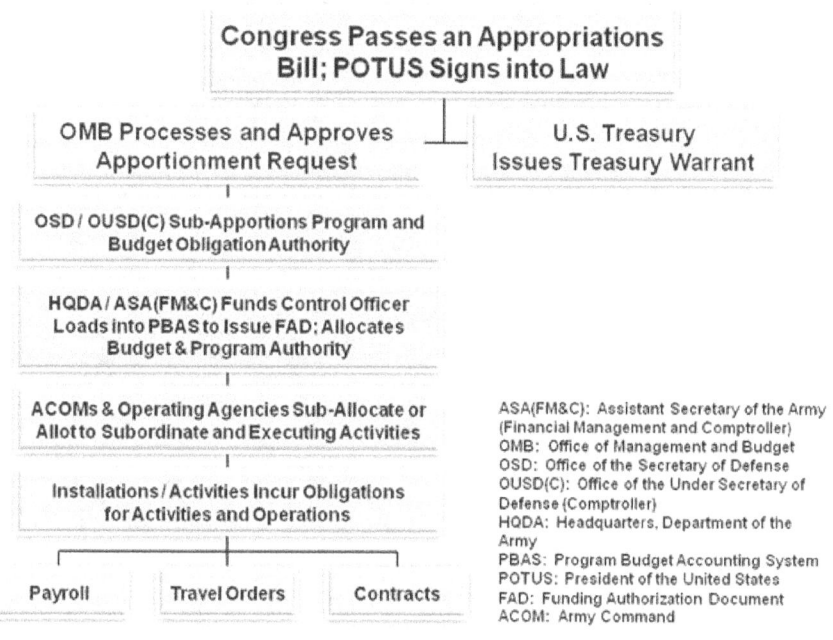

Figure 10-3. Fund Distribution Process

Section III
Allocate Resources to the Field

10-8. Fund Distribution and Control
"Pass funds through command channels and make the commander responsible for their control." This is the basic tenet by which the Army's funding distribution system operates. In this case the use of the term "funds" implies that the authority to create obligations, for which the U.S. Government has to pay, has been granted. Distribution of funds is any documented action that makes funds available for obligation. This distribution is made in a stated amount for specific purposes and to a specific organization for a specific time period. The commander's authority to incur obligations is received on a funding document, which specifies the appropriation and budget program for which the funds may be used, and identifies applicable statutory limitations. This process is used to facilitate control over funds and the reporting of

HOW THE ARMY RUNS

violations of laws (see below about Anti-deficiency Act (ADA) violations) and directives. Starting in FY03 however, the mission commander was no longer responsible for Base Operations (BASOPS) funding. BASOPS funding was centrally controlled by the Installation Management Activity (a FOA of the Office of the Assistant Chief of Staff for Installation Management (OACSIM)). And in 2006, the Installation Management Agency (IMA), the Community and Family Support Center, and the Army Environmental Center were consolidated under a single command, the Installation Management Command (IMCOM) a direct reporting unit to the Assistant Chief of Staff for Installation Management (ACSIM). Today, IMCOM centrally controls BASOPS funding.

   a. The Distribution Procedure. After obtaining OA from OMB and OUSD(C), HQDA directs major commands and other subordinate operating agencies to execute their approved budgeted programs (see Figure 10-3). Using the GFEBS, the HQDA Funds Control Officer in the OASA(FM&C) allocates program authority and OA to ACOMs and operating agencies based upon guidance from the appropriation sponsors. Army commands and operating agencies in turn sub-allocate or allot to the appropriate subordinate organization (for example, installation, major unit, PM, and so forth) where the program will actually be executed by obligating for such things as payroll, travel orders, contracts, purchase orders, and so forth. Although this funds distribution system is a means of controlling obligations and fixing responsibility, the policy is to minimize the formal distribution and to fund an operation at the highest practical level. As an example, the MPA appropriation is held and controlled centrally at HQDA, whereas the OMA appropriation is decentralized through the Army Commands to the installations.

   b. Funding Guidance. Along with program authority and BA moved out to Army activities through the PBAS, HQDA normally issues additional specific spending guidance at the beginning of the FY. The appropriation sponsors for OMA and AFHO issue annual funding letters to ACOMs with required or specialized fiscal guidance that is to be used in the execution of the budget for the FY. ACOMs and Operating Agencies may also issue specific funding guidance to their subordinate commanders and activities for the execution of their programs and budgets. The Chief of the Army Reserve issues a funding guidance letter to subordinate Army Reserve activities for executing the Operations and Maintenance, Army Reserve (OMAR) appropriation and the Reserve Personnel, Army (RPA) appropriation. Likewise, the Director of the Army National Guard issues a funding guidance letter to subordinate Army Guard activities, principally the State adjutants general, for executing both the Operations and Maintenance, Army National Guard (OMNG) appropriation and the National Guard Personnel, Army (NGPA) appropriation.

10-9. Fund Authorization Document (FAD)

Using the PBAS, the HQDA Funds Control Officer issues FADs to allocate OA and program authority to ACOMs and operating agencies. The ACOMs and operating agencies in turn use PBAS to issue FADs to their subordinate activities (for example, installations) to allot OA and program authority. For the procurement and RDT&E appropriations, an approved program document accompanies the FAD to provide further administrative limitations on the use of those funds.

10-10. Fund Allowance System

Some ACOMs and operating agencies have implemented a fund allowance system whereby the lowest formal distribution of funds is at the ACOM/Operating Agency level with funding allowances being issued to subordinate installation commanders or activity heads. The advantages of this system are that it allows more flexibility in fund control and lessens the possibilities of reportable statutory violations. Commanders are still responsible for assuring the execution of their mission remains within the provided fund allowance and violations of that guidance may warrant administrative disciplinary action. Exceeding this funding allowance does not constitute a statutory violation but could cause an over-obligation or over-expenditure of the ACOM allotment provided on the Funding Authorization Document. Nevertheless, individuals responsible for exceeding their allowances will be named responsible for any resultant ADA violations (see Para. 10-17).

10-11. Delegation of Funding Authority

Commanders to whom funds are made available may delegate authority to establish and maintain such administrative controls as may be necessary to comply with the provisions of federal fiscal law and Department financial management regulations. This may be done keeping these key points in mind:

RESOURCE MANAGEMENT

   a. Delegation of authority must be in writing. (Verbal or telephonic authorizations will not be recognized except in emergency circumstances (i.e., those jeopardizing health and/or safety of the command) and must be confirmed in writing as soon as possible).
   b. Authority may be delegated to a named individual or a position so long as the authority is vested in a readily identifiable person at all times.
   c. Delegation of authority does not relieve commanders of their fiscal responsibilities under the law.

10-12. Special Classified Programs
Classified programs, which are sensitive "need to know," may be compartmentalized for security reasons. Specific funding distribution procedures have been created to accommodate the unique security requirements of such programs. Generally, the Vice Chief of Staff, U.S. Army (VCSA) must approve the use of the procedures.

10-13. SECARMY Representation Funds
Congress gives the SECARMY a specific level of authority to be utilized for emergency and extraordinary expenses from within the OMA appropriation. These authorities are identified under limitations entitled with the limit code .0012, described in AR 37-47, Representation Funds of the Secretary of the Army. The utilization of these authorities are very closely monitored and fall under audit responsibilities of the Army Audit Agency to ensure that funds used under these authorities are solely for the purposes intended and approved by the SECARMY. The rules for using the authorities are very specific and exceptions to deviate should be obtained from higher headquarters. A brief description of these authorities is provided below.
   a. Limitation .0012 (Miscellaneous Expenses, Category A). For official representation expenses, as authorized by the SECARMY, in connection with official functions at times of national holidays; dedication of facilities; visits of distinguished guests; purchase of floral wreaths, decorations, and awards upon occasions of national holidays and similar observances in foreign countries; and gifts and mementos by the authorized host, costing not more than $200 each, used in connection with official ceremonies or functions. Commanders of ACOMs, their subordinate commanders, and installation commanders are authorized to present gifts or mementos in circumstances that they personally document as being a necessary part of the event or occasion being observed.
   b. Limitation .0014 (Miscellaneous Expenses, Category B). For miscellaneous expenses, other than for official representation, not provided for in other appropriations. Examples of these expenses are awards for emergency rescues, witness fees for the Armed Services Board of Contract Appeals, and settlement of meritorious claims.
   c. Limitation .0015 (Criminal Investigation Activities, AR 195-4). For emergency and extraordinary expenses in support of the worldwide expenses of the U.S. Army Criminal Investigation Command's activities.
   d. Limitation .0017 (Intelligence Contingency Funds, AR 381-141). For expenses related to worldwide intelligence activities.
   e. Limitation .0019 (Compartmented Special Operations, SECARMY Letter of Instruction (proponent HQDA, G-3/5/7). For emergency and extraordinary expenses related to worldwide-compartmented operations.

Section IV
Account for the Use of Resources

10-14. Legally Using the Resources to Accomplish the Mission
This section gives a brief overview of the controlling principles used in accounting for the use of fiscal resources. Title 31, USC, Section 1301(a) states that "Appropriations shall be applied only to the objects for which the appropriations were made except as otherwise provided by law." Congress initially enacted this statutory control in March 1809. The act, generally referred to as the "Purpose Statute," was passed as a part of a reorganization of the War, Navy, and Treasury Departments to limit the discretion of the executive branch in spending appropriations. Thus it becomes abundantly evident that the Congress, for close to two hundred years, has taken a keen interest in how the Army spends the funds that have been appropriated to it. To preclude the misappropriation/misspending of funds, a body of laws, regulations,

HOW THE ARMY RUNS

court decisions, and rules has evolved over many years to direct how fiscal resources will be used to accomplish the Army's missions and tasks. Because Congress provides funds in specific amounts for specific purposes through the enactment of public law, the expenditure of those funds must be within the boundaries established by the law. The term "administrative control of funds," as required by law is used to identify those actions, events, or systems that are required to ensure essentially three things:

    a. Funds are used only for the purposes for which they were intended.

    b. Amounts of funds in excess of that available, are neither obligated, neither disbursed nor further distributed.

    c. The agency head is capable of fixing responsibility in the event of violations of either of the first two.

10-15. Availability of Appropriations for Obligations

Congress determines how long an appropriation or fund may be used, that is, new obligations may be made against the specified appropriation or fund. Most appropriations used by the Army have a limited time period for which new obligations can be made against them. Note: In the past Congress has made exceptions to the normal periods of availability of appropriations such as making two year or "X" year O&M appropriations, three-year RDT&E appropriations, and so forth, as well as continuing with the "normal" periods of availability.

    a. Annual appropriations. These appropriations, generally having a one-year period of availability to be obligated, include:

        (1) Operation and maintenance appropriations like OMA; OMNG; OMAR; and AFHO.

        (2) Military personnel appropriations like MPA, NGPA, and RPA.

    b. Multi-Year Appropriations. These appropriations having a multi-year period of availability include:

        (1) The RDT&E,A appropriation is available for two years.

        (2) Procurement appropriations (e.g., Aircraft Procurement, Army; Missile Procurement, Army; Procurement of Weapons and Tracked Combat Vehicles (WTCV), Army; Procurement of Ammunition, Army; and Other Procurement, Army (OPA)) are available for three years.

        (3) MCA; Military Construction, National Guard (MCNG); Military Construction Army Reserve (MCAR); and Army Family Housing Construction (AFHC) are available for five years.

    c. "No-year" Appropriations. These appropriations and funds have an unlimited period of availability. Examples include the appropriation for Base Realignment and Closure (BRAC) and the Army Working Capital Fund (AWCF).

    d. Expired Appropriations. Once an appropriation's period of availability is over for incurring new obligations, it is considered "expired." For five years after an appropriation expires (i.e.no new obligations can be incurred) both obligated and un-obligated balances of that appropriation shall be available for adjusting and liquidating (that is, disbursing against a previously incurred obligation) obligations properly charged to the account. As an example, the FY 12 OMA appropriation has a period of availability for obligation from 1 October 2011 through 30 September 2012. The appropriation has a five-year expiration period from 1 October 2012 through 30 September 2017.

    e. Cancelled Appropriations. After the fifth year of expiration an appropriation is canceled on the books of the U.S. Treasury. The appropriation is no longer available for any purpose, for example, accounting adjustments. Obligated and un-obligated balances are canceled. Using the FY 12 OMA example above, it would cancel on 30 September 2017. Note: If an obligation adjustment, such as a final settlement to a disputed contract, has to be made from what is now a canceled appropriation, then the payment is made out of the activity's current year appropriation subject to several limitations such as total amounts of such transactions cannot exceed 1% of the current appropriation and cannot exceed the un-liquidated balance of the initial, now cancelled, appropriation.

10-16. Properly Obligating the Resources

An obligation is the action taken to establish a liability against the U.S. Government that will ultimately result in a disbursement from the U.S. Treasury. There are several principles that must be followed in executing and accounting for obligations. The foundations for these principles are contained in Title 31 Money and Finance of the USC. While only the most important "obligating" principles are outlined here, the entire listing is provided in the DOD Financial Management Regulation 7000.14-R or in DFAS-IN Regulation 37-1 (Finance and Accounting Policy Implementation).

    a. Bona fide need of the current FY. A determination must be made that supplies or services required pursuant to contracts entered into or orders placed obligating an annual appropriation are intended to fill a

RESOURCE MANAGEMENT

bona fide need of the current FY. There are provisions when lead-time is an important factor to obligate funds in the current year for a subsequent year delivery.

b. Intent of Performance. Contracts entered into or placed for supplies or services are executed only if there is a bona fide intent on the part of the contractor (or other performing activity) to commence work promptly or to perform the contract in accordance with its terms and conditions (to include beginning date).

c. Assure Availability. The responsible official must ensure that proper funds are available before binding the U.S. Government in an agreement with a second party, which will result in an obligation for which the Government is required to pay.

d. Documentary Evidence. Each obligation recorded in the official record must be supported by proper documentary evidence. These may be originals, duplicates, or copies of appropriate documents so long as signatures are visible. A memorandum of telephone conversation or an electronically received written message may be used temporarily until the actual document is received.

e. Charge Immediately. Obligations, when incurred, must be charged immediately to the applicable account. The recording of obligations incurred cannot be deferred until additional funds are received. The obligation must be recorded even if there are insufficient funds to cover it, thereby incurring a statutory violation, which must then be reported through command channels. Failure to record an obligation will not obviate a suspected violation of the ADA statute.

f. Prompt Adjustment. Any adjustment to previously recorded obligations, either as an increase or decrease, must be entered in the accounts as soon as the necessity for an adjustment is evident and the amount can be determined.

10-17. ADA

Chapters 13 and 15 of USC Title 31 contain prohibitions with respect to the legal use of funds and establish punitive provisions in the event there are violations. When the ADA was codified into the USC, its provisions were incorporated into a number of sections of Title 31. The sections that are most frequently cited are sections 1341, 1342, and 1517.

a. How Anti-deficiency Act Violations Occur. Generally, ADA violations may occur when:

(1) Funding authority is issued in excess of the amount available and the excess amount is obligated or expended.

(2) There are violations of the special and recurring statutory limitations or restrictions on the amounts for which an appropriation or fund may be used.

(3) There are violations of statutory or regulatory limitations on the purposes for which an appropriation or fund may be used.

(4) Obligations are authorized or incurred in advance of funds being available.

(5) Obligations or expenditures of funds do not provide for a bona fide need of the period of availability of the fund or account and corrective funding is not available.

b. Administrative and criminal penalties for ADA violations. The person who caused the violation may be subject to discipline, to include suspension without pay or removal from office (31 USC 1349 and 1518). The Army's implementation procedures of these statutes are contained in DFAS-IN Regulation 37-1 (Finance and Accounting Policy Implementation). If an action is taken knowingly and willfully and results in a conviction for violating the ADA, the person may be fined up to $5000, imprisoned for not more than two years, or both (31 USC 1350 and 1519).

10-18. Accounting for the Obligation

a. Legal Mandate to Account for Funds. By law the DOD is required to maintain accounting systems that provide:

(1) Complete disclosure of the financial results of the Department's activities.
(2) Adequate financial information the Department needs for management purposes.
(3) Effective control over, and accountability for, assets for which the Department is responsible.
(4) Reliable accounting results that will be the basis for:
(a) Preparing and supporting the Department's budget requests.
(b) Controlling the Department's budget execution.
(c) Providing financial information the President requires.
(d) Suitable integration of the Department's accounting with the central accounting and reporting responsibilities of the Secretary of the Treasury.

HOW THE ARMY RUNS

b. DFAS. As can be surmised, if the DOD is required to account for the ways it spends its funds, so too does the Army have to account in the same way for how it uses its funds. Most of the financial management accounting required by the Army is performed by DFAS. This organization was established in January 1991 to reduce the cost and improve the overall quality of DOD financial management through consolidation, standardization, and integration of finance and accounting operations, procedures, and systems. DFAS took over responsibility for five finance and accounting centers and 338 installation finance and accounting offices that belonged to the military services and Defense agencies. Through its mandated consolidation efforts, DFAS now consists of a headquarters located in Washington, D.C., five centralized sites located in Indianapolis (formerly the U.S. Army Finance and Accounting Center), Cleveland, Columbus, Denver, Kansas City, and 20 field sites or Operating Locations (OPLOCs). Personnel staffing levels were reduced from 31,000 in 1992 to the current level of 18,000. Since 1991 DFAS has consolidated and standardized 324 finance and accounting systems down to 109 systems in 1998. In the future DFAS expects to reduce down to 32 systems.

Accounting systems used by the Army. The Army and its subordinate activities use a number of the remaining accounting systems operated by DFAS. The principal system used is GFEBS (see Para. 10-40). GFEBS has been fully deployed to replace Standard Financial System (STANFINS) as the Army's primary accounting system. Other accounting systems are used by the Research, Development and Acquisition activities, the U.S. Army Corps of Engineers, and the Army National Guard.

10-19. The Army Management Structure (AMS)

The AMS provides a resource management language and coding structure that is based on congressional appropriations. It relates program dollars and manpower to a standard classification of activities and functions required and used by Congress as they deliberate on Army programs and budget requests. GFEBS has initiated a new term called functional area which combines the first six digits of the old AMS Codes (AMSCOs) and the Management Decision Package (MDEP) to help record data in the detail needed for budgeting, execution, and accounting. Army activities use the AMS to record obligations and disbursements in the requisite accounting system. The details for constructing the accounting and classification codes for all funds received by the Army are contained in DFAS-IN Manual 37-100-xx, where the "xx" indicates the last two digits of the FY. For instance the AMS for FY 2012 would be outlined in DFAS-IN Manual 37-100-12. Using the AMS coding structure assists Army activities to fulfill federal accounting requirements. A simple illustration translating an accounting classification code (as one could see on a purchase request, a set of Temporary Duty (TDY) orders, and so forth) would be the following accounting fund cite on a supply purchase transaction at Fort Sill: 21 2 2020 57-3106 325796.BD 26FB QSUP CA200 GRE12344019003 AB22 WORNAA S34031.

Table 10-1. Translating an Accounting Code

Code	Data Element Treasury Symbol:	Translation
21	Department Code	Department of the Army
2	Period Availability	FY 2002
2020	Basic Symbol	OMA Appropriation
57	Operating Agency	TRADOC
3106	Allotment Serial Number	(a locally assigned code)
325796.BD	AMSCO or Project Account	Base Operations (-), Director of Logistics
26FB	Element of Resource	Supplies - Army Managed / DWCF item
QSUP	MDEP	Installation Supply Operations
CA200	Functional Cost Account	Commercial Activities - contract furnished supplies
GRE1234019003	Standard Document Number	(a locally assigned code)
AB22	Account Processing Code	(a locally assigned code)
WORNAA	Unit Identification Code (UIC)	Fort Sill Garrison
S34030	Fiscal Station Number	DFAS OPLOC, Lawton, OK

10-20. Year-End Certification of Accounts

RESOURCE MANAGEMENT

Since DFAS was established, the subordinate Defense Accounting Office (DAO) has had the responsibility for preparing and monitoring "accounting reports" at the installation. Commanders who receive FADs authorizing them to incur obligations not in excess of certain amounts and for specific purposes have a legal requirement to "certify the status" of those funds as of 30 September, that is, the end of FY. Commanders may delegate the authority to certify FY-end reports to the Deputy Commander, Chief of Staff, Garrison Commander, or Director of Resource Management.

   a. The DAO will make the certification on the "accounting reports" substantially as follows: "I hereby certify that the attached reports and associated schedules include all transactions received which have been properly recorded and are supported by subsidiary accounting records."

   b. The DAO will forward the certification to the Commander or a designated representative, who, in turn, will make the following certification: "I hereby certify that the attached reports and schedules include all known transactions. Those meeting the criteria of 31 USC 1501(A) have been obligated and are so reported. All reports and schedules for all transactions for the fiscal year ended September 30, ____, are correct and are supported by subsidiary accounting records. All individual upward obligation and open allotment disbursement adjustments in excess of $100,000 of expired appropriations have been properly approved and are on file for audit purposes."

   c. Certifications are required for all appropriations and for any reimbursable activity performed by the command or agency. The ASA(FM&C) certifies all Army appropriations to the U.S. Treasury.

Section V
Analyze the Use of Resources

10-21. A Change in Responsibilities
The Chief of Staff, U.S. Army (CSA) charged Army leaders with the responsibility to evaluate or analyze and report on the effectiveness of program and budget accomplishment. These evaluations and reports relate funds and personnel inputs in output terms to the Army's Title 10 responsibilities. In 2003 DOD, the military departments, and agencies renamed their resource management processes to the PPBE process.

10-22. Execution Reviews
Using the information presented by the accounting systems and other data feeder systems, functional, programmatic and fiscal managers along with commanders track the course of program and budget execution in their organization or functional area. Inherent in this analysis is the need to judge program performance and effectiveness, to consider the need for more resources to accomplish the specified program, and finally to consider reallocation of resources to higher priority missions and programs. This process takes place at all of the resourcing echelons of the Army.

10-23. HQDA Quarterly Reviews
The Army conducts quarterly reviews of program performance and fiscal execution focusing on strategic priorities and performance metrics. The OASA(FM&C) is responsible for the conduct of the quarterly reviews.

10-24. Shifting Resources
During the course of analyzing the execution of resources, there often arises the need to shift resources outside the boundaries of programs for which Congress authorized and Appropriated Funds (APF) (see Para. 14-2a). Examples of such real life events may be an emerging contingency operation, storm damage to an installation, increasing cost of installation utilities, accelerating the procurement of an item to achieve an economic savings, new bills resulting from a newly assigned mission, and so forth. The congressional committees concerned with DOD's operations have generally accepted the view that rigid adherence to the amounts justified for budget activities, appropriations, or for subsidiary items or purposes may unduly jeopardize the effective accomplishment of planned programs in a businesslike and economical manner.

   a. Reprogramming procedures have been worked out with the congressional committees (House and Senate Appropriations and Authorization Committees (and for intelligence related items, the House and Senate Select Intelligence Committees)) to accommodate different degrees of interest in the

HOW THE ARMY RUNS

reprogramming of funds; that is, certain reprogramming requires prior approval by the appropriate committees of Congress, while others require advance notification, and still others are provided notice after the fact. Reprogramming reapplies funds from one project to another within the same appropriation or transfers funds from one appropriation to another to resolve financial shortfalls or to adjust programs to meet unforeseen requirements. The process is subject to designated dollar thresholds and congressional requirements for advance approval or notification. No transfers (shifts between appropriations) are allowed without prior consent of Congress and must be requested in writing by the submission of the Congressional Reprogramming Request (DD 1415).

b. Other flexibility is obtained through additional laws, committee reports, or by requesting supplemental appropriations. The OASA(FM&C) manages the reprogramming process for Army appropriations.

10-25. Analyzing the "Accounting Books"—Joint Reconciliation Program

The Joint Reconciliation Program is an effort combining the skills and expertise of accountants, budget and program analysts, contracting professionals, logisticians, internal review auditors, and DFAS personnel for the purpose of verifying the validity of un-liquidated obligations, contractor work in progress, billing status, and validating the continued need for goods and services that have not yet been delivered. The reconciliation must be performed by all commands and, when performed properly, will result in real dollar savings through the identification and cancellation of nonessential goods and services, reconciliation of current appropriations to ensure the correctness of amounts obligated, and liquidation of appropriations expiring at the end of the FY.

a. The primary objectives of the Joint Reconciliation Program are to "harvest" OA by:
(1) De-obligating funds supporting invalid obligations.
(2) Eliminating the use of current funds to pay liabilities arising from appropriations that expired.
(3) Reconciling and liquidating delinquent travel advances.
(4) Eliminating and avoiding Unmatched Disbursements (UMD).
(5) Eliminating and avoiding Negative Un-Liquidated Obligations (NULO).

b. As a result of performing effective joint reconciliation, commands increase their purchasing power which directly enhances mission accomplishment. Purchasing power is increased in that:
(1) Canceled account liabilities are reduced.
(2) Current OA is harvested for reutilization.
(3) Erroneous payments and over payments are identified and eliminated.
(4) Visibility over contractor Work In Process (WIP) and Contract In Process (CIP) is increased.
(5) Delinquent travel advances are eliminated.

c. Additionally, joint reconciliation increases the Army's stewardship credibility with Congress. The integrity and accuracy of financial records has improved and the cycle time for processing financial transactions has been reduced. History has proven that using a thorough and intense joint reconciliation program is an excellent investment of time and resources and adds value to financial management, logistics, and procurement activities.

Section VI
Improving Management and Business Practices in the Army

10-26. Efforts to Improve Army Management

Since the early 1980s, major legislative and Army management initiatives have introduced an unprecedented focus on performance and results. These initiatives all point to the transition to more outcome-oriented program management and performance budgeting.

10-27. Federal Manager's Financial Integrity Act (FMFIA) of 1982

a. This act requires all federal agencies to establish and maintain effective accounting and administrative controls to provide "reasonable assurance" that:
(1) Obligations and costs are in compliance with applicable laws.
(2) Funds, property, and other assets are safeguarded against waste, loss, unauthorized use or misappropriation.
(3) Revenues and expenditures are properly recorded and accounted for.

RESOURCE MANAGEMENT

b. The Act also requires agency heads to submit an annual statement to the President and the Congress indicating whether agency management controls are reasonable and, where they are not, material weaknesses are identified and corrective actions are taken.

10-28. CFO Act of 1990

a. The CFO Act was enacted to implement more effective financial management practices in the federal government. Its key purpose is to provide more accurate, timely, and reliable financial information for decision-makers through improved accounting systems, integrated functional and financial management, and strengthened internal controls. The law also establishes initial requirements for the "systematic measurement of performance" by shifting the management focus from resource acquisition to resource execution-not in terms of obligation and outlay rates, but in how well taxpayer dollars are spent.

b. A major provision of the Act mandated the preparation of audited annual financial statements for revolving funds, trust funds, and substantially commercial activities. The law designated ten federal agencies—including the DA—as pilots for comprehensive, agency-wide financial statements covering all operations and activities. As the first DOD pilot under the CFO Act, the Army broke new ground in a number of important areas-for example, physical inventory policy, valuation of assets, interface between military pay and personnel systems, the incorporation of outcome-oriented program performance measures in financial reports, and the restructuring of the management control process. The U. S. Government Accountability Office (GAO) and congressional committees have acknowledged Army efforts and improvements. However, the Army cannot by itself achieve full compliance with the standards of the CFO Act. The resolution of long-term problems with financial systems is a DOD-wide effort and there must be government-wide accounting principles and standards to support both management decision-making and public accountability.

10-29. Government Management Reform Act (GMRA) of 1994

a. GMRA implements the requirements for audited annual financial statements "covering all accounts and associated activities of each office, bureau, and activity of the agency" for all federal agencies. Beginning in 1998, and annually thereafter, the Secretary of the Treasury, in coordination with the Director of the OMB, is required to submit to the President and Congress government-wide audited financial statements that cover all accounts and associated activities of the executive branch of the federal government. With the end of the CFO Act pilot project and full implementation of reporting under the Act, the Army continues working to implement the letter and the spirit of the legislation and to improve all aspects of Army financial management and stewardship.

b. The most recent financial report for the U.S. Government can be viewed online at http://www.gao.gov/financial.html

c. The most recent financial statement for the Army can be viewed online at http://comptroller.defense.gov/cfs/index.html

10-30. Government Performance and Results Act (GPRA) of 1993

a. GPRA is major management reform legislation and a critical step in the inevitable transition to more outcome-oriented program management and performance budgeting. As noted above, the CFO Act intended to integrate financial and functional systems to provide better information for decision makers and shift management focus to how well taxpayer dollars are spent. Although implementation of the CFO Act and audited financial statements have led to significant improvements in financial reporting, the law itself provided only limited guidance with regard to its provisions for "the systematic measurement of performance".

b. The GPRA builds on the CFO Act and establishes the framework for full integration of financial and functional data in all phases of the resourcing cycle. GPRA was implemented to improve government-wide programs by linking resource expenditures to results achieved. OSD has implemented GPRA by establishing corporate and annual performance goals, and linking specific performance measures to each goal. The most recently completed Quadrennial Defense Review (QDR) serves as DOD's strategic plan in accordance with the GPRA requirements.

c. The purpose of the GPRA is to increase public confidence in the federal government and improve program effectiveness and public accountability by systematically holding agencies accountable for achieving program results. The law also is intended to improve congressional decision-making by providing more objective information on the relative effectiveness and efficiency of federal programs and

HOW THE ARMY RUNS

spending. DOD FY 2012 financial and performance reporting consists of three components: Agency Financial Report (AFR) published November 15, 2012; Annual Performance Report (APR) to be published February 6, 2013; and Summary of Performance and Financial Information to be published February 15, 2013. The AFR contains the Management's Discussion and Analysis section that provides executive- level information on the Department's history, mission, organization, key performance activities, analysis of the financial statements, controls and legal compliance and other challenges facing the Department. The APR will be included in the Congressional Budget Justification and provides the detailed performance information and description of results by performance measures. The Summary of Performance and Financial Information, formerly the DOD Citizen's Report, summarizes the Department's financial and performance information from the AFR and the APR, making the information more transparent and accessible to Congress, the public, and other key constituents. All three reports are available at the DOD Comptroller's website: http://comptroller.defense.gov/reports.html.

d. Through its PPBE process, the Army reviews and monitors its strategic plans and mission objectives. The PPBE process supports the Army's implementation of the GPRA by using:

(1) Army Strategic Planning Guidance (ASPG) that promulgates Army goals, strategies, objectives, and the required capabilities to achieve them.

(2) Army Planning Priorities Guidance (APPG) that leads to the preparation of capabilities-based action plans and, where needed, the prioritized allocation of resources to carry them out.

(3) Army Program Guidance Memorandum (APGM) that links operational tasks and their associated resources to the Secretary of the Army USC Title 10 functional responsibilities.

(4) Army Campaign Plan (ACP) that establishes nine campaign objectives incorporating Army transformation into the context of ongoing strategic commitments.

The Army POM/BES that results from the PPBE integrated programming and budgeting phase allows the Army to balance program and budget resources based upon more definitive resource objectives.

MDEPs, the building blocks of the Army program, are linked to objectives, sub-objectives, and prioritized resource tasks. Program resources that govern levels of accomplishment are adjusted according to affordability.

Appropriations approved by Congress in the budget phase are applied in the execution phase. Execution of programs is constantly monitored to ensure congressional and other legally mandated requirements are met.

10-31. Federal Financial Management Improvement Act (FFMIA) of 1996

This law builds upon and compliments the acts discussed above. It requires auditors to report as part of their report on agencies' annual financial statements whether the agencies' financial management systems comply substantially with three requirements: (1) federal financial management systems requirements; (2) applicable federal accounting standards; and (3) the U.S. Government Standard General Ledger at the transaction level. These requirements are critical for ensuring that agency financial management activities are consistently and accurately recorded, and timely and uniformly reported throughout the federal government.

10-32. Management Controls

a. Management controls are the procedures we establish to ensure that we accomplish our objectives and guard Army resources against fraud, waste, and abuse. Numerous audit and inspection reports, however, continue to find serious management control deficiencies in DOD and the Army. This damages our reputation as stewards of public resources and hinders our ability to compete effectively in Congress for additional resources. Congress has made clear that their emphasis on management controls will continue.

b. Army Regulation 11-2, Management Control, establishes policies and guidelines for implementing the provisions of the Federal Financial Management Improvement Act. It describes the Army's current management control process which was restructured effective in FY 95 to reduce the administrative burden, to provide commanders and managers with greater flexibility in scheduling and conducting their evaluations, and to make them directly accountable for the effectiveness of their management controls. The restructured process requires management control evaluations only for the most critical controls (the "key management controls") and encourages commanders and managers to use existing review and oversight processes wherever possible to accomplish evaluations.

RESOURCE MANAGEMENT

10-33. Improving Business Practices

a. An essential element of Resource Management is the process of reviewing, revising and reengineering the business practices of the Army to increase revenues, reduce costs, and leverage Army assets. Several tools have been developed to assist in furthering business practices improvements:

(1) The Business Practices Initiatives focus on Army operations to avoid or reduce costs, generate and collect revenues, leverage assets, streamline and consolidate functions, form partnerships, and use the latest technology to help the Army better utilize scarce resources.

(2) The development of initiatives under the focused leadership of the BSIT Forum is intended to support transformation of the business sides of the Department of the Army, resulting in a more efficient and effective business environment from which the total Army is supported.

(3) The Legislative Program expedites processing of viable, high payoff, reengineering legislative proposals through OSD, OMB, and Congress.

(4) The Non-appropriated Fund (NAF) Financial Oversight prepares policy guidance and conducts reviews of NAF finances and encourages NAF activities to operate more like a business.

(5) The Waiver Program facilitates preparation, coordination, and submission of waiver requests to gain exceptions to certain policies or regulations on a case-by-case basis to improve processes.

b. The Army is implementing new and improved business practices to bridge the gap between Army resources and Army requirements. Many private sector business practices "make sense" for the DOD and can potentially be applied to optimize the use of Army resources. The overall objective is to stretch available resources by generating revenues, reducing costs, leveraging assets, and improving the delivery of service.

c. A major example of the successful use of business practices to bridge the gap between Army resources and requirements is in the area of real property assets (land and facilities). Historically, the Army relied primarily upon APFs (MILCON Funds) to build, modify, and upgrade Army facilities. The Army also relied upon APFs (Operating Funds) to maintain and repair the real property assets. The lack of sufficient funds allows construction of only the most critical facilities and causes a backlog of maintenance and repair that ultimately reduces the useful life of Army assets. As the size of the Army was reduced during the 1990's, the Army began to dispose of real property assets that were underutilized and no longer needed. There is a significant cost associated with maintaining assets, even when the assets are maintained at a minimal level. This disposal effort is continuing. However, a problem surfaces when facilities are needed, but there are insufficient APFs to construct, modify, or maintain them.

d. To address this problem, the Army began using a new private sector tool – Public Private Ventures (PPVs). PPVs can take many forms - the Residential Communities Initiative (RCI) Program; Armament Retooling and Manufacturing Support Program (ARMS); leasing initiatives that use Title 10, Section 2267 authority; Morale, Welfare, and Recreation (MWR) Program initiatives; utilities privatization; and energy saving projects. What is unique about PPVs is (1) they involve a significant contribution of private capital and expertise to meet Army resource needs; and (2) the private sector requirements for successful business ventures must also be met. With the PPV approach, the Army is not buying a specified product in the traditional sense. The Army is selecting a private sector "partner" to work jointly on a solution that will line up both with Army requirements and those for commercial success.

e. The past several years have witnessed a quantum leap forward in the planned use of PPVs as a tool to bridge the gap between Army resources and requirements for real property assets. The Congress has repeatedly shown its general support for using this tool by passing very significant enabling legislation in areas such as housing privatization, utilities privatization, energy savings, and enhanced lease authority. These PPV efforts will have a prominent role in the way the Army manages its real property assets in the future. We will succeed if we (1) use PPVs as part of a sound strategic plan; (2) adequately weigh the long-term implications of our actions; and (3) realize that PPVs make new and different demands on program and financial managers.

f. The Army also is wrestling with similar resource management issues for activities supported by NAF. Base closures, troop realignments, and declining APF support create a challenging environment for NAF. Policy decisions for NAF must take into account a resource management strategy that considers the interrelationship between APFs and NAF. Coordination between the NAF and APF communities is essential to ensure appropriate execution of both the appropriated and NAF programs. For example, a facility built as a NAF major construction project may be authorized APFs for maintenance and repair support. In such instances, a one-time NAF expenditure could result in a significant and continuing APF

HOW THE ARMY RUNS

operating expense. Conversely, reduction of APF support for NAF activities can force dramatic changes in the level of quality-of-life programs available to Soldiers and their families.

g. Enabling and encouraging improved operating efficiency, better use of information, implementation of private sector practices, and enhanced utilization of Army resources through asset leveraging is essential to maximizing the use of The Army's scarce resources. Improving business and operating practices is not only complementary to financial reform, but is in the spirit of reinventing government and the "battle on bureaucracy", and is absolutely necessary to fully support Army transformation to meet future challenges.

10-34. Cost Management (CM)

a. CM must play a critical role in support of decision-making. Managers at all levels fight a war every day in resourcing and operating today's Army. It is a cost war. We are drawn into it and forced to fight it in order to maintain the maximum number of well-trained and properly equipped forces possible. In the cost war, we do not lose forces to an enemy on a conventional battlefield, but to the constant reduction of dollars available to resource the force. This is an unfamiliar war, fought on an unfamiliar battleground by commanders and leaders generally new to the weapons needed to win. CM, focused on the activities necessary to produce the products or services required for mission success, is the most important war-fighting "doctrine" available for employment. Given full understanding of the potential of CM and complete knowledge and use of its working parts, the cost war can be won.

b. The Army has chosen to implement Activity Based Costing (ABC) as a tool to assist the local manager in maximizing scarce resources and as a means of continuous process improvement. The Army Implementation Plan mandates CM/ABC implementation in the Army's eleven support business areas. These business areas are Acquisition, Base Operations, Civilian Human Resources (CHR) (see Chap. 14), Contracting, Depot Maintenance, Information Support, Institutional Training, Ordnance, R&D Laboratories, Supply Management, and Test & Evaluation.

10-35. Cost Modeling

CM/ABC focuses managerial skills and action at all levels on the results of a cost modeling process that presents useful, accurate cost data based on the activity (a product or service) that the manager wishes to accomplish. Traditional cost accounting systems and processes in DOD do not provide the same focus. Instead, they focus cost models on bags of money that are available to accomplish grossly defined categories of expenditures. Amounts of money are allocated to the bag by passing down a limit or budget, then managers at all levels use up the money until someone tells them that the budget is exhausted. This is and has been the conventional way of operating. In fact, using up the entire budget allocated down to low levels in the organization has generally been viewed as a good thing. The budget has come to be thought of as an entitlement to spend. This is far from a desirable way to operate at a functional level. The objective should be to use as little money as possible to achieve a defined level of quality and thereby have as much money as possible available to allocate to other command priorities. These available funds must be identified early in the FY to enable execution of other priority missions.

10-36. Planning

a. Managers at all levels should accurately plan their future resourcing needs just as tactical commanders plan combat engagements in order to win the next battle and the overall campaign. Relative CM/ABC success should be measured based on how much and how often that manager can reduce the resourcing need over time while accomplishing the required tasks to an acceptable level of quality. Resources saved in the production of one product or service are then available to commanders to redirect to high priority tasks otherwise destined to be unfunded. The CM/ABC process, focused on important activities, in conjunction with other leadership tools, provides the manager the information needed to know how much something needed really costs and provides a structure to do something about the unit cost of producing it.

b. Integration of CM/ABC practices into the twenty-first century Army is designed to enhance decision making at all levels. This requires a cultural change within the Army, recognizing that CM/ABC is a necessary discipline for all managers and decision makers both military and civilian. Effective CM/ABC practices will assist us in understanding the true costs of producing goods and services, improving operations, and linking execution to Army strategies. CM/ABC fully supports continuous improvement to achieve the most efficient organization. Therefore it is useful in streamlining cost competition

RESOURCE MANAGEMENT

(Competitive Sourcing), productivity and performance programs, and perhaps most of all, decision making by local managers. Executing CM/ABC doctrine controls costs and improves efficiency and effectiveness.

   c. The support business areas will continue to be vital to the mission of the Army. CM/ABC is the Army's tool to maximize the effectiveness of existing fiscal resources. Aggressive, proactive management of existing resources is the best way to provide resources for higher priority mission needs such as improved mission support services, quality of life, and force retention.

   d. Successful implementation of CM/ABC combines strong leadership support, a cycle of commitment and performance review, employee empowerment, and motivational incentives. With Army leadership serving as strong advocates, the CM/ABC culture establishes goals and encourages participative behavior to achieve improved performance.

10-37. Building an ABC Model

   a. An ABC model is needed because the traditional cost accounting system used by the DOD does not allow the assignment of all relevant costs to a product or service (activity). For example, a commander should know the total cost of activities under his control (e.g. the cost of overhauling a tactical vehicle, or training a Soldier in a new Military Occupational Specialty (MOS), or renovating a set of family quarters). More importantly, the manager that has the power to influence costs must know and understand them. By analyzing them and the process that produces them, the effective manager is prompted to discover numerous changes that will affect costs. The manager should expect subordinates to understand, explain, and improve cost performance. Unfortunately, a process of collecting and allocating costs that contribute to the creation of a product or service is not readily available. An ABC model needs to be built based on the real way the production mechanism functions in each business area and location. Building a specific model is a time consuming but necessary function to be able to deal with real data vice a template model, provided by others, that can produce only theoretical or standard costs. The creation and regular updating of a specific model is often viewed as too much work and therefore not attempted. The loser is the manager faced with more requirements than assets to get them done.

   b. A process to build a model has to be used to capture and allocate costs. A useful model is built by allowing the people who do the work to build their model using a simple question and answer walk-through of what they do each day in performing their mission. All relevant costs are then allocated to the product or service that the tasks produce. No salary or other relevant expense can be left out. Managerial tasks commonly referred to as overhead and other costs have to be considered. On the other hand, precision, carried to an extreme, can overly complicate the process and diminish usefulness of the results. This outcome has been observed in many initial attempts at creating a useful cost model. Together, CM and the ABC model give the manager a structure to be as cost effective as possible.

   c. A concrete example of the CM/ABC process at work: During the FY's first quarter CM performance review, the first-line manager in the vehicle maintenance shop presented his second quarter spending plan. During previous reviews under similar circumstances, he stated he would need many hours of overtime in the second quarter to immediately repair vehicles returning from an extended deployment. Instead for this review, because of his understanding and use of cost management and the cost model that represents what he does, he has become conscious of all costs and consistently tries to reduce them. The culture of the workforce has been changed to include reduced cost into the definition of mission success. To that end, he spent additional time and effort better allocating work throughout his workforce and managing the second quarter's employee leaves more carefully. He also gave priority to repair to only the vehicles that commanders told him were most critical to have repaired right away. This extra effort resulted in no overtime being required in the second quarter which he can now brief as a unit cost for vehicle repair that was below the planned level. This identified alternative process, discussed in the performance review, will be recognized for possible wider application throughout the organization.

10-38. Using the ABC Model

   a. Once a model is built and is repetitively presenting unit cost results, a managerial process to use the data has to be implemented. Leaders with power to change the way things function must view the unit cost data, be presented with managers' analyses, and approve or create new work processes and direct their implementation.

   b. A regularly scheduled performance review and planning meeting can be the single vehicle to do all these things. The manager is presented with the data, preferably by the individuals responsible for spending the money to produce the product, and its correctness is evaluated. The best results are

HOW THE ARMY RUNS

usually reached if the first line manager is the person explaining what the costs are and why his planned resource needs were either exceeded or improved upon. Since the overall goal is to reduce unit costs without sacrificing performance, that discussion ensues. It is important to remember that this same manager previously presented his spending plan, using his ABC model as the basis, for the quarter that is now being reviewed.

  c. The commander or senior manager should be the leader at the review as this is the person who has the ultimate authority to implement procedural changes that result in cost reductions in the process under scrutiny. The commander is also the one that will reallocate the savings produced to higher priorities. An integral part of the overall methodology must be to provide incentives for managers at all levels to think and work smarter.

  d. In the previous example, the commander may choose to divide the money now available for reallocation between his desire to pay for another need and to provide a reward to the manager that is helping him win the cost war. The commander might ask the first line manager and his supervisor what is needed to improve the function of the organization that produced this improvement. The commander could chose to buy that new forklift for Supply that they have needed for a while but have not had the funds to buy. All this can happen at the same performance review thereby reducing the number of subsequent meetings that need to take place.

  e. Commanders focus on the tactical component of CM/ABC by managing cost and performance throughout the cycle of planning and review to achieve continuous improvement. Leadership sets efficiency challenges to be achieved through the managing of activities (CM/ABC), processes, and cost. Gaining a better understanding of cost and performance will better enable managers to achieve the strategic goals set by Army leadership.

10-39 Cost Commitment and Review

  a. The cycle of commitment and review is the key for each business area to practice CM/ABC successfully. This process has been established through prototypes and is depicted in Figure 10-4.

  b. Managerial costing requires commanders and senior managers to provide the leadership support and need for CM/ABC information. The necessity to pull or lead the cost reconnaissance process creates an atmosphere of cost awareness throughout the command. A cycle of forecasting and after-action review provides frequent feedback and accountability that drives continuous improvement and allows for the most efficient use of resources.

  c. A good way to look at the cycle of commitment and review of cost managing in the future is by analogy to Command, Control, Communications, Intelligence (C3I) used in the tactical Army. The same principles can be applied to inform decision-makers in ways that lead to improved execution. This can easily fit the emerging requirements of better cost management.

  d. ABC represents the intelligence or information gathering process. In battlefield management, these are the intelligence technologies that acquire information for war fighters. Cost warrior pull recognizes the war fighter as the customer of the management information system. The cost warrior will command what needs to be measured and how to present the information. Cost forecasting recognizes the value and importance of projecting the current cost situation into the future in order to control future spending. In financial terms this means that the cost control system should facilitate forecasting, what if analysis, and simulation. After-action cost review completes the cycle by considering actual mission execution and communicating the results. In financial terms, this means that cost warriors must ultimately be measured and held accountable for cost performance. The trend of cost based performance metrics should be expected to show continuous improvement.

  e. Effective development of CM/ABC should provide an important weapon for winning the cost war. Strategies, tactics, and weapons that improve the command, control, and communication of cost will be important.

RESOURCE MANAGEMENT

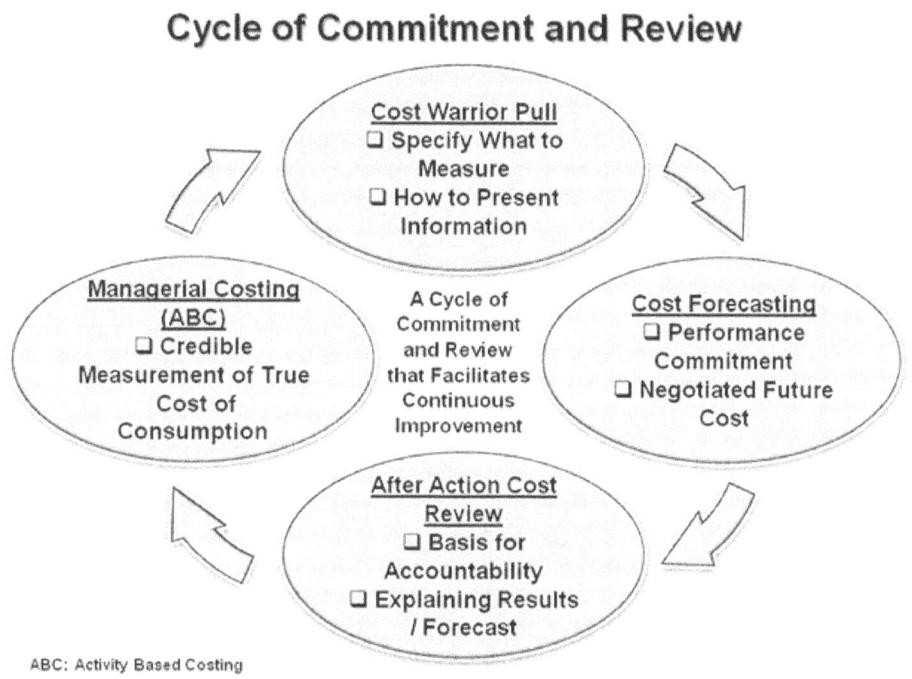

Figure 10-4. Cycle of Commitment and Review

10-40. GFEBS

a. GFEBS is a Chief Financial Officers Council certified Commercial Off The shelf (COTS) Enterprise Resource Planning (ERP) system that will provide the Army and the Department of Defense relevant, reliable, and timely financial information across the full spectrum of its operations. GFEBS is helping the Army standardize and streamline its financial business processes to provide continuous access to financial information, as well as contribute an important element in the development of an Army integrated enterprise-wide system.

b. The three ERP systems—GFEBS, the Logistics Modernization Program, and the Global Combat Support System-Army—provide the Army an integrated enterprise-wide system to provide decision-makers with data for better informed decision making and to comply with legal and mandatory reporting requirements. As "mixed systems," these three systems perform financial management functions to better support their primary missions and system functions. GFEBS replaces existing information systems: the Standard Army Finance System, the Defense Joint Accounting System, and the Standard Operation and Maintenance Army Research and Development System. GFEBS is a web-based system designed to integrate seamlessly into the Army's current information technology environment. The project also includes significant business process reengineering, change management, and business case analysis support components. The GFEBS solution includes Design, Build, Run, and Application Service Provider services for approximately 10 years. Ultimately, GFEBS will replace over 80 Army legacy accounting, financial and assess management systems.

c. GFEBS processes financial, real property, cost management, and performance data, and then integrates this data for decision support. GFEBS' primary objectives include improving performance; standardizing financial and business processes; ensuring capabilities exist to meet future needs; and complying with statutory and regulatory accounting requirements. Specifically, GFEBS' goals are to: provide decision support information to sustain Army capabilities; provide analytic data and tools to support institutional adaptation; reduce the cost of business operations; and Improve accountability and stewardship. Once fully implemented, GFEBS will be one of the largest ERP systems in the world, processing 1 million transactions a day for the active Army, Army National Guard, and Army Reserves from some 79,000 end-users at more than 200 sites worldwide. The system will standardize transactional input and business processes across the Army; provide accurate, reliable, online and real-time data; enable cost management activities; and tie budgets to execution. For the first time, the Army will have a single source for financial and related non-financial data, and a single system of record for the General Fund. GFEBS will enable the Army's workforce to focus its efforts on value-added tasks, such as analysis and decision making, as opposed to redundant data entry or extensive reconciliations, and empower leaders at all levels to determine the true costs of operations and the costs that affect their budgets. GFEBS is a complex initiative that blends expertise from many Army and Defense organizations in developing new enterprise business processes.

d. GFEBS complies with the Standard Financial Information Structure standard, which is the common business language that supports information and data requirements for budgeting, financial accounting, cost/performance management, and external reporting across the DOD enterprise (Para. 10-40 was taken from p.2-1 and 2-2, Army Funds Management Data Reference Guide, September 2012, see http://www.asafm.army.mil/offices/BU/afm.aspx?OfficeCode=1200).

10-41. CBA—A Key Decision-Making Tool

a. In today's resource-constrained environment, the Army must exercise wise stewardship of every dollar it manages. A key element in that stewardship is to develop and use sound CBA practices throughout all requirement/resourcing processes. For every proposed program, initiative, or decision point that is presented to decision makers, it is important to provide an accurate and complete picture of both the costs to be incurred and the benefits to be derived.

b. On March 14, 2011, the Secretary of the Army directed that "All issues, proposals, or requirements must address the costs and trade-offs against projected benefits". Secretary of the Army Memorandum, SUBJECT: Consideration of Costs in Army Decision-Making, dated 14 March 2011 at https://cpp.army.mil/portal/page/portal/Cost_Performance_Portal/CPP_Main_Page/CBA_Portal/About_CBA/SA%20MEMO%20-%20CONSIDERATION%20OF%20COSTS%20IN%20ARMY%20DECISION-MAKING.3Mar2011.pdf. Also in the memorandum, The Secretary identified the Assistant Secretary of the Army for Financial Management and Comptroller as "proponent for costs in Army decision-making, policy, and guidance." The Office of the Assistant Secretary of the Army (Financial Management and Comptroller) established the CBA Portal on the Cost and Performance Portal (CPP) (see https://cpp.army.mil for detailed information on CBA). The Portal provides information on a wide range of requirements, issues, tasks, and problems that require a deliberate analysis to arrive at the optimum course of action.

c. As shown in Figure 10-5, CBA is a structured methodology for forecasting and comparing the anticipated costs and benefits of alternative courses of action in order to identify the optimum solution for achieving a stated goal or objective. The goal is to produce a strong value proposition—a clear statement that the benefits more than justify the costs, risks, and bill payers (Para. 10-41 information was taken from the CBA Portal in the Cost and Performance Portal (see https://cpp.army.mil/portal/page/portal/Cost_Performance_Portal/CPP_Main_Page/CBA_Portal).

RESOURCE MANAGEMENT

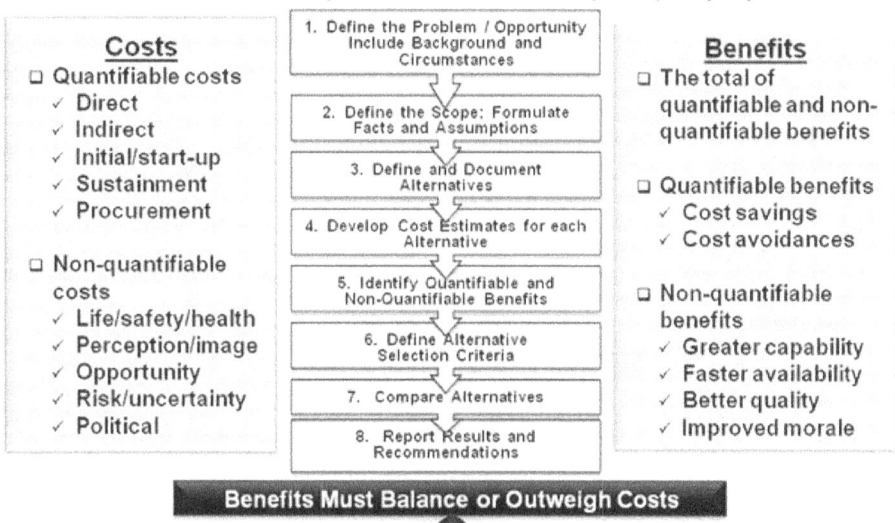

Figure 10-5. Cost Benefit Analysis (CBA)

10-42. Links to Principles
a. Visionary leadership. Commanders, leaders, and managers must determine the strategies for obtaining and managing costs. Their emphasis on mission accomplishment must be complemented by an emphasis on controlling mission costs.

b. Continuous improvement and learning. CM/ABC is not yet universally understood. Leaders must foster and encourage a continuous improvement and learning mentality within their organizations. The modeling concepts and cycle of commitment and review discussed in this chapter provide a starting point for the learning process.

10-43. Summary
CM principles offer Commanders greater flexibility in mission execution by providing more information in the decision-making process. Planning and the ABC model provide the foundation for CM. Use of the model in the commitment and review cycle enables Commanders and other senior leaders to conserve resources within individual operations. By reducing the costs of individual operations, the manager has flexibility with funds during the execution year. These available funds must be identified early in the FY to enable execution of other priority missions. CM/ABC provides a mechanism for accomplishing the mission within the funds provided.

Section VII
Non-Appropriated Funds

HOW THE ARMY RUNS

10-44. Non-Appropriated Funds Definitions
a. NAF. NAF are cash and other assets that are not appropriated by Congress. NAF come primarily from the sale of goods and services to authorized patrons, DOD military and civilian personnel and their family members, and are used to support MWR programs for the collective benefit of authorized patrons who generate them. NAF are government funds, but they are separate and apart from APF that are recorded on the books of the U.S. Treasury.

b. Non-Appropriated Fund Instrumentality (NAFI). A NAFI is a U.S. Government fiscal entity that performs an essential government function. It acts in its own name to provide, or assist other DOD organizations in providing, MWR, and other programs for military personnel, their families, and authorized civilians.

10-45. NAFI Management
a. Every NAFI is legally constituted as an "instrumentality of the United States." Funds in NAFI accounts are U.S. Government funds and NAF property including buildings and real estate is U.S. Government property. NAF are not commingled with APF and are managed separately, even when supporting a common program or activity. This means that:

(1) Each NAFI operates under the authority of the U.S. Government in accordance with applicable federal laws and departmental regulations.

(2) Because NAFIs operate under the authority of the federal government, they are entitled to the same sovereign privileges and immunities as the U.S. Government accorded by federal law.

(3) Applicable DOD directives and implementing Army regulations have the force and effect of law.

b. A NAFI is administered and managed by military or civilian personnel acting in an official capacity. The NAFI is generally immune from federal taxes and exempt from most direct state, local, and host country taxes. It must account for and report financial operations through command and department channels. NAFI operations are subject to review by Congress. AR 215-1, Military Morale, Welfare, and Recreation Programs and Non-appropriated Fund Instrumentalities, provides more information on management of Army NAFIs.

10-46. Fiduciary Responsibility for NAF (10 USC Section 2783)
NAF are U.S. Government funds entitled to the same protection as funds appropriated by the Congress.

a. Individual responsibility. There is an individual fiduciary responsibility to use NAF properly and prevent waste, loss, mismanagement, or unauthorized use. This responsibility extends to all DOD personnel to include members of the Armed Forces and appropriated funded and non-appropriated funded civilian employees.

b. Violations. Commanders are responsible for the prompt detection and proper investigation of possible violations and instituting appropriate corrective action. Individuals reporting NAF violations are protected from reprisal. Commanders will take appropriate administrative action against violators. Where evidence indicates criminal conduct, commanders will refer the matter to the appropriate criminal investigative organization. Penalties for violations of waste, loss, mismanagement, or unauthorized use of NAF apply to military, appropriated funded civilian personnel, and NAF civilian personnel. They include the full range of statutory and regulatory sanctions, both criminal and administrative, and are the same as those under provisions of federal law that govern the misuse of appropriations. Reporting of suspected violations at the lowest organizational level possible is encouraged. However, reports may be made to senior management, organizational inspectors general, or to the Defense Hotline.

10-47. Management of MWR and NAF
a. MWR and NAF are managed by a Board of Directors (BOD). Members of the BOD are the four-star commanders, the Sergeant Major of the Army, and the Assistant Secretary of the Army for Manpower and Reserve Affairs. The senior military member chairs the BOD. The MWR BOD develops goals and objectives, approves financing strategies, monitors performance, prioritizes NAF major construction requirements, and ensures fiduciary responsibility for MWR.

b. An Executive Committee (EXCOM) reports to the MWR BOD. The EXCOM is chaired by the G1. The BOD structure also includes Strategic Planning, Finance, and Audit Committees that report to the EXCOM. An Investment Subcommittee reports to the Finance Committee.

10-48. HQDA Oversight of NAF

RESOURCE MANAGEMENT

As part of the responsibility of overseeing NAF, the ASA(FM&C) participates in addressing non-appropriated fund issues to the SECARMY and CSA for decision. Applying various means, the ASA(FM&C) provides HQDA level financial management oversight of Army controlled NAF. One method is by participating in the various levels of the Soldier and Family Readiness Board of Directors' (SFRBOD) various forums. A representative from the Army Budget Office participates in all SFRBOD working group level meetings where major MWR financial policy issues can be addressed. The Military Deputy for Budget advises the SFRBOD and is a voting member of the SFRBOD three-star level Executive Committee. The Deputy Assistant Secretary of the Army for Financial Operations chairs the SFRBOD Audit Committee. A senior member of the Army Budget Office serves on the Investment Committee for the Army Banking and Investment Fund. The Military Deputy for Budget is also a voting member of the Army and Air Force Exchange System (AAFES) Board of Directors and its Finance Committee. The AAFES is a major revenue contributor to Army MWR. Through these positions, the ASA (FM&C) influences all aspects of MWR financial policy.

Section VIII
Summary and References

10-49. Summary

a. Resource management in our Army continues to evolve. New legislation, new requirements, new management initiatives, new missions, and the proviso to get the "biggest bang for the buck" out of Army resources continually force resource managers to develop new approaches to resource management. On top of this, the application of IT has literally revolutionized the resource management community. The power of the computer and its sophisticated software has provided decision makers at all levels with powerful tools to maximize the allocation and application of resources.

b. The real innovation lies, however, in the thrust of the entrepreneurial approaches being advocated in the resource management community. Recognition that Army budget levels in the 1990s were declining forced us to reexamine business practices, to integrate in a far more comprehensive manner programming and budgeting, and to look seriously at ways of enhancing the productivity of the people that constitute the Army team. The MDEP concept was a forerunner of this integration effort.

c. Third-party financing, value engineering, charge-back/direct-customer payment, self-sufficiency, organizational efficiency reviews, and output focus based on unit cost are some of the concepts that allow us to examine the way we manage our Army and to do so in a more productive way to enhance the efficiency and effectiveness of the resources that Congress and the American taxpayer provide to us to forge combat capabilities.

d. This chapter summarized the more pertinent features of resource management systems using a minimum of the complex terms associated with the process. We have identified the major players, the major steps they must take, and the various controls that guide their actions in the resource management process particularly during the execution stage.

10-50. References

a. Army Regulation 5-1, Total Army Quality Management, March 15, 2002
b. Army Regulation 11-2, Managers' Internal Control Program, January 4, 2010 with a Rapid Action Revision (RAR) 001, March 26, 2012
c. Army Regulation 37- 47, Official Representation Funds of the Secretary of the Army, September 18, 2012
d. Army Regulation 215-1, Military Morale, Welfare, and Recreation Programs and Non-appropriated Fund Instrumentalities, September 24,
e. USC, Titles as follows:
(1) Title 5 USC, Government Organization and Employees
(2) Title 10 USC, Armed Forces
(3) Title 31 USC, Money and Finance
(4) Title 32 USC, National Guard
(5) Title 41 USC, Public Contracts
f. DFAS-IN Regulation 37-1, Finance and Accounting Policy Implementation, December 10, 2012

HOW THE ARMY RUNS

g. DFAS-IN Manual 37-100-13,The Army Management Structure (AMS) for Fiscal Year 2013, Basic Complete Manual, January 2, 2013

h. DOD Regulation 7000.14-R, Financial Management Regulation (FMR), consisting of twenty volumes, 2010

MATERIAL SYSTEM RESEARCH, DEVELOPMENT, AND ACQUISITION MANAGEMENT

Chapter 11

Material System Research, Development, and Acquisition Management

Section I
Introduction

11-1. Department of Defense (DOD) and U.S. Army Capabilities Development and System Acquisition Management
This chapter describes the DOD and U.S. Army management systems used for capabilities development and Research, Development, and Acquisition (RDA) of materiel systems. These systems can be viewed simply as a combination of structure, process, and culture.
  a. Structure is the sum of the guidance provided by law, policy, or regulation, and the organization provided to accomplish the capabilities development and system RDA management functions.
  b. Process is the interaction of the structure in producing the output.
  c. Culture is the cumulative sum of past practices and their impact on interpretation of guidance and attitude toward institutional changes to the system.

11-2. System Focus
For the Army, the focus of the capabilities development and materiel system acquisition management systems is producing military units that are adequately trained, equipped, and sustained to execute the National Security Strategy (NSS), National Defense Strategy (NDS), National Military Strategy (NMS), and Quadrennial Defense Review (QDR) effectively by developing and acquiring warfighting systems that are affordable and support the national strategies. To facilitate an understanding of the process, this chapter will begin by highlighting some of the critical aspects of capabilities development.

Section II
Capabilities Integration and Development

11-3. Policy
The Chairman of the Joint Chiefs of Staff Instruction (CJCSI) 3170.01H mandates policy and the supporting Joint Capabilities Integration and Development System (JCIDS) Manual mandates procedural guidance for the JCIDS. The Army supports JCIDS through the Army's JCIDS process discussed in Army Regulation 71-9 and Training and Doctrine Command (TRADOC) Regulation 71-20.

11-4. JCIDS
  a. The JCIDS, the Defense Acquisition Management System (DAS), and the Planning, Programming, Budgeting, and Execution (PPBE) process form the DOD's three primary decision support systems/processes for shaping the military forces to support strategic guidance documents. The procedures established in JCIDS support the Chairman, Joint Chiefs of Staff (CJCS), and the Joint Requirements Oversight Council (JROC) in advising the Secretary of Defense (SECDEF) in identifying, assessing, and prioritizing joint military capabilities-based requirements (needs).
  b. JCIDS is a need driven joint capabilities-based requirements generation process. The objective is to develop a balanced and synchronized Doctrine, Organization, Training, Materiel, Leadership and Education, Personnel, Facilities, and Policy (DOTMLPF-P) solution approach that is affordable, militarily useful, supportable by outside agencies, and based on mature technology that is demonstrated in a relevant operational or laboratory environment. JCIDS implements an integrated, collaborative process, based on top-level strategic direction, to guide development of new capabilities through changes in DOTMLPF-P. Change recommendations are developed and evaluated in consideration of how to optimize the joint force's ability to operate as an integrated force. This integrated, collaborative approach requires a process that uses joint/Services concepts and integrated architectures to identify prioritized high-risk capability gaps and integrated joint DOTMLPF-P approaches (materiel and non-materiel) to resolve those capability gaps. Recent changes to the JCIDS have consolidated and institutionalized the

HOW THE ARMY RUNS

previous deliberate requirements generation process with the urgent operational requirements generation process into one standard JCIDS process with three requirement review and validation lanes-deliberate (standard), urgent (institutionalized), and emergent (new). See Sections IV and V.

11-5. DOD Science and Technology (S&T)
Since World War II, owning the technology advantage has been a cornerstone of our national strategy. Technologies such as radar, jet engines, nuclear weapons, night vision, global positioning, smart weapons, stealth, situational awareness, precision munitions, protection, robotics, and biotechnology have changed warfare dramatically. Maintaining this technological edge has become even more important as high technology weapons have become readily available on the world market. In this environment, it is imperative that joint forces possess technological superiority to ensure success and minimize casualties across the broad spectrum of engagements. The technological advantages enjoyed by the United States in Afghanistan and Iraq, which are still employed today, are the legacy of decades of wise investments in S&T. Similarly, our warfighting capabilities 10 to 15 years from now will be substantially determined by today's investment in S&T.

11-6. Army S&T
The Army's S&T investments support Army unified land operations focusing on the future force while, at the same time, seeking opportunities to provide advanced technology to the current force. This dual strategy requires a dynamic technology investment portfolio that is strategically aligned with the Army's future operational capability needs and that maintains an awareness of the lessons learned from current overseas contingency operations. Fundamentally, Army S&T programs are seeking to provide solutions that enable faster, lighter, and smarter systems.

   a. The S&T program supports Army unified land operations in three ways. First, Soldiers benefit today from technologies that emerged from the Army's past investments. Second, S&T exploits transition opportunities by accelerating mature technologies derived from ongoing efforts. Finally, Army S&T leverages the expertise of our scientists and engineers to develop solutions to unforeseen problems encountered during current operations, such as the slat armor applied to Stryker combat vehicles for enhanced Rocket-Propelled Grenade (RPG) protection.

   b. The ultimate goal of the Army's S&T program is to provide the Soldier with a winning edge on the battlefield. The accelerating pace of technological change continues to offer significant opportunities to enhance the survivability, lethality, deployability, and versatility of Army forces. High technology research and development is, and will remain, a central feature of The Army Plan (TAP). The key to the TAP strategy is the planned transition of promising technology developments into tomorrow's operational capabilities. Technology Demonstrations (TD), discussed later, which evolve into systems and system upgrades incorporated in the Army Modernization Plan (AMP), accomplish this transition.

   c. Army S&T programs are an integral part of capabilities development and system acquisition management. The S&T program consists of three stages – basic research (6.1), applied research (6.2), and advanced technology development (6.3). The identifiers—6.1, 6.2, etc.—are commonly used for identifying funds, but they are also used as a shorthand technique by members of the Research and Development (R&D) community to identify levels of research development. For example, instead of referring to a project as being "in applied research," it is often referred to as being "6.2." The 6.1, 6.2, and 6.3 categories are known as the "tech base." Basic research (6.1) includes all efforts of scientific study and experimentation directed toward increasing knowledge and understanding in those fields related to long-term national security needs. Applied research (6.2) includes all efforts directed to the solution of specific military problems, short of major development projects. Advanced technology development (6.3) includes all efforts directed toward projects, which have moved into the development of hardware for testing of operational feasibility. Initiatives, such as the DOD Joint Capability Technology Demonstrations (JCTD), discussed later in this chapter, obscure the distinction between S&T and development – pre- and post- acquisition Milestone (MS) B activities.

      (1) Army S&T has been at the forefront in adapting technology for urgent operational needs, as exemplified by the First Strike Ration, which reduces the weight of the daily combat food rations carried by Soldiers in initial periods of high intensity conflict by 40-50 percent. Likewise, DOD scientists and engineers continuously harvest materiel solutions from past investments, such as the development of mine detection ground penetrating radar. They also provide extraordinary technical expertise resulting in the development and integration of technologies, such as lightweight armor. This armor has dramatically

MATERIAL SYSTEM RESEARCH, DEVELOPMENT, AND ACQUISITION MANAGEMENT

enhanced Mine Resistant Ambush Protected (MRAP) vehicle survivability in the face of constantly evolving threats. Also, Army S&T provides the technology for many of the upgrade and modernization programs for existing systems.

(2) The S&T program will continue to invest in a diverse portfolio of technologies and research. A significant S&T investment is made in basic research areas such as advanced materials, nanotechnology, biotechnology, network science, science of autonomy, immersive technology, and quantum information science. Other large investment areas focus on protection technologies, where we are seeking to develop technologies for active and passive protection of the Soldier, ground vehicles, and air platforms. Army S&T continues to invest heavily in Command, Control, Communication, Computer, Information, Surveillance, and Reconnaissance (C4ISR), medical/force health protection, lethality, Soldier systems, logistics, rotorcraft, unmanned systems, and advanced simulation.

d. A mainstay of the Army strategy for military technology is a viable in-house research capability. Research, Development, and Engineering Command (RDECOM), Research, Development, Engineering Centers (RDEC) and laboratories are the key organizations responsible for technical leadership, scientific advancements and support for the capabilities development and system acquisition management processes. Activities of these organizations range from basic research to the correction of deficiencies in field systems. Academia and industry, as well as hands-on bench work contribute to the S&T mission. Technology insertion into systems is accomplished via the flow of patents, data, design criteria, and other information into TDs, Advanced Technology Demonstrations (ATD), JCTDs, new designs, and fielded systems.

e. Overall, the Army's S&T strategy and programs are committed to the maintenance of technological superiority, while preserving the flexibility to cope with a wide array of possible threat, technology, and budget environments. The Army's investment in S&T is paramount and is playing a greater role in acquisition than ever, particularly since the advent of DOD JCTDs.

f. A series of reviews of current and proposed S&T activities guide focused research. The first is an annual assessment of all proposed Army funded S&T projects. It is conducted based on an appreciation of current capabilities, ongoing S&T activities, and their applicability to the Force Operating Capability (FOC) described earlier in the chapter in TRADOC Pamphlet 525-66. Building from the S&T project review, a list of the top Army Technology Objectives (ATO) candidates—the Army's most important technology projects—are generated. There are three distinct types of ATOs. ATO-Research (ATO(R)) focuses on laboratory applications to determine feasibility and potentially provide technology options in the mid- and far- terms. ATO-Demonstration (ATO(D)) focuses on products and transition into the acquisition Engineering and Manufacturing Development (EMD) phase for warfighting capability. ATO-Manufacturing Technology (ATO(M)) is focused on improving affordability and producibility of new technology and reducing Operations and Support (O&S) cost for fielded systems. Based on formal developmental MSs and achievement measures, the Army Science and Technology Working Group (ASTWG) approves each ATO. The AMP provides the basis for ATDs, which showcase a variety of advanced technologies and their potential military merit. In addition to advancing the technology, these S&T activities aid TRADOC's Army Capabilities Integration Center (ARCIC) chartered Center of Excellence (CoE) standing Integrated Capabilities Development Teams (ICDT), previously discussed, to better understand the "art of the possible" and refine the many requirements associated with them (see Para. 5-5).

g. As with some concepts, S&T research occasionally produces an item that is recognizable as a defined requirement that should be documented and resourced. Most S&T products must be evaluated in warfighting experiments (previously discussed) before a decision is made to document them as materiel requirements.

h. Oversight of the S&T program is provided by the Army Science and Technology Advisory Group (ASTAG), which is co-chaired by the Army Acquisition Executive (AAE) and the Vice Chief of Staff Army (VCSA). The ASTWG, is co-chaired by the Army S&T executive (the Deputy Assistant Secretary of the Army for Research and Technology), and the Headquarters, Department of the Army (HQDA) Deputy Chief of Staff (DCS), G-8 Director, Force Development. The ASTWG provides the following: general-officer-level resolution of pressing S&T issues prior to meetings of the ASTAG; recommendations for ASTAG revisions to the Army's S&T vision, strategy, principles, and priorities; and review and approval of ATOs.

HOW THE ARMY RUNS

i. The Army S&T program is organized into investment portfolios that address challenges in six capability areas: four Army-wide areas (air; Soldier; ground; and Command, Control, Communications, and Intelligence (C3I)); and two areas unique to S&T (basic research and enduring technologies).

(1) The Air Portfolio includes technologies for the following: manned and unmanned systems; air-delivered lethality; and air-platform safety, survivability, and protection.

(2) The Soldier Portfolio includes the following: technologies for Soldier and Squad Lethality, Survivability, Mobility; Leader Development; Training; Combat Casualty Care; and Clinical and Rehabilitation Medicine capabilities.

(3) The Ground Portfolio includes the following: technologies for weapons systems; active and passive protection systems for ground vehicles; manned and unmanned ground platforms and mobility systems; countermine/counter- Improvised Explosive Device (IED) efforts; and deployable small base protection.

(4) The C3I Portfolio includes the following: technologies for ground, air, and Soldier communications devices and networks; air and space sensor and network payloads; and Mission Command.

(5) The Basic Research Portfolio provides a fundamental S&T foundation to enable Army-relevant technology capabilities.

(6) The Enduring Technologies Portfolio includes technology development associated with environmental quality and installations (e.g., sustainable ranges and lands, pollution prevention, military materials in the environment, and adaptive and efficient installations). It also includes the DOD High Performance Computing Modernization Program, which was devolved from OSD to the Army in FY12. This program supports all Services and DOD agencies, enables incorporating advanced computational capabilities as a solution of first resort to explore and evaluate new theories, reduces time and cost of acquiring weapons systems, and provides real-time calculations in support of military operations.

11-7. Army Technology Transition Strategy
The basic strategy of the S&T program is to transition mature technologies into operational systems that satisfy validated warfighting capabilities-based materiel requirements. The key to this strategy is demonstrations. TDs, ATDs, and JCTDs exploit technologies derived from applied research (6.2), which in turn build on new knowledge derived from basic research (6.1) programs. These TDs, ATDs, and JCTDs provide the basis for new systems, system upgrades, or advanced concepts which are further out in time. The critical challenge is to tie these programs together in an efficient and effective way. TDs are not new. What is new is the scope and depth of the TDs, the increased importance of their role in the capabilities development and system acquisition management processes, and the increased emphasis on user involvement to permit an early and meaningful evaluation of overall military capability. The following sections provide an explanation of technology maturity, TDs, ATDs, JCTDs as well as systems/system upgrades.

a. Technology Maturity. Technology maturity measures the degree to which proposed critical technologies meet program objectives. Technology maturity is a principal element of program risk. A Technology Readiness Assessment (TRA) examines program concepts, technology requirements, and demonstrated technology capabilities to determine technological maturity.

(1) TRAs for critical technologies occur prior to Defense Acquisition Management System (DAS) Milestone Decision Review (MDR) MS B and C to provide useful technology maturity information to the acquisition review process.

(2) The Deputy Assistant Secretary of the Army (Research and Technology) (DASA(R&T)), directs the TRAs and for Major Defense Acquisition Programs (MDAP), submits the findings to the AAE, who submits the report to the Deputy Under Secretary of Defense for Science and Technology DUSD(S&T) with a recommended Technology Readiness Level (TRL) (see Figure 11-1) for each critical technology. In cooperation with the DASA(R&T), the DUSD(S&T) evaluates the TRAs and, after concurrence, forwards the findings to the DOD Overarching Integrated Product Team (OIPT) leader and Defense Acquisition Board (DAB) or the Information Technology Acquisition Board (ITAB). If the DUSD(S&T) does not concur with the TRA findings, an independent TRA, under the direction of the DUSD(S&T), will be required. DOD OIPTs and acquisition boards will be discussed later in this chapter.

(3) TRLs are a measure of technical maturity that enables consistent, uniform, discussions of technical maturity, across different types of technologies. Decision authorities must consider the recommended TRLs when assessing program risk. TRL descriptions appear in the Defense Acquisition Guidebook.

b. Technology Demonstrations (TD). The primary focus of TDs is to demonstrate the feasibility and practicality of a technology for solving specific military requirements. They are incorporated during the

MATERIAL SYSTEM RESEARCH, DEVELOPMENT, AND ACQUISITION MANAGEMENT

various stages of the 6.2 and 6.3 development process and encourage technical competition. They are most often conducted in a non-operational (laboratory or field) environment. These demonstrations provide information that reduces uncertainties and subsequent engineering cost, while simultaneously providing valuable development and requirements data.

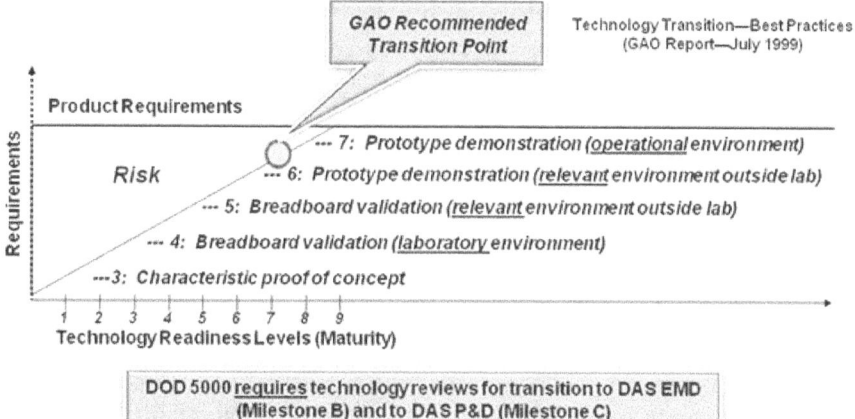

Figure 11-1. Technology Readiness Levels (TRL)

c. ATDs. ATDs are typically integrated demonstrations that are conducted to demonstrate the feasibility and maturity of an emerging technology. They provide a relatively low-cost approach for assessment of technical risks and uncertainties associated with critical technologies prior to the incorporation of these technologies into a system entering the formal acquisition process. They are conducted at the Service and DOD agency level with internal funding. They focus on evolving a specific element of technology nominally at the 6.3 advanced technology development point (typically TRL 5-6) to reduce its risk of implementation by an acquisition program or to feed into a JCTD.

d. JCTDs. DOD initiated the JCTD process to permit the early and relatively inexpensive evaluation of mature advanced technologies. The Soldier evaluates JCTDs to determine military utility of the technologies and to develop the Concept of Operations (CONOPS) that will optimize effectiveness. JCTDs are structured and executed so that, when successful, DOD can proceed rapidly into formal acquisition systems.

(1) By introducing new technologies in the field prior to the initiation of formal systems acquisition, DOD allows operators, who have experience in combat, to evaluate and assess the military utility and develop the tactics to ensure that we can realize the full potential of the substantial technology base that is available—both DOD and commercial. JCTDs are not a means by which to circumvent the formal acquisition process, but rather a means to enter that process based on a user assessment of the value of the new capability that reduces the user acceptance risk. This process helps DOD make more informed

HOW THE ARMY RUNS

acquisition decisions and improve its acquisition cycle time.

(2) The Deputy Under Secretary of Defense for Advanced Systems and Concepts (DUSD(AS&C)), designs JCTDs to transfer technology rapidly from the developers to the users. JCTDs are user oriented and represent an integrated effort to assemble and demonstrate a significant, new, or improved military capability based on mature advanced technologies. Also, they are on a scale large enough to demonstrate operational utility and end-to-end system integrity. As key participants, the operational user and materiel development communities jointly develop and implement a demonstration. JCTDs allow the Soldier to:
 (a) Evaluate a technology's military utility before commitment to a major acquisition effort
 (b) Develop CONOPS for employing the new technology
 (c) Retain a low-cost, residual operational capability, if desired
(3) When a JCTD has been completed, DUSD(AS&C) elects one of the following alternative actions based on the results of the exercises.
 (a) Based on demonstrated military utility, execute the transition of the successfully demonstrated technology directly to the Soldier making only necessary minor, or perhaps no modifications to the existing hardware or software. This transition approach is particularly appropriate where Soldiers require only small quantities of the new equipment.
 (b) Based on demonstrated military utility, enter the formal DAS at the appropriate MS B or C as per the appropriate Materiel Development Decision (MDD).
 (c) Terminate the efforts or restructure them based on the evolved CONOPS and lessons learned during the JCTD.
(4) Over the past six years, the Joint Staff, Combatant Commanders (CCDR), and military services have forwarded proposals for a number of JCTDs to DOD. Also, industry and many DOD research and development agencies have proposed candidate JCTDs. Some JCTDs are completed in less than one year and evaluate a very specific technology or address a particular mission area; others are several years long and include coordination of multiple developing technology programs into a series of specific demonstrations. The goal is to complete a JCTD within a 1 to 3 year period.
(5) DUSD(AS&C) coordinates all JCTD proposals, including recommendations on potential participants, with the Under Secretary of Defense for Acquisition, Technology, and Logistics (USD(AT&L) and the Vice Chairman of the Joint Chiefs of Staff (VCJCS), based on prioritization from the JROC and reviews by JCTD senior members of OSD, Service, agency, and the combatant command S&T community.

 e. Systems and System Upgrades.
(1) The development of the next set of materiel systems requires prior demonstration of the feasibility of employing new technologies. "New-start" systems are those next in line after the ones currently fielded or in production. For these systems, most technical barriers to the new capability have been overcome. Generally, these systems can enter the DAS EMD phase relatively quickly as a result of the successful demonstration of enabling technologies. Based on current funding guidance and support for Overseas Contingency Operations (OCO), the number of "new-start" systems has declined in recent years.
(2) The Army is pursuing incremental improvements to existing systems to maintain its technological edge. These improvements are designated as systems modifications. System modifications are brought about through technology insertion programs, Service Life Extension Programs (SLEP), Preplanned Product Improvements (P3I), and block improvement programs. These modifications are based primarily on the success of funded 6.3 TDs. The 6.3 TDs are the basis for the system modification or have a high probability of forming the basis for the system modification. If incremental improvements are significant or costly enough, they will be treated as separate programs with regard to acquisition, funding, and test and evaluation.

Section III
Materiel Capabilities Documents

11-8. Generating and Documenting Capabilities-Based Materiel Requirements
Materiel Capabilities Documents (MCD) establish the need for a materiel acquisition program, how the materiel will be employed, and what the materiel must be capable of doing. As the acquisition program progresses, statements of required performance and design specifications become more and more

MATERIAL SYSTEM RESEARCH, DEVELOPMENT, AND ACQUISITION MANAGEMENT

specific. The functional area focused Initial Capabilities Document (ICD) is the document that initiates the Defense Acquisition Management System (DAS). The Capability Development Document (CDD) and the Capability Production Document (CPD) are the documents that define the system capabilities needed to satisfy an approved materiel need (high risk capability gap).

  a. ICD. The ICD is a broad statement of functional required materiel capability (need) that can possibly support more than one developmental system. It documents the need for non-materiel and/or materiel solution approaches to resolve a specific high risk capability gap derived from the JCIDS Capabilities-Based Assessment (C-BA) process (previously discussed). It describes capability gaps that exist in warfighting functions as described in the applicable warfighting concepts and integrated architectures. The capability gap is defined in terms of the functional area, the relevant range of military operations, and timeframe under consideration.

  (1) The ICD summarizes the results of the C-BA analysis and identifies any changes in U.S. or Allied doctrine, operational concepts, tactics, organization, and training that were considered in satisfying the identified high risk capability gap. The ICD describes why such non-materiel changes have been judged to be inadequate in addressing the complete capability.

  (2) The ICD documents the evaluation of balanced and synchronized Doctrine, Organization, Training, Leadership and Education, Personnel, Facilities, and Policy (Non-Materiel) (DOTmLPF-P) approaches that are proposed to provide the Required Capabilities (RC). The ICD further proposes a recommended materiel approach based on analysis of the different materiel approaches and describes how the recommended approach best satisfies the desired RC.

  (3) Once validated, an ICD is not normally updated, but is archived to the Joint Staff, J-8 Knowledge Management/Decision Support (KM/DS) tool database, so that all validated MCDs are maintained in a single location. When validated, CDDs (described below) bring the desired capability specified in the ICD into the DAS EMD phase. The CDD then serves as the living document to carry the program and its increments through the acquisition process.

  (4) The ICD length is limited to 10 pages and the format and detailed content instructions are provided in the JCIDS Manual, B-9.

  b. CDD. The CDD is the warfighter's primary means of defining authoritative, measurable, and/or testable capabilities for the EMD phase of an acquisition program. The CDD is guided by the ICD and captures the information necessary to deliver an affordable and supportable capability using mature technology within a specific increment of an Acquisition Strategy (AS) – the framework (roadmap) for planning, directing, and managing an acquisition program to satisfy a validated materiel requirement.

  (1) A draft CDD is generated during the Materiel Solution Analysis (MSA) Phase and the final CDD is generated during the TD phase of the acquisition process prior to MS B (program initiation). The CDD describes a technically mature and affordable increment of militarily useful capability that was demonstrated in a relevant environment. The CDD supports entry into EMD phase.

  (2) In an evolutionary acquisition program, the capabilities delivered by a specific increment may provide only a partial solution of the ultimate desired capability therefore; the first increment's CDD must provide information regarding the strategy to achieve the full capability. Subsequent increments, leading to the full capability, are also described to give an overall understanding of the program strategy. This strategy is updated with each subsequent increment to reflect lessons learned from previous increments, changes in the warfighting concepts, or changes in the integrated architecture.

  (3) The CDD describes the operational capability; threat; integrated architectures; required capabilities; program support; supportability; force structure, DOTmLPF-P impact, and constraints; schedule; and program affordability for the system.

  (4) The CDD identifies the operational performance attributes (testable or measurable characteristics), in threshold-objective (minimum-desired) format, necessary for the acquisition community to design a proposed system and establish an Acquisition Program Baseline (APB). The CDD states performance attributes, including Key Performance Parameters (KPP) that guide the development, demonstration, and testing of the current increment. These parameters provide the "trade space" for the system as it goes through development and testing. The performance attributes and KPPs apply only to the current increment. Each increment must provide an operationally effective and useful capability in the intended mission environment that is commensurate with the investment and independent of any subsequent increment.

  (5) The CDD articulates the attributes, KPPs, and Key System Attributes (KSA) that are further refined in the CPD. The CDD is updated or appended for each MS B decision.

HOW THE ARMY RUNS

(6) The CDD page limit is 45 pages, and the format and detailed content instructions are provided in the JCIDS Manual, B-27.

c. CPD. The CPD is the warfighter's primary means of providing authoritative and testable capabilities for the Production and Deployment (P&D) phase of an acquisition program. A CPD is finalized after the Post Critical Design Review (CDR) Assessment and is validated prior to the MS C (Low-Rate Initial Production (LRIP)) decision. The CPD development is guided by the ICD, CDD, developmental and operational testing results, and the Post CDR assessment. It captures the information necessary to support production, testing, and deployment of an affordable and supportable increment within an AS.

(1) The CPD provides the operational performance characteristics necessary for the acquisition community to produce and field a single increment of a specific system. The CPD presents performance characteristics, including KPPs and KSAs, to guide the production and deployment of the current increment. Since a CPD applies to only a single increment of a program's development, the performance attributes, KPPs, and KSAs apply only to the increment described in the CPD. Each increment must provide an operationally effective and useful capability in the intended environment, commensurate with the investment.

(2) The CPD refines the threshold and objective values for performance attributes and KPPs that were validated in the CDD for the production increment. Each production threshold listed in the CPD depicts the minimum performance that the Program, Project, or Product Manager (PM) is expected to deliver for the increment based on the post-CDR system design. The refinement of performance attributes and KPPs is the most significant difference between the CDD and the CPD.

(3) The CPD is an entrance criteria item that is necessary to proceed to each MS C (LRIP) decision. The CPD page limit is 40 pages, and the format and detailed content instructions are provided in the JCIDS Manual, B-39.

d. MCD Performance Characteristics, KPPs, and KSAs. The CDD and CPD state the operational and support-related performance attributes of a system that provides the capabilities required by the Soldier – attributes so significant, they must be verified by testing or analysis. The CDD and CPD identify, in threshold-objective format, the attributes that contribute most significantly to the desired operational capability. Whenever possible, attributes are stated in terms that reflect the operational capabilities necessary to operate in the full range of military operations and the environment intended for the system, Family of Systems (FoS), or System of Systems (SoS). These statements guide the acquisition community in making trades decisions between the threshold and objective values of the stated attributes. Operational Testing (OT) assesses the ability of the system to meet the production threshold and objective values.

(1) Each attribute is supported by an operationally oriented rationale. Below the threshold value, the military utility of the system becomes questionable. The objective value for an attribute is the desired operational goal.

(2) KPPs are those system attributes considered most essential for an effective military capability. The CDD and the CPD contain a required number of KPPs that capture the minimum operational effectiveness and suitability attributes (testable or measurable characteristics) needed to achieve the overall desired capabilities for the system during the applicable increment. Failure to meet a CDD or CPD KPP threshold can result in the reevaluation of the selected system, program reassessment, or termination.

(3) KSAs are those system attributes considered most critical or essential for an effective military capability, but not selected as a KPP. KSAs provide decision-makers with an additional level of capability prioritization below the KPP, but with senior sponsor leadership control (authority is system dependent designated by the Acquisition Executive).

(4) Net-Ready Key Performance Parameters (NR-KPP)(interoperability compliance) is a required KPP. The NR-KPP assesses information needs, information timelines, information assurance, and net-ready attributes required for both the technical exchange of information and the end-to-end operational effectiveness of that exchange. The NR-KPP consists of measurable and testable characteristics and/or performance metrics required for the timely, accurate, and complete exchange and use of information to satisfy information needs for a given capability.

(a) A NR-KPP is developed for all Information Technology (IT) and National Security Systems (NSS) used to enter, process, store, display, or transmit DOD information, regardless of classification or sensitivity. IT and NSS interoperability is defined as the ability of systems, units, or forces to provide data, information, materiel, and Services to and accept the same from other systems, units, or forces and to

MATERIAL SYSTEM RESEARCH, DEVELOPMENT, AND ACQUISITION MANAGEMENT

use the data, information, materiel, and Services exchanged to enable them to operate effectively together.

(b) The NR-KPP should reflect the information needs of the capability under consideration and the needs of appropriate supported systems. It should cover all communication, computing, and electromagnetic spectrum requirements involving the exchange of products and Services between producer, sender, receiver, and consumer for the successful completion of the Soldier mission, business process, or transaction. The NR-KPP identified in CDDs and CPDs will be used in the Information Support Plan (ISP) to identify support required from outside the program.

(5) Force protection and survivability are Congressionally required KPPs for all manned systems and systems designed to enhance personnel survivability in an asymmetric threat environment. The Joint Staff Protection Functional Capabilities Board (FCB), in coordination with the lead FCB, assess these KPPs and their applicability for Joint Capabilities Board (JCB) Interest and JROC Interest CDDs and CPDs and make a recommendation to the JCB or JROC on validation. The sponsoring component validates the KPPs for non-JCB/JROC Interest CDDs and CPDs. A single KPP can be developed, provided it complies with the congressional direction pertaining to protection and survivability.

(a) Protection KPP. Protection attributes are those that contribute to the protection of personnel by preventing or mitigating hostile actions against friendly personnel, military and civilian. This may include the same attributes as those that contribute to survivability, but the emphasis is on protecting the system operator or other personnel rather than protecting the system itself.

(b) Survivability KPP. Survivability attributes are those that contribute to the survivability of a manned system. This includes attributes such as speed, maneuverability, detectability, and countermeasures that reduce a system's likelihood of being engaged by hostile fire, as well as attributes such as armor and redundancy or critical components that reduce the system's vulnerability if it is hit by hostile fire.

(6) Sustainment KPP. A sustainment KPP (materiel availability) and two mandatory supporting KSAs (materiel reliability and O&S cost) are developed for all JROC Interest programs involving materiel solutions. For non-JCB/JROC Interest programs, the sponsor determines the applicability of this KPP.

(a) Materiel reliability KSA is a measure of the probability that the system will perform without failure over a specific interval. Reliability must be sufficient to support the warfighting capability needed. Materiel reliability is generally expressed in terms of a Mean Time Between Failure (MTBF).

(b) O&S cost KSA provides balance to the sustainment solution by ensuring that O&S costs associated with materiel readiness are considered in making decisions.

(7) System training KPP ensures system training is addressed in the Analysis of Alternatives (AoA) and supporting analysis for subsequent acquisition phases and ensures projected training requirements and associated costs are appropriately addressed across the proposed acquisition program life-cycle.

(8) Energy efficiency KPP includes fuel efficiency considerations for fleet purchases and operational plans consistent with mission accomplishment. Life-cycle cost analysis will include the fully burdened cost of fuel during the AoA and subsequent analyses and acquisition program design trades.

e. Joint DOTmLPF-P Change Recommendation (DCR) Document. A joint DCR is a recommendation for changes to existing joint resources when such changes are not associated with a new defense acquisition program. The DCR page limit is 30 pages, and the format and detailed content instructions are provided in JCIDS Manual, B-21.

11-9. Capability Development Tracking and Management (CDTM) System

a. On June 6, 2011, the VCJCS signed a memorandum directing implementation of the CDTM for development of all JCIDS capability documents - ICDs, CDDs, CPDs, and DCRs. The purpose of CDTM is to move from a document-centric process to a data-centric process that enables data sharing and system interoperability. CDTM is a "turbo-tax" like web-based application to assist the Capability Developer (CAPDEV) in writing capability documents. The system presents a series of "wizard" pages that guide the user through data entry and complete document creation. Once data is entered, the system handles workflow within customized workgroups. When a capability document is ready for vetting by the Army Staff (ARSTAF) and Joint Staff (JS), CDTM automates transfer of a Microsoft Word version of the document to external systems like the Army's Capabilities and Army Requirements Oversight Council (AROC) Management System (CAMS) and the JS KM/DS for further processing. After document transfer, the document data is exposed to all CDTM users through search functionality.

b. Using CDTM, capability documents are no longer just documents, but structured information that can be aggregated, tabulated, and searched. What was once a document is now information broken down

HOW THE ARMY RUNS

into field-level data that is stored in the CDTM database. The data can be reassembled into a document at any time, but is workable in pieces, by any number of users. In the past, capability documents were created in a variety of formats and templates, the final result being multiple files that were non-standard and difficult to search. With CDTM, capabilities documents are created by dynamically assembling all the data elements into a standard format. Effective June 30, 2011, the CDTM format was required for the creation, reading, and editing of all JCIDS capability documents across all DOD organizations. CDTM is located on https://cdtm.js.mil/Default.aspx (NIPRNET) and https://cdtm.js.smil.mil (SIPRNET).

c. CDTM is not used for the drafting and submission of Joint Urgent Operational Needs (JUON) and Joint Emergent Operational Needs (JEON). These documents are submitted via memorandum to the Joint Staff J-8 Gatekeeper. CDTM is not used for the drafting and submission of Service, Combatant Command (Command Authority) (COCOM), or Component Urgent Operational Needs (UON). These documents are submitted internally. These documents are only submitted to the KM/DS system for information purposes after validation.

Section IV
Traditional Materiel Requirements Validation

11-10. Army Requirements Validation

In 2007, the Army revised its warfighting requirements validation process to adjust for rapidly changing technology, constraints on the Army budget, increased sustainment costs, the need to provide a concrete linkage between requirements and resources, and increasing emphasis on joint interoperability. Within the Army, the VCSA approves and the Chief of Staff of the Army (CSA) retains veto authority for all warfighting materiel requirements. Requirements meeting specific threshold criteria may be approved by the HQDA DCS, G-3/5/7, in order to facilitate timely processing, if delegated by VCSA.

a. In order to provide more effective management of the total requirements process for all aspects of Army needs, the requirements process was modified to consolidate all DOTMLPF-P requirements at HQDA for staffing and validation. This process ensures that the Army pursues requirements that can compete for and retain resources that are tied to the future Army and joint visions and goals. The process places increased emphasis on analysis of the requirement, potential alternatives, affordability, and joint interoperability. The goal is to evaluate all DOTMLPF-P requirements, regardless of origin, against the goals, vision, and needs of the current and future force. The lead organization for the implementation of the JCIDS process, within the Army is the DCS, G-3/5/7.

b. Within the DCS, G3/5/7, the Capabilities Integration, Prioritization, and Analysis Directorate (DAMO-CI), specifically the Current and Future Warfighting Capabilities Division (DAMO-CIC), is the single entry point for all Army and joint DOTMLPF-P requirements. DAMO-CIC is the proponent for policy development, Army JCIDS process oversight, and interface with the JCIDS process. Within DAMO-CIC, the Requirements Staff Officer (RSO) is directly responsible for leading HQDA staff integration and coordination efforts for all Army and joint DOTMLPF-P requirements issues. The RSO coordinates with the HQDA DCS, G-8 counterpart, the Staff Synchronization Officer (SSO), to facilitate the transition from capabilities-based requirements development and validation to requirements solutions (execution and resourcing).

11-11. AROC

a. The AROC was created in 2001 to provide a concrete linkage and synchronization between required capabilities and resources. The AROC, coordinated by DCS, G-3/5/7, Current and Future Warfighting Capabilities Division (DAMO-CIC), is responsible for advising the CSA/VCSA in the assessment and prioritization of capabilities integrated across DOTMLPF-P, to include the disposition of MCDs. DAMO-CIC schedules and executes the AROC forum. TRADOC ARCIC continues to be responsible for the balanced development of concepts, capabilities (requirements), and products in DOTMLPF-P.

b. The AROC process is used to validate:
(1) Proposals for rapid insertion of technologies to address current capability needs when the solution extends into the Program Objective Memorandum (POM)
(2) Strategies to resolve capability gaps and resultant changes to modernization
programs and plans
c. The AROC validates all JCIDS documents prior to submission to the Joint Staff, J-8 JCIDS

MATERIAL SYSTEM RESEARCH, DEVELOPMENT, AND ACQUISITION MANAGEMENT

"gatekeeper" – Deputy Director, Requirements. This encompasses all JCIDS efforts including Army annexes to joint and other Service MCDs and those where an Army proponent has been designated as a joint CAPDEV.

d. The AROC reviews JCIDS documentation for:

(1) Military need and risk. The AROC reviews and provides decisions and guidance on the capability gaps identified in JCIDS proposals presented for validation. This ensures identified gaps are linked with modernization investment priorities essential for maintaining land force dominance.

(2) Synchronization with Army and joint modernization strategies. The AROC validates that the recommended strategies to resolve capability gaps, including associated DOTMLPF-P changes, are consistent with Army modernization strategies. Proposals must contribute to a balanced and synchronized modernization program. The AROC reviews how the recommended strategies fit into related joint concepts, force modernization strategies, and investment portfolios to ensure interoperability and synergy.

(3) Estimated program affordability. The AROC reviews the affordability, based on the Deputy Assistant Secretary of the Army, Cost & Economics (DASA(CE)) approved Cost Benefit Analysis (CBA), of all proposed solutions to capability gaps and programs presented to ensure that, if pursued, they are within budgeting and programming limits for development, procurement, and sustainment. The AROC considers "trades" of capability and/or performance versus cost to ensure only affordable solutions are pursued. Affordability includes potential long-term supportability requirements for the concept or system.

(4) Capability definition and interoperability. The AROC ensures that the operational definition of the capability gap and the proposed solution is clear and consistent with Army and joint warfighting concepts. KPPs and KSAs serve as the pivot for AROC risk deliberations on operational improvements versus costs to field a capability at the appropriate time and in the appropriate quantities. Opportunities to integrate other Service programs or alternate technologies to improve joint interoperability are also addressed in the AROC presentation.

e. The AROC consists of the following permanent principal members:
(1) Vice Chief of Staff, Army (Chair)
(2) Principal Military Deputy, Office of the Assistant Secretary of Army (Acquisition, Logistics, and Technology)
(3) Chief Information Officer (CIO)/Deputy Chief of Staff, G-6
(4) Deputy Chief of Staff, G-1
(5) Deputy Chief of Staff, G-2
(6) Deputy Chief of Staff, G-3/5/7 (Secretary)
(7) Deputy Chief of Staff, G-4
(8) Deputy Chief of Staff, G-8
(9) Director, ARCIC
(10) DASA(CE)
(11) Commanding General (CG), Army Test and Evaluation Command (ATEC)

f. Permanent Advisors include: the Director of the Army Staff (DAS); Assistant Deputy Under Secretary of the Army, Test and Evaluation; the Military Deputy (MILDEP) to the Assistant Secretary of Army (Financial Management & Comptroller); Chief, Army Reserve; Chief, Army National Guard; Director, Force Development (DCS, G-8); Director, Program Analysis and Evaluation (DCS, G-8); and Director, Capabilities Integration, Prioritization, and Analysis (DCS, G-3/5/7, G-37).

g. The AROC Process Review Board (APRB) serves as the AROC intermediate review body inserted prior to and immediately following the initial staffing of JCIDS proposals and as required, to review and comment on other documentation, analysis, or actions. The APRB ensures topics are suitable and mature, in accordance with AROC objectives. Also, it determines the required method of presentation for validation of the submission (formal or paper AROC).

(1) The APRB meets weekly, or as required, to manage workload and ensure "value added" without unnecessarily slowing the Army JCIDS staffing process. The meeting date, time, and location supports an orchestrated staff battle rhythm and provides efficiency to the overall process by ensuring document readiness and identification of special coordination requirements prior to flag-level (1-Star) staffing, resolution of complex issues across the ARSTAF prior to moving the document into the AROC for review, and providing situational awareness to senior leaders for issues not resolved or jeopardizing successful staffing/review.

(2) The APRB is co-chaired by the Chief, Current and Future Warfighting Capabilities Division DCS, G-

HOW THE ARMY RUNS

3/5/7 (G-37); a Colonel/GS-15 representative from the DCS, G-8, Force Development Directorate; and a Colonel/GS-15 representative from TRADOC ARCIC. The APRB is composed of representatives of the AROC principals and permanent advisors. Other ARSTAF elements and external organizations provide subject matter expertise as required. The APRB makes recommendations to and executes the decisions of the AROC Secretary – DCS, G-3/5/7.

h. The AROC may not review all Army requirements. Validation of selected JCIDS proposals may be delegated to the DCS, G-3/5/7 by the VCSA. Disapproval authority remains at the VCSA level. In addition, a "paper or electronic AROC" may be used, at the discretion of the AROC chair, to staff non-contentious issues. The VCSA/CSA receive a copy of all approved issues by the DCS, G-3/5/7.

11-12. Army Requirements Validation Process

a. The process of obtaining validation of JCIDS proposals begins with the submission of a proposal by the TRADOC ARCIC Requirements Integration Directorate (RID) JCIDS Gatekeeper, into the Capabilities and AROC Management System (CAMS) database. CAMS is the HQDA DCS, G-3/5/7 database driven knowledge management decision support information technology system. CAMS supports AROC document staffing and commenting from numerous users and organizations within the Army into a centralized database repository. The system allows users to view document information and monitor document progress through AROC validation until submission to the JS staffing and validation process. Staffing continues until the document is validated.

b. All JCIDS proposals are entered into CAMS by the ARCIC gatekeeper. The ARCIC gatekeeper acts as the entry and exit point for all JCIDS capability documents forwarded by TRADOC and non-TRADOC proponents for validation and other Service capability documents sent to ARCIC for review. The gatekeeper manages the TRADOC staffing of the JCIDS capability documents and loads ARCIC-validated and CG, TRADOC-endorsed capability documents into the CAMS database for AROC/JROC validation. Submission of the proposal will trigger the Army gatekeeper process. The JCIDS proposal will be submitted for HQDA staffing and coordination. All proposals undergoing the review process are considered draft until they are validated by the designated validation authority.

c. All Army sponsored JCIDS proposals are submitted for HQDA JCIDS gatekeeper review to determine accuracy and completeness. Based on the content of the proposal, the gatekeeper will assign the proposal to the functional RSO and initiate Army staffing utilizing CAMS as the staffing tool.

d. The HQDA JCIDS staffing process includes the APRB, flag-level (1-Star) initial staffing, and flag-level (3-Star) AROC principal/advisor review phases. The Army validation process optimally takes 95 to 110 business days. JCIDS document flow to the AROC for validation is depicted in Figure 11-5.

e. At the conclusion of the AROC validation process, the Army JCIDS gatekeeper enters the document, using CDTM (previously discussed), into the KM/DS web-based staffing tool for JS staffing.

f. The HQDA JCIDS gatekeeper signals completion of Army and joint staffing and validation by publishing the DCS, G-3/5/7 approval memorandum with a Catalog of Approved Requirement Documents (CARDS) reference number. The CARDS reference number signifies an approved Army materiel requirement.

11-13. Cost Benefit Analysis (CBA)

a. In a December 30, 2009 memorandum, the Army senior leadership directed that each unfunded requirement and new or expanded program proposal submitted to the Secretary of the Army (SECARMY), CSA, Under Secretary of the Army (USA) or VCSA, must be accompanied by a thorough CBA. The CBA must identify the total cost of the proposal, the benefits that will result, the bill payers that would be used to pay for it, and the second and third order effects of the funding decision. A CBA enables Army senior leaders and managers to make better resource-informed decisions.

b. CBAs make the case for a project or proposal weighing the total expected costs against the total expected benefits over the near-term and life-cycle timeframes from an Army enterprise perspective, which means that initiatives should be evaluated based on the benefits they provide to the Army as a whole, not to any individual organization. Army elements are connected organizationally and what happens even at the lowest levels within the Army can impact/influence higher level organizations.

c. A CBA is a structured methodology of forecasting and comparing the anticipated costs and benefits of alternative Courses of Action (COA) in order to identify the most effective manner of achieving a stated goal or objective. A CBA is weighing the consequences, both good and bad, of potential actions.

d. All CBAs provide decision-makers with facts, data, and analysis required to make an informed

MATERIAL SYSTEM RESEARCH, DEVELOPMENT, AND ACQUISITION MANAGEMENT

decision. In its most basic form, the CBA is a tool to support resource informed decision-making. There is no prescribed length to a CBA. All that is required is that it fully supports the decision. CBAs are reviewed by a Cost Benefit Analysis Review Board (CBARB) for suitability of use by a decision-maker or decision-making body. The CBARB provides its recommendation on suitability of use to the Deputy Assistant Secretary of the Army for Cost and Economics (DASA(CE)) who forwards the final recommendation on suitability of use to the decision-maker or decision-making body.

e. In today's resource-constrained environment, the Army must exercise wise stewardship of every dollar it manages. A key element in that stewardship is to develop and use sound CBA practices throughout all requirement/resourcing processes. For every proposed requirement, program, initiative, or decision point that is presented to decision-makers, it is important to provide an accurate and complete picture of both the costs to be incurred and the benefits to be derived.

11-14. Joint Requirements Validation Process

a. The process of obtaining validation of JCIDS documents begins with the submission of an MCD proposal to the JS, J-8 KM/DS tool and continues until the document is validated by the appropriate authority.

b. Services, combatant commands, and other DOD organizations conducting a JCIDS C-BA analyses, previously discussed, may generate ideas and concepts leading to draft ICDs, CDDs, CPDs, and joint DCRs. Also, JCIDS initiatives may be generated within a JS FCB as a result of analyses conducted by, or in support of the FCB. As the initiative develops into proposed DOTLmPF or materiel solutions to provide the desired capabilities, a FCB may task a lead Service or component with sponsoring the initiative. Further development of the proposal then becomes the responsibility of the sponsor. The FCB is responsible for the organization, analysis, and prioritization of joint warfighting capability needs within assigned functional areas. The FCB is an advisory body to the JCB and the JROC for JCIDS initiatives assigned with Joint Staffing Designators (JSD) of JCB Interest or JROC Interest.

c. All JCIDS documents (ICDs, CDDs, CPDs, and DCRs) are submitted, using CDTM, to the JS, J-8 KM/DS tool by the sponsoring component. Submission of the document to the KM/DS tool triggers the JS and the gatekeeper process to determine whether the document has joint implications or is sponsor unique. Normally, the document has undergone an appropriate sponsor staffing process before submission to the JS J-8 KM/DS tool.

d. The Gatekeeper. The JS J-8 Deputy Director, Requirements, serves as the "gatekeeper" of the JCIDS process. The gatekeeper, with the assistance of the JS J-8 Requirements Management Division (RMD), and JS J-6 Requirements and Assessments Division (RAD), evaluate all JCIDS documents submitted through the J-8 KM/DS tool database.

(1) JCIDS documents are submitted for gatekeeper review to determine whether the proposal affects the joint force. The gatekeeper review is conducted for each document regardless of potential Acquisition Category (ACAT), previous delegation decisions, or previous JSD decisions. An ACAT is designated as ACAT I, II, or III when the materiel requirement and manner of acquisition have been identified. Title 10, Section 2430, identifies dollar criteria for determining the ACAT of a potential program. The ACAT designation determines the level of review, and who will make the milestone decisions. The three acquisition categories are defined in Figures 11-2a and 11-2b.

(2) Based on the content of the submission, the "gatekeeper" assigns a JSD of JROC Interest, JCB Interest, Joint Integration, Joint Information, or Independent to the ICD, CDD, CPD, or DCR submitted via the KM/DS tool.

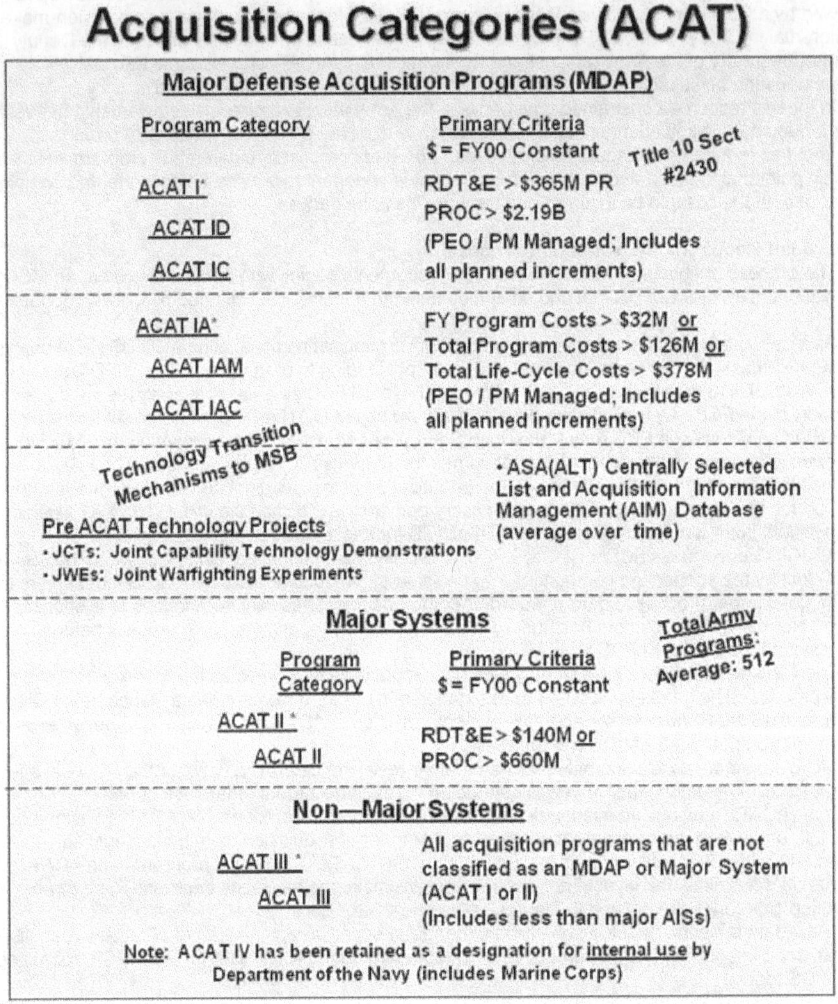

Acquisition Categories (ACAT)

Major Defense Acquisition Programs (MDAP)

Program Category	Primary Criteria $ = FY00 Constant
ACAT I* ACAT ID ACAT IC	RDT&E > $365M PR PROC > $2.19B (PEO / PM Managed; Includes all planned increments)
ACAT IA* ACAT IAM ACAT IAC	FY Program Costs > $32M or Total Program Costs > $126M or Total Life-Cycle Costs > $378M (PEO / PM Managed; Includes all planned increments)

Title 10 Sect #2430

Technology Transition Mechanisms to MSB

Pre ACAT Technology Projects
- JCTs: Joint Capability Technology Demonstrations
- JWEs: Joint Warfighting Experiments

• ASA(ALT) Centrally Selected List and Acquisition Information Management (AIM) Database (average over time)

Major Systems

Program Category	Primary Criteria $ = FY00 Constant
ACAT II* ACAT II	RDT&E > $140M or PROC > $660M

Total Army Programs: Average: 512

Non—Major Systems

ACAT III* ACAT III	All acquisition programs that are not classified as an MDAP or Major System (ACAT I or II) (Includes less than major AISs)

Note: ACAT IV has been retained as a designation for *internal use* by Department of the Navy (includes Marine Corps)

ASA (ALT): Assistant Secretary of the Army (Acquisition, Logistics, and Technology)
C: Component
D: Defense
IAM: Major Automated Information System
PEO: Program / Project / Project Manager
PROC: Procurement
RDT&E: Research, Development, Test, and Evaluation

Figure 11-2. Acquisition Categories (ACAT)

MATERIAL SYSTEM RESEARCH, DEVELOPMENT, AND ACQUISITION MANAGEMENT

(a) JROC Interest. This designation applies to all potential ACAT I/information assurance programs where the capabilities have a significant impact on joint warfighting or have a potential impact across Services or interoperability in allied and coalition operations. All joint DCRs will be designated as JROC Interest. A JSD of JROC Interest will be presumed for all capabilities documents within the following Joint Capability Area (JCA) portfolios: Battlespace Awareness; Command and Control; Logistics; and Net-Centric. Also, it may apply to intelligence capabilities that support DOD and national intelligence requirements. Capability documents designated as JROC Interest will be staffed through the JROC for validation. An exception may be made for ACAT IAM programs without significant impact on joint warfighting (such as business-oriented systems). These programs may be designated Joint Integration, Joint Information, or Independent.

(b) JCB Interest. This designation applies to all potential ACAT II and below programs where the capabilities and/or systems associated with the document affect the joint force and an expanded joint review is required. These documents will receive all applicable certifications, including a weapon safety endorsement when appropriate, and be staffed through the JCB for validation.

(c) Joint Integration. This designation applies to potential ACAT II and below programs where the capabilities and/or systems associated with the document do not significantly affect the joint force and an expanded review is not required. Staffing is required for applicable certifications (information technology and National Security Systems (NSS) interoperability and supportability and/or intelligence) and for a weapons safety endorsement, when appropriate. All weapons and munitions will be designated Joint Integration as a minimum. Once the required certification(s)/weapons safety endorsement are completed, the document may be reviewed by the FCB. Joint Integration documents are validated by the sponsoring component.

(d) Joint Information. This designation applies to potential ACAT II and below programs that have interest or potential impact across the Services or defense agencies, but do not have significant impact on the joint force and do not reach the threshold for JCB Interest or JROC Interest. No certifications or endorsements are required. Once designated Joint Information, staffing is required for informational purposes only and the FCB may review the document. Joint Information documents are validated by the sponsoring component.

(e) Independent. This designation applies to potential ACAT II and below programs, where the capabilities and/or systems associated with the document do not significantly affect the joint force, an expanded review is not required, and no certifications or endorsements are required. Once designated Independent, the FCB may review the document. Independent documents are validated by the sponsoring component.

(3) The JS J-8, using the KM/DS tool, maintains a database of JCIDS documents processed through the gatekeeper function. The database includes the JSD as defined above; which FCBs have equity in the proposal (if any); and the lead FCB for the proposal (if any). The database helps to ensure consistency of staffing as JCIDS proposals progress through the JCIDS process.

(4) Once the JSD has been assigned, the document moves into the staffing and validation process.

e. Staffing Process. The JS J-8 RMD staffs all JCB Interest and JROC Interest proposals before FCB review. During the review process, the FCB evaluates how well the proposed solution documented in an ICD, CDD, CPD, or DCR addressed the capability needs identified in the JCIDS C-BA analyses.

f. Certifications and Weapon Safety Endorsement. Applicable certifications and the weapon safety endorsement will be processed as part of the staffing process for each JCIDS document. If a certification/endorsement authority determines the content is insufficient to support a required certification/endorsement, it is the sponsor's responsibility to resolve the issue with the certification/endorsement authority. If resolution cannot be achieved, the sponsor may request a review of the issue by a higher authority.

(1) Threat Validation and Intelligence Certification—JS, J-2.

(a) Threat Validation. For all Joint Integration, JCB Interest, and JROC Interest ICDs, CDDs, and CPDs, the Defense Intelligence Agency (DIA) provides validation of threat information appropriate to the proposal through the intelligence certification process. DOD components may validate intelligence information for programs designated as Joint Information or Independent proposals using DIA-validated threat data and/or data contained in DOD Service Intelligence Production Program products and data.

(b) Intelligence Certification. JS J-2 provides intelligence certification as a part of the JCIDS staffing of ICDs, CDDs, and CPDs, regardless of ACAT level, unless a waiver has been granted by the JS J-2. J-2

HOW THE ARMY RUNS

will assess intelligence support needs for completeness, supportability, and impact on joint intelligence strategy, policy, and architectural planning. The JS J-2 certification will evaluate intelligence-related information systems with respect to security and intelligence interoperability standards.

(2) IT and National Security System (NSS) Interoperability and Supportability Requirements Certification – JS, J-6. The J-6 certifies all CDDs and CPDs designated as JROC Interest, JCB Interest, or Joint Integration for conformance with joint IT and NSS policy.

(3) Weapon Safety Endorsement. The JS J-8 Deputy Director, Force Protection (DDFP), provides a weapon safety endorsement coordinated through the Force Protection FCB as part of the JCIDS staffing of ICDs, CDDs, CPDs, and DCRs regardless of ACAT. A weapon safety endorsement is the means for documenting the extent to which weapon capabilities documents provide for safe integration into joint warfighting environments. Endorsement recommendations are prepared by the Joint Weapon Safety Technical Advisory Panel (JWSTAP) and submitted to the JS J-8 DDFP for appropriate staffing and coordination with the FP FCB. The endorsement indicates that required joint warfighting environment attributes and performance parameters, from a weapon safety perspective, are judged to be adequately prescribed in the ICD, CDD, CPD, or DCR. Also, the endorsement may convey identified limitations in the prescribed attributes or performance parameters that are deemed acceptable from a weapon safety perspective, yet foreseen as potential military utility hindrances or joint operation limitations. If the weapon safety endorsement identifies restrictions/limitations, the sponsor will coordinate with the FP FCB for resolution or acceptance of the restrictions/limitations.

Section V
Urgent Operational Need Validation

11-15. JUONs/JEONs

DOD and the Army continue to improve and adapt their capabilities and materiel developments processes in response to OCO. The deliberate JCIDS and DAS acquire weapons systems using traditional DOD processes, usually taking five to seven years even when the system uses maximum streamlining. Sometimes, the warfighter needs a new capability as soon as possible. When operational commanders, in a conflict or crisis, report situations that put life at risk or risk mission failure, every military Service has responded with its own rapid response approach. When the situation is a joint, theater-wide problem, the JUON process applies.

a. JUONs are urgent operational needs identified by a CCDR affecting two or more DOD components involved in an ongoing overseas contingency operation. The JUON purpose is to identify and subsequently gain JS validation and resourcing solution, usually within days or weeks, to meet a specific high priority CCDR need. Rapid validation and resourcing of a JUON is a time-sensitive process in support of a CCDR involved in a combat-related ongoing operation. The JUON rapidly validates resources and fields urgent operational solutions that fall outside of the established Service processes. This process is not intended to compete with any of the current Service processes, but rather to complement them. Also, it is not intended to replace any other JS process.

b. JEONs are UONs that are identified by a CCDR as inherently joint and impacting an anticipated or pending contingency operation.

c. The scope of a JUON/JEON will be limited to addressing urgent operational needs that fall outside of the established Service processes; and most importantly, if not addressed immediately, will seriously endanger personnel or pose a major threat to ongoing operations. They should not involve the development of a new technology or capability; however, the use of "off-the-shelf" items or the acceleration of a science and technology JCTD or minor modification of an existing system to adapt to a new or similar mission is within the scope of the JUON/JEON validation and resourcing. The JUON/JEON staffing/validation process is shown in Figure 11-3.

MATERIAL SYSTEM RESEARCH, DEVELOPMENT, AND ACQUISITION MANAGEMENT

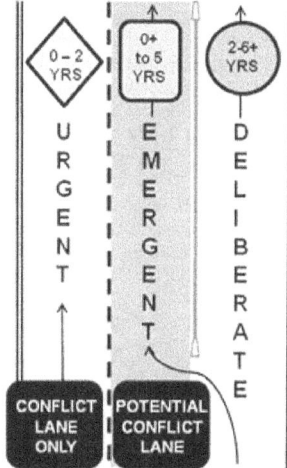

JUON/JEON Validation Process

- **Deliberate Requirements**
  - Service, CCMD, or Agency driven
  - Traditional route for capabilities that require significant technological development and / or are not urgent or compelling in nature
- **Emergent Requirements**
  - CCMD driven
  - Supports accelerated acquisition of capabilities needed for an anticipated or pending contingency operation
  - VCJCS verifies, JCB, or JROC validates
- **Urgent Requirements**
  - CCMD driven
  - Urgent and compelling to prevent loss of life and / or mission failure during current operations
  - Requires little technological development and can be resolved in less than two years
  - DDR validates

CCMD: Combatant Command
DDR: Deputy Director of Requirements, J-8
JCB: Joint Capabilities Board
JROC: Joint Requirements Oversight Council
VCJCS: Vice, Chairman of the Joint Chiefs of Staff

Figure 11-3. Joint Urgent Operational Need (JUON) / Joint Emergent Operational Need (JEON) Validation Process

11-16. JUON/JEON Process
The JUON/JEON process consists of four phases:
  a. Generation Phase: The operational force commander identifies the urgent/emergent need and the COCOM staff determines the most suitable solution process. New JUONs and JEONs, and modifications to the capability requirements in previously validated JUONs and JEONs, must be endorsed by the CCDR, Deputy Commander, or Chief of Staff. The COCOM-endorsed JUON/JEON is then submitted to the Joint Staff, via the KM/DS, to the Joint Staff J-8 Requirements Management Division (RMD).
  b. Vetting Phase: JUON and JEON staffing begins when the Joint Staff J-8 Requirements Management Division receives the JUON/JEON from the COCOM and verifies the document meets submission criteria. Following confirmation that the JUON/JEON meets the appropriate entry criteria, both are assigned directly to a Lead FCB for review. JEONs, however, are first confirmed by the VCJCS, via the Joint Staff J-8 JCIDS Gatekeeper and DJ-8. The VCJCS will identify the validation authority as the JCB or JROC. Once the VCJCS provides confirmation that the JEON may use the emergent process, JEONs are assigned to a Lead FCB and the Joint Rapid Acquisition Cell (JRAC) for collaborative review. The Lead FCB, in collaboration with the JRAC, assesses the validity of the JUON or JEON and identifies potential solution approaches which could satisfy the capability requirement in the requested timeframe. The Lead FCB updates the FCB Joint prioritization to reflect the placement of the new capability requirement(s) within their priority list. At the end of their assessment, the Chair of the lead FCB, with a JRAC representative makes a recommendation to the validation authority either for or against validation.
   (1) The validation authority will make one of the following decisions:
   (a) Validate the JUON/JEON. The validation authority validates that the urgency of satisfying the identified capability requirements to support ongoing or anticipated contingency operations precludes the

HOW THE ARMY RUNS

use of the deliberate requirements validation process. Validation of the JUON/JEON allows the JRAC to proceed with assigning a solution Sponsor to rapidly fund, develop, and field a capability solution.

(b) Validate part of the JUON/JEON. If it is clear that the Sponsor's capability requirement is best validated through a mix of urgent and deliberate requirements validation processes, the validation authority will validate part of the capability requirement as a JUON/JEON, and recommend the Sponsor resubmit the remainder of the capability requirement for validation in the deliberate requirements validation process.

(c) Reject the JUON/JEON. If the JRAC, FCBs, and/or validation authority anticipate technology challenges or other issues which would prohibit the fielding of a militarily useful solution in an appropriate timeline, or if the validation authority determines that the criteria for being a JUON/JEON are not met, the validation authority will reject the capability requirement with recommendation that the Sponsor accept risk, adopt a non-materiel approach, or pursue the capability requirement through the deliberate requirements validation process.

(2) After the Joint Staff J-8 receives the JUON/JEON, the FCB triages the JUON/JEON. After the triage analysis confirms the need is urgent and compelling, the Joint Staff J-8 validates the JUON/JEON and forwards it to the JRAC to determine the resourcing strategy, and then to the appropriate Service or Agency for action. IED challenges go directly to the Joint IED Defeat Office (JIEDDO). Senior Integration Group (SIG) is to be the single authority for prioritizing and directing action to fulfill DOD urgent needs.

c. Equipping Phase. This phase is the delivery of a JUON/JEON solution to the Warfighter. The Sponsor submits an abbreviated acquisition plan to JRAC and to the Joint Staff for approval. The Sponsor then procures and delivers a solution and support package to the warfighter.

d. Operations and Support Phase. The Sponsor sustains the JUON/JEON solution in the field and monitors performance, cost, and schedule for up to 24 months. The Sponsor and supported COCOM must provide an operational utility assessment to the Joint Staff within 90 days of initial fielding. The FCB, Interim sponsor, and COCOM prepare and conduct a capability review. This review informs the final disposition of the materiel solution.

11-17. JRAC/ SIG

a. In 2004, DOD initiated the JRAC emulating the success of the Army's Rapid Equipping Force (REF) program. The JRAC is chartered to break through the institutional barriers of providing timely, effective support to operational commanders. The cell is not attempting to introduce a new acquisition/procurement process; however, it is attempting to push critical JUONs/JEONs through the existing DOD process. The USD(AT&L) and the USD (Comptroller) established the JRAC based on Deputy Secretary of Defense (DEPSECDEF) guidance. Membership consists of 1-Star-level or senior executive representatives from the Joint Staff, COCOMs, and each of the Services, empowered to go back to their organizations and carry out the JRAC's decisions.

b. The cell works directly with the COCOMs to meet certified operational critical DOTMLPF-P (primarily materiel and logistics) requirements. The cell selects and focuses on high priority JUONs. The goal is to act on requests within 48 hours so that a contract is awarded and goods and services are delivered within four months to two years. All incoming requests for an urgent operational need must be validated and prioritized by the COCOM before forwarding to the JS via SIPRNET. The cell tracks how quickly the military responds and reports directly to the SECDEF through the DEPSECDEF and the Warfighter SIG.

c. Building on the previous establishment and success of the JRAC to resolve requests from operational forces for urgently needed capabilities, OSD, in August 2012, formally established the Warfighter SIG. The Warfighter SIG is responsible for leading the response to CCDR UONs, and must recognize, respond to, and mitigate the risk of operational surprise associated with ongoing or anticipated near-term contingency operations. The SIG is expected to help speed up the process of developing ways to fill JUONs/JEONs, focusing on solutions that are capable of being fielded within two years. The DEPSECDEF serves as the chair of the Warfighter SIG, with the director of the JRAC serving as executive secretary.

d. DOD's highest priority is to provide warfighters involved in conflict or preparing for imminent contingency operations with the capabilities urgently needed to overcome unforeseen threats, achieve mission success, and reduce risk of casualties. Responding to an urgent operational need occurs in three steps. The Warfighter SIG oversees, prioritizes, and facilitates these steps:

(1) First, the need or requirement is validated.

MATERIAL SYSTEM RESEARCH, DEVELOPMENT, AND ACQUISITION MANAGEMENT

(2) Second, a valid solution, consisting of a combination of materiel solution and Tactics, Techniques, and Procedures (TTP), is identified.

(3) Third, the solution must be rapidly executed, including completing any development (necessarily minimal, given the timeline), acquisition, identification, and prioritization of funding, training, and fielding.

e. The Co-Chairs of the Warfighter SIG will prioritize and direct actions to meet urgent requirements and to integrate DOD-wide efforts to manage the institutional response to operational surprise. The Warfighter SIG is the overarching entity through which OSD's previously established urgent needs organizations and task forces and any future OSD-level urgent needs task forces will report to the SECDEF regarding the status of JUONs/JEONs-related actions.

f. CCDRs will use the JUONs/JEONs processes to identify operational vulnerabilities that require resources and/or capabilities beyond those available through the global force management process and more rapidly than the traditional Planning, Programming, Budgeting and Execution System (PPBES) and Defense Acquisition Management System (DAS) allow.

11-18. Component UON: Army Operational Needs Statement (ONS) / Army Requirements and Resourcing Board (AR2B) Process

Services use various methods to shorten the acquisition timelines to meet urgent and compelling needs during crisis and conflict .(e.g.., Air Force's CCD, Marine's Urgent Universal Need statement (UUN), Navy's Rapid Deployment Capability (RDC), and USSOCOM's Combat-Mission Need Statement (C-MNS)). The ONS is the Army's UON process/approach.

a. An Army capability request to HQDA constitutes a request for a materiel and/or non-materiel solution to correct a deficiency or to improve a capability that impacts upon mission accomplishment. These capability requests come to HQDA via the SIPRNET-based Army "start to finish" Equipment Common Operating Picture (ECOP) database and fall into two general categories; authorized/pre-validated Equipment Sourcing Documents (ESD) and ONSs. The final validation, prioritization, and resourcing decision for these capability requests are made by the AR2B.

b. The AR2B is the mechanism (forum) for validating, prioritizing, and resourcing critical operational needs (ONSs and ESDs) for rapid senior leadership decision-making (accelerated fielding solutions) in support of an OCO named operation. The AR2B identifies solutions in the year of execution and/or budget year that require possible resource realignment. Established in December 2004, the AR2B replaced the Army Strategic Planning Board (ASPB) and Setting the Force Task Force. AR2B membership is shown in Figure 11-4.

c. Authorized/pre-validated equipment sourcing requests (equipment and quantities already validated by HQDA, ODCS G-3/5/7):

(1) Deployed and deploying units or other HQDA designated high priority units, may submit ESDs for authorized/pre-validated equipment (e.g., Modification Table of Organization and Equipment (MTOE) shortages, Table of Distribution and Allowances (TDA) shortages, Brigade Combat Team (BCT) Basis-Of-Issue Plan (BOIP) shortages, or other equipment shortages already validated by HQDA). The unit (05-level command) submits an ESD, via the ECOP database, through the chain of command to HQDA G-8/G-4 for resourcing.

(2) Other means are still available for units to request equipment resourcing of authorized/pre-validated equipment such as MTOE shortages. For example, units can and should continue to use the Unit Status Reporting (USR) process (In Accordance With (IAW) AR 220-1) to identify critical shortages affecting unit readiness.

d. ONSs. Operational field commanders use an ONS to document the urgent need for a materiel and/or non-materiel solution to correct a deficiency or to improve a capability that impacts upon mission accomplishment in overseas contingency operations.

(1) The ONS provides an opportunity for the operational field commander (06 level) to initiate the HQDA AR2B process via the Army ECOP database.

(2) The ONS is not an MCD. The CAPDEV, Training Developer (TNGDEV) or Materiel Developer (MATDEV) communities do not initiate or develop an ONS.

HOW THE ARMY RUNS

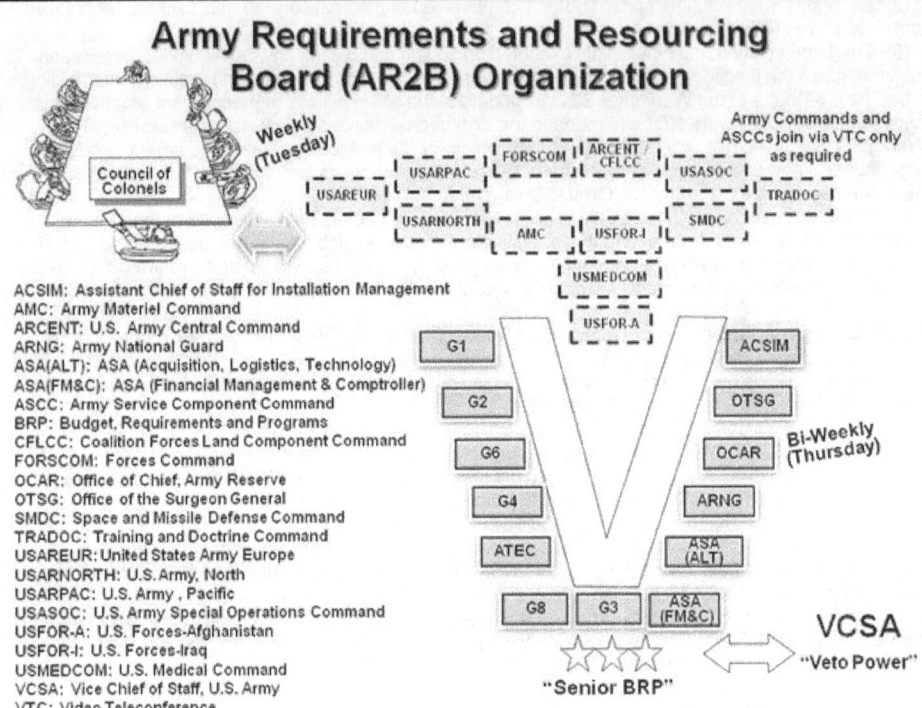

Figure 11-4. Army Requirements and Resourcing Board (AR2B) Organization

(3) Response to an ONS varies depending on the criticality of the need for the proposed item. Response can range from a HQDA-directed requirement and fielding of a materiel system to the forwarding of the action to TRADOC ARCIC for review and appropriate action. HQDA may decline to favorably consider an ONS for a variety of reasons, including conflicting needs, higher priorities for funding, existence of a similar system, or non-concurrence of the criticality of the need. The response to an ONS is based on an ARSTAF validation supported by TRADOC, Army Material Command (AMC), and MATDEV reviews. HQDA AR2B determines validity of the need, availability of technology, and sourcing of resources to fill the requirement. If the need is determined to be critical and can be resourced (at least for the present situation), a directed requirement may result.

(4) All ONS are reviewed by the CAPDEVs/TNGDEVs to determine applicability to future requirements or continuing need for which a standard requirement and acquisition is needed. If validation of the ONS indicates that the concept has potential for Army-wide application and development of a new system is appropriate, TRADOC ARCIC will initiate a functional area ICD and/or CDD/CPD as appropriate through the Capability Development for Rapid Transition (CDRT) program, discussed later in the chapter.

11-19. Directed Requirement

a. If operational analysis and assessment of an ONS or JUON solution or results of an ATD or JCTD, indicate a specific, limited but necessary, urgent need exists, HQDA, DCS G-3/5/7, Director, DAMO-CI may prepare and issue a directed requirement for a capability having application within the Army. Directed requirements must be approved in writing by the VCSA or HQDA, DCS G-3/5/7. While JCIDS capabilities compete in the Army prioritization process for program funding, the DCS G-3/5/7 will specify the funding source and priority for a directed requirement. Requests for directed requirements will be

MATERIAL SYSTEM RESEARCH, DEVELOPMENT, AND ACQUISITION MANAGEMENT

presented through the APRB, AR2B or AROC for decision.

b. The scope of a directed requirement will be limited to addressing urgent operational needs that, fall outside of the established JCIDS process, and if not addressed immediately, will seriously endanger personnel or pose a major threat to the success of ongoing operations. A directed requirement should not involve the development of a new technology or capability; however, the acceleration of an ATD or JCTD (previously discussed), is within the scope of the directed requirements process. The directed requirement format is provided in AR 71-9, Appendix D.

11-20. Rapid Acquisition Authority

a. Congressional legislation uses the term Rapid Acquisition Authority to describe measures with respect to procurement that the SECDEF can take to eliminate a combat capability deficiency that has resulted in combat fatalities. The legislation permits the SECDEF to waive statutes and regulations for testing and procurements (contracting) short of criminal statutes; and to move up to $100 million in authority, per fiscal year, regardless of the "color" (Research, Development, Test, and Evaluation (RDT&E), Procurement, O&M, Military Construction, Army (MCA)) of money. The $100 million is not appropriated funding by Congress for this purpose; it is the authority to expend up to $100 million of existing DOD funding, using this waiver authority.

b. The legislation granting the SECDEF this special authority is contained in section 806(c) of the Bob Stump National Defense Authorization Act for FY 2003, as amended by section 811 of the Ronald W. Reagan National Defense Authorization Act for FY 2005.

c. This Rapid Acquisition Authority, as well as the OCO funding, are the primary sources of funding for the accelerated capabilities and materiel development initiatives, discussed in this chapter, responding to unforeseen urgent operational needs of the military and coalition forces engaged in overseas contingency operations.

Section VI
Traditional Materiel Systems Acquisition

The Defense Acquisition Management System (DAS) establishes a management process to translate user needs (broadly stated functional high risk capability gaps developed in the JCIDS or business needs responding to new ways of doing business) and technological opportunities (developed or identified in the S&T program based on user needs) into reliable and sustainable systems that provide capability to the user.

11-21. DOD System Acquisition Policy

a. The basic policy is to ensure that acquisition of Defense systems is conducted efficiently and effectively in order to achieve operational objectives of the U.S. Armed Forces in their support of national policies and objectives within the guidelines of the Office of Management and Budget (OMB) Circular A-11, Part 3: Major System Acquisitions; DOD Directive 5000.01: The Defense Acquisition System; and DOD Instruction 5000.02: Operation of the Defense Acquisition System. There is a guidebook containing additional supporting discretionary best practices, lessons learned, and expectations posted to the Defense Acquisition Portal at http://dag.dau.mil. AR 70-1 provides Army acquisition policy for materiel and information systems. These documents establish an integrated management framework for a single, standardized DOD-wide acquisition system that applies to all programs including highly sensitive, classified programs. "Tailoring" is encouraged in the process to reflect specific program needs. In accordance with Department of Defense Directive (DODD) 5000.01, "There is no one best way to structure an acquisition program to accomplish the objective of the Defense Acquisition System." The essential features of the DOD materiel acquisition system are:

(1) A clear and stable requirement
(2) A clear AS
(3) A thorough program plan
(4) Risk management techniques
(5) Systematic program tracking against the plan

b. An acquisition program is defined as a directed, funded effort designed to provide a new, improved or continuing weapon system or IT system capability in response to a validated operational need.

HOW THE ARMY RUNS

Acquisition programs are divided into three ACATs, which are established to facilitate decentralized decision-making, execution, and compliance with statutory and regulatory requirements. Acquisition phases provide a logical means of progressively translating broadly stated mission needs into well-defined system-specific requirements and ultimately into operationally effective, suitable, and survivable systems. An acquisition program can enter the system at any phase or MS, based on the maturity of the needed technology or the demonstrated viability of possible materiel solutions under consideration. All the tasks and activities needed to bring the program to the next MS occur during acquisition phases. A MS is the major decision point that initiates the next phase of an acquisition program. MSs may include, for example, the decisions to begin technology development, or to begin LRIP.

11-22. Materiel Systems Acquisition Management
   a. In the broad sense, the event-driven materiel DAS consists of a series of management decisions made within DOD or the Services as the development of a materiel system progresses from a stated materiel requirement to a fielded system. Product Improvements (PI) to existing systems or acquisition of Non-Developmental Items (NDI) usually occur through acquisition streamlining. The system that is used is shown in Figure 11-5. A key aspect of the process is that it is divided into three distinct activities (pre-systems acquisition, systems acquisition, sustainment); five phases (materiel solution analysis, technology development, engineering and manufacturing development, production and deployment, and operations and support); and six work efforts (integrated system design; system capability and manufacturing process demonstration; LRIP; Full-Rate Production (FRP); and deployment, sustainment, and disposal). Entry into the DAS is at one of the formal MS decision points, dependent on the MDD.

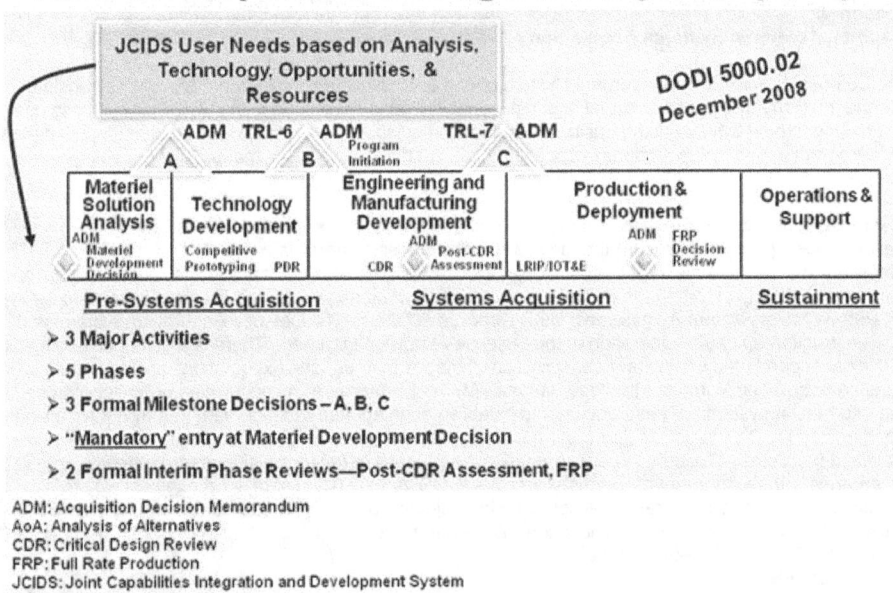

Figure 11-5. Defense Acquisition Management System (DAS)

MATERIAL SYSTEM RESEARCH, DEVELOPMENT, AND ACQUISITION MANAGEMENT

   b. Key policies and principles governing the operation of the DAS are (DODD 5000.01):
   (1) Flexibility. There is no one best way to structure an acquisition program to accomplish the objective of the DAS. Milestone Decision Authorities (MDA) and PMs tailor program strategies and oversight, including documentation of program information, acquisition phases, the timing and scope of decision reviews, and decision levels, to fit the particular conditions of that program, consistent with applicable laws and regulations and the time-sensitivity of the capability need.
   (2) Responsiveness. Mature technology is integrated into producible systems and deployed in the shortest time. Validated, time-phased capability needs matched with available technology and resources enable evolutionary acquisition strategies. Evolutionary acquisition is the DOD approach to satisfying operational needs.
   (3) Innovation. Throughout DOD, acquisition professionals continuously develop and implement initiatives to streamline and improve the DAS. MDAs and PMs examine and, as appropriate, adopt innovative practices (including best commercial practices), that reduce life-cycle time and cost, and encourage teamwork.
   (4) Discipline. PMs manage programs consistent with statutory and regulatory requirements. Every PM establishes program goals for the minimum number of cost, schedule, and performance parameters that describe the program over its life-cycle. Approved APB parameters serve as program control objectives. PMs identify deviations from approved APB parameters and exit criteria.
   (5) Streamlined and effective management. Responsibility for the acquisition of systems is decentralized to the maximum extent. The MDA provides a single individual with sufficient authority to accomplish MDA approved program objectives for development, production, and sustainment. The MDA ensures accountability and maximizes credibility in cost, schedule, and performance reporting.
   c. Technology projects (e.g., JCTDs, JWEs, concepts development, and capabilities development), are efforts that occur prior to acquisition program initiation. These are referred to as pre-ACAT technology projects. The MDA for projects which will likely result in a MDAP, if successful, will be the Under Secretary of Defense, Acquisition, Technology, and Logistics (USD(AT&L)).
   d. The DAS is initiated as a result of output—validated warfighting materiel capabilities-based requirements—from the JCIDS process. Identified warfighting requirements are first assessed to determine if they can be satisfied by non-materiel solutions. Non-materiel solutions include changes in DOTmLPF-P. If these non-materiel solutions do not satisfy the deficiency, a new materiel development program is initiated.

11-23. Acquisition Strategies and Program Plans
   a. The AS is the framework (roadmap) for planning, directing, and managing an acquisition program to satisfy a validated materiel requirement. Acquisition strategies and their supporting program plans are tailored to accomplish established program objectives and to control risk. Also, they must provide the information essential for MS decisions. In this regard, ASs are event-driven and explicitly link major contractual commitments and MS decisions to demonstrated accomplishments in development and testing.
   b. Evolutionary acquisition. Evolutionary acquisition is DOD's preferred strategy for rapid acquisition of a mature technology for the user. An evolutionary approach delivers capability in increments recognizing, up front, the need for future capability improvements. The success of the strategy depends on the consistent and continuous definition of capabilities-based requirements and the maturation of technologies that lead to disciplined development and production of systems that provide increasing capability towards a materiel concept.
   c. Program plans provide for a systems engineering approach to the simultaneous design of the product and its associated manufacturing, test, and support processes. This concurrent engineering approach is essential to achieving a careful balance among system design requirements (e.g., operational performance, producibility, reliability, maintainability, logistics and human factors engineering, safety, survivability, interoperability, and standardization). Maximum practicable use is made of commercial and other NDI. The Army's first preference is to use performance specifications; the next is to use Non-Government Standards (NGS); and as a last resort, Military Specifications and Standards (MILSPEC/STD) may be used. Use of MILSPECs/STDs requires a waiver from the MDA. Additionally, changes to DODI 5000.02, state that the AS should be tailored to the extent feasible to employ commercial practices when purchasing commercial products or other NDI.

HOW THE ARMY RUNS

d. CAIV. CAIV is the DOD cost reduction methodology utilized throughout the entire life-cycle of a programs acquisition process, to ensure operational capability of the total force is maximized for the given modernization investment. In other words, cost is treated as an independent variable along with others used to define a system. CAIV directly impacts the preparation of a program's materiel capabilities documents (ICDs/CDDs/CPDs), as well as acquisition documents (AS and APB).

11-24. Environmental Considerations

Environmental impact is always considered in Defense acquisitions. The National Environmental Policy Act (NEPA) of 1969, mandates analysis of potential environmental effects of proposed federal actions. For materiel acquisitions, NEPA applies to all "new starts," SLEP, P3I, and block modifications in all ACATs. NEPA analysis begins during the DAS Technology Development (TD) phase and continues through the EMD Phase and P&D Phase, accounting for all direct, indirect, and cumulative environmental impacts. NEPA compliance is key to support production, testing, and fielding of the system, as well as ensuring the system can be operated, maintained, and sustained throughout the remainder of its life-cycle. The NEPA documentation process can be lengthy and costly, but environmental issues and concerns represent a risk to the program that must be managed. Inadequate environmental analyses can lead to dramatic increases to overall program costs, can delay testing and fielding schedules, and may produce a system that cannot be operated or maintained at the location where Soldiers need it most. Early consideration of environmental impacts and NEPA requirements help protect not only the environment, but helps ensure a well-trained, protected Soldier.

11-25. Risk Assessments and Management

Program risks and risk management plans are explicitly assessed at each MS decision point prior to granting approval to proceed into the next acquisition phase. Risks must be well understood and risk management approaches developed before MDAs can authorize a program to proceed into the next phase of the acquisition process. To assess and manage risk, MATDEVs use a variety of techniques. They include TDs, prototyping, and Test and Evaluation (T&E). Risk management encompasses identification, mitigation, and continuous tracking and control procedures that provide feedback through the program assessment process to decision authorities. PMs develop a contracting approach appropriate to the type of system being developed and acquired and the risk of the program.

Section VII
Department of Defense Acquisition Organization and Management

11-26. DOD System Acquisition Management

a. The USD(AT&L), is the senior procurement executive and the principal staff assistant and adviser to the SECDEF and takes precedence in DOD for all matters relating to the DAS: research and development; test and evaluation; production; logistics; command, control, and communications, and intelligence activities related to acquisition; military construction; and procurement.

b. The USD(AT&L) serves as the Defense Acquisition Executive (DAE) with responsibility for supervising the performance of the entire DAS in accordance with the laws, Congressional guidance and direction, and OMB Circular No. A-11, part 3. The DAE establishes policy for all elements of DOD for acquisition. The basic policies of the DAE are established and implemented by DODD 5000.01 and DODI 5000.02. The DAE serves as the chairman of the DAB and ITAB, assisted by the OIPTs that relate to the acquisition process. As the DAB chairman, the DAE recommends to the SECDEF acquisition resource matters and other acquisition management matters required to implement acquisition MS decisions. A clear distinction exists between responsibility for weapon systems acquisition and budgetary authority. While the DAE, as DAB/ITAB chairman, makes recommendations whether to proceed with plans to acquire major materiel systems, the Senior Leader Review Group (SLRG), chaired by the DEPSECDEF, makes budgetary recommendations on the same programs. Acquisition programs must operate within the parameters established by the SLRG and the SECDEF through the PPBE process.

11-27. Defense Advanced Research Projects Agency (DARPA)

DARPA is a unique organization and management tool of the SECDEF. It consists of a mix of military and civilian scientists and engineers, and has a broad charter to conduct advanced research that fills R&D

MATERIAL SYSTEM RESEARCH, DEVELOPMENT, AND ACQUISITION MANAGEMENT

gaps between Service lines of responsibility or handles high priority problems that cross Service lines. DARPA's purpose is to review ongoing R&D, determine whether or not the concept is feasible, determine its usefulness, and transfer it to the appropriate Service. DARPA does not have its own in-house research facilities and relies on the Services and other government agencies for technical and administrative support. Once a decision to support a research proposal is made, responsibility for contracting is generally assigned to one of the Services. Examples of past DARPA contributions include the M-16 Rifle, Air Force F-117 Tactical Fighter (Stealth Fighter), Unmanned Aerial Vehicle (UAV), and the Advanced Research Projects Agency (ARPA) Net (current Internet).

11-28. Defense Acquisition University (DAU)
The DAU is a corporate university that includes the Defense Systems Management College (DSMC). Its operation and structure is designed to be similar to a state university with many campuses each specializing in certain acquisition disciplines. The Defense Acquisition Workforce Improvement Act (DAWIA) required the formation of the DAU with operation commencing in 1992.

11-29. DSMC
a. The DSMC is the USD(AT&L) institution for ensuring the up-to-date training of military and civilian professionals in the management of materiel acquisition programs in DOD. The DAWIA required the establishment of a senior course for personnel serving in Critical Acquisition Positions (CAP), which is equivalent to existing senior professional military education programs. The USD(AT&L) has oversight authority for the acquisition curriculum of the course.

b. The DSMC, founded 1971, is a joint military professional institution, operating under the direction of the DAU Executive Board, to support acquisition management as described in DOD Directive 5000.01, and to assist in fulfilling education and training requirements set out in appropriate DOD directives and public laws. The mission of the DSMC is to:

(1) Conduct advanced courses of study in defense acquisition management as the primary function of the college

(2) Conduct research and special studies in defense acquisition management

(3) Assemble and disseminate information concerning new policies, methods, and practices in defense acquisition management

(4) Provide consulting services in defense acquisition management

Section VIII
Army Acquisition Organization and Management

11-30. Army RDA Goals
a. The SECARMY is responsible for functions necessary for the research, development, logistical support and maintenance, preparedness, operation, and effectiveness of the Army. The SECARMY supervises all matters relating to Army procurement. The SECARMY executes his acquisition management responsibilities through the AAE.

b. Special emphasis is placed on medium and long-range materiel planning, product modification, and life extension programs. Major state-of-the-art advancements are sought only in carefully selected areas. Stability of materiel acquisition programs is a matter of utmost interest, especially after the system passes the DAS MS B program initiation decision. Reliability, Availability, and Maintainability (RAM) goals; manpower and personnel integration (MANPRINT); Integrated Logistics Support (ILS); survivability; effectiveness; safety; and product quality are incorporated into system performance objectives. Contractual incentives for the improvement of RAM and ILS are encouraged.

11-31. AAE
The Assistant Secretary of the Army (Acquisition, Logistics, and Technology) (ASA(ALT)) is the AAE. The AAE is designated by the SECARMY as the Component Acquisition Executive (CAE) and the senior procurement executive within HQDA. The AAE is the principal HQDA staff official for the execution of the AAE responsibilities. When serving as the AAE, the ASA(ALT) is assisted by a Principal MILDEP.

a. The MILDEP is assigned to the Office of the ASA(ALT) and provides staff support to the AAE in managing the R&D, Developmental Test (DT), and materiel acquisition for all Army weapon and support

HOW THE ARMY RUNS

systems. The MILDEP, delegated down from the AAE, is also the Army Director, Acquisition Career Management (DACM). The DACM is responsible for directing the Army Acquisition Corps (AAC), as well as implementation of the acquisition career management requirements set forth in the DAWIA legislation. The day-to-day management of Army acquisition programs is shown in Figure 11-6.

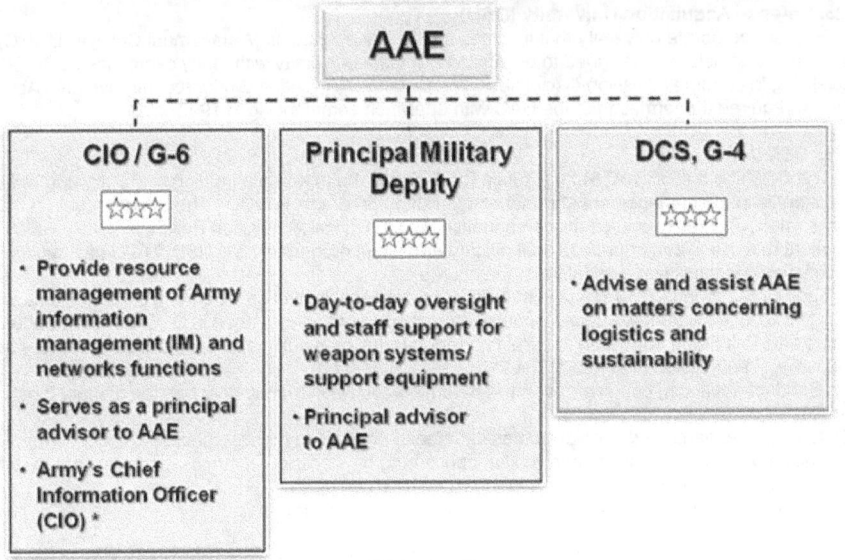

Figure 11-6. Army Acquisition Executive (AAE)

b. Similar to the DAE, the AAE develops Army acquisition policies and procedures and manages the Army's production base support and industrial mobilization programs. The AAE, acting with the full authority of the SECARMY, is responsible for administering acquisition programs according to DOD policies and guidelines, and exercises the powers and discharges the responsibilities as set forth in DODD 5000.01 for CAEs. In addition, the AAE:

  (1) Appoints, manages, and evaluates Program Executive Officers (PEO) and direct-reporting PMs.
  (2) Coordinates with Office of the DCS, G-3/5/7, to establish policy and guidance for the AoAs; for ACAT I and II programs; designates the organization responsible for performing system engineering trades analyses for the AoA; and provides issues and alternatives to the DCS, G-3/5/7 for inclusion in the AoA tasking document.
  (3) Carries out all powers, functions, and duties of the SECARMY with respect to the acquisition work force within the Army, subject to the authority, direction, and control of the SECARMY.
  (4) Develops guidance, in coordination with the HQDA DCS, G-3/5/7, and serves as co-proponent, with the HQDA DCS, G-8, for the Army's Research, Development, and Acquisition Plan (RDAP).
  (5) Formulates Army-wide S&T base strategy, policy, guidance, and planning.
  (6) Establishes and validates Army technology base priorities throughout the PPBES.
  (7) Acts as the final authority of all matters affecting the Army's acquisition system, except as limited by statute or higher-level regulation. Develops and promulgates acquisition, procurement, and contracting policies and procedures.

MATERIAL SYSTEM RESEARCH, DEVELOPMENT, AND ACQUISITION MANAGEMENT

(8) Chairs all Army System Acquisition Review Council (ASARC) meetings.
(9) Directs the Army Science Board (ASB).
(10) Appoints the Source Selection Authority (SSA) for specified programs. The Federal Acquisition Regulation (FAR) is the primary contracting regulation. It is the first regulatory source to which DA acquisition personnel refer. The ASA(ALT) issues the Army Federal Acquisition Regulation Supplement (AFARS) to implement and supplement the FAR and the Defense Federal Acquisition Regulation Supplement (DFARS) and to establish uniform policies and procedures for use in the Army.
(11) Reviews and approves, for ACAT ID programs, the Army position at each decision MS before the DAB review. This includes the review and approval of APBs. The AAE serves as the Milestone Decision Authority (MDA) for ACATs IC, IAC, selected ACAT II, and assigns the MDA for ACAT III programs to the PEOs. The MDA is the individual designated to approve entry into the next acquisition phase.
(12) Approves the establishment and termination of all Program Management Offices (PMO) and PEOs. The AAE has authority to designate a system for intensive, centralized management and prescribe the appropriate level of management at any point in the program management process.
    c. HQDA System Coordinator (DASC). The DASC is the primary acquisition staff officer at HQDA. The DASC is responsible for the day-to-day support of assigned programs and serves as the PM's representative and primary Point Of Contact (POC) within the Pentagon. The DASC reports to the ASA(ALT), Deputy for Acquisition and Systems Management. The DASC is responsible for keeping the acquisition chain of command informed of the status of assigned acquisition programs. In addition, the DASC assists the PM with issue resolution at HQDA and OSD levels. The DASC is the "eyes and ears" of the PM at the Pentagon and ensures that the PM is advised of any actions or circumstances that might negatively impact their program.
    d. HQDA logistics support officer (DALSO) is the HQDA representative of the logistics community, providing logistics coordination. The DALSO monitors the progress of the assigned system and ensures that all elements of ILS, as outlined in AR 700-127, are satisfactorily completed. Because of the interrelationships of assigned responsibilities in materiel acquisition, close and continuous coordination and cooperation is essential between the DALSO and his counterparts at TRADOC, AMC, and the ARSTAF. In addition to new items of equipment, DALSOs also have responsibility for existing weapons and materiel systems in the Army force structure. This responsibility covers all phases of logistics support to include readiness, redistribution, and disposal. The DALSO's primary mission is to provide HQDA general staff supervision over the ILS management of assigned commodity materiel/weapons systems from concept to disposal. Other responsibilities include:
(1) ARSTAF responsibility for logistical acceptability, deployability, and supportability of materiel systems, interoperability, ILS, materiel release, and logistics R&D programs for the Army
(2) Serving as the logistician in the DAS for other than medical equipment, and conducting surveillance over logistics aspects of materiel acquisition and modification programs to ensure supportable systems
(3) Providing policy guidance for logistics, medical, and engineer materiel acquisition

11-32. PEO
    a. The PEO system structure was implemented by the Army in 1987, in response to requirements established by the Goldwater-Nichols Reorganization Act of 1986; and the recommendation of the Packard Commission, under President Reagan, that was approved and then ordered by the National Security Decision Directive (NSDD) 219 (see Figure 11-7).
    b. The PEO, administering a defined number of AAE assigned MDAPs, major and/or non-major programs, is responsible for programmatics (materiel acquisition cost, schedule, and total system performance) and for the PPBE necessary to guide assigned programs through each DAS MS. In addition, the PEO provides program information to the AAE, HQDA, DOD, and Congress; defends assigned programs to Congress through the Army Office Chief of Legislative Liaison (OCLL); and participates in the development of data to support AAE programmatic decisions in the PPBE. Other PEO and direct-reporting PM responsibilities include assisting the CAPDEV and TNGDEV in developing MCD, by providing technical, availability, performance, anticipated materiel acquisition cost, and schedule type information as needed.

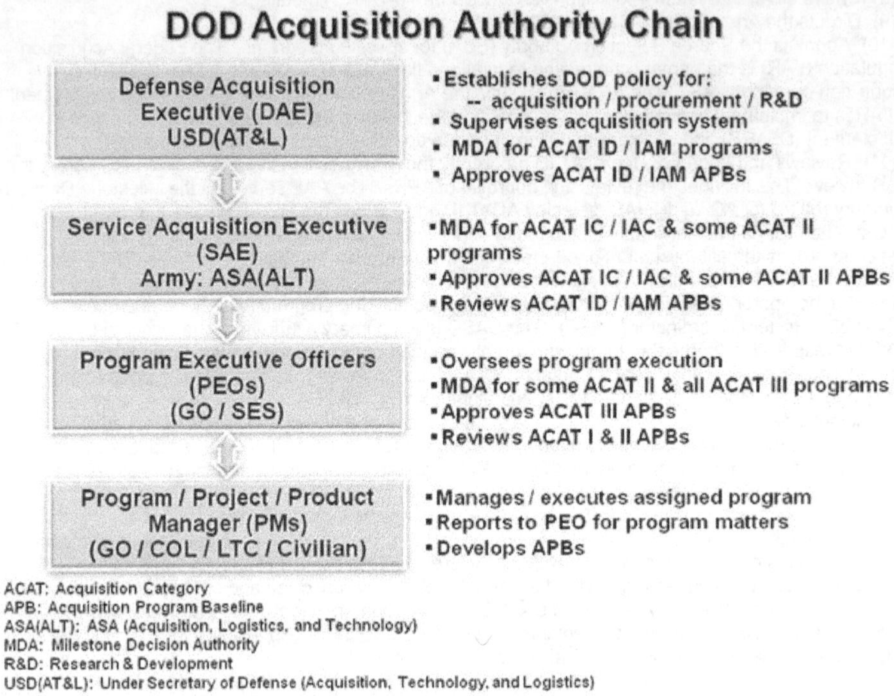

HOW THE ARMY RUNS

DOD Acquisition Authority Chain

Defense Acquisition Executive (DAE) USD(AT&L)
- Establishes DOD policy for:
  -- acquisition / procurement / R&D
- Supervises acquisition system
- MDA for ACAT ID / IAM programs
- Approves ACAT ID / IAM APBs

Service Acquisition Executive (SAE) Army: ASA(ALT)
- MDA for ACAT IC / IAC & some ACAT II programs
- Approves ACAT IC / IAC & some ACAT II APBs
- Reviews ACAT ID / IAM APBs

Program Executive Officers (PEOs) (GO / SES)
- Oversees program execution
- MDA for some ACAT II & all ACAT III programs
- Approves ACAT III APBs
- Reviews ACAT I & II APBs

Program / Project / Product Manager (PMs) (GO / COL / LTC / Civilian)
- Manages / executes assigned program
- Reports to PEO for program matters
- Develops APBs

ACAT: Acquisition Category
APB: Acquisition Program Baseline
ASA(ALT): ASA (Acquisition, Logistics, and Technology)
MDA: Milestone Decision Authority
R&D: Research & Development
USD(AT&L): Under Secretary of Defense (Acquisition, Technology, and Logistics)

Figure 11-7. Department of Defense (DOD) Acquisition Authority Chain

   c. The AAE has 11 PEOs—Missiles and Space; Aviation; Command, Control, Communications – Tactical/Joint Tactical Radio System (JTRS); Intelligence, Electronic Warfare (EW) and Sensors; Ground Combat Systems; Combat Support/Combat Service Support Systems; Simulation, Training, and Instrumentation; Ammunition; Soldier; Enterprise Information Systems, and JPEO, Chemical and Biological Defense – responsible for the intensive management of RDA weapon and information systems. Unless a waiver is granted by the DAE or AAE, a PEO must be certified in acquisition management.

   d. The Army's primary CAPDEV, referred to above, is the U.S. Army TRADOC. TRADOC formulates and documents operational concepts, doctrine, organizations, and/or materiel requirements for assigned Army functions. TRADOC serves as the user representative during acquisitions for their validated materiel requirements, as well as doctrine and organization developments.

   e. A MATDEV is located within the RDA command, agency, or office, assigned responsibility for the system under development or being acquired. The term may be used generically to refer to the RDA community in the materiel acquisition process (counterpart to the generic use of CAPDEV).

   f. A TNGDEV is located within a command or agency that formulates, develops, and documents or produces training concepts, strategies, requirements (materiel and other), and programs for assigned mission areas and functions. The TNGDEV serves as user (trainer and trainee) representative during acquisitions of their validated training materiel requirements and training program developments. TNGDEVs perform the following functions solely in support of training systems:

   (1) Fund and conduct concept formulations for all system Training Aids, Devices, Simulations, and Simulators (TADSS) in support of assigned systems

   (2) Program and budget resources for TADSS, as specified in the Training Support Requirements (TSR) annex of the CDD

MATERIAL SYSTEM RESEARCH, DEVELOPMENT, AND ACQUISITION MANAGEMENT

(3) Integrate system training capabilities into assigned materiel systems in accordance with the validated system MCD and in coordination with the CAPDEV

(4) Develop, acquire, and field the subsystem training package with the materiel system; plan and program resources for the execution of New Equipment Training (NET) using Distance Learning (DL) technology and/or contract NET as the desired training strategy in support of TRADOC developed/approved System Training Plans (STRAP)

(5) Provide TNGDEV perspective through input to the Army RDAP and the AMP

11-33. Program / Project / Product Manager (PM)

a. The program management approach to system acquisition management is a distinct departure from the Services' traditional practice of establishing functionally oriented organizations to carry out well-defined, repetitive, and continuous long-term tasks. Organization for program management is a tailored, task-oriented process. This approach requires the PM to establish management arrangements among the PMO, other military organizations, and various contractors to coordinate their efforts and to accomplish program objectives effectively, efficiently, and economically. A variety of PMO organizations have been established. They operate on the matrix management principle and must draw all functional support from a host command or installation. In addition to the formal PM organization, the PM directs the informal MATDEV/CAPDEV team to execute the assigned materiel acquisition program. MATDEV/CAPDEV team is the terminology used to describe the informal, but essential, close working relationship among the MATDEV, CAPDEV, and other players in the RDA management process.

b. The PM has authority and responsibility for all programmatic (cost, schedule, performance, and life-cycle sustainment) decisions to execute the assigned program within the approved APB and subject to functional standards established by regulation, secretarial direction, or law. Generically, all PMs are program managers, but they are chartered as a program manager, a project manager, or product manager generally based on the value and importance (visibility) of the program they manage. The criteria established for designation of a program manager are generally the same as those which cause a system acquisition to be designated as a MDAP, major, or non-major program—high defense priority, high dollar value, or major Congressional or OSD interest. Since 2001, all Army acquisition programs, regardless of ACAT, are managed by a PM overseen by a PEO or directly reporting to the AAE. All PEOs report directly to the Defense Acquisition Executive (ACAT ID programs) or to the SAE (for ACAT IC and below). Project managers report to a PEO or the AAE. All product managers report to a project manager. As a general rule, a program manager is a general officer or SES; a project manager is a Colonel or GS-15; a product manager is a Lieutenant Colonel or GS-14. This distinction between PMs is unique to the Army, and does not apply to the other Services or within industry.

c. Normally project managers of ACAT I programs are assigned for four years, with other program managers and product managers staying three years in position. Unless a waiver is granted by the DAE or AAE, a PM must be certified in acquisition management.

11-34. PEO Resource Control

The Army has revised its resource support system structure for the PEOs to improve their control over the funding and manpower resources they need to carry out their responsibilities. PEOs and subordinate PMs receive dollars and personnel authorization resources directly from HQDA rather than through the AMC Life-Cycle Management Commands (LCMC). The LCMCs continue to provide a variety of support services without duplicating any of the PEOs or PMs management functions. This enhanced resource control system ensures PEO and PM managed programs are managed with modern efficient techniques, without administrative burdens or materiel command layers being inserted into the chain of command.

11-35. HQDA

a. CSA. The CSA is responsible by law to the SECARMY for the efficiency of the Army and its preparedness for military operations. The CSA acts as the agent of the SECARMY in carrying out the plans or recommendations submitted by the ARSTAF and approved by the SECARMY. The VCSA, supports the CSA by managing the day-to-day operations of the Army. The VCSA chairs the AROC and in the area of RDA, the VCSA co-chairs the ASARC.

b. Assistant Secretary of the Army (Financial Management and Comptroller) (ASA(FM&C)). The ASA(FM&C) has secretariat responsibility for all financial management activities and operations for

HOW THE ARMY RUNS

appropriated funds. While the budget is in preparation, the ASA(FM&C) receives and consolidates procurement and RDT&E budget forms from Army commands and PEOs. The ASA(FM&C) also:

(1) Works with the AAE on all cost and Economic Analysis (EA) matters related to the acquisition process.

(2) Carries out all financial management responsibilities assigned under Title 10.

(3) Tasks the appropriate MATDEV to conduct Program Office Estimates (POE) and/or EA to MDR and PPBE requirements.

(4) Manages all budgeting activities in support of the Army materiel requirements processes and RDA modernization program, with the framework of PPBE.

(5) Develops statutory Independent Life-Cycle Cost Estimates (ICE) and Component Cost Estimates (CCE) for weapon and information systems. Chairs and oversees the Army Cost Review Board (CRB) and approves the Army Cost Position (ACP) for all major acquisition programs. The ASA(FM&C) Deputy for Cost & Economics, ensures that the ACP reflects the costs and risks associated with the program, in concurrence with the CAIV process.

(6) MILDEP, ASA(FM&C) is a regular member of the AR2B in support of OCO.

c. Assistant Chief of Staff for Installation Management (ACSIM). The ACSIM is responsible for developing criteria for the mitigation of environmental impacts, and reviewing emerging Army RDA systems for environmental effects. The ACSIM is a regular member of the AR2B.

d. Deputy Chief of Staff, G-1 (DCS, G-1). The DCS, G-1 has ARSTAF responsibility for personnel management. DCS, G-1 monitors planning for the manpower and personnel aspects of new systems. Also, the DCS, G-1 is the proponent and has primary ARSTAF responsibility for the DOD Human Systems Integration (HSI) program (MANPRINT program in the Army). The emphasis of the MANPRINT program is to enhance total system performance (Soldier in the loop) and to conserve the Army's Manpower, Personnel, and Training (MPT) resources. The DCS, G-1 is a regular member of the AROC, ASARC, and AR2B.

(1) The HQDA Personnel System Staff Officer (PERSSO) is the ARSTAF representative of the personnel community. The PERSSO provides for the continuous coordination necessary to ensure the smooth integration of new equipment, materiel systems, and new organizations. The PERSSO responsibilities include, but are not limited to: preparing and justifying force structure requests in conjunction with the DCS, G-3/5/7 Organization Integrator (OI) and DCS, G-8 SSO; reviewing and coordinating the development of force structure changes; personnel supportability architecture; officer and enlisted issues related to new organizational concepts and doctrine; and ensuring programming and budgeting of manpower spaces.

(2) The PERSSO participates in all HQDA actions to develop the staff position on CAPDEV proposals for potential MDAPs, the designation of a proposed system, the recommendations on the elements of system fielding, including the proposed BOIP, the Initial Issue Quantity (IIQ), and the Army Acquisition Objective (AAO). The PERSSO represents the DCS, G-1 at force modernization-related, HQDA-sponsored conferences, forums, and meetings on issues of supportability concerning the introduction of new and/or reorganized existing table of organization and equipment (TOE)/ TDA units.

e. Deputy Chief of Staff, G-2 (DCS, G-2). The DCS, G-2 provides scientific and technical intelligence and threat projections in support of all aspects of the Army RDA programs. The DCS, G-2 is a regular member of the ASARC, AROC, and AR2B. In addition, a HQDA Threat Integration Staff Officer (TISO) is designated by the DCS, G-2 to function as the HQDA threat integration coordinator for designated mission areas, programs, and systems. The TISO represents the DCS, G-2 on all aspects of threat support throughout the system life-cycle or study process. The TISO complements the DCS, G-3/5/7 RSO and DCS, G-8 SSO and is designed to foster closer coordination among the intelligence community, Army commands, and ARSTAF agencies to ensure the timely integration of the threat into the materiel acquisition process.

f. Deputy Chief of Staff, G-3/5/7 (DCS, G-3/5/7). As the Army's force manager, the DCS, G-3/5/7 serves as the HQDA proponent for all Army force structure related policies, processes, and actions. The DCS, G-3/5/7 is a regular member of the ASARC, AROC, and chairs the AR2B. The DCS, G-3/5/7:

(1) Integrates Army DOTMLPF-P capability-based requirements into structure;

(2) Develops and maintains force planning guidance and active and reserve component force structure through the Total Army Analysis (TAA) force accounting, force documentation and other force management forums; and

MATERIAL SYSTEM RESEARCH, DEVELOPMENT, AND ACQUISITION MANAGEMENT

(3) Oversees the force management, training, mission command simulations and experimentation, prioritization, and requirements validation processes for the Army. The DCS, G-3/5/7 is assisted by the Director, G-37 Capabilities Integration, Prioritization, and Analysis (DAMO-CI), who has supervisory responsibility for:
(a) Analysis, Experimentation, Testing and Technology Division (DAMO-CIA).
(i) Ensures key Army and DOD decisions regarding materiel requirements and materiel acquisition solutions are supported by sound analysis
(ii) Serves as HQDA proponent for experimentation oversight and policy
(iii) Serves as G-3/5/7 lead for T&E and S&T matters
(b) Army Requirements and Resource Division (DAMO-CIB).
(i) Accelerates urgent requirements to solutions for the Soldier through the AR2B
(ii) Synchronizes accelerated materiel solution efforts through the War Production Board (WPB)
(c) Current and Future Warfighting Capabilities Division (DAMO-CIC).
(i) Validates current and future Army warfighting capability requirements
(ii) Serves as the Army lead for validation and prioritization of ONS
(iii) Serves as Army lead for implementation of policy and procedures for the JCIDS process
(d) Portfolio Review and Integration Division (DAMO-CIP). Leads conduct of VCSA-directed capability portfolio reviews in order to identify trade-offs and to establish and revalidate priorities among programs.
(e) Resource Analysis & Integration Division (DAMO-CIR). Represents DCS, G-3/5/7 in all phases of the PPBE process (e.g., Program, Budget, Year of Execution, and OCO funds.
(4) DCS, G-3/5/7, Current and Future Warfighting Capabilities Division (DAMO-CIC). Within the DCS, G-3/5/7, DAMO-CIC is the single entry point, as the Army's JCIDS "gatekeeper," for all Army and joint DOTMLPF-P requirements. DAMO-CIC is the proponent for policy development and joint/Army JCIDS process oversight. Within DAMO-CIC, the RSO is directly responsible for leading HQDA staff integration and coordination efforts for all Army and joint DOTMLPF-P requirements issues within Army JCIDS. The RSO coordinates with the HQDA DCS, G-8 counterpart, the SSO, to facilitate the transition from requirements development and validation to requirements solutions (execution and resourcing). DAMO-CIC functions and responsibilities include:
(a) Proponent for Army's warfighting capabilities (requirements) determination policy (AR 71-9):
(i) Army implementation of JCIDS
(ii) Army policies and procedures for execution of the JCIDS UON process
(b) Provides support to ODCS, G-3/5/7 for equipment/system capability and employment issues:
(i) DAS process (ASARC/OIPT/DAB)
(ii) PPBE (POM/investment reviews with HQDA DCS, G-8)
(iii) Congressional inquiries and testimony
(c) Serves as the HQDA Gatekeeper for JCIDS documents to support:
(i) HQDA validation of TRADOC-generated documents by AROC
(ii) Development of the official Army position on other Service/COCOM documents during joint staffing
(iii) Configuration management of Army documents during joint staffing and JROC review for validation
(iv) AROC secretariat support to the HQDA DCS, G-3/5/7 and VCSA
(d) Conduct staff integration of modernization proposals to support force development planning:
(i) Execute JCIDS document staffing within ARSTAF/lead comment resolution process
(ii) Organize presentation of Army modernization proposals to AROC for validation
(iii) Assemble Army position/input on other Service JCIDS documents during joint staffing
(iv) Support joint review of Army proposals/input during FCB consideration
(e) Conduct staff integration of ONSs for urgently required warfighting capabilities:
(i) Serves as the HQDA Gatekeeper for ONS requests submitted by operational commanders
(ii) Develops validation recommendations/conduct execution planning for HQDA DCS, G-3/5/7 in support of overseas contingency operations missions
(5) RSOs. Within G-37 (DAMO-CI), RSOs, as the functional integrator for specific focus areas (e.g., Focus Logistics, Battlespace Awareness, Force Application, etc.), to facilitate the staffing, validation, and prioritization of all Army DOTMLPF-P requirements. Primary functions and responsibilities are:
(a) Represents HQDA DCS, G-3/5/7 equities in TRADOC CoE ICDTs for JCIDS analysis and documentation
(b) Responsible for integrated validation recommendations to the HQDA DCS, G-3/5/7 on urgent warfighting requirements (ONSs)

HOW THE ARMY RUNS

(c) Participates in Army/OSD DAS Integrated Product Teams (IPT) representing the validated operational requirement"

(d) Prepares congressional correspondence and testimony addressing operational requirements and future warfighting capabilities

(e) Provides PPBE support to the Budget, Requirements and Programs (BRP) Board regarding operational requirements and integration considerations for Army Programs

(f) Participates in FCB forums in support of the JROC review of JCIDS analysis and documentation

(g) Responsible for HQDA staffing of other Service capability documents

(h) Produces official Army Position on Army and other Service capability documents during joint staffing

(i) Responsible for HQDA staffing of Army capability documents, including comment resolution, in support of AROC validation decisions

g. Deputy Chief of Staff, G-4 (DCS, G-4). The DCS, G-4 assesses the logistical supportability of materiel systems during the DAS process. The DCS, G-4 participates in all phases of the RDA management process to ensure equipment is logistically reliable, supportable, and maintainable. DCS, G-4 is responsible for secondary item requirements, such as war reserve requirements. The DCS, G-4 is a regular member of the ASARC, AROC and AR2B. The DCS, G-4 has been designated the Principal Military Advisor to the AAE for logistics and sustainment. As the principal military advisor to the AAE for logistics, the DCS, G-4 is assisted by the Deputy ASA(ALT) for ILS, who is the HQDA focal point for a system's ILS program. h. Army CIO/Deputy Chief of Staff, G-6. The CIO/G-6 has ARSTAF responsibility for Army Automated Information Systems (AIS) and IT activities. These include establishing and approving policies, procedures, and standards for the planning, programming, life-cycle management, use of Army IT resources, and responding to and validating all warfighting requirements. The G-6 serves as the Army CIO as directed by the Clinger-Cohen Act (originally known as the Information Technology Management Reform Act (ITMRA) of 1996). The CIO's primary responsibility, under the Clinger-Cohen Act, is the management of resources for all Army information programs. The DCS, G-6 is a regular member of the ASARC, AROC, and the AR2B.

i. Deputy Chief of Staff, G-8 (DCS, G-8). The DCS, G-8 is the principal military advisor to the ASA (FM&C). The DCS, G-8 prepares the Army POM; integrates and synchronizes the POM process; and provides analysis and evaluation of Army programs to the senior Army leadership. The DCS, G-8 is a regular member of the ASARC, AROC, Army Marine Corps Board (AMCB), and the AR2B. The DCS, G-8 responsibilities include:

(1) Army program advocate to OSD, the JS, other military departments, government agencies and organizations

(2) Overseeing materiel fielding across the Army and ensuring integration of DOTMLPF-P into materiel solutions (IAW validated Army requirements

(3) Serving as principal advisor to the CSA on joint materiel requirements, representing the Army in the JS FCB, JCB, and JROC process

(4) Serving as the Army lead for all QDR activities

(5) Overseeing the Army Studies Program

(a) G-8, Director, Program Analysis and Evaluation (DPAE). Within DCS, G-8, the DPAE is responsible for reviewing and analyzing requirements and programs in force structure development; providing analytical support to the Army Resources Board (ARB) and subordinate committees; developing resource guidance; developing and compiling the POM; maintaining the Army portion of the DOD Future Years Defense Program (FYDP); and presenting an affordability analysis to the ASARC. Other responsibilities include conducting and presenting affordability assessments to support DOD and HQDA ACAT I programs, and managing the programming phase of the PPBE process.

(b) G-8, Director, Force Development (Director, FD). Within DCS G-8, the Director, FD translates validated Army DOTMLPF-P requirements into programs, within allocated resources, to accomplish Army missions and functions. In addition, the Director, FD exercises life-cycle management of materiel programs.

(i) The FD Directorate is organized with a Director of Materiel (DOM), Director of Joint & Integration (DJI), and Director of Resources (DOR).

(ii) SSOs. Within the FD Directorate, the SSOs focus on systems and fielding to deliver capabilities and functions to the warfighting force structure of the Army. SSOs are the single ARSTAF POCs for integration and synchronization of all Army materiel programs to achieve the TAP priorities, and the AMP. Generally, the SSO is responsible for the integration, synchronization, and coordination of hardware,

MATERIAL SYSTEM RESEARCH, DEVELOPMENT, AND ACQUISITION MANAGEMENT

software, and associated equipment in support of the TAP. All equipment is fielded using the Total Package Fielding (TPF) methodology, discussed later in the chapter, managed by DCS, G-8 Director, FD DJI (DAPR-FDH). SSOs responsibilities include:

(aa) Coordinates with TRADOC Capability Managers (TCM) and HQDA G-37 (RSOs/OIs) during the requirements phase on affordability and TAA/Force Feasibility Reviews (FFR) resourcing.

(bb) Programs money to support materiel programs and insertion into the Army in the POM years in the Force Development Investment Information System (FDIIS). FDIIS is the primary planning, programming, and budgeting decision support tool for SSOs to insert data into the POM. In addition, FDIIS produces charts to explain and defend Army programs to POM CoCs and General Officer Steering Committees (GOSC).

(cc) Works with ASA(ALT) DASC and ASA(FM&C) budget liaison (SAFM-BUL), to influence current year and budget year of execution. SAFM-BUL defends programs and the details of the President's Budget (PRESBUD) to the Congressional appropriations committees.

(dd) Submits requests for overseas contingency operations funding.

(ee) Works with HQDA G-37, ACOMS, and PMs to determine fielding plans IAW Army priorities.

(ff) Analyzes production and equipment on hand against requirements/authorizations.

(gg) Develops solutions to problems incurred due to changes in funding requirement/authorization, schedule, or performance.

(hh) Prepares justifications for defending current programmed money and funding Unfunded Requirements (UFR) to POM boards and other forums for resourcing and prioritization.

(ii) Coordinates with HQDA G-4 and AMC on life-cycle sustainment and disposition of materiel.

j. The Surgeon General (TSG). TSG has ARSTAF responsibility for medical research, development, test and evaluation, and is the Army medical MATDEV. The TSG is responsible for the medical aspects of all other development and acquisition programs ensuring functional area interface with CAPDEVs. The TSG serves as a member of the ASARC and AR2B for medical issues, including health hazard assessment, personnel safety, and hazards remediation. Other responsibilities include:

(1) Developing policy, responsibilities, and procedures to ensure implementation of systems acquisition policy as it applies to combat medical systems, medical readiness and health care programs, and other assigned Army and joint requirements

(2) Assigning support responsibilities for medical materiel development and acquisition to agencies and activities under TSG for command and control

(3) Recommending to TRADOC ARCIC capabilities-based materiel and non-materiel requirements and associated priorities for medical readiness and health care programs

(4) Establishing functional area interface with TRADOC ARCIC for all medical programs, ensuring that requirements and interests of each participating Service are provided full consideration in medical programs for which the Army has lead agency or executive agency responsibility.

k. Chief of Engineers (COE). The COE monitors requirements, research, and development necessary to provide construction design criteria, construction techniques, and construction material for the Army, Air Force, and other government agencies. The COE provides fixed-facility concealment, camouflage, and deception; real estate management techniques; and engineering support for maintenance of installation and facilities. It is the COE's mission to preserve and improve environmental quality associated with construction and facilities; Army environmental quality; and R&D activities covering atmospheric, terrestrial, and topographical sciences. The COE is responsible, under the general direction of the AAE, for the RDT&E of fixed and floating power systems, and high voltage generation applications (to include nuclear applications). The COE reviews all emerging Army systems for digital terrain data requirements and environmental effects such as climate, terrain, or weather. The review includes minimization of toxic and hazardous wastes and those hazardous wastes associated with normal system test, operation, use, and maintenance. The COE serves as a member of the AR2B.

l. The General Counsel (GC). The GC advises the AAE and the ASARC on any legal issue which arises during the acquisition of a weapon or materiel system. The GC reviews all Army acquisition policy and supervises all attorneys providing legal advice relating to programs within the Army RDA management system. The GC is responsible for all legal advice in the negotiation, oversight, and review of international cooperative RDA programs.

11-36. Army Commands (ACOM)

HOW THE ARMY RUNS

a. U.S. Army Materiel Command (AMC). AMC performs assigned materiel and related functions for logistics support of materiel systems, and other system acquisition management functions required by HQDA. AMC is a regular member of the ASARC and AR2B. The AMC mission, in support of RDA, is to:
(1) Equip and sustain a trained, ready Army
(2) Provide development and acquisition support to MATDEVs (PEOs and PMs)
(3) Provide equipment and services to other nations through the Security Assistance Program
(4) Define, develop, and acquire superior technologies
(5) Maintain the mobilization capabilities necessary to support the Army in emergencies
(6) Verify system safety; support developmental and operational tests; and participate in the continuous evaluation process
(7) Exercise delegated authority, under ASA(ALT) oversight, in the following areas: metrication; design to cost; production readiness reviews; manufacturing technology standardization; reliability, availability, and maintainability; quality; risk management; value engineering; parts control; and industrial modernization improvement
(8) Provide survivability, vulnerability, or lethality assessments and survivability enhancement expertise for all Army materiel programs
(9) Evaluate and recommend improvements to the industrial base
(10) Maintain responsibility for the logistics support of assigned materiel in response to validated capabilities-based materiel requirements
(11) Plan, coordinate, and provide functional support to PEOs and PMs. Support includes, but is not limited to, procurement and contracting, legal, managerial accounting, cost estimating, systems engineering, conducting system TADSS and embedded training concept formulation, developmental test, logistics support analyses, MANPRINT, environmental, intelligence and threat support, configuration management, and conducting various independent assessments and analyses;
(12) Provide overall management of the Army's technology base (less Class VIII), including identification of maturing technologies necessary to support acquisition of warfighting materiel systems;
(13) Provide RDA science and infrastructure information to HQDA for the Army RDAP; and
(14) Provide initial and updated cost and system performance estimates for battlefield and peacetime operations as inputs to supporting analysis and program decisions

b. U.S. Army TRADOC. TRADOC is the Army's primary "user representative" in the capabilities development and system acquisition management processes. As the Army's principal CAPDEV, TRADOC guides, coordinates, and integrates the total capabilities development effort of the Army. Capabilities developments are a major component of force development and encompass the formulation of concepts, doctrine, organization, materiel objectives, capabilities-based requirements, and OT of products of the Army's capabilities integration and development system (JCIDS). TRADOC is a regular member of the ASARC and the AR2B.

(1) As the Army's primary CAPDEV/TNGDEV, TRADOC is the Army's "Architect for the Future" and is charged to chart the future course for the Army. In doing so, CG, TRADOC:
(a) Guides and disciplines the Army JCIDS by:
(i) Providing capabilities-based requirements generation and documentation procedures and process guidance
(ii) Generating all Army warfighting DOTMLPF-P requirements prior to their submission to HQDA for validation and resourcing
(iii) Approving ICDT minutes or reports containing proposed solution sets for force level FOCs
(iv) Coordinating MCDs produced by the Army community and forwarded to HQDA DCS, G-3/5/7 Current and Future Warfighting Capabilities Division (DAMO-CIC) for staffing, validation, and prioritization
(b) Assists HQDA to prioritize and justify warfighting requirements by:
(i) Determining applicability of current force ONSs to future Army-wide requirements and assign to a CoE/proponent for requirement documentation
(ii) Providing insights and descriptive information for materiel programs
(iii) Supporting HQDA ODCS,G-37 (DAMO-CIC), by presenting documents and information to the JCIDS (C-BA) process and assisting in issue resolution
(c) Coordinates and integrates the total capabilities/training developments efforts of the Army by:
(i) Providing, with appropriate support from other Army commands, the capstone and subordinate operating and functional warfighting concepts and FOCs (the start point for the Army JCIDS)
(ii) Developing and maintaining the C4I Operational Architecture (OA)

MATERIAL SYSTEM RESEARCH, DEVELOPMENT, AND ACQUISITION MANAGEMENT

(iii) Being the primary source for determining the need for and preparing capabilities-based requirements and MCDs for TADSS and embedded training

(iv) Determining need for and obtain CSA approval for conduct of advanced warfighting experiments (AWE)

(d) Conducts AoAs for ACAT I, IA, and most ACAT II programs when required by HQDA. When required by the MDA, conduct AoA for all other ACAT programs.

(e) Serves as member of the ASTAG.

(f) Provides representative to Army S&T reviews and management teams.

(2) TRADOC is organized into integrating centers and functional area CoEs and schools. The principal integrating centers are ARCIC, Fort Eustis, VA ; the Combined Arms Center (CAC), Fort Leavenworth, KS; and the Combined Arms Support Command (CASCOM), Fort Lee, VA. The functional area CoEs are Mission Command CoE, Signal CoE, Intelligence CoE, Fires CoE, Aviation CoE, Sustainment CoE, Maneuver Support CoE, and Initial Military Training CoE. The CoE Capabilities Development & Integration Directorates (CDID) work very closely with the PEO community in the RDA management process.

(3) Director, ARCIC:

(a) Determines and integrates force requirements and synchronizes the development of DOTMLPF-P solutions across the Army.

(b) Leads joint and Army CD&E efforts through TRADOC and non-TRADOC proponents.

(c) Leads the execution of the JCIDS process by TRADOC and/or non-TRADOC proponents to determine capability requirements for the force. Identifies joint and Army gaps and redundancies in capability; proposes DOTMLPF-P solutions to resolve or mitigate gaps; and recommends divestitures to help fund new requirements.

(d) Leads Asymmetric Warfare (AW) efforts within TRADOC. Integrates and synchronizes proponent activities within the AW areas of electronic warfare, protection, and improvised explosive device – defeat.

(e) Validates research and development priorities for Army S&T needs (to include special access programs (SAP)), for the required capabilities outlined in Army concepts ICW the ASA(ALT). Conducts a review of SAP and new S&T initiatives, as required, to ensure technology is aligned with future needs.

(f) Provides guidance for the execution of TRADOC force design goals and objectives and recommends approval to release organizational changes and adjustments for Army-wide staffing.

(g) Supports the CG, TRADOC in his role as the operational architect of the Army.

(h) Manages, coordinates, develops, and maintains the Battle Lab Collaborative Simulation Environment (BLCSE) federation of Modeling and Simulation (M&S), and distributed simulation network in support of joint and Army capabilities development and experimentation.

(i) Serves as the Advanced Concepts and Requirements (ACR) domain agent for review and validation of ACR domain M&S capabilities. Manages the M&S requirements for concept development and experimentation.

(j) Leads the Army Brigade Combat Team Modernization Program (ABCTMP) strategic communications ICDT; ABCTMP Board Of Directors (BOD); and ABCTMP GOSC efforts to integrate ABCTMP into the Army.

(4) ARCIC. In 2006, the SECARMY directed the formation of the ARCIC from the resources and organization of the TRADOC Futures Center. The Director, ARCIC, through the CG TRADOC, is directly responsible to the SECARMY and CSA to ensure that the ABCTMP technologies are transitioned into the current force as soon as they are ready, and the ABCTMP is integrated and coordinated with co-evolution of joint warfighting doctrine.

(a) The ARCIC has four primary responsibilities:

(i) Using wargaming, experimentation, and concepts, develops and integrates force capability requirements for the Army from a comprehensive perspective of DOTMLPF-P

(ii) Identifies and integrates Army current and future force DOTMLPF-P requirements and synchronize the development of DOTMLPF-P solutions across the Army

(iii) Provides the management structure for identifying capability gaps and directing analytical support for DOTMLPF-P developments, including validating R&D priorities for key Army S&T needs, and the development and validation of integrated operational architectures depicting warfighting capabilities

(iv) Serves as the lead Army agency for coordination with joint agencies and other Services for identification and integration of joint RCs, including joint wargaming, concept development, and experimentation

HOW THE ARMY RUNS

(b) In support of these responsibilities, ARCIC is organized in four major directorates and one direct reporting command:

(i) Concept Development and Learning Directorate (CDLD) prioritizes, manages, and synchronizes TRADOC's efforts in joint and Army concept development and experimentation.

(ii) RID analyzes concepts and identifies tasks, capability gaps, and DOTMLPF-P solutions to achieve the concept driven RCs. RID works on long-term and near term needs.

(iii) Analysis and Integration Directorate (A&ID) ensures all DOTMLPF-P capabilities are integrated for both the current and future forces. The A&ID helps the Army develop its resourcing strategies, leads the development, integration, and validation of operational architectures that provide the underpinnings for land warfare concepts and capabilities and support experimentation, analysis, and DOTMLPF-P solutions. Within the A&ID the Force Design Division (FDD) is the TRADOC lead in developing operational force design and force structure solutions. FDD leads the organizational design efforts for TRADOC.

(iv) The Brigade Modernization Command (BMC), stationed at FT Bliss Texas, is ARCIC's MTOE unit which is used to test equipment and concepts in a live training environment. The Army has assigned the 2/1 AD, a Heavy Brigade, to the BMC as the unit to conduct the exercises. Currently the BMC is involved in a semi-annual, multi-year test and evaluation of equipment, called Agile Network Integrated Evaluation (NIE), which support the Tactical Network, a vision which will connect all Soldiers, leaders, and equipment on the battlefield in an environment which provides greater situational awareness and lethality. The network testing (NIE phase of the Agile process) is being supported by all TRADOC CoEs, ATEC, HQDA LandWarNet (LWN), and ASA (ALT).

(v) International Army Programs Directorate coordinates TRADOC activities with multinational partners across TRADOC CoEs.

(c) The ARCIC-Forward element stationed in Arlington, Virginia acts as the liaison between the Director ARCIC and the ARSTAF, JS, OSD, and others in the Washington DC area.

(5) CAC. CAC provides leadership and supervision for leader development and professional military and civilian education; institutional and collective training; functional training; training support; mission command; doctrine; lessons learned; and specified areas the CG, TRADOC designates in order to serve as a catalyst for change and to support developing relevant and ready expeditionary land formations with campaign qualities in support of the joint force commander.

(6) CASCOM. CASCOM, the Logistics CoE, has the mission to develop logistics leaders, doctrine, organizations, training, and materiel solutions. There are three major functions performed by CASCOM:

(a) Develops and evaluates sustainment warfighting function concepts, doctrine, organizations, systems, materiel concepts and requirements, and planning factors for the Army and in concert with joint logistics doctrine. CASCOM ensures the personnel service support, supply, maintenance, transportation, Services, and facilities systems designed for the Army in the field and the CONUS-based theater logistics systems, are compatible with the sustaining base system.

(b) Acts as the TRADOC proponent for CSS training and monitors and evaluates CSS training at TRADOC schools. CASCOM ensures CSS course content is consistent with approved doctrine and assesses the training evaluation process at associated schools.

(c) Serves as a principal adviser to HQDA, TRADOC, and AMC on all CSS matters. CASCOM provides direction, guidance, and tasks to assigned capabilities development activities, associated CoEs, other Army Commands, and HQDA staff agencies for their contribution to CSS development and training.

(7) CoE Capabilities Development and Integration Directorate (CDID). CDID represents the CoE in the execution of its responsibilities for concept development, experimentation, and requirements determination. CDID's purpose is to facilitate the development, assessment, management, validation, and synchronization of DOTMLPF-P-integrated combined arms capabilities that complement joint, interagency, and multinational capabilities. The CDID serves as the primary activity to develop proponent, Army and joint concepts; reviews Army and joint doctrine, support experimentation efforts, reviews requirements documentation, and reviews training material; assists in the development of training materials; and develops proponent equipment Operational Mode Summary/Mission Profiles (OMS/MP). The OMS/MP describes the anticipated missions; units (active, reserve, and institutional training base); or mix of units that will use the system overtime to include peacetime, crisis situations, national conflict, and war; in what environments and under what conditions (climate, terrain, battlefield environment, etc.), as well as how it will be supported and maintained.

MATERIAL SYSTEM RESEARCH, DEVELOPMENT, AND ACQUISITION MANAGEMENT

(8) TCM. The TRADOC counterpart to the PM, the TCM, is a central figure in the RDA process and a key member of the MATDEV/ CAPDEV team. The TCM is TRADOC's focal point for coordination of the CAPDEV/TNGDEV efforts in the development and acquisition of a materiel and/or AIS capability. The TCM is responsible for synchronizing all DOTmLPF domains that are impacted by the fielding of major materiel capability. A TCM is associated with a capability solution early in the development cycle, normally at the same time as the PM. The TCM is located in the CDID at the CoE proponent center or school.

11-37. Other HQDA Agencies
a. U.S. ATEC. The CG, ATEC is responsible for management of the Army's OT, DT, and System Evaluation (SE) processes. Their evaluations of materiel and IT systems' operational effectiveness, suitability and survivability are independent of the CAPDEV/MATDEV and are reported directly to the MDA. CG, ATEC is a member of the ASARC, AROC, and chairman of the Test Schedule and Review Committee (TSARC). The TSARC is the HQDA centralized management forum for user (operational) testing resources. ATEC provides advice and assistance to the CSA, the VCSA, other members of the ARSTAF, and other elements of HQDA in regard to Army T&E. Other responsibilities include:
(1) Reviewing all draft MCDs for T&E implications.
(2) Assisting TRADOC ARCIC in developing evaluatable, operationally relevant, and totally system focused Critical Operational Issues and Criteria (COIC). Provide advice concerning methods and measures to evaluate the system against the COIC and advise on the resources and ability to test and evaluate the system.
(3) Preparing and approving all ATEC Capabilities & Limitations (C&L) Reports in support of OCO rapid fielding.
(4) Supporting the TRADOC AWE program, Network Integration Evaluation (NIE) and Concept Experimentation Program (CEP).
b. U.S. Army Intelligence and Security Command (INSCOM). INSCOM is the CAPDEV for strategic signals intelligence (SIGINT) systems and INSCOM sole-user intelligence, EW systems used for formulating doctrine, concepts, organization, materiel requirements, and objectives. INSCOM responsibilities include:
(1) Preparing MCDs and serving as the Army CAPDEV during development and fielding of new SIGINT and Information Security (INFOSEC) systems under the purview of the National Security Agency (NSA) and having sole application to U.S. SIGINT and INFOSEC systems. INSCOM forwards warfighting concepts and MCDs to TRADOC ARCIC for review and appropriate action.
(2) Coordinating with the PEO/PM on matters pertaining to acquisition of INSCOM sole-user SIGINT and Intelligence, Security, and Electronic Warfare (ISEW) systems.
(3) Coordinating with the TRADOC ARCIC, on capabilities-based requirements generation for other INSCOM sole user ISEW systems and conduct capabilities and training developments for these Army systems when directed by HQDA, and/or Director, Central Intelligence (DCI), or at the request of TRADOC's ARCIC.
(4) Ensuring documentation of requirements for training support products, system TADSS, and/or embedded training for INSCOM systems.
(5) Providing threat documentation to HQ, TRADOC as validated by HQDA DCS, G-2.
(6) Recommending to TRADOC ARCIC capabilities-based materiel requirements and associated priorities for strategic intelligence and security readiness.
c. U.S. Army Special Operations Command (USASOC). In support of systems acquisition management, USASOC establishes functional area interface with TRADOC ARCIC for all programs, ensuring that requirements and interests of each participating agency are provided full consideration in programs for which the Army has lead agency or executive responsibility, and serves as the special operations trainer and user representative. The USASOC is a regular member of the Army AR2B. In addition, USASOC:
(1) Forwards all SOC unique and non-SOC unique warfighting capability requirements and documents to TRADOC ARCIC for appropriate action
(2) Monitors TRADOC projects and identifies needs that affect the USASOC mission and responsibility
(3) Supports TRADOC field activities, conducts and supports testing, and monitors RDA projects to include potential force standardization and interoperability
(4) Participates in warfighting experiments, as appropriate

HOW THE ARMY RUNS

d. U.S. Army Space and Missile Defense Command (USASMDC). USASMDC is the principal assistant and advisor to the SECARMY and the CSA for all matters pertaining to space and strategic defense. The USASMDC is responsible for technology development programs related to strategic and tactical missile defense, space defense, and satellite technology. The command conducts missile defense technology base research and development activities in support of the Missile Defense Agency (MDA); assures transfer of technology between MDA and Army systems; and provides matrix support to PEO Air and Missile Defense. USASMDC is also chartered by CSA to be the operational advocate and focal point for Theater Missile Defense (TMD) at Army level. The CG, USASMDC, assists in the development of Army TMD positions, reflective of work being done in TRADOC, and represents those positions at HQDA, OSD, MDA, JS, Congressional, and other high-level forums.

e. U.S. Army Medical Command (MEDCOM). MEDCOM is the medical CAPDEV, TNGDEV, trainer, and user representative. MEDCOM conducts medical capabilities and training development activities as assigned by CG, TRADOC and TSG; reviews and evaluates materiel and TADSS requirements documents to identify and assure that adequate consideration is given to the prevention of health hazards from operating or maintaining materiel systems, and conduct the Health Hazard Assessment (HHA) program, as required; conducts and supports assigned OTs; and forwards all medical warfighting concepts and requirements documents to TRADOC for review and appropriate action.

f. U.S. Army Surface Deployment and Distribution Command (SDDC). SDDC provides transportability engineering advice and analyses to the MATDEV, CAPDEV and TNGDEV; provides item, unit, and system transportability assessments for MDR; provides transportability approval and identifies corrective actions required to obtain approval for all transportability problem items; and reviews all MCDs to assess adequacy of transportability.

g. U.S. Army Medical Research and Materiel Command (USAMRMC). USAMRMC is the medical MATDEV, logistician, and developmental tester and is responsible for RDA and logistics support of assigned materiel in response to validated materiel capabilities-based requirements. In addition, USAMRMC:

(1) Plans, programs, budgets, and executes medical RDT&E tasks that support system RDA, to include required system training support products, TADSS, and/or embedded training

(2) Plans, coordinates, and provides functional support to USAMRMC organizations. Support includes, but is not limited to, procurement and contracting, legal, managerial accounting, cost estimating, systems engineering, conducting system TADSS and embedded training concept formulation, developmental testing, ILS, MANPRINT, environmental management, configuration management, and conducting various independent assessments and analyses

(3) Assists the medical CAPDEV/TNGDEV in the Army JCIDS process

(4) Reviews MCDs to determine their adequacy and feasibility and for logistical support aspects of materiel systems to include ILS

(5) Develops and maintains the physiological, psychological, and medical database to support the HHA, System Safety Assessments (SSA), and Human Factors Engineering Analysis (HFEA)

(6) Evaluates and manages the materiel readiness functions in the medical materiel acquisition process

(7) Functions as TSG agency for the materiel acquisition of medical NDI, Commercial Off-The-Shelf (COTS) items, and sets, kits, and outfits

h. U.S. Army Medical Department Center and School (AMEDDC&S). AMEDDC&S is the medical CAPDEV, TNGDEV, doctrine developer, and operational tester. In addition, AMEDDC&S develops doctrine, organizations, and systems requirements within the guidelines established by the TRADOC ARCIC and in accordance with Army health care standards established by TSG.

Section IX
Traditional Acquisition Phases and Milestones

11-38. Pre-Systems Acquisition Activity
Pre-system acquisition is composed of ongoing activities in development of user needs, in S&T, and in MSA and TD work specific to the development of a materiel solution to an identified, validated capabilities-based materiel requirement.

MATERIAL SYSTEM RESEARCH, DEVELOPMENT, AND ACQUISITION MANAGEMENT

a. The capability needs and acquisition management systems use joint/Service concepts, integrated architectures, and an analysis of DOTMLPF-P in an integrated, collaborative process to define needed capabilities to guide the development of affordable systems. The CJCS, with the assistance of the JROC, assesses and provides advice regarding military capability needs for defense acquisition programs. This JCIDS process, previously discussed, is described in CJCSI 3170.01H.

b. Representatives from the Services and multiple DOD communities assist the CJCS in formulating broad, time-phased, operational goals, and describing requisite capabilities in the ICD. When the ICD demonstrates the need for a materiel solution, the JROC or AROC recommends that the MDA convene a formal DAS MDD Review.

11-39. MDD Review

a. At the MDD review, the validated ICD is presented to the MDA. The ICD documents the need for non-materiel and/or materiel solution approaches to resolve a specific high risk capability gap derived from the JCIDS C-BA process. The ICD includes: the preliminary CONOPS; a description of the needed capability; the operational risk; and the basis for determining that non-materiel approaches will not sufficiently mitigate the capability gap. The OSD Director, Assessment & Program Evaluation (D, CAPE), (or Service equivalent), proposes study guidance for the MS AoA. The purpose of the AoA is to assess the potential system-level materiel solutions to satisfy the selected materiel concept (approach) documented in the validated ICD.

b. The MDA designates the lead agency to refine the initial materiel concept selected, approves the AoA study guidance, and establishes a date for a MS A review. The MDA decisions are documented in an acquisition decision memorandum (ADM). This effort normally is funded only for the MSA work. The MDA decision to begin the MSA phase does not mean that a new acquisition program has been initiated.

c. Following approval of the study guidance, the organization conducting the AoA immediately prepares an AoA study plan to assess preliminary materiel solutions, identify key technologies, and estimate life-cycle costs. Following the MDD, the MDA may authorize entry into the DAS at any point consistent with phase-specific entrance criteria and statutory requirements. Progress through the DAS depends on obtaining sufficient knowledge to continue to the next phase of development. The MDD review is the formal entry point into the DAS and is mandatory for all potential acquisition programs. The MSA phase begins with the MDD review.

11-40. MSA Phase

a. The purpose of this phase is to assess potential materiel solutions, to satisfy the phase-specific entrance criteria for the next program MS designated by the MDA, and develop a Technology Development Strategy (TDS). Entrance into this phase depends upon an validated ICD resulting from the analysis of potential materiel concepts (approaches) across the Services, international systems from Allies, and cooperative opportunities and MDA guidance for conducting an AoA for the selected materiel concept, documented in the validated ICD.

b. The ICD and the AoA study guidance guide the AoA and MSA phase activities. The AoA assesses the Critical Technology Elements (CTE) associated with each proposed system-level materiel solution, including technology maturity, integration, risk, manufacturing feasibility, and, where necessary, technology maturation and demonstration needs. A CTE is a technology element which is critical, if the system being acquired depends on this technology element to meet capability thresholds.

c. The results of the AoA provide the basis for the TDS, to be approved by the MDA at MS A. The TDS documents the following:

(1) The rationale for adopting either an evolutionary strategy (the preferred approach) or using a single-step-to-full-capability strategy (e.g., for common supply items or COTS items). For an evolutionary acquisition, the TDS includes a preliminary description of how the program will be divided into technology development increments, an appropriate limitation on the number of prototype units that may be produced and deployed during technology development, how these units will be supported, and specific performance goals and exit criteria that must be met before exceeding the number of prototypes that may be produced under the R&D program.

(2) A program strategy, including overall cost, schedule, and performance goals for the total R&D program.

(3) Specific cost, schedule, and performance goals, including exit criteria, for the first TD.

(4) A test plan to ensure that the goals and exit criteria for the first TD have been met.

HOW THE ARMY RUNS

d. MSA ends when the AoA has been completed, materiel solution options for the capability need identified in the validated ICD have been recommended, and the phase-specific entrance criteria for the initial review milestone have been satisfied.

11-41. MS A

At MS A, the MDA designates a lead agency, approves Technology Development (TD) phase exit criteria, develops and issues the ADM. The leader of the CAPDEV–led ICDT, working with the ATEC System Team (AST), develops an integrated evaluation strategy that describes how the capabilities in the MCD will be evaluated once the system is developed. For potential ACAT I programs, the integrated evaluation strategy is approved by the DOD Director, Operational Test and Evaluation (D,OT&E) and the cognizant OIPT. The MDA complies with the Congressionally directed certification requirements at MS A. This effort normally is funded only for the advanced technology development work. TD for a MDAP cannot proceed without MS A approval. A favorable MS A decision, **does not** mean that a new acquisition program has been initiated.

11-42. TD Phase

The purpose of this phase is to reduce technology risk, determine a mature appropriate set of mature technologies to be integrated into a full system, and to demonstrate CTEs on prototypes. TD is a continuous technology discovery and development process reflecting close collaboration between the S&T community, the CAPDEV, and the system MATDEV. It is an iterative process designed to assess the viability of technologies, while simultaneously refining user requirements.

a. Entrance into this phase depends on the completion of the AoA, a proposed materiel solution, and full funding for planned TD phase activity. Full funding is for the dollars and manpower needed for all current and future efforts to carry out the AS.

b. The TDS and associated funding approved at MS A provides for competitive prototyping (two or more competing teams (contractors), producing prototypes of the system and/or key system elements prior to, or through MS B). Prototypes are employed to reduce technical risk, validate designs and cost estimates, evaluate manufacturing processes, and refine requirements.

c. The ICD and the TDS guide, and Systems Engineering (SE) planning support this effort. Multiple technology development demonstrations may be necessary before the CAPDEV and MATDEV agree that a proposed technology solution is affordable, militarily useful, and based on mature, demonstrated technology. Initial life-cycle sustainment of proposed technologies is planned during this phase. Technology obtained within the S&T community or procured from industry or other sources is demonstrated in a relevant environment, preferably in an operational environment considered to be very mature.

d. A Preliminary Design Review (PDR) is conducted for each candidate design or capability to ensure that the system can proceed into a detailed design and meets performance requirements. All system elements (hardware and software) must be at a level of maturity commensurate with the PDR entrance and exit criteria. A successful PDR informs requirements trades; improves cost estimation; and identifies remaining design, integration, and manufacturing risks. The PDR is conducted at the system level and includes CAPDEV representatives and associated certification authorities. The PM provides a PDR report to the MDA at MS B and includes recommended requirements trades based upon an assessment of cost, schedule, and performance risk.

e. The proposed system-level solution exits the TD phase when an affordable program or increment of militarily useful capability has been identified, the technology for that program or increment have been assessed and demonstrated in a relevant environment, manufacturing risks have been identified and assessed, and a system or increment can be developed for production within a relatively short timeframe (normally less than five years for weapon systems), or when the MDA decides to terminate the effort. During TD, the CAPDEV prepares the CDD to support initiation of the acquisition program, refines the integrated architecture, and clarifies how the program will lead to warfighting capability. The CDD builds on the ICD and provides the detailed operational performance and support parameters necessary to complete the design of the proposed system. A MS B decision follows the completion of TD.

11-43. Systems Acquisition Activity

Systems acquisition is the process of developing system-level materiel solutions into producible and deployable products that provide capability to the user. The proposed system-level materiel solution to

MATERIAL SYSTEM RESEARCH, DEVELOPMENT, AND ACQUISITION MANAGEMENT

exploit in systems acquisition is based on the AoA conducted in the MS A phase to meet the military need, including commercial and non-developmental technologies and products and services determined through market research (a process for gathering data on product characteristics, suppliers' capabilities, and the business practices that surround them, plus the analysis of that data to make acquisition decisions). The responsible CAPDEV for the functional area in which a capability gap or opportunity has been identified, but not the MATDEV, normally prepares the AoA. The goal is to develop the best overall value solution over the system's life-cycle that meets the user's operational requirements. If existing systems cannot be economically used or modified to meet the operational capabilities-based requirement, an acquisition program may be justified.

11-44. MS B
MS B is the initiation of an acquisition program. The purpose of MS B is to authorize entry into the EMD phase.

  a. MS B approval can lead to integrated system design or system capability and manufacturing process demonstration. Regardless of the approach recommended, PMs and other acquisition managers continually assess program risks. Risks must be well understood before MDAs can authorize a program to proceed into the next phase of the acquisition process. The types of risk include, but are not limited to, schedule, cost, technical feasibility, risk of technical obsolescence, software management, dependencies between a new program and other programs, and the risk of creating a monopoly for future procurements.

  b. There is only one MS B per program or evolutionary increment. Each increment of an evolutionary acquisition has its own MS B, unless the MDA determines that the increment will be initiated at MS C. At MS B, the MDA approves the AS and the APB. The MDA decision is documented in an ADM.

  c. At MS B, the MDA determines the LRIP quantity for MDAPs and major systems. Without approval of the MDA, the LRIP quantity for an MDAP cannot exceed 10 percent of the total production quantity. For programs with OSD T&E oversight, the OSD D,OT&E, following consultation with the PM, determines the number of production or production-representative test articles required for Live-Fire Testing (LFT) and Initial Operational Testing and Evaluation (IOT&E). For a system that is not on the OSD Oversight List, the ATEC, following consultation with the PM, determines the number of test articles required for IOT&E.

  d. In general, MS B is planned when a system-level materiel solution and design have been selected, a PM has been assigned, requirements have been validated, and system-level integration is ready to begin. In no case will MS B be approved without full funding (e.g., inclusion of the dollars and manpower needed for all current and future efforts to carry out the AS in the budget and out-year program), which are programmed in anticipation of the MS B decision.

11-45. EMD Phase
The purpose of the EMD phase is to develop a system or an increment of capability; complete full system integration (technology risk reduction occurs during TD); develop an affordable and executable manufacturing process; ensure operational supportability with particular attention to minimizing the logistics footprint; implement MANPRINT; design for producibility; ensure affordability; and demonstrate system integration, interoperability, safety, and utility. The CDD, AS, systems engineering plan (SEP), and test and evaluation master plan (TEMP) guide this phase.

11-46. Entrance Criteria
  a. Entrance into the EMD phase depends on demonstrated technology maturity (generally TRL 6, including software), validated capabilities-based requirements, and full funding. Unless some other factor is overriding in its impact, the maturity of the technology determines the path to be followed. Programs that enter the acquisition process at MS B must have a validated ICD that provides the context in which the capability was determined and validated.

  b. The management and mitigation of technology risk, which allows less costly and less time-consuming systems development, is a crucial part of overall program management and is especially relevant to meeting cost and schedule goals. Objective assessment of technology maturity and risk is a continuous aspect of system acquisition. Technology developed within the S&T community or procured from industry or other sources must be demonstrated in a relevant environment or, preferably, in an operational environment to be considered mature enough to use for product development in systems integration. TRAs, previously discussed, and where necessary, independent assessments, are also

HOW THE ARMY RUNS

conducted. If technology is not mature, the MATDEV uses alternative technology that is mature and that can meet the user's needs.

c. Prior to beginning EMD, CAPDEVs identify and the requirements authority validates a minimum set of KPPs included in the CDD, that guide the efforts of this phase. These KPPs may be refined, with the approval of the requirements authority, as conditions warrant. Each set of KPPs only apply to the current increment of capability in EMD (or to the entire system in a single step to full capability). To maximize program trade space, the MATDEV, CAPDEV, and T&E communities work closely with the requirements authority to minimize KPPs and limit total identified program requirements. Performance requirements that do not support the achievement of KPP thresholds, are limited and considered a part of the engineering trade space during development. During OT, a clear distinction is made between performance values that do not meet threshold requirements in the user capabilities document and performance values that should be improved to provide enhanced operational capability in future upgrades. At MS B, the PM prepares and the MDA approves an AS that guides activity during EMD. In an evolutionary acquisition program, each increment begins with MS B, and production resulting from that increment begins with MS C.

d. Each program must have an APB establishing program goals—thresholds and objectives—for the minimum number of cost, schedule, and performance parameters that describe the program over its life-cycle.

e. The affordability determination is made in the process of addressing cost in the JCIDS process and included in each CDD, using life-cycle cost or, if available, total ownership cost. Transition into EMD requires full funding – e.g., inclusion of the dollars and manpower needed for all current and future efforts to carry out the AS in the budget and out-year program. Full funding (at least five years) should be done no later than MS B, unless a program first enters the acquisition process at MS C.

f. EMD effectively integrates the acquisition, engineering, and manufacturing development processes with T&E. T&E is conducted in a continuum of Live, Virtual, and Constructive (LVC) system and operational environments. Developmental and operational test activities are integrated and seamless throughout the phase. Evaluations take into account all available relevant data and information from contractor and government sources. The independent planning of dedicated IOT&E and Follow-on Operational Test and Evaluation (FOT&E), if required, is the responsibility of ATEC. The PM prepares and the MDA approves an AS to guide activity during EMD. The AS describes how the PM plans to employ contract incentives to achieve required cost, schedule, and performance outcomes.

g. The MDA selects the contract type for a development program at MS B. The contract type must be consistent with the level of program risk and normally is a fixed price contract.

h. EMD has two major work efforts – integrated system design and a system capability and manufacturing process demonstration. Additionally, the MDA (DDRE for ACAT I programs) conducts a Post-CDR Assessment to end integrated system design.

11-47. Integrated System Design Work Effort

This work effort is intended to integrate subsystems and reduce system-level risk. The program enters integrated system design when the PM has a technical solution for the system, but has not yet integrated the subsystems into a complete system. The CDD guides this effort. This effort typically includes the demonstration of prototype articles or Engineering Development Models (EDM).

11-48. Post-CDR Assessment

a. The MDA conducts a formal program assessment following system-level CDR. The system-level CDR provides an opportunity to assess design maturity as evidenced by measures such as: successful completion of subsystem CDRs; the percentage of hardware and software product build-to specifications and drawings completed and under configuration management; planned corrective actions to hardware/software deficiencies; adequate DT; the identification of key system characteristics; the maturity of critical manufacturing processes; and an estimate of system reliability based on demonstrated reliability rates; etc.

b. The PM provides a post-CDR report to the MDA that provides an overall assessment of design maturity and a summary of the system-level CDR results. The MDA reviews the post-CDR report and the PM's resolution/mitigation plans and determines whether additional action is necessary to satisfy EMD phase exit criteria. The results of the MDA's post-CDR assessment are documented in the ADM.

MATERIAL SYSTEM RESEARCH, DEVELOPMENT, AND ACQUISITION MANAGEMENT

Successful completion of the post-CDR assessment ends the integrated system design work effort and continues the EMD phase into system capability and manufacturing process demonstration work effort.

11-49. System Capability and Manufacturing Process Demonstration Work Effort
 a. This work effort is intended to demonstrate the ability of the system to operate in a useful way consistent with the approved KPPs, and that system production can be supported by demonstrated manufacturing processes. The program enters system capability and manufacturing process demonstration upon completion of the post-CDR assessment and establishment of an initial product baseline. This work effort ends when the system meets validated requirements and is demonstrated in its intended operational environment, using the selected production-representative article; manufacturing processes have been effectively demonstrated; industrial capabilities are reasonably available; and the system meets or exceeds exit criteria and MS C entrance requirements.
 b. Successful DT to assess technical progress against critical technical parameters, early operational assessments, and, where proven capabilities exist, the use of M&S to demonstrate system/SoS integration are critical during this effort. T&E assesses improvements to mission capability and operational support based on user needs and is reported in terms of operational significance to the user. The completion of the EMD phase is dependent on a decision by the MDA to commit to the program at MS C or a decision to end this effort.

11-50. P&D Phase
The purpose of the P&D phase is to achieve an operational capability that satisfies functional needs. OT determines the operational effectiveness, suitability, and survivability of the system. The MDA makes the decision to commit to production at MS C, and documents the decision in the ADM.
 a. MS C authorizes entry into LRIP for MDAPs and major systems; into production or procurement (for non-major systems that do not require LRIP); or into limited deployment in support of OT for Major Automated Information Systems (MAIS) programs or software-intensive systems with no production components.
 b. This phase has two major work efforts – LRIP and full-rate production and deployment, and includes a full-rate production decision review. MS C can be reached directly from pre-systems acquisition (e.g., a commercial product) or from the EMD phase.

11-51. Entrance Criteria
Regardless of the entry point, approval at MS C is dependent on the following criteria being met (or a decision by the MDA to proceed):
 a. Acceptable performance in DT
 b. An operational assessment
 c. Mature software capability
 d. No significant manufacturing risks
 e. Manufacturing processes under control (if MS C is full-rate production)
 f. A validated ICD, if MS C is program initiation
 g. Validated CPD. The CPD reflects the operational requirements resulting from EMD and details the performance expected of the production system
 h. Acceptable interoperability
 i. Acceptable operational supportability
 j. Demonstration that the system is affordable throughout the life-cycle, optimally funded, and properly phased for rapid acquisition

11-52. MS C
 a. Prior to making the MS decision, the MDA considers the CCE; and for MAISs, the CCE and economic analysis; the manpower estimate; the program protection for critical program information including anti-tamper recommendations; and an established completion schedule for the NEPA compliance covering testing, training, basing, and operational support.
 b. At MS C, the MDA approves an updated AS prior to the release of the final Request for Proposal (RFP) (if not already released) and approves an updated development APB, exit criteria for LRIP (if needed) or limited deployment, and the ADM.

HOW THE ARMY RUNS

c. The DOD D,OT&E and cognizant OIPT leader approve the TEMP for all OSD T&E oversight programs. IT acquisition programs (regardless of ACAT) that entered system acquisition at MS C are registered with the DOD CIO before MS C approval.

d. A favorable MS C decision authorizes the PM to commence LRIP or limited deployment for MDAPs and major systems. The PM is only authorized to commence full-rate production with further approval of the MDA.

11-53. LRIP Work Effort

a. This work effort is intended to result in completion of manufacturing development in order to ensure adequate and efficient manufacturing capability and to produce at least the minimum quantity necessary to provide production configured or representative articles for IOT&E; establish an initial production base for the system; and permit an orderly increase in the production rate for the system, sufficient to lead to full-rate production upon successful completion of operational (and live-fire, where applicable) testing.

b. Deficiencies encountered in testing prior to MS C are resolved prior to proceeding beyond LRIP (at the FRP decision review) and any fixes verified in IOT&E. Test Resource Plans (TRP) are provided to the D,OT&E for oversight programs in advance of the start of OT.

c. LRIP may be funded by RDT&E appropriation or by procurement appropriation, depending on the intended usage of the LRIP systems.

d. LRIP quantities are minimized. The D,OT&E determines the LRIP quantity for MDAPs and major systems at MS B, and provides rationale for quantities exceeding 10 percent of the total production quantity documented in the AS. Any increase in quantity after the initial determination, must be approved by the D,OT&E. When approved LRIP quantities are expected to be exceeded because the program has not yet demonstrated readiness to proceed to full-rate production, the MDA, in coordination with the D,OT&E, assesses the cost and benefits of a break in production versus continuing annual buys.

11-54. FRP Decision Review

a. An acquisition program may not proceed beyond LRIP without approval of the MDA at the FRP decision review. Before making the full-rate production and deployment decision, the MDA considers:
   (1) The CCE, and for MAISs, the CCE and economic analysis
   (2) The manpower estimate (if applicable)
   (3) The results of operational and live fire test (if applicable)
   (4) CCE compliance certification and certification for MAISs
   (5) C4I supportability certification
   (6) Interoperability certification

b. The MDA approves the AS prior to the release of the final RFP, the production APB, and the ADM. The decision to continue beyond low-rate to full-rate production, or beyond limited deployment of AISs or software-intensive systems with no developmental hardware requires completion of IOT&E, submission of the Beyond LRIP Report for D,OT&E oversight programs, and submission of the Live-Fire Test and Evaluation (LFT&E) Report (where applicable) to the USD(AT&L), to the SECDEF, and to Congress.

11-55. FRP and Deployment Work Effort

This work effort delivers the fully funded quantity of systems and supporting materiel and services to the users. During this work effort, units attain initial operational capability (IOC). The IOC is the first attainment of the capability by a MTOE unit and supporting elements to operate and maintain effectively a production item or system provided the following:

a. The item or system has been type classified as standard or approved for limited production.

b. The unit and support personnel have been trained to operate and maintain the item or system in an operational environment.

c. The unit can be supported in an operational environment in such areas as special tools, test equipment, repair parts, documentation, and training devices.

11-56. Sustainment Activity / O&S Phase

The objective of this activity/phase is the execution of a support program that meets materiel readiness and operational support performance requirements and sustains the system in the most cost-effective manner over its total life-cycle. When the system has reached the end of its useful life, it must be disposed of in an appropriate manner. Planning for this phase begins prior to program initiation and is

MATERIAL SYSTEM RESEARCH, DEVELOPMENT, AND ACQUISITION MANAGEMENT

documented in the Life-Cycle Sustainment Plan (LCSP). The O&S phase has two major work efforts – life-cycle sustainment and disposal.

11-57. Life-Cycle Sustainment Work Effort
  a. The life-cycle sustainment program includes all elements necessary to maintain the readiness and operational capability of deployed systems. The scope of support varies among programs, but generally includes supply, maintenance, transportation, sustaining engineering, data management, configuration management, manpower, personnel, training, habitability, survivability, safety (including explosives safety), occupational health, protection of Critical Program Information (CPI), anti-tamper provisions, IT (including National Security System (NSS)) supportability and interoperability, and environmental management functions. This activity includes the execution of operational support plans in peacetime, crises, and wartime. Programs with software components must be capable of responding to emerging requirements that will require software modification or periodic enhancements after a system is deployed. An FOT&E program that evaluates operational effectiveness, survivability, suitability, supportability, interoperability, and that identifies and ensures deficiencies are later corrected, is conducted, as appropriate.
  b. Evolutionary sustainment. Supporting the tenets of evolutionary acquisition, sustainment strategies must evolve and be refined throughout the life-cycle, particularly during development of subsequent blocks of an evolutionary strategy, modifications, upgrades, and re-procurement. The PM ensures that a flexible, performance-oriented strategy to sustain systems is developed and executed. This strategy includes consideration of the full scope of operational support, such as maintenance, supply, transportation, sustaining engineering, spectrum supportability, configuration and data management, manpower, training, environmental, health, safety, disposal, and security factors. The use of performance requirements or conversion to performance requirements are emphasized during re-procurement of systems, subsystems, components, spares, and services after the initial production contract.
  c. The PM works with the CAPDEV to document performance and sustainment requirements in performance agreements specifying objective outcomes, measures, resource commitments, and stakeholder responsibilities. The PM employs effective performance-based life-cycle product support planning, development, implementation, and management. Performance-Based Logistics (PBL) product support represents the latest evolution of performance based logistics. Both can be referred to as PBL. PBL offers the best strategic approach for delivering required life-cycle readiness, reliability, and ownership costs. Sources of support may be organic, commercial, or a combination, with the primary focus optimizing customer support, weapon system availability, and reduced ownership costs.

11-58. Disposal Work Effort
At the end of its useful life, a system must be demilitarized and disposed of in accordance with all legal and regulatory requirements and policy relating to safety (including explosives safety), security, and the environment. During the design process, PMs document hazardous materials contained in the system, and estimate and plan for demilitarization and safe disposal. The demilitarization of conventional munitions (including any item containing propellants, explosives, or pyrotechnics) shall be considered during systems design.

11-59. Additional Considerations
The above discussion examined the activities performed in each phase of the nominal life-cycle of an acquisition system according to the current DODD 5000.01, DODI 5000.02, and AR 70-1. This is not to imply that all system developments must follow this exact sequencing of life-cycle phases and activities. On the contrary, DODI 5000.02 specifically authorizes and encourages a PEO/PM to devise program structures and acquisition strategies to fit that specific program – an approach called "tailoring." Other aspects of acquisition planning and strategy (e.g., P3I and technology insertion) can also be accommodated under the broad guidance and direction contained in DODD 5000.01 and DODI 5000.02. What remains constant is the task to develop and deliver combat-capable, cost-effective, and supportable systems to our Soldiers.

Section X
Traditional Acquisition Oversight and Review

HOW THE ARMY RUNS

11-60. DAB

The Defense Acquisition Management System (DAS) is controlled by decisions made as the result of various acquisition programs MDRs conducted by appropriate management levels at program MSs. The reviews are the mechanism for checking program progress against approved plans and for developing revised APBs. Approval of APBs and plans in these reviews do not constitute program funding approval; and allocation of funds in the PPBE process is required.

a. The function of the DAB is to review DOD ACAT ID programs to ensure that they are ready for transition from one DAS program phase to the next. The DAB is the DOD senior-level acquisition forum for advising the USD(AT&L), as the DAE, on critical decisions concerning ACAT ID programs. DAB reviews focus on key principles to include interoperability, time-phased requirements related to an evolutionary strategy, and demonstrated technical maturity. The DAB is composed of DOD senior acquisition officials. The board is chaired by the USD(AT&L). Other principal members include: the VCJCS; Under Secretary of Defense (Comptroller); Under Secretary of Defense (Policy); Under Secretary of Defense (Personnel & Readiness); DOD Chief Information Officer; Director, Cost Assessment and Program Evaluation; Director, Operational Test and Evaluation; and the Secretaries of the Army, Navy, and the Air Force. The Director, Acquisition Resources and Analysis serves as the DAB Secretary.

b. Approximately one week prior to the DAB review, the OIPT meets to pre-brief the OIPT leader. The purpose of the meeting is to update the OIPT leader on the latest status of the program and to inform the senior acquisition officials of any outstanding issues and to insure the program is ready for a formal DAB review.

c. The JROC reviews all deficiencies that may necessitate development of ACAT I and ACAT IA systems prior to any consideration by the DAB or, as appropriate, the ITAB at MS B. The JROC validates an identified materiel need and forwards the MCD with JROC recommendations to the USD(AT&L). In addition, the JROC continues a role in validation of KPPs in program baselines prior to scheduled reviews for ACAT I and ACAT IA programs prior to all successive MDRs.

d. The OSD Director, Cost Assessment and Program Evaluation (D,CAPE), reviews the component (Army) ACP, prior to the scheduled MDR and determines if additional analysis is required. The product is an independent cost position assessment and recommendations based on its independent review of the life-cycle cost estimate(s), validation of the methodology used to make the cost estimate(s), and determination if additional analysis or studies are required.

e. A formal DAB review is the last step of the DAB review process. The PM briefs the acquisition program to the DAB and specifically emphasizes technology maturity, risk management, affordability, critical program information, technology protection, and rapid delivery to the user. The PM addresses any interoperability and supportability requirements linked to other systems and indicates whether those requirements will be satisfied by the AS under review. If the program is part of a system-of-systems architecture, the PM briefs the DAB in that context.

f. Following presentations by the PM and a full discussion, the USD(AT&L), as DAE, decides to continue, alter, or terminate the program. This decision is published in an ADM. With the approval of the DAE, other committee reviews may be held for special purposes, such as to develop recommendations for the DAE on decisions other than MS or program reviews (e.g., release of "withhold funds," baseline changes, AS changes).

11-61. DOD ITAB

a. The DOD ITAB provides the forum for ACAT IAM MSs, for deciding critical ACAT IAM issues when they cannot be resolved at the OIPT level, and for enabling the execution of the DOD ITAB's acquisition-related responsibilities for IT, including National Security Systems (NSS), under the Clinger-Cohen Act and Title 10. Wherever possible, these reviews take place in the context of the existing IPT and acquisition MDR process. Where appropriate, an ADM documents the decision(s) resulting from the review.

b. The ITAB is chaired by the USD(AT&L). Principal participants at DOD ITAB reviews include the JS J-8; the Deputy DOD CIO; IT OIPT leader; ACAT ID OIPT leaders; cognizant PEO(s) and PM(s); CAEs and CIOs of the Army, Navy, and Air Force. Also, participants include (as appropriate to the issue being examined) executive-level representatives from the following organizations: Office of USD(AT&L); Office of the Under Secretary of Defense (Comptroller); Office of the Joint Chiefs of Staff; Office of D,OT&E;

MATERIAL SYSTEM RESEARCH, DEVELOPMENT, AND ACQUISITION MANAGEMENT

Office of the Director, Cost Assessment and Program Evaluation (D,CAPE); and the Defense Information Systems Agency (DISA).

11-62. ASARC
a. The ASARC is the Army's senior-level acquisition advisory body for ACAT IC, IAC, and selected ACAT II programs, ACAT ID programs (DAB managed) prior to a DAB, and ACAT IAM programs prior to an ITAB. The ASARC convenes at formal MSs to determine a program or system's readiness to enter the next phase of the materiel acquisition cycle, and makes recommendations to the AAE on those programs for which the AAE is the MDA. An ASARC may be convened at any time to review the status of a program. The ASARC is chaired by the AAE.

b. ASARC membership includes the Assistant Secretary of the Army (Acquisition, Logistics and Technology) – AAE; Vice Chief of Staff of the Army; Deputy Under Secretary of the Army – Test and Evaluation Executive; Assistant Secretary of the Army (Financial Management and Comptroller); Assistant Secretary of the Army (Installations, Energy, and Environment); Assistant Secretary of the Army (Manpower and Reserve Affairs); CG, Army Materiel Command; CG, Training and Doctrine Command; Office of the General Counsel; DCS, G–1; DCS, G–2; DCS, G–3/5/7; DCS, G–4; DCS, CIO/G–6; and the DCS, G–8. Other organizations are invited to attend, if a significant issue is identified within their area of responsibility. The AAE makes the final decision as to the attendance at the ASARC.

c. The effectiveness of the ASARC review process results from presentation of a thorough analysis of all relevant issues and face-to-face discussion among the principals from the Army Secretariat, ARSTAF, AMC and TRADOC.

11-63. In-Process Review (IPR)
a. The IPR is a formal acquisition review forum for ACAT III programs. General policies for reviews for IPR programs are the same as for ACAT I and II programs. Reviews are conducted at MSs and at other times deemed necessary by the MDA. The MDA, usually the assigned PEO, chairs the IPR.

b. The IPR brings together representatives of the MATDEV, the CAPDEV, the trainer, the logistician, and the independent evaluators for a joint review and decision on proceeding to the next phase of development. Their purpose is to provide recommendations, with supporting rationale, as a basis for system concept, system development, type classification, and production decisions by the appropriate level of authority. They are the forums where agencies responsible for participating in the materiel acquisition process can present their views and ensure that those views are considered during development, test, evaluation, and production. Participation is extended to the appropriate testing agencies, HQDA representatives, and to others as designated by the IPR chairman.

11-64. Configuration Steering Board (CSB)
a. Section 814 of the 2009 National Defense Authorization Act (NDAA) requires the Secretary of each military department to establish a CSB for DAS post MS B ACAT I and IA programs. Meeting annually, the CSB is responsible for reviewing all requirements changes and any significant technical configuration changes for ACAT I and IA programs in development that have the potential to result in cost and schedule impacts to the program. Changes are not approved unless funds are identified and schedule impacts are mitigated. CSBs were designed to monitor programs and avoid requirements creep. The law does not limit the CSB process to ACAT I and IA only; it may be used for other ACAT programs.

b. The 2009 NDAA explicitly provides PMs with the authority to challenge new program requirements. The PM, in consultation with the PEO, identifies and proposes a set of de-scoping options, with supporting rationale addressing operational implications that reduce program cost or moderate requirements. The CSB recommends to the MDA which of these options should be implemented. The NDAA 2009 does not give the materiel development community the authority to unilaterally modify or delete requirements. Final decisions on de-scoping option implementation are coordinated with the appropriate Joint Staff and military department requirements officials. These checks and balances provide a framework for the acquisition executive to challenge requirements without sacrificing the Services' accountabilities to ensure user requirements are met.

c. In the Army, the CSB consists of the following principal members:
(1) Army Acquisition Executive (Chair)
(2) Vice Chief of Staff, Army (Vice-Chair)
(3) Principal Military Deputy, Office of the Assistant Secretary of Army (Acquisition, Logistics, and

HOW THE ARMY RUNS

Technology)
(4) PEO
(5) Senior executive representatives from the office of the Under Secretary of Defense (Acquisition, Technology, and Logistics), Joint Staff and the TRADOC ARCIC

11-65. IPT

DODD 5000.01 directs the DOD acquisition community to utilize IPTs to facilitate the management and exchange of program information. IPTs integrate all acquisition activities starting with capabilities development through production, fielding/deployment, and operational support in order to optimize the design, manufacturing, business, and supportability processes. The IPT is composed of representatives from all appropriate functional disciplines working together with a team leader to build successful and balanced programs, identify and resolve issues, and make sound and timely recommendations to facilitate decision-making. There are two levels of IPTs: OIPTs focus on strategic guidance, program executability (cost, schedule, risk), and issue resolution; and the Working-level Integrated Product Teams (WIPT), that identify and resolve program issues, determine program status, and seek opportunities for acquisition reform.

a. OIPTs. In support of all ACAT ID and IAM programs, an OIPT is formed to provide assistance, oversight, and review as that program proceeds through its acquisition life-cycle. The OIPT for ACAT ID programs is led by the appropriate OSD Principal Staff Assistant (PSA) or Technical Director. The DASD(C3ISR, Space, IT Programs) is the OIPT leader for ACAT IAM programs. Program OIPTs are composed of the PM, PEO, component staff, Joint Staff, USD(AT&L) staff, and the OSD staff principals or their representatives, involved in oversight and review of a particular ACAT ID or IAM program.

(1) In the Army, an ASARC OIPT is established at the direction of the MDA for ACAT IC, IAC, and most ACAT II programs. The ASARC OIPT is a team of HQDA staff action officers and the PEO/PM/TCM responsible for integration of oversight issues to be raised to the MDR forums.

(2) The secretary/facilitator of the ASARC OIPT for Army ACAT I and II programs is the DASC, in ASA(ALT), for that specific program. OIPT membership consists of empowered individuals appointed by ASARC members (ACAT IC, IAC, or selected ACAT II programs), and the MDA for ACAT III programs. Team membership is tailored based on the needs and level of oversight for the individual program. Typical ASARC OIPT responsibilities include:

(a) Meeting with the PEO/PM throughout program development to raise and resolve issues early, providing recommendations for tailoring and streamlining the program
(b) Linking vertically with the PM's WIPTs
(c) Helping the PM successfully achieve a MS decision
(d) Providing an independent assessment for the MDA in preparation for the MDR
(e) Developing a memorandum documenting the issues/risks to be raised to the MDA with a recommendation to the MDA

(3) The OIPT, at all levels, follow the general procedures that are described below for a typical ACAT ID and IAM program. Initially the OIPT meets to determine the extent of WIPT support needed for the potential program, who shall be members of the WIPTs, the appropriate MS for program initiation, and the minimum information needed for the program initiation review. The OIPT leader is responsible for taking action to resolve issues when requested by any member of the OIPT or when directed by MDA. The goal is to resolve as many issues and concerns at the lowest level possible, and to expeditiously escalate issues that need resolution at a higher level, bringing only the highest-level issues to the MDA for decision. The OIPT meets as necessary over the life of a program.

(4) The OSD OIPT PSA or Technical Director provides an Integrated Program Assessment (IPA) at MDRs, using data gathered through the IPT process. The OIPT leader's assessment focuses on core acquisition management issues and takes into account independent assessments that are normally prepared by OIPT members.

b. WIPTs. WIPTs are established for all acquisition programs. The number and membership of the WIPTs are tailored to each acquisition phase based on the level of oversight and the program needs. They are comprised of HQDA and/or Service/functional action officers and normally chaired by the PM or designee. WIPTs provide advice to the PM and help prepare program strategies and plans. Each WIPT focuses on a particular topic(s), such as T&E, cost/performance, risk management (both programmatic and safety), etc.

MATERIAL SYSTEM RESEARCH, DEVELOPMENT, AND ACQUISITION MANAGEMENT

Section XI
Traditional Acquisition Documentation

11-66. MCDs
Acquisition management documentation is designed to support the management process as the life-cycle development of a materiel system progresses. MCDs establish the need for a materiel acquisition program, how the materiel will be employed, and what the materiel must be capable of doing. As the acquisition program progresses, statements of required performance and design specifications become more and more specific. The ICD is the document that initiates the DAS. MCDs were discussed in section III.

11-67. Other Service Requirements
The CAPDEV/TNGDEV reviews other Service warfighting capability requirements documents for potential Army interest. When the Army chooses to participate in the RDA of another Service program, HQDA initiates action to validate the documentation. When another Service's MCD, to include an approved production RFP, adequately describes an Army requirement, the document may be validated as the Army requirement. The Army may acquire other Services' equipment with a National Stock Number (NSN) that has been identified through the MATDEV market investigation and meets an approved Army need. For joint programs, capabilities documents are prepared and processed in accordance with the lead Services' procedures. Service peculiar requirements may be documented in the other Service's capabilities documents.

11-68. CARDS
Army CARDS is an unclassified HQDA DCS, G-3/5/7 publication that provides information on the status of all validated MCDs. It includes both active and inactive requirement documents. An active document or assignment of a CARDS reference number does not automatically authorize the expenditure of funds. Each program must compete for funds in the Army prioritization and programming process. The HQDA DCS, G-37 Current and Futures Warfighting Capabilities Division (DAMO-CIC), assigns a CARDS reference number to each MCD after approval and prior to publication and distribution.

11-69. Program Review Documentation and Program Plans
The MDA is responsible for identifying the minimum amount of documentation necessary for MS review purposes. Only those mandatory formats called for by statute or DODI 5000.02 are required. All other formats are used as guidance only. Program plans are a description of the detailed activities necessary for executing the AS. Program plans belong to the PM and are used by the PM to manage program execution throughout the life-cycle of the program. The PM, in coordination with the PEO, determines the type and number of program plans, except those required by statute or DOD policy. Some of the typical program plans used to support the execution of a program are:
 a. System Threat Assessment Report (STAR). The STAR is the basic authoritative threat assessment that supports the development and acquisition of a particular ACAT I, IA, or II system. The STAR contains an integrated assessment of projected enemy capabilities (doctrine, tactics, hardware, organization, and forces) at IOC and IOC plus 10 years, to limit, neutralize, or destroy the system. It explicitly identifies Critical Intelligence Categories (CIC), which are a series of threat capabilities that could critically impact the effectiveness and survivability of the program. The STAR is a dynamic document that is continually updated and refined as a program develops. It is approved and validated in support of MDRs. This report is the primary threat reference for the CDD, the Modified Integrated Program Summary (MIPS), the AoA, and the TEMP developed in support of a MDR. The STAR is approved by HQDA DCS, G-2 and validated by the DIA for all ACAT I, IA, and DOTE Oversight List programs at MS B and updated at MS C.
 b. MIPS. The MIPS, with its annexes, is the primary Army decision document used to facilitate top-level acquisition MS decision-making. The MIPS provides a comprehensive summary of program structure, status, assessment, plans, and recommendations by the PM and the PEO. The primary functions of the MIPS include a summary of where the program is versus where it should be; a description of where the program is going and how it will get there; an identification of program risk areas and plans for closing risks; and a basis for establishing explicit program cost, schedule, and performance

HOW THE ARMY RUNS

objectives. Also, the MIPS include thresholds in the stand-alone APB and program-specific exit criteria for the next acquisition phase. The MIPS provides answers to the following five key MDR core issues:
(1) Is the system still needed?
(2) Does the system work from the viewpoints of the user, functional staffs, and the PM?
(3) Are major risks identified and manageable?
(4) Is the program affordable and is adequate programming in the POM?
(5) Has the system been subjected to CAIV?

c. AS. The AS is the framework (roadmap) for planning, directing, and managing a materiel acquisition program. It states the concepts and objectives that direct and control overall program execution from program initiation through post-production support. An AS is required for all Army acquisition programs regardless of ACAT. The AS documents how the acquisition program will be tailored and identifies risks and plans to reduce or eliminate risks. The AS, prepared by the PM-led WIPT, is a living document that matures throughout the program. It provides fundamental guidance to the functional elements of the MATDEV/CAPDEV organizations. Individual functional strategies leading to the preparation of detailed program plans required to implement the AS are depicted in Figure 11-8.

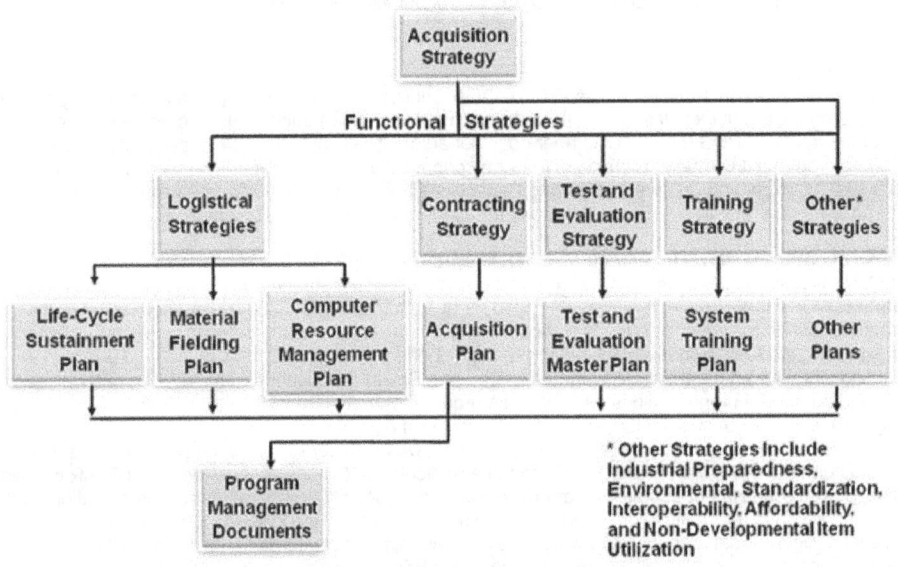

Figure 11-8. Acquisition Strategy (AS)

d. Environmental analysis. This is a Congressionally mandated analysis of the potential environmental impacts of weapons systems. It identifies land, sea, or air space requirements of the most promising alternatives and describes the potential effects on the land, sea, and air environment. It also describes the potential impacts on public health and safety by the development, test manufacturing, basing operation, and support of the proposed system. The environmental impact data is weighed against system cost, schedule, and performance (programmatics) in deciding how to best minimize environmental harm.

e. POE (life-cycle cost) and CCE. These documents are prepared in support of MS B and all subsequent MS reviews. The cost estimates are explicitly based on the program objectives, operational requirements, and contract specifications for the system, including plans for such matters as peacetime

MATERIAL SYSTEM RESEARCH, DEVELOPMENT, AND ACQUISITION MANAGEMENT

utilization rates and the maintenance concept. The estimates identify all elements of additional cost that would be entailed by a decision to proceed with development, production, and operation of the system. They are based on a careful assessment of risks and reflect a realistic appraisal of the level of cost most likely to be realized. Two cost estimates are prepared. The program office in support of MS A and all subsequent decision reviews prepare the POE. The other estimate is prepared by an organization that does not report through the acquisition chain. In the Army, this independent cost estimate, entitled CCE, is prepared by the Deputy Assistant Secretary of the Army, Cost and Economics (DASA(CE)) for MDAP systems. Both estimates are based on the Cost Analysis Requirements Description (CARD). The CARD is the document that provides estimators a complete description of the system whose costs are to be estimated. It is intended to define the program to a sufficient level of detail such that no confusion exists between the many parties who may be concerned with estimating the program's cost.

f. ACP. The ACP is the Army's approved life-cycle cost estimate for the materiel system. It is used for DOD MS reviews and is the basis for Army planning, programming, and budgeting. For all MDAP programs, the Army's CRB develops the proposed ACP after an intensive review of both the POE and CCE. This proposal becomes the ACP when it is approved by the ASA(FM&C) and then is provided to the AAE. DODI 5000.02 requires the component's cost position.

g. AoA.

(1) The independent AoA provides information to the decision authority at the MS A review to assist in determining whether any of proposed alternatives to an existing system offer sufficient military and/or economic benefit. AoA findings provide the analytical underpinning to support the recommendation to initiate, modify, or terminate a program. An AoA is required for potential ACAT I and most ACAT II programs and is typically conducted by the TRADOC Analysis Center (TRAC) during the acquisition MSA phase (previously discussed).

(2) The AoA focuses on broad operational capabilities, potential technology concepts, and materiel solutions that could satisfy the MCD. It examines the full range of materiel alternatives (including those identified in the Materiel Development Decision review ADM). AoAs illuminate the relative advantages and disadvantages of alternatives being considered by identifying sensitivities of each alternative to possible changes in key assumptions (e.g., threat) or variables (e.g., selected performance capabilities). The AoA provides insights regarding KPPs for preferred alternatives and indicates how these parameters contribute to increases in operational capability. It identifies opportunities for trades among performance, cost, and schedule and determines operational effectiveness and costs (including estimates of training and logistics impacts) for all alternatives.

(3) If a new program is approved (MS B), the AoA may be useful for identifying alternatives that will be refined by cost-performance trades during the EMD phase. The MDA may direct updates to the AoA for subsequent decision points, if conditions warrant (e.g., AoA may be useful for examining cost-performance trades at MS C).

h. APB. APBs consist of the concept baseline, the development baseline, and the production baseline approved at MS B, C, and FRP, respectively. The purpose of the baselines is to enhance program stability and to provide a critical reference point for measuring and reporting the status of program implementation. Each baseline contains objectives for key cost, schedule, and performance parameters. Key parameters must meet minimum acceptable requirements, known as thresholds, at each MS decision point. The thresholds establish deviation limits from which a PM may not trade-off cost or performance without authorization from the MDA. The APB must cross-walk to the program CDD or CPD for performance parameters. Failure to meet the threshold requires a reevaluation of alternative concepts or design approaches. APBs and deviation reporting are required for all ACAT programs.

i. TEMP. The TEMP is the executive-level planning document required for a system that focuses on the overall structure, major elements, and objectives of the T&E program. The TEMP is consistent with the AS as well as the validated CDD, CPD, and ISP. It is a reference document used by the T&E community to generate detailed T&E plans and to ascertain schedule and resource requirements associated with a given system. The TEMP provides a roadmap for integrated simulation, test, and evaluation plans, schedules, and resource requirements necessary to accomplish the T&E program. The TEMP describes what testing (e.g., developmental test and operational test) is required, who will perform the testing, what resources will be needed, and what are the requirements for evaluation. It relates program schedule, test management strategy and structure, and required resources to critical operational issues; critical technical parameters; Measures Of Effectiveness (MOE) and suitability; and MS decisions points. While the PM has the overall responsibility, each T&E WIPT member contributes to the TEMP

HOW THE ARMY RUNS

development and maintenance. The TEMP is initially developed at a system's first MS review and is updated before each subsequent MS, when the CDD/CPD/ISP has changed significantly, or when the APB has been breached. Upon approval, the TEMP serves as a contract between the CAPDEV, MATDEV and T&E community for executing the system's T&E program. The TEMP provides key management controls for T&E in support of the acquisition process. Detailed TEMP procedures and format are in DA Pamphlet 73-1.

j. LCSP. LCSP spans a system's entire life-cycle, from DAS MSA phase to disposal. It translates force provider capability and performance requirements into tailored product support to achieve specified and evolving life-cycle product support availability, reliability, and affordability parameters. Life-cycle sustainment planning is considered during MSA, and matures throughout the DAS TD phase. A LCSP is prepared for MS B. The planning is flexible and performance-oriented, reflecting an evolutionary approach, and accommodates modifications, upgrades, and re-procurement. The LCSP is part of the program's AS and is integrated with other key program planning documents. The LCSP is updated and executed during DAS P&D and O&S phases. Life-cycle sustainment considerations include supply; maintenance; transportation; sustaining engineering; data management; configuration management; HSI; manpower, personnel, training, habitability, survivability, environment, safety (including explosives safety), and occupational health; protection of critical program information and anti-tamper provisions; supportability; and interoperability.

k. Manpower Estimate Report (MER). This Congressionally directed report documents the total number of personnel (military, civilian, and contractor) that are or will be needed to operate, maintain, support, and train for a ACAT I program upon full operational deployment. The validity of the MER is dependent upon force structure, personnel management, and readiness requirements, as well as the acquisition decision on the size of the buy (procurement).

11-70. Typical Waivers and Reports

a. LFT&E report. The LFT&E is an independent OSD report to Congress that provides test results and assessment of realistic survivability testing on a covered major system, and realistic lethality testing on a major munition or missile program. Congress mandates this report.

b. Live-fire test and evaluation waiver. This certifies to Congress when live-fire survivability testing of a covered major system would be unreasonably expensive and impractical. However, some testing must still be accomplished at the subsystem level as described in the alternate LFT&E plan.

c. Developmental test report. This provides the results of developmental tests to include live-fire test results and reports.

d. Beyond low-rate initial production report. This provides Congress with an assessment of the adequacy of IOT&E and whether the test results confirm the items are effective, suitable, and survivable for combat prior to the FRP decision to proceed beyond LRIP. Congress mandates this report.

e. Defense Acquisition Executive Summary (DAES). The DAES is an early-warning report to DOD's USD(AT&L). The DAES describes actual or potential program problems and describes mitigating actions taken. The DAES is a multi-part document, reporting program information and assessments; PM, PEO, and AAE comments; and cost and funding data. The PM may obtain permission from USD(AT&L) to tailor DAES content. At a minimum, the DAES reports program assessments (including interoperability), unit costs, current estimates, exit criteria status, and vulnerability assessments.

f. Selected Acquisition Report (SAR). The SAR reports the status of total program cost, schedule, and performance; as well as program unit cost and unit cost breach information. For joint programs, the SAR reports the information by participant. Each SAR includes a full, life-cycle cost analysis for the reporting program. The SAR is provided to Congress.

g. Nunn-McCurdy unit cost breach report. A Nunn-McCurdy unit cost breach occurs when a MDAP experiences an increase of at least 15% in Program Acquisition Unit Cost (PAUC) or Average Procurement Unit Cost (APUC) above the unit costs in the current APB or 30% from the original baseline. For programs with unit cost increases of at least 25% of current or 50% of original baseline, a SECDEF certification is required. Certification responsibility has been delegated to the USD(AT&L). Unit cost reporting is required by 10 USC 2433.

11-71. Other Documentation

MATERIAL SYSTEM RESEARCH, DEVELOPMENT, AND ACQUISITION MANAGEMENT

a. ADM. The ADM documents the MDA's decision on the program AS goals, thresholds, and the exit criteria for the next phase of the program. The ADM is used to document the decision for all ACAT I, II, and III programs.

b. IPA. Information derived from the PM's MIPS allows the DOD OIPT to develop the IPA for program MDR. The IPA summarizes the DOD independent assessment of the PM's program. It identifies critical areas, issues, and recommendations for the MDA. For ACAT ID and IAM programs, the IPA is prepared by the OIPT, approved by the OIPT leader, and submitted to the USD (AT&L).

Section XII
Testing and Evaluation

11-72. T&E Process/Products

There are four major sub-processes that support the Defense Acquisition Management System (DAS). The first major sub-process is Testing and Evaluation (T&E).

a. All Army acquisition programs must be supported by a TEMP, previously discussed, that reflects an adequate and efficient T&E program. T&E is the principal tool with which progress in system development and acquisition is measured. T&E is structured to support the DAS and user by providing essential information to decision-makers, assessing attainment of technical performance parameters, and determining whether systems are operationally effective, suitable, and survivable for intended use. The primary reasons for conducting T&E are to facilitate learning, assess technical maturity and interoperability, facilitate integration into fielded forces, and confirm performance. Also, T&E can assess and reduce program risk (e.g., cost, schedule, technical feasibility, technical obsolescence, and software management). The primary product of the T&E sub-process is information (hard facts), plus an independent evaluation of all the credible data on a system, so that the MDA can make informed decisions.

b. The planning, programming, and budgeting for T&E begins early in the acquisition process, concurrent with coordination of the validated ICD. Early T&E integration is accomplished through the independent evaluator's involvement in the ICDT and the planning of the acquisition team within the T&E WIPT. The primary purpose of the T&E WIPT is to optimize the use of the appropriate T&E expertise, instrumentation, targets, facilities, simulations, and models to implement test integration, thereby reducing costs and decision risk to the Army. The primary product of the T&E WIPT is the TEMP. The Army Test and Evaluation Executive, within the office of the DUSA, is the TEMP approval authority for all ACAT I/IA, ACAT II, and any programs on the OSD T&E Oversight List prior to final OSD approval. The MDA approves TEMPs for ACAT II and III programs not on the OSD T&E Oversight List.

c. Continuous Evaluation (CE) is used to provide a continuous flow of information and data to decision-makers, MATDEV, and CAPDEVs. The data generated in early development phases is visible and maintained as the system moves into formal testing, thereby avoiding duplication of testing. Continuous evaluation continues through a system's post-deployment, to verify whether the fielded system meets or exceeds demonstrated performance and support parameters.

11-73. DT and OT

a. DT encompasses models, simulation, and engineering type tests that are used to verify that design risks are minimized, system safety is certified, achievement of system technical performance is substantiated, and to certify readiness for OT. DT generally requires instrumentation and measurements, is accomplished by engineers and technicians, is repeatable, may be environmentally controlled, and covers the complete spectrum of system capabilities. The PM designs DT objectives applicable to each phase and MS. Examples of key DTs are the LFT that is mandated for covered systems and the Production Qualification Test (PQT), the system-level test that ensures design integrity over the specified operational and environmental range.

b. OT is a field test of a system (or item) under realistic operational conditions with users who represent those expected to operate and maintain the system (or item) when fielded or deployed. Examples of key OTs are:

(1) Limited User Test (LUT). An LUT is a risk mitigation test normally conducted in the systems acquisition phase prior to MS C. Although not required by law, it is used to mitigate risk during follow-on OTs.

HOW THE ARMY RUNS

(2) IOT&E. It is conducted before the FRP decision and is structured to provide data to determine the operational effectiveness, suitability, and survivability of a system operated by typical users under realistic conditions (e.g., combat and representative threat). Before an IOT&E commences for all programs on the OSD T&E Oversight List, OSD D,OT&E usually approves the Operational Test Agency (OTA) Test Plan (OTA TP).

(3) FOT&E. FOT&E may be necessary during (or after) production to refine the estimates made during the IOT&E, provide data to examine changes, and verify that deficiencies in materiel, training, or concepts have been corrected. A FOT&E provides data to ensure that the system continues to meet operational needs and that it retains its effectiveness in a new environment or against a new threat.

c. The Army's TSARC is a high-level centralized management forum that reviews and coordinates the resource commitment (e.g., personnel, instrumentation, and equipment), required to support the tests included in the Army's Five-Year Test Program (FYTP). The TSARC is chaired by CG, ATEC and operates under AR 73-1. When approved for inclusion in the FYTP, a program's TRP becomes the authority for tasking in the current and budget years. The TRP is the acquisition system's formal T&E resource planning and tasking document.

Section XIII
Integrated Logistics Support

11-74. ILS Process
The second major sub-process in support of DAS is Integrated Logistics Support (ILS). TPF and the LCMC are also discussed in this section of the chapter.

a. ILS is a disciplined, unified, and interactive approach to the management and technical activities necessary to integrate logistics support into system and equipment design. ILS is the process used by the Army to implement the mandatory life-cycle logistics policies and procedures and includes all elements of planning, developing, acquiring, and supporting Army materiel throughout its life-cycle.

b. Supportability Integrated Product Team (SIPT).

(1) The SIPT is a working-level IPT to support both the capabilities development and system acquisition management processes. The CAPDEV proponent CoE establishes an SIPT at the DAS MSA phase for all potential ACAT I/II and selected ACAT III acquisition programs to coordinate overall ILS planning and execution. At MS B, or when the PM is assigned, the designated MATDEV Integrated Logistic Support Manager (ILSM) assumes responsibility to chair the SIPT.

(2) SIPT members develop PBL concepts and ILS program documentation and conduct supportability/tradeoff analyses to determine the optimum PBL strategy or ILS concepts. The SIPT make recommended ILS-related planning, programming, and execution decisions to the PM. The SIPT is a working body, and the roles and responsibilities of members are prescribed in the LCSP, formerly Supportability Strategy (SS). The SIPT must work with other functional groups, such as the T&E WIPT and the Training Support Work Group (TSWG) to ensure an integrated effort.

(3) The SIPT considers numerous alternatives and trades. The Supportability Analysis (SA) is required to identify the optimum support system requirements. Both the MATDEV and CAPDEV perform SA tasks (either in-house or through contractors) applicable to their respective mission responsibilities as defined in AR 700-127.

c. ILSM. The ILSM is established by the MATDEV prior to MS B or when a PM is assigned to serve as the focal point for all life-cycle management supportability actions related to the acquisition program. The ILSM assumes the responsibility to chair the SIPT from the CAPDEV.

d. PBL. PBL is the preferred Product Support Strategy (PSS) for weapon systems that employs the purchase of support as an integrated performance package designed to optimize system readiness. PBL objectives include optimizing total system availability while minimizing cost and logistics footprint. PBL is implemented on all Army ACAT programs where it is operationally and economically feasible. PBL is implemented on Army ACAT III programs at the discretion of the PM/PEO. A basic tenet of PBL is the use of high-level metrics that measures support outcomes both operationally and economically. Current overarching life-cycle metrics include: operational availability; mission reliability; cost per unit usage; logistics footprint; logistics response time; and total life-cycle cost per unit usage. PBL may be implemented on systems, subsystems, secondary items, components, assemblies, or subassemblies as well as processes that lead to business process improvements (for example, Lean or Six Sigma

MATERIAL SYSTEM RESEARCH, DEVELOPMENT, AND ACQUISITION MANAGEMENT

improvements on a depot line). PBL will meet performance goals for the system through a support structure based on performance agreements with clear lines of authority and responsibility, delineate outcome performance goals of weapon systems, ensure that responsibilities are assigned, provide incentives for attaining these goals, and facilitate the overall life-cycle management of system reliability, supportability, and total ownership costs. The PBL strategy must be addressed at each MDR and is tailored for each individual acquisition system with specific performance goals, roles, responsibilities that will be detailed in Performance-Based Agreements (PBA) prior to system fielding.

  e. Supportability Analysis (SA) and Logistics Management Information (LMI). Supportability is a design characteristic. The early focus of SA should result in establishment of support-related parameters in performance terms. As system design progresses, SA will address supportability requirements and provide a means to perform trades among these requirements and the system design. In order to be effective, SA will be conducted within the framework of the systems engineering process. Examples of these analyses are analysis use studies, repair-level analysis, task analysis, reliability predictions, Condition-Based Maintenance (CBM) analysis, reliability-centered maintenance, and life-cycle cost analysis. LMI is the support and support-related engineering and logistics data acquired from contractors and a product of SA. MIL-PRF-49506 is the specification that provides DOD with a contractual method for acquiring these data. DOD uses these data in existing DOD materiel management processes such as those for initial provisioning, cataloging, and item management. If there is a requirement for the contractor to provide data for loading into a government database, then it will be necessary to specify the required data file format and data relationships as performance requirements for electronic data interchange.

  f. LCSP (formerly supportability strategy). LCSP documents the PM's plan for the sustainment strategy of an acquisition program. The LCSP is based upon the ILS framework (ILS elements) and defines how supportability analyses will be used throughout the systems engineering process to design and support the system. The LCSP is a standalone document which is submitted for Milestone Decision Authority (MDA) approval as an appendix to the AS beginning with MS B. The PM will also include a summary of the LCSP in the main body of the AS. The initial LCSP is prepared by the CAPDEV ILS lead for the system during the Materiel Solution Analysis Phase and is provided to the PM's ILSM or PSM upon establishment of the PM SIPT.

  (1) The purpose of the LCSP is to methodically gather and review relevant logistics data (Supportability Analysis (SA)), assess alternative system design and support concepts using the SA, document decisions, coordinate plans, and execute the selected logistics support concept. The LCSP will serve as the official record to document the actions taken during the development and implementation of the ILS management process.

  (2) The LCSP is used to maintain an audit trail of changes that affect:
  (a) Support planning
  (b) Support budgets, including the LCC estimate and reduction in total ownership costs initiatives
  (c) Support concepts, support-related goals, and thresholds (including changes in definition)
  (d) Impacts or changes on system readiness objective (SRO), support costs, and ILS objectives
  (e) Strategy to achieve type classification-standard and Full Materiel Release (FMR) by FRP decision
  (3) The LCSP for all ACAT levels is managed by the PM SIPT and approved by the MDA. The SIPT utilizes the acquisition strategy for its foundation to ensure supportability is integrated into the acquisition.
  (4) The LCSP is updated by the PM; coordinated with CAPDEV, supporting LCMCs, Army Acquisition Logistician, the technical and operational testers/evaluators, and other program participants; and will be available 60 days prior to MS B.
  (a) When no PM exists prior to MS B, the PEO, who is assigned system responsibility, will lead the effort to develop the LCSP.
  (b) In cases where there was not a CAPDEV ILS lead, the PEO (or PM if assigned) will develop the initial LCSP.
  (c) Programs past MS B that do not have a LCSP will require one prior to MS C to address the ILS planning during development, production, fielding, and sustainment.
  (5) The LCSP will be updated:
  (a) Before MDRs
  (b) When new program direction is received
  (c) When programmatic or funding changes occur
  (d) Prior to development of solicitation documents

HOW THE ARMY RUNS

(e) Prior to requesting a materiel release position from any agency
(f) Not more than three years from the previous update if there have been any changes to the program that may have logistical impacts
(g) For substantial changes not easily handled by administrative notification
(h) When manpower, personnel, training, or logistics support plans change

(6) The minutes of the SIPT meetings will serve as interim updates to the LCSP. The approved LCSP, together with the SIPT minutes, will be the action guide for all ILS program participants.

(7) For joint Service acquisition programs for which the Army has lead responsibility, the ILSM or PSM will develop a LCSP in coordination with all participating Services. For other programs, the Army representative on the SIPT will coordinate Army input to the LCSP.

(8) A LCSP is not required for:
(a) Reprocurement of systems for which a LCSP has been previously developed and is still current, except when there is a new make, model, or manufacturer
(b) Engineering Change Proposals (ECP) resulting in modification work orders that do not change system configuration
(c) Components having minor logistics impact

(9) The LCSP will include the details of the plan, exit criteria, and the timeline to achieve all program decision points, key events, and MSs to include Type Classification (TC) and Full Materiel Release (FMR). (see AR 700-142).

(10) The LCSP will include an explanation why organic support cannot be provided for any system requiring contractor support personnel in the forward maneuver area (see AR 715-9).

(11) The format for the LCSP is provided in DA Pam 700-56.

(12) The LCSP will be utilized to develop the input to the PM's probability of success model.

11-75. TPF

a. TPF is currently the Army's standard fielding process. In 1984, the Army began using TPF on a test basis and made it the standard fielding process in 1987. It is designed to ensure a thorough planning and coordination between CAPDEVs, TNGDEVs, MATDEVs, fielding commands, gaining Army commands, and using units involved in the fielding of new materiel systems. At the same time, it is designed to ease the logistics burden of the using and supporting Army troop units. Regulatory and instructional guidance for materiel release, fielding, and transfer is contained in AR 700-142, and DA Pamphlet 700-142 respectively. The TPF process is shown in Figure 11-9.

b. Identification of the TPF package contents for a particular fielding is known as establishment of the Materiel Requirements List (MRL). It is the responsibility of the MATDEV/fielding command to identify everything that is needed to use and support the new system and coordinate these requirements with the CAPDEVs/TNGDEVs and the gaining Army commands. The total fielding requirements are documented, coordinated, and agreed on through the Materiel Fielding Plan (MFP), the Mission Support Plan (MSP) and the Materiel Fielding Agreement (MFA).

c. The Defense Logistics Agency (DLA) operates Unit Materiel Fielding Points (UMFP) in Pennsylvania, Texas, and California that support the Army. These three DLA UMFPs are sites where initial issue items are consolidated at Unit Identification Code (UIC) level to support TPF worldwide. The staging site is the facility or location where the total package comes together. It is usually here that all end items, support equipment, and initial issue spare and repair parts are prepared for handoff to the gaining units. To support TPF Outside the Continental United States (OCONUS), the AMC operates a number of central staging sites in Europe, and two sites in Korea.

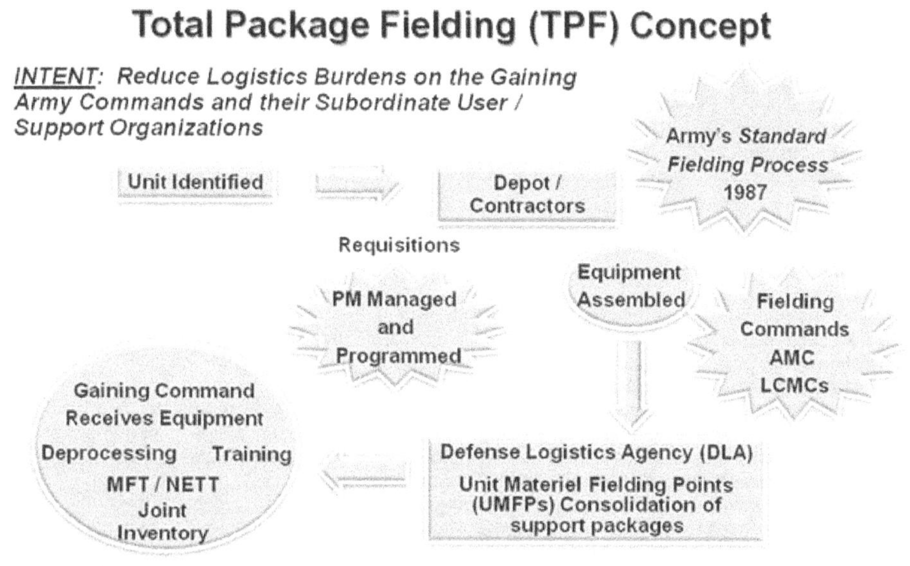

MATERIAL SYSTEM RESEARCH, DEVELOPMENT, AND ACQUISITION MANAGEMENT

Total Package Fielding (TPF) Concept

INTENT: *Reduce Logistics Burdens on the Gaining Army Commands and their Subordinate User / Support Organizations*

- Unit Identified
- Depot / Contractors
- Army's Standard Fielding Process 1987
- Requisitions
- PM Managed and Programmed
- Equipment Assembled
- Fielding Commands AMC LCMCs
- Gaining Command Receives Equipment — Deprocessing, Training, MFT / NETT, Joint Inventory
- Defense Logistics Agency (DLA) Unit Materiel Fielding Points (UMFPs) Consolidation of support packages

LCMCs: Life-Cycle Management Commands
MFT: Materiel Fielding Team
NETT: New Equipment Training Team

Figure 11-9. Total Package Fielding (TFP) Concept

d. A joint supportability assessment takes place about 90 days before the projected First Unit Equipped Fate (FUED) and 60 days before fielding to a unit in CONUS. The MATDEV/fielding command assures that those items requiring de-processing are inspected and made fully operational-ready before handoff to the gaining units. A joint inventory is conducted by the fielding and gaining commands to ensure all needed items are received, or placed on a shortage list for later delivery.

e. The MATDEV/fielding command provides, at the time of handoff, a tailored customer documentation package for each gaining unit that allows the unit to establish property accountability and post a receipt for TPF materiel. Logistics changes are helping the Army transform to the future force. Many of these changes apply directly to TPF.

11-76. LCMCs

a. Since the passage of the DAWIA in November 1990, the Army has continually attempted to reduce total life-cycle costs for warfighting systems, specifically sustainment costs which account for approximately 80% of system life-cycle costs. Under acquisition reform efforts, the PM is responsible and accountable for all system life-cycle phases, including sustainment; but the planning, programming, budgeting, and execution of sustainment funding resided in the AMC.

b. In an effort to improve system life-cycle management, a Memorandum of Agreement (MOA) was signed by the ASA(ALT) and the CG, AMC, to establish the LCMCs and bring the acquisition, logistics, and technology communities together to support the PM as the single total life-cycle manager or " the trail boss" for assigned warfighting systems. The LCMC MOA was signed on August 2, 2004 and the LCMC initiative was approved by the CSA on August 16, 2004. The LCMC MOA aligned AMC system "commodity" commands with their related PEOs into four product-focused LCMCs. The four LCMCs are:

(1) Aviation and Missile LCMC, Huntsville, Alabama, is aligned with the Aviation and Missile Command

(AMCOM) with PEO Tactical Missiles and Space and PEO Aviation.
 (2) TACOM (not an acronym) LCMC, Warren, Michigan is aligned with the PEOs Combat Support, Combat Service Support, Ground Combat Systems, Soldier, and Chemical Biological Defense.
 (3) Communications-Electronics Command (CECOM) LCMC, Aberdeen Proving Ground, MD is aligned with the Communications-Electronics Command with PEO Command, Control, Communications-Tactical and PEO Intelligence, Electronic Warfare, and Sensors.
 (4) Joint Munitions and Lethality (JM&L) LCMC, Picatinny Arsenal, New Jersey, is aligned with the Joint Munitions Command with PEO Ammunition.
 c. Numerous other PEOs were not affected under the initial construct regarding the LCMS initiative.

Section XIV
Manpower and Personnel Integration Program

11-77. Manpower and Personnel Integration (MANPRINT)
The third major sub-process in support of the DAS is the MANPRINT program. MANPRINT is the Army's application of the DOD HSI requirements in systems acquisition (DODD 5000.01 and DODI 5000.02), in compliance with Title 10. MANPRINT, described in detail in AR 602-2, is the Army's program to ensure that Soldier performance is the central consideration in system design, development, and acquisition. MANPRINT is the technical process of integrating the seven interdependent elements of manpower availability, personnel capabilities, training human factors engineering, system safety, health hazards, and Soldier survivability. There are seven MANPRINT domains.
 a. Manpower. Manpower is the personnel strength (military and civilian) available to the Army. It refers to the consideration of the net effect of Army systems on overall human resource requirements and authorizations (spaces) to ensure that each system is affordable from the standpoint of manpower. It includes the analysis of the number of people (including contractors) needed to operate, maintain, and support each new system being acquired, including maintenance and supply personnel, and personnel to support and conduct training. It requires a determination of the Army manpower requirements generated by the system, comparing the new manpower needs with those of the old system(s) being replaced. If an increase in personnel is required to support a new (or modified) system, "bill payers" must be identified from existing personnel accounts.
 b. Personnel capabilities. Personnel capabilities are military and civilians (including contractors) possessing the aptitudes, characteristics, and grades required to operate, maintain, and support a system in peacetime and war. Personnel refers to the ability of the Army to provide qualified people in terms of specific aptitudes, experiences, and other human characteristics needed to operate, maintain, and support Army systems. It requires a detailed assessment of the aptitudes that personnel must possess in order to complete training successfully, as well as operate, maintain, and support the system to the required standard. Iterative analyses must be accomplished for the system being acquired, comparing projected quantities of qualified personnel with the requirements of the new system, or any system(s) being replaced, and overall Army needs for similarly qualified people. Personnel analyses and projections are needed in time to allow orderly recruitment, training, and assignment of personnel in conjunction with system fielding.
 c. Training. Considerations of the necessary time and resources required to impact the requisite knowledge, skills, and abilities to qualify Army personnel for operation, maintenance, and support of Army systems.
 (1) It involves:
 (a) Formulating and selecting engineering design alternatives that are supportable from a training perspective
 (b) Documenting training strategies
 (c) Determining resource requirements to enable the Army training system to support system fielding
 (2) It includes analyses of the tasks that must be performed by the operator, maintainer, and supporter; the conditions under which the tasks must be performed; and the performance standards that must be met. Training is linked with personnel analyses and actions, because availability of qualified personnel is a direct function of the training process.

MATERIAL SYSTEM RESEARCH, DEVELOPMENT, AND ACQUISITION MANAGEMENT

d. Human factors engineering. Human factors engineering is the technical effort to integrate design criteria, psychological principles, and human capabilities as they relate to the design, development, test, and evaluation of systems. The human factors engineering goals are:

(1) To maximize the ability of the Soldier to perform at required levels by eliminating design-induced error.

(2) To ensure materiel maintenance, support, and transport are compatible with the capabilities and limitations of the range of fully equipped Soldiers who would be using such materiel. Human factors engineering provides an interface between the MANPRINT domains and system engineers. Human factors engineering supports the MANPRINT goal of developing equipment that will permit effective Soldier-machine interaction within the allowable, established limits of training time, Soldier aptitudes and skill, physical endurance, physiological tolerance limits, and Soldier physical standards. Human factors engineering provides this support by determining the Soldier's role in the materiel system, and by defining and developing Soldier-materiel interface characteristics, workplace layout, and work environment.

e. System safety. System Safety involves the design features and operating characteristics of a system that serve to minimize the potential for human or machine errors or failure that cause injury and/or accidents.

f. Health hazards. Health hazards are the inherent conditions in the use, operation, maintenance, support, and disposal of a system (e.g., acoustical energy, biological substances, chemical substances, oxygen deficiency, radiation energy, shock, temperature extremes, trauma, and vibration), that can cause death, injury, illness, disability, or reduce job performance of personnel.

g. Soldier survivability. Soldier survivability within the context of MANPRINT may refer to a military or a civilian.

(1) System. The characteristics of a system that can reduce fratricide, reduce detectability of the Soldier, prevent attack, if detected; prevent damage, if attacked; minimize medical injury, if wounded or otherwise injured; and reduce physical and mental fatigue.

(2) Soldier. Those characteristics of Soldiers that enable them to withstand (or avoid) adverse military action or the effects of natural phenomena that would result in the loss of capability to continue effective performance of the prescribed mission.

11-78. MANPRINT Objectives and Concept

a. The MANPRINT program has three primary objectives:

(1) Optimize both the quantity and quality of the personnel needed for systems

(2) Design systems that are easily useable by Soldiers, safe to operate, cause no unnecessary health problems, and maximize Soldier survivability

(3) Ensure acceptable trade-offs are made among performance, design, and Soldier capabilities and limits

b. This ensures that Soldier readiness is not compromised by equipment that is difficult to use or maintain. The implementation of MANPRINT impacts total system performance (both effectiveness and availability) by making explicit the role that Soldier performance plays and is shaped by design factors. MANPRINT addresses the MPT resources needed to achieve the required performance and, where possible, indicates more affordable configuration of MPT resources.

c. The engineering design philosophy of MANPRINT is focused on optimum system performance on the battlefield, which includes consideration of both Soldier and equipment capabilities and survivability. MANPRINT is an option-oriented process as opposed to an objective-oriented process. The MANPRINT process provides decision-makers information upon which to make trades in areas such as quality and numbers of people, training times, technology, conditions, standards, costs, survivability, safety, health hazard risks, design and interface features, and personnel assignment policy.

d. The body of MANPRINT expertise, formerly known as the MANPRINT joint working group, continues to function through the ICDT and IPT process, previously discussed. The MANPRINT members of the ICDT transition to the MANPRINT WIPT, when applicable. The purpose of this body is to:

(1) Assist the CAPDEV (or functional proponent) and PM to ensure MANPRINT principles are applied to the system

(2) Provide MANPRINT input to the MCDs

(3) Provide a tracking system and historical database of MANPRINT issues

e. In FY 2010, the Army responded to OSD USD(AT&L) "to conduct and provide comprehensive reviews and assessments of MANPRINT efforts within the department." The Army has the most

HOW THE ARMY RUNS

successful program of all the Services. For example, there are currently 48 ACAT I and II (complex, high dollar value) systems in the Army inventory, of which 80 percent are fully covered by MANPRINT analytic efforts. Current accomplishments include:

(1) Warfighter Information Network – Tactical (WIN-T). Current effort includes engagement with the PMs and engineers to make the user and maintainer task demands less complex, thereby increasing user friendliness and significantly reducing training requirements.

(2) Blackhawk. Changes to air crew seating, including dual-axis seat adjustment which now accommodates 40 percent more Soldiers.

(3) Fox Combat Vehicle. Crew reduced from four to three, amounting to cost savings of $2-4 million.

(4) Ground Tactical Vehicles Maintenance Concept. Streamlined the number of tasks to be performed barehanded as much as possible, which has resulted in fewer tools (10 tools) to track and less time to perform maintenance.

(5) Apache Longbow. Eighty MANPRINT problems, issues, and concerns were identified and resolved, so that a $2.7 million MANPRINT investment resulted in a $286 million cost avoidance to operations and support.

(6) Handheld GPS Receiver Operator Performance. An evaluation with dismounted Soldiers using the Defense Advanced GPS Receiver (DAGR) in the field revealed the presence of a fratricide issue: 38 percent of the Soldiers (6 out of 16) incorrectly reported their present position rather than the target's during a simulated call for fire scenario; MANPRINT recommended the use of a pop-up warning message, which was incorporated; and, in the retest, none of the Soldiers incorrectly reported their present position.

(7) Stryker. An added platform for the loader on the Mortar Carrier "B" enables the loader to "drop" mortar rounds more safely and reduce physical stress; increased room in the commander's station allows a larger portion of the Soldier population to fit into the crew station; redesigned gunner position now accommodates the body configuration of approximately 95 percent of Soldiers.

These and many other significant contributions to aviation, maneuver, weapons, and logistics programs have resulted in enhanced system performance, significant cost savings, cost avoidance, and increased personnel survivability.

f. The Army's combat effectiveness and readiness depend on equipping our Soldiers with equipment that meets their needs and allows them to accomplish their assigned missions rapidly, accurately, and efficiently.

g. The Army Research Laboratory's Human Research & Engineering Directorate serves as the MANPRINT focal point for coordinating domain support for CoE ICDTs and IPTs. Additional MANPRINT information and references are available online at http://www.manprint.army.mil.

Section XV
Training Development

11-79. TD Overview
The fourth major sub-process in support of the DAS is training development.

a. Training development is a vital component of TRADOC's mission to prepare the Army for war. TRADOC is responsible for developing training and providing support for individual and unit training. This responsibility includes determining requirements for range, ammunition, and training devices and facilities, as well as education/training courses, products, and programs.

b. The Army's TD process, the Army Training and Education Development Process (TEDP), is a systematic approach to making training/education decisions. TEDP is a systematic, spiral approach to making decisions about collective, individual, and self-development training for the Army. The TEDP involves five training related phases: evaluation; analysis; design; development; and implementation. Evaluation is continuous throughout the TEDP process and the entire process must operate within a given set of resources. DOTMLPF-P drive training and TD capabilities-based requirements.

c. The Army's implementation of DAS is a complex, lengthy process and training development is embedded throughout the process. The capabilities development and system acquisition management process provide a structure for system management. Training impacts and costs are vital to system performance. Coordination between the CAPDEV, MATDEV, and TNGDEV must be close and continuous to develop and field a complete material system that meets the CDD requirements (previously

MATERIAL SYSTEM RESEARCH, DEVELOPMENT, AND ACQUISITION MANAGEMENT

discussed).

11-80. STRAP
  a. The STRAP is the master training plan for a new, improved, or displaced materiel system. It establishes a basis for determining resources (manpower, equipment, facilities) to ensure training can be adequately conducted and supported. It outlines the development of the total training strategy for integrating a new system into the training base and gaining units; plans for all necessary training support, training products, and courses; and sets MSs to ensure the accomplishment of the training strategy. In addition, the STRAP supports development and validation of the system Materiel Requirements Documents (MRD) and establishes MSs for managing training development.
  b. The STRAP is developed by the proponent TNGDEV, and is approved by the commanding general of the proponent TRADOC or non-TRADOC CoE.

11-81. Army Modernization Training (AMT)
AR 350-1 provides policy and procedures and assigns responsibilities for the planning and execution of new systems training. The regulation provides a process for the expeditious integration of equipment into the force structure through NET, Displaced Equipment Training (DET), Doctrine and Tactics Training (DTT), and Sustainment Training (ST).
  a. NET. NET is designed to support force integration and modernization through identification of personnel, training, and training devices required to support new or improved equipment; by planning for the orderly transfer of knowledge from the MATDEV to the trainer, user, and supporter by documenting requirements in New Equipment Training Plans (NETP); and the deployment of New Equipement Training Teams (NETT) to train Soldiers to operate, maintain, and provide instruction on modernized equipment.
  b. DET. DET applies to systems that are being replaced by new equipment, but remain in the inventory. Planning for and executing DET is similar to the process used in NET.
  c. DTT. DTT is conducted in conjunction with NET or DET. DTT provides commanders, staffs, operators, and trainers with a doctrinal basis for employment of new or displaced materiel.
  d. ST. ST is a command responsibility. The training base shares the responsibility for ST by assuring that a pool of trained replacements is established to support the sustainment effort. The ultimate responsibility for ST, however, remains with the commander.

11-82. Training Requirements Analysis System (TRAS)
TRAS is a long and short-range planning and management process for the timely development of peacetime and mobilization individual training. It integrates the TD process with the PPBES, by documenting training strategies, courses, and related resource requirements. The TRAS ties together related acquisition systems for students, instructors, equipment and devices, ammunition, dollars and facilities.

11-83. TADSS
  a. TADSS are developed and acquired to support training at the unit and/or Combat Training Centers (CTC) and within the institutional training base.
  (1) Training aids are instructional aids to enable trainers to conduct and sustain task-based training in lieu of using extensive printed material or equipment. Examples are graphic training aids, models, and displays.
  (2) Training devices are three-dimensional objects and associated computer software developed, fabricated, stand-alone, embedded, or appended and procured specifically for improving the learning process and to usually support the live fire training environment. Examples are emplaced mines, Opposing Forces (OPFOR) weapons, pyrotechnics for training, and inert training rounds.
  (3) Simulators are devices, computer programs, or systems that allow simulation of an essential training task and allow for skill development in that task by providing repeatable drills in a controlled assessed training situation. They include physical models, mock ups, and simulations of weapon systems that replicate major training requirements. Examples include flight simulators, HMMWV Egress Trainer (HEAT), Conduct of Fire Trainers (COFT) with upgrades for canister munitions, and Virtual Combat Convoy Trainer (VCCT).
  (4) Simulations are the representation of salient features, operations, or environment of a system, subsystem, or scenario that usually supports the constructive environment. Examples are Brigade-

HOW THE ARMY RUNS

Battalion Battle Simulation (BBS), Corps Battle Simulation (CBS), and Joint Simulation Training.

b. TADSS are categorized as either system or non-system.

(1) System TADSS are designed for use with a system, family-of-systems or item of equipment, including sub-assemblies and components. They may be stand-alone, embedded, or appended. They are funded (HQDA DCS, G-8, Equipping Program Evaluation Group (PEG)) and documented as part of the weapon system they support. The weapon system PM is responsible to procure the system TADSS.

(2) Non-Standard Training Aids, Devices, Simulations, and Simulators (NSTD) are designed to support general military training and non-system specific training requirements. They are funded (HQDA DCS, G-3/5/7, Training PEG) and documented as a separate program under the Training Mission Area (TMA). The PEO Simulation, Training, and Instrumentation is normally responsible to procure and develop non-system TADSS. Stand-alone CDDs and CPDs, with supporting STRAPs, are developed by the TNGDEV.

Section XVI
Agile Acquisition

11-84. Network Integration Agile Acquisition Process

a. Acquisition, testing, assessment/evaluation, and fielding processes typically have taken several years to complete, which can take longer than several technology maturation cycles. Funding and timelines for Network-related programs were rarely aligned. Capabilities were fielded piecemeal and integration with existing technology was sometimes left to the user. Therefore, many recently fielded systems did not benefit from the latest mature technologies nor did they respond to the latest Army capabilities needs. This approach greatly challenged interoperability and training. The Army, however, had implemented improved business practices, namely Software Blocking (SB) and Unit Set Fielding (USF) to address specific problems, but did not holistically focus on the Army Enterprise Network.

b. To achieve its network objectives, the Army is radically changing the way it delivers capability to its operating forces from start (need or gap identification) to finish (fielding and sustainment). Consistent with Public Law 111-84 (National Defense Authorization Act (NDAA) FY2010), Section 804, and the OSD Report to Congress, the VCSA directed the ARSTAF to implement agile business solutions that would address current network acquisition shortcomings and bring efficiency, effectiveness, and affordability to these otherwise burdensome processes. Successful implementation of this process will result in early and continuous delivery of needed capabilities to leaders and Soldiers throughout the force with particular focus on the BCT. In order to ensure that new capability solutions are integrated with the network, constant adaptability and frequent changes are essential due to the swift maturation cycle of information technology and the rapid reaction required by the Army.

c. Two ongoing initiatives, one DOD and one Army, are being leveraged to improve acquisition efficiency and support rapidly evolving warfighter requirements. First, the Army is actively pursuing NDAA §804 initiatives to reform its cumbersome requirements, resourcing, and acquisition processes. Under NDAA §804, the Army intends to integrate its governance and management structure to accelerate decision-making and to transition from a program-centric approach to a capability-centric approach – all in order to speed delivery of needed capabilities to the user. Second, concurrent with NDAA §804 reforms, the Army is instituting the Agile Process to enable rapid technology insertion. The Agile Process focuses primarily on meeting identified and prioritized capability gaps by integrating emerging technological (materiel) solutions through iterative, pre-defined, predictable windows for testing and insertion that are aligned with Army force generation.

d. The Army Agile Process, depicted in Figure 11-10, consists of seven phases that start with the continuous evaluation and identification of potential capability gaps and capability solutions; includes an NIE by the BMC leaders/Soldiers within a field environment at Fort Bliss, Texas, and White Sands Missile Range (WSMR), New Mexico; and concludes with an acquisition/fielding decision. The seven phases of the Agile Process are:

(1) Phase 0–Define Gaps and Requirements
(2) Phase I–Solicit Potential Solutions
(3) Phase II–Candidate Assessment
(4) Phase III–Evaluation Preparation
(5) Phase IV–Integration Rehearsal (IR)
(6) Phase V–Integration Evaluation (IE)

MATERIAL SYSTEM RESEARCH, DEVELOPMENT, AND ACQUISITION MANAGEMENT

(7) Phase VI–Implementation Plan

e. In Phase 0, which will occur two times per year, TRADOC will define near-term requirements, using existing ONS, JEONs, JUONs, COCOM Integrated Priority Lists (IPL), existing requirements documents, and relevant assessments from ongoing and past analyses. In coordination with HQDA CIO/G-6 Cyber Directorate, TRADOC will then prioritize the requirements, taking into account technology maturity and cost. In Phase I, the Army will solicit potential solutions, followed by validating their maturity and recommending a way forward for each in Phase II. The Army will then prepare to and conduct assessments of systems and concepts through a Network Integration Rehearsal (NIR) (Phases III and IV). Subsequently, the Army will use a full NIE, executed by BMC, to generate user recommendations regarding system/concept continuance and DOTMLPF-P changes necessary to integrate systems/concepts into units and operations (Phase V). In Phase VI, the Army will finalize acquisition, resourcing, and fielding strategies for the selected solutions.

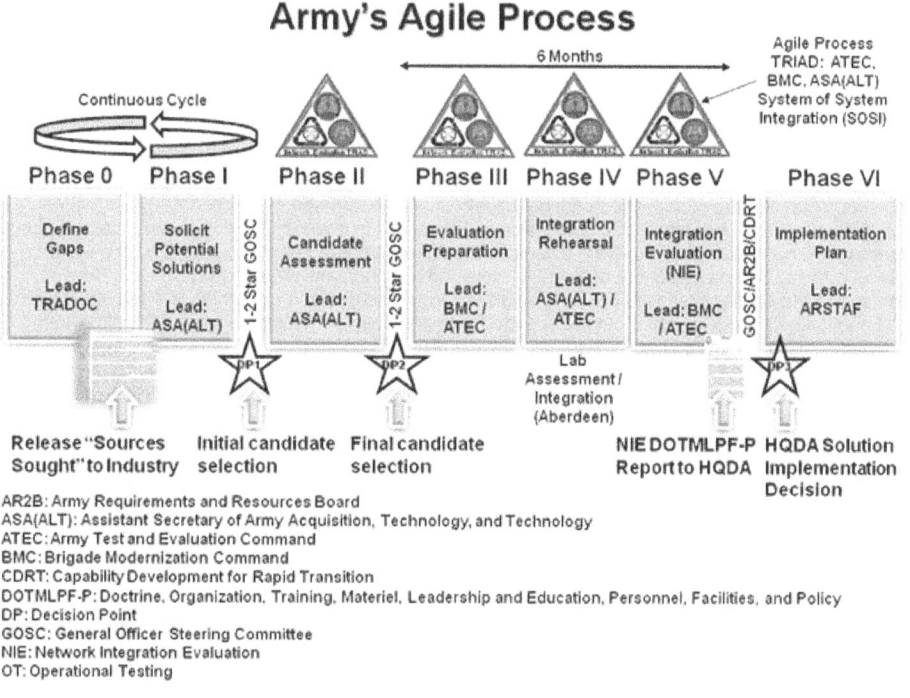

Figure 11-10. Army Agile Process

f. There are three network capability solution types to be assessed/evaluated during NIE; these include:

(1) <u>Type I</u> – Acquisition Programs (Systems Under Testing (SUT)) – capabilities ready for formal Technical Field Tests (TFT), <u>Force</u> Development Tests and Experimentation (FDTE), and OT to inform an acquisition decision.

(2) <u>Type II</u> – developing capabilities (Systems Under Evaluation (SUE)) – Theater Provided Equipment (TPE), rapid equipping initiatives to satisfy ONSs/JUONs, or existing acquisition programs with sufficient maturity levels (technology, integration, and manufacturing) to accelerate.

(3) <u>Type III</u> – emerging capabilities SUEs – next generation war-fighting technologies that have the potential for enhancement and could fill a known gap or improve current capabilities.

g. There are three core stakeholder organizations supporting the NIE. These include HQDA ASA(ALT),

HOW THE ARMY RUNS

TRADOC, and ATEC. The core stakeholders, in coordination with the ARSTAF, are the core team tasked by the VCSA with leading and executing the Agile Process lifecycle through Phase V. The core stakeholders plan and execute semi-annual integrated network test and evaluation events with resulting acquisition and DOTMLPF recommendations provided to Army leadership for networked and non-networked capability gap solutions.

11-85. Capability Set Management (CSM)

a. To achieve its Network objectives, the Army is radically changing the way it delivers capability to its operating forces, from start to finish. Until now, the Army has developed and fielded Network technologies asynchronously. Funding and timelines for network-related programs were rarely, if ever, aligned. Capabilities were fielded piecemeal and integration with existing technology was largely the responsibility of the user. In addition, in previous years, the Army pursued two network modernization tracks—the cancelled Future Combat System program and its follow-on Early Infantry Brigade Combat Team effort (which included only a small slice of the Army's BCTs) and another non-integrated strategy for the rest of the force.

b. In a rapidly changing operating environment, the Army must have the means to quickly evaluate and deliver resourced DOTMLPF-P solutions into the hands of Soldiers. The Army has created the adaptive capabilities process, which involves "buying less, more often." By doing this, the Army avoids equipping the entire force with equipment that often becomes obsolete in two or three years and can quickly get solutions in the hands of Soldiers of those units with the greatest need – deploying and global response force brigades. The Army meets Soldiers' requirements for adaptive capabilities by buying fewer quantities (only for Army force generation designated priority units), and seeking incremental improvements within regular defined periods (usually in two-year increments).

c. The Army is shelving this inadequate, disjointed process in favor of CSM. Treating tactical network capability as a cohesive portfolio, CSM evaluates the current operational environment, then designs a suite of systems and equipment to answer the projected requirements for a two-year period. Any elements of the set not already in the Army inventory then procured and everything is distributed together throughout a combat formation, from the brigade command post to the commander on the move to the dismounted Soldier – a significant departure from the previous practice of fielding systems individually and often to only one element of the operational force at a time (e.g., companies, battalions, or brigades). Within CSM, the Army will continue to upgrade, improve, and recapitalize existing capabilities and divest those capabilities deemed redundant or no longer required.

d. Especially significant, CSM is aligned with Army force generation requirements. CSs will go only to those units in the queue for deployment (the Army will no longer commit to acquisition objectives that cover the entire force) and will be fielded earlier in the force generation cycle so that forces are properly prepared for any possible deployment. The Army will buy less at any given instance, but buy more often in order to ensure that the force has the right capability at the right time.

e. CSM allows the Army to synchronize network development and fielding with the POM cycle, as well, thereby ensuring that the right amount of funding is in place at the right time for all components of the CS. By fully aligning fiscal resources, development and fielding, the Army ultimately will field a greater depth of capability to more formations than was possible before. For Capability Set 13/14, the increase will be fivefold; in that two-year period, the Army expects to fulfill the Network requirements of at least 20 brigades instead of just four, exponentially multiplying operational effectiveness.

f. CSM is a key element of the Army's transition to a BCT modernization strategy to build a versatile mix of mobile, networked, and combat effective brigades. These activities will support the accelerated delivery of select capabilities to the current force, reducing operational risk prior to delivery.

11-86. CDRT

a. The CDRT is the Army's mechanism designed to transition rapid acquisition systems and technologies proven in combat to the Army's deliberate Defense Acquisition Management System (DAS). During recent combat operations the Army developed new materiel systems and non-materiel capabilities to meet emerging requirements. Many of those that worked well in the operational theaters have value to the Army in the long term. To identify those valuable capabilities, the HQDA DCS, G-3/5/7 Current and Future Warfighting Capabilities Division (DAMO-CIC) and TRADOC ARCIC A&ID, Accelerated Capabilities Division (ACD), developed the CDRT process, formerly known as "Spiral to the Army at Large". CDRT is a quarterly assessment that identifies the very best non-standard materiel and non-

MATERIAL SYSTEM RESEARCH, DEVELOPMENT, AND ACQUISITION MANAGEMENT

materiel insertion the Army should incorporate into the future force. The goal is to significantly reduce the time needed to field selected systems or capabilities to the operational Army. The process recommends disposition for those capabilities not selected as enduring, either for retention (i.e., sustain) within the operational theaters or for termination of all Army support, saving critical resources. Operational Army unit input, through survey responses, is the basis for the recommendations.

(1) The CDRT eligibility for nomination criteria requires a capability to be operationally mature, in country for a minimum of 120 days, and have a complete Forward Operational Assessment (FOA). The intent of the selection criteria is to qualify each materiel system for entry into the formal JCIDS process at a later stage, either beginning with a CDD at DAS MS B or a CPD at MS C, bypassing the DAS pre-system acquisition activity. The CDRT process does not obviate the JCIDS process for materiel systems, but leverages a provision in JCIDS that provides for a Military Utility Assessment (MUA) to enable entry into the process at a later stage if a system has performed successfully in an operational environment. Once the HQDA AROC approves the CDRT recommendations, DAMO-CIC (through TRADOC headquarters) tasks a TRADOC CoE or other CAPDEV to produce the required JCIDS documentation. The Army incorporates non-materiel capabilities identified as enduring through standard DOTmLPF-P development processes and procedures. For example, an organizational capability change would require consideration by the Force Design Update (FDU) process.

(2) HQDA DCS, G-3/5/7 and DCS, G-8 are critical in processing JCIDS documentation and ensuring funding is aligned across the POM. A system is considered an acquisition program once it has a validated JCIDS document (CDD or CPD), a DAS MS decision, and funding in the base budget.

b. The TRADOC ACD and HQDA DCS, G-3/5/7 have concluded 14 iterations of the CDRT process to date, with iteration 15 in the final validation/approval phase, iteration 16 in the unit survey step, and iteration 17 gathering nominations. The process has evolved since 2004, from an annual consideration of only materiel systems to a semi-annual process considering both materiel systems and non-materiel capabilities, and now a quarterly overlapping cycle. Through iteration 14, the CDRT process has considered 657 capabilities (materiel and non-materiel); 44 (plus 16 merged into other programs) selected as enduring; 167 terminated; and 430 sustained in theater. Examples of acquisition programs include the IED Route Clearance Package, the Armored Security Vehicle (ASV), and the Common Remote Operated Weapons System (CROWS). Examples of non-materiel capabilities approved include the Weapons Intelligence Team (WIT), the Joint Trauma Analysis and Prevention of Injury in Combat Program (JTAPIC), and the most recent, the Company Intelligence Support Team (COIST) Training. The Army continues to conduct CDRT iterations, beginning a new iteration every three months. Iterations require six months to complete – resulting in overlapping iterations. The Army institutionalized the process in AR 750-1, AR 71-9, and TR 71-20.

c. The CDRT process is an example of generating force responsiveness to operational Army requirements by reducing the time to meet Army requirements for materiel and non-materiel capabilities. The process identifies, through operational Army unit input, those systems working well in operational theaters and speeds the process to get them into the hands of Soldiers throughout the Army for the long term.

Section XVII
Acquisition Resource Management

11-87. Appropriations
The "color of money," or kind of appropriation, is an important factor in system acquisition management. An appropriation provides limited amounts of budget authority that agencies may obligate during a specific time period for the purposes specified in the legislation that provides the appropriation. Budget Authority provides the power to obligate the U.S. government to pay a bill. In general, a particular appropriation can be expended only for specified activities and budget authority cannot be moved from one appropriation to another without transfer authority. Acquisition management involves at least two to four appropriations. The two-year RDT&E appropriation provides funds for research, design engineering, prototype production, LRIP for OT, and T&E activities in the course of developing a materiel system. The three-year procurement appropriation provides funds for procuring materiel that has been fully tested and type classified. Procurement funds are used to procure LRIP for initial spares, support, and training equipment. The one-year Operations and Maintenance, Army (OMA) appropriation, provides funds for

HOW THE ARMY RUNS

retiring and retrograding the old equipment being replaced; for repairing systems after fielding; for fuel and ammunition for training and operations; for periodic system rebuild; for training both system operators and maintainers, except new equipment training; and, in general, anything else to keep a system in the field and operating. Some systems may require five-year MILCON appropriated funds for the construction of special facilities required for fielding that system. The period of years identified for each appropriation refers to the time period that the appropriation is available to be obligated.

11-88. Program and Budget Process

Funds of the correct amount and appropriation must be planned and programmed into the Army budget, in general, two years before they are needed. In the program and budget process, funding requests are initiated and reviewed annually. Congress appropriates funds for RDT&E (Title IV, DOD Appropriations Act) and Procurement (Title III, DOD Appropriations Act), as part of the annual Defense Appropriation Act. The RDT&E and procurement budget requests must first be approved by DOD, submitted to Congress by the President, and then be authorized and appropriated in two separate Congressional actions before any money can be spent. In the year of budget execution, the Army may reprogram funds, except for Congressional-interest items, within an appropriation subject to budget authority dollar limits or in excess of dollar limits with prior Congressional approval. Below $10 million of RDT&E and below $20 million of procurement may be reprogrammed from a lower priority program to a higher priority program without prior Congressional approval (see Table 11-1). The PM is responsible for planning and programming the RDT&E and procurement funds to cover a program, and the MILCON funds, when required. The PM is responsible for programming all life-cycle system costs for the system, while the system remains under his management control. This includes programming for out-year sustaining resources, as well as RDT&E and procurement. Once the management responsibility transitions to the AMC LCMCs, it becomes that command's responsibility to continue the depot-level sustaining program. The field user Army command is responsible to program day-to-day system below-depot operational support. The field user Army command is responsible for planning and programming of OMA funds needed to ensure continued readiness of the fielded system. Responsibility for planning and programming funds for product improvements and sustaining supply spare parts is complex and divided between the LCMCs and the field Army command.

11-89. RDT&E Appropriation Activities

To assist in the overall planning, programming, budgeting, and managing of the various R&D activities, the RDT&E appropriation is divided into seven R&D budget activities. These categories are used throughout DOD. The current RDT&E budget activities are as follows:

   a. Budget Activity 1 – Basic Research. Basic research includes all efforts and experimentation directed toward increasing fundamental knowledge and understanding in those fields of the physical, engineering, environmental, and life sciences related to long term national security needs.

   b. Budget Activity 2 – Applied Research. This activity translates promising basic research into solutions for broadly defined military needs, short of development projects. This type of effort may vary from systematic mission-directed research, which is beyond that in Budget Activity 1, to sophisticated breadboard hardware, study, programming, and planning efforts that establish the initial feasibility and practicality of proposed solutions to technological challenges. These funds are normally applied during the MSA phase of the DAS life-cycle.

   c. Budget Activity 3 – Advanced Technology Development. This activity includes all efforts that have moved into the development and integration of hardware for field experiments and tests. The results of this type of effort are proof of technological feasibility and assessment of operability and production rather than the development of hardware for Service use. These funds are normally applied during the TD phase of the DAS life-cycle.

MATERIAL SYSTEM RESEARCH, DEVELOPMENT, AND ACQUISITION MANAGEMENT

Table 11-1. Prior Approval Threshold Reprogramming Levels*

APPN	CUM INC	CUM DEC	Level of Control	OBL AVAIL
RDT&E	$10M or more or 20% of the program base amount whichever is less	$10M or more or 20% of the program base amount whichever is less	Program Element	2 Years
PROC	$20M or more or 20% of the program base amount whichever is less	$20M or more or 20% of the program base amount whichever is less	Budget Line Item	3 Years
OMA	$15M or more	$15M or more	Budget Activity	1 Year
MILCON	Any increase exceeding 25% or $2M to a project whichever is less	No Congressional restrictions	Project	5 Years

* See DOD Financial Management Regulation (FMR) 7000.14-R Vol. 3 Chapter 6 and 7 for details

    d. Budget Activity 4 – Advanced Component Development and Prototypes. This budget activity includes all efforts necessary to evaluate integrated technologies in as realistic an operating environment as possible, to assess the performance or cost reduction potential of advanced technology. These funds are normally applied during TD, but could be applied throughout the acquisition life-cycle.
    e. Budget Activity 5 – System Development and Demonstration. This budget activity includes those projects in system development and demonstration, but not yet approved for LRIP at MS C. These funds are normally applied during the EMD phase of the DAS life-cycle.
    f. Budget Activity 6 – RDT&E Management Support. Includes efforts directed toward support of RDT&E installations or operations required for use in general R&D and not allocable to specific R&D missions. Included are technical integration efforts, technical information activities, space programs, major test ranges, test facilities and general test instrumentation, target development, support of operational tests, international cooperative R&D, and R&D support.
    g. Budget Activity 7 – Operational System Development. This activity includes R&D efforts directed toward development, engineering, and test of changes to fielded systems or systems already in procurement which alter the performance envelopes. Operational system development may include OT costs.

11-90. Procurement Appropriations
Procurement is used to finance investment items, and covers all costs integral and necessary to deliver a useful end item intended for operational use or inventory. The Army budget includes five separate procurement appropriations:
    a. Aircraft Appropriation. Aircraft procurement includes the procurement of aircraft, aircraft modifications, spares, repair parts, and related support equipment and facilities.
    b. Missile Appropriation. Missile procurement includes the procurement of missiles, missiles modifications, spares, repair parts, and related support equipment and facilities.
    c. Weapons and Tracked Combat Vehicles (WTCV) Appropriation. WTCV procurement includes tracked and combat vehicles, weapons, other combat vehicles, and repair parts.
    d. Ammunition Appropriation. Ammunition procurement includes procurement of ammunition end items, ammunition production base support, and ammunition demilitarization.
    e. Other Procurement, Army (OPA) Appropriation. OPA covers four major categories:
        (1) Tactical and support vehicles
        (2) Communications and electronic equipment

HOW THE ARMY RUNS

(3) Other support equipment
(4) Initial spares

11-91. MILCON Appropriation
MILCON funds the cost of major and minor construction projects such as facilities. Major or specified military construction projects exceed $2.0M and require congressional line-item authorization. Unspecified military construction projects are $2.0M or less, but can be increased to $3M if the project is intended to correct a life, health, or safety deficiency. Each military department receives an appropriation for minor military construction. The military department Secretary controls expenditure of minor military construction funds and is required to notify Congress of minor military construction projects that exceed $750K. A 21-day waiting period is required after notification before work begins. Project costs include architecture and engineering services, construction design, real property acquisition costs, and land acquisition costs necessary to complete the construction project. The OMA appropriation can be used to fund unspecified minor military construction projects up to $750K or up to $1.5M, if the project is intended to correct a life, health, or safety deficiency.

11-92. Operations and Maintenance Appropriation (OMA)
OMA finances those things that derive benefits for a limited period of time, such as expenses, rather than investments. Examples are Headquarters operations, civilian salaries, travel, fuel, minor construction projects of $750K or less, expenses of operational military forces, training and education, recruiting, depot maintenance, purchases from Defense Working Capital Funds, and base operations support.

11-93. Capability Portfolio Reviews (CPR)
a. On February 22, 2010, the SECARMY directed the USA and the VCSA to implement a CPR pilot process to conduct an Army-wide, all components revalidation of the operational value of Army requirements within and across capability portfolios to existing joint and Army warfighting concepts. The intent of this revalidation is to eliminate redundancies and to ensure that funds are properly programmed, budgeted, and executed against the programs that yield the most value to the Army.

b. CPRs focused on two categories - materiel CPRs and non-materiel CPRs. Materiel CPRs include: Tactical Wheeled Vehicles; Precision Fires; Air and Missile Defense; Combat Vehicle Modernization; Radios; The Network; Engineer; Soldier Systems; Intelligence, Surveillance, and Reconnaissance (ISR); Aviation (Rotary, Fixed, UAS); Information Technology; and Training Ammunition. Non-materiel CPRs include; Installation Management; Work Force Composition; Army Training Strategy; Sustainment Accounts; and organizational Structure.

c. The review process revalidates the requirement in each portfolio using a wide-range of criteria, including: CCDR requests; wartime lessons learned; the ability to support the Army force generation model; the potential for leveraging emerging technologies; and affordability.

d. The output of the two-phased (session) CPR process is actionable recommendations to the SECARMY to make decisions that established the current Army FY POM priorities for investment in research and development, acquisition, and life-cycle sustainment, to include force structure and training across each Army capability portfolio. HQDA, DCS G-3/5/7 is the lead agency for CPR coordination and synchronization.

(1) Phase #1 – The VCSA chairs session #1. The purpose is revalidation of the operational value of Army requirements to include cost, schedule, performance, life-cycle sustainability, and the Army's plan to manage the totality of the requirement. The product is actionable recommendations that can be addressed by Army senior leadership during phase 2.

(2) Phase #2 – The USA, as the Army Chief Management Officer, chairs session #2. The purpose is to address follow-on analysis from phase #1 and the programmatics (cost, schedule, performance, life-cycle sustainment) implications of the recommendations presented. The product is actionable recommendations to the SECARMY to validate, modify, or terminate R&D investment, procurement, and/or life-cycle sustainment requirements within capability portfolio accounts for the current POM in development based on the results of the CPRs.

e. The analysis that has resulted from the CPRs conducted under the program has clearly highlighted the utility of this process in building an effective and affordable modernization strategy. The resulting recommendations will continue to assist the SECARMY in establishing future priorities for investment, research, development, acquisition, and life-cycle sustainment. The SECARMY will continue to rely on

MATERIAL SYSTEM RESEARCH, DEVELOPMENT, AND ACQUISITION MANAGEMENT

this process to help him make informed decisions on behalf of the Army.

f. CPR's operate concurrently with, but do not supplant the authority of, the AROC, ASARC, or CSB forums, previously discussed.

11-94. Research, Development, and Acquisition Plan (RDAP)

a. Overview. The Army RDAP is a 15-year plan for the development and production of technologies and materiel to advance Army modernization. Modernization is "the continuous process of integrating new doctrine, training, organization, and equipment to develop and field warfighting capabilities for the total force." Under ideal circumstances, Army modernization would be fully supported by an unconstrained RDAP. However, the realities of limited resources restrict modernization to those efforts that are both technically and fiscally achievable. The RDAP, therefore, is the result of a process that converts the Army's unconstrained planning environment into a constrained RDAP that maximizes warfighting capabilities and supporting infrastructure requirements within limited resources.

b. The RDAP assumes the form of a 1-N priority list of RDT&E and procurement program packages called Management Decision Packages (MDEP), with funding streams for the entire 15-year planning period. An MDEP represents a particular program, function, or organization and displays the resources (dollars, civilian, and military manpower) needed to achieve an intended goal. An MDEP may receive its resources (funding streams) from any number of appropriations; the RDAP, however, includes only the RDT&E and procurement funding streams of its MDEPs. There is no limitation to the number of commands to which the resources of an MDEP may be assigned. The RDAP is recorded in and represented by the HQDA DCS, G-8 RDA database.

c. RDA Database. The HQDA DCS, G-8 RDA database represents the RDAP. The principal elements of the RDA database, MDEPs, are grouped by JCA. A JCA is a set of MDEPs that represent a common function on the battlefield or a common activity of the supporting Army infrastructure (e.g., aviation, ammunition). JCAs were formerly called budget operating systems (BOS). In fact, JCA data is still named BOS in Army databases. Most JCAs are managed by a HQDA DCS, G-8 division. The division chief (known as the JCA manager), assisted by his staff and his ASA(ALT) counterpart, determines required capabilities for each of the MDEPs within his or her JCA. The Equipping (EE) PEG co-chairs, determine EE PEG priority ranking of MDEPs. The EE PEG prioritization is forwarded to HQDA DCS, G-3/5/7 for Army-wide prioritization.

d. The RDAP is a continual process comprising periodic revisions to the 15-year planning period of the RDA database. The revisions occur during the fiscal year POM/BES cycle. During the POM/BES cycle, the Army adjusts the first five years (FYDP) of the 15-year planning period. These five years are referred to as the POM years. After each cycle, the Army's RDA community adjusts the final nine years, called the Extended Planning Period (EPP), to ensure a smooth and reasonable progression from the POM to EPP. The 15-year planning period of the RDA database moves forward by one year in January annually. For example, the FY15-28 RDAP began in January 2013.

11-95. Program Stability

Achieving early program objective consensus and following a good investment strategy will yield a stable program, clearly showing where we are today and where we want to be when we bring on the new system. To be successful, new systems acquisition programs must be developed and acquired in a timely and economical manner. Life-cycle cost estimates and changes to programs and schedules must be controlled. Changes to programs affecting established goals will be fully documented in the program management documentation, providing the justification for change (e.g., budget cut, design change). After entering the DAS EMD phase, design changes in system components that are meeting the validated requirement are discouraged and must be individually justified. The design should be frozen in sufficient time prior to DT and OT to provide an adequate system support package for testing. Changes to programs as a result of DT/OT must be of the "objective" nature to satisfy the requirement and not a "threshold" type of change, unless it can be demonstrated that the change will not have a significantly negative impact on the cost, schedule, producibility, and ILS aspects of the program.

HOW THE ARMY RUNS

Section XVIII
Summary and References

11-96. Summary
a. This chapter provided a basic introduction to the management process, organization, and structure of the JCIDS and system acquisition management process. Through the chapter description, the reader should have gained an appreciation of the logic of the process, its organization and management, including recent changes. This chapter highlights the current basic DOD and Army policies for capabilities development, materiel systems acquisition, and descriptions of capabilities development and system acquisition managers.

b. Difficult decisions, overseas contingency operations, a scarcity of dollar resources, and honest differences of opinion cause disruptions and delays. It is unlikely that there will be total agreement on the best technical approach to satisfy a need—or, indeed, on the need itself. The annual budget cycle and budget constraints almost ensure that some projects will not be funded at the level desired—if at all. Tests are not always successful. Estimates of time, costs, effectiveness, and technical feasibility are often "wide of the mark" for complex systems. After all, they are estimates that are projected well into the future based on sketchy data. These real-world problems reinforce the fact that capabilities development and system acquisition management are complex tasks of great importance to national defense. Capabilities development and system acquisition can be a wellspring of new and effective weapons systems, where effective management and professionalism can make the difference in overseas contingency operations. As with any activity involving the use of scarce resources to meet organizational goals and objectives, the people involved—the capability developers, acquisition managers and the Soldier users and maintainers—constitute the most vital link to mission accomplishment.

11-97. References
a. 2013 Army Strategic Planning Guidance
b. Army G-8 Standard Operating Procedures (SOP) for Joint Capabilities Integration and Development System (JCIDS) Document Review Staffing and Affordability Assessments, March 2011.
c. Army Materiel Command Logistics Support Activity (LOGSA) Pamphlet 700-3, Total Package Fielding (TPF)
d. Army Regulation 350-1, Army Training and Leader Development, 18 December 2009
e. Army Regulation 5-22, The Army Force Modernization Proponent System, (Rapid Action Revision (RAR), 25 March 2011
f. Army Regulation 525-29, Army Force Generation, 14 March 2011
g. Army Regulation 602-2, Manpower and Personnel Integration (MANPRINT) in the System Acquisition Process, 1 June 2001
h. Army Regulation 700-127, Integrated Logistics Support, 17 July 2008
i. Army Regulation 700-142, Materiel Release, Fielding, and Transfer, 26 March 2008
j. Army Regulation 70-1, Army Acquisition Policy, 22 July 2011
k. Army Regulation 71-9, Warfighting Capabilities Determination, 28 December 2009
l. Army Regulation 73-1, Test and Evaluation Policy, 1 August 2006
m. Army Standard Operating Procedures (SOP) for Agile Capabilities Life-cycle Process, 7 August 2012
n. Capstone Concept for Joint Operations (CCJO), Joint Forces 2020, 10 September 2012
o. CJCS Capability Development Tracking and Management (CDTM) User Manual, version 1.3, June 2011
p. CJCSI 3010.02C, Joint Concept Development and Experimentation (JCD&E), 15 January 2012
q. CJCSI 3170.01H, Joint Capabilities Integration and Development System (JCIDS) 10 January 2012 with supporting JCIDS Manual, 19 January 2012. Manual is found online at https://www.intelink.gov/wiki/JCIDS_Manual
r. CJCSI 5123.01F, Charter of the JROC, 10 January 2012
s. DA Pamphlet 700-142, Instructions for Materiel Release, Fielding, and Transfer, June 2010
t. DA Pamphlet 700-56, Logistics Supportability Planning and Procedures in Army Acquisition, 5 December 2005
u. DA Pamphlet 70-3, Army Acquisition Procedures, 28 January 2008
v. DA Pamphlet 73-1, Test and Evaluation in Support of Systems Acquisition, 30 May 2003

MATERIAL SYSTEM RESEARCH, DEVELOPMENT, AND ACQUISITION MANAGEMENT

w. Defense Acquisition University (DAU), Introduction to Defense Acquisition Management, 10th Edition, August 2010
x. Defense Strategic Guidance (DSG), January 2012
y. DOD Directive 5000.01, The Defense Acquisition Management System,12 May 2003 (certified current as of 20 November 2007)
z. DOD Directive 5000.52, Defense Acquisition Education, Training and Career Development Program, 25 October 1991
aa. DOD Directive 5000.71, Rapid Fulfillment of CCDR Urgent Operational Needs, 24 August 2012
bb. DOD Directive-Type Memorandum (DTM) 09-027, Implementation of the Weapon Systems Acquisition Reform Act of 2009 (Public Law 111-23), 4 December 2009
cc. DOD Instruction 5000.02, Operation of the Defense Acquisition Management System, 2 December 2008
dd. DODD 7045.20, Capability Portfolio Management, 25 September 2008
ee. Federal Acquisition Streamlining Act of 1994, 13 October 1994
ff. HQ TRADOC, ARCIC Memorandum, Subject: Implementing Cost Benefit Analysis (CBA) Guidance for JCIDS Capabilities Documents, 15 June 2012
gg. HQ TRADOC, Army Capabilities Integration Center (ARCIC) Alternate Format Initial Capabilities Document (ICD) Instruction Guide, version 3.0, 16 August 2012
hh. HQ TRADOC, Army Capabilities Integration Center (ARCIC) Capability Development Document (CDD) Writer's Guide, version 3.31, 13 May2013
ii. HQ TRADOC, Army Capabilities Integration Center (ARCIC) Capability Production Document (CPD) Writer's Guide, version 3.41, 13 May 2013
jj. HQ TRADOC, Army Capabilities Integration Center (ARCIC) DOTmLPF Integrated Capabilities Recommendation (DICR) Guide, 25 May 2011
kk. HQ, TRADOC Memorandum, Subject: Doctrine 2015 Guidance, 23 August 2011
ll. HQDA (G37 DAMO-CIC), Capabilities and AROC Management System User's Guide, 23 March 2010
mm. HQDA DCS, G-3/5/7, ECOP User's Guide, version 2.3, 20 July 2011
nn. HQDA DCS, G-8 Army Equipping Strategy, 27 July 2011
oo. HQDA DCS, G-8 Memorandum, Subject: Conduct of Review and Affordability Assessments for Joint Capabilities Integration and Development System (JCIDS) and other Emerging Equipment Requirement Documents, 4 March 2011
pp. HQDA G-3/5/7, The 2012 Army Campaign Plan, 1 June 2012
qq. HQDA, 2010 Army Science and Technology Master Plan, 14 July 2010
rr. HQDA, 2013 Army Posture Statement
ss. HQDA, 2013 Weapon Systems Handbook
tt. HQDA, Assistant Secretary of the Army for Financial Management and Comptroller (ASA(FM&C) Memorandum, Subject: Cost-Benefit Analysis Guidance and Training, 1 February 2010
uu. HQDA, Deputy Assistant Secretary of the Army Cost and Economics (DASA(CE)) Memorandum, Subject: U.S Army Cost-Benefit Analysis Guide, version 1.0, 12 January 2010
vv. HQDA, The United States 2014 Army Equipment Modernization Plan, 13May 2013
ww. JCS J-8 Force Structure, Resources, and Assessments Directorate, Capabilities-Based Assessment (C-BA) User's Guide, version 3, March 2009
xx. JROC Memorandum (JROCM), Subject: JROC, and JCIDS Changes, 3 February 2012
yy. National Defense Strategy (NDS), 16 June 2008
zz. National Military Strategy (NMS), 8 February 2011
aaa. National Security Strategy (NSS), May 2010
bbb. Office of the Under Secretary of the Army and Vice Chief of Staff, Army Memorandum, Subject: Cost-Benefit Analysis to Support Army Enterprise Decision Making, 30 December 2009
ccc. Office of the Under Secretary of the Army and Vice Chief of Staff, Army Memorandum, Subject: Secretary of the Army-Designated Capability Portfolio Reviews (Expanded Army Requirements Oversight Council) Terms of Reference, 22 February 2010
ddd. SECARMY Memorandum, Subject: Army Directive 2010-07, Non-Standard Equipment Interim Policy, 4 August 2010
eee. SECARMY Memorandum, Subject: The SECARMY's Capability Portfolio Review Strategy, 22 February 2010

fff. The Defense Acquisition Workforce Improvement Act (DAWIA), Title 10 USC Sections 1701-1764, Defense Acquisition Workforce Improvement Act of 1990, as amended by Section 808, Public Law (PL) No. 106-398, National Defense Authorization Act for Fiscal Year 2001, October 30, 2000: Section 824, PL No. 107-107, December 28, 2001

ggg. TRADOC Army Capabilities Integration Center (ARCIC), Capabilities-Based Assessment Guide, Version 3.1, 10 May 2010

hhh. TRADOC Pamphlet 525-3-0, The U.S. Army Capstone Concept (ACC), 19 December 2012

iii. TRADOC Pamphlet 525-3-1, The U.S. Army Operating Concept (AOC) 2016-2028, version 1.0, 19 August 2010

jjj. TRADOC Regulation 350-70, Army Learning Policy and Systems, 8 December 2011

kkk. TRADOC Regulation 71-20, Concept Development, Capabilities Determination, and Capabilities Integration, 23 February 2011

lll. U.S. Army War College, How the Army Runs: A Senior Leader Reference Handbook, 2011-2012

mmm. USD(AT&L) Memorandum, Subject: Configuration Steering Boards, 30 July 2007

nnn. USD(AT&L) Memorandum, Subject: Prototyping and Competition, 19 September 2007

ooo. Weapon Systems Acquisition Reform Act of 2009 (Public Law 111-23), 22 May 2009

LOGISTICS

Chapter 12

Logistics

Army sustainment forces provide unique support to the Joint Forces Commander and enable freedom of action across the range of military operations. Therefore, during this austere fiscal environment and known strength reductions, we must continue to provide sustainment capabilities for Globally Integrated Operations.

Our decisions must balance the essential Force Structure, Modernization, and Readiness needs within the Total Army to support both Conventional and/or Special Operations Forces for any mission area. We must invest in and advocate for essential capabilities to provide equipment, infrastructure, and training to guarantee success.

What the LOG Nation has done over the past ten years is nothing short of brilliant. The American Army and other services are the best-fed, best-equipped, best-maintained military in the history of the world.

LTG Raymond Mason, Deputy Chief of Staff, G-4

Section I
Introduction

12-1. Chapter Content
This chapter provides an executive overview of the nature and structure of the Army's national and theater logistics systems and includes: key concepts and definitions; the principles of logistics; selected logistic terms; and the Army's national logistics organizations' roles and responsibilities – Assistant Secretary of the Army (Acquisition, Logistics, and Technology) ASA(ALT), Army G-4, Army G-8, and Army Materiel Command (AMC). The chapter underscores other national logistics organizations and Department of Defense (DOD) agencies that directly impact Army sustainment: U.S. Army Corps of Engineers (USACE); U.S. Army Combined Arms Support Command (CASCOM); the Army and Air Force Exchange Service (AAFES); Defense Logistics Agency (DLA); and the Defense Contract Management Activity (DCMA).

12-2. Key Concepts and Definitions
   a. Fundamentals of Sustainment. For the Army, sustainment is the provision of logistics, personnel services, and health service support necessary to maintain operations until successful mission completion (ADP 4-0). This is accomplished through the integration of national and global resources and ensures Army forces are physically available and properly equipped, at the right place and time, to support the Combatant Commander (CCDR). The concept leverages multinational and Host Nation Support (HNS), Operational Contract Support (OCS), and other available capabilities to reduce overburdening military resources and at the same time maintaining a quality Army. Army sustainment is based on an integrated process (e.g., people, systems, materiel, health services, and other support) inextricably linking sustainment to operations. The concept focuses on building a combat ready Army, delivering it to the CCDR as part of the joint force, and sustaining its combat power across the depth of the operational area and with unrelenting endurance.
   b. Logistics. Logistics is planning and executing the movement and support of forces. Logistics involves both military art and science. Knowing when and how to accept risk, prioritizing a myriad of requirements, and balancing limited resources all require military art while understanding equipment capabilities incorporates military science. Logistics integrates strategic, operational, and tactical support of deployed forces while scheduling the mobilization and deployment of additional forces and materiel. Army logistics include the following:
   (1) Maintenance. Maintenance is all actions taken to retain materiel in a serviceable condition or to restore it to serviceability. The Army's two levels of maintenance are field maintenance and sustainment

HOW THE ARMY RUNS

maintenance (ATTP 4-33). Maintenance is necessary for endurance and performed at the tactical through strategic levels of war.

(a) Field maintenance is repair and return to user and is generally characterized by on-(or near) system maintenance, often utilizing line replaceable unit, component replacement, battle damage assessment, repair, and recovery (ATTP 4-33). It is focused on returning a system to an operational status. Field level maintenance is not limited to remove and replace, but also provides adjustment, alignment, and fault/failure diagnoses. Field maintenance also includes battlefield damage and repair tasks performed by either the crew or support personnel to maintain a system in an operational state.

(b) Sustainment maintenance is generally characterized as "off system" and "repair rear" (ATTP 4-33) The intent is to perform commodity-oriented repairs on all supported items to one standard that provides a consistent and measurable level of reliability. Off-system maintenance consists of overhaul and emanufacturing activities designed to return components, modules, assemblies, and end items to the supply system or to units, resulting in extended or improved operational life expectancies.

(2) Transportation Operations. Army transportation units play a key role in facilitating endurance. Transportation units move sustainment from ports to points of need and retrograde materiel as required. Transportation operations encompass the wide range of capabilities needed to allow joint and Army commanders to conduct operations. Important transportation functions are movement control, intermodal operations (terminal and mode), and container management.

(a) Movement control is the dual process of committing allocated transportation assets and regulating movements according to command priorities to synchronize distribution flow over lines of communications to sustain land forces. Movement control balances requirements against capabilities and requires continuous synchronization to integrate military, host nation, and commercial movements by all modes of transportation to ensure seamless transitions from the strategic through the tactical level of an operation. It is a means of providing commanders with situational awareness to control movements in their operational area. Movement control responsibilities are imbedded in an infrastructure that relies on coordination for the planning and execution to ensure transportation assets are utilized efficiently while ensuring lines of communications (LOCs) are deconflicted to support freedom of access for military operations.

(b) Intermodal operations is the process of using multiple modes (air, sea, highway, rail) and conveyances (truck, barge, containers, pallets) to move troops, supplies and equipment through expeditionary entry points and the network of specialized transportation nodes to sustain land forces. It uses movement control to balance requirements against capabilities against capacities to synchronize terminal and mode operations ensuring an uninterrupted flow through the transportation system. It consists of facilities, transportation assets and material handling equipment required to support the deployment and distribution enterprise.

(i) Terminal operations consist of the receiving, processing, and staging of passengers; the receipt, transit storage and marshalling of cargo; the loading and unloading of transport conveyances; and the manifesting and forwarding of cargo and passengers to a destination (JP 4-01.5). Terminal operations are a key element in supporting operational reach and endurance. They are essential in supporting deployment, redeployment and sustainment operations. There are three types of terminals: air, water, and land.

(ii) Mode operations are the execution of movements using various conveyances (e.g., truck, lighterage, railcar, and aircraft) to transport cargo. It includes the administrative, maintenance, and security tasks associated with the operation of the conveyances.

(c) Container management is the process of establishing and maintaining visibility and accountability of all cargo containers moving within the Defense Transportation System (DTS). In theater, container management is conducted by commanders at the operational and tactical levels. The Theater Sustainment Command (TSC) distribution management center coordinates intermodal operations with the movement control battalion at transportation, storage, and distribution nodes. The TSC maintains information on the location and status of containers and flatracks in the theater. The movement control battalion provides essential information on container location, use, flow, and condition. They assist with control of containers by indentifying that they are ready for return to the distribution system. The distribution management center sets priorities for container shipment and diversion.

(3) Supply. Supply is essential for enhancing Soldiers' quality of life. Supply provides the materiel required to accomplish the mission. Supply includes the following classes:

(a) Class I—Subsistence, including health and welfare items.

LOGISTICS

(b) Class II—Clothing, individual equipment, tentage, tool sets and tool kits, hand tools, administrative, and housekeeping supplies and equipment (including maps). This includes items of equipment, other than major items, prescribed in authorization/allowance tables and items of supply (not including repair parts).

(c) Class III—Petroleum, Oils, Lubricants (POL). Petroleum and solid fuels, including bulk and packaged fuels, lubricating oils and lubricants, petroleum specialty products; solid fuels, coal, and related products.

(d) Class IV—Construction Materials, to include installed equipment and all fortification/barrier materials.

(e) Class V—Ammunition of all types (e.g., chemical, radiological, and special weapons), bombs, explosives, mines, fuses, detonators, pyrotechnics, missiles, rockets, propellants, and other associated items.

(f) Class VI—Personal Demand items (e.g., nonmilitary sales items).

(g) Class VII—Major End items. A final combination of end products which is ready for its intended use: (principal item) for example, launchers, tanks, mobile machine shops, vehicles.

(h) Class VIII—Medical Materiel, including medical peculiar repair parts.

(i) Class IX—Repair Parts and components, including kits, assemblies and subassemblies, reparable and nonreparable, required for maintenance support of all equipment.

(j) Class X—Material to support nonmilitary programs such as, agricultural and economic development, not included in Class I through Class IX.

(4) Field Services. Field services maintain combat strength of the force by providing for its basic needs and promoting its health, welfare, morale, and endurance. Field services provide life support functions.

(a) Shower and Laundry. Shower and laundry capabilities provide Soldiers a minimum of one weekly shower and up to 15 pounds of laundered clothing each week (comprising two uniform sets, undergarments, socks, and two towels). The shower and laundry function does not include laundry decontamination support.

(b) Field Feeding. Food preparation is a basic unit function and one of the most important factors in Soldiers' health, morale, and welfare. The standard is to provide Soldiers at all echelons three quality meals per day (AR 30-22). Proper refuse and waste disposal is important to avoid unit signature trails and maintain field sanitation standards.

(c) Water Production and Distribution. Water production and distribution are essential for hydration, sanitation, food preparation, medical treatment, hygiene, construction, and decontamination. The water production is both a field service and a supply function. Quartermaster supply units normally perform purification in conjunction with storage and distribution of potable water.

(d) Clothing and Light Textile Repair. Clothing and light textile repair is essential for hygiene, discipline, and morale purposes. Clean, serviceable clothing is provided as far forward as the brigade area.

(e) Aerial Delivery. Aerial delivery includes parachute packing, air item maintenance, and rigging of supplies and equipment. This function supports airborne insertions, airdrop and airland resupply. It is a vital link in the distribution system and provides the capability of supplying the force even when land LOCs have been disrupted or terrain is too hostile, thus adding flexibility to the distribution system. See FM 4-20.41 for details.

(f) Mortuary Affairs. Mortuary affairs is a broadly based military program to provide for the necessary care and disposition of deceased personnel. The Army is designated as the Executive Agent for the Joint Mortuary Affairs Program (JP 4-06, Mortuary Affairs).

(5) Distribution. Distribution is the primary means to prolong endurance. Distribution is the operational process of synchronizing all elements of the logistics system to deliver the "right things" to the "right place" at the "right time" to support the Geographic Combatant Commander (GCC). Distribution is more than just transportation; it is the integration of supply stockage, transportation resources, and materiel management. Additionally, it is also the process of assigning military personnel to activities, units, or billets (JP 4-0). The distribution system consists of a complex of facilities, installations, methods, and procedures designed to receive, store, maintain, distribute, manage, and control the flow of military materiel between point of receipt into the military system and point of issue to using activities and units.

(a) Global Distribution. The Joint segment of the distribution system is referred to as global distribution. It is defined as the process that synchronizes and integrates the fulfillment of joint requirements with the employment of joint forces (JP 4-09). It provides national resources (personnel and materiel) to support the execution of joint operations.

(b) Theater Distribution. The Army segment of the distribution system is referred to as theater distribution. Theater distribution is the flow of equipment, personnel, and materiel within theater to meet the CCDR's mission. The Theater segment extends from the ports of debarkation or source of supply (in theater) to the points of need (Soldier). It is enabled by a distribution management system that synchronizes and coordinates a complex of networks (physical, communications, information, and resources) and the sustainment warfighting function to achieve responsive support to operational requirements. Distribution management includes the management of transportation and movement control, warehousing, inventory control, order administration, site and location analysis, packaging, data processing, accountability for equipment (materiel management), people, and communications. See ATTP 4-0.1, Army Theater Distribution for details. The distribution management of medical materiel is accomplished by a support team from the Medical Logistics Management Center (MLMC). The MLMC support team collocates with the Distribution Management Center (DMC) of the TSC/Expeditionary Sustainment Command (ESC) to provide the Medical Command (Direct Support) MEDCOM (DS) with visibility and control of all Class VIII.

(c) In-Transit Visibility. In-transit visibility is the ability to track the identity, status, and location of DOD units, and nonunit cargo (excluding bulk petroleum, oils, and lubricants) and passengers, patients and personal property from origin to consignee, or destination across the range of military operations (JP 3-35). This includes force tracking and visibility of convoys, containers/pallets, transportation assets, other cargo, and distribution resources within the activities of a distribution node. In-transit visibility (ITV) provides the distribution manager the ability to assess how well the distribution process is responding to supported force needs. Distribution managers gain and maintain visibility (items, personnel, units, transition hubs, and transport modes) at the earliest practical point in the management process. This allows managers to operate with timely information to effectively assess the status of resources, adapt and rapidly respond to immediate distribution requirements.

(d) Retrograde of Materiel. Another aspect of distribution is retrograde of materiel. Retrograde of materiel is the return of materiel from the owning/using unit back through the distribution system to the source of supply, directed ship-to location, and/or point of disposal (ATTP 4-0.1). Retrograde includes turn-in/classification, preparation, packing, transporting, and shipping. To ensure these functions are properly executed, commanders must enforce supply accountability and discipline and utilize the proper packing materials. Retrograde of materiel can take place as part of theater distribution operations and as part of redeployment operations. Retrograde of materiel must be continuous and not be allowed to build up at supply points/nodes. Early retrograde planning is essential and necessary to preclude the loss of materiel assets, minimize environmental impact, and maximize use of transportation capabilities. Planners must consider environmental issues when retrograding hazardous materiel. Contractor or HNS may be used in the retrograde of materiel. This support is planned and negotiated early in the operation. HNS must be identified early enough to ensure they are properly screened and present no security risk. Leaders at all levels are responsible for the adherence of all policies and safety measures by contractors and HNS. Retrograde materiel flows through the distribution system from the tactical to strategic levels. Retrograde materiel is consolidated at the lowest supply support activity and reported up through the support operations for distribution instructions. When released by the maneuver commander, AMC assumes responsibility for providing disposition instructions, accounting, and shipment of retrograde materiel from the theater. An approved military customs inspection program must be in place prior to redeployment to preclear not only redeployment materiel but also the shipment of battle damaged equipment out of theater. The Theater Army is responsible for establishing the customs inspection program to perform U.S. customs preclearance and United States Department of Agriculture (USDA) inspection and wash down on all materiel retrograded to the United States in accordance with Defense Transportation Regulation (DTR) 4500.9-R.

(6) Operational Contract Support. Operational contract support is the integration of commercial sector support into military operations. This is commanders business, not something relegated to contracting officers. Operational contract support consists of two complementary functions: contract support integration and contractor management. Operational contract support has three types of contract support: theater support, external support, and systems support. See ATTP 4-10 for full discussion on operational contract support.

LOGISTICS

(a) Contract support integration is the process of synchronizing operational planning, requirements development and contracting in support of deployed military forces and other designated organizations in the area of operations (ATTP 4-10). The desired end state of contract support integration actions include:
  (i) Increased effectiveness, efficiencies, and cost savings of the contracting effort.
  (ii) Increased visibility and control of contracting functions.
  (iii) Minimized competition for scarce commercial resources.
  (iv) Increased ability for the Army force commander to enforce priorities of support.
  (v) Decreased and/or mitigated contract fraud.
  (vi) Limiting sole source (vice competitively awarded) and cost-plus contracts (vice fixed price) as much as practical.
  (vii) Enhanced command operational flexibility through alternative sources of support.

(b) Contractor management is the process of managing and integrating contractor personnel and their equipment into military operations (ATTP 4-10). Contractor management includes planning and deployment/redeployment preparation; in-theater management; force protection and security; and executing government support requirements. Integrating the two related operational contract support functions is a complex and challenging process. Multiple organizations are involved in this process including commanders, their primary/special staffs (at the Army Service Component Command (ASCC) down to, and including, battalion levels) and the supporting contracting organizations.

(c) Types of Operational Contract Support. There are three types of operational contract support: theater support contracts; external support contracts; and system support contracts.

  (i) Theater support contracts are a type of contingency contract awarded by contracting officers deployed to the area of operation (AO) serving under the direct contracting authority of the designated head of contracting activity for that particular contingency operation. These contracts, often executed under expedited contracting authority (reduced time frames for posting of contract solicitations; allowing for simplified acquisition procedures for higher dollar contracts, etc.), provide goods, services, and minor construction from commercial sources, normally within the AO. Also important from a contractor management perspective are local national employees that often make up the bulk of the theater support contract workforce.

  (ii) External support contracts are awarded by contracting organizations whose contracting authority does not derive directly from the theater support contracting head(s) of contracting activity or from systems support contracting authorities. External support contracts provide a variety of logistics and other noncombat related services and supply support. External support contracts normally include a mix of U.S. citizens, host nation, and local national contractor employees. Examples of external support contracts are:
    (aa) Service (Air Force, Army, and Navy) civil augmentation programs
    (bb) Special skills contract (staff augmentation, linguists, etc.)
    (cc) DLA prime vendor contract
    (dd) The largest and most commonly known external support contract is the Army's Logistics Civil Augmentation Program (LOGCAP). LOGCAP can provide a complete range of logistics services, including supply services (e.g., storage, warehousing, distribution, etc.) for the nine classes of supplies, but the Services source the actual commodities. LOGCAP does not provide personal services type contracts

  (iii) System support contracts are prearranged contracts awarded by and funded by acquisition program executive officers (PEOs) and project/product management (PM) officers. These contracts provide technical support, maintenance support and, in some cases, Class IX support for a variety of Army weapon and support systems. System support contracts are routinely put in place to provide support to newly fielded weapon systems, including aircraft, land combat vehicles and automated command and control information systems. System support contracting authority and contract management resides with the Army Contracting Command (ACC), while program management authority and responsibility for requirements development and validation resides with the system materiel acquisition program executive officers and project/product management offices. The Army Field Support Brigade (AFSB) assists in systems support integration. System support contractor employees, made up mostly of U.S. citizens, provide support both in garrison and in contingency operations. Operational commanders generally have less influence on the execution of system support contracts than other types of contracted support. For more information on operational contract support see ATTP 4-10 and JP 4-10.

HOW THE ARMY RUNS

(7) Operational Energy. As we operate across the spectrum of missions, we must conserve energy and reduce risk. Energy consumption is a burden on the unit, as well as a huge funding and resource requirement. Most importantly, it leaves our operations vulnerable. Every time we deliver fuel or batteries on the battlefield we put Soldiers at risk. As volumes increase, more storage is required, making our forward operating bases larger and harder to protect. We are examining every way possible to be more effective with our energy use, to employ renewable resources, and lower our costs. All of this will reduce the number of convoys on the roads. But it requires us to change our behavior. When Soldiers start thinking, "How can I use energy smarter?" then we know we are on our way. Soldiers have speed, agility, endurance, and a lethal edge on the battlefield thanks to Operational Energy, but it comes at a cost. Today in combat, it takes more than 20 gallons of fuel per day to sustain each Soldier. Every Soldier in an Infantry squad carries 23 batteries just to power equipment on a 72-hour mission. We must learn to use energy smarter. Just as consumers check fuel economy of cars and energy performance of appliances before buying them, we too must make more energy-informed decisions. If we do, we can grow our operational capabilities, while reducing risks to our Soldiers and the costs of providing that energy. Operational Energy touches every aspect of the Army from the factory to the foxhole. Successful missions require us to consider energy from planning through execution. Operational Energy efforts are already enabling the Army to Prevent, Shape, and Win (Operational Energy White Paper).

(8) General Engineering Support. The Army has a broad range of diverse engineer capabilities, which commanders can use to perform various tasks for various purposes. One such purpose is to provide support that helps ground force commanders enable logistics. To accomplish this purpose, engineers combine and apply capabilities from all three engineer disciplines (combat, general, and geospatial engineering) to establish and maintain the infrastructure necessary for sustaining military operations in the AO. This involves primarily general engineering tasks that consist largely of building, repairing, and maintaining roads, bridges, airfields, and other structures and facilities needed for Aerial Port of Debarkations (APODS), Sea Port of Debarkations (SPODS), main supply routes, and base camps. Depending on the range of military operations, other tasks include the planning, acquisition, management, remediation and disposition of real estate, supplying mobile electric power, utilities and waste management, environmental support and firefighting (see FM 3-34.400). Although engineering tasks that help enable logistics are primarily considered general engineering tasks, engineers also use capabilities from the other engineer disciplines to enable logistics. Similarly, although general engineering tasks are often used to enable logistics, engineers also use capabilities from the general engineering discipline for other purposes and to support other warfighting functions. FM 3-34 provides additional information about all three engineer disciplines and how they are used for various purposes and to support all the warfighting functions. FM 3-34.400 provides additional information about general engineering. ATTP 3-34.80 and JP 2-03 provide additional information about geospatial engineering.

12-3. Principles of Logistics

The principles of logistics are essential to maintaining combat power, enabling strategic and operational reach, and providing Army forces with endurance. While these principles are independent, they are also interrelated. The principles of logistics and the principles of sustainment are the same.

a. Integration. Integration is combining all of the sustainment elements within operations assuring unity of command and effort. It requires deliberate coordination and synchronization of sustainment with operations across all levels of war. Army forces integrate sustainment with joint and multinational operations to maximize the complementary and reinforcing effects of each Service component and national resources. One of the primary functions of the sustainment staff is to ensure the integration of sustainment with operations plans.

b. Anticipation. Anticipation is the ability to foresee operational requirements and initiate necessary actions that most appropriately satisfy a response without waiting for operations orders or fragmentary orders. It is shaped by professional judgment resulting from experience, knowledge, education, intelligence, and intuition. Commanders and staffs must understand and visualize future operations and identify appropriate required support. They must then start the process of acquiring the resources and capabilities that best support the operation. Anticipation is facilitated by automation systems that provide the common operational picture upon which judgments and decisions are based. Anticipation is also a principle of personnel services.

c. Responsiveness. Responsiveness is the ability to react to changing requirements and respond to meet the needs to maintain support. It is providing the right support in the right place at the right time. It

LOGISTICS

includes the ability to anticipate operational requirements. Responsiveness involves identifying, accumulating, and maintaining sufficient resources, capabilities, and information necessary to meet rapidly changing requirements. Through responsive sustainment, commanders maintain operational focus and pressure, set the tempo of friendly operations to prevent exhaustion, replace ineffective units, and extend operational reach.

d. Simplicity. Simplicity relates to processes and procedures to minimize the complexity of sustainment. Unnecessary complexity of processes and procedures leads to the confusion. Clarity of tasks, standardized and interoperable procedures, and clearly defined command relationships contribute to simplicity. Simplicity enables economy and efficiency in the use of resources, while ensuring effective support of forces. Simplicity is also a principle of financial management (FM 1-06).

e. Economy. Economy is providing sustainment resources in an efficient manner that enables the commander to employ all assets to the greatest effect possible. Economy is achieved through efficient management, discipline, prioritization, and allocation of resources. Economy is further achieved by eliminating redundancies and capitalizing on joint interdependencies. Disciplined sustainment assures greatest possible tactical endurance and constitutes an advantage to commanders. Economy may be achieved by contracting for support or using host nation resources that reduce or eliminate the use of limited military resources.

f. Survivability. Survivability is all aspects of protecting personnel, weapons, and supplies while simultaneously deceiving the enemy (JP 3-34). Survivability consists of a quality or capability of military forces to avoid or withstand hostile actions or environmental conditions while retaining the ability to fulfill their primary mission. This quality or capability of military forces is closely related to protection (the preservation of a military force's effectiveness) and to the protection/force protection warfighting function (the tasks or systems that preserve the force). Hostile actions and environmental conditions can disrupt the flow of sustainment and significantly degrade forces' ability to conduct and sustain operations. In mitigating risks to sustainment, commanders often must rely on the use of redundant sustainment capabilities and alternative support plans.

g. Continuity. Continuity is the uninterrupted provision of sustainment across all levels of war. Continuity is achieved through a system of integrated and focused networks linking sustainment to operations. Continuity is achieved through joint interdependence; linked sustainment organizations; a strategic to tactical level distribution system, and integrated information systems. Continuity assures confidence in sustainment allowing commanders freedom of action, operational reach, and endurance.

h. Improvisation. Improvisation is the ability to adapt sustainment operations to unexpected situations or circumstances affecting a mission. It includes creating, inventing, arranging, or fabricating resources to meet requirements. It may also involve changing or creating methods that adapt to a changing operational environment. Sustainment leaders must apply operational art to visualize complex operations and understand additional possibilities. These skills enable commanders to improvise operational and tactical actions when enemy actions or unexpected events disrupt sustainment operations. In regards to financial management, it includes task organizing units in non-traditional formations, submitting fiscal legislative proposals to acquire new fiscal authorities, and applying existing financial and communication technologies (FM 1-06).

Section II
National Logistics Organization—Assistant Secretary of the Army (Acquisition, Logistics, and Technology), Army G-4, Army G-8, and Army Materiel Command

12-4. ASA(ALT)

The ASA(ALT) is the principal adviser to the Secretary of the Army (SECARMY) on all matters relating to acquisition, logistics and technology. The ASA(ALT) is responsible for the overall supervision of the acquisition, logistics and technology matters of DA and has sole responsibility for performing the acquisition function within HQDA. The ASA(ALT) is designated as the Army Acquisition Executive (AAE), Senior Procurement Executive and Senior Official responsible for the management of acquisition of contract services, Science Adviser to the SECARMY and senior research and development official for DA. The ASA(ALT) is responsible for setting the strategic direction for and ensuring that DA policies, plans and programs related to acquisition, logistics, technology, procurement, the industrial base, materiel related security cooperation (including security assistance and armaments cooperation), and the Army's

HOW THE ARMY RUNS

portion of the Chemical Demilitarization Program are executed consistent with law, regulation and policy. The Office of the ASA(ALT) is designated the single office for the
acquisition function in HQDA and, subject to the authority, direction and control of the SECARMY, provides the CSA such staff support for acquisition matters as the CSA considers necessary to perform his duties and responsibilities. The ASA(ALT) is assigned responsibility for:

    a. Establishing strategic direction for aspects of the Planning, Programming, Budgeting, and Execution (PPBE) process within the ASA(ALT)'s assigned functions and responsibilities, including acquisition, logistics, technology, procurement and associated resource allocation decisions and policies and, when appropriate, coordinating and integrating that direction with the ASA Financial Management and Comptroller (FM&C); Chief Information Officer (CIO); DCS, G-4; DCS, G-3/5/7; DCS, G-8; and other DA officials and organizations.

    b. Providing strategic guidance and supervision for policies and programs for any procurement, logistics and technology initiatives executed by DA officials, organizations and commands.

    c. Exercising sole authority for providing material solutions to equipment modernization requirements.

    d. Developing and executing the Army's acquisition function and the acquisition management system, including Army acquisition programs and Army acquisition policy, and chairing the Army Systems Acquisition Review Council (ASARC) and Configuration Steering Board.

    e. Supervising the research and development function for DA and directing the Army Science Board (ASB).

    f. Carrying out, as the AAE and consistent with DA requirements for appointing executive or senior professionals, the functions and duties of the SECARMY with respect to the acquisition workforce, including managing the Army Acquisition Corps and Army Acquisition Workforce; appointing those personnel below the executive level; and managing and evaluating acquisition program executive officers and direct-reporting program, project and product managers.

    g. Executing the authorities of the agency head for contracting procurement matters pursuant to laws and regulations.

    h. Supervising logistics, including acquisition fielding, sustainment and disposal logistics management, and administering life cycle logistics support planning and execution.

    i. Supervising the development, coordination and implementation of policy and programs for the Army's materiel related security cooperation activities, to include foreign military sales (FMS), foreign military training (FMT), allocation of excess defense articles (EDA) to foreign countries, armaments cooperation, technology transfer, direct commercial sales, and munitions case processing.

    j. Providing export policy supervision and chairing and directing the Technology Transfer Security Assistance Review Panel.

    k. Supervising the Director, U.S. Army Chemical Materials Agency and the activities of the Army portion of the Chemical Demilitarization Program, including chemical stockpile emergency preparedness efforts.

    l. Representing the Army in relevant matters to DOD and non-DOD partners.

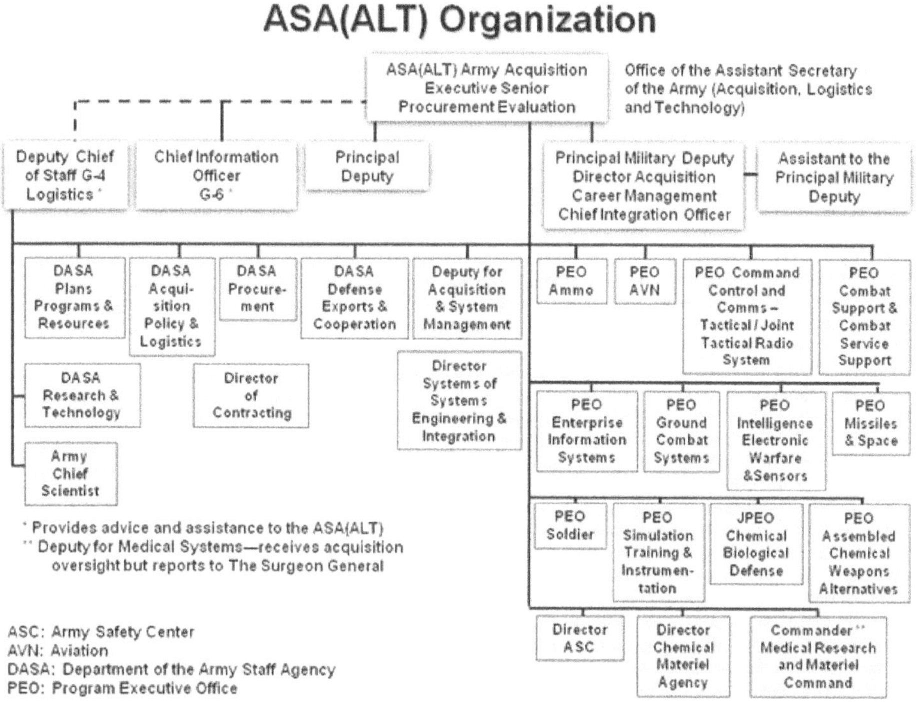

LOGISTICS

ASA(ALT) Organization

[Figure showing organizational chart with the following structure:]

- ASA(ALT) Army Acquisition Executive Senior Procurement Evaluation
- Office of the Assistant Secretary of the Army (Acquisition, Logistics and Technology)

Reporting/related boxes:
- Deputy Chief of Staff G-4 Logistics *
- Chief Information Officer G-6 *
- Principal Deputy
- Principal Military Deputy Director Acquisition Career Management Chief Integration Officer
- Assistant to the Principal Military Deputy

Sub-organizations:
- DASA Plans Programs & Resources
- DASA Acquisition Policy & Logistics
- DASA Procurement
- DASA Defense Exports & Cooperation
- Deputy for Acquisition & System Management
- PEO Ammo
- PEO AVN
- PEO Command Control and Comms – Tactical/Joint Tactical Radio System
- PEO Combat Support & Combat Service Support
- DASA Research & Technology
- Director of Contracting
- Director Systems of Systems Engineering & Integration
- PEO Enterprise Information Systems
- PEO Ground Combat Systems
- PEO Intelligence Electronic Warfare & Sensors
- PEO Missiles & Space
- Army Chief Scientist
- PEO Soldier
- PEO Simulation Training & Instrumentation
- JPEO Chemical Biological Defense
- PEO Assembled Chemical Weapons Alternatives
- Director ASC
- Director Chemical Materiel Agency
- Commander ** Medical Research and Materiel Command

* Provides advice and assistance to the ASA(ALT)
** Deputy for Medical Systems—receives acquisition oversight but reports to The Surgeon General

ASC: Army Safety Center
AVN: Aviation
DASA: Department of the Army Staff Agency
PEO: Program Executive Office

Figure 12-1. Assistant Secretary of the Army (Acquisition, Logistics, and Technology) (ASA(ALT)) Organization

12-5. Deputy Chief of Staff, G-4

The DCS, G-4 is the principal military adviser to the ASA(ALT) for logistics. The DCS, G-4 is the principal ARSTAF adviser to the CSA on logistics and assists the CSA in acting as the agent of the SECARMY in carrying into effect approved plans and recommendations. Under the supervision of ASA(ALT), for Army logistics and sustainment issues, the DCS, G-4 develops and executes Army strategy, policy, plans and programs for logistics and sustainment; ensures the execution of policies, plans and programs consistent with law, regulation and policy by other DA officials and organizations; and reviews and assesses the execution of Army logistics policies, plans and programs. The DCS, G-4 is assigned responsibility for:

   a. Collaborating on logistics operations in support of security cooperation and representing the Army on coalition sustainment standardization actions.

   b. Maintaining current logistics operations, contingency plans and resource programs that support Armywide logistics operations.

   c. Executing staff proponency for the logistics civil augmentation program and coordinating the development of multinational interoperability policy and practice for the use of allied civil augmentation programs.

   d. Serving as proponent for Army equipment safety and Army airworthiness.

   e. Advising on and monitoring the Army's materiel readiness to determine Armywide readiness trends.

   f. Ensuring that supportability requirements are incorporated into acquisition and fielding requirements for new systems.

12-9

HOW THE ARMY RUNS

g. Assisting in the supervision of the execution of Army logistics policies, programs, budgetary inputs and activities.

h. Coordinating with and supporting the ASA Installations Energy and Environment (IE&E) on issues, policies and programs related to energy security, including operational and tactical energy, and contingency bases.

i. Supporting the ASA(ALT) in the Army's organic industrial base matters and activities.

j. Ensuring sustainment functions and related logistics automated information systems management are fully integrated and properly balanced between acquisition and sustainment.

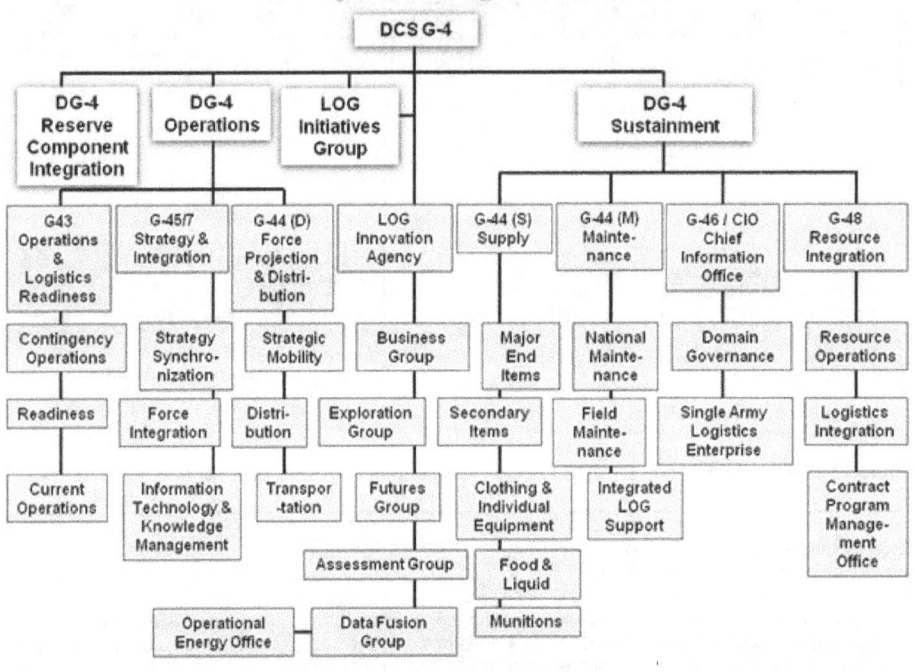

Figure 12-2. Army G-4 Organization

12-6. Deputy Chief of Staff, G-8

The DCS, G-8 is the principal military adviser to the ASA(FM&C) for program development and justification. In performing this function, the DCS, G-8 coordinates with the ASA(ALT) on all proposed programming recommendations that are related to ongoing acquisition program and science and technology initiatives. The DCS, G-8 is the principal ARSTAF adviser to the CSA on all materiel requirements, integration and programming of Army and joint materiel capabilities. The DCS, G-8 is assigned responsibility for:

a. Supervising the Director, Program Analysis and Evaluation, who is:

(1) Responsible for developing and defending the Army Program under the guidance and direction of the ASA(FM&C) and the DCS, G-8. This includes managing the programming phase of PPBE to facilitate the development and defense of the Army Program and the Future Years Defense Program, developing

LOGISTICS

and maintaining the Army's authoritative resource position database and ensuring the coordination of the programming and budgeting phases of PPBE and an effective transition to an Army budget estimate.

(2) Directly responsible to the SECARMY and CSA, including for developing and providing an independent assessment of the Army Program.

b. Managing the Center for Army Analysis (CAA) and other HQDA studies and providing analytic support to HQDA.

c. Developing plans, in coordination with the ASA(ALT), for equipping the future Army through programming, materiel integration and studies.

d. Coordinating Army input and participation in joint requirements matters considered by DOD bodies and supporting the CSA and VCSA in their related responsibilities.

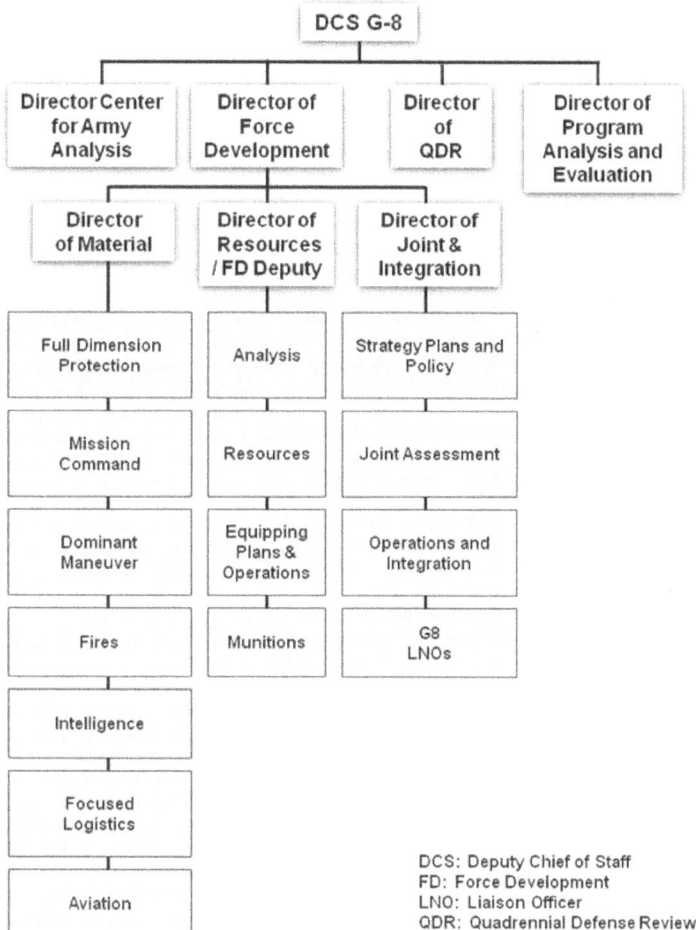

Figure 12-3. Army G-8 Organization

HOW THE ARMY RUNS

12-7. AMC
The AMC is the Army's premier provider of materiel readiness – technology, acquisition support, materiel development, logistics power projection, and sustainment – to the total force, across the spectrum of joint military operations. If a Soldier shoots it, drives it, flies it, wears it, eats it or communicates with it, AMC provides it. AMC is headquartered at Redstone Arsenal, Alabama, and impacts or has a presence in all 50 states and 150 countries. Manning these organizations is a work force of more than 70,000 dedicated military and civilian employees, many with highly developed specialties in weapons development, manufacturing, and logistics. To develop, buy, and maintain materiel for the Army, AMC works closely with PEOs, the AAE, industry, academia, and other related agencies. The command's complex missions range from development of sophisticated weapons systems and cutting-edge research, to maintenance and distribution of spare parts. The command's maintenance depots and arsenals overhaul, modernize, and upgrade major weapons systems – not just making them like new, but inserting technology to make them better and more reliable. AMC operates the research, development and engineering centers; Army Research Laboratory; depots; arsenals; ammunition plants; and other facilities; and maintains the Army's Prepositioned Stocks (APS), both on land and afloat. The command is the DOD Executive Agent for the chemical weapons stockpile and for conventional ammunition. AMC includes global surface transportation experts who provide the Warfighter with a single surface distribution provider for adaptive solutions that deliver capability and sustainment on time. AMC also handles the majority of the Army's contracting including a full range of contracting services for deployed units and installation-level services, supplies, and common-use information technology hardware and software. It operates a network of Army field support brigades and battalions, logistics support elements, and brigade logistics support teams, all of which identify and resolve equipment and maintenance problems, and materiel readiness issues for combatant commands. AMC handles diverse missions that reach far beyond the Army. For example, AMC manages the multibillion-dollar business of selling Army equipment and services to friends and allies of the United States and negotiates and implements agreements for co-production of U.S. weapons systems by foreign nations. AMC provides numerous acquisition and logistics services to the other components of the DOD and many other government agencies. The AMC subordinate commands are:

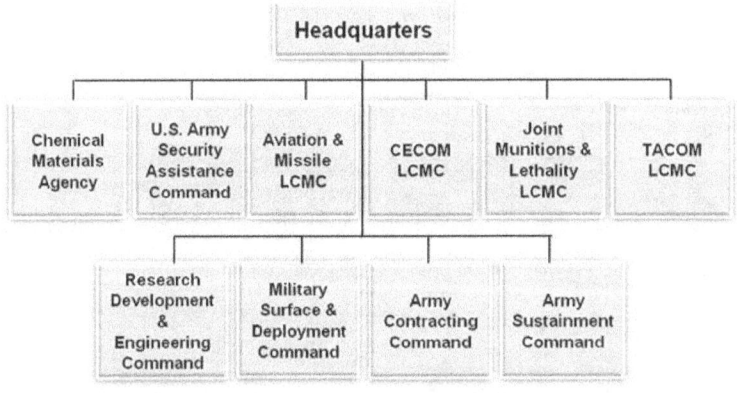

CECOM: Communications-Electronics
LCMC: Life Cycle Management Command
TACOM: Tank-Automotive and Armaments

Figure 12-4. Army Materiel Command (AMC) Organization

LOGISTICS

a. **U.S. Army Chemical Materials Activity (CMA).** CMA is the world leader in programs to store, treat, and dispose of chemical weapons safely and effectively. The activity developed and used technologies to safely store and eliminate chemical weapons at seven stockpile sites while protecting the public, its workers and the environment. CMA also has the storage mission at the Nation's final two stockpile sites.

b. **U.S. Army Security Assistance Command (USASAC).**

(1) USASAC is responsible for managing security assistance programs and Foreign Military Sales (FMS) for the Army. USASAC is known as the "Army's Face to the World," because it serves as the primary entry point for U.S. Army materiel-and service-related FMS requirements. The mission of USASAC is leading the AMC Security Assistance Enterprise, developing and managing security assistance programs and FMS cases to build partner capacity, supporting Combatant Command (COCOM) engagement strategies, and strengthening U.S. global partnerships. USASAC is responsible for Army security assistance information management and financial policy; provides policy, procedure, and guidance to the Army security assistance community; and manages the Army's co-production program. The U.S. Army Security Assistance Training Management Organization (USASATMO) is a subordinate command of USASAC that can deploy teams throughout the world to provide training tailored to a country for equipment purchased through FMS. USASATMO's motto is "Training the World, One Soldier at a Time." Locations: Headquarters, Redstone Arsenal, Alabama; New Cumberland, Pennsylvania; Washington Field Office, Fort Belvoir, Virginia; U.S. Army Security Assistance Training Management Organization, Fort Bragg, North Carolina; Office of the Program Manager, Saudi Arabian National Guard Modernization Program (SANG), Riyadh, Saudi Arabia; Liaison Officers at each Combatant Commands (COCOMs), Kuwait and Afghanistan.

(2) Security assistance is a national program supervised and directed by the State Department. In conjunction with the White House, Congress, and the Treasury Department, military security assistance programs are executed by the DOD. The FMS program is the U.S. government's program for transferring defense articles, services and training to other sovereign nations and international organizations. Under FMS, the U.S. government procures defense articles on behalf of the foreign customer. The President of the United States designates countries and international organizations eligible to participate in FMS. The Department of State makes those recommendations and approves individual programs on a case-by-case basis. Countries approved to participate in this program may obtain defense articles and services by paying with their own national funds or with funds provided through U.S. government-sponsored assistance programs. In certain cases, defense articles, services and training may be obtained on a grant basis. The Defense Security Cooperation Agency (DSCA) administers the FMS program for DOD. USASAC implements approved U.S. Army security assistance programs, including FMS of defense articles and services to eligible foreign governments. In carrying out the Army security assistance mission, USASAC calls on all AMC Life Cycle Management Commands (LCMC), as well as other DOD agencies and U.S. industry. Each sale of equipment to overseas customers comprises the same "total package" of quality materiel, facilities, spare parts, training, publications, technical documentation, maintenance support, and other services that AMC provides to U.S. Army units. USASAC is responsible for life cycle management of FMS cases, from preletter of request, development, execution, and closure. The command manages approximately 4,600 FMS cases valued greater than $134 billion. USASAC encourages strength in cooperation with 145 countries and 11 agencies by providing security assistance and FMS, and interfaces with 119 Security Cooperation Offices worldwide.

HOW THE ARMY RUNS

Figure 12-5. Foreign Military Sales (FMS) Process

c. Aviation and Missile LCMC. Aviation and Missile LCMC, a major subordinate command of AMC, unites all of the organizations that work to design, acquire, integrate, field, and sustain Army aviation, missile, and unmanned aircraft weapon systems. Headquartered at Redstone Arsenal, AL, home to some of the world's most advanced missile and rocket research, development, and test facilities, the Aviation and Missile Materiel Enterprise is comprised of the Aviation and Missile Command (AMCOM), the Aviation and Missile Research, Development and Engineering Center (AMRDEC), the Army Contracting Command-Redstone, the Program Executive Officer (PEO) Aviation, and the PEO Missiles and Space. AMCOM also supports PEO Aviation and the PEO Missiles and Space as they execute their missions of acquiring and managing the Army's aviation and missile systems. AMCOM performs several steps in the life cycle of Army aviation and missile systems, including procurement of spare parts, flight safety, maintenance and overhaul, Foreign Military Sales, and, eventually, retirement or demilitarization. AMCOM provides depot-level support to the Army's aviation and missile systems at Corpus Christi Army Depot (CCAD) and Letterkenny Army Depot (LEAD). Depot support comprises specialized, complex maintenance and overhaul activities, performed by skilled artisans who are essential to keeping the Army's systems ready for service. Resetting equipment, along with repairing crash and battle-damaged aircraft, are two key missions performed at AMCOM's depots.

d. Communications-Electronics Command (CECOM) Life Cycle Command. CECOM is the Warfighter's "one-stop-shop" for life cycle support of communications-electronics systems and equipment they carry. CECOM's mission is to develop, acquire, provide, and sustain world-class Command, Control, Computers, Intelligence, Surveillance and Reconnaissance (C4ISR) systems and battle command capabilities for the joint Warfighter. As an LCMC, CECOM conducts training missions; provides field

LOGISTICS

support for equipment and systems modifications and upgrades; and provides logistical expertise to ensure the on-time delivery of equipment, services, and capabilities to the Warfighter. CECOM also plays an integral part in the establishment and optimization of the Army's C4ISR Materiel Enterprise and C4ISR Center of Excellence (CoE), also located at Aberdeen Proving Ground (APG), MD. The C4ISR Materiel Enterprise is co-chaired by AMC and the ASA(ALT). Together, these organizations develop, acquire, provide, field, and sustain world-class C4ISR systems and battle command capabilities for the joint Warfighter. CECOM is comprised of approximately 8,500 military, civilian, and contract personnel. CECOM provides depot level support at Tobyhanna Army Depot (TYAD), Tobyhanna, PA. TYAD is the Army's premier depot providing maintenance, manufacturing, integration, and fielded repair to C4ISR systems worldwide, including more than 80 forward repair activities. TYAD accomplishes maintenance, fabrication, and system integration for Army, Navy, and Air Force C4ISR systems.

  e. Joint Munitions & Lethality LCMC. JM&L LCMC is a life cycle management command that manages research, development, production, storage, distribution, and demilitarization of all conventional ammunition and the personnel, organizations, infrastructure, and processes required for effective life cycle management of conventional ammunition within the DOD. JM&L LCMC is headquartered at Picatinny Arsenal, NJ, with major components located at Rock Island Arsenal (RIA), IL, and at Picatinny. While the objectives of the JM&L LCMC are to facilitate product responsiveness, minimize life cycle costs, and enhance the effectiveness and integration of munitions and lethality acquisition, logistics, and technology, its overarching objective is to deliver the best munitions to the right place, at the right time, and at the right cost. The JM&L LCMC brings together the resources and expertise of its three component organizations: the Program Executive Office for Ammunition located at Picatinny Arsenal, Joint Munitions Command (JMC) at Rock Island, and the Armament Research, Development and Engineering Center (ARDEC), also at Picatinny. It also oversees a nationwide network of installations and facilities that produce and store conventional ammunition under the direction of JMC. JMC manages the Army's ammunition plants and depots and serves as the logistics arm of the LCMC. JMC installations produce, store, issue, and demilitarize conventional ammunition for all U.S. military services, and for other U.S. agencies and allied nations as directed. JMC manages the Army's 14 ammunition production plants and storage depots and the Defense Ammunition Center, a technical center for munitions where the next generations of civilian ammunition specialists are trained. JMC also serves as the logistics and readiness arm of the LCMC, ensuring that munitions are delivered at the right place and time to support unit training and deployments.

  f. TACOM (not an acronym) LCMC. The TACOM LCMC, a major subordinate command of the AMC headquartered in Warren, MI, unites all of the organizations that focus on Soldier and ground systems throughout the entire life cycle. The TACOM LCMC mission is to develop, acquire, field, and sustain Soldier and ground systems or America's warfighters. If a Soldier eats it, wears it, drives it, or shoots it, TACOM LCMC develops, provides, or sustains it. The TACOM LCMC consists of the Integrated Logistics Support Center, Program Executive Office (PEO)-Combat Support and Combat Service Support, PEO-Ground Combat Systems, and PEO-Soldier. The TACOM LCMC is also aligned with several business partners: U.S. Army Tank Automotive Research, Development and Engineering Center; Army Contracting Command-Warren; U.S. Army Armaments Research, Development and Engineering Center; Natick Soldier Research, Development and Engineering Center; Edgewood Chemical and Biological Center; Joint Program Executive Office for Chemical and Biological Defense; and System of Systems Integration Directorate. Successful execution of TACOM LCMC's mission requires effective communication and coordination among the acquisition, logistics, and technology (ALT) organizations that are part of the TACOM LCMC and the Army's Materiel Enterprise. TACOM's arsenal and depots are: Watervliet Arsenal (WVA), Watervliet, NY; Anniston Army Depot (ANAD), Anniston, AL; Red River Army Depot (RRAD), Texarkana, TX; and Sierra Army Depot, Herlong, CA.

  g. U.S. Army Research, Development, and Engineering Command (RDECOM). RDECOM is headquartered at Aberdeen Proving Ground, Maryland. As an AMC major subordinate command, RDECOM's mission is to empower, unburden and protect our joint forces to enable the dominance of the Army. RDECOM is the Army's largest technology developer and it provides the Army a critical system engineering capabilities. The command has more than 17,600 scientists, engineers and other professionals. RDECOM works to create balance between developing technology solutions for the current fight and investing in future capabilities for tomorrow's challenges. The command uses its expansive working relationships with university-level institutions, its small business innovative research agreements and its cooperative research and development agreements with industry as well as

HOW THE ARMY RUNS

international agreements with more than two dozen countries to improve the capabilities of the Army's research, development and engineering processes.

h. Military Surface Deployment and Distribution Command (SDDC). SDDC is headquartered at Scott AFB, IL. SDDC's mission is to provide expeditionary and sustained end-to-end deployment and distribution to meet the Nation's objectives. SDDC is the ASCC of the U.S. Transportation Command (USTRANSCOM) and is a major subordinate command to AMC. This relationship links USTRANSCOM's Joint Deployment and Distribution Enterprise and AMC's Materiel Enterprise. The command also partners with the commercial transportation industry as the coordinating link between DOD surface transportation requirements and the capability industry provides. SDDC's success in deploying and redeploying the Defense Department's personnel and assets is achieved by coordination and leveraging the capability of the commercial transportation industry and other military assets to create an efficient flow of materials worldwide. SDDC averages about 20 million square feet of deployment and redeployment cargo movements each year or roughly 314 vessel operations per year. SDDC operates 24 ports spread throughout the continental U.S. and the world. Their support teams are able to deploy to virtually any port in the world. SDDC manages and coordinates all surface moves in support of door-to-door container and break bulk cargo movements around the globe and provides domestic routing services for rail and highway movements in the continental U.S., including arms, ammunition and explosives. SDDC also manages the assets of the Defense Rail Interchange Fleet and the Army's Containerized Ammunition Distribution System. In addition, SDDC manages household goods, privately owned vehicles and bus charters for Soldiers.

i. U.S. Army Contracting Command (ACC). A Major Subordinate Command (MSC) of the AMC, the ACC's Soldiers, civilians, and contractors support Soldiers worldwide by acquiring equipment, supplies, and services vital to Soldiers' mission and well-being. ACC ensures contracting support to the Warfighter as mission requirements emerge and as the Army transforms and moves within the continental United States and throughout the globe. Headquartered at Redstone Arsenal, AL, ACC is a two-star level command with two subordinate one-star commands – the Expeditionary Contracting Command (ECC) (for locations outside the continental United States) and the Mission and Installation Contracting Command (MICC) – and six major contracting centers that provide support to AMC's life cycle management commands and MSCs. These centers also provide contracting support to several program executive offices and program managers supporting the U.S. Army's major acquisition programs. The ECC provides effective and agile contracting service across the full spectrum of military operations for U.S. Army Service Component Commanders in support of Army and joint operations as well as to other defense organizations at locations outside the continental United States. ECC accomplishes this vital mission through seven contracting support brigades, eight contingency contracting battalions, and 83 contingency contracting teams throughout the world. The MICC provides contracting support for the Warfighter across Army commands, installations, and activities located throughout the continental United States, Alaska, and Puerto Rico. Its customers include the U.S. Army Installation Management Command, U.S. Army Forces Command, U.S. Army Training and Doctrine Command (TRADOC), U.S. Army North, U.S. Army Reserve Command, and U.S. Army Medical Command.

j. U.S. Army Sustainment Command (ASC). The ASC organizes, trains, and sustains a quality deployable force and integrates materiel and services to the Soldier. Rock Island Arsenal, ASC, is a two-star command providing support through the Lead Materiel Integrator (LMI) program, Materiel Management, the LOGCAP, APS, and the Directorates of Logistics. Major ASC responsibilities include:

(1) Lead Materiel Integrator (LMI). The AMC has developed a new materiel management approach to effectively and efficiently distribute and redistribute materiel to support the generation of trained and ready force. As AMC's executing agent for LMI, ASC becomes the single integrator to ensure Soldiers have the right equipment at the right time to accomplish their missions. Using the decision support tool developed by Logistics Support Activity (LOGSA), LMI represents a powerful new approach to implementing the Army's equipping priorities, policies, and programs to meet the demands of the 21st century Army. Materiel Management: ASC provides materiel readiness visibility and management, including property accountability and source of repair work loading. The Distribution Management Center works contracting requirements, supply management, Army Force Generation equipping strategy, and Directorate of Logistics realignment.

(2) LOGCAP. The Logistics Civil Augmentation Program is an Army program that uses contractors in wartime to support global contingencies for Department of Defense missions. They deliver a wide range

LOGISTICS

of support services such as dining facilities, laundry, and lodging to deployed forces worldwide, freeing Soldiers for combat missions.

(3) Army Prepositioned Stocks (APS). ASC maintains, accounts for, and cares for stocks in storage worldwide. These stocks include combat equipment and supplies, and humanitarian mission stocks, at land- and sea-based positions strategically located around the globe. Sites include the continental United States, Italy, Korea, Japan, Kuwait, Qatar, and Afghanistan.

(4) Directorates of Logistics (DOL). Transferring all functions and responsibilities of the DOLs around the globe from the Installation Management Command to AMC, with full operational control in fiscal year 2013 to ASC's Army Field Support Brigades, aligns logistics support with core competencies. The objective is to provide good or better service at the best value, by increasing quality, efficiency, and standardizing performance across the Materiel Enterprise. This transfer essentially places the Army's field-level maintenance and supply capabilities under the command and control of one single command structure, the ASC.

12-8. Theater Sustainment

a. The Theater Sustainment Command (TSC) serves as the senior Army sustainment HQ (less medical) for the Theater Army. The TSC provides mission command of units assigned, attached, or OPCON. The mission of the TSC is to provide theater sustainment (less medical) (FM 4-94). The TSC is capable of planning, preparing, executing, and assessing logistics and human resource support for Army forces in theater. It provides support to unified land operations. As the distribution coordinator in theater, the TSC leverages strategic partnerships and joint capabilities to establish an integrated theater-level distribution system that is responsive to Theater Army requirements. It employs sustainment brigades to execute theater opening (TO), theater sustainment, and theater distribution operations. The TSC includes units capable of providing multifunctional logistics: supply, maintenance, transportation, petroleum, port, and terminal operations. Other specialized capabilities, such as mortuary affairs (MA), aerial delivery, human resources, sustainment to internment/resettlement operations, and financial management, are available from the force pool. The combination of these capabilities gives the TSC commander the ability to organize and provide tailored support.

b. The Expeditionary Sustainment Commands (ESC) are force pooled assets. They are normally under the mission command of the TSC. The ESC provides mission command of sustainment units (less medical) in designated areas of a theater. The ESC plans, prepares, executes, and assesses sustainment, distribution, theater opening, and reception, staging, and onward movement operations for Army forces in theater. It may serve as a basis for an expeditionary command for joint logistics when directed by the Geographical Combat Commander (GCC) or designated multinational or joint task force commander. It normally deploys when the TSC determines that a forward command presence is required. This capability provides the TSC commander with the regional focus necessary to provide effective operational-level support to Army or JTF missions.

c. The Army Field Support Brigade (AFSB) is assigned to the ASC, and when deployed, is placed OPCON to the supported Theater Army. This OPCON relationship is normally delegated to the supporting TSC or ESC as appropriate. An AFSB provides materiel readiness focused support to include coordination of acquisition logistics and technology actions, less theater support contracting and medical, to Army operational forces. AFSBs serve as ASC's link between the generating force and the operational force. AFSBs are also responsible to integrate LOGCAP support into contract support integration plans, in coordination with the theater Army G-4 and the supporting CSB (ATP 4-91).

d. The Sustainment Brigade (SB), when deployed, is a subordinate command of the TSC, or by extension the ESC. The sustainment brigade is a flexible, multifunctional sustainment organization, tailored and task organized according to mission, enemy, terrain and weather, troops and support available, time available, and civil considerations (METT-TC). It plans, prepares, executes, and assesses sustainment operations within an area of operations. It provides mission command of sustainment operations and distribution management.

e. The Combat Sustainment Support Battalion (CSSB) is a flexible and responsive unit that executes logistics throughout the depth of an area of operations including transportation, maintenance, ammunition, supply, MA, airdrop, field services, water, and petroleum. The CSSB is attached to a sustainment brigade and is the building block upon which the sustainment brigade capabilities are developed. The CSSB is tailored to meet specific mission requirements. Employed on an area basis, the CSSB plans, prepares, executes, and assesses logistics operations within an area of operations. The

HOW THE ARMY RUNS

CSSB also supports units in or passing through its designated area. The CSSB may operate remotely from the sustainment brigade and therefore must maintain communications with the sustainment brigade. The CSSB establishes voice communications to support mission command and convoy operations as well as to monitor, update, and evaluate the logistics posture.

f. The Sustainment Brigade (Special Operations) (Airborne) is a subordinate command of the U.S. Army Special Operations Command. Its mission is to provide limited sustainment, medical, and signal support to Army Special Operations Forces (ARSOF). ARSOF are not logistically self-sufficient. ARSOF units rely upon the GCC theater infrastructure for virtually all of their support above their organic capabilities. The planning and execution of logistics support to ARSOF must be nested within the GCC's concepts of operation and support, as well as tailored to interface with the theater logistics structures. For further information on ARSOF logistics capabilities refer to FM 3-05.140.

g. The Brigade Support Battalion (BSB) is an organic component of BCT, fires, and maneuver enhancement brigades. The BSB is tailored to support the particular brigade to which it is organic. For example, the BSB of an armor brigade combat team (HBCT) has more fuel distribution capabilities and maintenance than does a fires brigade BSB. The BSB provides supply, maintenance, motor transport, and medical support to the supported brigade. The BSB plans, prepares, and executes, logistics operations in support of brigade operations (FM 4-90).

h. The Aviation Support Battalion (ASB) is the primary aviation logistics organization organic to Combat Aviation Brigade and the Theater Aviation Brigade. The ASB performs the BSB mission. It provides aviation and ground field maintenance, brigade-wide satellite signal support, replenishment of all supplies, and medical support to the aviation brigade. The Aviation Support Battalion has been optimized to support the Combat Aviation Brigade's forward support companies, aviation maintenance companies, and the brigade HQ and HQ company (FM 3-04.111).

i. In an environment of rapid change and limited resources, the military must respond quickly and efficiently to situations around the world. To deal with this, the U.S. Transportation Command (USTRANSCOM) developed Joint Task Force – Port Opening (JTF-PO) in 2005 to rapidly open and establish ports of debarkation and initial distribution networks to support joint operations and multinational operations. The command is stationed at Fort Eustis, VA, and assigned to TRANSCOM, with OPCON or TACON to the GCC upon employment.

Section III
National Logistics Organizations—Other

12-9. Other Logistics–Related Organizations

a. USACE. Designated a Direct Reporting Unit (DRU), the USACE plays a major role in the Army logistics system to include the Army's responsibility in supporting joint operations. USACE performs MILCON, installation support, real estate, R&D, and civil works missions. It provides an organizational structure for rapid conversion of its resources to support general war and other national emergency conditions. The six components of the USACE mission are:

(1) Manage and execute engineering, construction, and real estate programs for the U.S. Army and Air Force and perform R&D in support of these programs.

(2) Manage and execute installation support programs for Army installations.

(3) Manage and execute civil works programs, including the design, planning, engineering, construction, and R&D functions in support of this program.

(4) Perform R&D through non-system-specific advanced development in systems, specialized equipment, procedures, and techniques relevant to engineer support of combat operations.

(5) Develop and maintain a capability to mobilize readily in response to national security emergencies, domestic emergencies, and emergency water planning programs.

(6) Develop technology, and design and construct facilities and structures in support of Army space initiatives.

b. TRADOC. TRADOC develops, educates and trains Soldiers, civilians, and leaders; supports unit training; and designs, builds and integrates a versatile mix of capabilities, formations, and equipment to strengthen the U.S. Army. TRADOC oversees 32 Army schools organized under eight Centers of Excellence (CoE), each focused on a separate area of expertise within the Army (such as Sustainment).

LOGISTICS

c. CASCOM. CASCOM, a subordinate command of TRADOC, has the mission to train, educate and grow adaptive sustainment professionals; develop and integrate innovative Army and Joint Sustainment capabilities, concepts and doctrine to enable Unified Land Operations (ULO). CASCOM transformed into the Sustainment CoE in September 2009. CASCOM's three core competencies are to:
 (1) Execute Initial military training for sustainment of Soldiers and civilians.
 (2) Prepare the Army to sustain FSO in a Joint Interagency Intergovernmental Multinational (JIIM) environment.
 (3) Design, develop, and integrate sustainment capabilities into warfighting requirements, foster innovation, and lead change for the future force.
 d. U.S. Army Forces Command (FORSCOM). FORSCOM is responsible for the administrative control of all Army forces in CONUS.
 e. Commander of an Army Service Component Command (ASCC). Logistics in a theater of operations is tailored to support the Joint Force Commander's (JFC) requirements for each situation. Consideration is given to the variety of missions, which tend to make each logistics requirement different in terms of amounts and types of supplies, maintenance, transportation, and services needed. Consequently, organizations are tailored to each theater to cover a full spectrum of possibilities ranging from a large theater of operations comprised of one or more corps to support levels required by a division or separate brigade. The ASCC is responsible for providing administrative control (that includes logistics support) to all Army units and contractors in the theater. This responsibility is executed through one or more subordinate TSCs or a functional command such as personnel, transportation, medical, or engineer commands. The Army commander manages theater logistics support by establishing broad policies, allocating critical supplies, and assigning missions in concert with the JFC's guidance. Additionally, the Army theater commander manages and controls supply, maintenance, and other logistics services through the TSC and provides for centralized movements control for U.S. Army forces through the Theater Movement Control Agency (TMCA).
 f. Army and Air Force Exchange Service (AAFES). AAFES is the provider of supply Class VI (personal demand items) for the Army and Air Force. It is a joint command of the Departments of the Army and Air Force. The AAFES commander is a general officer responsible to the AAFES Board of Directors (BOD). In turn, the BOD is responsible to the Secretaries of the Army and Air Force through their respective chiefs of staff. The chairmanship of the BOD alternates between the two Services approximately every three years. The AAFES positions of commander and vice commander alternate between the Army and the Air Force. Primarily a civilian-run organization under military leadership, AAFES employs about 52,400 people, and operates approximately 1,500 facilities worldwide. AAFES worldwide headquarters is located in Dallas, Texas and two subordinate headquarters manage operations within the Europe and Pacific Regions. The mission of AAFES is to provide merchandise and services of necessity and convenience to authorized patrons at uniformly low prices, and to generate funds to supplement Appropriated Funds (APF) for the support of MWR programs. AAFES does this in peace and wartime. To accomplish its mission, AAFES:
 (1) Operates retail, food, personal service, vending centers, theaters, automotive facilities, and Army military clothing sales stores on military installations.
 (2) Provides basic exchange support to military personnel engaged in contingency operations or field exercises by establishing military-run tactical field exchanges (TFEs) where regular AAFES operations are not possible. Class VI support in the field can be limited to basic health and hygiene needs or expanded to include food, beverages, and other comfort items based upon the requested needs of the theater commander.
 (3) Generates earnings that support MWR programs. AAFES pays dividends to the Army, which in turn allocates funds to specific MWR programs on installations. The Army MWR BOD, which is formed under the Army Community and Family Support Center (CFSC), controls the allocation of AAFES-generated MWR funds within the Army.
 g. General Services Administration (GSA). The GSA provides general supplies and services that are common to more than one department of the Government. The GSA has multi-mission responsibility to manage the varied business activities of the Federal Government. GSA provides an extensive amount of supply support to the DOD for such commonly used items as leased commercial-style vehicles, office furniture and supplies, machine and hand tools, photo supplies, etc.

HOW THE ARMY RUNS

12-10. Defense Logistics-Related Organization
  a. DLA.
  (1) As America's combat logistics support agency, the DLA provides the Army, Navy, Air Force, Marine Corps, other federal agencies, and combined and allied forces with the full spectrum of logistics, acquisition and technical services. The Agency sources and provides nearly 100 percent of the consumable items America's military forces need to operate, from food, fuel and energy, to uniforms, medical supplies, and construction and barrier equipment. DLA also supplies more than 84 percent of the military's spare parts. In addition, the Agency manages the reutilization of military equipment, provides catalogs and other logistics information products, and offers document automation and production services. The DLA is headquartered at Fort Belvoir, VA. As a global enterprise, wherever the United States has a military presence, DLA is likely there as well.

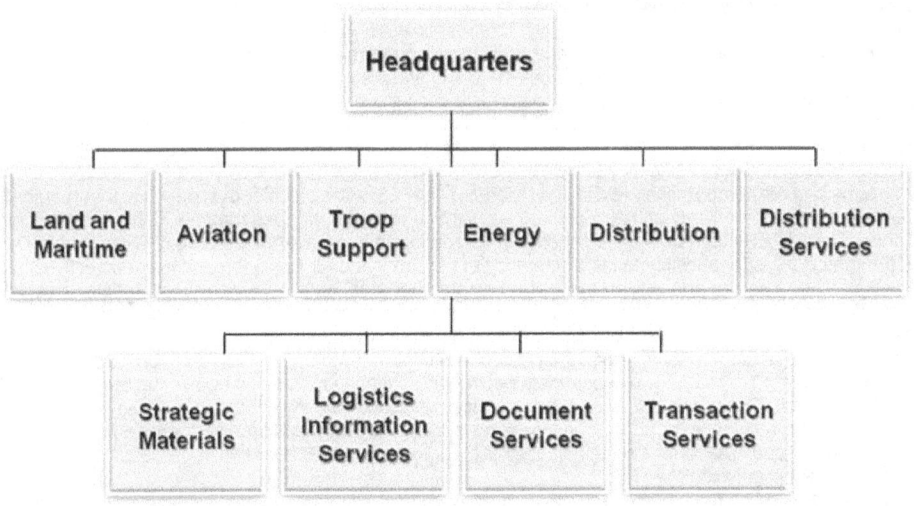

Figure 12-6. Defense Logistics Agency (DLA) Organization

  (2) The DLA primary activities are:
  (a) DLA Land and Maritime, Columbus, OH. Manages weapons system supply chains and is the largest Inventory Control Point (ICP). DLA Land and Maritime core functions include monitoring inventory levels, maintaining technical data, and assuring quality of more than two million spare and repair parts. DLA Land and Maritime manages more than two million different items for approximately $5 billion in annual sales. DLA Land manages wheeled, tracked and heavy vehicle parts; vehicle maintenance kits, power transmission, engine, suspension components, tires, batteries and small arms parts.
  (b) DLA Aviation, Richmond, VA. DLA Aviation operates in 19 stateside locations, supporting more than 1,400 major weapon systems and is the U.S. military's integrated materiel manager for more than 1.4 million repair parts and operating supply items. DLA Aviation manages aviation parts, including spares for engines on fighters, bombers, cargo aircraft and helicopters; airframe and landing gear parts; flight safety equipment; and propeller systems.
  (c) DLA Troop Support, Philadelphia, PA. DLA Troop Support supplies and manages food, clothing and textiles, pharmaceuticals, medical supplies, and construction and equipment supplies in support of

LOGISTICS

America's warfighters worldwide and their eligible dependents. Other customers include America's school children participating in federal school lunch programs, and other non-Defense Department customers. DLA Troop Support supports nearly every contingency operation, humanitarian relief effort, and every theater of operation.

(d) DLA Energy, Ft. Belvoir, VA. DLA Energy provides the Department of Defense and other government agencies with comprehensive energy solutions and is designated as the executive agent for bulk fuel. DLA Energy's mission continues to expand, incorporating emerging areas of renewable and alternative methods for satisfying customers' energy needs. Its mission is expanding beyond the role of traditional fuel and energy support as it leverages new technologies. Its business units continue to pursue solar power, hydrogen power, synthetic fuels and other alternative fuel and renewable energy sources as new procurement, research and development initiatives materialize.

(e) DLA Distribution, New Cumberland, PA. DLA Distribution is a combat support agency and the Lead Center for Distribution. DLA Distribution's 26 sites around the world are responsible for the receipt, storage, issue, packing, preservation and transportation of more than four million items.

(f) DLA Disposition Services, Battle Creek, MI. In support of the DLA mission, DLA Disposition Services supports the Warfighter and protects the public by providing worldwide disposal management solutions. DLA Disposition Services' (formerly known as the Defense Reutilization and Marketing Service) mission is to support customers through the reuse, transfer, donation, sale or disposal of excess property.

(g) DLA Strategic Materials, Fort Belvoir, VA. DLA Strategic Materials is the U.S. leading agency for the analysis, planning, procurement and management of materials critical to national security. They are responsible for providing safe, secure and environmentally sound stewardship for strategic and critical materials in the United States National Defense Stockpile (NDS). The stockpile of materials is intended to decrease dependence upon foreign sources of supply during national emergency. DLA Strategic Materials stores 28 commodities with a current market value of over $1.4 billion at 15 locations in the U.S. Commodities range from base metals such as zinc, cobalt, and chromium to the more precious metals such as platinum, palladium, and iridium. The Congress of the United States has authorized DLA Strategic Materials to sell commodities that are excess to Department of Defense needs. Since 1993, DLA Strategic Materials sales have totaled approximately $6.6 billion. Sales of excess NDS materials produce revenue for the Treasury General Fund and a variety of defense programs such as the Foreign Military Sales program, military personnel benefits, and the buy-back of broadband frequencies for military use. The sale revenues also fund DLA Strategic Materials operations to make it a self-sustaining organization.

(h) DLA Logistics Information Services, Battle Creek, MI. DLA Logistics Information Service provides interoperable, integrated, quality logistics data and enterprise IT solutions for the Military Services, the DOD, other federal agencies. DLA Logistics Information Services Cataloging Directorate is the centralized and consolidated cataloging activity for all DOD cataloging. It performs all 12 DOD cataloging functions and provides direct cataloging services in support of Warfighters, all DOD agencies (both at the wholesale and retail levels), and approximately 50 NATO and other allied nations. It is responsible for operational assignment, life cycle maintenance and collaboration with each of the Services for the 7.4 million National Stock Numbers and all the descriptive data associated with each item of supply.

(i) DLA Document Services, Mechanicsburg, PA. DLA Document Services provides a full portfolio of document services ranging from traditional offset printing, through on-demand output to on-line document services. Further, DLA Document Services is recognized as a transformation agent actively moving the DOD toward the use of on-line documents and services. Initiatives include an on-line customer eBusiness interface, Electronic Document Management CoEs for customer shared capability, Distribute and Print services (e.g., distribution of a digital file to multiple production facilities and print on demand), Equipment Management Solutions (e.g., best-value document support equipment in customer workspaces), and document conversion services (e.g., one of the largest providers in the federal government).

(j) DLA Transaction Services, Wright-Patterson AFB, OH. DLA Transaction Services receives, edits, and routes logistics transactions for the military services and federal agencies for standard Military Supply (MILS) transactions and provide information about anything, anywhere, anytime, to anyone in the DOD and Federal Logistics Community.

b. Defense Contract Management Agency (DCMA). DCMA is the DOD component that works directly with Defense suppliers to help ensure that DOD, Federal, and allied government supplies and services

HOW THE ARMY RUNS

are delivered on time, at projected cost, and meet all performance requirements. DCMA provides Contract Administration Services to the DOD Acquisition Enterprise and its partners to ensure delivery of quality products and services to the warfighter; on time and on cost. These services include: Acquisition Planning Support, Contract Management, Financial Services, Engineering Support Services, Property Management, Quality Assurance & Product Acceptance, Software Acquisition Management, Small Business, and Specialized Safety Support. DCMA professionals serve as "information brokers" and in-plant representatives for military, federal, and allied government buying agencies -- both during the initial stages of the acquisition cycle and throughout the life of the resulting contracts. Before contract award, DCMA provides advice and information to help construct effective solicitations, identify potential risks, select the most capable contractors, and write contracts that meet the needs of our customers in DOD, federal and allied government agencies. After contract award, DCMA monitors contractors' performance and management systems to ensure that cost, product performance, and delivery schedules are in compliance with the terms and conditions of the contracts.

12-11. Department of the Army Systems

a. Logistics Management Program (LMP). The LMP provides a comprehensive, modernized logistics solution that allows AMC to provide world class logistics readiness to the warfighter. Operational since July 2003, LMP delivers a fully-integrated suite of software and business processes that streamlines the Maintenance, Repair, and Overhaul (MRO), planning, finance, acquisition, and supply of weapon systems, spare parts, services, and materiel to the warfighter. Fundamental to the Army's transformation efforts, LMP replaces a stove-piped legacy systems environment and enables the Army to leverage the power of precise, up-to the minute Enterprise-wide data and improved business processes. This state-of-the-art Enterprise Resource Planning (ERP) solution moves the Army's logistics capabilities squarely into the 21st century and sets the stage for achieving a state of excellence in joint interoperability. Today, LMP is operational at all the AMC LCMCs, Army Sustainment Command (ASC), Defense Finance and Accounting Service (DFAS), and other Army locations. The program manages a multi-billion dollar inventory with tens of thousands of vendors and integrates with more than 70 DOD systems. Now fully fielded, LMP operates at more than 50 locations worldwide with approximately 25,000 users.

b. Global Combat Support System (GCSS-Army). GCSS-Army oversees the implementation of the tactical logistics and financial ERP program to integrate business processes and offer an Army-wide view of logistics information from the battlefield. GCSS-Army will allow commanders to anticipate, allocate, and synchronize the flow of resources across all areas of operations. Army logisticians will realize significant improvements in mission performance over the current tactical logistics management information systems. GCSS-Army will replace aging, stove-piped tactical logistics systems and associated financial capabilities and interface with applicable Army C2 systems and Joint systems as a follow-on initiative. This Web-based system, supported by laptops and Automatic Identification Technologies (AIT) devices, provides functionality for limited disconnected operations and for connected operations using robust deployable communications to connect to a centralized database for all users at all echelons.

c. Army Enterprise Systems Integration Program (AESIP). The Army continues to modernize its ERP business systems to simplify operations, optimize processes, and provide an accurate, Enterprise view of business information to all users. AESIP is a key component of this initiative. AESIP integrates business processes and systems by serving as the Enterprise hub for the Army's logistics and financial ERP business systems, to include: LMP, the national logistics system; GCSS-Army, the tactical logistics system; and General Fund Enterprise Business System (GFEBS), the Army's financial system. AESIP enables integration by linking business processes and data across existing IT systems. This integration optimizes business processes and supports Enterprise level information requirements. AESIP has successfully delivered a Web-based solution for the creation and management of customer and vendor master data and implemented an optimized messaging and hub services capability. AESIP houses and enables the Army Enterprise material master which provides the Army a single authoritative source for material data supporting all Army constituent (modernized and legacy) systems. This Army Enterprise material master provides the catalyst to manage, control, create, change, archive, and validate data, while providing a single global view of material thus, providing the basic building blocks for Product Lifecycle Management/Weapon System Management. Implementation of the Enterprise material master has enabled inventory management, accountability, pricing, accounting functions, and Material Requirements Planning (MRP) operations to be seamlessly integrated into the Army Enterprise vision.

LOGISTICS

Section IV
Summary and References

12-12. Summary
Army sustainment processes, organizations, and management enterprises continue to transform to meet our Nation's challenges and provide unique logistics support to the Joint Force Commander; enabling freedom of action across the range of military operations. Logisticians provide essential capabilities for the force enabling Prevent, Shape, and Win.

12-13. References
  a. Publications. Field manuals and selected joint publications are listed by new number followed by old number.
    (1) Joint Publications. Most joint publications are available online: http://www.dtic.mil/doctrine/
      (a) JP 1, Doctrine for the Armed Forces of the United States, 20 March 2009
      (b) JP 1-02, Department of Defense Dictionary of Military and Associated Terms, 8 November 2010
      (c) JP 1-06, Financial Management Support in Joint Operations, 2 March 2012
      (d) JP 2-03, Geospatial Intelligence Support to Joint Operations, 22 March 2007
      (e) JP 3-0, Joint Operations, 11 August 2011
      (f) JP 3-08, Interorganizational Coordination During Joint Operations, 24 June 2011
      (g) JP 3-28, Civil Support, 14 September 2007
      (h) JP 3-33, Joint Task Force Headquarters, 30 July 2012
      (i) JP 3-34, Joint Engineer Operations, 30 June 2011
      (j) JP 3-35, Deployment and Redeployment Operations, 31 January 2013
      (k) JP 4-0, Joint Logistics, 18 July 2008
      (l) JP 4-01.5, Joint Terminal Operations, 6 April 2012
      (m) JP 4-02, Health Service Support, 26 July 2012
      (n) JP 4-06, Mortuary Affairs, 12 October 2011
      (o) JP 4-08, Logistics in Support of Multinational Operations, 21 February 2013
      (p) JP 4-09, Distribution Operations, 5 February 2010
      (q) JP 4-10, Operational Contract Support, 17 October 2008
      (r) JP 5-0, Joint Operation Planning, 11 August 2011
    (2) Army Publications. Most Army doctrinal publications are available online: http://www.apd.army.mil/
      (a) ADP 3-0 (FM 3-0), Unified Land Operations, 10 October 2011
      (b) ADP 4-0 (FM 4-0), Sustainment, 31 July 2012
      (c) ADP 5-0, The Operations Process, 17 May 2012
      (d) ADP 6-0, Mission Command, 17 May 2012
      (e) ADRP 3-0, Unified Land Operations, 16 May 2012
      (f) ADRP 5-0, The Operations Process, 17 May 2012
      (g) AR 10-25, United States Army Logistics Innovation Agency, 5 April 2012
      (h) AR 11-2, Managers' Internal Control Program, 26 March 2012
      (i) AR 27-10, Military Justice, 3 October 2011
      (j) AR 30-22, The Army Food Program, 10 May 2005
      (k) AR 700-8, Logistics Planning Factors and Data Management, 15 March 2011
      (l) AR 700-80, Army IN-Transit Visibility, 24 September 2008
      (m) AR 700-131, Loan, Lease, and Donation of Army Materiel, 23 August 2004
      (n) AR 700-137, Logistics Civil Augmentation Program (LOGCAP), 28 December 2012
      (o) AR 702-6, Ammunition Stockpile Reliability Program, 23 June 2009
      (p) AR 710-2, Supply Policy Below the National Level, 28 March 2008
      (q) AR 711-6, Army Participation in the Defense Logistics Agency Weapon System Support Program, 15 May 2009
      (r) AR 715-9, Operational Contract Support Planning and Management, 20 June 2011
      (s) AR 735-5, Policies and Procedures for Property Accountability, 28 February 2005
      (t) ATP 4-91, Army Field Support Brigade, 15 December 2011
      (u) ATTP 1-19, U.S. Army Bands, 7 July 2010
      (v) ATTP 3-34.80, Geospatial Engineering, 29 July 2010
      (w) ATTP 4-0.1, Army Theater Distribution, 20 May 2011

HOW THE ARMY RUNS

    (x) ATTP 4-02, Army Health System, 7 October 2011
    (y) ATTP 4-10, Operational Contract Support Tactics, Techniques, and Procedures, 20 June 2011
    (z) ATTP 4-15, Army Water Transport Operations, 11 February 2011
    (aa) ATTP 4-33, Maintenance Operations, 18 March 2011
    (bb) FM 1-0, Human Resources Support, 6 April 2010
    (cc) FM 1-01, Generating Force Support for Operations, 2 April 2008
    (dd) FM 1-02, (101-5-1). Operational Terms and Graphics, 21 September 2004
    (ee) FM 1-04, Legal Support to the Operational Army, 26 January 2012
    (ff) FM 1-05, Religious Support, 18 April 2003
    (gg) FM 1-06, Financial Management Operations, 4 April 2011
    (hh) FM 3-04.111, Aviation Brigades, 7 December 2007
    (ii) FM 3-05, Army Special Operations Forces, 1 December 2010
    (jj) FM 3-05.140, Army Special Operations Forces Logistics, 12 February 2009
    (kk) FM 3-28, Civil Support Operations, 20 August 2010
    (ll) FM 3-34, Engineer Operations, 4 August 2011
    (mm) FM 3-34.400, General Engineering, 9 December 2008
    (nn) FM 3-35, Army Deployment and Redeployment, 21 April 2010
    (oo) FM 3-35.1, Army Prepositioned Operations, 1 July 2008
    (pp) FM 3-93, Theater Army Operations, 12 October 2011
    (qq) FM 4-02.1, Army Medical Logistics, 8 December 2009
    (rr) FM 4-02.7, Multiservice Tactics, Techniques, and Procedures for Health Service Support in a Chemical, Biological, Radiological, and Nuclear Environment, 15 July 2009
    (ss) FM 4-02.12, Army Health System Command and Control Organizations, 26 May 2010
    (tt) FM 4-20.41, Aerial Delivery Distribution in the Theater of Operations, 29 August 2003
    (uu) FM 4-90, Brigade Support Battalion, 31 August 2010
    (vv) FM 4-92, Contracting Support Brigade, 12 February 2010
    (ww) FM 4-94, Theater Sustainment Command, 12 February 2010
    (xx) FM 27-10, The Law of Land Warfare, 18 July 1956
    (yy) FMI 4-93.2, The Sustainment Brigade, 4 February 2009
    (zz) PAM 735-5, Financial Liability Officer's Guide, 9 April 2007
  (3) Other Publications.
    (a) Allied Land Publication 4.2, (Standardization Agreement 2406), Land Forces Logistics Doctrine, 4 February 2010
    (b) DODD 5100.1, Functions of the Department of Defense and its Major Components, 21 December 2010
    (c) DODD 5101.9, DOD Executive Agent for Medical Materiel, 23 August 2004
    (d) DTR 4500.9-R, Defense Travel Regulation, http://www.transcom.mil/dtr/part-i/ Military Justice (Preamble, Manual for Courts-Martial), http://www.loc.gov/rr/frd/Military_Law/pdf/MCM-2012.pdf
    (e) NATO Military Committee Decision 319/1, NATO Principles and Policies for Logistics http://nsa.nato.int/nsa/
    (f) Title 10 United States Code (USC), Armed Forces
    (g) Title 32 USC, National Guard

MILITARY HUMAN RESOURCE MANAGEMENT

Chapter 13

Military Human Resource Management

Our mission is to develop, manage, and execute all manpower and personnel plans, programs, and policies—across all Army Components—for the entire Army team. Our vision for the Human Resources (HR) enterprise is a team of HR professionals dedicated to supporting and empowering Soldiers, civilians, families, and veterans worldwide in an era of persistent conflict. We will recruit, retain, and sustain a high-quality volunteer force through innovative and effective enterprise solutions. We will ensure HR readiness of the Total Army across the full spectrum of operations.

Deputy Chief of Staff, Army G-1

Section I
Introduction

13-1. Military Human Resource Management (MHRM)
The term Human Resource Management (HRM) has been accepted by the Army leadership and, over time, has been integrated into policy and doctrine formerly used to describe the functions of personnel management and personnel administration. In the most general sense, HRM is a series of integrated decisions about the employment relationship that influences the effectiveness of employees and organizations. MHRM is the major component of the Army's overall HRM operations. It has evolved from a supporting role to that of a strategic enabler for the Army. Today's challenges require informed decisions on force structure requirements, recruiting and retention programs, well-being programs, and personnel readiness from both individual and unit perspectives. HR leaders must possess professional and specialized skills to meet these challenges and manage the programs that comprise the functions and integrating systems of the HR life cycle model.

13-2. Military HR Life Cycle Functions
In a broad sense, MHRM describes the process of managing people by performing the essential functions of planning, organizing, directing, and supervising effective procedures necessary in administration and operation of personnel management. The life cycle HR management functions are derived from the Army's life cycle, as follows.
  a. Personnel Structure. The HR portion of the Army's force development function where personnel requirements and authorizations are determined and documented.
  b. Acquisition. This function ensures the Army is staffed with the correct grades and skills in numbers sufficient to satisfy force requirements, and has three components.
    (1) Manpower Management. The process of linking accession, retention, and promotion targets to Army requirements as measured against the military manning program in the Planning, Programming, Budgeting, and Execution (PPBE).
    (2) Accession and Retention Management. The process that converts manpower targets to missions and oversees execution.
    (3) Training Integration. The establishment of a demand for training programs and a system to control input and tracking of trainees and students.
  c. Distribution. The function of assigning available Soldiers to units based on Army requirements and priorities.
  d. Development. This function begins with accession training and continues throughout a Soldier's entire period of service. It includes institutional training, self-development, leader development, and supporting programs such as the voluntary education, evaluation, promotion, and command selection systems.
  e. Deployment. This function enables the Army to transition from the "prepare mode" to the "conduct of military operations" mode. Deployment includes mobilization, deployment, redeployment, demobilization, reset, non-combatant evacuation, and repatriating.

HOW THE ARMY RUNS

f. Compensation. This function encompasses the management of all pay, allowances, benefits, and financial entitlements for Soldiers, retirees, and annuitants. The dollars involved exceed one-third of the Army's total obligation authority.

g. Sustainment. This function involves the management of programs to maintain and advance the well-being of Soldiers, civilians, retirees, and family members.

h. Transition. As individuals leave the Active Component (AC) for either the Reserve Components (RC) or civilian life, this function provides assistance to Soldiers, Army civilians, and family members.

13-3. HR Leadership

a. Assistant Secretary of the Army (Manpower and Reserve Affairs) (ASA(M&RA)) has principal responsibility for the overall supervision of manpower, personnel, and RC affairs.

b. The Deputy Chief of Staff, G-1 (DCS, G-1), as the Army's personnel proponent, determines the broad objectives of the military personnel management system. The DCS, G-1 establishes policy for and exercises Army staff (ARSTAF) proponent supervision of the system's functions and programs.

c. The Commanding General (CG), U.S. Army Human Resources Command (AHRC) is the Army's functional proponent for the military personnel management system and operates the Army's military HR systems within the objectives set by the DCS, G-1. The CG, AHRC also supports the MHRM system's automation requirements in the design, development, and maintenance of personnel databases and automation systems.

d. The CG, U.S. Army Soldier Support Institute (USASSI) develops and coordinates operational concepts, materiel requirements, organization and force design requirements, and integrates training into courses of instruction at the Adjutant General School.

13-4. Key Military HR Publications

a. Army Regulation (AR) 600-8, Military Personnel Management. This regulation establishes the military personnel management system. It describes the functional structure of the system and sets forth the organizational structures that direct, integrate, and coordinate the execution of the system. The AR 600-8 series addresses specific subjects within the military personnel management arena.

b. Field Manual (FM) 1-0, Human Resource Support. This field manual describes the Army's personnel doctrine and how it fits into the Army's operational concept across the full spectrum of conflict, as well as how it supports unit commanders and Soldiers. It provides a common understanding of HR support and encompasses the management concepts of personnel information and readiness; replacement, casualty, and postal operations; personnel accounting and strength reporting; mobilization and demobilization; and other essential personnel services.

c. AR 600-3, The Army Personnel Proponent System.

(1) The Human Resources Command (HRC) manages the personnel proponent system, designating personnel proponents, assigning their basic responsibilities, and defining the personnel life cycle management functions. The objectives of the personnel proponent system are as follows.

(a) Identify a single agent (proponent) responsible for all personnel matters for each career field (officer, warrant, enlisted, and civilian).

(b) Fix responsibility for all career field-related matters.

(c) Ensure the civilian work force is integrated into the personnel proponent system.

(d) Ensure personnel management policies and programs established by Headquarters, Department of the Army (HQDA) incorporate career field-related considerations.

(e) Foster awareness and achievement of the objectives of the Officer Personnel Management System (OPMS), the Total Warrant Officer System (TWOS), the Enlisted Personnel Management System (EPMS), and the Civilian Integration into the Personnel Proponent System (CIPPS).

(2) The functions of personnel proponency are accomplished through approximately 54 personnel proponent offices in conjunction with HRC. Together the proponents assist the DCS, G-1 in all personnel-related matters.

(3) The framework for proponency consists of the eight life cycle management functions. The personnel proponent system serves as the honest broker, ensuring fairness, completeness, accuracy, and timeliness of all aspects of the personnel system.

MILITARY HUMAN RESOURCE MANAGEMENT

13-5. Military Occupational Classification and Structure (MOCS) System

a. The MOCS system translates manpower requirements into specific skills and grade levels. System policy is set forth in AR 611-1, Military Occupational Classification and Structure Development and Implementation. Department of the Army Pamphlet (DA PAM) 611-21, Military Occupational Classification and Structure, contains the procedures and detailed officer, warrant officer, and enlisted classification and structure guidance. Both publications are available as electronic publications on the U.S. Army Publishing Agency (USAPA) web site (www.usapa.army.mil).

b. Changes to occupational identifiers within the MOCS are generally driven by the requirements determination process. Personnel proponents submit proposed changes to the system in accordance with responsibilities in AR 600-3 for recommending classification criteria. The Personnel Occupational Specialty Code Edit (POSC-Edit) System, an automated system maintained by HRC Deputy Chief of Staff, Operations (DCSOPS), is the official military occupational edit file used to edit and update data on authorized automated personnel systems. The file is updated based on approved revisions to the MOCS. It contains a listing of all authorized commissioned officer, warrant officer, and enlisted identifiers; grades associated with those identifiers; and other personnel information.

13-6. Key Terms and Interrelated Documents and Systems at the Heart of HR Process

a. End Strength. The total number of personnel authorized by the Congress to be in the Army on the last day of the Fiscal Year (FY) (30 September). This is normally provided in the National Defense Authorization Act (NDAA).

b. Force Structure Allowance (FSA). The sum of authorized spaces contained in all Modification Tables of Organization and Equipment (MTOE) units and Table of Distribution and Allowances (TDA) type organizations.

c. Total Strength. The total of all personnel serving on active duty in the Army, including Soldiers in units and organizations and those in the individuals account.

d. Operating Strength (OS). Those Soldiers available to fill spaces in MTOE units and TDA organizations, sometimes referred to as the distributable inventory.

e. Individuals Account. This account, often referred to as the Trainee, Transient, Holdee, and Student (TTHS) account, is comprised of those personnel unavailable to fill spaces in units. The six sub-accounts are trainees, officer accession students, transients, holdees, students, and U.S. Military Academy (USMA) cadets.

f. The Active Army Military Manpower Program (AAMMP). The manpower program is produced as monthly updates and as decision programs for the Program Objective Memorandum (POM), Office of the Secretary of Defense (OSD) budget submission, and President's Budget. It is the report produced by the Enlisted Grades (EG) Model. Using a linear program, the EG Model operates within constraints such as end strengths, man years, and recruiting capability to develop an OS that matches the FSA as closely as possible. It also carries up to seven years of historical loss behavior to use as a projective (predictive) database. Inputs are the latest available strength, gains, and loss data. Vital data for the AAMMP comes from (or will come from) several manpower systems, most of which are discussed later in this chapter. These systems include the suite of forecasts that constitute the Officer Forecasting Model (OFM); Enlisted Specialties Model; the Individual Account (IA) Model; and the Army Training Requirements and Resources System (ATRRS). The AAMMP records and/or projects strength of the Army; losses and gains; FSA; training inputs; officer, cadet, and female programs; and the TTHS account.

g. Total Army Personnel Database (TAPDB). An automated, standardized database containing military personnel data to fully support manning and sustaining functions during peacetime and under mobilization required by HRC and the National Guard Bureau (NGB). It consists of integrated but physically distributed databases (Active Officer (TAPDB-AO), Active Enlisted (TAPDB-AE), United States Army Reserve (USAR), Army National Guard (ARNG), and Core). TAPDB core contains selected data elements from each component database needed to support mobilization.

h. Electronic Military Personnel Office (eMILPO). This web-based automated personnel information system is the Army's database of record and primary HR system. eMILPO provides commanders with management information reports; performs automated field records maintenance; and provides automated personnel information to TAPDB (AE, AO), the Enlisted Distribution and Assignment System (EDAS) Active Enlisted (AE) and Total Officer Personnel Management Information System (TOPMIS) (AO). eMILPO is web based, uses a centralized database and provides near real-time, Army-wide visibility on personnel information.

HOW THE ARMY RUNS

i. Enlisted Specialties Model. This is part of the HQDA decision support system. It is personnel planning optimization model that computes recommended Military Occupational Specialty (MOS) and grade mix, enlisted accessions, training to support accessions, and in-service reclassification/reenlistment and promotions to maintain force alignment through the POM cycle.

j. OFM. The OFM uses time-series forecasting techniques to demonstrate the aggregate impact of current proposed manpower policies. It maintains force alignment by minimizing the difference between the desired and projected OS in each competitive category and grade. The major inputs are authorizations data, inventory data, loss rates, and promotion targets. The model provides output data that can be imported into spreadsheets or word processing documents for analysis and reporting. The OFM outputs support program and budget development, policy analysis, and other management activities and serves as an input or constraint into EG.

k. Active Army Strength Forecaster (A2SF). This system developed and used by DCS, G-1, replaced several legacy systems used in forecasting officer and enlisted strengths, gains, losses, and force manning. Using updated methodologies, the object-oriented design of this system provides more accurate and timely forecasting, as well as significantly enhanced detail (rates for specific populations, gender, etc.) to support DCS, G-1 decisions. It draws upon TAPDB for personnel source data and produces the AAMMP as one of its primary reports.

l. ATRRS. ATRRS is the Army's system of record for training. It is an automated information system that provides personnel input to training management information for HQDA, commands, schools, and training centers during both peacetime and mobilization operations. The system contains information at the course level of detail on all courses taught by and for the Army. A major product of ATRRS is the Army Program for Individual Training (ARPRINT).

m. ARPRINT. The ARPRINT is a mission document that provides officer and enlisted training requirements, objectives, and programs for the Active Army (AA), Army RC, Department of the Army (DA) civilians, other U.S. Services, and foreign military. Training is planned and executed on a FY basis and the goal is to train sufficient numbers in each MOS/branch and functional area to equal the projected authorizations as of the end of the FY.

Section II
The Structure Function

13-7. Military Manpower Management
In Chapter 5, we addressed unit structure and force planning, describing how the force is sized and configured and how that force is accounted for in the documentation system. This paragraph, which should be viewed as an extension of Chapter 5, will focus on how the Army manages manpower and personnel once the force is configured and sized.

a. Manpower management at the macro level is the function of determining requirements, obtaining manpower, and allocating resources. It includes the determination of minimum-essential requirements, alternative means of providing resources, and policies to be followed in utilization of manpower. It involves the development and evaluation of organizational structure and review of utilization. It includes Soldiers in the AC, ARNG, and USAR, Army civilian manpower assets, and certain contractor assets when a requirement is satisfied by contractual services rather than by Army military or civilian personnel.

b. Manpower managers deal with HR requirements from the perspective of the organizational structure in which they will be most efficiently and economically used. First, they focus on requirements demanding explicit grades and skills to perform specific tasks. Then, they focus on determining which requirements will be supported with authorizations (spaces). Finally, they combine force structure authorizations with requirements in the TTHS Account, also referred to as the IA, to determine the needs of the Army by grade and skill within constraints that exist. Simultaneously, HR managers focus on supporting requirements through the acquisition, training, and assignment of personnel (faces) to authorized positions.

c. The Congress, the Office of Management and Budget (OMB), OSD, and the Office of the Secretary of the Army (OSA) are not directly involved in the management of individual military personnel. They do, however, establish policies that prescribe the availability of this resource and the management latitude available to those involved in personnel management. For example, policies which limit Permanent Changes of Station (PCS), establish tour lengths, set officer grade limitations, or place a ceiling on the

MILITARY HUMAN RESOURCE MANAGEMENT

hire of local national personnel affect the flexibility of personnel managers. OSD and, to a more limited extent, OMB, are involved in the force-structuring process. Managers, above the DA level, are concerned primarily with the management of spaces, while at descending levels below HQDA, they are increasingly concerned with the management of people and their associated costs. Much of the work at the departmental level involves decisions dealing with the aggregate of the force structure and inventory rather than the subsets of grade and skill. At lower levels, the HR process turns its focus more toward the faces and the management of people. Whenever the force structure changes, there is a significant cause and effect relationship on the many systems that support manpower planning and HR management.

13-8. Manpower Management at HQDA

   a. In managing military manpower at the macro level, the key measurement used by HR managers is the Operating Strength Deviation (OpSD). OpSD is a measurement of how much the OS (faces) is deviating from the FSA (spaces). The OS must not be confused with the FSA. The anticipated size of the OS, however, gives a good idea as to how large a structure can realistically be manned. Throughout the year there can be many causes for these deviations, such as unpredicted changes in retention rates and seasonal surges in acquisitions. Personnel managers must constantly monitor the OpSD and adjust personnel policies to ensure the Army has an optimum match of faces to spaces. At the same time, the Army must comply with the congressional mandate to be at the authorized end strength on the last day of each FY.

   b. Although the goal is to minimize the difference (delta) or deviation between the FSA and the OS, some deviation, the OpSD, almost always exists. A positive deviation (OS greater than FSA) means personnel are present in units in excess of structure requirements. A negative deviation (FSA exceeds OS) means the structure is larger than the quantity of personnel available to fill it. The OS is easily computed by subtracting TTHS personnel from the total strength. The OpSD is computed by subtracting the FSA from the OS.

   c. The size of the OS is affected by fluctuations in the two elements employed in its calculation: the total strength (End Strength (ES) at year end) and total TTHS at any particular time. Changes in the OS over time and the magnitude of the FSA affect the OpSD. Often these quantities are compared only at the end of the FY (end strength). It is, however, often much more meaningful to view the situation on an average throughout the year by calculating man year values for each of these quantities. This provides more information than the frequently atypical and skewed end strength picture, which represents only one day in the entire year. Figure 13-1 illustrates the relationships between the components of the force just discussed.

   d. The total number of personnel in TTHS will fluctuate considerably throughout the year due to a variety of reasons, such as the seasonal increase in transients during the summer and in trainees during the fall and winter. Past experience and estimates of the effects of policy changes make the number of personnel in this account fairly predictable. In the recent past, it has averaged about 13% of the total strength.

   e. By knowing the TTHS and total strength projections, manpower planners can easily determine the size of the OS and use that as a basis for developing a FSA for building authorized units. TTHS, FSA, and OSD projections are all contained in the AAMMP.

   f. The number of personnel in the TTHS is often directly attributable to the personnel policies in effect. Soldier casualties, fill of projected deploying units, and training requirements and policies are but a few examples of policies which affect the size of TTHS. Since TTHS has a direct effect on the faces available for FSA manning, these same policies have a direct impact on the number of units and organizations which the Army can field. Thus, manpower and personnel managers face a constant challenge to ensure a balance exists between the use of authorized spaces and the acquisition, training, and distribution of personnel assets to meet the needs of the Army. The stated personnel needs of the Army as expressed in its various organizational documents change on a daily basis as different units and organizations are activated, inactivated, or changed. However, the process of providing personnel to meet these changing needs is much slower.

HOW THE ARMY RUNS

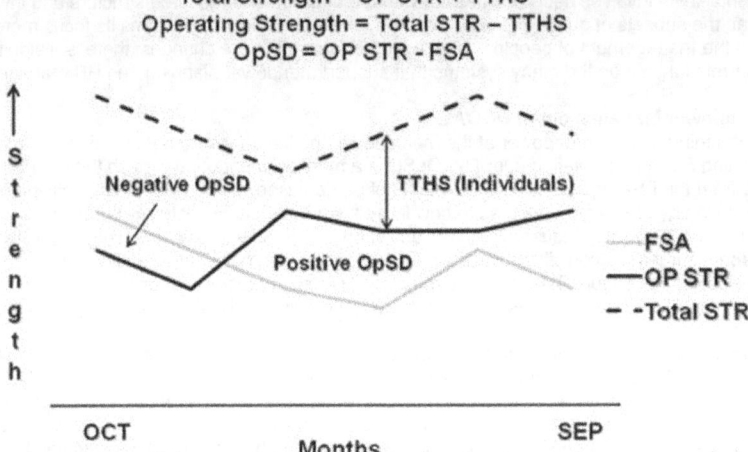

Figure 13-1. Manpower Strength Relationships

13-9. Personnel Management Authorizations Document (PMAD) and Updated Authorizations Document (UAD)

a. The PMAD and UAD are the Army's documents of record for active component military authorizations. The PMAD and UAD provide authorizations data at the Unit Identification Code (UIC), MOS, and grade level of detail for the current year through the end of the program. The PMAD and UAD support the distribution of personnel, strength forecasting, programming, budgeting, accessions, promotions, and training.

b. The primary inputs to the PMAD and UAD are is built from annual updates of the force structure files reflected in the HQDA Deputy Chief of Staff, G-3/5/7 (DCS, G-3/5/7) Force Management Division, to include: Structure and Manpower Allocation System (SAMAS) and Army authorization documents files. A PMAD is based on a locked SAMAS file. A normal year sees two locked SAMAS files and two corresponding PMADs. In between command plans, decisions are often made which cause significant changes to authorizations. A UAD which makes adjustments to PMAD authorizations is produced periodically to capture such changes. The Army will publish UADs to capture emerging changes to personnel structure. A normal year sees the publication of two UADs. The personnel community uses PMAD and its most current UAD as the sole source of AC authorizations to UIC, MOS, grade, and Additional Skill Identifier (ASI) level of detail for the current and budget years. The focus of the PMAD and UAD is on detail for near-term distribution. The PMAD is the basis for decisions regarding accessions, training, force alignment, promotions, and distribution of personnel. Throughout this text the term PMAD refers to the PMAD itself or its most current UAD.

13-10. Notional Force (NOF) System

As needed the Army may also publish a NOF. A NOF provides the same authorizations data as a PMAD or UAD–active component military authorizations at the UIC, MOS, and grade level of detail for the current year through the end of the program. The difference is that a NOF reflects force structure or

MILITARY HUMAN RESOURCE MANAGEMENT

personnel structure decisions that have not received approval. The purpose of a NOF is to support analysis only and its distribution is limited.

13-11. Military Force Alignment

Force alignment is managing changing faces and spaces simultaneously by grade level and Career Management Field (CMF)/MOS–reshaping a force today to also meet tomorrow's needs. The always changing AAMMP, PMAD, and budget are intensively managed monthly for the PPBE six-year cycle; ensuring military personnel strength is skill-qualified and available for distribution. Force alignment strives to synchronize military personnel programs: promotions, recruiting, accessions, training, reenlistment, reclassification, and special and incentive discretionary pay. Simultaneously, every effort is made to provide professional career development consistent with Army force manning levels for qualified Soldiers. Management forums are the Functional Review (FR), personnel functional assessment (PFA), Structure Manning Decision Review (SMDR), Monthly Military Personnel Review (M2PR), Training Requirements Arbitration Panel (TRAP), and CMF reviews. Representation in shaping the officer and enlisted forces involves the entire personnel community in varying degrees of programming and execution. Enlisted Strength Model is a major planning tool for enlisted force alignment analysis. The goal: to achieve a PMAD grade-CMF/MOS match to OS for the current year, budget year, and program years.

Section III
The Acquisition Function

13-12. Enlisted Procurement

a. Based on input from the PMAD (authorizations by skill and grade), TAPDB-AE (skills and grades on hand), and the AAMMP (projected accessions in the aggregate), the Enlisted Specialties Model projects the numbers and training requirements for the various MOSs. This in turn is used to develop the annual program (ANNPRO) and the ARPRINT and feeds the personnel input to the ATRRS which is linked to the Recruit Quota Enlistment System (REQUEST) and the Reenlistment/Reclassification System (RETAIN) (Figure 13-2).

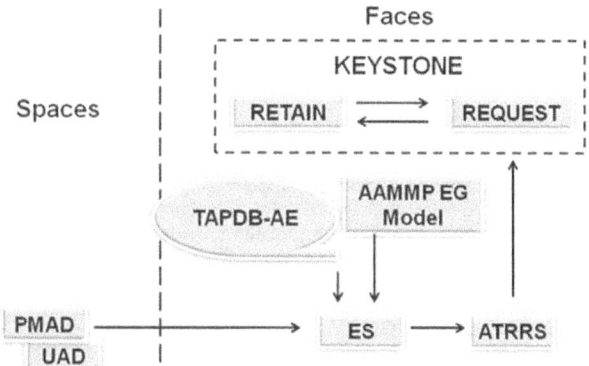

Figure 13-2. Enlisted Procurement

HOW THE ARMY RUNS

b. The mission of the U.S. Army Recruiting Command (USAREC) is to obtain the quantity and quality of recruits to meet both AC and USAR requirements. Active Component enlistment options provide the vehicle by which Army applicants are attracted. The option packages vary and contain such incentives for applicants as training guarantees, unit/station of choice assignments (used primarily for prior service applicants), and payment of bonuses or education incentives. Additionally, the length of the enlistment period varies for certain options and skills.

(1) Quality Constraints. The recruiter is constrained by quality standards, which must be met. A potential enlistee is classified as a result of an Armed Services Vocational Aptitude Battery (ASVAB) which has 10 aptitude areas. ASVAB results place individuals into test score categories and determine both basic enlistment and specific MOS eligibility. Both law and Army policy constrain the number of certain test categories the recruiting force may enlist. The Army Non-Prior Service (NPS) accession quality program seeks to maximize the number of high school diploma graduates and those in the upper test score categories, with a ceiling established for the lower test score categories.

(2) MOS Training Targets. All new Soldiers receive a minimum of 12 weeks of Initial Entry Training (IET) prior to becoming available for deployment. All new Soldiers recruited by USAREC contract for a specific MOS, which is supported by a resourced training seat. Using projections from Enlisted Specialties Model, HRC projects annual IET requirements for new Soldiers in the ANNPRO for each MOS. These requirements then feed into the ATRRS. In ATRRS, IET requirements combine with professional development and other training requirements and are presented at the SMDR for resourcing. Once approved by the Army leadership, all training requirements and approved training programs are identified in the ARPRINT.

(3) Management of Recruiting Objectives. REQUEST is an automated enlistment and training space management system designed to support the Army's recruiting and RC retention missions. The system is a worldwide, real-time, interactive system and is the controlling element for recruiters and RC retention Noncommissioned Officers (NCO) in translating aggregate mission objectives to the MOS needs of the Army. It uses a worldwide telecommunications network with remote data terminals accessing a common data bank containing the Army's training programs determined by the ARPRINT and modified in the year of execution by TRAPs which either increase or decrease the SMDR ANNPRO to meet current requirements. ATRRS provides class schedules and quota allocations to REQUEST, which becomes visible to Army recruiters to enlist Soldiers to fill those quotas. The system provides reservation processing for enlistment options, accession controls, and management information reports from remote data terminals.

(a) REQUEST, designed to enhance the efficiency of Army recruiting, provides the Army with a means of allocating training resources to accessions. Enlistment options during periods of non-mobilization result from a review of the applicant's qualifications based on the ASVAB, physical testing, individual preference, and Army MOS requirements. An automated matching algorithm aligns the applicant's qualifications, desires, and aptitudes to the Army's needs. Qualification checks and other features of the system preclude erroneous enlistments into skills for which the applicant does not qualify.

(b) The REQUEST Unit Distribution Program (RUDIST) adds a unit vacancy and distribution guidance file to the REQUEST System. A portion of the training spaces for MOSs available under an enlistment option guarantees a first assignment is allocated to specific units and stations. Allocations of first assignment are based upon projected unit requirements and distribution policies. This is primarily used for Prior Service Soldiers. For Non-Prior Service applicants, the majority are contracted as uncommitted, providing maximum flexibility to the distribution system to assign them to a unit where they best meet an army requirement.

(c) The REQUEST System is the controlling element for recruiters in translating aggregate recruiting objectives to the MOS needs of the Army.

(4) Military Entrance Processing Station (MEPS).

(a) The MEPS is a jointly staffed Service activity charged with aptitude testing, medical examination, moral evaluation, and administrative processing of applicants for the Armed Forces. DA is the Department of Defense (DOD) Executive Agent for the MEPS. The Military Entrance Processing Command (MEPCOM) commands and controls the MEPS.

(b) Once the recruiter has determined the applicant's desire to enlist and his or her areas of interest, he or she can administer an enlistment screening test which gives an informal indication of how the applicant might fare on the ASVAB. If the applicant continues his or her interest, he or she goes to MEPS for processing.

MILITARY HUMAN RESOURCE MANAGEMENT

13-13. Warrant Officer (WO) Procurement

a. WOs are highly specialized officers, appointed based on technical competence and leadership abilities. USAREC procures warrant officer candidates for the AC. DCS, G–1 develops a recruiting goal by MOS for each FY. USAREC uses this and an internally created lead refinement list, to direct recruiting efforts, especially for hard-skill MOSs with existing or projected critical shortages. Applicants come from the best of the NCO ranks, outside the Army (primarily aviation applicants), other in-service sources such as other Services, commissioned officers, and members of the RC.

b. Applications of all eligible individuals are evaluated by a HQDA selection board. USAREC conducts the board which is composed of a field grade officer president and warrant officer members from each branch with applicants to be considered. Those recommended by the board on an order of merit list are slated to attend the Warrant Officer Candidate School (WOCS), in a candidate status, as procurement openings present themselves. Each new WO1 then attends the appropriate Warrant Officer Basic Course (WOBC) to complete certification training.

c. The recruitment, application processing, and selection of warrant officers for the USAR is performed in a similar manner as the AC. However, USAREC recruits warrant officer candidates against specific USAR unit vacancies. In addition, USAREC accepts and processes applications for Active Guard Reserve (AGR), Individual Mobilization Augmentee (IMA), and Individual Ready Reserve (IRR) vacancies. The USAR uses boarding and school-slating procedures similar to those used by the AC. The ARNG solicits applications through announcement of vacancies via an internal recruiting effort. The boarding and school-slating procedures are as determined by each individual State Adjutant General. All RC WO applicants attend WOCS and WOBC. RC versions for many WOBCs are available.

13-14. Commissioned Officer Procurement

a. The PMAD is the authoritative source for officer requirements. Authorizations are defined by unit, by Area of Concentration (AOC), and by grade for all grades except WO1. There are no authorizations for WO1s in the U.S. Army. Procurement each year is based on an analysis of the current inventory and the losses projected by the DCS, G-1. This annual procurement number is then disaggregated by HRC into an allocation for each branch. The G-1 then distributes an allocation of branches to each commissioning source. Sufficient officers must be procured each year to ensure an adequate number of trained individuals by grade, AOC, and skill is available for utilization in the future. There are constraints associated with the management of officer end-strength contained in Title 10 United States Code (USC). There is no specific force structure allowance for the officer corps within the authorized end strength of the Army. However, for field grade officers, Title 10 USC restricts the number of officers serving at each grade as a proportion of the size of the officer corps. Training constraints limit the number of officers that can be procured in each branch.

b. Officer Sources. The sources of officer procurement for the basic branches are Officer Candidate School (OCS), Reserve Officers' Training Corps (ROTC), and USMA. Requirements are determined by the DCS, G-1 and filled through the various commissioning programs and special branch programs. To supplement these appointments, recall of reserve officers, recall of retired officers, direct appointments, and inter-service transfers are also used. The inter-service transfer program allows the Army to access members of the Air Force, Navy, Marine Corps, or Coast Guard to fill shortages in the mid-grade ranks and has proven effective as the other services have been decreasing officer strength. All commissioned officers incur a statutory eight-year Military Service Obligation (MSO), which may be supplemented by concurrent or consecutive obligations like those described in AR 350-100. Officers may serve their MSO it in a variety of ways depending on the source of their commission as outlined below.

(1) The OCS.

(a) OCS at Fort Benning, Georgia, trains and commissions officers for both the AC and RC. AC OCS graduates incur a three-year Active Duty Service Obligation (ADSO) and may serve the remainder of their eight-year MSO on active duty or in the RC. RC graduates receive a reserve appointment and return to reserve status after completing their initial officer training requirements such as Basic Officer Leaders Course (BOLC) or Airborne or Ranger School. RC graduates not only incur the statutory MSO but must serve six years of that in a Troop Program Unit (TPU) as a drilling reservist.

(b) In-service candidates are enlisted Soldiers serving on active duty. Semi-annual selection boards at HRC select qualified Soldier applicants for OCS. Branches are assigned based on the needs of the Army and candidate's preferences. In-service candidates incur a three-year ADSO within their eight-year MSO.

(c) Enlistment option candidates are qualified college graduates who elect to enlist in the Army in order to attend the OCS. These candidates enlist in the Army and attend basic training followed by the 12-week OCS course. Enlistment option candidates incur a three-year ADSO within their eight-year MSO.

(d) Additionally, each state runs a National Guard OCS to commission officers into the RC.

(2) ROTC. The ROTC trains and commissions officers for both the AC and the RC. Branching is accomplished through Cadet Command and HQDA boards based on the needs of the Army and the cadet's qualifications, standings on the Order of Merit List, and individual preferences.

(a) AC. Upon accession, scholarship cadets incur a four-year ADSO within their eight-year MSO, while non-scholarship cadets incur a three-year ADSO with their eight-year MSO. The remainder of any MSO may be served in the AC or in the RC.

(b) RC. Scholarship cadets must serve in a TPU all eight years of their MSO, while non-scholarship cadets must serve at least six years in a TPU. The remainder of the MSO may be spent in the IRR.

(3) USMA. The USMA trains and commissions officers for the AC. A formal branch selection process matches the needs of the Army with cadet preferences based on a strict order of merit list. The active duty service obligation for USMA graduates is five years and the remainder of the MSO may be spent in the AC or RC.

(4) Special Branches. The special branches–Judge Advocate General's Corps (JAG), the medical branches, and the Chaplains Corps–procure officers through their individual programs, and service obligations vary depending upon the program. Procurement for most medical officers and Chaplains has been assigned to USAREC while JAG is responsible for its own recruiting.

Section IV
The Compensation Function

13-15. Compensation Overview

a. Compensation is a relatively recent addition to the military HR life cycle. Over one third of the Army's total obligation authority relates to compensation and only through controlling the cost drivers (number, grade, and skill of Soldiers) can the Army manage the dollars appropriated by Congress.

b. The Army's personnel assets are centrally managed as are Army resources tied to these assets. The Army pays against the inventory (assigned strength), but authorizations and personnel policies are the cost drivers.

c. Personnel management policies, force structure decisions, and content of the force influence the Military Personnel, Army (MPA) appropriation requirement. Among these cost drivers are the following.

(1) Pay rates
(2) Retirement rates, including number of medical retirements vice normal retirements, and early retirements (less than 20 years of service)
(3) Cost of food
(4) Social Security and Medicare rates
(5) Basic Allowance for Housing (BAH), including programs similar to
(6) Residence Communities Initiative (RCI), privatize housing, privatize barracks
(7) Military Health Care
(8) Stationing plans and manpower.
(9) Clothing bag
(10) Entitlements
(11) Special Pays (Medical, Aviation, Special Duty Assignment Pay (SDAP), etc.)
(12) Assignment Incentive Pay (AIP)
(13) Enlistment bonuses
(14) State of the Economy
(15) Reenlistment rates/bonuses
(16) Separation Pays
(17) Marital status
(18) Size of the Army Outside of the Continental United States (OCONUS) and overseas station allowances
(19) Tour lengths
(20) Force changes

MILITARY HUMAN RESOURCE MANAGEMENT

(21) Grade and skill content
(22) Active Duty Operational Support (ADOS)
(23) Unemployment Compensation
(24) ROTC pay/scholarships
(25) Junior ROTC (JROTC) support

d. The MPA account pays the force, moves the force, subsists the force, and supports the force. Pay includes pay and allowances for officers, enlisted, and cadets. Movement is managed under the PCS account, which is sub-divided into accessions, separations, training, operational, rotational, and unit moves. Subsistence provides payment for the basic allowance for subsistence and subsistence in kind. Finally, support comes in other military personnel costs such as education, adoption, unemployment, death gratuities, and survivor benefit programs.

13-16. Manning Program Evaluation Group (PEG)
At the departmental level, all personnel-related programs are contained within the Manning PEG. The Manning PEG has responsibility to determine the valid requirements for those programs in Figure 13-3. All should come together in providing the right skills, at the right place and time.

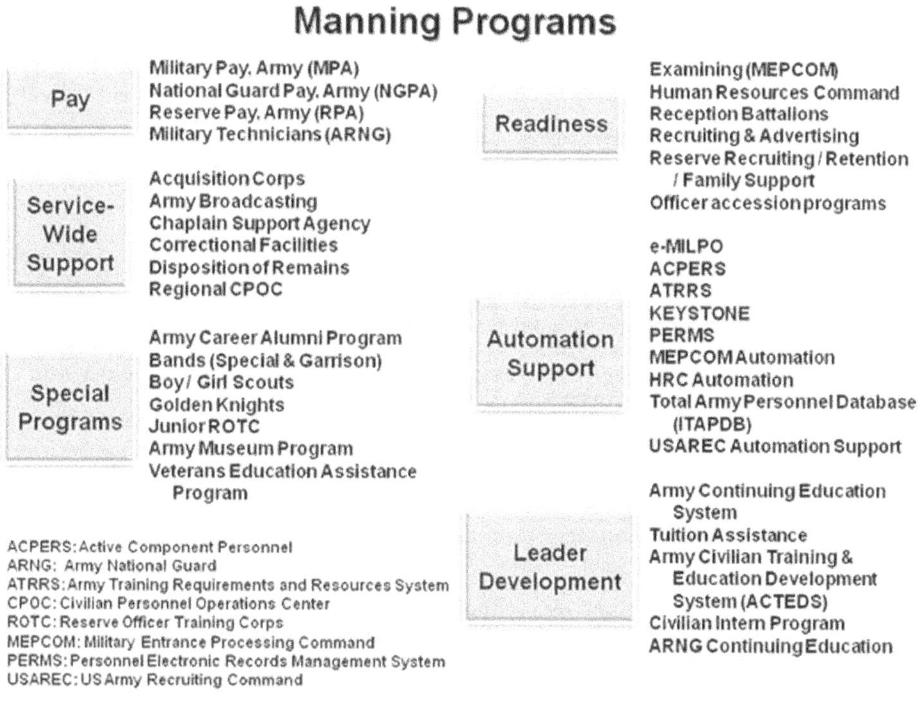

Manning Programs

Pay
- Military Pay, Army (MPA)
- National Guard Pay, Army (NGPA)
- Reserve Pay, Army (RPA)
- Military Technicians (ARNG)

Service-Wide Support
- Acquisition Corps
- Army Broadcasting
- Chaplain Support Agency
- Correctional Facilities
- Disposition of Remains
- Regional CPOC

Special Programs
- Army Career Alumni Program
- Bands (Special & Garrison)
- Boy/ Girl Scouts
- Golden Knights
- Junior ROTC
- Army Museum Program
- Veterans Education Assistance Program

Readiness
- Examining (MEPCOM)
- Human Resources Command
- Reception Battalions
- Recruiting & Advertising
- Reserve Recruiting / Retention / Family Support
- Officer accession programs

Automation Support
- e-MILPO
- ACPERS
- ATRRS
- KEYSTONE
- PERMS
- MEPCOM Automation
- HRC Automation
- Total Army Personnel Database (ITAPDB)
- USAREC Automation Support

Leader Development
- Army Continuing Education System
- Tuition Assistance
- Army Civilian Training & Education Development System (ACTEDS)
- Civilian Intern Program
- ARNG Continuing Education

ACPERS: Active Component Personnel
ARNG: Army National Guard
ATRRS: Army Training Requirements and Resources System
CPOC: Civilian Personnel Operations Center
ROTC: Reserve Officer Training Corps
MEPCOM: Military Entrance Processing Command
PERMS: Personnel Electronic Records Management System
USAREC: US Army Recruiting Command

Figure 13-3. Manning Programs

HOW THE ARMY RUNS

Section V
The Distribution Function

13-17. Enlisted Distribution and Assignment
   a. Distribution Challenge. In theory, the distribution planning and assignment processes place the right Soldier with the right skills at the right place at the right time. In fact, the system does a very credible job for those MOSs and grades which are nearly balanced, those for which the overseas-to-sustaining base ratio is supportable, and for those in which there is a high density of personnel in substitutable skills. The problem arises in the MOSs where these conditions do not exist, and a sharing of shortages is required for all commands. When certain commands, or organizations, are exempted from "shortage-sharing" based upon special guidance, it compounds shortages to be shared by the organizations lower in priority. The readiness cost of this compounded shortage-sharing comes to light when each organization must assess its mission capable status in the monthly readiness reporting. The personnel component of the report involves several calculations, but its principal factors are assigned strength, available strength, available senior grade personnel (Sergeant (SGT) and above), and MOS qualification.
   (1) Enlisted personnel distribution is a very complex business, replete with pitfalls and shortcomings because of the rapidly changing variables that exist–force structure changes, recruiting success, training attrition rates, retention rates, military personnel authorizations, dollar constraints, and most of all, the unpredictability of the individual Soldier, his or her health, and his or her family. All of these variables point up the critical factors which govern successful distribution–the accuracy and timeliness of the databases being used for analysis. Authorizations not approved and posted expeditiously to PMAD and individual change data not properly reported for posting on the TAPDB-AE make the already complicated distribution system less responsive.
   (2) Soldiers have the ability to influence their assignment in several ways. One is by submitting an assignment preference. They do so via a web-based application called Assignment Satisfaction Key (ASK), which allows the Soldier to update his/her assignment desires and volunteer for valid requirements directly with HRC in real time.
   b. Distribution Planning and Priorities.
   (1) The Army introduced the program of Force Stabilization in FY 2004, in order to provide Soldiers and their families more predictability and stability during periods of high Operating Tempo (OPTEMPO), and build more cohesive, combat-ready units. This program has two primary components: stabilization and unit-focused stability. Stabilization is designed to assign Soldiers, on their initial assignment, for much longer periods of time than in the past. During this extended period, the Soldier may deploy several times, but his/her family would enjoy a level of stability. Also during the Soldier's career, he/she would return to that installation repeatedly, if possible. Unit-focused stability synchronizes the Soldier's tour with the unit's operational cycle but also allows commanders flexibility to manage turbulence within their unit by focusing training around replacement periods.
   (2) The basic document that defines priorities for the distribution of enlisted personnel to all units/activities is the FY HQDA Manning Guidance. DCS, G-1 publishes and distributes this guidance to HRC and to Army commands for implementation after the Chief of Staff, U.S. Army (CSA) approves it. The guidance provides responsibilities at all levels for manning units and expected level of fill commands can expect. Distribution is driven by requirements to fill approved authorizations documented in PMAD/UAD, Directed Military Overstrength (DMO), and overstrengths in specific high priority units. Distribution is affected by recruiting and retention goal achievement; unprogrammed losses; and fiscal constraints affecting promotions, PCS movements, and end strength. Special priorities are based on operational and training requirements for special skills, such as Ranger qualifications and linguists.
   (3) In 1999, the CSA dramatically changed the distribution priorities in the Army, by establishing four general priorities. The priorities were: 1) AC divisions, Armored Cavalry Regiments (ACR), and other high-priority organizations/positions (e.g. drill sergeants, prison guards, recruiters, 75thRanger Regiment, Active/Reserve Component (AC/RC) positions, Combat Training Centers (CTC), etc.); 2) early deploying units; 3) the remainder of the MTOE Army not previously filled; 4) TDA Army. These priorities were designed to first fill warfighting formations but had to be accomplished without breaking any organizations in the process. Manning the Force in accordance with the CSA priorities, a key ingredient of the Personnel Transformation initiative, postured the Army very well to respond to Operation Enduring Freedom (OEF) and Operation Iraqi Freedom (OIF). As these operations became more protracted, enlisted distribution guidance changed in FY 2004 to focus primarily on units that were deployed, units

MILITARY HUMAN RESOURCE MANAGEMENT

preparing to deploy, and other high-priority units based on policy or statute, and the guidance has been adjusted almost annually. FY 2010-2011 G-1 distribution guidance employs a phased readiness methodology and is reflected in Figure 13-4.

(4) The HQDA AC Manning Guidance for FY 2011 establishes AC manning priorities, manning goals, and responsibilities at all levels for the accomplishment of these goals. The Army remains in an environment of high demand with critical shortages preventing the meeting of all manning requirements. Manning priorities, strategies, and goals are designed to support our Army in this environment. Personnel distribution decisions continue to be a function of a unit's mission and deployment status: deployed; preparing to deploy; or not expected to deploy. The current manning methodology is reflected in Figure 13-4.

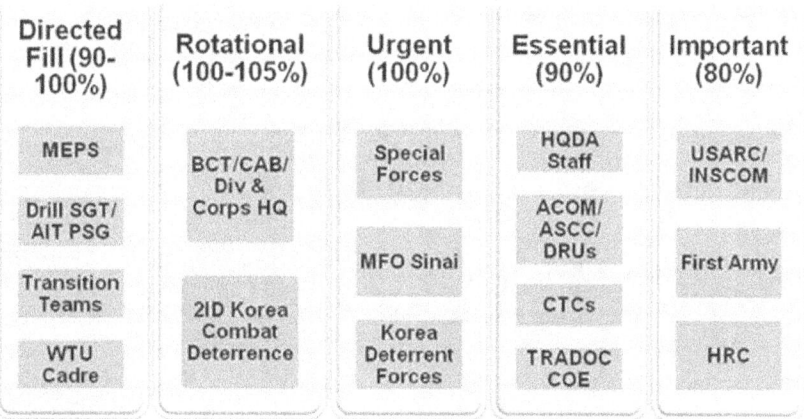

Figure 13-4. Headquarters, Department of the Army (HQDA) Fiscal Year (FY) 13-15 Active Component (AC) Manning Guidance

c. Enlisted Distribution Target Model (EDTM).

(1) The EDTM is an automated system that creates enlisted distribution targets by MOS, grade, and UIC. The model fills each UIC reflected in the PMAD with projected available inventory from the Enlisted Specialties Model in accordance with the DCS, G-1 distribution policy. This results in an optimum distribution of scarce resources consistent with distribution policy fill priorities. The EDTM constrains the assignment process to coincide with the projected OS targets. It represents the assets the Army realistically expects to be available for distribution.

(2) The EDTM is maintained by the Enlisted Readiness Division, Enlisted Personnel Management Directorate (EPMD), HRC. The targets are produced monthly with EDTM targets for grade bands E1-4,

HOW THE ARMY RUNS

E5-8, and E9. Current Month (CM) through CM+18 are visible to field personnel managers via Personnel Network (PERNET) using the EDAS.

   d. Management Systems. HRC uses several automated data-processing systems to distribute, manage, and develop active duty enlisted personnel. These systems are described below and reflected in Figure 13-5.

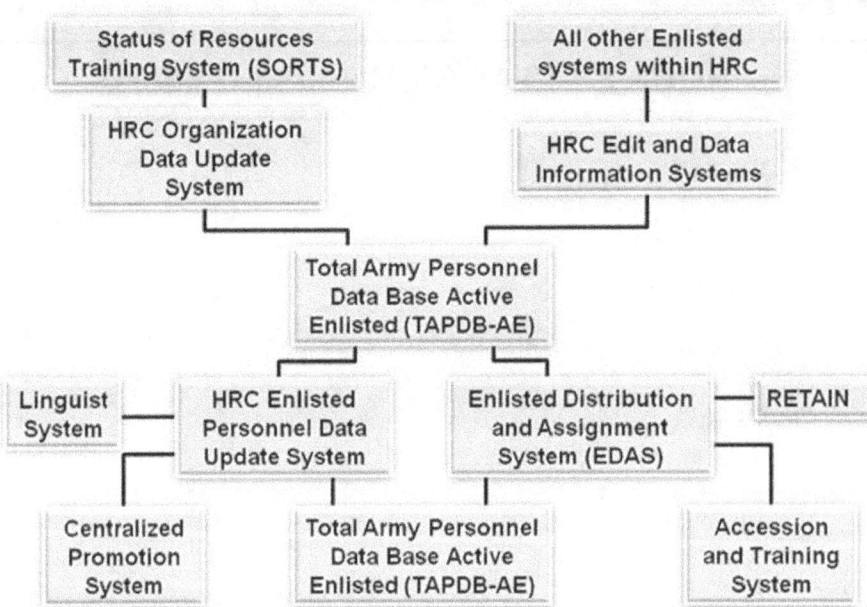

Figure 13-5. Enlisted Automation Management System

   (1) TAPDB is the heart of the overall system. It consists of three logical components containing personnel, requisition, and organizational data. The Personnel (Component of TAPDB) (PER DB) contains personnel information on every active duty Soldier. HRC and DCS, G-1 use this information to determine Army readiness, strength, promotion eligibles, reassignable personnel, and training requirements. The Requisition (Component of TAPDB) (REQ DB) contains information on requirements to move individuals and information on those who have been directed to move (assignments). The Organization (Component of TAPDB) (ORG DB) contains information on location and status of Army units; it does not contain any authorization or unit strength information.
   (2) HRC Enlisted Personnel Data Update System (PEPDUS) is one of the major systems used to update the data on the TAPDB. It consists of two components, a batch component and an online, interactive component that allows managers worldwide to query and update personnel data.
   (a) The batch component receives transactions daily from other systems. The primary source is eMILPO, but other sources such as the Centralized Promotion System and the EDAS submit transactions. PEPDUS is also designed to support mobilization. During a mobilization scenario it is able to process over 500,000 transactions daily. As PEPDUS updates the TAPDB, it also creates transactions

MILITARY HUMAN RESOURCE MANAGEMENT

that are passed back to eMILPO (receipt notices, update transactions, DA error notices, etc.), in order to update the TAPDB-Mobilization (TAPDB-MOB), and provide feedback to other systems.

(b) The on-line interactive component allows EPMD managers to update data items on the PER DB. Some examples are Continental United States (CONUS) and OCONUS assignment preferences, assignment eligibility, and Date Eligible for Return from Overseas (DEROS). As EPMD managers update, PEPDUS updates the eMILPO Personnel File.

(3) EDAS is an on-line system which allows EPMD managers to create, review, and update requisition and assignment data. It also provides reports for those managers for strength management of the force. It has several batch programs that exchange information with external systems. EDAS allows EPMD distribution and assignment managers to work with one collection of information on the same computer. Under previous systems, updates to information occurred only during the weekend; updates are now instantaneous. Consequently, decisions made by one manager are immediately available to all other managers. Moreover, EDAS provides field users the capability to view and in some cases update the same information that distribution and assignment managers use to make decisions. Finally, EDAS reduces the time to validate a requirement, select a Soldier to fill the requirement, and transmit the assignment instructions to the field. A more detailed explanation on how EDAS is used in distributing and assigning Soldiers is presented in a subsequent section.

(4) Assignment of Newly Trained Personnel.

(a) Permanent unit assignments are based on input to HRC from basic and advanced individual training centers via the Student/Trainee Management System-Enlisted (STRAMS-E), a module within the ATRRS. Information is passed by ATRRS to EDAS which processes newly trained personnel for assignment.

(b) If an individual has an enlistment agreement for a unit in an area, he or she is assigned according to the enlistment contract upon satisfactory completion of training. Soldiers who have no unit/area options are assigned against requirements in accordance with a distribution plan prepared by HRC. Assignment instructions are generated by EDAS and sent directly to losing commands. The transaction is processed through EDAS and is posted to the TAPDB. EDAS advises the gaining command of the assignment.

e. Enlisted Distribution Management. HRC Enlisted Readiness Division manages the strengths of major overseas commands, Army commands, and special management and functional commands worldwide. HRC established a direct requisition authority to each of the brigade combat teams Brigade Combat Team (BCT)/ACRs to ensure projected gains to those organizations were not diverted by installation strength managers. Under modularity and brigade centric organizations, brigades with organic military HR assets will requisition and receive replacements directly from HRC. Strength managers at HRC project the assigned strength of an activity ranging from the current month's strength out to 12 months, and determine how many Soldiers are needed each month to ensure the commands meet targets established by the FY enlisted distribution policy (Figure 13-4). These aggregate totals (arranged by individual rank and rank bands, i.e., private-specialist, sergeant-staff sergeant, sergeant first class-master sergeant, and sergeant major) are the basis for transition into individual MOS requirements. These top-of-the-system strength managers then determine how many requisitions for replacements should be placed in EDAS, by either directly building the requisitions or coordinating with field commanders.

f. Overseas Requisitions. Requirements for Korea, U.S. Army, Europe (USAREUR), and U.S. Army, Pacific (USARPAC) are analyzed 10 months into the future (eight months for USARPAC). Using the EDTM targets, distribution managers allocate requisitions to each command at the four-character MOS level, allowing commands two weeks to submit requisitions at the nine-character MOS level, including any other special requirements.

g. CONUS Requisitions.

(1) For CONUS installations, requisitioning is partially constrained through a process known as Requisition Allocation Plan-CONUS (RAP-C). Since fill of vacancies in CONUS commands is partially based on eligible overseas returnees, RAP-C keys on DEROS data in the TAPDB-AE and calculates the number of Soldiers in an MOS and grade who are expected to return to CONUS in a requisition month (two months after DEROS month). CONUS requisitions are normally validated 12 months out. Distributors at HRC, using the EDTM, allocate these Soldiers. If the EDTM requires more requisitions than Soldiers returning from overseas, additional requisitions are loaded, which will require CONUS-to-CONUS moves.

HOW THE ARMY RUNS

(2) The next effort for HQDA distribution managers is validation, whether for CONUS or OCONUS. If an apparent over or under requisitioning exists, the manager attempts to resolve the discrepancy with the command/installation prior to making a decision to validate, or not validate, requisitions. Discrepancies in the two projections may be caused by a proponent-approved authorization change at the unit level not yet recorded in the Personnel Structure and Composition System (PERSACS), or by more current authorizations data available to HRC through the use of the PMAD, or by more current gain and loss data. The problem is resolved prior to the submission of the validated requisitions for assignment processing in the EDAS.

(3) Distribution managers continually monitor command and installation strength projections and adjust accordingly. Deletions, authorization changes, and other variables may create need for top loading or canceling requisitions.

h. EDAS. EDAS consists of several major subsystems: management information, requisition, policy, assignment, and personnel.

(1) EPMD distribution managers use the management information subsystem to determine an organization's authorized, assigned, and projected strength. Managers can obtain this information by MOS, skill, CMF, grade, Special Qualification Identifier (SQI), ASI, language, Distribution Management Level/Sub-Level (DML/DMSL), location (installation, state, and country), command, requisition activity code, Troop Program Sequence Number (TPSN), and/or UIC. This information is used to determine the number of valid requisitions needed to maintain that organization at an acceptable strength level.

(2) After the distribution managers determine the number of valid requisitions, the assignment managers must fill them. The policy and nomination subsystems assist assignment managers by recommending which Soldier should be assigned to each requisition and also provide alternate recommendations.

(3) The policy subsystem allows EPMD managers to enter assignments into EDAS that are in accordance with current policies. For example, Soldiers with Homebase/Advanced Assignment Program (HAAP) agreements can only be recommended for assignments which fulfill HAAP agreements.

(4) In addition to making assignments, the assignment subsystem provides the capability to delete or defer Soldiers. If field users have the authority to approve a deletion or deferment, they can complete the action interactively through the assignment subsystem as an alternative to submitting it through eMILPO. If field users do not have the authority to approve the action, they can request a deletion or deferment electronically through EDAS. Throughout this entire process, the field user can interactively monitor the current status of the request.

(5) One important aspect of EDAS is that the system tightly controls access and what the user can do in the system. Some modules allow users to query data, while others allow updates. EDAS controls access by individual user and provides system managers with audit trails which can be used to determine who accessed or changed data in the system. Additionally, EDAS controls which records a user can query and/or update.

(6) The EDAS promotion points update module allows field personnel managers to post promotion point data for Soldiers in grades E4 and E5 directly to the TAPDB. This function allows personnel managers to review and update the information that is resident on the TAPDB. This information is then used by HRC to determine the numbers of promotions for each month by MOS. By using the promotion subsystem, field managers can see those Soldiers, by name, who were considered eligible for promotion when the calculations were performed. If the data on the Soldiers is incomplete or in error, field managers use the EDAS promotion point update and promotion update functions to update the data, promote the Soldier, or alert HRC managers as to why Soldiers will not be promoted. EDAS returns the promotion on the Soldier to eMILPO which then updates local databases and the Defense Finance and Accounting Service (DFAS).

(7) EDAS fully supports mobilization scenarios. The policy subsystem can store and maintain any number of scenarios (peace, limited mobilization, full mobilization, etc.) and the user can invoke any one of the scenarios in seconds. The system can also evaluate "what if" questions.

i. The Army Automated RETAIN. RETAIN is a real-time automated system that identifies and reserves training spaces or assignment vacancies for potential reenlistees and determines MOS availability for Soldiers undergoing reclassification based upon the individual's qualifications and the needs of the Army. It is also used to process enlisted Soldiers for reenlistment or reclassification assignments.

(1) If the Soldier is requesting a MOS training space, RETAIN accesses the REQUEST system to determine if there are any AC in-service quotas available for the school the Soldier desires. If the seat is

MILITARY HUMAN RESOURCE MANAGEMENT

available, it allows the retention NCO or reclassification authority to make a reservation and puts the record on the RETAIN wait list for an ultimate assignment in the new MOS upon completion of training. The wait list manager is required to give the Soldier an ultimate assignment 120 days prior to the start date of the school. RETAIN is also used to process potential reenlistees for assignments. RETAIN will determine if there are any vacancies available for the installation/overseas area the Soldier desires. If a vacancy exists, it will be offered to the Soldier. If a vacancy does not exist, the Soldier may elect to be put on the RETAIN wait list.

(2) The RETAIN wait list is for those Soldiers desiring an installation/overseas area which was not available and no other area/location was available at the time of entry into RETAIN. Weekly, the RETAIN system attempts to match Soldiers on the wait list to the place they desire to go.

(3) RETAIN is a valuable tool that commanders, career counselors, and personnel service centers use in counseling Soldiers for reenlistment and reclassification. Since RETAIN is a real-time automated system it can provide current, accurate information to the potential reenlistee or Soldier involved in reclassification.

j. Reclassification. RETAIN also addresses reclassification. Reclassification is a process which provides for migration from one MOS to another. It supports policies and goals to reduce MOS overstrength and alleviate shortages. In addition to individual voluntary requests, mandatory reclassifications are necessary when a Soldier loses qualification, for example, loss of security clearance, or disqualifying medical condition. Special reclassification programs, such as Fast Track, realign MOS overages through reenlistment and reclassification. Soldiers possessing the overstrength MOS may be allowed to reclassify or reenlist for retraining without regard to Expiration of Term of Service (ETS).

13-18. Officer Distribution and Assignment

The Army continues to adapt and change its officer assets by branch, functional area, and grade equal the sum total found in authorization documents, taking into consideration Professional Military Education (PME) schools and training programs for each branch and functional area. In fact, force structure change and growth due to modularity is by far outpacing the Army's ability to meet authorizations in certain skills and grades.

a. Distribution Planning. The officer distribution planners and managers at HRC are influenced by three principal factors: officer assets (inventory), authorizations, and priorities. All three are in a constant state of change. Therefore, there is a need for a master distribution plan that will ensure that all commands, agencies, and activities receive, according to priority, an appropriate share of the available officer assets/inventory. The foundation of this master plan is a management tool known as the Dynamic Distribution System (DDS), formerly the Officer Distribution Plan (ODP), and also formerly the Officer Distribution System (ODS). The DDS brings assets/inventory, authorizations, and priorities into balance and is one of the Army's most important systems for officer distribution planning. DDS allows the Army to be more flexible during times of war and transformation, as DDS allows us to shift with the Army's changing priorities.

b. The DDS Process. If available officer assets matched the requirements identified through the PMAD, by branch, functional area, and grade, officers would simply be assigned against authorizations. However, this is rarely the case. As with most resources, there is generally a greater demand than there is a supply, and officer shortages in certain units is a result. Some system of priorities is needed to help manage these shortages. After the available officer inventory has been compared with the authorizations in the PMAD, a computer system, Statistical Analysis Software (SAS) runs a program model to determine officer needs based on current Army Manning Guidance initiatives and any special distribution guidance as determined by HQDA (Figure 13-6). Under DDS, an available officer fits into one of two categories: non-discretionary or discretionary. An important concept to keep in mind is what defines an available officer. An available officer is defined differently for each type of unit. Generally speaking, a deploying brigade needs a non-dwell restricted, deployable, PME graduate that needs key development time. The opposite is true for the National Training Center which needs a Key Developmental (KD) complete officer with recent deployment experience. A non-discretionary move includes those moves that involve hard dates in an officer's career, e.g., a DEROS from an overseas assignment, a report date to a professional school, a graduation date from a school, a command selection, a Personnel Management System (PMS) selection, a joint tour completion, a sequential assignment report date, or a retirement date. These can generally be determined from data analysis from TOPMIS. A discretionary move includes those moves that are triggered by an assignment officer working to ensure an officer continues appropriate career

HOW THE ARMY RUNS

development e.g., an officer needs a new skill set (Joint or Army Staff), an officer's skills are no longer applicable to the current assignment, or where an officer is pre-positioned for a career enhancing position (Command, Schools, etc.). Moves driven by the individual needs of the officer are also included in this category e.g. Exceptional Family Member Program (EFMP), joint domicile, and compassionate reassignments and personal preference.

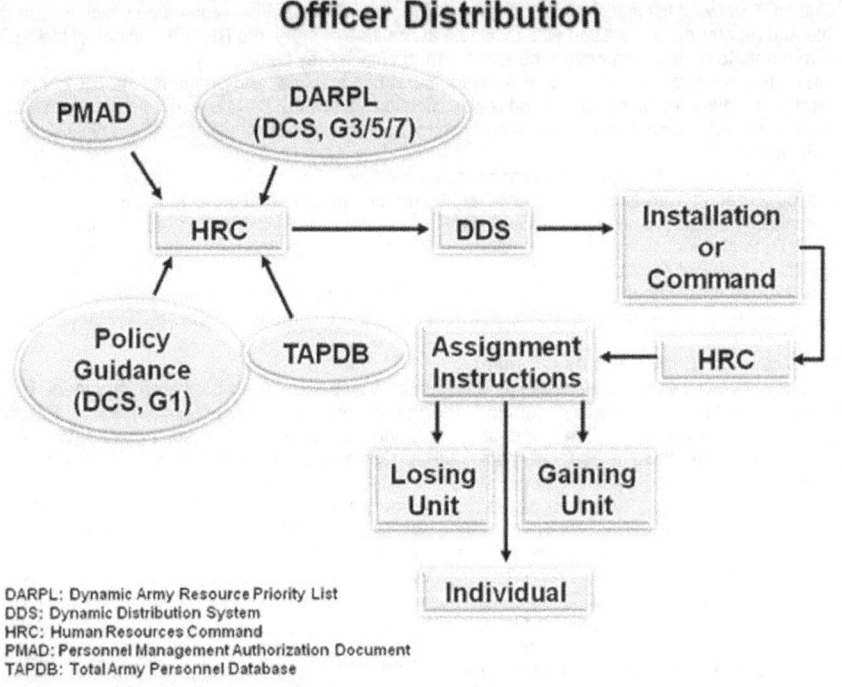

Figure 13-6. Officer Distribution

c. Officer Requisition System. The officer requisition system is designed to fill the officer requirements of all commands and activities.

(1) TOPMIS. This is a fully integrated management information system that supports the officer management process within HRC and at worldwide requisitioning activities. TOPMIS is composed of seven operational modules:

(a) The control module provides security of access and updating, creates individual user profiles, and provides on-line electronic mail service to all TOPMIS users.

(b) The strength module displays operating and projected strength down to the CMF level for requisitioning activities in various report formats.

(c) The goaling and monitoring module displays assignment goals for the FY by grade and CMF. It is also used to plan the DDS and monitor its progress.

(d) The requisition module allows distribution managers and the requisition activity managers to generate, edit, validate (based on the DDS), and update requisitions. This module generates and maintains requisitions based on projected strength. The final product is a list of requisitions for career managers to fill.

MILITARY HUMAN RESOURCE MANAGEMENT

(e) The asset/Officer Record Brief (ORB) module provides an online version of the ORB and the capability for on-line updating of ORB fields by career managers. This module also provides access to by-name reports of officers assigned and/or on orders.

(f) The assignment module provides access to personnel, requisition, and organization data; provides online extract/update capability from the TAPDB-AO via TOPMIS; and processes assignments generated by HRC managers in the Officer Personnel Management Directorate (OPMD). Assignment instructions are transmitted electronically on a daily basis to the gaining and losing requisition activity.

(g) The user assistance module allows users to review data name definitions and tables of valid codes used in officer management.

(h) TOPMIS interacts with the TAPDB-AO and is used by assignment and distribution managers of the basic branches, medical department branches, the Chief of Chaplains, and JAG offices. Worldwide requisition/officer management activities can access TOPMIS through the Defense Data Network (DDN) or a variety of host-to-host systems.

(2) Requisition Cycles. Officer requisitions are generated on an alternating bimonthly basis for either overseas or CONUS. As a general goal, requisitions are validated so that officers will arrive 12 months after validation, which also allows a 12-month notification to the officer concerned. As a normal rule, overseas returnees, school requirements and units preparing to deploy drive the assignment system because these officers must move on time and deploying units must have necessary officer assets. Overseas returnees and various school requirements are largely due to tour length policies and graduation dates respectively. Others are assigned to replace these personnel and the cycle continues.

(3) Assignment Challenge. Assignment officers within the divisions and branches of OPMD must take into consideration a wide variety of competing factors in the process of identifying the right officers to fill valid requisitions. Some, but by no means all, of these factors are listed below. They are in no particular order, because each assignment action is unique.
   (a) Army requirements
   (b) Gaining and losing organizations' requirements
   (c) Tour equity (CONUS vs OCONUS)
   (d) Time-on-station and Dwell time
   (e) Professional development
   (f) Officer preference
   (g) Joint domicile
   (h) Compassionate situations
   (i) CTC experience
   (j) Joint duty

Section VI
The Development Function

13-19. Enlisted Development
There must be a way of developing leadership, evaluating, and rewarding those who do well, and eliminating those who do not measure up. This section will address some of the programs designed to accomplish these tasks and to create an environment which will motivate men and women to become career Soldiers.

13-20. EPMS
a. The EPMS provides a logical career path from private to sergeant major, career-long training, and performance-oriented evaluation. Additionally, it is designed to eliminate promotion bottlenecks, provide all Soldiers with promotion opportunities, make assignments more flexible, and provide greater challenge by making MOSs more multi-functional.

b. A key feature of EPMS is to associate five standardized skill levels for the enlisted ranks, with privates and specialists having skill level 1 and master sergeants and sergeants major having skill level 5. EPMS skill levels were selected so that the vital middle-grade NCOs would be distinct and visible for management purposes.

c. Another major feature of EPMS is the Noncommissioned Officer Education System (NCOES). EPMS and NCOES are part of the same continuum.

HOW THE ARMY RUNS

13-21. Enlisted Evaluation System (EES)
At the heart of EPMS is the EES. It is used to assist in the identification of Soldiers for assignment, promotion, reenlistment, reclassification, special training, elimination, and other personnel management actions. The EES consists of Academic Evaluation Reports (AER) and a NCO Evaluation Report (NCOER) for sergeant and above. Both reports serve as the official evaluation of duty performance and academic success and provide a record of each individual NCO's potential.

13-22. The NCO Leader Self-Development Career Model
  a. The NCO Leader Self-Development Career Model provides enlisted Soldiers a guide in the selection of self-development activities recommended by CMF proponents. Career models have been developed by subject matter experts (SME) for each CMF and are published in DA PAM 600-25.
  b. The career models correspond to the Army's leader development process relating self-development activities to institutional training and operational assignments. The models can help Soldiers establish planned, progressive, and sequential self-development programs, which enhance and sustain military competencies as well as required Skills, Knowledge, and Attributes (SKA). The career models also contain CMF-proponent recommended goals, e.g., licensure, certification, or academic degree, and allow Soldiers to combine experience and training with self-development activities for career progression as well as goal achievement.
  c. Activities and goals are recommendations, not requirements, and do not preclude mission assignments and training. Completion does not guarantee advancement. The career models are tools for use by supervisors and professional education counselors to help guide Soldiers in their professional and personal growth. They also may be used to help Soldiers prepare for NCOES and NCO functional resident courses.
  d. The elements in the leader development process--education, training, experience, assessment, feedback, and reinforcement--create a dynamic synergy to prepare Soldiers for increasing responsibilities. Self-development is the only aspect of that process over which the Soldier has direct control. The career model can stimulate involvement in this vital imperative, which should be the goal of every career Soldier. To foster this desire requires close cooperation between commanders, supervisors, education counselors, and the Soldier.

13-23. Enlisted Promotions
  a. The objectives of the enlisted promotion system are to ensure advancement of the best qualified Soldiers, to provide career incentive, to promote Soldiers based on potential rather than as a reward for past service, and to identify and preclude promotion of Soldiers who are nonproductive and ineffective. Three programs make up the promotion system: the decentralized program which controls advancements from private through specialist; the semi-centralized program which controls promotions to SGT and Staff Sergeant (SSG); and the centralized program which controls promotions to Sergeant First Class (SFC) through Sergeant Major (SGM)/Command Sergeant Major (CSM).
  b. Under the decentralized program, authority to appoint and promote Soldiers is delegated to local commanders, but there must be compliance with standard policies and procedures established by HQDA. Promotion boards are not required.
  c. Authority to promote Soldiers under the semi-centralized program is delegated to field commanders who are serving in an authorized lieutenant colonel or above command position in accordance with guidance from HQDA. In this case, eligible Soldiers compete Army-wide on the basis of relative standings by points attained on a standardized point system. Soldiers recommended for promotion are required to appear in person for evaluation by a selection board. Names of Soldiers recommended for promotion by the board are placed on a locally maintained recommended list and grouped by MOS in an order of merit based on the total points attained under the point system. HQDA controls the number of Soldiers who can be promoted in each MOS by establishing cut-off scores according to the needs of the Army. Soldiers whose scores equal or exceed the announced cut-off scores are promoted without regard to assignment. Those not immediately promoted remain on the recommended list until promoted, unless they are removed for administrative reasons or for cause. Soldiers on a recommended list may request reevaluation to improve their standing. Recent program changes due to SGT shortages mandate that Specialists and Corporals (E-4) meeting minimum time-in-grade and time-in-service requirements for

MILITARY HUMAN RESOURCE MANAGEMENT

promotion to SGT be automatically integrated on the promotion standing list without local board action unless his/her commander takes action to prevent such action.

    d. Promotions to sergeant first class through sergeant major are centralized and a board, convened by HQDA, makes selections. Selections are based on the whole person concept. No one single factor should be considered disqualifying but rather an individual's entire record is given careful consideration. Selections are made on a best-qualified basis in conjunction with Army needs.

13-24. Command Sergeants Major Program
This program ensures the selection and assignment of the best-qualified sergeants major, first sergeants, and master sergeants for command sergeant major positions. These positions are the principal enlisted assistants to commanders of organizations with enlisted troop strength equivalent to a battalion or higher level and commanded by a lieutenant colonel or above. Boards convened by HQDA make selections. A list of those selected is published and maintained within HRC for use in appointing personnel to fill vacancies. Command sergeants major are assigned only to positions that have been designated by the DCS, G-1.

13-25. Total Army Retention Program
This program consists of the AA Retention and RC Transition Programs and is responsible for assisting in manning the force with quality Soldiers by achieving and maintaining a balanced career content in the regular Army enlisted force. The retention program also focuses on improving quality through the retention of trained, qualified, and experienced enlisted Soldiers in the correct MOS and grade. Those not retained in the Active Force, being otherwise qualified, are recruited to serve in USAR or ARNG units. AC retention and RC transition program objectives are assigned to commands by DCS, G-1 while HRC provides overall program and personnel management of the programs. Personnel and fiscal support of the RC Transition Program is provided by the ARNG and USAR.

13-26. Qualitative Management Program (QMP)
    a. This program was developed as a means of improving the enlisted career force and consists of two subprograms–qualitative retention and qualitative screening.

    b. The qualitative retention subprogram specifies that a Soldier cannot reenlist beyond the time-in-service limits established for the Soldier's rank. These limits are called Retention Control Points (RCP). The qualitative screening subprogram is the DA bar to reenlistment aspect of the QMP. Regularly scheduled, centralized promotion/selection boards for sergeant first class, master sergeant, sergeant major/command sergeant major select individuals for promotion or retention in grade, as well as those Soldiers to be barred. These boards consider the Soldier's entire record using the whole person concept, not just his or her current job or term of service. Soldiers separated with a DA bar receive a reenlistment eligibility code of 4 (no further military service authorized, any branch of Service). Bars to reenlistment were designed as a personnel management tool to assist commanders in denying further service to Soldiers whose separation under administrative procedures is not warranted but where service beyond current ETS is not in the best interest of the Army. There are two types of bars to reenlistment: field imposed and DA imposed (QMP). Locally imposed bars and DA-imposed bars to reenlistment are two distinct and separate actions. Imposition of one does not preclude imposition of the other. Reenlistment is deemed a privilege and not a right. It is the responsibility of commanders, at all levels, to ensure that only those Soldiers of high moral character, personal competence, and demonstrated performance are allowed to reenlist in the Army. Reenlistment should be denied Soldiers who by their performance, conduct, and potential indicate further service will be non-progressive and unproductive. Under QMP, commanders must initiate separation actions not later than 60 days following the date the Soldier is notified of the bar unless the Soldier elects to retire or appeal or requests voluntary discharge. If an appeal is denied, commanders will initiate separation action not later than 60 days from the date of notification of denial. Appeals must be submitted within 90 days of completion of the option statement. Soldiers who have less than 90 days to ETS and who submit appeals may be extended until results of the appeal have been received from CG, HRC. Soldiers who have a DA-imposed bar to reenlistment must separate within 90 days of decision not to appeal or denial of appeal. Soldiers who have 18 but less than 20 years of service on that date may remain on active duty to attain retirement eligibility.

    c. Under the Army Mobilization Operation Plan, Annex E, Personnel, the QMP program can be suspended for the period the Army is under partial mobilization.

HOW THE ARMY RUNS

13-27. Warrant Officer Development
   a. The implementation of TWOS in 1986, the Warrant Officer Management Act (WOMA) of 1991, the Warrant Officer Leader Development Action Plan (WOLDAP) in 1992, the Warrant Officer Education System (WOES) in 1993, and the Army Training and Leader Development Panel (ATLDP) decisions in 2002, have had a major impact on the management and professional development of warrant officers. The Army's current goal is to recruit warrant officers earlier in their careers, train them better, and retain them longer. About half of all warrant officers retire after 23 years of combined (enlisted and warrant officer) active federal service. Under WOMA, decisions on promotions, training, and assignments are based on years of Warrant Officer Service (WOS). A careerist will have an opportunity to serve 30 years of WOS if selected for CW5. All others will have an opportunity to serve up to 24 years of WOS unless twice nonselected for promotion to the next higher grade.
   b. Every Active Army warrant officer position in authorization documents is classified by rank based on the skills, knowledge, abilities, and experience needed in that position. Formerly there was no rank differentiation in warrant officer positions.

13-28. WOMA
   a. WOMA provided a comprehensive and uniform personnel management system, similar to Defense Officer Personnel Management Act (DOPMA), for warrant officer appointments, promotions, separations, and retirements. The key provisions of WOMA include the following.
      (1) Authorized the grade of CW5, to include pay and allowances. Maximum number of CW5s on active duty is limited to 5% of the total number of warrant officers on active duty.
      (2) Eliminated the dual promotion system and established a DOPMA-style promotion system for warrant officers.
      (3) Established minimum Time in Grade (TIG) requirement for consideration for promotion.
      (4) Established authority to convene Selective Retirement Boards (SRB) to consider retirement eligible warrant officers for involuntary retirement.
      (5) Established the management of warrant officers by years of WOS rather than by Active Federal Service (AFS). A CW5 may serve for 30 years WOS. Retirement eligibility at 20 years AFS remains unchanged.
      (6) Established selective continuation for warrant officers twice nonselected for promotion (very limited use and normally in shortage skills).
      (7) Modified the involuntary separation date from 60 days to the first day of the seventh month after board results are approved. This provision applies to warrant officers twice nonselected for promotion and those selected for involuntary retirement.
   b. WOMA modernized warrant officer life cycle management, offers all warrant officers the potential for a full career, provides tools to shape the force, and enhances readiness by providing the Army with a highly qualified and experienced WO cohort.

13-29. WOES
Warrant officer education is integrated within the Officer Education System (OES). Warrant officer specific courses are depicted in Figure 13-7. Chapter 15 provides additional information on these courses and other warrant officer training and education.
   a. The WOBC is the first course encountered by all newly appointed WO1s. WOBC certifies the new WO1 within his branch and specialty.
   b. The Warrant Officer Advanced Course (WOAC) is a combination of common core and MOS proponent training that prepares warrant officers to serve in CW3 level positions. WOAC is provided in a non-resident common core phase and a resident phase, which includes a common core module and a MOS-specific module. Completion of the Action Officer Development Course (AODC) is a prerequisite for WOAC attendance
   c. The Warrant Officer Staff Course (WOSC) provides senior CW3s and new CW4s with the intermediate-level education and influential leadership skills necessary to apply their technical expertise in support of leaders on tactical and operational level Joint, Interagency, Intergovernmental, and Multinational (JIIM) staffs during full spectrum operations.
   d. The Warrant Officer Senior Staff Course (WOSSC) is the capstone for WO PME conducted at the Warrant Officer Career Center (WOCC), Fort Rucker, Alabama. WOSSC provides senior CW4s and new

MILITARY HUMAN RESOURCE MANAGEMENT

CW5s with the senior level education, knowledge, and influential leadership skills necessary to apply their technical expertise in support of leaders on strategic level JIIM staffs during full spectrum operations.

e. The WOCC serves as the Training and Doctrine Command (TRADOC) executive agent for warrant officer common core education. The WOCC evaluates common core instruction within the proponent specific program of instruction for WOBC and WOAC.

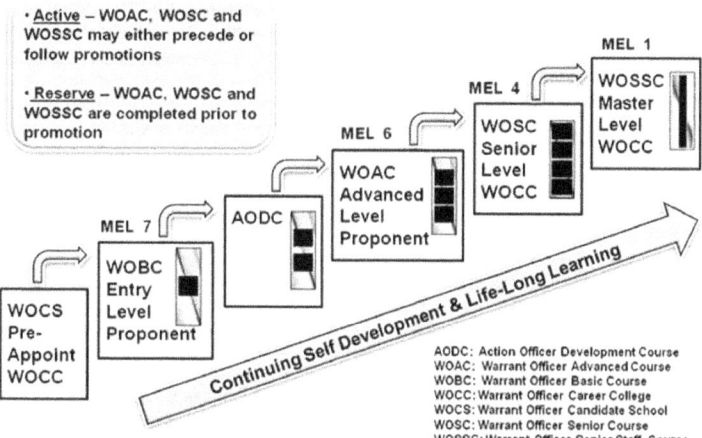

Figure 13-7. Warrant Officer Training and Education

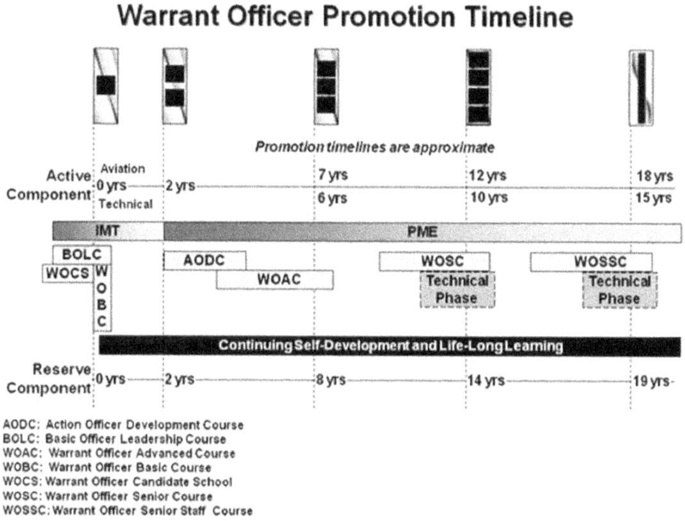

Figure 13-8. Warrant Officer Promotion Timeline

HOW THE ARMY RUNS

13-30. Warrant Officer Promotions
Warrant officers are promoted under a single permanent promotion system similar to the commissioned officer system.

    a. Promotions to CW3, CW4, and CW5 for warrant officers on the Active Duty List (ADL) are administered at HQDA. Promotion authority to CW2 is delegated to commanders in the rank of lieutenant colonel and above. Warrant officers may be promoted to CW2 after completion of 24 months in the grade of WO1 under current policy. WOMA allows CW2 promotion consideration after 18 months in grade. Time in grade for promotions to CW3, CW4, and CW5 are depicted in Figure 13-8 and Table 13-1, but vary with Army requirements.

    b. Warrant officers twice nonselected for promotion to the next higher grade will be discharged or retired, if eligible, unless selectively continued on active duty to meet a valid Army requirement.

Table 13-1. Warrant Officer Promotion Goals

To grade	Promotion opportunity	Years AWOS
W2	Fully qualified	2
W3	80%	7 +1/-0
W4	74%	12 +/-1
W5[1]	44%	17 +/-1

Note: 1. By law the number of CW5s is limited to 5% of the warrant officer force.

13-31. Warrant Officer Retention Programs
    a. Regular Army integration and commissioning is concurrent with promotion to CW2. Officers who decline regular Army integration will not be promoted and shall be separated 90 days after the declination date or upon completion of any active duty service obligation, whichever is later.

    b. Separate regular Army integration boards were discontinued during the Army drawdown. Future boards are planned to only consider exceptions; for example, a USAR CW3 who requests and is called to active duty to fill a valid requirement.

    c. Warrant officers are released from active duty after being twice non-selected for promotion to the next higher grade unless they are selectively continued.

13-32. Officer Development
The OPMS provides a framework for developing the required number of officers with the necessary skills and for managing the careers of all commissioned officers, except those assigned to the special branches (Army Medical Department (AMEDD), JAG, and Chaplain Corps). This framework consists of all OPMS functional categories, with each one being a grouping of duty positions whose skill, knowledge, and job requirements are mutually supportive in the development of officers to successfully perform in the functional category. Each functional category contains sufficient duty positions to support progression to the grade of colonel. Military and civilian educational opportunities are also geared to the officer's functional category. Army requirements and an individual's qualifications and preference are the major considerations in determining the designation of functional categories. OPMS consists of three major and interrelated subsystems: strength management, professional development, and evaluation.

13-33. OPMS
In May 1997, the CSA approved implementation of several changes in OPMS as a result of the recommendations of the OPMS XXI Task Force. During 2002, the DCS, G-1 changed the name to OPMS III (vice OPMS XXI) to reflect the system as progressive and evolving to support emerging needs for the 21st century. In 2006 the DCS, G1 eliminated the numerical designation in recognition that OPMS was designed to be a continual evolution.

    a. Historical Perspective.

    (1) OPMS exists to balance the needs of the Army with the aspirations and developmental requirements of the officer corps. OPMS was instituted in 1972 as a result of the U.S. Army War College Study on Military Professionalism and a follow-on analysis directed by the DCS, G-1. After passage of the DOPMA by Congress in 1981, the CSA ordered a major review to examine the impact of the

MILITARY HUMAN RESOURCE MANAGEMENT

legislation on OPMS policies. As a result, OPMS II was developed in 1984 to accommodate the changes brought about by DOPMA, including the creation of functional areas, dual tracking and regular Army integration. In 1987, the CSA directed a review of officer leader development to account for the changes in law, policy, and procedures that had occurred since the creation of OPMS II. As a result of the study, the leader development action plan was approved for implementation in 1989.

(2) During the last decade plus, the Army has undergone significant changes with widespread affect on the officer personnel system, brought about by the drawdown at the end of the Cold War and by major legislative initiatives. The DOD Reorganization Act of 1986 (Goldwater-Nichols) required the Services to improve interoperability and provided the statutory requirements for joint duty assignments, joint tour credit and joint military education. In 1986, Congress also passed Public Law 99-145, which specified the acquisition experiences and education necessary for an officer to be the project manager of a major weapons system. This law later led to the creation in 1990 of the Army Acquisition Corps (AAC). The Defense Acquisition Workforce Improvement Act (DAWIA) of 1990 placed additional requirements on Acquisition Corps officers and directed them to single track in their functional area. Congressional Title VII (1992) and XI (1993) legislation placed additional officer requirements on the AA in their support of the RC. The Reserve Officer Personnel Management Act (ROPMA) of 1996 brought the RC officer promotion systems in synchronization with the AC. This legislation established a best-qualified promotion system for RC officers, thereby replacing the fully qualified system previously used.

b. Initiation of OPMS III.

(1) In 1994, a team of senior field grade officers was assembled to examine a series of OPMS-specific issues and to determine whether a general review of the OPMS was warranted. This OPMS XXI Precursor Study Group ultimately reviewed more than 60 individual issues. Based on the collective body of these issues, the OPMS XXI Task Force convened in July 1996 to review and revise the personnel management system as necessary to ensure its viability for meeting future challenges. The Task Force focused on the development and career management of officers of the Army Competitive Category (ACC). The special branches (Chaplain, JAG, and the branches of the AMEDD) were not specifically addressed although some OPMS XXI issues and solutions dealing with education, officer evaluation, and general promotion policies will apply to them as well.

(2) The Task Force linked its work with other ongoing Army planning efforts: Force XXI for the near-term, Army XXI initiatives for the mid-term, and Army after next projections for the long-term planning environment. In designing the personnel system for the future, the CSA directed the task force to also create a conceptual framework that integrated OPMS with the leader development system, ongoing character development initiatives and the then new officer evaluation report.

(3) The task force concluded that, in order for OPMS III to work effectively, three sets of strategic recommendations for change must be jointly addressed.

(a) The first recommendation called for the creation of an Officer Development System (ODS) as part of an overall Army development system. ODS will encompass and integrate officer leader development, character development, evaluation, and personnel management.

(b) The second recommendation recognized the need to adopt a holistic, Strategic Human Resource Management (SHRM) approach to officer development and personnel management for the 21st Century.

(c) The final strategic recommendation by the task force called for the creation of an officer career field-based management system composed of four career fields: Operations, Operational Support, Institutional Support, and Information Operations. Under OPMS III, officers are designated into a single career field after selection for major and serve and compete for promotion in their designated career field from that point on.

(d) The results of these strategic recommendations, approved by the CSA in December 1997, formed the basis for the changes to OPMS until 2005.

(e) In 2005 the CSA directed that OPMS be reviewed to determine if the system met the developmental needs of the officer corps for the future. After study by a new OPMS task force, and a vetting process for recommendations with subject matter experts, a Council of Colonels representing all stakeholders, and General Officer Steering Committees, many changes have been approved or are under consideration at this writing. Driving many of the changes is the Army leadership's view that the future officer corps needs to be more multi-skilled and afforded assignment and educational opportunities that foster this end. Among the changes approved was changing the four career fields to three functional categories as depicted in Figure 13-8. The new design is considered more conducive to bringing balance to the officer corps–breadth and depth, was less prescriptive, and provided multiple career paths. There have been

HOW THE ARMY RUNS

some changes to this initial construct as functional areas were eliminated or consolidated (e.g. Comptroller, HR) and other created (e.g., Logistics Corps).

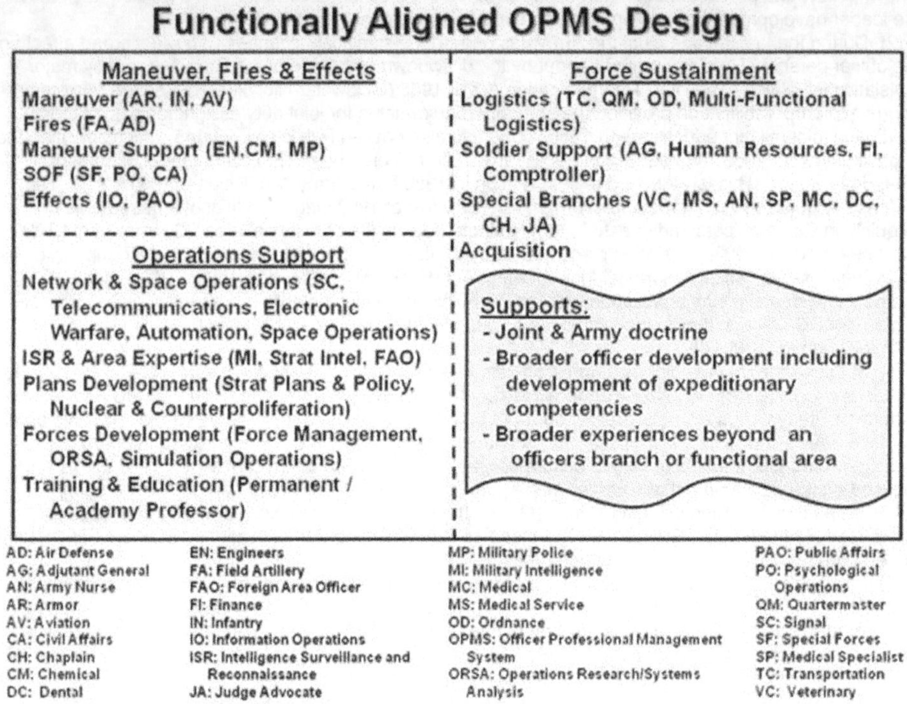

Functionally Aligned OPMS Design

Maneuver, Fires & Effects
- Maneuver (AR, IN, AV)
- Fires (FA, AD)
- Maneuver Support (EN, CM, MP)
- SOF (SF, PO, CA)
- Effects (IO, PAO)

Operations Support
- Network & Space Operations (SC, Telecommunications, Electronic Warfare, Automation, Space Operations)
- ISR & Area Expertise (MI, Strat Intel, FAO)
- Plans Development (Strat Plans & Policy, Nuclear & Counterproliferation)
- Forces Development (Force Management, ORSA, Simulation Operations)
- Training & Education (Permanent / Academy Professor)

Force Sustainment
- Logistics (TC, QM, OD, Multi-Functional Logistics)
- Soldier Support (AG, Human Resources, FI, Comptroller)
- Special Branches (VC, MS, AN, SP, MC, DC, CH, JA)
- Acquisition

Supports:
- Joint & Army doctrine
- Broader officer development including development of expeditionary competencies
- Broader experiences beyond an officers branch or functional area

AD: Air Defense
AG: Adjutant General
AN: Army Nurse
AR: Armor
AV: Aviation
CA: Civil Affairs
CH: Chaplain
CM: Chemical
DC: Dental
EN: Engineers
FA: Field Artillery
FAO: Foreign Area Officer
FI: Finance
IN: Infantry
IO: Information Operations
ISR: Intelligence Surveillance and Reconnaissance
JA: Judge Advocate
MP: Military Police
MI: Military Intelligence
MC: Medical
MS: Medical Service
OD: Ordnance
OPMS: Officer Professional Management System
ORSA: Operations Research/Systems Analysis
PAO: Public Affairs
PO: Psychological Operations
QM: Quartermaster
SC: Signal
SF: Special Forces
SP: Medical Specialist
TC: Transportation
VC: Veterinary

Figure 13-9. Functionally Aligned Officer Personnel Management System (OPMS) Design

13-34. Fundamentals of Officer Management
The Army needs, and will continue to need, the finest officers imbued with the warfighting ethos and with the right skills, knowledge and experience to effectively meet any challenges. Further, the Army continues to be a values-based organization, steeped in core principles and beliefs that set the muddy boots Soldier apart as a unique professional. In order to grow an Officer Corps with the right SKA to respond to evolving future challenges–to remain ready not only today but also tomorrow—OPMS changed many aspects of how officers are managed, developed, and promoted.

   a. Functional Category Based Management. Officers are developed in only one branch, and the branch remains primary for approximately the first 10 years of an officer's career (an exception exists for those officers being branch detailed as a new lieutenant and a small number of officers in selected functional areas). Career field or functional category designation will occur at four years of service for a small number of officers and at seven years of service for the remainder. Officer preference will be a key factor in terms of board selection criteria in the functional category designation process, but Army requirements are always paramount.

   b. Functional Areas. Functional areas are not directly related to any specific branch. Incorporating what are referred to as non-accession specialties, functional areas provide a management and development system to effectively use the vast talents of a diverse officer corps and meet Army requirements.

MILITARY HUMAN RESOURCE MANAGEMENT

13-35. Functional Categories

Officers compete for promotion only with other officers in the same functional category. Each functional category, or branch or functional area within a functional category, has its own unique characteristics and development track for officers that reflects the readiness requirements of the Army today and into the 21st century. DA PAM 600-3 outlines all aspects of OPMS, officer training, education and development. Officers from every branch and functional area will also fill officer generalist and combat arms generalist (01A/02A) positions across the Army. Functional categories are depicted in Figure 13-9. As of this writing, there are numerous actions and pending decisions relative to these new functional categories that will impact promotion consideration, command opportunity, and education.

13-36. Functional Category Assignment

Functional categories are assigned through a career field or functional category designation process, under the direction of HRC. An important part of the process is the convening of a formal board to recommend functional categories for individual officers. HRC identifies officers in the window for functional category designation and notifies them of required actions to be taken in advance of the board. HRC also provides the board with the number of officers to be designated into each functional category, as well as the branches from which these officers will be drawn, based on Army requirements. This process is similar to the way in which promotion requirements by branch and functional area are determined. The board is charged to identify and take into consideration officer preference, aptitudes, and abilities in order to best meet the needs of the Army. The functional category designation process includes the following considerations:

13-37. Centralized Selection for Command and Key Billet Positions

OPMS III changed the name of this process from Command Designated Positional List (CDPL) to Centralized Selection List (CSL). This process emphasizes the preference-based approach to an officer's career pattern. The CSL includes four functional categories of commands and key billets as depicted in Figure 13-10. The CSL commands include all Lieutenant Colonel (LTC) and Colonel (COL) command positions approved by the Army. The list of centrally selected command positions changes regularly. In FY 2004 key division staff positions (G1, G2, and G6) were added to the list of centrally selected positions. Prior to convening each command selection board, officers being considered will be given the opportunity to indicate the functional category (or categories) in which they desire to compete for selection. The board selects officers for command within the given categories and HRC conducts the slating process and recommends the specific unit or organization for the officer to command. The CSA has the final decision on the command slate.

Centralized Selection List (CSL) Categories

Operations (OPS)
- Table of Organization and Equipment (TOE)
- Echelon Corps & Below (ECB)— Combat Arms
- Echelon Corps & Above (EAB)— Combat Service Support

Strategic Support (SS)
- Strategic: TOE/Table of Distribution and Allowances (TDA) Echelons Above Corps (Army Command / Direct Report Unit / Army Service Component Command-Level)

Officer Professional Management System CSL

Installations (INSTL)
- Garrison / Brigade Support Battalion Commands

Boards select for each category with separate Order of Merit Lists (OML)

Key Billet (KB)
- Includes both Operational and Strategic Support Type Organizations

Recruiting and Training (RT)
- US Army Recruiting Commands
- Training: Training Base (Training and Doctrine Command) and Training Support Brigades (Active / Reserve Component)

Figure 13-10. Centralized Selection List (CSL) Categories

13-38. AAC

a. The mission of the AAC is to create a corps of dedicated military and civilian acquisition managers capitalizing on their operational experience and technical skills. Successful weapon system development, and all the support activities required throughout its life cycle, requires a balance between keen regard for current operational realities and technical knowledge.

b. The AAC program develops world-class acquisition specialists to fill approximately 3,850 critical positions. Critical positions require the level of education, training, and experience stated in the DAWIA and the DOD implementing instructions. The positions include Program Managers (PM), Program Executive Officers (PEO) (general officer/ Senior Executive Service level), deputy or assistant PEOs/PMs, senior contracting officials, and selected positions in procurement commands, matrix support commands, and headquarters staffs.

c. The Army Acquisition Executive (AAE), Assistant Secretary of the Army (Acquisition, Logistics, and Technology) (ASA(ALT)), (which is dual-hatted as the AAE), acting for the Secretary of the Army (SECARMY) through established structure, implementing DOD Acquisition Workforce policy and tailoring the Army program. The Director, Acquisition Career Management (military deputy to the AAE) provides requirements to the DCS, G-1.

d. DCS, G-1 provides personnel policy management for the AAC as for the rest of the Army. The AAC Management Office (AACMO), OPMD, HRC, centrally manages all officer and civilian AAC members. The AACMO consists of a Military Acquisition Management Branch and a Civilian Acquisition Management Branch. Each branch manages members of its component from accession through the members' entire career life cycle.

e. Only qualified officers and civilians may fill critical positions. The AAC targets branch-qualified captains and civilians in grade General Schedule (GS)-13 as candidates for competitive entry into the

MILITARY HUMAN RESOURCE MANAGEMENT

AAC. Once accessed into the AAC, members attend schooling and obtain acquisition experience to meet acquisition certification requirements for critical positions.

f. Recognizing the difficulty in pursuing branch qualification for battalion and brigade command and at the same time achieving the acquisition requirements, AAC members are precluded from Table of Organization and Equipment (TOE) command. AAC officers compete for acquisition-related TDA commands and product manager (battalion-level command equivalent) and project manager (brigade-level command equivalent) positions.

g. DA Acquisition Selection Boards select AAC commanders and product and project managers. Commanders normally serve three-year tours and product/project managers four years.

h. AAC TDA commands include the research & development centers and laboratories, and procurement and contracting offices. Product/project managers are charged with managing and executing the day-to-day activities for development, production, and fielding of a system in accordance with approved performance, schedule, and cost requirements.

i. DA PAM 600-3 details the professional development requirements for commissioned officers within the AAC. AR 690-950 and the Army Civilian Training, Education, and Development System (ACTEDS) list requirements for AAC civilians.

13-39. Officer Evaluation System

a. The Officer Evaluation System is the Army's method of identifying those officers most qualified for advancement and assignment to positions of increased responsibility. The system includes assessments of officer performance and potential accomplished in the organizational duty environment; in an academic environment, both military and civilian; and at joint and departmental levels.

b. The potential assessment of an officer is a subjective judgment as to the officer's capability to perform at a specified level of responsibility, authority, or sensitivity. Although potential is normally associated with the capability to perform at a higher grade, judgments are also made by DA on retention and increased responsibility within a specified grade. The assessment is based on three major factors: the Army's officer requirements, the individual officer's qualifications, and a summation of the individual officer's performance.

c. The performance assessment by DA differs significantly from that accomplished in the organizational duty environment. Whereas the organizational duty assessment involves a personal knowledge of the situations surrounding a specific period of time, DA assessment is accomplished by an after-the-fact assessment of a series of reports on performance over a variety of duty positions and covering the officer's entire career.

13-40. Officer Evaluation Report (OER) System

a. The OER System is a subsystem of the Officer Evaluation System. It includes the methods and procedures for organizational evaluation and assessment of an officer's performance and an estimation of potential for future service based on the manner of that performance. The official documentation of these assessments is the OER and the AER.

b. The primary function of the OER System is to provide information from the organizational chain to be used by DA for officer personnel decisions. The information contained in the OER is correlated with the Army's needs and individual officer qualifications providing the basis for personnel actions such as promotion, elimination, retention in grade, retention on active duty, reduction in force, command designation, school selection, assignment, and functional category designation.

c. A secondary function of the OER System is to encourage the professional development of the officer corps. To enhance this, emphasis is placed on the responsibility of senior officers to counsel their subordinates. While this has always been a major aspect of leadership, continual reemphasis is necessary. The OER System contributes significantly by providing a natural impetus to continual two-way communication between senior and subordinate. It is through this communication that the rated officer is made aware of the specific nature of his or her duties and is provided an opportunity to participate in the process. The rater uses the communication to give direction to and develop his or her subordinates, to obtain information as to the status and progress of his or her organization, and to plan systematically for the accomplishment of the mission. The senior/ subordinate communication process also facilitates the dissemination of career development information, advice, and guidance to the rated officer. This enables the rated officer to take advantage of the superior's experience when making functional category or assignment-related decisions.

HOW THE ARMY RUNS

d. There have been nine OER systems since WWII. The first seven experienced a relatively rapid system turnover because inflation had gotten out of hand. The eighth (DA Form 67-8), which introduced the support form process and senior rater concept, was effective far longer (18 years, one month) than any previous system. The current OER, (DA Form 67-9), is an evolution of the 67-8 and has been in use even longer. The Army is preparing to revise the OER again to accommodate changes in officer career development processes and goals.

13-41. Officer Promotions

As of 15 September 1981, the DOPMA amended Title 10 for officer promotions. DOPMA, as implemented, is applicable to all officers on the ADL. It does not apply to warrant officers. The act provides for a single promotion system for all officers (regular Army and Other than Regular Army (OTRA)), thus eliminating the previous dual (Army of the United States (AUS)/RA or AUS/USAR) system of promotions. The intent is for promotions to be made within fairly uniform promotion timing and opportunity goals, as vacancies occur. Eligibility for consideration for promotions is based on minimum TIG and Time in Service (TIS) with the below-the-zone selection rate established at a maximum of 10% (or 15% when so authorized by the Secretary of Defense (SECDEF)) of the list for any grade above captain. Goals for promotion opportunity and phase point (i.e., TIS when most officers are promoted) are listed in Table 13-2, as found in DOD Instruction (DODI) 1320.13 dated 13 July 2009. (Actual promotion percentages and TIG/TIS may vary considerably.)

Table 13-2. Career Progression Pattern

To grade	Promotion opportunity	DOPMA phase point
First Lieutenant	Fully Qualified	18 MOS TIS/TIG min
Captain	90%	Not less than 2 years TIG
Major	80%	10 +/-1 year
Lieutenant Colonel	70%	16 +/-1 year
Colonel	50%	22 +/-1 year

Note: Opportunity and TIS are set by policy. TIG for promotion to 1LT and CPT is set by law.

13-42. Officer Quality Management

a. The goal of the officer management program is to ensure that only those individuals demonstrating satisfactory performance and possessing acceptable moral and professional traits be allowed to serve on active duty, retain their commissions, and remain on DA promotion lists.

b. Commanders and DA agencies are continually striving to maintain the quality of the officer corps by identifying and processing for involuntary separation those officers whose performance or professional or moral traits are deficient. To this end, the records of officers are screened continually to identify those whose degree of efficiency and manner of performance and/or misconduct, moral, or professional dereliction require separation.

c. Whenever an officer is identified to show cause, the officer is afforded the opportunity to resign in lieu of undergoing the entire process. Similarly, DA agencies are tasked to review promotion lists and CSLs to ensure that no officer is promoted or allowed to command who has become mentally, physically, morally, or professionally disqualified after being selected. The records of officers whose fitness for promotion or command has become suspect are referred to a DA Promotion/Command Review Board, which will recommend to the SECARMY whether the officer should be retained on or removed from the promotion/CSL.

d. The promotion system also serves as a qualitative management tool through the mandatory separation from active duty of officers who fail to be selected for promotion to certain grade levels. However, an officer non-selected for promotion may be selectively continued in his current rank upon recommendation by the DA promotion board that non-selected him for promotion.

e. No person has an inherent right to continue service as an officer. The privilege of service is his or hers only as long as he or she performs in a satisfactory manner. Responsibility for leadership and example requires officers accomplish their duties effectively and conduct themselves in an exemplary manner at all times.

MILITARY HUMAN RESOURCE MANAGEMENT

13-43. Officer Strength Management
When manpower reductions are necessary, the Army has several programs that may be applied to reduce the number of officers on active duty. When possible, reductions are accomplished through normal attrition and voluntary release programs coupled with reduced officer accessions. In the past, Congress directed the Services to include senior as well as junior officers when implementing officer strength cuts, Selective Early Retirement Boards (SERB) and Reductions-in-Force (RIF) may be implemented when required. RIFs target all officers by year while SERBs select a fixed number of retirement-eligible officers for involuntary early retirement. RIFs and SERBs are quantitative measures that are qualitatively administered.

13-44. DOPMA
DOPMA evolved from the continued inability of the Officer Personnel Act (OPA) of 1947, as changed by the Officer Grade Limitation Act (OGLA) of 1954, to meet the changing requirements for a modern and equitable officer management system for the active forces. The intent of DOPMA was to provide all Services with an equitable, effective, and efficient system to manage their officer corps below the brigadier general level.

    a. The management objective is to provide consistent career and promotion opportunities across all Services in order to attract and retain high-caliber officers, and promote them at a point in service conducive to effective performance. The integration into a single promotion and grade authorization system of the dual-track Regular Army/Reserve system mandated by OGLA and OPA provided a more favorable environment in which to achieve this goal.

    b. The provisions for selective continuation of captains and majors, combined with the capability to instruct promotion boards on skill needs, provides a mechanism through which specialty needs can be filled, while enhancing an officer's opportunity to stay on active duty until retirement. Under DOPMA, a first lieutenant who twice fails to be selected for promotion to captain is involuntarily released from active duty. By law, captains and majors may be selectively continued to remain on active duty until 20 and 24 years respectively. DOPMA establishes uniform, general constructive provisions for all Services, thus recognizing that special skills acquired are essential for effective performance in special branches. This provision impacted AMEDD, Chaplain, and the JAG accessed after the effective date of the act.

13-45. DOD Reorganization Act of 1986 (Goldwater-Nichols)
The congressional goal of this act was to improve the performance of officers in joint duty positions by establishing management procedures for their selection, education, assignment, and promotion. Key provisions of the law are listed below.

    a. Assignments. The qualifications of officers assigned to joint duty assignments will be such that they are expected to meet certain specified promotion rates comparable to their Service headquarters and the overall board selection rate. Officers assigned to joint duty assignments will be assigned in anticipation that they will serve the prescribed tour length for their grade: two years for general officers and three years for others. Assignments for officers possessing critical occupational specialties, which for the Army are defined as the combat arms branches, may be curtailed to a minimum of 24 months under certain conditions. All graduates of professional joint education (e.g., National War College and Industrial College of the Armed Forces (ICAF)) who are designated as Joint Specialty Officers (JSO), and a high proportion (greater than 50%) of those graduates not designated as JSO, will be assigned to a joint duty assignment immediately following graduation.

    b. Promotions. Selection boards considering officers serving in, or who have served in, joint duty assignments will include at least one officer designated by the Chairman of the Joint Chiefs of Staff (CJCS) who is currently serving in a joint duty assignment. The letter of instruction for selection boards includes the following guidance: "You will give appropriate consideration to the performance in joint duty assignments of officers who are serving in, or who have served in such assignments." Prior to approval by the Secretary of the Military Department, the results of selection boards considering officers who are serving in, or who have served in, joint duty assignments will be forwarded by the Secretary to the CJCS. The CJCS will review the results to determine whether appropriate consideration was given to performance in joint duty assignments.

    c. Reports. Each Secretary of a Military Department must provide periodic progress reports on their promotion rates in relation to the promotion objectives specified above.

HOW THE ARMY RUNS

d. General/flag officer actions. In the absence of a waiver (waiver authority was eliminated in the 2007 NDAA) by the SECDEF, officers selected to the grade of 0-7 subsequent to 1 January 1994 must have completed a full joint duty assignment before selection or their first assignment as a general/flag officer will be in a joint duty assignment. A capstone military education course has been created and all newly promoted general/flag officers must attend this course within two years after selection, unless such attendance is waived by the SECDEF.

Section VII
The Sustainment Function

13-46. Sustainment Function Overview
The sustainment function includes a broad range of activities that are focused on the well being of Soldiers, retirees, and their families. The range includes but is not limited to quality of life activities, awards, and decorations, casualty and memorial affairs, housing, morale, recreation, personnel actions, and Soldier readiness.

13-47. Army Continuing Education System (ACES)
a. ACES is a critical element in the recruitment and retention of a quality force. ACES exist to ensure Soldiers have opportunities for personal and professional self-development. Education opportunities are offered through education centers, regional and state education offices, and learning centers located worldwide. Educational programs include the following.
   (1) On-duty functional academic skills training, which provides job-related instruction in the academic areas of reading, mathematics, and English grammar at no cost to the Soldier or adult family member.
   (2) High school completion programs for Soldiers without a high school diploma.
   (3) Undergraduate and graduate college courses and programs which provide financial assistance, such as the Tuition Assistance Program.
   (4) Foreign language programs for qualified Army linguists assigned overseas.
   (5) Skill development programs to prepare non-commissioned officers for NCOES training.
   (6) Counseling to establish challenging yet attainable short and long-term goals
   (7) Academic testing through the Defense Activity for Non-Traditional Education Support (DANTES).
   (8) Army personnel testing, and training support for skill specific and unit training, leaders self-development and language and computer laboratories.
   b. In addition, the Service members Opportunity College Army degree system of college and university networks promoting credit transferability and the Army/American Council on Education Registry Transcript System (AARTS) documenting recommended credit for Soldier training and experience help Soldiers earn degrees despite frequent transfers and rotations. The ACES, focused on Soldiers, family members, and available to DA civilians, represents a primary family covenant program.
   c. To further enable Soldiers to continue their education, the Army has implemented a web-based portal, GoArmyEd.com, so that Soldiers and family members have anytime, anywhere access to education programs and services. Soldiers use GoArmyEd to request funding for college level courses wherever they are in the world. GoArmyEd.com provides Soldiers maximum flexibility to continue to pursue their individual educational goals.

13-48. Equal Opportunity Program
a. Army's Military Equal Opportunity (MEO) Program formulates, directs, and sustains a comprehensive effort to maximize human potential and to ensure fair treatment for all persons based solely on merit, fitness, and capability in support of readiness. This program strives to eliminate incidents of discrimination based on race, color, gender, religion, or national origin and provide an environment free of unlawful discrimination or offensive behavior. Army Equal Opportunity Program is resonant in leadership that is rooted in taking care of Soldiers and is crucial to unit cohesion, readiness, and mission accomplishment. Ensuring Soldiers are treated with fairness, justice, and equity is central to an Army culture dedicated to the highest professional and personal standards and to sustaining our most important resource-people.
   b. The Army reorganized the Prevention of Sexual Harassment (POSH) to the Sexual Assault Prevention Response (SAPR) Program in March 2009. The new office is Sexual Harassment/Assault

MILITARY HUMAN RESOURCE MANAGEMENT

Response Prevention (SHARP) Program. This initiative transferred POSH from MEO to infuse the full spectrum of Army Operations and strategically focused on the interrelationship in one program (SHARP) within the Army. The Equal Opportunity (EO) Program is currently in the process of transforming by integrating diversity and other human relations programs to better serve the Total Army Family.

    c. Commanders are assisted in sustaining MEO goals and objectives by an Equal Opportunity Program Manager (EOPM) at division level and above, Equal Opportunity Adviser (EOA) at brigade level and above, and an EO leader (EOL) collateral duty at battalion and company level. These MEO practitioners assist the commander in EO training, reporting and continuously assess the command climate to identify indicators of individual and institutional barriers. Soldiers volunteer or selected as EOPMs and EOAs receive 10 weeks of intensive training at Defense Equal Opportunity Management Institute (DEOMI), receive an ASI of "T" for officers and a SQI of "Q" for NCOs, and serve a 24 month tour as an EOPM or EOA. EOL receives 80 hours of training at the installation. The EO practitioner provides the commander a valuable subject matter resource for sustaining a positive EO climate, training, and developing remedies to eliminate practices or treatment, which affects readiness.

13-49. The Army Casualty System

    a. The casualty operations functions include casualty reporting, notification, assistance, and fatal accident family brief program. Casualty reporting is the source of information provided to the Next of Kin (NOK) concerning a casualty incident. It is of the utmost importance to provide that information accurately, promptly, and in as much detail as possible so that the NOK receive as full an accounting as possible of the casualty incident.

    b. Defense Casualty Information Processing System (DCIPS) provides casualty, mortuary affairs, personal effects tracking and processing, remains tracking, Line of Duty (LOD) and Freedom of Information Act (FOIA) management capability for casualties from current and prior conflicts for all Services. DCIPS is the DOD required system for casualty management (DODI 1300.18). All information contained in the DCIPS data base is classified For Official Use Only (FOUO). This information is governed under the Privacy Act Laws and should not be discussed with those not having a need to know.

Section VIII
The Transition Function

13-50. Transition Function Overview

The transition function includes a broad range of activities focused on ensuring Soldiers and their families are treated with dignity and respect and assisted in every way possible as they transition from the AC to a RC and/or civilian status. Selected transition activities are described in greater detail below.

13-51. The Army Career and Alumni Program (ACAP)

    a. The ACAP orchestrates a broad spectrum of programs and services designed to assist Soldiers in making critical career and transition decisions. ACAP provides transition services to Soldiers, DA civilians, retirees, and their family members. RC personnel are also eligible to receive ACAP services upon serving a minimum of 180 consecutive days of active duty immediately prior to separation.

    b. ACAP is not a job placement service but instead a program through which a wide range of services are made available to users through a combination of DOD, Department of Labor, Department of Veteran Affairs, U.S. Army, and contractor provided services. Transition counseling and career planning are the cornerstone services that assist the user to properly focus on their career path and the value of their experience should they remain on active duty or transition to civilian life. Individuals using ACAP services have access to an abundance of reference materials and a wealth of information about benefits, civilian employment opportunities, career planning and services available through many federal, state, and local government agencies.

    c. Participation in ACAP is mandatory for all active duty Soldiers who are separating or retiring. Individuals are encouraged to start using ACAP services 180 days before their separation date. Eligible individuals may continue to use ACAP for up to 90 days after separation. Retirees and their families are eligible to use ACAP services for life on a space available basis. Referral to ACAP is mandatory for civilians who are departing because of force alignments, RIFs, or base closures. ACAP participation is optional for transition of family members and eligible RC Soldiers.

HOW THE ARMY RUNS

d. ACAP establishes a strong partnership between the Army and the private sector, creates a recruiting multiplier, improves employment prospects for transitioning personnel, reduces unemployment compensation costs to the Army, and allows career Soldiers to concentrate on their mission. ACAP is an enduring program, institutionalized into the Army culture and life cycle functions.

13-52. Army Retirement Services Program

a. The DA has a worldwide network of retirement services offices to assist retiring Soldiers and their families make a smooth and successful transition into retirement. Each major Army installation has a full-time, paid employee, called a Retirement Services Officer (RSO), to administer this program. The program prepares Soldiers and family members for retirement by providing assistance and information on their benefits and entitlements. These services are available to the surviving spouses of retired Soldiers.

b. The RSO conducts a periodic pre-retirement briefing, which covers subjects from computation of retired pay to survivor benefits. Soldiers must attend a pre-retirement briefing between submission of their retirement application and no later than 120 days before retirement. Spouses are encouraged to attend. The RSO also provides mandatory Survivor Benefit Plan (SBP) counseling to these individuals. By law, retired pay stops with a Soldier's death unless the Soldier is enrolled in SBP. The Soldier must make the SBP decision before retirement.

c. The DA RSO provides policy guidance and program oversight to the installation RSOs and is also responsible for publishing Army Echoes, the newsletter sent (also available online) to all retirees, surviving spouses, and retirement-eligible RC personnel. The DA RSO also administers the Army Chief of Staff's Retiree Council, the SBP, and RC SBP Programs and monitors the operation of the Armed Forces Retirement Homes.

13-53. Separation

Separation includes voluntary and involuntary release from active duty, discharge, non-disability retirement, and physical disability retirement. Because the type of discharge and character of service are of such great significance to the Service member, it must accurately reflect the nature of service performed. Eligibility for veterans' benefits provided by law, eligibility for reentry into service, and acceptability for employment in the civilian community may be affected by these determinations.

13-54. Enlisted Separation

a. An enlisted Soldier may be separated upon ETS or prior to ETS by reason of physical disability (see below), sentence of general or special court-martial, or one of the administrative separation programs prescribed in AR 635-200. Both voluntary and involuntary administrative separation actions are outlined in AR 635-200.

b. Voluntary separations are initiated by the Soldier. Reasons include hardship/dependency, surviving family members, acceptance into an ROTC program, orders to active duty as an officer or warrant officer, defective enlistment, pregnancy, for the good of the service in lieu of trial by court-martial, and early separation when denied reenlistment. Soldiers who have tested positive for the Human Immunodeficiency Virus (HIV) antibody may request discharge under Secretarial authority. Soldiers may also be allowed to separate early to further their education.

c. Commanders may initiate involuntary separation proceedings for parenthood, personality disorder, concealment of an arrest record, fraudulent or erroneous entry, alcohol or drug abuse rehabilitation failure, failure to meet body composition/weight control standards, entry-level performance and conduct, unsatisfactory performance, or misconduct. To separate a Soldier involuntarily, the unit commander must notify the Soldier in writing. Any involuntary separation action involving a Soldier with six or more years of total active and reserve military service entitles the Soldier to a hearing by an administrative separation board. If the Soldier has 18 or more years, the board is mandatory and cannot be waived. Administrative discharges of Soldiers with 18 or more years of AFS must be approved at the Army Secretariat level.

d. Discharge certificates are furnished only to Soldiers who are honorably discharged or discharged under honorable conditions. All Soldiers leaving active duty are issued a Department of Defense (DD) Form 214, Certificate of Release or Discharge from Active Duty. The DD Form 214 documents the characterization of service, except when a Soldier is separated while in an entry-level status. Entry-level separations normally have service described as uncharacterized. Honorable, general, and under other than honorable conditions characters of service are assigned administratively. Bad conduct and dishonorable discharges are issued upon conviction by a court-martial.

MILITARY HUMAN RESOURCE MANAGEMENT

13-55. Enlisted Non-Disability Retirement System
To qualify for voluntary retirement, an enlisted Soldier must be on active duty and have completed 20 or more years of AFS on the retirement date. A Soldier who has completed 20 years, but less than 30 years AFS and who has completed all required service obligations may be retired at his or her request. Enlisted Soldiers who have completed 30 years AFS have the vested right under law to retire and may not be denied unless other provisions of law are invoked (e.g., stop loss). DA policy requires that all service obligations incurred by promotion, schooling, or PCS be completed prior to approval of voluntary retirement of Soldiers with less than 30 years' service. However, a Soldier may request waiver of a service obligation, and approval would depend upon whether the best interests of the Service are involved or whether a substantial hardship might exist should retirement be denied. Enlisted retirements are normally approved by field commanders of general officer rank. Enlisted Soldiers retire in the grade they hold on the date of retirement unless they have 10 years active commissioned service. Additionally, enlisted Soldiers who have completed 30 years' combined active and retired list service may be eligible for advancement on the retired list to the highest grade held satisfactorily. Requests for grade determination are acted upon by HQDA.

13-56. Officer Non-Disability Retirement System
a. There are two types of retirement–voluntary and mandatory. To qualify for voluntary retirement, officers must have completed at least 20 years AFS on their retirement date. All service obligations incurred must be completed unless waived by HQDA. Mandatory retirement dates are established by law and only in very rare cases are individuals retained on active duty beyond these dates. Majors, lieutenant colonels, and colonels may remain until 24, 28, and 30 years of Active Federal Commissioned Service (AFCS) respectively, unless involuntarily retired through the SERB process.

b. While majors and below must have served six months in their grade to retire at that grade, lieutenant colonels and colonels must serve three years in grade to retire in that grade unless waived by HQDA. Some programs like the Voluntary Early Release and Retirement Program (VERRP) can waive one year of the three-year obligation, subject to limitations and provisions imposed by Congress. Officers who are selected by SERB retain their grade regardless of time held.

13-57. Physical Disability Separation
The laws governing physical disability separation from the Army provide for the medical retirement or separation of a Soldier who is determined to be unfit by reason of physical disability when the physical/mental condition(s) significantly interferes with their ability to perform the duties of his or her office, grade, rank, or rating. The severity of the condition(s) determines eligibility for disability benefits, disability retirement, and severance pay. It is possible to receive a non-disability separation and still have physical disabilities, which could affect potential for civilian employment and retirement benefits. Disability compensation for any medical condition that affects a Soldier's quality of life may be determined by Department of Veteran Affairs and is separate from the service separation.

Section IX
Summary and References

13-58. Summary
a. The primary purpose of the MHRM system is to satisfy valid Army requirements and, insofar as practicable, accommodate the legitimate needs of its members. The system is a complex, dynamic, multifaceted mosaic of interacting subsystems, which interface in a variety of ways with all other major Army systems. It must keep up with the rate of change occurring in the Army so that Soldiers are properly supported, and commanders have timely, relevant information on which to base operational decisions.

b. The processes designed to structure, acquire, train, educate, distribute, sustain, professionally develop, and separate Soldiers must be continuously evaluated and refined to ensure they support current and future Army requirements. The subsystems within these processes must have flexibility to meet the needs of the Army. Whether the Army is reducing or expanding, there are a few critical operating principles to guide decision makers as they choose between difficult, challenging options in

HOW THE ARMY RUNS

either scenario: maintain force readiness at the prescribed levels; maintain quality in recruiting, retention, and development programs; make changes in a balanced and orderly way throughout all grades and specialties, both officer and enlisted; maintain current board selection functions to continue to build on the best; rely on RC; protect well-being; and, finally, in order to reduce uncertainty, ensure there is an understandable, comprehensive plan.

c. This chapter was designed to provide a broad overview of major personnel management systems. During the next several years, the policies, functions, and processes within every one of the subsystems will be continuously challenged to ensure Army requirements are satisfied and to care for its most important resource: people.

13-59. References
  a. Regulations:
  (1) Army Regulation 600, Personnel—General
  (2) Army Regulation 601, Personnel Procurement
  (3) Army Regulation 614, Assignments, Details, and Transfers
  (4) Army Regulation 621, Education
  (5) Army Regulation 623, Evaluations
  (6) Army Regulation 624, Promotions
  (7) Army Regulation 635, Personnel Separations
  (8) Army Regulation 680, Personnel Information Systems
  (9) Field Manual 1-0, Human Resources Support
  b. Useful Links:
  (1) www.army.mil
  (2) www.armyg1.army.mil/
  (3) www.asamra.army.pentagon.mil
  (4) www.usarec.army.mil
  (5) www.goarmy.com
  (6) https://www.hrc.army.mil/
  (7) https://www.goarmyed.com/

CIVILIAN HUMAN RESOURCE MANAGEMENT

Chapter 14

Civilian Human Resource Management

Section I
Introduction

14-1. Chapter Content

   a. Civilians have been an important component of the Army since the Revolutionary War. They are an integral part of the force utilized to accomplish today's multiple complex missions. On 19 June 2006 the Secretary of the Army (SECARMY) established the Army Civilian Corps and the Army Civilian Corps Creed. This name unifies the Army civilian service and embodies the commitment of the dedicated individuals who serve as a fundamental part of the Army team. Army civilians serve in all theaters and are deployed worldwide to support the Army mission and the Overseas Contingency Operations. The purpose and role of the Army civilian is defined by the Army Civilian Corps Creed:

   (1) I am an Army Civilian–a member of the Army team.
   (2) I am dedicated to our Army, our Soldiers and civilians.
   (3) I will always support the mission.
   (4) I provide stability and continuity during war and peace.
   (5) I support and defend the Constitution of the United States and consider it an honor to serve our nation and our Army.
   (6) I live the Army values of loyalty, duty, respect, selfless service, honor, integrity, and personal courage.
   (7) I am an Army civilian.

   b. The Army Civilian Corps includes both Appropriated Fund (APF) and Non-Appropriated Funds (NAF) employees, as well as foreign or local national employees (see Figure 14-1 for details). These civilians are employed in over 530 different occupations with the highest concentrations in logistics, research and development, and Base Operations (BASOPS) functions. Civilians are excluded from positions that by law require military incumbents but are increasingly being used in combat service support functions as formerly military positions are being converted to civilian occupancy.

   c. An understanding of the types of employees and the rules and regulations that govern each of them is necessary to understand the management and administrative environment within which civilian personnel management systems operate. The laws, regulations, personnel policies, and practices differ for Army civilian employees based on their fund source.

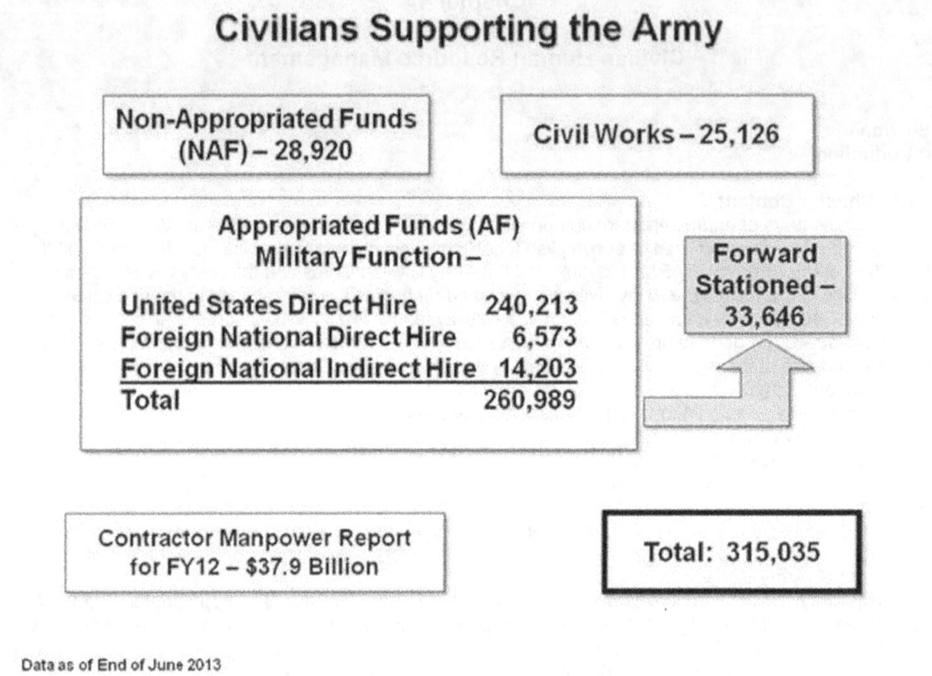

HOW THE ARMY RUNS

Civilians Supporting the Army

Non-Appropriated Funds (NAF) – 28,920

Civil Works – 25,126

Appropriated Funds (AF) Military Function –

United States Direct Hire	240,213
Foreign National Direct Hire	6,573
Foreign National Indirect Hire	14,203
Total	260,989

Forward Stationed – 33,646

Contractor Manpower Report for FY12 – $37.9 Billion

Total: 315,035

Data as of End of June 2013

Figure 14-1. Civilians Supporting the Army

14-2. Categories of Civilian Personnel

a. APF Civilians. The term appropriated funds refers to those funds provided by Congress, normally in annual Defense Appropriations Act legislation. U.S. citizens and eligible U.S. aliens are paid from APFs and are managed within a structure of federal civil service laws. APF employees are further divided into two categories based on the nature of work performed. Military-function civilians perform support duties associated directly with the Army's National Military Strategy (NMS) objectives. Civil-function civilians perform duties associated with the Army's civil works program, administered by the Army Corps of Engineers. Civil works includes planning, design, construction, operation, and maintenance of projects that improve the nation's water resource infrastructure (e.g., navigation, flood control, and hydroelectric power, plus other civil functions prescribed by law). The laws governing APF employees are administered by the U.S. Office of Personnel Management (OPM) and will be discussed in more detail in subsequent sections of this chapter.

b. NAF Civilians.

(1) NAF employees are paid from funds generated from sales, fees, and charges to authorized patrons. This category is comprised of U.S. civilians, foreign nationals (usually from the local labor market), and enlisted service personnel working part time during off-duty hours. All compete for employment on the basis of merit.

(2) NAF employees play an important role in providing Family and Morale, Welfare and Recreation (FMWR) services to military personnel and their family members. Army clubs, guest houses, child care centers, craft shops, bowling centers, swimming pools, gymnasiums, and many other NAF activities employ a considerable number of employees at most Army installations and contribute to the overall quality of life.

c. Foreign/local national civilians. The Army also employs foreign and local nationals in both APF and NAF positions in overseas areas. The Status of Forces Agreement (SOFA) in effect with a given host

CIVILIAN HUMAN RESOURCE MANAGEMENT

country forms the basis of the employment systems for these employees. Within this framework, employee administration must be consistent with host country practice, U.S. law, and the management needs of the Army. In some cases the host government may reimburse the salary and associated personnel costs in whole or in part.

14-3. Army Workforce Mix

a. The Army's fighting environment has changed, causing the Army to transform. The number and scope of the missions that the Army must perform has grown significantly since the end of the Cold War. Following the post-Cold War drawdown that ended in 1999, the number of Army civilian employees increased modestly through Fiscal Year (FY) 2004. During FY 2005 to FY 2010, the numbers increased significantly due to migration of Overseas Contingency Operations missions to base missions, Grow the Army budget initiatives such as increases for base support functions, contractor to civilian conversions, military pay re-capitalization, and conversion of military billets to civilian positions. Civilian increases are not likely to continue into the future, considering budget and deficit reduction deliberations currently underway.

b. The Army is undergoing a fundamental change in how it defines its total manpower. The challenge is achieving the right balance of civilian employees, contractors, and Soldiers in our Army.

14-4. Decentralized Management

The systems for recruiting, utilizing, developing, and sustaining Department of Army (DA) civilians are in large part decentralized. Decentralized management of civilians is very different from the centralized management of military personnel (Figure 14-2). Most authorities for the supervision and management of civilians have been delegated through the chain of command to the lowest practicable level. Certain civilian personnel functions are performed on a regional, command-wide, or DA-wide basis when doing so results in more efficient operations (e.g., the Army Benefits Center-Civilian (ABC-C) at Fort Riley provides individual employees across the Army with counseling on their benefits and automated support for benefits changes) or when a managerial perspective above the local level is required to meet program objectives (e.g., Headquarters, Department of the Army (HQDA) manages the intake and training of interns in DA career programs). The management of Senior Executive Service (SES) employees is also centralized.

Differences Between the Military and Civilian Systems

Category	Military	Civilian
Statute	Title 10, United States Code	Title 5, United States Code
Authority	Rank in Person	Rank in Job
Acquisition	Fill based on structure and authorizations; managed by United States Army Recruiting Command, United States Military Academy, Cadet Command, Human Resources Command, Army G-1	Fill based on position vacancy; managed by supervisor, Commander, Civilian Personnel Advisory Center, Career Program Manager, Assistant Secretary of the Army for Manpower & Reserve Affairs
Individual Training	Hierarchy of schools for military and leadership skills	Functional training primarily occupation-related
Distribution	Mandatory movement to meet worldwide requirements	Voluntary mobility (generally)
Deployment	Involuntary (based on Army requirements)	Voluntary (unless part of job criteria)
Professional Development	Central selection and management	Heavy decentralized management
Transition	Contractual obligation and forced separation / retirement	More individual choices and longer tenure

Figure 14-2. Differences Between the Military and Civilian Systems

HOW THE ARMY RUNS

Section II
Organization of Civilian Personnel Management

14-5. Merit System Principles

a. The Merit System Principles are nine basic standards governing the management of the executive branch workforce. The principles are part of the Civil Service Reform Act of 1978 and can be found at Title 5 United States Code (USC) § 2301. The following merit principles govern all personnel practices.

(1) Recruitment should be from qualified individuals from appropriate sources in an endeavor to achieve a workforce from all segments of society. Selection and advancement should be determined solely on the basis of relative ability, knowledge, and skills, after fair and open competition which assures that all receive equal opportunity.

(2) All employees and applicants for employment should receive fair and equitable treatment in all aspects of personnel management without regard to political affiliation, race, color, religion, national origin, sex, marital status, age, or handicapping condition (sic - the preferred term is disability), with proper regard for privacy and constitutional rights.

(3) Equal pay should be provided for work of equal value, with appropriate consideration of both national and local rates paid by employers in the private sector, and appropriate incentives and recognition should be provided for excellence in performance.

(4) All employees should maintain high standards of integrity, conduct, and concern for the public interest.

(5) The federal work force should be used efficiently and effectively.

(6) Employees should be retained on the basis of adequacy of their performance. Inadequate performance should be corrected. Employees should be separated who cannot or will not improve their performance to meet required standards.

(7) Employees should be provided effective education and training in cases in which such education and training will result in better organizational and individual performance.

(8) Employees should be protected against arbitrary action, personal favoritism, or coercion for partisan political purposes, and prohibited from using their official authority or influence for the purpose of interfering with or affecting the result of an election or a nomination for an election.

(9) Employees should be protected against reprisal for the lawful disclosure of information which an employee reasonably believes evidences a violation of any law, rule, or regulation, or evidences mismanagement, a gross waste of funds, an abuse of authority, or a substantial and specific danger to public health or safety.

b. Twelve prohibited personnel practices are defined by law at, § 2302(b) of Title 5 of the U.S.C. Generally stated, § 2302(b) provides that a federal employee may not authorize to take, direct others to take, recommend, or approve any personnel action that may–

(1) Discriminate for or against an employee or applicant based on race, color, religion, sex, or national origin

(2) Solicit or consider employment recommendations based on factors other than personal knowledge or records of job-related abilities or characteristics

(3) Coerce the political activity of any person (including the providing of any political contribution or service), or take any action against any employee or applicant for employment as a reprisal for the refusal of any person to engage in such political activity

(4) Deceive or willfully obstruct anyone from competing for employment

(5) Influence anyone to withdraw from competition for any position so as to improve or injure the employment prospects of any other person

(6) Give an unauthorized preference or advantage to anyone so as to improve or injure the employment prospects of any particular employee or applicant

(7) Engage in nepotism (i.e., hire, promote, or advocate the hiring or promotion of relatives)

(8) Engage in reprisal for whistle blowing (i.e., take, fail to take, or threaten to take or fail to take a personnel action with respect to any employee or applicant because of any disclosure of information by the employee or applicant that he or she reasonably believes evidences a violation of a law, rule or regulation; gross mismanagement; a gross waste of funds; an abuse of authority; or a substantial and specific danger to public health or safety (if such disclosure is not barred by law and such information is not specifically required by Executive Order (EO) to be kept secret in the interest of national defense or

the conduct of foreign affairs–if so restricted by law or EO, the disclosure is only protected if made to the Special Counsel, the Inspector General, or a comparable agency official))

(9) Take, fail to take, or threaten to take or fail to take a personnel action against an employee or applicant for exercising an appeal, complaint, or grievance right; testifying for or assisting another in exercising such a right; cooperating with or disclosing information to the Special Counsel or to an Inspector General; or refusing to obey an order that would require the individual to violate a law

(10) Discriminate based on personal conduct which is not adverse to the on-the-job performance of an employee, applicant, or others

(11) Take or fail to take, recommend, or approve a personnel action if taking or failing to take such an action would violate a veterans' preference requirement

(12) Take or fail to take a personnel action, if taking or failing to take action would violate any law, rule or regulation implementing or directly concerning merit system principles at Title 5 USC § 2301.

14-6. U.S. OPM

a. OPM is the personnel agency of the executive branch charged with the mission to administer most federal laws and EOs dealing with all aspects of civilian personnel management and administration in the federal sector. Some laws and EOs place certain personnel management responsibilities directly on agency and department heads, subject to OPM policy and review. In other cases, OPM retains the authority to establish specific program standards and regulate and control the means of carrying out major aspects of agency or departmental personnel management operations.

b. OPM develops proposals for federal personnel legislation and EOs and develops and publishes specific policies, procedures, and regulations implementing federal personnel laws and EOs. It also provides testing, evaluation, and referral of job applicants to agencies; evaluates agency personnel management systems; and provides advice and assistance to agencies in the development of effective personnel management programs and provides oversight on Department of Defense (DOD) evaluations and assessments of human capital policies, programs, and practices. In addition, OPM develops standards by which jobs are classified (i.e., pay systems, title, job series, and grades); administers retirement, health, and life insurance programs; and adjudicates position classification appeals.

c. OPM executes, administers, and enforces civil service rules and regulations through audits, reviews and inspections. Failure on the part of agencies to observe the prescribed standards, requirements, and instructions may result in the withdrawal of personnel management authority delegated by OPM.

14-7. Other Agencies with Federal Government-Wide Authority

In addition to OPM controls and procedures, four separate, independent federal agencies also provide oversight to ensure that agencies adhere to principles of merit, labor relations guarantees, and equal employment rights:

a. U.S. Merit Systems Protection Board (MSPB). The MSPB is an independent, quasi-judicial agency in the executive branch that serves as the guardian of federal merit systems. The board's mission is to protect federal merit systems and the rights of individuals within those systems. MSPB carries out its statutory responsibilities and authorities primarily by adjudicating individual employee appeals and by conducting merit systems studies. In addition, MSPB reviews the significant actions of the OPM to assess the degree to which those actions may affect merit.

(1) Cases arising under the MSPB jurisdiction include the following.

(a) Employee appeals of agency adverse actions, including removals, suspensions of more than 14 days, reductions in grade or pay, furloughs of 30 days or less, reduction-in-force actions, denials of within grade salary increase

(b) OPM suitability determinations

(c) OPM determinations in retirement matters

(d) Disciplinary actions brought by the Office of Special Counsel (OSC) alleging violations of the Hatch Act (coercion of government employee political activity)

(e) Corrective and disciplinary actions brought by the OSC against agencies or federal employees who are alleged to have committed certain prohibited personnel practices, or to have violated certain civil service laws, rules, and regulations

(f) Requests for stays of personnel actions alleged by the OSC to result from certain prohibited personnel practices

HOW THE ARMY RUNS

(g) Requests for review of regulations issued by OPM or of implementation of OPM regulations by an agency

(h) Informal hearings in cases involving proposed performance-based removals from the Senior Executive Service

(2) The MSPB also has jurisdiction over allegations of employment discrimination in connection with actions otherwise appealable to the MSPB and certain employee allegations subject to a negotiated grievance procedure covering actions otherwise appealable to the MSPB.

b. OSC. The OSC is an independent federal investigative and prosecutorial agency. OSC's authority comes from four federal statutes: the Civil Service Reform Act (CSRA), the Whistleblower Protection Act, the Hatch Act (legal restrictions on government employee political activity), and the Uniform Services Employment and Reemployment Rights Act (USERRA). OSC's primary mission is to safeguard the merit system by protecting federal employees and applicants from prohibited personnel practices, especially reprisal for whistle blowing. Sexual orientation and parental status employment discrimination have been designated as prohibited personnel practices by EO. Allegations of employment discrimination on these bases may be filed with and subject to investigation by the OSC.

c. Federal Labor Relations Authority (FLRA). The FLRA is an independent administrative federal agency which adjudicates federal employee collective bargaining disputes, including resolving complaints of unfair labor practices, determining appropriateness of units for labor organization representation, adjudicating exceptions to arbitrator's awards, adjudicating legal issues relating to duty to bargain and negotiability, and resolving impasses during negotiations.

d. The Equal Employment Opportunity Commission (EEOC). EEOC is an independent federal agency responsible for enforcing federal laws which prohibit employment discrimination in both the private and public sector based on race, color, national origin, sex, age (40 and older), religion, genetic information, mental or physical disability or in reprisal for engaging in protected activity such as opposing discrimination or participating in a discrimination complaint or lawsuit. The EEOC provides oversight and coordination of all federal sector equal employment opportunity regulations, practices and policies, and submits an annual report on the federal workforce to the President of the United States (POTUS), Congress, and appropriate congressional committees. The EEOC's regulation implementing the federal sector Equal Employment Opportunity (EEO) program (29 Code of Federal Regulations (CFR) 1614), requires each federal agency to implement and maintain effective EEO programs. The EEOC Administrative Judges (AJ) play an adjudicative role in formal federal sector EEO complaints as well as at the appellate level of the administrative complaint process. EEOC findings of discrimination are not appealable by agencies in federal court.

14-8. DOD

Under EO 9830, the POTUS has delegated authority to agency heads, including the Secretary of Defense (SECDEF), to act in civilian human resource matters in accordance with applicable policies, program requirements, standards, and instructions.

a. Office of the Secretary of Defense (OSD). Within OSD, the Under Secretary of Defense (Personnel and Readiness) (USD(P&R)) and the Deputy Assistant Secretary of Defense (Civilian Personnel Policy) (DASD(CPP)) have responsibility for DOD-wide Civilian Human Resource (CHR) policy. The DASD(CPP) develops plans, policies, and programs to manage the DOD civilian workforce, including NAF and local national employees in coordination with the services and within the framework established by federal law, EOs, and government-wide regulations. Through its Defense Civilian Personnel Advisory Services (DCPAS), the DASD(CPP) also provides certain civilian human resource services on a DOD-wide basis.

b. DOD Investigations and Resolutions Division (DOD IRD). The IRD investigates and facilitates the resolution of EEO complaints and formal employee grievances not covered by negotiated grievance procedures. In a complex formal grievance of a NAF employee, or a formal grievance of an APF employee under the Administrative Grievance System, the deciding official may elect to retain the services of the IRD to review the facts and make recommendations.

14-9. Assistant Secretary of the Army (Manpower and Reserve Affairs) (ASA(M&RA))

a. DA authority for civilian personnel management is further delegated by the SECDEF to the SECARMY. The SECARMY in turn has delegated some of the civilian personnel management responsibilities including responsibility for personnel policy, programming, and oversight to the

CIVILIAN HUMAN RESOURCE MANAGEMENT

ASA(M&RA) through General Order No. 2012-01, 11 June 2012. The SECARMY retains appointing and pay setting authority for civilian Executive and Senior Professional (ESP) personnel (except for those appointed by the POTUS or other higher level authority). This includes positions in the SES, Defense Intelligence Senior Executive Service (DISES), Scientific and Technical (ST) Professionals, Senior Level (SL) and Defense Intelligence Senior Level (DISL), as well as Highly Qualified Expert (HQE) positions. By memo dated 3 August 2009, the SECARMY delegated to the ASA(M&RA) authority, direction, and control over missions, functions, and personnel of the Civilian Senior Leader Management Office (CSLMO). The Deputy Chief of Staff, G-1 (DCS, G-1), is the responsible official to the ASA(M&RA) in developing, coordinating, and implementing programs and policies directly associated with accession, development, distribution, and sustainment of military and civilian personnel. The Assistant G-1 for Civilian Personnel (AG-1 CP) has responsibility for supervision of civilian personnel policy, management, and related civilian personnel functions.

   b. Appointing authority, which is the authority to approve personnel actions, is delegated to the Commanders of the Army Commands, the Commanders of the Army Service Component Commands, the Commanders/Superintendent of the Direct Reporting Units and the Administrative Assistant to the SECARMY. In order to streamline the execution of the DA's civilian personnel program, the Army's Civilian Human Resources Agency (CHRA), through the CHRA Regional Directors or their designees, authenticates civilian personnel actions for their serviced organizations. Such personnel officials will act for the appointing authorities in authenticating actions. Authenticating officials may electronically approve a personnel action only after the responsible management official has approved the action, determined its accordance with law and regulation, as well as exercised appropriate fiduciary responsibility to ensure fiscal soundness. The authenticating official is responsible for ensuring that personnel actions are in compliance with applicable civilian personnel laws, rules, regulations, and governing policies before processing the actions and thus serves as the appointing official. An example is provided to illustrate the act for relationship: whenever the regional processing center approves and processes an official personnel action (such as the appointment of someone to a position), it is doing so on behalf of the commander of the serviced organization, exercising that commander's personnel management authority. Regional and Civilian Personnel Advisory Center (CPAC) directors are directly responsible to each of the commanders they service for the proper exercise of this authority.

14-10. Other Army Organizations with Civilian Personnel Responsibilities

   a. U.S Army Family and Morale, Welfare, and Recreation Command (FMWRC). FMWRC is a subordinate command to Installation Management Command (IMCOM). FMWRC's mission is to develop and administer systems and programs for the Army family and community activities under the general heading of Family and Morale, Welfare, and Recreation (MWR). The FMWRC administers a central referral program for specified MWR managerial jobs (both APF and NAF) and a benefits program for all Army NAF employees.

   b. Intelligence Personnel Management Office (IPMO). The IPMO is a subordinate element of the Office, Deputy Chief of Staff, G-2, HQDA. It serves as the focal point in the Army for policy and management of the Defense Civilian Intelligence Personnel System (DCIPS) and reports jointly to the Army Deputy Chief of Staff for Intelligence (G-2) and the ASA(M&RA). It maintains liaison with the rest of federal intelligence on civilian personnel management issues, develops policies and programs, and develops and provides training and guidance. The IPMO also provides personnel management advice and assistance to CPACs that, in turn, provide civilian personnel management support to intelligence organizations or those with DCIPS employees.

Section III
Civilian Human Resource Service Delivery

14-11. CPACs

   a. Advisory functions requiring face-to-face interaction between personnel specialists and managers and employees typically reside at the CPAC (installation/activity level). Action processing, record keeping, and database management functions are centralized at regional processing centers. The Army has established seven geographically based regions, each with a regional processing center. The two Outside of the Continental United States (OCONUS) regions and their regional processing center

HOW THE ARMY RUNS

locations are: Europe Region-Germany and Far East Region-Korea. Five regions are in the Continental United States (CONUS): Southwest Region-Fort Riley, Kansas; Northeast Region-Aberdeen Proving Ground, Maryland; North Central Region-Rock Island Arsenal, Illinois; South Central Region-Redstone Arsenal, Alabama; and the West Region-Fort Huachuca, Arizona. Within the regions are a total of 99 CPACs. Each CPAC is typically located at or near the installation(s) to which it provides advisory services.

b. Specific responsibilities of the CPACs are as follows.

(1) Providing the civilian personnel service and assistance necessary to obtain, compensate, develop, use, and retain an effective civilian workforce.

(2) Promoting equality of opportunity in the organizational units serviced.

(3) Coordinating personnel management requirements and needs of the organizations serviced.

(4) Providing information and staff assistance and guidance to managers and supervisors to assist them in obtaining the most effective use of civilians through improved management.

(5) Establishing labor management relationships focused on supporting and enhancing the Army's national security mission and creating and maintaining a high-performance workplace that delivers the highest quality products and services at the lowest possible cost. Such relationships should be committed to pursuing solutions that promote increased quality and productivity, customer service, mission accomplishment, efficiency, quality of life, employee empowerment, organizational performance, and military readiness. Consensual means of resolving disputes, such as alternate dispute resolution and interest based bargaining, should be sought.

14-12. Automation Tools

a. The Defense Civilian Personnel Data System (DCPDS) is an automation tool used throughout DOD. DCPDS contains the world's largest relational database; housing and processing all of DOD's civilian Human Resources (HR) data. The system is designed to support APF, NAF, and local national HR operations. It offers a comprehensive array of state-of-the-art personnel processing capabilities. Managers can access organizational, historical, and employee data through a variety of reports and individual screens. Human Resource Specialists can process personnel actions, automatically interface with APF payroll, and generate confirming documents that can print at the originating manager's office printer. Along the way, the personnel action can be acted upon by those with the need and access, such as resource management for coding and budgetary data.

b. Automated tools have been developed to support remote processing and enable fewer human resource specialists to provide the same or better customer service. These tools include the following.

(1) Personnel Management Information and Support System (PERMISS). The PERMISS is an online supervisors' and employees' handbook. It contains over 800 articles providing general civilian personnel guidance and information, with links to source and reference documents (e.g., applicable laws and regulations). PERMISS may be accessed through the Army Civilian Personnel Online Library (CPOL) web site on the Internet. Although PERMISS is not designed to answer questions pertaining to a specific individual's entitlements or job status, it does provide access to many of the general concepts and logic involved in making personnel decisions. It is not a forum for raising situation-specific questions, which should be answered through the supervisory chain of command or by the servicing CPAC.

(2) CPOL. The CPOL system contains policy and guidance documents on the management and administration of the Army civilian workforce, including newsletters, bulletins, operating manuals, directives, forms, per diem rates, and salary schedules.

(3) CPOL-Portal. CPOL-Portal is a one-stop secure site which provides Army civilian employees and HR specialists access to a private portal with a complete set of employment-related resources, links, and web-based applications that require Army Knowledge Online (AKO) Common Access Card (CAC) single sign-on. CPOL-Portal provides an Integrated Management System (IMS) in support of Civilian Workforce Transformation (CWT). CPOL-Portal provides the full spectrum of Information Technology (IT) application support and access to Acquire, Develop, Distribute, and Sustain components of the Army Civilian Human Capital Management (HCM) Life Cycle and link to G3 Structure IT Enterprise Applications.

(4) Fully Automated System for Classification (FASCLASS). FASCLASS delivers position classification and position description information to the customer's desktop. It provides online access to active position descriptions and organizational information.

CIVILIAN HUMAN RESOURCE MANAGEMENT

(5) ABC-C. ABC-C enables customers to access and change their civilian benefits, such as health and life insurance, over the telephone or on the internet using the Employee Benefits Information System (EBIS). ABC-C processes employee retirements. ABC-C also has skilled and knowledgeable operators to provide counseling over the phone.

(6) Civilian Human Resource Training Application System (CHRTAS)/ Army Training Requirements and Resources System (ATRRS). CHRTAS and ATRRS provide a web-based training tool for supervisors, employees, and training course managers. Capabilities include training registration and approval, Individual Development Plans (IDP), and Training History Management. Completed training is recorded in CHRTAS, ATRRS, and DCPDS. All three systems are utilized for training provided by CHRA, Regional Human Resources Development (HRD) Divisions, as well as the Civilian Education System (CES) leadership courses managed by the Army Management Staff College. CHRTAS is evolving to become Army's enterprise Competency-Based Career Development System.

Section IV
Personnel Management at Installation / Activity Level

14-13. Personnel Management Responsibility and Authority
The responsibility for providing day-to-day leadership of Army civilians resides primarily at installation and activity level with the supervisor, manager, and commander. The SECARMY has delegated personnel management authority, except for management of ESP resources, to commanders with authority to further delegate to commanders of independent field activities. Thus, the actual management of DA civilians, including professional development, incentive awards, discipline, evaluation, labor relations, and almost all other life cycle personnel functions is decentralized to installation and activity commanders and local managers and supervisors. The CPAC assists the chain of command in exercising this responsibility. In the case of ESPs, centralized management is the responsibility of CSLMO.

14-14. Commander Responsibilities
Installation commanders are responsible for leading and managing civilian employees and are held accountable for effective utilization of their HR assets. Responsible commanders develop, empower, and utilize subordinate supervisors, managers, and the CHR staff to establish a work environment for positive employee motivation and high performance. Specific command responsibilities are to carry out civilian personnel management policies, procedures and programs as set forth in Title 5 USC Government Organizations and Employees; Title 5 Code of Federal Regulations Administrative Personnel; and DOD 1400.25-M DOD Civilian Personnel Manual; 5 CFR Parts 410 and 412, Training; Supervisory, Management and Executive Development, and other applicable laws and regulations, consistent with applicable negotiated agreements.

14-15. Supervisor Responsibilities
   a. Commanders generally delegate authority for leading and managing civilian employees to subordinate managers and supervisors. This carries with it specific responsibilities to do the following.
     (1) Maintain accurate position descriptions.
     (2) Recruit, select, assign, and set pay for employees.
     (3) Evaluate employee performance, and train and develop employees.
     (4) Administer award and incentive programs.
     (5) Maintain management-employee communications.
     (6) Communicate employee expectations, administer constructive discipline, and promptly address employee performance deficiencies.
     (7) Maintain a positive labor-management relations program.
   b. Supervisor responsibilities in each of these areas and the functional systems established to assist in carrying out these responsibilities are described below.
   c. The Army has an informal civilian mentoring program for mentoring civilians. The Army Mentorship Program was created to reemphasize, reinvigorate, and increase mentorship throughout the Army. The Army's Mentorship Resource Center is located at http://www.armyg1.army.mil/hr/mentorship/default.asp
     (1) Supervisors should motivate employees to seek mentors through the Army's Mentorship Resource Center.

HOW THE ARMY RUNS

(2) DA pamphlet 690-46 Mentoring for Civilian Members of the Force provides further guidance.

14-16. Position Classification and Pay
a. Position Classification and Pay for APF Positions.

(1) Position classification authority is delegated to managers and supervisors within the Army, who may further delegate to CHRA for day to day operation. Individual positions are classified by comparison with the appropriate classification standards or guides. These are developed by OPM or DOD based on comprehensive occupational studies of representative work found in the federal service. Army regulations assign responsibility for maintaining accurate job descriptions to supervisors. Differences in grades and pay must be attributed to differences in the difficulty, responsibility, and skill requirements of jobs.

(2) Most positions are covered by the following pay systems: the General Schedule (GS); Personnel demonstration projects (which cover white-collar workers in professional, administrative, technical, clerical, and protective occupations); and the Federal Wage System (FWS), which covers workers in trades, crafts, labor, and similar occupations. Salary rates for most GS positions, including locality pay, are based on surveys of private sector salary rates conducted by the Department of Labor. FWS wage rates are established based on local surveys of private sector rates conducted by federal agencies in accordance with OPM policies. Personnel demonstration projects operate under broad pay band systems rather than the GS. The National Security Personnel System (NSPS) covered some workers but was repealed by the National Defense Authorization Act for Fiscal Year 2010. It is no longer in use as of 1 January 2012.

(3) Personnel demonstration projects authorized by the Defense Authorization Acts of FY 1995, FY 1996, and FY 1998, operate under broad pay band systems rather than the GS schedule. Classification authority in these systems is delegated only to appropriate management officials. These officials classify positions by a comparison of duties and responsibilities with the appropriate broadband or factor-level descriptors as outlined in the demonstration projects' federal register notices. Typically occupations with similar characteristics are grouped together into career paths, such as Engineering/Science, Business/Technical and General Support. Depending on the demonstration project, each career path may have two to six pay bands. Pay bands allow managers flexibility in setting pay within a band. Salary rates for personnel demonstration project employees generally include staffing supplements, which are usually administered in the same manner as locality pay for GS. Employees progress through pay bands according to job performance. Management officials may also use recruitment, retention, and relocation incentives and other pay flexibilities as discussed in paragraph 14-17 below.

b. Position Classification and Pay for NAF Positions.

(1) The DOD NAF uses a pay band system for position classification and pay. Pay banding involves the establishment of several broad salary bands and allows managers to set individual salaries within an established pay band. It is easier for managers to provide high-performing NAF employees with greater compensation short of a promotion action or performance award. The DOD pay band system includes all NAF clerical, administrative, sales, technical, managerial, executive, professional, and personal service positions, exclusive of child care giving and crafts and trades positions.

(2) There are six pay bands, which are referred to as pay levels and identified using codes Nonappropriated Fund (NF)-1 through NF-6. They have minimum and maximum pay rates that are overlapping. The minimum and maximum rates for the first two levels and minimum level for NF-3 are determined by locality-based wage surveys of comparable private sector jobs. The maximum rates for NF-3 and the rates for NF-4 through NF-6 are related to the GS and SES pay range.

(3) Child caregiving pay band positions are covered by a separate pay band system implemented in consonance with the DA Caregiving Personnel Pay Program. There are two pay bands, also referred to as pay levels, and they are distinctly identified through use of terms Pay Band I or Pay Band II. The range in pay for child care giving pay band positions is equal to the hourly rate of pay for a GS-2, Step 1, through GS-5, Step 10, and pay rates prescribed for GS child care giving positions also apply. The DA Caregiving Personnel Pay Program (CPPP) was expanded in February 1999 to include positions in Youth Services that had similar duties and responsibilities. The program continues to follow the same guidelines that were established for the CPPP and is now known as the Child and Youth Personnel Pay Program (CYPPP).

(4) Crafts and trades positions are not affected by pay banding. Pay is determined through the prevailing rate system used for those positions covered under the FWS.

CIVILIAN HUMAN RESOURCE MANAGEMENT

c. Position Classification and Pay for Foreign National Positions. These positions are generally not included in either of the pay systems described above. Employees in these positions are paid under local host-nation pay scales and conditions.

14-17. Recruitment, Selection, and Assignment
   a. Management has the right to consider candidates from all appropriate sources, including but not limited to merit promotion, reinstatement and transfer eligibles, Veterans Employment Opportunity Act (VEOA) eligibles, individuals with severe physical or mental disabilities, family member eligibles under EO 12721 and 13473, and those certified as eligible for appointment by OPM or under a delegated examining authority. In deciding which sources to tap, consideration should be given to those which are expected to produce candidates who will meet the agency's mission requirements, contribute new ideas and viewpoints, and meet the agency's affirmative action and special employment programs. Recruitment sources also encompass the Pathways Programs created under Executive Order 13562, Recruiting and Hiring Students and Recent Graduates. The Pathways Programs includes the Internship Program, Recent Graduates Program and the Presidential Management Fellows (PMF) Program and are described below. Persons with statutory or priority placement rights to a vacancy must be given appropriate consideration before the normal recruitment process may proceed.
   (1) Recent Graduates Program. This program targets recent graduates of trade and vocational schools, community colleges, universities, and other qualifying institutions. To be eligible, applicants must apply within two years of degree completion (except for veterans precluded from doing so due to their military service obligation, who will have six years after degree completion). Successful applicants will be placed in a two-year career development program. Those who successfully complete the program may be considered for noncompetitive conversion to career/career conditional appointments.
   (2) Internship Program. The program provides students in high schools, community colleges, four-year colleges, trade schools, career and technical education programs, and other qualifying educational institutions and programs with paid opportunities to work in agencies and explore federal careers while still in school. Students that successfully complete the program may be eligible for noncompetitive conversion to career/career conditional appointments.
   (3) PMF Program. This program aims to attract to the federal service outstanding men and women from a variety of academic disciplines at the graduate level who have a clear interest in, and commitment to, the leadership and management of public policies and programs. Successful completion may lead to noncompetitive conversion to a career/career conditional appointment. Personnel selection decisions must be based solely on merit based and job-related reasons.
   b. In recent years, the DA, like other employers, has found the recruitment and retention of highly skilled employees a challenge, particularly for jobs in shortage occupations or in locations with an especially tight labor market. Due to an anticipated wave of retirements, completion of the Base Realignment and Closure (BRAC) process, and the proposed downsizing of the federal government, for the next several years DA anticipates difficulty in filling mission critical vacancies in a highly competitive environment. It is important that supervisors and managers are aware that special incentives are available for staffing positions with unusual recruitment and retention problems. These incentives may include recruitment incentives, relocation incentives, retention incentive superior qualifications appointments (appointment at a rate above the minimum for the GS grade because of superior qualifications or a special need for the candidate's services), and special salary rates (minimum rates and rate ranges above those of the GS). In addition, activities may identify local shortage positions for purposes of paying first duty station and pre-employment interview travel expenses for permanent positions. Information about these and other incentives is available in PERMISS. Army employment also offers attractive leave, insurance, and retirement benefits, and typically provides a family friendly environment, meaningful public service work, and good opportunities for training and advancement based on merit. All of these can be important tools in marketing the Army as an employer.

14-18. Evaluation of Employee Performance and Administration of Awards / Incentives Programs
   a. Administration of the evaluation and performance incentive functions of civilian personnel management requires managers and supervisors to exercise both leadership and fiscal responsibilities. It also requires an appreciation of the workplace environment and an understanding of individual needs for counseling, recognition, and reward. The civilian incentive awards program includes monetary and honorary awards. Civilian incentive award decorations and award approval authority are aligned with the

HOW THE ARMY RUNS

military awards system to the extent practicable. The following Army civilian performance management programs are detailed in regulations, pamphlets, and DOD and OPM guidance listed in the reference section of this chapter.

(1) Performance planning and evaluation programs for ESPs, white-collar, blue-collar, and NAF employees.

(2) Base pay adjustment policy and procedures for all civilian employees (ESP pay increases; GS and FWS within-grade increases; and NAF pay increases).

(3) Cash and honorary award programs to recognize significant individual and group contributions (SES performance bonuses; GS, NAF, and FWS performance awards; GS quality step increases; and time-off and honorary awards).

(4) Policy and procedures for dealing with employees who fail to meet performance expectations.

(5) Personnel demonstration projects and ESPs use systems that reward high performance or contributions to mission, and place less emphasis on longevity for pay and retention.

b. As with the military performance evaluation systems, the civilian evaluation process is designed to enhance supervisory/employee communications and day-to-day relationships to improve overall performance. At the beginning of each rating period, the rating supervisor and the employee determine job requirements and develop a performance plan for the year. The performance plan should reflect the organization's mission and goals and the duties and responsibilities of the employee in concert with individual position descriptions. The performance plan may change during the year if the mission requires a re-ordering of responsibilities and priorities. At least once during the performance cycle (usually at the midpoint of the rating period), the rating official must conduct an in-progress review of employee performance. This typically involves discussion of employee achievements, any changes to expectations, and ways to improve performance, if applicable. At the end of the rating period, the rating chain compares the individual's contributions to the requirements in the performance plan and renders a rating of record. The rating of record is used to make promotion/pay increase and training decisions, document justification for performance-based cash awards and honorary awards, and give additional credit for reduction-in-force/workforce shaping purposes. The evaluation process is also used to assist employees who experience performance problems. Performance counseling sessions may be used to help employees improve to an expected level or the evaluation can serve to support removal from the position if employees fail to meet standards. The keys to successful performance management are frequent, two-way communication and timely, appropriate action to either recognize significant contributions or correct performance which fails to meet expectations.

14-19. Training and Development of Employees

On 10 December 2009, significant federal changes governing the training, supervisory, management, and executive development of employees went into effect. These changes were published by OPM in the federal register and they pertain to 5 CFR Parts 410 and 412 (Training; Supervisory, Management, and Executive Development). Based on these new requirements, the Army is developing and maintaining training programs to include all types of training activities in support of organizational missions and to support the very first of this federal requirement to evaluate on a regular basis, Army training programs and plans with respect to the accomplishment of our agency's specific performance plans and strategic goals. Coordinating with the CPAC's, the CHRA and Regional Human Resources Development Divisions aide organizational managers and supervisors to develop, coordinate, and administer their training and development programs. Army executives, managers, and supervisors are required to define their training requirements in support of the life cycle management of employee development through competency-based training.

a. Training Programs. Training categories cover a broad field from executive and management courses to adult basic education. Training is classified as either short- or long-term (more than 120 days). The actual training can be delivered through on-the-job training at local activities, Army schools, DOD schools, CHRA locations, interagency schools, formal schools, and a host of other government and non-government sources as well as online sources. Civilians can also compete for attendance in formal training programs such as Senior Service Colleges and other training opportunities. The Army Regulation (AR) 215 series of documents establishes training requirements for both APF and NAF employees in MWR activities. This training is met largely through courses sponsored and/or conducted by the FMWRC at the MWR Academy.

b. Career Management System.

CIVILIAN HUMAN RESOURCE MANAGEMENT

(1) To establish basic policies and program requirements for the intake, assignment, training, and development of employees in designated occupations, the Army developed The Army Civilian Training, Education and Development System (ACTEDS) as outlined in AR 690-950, Career Management. These systems support supervisors in recruiting candidates for long-term career opportunities and ensure a steady flow of capable, fully qualified, and trained personnel for Army positions in 23 civilian career professional, technical, and administrative fields. The relative strength in these fields is shown in Figure 14-3.

Annual Civilian Personnel Strength Review

by Career Program	FY2012
10 Civilian Human Resource Management	3,893
11 Comptroller	12,304
12 Safety & Occupational Health Management	4,620
13 Supply Management	14,438
14 Contract / Acquisition	8,731
15 Quality and Reliability Assurance	1,460
16 Engineers & Scientists (Non-Construction)	20,201
17 Materiel Maintenance Management	28,301
18 Engineers & Scientists (Resources & Construction)	23,906
19 Physical Security & Law Enforcement	7,442
20 Quality Assurance Specialist (Ammunition Surveillance)	500
22 Public Affairs & Communications Media	1,443
24 Transportation & Distribution Management	4,631
26 Manpower & Force Management	3,176
27 Housing Management	394
28 Equal Employment Opportunity	474
29 Installation Management	4,693
31 Education Services	1,079
32 Training, Capabilities & Doctrine Warfighting Development	9,767
33 Ammunition Management	2,614
34 Information Technology Management	14,782
35 Intelligence	5,039
36 Analysis, Modeling and Simulation	2,288
50 Military Personnel Management	5,825
51 General Administration & Management	22,240
53 Medical	32,226
55 Inspector General	396
56 Legal	2,346
60 Foreign Affairs & Strategic Planning	334
61 Historian, Museum Curator	382
64 Aviation	1,181
96 Administrative	3,874
97 Clerical	1,831
98 Program Management	225
Grand Total	247,036

Figure 14-3. Annual Civilian Personnel Strength Review

HOW THE ARMY RUNS

(2) The career management system provides clear lines of progression to successively more responsible positions and a coordinated training and development program for occupational specialties, using both Army and outside facilities. Procedures are provided for counseling employees; planning individual development programs; and appraising employee competencies. New employees participate in planned work or rotational assignments designed to develop technical and leadership competencies to prepare for future managerial responsibilities. The ACTEDS is the DA-wide program by which these objectives are accomplished and funded.

(3) At the higher-grade levels, typically for promotion to grades GS-13 through GS-15, candidates are considered on an Army-wide basis. Application procedures depend on the particular career program.

(4) The above procedures apply to APF personnel, including those working in MWR programs. NAF employees also benefit from a central referral program. FMWRC is the executive agent for NAF MWR career programs and maintains a central roster of NAF pay band employees eligible for level NF-4 and above positions. Outside applicants may also register in the program. The system provides selecting officials with names and information on employees who are interested in being considered for a given NAF position.

14-20. Workers Compensation Program

a. Federal employees who are injured or become ill as a direct result of their employment are entitled by the Federal Employees Compensation Act (FECA) to medical care and also salary replacement (compensation) while they are not working. Benefits are also available for a surviving spouse and dependents if the death is job related. Additionally, employees are entitled to a lump sum if there is a permanent loss or impairment of a body part because of their employment. The Workers Compensation program is very expensive to the Army, both in dollars and in lost human potential. The majority of the cost stems from workers who never return to Army employment and continue to draw salary replacement for their lifetime.

b. To maintain control of these costs, each installation is required to have a FECA working group, established by the Senior Commander, and including the Injury Compensation Program Administer (ICPA) and representatives of management, medical, safety, and investigative service staff. The FECA working group is required to meet at least quarterly to analyze trends and develop cost-containment initiatives. Managers and supervisors have the obligation to ensure that all workplaces are as safe as possible, that employees are trained on safe work practices, issued appropriate safety equipment, and that safety standards are constantly enforced. All workplace injuries and illnesses should be investigated by the supervisor and by the safety office to ensure the cause of the injury or illness is corrected. The ICPA, located in the CPAC, has the lead in administering the workers compensation program at the installation level. The ICPA has the dual responsibility of seeing that the injured or ill worker receives the medical care needed to recover and that the worker returns to employment, either to the same position held at the date of injury position, light duty, or a new position if necessary. Every employee who is never returned to productive employment is entitled to salary replacement (compensation) for the employee's lifetime. The ICPA also is responsible for ensuring that all questionable claims of injury or illness are challenged so that Army is not charged for undue expenses. The ICPA should be in frequent contact with all injured employees, and ensure that each treating physician understands that Army is eager to offer light duty or modified employment.

c. NAF employees are entitled to worker's compensation benefits established under provisions of the Non-Appropriated Funds Instrumentalities (NAFI) Act of 1958 (5 USC Sections 8171-8173), which extends the provisions of the Longshore and Harbor Workers Compensation Act (LHWCA) (33 USC 901 et seq.). Worker's compensation provides benefits to NAF employees who are disabled because of job-related illness or injury or to surviving spouse and dependents in cases of death from job-related causes. Benefits apply to employees of NAFI/entities employed inside the continental United States; or employees of NAFIs/entities who are U.S. citizens, permanent residents of the U.S. or a territory or possession of the U.S., and employed OCONUS. Benefits will not apply to active duty military personnel employed by NAFIs/entities or local civilians employed by NAFIs/entities overseas. AR 215-3, Nonappropriated Funds Personnel Policy and AR 215-1, Morale, Welfare, and Recreation Activities and Nonappropriated Instrumentalities outline established processes and procedures related to Worker's Compensation for NAF employees.

CIVILIAN HUMAN RESOURCE MANAGEMENT

14-21. Communication, Discipline, and Labor-Management Relations
Supervisors are responsible for striving to develop a cooperative labor-management relationship: administering labor-management agreements; communicating management objectives, decisions, and viewpoints to their subordinates; and communicating their subordinates' views to higher-level management. Supervisors must analyze problems, develop solutions, and evaluate the results of decisions. The CPAC is responsible for assisting management in the day-to-day business of employee performance, discipline, individual adverse actions, effective use of recognition and awards, labor-management-employee relations, administration of leave, hours of work, and monitoring of health and safety conditions.

   a. If an employee believes that his or her rights have been denied, or that improper procedures have been followed, or that an action taken by management is unwarranted, he or she may utilize appropriate forums for relief. Such forums may include, but are not limited to Administrative Grievance Procedures, Negotiated Grievance Procedures, Alternative Dispute Resolution (ADR), MSPB, and EEO channels. The MSPB may be used for adverse actions (except in cases of a short suspension defined as 14 days or less). Short suspensions and reprimands may be contested through the Administrative Grievance System or Negotiated Grievance Procedures. Subsequently the courts may also be used.

   b. The grievance procedures (both in policy and through negotiated agreements) set forth specific steps to be followed for resolving employee dissatisfaction with any aspect of working conditions, working relationships, or employment status. Army policy encourages timely resolution at the lowest level practical; however, grievances can escalate up the chain of command, or, if under a negotiated grievance procedure, to binding arbitration.

   c. Negotiated grievance procedures are outlined in labor contracts which are jointly developed by management and the local labor union granted exclusive recognition to represent all bargaining member employees (whether or not the employees are union members). The legal basis for the labor-management relations program for federal employees is 5 USC Chapter 71. It states that labor organizations and collective bargaining in the civil service are in the public interest. The rights and obligations of employees, unions, and agency management are also established in AR 215-3, which provides the framework for addressing labor-management relations for NAF employees.

   d. Supervisors are obliged to maintain a willingness to bargain collectively with labor organizations. Despite earnest efforts, there may be a time when an impasse will result, and if both parties fail to resolve their differences, the law provides for a neutral third party to resolve the impasse. This is the job of the Federal Mediation and Conciliation Service (FMCS) and the Federal Service Impasses Panel (FSIP). The FMCS assists the parties in reaching a voluntary agreement. Failing this, the FSIP may impose a settlement on the parties.

   e. Management should strive to ensure that non-adversarial labor-management relationships are nurtured so mission accomplishment is enhanced rather than inhibited by the labor relations process. Management is also responsible for the following.

   (1) Negotiating in good faith regarding conditions of employment (e.g., personnel policies, practices, and matters affecting working conditions).

   (2) Furnishing official time to union representatives for negotiating collective-bargaining agreements and for other representational purposes as provided for by negotiated agreement.

   (3) Deducting union dues from the pay of eligible employees who authorize such deductions and allotting those deductions to recognized unions.

   (4) Notifying recognized unions and giving them the opportunity to be present at formal discussions between management and one or more employees.

   (5) Allowing the union the opportunity to be represented at any examination of an employee pursuant to an investigation if the employee reasonably believes that the examination may result in disciplinary action and if the employee requests representation (this is called the Weingarten Right).

   f. Certain ground rules are established to safeguard the basic intent of the law. The FLRA is an independent, administrative agency presided over by three members appointed by the POTUS. The FLRA is the central policymaking body of the federal labor-management relations program. It decides representation questions (whether a union is eligible to represent certain groups of employees or whether particular employees fall within the certified bargaining unit), adjudicates negotiability disputes (whether there is an obligation to negotiate on specific proposals), adjudicates Unfair Labor Practices (ULP) (i.e., a violation of the provisions of Title VII), and decides appeals to arbitrators' awards.

HOW THE ARMY RUNS

g. Responsibilities of CPAC Directors. The CPAC Director is the designee of the installation/activity commander and, as head of the CPAC, is responsible for administering the civilian personnel program. Note that the commander retains overall responsibility for management and leadership of the civilian work force. The CPAC director has responsibility for the implementation, maintenance, and evaluation of local personnel programs designed to assist supervisors with their personnel management responsibilities and achieve activity mission objectives. The CPAC Director interprets personnel policies and regulations and provides guidance and assistance in personnel matters in his or her assigned areas of responsibility. The CPAC Director must seek to ensure that management actions affecting civilian employees will enhance the Army's reputation as a good and fair employer, ensure employee productivity, support EEO, and maintain effective community relations. The CPAC Director also has oversight of the local NAF personnel program. The CPAC director is assisted in the administration of the NAF discipline and labor relations programs by a NAF Human Relations Officer as well as the NAF personnel program in general.

h. Executive Order 13522. On December 9, 2009, President Obama signed EO 13522, Creating Labor-Management Forums to Improve Delivery of Government Services. Among other things, this EO provides for the establishment of labor-management councils at the level of recognition and other appropriate levels agreed to by labor and management. These councils are intended to help identify problems and propose solutions to better serve the public and the agency mission. In addition to councils, the EO provides for employees and their union representatives to have pre-decisional involvement in all workplace matters to the fullest extent practicable. The CPAC can provide additional guidance and instruction on the local implementation of the provisions of the EO.

14-22. Army Civilian Wellness Program

The Army's Civilian Wellness program helps employees enhance mental and physical well-being, prevent health problems, engage in health promoting behaviors, and find assistance and support in times of need. Studies show that on average, employees who are healthy, and personal and professionally satisfied, are more productive, spend fewer days away from work due to illness, and are more engaged in their work. The Army's Wellness Vision statement is as follows: To improve the health and well-being of DA employee's lives through health education and activities that encourage and support positive lifestyle and healthy living changes thereby resulting in improved employee productivity and morale and healthcare costs savings for the Army. The wellness program is covered by AR 600-63, Army Health Promotion.

Section V
Equal Employment Opportunity in the Army

14-23. EEO and Diversity in the Army

a. Discrimination in the workplace negatively affects employee morale, productivity, and teamwork, increases employee absenteeism and turnover, and takes focus away from mission readiness.

b. To ensure full implementation and intent of the law, the DA willfully complies with requirements set forth in, to include but not limited to, Title VII of the Civil Rights Act of 1964, as amended; 29 CFR Part 1614, The Rehabilitation Act of 1973 (as amended), Sections 501, 504, 508 of Title VI, The Equal Pay Act of 1963 (as amended), The Age Discrimination in Employment Act of 1967 (as amended), The Architectural Barriers Act of 1968 (as amended), The Genetic Information Nondiscrimination Act (GINA) 42 USC 2000, and all applicable implementing instructions from the DOD, the EEOC, and the OPM.

c. The Policy of the DA is to provide equal opportunity in employment for all persons, to prohibit discrimination in employment because of race, color, religion, sex, national origin, age, disability, or genetic information, and to promote the full realization of EEO, diversity and inclusion principles in managing all human resources. No person shall be subject to retaliation for opposing any practice made unlawful or for participating in any stage of an administrative or judicial proceeding under those statutes.

d. The EEOC has authority and oversight for the federal sector EEO program and provides federal agencies instruction and direction on how to obtain model EEO programs, practices, and processes through affirmative employment planning models, identifying barriers that prevent employment and implementing strategies for diversity and inclusion. EEOC also provides for the EEO Complaint Process which encourages and enables opportunities to resolve allegation s of employment discrimination quickly and administratively. The Army's authority to administer, manage and direct Army's EEO & Diversity

CIVILIAN HUMAN RESOURCE MANAGEMENT

Programs is delegated to the Deputy Assistant Secretary of the Army for Diversity and Leadership (DASA DL).

e. Within the Office of the DASA DL, the Policy and Programs Directorate is responsible for the administrative oversight of the Army's EEO and Diversity Program and is the proponent for AR 690-12.

f. Responsibility for EEO, Affirmative Employment, Diversity, Inclusion, Education and Training extends from the Secretary of the Army to the ASA(M&RA), to the Deputy Assistant Secretary of the Army for Diversity and Leadership, to Commanders and Leaders at all levels. The Army's EEO & Diversity Programs focus on evaluating and assessing the Army's workforce (civilian and military) demographics compared to appropriate labor force statistics, identifying trends and/or barriers to employment, less than expected participation rates of groups and implementing strategies that address both internal training & development and external outreach to ensure a talent pool motivated and capable of accomplishing the mission. The Army documents progress, strengths and weaknesses annually in the federal EEO Progress Report - Management Directive 715, The State of the Agency Briefing and through the administration of all 31 Career Programs in the Army.

g. The ASA(M&RA) serves as the Agency Director for EEO with responsibility for EEO, Diversity and EEO Compliance and Complaints Review/Adjudication Policy.

h. The DASA DL develops directs and implements Army wide EEO, Diversity, EEO Compliance and Complaints policy and program evaluation and reporting requirements.

i. Commanders are responsible and accountable for the effective execution of EEO programs and creating a climate in which it is clear to all Soldiers and civilians that unlawful discrimination and harassment (sexual/non-sexual) will not be tolerated. All allegations of discrimination will be dealt with seriously, swiftly, and effectively in accordance with all applicable laws, regulations, and procedures. Commanders' EEO policy statements expressing support of Army EEO and diversity policy will be signed upon assumption of command and disseminated annually. The Commander serves as the senior rater of the EEO Official in the performance evaluation and review process.

j. The EEO Official is a member of the Commander's personal/special staff. EEO Officials are a part of the management team, not an advocate for employees, yet an advocate for leadership, federal civil rights, due process, employee's rights, the EEO complaints process, and strategic management of human capitals. A reporting structure will be maintained that provides the EEO Official direct access to the Commander and senior leaders as a trusted and confidential advisor for effective management and resolution, reporting, compliance, efficiency, and resources for the EEO Program. The EEO Official and staff will be utilized as a valued partner/advisor on all matters in the management and implementation of the civilian personnel human resources arena and decision making models and processes within the command.

14–24. The EEO Complaints Program and Process

a. Within the office of the DASA DL, the Equal Employment Opportunity Compliance and Complaints Review (EEOCCR) Directorate is responsible for the administrative oversight of the Army's EEO Complaints Program, and is the proponent lead for AR 690-600, Equal Employment Opportunity Discrimination Complaints which implements the complaints program. DL-EEOCCR monitors Army compliance with laws, statutes, and regulations governing EEO complaint processing, reports the Army's compliance status to the EEOC annually, and is the complaint records custodian for the Army. DL-EEOCCR is also the Army's adjudicator of the merits of formal EEO complaints when final agency decisions are requested or required.

b. EEO offices generally have one of two roles: operational and administrative. Operational EEO offices are responsible for processing EEO complaints and providing training and information to the workforce. Many operational EEO offices are located on Army installations and provide services to tenant commands on the installations as well as their own commands. Administrative EEO offices are responsible for monitoring complaint activity within their area of responsibility but generally do not process EEO complaints themselves. Army Commands (ACOM), Army Service Component Commands (ASCC), and Direct Reporting Units (DRU) headquarters EEO offices are generally administrative. Some administrative EEO offices have oversight and support responsibilities for operational EEO offices.

c. On behalf of the Commander, the EEO Officer is charged with the duty to impartially execute the EEO Complaints Program and ensure that due process is preserved. Commanders should be briefed on the status of current complaints within the command, the use of ADR, the timeliness of complaint processing, the office complaint load overall (if the EEO office processes complaints for tenant

HOW THE ARMY RUNS

organizations as well as the command), and trends in complaints that impact the command. Other senior leaders should also be briefed on the status of complaints within their area of responsibility as appropriate.

  d. The Complaints Process. Army employees, former employees, applicants for employment, and contractors who believe they have been discriminated against by the Army with respect to a term, condition, or benefit of employment on the basis of race, color, national origin, religion, sex, age (40 and over), mental or physical disability, genetic information, or in reprisal or retaliation for having engaged in protected EEO activity have the right to initiate an EEO complaint with the Army. Examples of employment actions that may give rise to a complaint include, but are not limited to, hiring and promotion decisions, performance evaluations, reassignments, disciplinary actions, and harassment.

  e. Individuals must contact the EEO office, or anyone reasonably connected to EEO, to initiate a precomplaint. Contact must be made within 45 calendar days from the date the individual knew or should have known of the alleged discrimination. An employee from the EEO office will conduct a precomplaint intake interview with the individual, called the aggrieved, and document the claim and the narrative information. An EEO Counselor will be assigned to conduct a limited inquiry into the claims alleged. When deemed appropriate by the EEO officer, and after coordination with Labor and Management Employee Relations (LMER), legal officials, and Army management, ADR may be offered to the aggrieved as a means of trying to settle the complaint. If resolution of the complaint is reached at any point in the process, the terms of the resolution will be documented in a written negotiated settlement agreement. Commanders and other senior leaders can promote ADR programs and encourage managers and supervisors in their organizations to participate in ADR. If the complaint cannot be resolved, the aggrieved will receive a Notice of Right to File a Formal Complaint of Discrimination, and will have 15 calendar days from the date of receipt of the notice to file a formal complaint.

  f. Upon receipt of a written formal complaint, the EEO officer will determine if the claim(s) alleged can be dismissed for procedural reasons provided in 29 CFR 1614 and AR 690-600. Any claim(s) that cannot be dismissed will be accepted. The EEO officer will issue a letter accepting and/or dismissing claims identified in the complaint within 15 calendar days of receipt of the formal complaint. If a claim is accepted, a formal investigation is arranged and ADR may be offered again. The EEO office will request the assignment of an investigator from the DOD IRD. IRD charges a flat administrative processing fee for requests for investigators. The activity where the discrimination is alleged to have occurred is responsible for paying the IRD fee and identifying the activity Point of Contact (POC) who will make the payment. Once an investigator is assigned, the EEO office will coordinate the investigation. IRD investigations are conducted via Fact Finding Conference (FFC), the Army's preferred method of investigation. The FFC is attended by the investigator, the complainant and complainant's representative, and any responding management officials, witnesses, agency representatives, and a certified court reporter. Commanders and other senior leaders are required to ensure that their organizations cooperate with any request from an EEO for documentation or the testimony of a Soldier or civilian within the command identified as a witness. Testimony is taken under oath and on the record from the complainant, the responding management official, and other witnesses. The activity where the discrimination is alleged to have occurred is also responsible for paying for a certified court reporter to take a verbatim transcript of the investigation. The investigator will use the verbatim transcript and complaint documents to draft a Report of Investigation (ROI). The ROI is a compilation of facts and evidence taken under oath to be used to make a decision on the merits of the complaint at a later time. The Army is responsible for ensuring that investigations are completed within 180 calendar days of the formal filing date or within 120 calendar days where the complaint involves an issue appealable to the MSPB. The investigation officially ends when the EEO office receives the ROI.

  g. Once the EEO office receives the ROI, a copy is sent to the complainant, along with a Post-Investigative Options Notice. This notice provides the complainant the option of either requesting a hearing before an EEOC Administrative Judge (EEOC AJ), or requesting a Final Agency Decision (FAD) from the EEOCCR. If the complainant fails to select an option, the EEO office will request a FAD on the complainant's behalf. If the complaint involves an issue appealable to the MSPB, the complaint will be sent to the EEOCCR for a FAD. If the complainant elects to request a hearing, the hearing request, along with a copy of the complaint file, is sent to the appropriate EEOC regional or field office, and the EEOC AJ is appointed to hear the complaint. Once the hearing is scheduled, witnesses will be required to attend and provide sworn testimony at the hearing. The activity where the discrimination is alleged to have occurred will again be required to pay for the services of a court reporter to take a verbatim

CIVILIAN HUMAN RESOURCE MANAGEMENT

transcript of the hearing. After the hearing, the EEOC AJ will issue a decision stating if discrimination was or was not found to have occurred. The EEOC AJ decision is forwarded to the Army (EEOCCR) for issuance of a Final Agency Action (FAA) implementing the AJ's decision. The complainant has the option of appealing a FAA or a FAD to the EEOC Office of Federal Operations (OFO) or filing suit in federal court. The Army may choose to appeal an EEOC AJ's finding of discrimination to the EEOC OFO instead of issuing a FAA.

h. Failure to cooperate with the complaint process places the Army at risk. A finder of fact, such as an EEOC AJ or EEOCCR, may determine that the failure to cooperate constitutes sufficient grounds to presume that unlawful discrimination occurred. This is called an adverse inference, and essentially means that a prima facie case of discrimination is established, and the agency bears the burden of providing evidence to rebut the adverse inference. When a finder of fact determines that discrimination has occurred, the activity where the discrimination occurred is responsible for providing any relief the complainant is deemed entitled to, such as money damages (including attorney fees), initiating personnel actions, and conducting a culpability study of management officials found to have discriminated to determine what, if any, disciplinary action should be taken. A management official found to have discriminated against an employee may be subject to discipline, including termination, in accordance with AR 690-700, Chapter 751 Table of Penalties. A finding of discrimination may also prevent a management official from being eligible for certain awards and prevent an officer from promotion into or up through the General Officer ranks.

Section VI
Executive and Senior Professional Personnel

14-25. ESP Structure and Composition

a. Civilian senior leadership is crucial to the support of military operations in a wide range of functions that are necessary for the Army to achieve battlefield success. This includes roles in procurement, logistics, research and development, finance, and human capital management. Executive and Senior Professional (ESP) positions are above the GS-15 level, and salaries can range as they do for general officers. OPM establishes the regulations and allocations for ESP positions. DA requests allocations through the OSD. Army's authorized ESP positions include a broad range of occupational series which span across the U.S. and overseas. However, almost half of the Army's ESP positions are located in the Washington, DC Metro area.

b. On 9 August 2010 the SECARMY signed the Executive Resources Board (ERB) Charter. The ERB plays an active, robust role in formulating policies for, and in the management, governance and oversight of all Army ESP programs, and reviews and renders decisions or opinions on certain actions affecting ESP members and positions, including ESPs assigned to combatant commands (COCOM) to which the Army provides administrative and logistical support. The ERB advises the SECARMY on matters relating to the hiring, training and development, utilization, performance evaluation, and compensation of the Army's ESP workforce, which includes career SES, SL, ST, DISES, and DISL personnel. The ERB may also provide advice on, and oversight of, matters relating to other Army executive-level positions.

Table 14-1. Executive Service Personnel

Acquisition/Contracting	53
Comptroller	32
Engineer & Science	103
General Administration	47
Human Resources, EEO & Manpower	21
Intelligence	30
International Relations	4
IT, Record Management	6
Legal	15
Medical	14
Military Human Resources	3

HOW THE ARMY RUNS

Morale, Welfare & Recreation	2
Operations and Plans	5
Public Affairs	1
Real Estate	3
Installation/Business Management	15
Safety/Occupational	3
Transportation/Supply	17
Training	3

Table 14-2. Executives by Organization

OSA	96
AMC	94
USACE	40
ARSTAF	74
TRADOC	17
JOINT ACT	11
IMCOM	9
USAREUR	7
SMDC	7
MEDCOM	19
FORSCOM	5

14-26. Qualifications of SES Members

a. There are five Executive Core Qualifications (ECQ) that all potential SES members must possess the following.

(1) Leading Change. This core qualification involves the ability to bring about strategic change, both within and outside the organization, to meet organizational goals. Inherent to this ECQ is the ability to establish an organizational vision and to implement it in a continuously changing environment.

(2) Leading People. This core qualification involves the ability to lead people toward meeting the organization's vision, mission, and goals. Inherent to this ECQ is the ability to provide an inclusive workplace that fosters the development of others, facilitates cooperation and teamwork, and supports constructive resolution of conflicts.

(3) Results Driven. This core qualification involves the ability to meet organizational goals and customer expectations. Inherent to this ECQ is the ability to make decisions that produce high-quality results by applying technical knowledge, analyzing problems, and calculating risks.

(4) Business Acumen. This core qualification involves the ability to manage human, financial, and information resources strategically.

(5) Building Coalitions. This core qualification involves the ability to build coalitions internally and with other federal agencies, state and local governments, nonprofit and private sector organizations, foreign governments, or international organizations to achieve common goals.

b. The executive development of employees in GS-14 and 15 grade levels or equivalent is an important command responsibility. ESP members are expected to possess leadership competencies that parallel those of Army general officers. Therefore, attendance at a Senior Service College program is a highly desirable experience for civilians who aspire to ESP positions. Appointment to the ESP marks achievement of the highest nonpolitical civilian executive position. These positions are given protocol precedence equivalent to lieutenant general, major general, and brigadier general.

c. For more information on these positions go to http://www.opm.gov/ses/index.asp.

CIVILIAN HUMAN RESOURCE MANAGEMENT

Section VII
Defense Civilian Intelligence Personnel System

14-26. Structure and Composition of the DCIPS

a. DCIPS employees are U.S. citizens paid from APFs. Unlike most other APF civilians, they are managed through a statutorily based excepted personnel service administered by the OSD for the DOD Intelligence Community.

b. There are currently approximately 6,800civilians in the Army under this personnel system. The Army has included in DCIPS all employees in series and specialties with clear ties to intelligence wherever they are found. Some examples are intelligence specialists in the 132 series and intelligence assistants in the 134 series regardless of function as well as security specialists in the 080 series and security assistants in the 086 series where 51% or more of their duties are intelligence related (not law enforcement related). DCIPS coverage by series/function has resulted in most major commands having at least some DCIPS employees. The Army has also included in DCIPS all employees (except local nationals) in commands that have a primary intelligence mission. Many of the administrative, technical, and support series, and a few wage grade employees in DCIPS, as well as the Army's intelligence and security professionals, are found in such commands as the U.S. Army Intelligence and Security Command.

14-27. Relationship of DCIPS to the Army Civilian Personnel Program

a. DCIPS is considered a part of the Army's overall civilian personnel program and has tested innovative personnel management features for Army and the DOD. As a statutory alternative personnel system, DCIPS is exempt from Title VII job classification provisions and has adopted the use of the National Security Agency's (NSA) classification system to better align grades with the rest of the intelligence community. It is also exempt from many OPM hiring provisions and can directly consider applications from non-government employees through its own merit system. In 2009, DCIPS was revised by DOD to encompass all of DOD's intelligence community and not just the military services.

b. Civilian personnel servicing support for CONUS intelligence activities are consolidated at the Fort Huachuca CPAC and West Regional Processing Center at Fort Huachuca, Arizona. This consolidation improved HR understanding and system expertise and increased servicing effectiveness and efficiency.

c. DCIPS was implemented in FY 1990, first as a tri-service system known as the Civilian Intelligence Personnel Management System (CIPMS), and then evolving into DCIPS when a provision of the DOD Authorization Act of 1997 (known as the DOD Civilian Intelligence Personnel Policy Act of 1996) combined all civilian personnel management systems for intelligence components in DOD into one broad excepted service system. DCIPS legislation and supporting initiatives continually strive to achieve a broad common architecture of policies, systems and standards while protecting individual Service and agency prerogatives. Common employment and compensation architectures are planned along with inter-community rotational and development programs. Common senior executive and leader programs have also been developed. These include the DISES for intelligence executives and the DISL program for senior experts Section VIII Civilian Expeditionary Workforce (CEW).

14-28. CEW

a. On 23 January 2009, DOD issued a new DOD Directive (DODD), 1404.10, DOD Civilian Expeditionary Workforce. This new Directive reissued the previous DODD 1404.10, Emergency-Essential (E-E) DOD U.S. Citizen Civilian Employees (dated April 10, 1992) under a new title to establish the policy through which an appropriately sized subset of the DOD civilian workforce is pre-identified to be organized, trained, and equipped in a manner that facilitates the use of their capabilities for operational requirements. These requirements are typically away from the normal work locations of DOD civilians, or in situations where other civilians may be evacuated to assist military forces where the use of DOD civilians is appropriate. These employees are collectively known as the DOD Civilian Expeditionary Workforce. The DODD 1404.10 also superseded any conflicting portions of other DOD issuances. Members of the DOD CEW are to be organized, trained, cleared, equipped, and ready to deploy in support of combat operations by the military; contingencies; emergency operations; humanitarian missions; disaster relief; restoration of order; drug interdictions; and stability operations of DOD in accordance with DODD 3000.05.

b. The DODD 1404.10 updates policies and responsibilities for the designation of part of the DOD CEW using the existing category of E-E civilian employee positions, and establishes policies and responsibilities for the designation of part of the DOD CEW using new categories of Non-Combat Essential (NCE) positions and Capability-Based Volunteer (CBV) employees and former DOD employees.

c. Implementation of the CEW program within the Army requires that commands identify and designate a portion of their workforce as CEW. Additionally, Commanders of commands will be responsible for ensuring all designated CEW employees are properly trained, equipped, and ready to deploy. This also includes the assurance that all employees returning from a deployment complete the required Post Deployment Health Assessments (i.e., 30, 90, and 180 days after deployment). To aid Commanders in ensuring the readiness of their designated CEW employees various readiness processing centers are available to validate readiness prior to deployment. The majority of the Army's employees are to be processed through the CONUS Replacement Center (CRC) located at Fort Benning, Georgia. The U.S. Army Corps of Engineers (USACE) has a readiness processing center located in Winchester, Virginia. The USACE processing center is primarily established to process USACE employees, but others can be processed via a Memorandum of Agreement/Understanding between the requesting command/organization and the USACE. A third processing center is located at Camp Atterbury, Indiana. This processing center has been established by the OSD as a primary means of processing employees who have volunteered to deploy in support of CEW positions advertised and sponsored by OSD.

d. CEW Designations and Definitions.

(1) E-E. Position-based designation to support the success of combat operations or the availability of combat-essential systems in accordance with USC section 1580 of Title 10 and designated as key.

(2) NCE. A position-based designation to support the expeditionary requirements in other than combat or combat support situations and designated as key.

(3) CBV. An employee who may be asked to volunteer for deployment, to remain behind after other civilians have evacuated, or to backfill other DOD civilians who have deployed to meet expeditionary requirements in order to ensure that critical expeditionary requirements that may fall outside or within the scope of an individual's position are fulfilled.

(4) Capability-Based Former Employee Volunteer Corps. A collective group of former (including retired) DOD civilian employees who have agreed to be listed in a database as individuals who may be interested in returning to federal service as a time-limited employee to serve expeditionary requirements or who can backfill for those serving other expeditionary requirements.

(5) Key Employees. DOD civilian employees in positions designated as E-E and/or NCE are to be designated key in accordance with DODD 1200.7.

Civilian Expeditionary Workforce (CEW) Model

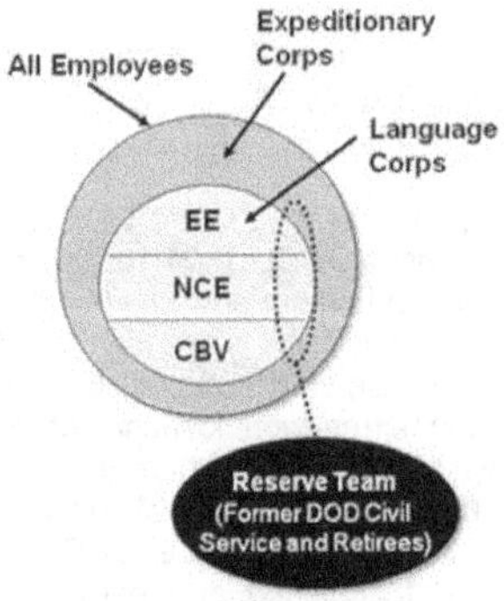

Features:

- Designated subset of employees to respond within 72 hours to 30 days of notification
  - <u>**EE—Emergency Essential**</u>: a position-based designation to support combat operations or combat-essential systems in a combat zone (10 U.S.C. 1580). Deployability required as condition of employment
  - <u>**NCE—Non-Combat Essential**</u>: a position-based designation to support non combat missions. Deployability required as condition of employment
  - <u>**CBV—Capability Based Employee Volunteers**</u>: a personnel-based designation to support voluntary identification of capabilities outside scope of an employee's position for EE and NCE requirements
  - <u>**Reserve Team—Inventory of Former or Retired DOD Employees**</u>: prepared to support backfill or deployed requirements

Figure 14-4. Civilian Expeditionary Workforce (CEW) Model

CIVILIAN HUMAN RESOURCE MANAGEMENT

Section VIII
Army Personnel Transformation

14-29. Current and Transforming CHR Administration
The current CHR force is vital to the Army's mission. Each CPAC staff member is a strategic partner with serviced commands, managers, and supervisors. Today, the Army faces significant challenges as it transforms to a more agile and technology-based force. With both external and internal drivers such as BRAC, Global Defense Posture Strategy (GDPS), Joint Basing, and OPM HR Lines of Business (LOB), the CHR workforce must also transform as it positions to be the premier HR provider for all DOD. The CHR community will utilize Lean Six Sigma methodology to redesign business processes and delivery of services and reinvest those savings into the organization to continue to provide world-class customer service.

14-30. Transforming CHR Administration
The establishment of NSPS changed the administration of HR in DOD and the Army with its initial implementation in 2006. In October 2009, the National Defense Authorization Act for FY 2010 (NDAA 2010) was passed, repealing NSPS as of 1 January 2012, and directing the return of NSPS employees to the personnel systems that last applied to them prior to the establishment of NSPS. NDAA 2010 also directed DOD and OPM to develop a new hiring system and an enterprise performance management system for DOD. DOD began efforts to develop these new systems in 2010; their completion and implementation are expected to bring about comprehensive change in human resources administration in DOD and Army.

14-31. Career Management
In 2011, the Army undertook transformation initiatives to expand career program coverage to encompass 100% of the civilian population, both appropriated and nonappropriated fund, except for National Guard Bureau technicians and indirect hire foreign nationals. Functional Chief and Functional Chief Representative roles and responsibilities were expanded for exercise in an evolving strategic and competency-based, life-cycle management planning environment and to address occupational and career program management matters across command lines.

14-32. Hiring Reforms
Army's HR community will continue to support recruitment and hiring reform objectives developed to improve the quality and speed of the hiring process. In addition, these hiring reforms require managers and supervisors to assume a greater responsibility and accountability in the planning, recruitment, and selection of the employees under them.

Section IX
Summary and References

14-33. Summary
  a. The purpose of the Army Civilian Personnel Management System is to provide a motivated and technically qualified work force to meet Army requirements. The civilian workforce is an integral part of the Army team. Army civilians play an important role in all our missions and share in the organization's accomplishments. The Army employs civilians because they possess unique skills, ensure operational continuity, are economical, and permit military personnel to perform purely military duties. The civilian personnel management system and its supporting policy and service organizations contribute to the overall mission.
  b. More than half of Army civilian positions are bargaining unit positions represented by labor unions. Army leaders, both civilian and military, must accept their labor-management responsibilities. The efficiency of our operations cannot be allowed to fail due to an unhealthy labor climate where leaders did not accept obligations to advise, consult, and bargain, as the law requires.
  c. As the force downsized and underwent initiatives to convert formerly military positions to civilian occupancy, more and more civilians have assumed key roles in headquarters and support activities,

HOW THE ARMY RUNS

schools and training centers, and BASOPS. For many of these important positions it may not be possible to hire people with the necessary skills. Therefore, the Army must develop civilians from within the current ranks.

d. This chapter was designed to provide only a broad overview of the Civilian Personnel Management System in order to describe how the major processes are designed to support Army leaders. It is important to understand the legal basis for the federal civil service, how the Army's system works within the federal system and also the regulatory basis and practices for the Army's NAF Personnel System. Furthermore, commanders and managers at all levels must have a clear understanding of the nature of the civilian personnel structure, programs, and mission, as well as their responsibilities to provide effective leadership and management. DA civilians are part of an Army team comprised of a diverse workforce dedicated to doing the best job possible to ensure Army missions are accomplished effectively. The Army and DOD civilian personnel web sites contain a great deal of helpful information and may be accessed at www.cpol.army.mil and www.cpms.osd.mil, respectively. The CSLMO also has a secure web site which may be accessed by anyone holding a CAC registered with AKO at https://www.cslmo.army.mil.

14-34. References

a. 5 CFR Parts 410 and 412, Training; Supervisory, Management, and Executive Development
b. Age Discrimination in Employment Act of 1967
c. Americans with Disabilities Act of 1990
d. Architectural Barriers Act of 1968
e. Army Regulation 10-89, U.S. Army Civilian Personnel Evaluation Agency
f. Army Regulation 215-1, Morale, Welfare, and Recreation Activities and Nonappropriated Fund Instrumentalities
g. Army Regulation 215-3, Nonappropriated Funds Personnel Policy
h. Army Regulation 570-4, Manpower Management
i. Army Regulation 600-3, The Army Personnel Proponent System
j. Army Regulation 600-7, Nondiscrimination on the Basis of Disability in Programs and Activities Assisted or Conducted by the Department of the Army
k. Army Regulation 600-63, Army Health Promotion
l. Army Regulation 672-20, Incentive Awards
m. Army Regulation 690-11, Use and Management of Civilian Personnel in Support of Military Contingency Operations
n. Army Regulation 690-12, Equal Employment Opportunity Program and Affirmative Action
o. Army Regulation 690-13, CIPMS - Policies and Procedures
p. Army Regulation 690-400, Chap.432, Reduction in Grade and Removal Based on Unacceptable Performance
q. Army Regulation 690-400, Chap. 4302, Total Army Performance Evaluation System (TAPES)
r. Army Regulation 690-600, Equal Employment Opportunity Discrimination Complaints
s. Army Regulation 690-700, Chap.751, Discipline
t. Army Regulation 690-900, Chap. 920, Senior Executive Service
u. Army Regulation 690-950, Career Management
v. Army's Mentorship Resource Center is located at http://www.armyg1.army.mil/hr/mentorship/default.asp
w. Civil Rights Act of 1991
x. Civil Service Reform Act of 1978
y. DA Pamphlet 672-20, Incentive Awards Handbook
z. DA Pamphlet 690-11, Guide to Civilian Personnel Management
aa. DA Pamphlet 690-46, Mentoring for Civilian Members of the Force
bb. DA Pamphlet 690-47, DA Civilian Employees Deployment Guide
cc. DOD Civilian Intelligence Personnel Policy Act of 1996
dd. DOD Authorization Act of 1997
ee. DOD Manual 1400.25 Subchapter 920, Executive and Senior Professional Pay and Performance.
ff. DOD 1400.25-M, Civilian Personnel Manual
gg. DODD, 1404.10, DOD Civilian Expeditionary Workforce

CIVILIAN HUMAN RESOURCE MANAGEMENT

hh. DOD Instruction (DODI), 1400-25, DOD Civilian Personnel Management Systems: Volume 250, Civilian Strategic Human Capital Planning (SHCP)

ii. Equal Employment Opportunity (EEO) Act of 1972

jj. Equal Employment Opportunity Commission Management Directive 715 (EEOC MD 715)

kk. Equal Pay Act of 1963

ll. Executive Order 9830, Amending the Civil Service Rules and providing for Federal personnel administration

mm. Executive Order 12721, Eligibility of Overseas Employees for Noncompetitive Appointments

nn. Executive Order 13473, To Authorize Certain Noncompetitive Appointments in the Civil Service for Spouses of Certain Members of the Armed Forces

oo. Executive Order 13522, Creating Labor-Management Forums to Improve Delivery of Government Services

pp. Executive Order 13562, Recruiting and Hiring Students and Recent Graduates

qq. Federal Anti-Discrimination and Retaliation Act of 2002

rr. Genetic Information Nondiscrimination Act of 2008

ss. Hatch Act of 1939

tt. HQDA General Orders No. 3, 9 July 2002, and amendment No. 2002-03

uu. Longshore and Harbor Worker's Compensation Act (33 USC, 901 et seq.)

vv. Management Directive 715 State of the Agency Report

ww. Nonappropriated Fund Instrumentalities Act of 1958 (5 USC, Sec 8171 – 8173)

xx. Rehabilitation Act of 1973

yy. Title 5 USC, Government Organizations and Employees

zz. Title 10 USC, Section 1580: Emergency Essential Employees: Designation

aaa. Title 33 USC, Navigable Waters

bbb. Uniformed Services Employment & Reemployment Rights Act of 1994

ccc. Whistleblower Protection Act of 1989

HOW THE ARMY RUNS

This page is intentionally left blank

ARMY TRAINING AND LEADER DEVELOPMENT

Chapter 15

Army Training and Leader Development

To better prepare Soldiers and leaders for decisive action, Army training has refocused on our core competencies of combined arms maneuver and wide area security, set in a challenging joint, interagency and multinational environment, supplemented by an expanded range of virtual, constructive and gaming tools.

GEN Raymond T. Odierno, Chief of Staff, U.S. Army (CSA)
"38th CSA Marching Orders: Waypoint # 1, January 2013"

Section I
Introduction

15-1. The Army Training Strategy
  a. The Army Training Strategy provides vision and guidance on ends, ways, and means for training and educating Soldiers, civilians, leaders, and units to support operational adaptability and sustain readiness to conduct unified land operations. This strategy focuses on near-term requirements of execution and budget years (FY 2013-2014) through the mid-range requirements of the Program Objective Memorandum (POM) years FY 2015-2019. It informs the training strategies and detailed training guidance of subordinate commanders, supervisors, leaders, and trainers of all components in Army Commands (ACOM), Army Service Component Commands (ASCC), Direct Reporting Units (DRU), the Army Staff, and other activities involved in the planning, programming, preparation, and execution of Army Training.
  b. The Army Training Vision states that Army training must balance current operational missions while simultaneously preparing forces to meet future requirements. The future requires the Army to be regionally responsive and globally engaged. Army training will provide the critical depth and versatility needed to support the three strategic roles of Prevent—Shape—Win by conducting unified land operations executed through decisive action by means of the Army core competencies of combined arms maneuver and wide area security, guided by mission command. Achieving this balance will be accomplished by focusing on following three strategic ends described below.
  (1) Hold commanders responsible for training units and developing leaders through the development and execution of progressive, challenging, and realistic training.
  (2) Develop leaders, both military and civilian, to be competent, confident, agile, and adaptive in order to lead units and organizations in the complex and uncertain operational environments of the 21st century.
  (3) Train units to be versatile and to the required level of readiness in order to provide ready forces to combatant commanders worldwide.
  c. The primary management tool for the Army Training Strategy is the Training General Officer Steering Committee (GOSC), which meets semi-annually (see AR 350-1, Army Training and Leader Development), with the Department of the Army G-3/5/7 approving changes within this forum. Concurrently, the Department of the Army Secretariat oversight of the Army Campaign Plan (ACP) may impact strategic training-related programs and initiatives.

Section II
Army Training Overview

15-2. Army Training
  a. Future Force Generation Model.
  (1) The proposed Future Force Generation Model is designed to provide the required capabilities for Army missions. U.S. Army Forces Command is the supported command for the Future Force Generation Model and it will ensure that every deploying unit is the best trained, led, and equipped force

HOW THE ARMY RUNS

possible. It is a continuous and structured process for generating active Army and reserve component forces that provide increasing unit readiness over time.

(2) Force pools. The Mission Force Pool (MFP), Rotational Force Pool (RFP), and the Operational Sustainment Force Pool (OSFP) provide a framework for the structured progression of increasing readiness in Future Force Generation. Each force pool is defined by designated unit activities, capability levels, and the period of time allocated to each force pool. The Army uses the force pools in addition to mission requirements to prioritize resources over time, and to synchronize unit manning, equipping, resourcing, and training.

(3) Mission Essential Task Lists (METL). The CSA directed Army-wide implementation of Standardized METL down to brigade level. The Standardized METL is based on the tasks the unit is designed and organized to perform.

(4) Army Doctrine Publication (ADP) 7-0, Training Units and Developing Leaders, 23 August 2012, provides training doctrine within the context of the Future Force Generation process. Future Force Generation training is supported by the Combined Arms Training Strategy (CATS). CATS provides strategies to train brigade and higher level organizations through Standardized METLs, as well as battalion and lower level units through METLs. Progress on the Standardized METL is assessed and reported by unit commanders after priorities have been established. CATS events ranging from individual/crew/squad levels through company/battalion/brigade/division and corps are scheduled and resourced in accordance with the expectations of each force pool and any other specified guidance. Standardized METL focused training will conclude with a CTC or Culminating Training Event (CTE) event prior to transitioning to the Available pool.

b. Leader development. Leader development is the deliberate, continuous, and progressive process founded in Army values that grows Soldiers and Army civilians into competent, committed professional leaders of character. The Army Leader Development Model (Figure 15-1) portrays the process and its major components. Leader development is achieved through the life-long synthesis of the training, education, and experiences acquired through opportunities in the operational, institutional, and self-development domains. The Army adheres to five leader development imperatives that guide policy and actions in order to develop leaders to meet the challenges of the 21st Century. These guiding principles remain consistent from initial service to departure from the Army, creating a leader development process that is deliberate, continuous, and progressive:

(1) Select and develop leaders with positive leader attributes and proficient in core leadership competencies.

(2) Prepare adaptive leaders for unified land operations capable of operating with unified action partners and across joint, interagency, intergovernmental, and multinational (JIIM) settings.

(3) Reinforce the Army Profession and encourage life-long learning and development.

(4) Embed mission command principles in leader development.

(5) Value a broad range of leader experiences/opportunities.

c. The basic concepts, techniques of training, and methods of measuring and evaluating training have constantly evolved over the years and continue to do so today. ADP 7-0, supplemented by the Army Training Network (ATN), contains the Army's standardized training doctrine and other information applicable to all levels of leaders and organizations. They provide the necessary guidelines on how to plan, prepare, execute, and assess training at all levels. ADP 7-0 and the ATN provide authoritative foundations for Soldier, leader, and collective training. Army Regulation 350-1, Army Training and Leader Development, prescribes how the Army will create efficient and effective education and training.

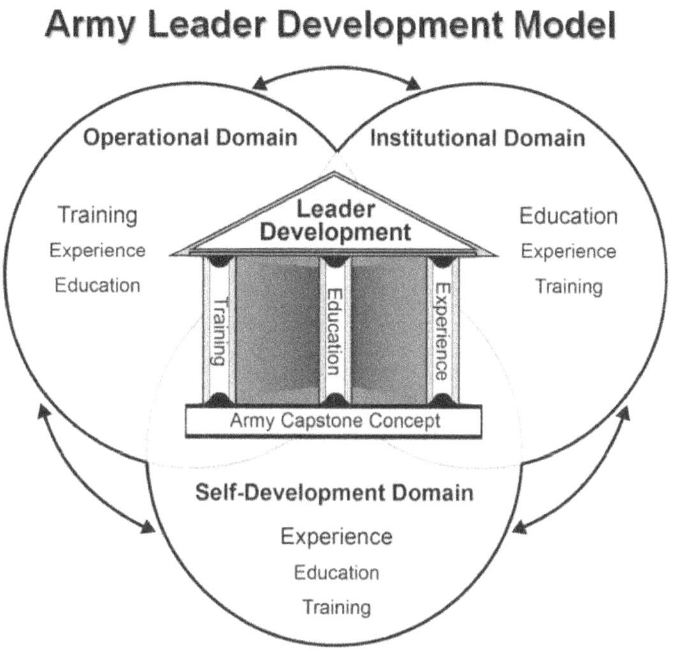

ARMY TRAINING AND LEADER DEVELOPMENT

Army Leader Development Model

Source: Army Doctrine Reference Publication (ADRP) 7-0, August 2012

Figure 15-1. Army Leader Development Model

15-3. CATS

a. Overarching strategy. CATS are a start point for determining events for long-range training plans. Within CATS, the commander consults various resources such as training templates, event menus, and unit-specific and functional strategies. CATS provides options and menus for the training events that can go into the training plan to achieve Standardized METL readiness. CATS is a digitized publication that provides commanders with a template for task-based, event-driven organizational training. It can be adapted to the unit's requirements based on the commander's assessment. CATS states the purpose, outcome, execution guidance, and resource requirements for training events. Commanders can modify these to meet unit training objectives. Each CATS describes how a particular unit type can train to and sustain the Army standard. CATS identifies and quantifies training resources required to execute long- and short-range collective training.

(1) There are two types of CATS: those that are unique to a unit type (unit CATS); and those that address a functional capability common to multiple units (functional CATS). Unit CATS is based on the core capabilities described in a unit's authorization document and doctrine. The unit Standardized METL is published in the CATS for that unit type. Functional CATS is based on standard capabilities performed by most Army units, such as command and control, protection, and deployment.

(2) Each CATS is a training management tool for commanders, leaders, and other unit trainers. A variety of links takes the user directly to applicable supporting individual and collective tasks. This automation capability decreases the need to sort through training materials used to develop training plans, schedules, and resource cost estimations (such as fuel and ammunition) and allows more time to design challenging training. CATS identifies and groups the supporting collective tasks into task groups for each mission-essential task. The discussion of each task group includes guidance for training the task group, resource requirements, and training support requirements for each proposed training event.

HOW THE ARMY RUNS

(3) CATS supports both short-term and long-term training development efforts. Short-term training is intended to allow for planning over a roughly two-year cycle. It is task-based and focused on the unit's Army Training and Evaluation Plan Mission Training Plan. It describes one way of organizing task-based, multi-echelon training into a set of events that will achieve and maintain a high state of readiness in today's environment of high personnel turbulence and leader turnover. Long-range planning is based on the third year and beyond. Its focus is on who (individuals and units) needs training, the type of training required and when/where training will take place.

a. Training strategies development by units. The development of training strategies is the first step in designing training. A training strategy describes the ways and means the commander intends to use to achieve and sustain training proficiency on mission-essential tasks, the ends. The strategy is based on the commander's assessment and discussions with the higher commander. Training strategies include:
(1) Tasks to be trained
(2) Training audience
(3) Training objectives
(4) Sequence in which the tasks are to be trained, given limited time and other resources
(5) Frequency at which tasks are trained
(6) Types of events used to create conditions for training tasks
(7) Conditions under which the tasks are to be trained
(8) Resources required to execute the training strategy
(9) Alternative ways of training tasks

b. There are both long and short-range individual and collective training strategies. Development of these strategies involves decisions on who (unit), what (job or task), where (site) when, why (higher guidance, commander's assessment) and how (media, method) to attain and sustain critical task performance proficiency. They establish the need for training programs, courses, products, and materials. These decisions are identified in supporting plans/models. A process overview would appear as follows: long-range strategies (3-10 years after current year); short-range strategies (current plus 2 years); and program/product design (current year).

c. Long-range Training Strategies. Long-range training strategies include initial determination of who (individuals or units) needs training, what type of training is needed, and where and when the training will take place. They cover the third year following the execution year and beyond. Training proponents add these requirements to appropriate plans/models to ensure resources are available for product development and/or training support. At the unit level, long-range plans identify the major training events for the unit along with the resources required to execute the training events. A long-range plan normally covers 12 months for Active Component (AC) and mobilized Reserve Component (RC) units. It covers two years to an entire Army force generation cycle for other Reserve Component units.

d. Short-range or current training strategies. Short-range or current training strategies emphasize task analysis data. They include the training design (plan) to attain and sustain the desired level of performance proficiency on each critical task contained in the unit Standardized METL. Units refine and expand the appropriate portions of a long-range plan by tying training events together with specific objectives during near-term planning. Normally done at battalion equivalent level and below, the strategy drives specific detail refinement, resource allocation, and training schedule publication.

e. Self-development. Self-development strategies are part of a lifelong learning culture that enable Soldiers and Army civilians to supplement their professional growth in the skills and competencies they need as leaders and technical specialists. Self-development is the individual's responsibility to acquire and sustain the skills, knowledge, and experienced needed to successfully perform the duty position requirements of current and future assignments. Self-development is not reserved for institutional training. Rather, it is a continuous process that takes place during institutional training and operational assignments.

15-4. The Future of Army Training

a. Overview. Army education and training is changing from the traditional classroom, instructor presented lessons to a combination of resident, Distributed Learning (dL), and unit training. This approach leverages automation technologies to improve the efficiency of producing, distributing, and implementing instruction. This change affects individual and collective training. The automation network serves as the conduit for producing and distributing learning material to Soldiers, leaders, and units to meet their specific needs to train and prepare for a broad spectrum of global contingencies. The use of

ARMY TRAINING AND LEADER DEVELOPMENT

automation technologies does not change performance standards expected of Soldiers, Army civilians, and units. Reliance on traditional training methods will continue, but will be enhanced by the availability and communications power of the commercial world-wide web, internet, and other information transfer systems. To attain this vision, the Army launched a number of projects to provide a solid education and training information foundation. Registration for formal Army education/training including dL courses will be accomplished in the Army Training Requirements and Resources System (ATRRS). Beginning in FY14, registration for training and education for Army civilians will be accomplished through the use of GoArmyEd, a system currently in use by the Army Continuing Education System for Soldier tuition assistance. ATRRS facilitates student enrollment, class scheduling, registration, tracking of training records and financial tracking for most training and education courses used by Army civilians.

   b. Learning Environment. Classroom learning is shifting from instructor-centered, lecture-based methods, to a learner-centered, experiential methodology. Knowledge and comprehensive learning objectives and individual learning activities such as reading, self-paced technology-delivered instruction, or research will be done outside the classroom. Students and trainees will participate in discussion, collaborative learning activities, problem identification, and small-group problem solving. Engaging the learner in collaborative practical and problem-solving exercises relevant to their work environment provides an opportunity to develop critical competencies--initiative, critical thinking, teamwork, and accountability in addition to specific knowledge content.

   c. dL. To meet the challenge of the future, the Army is implementing dL to deliver education and training to the Soldier when and where needed. Types of dL include interactive multimedia instruction (individualized self-paced instruction), video teleconferencing, web-managed instruction, and simulations. Army dL does not fundamentally change the way the Army trains, it enhances training by using current and emerging technologies for management and delivery of training to the Soldier at the point of need. Exploiting these technologies takes the classroom to the unit, and the unit to the classroom, providing training in a worldwide virtual Training Environment (TE). Soldiers in the field, in units, at institutions, and at home can train by accessing the informational databases through the Army Knowledge Online (AKO) website. Units can select training options (resident and non-resident) based upon their need, time available to train, distance from the "on-site" training site, and other resource constraints. The Distributed Learning System (DLS) uses an integrated learning management support system, which automates student enrollment, scheduling, and training records. DLS delivers digital courseware to include real-time Video Teletraining (VTT), video and audio recordings, web- and computer-based training materials, and simulations. Army dL documents and related materials are available on the internet at http://www.atsc.army.mil/tadlp/index.asp. Types of dL include:

   (1) Army Learning Management System (ALMS). ALMS is the heart of the Army's Distributed Learning System. ALMS streamlines, consolidates, and provides overall direction to the Army's training processes. ALMS is a Web-based information system that: delivers training to Soldiers; manages training information; and provides training collaboration, scheduling, and career planning capabilities in both resident and non-resident training environments. The ALMS also assists Army trainers and training managers in conducting and managing the training of Soldiers and Army civilians throughout their Army careers.

   (2) Digital Training Facilities (DTF). DTFs provide training access for the Army's Soldiers and civilians at Active Army installations and US Army Reserves (USAR) training sites.

   (3) Deployed Digital Training Campus (DDTC). The DDTC is a deployable networked classroom that delivers proponent approved dL training using satellite communications (SATCOM), wireless connectivity, and VTT equipment. SATCOM provides linkage to deployed forces worldwide through the following: VTT; Video Teleconference (VTC); World-Wide Web (WWW); Non-Classified Internet Protocol Router Network (NIPRNET); and schoolhouse resources not reachable through other means.

   (4) Army National Guard (ARNG) Distributed Learning Classrooms (DLC) and Mobile Distributed Learning Classrooms (MDLC). The ARNG dL Program is a component of the Army dL Program. It provides multiple distributed learning methods and technology-enabled standardized individual and collective training relevant to the readiness requirements of Soldiers and units throughout the ARNG.

   (5) TRADOC Enterprise Classroom Program. The program includes Classroom XXI (CRXXI), Mission Command Art and Sciences Program (MCASP), Basic Combat Training (BCT)/One Station Unit Training (OSUT), and the Institutional Training Technology Program (ITTP). Enterprise Classroom Programs

sustain instructional capabilities that support approved training requirements and priorities that enable Army Learning Model 2015. Some of the program's capabilities include:

(a) Data/video projection systems with audio for display of instructor-led computer training and VTT. VTT capability will be two-way video/audio.

(b) Classroom control panels allowing instructors to operate equipment, electronically group students, and control and assist students at the desktop.

(c) Fully-networked classrooms providing internet access to worldwide sources of information as well as deliver multimedia to the user's desktop.

(d) Foundations for collaborative training among branches and schools; alternative training strategies using governmental, educational, industrial, and commercial sources; and the platform to support the delivery of distance learning.

(e) Full-motion video-on-demand and digital video over the Local Area Network (LAN), to include the Commander's channel, national news channels or video teletraining for one-way receive to each user's desktop. Users can view the same multimedia at the same time or each student can view different training courseware simultaneously.

(f) Instructor and students with multimedia computer workstations, giving both the capability to access Interactive Multimedia Instruction (IMI) courseware designed for student interaction and participation from the Digitized Training Access Center (DTAC), a centralized storage facility for proponent-approved courseware.

d. Training Information Infrastructure (TII). The TII Program consists of two primary components: the Army Training Information System (ATIS) and Point of Delivery systems for distributed learning.

(1) ATIS Program. The ATIS Program is a formal governance and acquisition program that integrates and synchronizes existing and evolving training information system capabilities in five enterprise capabilities to facilitate the following: improved IT governance; net-centric sharing among training applications; and centralized access to all training systems and services. The five enterprise capabilities include:

(a) Training Enterprise Scheduling Capability (TESC)
(b) Army Training Development Capability (ATDC)
(c) Army Learning Content Management Capability (ALCMC)
(d) Army Training Management Capability (ATMC)
(e) Training Resource Management Capability (TRMC)

(2) Point of Delivery (POD) infrastructure program. POD programs include Digital Training Facility (DTF), ARNG Facilities (dL classrooms and mobile dL classrooms), Digital Deployed Training Campus (DDTC), and Classroom XXI.

e. Embedded training. Embedded training is technology that shows great promise which currently has limited practical application. By adding simulation hardware and software to a combat vehicle, the crew would have training capability onboard their vehicle similar to that of the large simulators like the Close Combat Tactical Trainer (CCTT) or the Advanced Gunnery Training System (AGTS). By being embedded in the vehicle, training would be available anytime or anywhere, and would deploy as an integral part of the vehicle. An Embedded Simulation (ES) has application beyond training for testing, situational awareness, mission planning and rehearsal, and after action review and reporting.

f. Integrated Training Environment. The integrated training environment is one solution to unit training required capabilities. It links selected Training, Aids, Devices, Simulators, and Simulations (TADSS), infrastructure, mission command systems, and a training framework that approximates the conditions of the operational environment for full spectrum operations. The Army uses live, virtual, constructive and gaming (LVCG) training environments. Currently, these environments are partially interoperable, but not fully integrated among themselves or with the Army's Mission Command Systems. By 2013, the training environment will begin incorporating training enablers at select locations that are integrated and seamless to execute Army force generation multi-echelon training requirements.

g. Digital Training Management System (DTMS). DTMS is a Web-based, commercial, off-the-shelf software application customized to provide the ability to plan, resource, and manage individual and unit training. DTMS provides access to proponent approved CATS, comprised of both collective and individual tasks. Additional information is provided at the DTMS web site at http://dtms.army.mil/dtms.

ARMY TRAINING AND LEADER DEVELOPMENT

Section III
The Policy, Requirements, and Resourcing Process

15-5. General
Input is provided by manpower programs (Chapter 5), force structure changes (Chapters 4, 6, and 7), and resourcing actions (Chapters 9, and 10). Training activities draw Operations and Maintenance, Army (OMA) appropriation funds from Budget Activity 1 (Operating Forces), Budget Activity 2 (Mobilization), Budget Activity 3 (Training and Recruiting), and Budget Activity 4 (Administration and Service-wide Activities). Other contributing appropriations include the following: National Guard Personnel, Army (NGPA); Operations and Maintenance, ARNG (OMNG), Reserve Personnel, Army (RPA); and Operations and Maintenance, Army Reserve (OMAR).

15-6. Organization
The Deputy Chief of Staff (DCS), G-3/5/7 combines the functions of institutional and unit training and training support. The DCS, G-3/5/7 approves and manages Army military individual, collective, and modernization training and education programs and Army civilian training and education programs. It provides the Army a single point of entry for issues which impact training. The DCS, G-3/5/7, exercises Headquarters, Department of the Army (HQDA) supervision for defining concepts, strategies, resources, policies, and programs for Army training, education, and leader development. Other HQDA staff elements having direct or indirect impact on the training systems include:

 a. The Assistant Secretary of the Army (Manpower and Reserve Affairs) (ASA(M&RA)). ASA(M&RA) has a training division to assist in the development, implementation, and review of policies and programs related to achieving the Army goal of effective and efficient training and education for the Army. The ASA(M&RA) advises the Secretary of the Army (SECARMY) on all matters relating to human resources and reserve affairs, to include, readiness and training.

 b. The Assistant Secretary of the Army (Financial Management and Comptroller) (ASA (FM&C)). The ASA(FM&C) formulates the Army budget, issues manpower and dollar guidance, distributes funds to commands and agencies, and monitors obligation rates and reprogramming actions (Chapter 9).

 c. The Assistant Secretary of the Army (Acquisition, Logistics, and Technology) (ASA(ALT)). The ASA(ALT) manages the life cycle of materiel and non-materiel items used by individuals and units in mission performance (Chapter 11). The ASA(ALT) provides policy and guidance to research, develop, and procure system and non-system TADSS and other approved requirements for training support materials. Additionally, the ASA(ALT) funds and coordinates New Equipment Training.

 d. The Assistant Secretary of the Army (Installations and Environment) (ASA(I&E)). ASA(I&E) provides secretariat-level management for the formulation, execution, and review of policies, plans, and programs relating to the following: the Range and Training Land Program (RTLP); environment, safety and occupational health concerns or requirements; the National Environmental Policy Act; and Land Use Requirements Studies.

 e. DCS, G-1. The DCS, G-1 is responsible for integrating personnel readiness and training, and manages ATRRS, the system that supports the Army's Program for Individual Training (ARPRINT) management process. The DCS, G-1 manages execution-year training program change requests driven by personnel readiness requirements through the Training Resources Arbitration Panel (TRAP). The DCS, G-1 also manages the administration of the manpower requirements of the pre-commissioning programs for officers (USMA, ROTC, and OCS); and training for equal opportunity, and alcohol and drug abuse (Chapter 13 and 14).

 f. Army Human Resources Command (AHRC). The AHRC projects training requirements, by FY based on training spaces allocated by the G-3/5/7 for AC officers and enlisted personnel. The DCS, G-3/5/7 allocates training spaces for AC based on projected unit requirements and distribution policies informed by the Army force generation cycle.

 g. Human Resources Command (HRC)-Army Reserve. HRC commands and controls all Individual Ready Reserve (IRR) members. HRC also provides individual training management to the IRR, officers and enlisted (Chapter 7). It is responsible for the Officer Professional Management System (OPMS)-USAR and the Enlisted Professional Management System (EPMS)-USAR, and projects officer and enlisted training requirements for the USAR by FY. The HRC allocates training spaces for USAR officers and enlisted based on projected training requirements and in accordance with applicable Army force generation cycles.

HOW THE ARMY RUNS

h. Assistant Chief of Staff, Installation Management (ACSIM). ACSIM provides the following: policy and guidance for facility engineering programs and environmental compliance, restoration, pollution prevention, conservation, environmental program management, and real property master planning; direction and assistance in land acquisition in support of the RTLP; utility and manpower infrastructure facility support for installation Training Support Centers (TSC) operations.

i. DCS, G-2. The DCS, G-2 is responsible for the Opposing Force (OPFOR) program and assisting the DCS, G-3/5/7 on intelligence training policy.

j. DCS, G-4. The DCS, G-4 is responsible for logistics readiness of Army forces, to include supportability/maintainability of equipment (to include training assets) in troop units (Chapter 12).

k. The Army Chief Information Officer (CIO)/G-6. The CIO/G-6 provides policy and procedural guidance for Army visual information and multimedia support. CIO/G-6 oversees the Information Management Program Evaluation Group (PEG) which resources ACOMs, ASCCs, DRUs and installation Visual Information/Training Support Center (VI/TSC) operations.

l. The Inspector General (IG). The IG conducts Army-wide assessments of training development and training management to evaluate the implementation of training policy and impacts of training on readiness, sustainability, and units' ability to fight and win. Assessments focus on training resources and provide feedback to commanders in order to promote efficiency in training.

m. Office of The Surgeon General (OTSG). The OTSG projects training requirements and allocates course spaces internal to the Army Medical Department (AMEDD).

n. Chief, National Guard Bureau (CNGB). The CNGB promulgates training policy for ARNG units through National Guard Regulation 350-1. The CNGB also programs the resources for NG training and allocates training spaces to each State, Territory, and the District of Columbia. NG unit commanders are responsible for their units' training. U.S. Army Forces Command (FORSCOM) establishes training criteria and supervises training of ARNG units. Policy and guidance are contained in FORSCOM/ARNG Regulation 350-2.

o. Chief, Army Reserve (CAR). The CAR programs training resources for the Army Reserve and monitors USAR training activities. The CAR manages professional development training for USAR officers, warrant officers, and senior NCO through HR (Chapter 7).

15-7. Requirements and Resourcing

a. Training (TT) PEG. As one of the Army's six Title 10 PEGs, the TT PEG programs Army resources each year. The TT PEG manages all aspects of training dollars within components, individual through unit. The TT PEG has 124 Management Decision Packages (MDEP). The Deputy Director of Training, ODCS, G-3/5/7 and the ASA(M&RA) co-chair the TT PEG. MDEP managers articulate and defend resource requirements to the PEG during the POM build. The MDEP managers use various costing models to determine requirements.

b. ATRRS. ATRRS is the Army's Management Information System of record for student input to training. The on-line system integrates manpower requirements for individual training with the process by which the training base is resourced and training programs execution is recorded. This automation support tool contains: training requirements; training programs; class schedules; class quotas; student reservations; and student input and graduation data. It supports numerous Army processes to include the Structure Manning Decision Review (SMDR). The product of the SMDR (see Figure 5-2) is the ARPRINT, the mission document and input factor for resourcing the institutional training base during peacetime and mobilization. ATRRS supports the Training Requirements Division of the Office of the DCS, G-1 in its army wide mission of integrating all phases of input to training management, during peacetime and mobilization. The system supports the planning, programming, and budgeting processes.

c. Analysis of Change Cell (AOCC). The AOCC addresses issues impacting institutional training, across the budget and execution years that are too complex for the TRAP. The AOCC Action Officer forum vets its recommendations, through the AOCC COC, to the Input to Training (AOCC) GOSC to resolve the issues. These issues include changes in training loads generated as a result of changes in the following: current authorizations documents; Army policies; current manpower inventory; projected gains and losses; training attrition rates; training strategies; and availability of resources. HQDA convenes the AOCC on an "as needed" basis--usually annually—after assessing the ARPRINT mission against POM funding. The Army G-3 Training Directorate and the Army G-1 Military Personnel Management Directorate announce the date and specific purpose of convening an AOCC. The Director of Military Personnel Management (G-1/MP) and the Director of Training (G-37/TR) co-chair the AOCC.

ARMY TRAINING AND LEADER DEVELOPMENT

Additional members include: Director of Plans and Resources (G-1/PR); Director of Force Management (G-37/FM); Chief, OCAR; and Director, ARNG. Regular advisory members include representatives of the training commands (TRADOC, U.S. Army Medical Command (MEDCOM), U.S. Army Materiel Command (AMC)), as well as representatives from HRC.

15-8. Development of the Army Individual Training Requirements

a. Development of individual training requirements. The development of individual training for the Active Component (AC) begins with the identification of force structure authorizations from the Personnel Management Authorizations Document (PMAD) and AA Military Manpower Program (AAMMP). The Army G-1 produces the PMAD semiannually, usually in August and January. PMAD displays authorizations at the Military Occupational Specialty (MOS) and grade level. The Army G-1 also produces the AAMMP on a monthly basis. It contains manning data such as AC end strength, monthly recruiting requirements, and inputs to training for seven fiscal years.

b. MOS Level System (MOSLS). Using the PMAD, the MOSLS process predicts AC (enlisted) skill requirements. MOSLS compares MOS and grade inventory, aged to the fiscal year under consideration by applying gain, loss, and promotion factors. The difference between the authorizations and the aged (to the FY) inventory constitutes the number of trained Soldiers, by skill that the training base must produce (output). Applying training attrition rates at the skill level provides the number of Soldiers required to begin training (input).

c. Other training requirements. HRC identifies other training requirements for officer and enlisted in-service personnel who require training and education to support professional development, reenlistment or reclassification programs, and mission requirements. The Army G-1 identifies training requirements for Army civilians. Additionally, HRC solicits in-service training requirements from other ACOM, ASCC, DRUs, States' Adjutant Generals, and other services and agencies via the Total Army Centralized Individual Training Solicitations (TACITS). HRC conducts the TACITS survey annually. The accession-driven, in-service, and other task based training requirements are combined as total raw training requirements within the ATRRS. The ATRRS' automated databases include a list of Army task-based training courses that includes length, capacity, frequency, and location. It also includes other Services' courses attended by Army personnel. The task-based requirements are translated into course requirements and become the Army's training requirements at the course level of detail by component and fiscal year.

d. Training program development for each MOS/Area of Concentration (AOC). After the training requirements for courses are developed, the next major task in the process is the development of the training program for each MOS/AOC. The first step in establishing a training program is the SMDR, co-chaired by ODCS, G-1 and ODCS, G-3. It includes representatives from: ODCS (G-1, G-3/5/7, and G4); OTSG; TRADOC; AMC; AMEDD Center and School; HRC; FORSCOM; NGB; OCAR; USAREC; Office of the Chief of Engineers (OCE); other services; FMS; International Military Education and Training (IMET); and the individual proponent schools. The purpose of the SMDR (Figure 15-2) is to reach a consensus within the Army for the institutional training program for the first and second POM years and any major changes for the upcoming budget year. Additionally, the SMDR validates training requirements (Soldiers and civilians to be trained in formal education/training courses), compares training requirements with schoolhouse current resource capabilities (facilities, billeting, manpower), and adjusts training requirements or training resources to form recommended training programs. The SMDR is conducted annually in October. Individual training requirements are initially established for the third POM year, validated for the second POM year (the primary focus of the SMDR), and "fine tuned" for the first POM year.

HOW THE ARMY RUNS

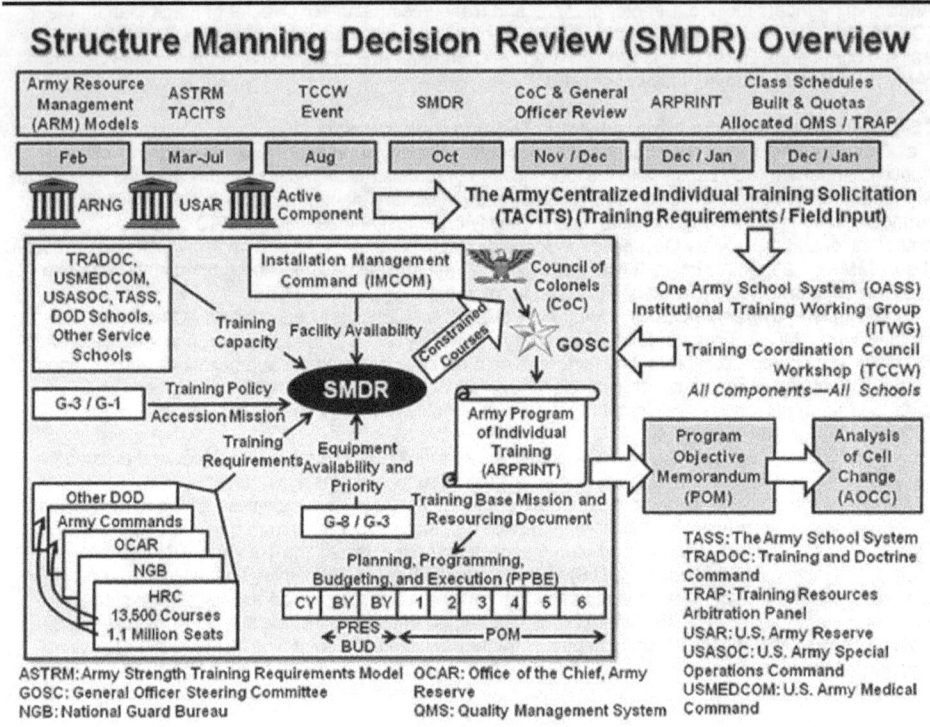

Figure 15-2. Structure Manning Decision Review (SMDR) Overview

e. SMDR categorization by course. The SMDR categorizes each course. The first category is composed of those courses where the total training requirement can be trained with available resources. The second category consists of courses where the requirements exceed the resourced capability of the training base. In the second category, resources can be provided or requirements reduced to the resourced level without significant impact on the manning program. The third category represents those courses where the requirement exceeds the capacity, requires significant resources, and cannot be reduced without significant impact on the manning program. These courses are termed "constrained." The results of the SMDR are briefed to a Council of Colonels (COC) which attempts to confirm category two adjustments/resources and move as many courses as possible from category three to category two.

f. GOSC. The courses in categories two and three are then referred to a GOSC co-chaired by the Director of Training (DOT) and the Director of Manpower and Personnel (DMP). At this meeting, general officers take action on the recommendations of the COC. Each course remaining constrained is reviewed as to current authorizations, projected operating strength, training requirements, training capability, source of constraint, resources required to eliminate the constraint, availability of required resources, and a recommended course of action. That review results in a resourced training requirement that is called an approved training program for each course for that fiscal year.

g. ARPRINT. After the GOSC is completed, the ODCS, G-1, Training Requirements Division publishes both the training requirement and the training program in the ARPRINT. The ARPRINT is a mission document for the training base as well as the Army in terms of recruitment and professional development education. The ARPRINT identifies, by fiscal year, projected individual training requirements for established courses and for task-based courses for new course requirements. Based on identified training requirements, subsequent actions are taken to provide resources (manpower, money, facilities,

ARMY TRAINING AND LEADER DEVELOPMENT

ammunition, and equipment) to train the required number of Soldiers and Army civilians. The desired flow of Soldiers into the schools and training centers aids in development of class schedules to support the ARPRINT-approved training requirements for each course. The class schedules are entered into ATRRS. TRADOC reviews the class schedules to ensure they support the ARPRINT requirement and TRADOC scheduling policy.

  h. Mobilization Planning System (MPS). The MPS is a subsystem of ATRRS. It provides training managers, at or above installation level, prompt access to information necessary to plan for implementation of the mobilization of the Army training base. The MPS helps produce the Mobilization (MOB) ARPRINT which provides a projection of trainee and student inputs, by task-based course, to satisfy post mobilization requirements for trained manpower as determined by Mobilization Manpower Planning System (MOBMAN).

Section IV
Training and Doctrine Command Organization and Training Development Systems

15–1. Training in Institutions—General
The HQDA authorizes direct communication between ACOM, ASCC, DRUs and U.S. Army Training and Doctrine Command (TRADOC). HQDA also authorizes TRADOC to task non-TRADOC commands, schools, and agencies (except the Army Medical Department Center and School (AMEDD C&S) and the U.S. Army John F. Kennedy Special Warfare Center and School (USAJFKSWCS)) to provide specialized subject materials for instruction with the TASS. The AMEDD C&S provides training on medical tasks and JFKSWCS provides training on special operations tasks to TRADOC. The CG, TRADOC, administers training functions outlined in AR 350-1, AR 600-100, AR 140-1, and AR 10-87 and is responsible for developing training doctrine, policy and procedures for approval by HQDA. Most institutional training (proponent schools) is managed by TRADOC.

  a. TRADOC, http://www-tradoc.army.mil. TRADOC is the Army's institutional base for education and training. TRADOC develops the Army's Soldier and civilian leaders and designs, develops and integrates capabilities, concepts and doctrine in order to build a campaign-capable expeditionary Army in support of joint warfighting commanders through Army force generation. TRADOC commands and directs more than 27,000 Soldiers and 11,000 civilians working daily to accomplish its mission. It consists of 32 schools and centers, and trains more than 600,000 Soldiers and civilians a year. Their footprint spreads throughout the Continental U.S. (CONUS) at 20 different locations. HQ, TRADOC, is located at Fort Eustis, VA. Headquarters TRADOC has several Deputy Commanding Generals (DCG):

  (1) DCG-Combined Arms/Combined Arms Center (CAC) Commanding General. TRADOC's DCG-Combined Arms is dual-hatted as the CG of CAC, Fort Leavenworth, KS. CAC's CG serves as the TRADOC proponent for leader development; professional military education (officer, warrant officer, noncommissioned officer and civilian); battle command and command, control, communications, computers, intelligence, surveillance and reconnaissance (more commonly known as C4ISR); collective training; Army doctrine; and dissemination of observations/lessons learned. The CAC commander is responsible for providing guidance, leadership, and command supervision to the branch centers/schools to ensure that training remains safe, relevant, realistic, and executed to Army standards. CAC's CG is also responsible for the Army's Combat Training Center (CTC) Program.

  (2) DCG-Futures/Army Capabilities Integration Center (ARCIC) Director. The DCG-Futures is dual-hatted as the Director, ARCIC. ARCIC develops and integrates into a joint warfighting environment, from concept to capability, all aspects of the future force. This DCG and his team perform the following functions: develop and integrate Joint and Army concepts, architectures and Doctrine, Organization, Training, Materiel, Leadership and Education, Personnel, Facilities, and Policy (DOTMLPF-P) capabilities; validate science and technology priorities; and lead future-force experimentation. The DCG-Futures synchronizes and integrates Army capabilities with Joint, Interagency, Intergovernmental and Multinational (JIIM) capabilities.

  (3) DCG-Initial Military Training (IMT). The DCG-IMT is the TRADOC executive responsible for the Army's officer, warrant officer and enlisted training process through completion of IMT. The DCG-IMT is also responsible for providing IMT policy and execution guidance to TRADOC commanders and staff outside the IMT chain of command. IMT encompasses reception-battalion operations that support IMT; BCT; Advanced Individual Training (AIT); OSUT; Reserve Officer Training Corps (ROTC); Officer

HOW THE ARMY RUNS

Candidate School (OCS); Warrant Officer Candidate School (WOCS); Basic Officer Leader Course (BOLC) Phases A and B; and recruiter, drill sergeant, and other IMT cadre training.

(4) DCG-Army Reserve. The DCG-Army Reserve assists TRADOC's CG in executing missions that require integration of Reserve Soldiers.

(5) DCG-ARNG. The DCG-ARNG assists TRADOC's CG in DOTMLPF-P matters impacting the training and readiness of ARNG Soldiers and champions TRADOC programs and future initiatives through existing senior-level forums.

b. The TRADOC mission. Central to the TRADOC mission are the following functions:

(1) Recruiting and Training Soldiers. TRADOC builds the Army on a solid foundation of quality people by selecting recruits and transforming them into Soldiers, who are physically tough, mentally adaptive, and live the Warrior Ethos. The ultimate asymmetric advantage of our Army is our Soldiers, and they cannot be matched by our adversaries—current or future.

(2) Developing Adaptive Leaders. TRADOC trains leaders for certainty and educates for uncertainty. Leader development produces innovative, flexible, culturally astute professionals—expert in the art and science of the profession of arms and able to quickly adapt to the wide-ranging conditions of decisive action operations.

(3) Designing today's Army Modular Force and the Future Combat Force. TRADOC identifies and integrates comprehensive solutions for the Army Modular Force, both today and tomorrow.

(4) Maximizing Institutional Learning and Adaptation. As an integral component of an innovative Generating Force, TRADOC shapes and links seamlessly with the operating force to maximize Army Learning and Adaptation.

c. DCS, G-3/5/7, Operations, Plans, & Training. The DCS, G-3/5/7 is the single manager for training in TRADOC. G-3/5/7 is the largest staff element within HQ, TRADOC. It consists of 15 directorates with over 500 personnel. The DCS, G3/5/7, through the Training Operations Management Activity (TOMA), provides oversight for technical training on 132 Army military specialties with over 1400 specialized courses for approximately 377,000 students annually. The DCS, G-3/5/7, has 281 leader development courses for officers, warrant officers, NCOs and civilians. Within TRADOC, the DCSOPS&T interfaces with the following: the G-3/5/7; DCS, G-1/4 (Personnel and Logistics); DCS, G-2 (Intelligence); DCS, G-6 (Command, Control, Communications, and Computers (C4)); and DCS, G-8 (Resource Management). The DCS, G-3/5/7 also coordinates with HRC for management of trainee accessions, as well as with other TRADOC staffs.

d. The DCS, G-3/5/7 is comprised of the following directorates and activities:

(1) Army Civilian Training, Education, and Development System (ACTEDS). Training, Combat, and Doctrine Warfighting Developers Career Program (CP-32), or the Career Program ACTEDS Plan, identifies the professional development assignments, training, and education that enable Army civilians to support Army Transformation, and enhances career development.

(2) Individual Training Directorate (ITD)
(3) Command Provost Marshal Directorate (CPMD); Current Operations Division, G-33
(4) Priorities, Analysis and Requirements Directorate (PARD)
(5) Training Integration Directorate (TID)
(6) Reserve Component Training Integration Directorate (RCTID)
(7) Security Assistance Training Field Activity (SATFA) (FOA)
(8) Training Operations Management Activity (TOMA) (FOA)

e. CAC. CAC has the primary mission of preparing the Army and its leaders for war http://usacac.army.mil/cac2/overview.asp. At present, this mission is divided between preparing the Army for the Overseas Contingency Operations (OCO) and transforming it to meet future threats. In order to accomplish these critical missions, CAC provides the following: Army-wide leadership and supervision for leader development and professional military and civilian education; institutional and collective training; functional training; training support; battle command; doctrine; lessons learned; and other specified areas that the TRADOC CG designates. These are focused toward making CAC a catalyst for change and to support the development of a relevant and ready ground force to support joint, interagency and multinational operations anywhere in the world. CAC is comprised of the following organization (for detailed descriptions, go to: http://usacac.army.mil/cac2/):

(1) CAC- Leader Development and Education (LD&E)
(a) LD&E/Command and General Staff College (CGSC)
(b) Center for Army Leadership (CAL)

ARMY TRAINING AND LEADER DEVELOPMENT

      (c) Center for the Army Profession and Ethic (CAPE)
      (d) Combined Arms Research Library (CARL)
      (e) Combat Studies Institute (CSI)
      (f) Defense Language Institute (DLI)
      (g) Military Review
      (h) Warrant Officer Career College (WOCC)
      (I) Western Hemisphere Institute for Security Cooperation (WHINSEC)
    (2) Army Management Staff College (AMSC)
    (3) Mission Command (MC) Center of Excellence (CoE)
      (a) Army Irregular Warfare Fusion Center (AIWFC)
      (b) Center for Army Lessons Learned (CALL)
      (c) Combined Arms Doctrine Directorate (CADD)
      (d) Capability Development Integration Directorate (CDID)
    (4) CAC-Training (T)
      (a) Army Joint Support Team (AJST)
      (b) Army Training Support Center (ATSC)
      (c) CTC Directorate (CTCD)
      (d) MC Training Program (MCTP) (formerly BCTP)
      (e) National Simulation Center (NSC)
      (f) TRADOC Capability Manager (TCM) for the Virtual Training Environment (Virtual)
      (g) Joint Center for International Security Force Assistance (JCISFA)
  f. Training Management Directorate (TMD) (location of ATN) TPO OneSAF
  g. ARCIC, http://www.arcic.army.mil. Since its inception, ARCIC has supported the CG, TRADOC in the design, development, and integration of force capability requirements for the Army. ARCIC is responsible to the SECARMY and CSA for determining and integrating force requirements and synchronizing the development of DOTMLPF-P solutions across the Army. ARCIC leads the development and integration of force capabilities across the DOTMLPF-P for the Army within a JIIM environment to support Joint Force Commanders. ARCIC is the Army's leader in the identification, design, development, and synchronization of capabilities into the Army current modular force and the future modular force, bringing together all Army agencies as well as JIIM and other Department of Defense (DOD) agencies to manage rapid change. ARCIC supports TRADOC in providing adaptive Soldiers, leaders and units by contributing to execute the following: doctrine development; Tactics, Techniques, and Procedures (TTP) codification; and collective training experience formalization.
  h. Combined Arms Support Command (CASCOM), http://www.cascom.lee.army.mil/default.asp. CASCOM provides training and leader development, and develops concepts, doctrine organizations, life-long learning, and materiel solutions, to provide the combat service support to sustain a campaign quality Army with joint and expeditionary capabilities. CASCOM trains, educates, and grows adaptive sustainment professionals; and develops and integrates innovative Army and Joint sustainment capabilities, concepts, and doctrine to enable Unified Land Operations.
  i. U.S. Army TRADOC Analysis Center (TRAC), http://www.trac.army.mil. TRAC conducts research on potential military operations worldwide to inform decisions about the most challenging issues facing the Army and the DOD. TRAC conducts Operations Research (OR) on a wide range of military topics, some contemporary, but most often set 5-to-15 years in the future. TRAC directly supports the mission of the Army's major commands and TRADOC to develop future concepts and requirements while also serving the decision needs of military clients. The TRAC program of operations research and analysis is forward-looking and addresses a wide range of military topics. TRAC leads TRADOC's major studies of new warfighting Operations and Organization (O&O) concepts and requirements, as well as the Army's analysis of Advanced Warfighting Experiments (AWE), and the Army's Analysis of Alternatives (AoA). The analysis topics span doctrine, training, leader development, organization, materiel, and Soldier support. Scenarios are used by the Army for education, training, and force development. TRAC develops scenarios of future potential military operations for use in modeling and analysis informed by intelligence estimates. The family of scenarios undergoes continual review and change in anticipation of emerging threats and new operational environments around the world.
  j. CALL, http://usacac.army.mil/cac2/call/about.asp. CALL collects and analyzes data from a variety of current and historical sources, including Army operations and training events, and produces lessons for military commanders, staff, and students. CALL disseminates lessons learned and other related research

HOW THE ARMY RUNS

materials through a variety of print and electronic media. Individuals requiring additional information, articles, publications, research material, etc., may request them at the CALL Request for Information (RFI), https://call-rfi.leavenworth.army.mil/rfisystem.

k. Army learning policy and systems and the Analyze, Design, Develop, Implement, and Evaluate (ADDIE) process.

(1) The purpose of the Army learning policy and systems is to support the Army by regulating practices in effective learning management and to specify required enabling systems.

(2) The Army is intentionally moving away from the older term of "Systems Approach to Training" in order to emphasize learning. The Army's Instructional Systems Design (ISD) process emphasizes the ADDIE process. Managers at all levels must have an understanding of the ADDIE process and the components of the Army's ISD process.

(3) The ADDIE process provides for effectiveness and efficiencies by developing continuous awareness of the relationships among the component parts, rather than a systematic and linear approach. The five phases of ADDIE—Analysis, Design, Development, Implementation, and Evaluation—enable the creation of integrated, mission essential products that support any type of learning and professional growth.

(4) The Army's ISD process allows for the organization, development and management of learning programs and products. This process organizes all course and curriculum development activities that ensure classroom instruction accomplishes the institution's educational purpose.

15-10. Education and Training Automation

a. AKO. Soldiers and Army civilians have individual accounts through which they can access education, training, doctrine, and other data and information.

b. ATN. ATN is the newest online tool designed for trainers and educators to provide best practices, and includes a database of training solutions and collaborative tools such as a Blog and Battle Command Knowledge System forum. Accessible through a secure AKO sign-in, ATN is an important source of information for the many Army training resources available.

(1) ATN replaces FM 7-1, Battle Focused Training. The ATN is not doctrine; rather, it provides an intuitive, easy to navigate website focused on Army training best practices, solutions and collaborative tools. Through Army-wide calls for training products, the ATN team has collected over 500 products from the field, and posted the best of them to the products portion of the web site. The ATN is growing and will mature with time.

(2) Because the ATN is online, it is available to the Army 24/7. Because it is virtual, it will remain current with no physical copy to maintain. Training solutions are at the fingertips of trainers by downloading text documents and training examples with embedded links for easy use. Training management is streamlined to provide best practices and unit-provided examples. CAC manages the ATN.

(3) Training techniques must adapt at least as rapidly as operations change. The Army wants leaders who are adaptive to the operational environment. Decisive operations, modular forces, versatile adversaries and the reality of persistent conflict, forces the Army to think differently about training. A web-based system allows Army leaders to share best ideas on training more intelligently, more effectively, and more efficiently.

c. Automated Systems Approach to Training (ASAT)/Training and Doctrine Development Tool (TDDT). ASAT/TDDT provides the capability to produce education/training and doctrine products. TDDT is the next generation (web-based) training developmental tool, which will replace the ASAT in all schoolhouses and other organizations producing Army education/training (e.g., contractors). This program will provide standardized products such as field manuals, Mission Training Plans (MTP) drill books, courses, and Soldier Training Publications (STP). It also produces unlimited ad hoc outputs like task analysis matrices and CATS when fully programmed. This program provides an electronic staffing capability.

d. DTMS. DTMS is a web-based Commercial off the Shelf COTS) software application customized to facilitate unit training management. Optimized for use at brigade and below, the DTMS provides the ability to plan, resource, and manage unit and individual training at all levels. The DTMS is used for METL development and can track separate METL for a unit, the unit's HHC, and unit staff. The DTMS has the ability to develop After Action Reviews (AAR) and commanders' assessments of training events. It compiles and displays a unit roll-up of training conducted through a series of customizable tabs to track weapons qualification, the Army Physical Fitness Test (APFT), Army Warrior Training, AR 350-1 common military training, MOS training, and deployment tasks from enlistment to retirement. DTMS is an

ARMY TRAINING AND LEADER DEVELOPMENT

unclassified (For Official Use Only (FOUO)) system that requires both AKO logon and user permissions (managed by units) to access training data.

 e. Digital Libraries. Reimer Digital Library (RDL) and Army Publishing Directorate (APD), https://rdl.train.army.mil/soldierPortal/soldier.portal and http://www.apd.army.mil. The digital libraries store education, training, and doctrinal data. Data stored is generated by the other ATIA supporting programs. They can be accessed through AKO/DOD Knowledge Online (DKO) website (https://www.us.army.mil) or through the Army Home Page (http://www.army.mil).

 f. Army proponent school web-sites are available to enhance one's professional education. The link, https://www.us.army.mil/suite/portal/index.jsp, provides a consolidated list of websites.

 g. Other training development and training resource support systems include:

  (1) Individual Training Resource Module (ITRM). Collects individual training implementation resource requirements for budgeting and POM submission. It uses ASAT/TDDT information.

  (2) Training and Doctrine Development (TD2) Management System. Used to plan for the education/training and doctrine development. It calculates the training development manpower requirements by school for building TDA and POM submission.

  (3) Training Resource Module (TRM). Collects resource data for unit training which is used to build the budget resource requirement which includes resources required to conduct and support unit training, maintain unit equipment and sustain routine day to day unit operations.

 h. Army Career Tracker (ACT). TRADOC has developed ACT in response to the need for a comprehensive leader development tool designed for use by all cohorts, to include: Active Army; USAR; ARNG; and Army civilians. The DCS, G-37/TRV is the HQDA lead for the development and implementation of ACT for Army civilians. ACT is an automated tool that integrates data on training, education, and experiential learning from a number of source systems into one personalized and easy to use system. It provides civilians an effective and efficient way to monitor their career development, allows supervisors and career program managers to track and advise employees on their leadership development.

Section V
The Army School System

15-11. Overview of The Army School System (TASS)

 a. TASS is a composite school system made up of AC, USAR, ARNG, and Army civilian institutional training systems. TASS conducts IMT (e.g., BCT, AIT, BOLC A and B); reclassification training (e.g., MOS and officer branch qualification); officer, warrant officer, NCO and Army civilian professional development training and education (e.g., Officer Education System (OES), Noncommissioned Officer Education System (NCOES), and Civilian Education System (CES)); and functional training (e.g., Additional Skill Identifier (ASI), Skill Qualifications Identifier (SQI), Skill Identifier (SI), Language Identification Code (LIC)). This is accomplished through both standard resident and dL courses. The RC TASS units are functionally aligned and linked to appropriate training proponents.

 b. The Army training proponents (e.g., TRADOC, U.S. Army Special Operations Command (USASOC), MEDCOM, U.S. Army Intelligence and Security Command (INSCOM), U.S. Army Space and Missile Defense Command/Army Forces Strategic Command (SMDC/ARSTRAT), ARNG, and USAR provide the structure to establish, maintain, and operate TASS education system from a common automated management system. The AC training proponents provide operational links to the RC instructor groups. This ensures quality assurance, instructor certification, The Army Training System (TATS) courseware, use of the learning product development process, and a dL strategy. TATS courseware ensures that all Army Soldiers, regardless of component, are trained to the same standard regardless of what component school conducts the training.

 c. The USAR provides component infrastructure organized into training commands with brigades and battalions. These elements deliver institutional training at multiple geographic resident and dL locations using TATS courseware approved and distributed by the Army training proponents through USARC. The USAR TASS conducts MOS reclassification, NCOES, OES, ASI/SQI, and functional courses.

 d. The ARNG TASS training regiments, battalions, companies, and batteries have transformed and approached training requirements on a national basis in support of Army force generation. Training battalions have been relocated or established geographically based on density of MTOE structure.

HOW THE ARMY RUNS

  e. All RC training battalions and regiments and AC institutions teach courses to the same standards.
  f. TASS training missions are validated during the SMDR process, reflected in the ARPRINT, and documented in ATTRS.

15-12. The Army Training System (TATS)
A TATS course is a single course designed to train the same MOS/AOC skill level or ASI, LIC, and SQI within the Army. It also includes MOS-Transition (MOS-T) (formerly known as reclassification), Army leadership, and functional and professional development courses. The TATS course structure (phases, modules, tracks, lessons, and tests) and media ensure standardization by training all Soldiers, regardless of component, on course critical tasks to task performance standard. Method of presentation and conditions may vary IAW TR 350-70.

15-13. Enlisted IMT/Initial Entry Training (IET)
  a. IET. IET is the introductory training given to all personnel upon initial entry into the Army and is governed by TRADOC Regulation 350-6 (Nov 10). The mission of enlisted IET is to transform volunteers into Soldiers who demonstrate the requisite character and values, possess a warrior spirit, are competent and confident in their warfighting and technical skills, and who can successfully contribute to their first unit of assignment. As a result, IET transforms civilians into Soldiers. Transformation is the deliberate physical and psychological development/progression of a person with an uncertain set of values and level of commitment, discipline, and knowledge of the Army into a contributing member of the Army profession who demonstrates an appropriate level of commitment, discipline, task proficiency, and adherence to the Army values. IET provides an orderly transition from civilian to military life, and motivates trainees to become dedicated and productive members of the Army. They become proficient in warrior tasks, battle drills, and selected MOS-related technical skills, and understand, accept, and live by the Army values and Warrior Ethos. At HQDA, the DCS, G-3/5/7, exercises general staff supervision IET except for AMEDD personnel. The CG, TRADOC, is responsible for conducting IET, which is accomplished by: the DCG, IMT; Commandants of the TRADOC schools; and commanders of the U.S. Army Training Centers (USATC). The CG, USAAC/DCG IMT's focus is to ensure that IET remains challenging, safe, relevant, realistic, and executed to Army standards. The AMEDD Center and School performs this function for AMEDD personnel.
  b. BCT. The CG, BCT CoE, Fort Jackson is the proponent for BCT. BCT is ten weeks of training in basic military skills given to all newly enlisted personnel who have no or limited prior military service. BCT provides a logical progression of training to transition civilians into Soldiers who are well disciplined, motivated, physically fit, and proficient in basic combat survivability skills. All Soldiers receive TRADOC Pam 600-4 (IET Soldier's Handbook) and STP 21-1 (Soldier's Manual of Common Tasks (SMCT) Soldier's Manual of Common Tasks Warrior Skills Level 1). The two publications provide Soldiers with pocket references for subjects taught and tested in BCT/OSUT, along with Warrior skills needed upon arrival at their first unit of assignment.
  c. AIT. AIT occurs after completion of BCT. AIT builds on the Soldier skills acquired in BCT while developing each Soldier to the level of proficiency required for the award of an MOS. Soldiers take one of two AIT paths: MOS training at a USATC; or MOS training at a school.
  d. OSUT. OSUT is conducted at one installation, in the same company-size unit, with the same cadre, and with one program of instruction. The OSUT model is used for most combat arms MOSs (except Air Defense and Aviation) and selected combat support MOSs. OSUT integrates common skill and MOS-specific training into a single program.
  e. Split Training Option (STO). The STO permits selected individuals to enlist in the ARNG or USAR and complete Initial Active Duty for Training (IADT) in two phases separated by a period of not more than 12 months. The program is designed to attract students and seasonal workers to enlist in the ARNG or USAR by minimizing the time lost from education or employment.

15-14. Noncommissioned Officer (NCO) Education System
The primary source of the formal military training and education that NCOs receive throughout their military career is institutional training. NCOs train to perform critical tasks to standard and develop supporting skills and knowledge essential for developing high-quality leaders. NCOs are continuously developed and trained through a train-ahead approach. Institutional training and education provides the foundation upon which leader development rests. The purpose of institutional training is to develop the

ARMY TRAINING AND LEADER DEVELOPMENT

values, attributes, critical warfighting skills, and actions that are essential to quality NCO leadership. When these same values, attributes, skills, and actions are tested, reinforced, and strengthened by follow-on operational assignments and meaningful self-development programs, NCOs attain and sustain competency and confidence in their profession of arms. The NCOES with Structured Self-Development (SSD) as a course prerequisite and certain other functional courses (e.g., First Sergeant Course and Battle Staff Course) form the institutional training pillar of NCO leader development. The NCOES is designed to prepare NCOs to lead and train Soldiers who work and fight under their direct leadership, and to assist their assigned leaders to execute unit missions. The NCOES accomplishes this preparation through progressive and sequential training using small group instruction throughout four levels of schooling—primary, basic, advanced, and senior. Functional courses are based on specific skills required for special assignments or duties. The Army uses resident and distance learning instruction to deliver institutional training. AR 350-1 prescribes how the Army will create efficient and effective education. The Basic NCO Leader Development Timeline is shown in Figure 15-3.

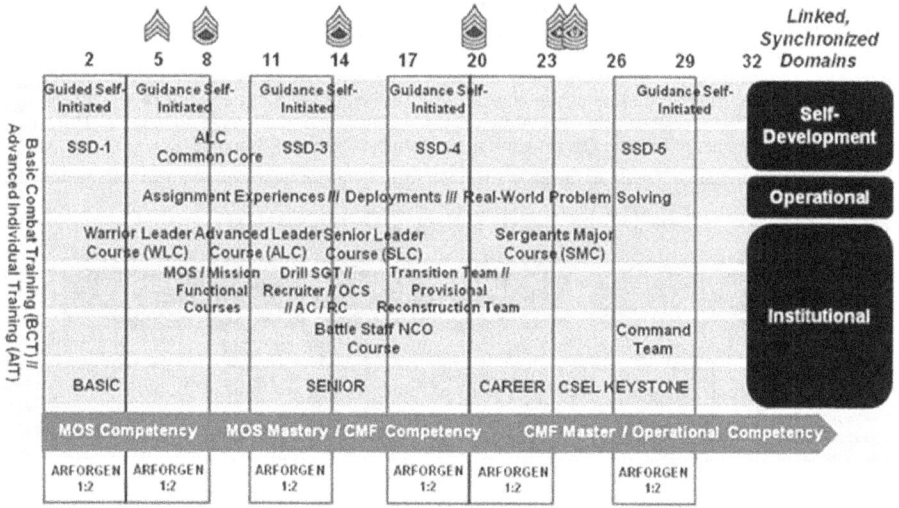

Figure 15-3. Basic Noncommissioned Officer (NCO) Leader Development Timeline

15-15. OES

a. The goal of the OES is to produce a corps of leaders who:
   (1) Are fully competent in technical, tactical, and leadership skills, knowledge, and experience
   (2) Are knowledgeable of how the Army runs
   (3) Are prepared to operate in JIIM environments
   (4) Can demonstrate confidence, integrity, critical judgment, and responsibility
   (5) Can operate in an environment of complexity, ambiguity, and rapid change
   (6) Can build effective teams amid organizational and technological change
   (7) Can adapt to and solve problems creatively.

HOW THE ARMY RUNS

    b. OES also produces warrant officers who are:
    (1) Highly specialized experts, trainers, and leaders fully competent in technical, tactical, and leadership skills
    (2) Creative problem solvers able to function in highly complex and dynamic environments
    (3) Proficient operators, maintainers, administrators, and managers of Army equipment, support activities, and technical systems.
    c. Officer leader development is a continuous process that begins with pre-commissioning/training and education.
    d. OES is a sequence of Professional Military Education (PME) for professionals in subjects that enhance knowledge of the science and art of war. PME is a progressive education system that prepares leaders for increased responsibilities and successful performance at the next higher level by developing the key knowledge, skills, and attributes required to operate successfully at the next level in any environment. PME is linked to promotions, future assignments, and career management models. It applies to all officers.
    e. The OES prepares officers and warrant officers for increased responsibilities and successful performance at the next higher level. It provides pre-commissioning, branch, functional area, leader-development and pre-command training and education that prepares officers to lead platoon, company, battalion, and higher level organizations. It also produces technically and tactically competent commissioned warrant officer leaders for assignment to platoon, detachment, company, battalion, and higher-level organizations. The OES consists of branch-immaterial and branch-specific courses that provide progressive and sequential training throughout an officer's career. Regardless of branch affiliation, functional area, or specialty, the common thread which ties all OES courses together is common-core training. Common-core training is approved by TRADOC and incorporated into OES courses. Army Regulation 350-1 prescribes how the Army will create efficient and effective education. Army Regulation 350-1 prescribes how the Army will create efficient and effective education. The O-grade and Warrant Officer Learning Continuums are shown in Figures 15-4 and 15-5.

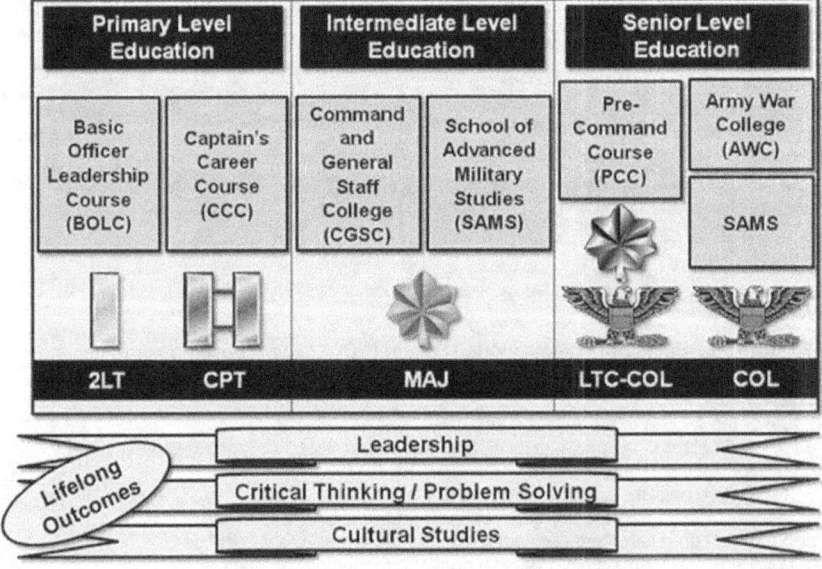

Figure 15-4. Officer Learning Continuum

ARMY TRAINING AND LEADER DEVELOPMENT

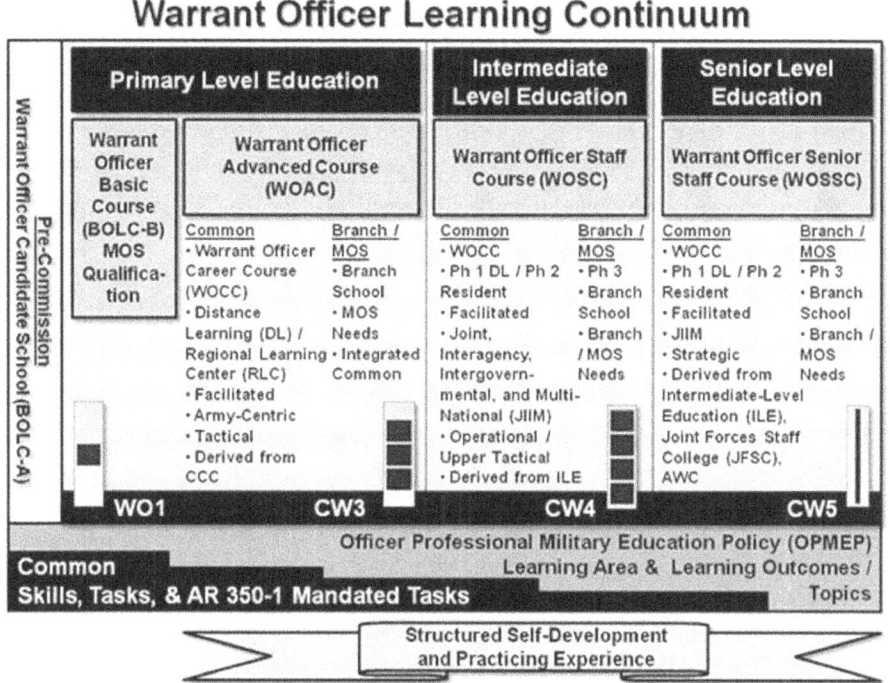

Figure 15-5. Warrant Officer Learning Continuum

15-16. Civilian Training and Leader Development
Civilian leader development is a continuous process accomplished through a blend of experience and work assignments, formal training and education, and self-development as individuals progress from entry to senior level positions. The Army develops the members of the Civilian Corps so they can effectively lead and operate in the Army's complex environment, as integral partners in the Army profession. Civilians provide mission-essential capability, stability, continuity, and leadership and are committed to Army values in the performance of their duties. Civilians serve and lead in the generating and operating force in garrison or deployed, manage significant programs at the highest levels, and make decisions that impact the overall success of the Army on a daily basis.

    a. Civilian functional training is the process of providing Army employees the opportunity to enroll in a planned and coordinated course or program of study. Programs available include: scientific; professional; technical; mechanical; trade; clerical; fiscal; administrative; or other fields. The purpose is to improve individual and organizational performance and assist in achieving the Army's mission and performance goals.

HOW THE ARMY RUNS

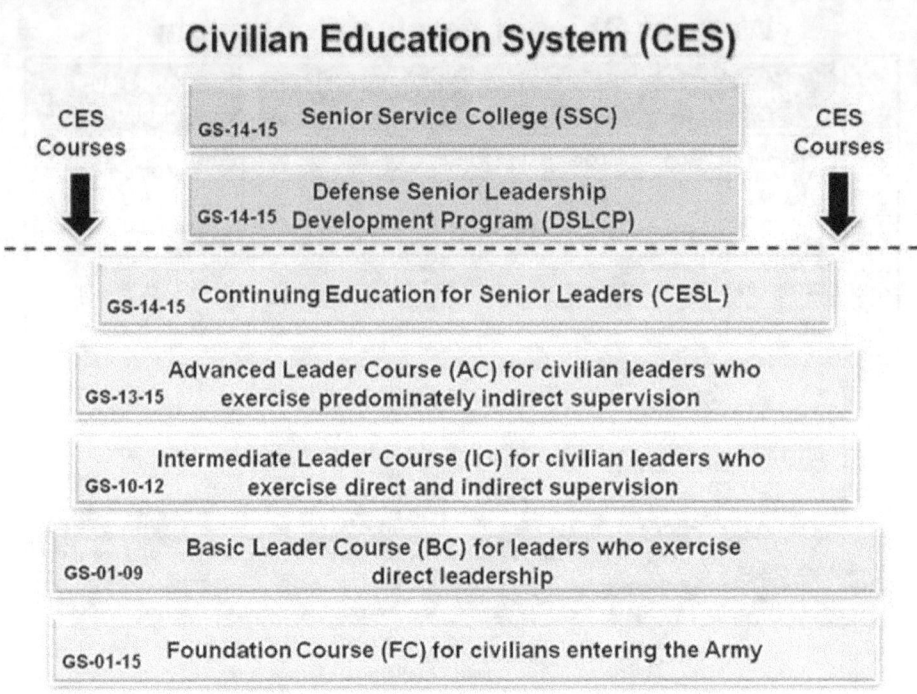

Figure 15-6. Civilian Education System (CES)

b. Functional training includes Competitive Professional Development (CPD). CPD is a planned, systematic, and coordinated program of professional development that supports the Army's organizational goals and mission. It encompasses functionally tailored developmental opportunities in academia, business/industrial settings, or in other strategically planned career enhancing developmental assignments that have been identified in an approved Career Program Master Training Plan (MTP) or Individual Development Plan (IDP). Training may be identified as short- or long-term and funded from various sources. Short-Term Training (STT) is training of 120 calendar dates or less. It includes professional workshops, seminars, and university courses. Long-Term Training (LTT) is training that exceeds 120 calendar days. It encompasses training or education to which an employee is assigned on a continuous, full-time basis for more than 120 calendar days. The assignment may be at either government or non-government facilities. They may include both formal training programs and strategically planned career assignments.

c. The CPD program includes Academic Degree Training (ADT), developmental assignments, Training-with-Industry (TWI), and various other G-37/TRV and/or Functional Chief Representatives' sponsored training and developmental opportunities. ADT must be related to the performance of the employee's official duties and part of a planned, systematic, and coordinated program of professional development, endorsed by the Army, and received from an accredited college or university. Developmental assignments provide employees an opportunity to enhance their competencies by performing duties in other occupational, functional, or organizational elements. Such assignments enhance employees understanding of other operations, systems, and relationships. The length of assignments may vary, but must have a well-defined learning objective and be established in conformance with all applicable civilian personnel management regulations. TWI is a non-degree producing program designed to provide

ARMY TRAINING AND LEADER DEVELOPMENT

training and/or skills in best business procedures and practices not available through existing military or advanced civilian schooling programs for identifiable DOD requirements.

d. CES (Figure 15-6) offers a series of progressive and sequential leader education courses. The courses are targeted towards the civilian's grade, and are intended to be completed through the entirety of the civilian's career. The program, requirements and eligibility are codified in AR 350-1. The goal of the CES is to prepare agile and innovative civilians who can lead during times of change and uncertainty; are prepared for the rigors of service as multi-skilled leaders; and are armed with the values, skills, and mindset to serve as competent, resilient supervisors and managers. A brief description of CES courses follows:

(1) Supervisor Development Course (SDC). SDC is an online course that is required for all supervisors of Army civilians. It provides supervisors and managers with personnel administration skills such as work management and basic supervision. New supervisors are required to take the course within 1 year of appointment, and experienced supervisors are required to take the course as refresher training every 3 years.

(2) Action Officer Development Course (AODC). AODC is an online course that describes "staff work" as it is generally practiced Army-wide. The AODC covers the following topics:
(a) Organization and management
(b) Conducting completed staff work
(c) Managing time and priorities
(d) Conducting meetings and interviews
(e) Solving problems and making decisions
(f) Communications
(g) Writing to the Army standard
(h) Coordination
(i) Conducting briefings
(j) Ethics

(3) Manager Development Course (MDC). MDC includes modules in the following: organizational culture; time management; objectives and plans; problem solving and decision making; planning, programming, and budgeting; manpower management; communications; information technology applications; the Army Environmental Program (AEP); Equal Employment Opportunity (EEO); professional ethics; internal management control; and Army family team building.

(4) The Foundation Course (FC) is an on-line course. The course focuses on "lead self" competencies and has important information for new Army civilians. This course is required for all Army civilians hired after 30 September 2006.

(5) The Basic Course (BC) is a blended learning course, with an on-line and resident phase (2 weeks). The course focuses on "lead teams/projects" competencies, and is the primary leader development course for civilians in grades GS 1-9 and comparable pay grades and bands.

(6) The Intermediate Course (IC) is a blended learning course, with an on-line and resident phase (3 weeks). The course focuses on "lead people" competencies, and is the primary leader development course for civilians in the grades GS 10-12 and comparable pay grades and bands.

(7) The Advanced Course (AC), is a blended learning course, with an on-line phase and resident phase (4 weeks). The course focuses on "lead organizations/programs" competencies, and is the primary leader development course for civilians in the grades GS 13-15 and comparable pay grades and bands.

(8) Continuing Education for Senior Leaders (CESL). CESL is designed to meet the needs of senior civilians who want continuing education on major Army issues, hot topics, and strategic direction. The course focuses on "lead the institution" competencies, and also emphasizes strategic thinking, external awareness, vision, and a global perspective. CESL consists of a dL phase and a 4.5 day resident phase.

(9) Senior Service College (SSC). SSC is at the apex of CES and prepares civilians for positions of greatest responsibility in the DOD. SSC provides advanced level educational opportunities for those who have completed CES training through the AC or equivalent training. Eligible candidates are Army civilians in a permanent appointment to GS-14/15, or pay band equivalent, with career status and at least 3 years as a full-time Army civilian. Attendance is a competitive process and a HQDA Board makes selections. Like the officer corps, civilians graduating from SSC are centrally placed in a position of greater responsibility in another assignment or organization where they can apply the advanced education they have received.

HOW THE ARMY RUNS

(10) Defense Executive Leader Development Program (ELDP). ELDP provides department and interagency personnel the opportunity to participate in an exceptional joint and enterprise-wide civilian leadership training and development experience. The objective of this 10-month program is to promote greater understanding of the overall DOD mission and culture, provide hands-on leadership training that parallels selected military training, and ensure cross-component exposure. The program is offered annually, and provides a series of learning and training experiences that blend experiential and academic learning, with hands-on exercises focused on the role of the warfighter. Program activities are conducted both in the U.S. and overseas.

(11) Defense Senior Leader Management Program (DSLDP). DSLDP is the premier civilian leader development program for DOD. DSLDP institutes a competency-based approach to the deliberate development of senior civilian leaders with the enterprise-wide perspective needed to lead organizations and programs, and achieve results in the JIM environment.

15-17. Self-Development

Learning is a lifelong process. Institutional, organizational, and operational training alone cannot provide the insight, intuition, imagination, and judgment needed in combat. The gravity of the Army profession requires comprehensive self-study and training. In no other profession is the cost of being unprepared so high. Soldiers, civilians and leaders at all levels continually study the profession in preparation to fight and win our Nation's wars. This requires commanders at all levels to create an environment that encourages subordinates to establish personal and professional development goals. Further refinement of those interests should occur through personal mentoring by commanders and first line leaders. Applications of battle-focused officer, NCO, and civilian professional development programs are essential to leader development. Exploiting reach-back, dL, and continuing education technologies support these programs. Self-development is continuous and should be emphasized in both institutional and operational assignments. Successful self-development requires a team effort. Self-development starts with an assessment of individual strengths, weaknesses, potential, and developmental needs. Commanders and leaders provide feedback to enable subordinates to determine the reasons for their strengths and weaknesses. Together, they prioritize self-development goals and determine courses of action to improve performance.

   a. Self-development is a planned process involving the leader and the subordinate being developed. Self-development focuses on maximizing individual strengths, minimizing weaknesses, and achieving individual development goals. Self-development:
   (1) Enhances previously acquired skills, knowledge, behaviors, and experience
   (2) Contributes to personal development
   (3) Highlights the potential for progressively more complex and higher-level assignments.
   b. Initial self-development is very structured and generally narrow in focus. The focus broadens as individuals understand their strengths and weaknesses, determine their individual needs, and become more experienced. Each Soldier's and civilian's knowledge and perspective increases with experience, institutional training, and operational assignments. It is accelerated and broadened by specific, goal-oriented self-development actions.

15-18. Mobilization Training Base

The mobilization training base is tasked to ensure that Soldiers arrive in theater, ready to fight as teams or individual replacements. It must provide combat-ready Soldiers proficient in those skills that ensure their immediate contribution and survival as members of teams, crews, or units in a theater of operations. A detailed process for the execution of the mobilization training base is discussed in Chapter 6 (Planning for Mobilization and Deployment).

   a. Levels of Mobilization. The training base will accomplish its task by planned expansion geared to varying levels of mobilization. During Presidential Reserve Call-Up (PRC) and partial mobilization, existing USATCs and service schools are augmented by elements of USAR Divisions (institutional training). Reserve reception battalions are also activated during phased mobilization to augment reception stations. USAR assets scheduled to expand or augment the training base are under the peacetime control of USARC, but placed under the command of TRADOC during the establishment and execution of the mobilization training base. Primary planning emphasis for mobilization expansion of the training base is on partial mobilization, with pre-deployment MOS/AOC certification of mobilized IRR members the primary mission.

ARMY TRAINING AND LEADER DEVELOPMENT

   b. PRC and Partial Mobilization. During PRC and Partial Mobilization, all peacetime training programs continue, with the IRR in-processing certification training mission being added.
   c. Mobilization Planning Guidance. Detailed planning guidance for mobilization is contained in the Army Mobilization and Operation Planning and Execution System (AMOPES) and TRADOC Mobilization and Operations Planning and Execution System (TMOPES). AMOPES provides a source document for issuing policies, procedures, guidance, and planning assumptions for the functional areas of training, exercises, mobilization, deployment, employment, sustainment, and expansion of forces beyond the approved force structure, redeployment, demobilization, and reconstitution of Army forces.

Section VI
Training in Units

15-19. General
   a. The Army's mission is to provide trained and ready forces and capabilities to the Combatant Commanders (CCDR) in support of the National Security and Defense Strategies. The Army's strategic goals are to remain relevant and ready by providing the Joint Force Commander with essential capabilities to dominate across the full range of military operations. Army leaders and units must be ready to perform with JIIM team members in a contemporary operating environment against an adaptive enemy. In the absence of a directed mission, commanders must prepare their unit to perform those core missions for which the unit was doctrinally designed to execute across the full range of military operations. The Army's training challenge is to optimize, synchronize, and support training in schools, training in units, and self-development to produce forces ready to respond across the full range of military operations. Unit commanders have two major training responsibilities:
   (1) Develop Soldiers/leaders for future responsibilities
   (2) Prepare their unit to accomplish the assigned mission.
   b. The challenges of today's operational environments require a change in the Army mindset. Army forces must be trained to conduct full spectrum operations under the conditions of any operational environment, anywhere along the spectrum of conflict. The Army must train, organize, and develop capabilities for stability operations with the same intensity and focus that it does for combat operations.
   c. To be successful in future operations, the Army cannot look at operations today as temporary interruptions in preparing for major combat operations against a near-peer enemy. Nor can it afford to view operations dominated by the offense and defense and those dominated by stability as either/or propositions. They usually occur simultaneously. Army forces must be well-trained and able to deploy rapidly to conduct and win engagements and wars while remaining ready to conduct sustained stability operations. Similarly, in operations dominated by stability they must remain prepared to conduct offensive and defensive operations. The predominate operation; offense, defense, or stability, is determined by the situation, objectives, or conditions to be achieved, desired end state, and level of violence. Commanders consider the simultaneous execution of these three elements of full spectrum operations in their mission analysis.
   d. Leaders in joint units (e.g., Joint Task Forces (JTF), Joint Force Land Component Commands (JFLCC), and CCMD HQ) manage training using procedures in the Chairman of the Joint Chiefs of Staff Training Manual (CJCSM) 3500.03. Leaders in Army units (e.g., TDA units and MTOE units within ACOMs and ASCCs) manage training using procedures in ADP 7-0 and the ATN, which support and are consistent with joint training management procedures. Training and readiness oversight/support is provided through the Administrative Control (ADCON) chain. Leaders in Army units will:
   (1) Use an Army-approved automated system, like the Digital Training Management System, to manage training.
   (2) Focus training on the Standardized METL.
   (3) Plan and execute training events that enable the unit to build and sustain Soldier, leader, and unit proficiency in mission essential tasks. The CATS and STRAC strategies are the doctrinal templates of training events, frequency, and duration that a commander uses in developing unit training guidance, strategy, and calendars. The critical training events in CATS and STRAC are the common building blocks for the commander's plan.
   (4) Minimize risk in training activities by conducting a composite risk assessment when planning all training events.

HOW THE ARMY RUNS

(5) Manage activities so that training land is protected, rehabilitated, and maintained.
(6) Given a directed mission, use available time to rehearse mission execution.
(7) Assess performance in training and operations, and provide feedback to unit personnel and Army lessons learned processes.

15-20. Organization for Training in Units

a. Troop units (e.g., FORSCOM; U.S. Army Europe (USAREUR); Eighth U.S. Army (EUSA); U.S. Army South (USARSO); USASOC; and U.S. Army Pacific (USARPAC) are all tasked to organize, equip, station, train, and maintain the readiness of assigned units.

b. AMC. AMC's mission is to provide superior technology, acquisition support, and logistics to ensure dominant land force capability for Soldiers, the U.S. and our allies. The training mission for AMC is directed toward specialized training of personnel in the materiel area, to include planning for and conducting NET in coordination with FORSCOM, TRADOC, and other commands. AMC is further tasked to assist TRADOC and FORSCOM on matters associated with supply and maintenance concepts, doctrine, training, and individual and collective training products. The education and training products produced must be IAW TRADOC policy.

c. MEDCOM. The MEDCOM's mission is to provide, sustain, and enhance Soldier health. The command is responsible to train, develop, and equip the medical force supporting the Army and to deliver leading edge health services. The AMEDD center and school is responsible for the execution of the training management function for the AMEDD. It provides training and education to all AMEDD personnel, on a worldwide basis and provides standardized Training Support Packages (TSP) on common medical tasks for use throughout the Army.

15-21. Training of Soldiers and Leaders in Units (ADP 7-0, Training Units and Developing Leaders, August 2012)

a. There are 11 principles of training.
(1) Commanders and other leaders are responsible for training
(2) NCOs train individuals, crews, and small teams
(3) Train to standard
(4) Train as you will fight
(5) Train while operating
(6) Train fundamentals first
(7) Train to develop operational adaptability
(8) Understand the operational environment
(9) Train to sustain
(10) Train to maintain
(11) Conduct multi-echelon and concurrent training

b. There are seven principles of leader development
(1) Lead by example
(2) Take responsibility for developing subordinate leaders
(3) Create a learning environment for subordinate leaders
(4) Train leaders in the art of mission command
(5) Train to develop adaptive leaders
(6) Train leaders to think critically and creatively
(7) Train your leaders to know their subordinates and their families

15-22. STP

Training Publications (TP) are Army Doctrine and Training Literature Program (ADTLP) publications that contain critical tasks and other training information used to: train Soldiers and serve to standardize individual training for the whole Army; provide information and guidance in conducting individual training in the unit; and aid the Soldier, officer, NCO, and commander in training critical tasks. STPs consist of Soldier's Manuals (SMs) (common task and branch specific) and Soldier's Manuals/Trainers Guides (SM/TG). STP 21-1 is the only SM projected to be printed under the ADTLP in the future. Training/Task (TD) proponents may publish branch-specific STPs. All other STPs can be published in electronic form through the ADTLP.

ARMY TRAINING AND LEADER DEVELOPMENT

a. STP. STPs support training of common, shared, and branch-specific individual critical tasks in the unit. Each task summary describes the minimum acceptable standard and the operational conditions under which the task must be performed, lists the references Soldiers need to master the task, and provides a guide to assess hands-on performance. Proponent schools develop branch-specific STPs that provide conditions, standards, and performance information to support training and evaluation of tasks at each skill level.

b. Training Guide (TG). The TG is a tool to guide the unit trainers and individual Soldiers in establishing an individual training plan. TGs give commanders and unit trainer's information needed to plan and conduct Soldier training and evaluations in the unit.

15-23. Collective Training

a. Collective training requires interaction among individuals or organizations to perform tasks, actions, and activities that contribute to achieving mission-essential task proficiency. Collective training includes performing collective, individual, and leader tasks associated with each training objective, action, or activity. Unit training occurs at home station, maneuver CTCs, and mobilization training centers. It also takes place in joint training exercises and while operationally deployed. Unit training develops and sustains an organization's readiness by achieving and sustaining proficiency in performing mission-essential tasks. Installations ensure units have access to the training enablers needed to enhance readiness. This training can be conducted in any or all of the live, virtual, constructive, or gaming environments.

b. Collective training refers to developing in a group of Soldiers those interdependencies and teamwork that go to make up team performance. The terms "collective training" and "unit training" cannot be used interchangeably. Unit training includes collective and individual training (the training of Soldiers and leaders). The primary features of collective training are that it is decentralized and performance-oriented. Performance-oriented collective training prepares units to perform the same tasks or missions that they will do in wartime, and execute them well enough to ensure success on the battlefield. The performance objective is the basis of the performance-oriented approach. Leaders conduct collective training to attain the objective, to include the tasks, conditions, and evaluation standards. Leaders use standards to determine the unit's ability to accomplish the task and measure standards in GO/NO GO terms. Leaders use the evaluation to develop timely remedial training programs. The Army provides units with training products (e.g., CATS, battle drills, exercises, TSPs, short-range unit training strategies, and training aides, devices, simulators, and simulations) to assist in this training.

15-24. Composite Risk Management (CRM)

a. FM 5-19, CRM, defines CRM as the Army's primary decision-making process for identifying hazards and controlling risks across the full spectrum of Army missions, functions, operations, and activities.

b. Unidentified and unmanaged threats and risks impede successful Army missions, undermine readiness, decrease morale, and deplete resources. The holistic approach of CRM provides commanders a tool to recognize, evaluate, eliminate, and control all the diverse threats and risks to mission execution. The underlying principle of CRM is that a loss is a loss. The loss can be either one of the following:

(1) Tactical (threat-based) loss.
(2) An accidental (hazard-based) loss.
(3) A loss due to terrorism, suicide, homicide, assault, sexual assault, illness, or even substance abuse.

c. The training mission cannot be considered fully successful if it is not accomplished with appropriate risk mitigation. The principles of integration and composite risk management have special relevance to the training situation. Commanders must integrate safety as a training management factor from the moment the mission is defined and the Standardized METL developed. When safety is realistically integrated in training, the benefits extend to the garrison environment, off-duty activities, and most importantly, to the combat theater. The Mishap Risk Management Process is used to identify, evaluate, and manage risks to missions, personnel, equipment, and the environment during peacetime, contingency operations and wartime due to safety and occupational health factors, design and construction of equipment, and other mishap factors

d. The Mishap Risk Management Process is the process of: identifying and assessing hazards; determining their risk; developing, evaluating and selecting controls; making risk decisions; and

HOW THE ARMY RUNS

implementing and managing those decisions to improve operational effectiveness and conserve Army resources. The process consists of the following five steps:
  (1) Identify hazards
  (2) Assess hazards to determine risk
  (3) Develop possible countermeasures and make risk decisions
  (4) Implement controls
  (5) Supervise and evaluate

  e. The risk assessment consists of the first two steps of the risk management process. In Step 1, individuals identify the hazards potentially encountered in executing an activity. In Step 2, leaders determine the impact of each hazard on the activity. The risk assessment provides for enhanced situational awareness. This awareness builds confidence and allows Soldiers, civilians, and organizations to implement timely, efficient, and effective protective control measures.

  f. Steps 3 through 5 are the essential follow-through actions to manage risk effectively. In these steps, leaders balance risk against costs and take appropriate actions to eliminate unnecessary risk. During execution, leaders continuously assess the risk to the overall mission and to those involved in the task. Finally, leaders and individuals evaluate the effectiveness of controls and provide lessons learned so that others may benefit from their experience.

  g. The U.S. Army Combat Readiness/Safety Center is the Army Lead Agent for Safety. Their website is at https://safety.army.mil/Default.aspx.

15-25. MTPs and Drills
There are MTPs for each type of Table of Organization and Equipment (TOE) platoon, company, battalion, and combined arms task force, and brigade, division, and corps staffs. The MTPs provide a clear description of "what" and "how" to train to achieve critical wartime mission proficiency for each unit echelon. Each MTP contains mission outlines, sample situational and field training exercises (STXs and FTXs), and comprehensive detailed training and evaluation outlines. The MTPs provide other training management aids such as leader tasks, resource requirements, and evaluation methods. They also include matrices linking collective tasks to missions, references to collective tasks, drills/ collective tasks to individual tasks, and STXs to missions. These products are also available in digitized format in the digital library.

15-26. CTC Program
  a. Mission. The CTC program consists of: the National Training Center (NTC), Fort Irwin, CA; the Joint Readiness Training Center (JRTC), Fort Polk, LA; the Joint Multinational Readiness Center (JMRC), Hohenfels, Germany; and the Mission Command Training Program at Fort Leavenworth, KS. The CTC Program objectives are to: increase unit readiness; develop battlefield leaders; embed doctrine; provide feedback on unit tactical effectiveness to participants; and provide data to improve DOTMLPF-P input to the combat and training development processes. AR 350-50, The CTC Program, establishes Army policies for the management of the CTC program. The CTC program provides realistic joint and combined arms training, according to Army and joint doctrine and approximates actual combat. CTC rotations are integrated into operationally deploying unit training schedules in synchronization with the Army force generation cycle and often serve as mission rehearsal sites. The CTC Program:
  (1) Provides commanders, staffs, and Soldiers an operational experience focused on leader development.
  (2) Produces bold, innovative leaders through stressful tactical and operational exercises.
  (3) Increases unit readiness for deployment and warfighting.
  (4) Embeds doctrine throughout the Army.
  (5) Provides feedback to the Army and joint participants to improve warfighting.
  (6) Provides a data source for lessons learned to improve DOTMLPF-P domains to win in combat.
  b. Rigor. During a CTC experience, commanders will fight with the equipment they would expect to take to war during their command tenure. CTC's achieve rigor by:
  (1) Training to standard.
  (2) Conducting doctrinally based AARs focused on performance, which enable Soldiers and leaders to discover for them what happened, why it happened, and how to sustain strengths and improve weaknesses.
  (3) Stressing all Battlefield Operating Systems (BOS) in decisive ground combat operations.

ARMY TRAINING AND LEADER DEVELOPMENT

 (4) Providing a freethinking, opportunities-based, OPFOR with an equal chance to win.
 (5) Developing tactical scenarios where the outcome is not assured.
 (6) Ensuring consequences of tactical decisions are fully played out.
 (7) Retraining to underscore the unit's adherence to standards and mastery of the task. Retraining is not an indication of failure.
  c. NTC. NTC provides realistic joint and combined arms training focused on developing Soldiers, leaders, and units of America's Army for success on the 21st Century battlefield. The NTC trains brigade combat teams and elements of functional and multi-functional brigades in full-spectrum operations against a hybrid threat. It also provides DOTMLPF-P feedback to improve the Army's practices and policies.
  d. JRTC. The JRTC provides realistic joint and combined arms training focused on developing Soldiers, leaders, and units of our nation's joint contingency forces for success on future battlefields. JRTC trains up to a brigade combat team and elements of functional and multi-functional brigades, and special operations forces in full-spectrum operations against a hybrid threat. Training occurs under tough, realistic, combat-like conditions across a wide range of likely tactical operations and mission rehearsal exercises capable of full integration into higher level exercises and scenarios. It also provides DOTMLPF-P feedback to improve the Army's practices and policies.
  e. JMRC. The JMRC provides realistic joint and combined arms training focused on developing Soldiers, leaders, and units for success on current and future battlefields. The JMRC trains up to a brigade combat team and elements of functional and multi-functional brigades in full spectrum operations. Although not part of the CTC program, JMRC trains allied military units deploying to support Operation Enduring Freedom (OEF) and as part of USAREUR theater engagements. It also provides DOTMLPF-P feedback to improve the Army's practices and policies.
  c. MCTP. MCTP is the Army's capstone CTC. MCTP supports realistic, stressful training and leader development for Army Force/ASCCs and corps, division, and brigade commanders and their staffs to assist the CSA in fulfilling his obligation to provide trained and ready units to win decisively on the modern battlefield and to conduct contingency operations worldwide. MCTP conducts full spectrum operations and mission rehearsal computer-assisted command post exercises at the mid-to-high intensity level of combat. The MCTP also provides a vital source of experience-based information and data essential to DOTMLPF-P to improve the Army's practices and policies, and supports contingency operations and deployed unit training.
  g. CTC Training Strategy. Unit CTC rotations are linked to the Army force generation cycle. Generally, all Deploying Expeditionary Forces (DEF) units execute a CTC rotation approximately 90 days prior to their Latest Arrival Date (LAD). Contingency Expeditionary Forces (CEF) brigade combat teams execute a CTC rotation nine to twelve months into the Army force generation cycle. Corps and division headquarters execute a maneuver CTC supported full spectrum exercise once in their Army force generation cycle.

15-27. Unit Training Management

  a. The foundation for Army training and education is found in Army Doctrine Reference Publication (ADRP) 3-0, which augments the unified land operations doctrine established in Army Doctrine Publication (ADP) 3-0, Unified Land Operations. This manual expands the discussion on the overarching guidance on unified land operations and the Army's core competencies of combined arms maneuver and wide area security. It accounts for the uncertain and ever-changing nature of operations and recognizes that military operations are foremost a human undertaking. It constitutes the Army's view of how to conduct prompt and sustained operations on land and sets the foundation for developing the other principles, tactics, techniques, and procedures detailed in subordinate doctrine publications.
  b. Effective training programs and exercises must be designed to get the most use from available resources. The central challenge for the next several years is to get the Army back in balance, where it generates forces trained and ready for decisive operations at sustainable levels. According to Army doctrine, decisive operations require versatile, adaptive units and tough, flexible leadership. These qualities develop first and foremost from training that prepares individuals and units for challenging operational environments. Managing training for unified land operations challenges leaders at all echelons.
  c. Training for offensive and defensive tasks develops discipline, endurance, unit cohesion, tolerance for uncertainty, and mutual support. It prepares Soldiers and units to address ambiguities inherent in

HOW THE ARMY RUNS

stability and defense support of civil authorities tasks as well. However, operational experience demonstrates that forces trained exclusively for offensive and defensive tasks are not as proficient at stability tasks as those trained specifically for stability tasks. For maximum effectiveness, tasks for stability and defense support of civil authorities require dedicated training, similar to training for offensive and defensive tasks. Likewise, forces involved in protracted stability or defense support of civil authorities require intensive training to regain proficiency in offensive or defensive tasks before engaging in large-scale combat operations. Effective training reflects a balance among the elements of decisive action that produce and sustain proficiency in all the tasks.

d. Training Management. Training management is the process used by Army leaders to identify training requirements and subsequently plan, prepare, execute, and assess training. It identifies the related resources needed to conduct and evaluate training. It involves all echelons and applies to every unit in the Army regardless of strength, mission, organization, or equipment. Training management must work in unison with other unit programs to achieve excellence in training. ADP 7-0 applies to all leaders at all organizational levels. Leaders include officers, warrant officers, NCOs, and Army civilians in leadership positions. ADP 7-0 applies to the Active Army, ARNG/ARNG of the U.S., and USAR unless otherwise stated. It has application for every type of organization.

e. Army Training Management Publications. The ADP 7 series manuals, TRADOC PAM 350 series pamphlets, and AR 350-1 establish the doctrine and provide guidance for the Army unit training management system. The manuals provide commanders with a management system they can use to: plan training; take necessary resource actions; and evaluate Soldier and unit proficiency, training, and training management. They describe long-range, short-range, and near-term planning and related resource actions. Execution of training, evaluation, and organizational assessment are also described. The methods and examples presented in these manuals have proved successful in units throughout the Army

f. Standardized METL. Units will have only one Standardized METL, and units will train to only one Standardized METL at a time. Non-deployed commanders, in dialogue with their commander, will determine the Standardized METL supporting tasks and the operational environment in which they will train during their Army force generation cycle.

g. DTMS. DTMS provides unit commanders with automation support to facilitate the execution of the training management process described in FM 7-0, ADP 3-0, and other related documents. It integrates key management functions, which support developing the Standardized METL to determine training requirements, planning, resourcing, scheduling, and the assessment of training in units. It assists in the management of training from company through corps, and serves as the Army's single, standard training management tool. Army organizations often provide Army forces within joint force formations. The DTMS accomplishes this by enabling unit commanders to use their existing office and tactical automation systems to:

(1) Access relevant training management documents and records, such as CATS, STPs, and drills.

(2) Perform nearly all analyses inherent in the training management process, such as ammunition forecasts and assessments.

(3) Identify resource requirements for training activities.

(4) Prepare and print required schedules, calendars, and reports.

h. Automated Systems Approach to Training. The DTMS uses data created by the ASAT/Training and Doctrine Development Configuration (TDDC) software application. The ASAT/TDDC is used by proponent developers to create task-based data and associated information necessary for units to effectively and efficiently conduct training. It compiles and displays a unit roll-up of training conducted through a series of customizable tools to track such things as weapons qualification, APFT scores, AR 350-1 mandated training, and deployment tasks from enlistment to retirement.

i. Battle Focus. The DTMS supports the Battle Focus concept by providing CATS, the Universal Joint Task List (UJTL), the Army Universal Task List (AUTL), Standardized METL, assignment of Battle Tasks, and supporting collective and individual tasks. It also provides for the development of non-documented local missions and tasks that may not appear in CATS. Further, it facilitates the synchronization of individual Soldier common and MOS tasks with each approved METL task as well as other supporting collective tasks associated with the METL.

ARMY TRAINING AND LEADER DEVELOPMENT

j. Planning. Training strategies, long and short-range plans, training calendars, coordination details, training schedules, and training resource projections are also developed based on proponent provided data and UTMC.

k. Execution/Assessment. Training and Evaluation Outlines (T&EOs) may be printed to assist in unit evaluations. Training Execution Matrices (TEM) can be exported to the Training Feedback Module (TFM), allowing evaluation of training either using paper T&EOs or the automated TFM. Evaluation results are then input fed back into the system. The commander's subsequent assessment of task preparedness and the recording of the actual resource expenditures are then completed in DTMS.

l. TSP. The TSP automatically extracts task, unit, and planning data from DTMS for the creation of a unit TSP to support all forms of training. TSPs developed with this module can be created at any level and shared with other units Army wide using this module. The TFM also extracts the same type of data for the purpose of providing an automated observer/controller tool. The TFM will provide task evaluation and after-action reporting data back into DTMS for unit commander assessments, to the CALL for archive and general information, and to the ASAT/TDDC for product improvement.

m. School. The DTMS has a schools management tool to resource and allocate seats for training events such as NET, digital systems training, safety courses, etc.

n. Reserve Component Automation System (RCAS). The RCAS is an automated information system that supports the decision-making needs of all commanders, staffs, and functional managers responsible for RC forces. The RCAS uses state-of-the-art office automation, telecommunications, databases, and processing capability to provide timely and accurate information for planning, preparation, and execution of mobilization and to improve the accomplishment of routine administrative demands. It is a self-sufficient system capable of exchanging data with related information systems. The RCAS will link all Army Reserve Component (ARNG and USAR) units, mobilization stations, and ACOM, ASCC, and DRUs. It will be able to interface with ATRRS.

15-28. Army Modernization Training (AMT)

Chapter 6 of AR 350-1 provides policy and procedures and assigns responsibilities for the planning and execution of new systems training. The regulation provides a process for the expeditious integration of equipment into the force structure through New Equipment Training (NET), displaced equipment training (DET), Doctrine and Tactics Training (DTT), and Sustainment Training (ST). New, improved, and displaced equipment is provided to Army units by planning, acquiring, and fielding a unit set (to include training capability) to a designated AC or RC unit (usually a brigade combat team) during a single modernization window. Doing so synchronizes all DOTMLPF-P activities required to field and support the individual systems that comprise unit sets. To the extent possible, a system-of-systems approach is used for capabilities/ requirements generation, materiel development and acquisition, manpower and personnel, funding, testing, fielding, transfer, training, sustainment, and support facilities. The Army Modernization Schedule, published biennially, identifies units being modernized and corresponding infrastructure and training base requirements. Unless exigencies require otherwise, lifecycle units are modernized when the unit reconstitutes, with training for operators provided previously in MOS-producing schools and training for unit leaders exported to their home station.

a. NET. NET is designed to support force integration and modernization through identification of personnel, training, and training devices required to support new or improved equipment. NET provides the initial transfer of knowledge on the operation and maintenance of this equipment from the materiel developer to the tester, trainer, supporter, and user. NET will assist commanders in achieving operational capability in the shortest time practical by training Soldiers/crews how to operate and maintain the new/improved equipment and by providing unit leaders with training support components needed to sustain proficiency of operators and maintainers on the new/improved equipment after NET. NET is tied to the System Acquisition Management Process (Chapter 11).

b. DET. DET applies to systems that are being replaced by new equipment, but remain in the inventory. Displaced equipment and its software, while not new to the Army, are new to the receiving unit. Because displaced equipment has established training base schools for operators and maintainers, units receiving displaced equipment may not need extensive training and may not need extensive formalized planning for that training. This determination will be made by the training developer, in coordination with the gaining command and the PM of the displaced system. Planning for and executing DET is similar to the process used in NET.

HOW THE ARMY RUNS

c. DTT. DTT is conducted in conjunction with NET or DET. The requirement for DTT will be based on two determinations- does the new/improved system significantly change the unit's how-to-fight doctrine, and does the unit need help learning how to employ the new/improved system to accomplish its wartime/design mission? DTT provides commanders, battle staffs, operators, and trainers with a doctrinal basis for employment of new or displaced materiel.

d. ST. ST sustains the proficiency of operators and maintainers of the new/improved system achieved during NET/DET or during training-base schools and sustain any proficiency of unit leaders to employ the new improved system achieved during DTT or training-base schools. Accordingly, it builds on the training and training support used for NET/DET and DTT. The training base shares the responsibility for ST by assuring that a pool of trained replacements is established to support the sustainment effort. The ultimate responsibility for ST, however, remains with the commander.

15-29. The Security Assistance Training Program (SATP)

a. SATP. Security assistance includes all training of international military personnel conducted within DOD activities under the Foreign Assistance Act (FAA) of 1961, as amended, and the Arms Export Control Act (AECA) as amended. The components of the SATP are the following:

(1) International Military Education and Training (IMET) program (under the FAA) represents education and training provided for which the military departments are reimbursed from foreign assistance appropriations.

(2) Foreign Military Sales (FMS) (under AECA) covers the sale of defense articles, services, and training to eligible foreign governments and international organizations. These sales are reimbursed as required by law.

(3) The Professional Military Exchange (PME) program, also under the FAA, authorizes the exchange of U.S. and foreign personnel on a one-for-one basis at MILDEP command and staff and war colleges.

(4) Unit Exchange, under the AECA, authorizes the provision of informal training and related support on a reciprocal basis.

b. HQDA Proponent. Deputy Assistant Secretary of the Army for Defense Exports and Cooperation is responsible for the development, coordination and implementation of policy and programs for the Army's security cooperation activities that include foreign military training. The CG, TRADOC, serves as implementing agent for development and implementation of the SATP. TRADOC is responsible for the central financial management and distribution of decentralized IMET and FMS training funds for all operating agencies as required by HQDA (AR 12-1, Security Assistance Training and Export Policy). The CG, TRADOC, will oversee, through the CAC Commander, the operation of WHINSEC. The CG, TRADOC, operates and administers the SATP through the Director, Security Assistance Training Directorate (SATD), dual-hatted as Director, Security Assistance Training Field Activity (SATFA).

c. Objectives of the SATP. The objectives of the SATP are to:

(1) Assist the foreign country in developing expertise and systems needed for effective management and operation of its defense establishment.

(2) Foster the foreign country's development of its own professional and technical training capability.

(3) Promote U.S. military rapport with the armed forces of foreign countries to operate in peacekeeping missions and in coalition environments.

(4) Promote better understanding of the United States, its people, political system, institutions, and way of life.

(5) Increase the international military student's (IMS) awareness of the U.S. commitment to the basic principles of internationally recognized human rights.

(6) Develop skills needed for effective operation and maintenance of equipment acquired from the United States.

ARMY TRAINING AND LEADER DEVELOPMENT

Section VII
The Training Support System

15-30. Training Support System (TSS)
   a. The TSS provides the foundation on which the Army training system runs. As described in AR 350-1, and ADP 7-0, it is the system of systems that provides networked, integrated, and interoperable training support capabilities that are necessary to enable operationally-relevant, Joint, Interagency, Intergovernmental, and Multinational (JIIM) training for Soldiers, units, and Army civilians anytime and anywhere. The TSS includes products (instrumentation and training aids, devices, simulators and simulations), services (training support operations and manpower) and facilities (ranges, simulation centers, mission training centers, training support centers) that are necessary for creating the conditions to realistically portray the operational environment and enable training strategies focused on a Standardized METL. These training enablers underpin the Army training strategies and institutional POIs by providing commanders with tools to execute Soldier, leader, battle staff, and unit collective training to standard at home station, CTCs, TRADOC Schools/CoEs, and while deployed.
   b. The TSS consists of five primary programs that complement each other and together generate the Army's TSS capability. The programs include the Sustainable Range Program (SRP), Mission Command Training Support Program (MCTSP), CTC Modernization (MOD), the Soldier Training Support Program (STSP), and the Training Information Infrastructure (TII) Program. Each TSS program will be defined by supporting functions or components that may include program policy and procedures, manpower, and Table of Distribution and Allowances (TDA) structure, modernization strategy, operations support functions and resources, facilities, connectivity, and management support systems.
      (1) The SRP is the Army's overall approach for improving the design, management, usage, and long-term sustainability of ranges. SRP is defined by its two core programs. The Range Program includes range modernization and range operations. The Training Land Program focuses on land management and maintenance through the Integrated Training Area Management (ITAM) process, training land acquisition, and SRP Outreach, which provides support to both SRP core programs. ITAM provides a Geospatial Information System (GIS) capability to support range modernization, range operations, and ITAM needs.
      (2) The MCTSP provides virtual and constructive training environments in support of combined arms training that replicates Army operations across the spectrum of conflict. This program supports MC training for individuals and for units ranging from company to corps, and at levels from tactical to JTF, ASCC, and JFLCC levels of command. The MCTSP creates training that helps the Army's leaders develop current, relevant MC instincts and skills. It supports Army Mission Command System (AMCS) training and battle command essential capabilities that empower individuals and small units and that allow junior leaders to prevail during decentralized operations. The MCTSP program provides the staff and trainers, facilities, infrastructure, and other resources necessary to support battle command training of Army, USAR, and ARNG formations. The MCTSP includes MC Training Capability operations and facilities, virtual and constructive TADSS, Army Games for Training (GFT), and Live, Virtual, Constructive (LVC) integration.
      (3) The STSP includes individual Soldier through crew level virtual and live TADSS, Training Support Center (TSC), and Virtual Training Facility (VTF) operations. STSP manages TADSS production and fabrication of training devices, manages loan and issuance of TADSS, provides instructor/operator support for specific virtual TADSS, and provides other TADSS support that enables the Mission Commander to execute individual and collective training at installations and TRADOC schools.
      (4) The CTC MOD provides modernization and life cycle technology refreshment of the Maneuver CTCs (NTC, JRTC, JMRC, and the Exportable Training Capability (ETC)) in support of Army Transformation. Modernization includes Opposing Forces (OPFOR), instrumentation, TADSS, and facilities to provide a realistic training environment for brigade combat teams in force-on-force and live fire scenarios. The CTC MOD ensures CTCs remain relevant by providing joint context to the operational environment and provides the doctrinally-based feedback, facilitating leader and unit training dictated in the Army force generation training cycle. Resultant training capability output produces trained and ready combat units, leaders, and Soldiers prepared for the spectrum of conflict in a Contemporary Operational Environment (COE) against a hybrid threat (Wide Area Security/Combined Arms Maneuver).
      (5) The TII Program consists of two primary components: the Army Training Information System (ATIS); and point of delivery systems for dL. ATIS includes the integration of Army training information

HOW THE ARMY RUNS

systems and provides an integrating architecture. Point of delivery systems for dL maintain and upgrade these systems.

15-31. Training Support System Management

a. The DCS, G-37 Training Simulations Division (DAMO-TRS) provides overall management and policy for TSS plans, programs, and budget. TRADOC manages the TSS Enterprise and provides executive agency support, to include TSS requirements validation. The IMCOM garrisons execute TSS in coordination with the TRADOC TSS Enterprise. The IMCOM HQ and regions oversee execution. USAREUR, USARPAC, and the ARNG execute TSS in coordination with the TRADOC Enterprise. The ACOMs/ASCCs/DRUs that are responsible for operational and institutional training maintain a staff that validates and prioritizes TSS requirements from their subordinate commands.

b. Enterprise Organization. The TRADOC organizations listed below represent the core of the TSS Enterprise and support DAMO-TRS in the following areas: policy development and dissemination; requirements development; integration validation and prioritization; resource allocation; and execution oversight and tasking.

(1) TRADOC's ATSC is the overall integrator of TSS. It manages the TSS Master Plan and database, and provides analytical support capability.

(2) TCMs (e.g., live, virtual, constructive, and gaming), aligned with each major TSS program, identify program requirements and support the planning, programming, budgeting, development and acquisition of products, facilities, and services to the field.

(3) TRADOC Schools/CoEs develop requirements that support their institutional/school Program of Instruction (POI) training, and, as a proponent, identify TSS requirements to support operational unit training.

c. Management Process. The TSS Management Process includes periodic Program Management Reviews to ensure TSS planning, programming, and execution is synchronized with current and future training needs. The Training Support Working Group (TSWG) provides oversight and facilitates the integration and decision forum for major TSS programs. The TSWG considers issues generated by management reviews and modernization reviews of each TSS program and identifies issues that must go forward to the DCS, G-3/5/7 TGOSC Council of Colonels or the TGOSC itself for review and action. The TSWG is co-chaired by the DCS, G-3/5/7 and TRADOC's Army Training Support Center. Voting members include TSS representatives from the ACOMs/ASCCs/DRUs TRADOC capability managers, and PEO STRI, TSS Modernization Reviews and Program Management Reviews meet semiannually. The TSWG meets immediately following the Program Management Reviews.

d. TSS Capability Assessment. The TSS undergoes continuous assessment to ensure capabilities support Army training strategies and the ACP.

(1) Assessment Metrics include:

(a) Mission Essential Requirements (MER) are products, services, facilities, and sustainment identified by the major TSS programs. The MERs define what is needed to support training strategies.

(b) Use Cases define the level of MER delivered to each location where TSS is executed. Each TSS major program sets the parameters by which use cases are determined.

(c) Bench Marks are derived from the ACP and reflect applicable PPBE cycles, normally by the fiscal year in which the MER is required at each Use Case.

(2) Assessment Process entails:

(a) Major assessments conducted biennially to support POM development. They are done by conducting TSS Theater In-process Reviews (IPRs) to determine TSS requirements based on the above metrics.

(b) The TRADOC TSS agencies biennial installation site visits.

(c) Proponent Service Schools' annual TSS Reviews to determine broad functional approaches to TSS by battlefield function.

ARMY TRAINING AND LEADER DEVELOPMENT

Section VIII
Summary and References

15-32. Summary

a. ADP 7-0, Training Units and Developing Leaders. This publication establishes the Army's key doctrine for training units and for developing leaders, on a rotational cycle and informed by the Army force generation priorities. It addresses the fundamentals of training modular, expeditionary, Army forces in an era of significant fiscal constraints.

b. Training mission and focus. Decisive action requires mentally agile leaders able to operate in any operational theme across the spectrum of conflict. Effective command and control focuses on commanders rather than staffs. Commanders, not staffs, drive effective decision-making. Commanders must be able to mass effects at decisive points and times and to accomplish assigned missions over time. Decentralized rather than centralized operations are the norm today and will likely remain so. All leaders, from the highest to the lowest levels, must understand the art and the science of operations and battle command. The training must focus on the unit's METL. Realistic, sustained, multi-echelon, integrated combined arms training must be continuously stressed at all levels. Every individual training and collective training program must be thoughtfully planned, aggressively executed, and thoroughly assessed.

(1) Battle Focus. Battle focus is the concept used to derive peacetime training requirements from wartime missions. Battle focus guides the planning, execution, and assessment of each organization's training program to ensure its members train as they are going to fight. Battle focus is critical throughout the entire training process and is used by commanders to allocate resources for training based on wartime mission requirements. METL provides a shared start point for training.

(2) Five training systems. This chapter discussed five training systems: policy, requirements, and resourcing; training development; training in schools; training in units; and training support. Training policy, requirements, and resourcing are the responsibility of the DCS, G-3/5/7, specifically the Director of Training (DAMO-TR). Resourcing necessitates some historically-related interfaces with other systems. The ARPRINT, for example, relies on input from ODCS, G-1 as well as DCS, G-3/5/7.

(3) TRADOC. TRADOC is the proponent for leader development and the center for establishing Army training standards worldwide. It develops policy and procedures for creating, implementing, and evaluating training and provides ongoing resident/nonresident training to AC and RC alike. This influence impacts the institutional, operational, and self-development training domains, following the guidance set forth in FM 7-0 and the 350-series regulations and pamphlets.

(4) FORSCOM. FORSCOM trains, mobilizes, deploys, sustains, transforms, and reconstitutes conventional forces. They are the lead for the Readiness Core Enterprise and manage the Army force generation process and its outputs. In addition, FORSCOM commands two CTC—NTC and JRTC.

(5) Training Support. The TSS ensures the provision of the materials, personnel, equipment, and facilities when and where needed to implement the training. It includes such functions as the reproduction and distribution of training products and materials, scheduling and resourcing training across all domains, and student record maintenance. Training support manages the distribution of training materials and services supporting the training base and unit training programs. It provides for the ability of Commanders and leaders to train their Soldiers.

(6) The future challenge.

The Army must prepare for a changing and uncertain future during a time of fiscal austerity… the focus on building that future force must be on developing adaptive and flexible leaders at all levels who are "the stewards" of Army professionalism and standards… while equipping them with advanced technology that brings greater mobility, lethality and survivability. Despite the more austere financial future, it is "essential" that the Army prepare to operate across a broader range of missions and regions in an environment that will require it to handle cultural and social challenges as much as its ability to physically dominate the battlefield.

GEN Raymond Odierno, CSA, 23 October 2012

HOW THE ARMY RUNS

15-32. References
a. Publications:
(1) Army Doctrine Publication (ADP) 3-0, Unified Land Operations, October 2011
(2) ADP 7-0, Training Units and Developing Leaders, August 2012
(3) Army Doctrine Reference Publication (ADRP) 3-0, Unified Land Operations, May 2012
(4) Army Regulation (AR) 5-13, Total Army Munitions Requirements Process and Prioritization System, December 2009
(5) AR 12-15, Joint Security Cooperation, Education and Training, January 2011
(6) AR 25-1, Army Knowledge Management and Information Technology, December 2008
(7) AR 25-30, The Army Publishing Program, March 2006
(8) AR 220-1, Army Unit Status Reporting and Force Registration, April 2010
(9) AR 350-1, Army Training and Leader Development, December 2009
(10) AR 350-2, Opposing Force (OPFOR) Program, April 2004
(11) AR 350-10, Management of Army Individual Training Requirements and Resources, September 2009
(12) AR 350-19, The Army Sustainable Range Program, August 2005
(13) AR 350-38, Policies and Management for Training Aids, Devices, Simulators and Simulations, March 2013
(14) AR 350-50, Combat Training Center Program, April 2013
(15) AR 525-29, Army Force Generation, March 2011
(16) AR 600-100, Army Leadership, March 2007
(17) AR 600-8-19, Enlisted Promotions and Reductions, April 2010
(18) AR 600-8-29, Officer Promotions, February 2005
(10) DA Pamphlet (DA Pam) 350-38, Standards in Training Commission, November 2012
(11) DA Pam 600-3, Commissioned Officer Professional Development and Career Management, February 2010
(12) DA Pam 600-25, U.S. Army Noncommissioned Officer Professional Development Guide, July 2008
(13) TRADOC Regulation 350-18, The Army School System (TASS), July 2010
(14) TRADOC Regulation 350-70, Systems Approach to Training Management, Processes, and Products, March 1999
(15) Army Training Strategy, 15 October 2012
(16) Army Leader Development Strategy 2013
(17) The U.S. Army Training Concept 2012-2020, 23 November 2010
(18) The U.S. Army Learning Model for 2015, 14 September 2010
(19) CSA Article, The Next Decade, Army Magazine, October 2010
b. Useful Links
(1) http://www.tradoc.army.mil
(2) http://www.apd.army.mil/
(3) http://www.tradoc.army.mil/dcsopst/sites.htm
(4) http://www.tradoc.army.mil/tpubs/pamndx.htm
(5) http://www.atsc.army.mil/ATSCnav.asp
(6) http://www.tradoc.army.mil/tadlp/index.htm
(7) http://www.adtdl.army.mil/
(8) http://www.dls.army.mil/
(9) https://rdl.train.army.mil/soldierPortal/soldier.portal
(10) http://www.army.mil/usapa/index.html
(11) https://forums.bcks.army.mil/secure/communitybrowser.aspx
(12) https://www.us.army.mil/suite/portal/index.jsp
(13) https://atn.army.mil
(14) https://www.atrrs.army.mil
(15) http://usacac.army.mil/cac2-t/index.asp

ARMY KNOWLEDGE MANAGEMENT

Chapter 16

Army Knowledge Management

Section I
Introduction

16-1. The Army Network and LandWarNet
LandWarNet must be capable, reliable, and trusted and to get there it has to be a single, secure, standards-based environment that ensures access at the point of need and enables global collaboration. The Chief Information Officer (CIO)/G-6 leads the LandWarNet modernization which will deliver timely, trusted, and shared information. The CIO/G-6 mission includes creating an environment where innovation and service empower Army and mission partners through an unsurpassed responsive, collaborative, and trusted information enterprise.
   a. End-to-End Capability. The Army Network is comprised of the operational network enterprise and installation components to create the end-to-end LandWarNet capability. Over the last decade, the Army invested heavily in augmenting and integrating LandWarNet's operational capabilities. During this same period, the enterprise and installation components of the network, which together comprise the institutional component of LandWarNet, have remained relatively stagnant, fostering significant disparities. As the Army shifts to a CONUS-based fighting force, the requirement to train with the same technology and procedures used in theater and the requirement for a smaller footprint in the area of operations mandate transformation of LandWarNet's institutional components. The Army must rebalance LandWarNet into an end-to-end network while maintaining readiness, guaranteeing interoperability, and minimizing cost.
   b. Modernize the Network. The network must be treated as a single entity, unified from the Global Information Grid (GIG) to the installation and to the farthest tactical edge. It must provide the same basic capabilities from home station to the dismounted Soldier in theater. The ultimate goal is to enable mission command, which empowers formations with unmatched lethality, protection and situational awareness to achieve tactical dominance. Achieving tactical dominance requires an overarching network architecture that connects all echelons from squad through Joint Task Force to ensure that leaders have the right information at the right time to make the best possible decisions. The Army must design, develop, acquire and field the network in a comprehensive, synchronized manner. The Army's CIO/G-6, in conjunction with the Assistant Secretary of the Army (Acquisition, Logistics and Technology) (ASA(ALT)), will modernize the network through Information Technology Management Reform (ITMR) initiatives that will achieve significant efficiencies and cost savings. The reforms will support the vision of a single, secure, standards-based network that aligns with the Joint Information Environment (JIE) White Paper (22 January 2013).
   c. LandWarNet 2020 & Beyond. Following the successful capability set approach used in the Mission Command (MC) domain, the Army will incrementally upgrade the institutional component of LandWarNet while synchronizing capabilities with the operational network. These upgrades, often transparent to end users, will provide significant capability improvements for Army leaders, network users, and network operators, while enhancing the security posture of the network. LandWarNet 2020 & Beyond will increase effectiveness (e.g., single sign-on access to applications and data repositories, and robust and always available collaborative capabilities), efficiency (e.g., command and control of the network through centralized network operations and synchronized network funding), and security (e.g., assured identity and access management, and continuous monitoring and risk assessment of the network security posture).

16-2. Information Management Transformation Implementation
   a. Network Capability Sets. The Army will pursue a capability set management construct for the network that will cut across functional areas. To realize the full operational capabilities of LandWarNet 2020 & Beyond, it is essential that Network Capability Sets (NCS) integrate operational and institutional requirements defined as Operational Capability Sets (OCS) and Institutional Capability Sets (ICS) respectively. The Army began fielding OCS in fall 2012. They are defined as MC hardware, applications,

HOW THE ARMY RUNS

communication transport, and services that support units and organizations while deployed. ICSs are defined as the hardware, applications, services and communications transport that support the Army business, installation management, and Army units and organizations. The ICS supports both Generating Forces and operational units as they train, prepare to deploy, and deploy. The operational units receive responsive support, while en route and forward deployed, from capabilities resident across various Army/DOD installations.

b. In the near term. NCS will focus on three Lines of Effort (LOE)—building capacity, improving security, and expanding enterprise services across the Army. Supporting each of these is a cross-cutting priority—implementation of network standards. To construct a single, secure, standards-based platform that reaches from every installation to the remotest operational location, uniform, Army-wide network standards are necessary and will aid integration of network solutions, serving as the foundation. Implementing network standards will help simplify operation, maintenance, and defense of the network.

(1) Build Capacity. This LOE is the backbone of the Army network and is focused on improving the Army's data processing and transmission capabilities. It is the foundation for all future ICS upgrades and the element on which nearly all other network modernization efforts will rely – to include operational (Joint/coalition/Army) and business perspectives. Proper capacity will ensure uniform accessibility, throughput, transmission speed, and reliability, no matter the location (operational theater, home station, Army and Joint training centers, and all data repositories).

(2) Improve Security. This LOE includes expanding visibility of the network (asset visibility and device control), defending the network against attack, mitigating security breaches, and defining command-and-control responsibilities for network defense.

(3) Enterprise Services. This LOE assures availability of information (data, voice, and video) and services to all authorized users across the Force. The Army must simplify and extend access to data, applications, collaboration tools, services and communications, and ensure that the network interoperates with all Joint, interagency, intergovernmental, and multinational (JIIM) partners. Enterprise services combine to provide capabilities to operational organizations.

Section II
Chief Information Officer / G-6 Roles and Responsibilities

16-3. Office of the CIO/G-6

The Army has consolidated the Army's CIO and the Army Staff G-6 as the Army CIO/G-6 to achieve enhanced standardization, compatibility, interoperability, security, compliance, and fiscal discipline to deliver a joint, Net-centric information enterprise enabling decision superiority Army-wide.

a. The Army CIO/G-6 is the principal staff assistant and advisor to the Secretary of the Army (SECARMY) and Deputy Secretary of the Army on Army Information Management (IM), pursuant to 10 U.S.C. 3014(c)(1)(D), including but not limited to the following: Information Enterprise (IE) networks and network-centric policies and concepts; Command, Control, Communications, and Computers (C4); non-intelligence space matters; and enterprise-wide integration of Army information matters. The CIO/G-6 sets the strategic direction for and supervises the execution of Army IM policies and programs, including the global network, network architecture, and information sharing policy. The CIO directs information resources management, including the allocation and obligation of IT capital assets in accordance with 40 USC, Subtitle III; and 44 USC 35 and 44 USC 36. The CIO is the principal official within Headquarters, Department of the Army (HQDA) with oversight responsibilities for all IT resources under the provisions of the Clinger-Cohen Act (CCA).

b. The Army CIO/G–6 is the principal advisor to the Chief of Staff of the Army, the Army Staff, Army Service Component Commands (ASCC), Army Cyber Command/Second U.S. Army, and combatant commands of unified and specified commands for IM, IT, and their impact on current and future Warfighting capabilities. This includes advice on all matters concerning enterprise information activities required to ensure the standardization, compatibility, security, interoperability, and fiscal discipline of enterprise information services supporting the Warfighter. CIO/G-6 responsibilities include:

(1) Serve as the Army's executive agent for LandWarNet to enhance the ability to reconcile current to future force LandWarNet capabilities, improve business agility, and achieve Warfighter decision superiority. The CIO is the single authority responsible and accountable for:

ARMY KNOWLEDGE MANAGEMENT

(a) Delivering structured, controlled, repeatable, and measurable processes that drive accountability and compliance for the management of the Army's information technology enterprise.
(b) Ensuring secure LandWarNet capabilities and services to Army leadership and Warfighters.
(c) Enabling agile responses to rapidly changing operational requirements for Army and Joint missions.
(2) Direct IM function within the DA, including:
(a) Develop the DA's IM strategy, policies, and guidance that are in compliance with laws, regulations, and standards.
(b) Oversee IM and IT resources planning, programming, budgeting, and execution;
(c) Develop and implement the IM and IT capital planning and investment-control strategy, including the design and operation of all major information resources management processes.
(d) Develop, coordinate, and implement an assessment process for Army IM programs, including compliance with IM policies, guidance, standards, and monitoring
(3) Develop and execute the Army's IM and IT strategy, policy, plans and programs; and oversee the execution of IM and IT policies and plans by other Army organizations.
(4) Monitor and advise on information and signal operations, network and communications security, force structure, and the equipping and employment of signal forces. Assess the impacts to the Warfighter of IM-related strategy, policies, plans, services, and programs. Advocate for and monitor the implementation of IM requirements on behalf of the Warfighter.
(5) Oversee the implementation and enforcement of Army global network requirements and operations to achieve standardization, compatibility, security, interoperability, and fiscal discipline of IM and IT services supporting the Warfighter.
(6) Provide policy, guidance, and resourcing for the Army's communication needs for all network layers, including top secret and higher levels of security, as well as access to coalition networks.
(7) Support ASA(ALT) through the development of policy on the acquisition of IM, IT, and information resources. Ensure that acquisitions are managed in a manner that implements CIO/G–6 policies and procedures to maximize value while assessing and managing the risks for acquiring IT.
(8) Establish, maintain, facilitate, and guide the implementation of the Army-wide Enterprise Architecture (EA).
(9) Prescribe Army strategy, policy, and portfolio management for Army bandwidth capabilities and activities.
(10) Serve as member of the Federal CIO Council and the DOD CIO Executive Board (EB).
(11) Chair the Army CIO EB.
(12) Develop, promulgate, and direct compliance with information security and information assurance policy.
(13) Review, coordinate, and co-certify the IT Budget in conjunction with the Assistant Secretary of the Army (Financial Management & Comptroller) (ASA(FM&C)).
(14) Represent the Army on the Committee on National Security Systems.
(15) Oversee the Army-wide implementation and modernization of LandWarNet.
(16) Prescribe Army Information Enterprise strategy, policy, portfolio management, architecture, and strategic communications that result in effective IT investments Army-wide.
(17) Serve as the Army-designated approval authority (DAA) for the certification and accreditation (C&A) of collateral top secret and below Army information systems.
(18) Provide policy and guidance to develop and maintain a competent military and civilian IT and cybersecurity workforce to support the Army's mission. Duties include serving as the functional chief for the ITM Career Program 34 (CP–34) and identifying strategic workforce issues that are critical to the life-cycle management and readiness of the Army's IT and cybersecurity professionals.
(19) Prescribe IT Portfolio Management (PfM) policy and oversee implementation of Mission Area (MA) IT portfolios to ensure they are aligned with Army enterprise solutions.
(20) Serve as the Army's lead for the Enterprise Information Environment Mission Area (EIEMA) to support the DOD EIEMA lead and ensure enterprise information environment efforts are traceable to, and fully enable, the required capabilities for the Warfighting and business MAs.
(21) Reduce the introduction of vulnerabilities and system interoperability performance problems by controlling and approving changes to the Army's authorized software baseline that constitutes its operational network.
(22) Serve as functional proponent for the Army enterprise portals.

HOW THE ARMY RUNS

(23) Serve as the functional proponent of Army Enterprise Architecture (AEA), to include establishing, implementing, leading, and managing AEA.

(24) Establish and oversee the Army Data Management Program (ADMP) to include the appointment of the Army Chief Data Officer.

(25) Provide oversight and direction for network-centric concepts and management, including the Army Networthiness Program.

(26) Serve as the functional proponent and primary interface with the Defense Information Systems Agency (DISA) on existing and emerging DOD enterprise services such as email, data center consolidation, collaboration, and unified communications.

(27) Serve as the proponent for the information systems supporting C4 and IT programs, including, but not limited to:

(a) Serve as the Army focal point for IT system issues (to include NSS). Receive, coordinate, and integrate these issues, ensuring the integration of systems-development efforts with cross functional or technical lines.

(b) Participate in and provide representation for Planning, Programming, Budgeting, and Execution (PPBE) process decision group; and exercise centralized oversight of IT expenditures for all appropriations, including formulating and defending the resources necessary to provide C4/IT to the Warfighter.

(c) Develop, coordinate, and manage the IT capital planning and investment management program.

(d) Recommend and coordinate new standards and ensure IT system conformance to the approved DOD IT Standards Registry (DISR); coordinate and support the priorities within IT for information system development-related activities; and secure adequate resource support.

(e) Coordinate resource requirements for IT support activities.

(f) Coordinate IT requirements relevant to Army Continuity of Operations (COOP) plans and systems that support survival, recovery, and reconstitution; and ensure essential information services in support of DA COOP are available to alternate sites of HQDA agencies, Army commands (ACOMs), and installations.

(g) Prescribe, in conjunction with the Office of the Administrative Assistant to the SECARMY (AASA), records management requirements in the life cycle of ISs, beginning at the initial milestone.

(h) Collaborate with the Deputy Chief of Staff, G–8 in the development of Command, Control, Communications, Computers, Intelligence, Surveillance, and Reconnaissance (C4ISR) positions presented at Functional Capabilities Boards, the Joint Capability Board, and the Joint Requirements Oversight Council.

(28) Lead and manage the Army Net-Centric Data Management Program and serve as the Army component data administrator under the DOD Data Administration Program.

(29) Ensure Army interoperability processes are structured to allow seamless transition for obtaining Joint Inter-operability Certification and synchronize the Army Portfolio Management Solution (APMS) with the DOD IT Portfolio Repository (DITPR).

(30) Establish annually, in coordination with Army Cyber Command and U.S. Army Network Enterprise Technology Command (NETCOM), the vision, direction, and architecture of Installation-Information Infrastructure Modernization Program (I3MP) for use by NECs in their requirements development efforts.

16-4. Army IT Governance

a. The Army CIO/G-6 hosts two primary governance boards that support the enterprise information environment mission area: the CIO EB and the CIO/G-6 Network Mission Area (NMA) general officer steering committee.

b. The CIO EB serves as a platform to share Army CIO/G-6 strategies, policies, actions, and guidance with ACOMs, ASCCs, Direct Reporting Units (DRU), and HQDA, as well as receive feedback and questions from the field. In addition, the CIO EB is a platform used to advocate the NMA decisions. Board membership consists of General Officers, Senior Executive Service, and other senior-level participants from Army Staff, ACOMs, ASCCs and DRUs.

c. The Network Mission Area General Officer Steering Committee (NMA GOSC) is chaired by the Army CIO. The NMA GOSC serves as a senior decision-making forum, ensuring that the strategic objectives of Army EIEMA support DOD's Joint Information Environment (JIE). The NMA GOSC ensures that validated requirements are traceable to and fully support the required capabilities of the Warfighting and Business Mission Areas. The NMA GOSC is a three-tiered structure with of two subcommittees:

ARMY KNOWLEDGE MANAGEMENT

(1) The NMA GOSC provides strategic guidance, enable the operational capabilities of, and recommend decisions encompassing three areas: Network security, Army Core Enterprise Services, and building Network capacity. The NMA GOSC conducts portfolio reviews in order to align requirements with the PPBE process. During the portfolio reviews, requirements will be validated against adherence to and compliance with strategic priorities, architecture integration, CCA criteria, capability gap and/or redundancy analysis, cost-benefit analyses, and/or other criteria. These reviews will inform processes such as Joint Capability Integration Development System (JCIDS), Defense Acquisition System, or other processes for appropriate action.

(2) The Director, CIO/G6 Architectures, Operations, Networks, and Space (AONS) chairs the Network Mission Area 1/2-Star Council.

(3) The Chief Integrator, CIO/G-6 AONS chairs the Network Mission Area Council of Colonels.

16-5. C4/IT Investment Strategy

The efficient and effective use of IT resources has a direct effect on the Army's ability to perform its missions. The Army CIO/G-6 manages IT investments and develops a coordinated, consolidated investment strategy. The IT planning process develops the IT Investment Strategy, recommending a prioritized list of IT investments and/or whether to continue, modify, or terminate an IT program/project according to mandates from the CCA. The recommended prioritization listing is a reference and support tool within Program Evaluation Groups (PEG) throughout the PPBE and acquisition processes. The prioritization process addresses capability gaps, investment risks, IT interdependencies and timing issues across all areas of IT investments. This helps the Army maximize how limited IT investment funding is used and ties investments to strategic priorities.

Section III
Army Enterprise Management

16-6. Army Enterprise Management

The Army is moving toward LandWarNet 2020 and the Joint Information Environment (JIE). As it moves toward this holistic enterprise concept the CIO/G-6 Information Infrastructure Integration Division (SAIS-AOI) synchronizes requirements and delivers capabilities to the enterprise, ensuring LandWarNet 2020 provides capability to the edge. As capabilities are delivered, the Army collapses local systems and delivers enterprise services bringing the full complement of LandWarNet to the edge.

16-7. LandWarNet 2020 and the Joint Information Environment—Army Data Management

As the Army moves toward this holistic enterprise concept the CIO/G-6 Information Infrastructure Integration Division (SAIS-AOI) synchronizes requirements and delivers capabilities to the enterprise, ensuring LandWarNet 2020 provides capability to the edge. As the Army delivers capabilities, local systems collapse and deliver enterprise services bringing the full complement of LandWarNet 2020 to the edge.

a. Data Management. Data is a strategic asset. The Army CIO is responsible for and prescribes the Army's information management policy at the strategic level. Consistent with this responsibility the Army CIO establishes and oversees data transformation through the Army Data Management Program. The Army CIO appoints the Army's Chief Data Officer (CDO); the CDO is responsible for developing, implementing, and enforcing Army and federal data standards and strategy for the Army. Each Mission Area/Joint Capability Area will identify a Data Steward, who is empowered by the Army CIO to perform the same Chief Data Officer responsibilities within their functional areas. As a team, they will lead the data transformation that is fundamental to Net-Centricity.

b. The Army Data Management Program (ADMP). The ADMP establishes required policies and procedures for the production of data standards to ensure enterprise-wide machine process ability of Army information resources and interoperability for all pertinent data exchanges among Army ISs. The ADMP addresses the creation and implementation of data standards applicable to automated systems, software applications, data exchanges, databases, record and document management, and information presentation within and across warfighting and business systems. Army Data Board structure, positions, responsibilities, and other information is also referenced in AR 25-1. The ADMP facilitates the dissemination and exchange of information among organizations and ISs throughout the Army, DOD, and the federal government. The ADMP implements the information standards portion of the DISR and supplements the DOD Net-Centric Data Strategy. Net-centricity is dependent upon the ability to locate and retrieve information and services regardless of where they are stored. A common data management strategy is essential to allowing authorized users to access required information. (See DoDD 8260.1 for information sharing restrictions.)

c. The Army Data Strategy, aligned to the DOD Data Strategy, guides the Army towards ensuring data and information is visible, accessible, understandable, trusted (to include protection, assurance, and security), and interoperable throughout the data life-cycle to any authorized DOD consumer or mission partner to the maximum extent allowed by law and DOD policy. The Army Data Strategy will provide guidance to data producers to maximize information availability to authorized consumers. This will allow Commanders and their organizations to have broad and efficient access to data-reducing duplication of efforts by leaders/Soldiers and their joint/multinational partners. It will also increase interoperability amongst systems and reduce development costs. The Army Data Strategy consists of the following components:

(1) Army Information Architecture (AIA). The AIA provides the foundation to accelerate Army transformation to net-centric information sharing in two ways. The first is design and development guidance for enabling information sharing. The second is a set of compliance requirements for assessing the level to which systems meet net-centric information sharing objectives.

(2) Authoritative Data Sources (ADS). This allows Commanders, decision makers, and stakeholders to target recognized systems for obtaining specific trusted information such as social security numbers, unit readiness, etc., without having to choose from several systems for the correct data.

(3) Information Exchange Specifications (IES). Enables efficient exchange of information between systems and saves resources, with agreed upon definitions and formats, for reuse by a larger group of systems. In other words, it will be easier for systems to exchange data because they speak the same language.

(4) Governance. In large enterprises such as the Army, data is produced by many different organizations, directed toward their specific needs and requirements. However, when data needs to be shared across the enterprise, as is certainly the case for the Army, there are considerations beyond the specific needs of the organization. These include issues of trust, security, policy, understandability, quality, and so on. Data governance is the means to address these issues. In compliance with Army Directive 2009-03, Army Data Management, the Chief Data Officer has developed a governance approach that provides a collaborative environment with active participation from across the Army. The Chief Data Officer recognizes that the individual proponents, as identified by the Assistants SECARMY, ACOMs, and Deputy Chiefs of Staff, are responsible for the operational success of their areas and are ideally suited to identify how data can best be exploited to support them in achieving mission success.

16-8. Enterprise Services

a. Enterprise services span the warfighting, business, and intelligence mission areas to support both the Current and Future Force. Enterprise services allow the widespread use of standardized capabilities (e.g., services, tools, or applications) to facilitate end-to-end linkage of the Army's operational and institutional processes. The CIO/G-6 is responsible for overseeing the Army's integrated approach to delivering Enterprise services. CIO/G-6 integrates plans, policy and resources to ensure the business and warfighting requirements of the Army are met. Enterprise services provide an array of critical enablers for executing the Army's mission. These include general-use services, services for specific functional communities, and services to support Army missions in JIIM environments.

b. CIO/G-6 serves as an integrator for enterprise services while ensuring compliance with applicable law, federal, DOD, and joint guidance. The CCA requires CIO/G-6 to perform management, integration, and accountability for use of IT resources in performing Army missions and functions (see Para. 16-5 above). Consistent with the LandWarNet 2020 & beyond strategy, the Army will deploy enterprise services as a part of capability set fielding.

c. The Army's network modernization efforts include investments in enterprise services that support implementation of the JIE. Managing IT capabilities as enterprise services reduces the total cost of ownership through bulk buying capacity and reduces security risks related to managing multiple individual solutions. Modernization investments include enterprise email, enterprise content management and collaboration services, and enterprise resource planning capabilities such as the General Fund Enterprise Business System (GFEBS).

ARMY KNOWLEDGE MANAGEMENT

16-9. Army's Network Modernization
Modernization efforts include investments in enterprise services that support implementation of the JIE. Managing IT capabilities as enterprise services reduces the total cost of ownership through bulk buying capacity and reduces security risks related to managing multiple individual solutions. Modernization investments include Enterprise Email, Enterprise Content Management and Collaboration Services, and enterprise resource planning capabilities such as the GFEBS.

   a. AEA Overview. Army Enterprise Architecture refers to either an architecture description or an architecture implementation. As an architecture description defined in DOD Architecture Framework (DODAF) 2.0, the AEA provides a representation of a current or future real-world configuration of resources, rules, and relationships. Once the representation enters the design, development, and acquisition portion of the system development life cycle process, the AEA is transformed into a real implementation of capabilities and assets in the field. The AEA Framework supports this transformation process. The AEA:

   (1) Provides policy and guidance governing the composition and use of architecture documentation within the Army and unique architecture responsibilities. Information about Army architecture can be found at http:// architecture.army.mil.

   (2) The Army uses AEA to analyze operational concepts and systems and to support new capabilities and requirements as required by the following: Chairman of the Joint Chiefs of Staff Instruction (CJCSI) 3170.01, JCIDS; the DOD 5000 series of acquisition documents; Information Support Plan (ISP) process; and other authorities.

   (3) Supports the key requirement and solution development processes of JCIDS in the following: Warfighting Mission Area (WMA); Business Capability Lifecycle (BCL) in the Business Mission Area (BMA); and Network Capability Set fielding in the EIEMA.

   (4) Defines the mission, the technologies necessary to perform the mission, and the transition processes for implementing new organizations, processes, and technologies in response to changing mission needs.

   (5) Helps drive the Army's IT investment strategy by providing the right data in useable formats to decision makers to address capability gaps, investment risks, interdependencies, and alignment with key Army and Joint doctrine.

   (6) Supports the design, development, acquisition and fielding of the network in a comprehensive, synchronized manner.

   (7) Supports acquisition, implementation, and management of integrated and interoperable systems that provide required operational capabilities to the operating force and the generating force as well as institutional business operations.

   (8) Provides the foundation for Army IT transformation by providing the information needed for data-driven decision making as relates to the current and future state LandWarNet. The AEA will also provide the necessary information to the CIO/G-6 to track progress on ITMR implementation and the related efficiencies, cost savings and avoidances.

   (9) Will depict the end-to-end architecture connecting the force from squad to Joint Task Force, to ensure our leaders have the right information, at the right time, to determine the best course of action for a given mission.

   b. AEA Composition. The AEA describes all aspects of the Army enterprise. Three segments comprise the AEA that contribute to the overall design of the Army and support the ability to operate in a joint and coalition environment: operating force, generating force, and network. The Army manages AEA using a tiered approach and its architectures will be developed in accordance with a rules-based framework approved by the CIO/G–6 and aligned with DOD IT standards. The AEA is composed of:

   (1) Unit, segment, or domain architecture guidance. Segment and organizational architectures are components of the AEA. It includes reference models and federated architecture concepts that describe the relationship between architectures at different levels (such as unit, segment, and domain architectures) by using fit-for-purpose architecture models as required. Domain architecture is developed or sponsored by the domain data stewards.

   (2) Three IT mission areas are Warfighting (WMA), Business (BMA), and Network (EIEMA). Mission areas describe the IT portfolio of services, capabilities, and material investments in support of various Army operations:

   (a) IT enabling the operating force is compiled in the WMA.

HOW THE ARMY RUNS

(b) IT enabling the generating force and the 15 end-to-end business processes are in the BMA.

(c) IT enabling and supporting the institutional Army, installations, and enabling the provision of enterprise services is in the EIEMA.

(3) Processes by framing capabilities and supporting analysis. IT/network requirements in the WMA and BMA are enabled through the enterprise services provided by the EIEMA.

(4) Rules and guidance for AEA relationships to external architectures. The AEA must conform to DOD Information Enterprise Architecture (IEA) and federal architecture policies and directives. When interfacing with other DOD external components' architectures, the vertical and horizontal alignments must be depicted.

c. AEA Executive Architects. The executive architects are responsible for the operating force, generating force, and network segments that together constitute the Army enterprise. They verify, validate, certify, approve and assess architectures within their area of responsibility. The current executive architects for the AEA are:

(1) The Under Secretary of the Army (Business Transformation) (DUSA(BT) for the generating force.

(2) The ASA(ALT) for mission command solution architectures.

(3) The CIO/G-6 for IT, network, and technical architecture, and network/technical standards.

(4) The Deputy Chief of Staff, G-3/5/7 for operating force structure architecture.

(5) The Commander, Training and Doctrine Command (TRADOC) for Warfighting operational architecture.

d. Architecture Views and Approved Frameworks. The diverse nature of the architecture describing the generating force, operational force and network architecture of the Army, and the need to support Joint, Office of the Secretary of Defense (OSD) and federal government architecture requirements and best practices, require that architecture products are developed under a variety of frameworks.

(1) These frameworks may be expressed in rule sets, reference architectures, ontology's, common operating environments, or standards.

(2) If however, a specific architecture artifact is mandated in support of a major DOD or Joint process, such as JCIDS or PPBE, the AEA will have the authoritative data and tools available to develop the required products.

(3) Views, artifacts and other products will be dictated by the questions to be answered by the architecture, decisions to be made, process reporting requirements, the architecture tools being used and most importantly the data underpinning the architecture.

16-10. Information Assurance

a. Cyber attacks threaten the Army network and its information every day putting operations and personnel at risk. Commanders require operational freedom to maneuver in cyberspace with the capability to identify vulnerabilities while minimizing risk. Network security and information assurance are therefore paramount for protecting and safeguarding our information and communications systems ensuring the integrity of operational Warfighting networks and business information systems critical to Army mission success.

b. The Army CIO/G-6 is responsible for overseeing and managing the Army Information Assurance program. The Army Information Assurance program protects information and its critical elements, including the systems and hardware that use, store, and transmit that information by identifying, measuring, and mitigating risk. Information assurance incorporates functions from Operations Security (OPSEC), Communications Security (COMSEC), Transmission Security (TRANSEC), Information Security (INFOSEC), personnel security, and physical security to protect and safeguard our information and communication technologies as well as our warfighting and business capabilities.

c. Information assurance is everyone's responsibility. Leaders must incorporate information assurance into their risk management programs; make certain their personnel are accountable for their daily practices that put our information and communication technologies at risk, and link information assurance to readiness. All personnel must be aware of the potential risks they present and take proper precautions to protect the information entrusted to them.

ARMY KNOWLEDGE MANAGEMENT

Section IV
Chief Information Officer / G-6 Organization

16-11. Chief Integration Office (CXO)

a. The CXO Directorate integrates of Army IM and IT initiatives. The CXO incorporates vision, strategic planning, and elements of quality management into the full range of its functions to encourage creative thinking and innovation, influence others toward a spirit of service, and design and implement new or cutting-edge programs and processes.

b. The CXO Directorate performs the following functions:

(1) Leads the development and integration of CIO/G-6 input into the Army's strategic planning documents, to include the synchronization of the supporting IM and IT strategies with Army strategic vision, goals, and objectives.

(2) Provides overall framework and management of strategic communications initiatives to enhance awareness of Army-wide IM/IT objectives. Responsibilities also include media relations, and the management of social media congressional responses.

(3) Serves as the CIO/G-6 contact office for requests for resource information from the Office of the President, the Congress, and the Office of the Secretary of Defense.

(4) Serves as the CIO/G-6 contact for all USA Audit Agency Inspections of IM/IT related areas and for the coordination for implementation of resulting recommendations.

(5) Serves as the principal agent for oversight of all Army Enterprise License Agreements (ELAs), in coordination with the ASA(ALT) and the Defense Information Systems Agency (DISA) for Joint ELA requirements.

(6) Acts as the Executive Secretary to the CIO/G-6 in its capacity as the sub-sponsor under the OSD's sponsorship of the National Security Engineering Center (NSEC) Federally Funded Research Development Corporation (FFRDC) MITRE. CXO administers and manages the CIO/G-6 MITRE program and has oversight of all Army MITRE programs.

(7) Provides management and oversight of CIO/G-6 Performance Management processes in accordance with the Government Performance Results Act (ACT). CXO administers the Strategic Management System (SMS) to report mandated OSD requirements for the Army Senior Leader Performance Budget Dashboard (ASLPBD), the CIO/G-6 input to the Army Campaign Plan, the Integrated Disability Evaluation System, and performance of the LandWarNet 2020 & Beyond strategic plan.

16-12. Policy and Resources (P&R)

a. The P&R Directorate oversees development of Army IM/IT policies and governance processes in coordination with OSD, the Joint Staff (JS), Services, Combatant Commands (CCMDs), components, and other federal agencies that are in compliance with laws, regulations and standards. It assists in developing and coordinating assessment processes for Army IM programs.

b. The directorate ensures the integration of C4/IT resource requirements across the Army by supervising the PPBE process for IM resources, and reviewing budget requests for all IT national security systems. It efficiently and effectively manages the integration of internal and external C4/IT resources to achieve organizational and Army Enterprise goals in accordance with CCA and USC Title 10. By overseeing decision-making at the enterprise level, the P&R Directorate transforms the Army IT workforce, processes, and information infrastructure by providing accountability, standardization, and efficiencies. Strategic resourcing decisions are made through the IT investment strategy process in coordination with Army Cyber Command and NETCOM, ACOMs, CCMDs, and HQDA stakeholders.

c. The P&R Directorate performs the following functions:

(1) Establishes policies and procedures that align resources in an effort to oversee the delivery of Army enterprise services. This function enables mission-critical applications and processes. Enterprise Services include the set of capabilities that enable information and information assets to be used within and across mission areas.

(2) Collects and manages Enterprise Service requirements, which shape conditions for resourcing the gathered requirements and drive recommendations for funding.

(3) Serves as Secretariat for CIO/G-6 Boards, focal point for all CIO/G-6 policies and related federal policy, standards, and initiatives.

HOW THE ARMY RUNS

(4) Develops and implements IT portfolio management guidance for issuance to the Army by the CIO/G-6, in accordance with SECARMY directives.

(5) Oversees IT resources and assessment, and develops and coordinates investment decisions at the enterprise level for IT expenditures.

(6) Represents the CIO/G-6 on the PPBE process, and is responsible for resource expenditures for any IT systems and programs not otherwise managed by an Army PEO. Specific oversight functions include compliance with CCA requirements, Army enterprise initiatives, and financial management guidelines. Activities include:
   (a) Serves as focal point for CIO/G-6 on resource matters
   (b) Guides CIO/G-6 participation in the PPBE events
   (c) Coordinates CIO/G-6 participation on PEG resourcing meetings

(7) Oversees the execution of current year financial resources, and initiatives directly related to the acquisition of IT hardware, software, and services across the Army. Activities include:
   (a) Manages the Other Procurement Army-2 (OPA-2) communications and electronics procurement programs.
   (b) Executes the internal CIO/G-6 Operations and Maintenance, Army (OMA) budget.
   (c) Leads the implementation of the Army Request for Information Technology (ARFIT) initiative to improve visibility of IT expenditures in the Army, develop a capability to measure and assess compliance with Army IT policies, and generate efficiencies in IT spending.

(8) Manages the IT Career Program 34 with competency-based career plans, training and education programs.

(9) Guides IT and cyber-security workforce development by working with Army, DOD, and federal agencies to build programs, assessments, and tools that support strategic human capital planning.

16-13. Architecture, Operations, Networks and Space (AONS)

a. The AONS Directorate establishes and maintains strategy, policy, and guidance for building, integrating, and facilitating the seamless implementation of LandWarNet in a joint and coalition environment, while ensuring compliance with statutory and regulatory mandates. AONS employs the Army Architecture Integration Center to develop the Enterprise Architecture, identify and coordinate technical standards, and create and maintain architecture processes for Army transformation. In addition, AONS manages Army radio frequencies spectrum access and requirements; establishes and maintains the Army Network Baseline Architecture; shapes the modernization approach and priorities for Network Capabilities within the EE, II, and TT PEGs; manages the Network Services, Application/Data and Network Transportation portfolios; provides HQDA G-6 support for current Army missions, including contingency operations and man-made/natural disaster relief efforts; and provides C4/IT oversight and support for COOP, Special Access Programs, and Sensitive Activities.

b. The AONS Directorate responsibilities include the following:

(1) Set the strategic direction for and supervise the execution of Army IM policies for Network Architecture creation. Synchronize Army Network activities.

(2) Advocate for and monitor the implementation of IM requirements on behalf of the Warfighter.

(3) Serve as the Army G-6 advisor for information and signal operations, network and communications security, force structure, equipping, and employment of signal forces.

(4) Coordinate with the JS and CCMDs regarding IT and National Security Systems.

(5) Develop enterprise architecture to support Army Generating and Operating Force information needs. Develop a single network architecture from Post/Camp/Station to the tactical edge, including developing the Army Technical Architecture, integrating the Army Enterprise Architecture, and identifying and coordinating technical standards

(6) Monitor implementation of the LandWarNet 2020 & Beyond strategy.

(7) Serve as the senior authority for telecommunications programs and committees, including:
   (a) JS-controlled mobile/transportable telecommunications assets
   (b) The Spectrum Certification Program
   (c) Support to Contingency Operations, disaster relief, and humanitarian assistance
   (d) Network Integration Evaluation (NIE) planning and support requirements
   (e) Oversight for tactical mobile switched systems and joint network management
   (f) Voting member of the Military Communications-Electronics Board (MCEB) and participant in MCEB activities

ARMY KNOWLEDGE MANAGEMENT

(g) Member of the Committee on National Security Systems

(h) Army lead for Joint Transformation Communication Program

(8) As the HQDA proponent for the information systems supporting C4/IT programs:

(a) Serves as the Army focal point for C4/IT system (to include NSS) issues; receives, coordinates, and integrates these issues; and ensures the integration of systems and development efforts that cross functional and/or technical lines

(b) Participates and provides representation in PPBE process decision groups; exercises centralized oversight of C4/IT expenditures for all appropriations

(c) Develops, coordinates, and implements a C4/IT capital planning and investment program with the CIO/G-6 CFO, P&R Division

(d) Ensures C4/IT system conformance to the approved Joint Technical Architecture–Army (JTA–A), Operational Architecture (OA), Technical Architecture (TA), and Systems Architecture (SA); coordinates and supports the priorities within C4/IT for information system development related activities; and securse adequate resource support

(e) Promotes the application of proven advanced technology techniques, procedures, and methodologies across the Army's corporate management processes and their associated information systems

(f) Provides CIO validation of requirements for warfighting, base operations (BASOPS), administrative processes, and other mission-related processes associated with an IT impact

(g) Coordinates resource requirements for C4/IT support activities

(h) Facilitates adoption of approved standards for information and information system Interoperability with joint, unified, combined federal government, and other Army systems, as required

(i) Ensures interoperability among Special Access Programs and coordinate Army survival, recovery, and reconstitution system and COOP support requirements

(j) Ensures that essential information services in support of Department of the Army (DA) COOP are available to alternate sites of HQDA agencies and ACOMs, ASCCs (Army Service Component Commands), and installations

(9) Provides oversight of the planning and programming for the Army Spectrum Management Program.

16-14. Cybersecurity Directorate

a. The mission of the Army CIO/G-6 Cybersecurity Directorate is to integrate and synchronize Army efforts across the federal, DOD, and Joint Staffs (JS) to provide policy, oversight, and guidance that ensure secure and trusted access to Army and DoD networks and the confidentiality, integrity, authentication, availability and non-repudiation of the Army data personal information.

b. The Cybersecurity Directorate responsibilities include the following:

(1) Oversees and manages the Army Information Assurance program; establishes and issues Army information assurance policy and procedures for achieving acceptable levels of Information Assurance in engineering, implementation, operation, and maintenance for all IT connecting to or crossing any Army-managed network.

(2) Develops strategy, plans, policies and guidance for Army cyber-security and information assurance activities, including certification and accreditation, training, workforce certification, key infrastructure, common access card, cross domain solutions, wireless, communications security, key management, and other technology programs.

(3) Determines the levels of information security appropriate to protect information/information systems, assess the risk, and provide information security protections.

(4) Ensures Army compliance with IT and national security systems standards as well as federal government and DOD directives/mandates.

(5) Designs, develops and promotes Army enterprise cyber-security and information assurance awareness, training, and education programs; oversees and manages the Army portion of the National Security Agency (NSA) Information Assurance Scholarship program for Army military and civilian personnel.

(6) Oversees the cyber-security and information assurance workforce; manages Army implementation of DOD Directives, Instructions and Manuals for information assurance and cybersecurity training and certifications for the civilian, military, and contractor workforce.

(7) Manages civilian, military, and contractor workforce compliance for baseline and computing environment certifications.

HOW THE ARMY RUNS

(8) Manages cybersecurity career roadmap.
(9) Ensures the interoperability and configuration management of all Army IT systems to meet DOD, joint, and coalition partners security certifications.
(10) Reviews all information assurance budget requests, and prioritizes and defends Army Information Assurance resource requirements in the planning, programming, and budgeting process.
(11) Manages resources for network operations in a manner that implements policies and procedures of applicable laws and regulations.
(12) Manages and reports privacy effect assessment compliance to DOD CIO and the Office of Management and Budget (OMB).
(13) Oversees and manages cross-domain solutions for the Army.
(14) Serves as the Army Senior Information Assurance Officer and Army Certification Authority.
(15) Manages appointment of Army Designated Approving Authorities (DAA).
(16) Oversees Army Agents of the Certification Authority (ACA).

Section V
Other Strategic Partnerships with the Army Chief Information Officer / G-6

16-15. Army Partnerships

Given the cross-cutting missions of CIO/G-6 to provide an integrated, secure, standards-based information environment that address the mission needs of the Army, internal and external partnerships are critical. Partnerships are required to accurately define, develop, execute and share critical information securely to meet the changing needs of the Army, DOD, other federal agencies and missions partners.

a. Principal Headquarters, Department of Army (HQDA) officials. Within their respective areas, principal HQDA officials serve as the proponent for information requirements and associated capabilities within their assigned functional areas of responsibility. As the proponent, the principal official oversees functional processes within respective portfolio areas to maximize end-to-end enterprise processes and improve efficiencies of information systems. The principal requests and defends the capabilities and supporting resources needed for the development, deployment, operation, security, logistics support, and modification of information systems through the PPBE process.

b. ASA(ALT). Army CIO/G-6 and ASA(ALT) are strategic partners in transforming Warfighter-required capabilities into standardized, compatible, interoperable, secure, and resourced data management and portfolio management solutions. Working with CIO/G-6, ASA(ALT) serves as the source selection authority for acquiring IT systems. In addition, ASA(ALT) oversees project managers and program executive offices (PEO) to ensure that IT and NSS systems successfully meet Army IT requirements. CIO/G-6 works closely with the PEOs on IT related programs, including:

(1) PEO Enterprise Information Systems (EIS). PEO EIS provides joint and Army organizations with information dominance by developing, acquiring, integrating, deploying, and sustaining net-centric knowledge-based IT and business management systems, communications, and infrastructure solutions through leveraged commercial and enterprise capabilities. The PEO EIS oversees the management of Computer Hardware, Enterprise Software Solutions (CHESS) and Army Knowledge Online (AKO).

(a) The CHESS office provides a full range of IT, IT infrastructure, and information systems (hardware, software, peripherals, networking, and infrastructure support services) to Army, DoD, foreign military, Soldiers, and federal agencies consistent with DOD and DA policy on standardization and interoperability.

(b) AKO is the Army's current enterprise portal for accessing information (see Para. 16-8). The Army is transitioning to enterprise services and enterprise email, the approved enterprise solutions and tools may change.

(2) PEO Command Control Communications-Tactical (C3T). PEO C3T provides the computer systems, radios and communications networks required to fight and win the Nation's wars. PEO C3T oversees the management of the MilTech Solutions and the Warfighter Information Network-Tactical (WIN-T).

(a) MilTech Solutions provide web-based tools and technologies that improve workforce collaboration and enable faster, more effective support to the Warfighter. MilSuite, one of the MilTech Solutions, provides a professional, behind-the-firewall version of familiar sites like Facebook and Wikipedia. Sites include milBook, milWiki, milBlog and milTube,

ARMY KNOWLEDGE MANAGEMENT

(b) PM WIN-T provides the communications network (satellite and terrestrial) and services that allow the Soldier to send and receive information to execute the mission. WIN-T incrementally develops and delivers products that simplify network initialization and management and significantly increase capabilities.

c. Deputy Chief of Staff (DCS), G-2. DCS, G-2, as the functional lead for intelligence IT purchases, systems, and leases, works with CIO/G-6 to ensure that IT investments in the intelligence community align with Army IT investment strategies.

d. Deputy Chief of Staff, G-3/5/7. CIO/G-6 and DCS, G-3/5/7 are strategic partners in delivering Warfighter-required capabilities. DCS, G-3/5/7 validates, synchronizes, and prioritizes Army network requirements to meet current, emerging, and future needs of operational commanders. DCS, G-3/5/7 ensures that all network-related requirements fit within the Army's enterprise network as part of the LandWarNet capabilities set.

e. Deputy Chief of Staff, G-8. CIO/G-6 and DCS, G-8 work closely to develop and defend Army IT programs. CIO/G-6 collaborates with DCS, G-8 in the development of command, control, communications, computers, intelligence, surveillance, and reconnaissance (C4ISR) positions presented to relevant governance boards. In addition, APMS (a CIO/G-6 system) is housed in the G-8 data warehouse to enable closer alignment with GFEBS (a DCS, G-8 financial, asset and accounting management system).

f. Army Cyber Command/Second U.S. Army. As the single command and control authority for all collateral top secret and below Army network operations, Army Cyber Command works closely with CIO/G-6 to establish the vision, direction, and architecture of I3MP. Army Cyber Command is the single authority for the operation, management and defense of the LandWarNet.

g. U.S. Army Network Enterprise Technology Command (NETCOM). As directed by the CIO/G-6, NETCOM serves and the Designated Approving Authority for the Army enterprise. NETCOM is the Army IT integrator advising the end-to-end management of the Army's enterprise service area to ensure the CIO/G-6 achieves a single, virtual, enterprise network.

16-16. External Partnerships

a. Federal Chief Information Officer Council. The CIO/G-6 serves as a member of the Federal CIO Council. The Federal CIO Council in partnership with all federal agencies serves as a forum for CIOs to improve practices in the design, use, sharing and performance of federal information resources and cross-agency challenges.

b. Department of Defense Chief Information Officer. The DOD CIO is the principal staff assistant and advisor to the Secretary of Defense on information resources management. The DOD CIO sets the vision, strategic goals and provides direction to DOD in executing policies and practices to deliver agile and secure information capabilities to enhance decision-making and combat mission needs. The DOD CIO and the Army CIO/G-6 are partners in addressing DOD-wide IM, IT business and warfighting information capabilities essential for enterprise-wide solutions and operational effectiveness. CIO/G-6 is a member of the DOD CIO Executive Board and Military Department CIO Executive forums to advise the DOD CIO on strategic direction, requirements and implementation strategies to meet Army's critical information mission needs.

c. Other DOD Partnerships. The Army CIO/G-6 also has an information capability delivery partnership with other DOD components such as the Defense Information Systems Agency, the Joint Staff and the other military department CIOs to address cross-cutting information and service delivery requirements to enable communication, collaboration and sustaining of secure trusted environments. This includes how information will be made available and how to develop and deliver enterprise service solutions.

d. Industry. Industry partners play an important role in supporting the mission of the CIO/G-6. These businesses offer technology and strategy consulting that provide IT solutions for current and future forces. In addition, CIO/G-6 works with industry partners to develop and implement enterprise licenses that use the Army's buying power to realize cost savings and efficiencies.

16.17. Cultural Changes

a. In the current economic climate, the Army expects significant budget cuts while potential threats to national security continue to evolve. At the same time, the Army is becoming primarily CONUS-based, while the threat environment demands the ability to deploy globally with little-to-no notice. To fulfill the United States' national security objectives, the Army must be agile and prepared to fight upon arrival.

HOW THE ARMY RUNS

Further, the Army must create a smaller footprint in theater while providing every type of required support to the Soldier at the tactical edge, and it must be capable of operating with all mission partners. While the Army transitions to an expeditionary Army that is smaller yet more capable, the network is the core of that smaller, capable Army.

b. The Army is supporting network modernization efforts through participation in the development and maturation of the DOD JIE. JIE is DOD's construct to provide a single, secure, reliable, timely, effective, and agile C4 enterprise information environment for use by Joint Forces and non-DOD mission partners across the full spectrum of operations, at all echelons, and in all operational environments. The CIO/G-6 has aligned its top IT initiatives to support the JIE effort, without being dependent on it.

c. Other key modernization efforts include:

(1) Modernizing the network as a platform by improving governance, enforcing compliance, implementing agile IT acquisition, and ensuring transparent IT spending

(2) Standardizing a basic architecture called the common operating environment – a centrally approved, commercially based set of computing technologies and standards to which the network itself and all applications and systems riding the network must adhere

(3) Updating and consolidating network infrastructure

(4) Consolidating and securing networks

(5) Moving to a capability set management construct to foster end-to-end network modernization

Section VI
Summary and References

16-18. Summary

a. Army transformation will enhance the Service's ability to conduct operations. The goal of the CIO/G-6 is to provide the strategy to enable better and faster decisions than U.S. adversaries.

b. IT/IM strategy provides for the integration and the interoperability of processing, storing, and transporting information over a seamless network, allowing access to universal and secure Army knowledge across the enterprise. As the Army moves toward building a single, secure, standards-based network that ensures access at the point of need and enables global collaboration, current operational systems are examined for the results they achieve and benefits they provide to the Army. If the systems do not contribute to a world-class net-centric knowledge system, they face elimination or migration to systems that do.

c. The CIO/G-6 commits to meeting the challenges that come with transforming the Army into a force that is strategically responsive and dominant. To that end, the CIO/G-6 is investing in today's technology to stimulate the development of doctrine, organizational design, and leader training to improve the future force. Doing so will extend the Army's technological overmatch.

16-19. References

a. Army Regulation 10-87, Army Commands, Army Service Component Commands, and Direct Reporting Units.

b. Army Regulation 25-1, Army Knowledge Management and Information Technology.

c. Army Regulation 25-2, Information Assurance.

d. Army Regulation 70-1, Army Acquisition Policy.

e. Department of the Army Pamphlet 25-1-1, Information Technology Support and Services.

f. General Order 2012-01, Assignment of Functions and Responsibilities Within the HQDA.

g. General Order 2002-05, Establishment of the U.S. Army Network Enterprise Technology Command/9th Army Signal command; Transfer and Re-designation of the Headquarters and Headquarters Company, 9th Army Signal Command; Discontinuance of the Communications Electronics Services Office and the Information Management Support Agency.

h. Office of the Chairman of the Joint Chiefs of Staff. Joint Information Environment White Paper. Washington D.C.: Joint Chiefs of Staff, 2013.

i. SECARMY, "Information Technology Management Reform (ITMR) Implementation Plan," Washington, D.C.: Office of the SECARMY, 2013.

INSTALLATION MANAGEMENT COMMUNITY

Chapter 17

Installation Management Community

The Installation Management Community's Vision: "We Are The Army's Home"

Section I
Introduction

17-1. Chapter Content
This chapter describes how the Army manages installations. It includes history, hierarchy, roles and missions, and initiatives and programs.

17-2. History
a. In the 1980s and early 1990s, findings from a host of inspections, studies, and surveys determined that installations could be managed far more efficiently and effectively. As a result, the Army leadership took these major actions:
  (1) Established ACSIM in 1993
  (2) Established centrally selected garrison commanders in 1993
b. Published the first installation management doctrine, FM 100-22, *Installation Management,* in 1994. These actions were taken to improve integration of the widely varying, often competing, installation management functions and to better prepare commanders for the increasingly complex and important work of running Army and Department of Defense (DOD) installations.
c. On 1 October 2002, the Installation Management Agency (IMA) was activated to support the Transformation of Installation Management (TIM). IMA was structured to provide efficient installation management worldwide through 'best practice' management programs; to establish quality installations; and to maintain the well-being of the Army family. The Secretary of the Army's (SECARMY) intent for TIM was to:
  (1) Provide corporate structure focused on installation management
  (2) Support and enable Mission Commanders
  (3) Enable Major Army Command (MACOM) now, Army Command (ACOM), Commanders to provide strategic guidance through the Installation Management Board of Directors (IMBOD)
  (4) Eliminate migration of installation support funds [(Base Operations (BASOPS) Environment, Family Programs, Base Communications, Sustainment, Restoration and Modernization (SRM)]
  (5) Achieve regional efficiencies
  (6) Provide consistent and equitable services through established standards
  (7) Integrate Reserve Components
  (8) Enhance Army Transformation
  (9) Support Information Technology (IT) and contracting centralization efforts
d. In October 2006, the Army reorganized its structure for managing installations with the activation of the IMCOM. The Army established IMCOM to improve its ability to provide critical support programs to Soldiers and their families. IMCOM is one of several land-holding commands of installations.

17-3. Hierarchy
The installation management community operates at four levels. These intertwined and complementary levels govern key levels of efforts by commands and staffs as shown in Figure 17-1.

HOW THE ARMY RUNS

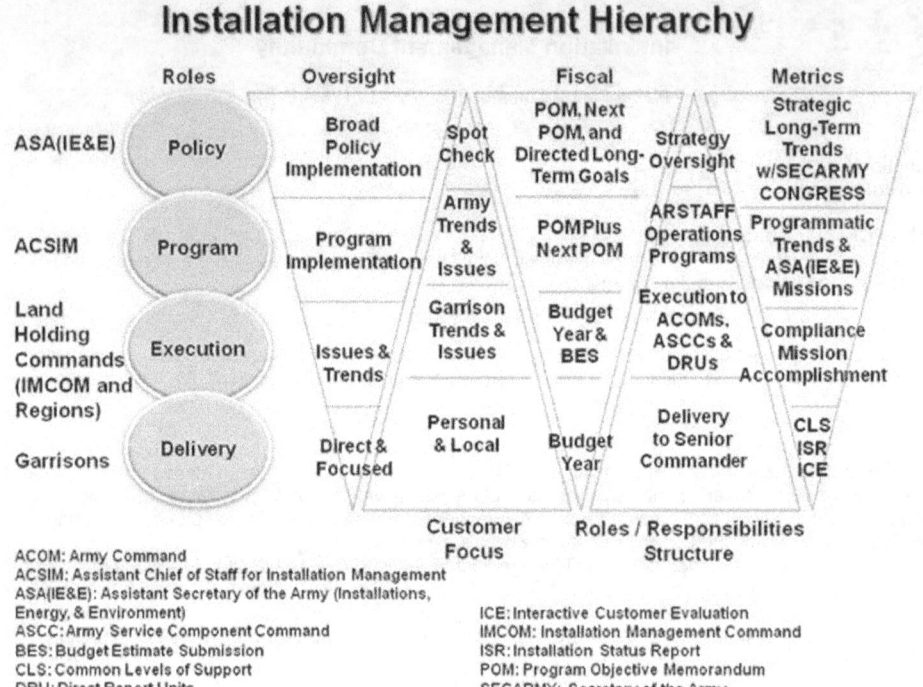

Figure 7-1. Installation Management Hierarchy

Section II
Roles and Missions

17-4. Assistant Secretary of the Army (Installations, Energy and Environment)
  a. The ASA (IE&E) is the principal adviser to the Secretary of the Army on matters related to Army installations, energy security and the Army's impact on the environment, safety and occupational health. They set the strategic direction and ensure Army efforts are executed consistent with law, regulation and policy. The ASA (IE&E) has responsibility for:
  (1) Establishing strategic direction for aspects of the Planning Programming and Budget Execution (PPBE) process within the ASA (IE&E)'s areas of responsibility, including facilities investment, military construction, installations, Army real estate, energy security, operational energy, water security, sustainability, the environment, safety and occupational health, and the associated resource allocation decisions and policies; and coordinating and integrating that direction with the Assistant Secretary of the Army (Financial Management & Comptroller) (ASA (FM&C)); Chief Information Officer (CIO); Deputy Chief of Staff (DCS), G–3/5/7; DCS, G–4; DCS, G–8; ACSIM; and other Department of the Army (DA) officials and organizations. ASA (IE&E) serves as the Co-Chair with the ACSIM for the Installations Program Evaluation Group (II PEG).
  (2) Providing strategic guidance and supervision for policies, plans and programs for facilities investments, military construction, energy security, operational energy, water security, contingency bases

INSTALLATION MANAGEMENT COMMUNITY

and environmental initiatives executed by the Army Staff (ARSTAF), including the ACSIM; DCS, G–4; other DA officials, organizations and commands, including the U.S. Army Corps of Engineers (USACE).

(3) Supervising and facilitating the development and management of Army installations, including facilities investments to support readiness, design, construction, physical security and critical infrastructure protection of installations to ensure continuity of operations, energy security, environmental, safety and occupational health; and advising the Secretary of the Army and the Chief of Staff of the Army (CSA) on installations for stationing.

(4) Supervising the development and implementation of policies and programs for Army real property, including acquisition, management, disposal, exchanges, public domain withdrawals, condemnation and donations. Setting policy for and supervising the management of historic properties under the Army's purview and the Army homeowners' assistance program.

(5) Developing policies for and supervising the implementation of policies for base closures, realignments, stationing, planning and utilization, reuse and economic adjustment programs.

(6) Supervising Army privatization initiatives and their implementation.

(7) Supervising and developing policies and budget requests for Army military construction, including overseas military construction agreements, and ensuring consistency with statute, regulation, and Army and DOD policy.

(8) Supervising Army energy security and sustainability, including the development of strategy and policy, coordination of initiatives, supervision of Headquarters, Department of the Army (HQDA) councils and committees and representation of Army environmental and sustainability interests in coordination with Federal regulatory agencies and State and local governments.

(9) Supervising and developing policies and programs for Army environmental efforts, including environmental compliance; pollution prevention; environmental impact analysis; stewardship of natural, cultural and historic resources; and environmental cleanup and restoration, including Formerly Used Defense Sites (FUDs).

(10) Coordinating with the Assistant Secretary of the Army (Acquisition, Logistics, and Technology) (ASA(ALT)) to ensure that environmental, safety, health, energy security, operational energy efficiency, green procurement, and installation management issues are appropriately addressed by materiel developers; integrated into acquisition program planning and documentation; and addressed as risk areas during milestone decision reviews.

(11) Providing policy and supervising Army-wide safety, occupational and environmental health risk management, including sanitation and hygiene.

(12) Supervising the development of Army policy for environmental, safety and occupational health aspects of DOD's Chemical Demilitarization Program and, in coordination with the ASA(ALT) and DCS, G–3/5/7, serving as the Army's Chemical, Biological, Nuclear, and Conventional Treaty Verification and Compliance Official.

b. Deputy Assistant Secretaries of the Army (DASA). The ASA(IE&E) has a Principal Deputy Assistant Secretary of the Army (PDASA) and four DASAs.

(1) DASA (Energy &Sustainability) is the Senior Energy Executive for the Army. This office provides guidance and direction on utilities privatization, policy review, The Army's Net Zero Program, energy partnerships and the Energy Initiatives Task Force (EITF).

(2) DASA (Environment, Safety and Occupational Health) provides strategic guidance on restoration, sustainability, compliance, conservation, pollution prevention and historic properties. In addition, this office provides safety and occupational health guidance, explosives, chemical safety and munitions response and chemical warfare response.

(3) DASA (Installations, Housing and Partnerships) provides secretarial direction on military construction, engineering, housing, base realignment and closure (BRAC), partnerships, Residential Communities Initiative (RCI) and privatization of Army lodging.

(4) DASA (Strategic Direction) is the ASA(IE&E) representative to the Army Campaign Plan. The office develops strategy, executes business transformation at the secretariat level and conducts day-to-day operations for the ASA(IE&E) in the Installation Program Evaluation Group (II PEG).

17-5. ACSIM

a. The ACSIM is the principal military adviser to the ASA (IE&E) for installation management, military facilities investment requirements and strategy, housing, installation environmental management and stewardship, privatization and energy security and sustainability. In the ACSIM's areas of functional

HOW THE ARMY RUNS

responsibility, the ACSIM assists and supports the ASA (IE&E) in the development, execution and evaluation of Army policy, plans, strategy and programs; executes and ensures the execution of policies and plans by other Army organizations; and assists the ASA (IE&E) in reviewing the execution of Army policies, plans and programs. The ACSIM is also the principal military adviser to the Assistant Secretary of the Army (Manpower & Reserve Affairs) (ASA (M&RA)) for morale, welfare, recreation and Family support programs and is responsible for assisting and supporting the ASA (M&RA) in the planning, development, budgeting, implementation and evaluation of installation morale, welfare and recreation and non-appropriated fund instrumentalities. The ACSIM is the principal ARSTAF adviser to the CSA on installation and family support matters and serves as the Co-Chair with the ASA (IE&E) for the II PEG. The ACSIM has responsibility for:

(1) Supervising and coordinating the development, implementation and evaluation of policies, plans and strategies for military facilities investment requirements, privatization, installation, environmental, water management and energy security and sustainability programs.

(2) Supervising and coordinating the development, validation and execution programs for the resourcing of environmental programs, privatization, water management and energy security and sustainability programs on assigned Army installations.

(3) Developing standards to evaluate installation and base operations, including compliance with environmental requirements and energy efficiency.

(4) Serving as the proponent for installation management doctrine and the professional development of installation and garrison commanders and staff.

(5) Serving as the ARSTAF proponent and execution authority for Army wide installation-related environmental programs and the execution authority for installation environmental programs assigned to the Army by DOD.

(6) Ensuring execution of approved operational programs for the reorganization, realignment and closure of installations.

(7) Developing infrastructure and monitoring the execution of programs for installation services and management that support readiness and enhance the well-being of Soldiers and families.

(8) Assisting and supporting the ASA (M&RA) in the planning, development, budgeting, implementation and evaluation of installation morale, welfare and recreation programs and non-appropriated fund instrumentalities.

b. ACSIM Directorates. The ACSIM is supported by four major directorates; Installation Services, Information Technology, Operations, and Resources.

(1) Installation Services directorate interprets strategic guidance, provides policy and creates priorities for resources in order to create a supportive and sustainable environment through world class housing, environmental stewardship, responsive logistics, collaborative partnerships and enhanced quality of life programs for Soldiers, civilians and their families. The directorate is made up of five divisions. The Housing Division focus is training personnel and developing permanent party barracks buyouts/upgrades and program requirements to sustain barracks. Logistics Service Division works to reduce fossil fuel consumption, transform the Non-Tactical Vehicle (NTV) fleet, and develop and implement standardized firefighter qualifications, duty descriptions and training requirements. Public Private Initiatives Division is the ACSIM center of excellence for privatization ensuring maximization and sustainability of Army assets and services via privatization. Key programs are the Residential Communities Initiative, Privatization of Army Lodging and the Barracks Privatization Initiative. Soldier and Family Readiness Division implements strategies that support Soldier and family programs and provide guidance and direction for the Army Family Covenant, Army Community Covenant, Army Family Action Plan, Survivor Outreach Services, Army Community Service (ACS), Sexual Harassment/Assault Response and Prevention (SHARP), health promotion programs, and the risk reduction and Suicide prevention program. The Environmental Division develops and monitors the Army Sustainability Campaign Plan, allocates resources to meet environmental cleanup targets and works to strengthen community environmental partnerships.

(2) Information Technology Directorate primary functions are to manage the Installation Energy and Environment (IE&E) domain systems; participate in the Army IT governance Board and request and defend ACSIM related capabilities and support resources. The Directorate works to integrate the Command, Control, Communications, Computers, and Information Management (C4IM) services list and measurements contained in the Army's Metrics Program into the Common Levels of Support (CLS) process. It also continues to deploy the SharePoint program across the ACSIM. The directorate is made

INSTALLATION MANAGEMENT COMMUNITY

up of three divisions. The IT Governance Division promulgates IT governance procedures and trains ACSIM personnel in the governance program. It also develops metrics to assess the ACSIM IT systems. The Strategy and Policy Division integrates CIO G6 policy into ACSIM operations and ensures ACSIM synchronizes the IT portion of the Army Campaign Plan. The division also develops the ACSIM Knowledge Management program. The Enterprise Integration Division monitors, assesses and reports on the performance of ACSIM databases. In addition, it conducts comprehensive business analysis of end-to-end IT needs to improve alignment with the Army force generation process and gain cost savings.

   (3) Operations Directorate has five divisions. The Base Realignment and Closure Division (BRAC) recently completed the BRAC 2005 realignment of Army forces. As it readies for potential future BRACs, it continues to execute cleanup and transfer of BRAC and assigned non-BRAC excess Army property. The Construction Division manages the Army military construction (MILCON) program and provides interface for the Non Appropriated Fund (NAF) construction program. The division also provides oversight and participates in regular updates from the Army Corps of Engineers on the execution of the Army construction program. The Facilities and Policy Division manages the Army energy program and develops policies and standards for facilities engineering and infrastructure. The division manages the Army Facilities Standardization Committee (AFSC) and operates the Army Energy and Water Report System (AEWRS), PAVER, RAILER, ROOFER and the emerging BUILDER databases. The operations division, organized into three branches, performs the following functions: assesses the readiness of Army facilities; is the ACSIM representative to the Strategic Readiness Update (SRU) and the Joint Forces Readiness Review (JFFR); reviews multiple regulations and policies; and operates, manages and executes multiple databases in support of Army operations. These databases include Real Property Planning and Analysis System (RPLANS), Installation Status Report (ISR), Installation Geospatial Information & Services (IGI&S), and the Army Stationing and Installation Plan (ASIP). The Strategic Plans Division is the ACSIM connection to the Army G-3/5/7 and the Army Campaign Plan (ACP). The division coordinates force structure stationing and joint basing requirements, and develops and manages the Army Facility Strategy 2020 (AFS 2020) and the Facility Investment Strategy (FIS).

   (4) Resources Directorate is made up of three divisions: Program Integration, Requirements Modeling and Financial Management. The directorates prime functions are as follows: analyzing and validating II PEG program requirements; providing baseline requirements for Base Operations Support (BOS) in support of the annual Program Objective Memorandum (POM) development; program resource distribution; defending the installation management communities' budget request; supporting emergent installation management requirements in the year of execution; and drafting guidance to address expenditures of resources for the Installation Management community. The modeling division develops defendable cost models, is the owner of the BOS Requirements Model (BRM), and regularly interfaces with the Deputy Undersecretary of Defense (Installations and Environment) Facility Sustainment Model (FSM). The financial management division executes the Managers Internal Control Program (MICP), provides interface for ACSIM with General Accounting Office (GAO) and the Army Auditing Agency and supports ACSIM for the financial portion of Lean Six Sigma and the Strategic Plans division of Operations for the resources portion of the AR 5-10 (Stationing) process.

17-6. Land Holding Commands Including IMCOM

   a. Land Holding Commands are commands with real property maintenance responsibilities that execute installation management and base operations activities. These Commands direct installations and include Army Central Command (ARCENT-3 installations), Army Material Command (AMC-27 installations), Army National Guard (ARNG-48 installations), Defense Logistic Agency (DLA-5 installations), Installation Management Command (IMCOM-66 installations), and United States Army Reserve (USAR-3 installations). The Arlington National Cemetery (ANC) is a virtual installation.

   b. The Army National Guard (ARNG) executes installation management separately from IMCOM and it occurs at the State-level (e.g., the 50 States, District of Columbia, Puerto Rico, Guam and the Virgin Islands). Each state, district, and territory contracts with the federal government to support the ARNG mission by providing services and facilities. This administration of support contract is through cooperative agreements, whereby the federal government funds the state to provide services in support of the federal share of the mission; the state is responsible for funding their share of costs. The organizational interface between the federal government and the State is provided through the National Guard Bureau. Each state has an assigned, National Guard Bureau, Title 10 Officer (United States Property and Fiscal Officer – USPFO) who works closely with the state's leadership to assure proper federal reimbursement for state-

HOW THE ARMY RUNS

provided services. Further, each state assigns a Construction and Facility Management Officer (CFMO) that generally manages the state's ARNG facilities and related services. (Note: For all intents and purposes related to this document, the ARNG is comprised of 55 Installations; ie.,50 States, District of Columbia, Puerto Rico, Guam, Virgin Islands and the ARNG Readiness Center in Arlington, VA). IMCOM is the primary active land holding command described below.

c. History. Army installation "ownership" transferred from some of the functional Major Army Commands (MACOMs) to the IMA effective 1 October 2002. On 24 October, 2006 the IMA was deactivated and its installation management role was assumed by the IMCOM, which was activated on the same day. IMCOM is commanded by a lieutenant general who is also the ACSIM on the Army staff. Other leadership position changes designated the former IMA director, a major general, as the IMCOM's Deputy Commanding General/Chief of Staff (DCG/CofS) and the former Family and Morale, Welfare, and Recreation (FMWRC) Commander as a second Deputy Commanding General (DCG). The deputy ACSIM remained a Senior Executive Service civilian. In activating the IMA and subsequently IMCOM, a HQ and Regional organizational structure was established to exercise management and supervision of Army installations.

(1) HQ IMCOM is currently located at Joint Base San Antonio, Texas. There are four geographically based regions, two of them are overseas: Europe, and Pacific. The two CONUS regions are the Atlantic and Central Regions. All regions report to HQ IMCOM and are led by a Senior Executive Service (SES) Region Director (RD). In addition, there are several garrisons that report directly to HQ IMCOM. The IMCOM's mission is to synchronize, integrate, and deliver installation services and facilities in support of Senior Commanders in order to enable a ready and resilient Army. This requires fast, efficient and agile support to commanders in the performance of their tactical, operational, and strategic missions.

(2) As a Direct Report Unit (DRU), IMCOM is accountable to the ACSIM for effective garrison support of mission activities, and serves as the active Army's primary provider of base support services. HQ IMCOM accomplishes integrated program execution of installation management related policies, plans, and programs as developed and promulgated by the ACSIM. It directs and oversees regional program execution. IMCOM functions include: funding the garrisons; disseminating planning, programming and budgeting guidance as prepared by the ARSTAF; implementing operational plans & Army-wide standards; and seeking Army-wide installation management initiatives and standardizing implementation of those initiatives. IMCOM, in coordination with ACSIM and ASA (IE&E), also provides liaison with Congress.

(3) The Regions implement, direct, and oversee policy and program execution. The Regions support garrisons by being responsible for: enforcing Army-wide standards and ensuring equity among installations; adopting best business practices; identifying and implementing regional efficiencies and partnerships; and interfacing with ACOMs, ASCCs, DRUs and other services/agencies.

(4) Each Army installation has a garrison command reporting to its geographic region (or directly to HQ, IMCOM). Garrison commanders (GCs) support and enable Senior Commanders (SC) by providing the full range of installation and base support services to all local units, tenants and customers. The mission of GCs is to command, control, and operate a garrison to support and enable missions and readiness of stationed units and care for people; conduct daily operations to provide installation support to mission commanders; maintain and improve installation services, infrastructure and environment; plan for and, on order, conduct contingency operations; maintain garrison operational and situational awareness and maintain liaison with mission commanders and leaders. Garrison commanders are responsible for local program execution, implementing and managing to Army-wide standards, and maintaining real property. In October 2012, IMCOM transferred its Directorates of Logistic (DOL) to Army Sustainment Command (ASC), a major subordinate command of the Army Material Command (AMC). All Base Operations Support (BASOPS) logistics services are now furnished by ASC.

(5) The Garrison commander roles and duties are described in AR 600-20 (Army Command Policy) and further described below as it relates to the Senior Commander. The GC is supported by the Deputy Garrison Commander (DGC), retained as a civilian position, to provide continuity for the garrison and its supported population. The DGC may act in the absence of the commander on all matters except that involving command authority. A civilian deputy is generally responsible for the overall administrative management within the garrison, coordination of requirements and activities between the garrison and multiple clientele, and assistance to the commander in implementing all policies, programs and services in support of BASOPS. This position may serve as a target assignment for BASOPS civilian employees engaged in cross-functional professional development.

INSTALLATION MANAGEMENT COMMUNITY

d. Standard Garrison Organization (SGO). The Standard Garrison Organization (SGO) was approved by the Army G3 in 2004. Modifications are primarily associated with organizational realignments (e.g., the 2012 transfer of Logistics (DOL) to AMC). SGO supports the Army's warfighting mission by affording a standard structure to provide Soldiers, civilians, and families effective and efficient services, facilities, and infrastructure. SGO provides a common method of managing installations, creates optimal professional relationships among related functions, eliminates redundancy in garrison staffing, sets the stage for implementation of common standards, facilitates training and professional development among garrison workforces, and fixes garrison Table of Distribution and Allowances (TDAs) in accordance with an Army standard. Exceptions to SGO must be approved by the CG, IMCOM. Regardless of command authorities, the Garrison Commander remains the single integrator of support services for the Senior Commander on the Installation. There are different types of Directorates or Offices, which directly report to or are under operational control of the GC.

(1) Garrison Management & Control Office
 (a) Resource Management Office (RMO)
 (b) Plans, Analysis, & Integration Office (PAIO)
 (c) Information Management Office (IMO)
 (d) Headquarters Company/Detachment (HHC/HHD)
(2) Installation Support Directorates
 (a) Human Resources (DHR)
 (b) Family, Morale, Welfare & Recreation (DFMWR)
 (c) Plans, Training, Mobilization & Security (DPTMS)
 (d) Emergency Services (DES)
 (e) Public Works (DPW)
(3) Installation Support Offices
 (a) Consolidated Legal Office (CLO)
 (b) Public Affairs (PAO)
 (c) Religious Support (RSO)
 (d) Equal Employment Opportunity (EEO)
 (e) Safety (ISO)
 (f) Internal Review (IRACO)
(4) Under Operational Control to the GC
 (a) Civilian Personnel Services (CPAC)
 (b) Network Enterprise Center (NEC)
 (c) Contractor (ICO)

e. Senior Commander/Garrison Commander Roles and Responsibilities. The senior assigned United States Army officer present for duty normally has responsibility for the command of units, platoon level and above. Command of Army installations is exercised by a Senior Commander (SC). The SC is designated by senior Army leadership. The SC's command authority over the installation is derived from the Chief of Staff, Army (CSA) and Secretary of the Army's (SA) authority over installations. This is a direct delegation of command authority for the installation to the SC. The SC's command authority includes all authorities inherent in command including the authority to ensure the maintenance of good order and discipline for the installation. Senior Commanders will coordinate with Region Directors or the DCG of IMCOM while accomplishing their installation duties. Senior Commander (normally the senior general officer at the installation) roles and responsibilities include:

(1) Care of Soldiers, families, and civilians, and to enable unit readiness.
(2) Use of the garrison as the primary organization to provide services and resources to customers in support of accomplishing this mission.
(3) Being dual-hatted as a mission commander. When this occurs the commander exercises discrete authorities as the SC and as a mission commander. The SC responsibilities and authorities are installation focused; the responsibilities and authorities as the mission commander are mission focused.
(4) Responsibility for synchronizing and integrating Army priorities and initiatives at the installation.
(5) Establishing installation priorities among all resident and supported units.
(6) Prioritizing base operations support consistent with HQDA priorities and Commanding General (CG) IMCOM approved Common Levels of Support (CLS) service support program (SSP) capability levels (CLs).

HOW THE ARMY RUNS

(7) Overseeing CLS services and capabilities provided to customers ensuring that those services are provided within the HQDA and/or IMCOM guidance, designated priorities, and CG IMCOM approved CLS SSP CLs and coordinates with the IMCOM Regions and/or HQ IMCOM proponent to obtain approval to lower CLS SSP CLs.

(8) Approving and submitting the installation master plan consistent with HQDA long-range plans and goals through the ACOMs, ASCCs or DRUs, and IMCOM.

(9) Approving the military construction, Army (MCA) and military construction (MILCON), Army Reserve (MCAR) project priority lists at the installation level. The U.S. Army Corps of Engineers executes MCA/MCAR projects for the Army.

(10) Reviewing and approving the prioritization of Family and installation programs.

(11) Installation force protection (FP) as follows:

(a) Continental United States (CONUS) SC as directed by U.S. Army North (USARNORTH) and in coordination with the installation management headquarters (IMCOM and Non-IMCOM), oversees FP on the installation

(b) Outside Continental United States (OCONUS) SC in coordination with the ASCC and IMCOM is responsible for FP oversight on the installation

(12) Normal designation as a General Court-Martial Convening Authority (GCMCA). The GCMCA orders will specify the appellate and review channels for SC GCMCA actions.

(13) Serving as the senior Army representative to the surrounding community.

(14) Senior rating the Garrison Commander.

f. Garrison Commander (GC). The GC is a military officer, lieutenant colonel or colonel, selected by HQDA. The GC commands the garrison, is the SC's senior executive for installation activities, is rated by the IMCOM RD (or DCG as applicable) and is senior rated by the SC. The GC is responsible for day-to-day operation and management of installations and base support services. The GC ensures that installation services and capabilities are provided in accordance with HQDA directed programs, SC guidance, CLS, and IMCOM guidance. The GC provides additional service support in accordance with HQDA directives and provides reimbursable services in accordance with memorandum of understanding or agreement (MOU/MOA). The GC is responsible to deliver Family and installation programs, coordinates and integrates the delivery of support from other service providers, and obtains SC approval of the installation master plan. The GC may be appointed as a Summary Courts-Martial Convening Authority or the Special Courts-Martial convening authority for the installation and its support area; in rare cases the GC may be appointed as GCMCA. In some cases, the senior official on an installation may be the garrison manager. A garrison manager (the civilian equivalent of a GC) has the same responsibility and authority as the military counterpart with the exception of the Uniform Code of Military Justice (UCMJ) and command authority. Prior to the appointment of the garrison manager, command and UCMJ authorities for the garrison will be specified. The GC responsibilities are:

(1) Representing the Army and the installation in the surrounding community as directed by the SC.

(2) Approving and issuing garrison policies in accordance with respective Army regulations or installation level policies involving tenant units as directed by the SC

(3) Approving and issuing policies for IMCOM civilian workforce

(4) Developing and implementing the Force Protection Program

(5) Supporting mobilization station requirements

g. Installation Environment.

(1) Installations are platforms of readiness supporting Senior Commanders' current and future requirements through regular modernization and new construction of standardized facilities to maintain efficient and sustainable operations and enable the provision of effective services to Soldiers, families and civilians. Installations are the Army's "face" to the nation and the world. Although the focus is on installations, the Senior and Garrison Commander play an important role interfacing with the civilian community. Garrison Commanders are expected to be involved in community relations events and may represent the command in business and civic organizations, such as Chamber of Commerce, Rotary and Lions Clubs, etc. Installations in the continental United States (CONUS) are the only Army installations most Americans see on a regular basis, while outside the continental United States (OCONUS) installations provide a unique perspective of our culture to the international community.

(2) To foster effective CONUS state and community partnerships while improving the quality of life for Active and Reserve Component Soldiers, civilians, and their families, the Secretary of the Army launched the Army Community Covenant (ACC). The ACC is tailored at the local level, with leaders at both local

INSTALLATION MANAGEMENT COMMUNITY

and state levels participating in covenant signings that started in April 2008. The covenant recognizes the strength of the Army, its Active, Reserve, and Civilian Components, its Army Families, and the support of the civilian community in which Soldiers and their families live. To highlight community initiatives around the country that focused on support for Soldiers and families, selected initiatives known as "best practices" are featured from local, state, and national organizations. IMCOM, National Guard Bureau through each state headquarters, Army Reserve Ambassadors, and Civilian Aides to the Secretary of the Army identified and reported best practices to the ACC Task Force for consideration across the Army. The current list of best practices can be found at www.communitycovenant.army.mil.

h. Installation Readiness.

(1) Installation Readiness is achieving mission excellence through streamlined processes, strategic partnerships, and good stewardship of resources that address Army priorities and meet the mission requirements of senior commanders. It translates into the ability to provide a growing and transforming Army with the infrastructure and support services it needs to remain a highly effective, expeditionary and campaign-quality force, today and in the future.

(2) Sustainability is a major facet of installation readiness. Today, the interdependence between mission excellence, energy security, environmental stewardship and community relations has never been more important. The installation community has produced an Energy Portfolio, Water Portfolio, and Environmental Portfolio which recognizes successes at installations in each of these areas. The community has emplaced a strategy of environmental sustainment through everyday actions and through education, incentives and alternatives. The efforts to support installation sustainability will yield multiple benefits for the Army. IMCOM collaborates with industry and Army Commands to establish installations that are more energy efficient and self-sustaining than in the past. Keys to this effort are the Army Net Zero Program. IMCOM continues to work with community partners as it pursues sustainability in long range goals, addresses encroachment issues and reaffirms installations as valued neighbors. IMCOM will continue to build healthy, inviting communities and quality housing that allow Soldiers and families to thrive and will continue to modernize installation training facilities to support unified land operations training creating training conditions that realistically portray the operational environment. IMCOM provides training areas and facilities that provide Soldiers with realistic experiences, thoroughly preparing them for all contingencies. IMCOM will continue to focus attention on current and emerging technologies, leveraging opportunities to conserve energy, promote water conservation, reduce waste, preserve natural resources, enhance training realism, and reduce supply chain vulnerability.

(3) A fully integrated Installation Protection Program will not only protect but enable readiness and resilience of loved ones, facilities, information and equipment at all locations and in all situations. Leaders will ensure adequate prioritization of efforts and funding for all facets of installation protection/emergency management activities (prevention, preparedness, response, recovery and mitigation) as reflected in the National Response Framework. In addition, a fully capable Emergency Services program will provide a safe and secure environment for Soldiers, family members, and civilians working and living on our installations. Trained first responders and maintained equipment are critical requirements. Risk assessments will be conducted in order to prioritize and fund programs. Community leaders outside our installation boundaries will be engaged to improve the quality of services available to Soldiers, families and Army civilians, improve public awareness and involvement in quality of life issues, and complete joint long-range planning to ensure mutual long-term growth and viability.

i. Establishing Standards. The Army's installation long-range plan conveys direction for installation management during the next 20-plus years. The plan identifies efficiency programs, determines funding requirements, and describes the metrics used to measure success. The goal of the plan is to provide quality, cost-effective, and efficient mission-ready installations that are the right size, in the right place, and available when needed. Management planning for installations focuses on streamlining, realigning and standardizing services and the workforce, recapitalizing investments and reducing costs. For this purpose, ACSIM acts for and exercises authority of the CSA in dissemination of policy and integration of doctrine pertaining to the operation of Army installations. The ACSIM/IMCOM is responsible for establishing performance metrics and implementing Army-wide standards for installation management and BASOPS.

j. The ACOE Program.

(1) The ACOE program is conducted by the three Army components: Active Army (IMCOM), National Guard (National Guard Bureau (NGB)) and the Army Reserve (Army Reserve Command (USARC)). The ACOE program is sponsored by the Chief of Staff of the Army (CSA). The ACOE program recognizes

HOW THE ARMY RUNS

excellence at Army installations by assessing all components and dimensions of installation management consistent with the Army mission, Army Campaign Plan, the Army's Imperatives, and AR 5-1. The program uses the Malcolm Baldrige Criteria for Performance Excellence published by the National Institute for Standards and Technology. The ACOE program is a commander's self-assessment that is broad enough to accommodate a variety of approaches that can be tailored to any organization, command or installation.

(2) The ACOE Program's goal is to improve operations and readiness of installations by implementing business transformation processes. The program utilizes an integrated management system that enables leadership to make resource-informed decisions and provide trained and ready forces at best value by identifying management strengths and key areas for improvement that are essential to achieving high levels of performance as part of Army-wide transformation to business excellence initiatives. The ACOE program is a multiyear/component program that spans the current year, prior year, and one out year.

(3) The ACOE program culminates with an ACOE Award Program. The ACOE Award honors the top Active Army, National Guard, and Reserve garrisons and installations that have achieved high level of excellence in building a quality environment, outstanding facilities, and superior services. During a year long process, ACOE Award applicants are assessed and evaluated against Army priorities and Malcolm Baldrige Criteria for Performance Excellence.

(4) Each of the three Army components is responsible for evaluating ACOE submissions and arranging attendance for the ACOE Award ceremony. Out-year dollars are presented to the winning communities in the first quarter following the competition. The mission of the ACOE Program is to provide in a quality environment, excellent facilities and services. Continuing to strive for greater excellence in customer service and facilities will contribute significantly to the improvement of Army readiness. ACOE has three important roles in strengthening mission performance:

(a) To help improve organizational performance practices, capabilities, and results
(b) To facilitate communication and sharing of best practice information among organizations of all types
(c) To serve as a working tool for understanding and managing performance and for guiding planning and opportunities for learning

k. Army Base Operations (BASOPS).

(1) A viable standard process for determining Mission/Base Operations military construction projects is a fundamental condition for the success of managing installations to standards. The streamlined components of this process include the following actions:

(a) Garrison Commander forwards the Senior Commander's (SC) prioritized listing of all projects to the IMCOM Region
(b) Region prioritizes all BASOPS projects within their Region and forwards to HQ IMCOM
(c) HQ IMCOM prioritizes all BASOPS projects and forwards to ACSIM
(d) ACOM, ASCC, DRU prioritize their mission projects and forward prioritizations to ACSIM
(e) ACOM, ASCC, DRU may offer their suggested prioritization of BASOPS projects for installations where the SC reports to the ACOM, ASCC or DRU. This suggested prioritization would be forwarded to ACSIM and IMCOM

(2) Upon receipt of prioritized project listing from the ACOMs, ASCCs and DRUs and HQ IMCOM, and using guidance provided by Senior Army Leadership, ACSIM builds the corporate Army prioritized project listing. ACSIM forwards the corporate Army prioritized project listing through the Army G-3 to the VCSA for approval. This listing will contain the ACOMs, ASCCs or DRUs mission project prioritizations and their suggested prioritization of BASOPS projects. The IMCOM's prioritization of BASOPS projects will also be included.

(3) Installations remain a big business. As of 2013, ACSIM and HQDA, manages Defense and Army budget and resources in excess of $20.8 billion. Approximately 75,000 persons, paid by military funds, appropriated funds (APF), and non-appropriated funds (NAF), perform installation management functions. Installations cover over 13.5 million acres of land, more than the combined acreage of the States of Maryland, Connecticut and Rhode Island. Installations maintain well over than 120,000 buildings covering more than 925 million square feet. Army facilities represent a replacement value of more than $315 billion. Installations are home to the Force and home to the Army family - where the Army lives, works, trains, deploys, sustains and prepares to meet tomorrow's challenges. Army posts and surrounding communities are home to well over one million service members and their families. Installations house half of Army families and nearly 200,000 single Soldiers. Army installations are where

INSTALLATION MANAGEMENT COMMUNITY

a quarter of a million civilian employees and tens of thousands of contract employees come to work every day.

17-7. Services and Infrastructure Core Enterprise (SICE) Board
   a. In an effort to improve Army force generation, adopt an enterprise approach to strategic decision-making and reform the requirements and resource processes, the Army has organized around core enterprises. This effort enhances the Army's versatility in response to a complex strategic environment. It isn't a change to organizational structure but is instead a drive to improve collaboration, synchronization and integration across the entire force. Improved cooperation will yield better decisions faster and lead to increased predictability and reduced turbulence for our Soldiers and families.
   b. The SICE board provides essential services, infrastructure, and operational support worldwide to enable an expeditionary Army and sustain Soldiers and their families. The SICE board also integrates Army services, infrastructure, and operational support functions and organizations to gain economies of scope and scale, increased efficiency, and improved effectiveness in support of Army force generation. Co-Chaired by the ASA (IE &E) and ACSIM/CG IMCOM, the board's outputs are:
   (1) Strategic: develop and subsequently use an Army Services and Infrastructure Strategy to advise the SA on services and infrastructure issues that sustain readiness and preserve the All Volunteer Force
   (2) Operational: provide essential services, infrastructure, and operational support enabling an expeditionary Army to support Army force generation and sustain Soldiers and their families
   c. Key Stakeholders in the SICE are:
   (1) U.S. Army Reserve Command (Office of the Chief of the Army Reserves)
   (2) U.S. Army National Guard (Director, ARNG)
   (3) U.S. Army Medical Command, (Office of the Surgeon General)
   (4) U.S. Army Corps of Engineers (Office of the Chief of Engineers)
   (5) U.S. Army Intelligence and Security Command (G2)
   (6) U.S. Army Network Enterprise Technology Command (G6)
   (7) U.S. Army Criminal Investigation Command (Office of the Provost Marshal General)
   (8) Army Corrections Command
   (9) U.S. Army Combat Readiness Center (Tentative)
   (10) Office of the Judge Advocate General (OTJAG)
   (11) Finance Command (Tentative)
   (12) EEO Civil Rights Office (Tentative)

Section III
Initiatives and Programs

17-8. Major Installation Management Initiatives and Programs
   a. Common Levels of Support (CLS). CLS is a decision process that enables successful uniform delivery of the Army's highest priority installation services, within available funds. The Installation CLS process is based on a comprehensive understanding of the Army's Base Operations Support (BOS) services, standards, and costs. CLS provides the Army with the ability to:
   (1) Provide definitive performance guidance to Garrisons for the execution of core services delivered to standard, based on available funding
   (2) Distribute available resources among installations to execute the guidance
   (3) Measure Garrison performance to make sure that expected performance is being achieved
   (4) Inform customers on the levels of support they can expect from Garrisons across the Army
   b. CLS is built on the principle that IMCOM installations will provide non-reimbursable Base Operations Support (BOS) to Army customers across all its installations. This support will be standard but adaptable to local realities for the installation (e.g., requirements of mission, demography, or geography). Garrisons are required to deliver installation management support services IAW with the Army's Installation Status Report (ISR) - Services program, which specifies content and pacing measures for each service component. The total dollar requirement for garrisons to deliver these services is calculated to fund the full scope of service as defined in the ISR. However, garrisons historically do not receive 100% of the required dollars for each service. Garrisons therefore cannot deliver the full scope of services, and must have some way of determining which service components can be delivered with the dollars available.

HOW THE ARMY RUNS

CLS provides the approach for making this decision across the Army, in a way that will lead to quality, consistency, and predictability.

   c. Army Baseline Standards. The effort to develop performance-based measures initially focused on those ISR services where the quality of the service provided was key to determining required resources and potential performance measures could easily be identified. For these services, quality played a significant role and needed supplemental data from Army Service Based Costing (SBC) - a model to capture the cost of base operations at the service level - to facilitate development of good cost estimating relationships (CERs) for resource program development purposes. That effort resulted in performance measures and standards for almost all 95 standard services developed by the Army Baseline Standards Task Force appointed by the ACSIM in late FY03. The resulting standards have been developed into performance measures that are included in the Installation Status Report.

   d. Joint Bases [Common Output Level of Standards (COLS)]. COLS is a DOD initiative intended to create common language and toolsets for common delivery of installations support applicable across all U.S. military installations in a host-tenant relationship. The COLS framework assists DOD Components in apportioning and managing limited resources and is similar to the Army CLS. The military components have different service delivery expectations and standards. As a result, the service delivery is measured by different metrics. OSD evaluates and establishes common service delivery standards for operations in a joint environment to meet each component's mission-specific and base support requirements. COLS are the framework for common delivery standards, metrics, and costs for installation services in a high-level host-tenant relationship in a joint military component environment. This support includes professional program management services, data collection, and data analysis. As joint bases have continued to evolve, all services have seen their funding decrease. While OSD remains committed to "green levels" for COLS, Joint Base Commanders will continue to use the Joint Management Oversight Structure to ensure a collaborative approach to installation management at joint bases while determining priorities for applying resources.

INSTALLATION MANAGEMENT COMMUNITY

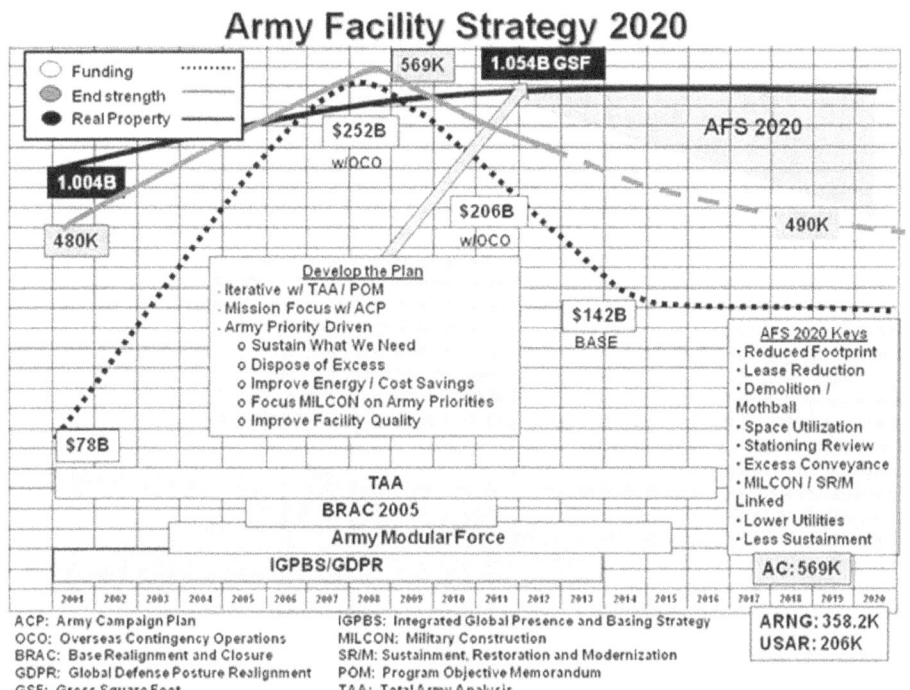

Figure 17-2. Army Facility Strategy 2020

e. Army Facility Strategy 2020 (AFS 2020). AFS 2020 recognizes as current operations end in Afghanistan and the Global Defense Posture Realignment Strategy (GDPRS) ends, the preponderance of Soldiers in Army units will be stationed in the continental United States (CONUS). Further, after more than a decade of increased funds to support two wars, the Army's funding and Overseas Contingency Operations (OCO) funds will decrease. AFS 2020 is a coordinated strategy focused on the Army mission ensuring the Army has the right facilities, for the right units, at the right location, for the long term (2020 and beyond). It will recognize that as the Army Staff analyzes force structure, funds and facilities, it needs a longer range view—out beyond the POM – as facilities are costly, take a long time for approval and once complete – the Army lives with them for many years. AFS 2020 seeks to size installations appropriately. Units will occupy authorized space. Excess facilities will be apportioned to: units in leases (driving down lease costs); on post units to ensure best facilities are used: be considered for renovation; be mothballed and taken off the utilities grid to reduce utility and SRM costs.

f. Facility Investment Strategy (FIS). FIS is a holistic approach to improve facility quality which includes investments to sustain enduring facilities/ improve existing facility conditions particularly energy and utility efficiencies, to demolish facilities no longer needed and to build to address critical shortfalls. The Army will use all forms of facility investment to include Unspecific Minor MILCON, O&M (R&M) and focus its MILCON on Army shortfalls. Over the next 15 years, the Army will concentrate investment on six Focus Areas: Energy/Utilities, Organic Industrial Base, Organizational Vehicle Maintenance, Ranges/Training Support Systems, Reserve Component Readiness Facilities, and Trainee Barracks. The Army will use the Installation Status Report and Real Property Planning and Analysis systems to measure investment results.

HOW THE ARMY RUNS

g. Installation 2020. Installation 2020 is emerging installation doctrine that operates at echelon providing guidance and direction to the installation community. It provides a shared vision and the strategic imperatives of the Army's Installation Community leadership, which includes the Active and Reserve components of the Army, AMC, Space and Missile Defense Command (SMDC), USACE, the Army Staff, OASA (IE&E) and OASA (M&RA). It guides the planning efforts for the activities which must occur on our installations (including garrisons, readiness centers, camps, posts, stations, joint bases, casernes, barracks, depots, arsenals, laboratories and other Army real property holdings and Army Contingency Bases to support the Army Vision and the Army Campaign Plan

h. Core Capabilities.

(1) Installation Services. We will provide a quality of life commensurate with the quality of service provided by Soldiers and their families. We plan for a future of delivering services that are flexible and adaptive to support the Operating and Generating Forces. Army-wide standards for service delivery will be customer-driven, leverage successful partnerships with communities and the private sector, enable mission accomplishment by Senior Commanders, and enable well-being and readiness for Service members and Families. Services will be provided based on an enterprise business model and reflect enterprise standards, priorities, and funding strategies intended to eliminate redundancies.

(2) Installation Infrastructure. We will provide infrastructure to enable the Army to accomplish its mission on a global scale and achieve Army standards for quality and capacity at least cost. In 2020, Army installation infrastructure will be secure and sustainable. Energy and environmental programs will be models for surrounding communities across the globe. Our facilities will enable a quality of life commensurate with the quality of service provided by our Soldiers and their families and help to mitigate the stress of repeated operational deployments on people, equipment, and infrastructure. We will work as an enterprise to properly station the force and adjust the Army's global infrastructure to enable the Army to fulfill its training and operational mission, and execute the requirements of the Defense Strategy.

(3) Installation Synchronization—People, Processes, and Tools. Inspired installation leaders will seek to use innovative approaches built on lessons learned and institutionalize the best practices of benchmark organizations within and outside of Army and DOD. Installation Leaders will use performance management, geo-spatial, financial management, and strategic communications tools to meet Army requirements and facilitate enterprise management. Internal installation functions will be streamlined and focus on the core competencies of installation services and installation infrastructure. Installations will work within the Army Management system, pursue vigorously public-public and public-private partnership opportunities, and will employ processes that develop and sustain the workforce and create a true Installation Profession. Installations will have many organizations responsible for providing services as an enterprise, and installation leaders will coordinate and synchronize all service providers to ensure integrated, balanced and efficient service delivery.

Section IV
Summary and References

17-9. Summary

The Installation Management Community concept provides effective Army-wide installation management through use of best corporate business models, development of relevant standards and comprehensive adherence to Army standards, and partnership with ACOMs, ASCCs, and DRUs, senior and mission commanders, who receive focus on their unique issues, while geographic efficiencies are realized through economies of scale. The concept cares for people while ensuring readiness is not compromised; it positions installations for Army and DOD transformation initiatives and represents the Army's commitment to improve installations, preserve the environment, enable well-being of Soldiers, civilians and family members, and support mission readiness of all stakeholder units.

17-10. References

a. Publications:

(1) Army Campaign Plan (ACP)
(2) Army Regulation 1-1, Planning, Programming, Budgeting, and Execution System
(3) Army Regulation 5-1, Total Army Quality Management
(4) Army Regulation 5-3, Installation Management and Organization

INSTALLATION MANAGEMENT COMMUNITY

    (5) Army Regulation 5-9, Area Support Responsibilities
    (6) Army Regulation 5-20, Competitive Sourcing Program
    (7) Army Regulation 115-11, Geospatial Information and Services
    (8) Army Regulation 200-1, Environmental Protection and Enhancement
    (9) Army Regulation 210-14, Installation Status Report Program
    (10) Army Regulation 210-20, Master Planning for Army Installations
    (11) Army Regulation 210-35, Civilian Inmate Labor Program
    (12) Army Regulation 405-70, Utilization of Real Property
    (13) Army Regulation 405-90, Disposal of Real Estate
    (14) Army Regulation 420-1, Army Facilities Management
    (15) Army Regulation 420-41, Acquisition and Sales of Utilities Services
    (16) Army Regulation 600-3, The Army Personnel Proponent System
    (17) Field Manual 100-22, Installation Management
    (18) General Order Number 4, Assignment of Functions and Responsibilities within Headquarters, Department of the Army (as pertains to Assistant Chief of Staff for Installation Management (ACSIM), 09 July 2002
    (19) Installation Management Community Campaign Plan
    (20) IMCOM Strategic Plan
    (21) Office of Management and Budget (OMB) Circular A-76 (Revised), Performance of Commercial Activities

  b. Useful Links:
    (1) Deputy Under Secretary of Defense for Installations & Environment (DUSD(I&E)) http://www.acq.osd.mil/ie/index.shtml.
    (2) Assistant Secretary of the Army for Installations & Environment (ASA(I&E)) http://www.asaie.army.mil/Public/IE/default.html.

HOW THE ARMY RUNS

This page is intentionally left blank

ARMY HEALTH SYSTEM

Chapter 18

Army Health System

"While the wounds of war have been and will continue to be ours to mend and heal, Army Medicine must now look forward and chart a new course for medicine and health. Army Medicine will set the example for the nation in quality healthcare, wellness, prevention and collective health for all those entrusted to our care and complements what we execute today, healthcare at home and abroad. This does not change our noble mission to care for Soldiers, families and retirees. Instead, it broadens our mission, to include engaging the Army (Soldiers, retirees, family members and civilians) in multiple ways to influence health, and achieve more holistic outcomes to include greater readiness and better living. This is a call to action to enable health. Together we will set the conditions to better understand the needs of the Army family and improve Army health and readiness. To do this, Army Medicine must create capacity to influence and enable individual, unit and organizational health; enhance diplomacy by strengthening existing partnerships and building new partnerships to promote unity of effort in the pursuit of health; and improve organizational and individual stamina – an essential element in our transition from healthcare to health that will increase organizational depth, resilience and endurance. These are the three strategic imperatives: create capacity, enhance diplomacy, and improve stamina."

LTG Patricia D. Horoho, The Surgeon General (TSG), U.S. Army, 2011-Present

Section I
Introduction

18-1. The Evolution in Military Medicine
The strategic environment is one of complex interdependence and contains two major parts. First, is the environment in general which includes various political, economic, and social forces that are not unique to Army Medicine or the federal government. Second, is the Army Medicine organizational context which includes both the Army and the Military Health System (MHS). Healthcare in the United States is at a critical juncture, and there is an opportunity for Army Medicine to lead the Nation away from the status quo. Advances in technology not only provide promise for improving the efficacy and delivery methods of healthcare, but new methods of communication will redefine how individuals connect with one another, with partners, and with patients; and increased data-collection and analysis provides new opportunities for intervention and understanding. The Army Medicine strategy considers how to support the Army as it transitions from continuous support of persistent conflicts to a peacetime setting which will include a strategic reset of the military. To move from a healthcare system to a system for health, Army Medicine must impact the determinants of health – those lifestyle choices, social and environmental factors that contribute to overall health – that are at the heart of the Lifespace. Success in doing this rests upon the ability to create capacity, enhance diplomacy and improve stamina.

18-2. Scope of the Army Medical Department (AMEDD)
 a. The AMEDD encompasses those Army special branches that are under the supervision and management of The Surgeon General. Specifically, these special branches are the Medical Corps (MC), Dental Corps (DC), Veterinary Corps (VC), Medical Service Corps (MS), Army Nurse Corps (NC), and Army Medical Specialist Corps (SP). The AMEDD is one of the world's largest health systems and includes all roles of medical, dental, veterinary, and other related healthcare from policy and decision-making to the combat medic in the field.
 b. The Surgeon General directs health services within the Army and commands AMEDD units and facilities of the U.S. Army Medical Command (MEDCOM), a Direct Reporting Unit (DRU) to Headquarters Department of the Army. MEDCOM has about 16,000 Soldiers and 44,000 civilian employees. Another 20,000 active-duty medical Soldiers are in field units. The National Guard and Army Reserve have over 30,000 medical Soldiers. MEDCOM currently manages an $11.9 billion budget and cares for more than five million beneficiaries, including active-duty members of all services, retirees and their family members.

HOW THE ARMY RUNS

c. The Surgeon General also monitors and manages health services Army-wide through the Office of the Surgeon General (OTSG), the AMEDD-element of the Army Staff. Hand-in-hand with other Army management processes (Total Army Analysis, Planning, Programming, Budget, and Execution), the AMEDD conducts various programs specifically designed to meet the force modernization, unit readiness, research and development, preventive medicine, and patient care missions for the armed forces.

d. Through the Warrior Transition Command, the AMEDD is responsible for every aspect of the Army's Warrior Care and Transition Program which provides a holistic patient and family centered approach to recovery, rehabilitation, and reintegration of wounded, ill, and injured Soldiers.

18-3. Army Health System Support

The Army Health System (AHS) and Army medical and dental benefits are an important element of overall military compensation. Providing comprehensive and quality healthcare to military personnel is required by law. Other eligible Army Medicine beneficiary categories, such as retirees and family members, are entitled to medical and dental care subject to availability of space, facilities, and medical and dental staff as defined by Title 10 of the United States Code (USC) and other regulatory requirements. Health services are essential to recruiting and retaining a quality force. Soldiers' confidence on the battlefield is enhanced by the knowledge that they and their families are supported by a superb medical evacuation and treatment system. The Army Medicine System for Health (AMSH) is a comprehensive, synchronized, integrated, responsive and reliable system to improve readiness, save lives, and optimize health in support of the force, military families, and all those entrusted to our care. The concept of complete Soldier "life cycle health management" begins during accession and initial training then extends throughout the cycles of stationing and deployment/redeployment until transition or separation from the Army. AMSH embodies the concept that the Army cares for its own and is capable of strengthening the health of the nation by improving the health of the Army.

18-4. Medical Support to the Transforming Army

a. Army Medicine is transforming from a healthcare system to a system for health. Army Medicine consistently delivers evidenced-based value-added services to our beneficiaries, improve existing healthcare programs and services, and develop new processes and initiatives to improve the health of the populations entrusted to our care. This includes engaging people where they live, work, and socialize (i.e., the Lifespace) in addition to traditional patient care settings, affecting the determinants of health and improving Army readiness. Of the 525,600-minutes in a year, a Soldier interacts with a healthcare provider for an average of 100-minutes. Through engagement in the Lifespace, Army Medicine will make the biggest impact on health and readiness.

b. The Army Medicine Strategic Framework – create capacity, enhance diplomacy, and improve stamina – will be used to move from a healthcare system to a system for health. Creating capacity is the collective ability to develop the capabilities and core competencies necessary to deliver services and programs that improve healthcare, influence overall health, and make Army Medicine a strategic enabler for the Army in the future environment. This includes optimization, innovation, and organizational learning. Creating capacity includes the delivery of healthcare and the development of new methods to impact beneficiaries' Lifespace. Creating capacity also includes ground-breaking research, innovative training and education, and the global reset of healthcare forces to support the Army's and the nation's strategic defense priorities. Building capacity is not about simply doing more, it is about doing things better. In a fiscally constrained environment, building more facilities or hiring more people is not tenable. Army Medicine must provide innovative solutions.

c. Enhancing diplomacy requires participating and shaping dialogue on healthcare delivery and individual health in Army, DOD, national and international communities. Shaping the dialogue will help nurture enduring Federal, national, and international relationships that use medical diplomacy to advance Army values, interests, and objectives. Diplomacy consists of three facets: Partnering, Active Engagements, and Marketing Initiatives. The Army Medicine team is critical to diplomacy and must partner internally and externally to enhance communication, collaboration, and innovation; all of which will ensure long-term sustainability of Army Medicine and advance the Army agenda.

d. Improving stamina requires the ability to increase operational depth, resilience and endurance in order to withstand periods of intense change and unexpected challenges, and ensure that the AMSH is sustainable over the long-term. Army Medicine must improve its own organizational stamina to withstand this intense period of transformation from a healthcare system to a system for health, ensuring long-term

ARMY HEALTH SYSTEM

sustainability for Army Medicine. Organizational stamina is built by improving and refining infrastructure, training, leader development, knowledge sharing, and the ability to innovate.

e. At the individual-level, improved health and resilience translate into improved stamina. The World Health Organization defines health as the "complete physical, mental and social well being, and not merely the absence of disease or infirmity." Health is an integral component of readiness and Army Medicine and Army leaders must prepare Soldiers and their families to negotiate the health risks facing them every day, and improve physical and mental fitness. Army Medicine must look for opportunities to educate and influence the health of its patients, starting with the basics of activity, nutrition, and sleep. Army Medicine's operational approach to improve Soldier and family health and stamina will focus upon Activity, Nutrition, and Sleep Management (ANS).

Section II
Army Medical Department Mission and Support to Commanders

18-5. Mission of the Army Medical Department

The mission of the AMEDD is to "maintain the health of members of the Army, to conserve the fighting strength, to provide healthcare for eligible personnel, and to provide health support to members of the Army in war, international conflict, or natural disaster." This mission relates directly to Army combat readiness. The AMEDD is responsible for maintaining the clinical, technical, and combat readiness of medical units and personnel to support forces in the theater of operations. The AHS is a component of the Military Health System (MHS) that is responsible for operational management of the health service support (HSS) and force health protection (FHP) missions for training, predeployment, deployment, and postdeployment operations. The AHS includes all mission support services performed, provided, or arranged by the AMEDD to support HSS and FHP mission requirements for the Army and as directed, for joint, intergovernmental agencies, coalition, and multinational forces. There will be significant changes between now and '15 however as the governance of DOD medical services changes to more DOD direct control – Initial Operational Capability (IOC) is later this year and has few effects but they will move to Full Operational Capability (FOC) by Oct '15 –so the next two years will be very interesting for the AMEDD.

a. Health service support is defined as all support and services performed, provided, and arranged by the AMEDD to promote, improve, conserve, or restore the mental and physical well being of personnel in the Army and as directed in other Services, agencies, and organizations. This includes casualty care, medical evacuation, and medical logistics, which encompass a number of AMEDD functions—organic and area medical support, hospitalization, the treatment aspects of dental care and behavioral health (BH)/neuropsychiatric (NP) treatment, clinical laboratory services, and the treatment of Chemical, Biological, Radiological, Nuclear, and High-Yield Explosive (CBRNE) patients.

b. Force Health Protection is defined as measures to promote, improve, or conserve the mental and physical well-being of Soldiers. These measures enable a healthy and fit force, prevent injury and illness, and protect the force from health hazards. This includes the prevention aspects of a number of AMEDD functions: preventive medicine such as medical surveillance and occupational and environmental health surveillance; veterinary services including the food inspection and animal care missions; the prevention of zoonotic diseases transmissible to man; combat and operational stress control; dental services (preventive dentistry); and laboratory services (area medical laboratory support).

(1) The deployable medical units of the Army carry out this task, with a heavy reliance on the Reserve Components (which constitute approximately 68 percent of the Army's medical forces). These units are apportioned to combatant commands around the world.

(2) The AMEDD mission as described in the Table of Distribution Allowances (TDA) includes the delivery of healthcare to Soldiers and family members at Medical Centers (MEDCEN), community hospitals, and medical clinics; dental clinics; veterinary services; medical research and development; education and training, rehabilitative care and training; and health promotion and preventive medicine. Fixed installation TDA medical units assigned to the AMEDD directly support operational units, on an area basis, as it relates to medical equipment and training of assigned medical personnel.

(3) The recruitment and retention of healthcare professionals and sustainment of their skills are central to the maintenance of a high quality medical force. Deploying the medical force is one of the AMEDD's primary missions. In peacetime, the vast majority of healthcare professionals and technical support personnel who deploy with medical units are employed within the Army's fixed hospitals, MEDCENs and

HOW THE ARMY RUNS

other healthcare facilities. The day-to-day practice of healthcare professionals and their support staff in these environments is the basis for maintaining the clinical skills and teamwork necessary to care for sick and wounded Soldiers during operations.

(c) Beneficiary Care and TRICARE. The second but equally important aspect of the AMEDD mission is to help maintain the personnel readiness of the Total Army by maintaining the health of individual Soldiers and their families.

(1) Quality healthcare for Soldiers, retirees, and their families is an essential and valuable benefit. Physical readiness, good health and the knowledge that family members will be cared for contribute to the ability of each Soldier to deploy and perform their mission in the operational environment.

(2) To meet readiness requirements and serve Soldier and family health needs better, Congress directed the DOD to develop and implement a new model for military healthcare that would improve patients' access to healthcare, assure high quality of care, and control rising healthcare costs. The result, TRICARE, is now the medical program for active duty service members, retirees, and their families, and eligible survivors of all uniformed Service Members. TRICARE relies on inter-service and civilian-military sharing of medical resources to improve accessibility of care and achieve efficiencies. A DOD program under the oversight of the Assistant Secretary of Defense(ASD) Health Affairs (HA), it is managed by the military in partnership with civilian contractors. Each TRICARE region has an Army, Navy, or Air Force lead agent (usually the commander of a Military Treatment Facility (MTF) or RMC (RMC)) responsible for the program. Details for each TRICARE program is available at http://www.tricare.mil.

18-6. AMEDD Support to Commanders

a. Commanders are responsible for the health and physical fitness of their Soldiers. The AMEDD supports commanders by acting as the proponent for medical doctrine, advising commanders in all health related matters, and executing command policy in the area of AHS. The AMEDD:

(1) Advises the command of measures to assure the health, fitness, and vigor of all members of the Army

(2) As directed, acts as the proponent to provide those measures needed to assure health and fitness

(3) Develops, trains, and maintains forces necessary for medical force health protection (FHP) to the Army in an operational environment

(4) Conducts routine Medical Surveillance to identify leading injury and disease trends affecting Soldier's readiness and health

(5) Conducts field investigations of outbreaks of potential health threats from disease, environmental hazards and injuries

(b) The importance of the AHS in the operational environment is paramount. It supports the prevention of disease and non-battle injury to ensure maximum operational capability. When casualties occur, the medical system provides rapid initial treatment, stabilization and evacuation to medical treatment facilities.

18-7. AMEDD Support to Emergency Management and Installation Commanders

a. AMEDD supports the National Preparedness Goal (NPG) to achieve, "A secure and resilient nation with the capabilities required across the whole community to prevent, protect against, mitigate, respond to, and recover from the threats and hazards that pose the greatest risk." TSG/MEDCOM provides overarching policy on the medical and human health aspects of Army installation activities and operations associated with the Army Installation Preparedness (IP) and Emergency Management Program (EMP), including consideration of potential and residual all-hazards contamination. TSG is responsible for ensuring all Continental United States (CONUS) medical headquarters develop applicable all-hazard plans that are procedurally compliant and interoperable with the National Incident Management System (NIMS).

b. MEDCOM, the RMCs, MTFs, and subordinate medical commands develop comprehensive, integrated, synchronized, interoperable, all-hazards and capabilities-based emergency management planning processes focused upon pre-incident planning, organization, equipping, training, coordination and testing of all IP-, Army Prevention Program (APP)-, EMP-, Installation EMP (IEMP)-, and Interagency EMP (IAEMP)public health and medical services emergency management requirements. Governing documents (addressing guidance, instructions, policies, competencies and performance objectives) are used to plan, execute, sustain, manage and report the tactical-level units' protection, emergency response, and recovery efforts utilizing a resource-balanced, phased implementation approach in support

ARMY HEALTH SYSTEM

of emergency management requirements (including Incident Management-, Crisis Management-, and Consequence Management-operations).

c. All governing documents, Standard Operating Procedures (SOPs), and Operational Plans (OPLANs) support rapid deployment and seamless employment of AMEDD-assets and resources in-compliance-with (ICW) Presidential-, DOD-, HQDA-, TSG/MEDCOM-, Installation- (including joint bases, where a sister-service is the lead agency), and IA-partner issuances and directives that established policy, assigned responsibilities, and prescribed procedures for developing, implementing, and sustaining IPs-, APPs-, EMPs, IEMPs-, and IAEMPs (i.e., federal, state, local, tribal jurisdiction, territorial government, private and nonprofit sectors, and the public). They are compatible with and capable of supporting Federally-mandated programs and processes such as the National Preparedness Guidelines, National Preparedness System, National Response Framework, NIMS, National Disaster Medical System, Incident Command System (ICS), and Hospital ICS; and all contingency plans for specified operations, any other national plans (approved by the President of the U.S. (POTUS) or Secretary of Defense (SECDEF)), or DOD-issuances governing Defense Support of Civil Authority (DSCA)-operations contributing to achieving and maintaining the NPG.

d. OPLANs address a series of integrated planning frameworks that will be used to govern prevention, protection, mitigation, response, and recovery; built upon scalable, flexible, and adaptable coordinating structures to align key roles and responsibilities; and be coordinated using a common terminology and approach. Coordinating activities address detailed concepts of operations, a description of critical tasks and responsibilities, detailed requirements (e.g., resources, personnel, and sourcing), and specific provisions for rapid integration. Plans identify resource guidance, such as arrangements enabling the ability to share personnel, equipment guidance aimed at nationwide interoperability, and guidance for national training and exercise programs.

Section III
The Army Health System

18-8. Key Elements

a. TSG/OTSG: TSG is responsible for development, doctrine, policy direction, organization, and overall management of an integrated AHS; is the medical materiel developer for the Army; and is the Secretary of the Army's (SECARMY) representative for diverse DOD joint medical training, research and health services executive agencies. OTSG is the Army Staff (ARSTAF) element that develops doctrine, policy and regulations for the AHS, health hazards assessment, the establishment of health standards, and medical materiel. TSG also has proponency for personnel management within the AMEDD.

b. Health Services. Health services are all services performed, provided, or arranged for (regardless of location) which promote, improve, conserve, or restore the physical or behavioral health of individuals or groups, and those services which contribute to the maintenance or restoration of a healthy environment. Health services include, but are not limited to, preventive, curative, and restorative health measures; medical doctrine; medical aspects of CBRNE defense; health promotion and injury prevention; assessment of health threats and countermeasures; medical operations planning; medical intelligence; health professional education and training; health-related research; transportation of the sick and wounded; selection of the medically fit and disposition of the medically unfit; administration; medical logistics; medical equipment maintenance; medical facility life cycle management; and the delivery of medical, nursing, dental, veterinary, laboratory, optical, and other specialized services.

c. Programming and Budgeting. Since 1991, military funding was secured through the DOD Unified Medical Program and the Defense Health Program (DHP) Appropriation, rather than the services' budgets. The ASD (HA) issues policy guidance and TRICARE manages and monitors Service execution of the DHP Appropriation and the DOD Unified Medical Program. The DHP appropriation consists of operation and maintenance; research, development, test, and evaluation; and procurement funds designed to finance the non-military personnel requirements of the MHS. In FY 2003, the Department implemented the DOD Medicare Eligible Retiree Healthcare Fund, an accrual-type fund to pay for healthcare provided to Medicare eligible retirees, retiree family members and survivors.

(1) The OTSG/MEDCOM Staff (see "One Staff," below) programs funds and manpower using both the DHP and Army appropriations. DHP funds provide for most peacetime healthcare operations in TDA units such as Army MEDCENs and community hospitals and for TRICARE Managed Care Support Contracts.

HOW THE ARMY RUNS

The vast majority of AMEDD manpower is funded by the DHP. Army funding supports deployable medical TOE units and medical readiness missions.

(2) The OTSG/MEDCOM Staff programs for Army funds and provides its input to the Army's Program Objective Memorandum(POM). It programs for DHP funds and provides input to the DHP POM through the TRICARE. Military personnel costs are programmed by TRICARE in the DHP POM and the programmed total obligation authority (TOA) transfers to the MPA appropriation when the budget estimate submission is prepared. Civilian personnel costs are reimbursable from DHP Operations and Maintenance Defense funds during the year of execution. Authorizations for both military and civilian personnel are on Army manpower documents.

18-9. Staff Relationships and Responsibilities

a. Office of the Assistant Secretary of Defense (ASD) Health Affairs (HA): The ASD (HA) has statutory responsibility for overall supervision of health affairs within DOD and is the principal staff assistant and adviser to SECDEF for all DOD health policies, programs, and activities.

(1) TRICARE Management Activity (TMA): The TRICARE is a DOD field activity of the Under Secretary of Defense (USD) for Personnel and Readiness (P&R) that operates under the authority, control, and direction of the ASD (HA). The mission of TRICARE is to administer and manage TRICARE and administer, manage, and monitor Service execution of the DHP appropriation and the DOD Unified Medical Program.

(2) TRICARE regional offices coordinate healthcare within the various geographic health service regions. Each region has a contractor that administers and helps coordinate the healthcare services available through MTFs and a network of civilian hospitals and providers. Each TRICARE regional office:
   (a) Provides oversight of regional operations and health plan administration at the regional level
   (b) Manages the contracts with regional contractors
   (c) Supports MTF Commanders;
   (d) Develops business plans for non-MTF areas (e.g. remote areas)
   (e) Funds regional initiatives to optimize and improve delivery of healthcare

b. OTSG has the following Army Staff (ARSTAF) responsibilities:

(1) Assisting the Secretary of the Army (SECARMY) and the Chief of Staff of the Army (CSA) in discharging Title 10 responsibility for health services for the Army and other agencies and organizations entitled to military health services

(2) Representing the Army to the executive branch, Congress, DOD agencies, and other organizations on all health policies affecting the Army

(3) DOD focal point for North Atlantic Treaty Organization (NATO) Medical Chemical, Biological, Radiological, and Nuclear (CBRN) actions. Provides U.S. Head of Delegation for the NATO CBRN Medical Working Group and General Medical Working Group

(4) Manage all aspects of medical CBRNE defense programs

(5) Advising and assisting the SECARMY and CSA and other principal officials on all policy issues pertaining to health and military health service support to include:
   (a) Policies and regulations concerning the health aspects of Army environmental programs
   (b) Health professional education and training for the Army, to include training programs for all medical, nursing, dental, and veterinary specialty areas
   (c) Research and development activities for nutrition and wholesomeness in support of the DOD Food Service
   (d) Medical materiel life-cycle management
   (e) Medical materiel in the Army War Reserves Program
   (f) Medical materiel concepts, requirements, validity and viability
   (g) Technical review and evaluation of medical and nonmedical materiel to determine the existence of possible health hazards
   (h) Program management for Army healthcare automation
   (i) Electronic health records
   (j) Army execution of the Defense Medical Systems Support Center (DMSSC)
   (k) Medical aspects of the Security Assistance Program
   (l) Program sponsor for Operations and Maintenance, Army - Program 84 (Medical)
   (m) Executive Agent (EA) of the SECARMY for all DOD veterinary services
   (n) Medical facility life cycle management

ARMY HEALTH SYSTEM

(o) Field medical support concepts, doctrine, training and leader development programs and user test
(p) Medical intelligence training
(q) Medical mobilization training

Section IV
Command and Management

18-10. AMEDD Organization

In 1998, TSG directed the implementation of the One Staff concept, consolidating the staffs at OTSG and Headquarters, MEDCOM, Fort Sam Houston, Texas. Personnel at both locations now function as a single staff with one set of leaders who coordinate ARSTAF functions, along with Army command functions (Figure 18-1).

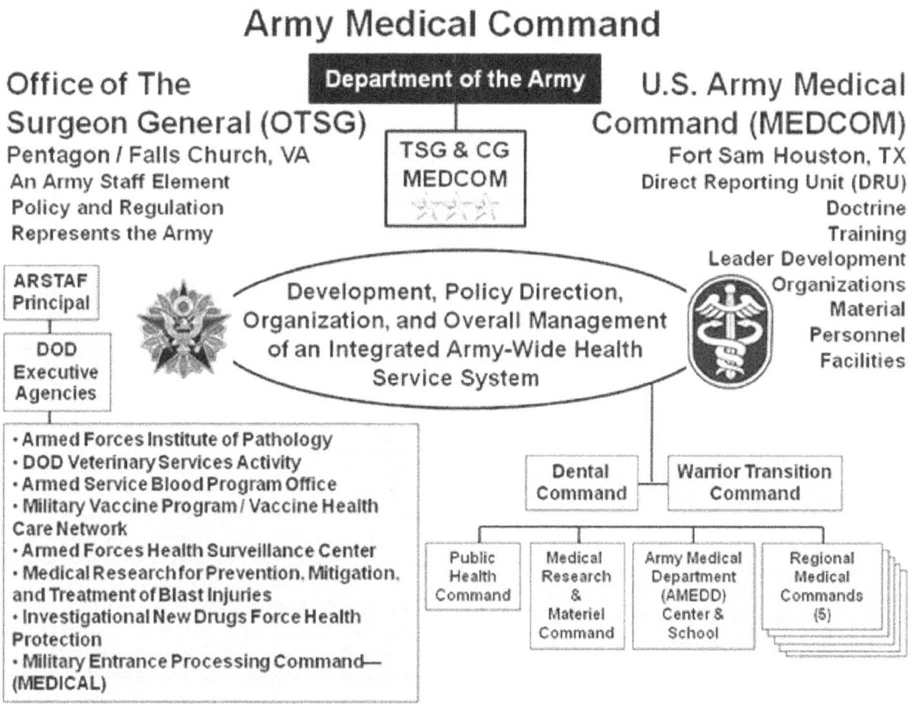

Army Medical Command

Office of The Surgeon General (OTSG)
Pentagon / Falls Church, VA
An Army Staff Element
Policy and Regulation
Represents the Army

Department of the Army
TSG & CG MEDCOM

U.S. Army Medical Command (MEDCOM)
Fort Sam Houston, TX
Direct Reporting Unit (DRU)
Doctrine
Training
Leader Development
Organizations
Material
Personnel
Facilities

ARSTAF Principal
DOD Executive Agencies

Development, Policy Direction, Organization, and Overall Management of an Integrated Army-Wide Health Service System

- Armed Forces Institute of Pathology
- DOD Veterinary Services Activity
- Armed Service Blood Program Office
- Military Vaccine Program / Vaccine Health Care Network
- Armed Forces Health Surveillance Center
- Medical Research for Prevention, Mitigation, and Treatment of Blast Injuries
- Investigational New Drugs Force Health Protection
- Military Entrance Processing Command—(MEDICAL)

Dental Command
Warrior Transition Command
Public Health Command
Medical Research & Materiel Command
Army Medical Department (AMEDD) Center & School
Regional Medical Commands (5)

Figure 18-1. Army Medical Command

18-11. U.S. Army Medical Command (MEDCOM)

a. RMCs oversee day-to-day operations in MTFs, exercising command and control over the medical treatment facilities in their regions. RMCs:
(1) Europe RMC
(2) Southern RMC
(3) Northern RMC
(4) Pacific Region Medical Command
(5) Western Region Medical Command

HOW THE ARMY RUNS

b. The major subordinate commands of the MEDCOM include:
(1) U.S. Army Medical Research and Materiel Command (USAMRMC)
(2) U.S. Army Dental Command (DENCOM)
(3) U.S. Army Public Health Command (USAPHC)
(4) U.S. Army Medical Department Center and School.(AMEDDC&S)
(5) Warrior Transition Command (WTC)

c. The consolidation of worldwide medical assets under the MEDCOM in 1996 greatly enhanced command and control efficiency to meet the needs of the Army of the 21st Century. Implementation of the One Staff concept to achieve the most efficient and effective mission command structure underscored the AMEDD's commitment to continuous quality improvement and poised the AMEDD for its role in the Army Transformation.

d. The One Staff is responsible for AMEDD policy, planning, and operations worldwide, with a focus on strategic planning. Its mission is to:
(1) Provide the vision, direction, and long-range planning for the AMEDD
(2) Develop and integrate doctrine, training, leader development, organization, materiel, and Soldier support for the AHS
(3) Allocate resources, analyze health services utilization, and conduct assessments of performance worldwide
(4) Coordinate and manage graduate medical education programs at the Army MEDCENs
(5) MEDCOM is designated by the Chairman, Joint Chiefs of Staff as the Theater Lead Agent for Medical Materiel (TLAMM) to NORTHCOM

18-12. U. S. Army Medical Research and Materiel Command (USAMRMC)

a. USMRMC is the Army's medical materiel developer, with responsibility for medical research, exploratory testing, engineering development, development for medical materiel systems, acquisition and medical logistics management; performing research, development, testing, and evaluation under four critical Research Area Directorates (RADs) areas: military infectious disease research program; combat casualty care research program; military operational medicine research program and medical chemical and biological defense research program. USAMRMC also functions as the DOD Executive Agent for medical research and development in the areas of biological and chemical defense, infectious diseases, combat dentistry, nutrition, HIV research, global emerging infections, accession standards and research, Gulf War research, and investigational new drugs; operate the National Maintenance Program (NMP) for medical equipment and provide the Army Service Item Control Center for medical, dental, and veterinary equipment and supplies. They also plan and execute medical logistics mobilization support and management of the Medical War Reserves Materiel Program.

b. Six medical research laboratory commands execute the science and technology program to investigate medical solutions for the battlefield with a focus on various areas of biomedical research, including military infectious diseases, combat casualty care, military operational medicine, medical chemical and biological defense, and clinical and rehabilitative medicine. The command manages a large extramural research program with numerous contracts, grants, and cooperative research and development agreements to provide additional science and technology capabilities from leading academic, private industry, and other government organizations.

c. Five additional commands focus on medical materiel advanced development, strategic and operational medical logistics, and medical research and development contracting, to complete the full life cycle of medical materiel acquisition.

18-13. U.S. Army Dental Command (DENCOM)

The mission of the Dental Command (DENCOM) is to provide responsive and reliable oral health services and influences Health to improve readiness and advance wellness in support of the force, military families, and all those entrusted to our care by:
a. Serving as the proponent for meeting the dental health needs of the Army and eligible beneficiaries.
b. Providing mission command of the Army Dental Laboratory, Regional Dental Commands, Dental Activities, Dental Clinic Commands, and Dental Treatment Facilities worldwide.
c. Developing leaders to ensure accomplishment of the MEDCOM and DENCOM missions.
d. Allocating resources, analyzing utilization trends, and assessing performance across the DENCOM.
e. Training and providing qualified dental personnel for contingency operations.

ARMY HEALTH SYSTEM

Supporting mobilization of the total force by integrating Reserve Components into the Command and expanding dental capacity, as required, to receive and treat dental casualties at all levels of care.

18-14. U.S. Army Public Health Command (USAPHC)
   a. The mission of USAPHC is to promote health and prevent disease, injury, and disability of Soldiers and retirees, their families, and Department of the Army Civilian employees; and assure effective execution of full spectrum veterinary services for Army and Department of Defense Veterinary missions. USAPHC provides operational oversight for TSG to the Military Vaccine (MILVAX) Agency and the Armed Forces Health Surveillance Center (AFHSC). Public Health mission responsibilities include but are not limited to:
   (1) Disease & Injury Prevention Control
   (2) Health Promotion & Wellness
   (3) Occupational & Environmental Medical and Health Surveillance
   (4) Health Risk Assessment and Risk Communication
   (5) Health Hazard Assessment
   (6) Medical, Occupational, and Environmental Epidemiology
   (7) Population Health Risk Assessments
   (8) Health Policy Development and Review
   (9) Graduate and Continuing Medical Education
   (10) Disease Outbreak Investigation
   (11) Veterinary Clinical Medicine
   (12) Food and Water Protection
   b. Major Disciplines include:
   (1) Animal Medicine
   (2) Deployment & Environmental Health
   (3) Diseases & Conditions
   (4) Emergency Preparedness & Response
   (5) Food & Drinking Water Protection
   (6) Health Surveillance & Evaluation
   (7) Healthy Living
   (8) Laboratory Sciences
   (9) Public Health Command Region-Specific Information
   (10) Workplace Safety & Health
   c. The Commander, USAPHC is designated as the Army's Functional Proponent for Preventive Medicine (FPPM). The Proponency Office for Preventive Medicine (POPM) is the OneStaff element that supports the FPPM in all issues of preventive medicine policy and strategy development.
   d. MEDCOM Public Health (PH) services, as part of the Army Public Health Program, will be delivered through an enterprise approach. The Commander, MEDCOM, designated the Commander, USAPHC, as the accountable agent for the MEDCOM Public Health Enterprise (PHE) with the other MSC commanders sharing responsibility. All PH assets throughout the MEDCOM, including those in HQ MEDCOM staff directorates, the MSCs, and their subordinate organizations, constitute the MEDCOM PHE.
   e. The MEDCOM PHE will pursue unified, standardized, and cohesive PH planning, resourcing, distribution, and use of PH assets across the MEDCOM to improve efficiencies, responsiveness, effectiveness, and timeliness of appropriate PH support locally, regionally, and corporately across the Army.

18-15. U.S. Army Medical Department Center and School (AMEDDC&S)
The mission of the AMEDDC&S is to:
   a. Develop, integrate, coordinate, implement, evaluate and sustain training and training products for active and reserve medical forces worldwide in accordance with AR 350-1
   b. Develop, integrate, analyze, test, validate, and evaluate concepts, emerging doctrine and medical systems, and doctrine and training literature
   c. Conduct all AMEDD officer, enlisted, and civilian proponency functions, personnel inventories, and life-cycle management of all career fields
   d. Develop concepts, systems, and force structure for combat health service support

e. As the integration center for all doctrine and training requirements; systematically develop courses, training devices, manuals and sustainment materials for readiness

f. Provide training, education, and evaluation of AMEDD personnel

g. Test and evaluate new and replacement items of medical equipment

h. Serve as proponent for Force Health Protection (FHP) in operational areas

i. Plan, program, perform, and publish complex, organized analytical assessments and evaluations in support of decision- and policy-making, management, and administration of Army Medicine

j. Provide statistical and analytical consultation to the AMEDD, with secondary support to subordinate organizations within the MEDCOM; provide decision support expertise to AMEDD senior leadership; promote data quality, integrity, and standardization across the AMEDD; provide biometric database management and programming expertise to the AMEDD; provide the AMEDD with medical record coding guidance and training for medical records personnel

k. Function as the DOD EA's representative for joint training and pharmaceutical standardization in the areas of defense medical readiness training, joint medical executive skills, and the pharmacoeconomic center

18-16. Warrior Transition Command (WTC)

The mission of the WTC is to successfully transition Soldiers and their families back to the Army, or to civilian life, through a comprehensive program of medical care, rehabilitation, professional development, and personal goal-setting. The core competencies of the command include:

a. Serving as the proponent for the execution of the Army's Warrior Care and Transition Program

b. Providing command and control oversight to ensure full execution of the Army Wounded Warrior Program

c. Coordinating with DA staff, other Services, other Departments of Government, and Congress

d. Establishing and executing a program of standardization and evaluation to ensure optimization of compliance with established policy governing the operation of Warrior Transition Units (WTUs) and Community-Based Warrior Transition Units (CBWTUs)

e. Assuming responsibility for the movement of Warriors in Transition between MTFs WTUs, Veterans Affairs Medical and Poly-Trauma Centers, CBWTUs, and civilian healthcare providers

f. Ensure that all Warriors in Transition receive the same level and scope of care and support regardless of Component through enforcement of fair and comprehensive policy and capable Reserve Component management

18-17. RMCs

a. RMCs are the key operational element for the delivery of healthcare services for geographical regions within MEDCOM. RMCs are Major Subordinate Commands (MSCs) operating under the supervision of the commander. Mission responsibilities include:

(1) Regional mission command of an affordable, multidisciplinary, customer-focused, quality military health service system

(2) Supporting the readiness requirement of the Army

(3) Developing and sustaining technical healthcare and leader skills in support of MEDCOM readiness goals

(4) Allocating resources, analyzing utilization, and assessing performance across the RMC

b. As the primary integrator of medical readiness, the RMC is responsible for:

(1) Daily utilization of Table of Organization and Equipment /Table of Distribution and Allowances (TOE/TDA) medical assets, integrating Active and Reserve training, and development of mobilization requirements

(2) Budgeting, defending, and allocating readiness costs and funding

(3) Preplanning MTF professional backfill requirements during deployment by expanding network coverage, shifting RMC assets, and coordinating Reserve Component coverage

(4) Ensuring that Army medical readiness requirements are fully integrated into the activities of DOD healthcare regions

(5) Conducting training exercises in MTF mobilization, professional backfill activities, and deployment actions

(6) Providing medical planning and preparation programs for worldwide contingency operations

(7) Sponsoring readiness-based clinical research

ARMY HEALTH SYSTEM

18-18. AMEDD Role in Sustainment Units

a. In addition to its fixed MTFs, the Army maintains medical units with a sustainment mission within all deployable commands. These medical units work in concert with logistics and personnel units to form the sustainment core for Army forces. The deployable medical assets consist of TOE units in both the Active and Reserve Components. Continental United States (CONUS) AC medical units are assigned to United States Forces Command (USFORSCOM). Outside the Continental United States (OCONUS) medical units are assigned to the Army Service Component Command. Deployable medical units range in size, scope of mission, and capacity from medical detachments to theater hospitals. Collectively they establish an integrated continuum of medical evacuation and treatment from point of injury on the battlefield, to the echelons above corps, and eventually to specialized treatment in CONUS.

b. In the event of mobilization, AMEDD Reserve Component medical units will often be among the earliest deploying forces. With approximately 68 percent of the medical force in the Reserve Components, the AMEDD truly exemplifies the Army. Well-trained and combat ready Reserve Component medical units are absolutely essential for ensuring that the FHP missions of the Army are accomplished during periods of mobilization. Under the Professional Filler Information System (PROFIS) qualified Active Army personnel serving in TDA units are designated to fill USFORSCOM deploying Modified Table of Organization and Equipment (MTOE) units, United States Army Pacific (USARPAC), United States Army Europe (USAREUR), and Eighth United States Army (EUSA) forward deployed units upon execution of an approved Joint Chiefs of Staff (JCS) OPLAN or upon execution of a contingency operation. Individuals pre-designated from fixed Army healthcare facilities will provide a large portion of the professional personnel to units deploying to and already stationed in the operational area.

c. A key operational enabler is the Medical Communications for Combat Casualty Care (MC4). MC4 integrates a medical information management system for Army tactical medical forces, enabling a comprehensive, lifelong electronic medical record for all Service Members, and enhancing medical situational awareness for operational commanders. MC4 integrates Theater Medical Information Program (TMIP); the Battlefield Medical Information-Theater (BMIS-T); Armed Forces Healthcare Longitudinal Application (AHLTA); the U.S. Transportation Command (TRANSCOM) Regulating and Command and Control Evacuation System (TRAC2ES); the Defense Medical Logistics Standard Support (DMLSS); and the Defense Medical Surveillance System (DMSS). MC4 integrates the global medical network with a fully integrated operational architecture and a Global Information Grid (GIG) infrastructure. MC4 will enable commanders to effectively synchronize medical care on any battlefield, worldwide.

18-19. Staff Surgeons

a. The senior AMEDD officer present for duty with a headquarters (other than medical) will be officially titled:

(1) The "Command Surgeon" of the ACOM and ASCC
(2) The "Surgeon" of the field command (e.g., corps, CONUSA)
(3) The "Director of Health Services (DHS)" at the installation level
(4) The surgeon and DHS are responsible for the staff supervision of all health matters and policies, except dental and veterinary matters. The DHS and the Director of Dental Services (DDS) will serve on the installation commander's staff. Normally, the commander of the MEDCEN or medical department activity (MEDDAC) is the DHS, and the commander of the Army dental activity (DENTAC) is the DDS.

18-20. Health Service Logistics

a. Health service logistics is integral to the AHS and is managed by the AMEDD as a core functional area of MHS. This gives the command surgeon the ability to influence and control the resources needed to save lives. TSG establishes medical logistics policies and procedures within the framework of the overall Army logistics system. Health service logistics includes the management, storage, and distribution of medical materiel (to include medical gases), blood and blood products, optical fabrication, medical material war reserves, and medical equipment maintenance which are inherent to the provision of healthcare. The medical commodity (Class VIII) has characteristics that make it distinctly different from other classes of supply. Medical materiel includes pharmaceuticals, narcotics, and blood products that are potency and shelf life (dated) that require special handling and security. Most items are subject to the regulations and standards of external agencies such as the Food and Drug Administration (FDA), the Environmental Protection Agency (EPA), the Drug Enforcement Agency (DEA) and The Joint Commission

HOW THE ARMY RUNS

(JTC). Medical logisticians have extensive knowledge of those requirements as they relate to health service support.

b. The Single Integrated Medical Logistics Manager (SIMLM) mission designates a single organization or Service component to manage and provide health service logistics support to joint forces operating in the theater. Blood is the only medical material not directly under control of the SIMLM. Blood supplies are coordinated and managed by the Joint Blood Program Officer in each of the Combatant Unified Commands.

c. The Theater Lead Agent for Medical Materiel (TLAMM) provides a single theater medical materiel distribution and supply chain management, providing the intensive management required for the medical commodity in close concert with FHP operations and industry partners at the national level.

d. MEDCOM established Medical Equipment Reset operations for medical equipment and sets for re-deploying units and Theater Provided Equipment (TPE)-Medical. Redeploying units conduct field-level Reset operations at home station in coordination with the RMCs and their Installation Medical Supply Activities. Sustainment Reset (Depot Level) activities occur at one of three depot locations: Hill AFB, UT; Tracy Army Depot, CA; and Tobyhanna Army Depot, PA. TPE-Medical Reset is provided to units in theater in order to reduce equipping requirements for deploying units and to maintain continuity of care in support of operations. High utilization and harsh conditions result in increased maintenance requirements and accelerated wear-out rates. TPE-Medical is owned by theater and life-cycle managed by theater stakeholders in partnership with MEDCOM.

e. Army Medical Logistics Enterprise (AMLE). In 2009, TSG established the AMLE comprised of generating and operating Medical Logistics (MEDLOG) organizations that work within a collaborative and networked framework to meet the medical logistics needs of the AHS in delivering medical support to the Army and/or JFC.

18-21. Secretary of the Army's (SECARMY) Executive Agent (EA) Representative for DOD Executive Agencies (DOD EA)

a. Executive Agent representative. An EA is the Head of a DOD Component (SECARMY) to whom the SECDEF or the Deputy SECDEF (DEPSECDEF) has assigned specific responsibilities, functions, and authorities to provide defined levels of support for operational missions, or administrative or other designated activities that involve two or more of the DOD Components. The DOD EA may delegate, to a subordinate designee within that official's Component (TSG), the authority to act on that official's behalf for any or all of those EA, functions, and authorities assigned by the SECDEF or the DEPSECDEF.

b. In addition to the DOD EAs embedded in AMEDD Major Subordinate Commands, TSG serves as the EA's representative for other essential joint medical agencies, to include:

(1) Accession Medical Standards Analysis and Research Activity
(2) Armed Forces Epidemiological Board
(3) Armed Forces Medical Library
(4) Armed Forces Pest Management Board
(5) Armed Services Blood Program
(6) Civilian Employee Occupational Health and Medical Services Program
(7) Defense Medical Readiness Training Institute
(8) DiLorenzo TRICARE Health Clinic
(9) DOD/VA Clinical Practice Guidelines Development
(10) DOD Pharmacoeconomic Center
(11) DOD Veterinary Services Activity
(12) Joint Readiness Clinical Advisory Board
(13) Joint Medical Executive Skills Institute
(14) Military Infectious Disease Research Program
(15) Medical Materiel Enterprise Standardization Office

ARMY HEALTH SYSTEM

Section V
Summary and References

18-21. Summary
This chapter has discussed the mission, organization, functions, and staff relationships of the AMEDD. The AHS encompasses all roles/levels of medical, dental, veterinary, and other related from the policy and decision-making level to the combat medic in the field. Health services within the Army are directed and monitored by TSG through MEDCOM and the OTSG. TRICARE has markedly altered the peacetime military health system and continues to evolve to ensure the provision of world class healthcare to all beneficiaries. After 12 years of sustained conflict the AHS continues to transform in order to meet the needs of the Army and the nation.

18-22. References
   a. Army Doctrine Publication 3-37, Protection
   b. Army Doctrine Publication 3-0, Unified Land Operations
   c. Army Doctrine Publication 4-0, Sustainment
   d. Army Doctrine Reference Publication 3-0, Unified Land Operations
   e. Army Doctrine Reference Publication 3-37, Protection
   f. Army Doctrine Reference Publication 4-0, Sustainment
   g. Army Regulation 10-87, Organization and Functions Army Commands, Army Service Component Commands, and Direct Reporting Units
   h. Army Regulation 40-1, Composition, Mission, and Functions of the Army Medical Department
   i. Army Regulation 40-4, Army Medical Department Facilities/Activities
   j. Army Regulation 40-61, Medical Logistics Policies
   k. Army Tactics, Techniques, and Procedures 4-02, Army Health System
   l. Call to Action: 43rd Surgeon General, United States Army, 2012
   m. DOD Directive 5101.1 DOD Executive Agencies
   n. DOD Directive 5136.1, (ASD[HA])
   o. MEDCOM Memorandum 10-2, Organizations and Functions, Headquarters
   p. MEDCOM/OTSG Regulation 10-32
   q. MEDCOM Regulation 10-1, Organization and Functions Policy
   r. U.S. Army Medical Department Website, www.armymedicine.mil

This page is intentionally left blank

CIVIL FUNCTIONS OF THE DEPARTMENT OF THE ARMY

Chapter 19

Civil Functions of the Department of the Army

I am firmly convinced that but for the existence of the Corps of Engineers peacetime organization and its resources of men, methods, training and supply and its close association with the military through the years, the history of the Pacific area in World War II would have been written more in blood than in achievement.

GEN Dwight D. Eisenhower, Chief of Staff, U.S. Army Testimony before the House Armed Services Committee on H.R. 3830, 1947

Section I
Introduction

19-1. Civil Functions Defined
A number of activities traditionally carried out by the Department of the Army (DA) are commonly referred to as civil functions. The most extensive of these is the Civil Works Program managed by the U.S. Army Corps of Engineers (USACE, or "the Corps"). The Civil Works Program focuses on responsible development, protection, and restoration of the Nation's water and related land resources. Civil Works projects are implemented and operated for commercial navigation, flood risk management, environmental restoration, hydroelectric power, recreation, municipal and industrial water supply, and allied purposes. Civil functions also include USACE engineering and construction support to non-defense-related activities of the federal government, state and local agencies; and USACE overseas activities not exclusively in support of U.S. forces overseas.

19-2. Authorization, Congressional Oversight, and Funding
Financial and personnel resources associated with the Civil Works Program are principally authorized under Water Resources Development Acts (WRDA) and funded separately by annual Energy and Water Development Appropriations Acts, not the Defense appropriation. Program funding under these acts is generally $5 to $6 billion a year. Additional funds may be provided through Supplemental Appropriation Acts. One for fiscal year (FY) 2012 provided over $1.7 billion for reconstruction and improvement of flood protection works in the Mississippi and Missouri River Basins damaged by record flooding in 2011. Funding for FY 2010 included a regular appropriation of $5.002 billion, a supplemental appropriation of $1.724 billion, and use of funds carried over from prior years. The WRDA of 1986 and subsequent WRDAs require cost-sharing contributions from State and local government project sponsors for most Civil Works activities. USACE support activities for other, non-defense agencies are reimbursed by those agencies - to include emergency response activities funded by the Federal Emergency Management Agency (FEMA). Congressional committees like the Subcommittee on Water Resources and Environment of the House Transportation and Infrastructure Committee or the Subcommittee on Transportation and Infrastructure of the Senate Environment and Public Works Committee provide legislative oversight and authorizing legislation, while the Energy and Water Development Subcommittees of the House and Senate Appropriations Committees provide funding. Although they differ from other Army programs in financing and oversight, the civil functions are an integral part of the overall mission of the Army and the service it provides to the Nation.

19-3. Relationship to Warfighting Competencies
The civil functions complement and augment the Army's warfighting competencies, providing the capability to respond to a variety of situations across the spectrum of conflict. They provide a valuable tool to support the National Security Strategy (NSS) by maintaining a trained and ready engineer force at virtually no additional expense to the Department of Defense (DOD) military budget and at minimum expense to personnel allocations. More than 10,000 Corps of Engineers employees in jobs funded by the Civil Works program have deployed for short tours in Iraq, Afghanistan, and other overseas areas. Expertise resident in the Civil Works program is also made available to Combatant Commanders (CCDR)

HOW THE ARMY RUNS

through USACE's "Reachback" programs which link subject matter experts within the government, private industry, and academia to obtain engineering solutions to complex problems.

19-4. Leadership and Organization

a. The Assistant Secretary of the Army (Civil Works) (ASA(CW)). Through specific statutory provisions, General Orders from the Secretary of the Army (SECARMY), and internal DA regulation, the ASA(CW) has been assigned responsibilities for the civil functions. Congress established the position of the ASA(CW) in Section 211 of the Flood Control Act of 1970, Public Law (PL) 91-611, and reaffirmed it in Section 501 of the Goldwater-Nichols Department of Defense Reorganization Act of 1986, PL 99-433. The Goldwater-Nichols Act specifies that the Assistant Secretary's duties include overall supervision of the functions of the DA relating to programs for conservation and development of water resources, including flood risk management, navigation, environmental restoration and stewardship, and related purposes. The ASA(CW) reports directly to the SA.

b. USACE. Most of the Army's civil functions are executed by the USACE, an executive branch agency within DOD and a Major Command within the Army consisting of about 800 military and 35,300 civilians, who also: provide real estate services; conduct research & development; conduct planning & engineering studies (Civil Works), and design and build military facilities for the Army, Air Force, other federal agencies, and foreign governments. Approximately 300 military personnel and 23,000 civilian employees in the USACE are involved in civil functions, making it the world's largest public engineering, design, and construction management agency.

c. The Chief of Engineers. The Chief of Engineers holds positions as both a principal Headquarters, Department of the Army (HQDA) Staff officer and as commander of the USACE. The Chief of Engineers and the Corps' Deputy Commanding General (CG) for Civil and Emergency Operations report to the ASA(CW) on the Civil Works Program.

d. Divisions and Districts. Under the Chief's command are nine divisions, eight of which have Civil Works missions. Under the divisions are 45 districts, 38 of which are within the United States. Division and district boundaries for the Civil Works Program within the Continental U.S. (CONUS) generally follow watersheds and drainage basins, as shown in Figure 19-1. These delineations reflect the water resources mission of USACE. Military Construction (MILCON) districts, on the other hand, generally follow State boundaries, and not all stateside districts have a MILCON mission.

e. Overseas Offices. USACE also includes a number of overseas offices with missions in construction in support of U.S. forces, assistance to other countries and international organizations, and support to other U.S. agencies.

(1) The Pacific Ocean Division, headquartered in Honolulu, HI, includes subordinate districts in Japan and Korea as well as Hawaii and Alaska.

(2) The North Atlantic Division includes the Europe District as well as five stateside districts.

(3) In October 2009, USACE stood up the Transatlantic Division, with headquarters in Winchester, VA, two subordinate districts in Afghanistan, one in Iraq, and one responsible for USACE activities elsewhere in the Middle East and Africa.

(4) Several CONUS-based districts also carry out overseas missions, such as Mobile District's support of U.S. Southern Command (USSOUTHCOM).

f. Other USACE Organizations. There are several other organizations within the Corps of Engineers:

(1) U.S. Army Engineer Research and Development Center (ERDC), Vicksburg, MS - the Corps of Engineers research and development command. ERDC consists of seven laboratories (see Para. 19-6a).

(2) U.S. Army Engineering and Support Center, Huntsville, AL - provides engineering and technical services, program and project management, construction management, and innovative contracting initiatives for programs that are national or broad in scope or not normally provided by other Corps of Engineers elements. Huntsville is also USACE's major training center.

(3) USACE Finance Center, Millington, TN - provides operating finance and accounting functions throughout the Corps of Engineers.

(4) Humphreys Engineer Center Support Activity, Fort Belvoir, VA - provides administrative and operational support for Headquarters, U.S. Army Corps of Engineers and various field offices.

(5) Marine Design Center, Philadelphia, PA - provides planning, engineering, and shipbuilding contract management in support of Corps, Army, and national water resource projects in peacetime, and augments the military construction capacity in time of national emergency or mobilization.

CIVIL FUNCTIONS OF THE DEPARTMENT OF THE ARMY

(6) Institute for Water Resources, Fort Belvoir, VA - supports the Civil Works Directorate and other Corps of Engineers commands by developing and applying new planning evaluation methods, polices and data in anticipation of changing water resources management conditions. Subordinate to the Institute are the Hydrologic Engineering Center in Davis, CA; the Waterborne Commerce Statistics Center in New Orleans, LA; the Risk Management Center in Lakeland, CO; and, at Fort Belvoir, the International Center for Integrated Water Resources Management, the Navigation and Civil Works Decision Support Center, and the Conflict Resolution and Public Participation Center of Expertise. The Institute also provides support to the U.S. Section of the World Association for Waterborne Transport Infrastructure (PIANC-USA). PIANC USA works with members from 40 other nations to address policy, engineering and environmental issues for the advancement of waterborne transportation.

(7) USACE Logistics Activity, Millington, TN - provides logistics support to the Corps including supply, maintenance, readiness, materiel, transportation, travel, aviation, facility management, integrated logistics support, management controls, and strategic planning.

(8) Enterprise Infrastructure Services (EIS) - designs information technology standards for the Corps, including automation, communications, management, visual information, printing, records management, and information assurance. EIS outsources the maintenance of its Information Technology (IT) services, forming the Army Corps of Engineers Information Technology (ACE-IT). ACE-IT is made up of both civilian government employees and contractors.

(9) Deployable Tactical Operations System (DTOS) - provides mobile mission command platforms in support of the quick ramp-up of initial emergency response missions for the Corps. DTOS is a system designed to respond to District, Division, National, and International events.

(10) 249th Engineer Battalion (Prime Power) - generates and distributes prime electrical power in support of warfighting, disaster relief, stability and support operations as well as provides advice and technical assistance in all aspects of electrical power and distribution systems. It also maintains Army power generation and distribution war reserves.

(11) 911th Engineer Company - provides specialized technical search and rescue support for the Washington, DC metropolitan area. It is also a vital support member of the Joint Force Headquarters National Capital Region, which is charged with the homeland security of the United States Capital Region.

(12) 412th Theater Engineer Command, U.S. Army Reserve, located in Vicksburg, MS.

(13) 416th Theater Engineer Command, U.S. Army Reserve, located in Darien, IL.

g. The Role of the Private Sector. The private sector is an essential element of the Engineer team. Private construction firms carry out practically all of its construction work, employing about 300,000 people at a time on Corps activities. The Corps also employs private architectural, engineering and construction firms for over half of its design work. In FY 2012, the USACE let about $4.76 billion in contracts for Civil Works activities. Of this amount, $2.31 billion (48.5%) went to small businesses, including $898 million (18.9%) to small disadvantaged firms. The partnership between the USACE and the private sector represents a force multiplier of several hundred thousand architects, engineers, and builders, ready to support the Nation in times of emergency.

Section II
Civil Works Program

19-5. Civil Works Program Activities

a. The Program. The Civil Works Program provides nationwide development and management of water and related land resources, including the planning, design, construction, rehabilitation, operation and maintenance of flood risk management, navigation, and ecosystem and other environmental restoration, and multiple-purpose water resource projects. The Civil Works Planning function is the foundation of the overall Corps of Engineers Civil Works Program in the development and authorization of new water resources projects. In addition to the project purposes listed above, completed Corps projects may include hydroelectric power, water supply, recreation, and natural and cultural resource management. Collectively, they include approximately 12 million acres of land and water. In addition to this direct federal investment program, the Civil Works Program includes an important regulatory mission in which the Corps regulates construction in navigable waters under the Rivers and Harbors Act of 1899. The Corps also regulates the deposition of dredged and fill material in waters of the United States,

HOW THE ARMY RUNS

including many wetlands, under the Clean Water Act of 1972. In addition, the Civil Works Program includes emergency flood fighting, recovery operations, and repair and restoration of flood control works -- all performed under the USACE's own authority as specified in PL 84-99. USACE also carries out DOD's responsibilities under the National Response Plan (NRP) (refer to Chap. 22) as the lead planning and operating agent for public works and engineering (Emergency Support Function #3) (refer to Chap. 22), in support of FEMA and other federal agencies.

b. Funding Sources. The Civil Works Program receives its principal funding through the annual Energy and Water Development Appropriations Acts, which include funds from the Inland Waterways and Harbor Maintenance Trust Funds as well as general revenues. The program also receives funding from non-federal project sponsors who share in feasibility study and construction costs according to formulas established by Congress in PL 99-662, the WRDA of 1986, and subsequent water project authorization acts. The Civil Works Program funding in FY 2012 totaled $7.361 billion. Of this amount, $5.002 billion was appropriated by Congress in the regular appropriation, $1.724 billion in Supplemental Appropriations; about $540 million by non-federal project sponsors, $85 million from the Coastal Wetlands Trust Fund for work in Coastal Louisiana, and $15 million from license and use fees. This figure does not include $1.6 billion in reimbursable support to other agencies.

c. Economic Infrastructure.

(1) USACE has been the Nation's major contributor to the development, construction, and maintenance of a sound water resources infrastructure. Commercial navigation and flood risk management are long-standing missions of the Civil Works Program. The navigation function includes improvement and maintenance of harbors handling all of the Nation's seaborne commerce and that of the Great Lakes. With funds from the Harbor Maintenance Trust Fund, the Corps maintains navigability in 178 harbors handling more than 250,000 tons of cargo per year, and 748 smaller harbors. With more than 15 million American jobs dependent on U.S. import and export trade, the Nation's commercial ports are vital to the economic security of the United States. The Corps has built an intracoastal and inland commercial waterway network of 12,000 miles, and operates 242 lock chambers at 198 sites. Major improvements to inland waterway facilities are financed in part by the Inland Waterway Trust Fund. More than 600 million tons of commerce moves every year on these waterways. Maintaining the system of ports and inland waterways involves removing more than 220 million cubic yards of dredged material each year. Major segments of this network include:

(a) The lower Mississippi River (1,015 miles)
(b) The upper Mississippi River (936 miles)
(c) The Ohio River (981 miles)
(d) The Tennessee River (785 miles)
(e) The Missouri River (735 miles)
(f) The Arkansas and White Rivers (706 miles)
(g) The Columbia-Snake River System (468 miles)
(h) The South Atlantic Coast (1,111 miles)
(i) The Gulf Intracoastal Waterway (GIWW)-West (1,501 miles)
(j) GIWW-East (431 miles)

(2) USACE shares with the U.S. Department of Homeland Security's (DHS) FEMA both the expertise and mandate to address the nation's vulnerabilities to flood related disasters and damages. USACE has been involved in flood control activities, largely on the Ohio and Mississippi Rivers, since the 19th Century. The levees protecting St. Louis, MO, were designed by none other than Engineer LT Robert E. Lee in 1837. This involvement was ramped up with the Mississippi River & Tributaries Flood Control Project in 1928, in the aftermath of widespread flooding in the Mississippi Basin the year before. The Flood Control Act of 1936 established a nationwide federal role in flood management, and since then the Corps' authorized responsibilities have expanded to include developing structural and non structural solutions to managing flood risks, inspecting the condition of existing flood management infrastructure, providing technical and planning support to States and communities, conducting advance emergency measures to alleviate impending flooding, and rehabilitating levees and other flood management infrastructure damaged by flooding. The Nation's investment in flood risk management has prevented almost eight dollars in flood damage reduction for each dollar invested, even after adjusting for inflation. In August, 2011, the USACE completed reconstruction of the New Orleans Hurricane and Storm Damage Risk Reduction System (HSDRRS) to the "100 year" level of protection (able to withstand a storm with a one percent chance of happening in a given year). HSDRRS was highly successful in preventing

CIVIL FUNCTIONS OF THE DEPARTMENT OF THE ARMY

damage and loss of life during Hurricane Isaac in August 2012 - the $14.7 billion spent to build system prevented about $90 billion in damages - a 6:1 return on investment in the first year! Civil works projects seek to reduce flood-related damages with structural measures such as reservoirs, levees, improved channels, and floodwalls. Nonstructural measures, such as advice and encouragement for local zoning regulations, flood proofing of individual homes, and setting aside land in the floodplain as open space, also contribute to this mission. Flood risk management efforts range from small, local protection projects to large lakes and dams. Today, 383 dams and reservoirs are maintained and operated by the Corps for the purpose of flood damage prevention. Since passage of the WRDA of 1986, most of these projects have been constructed as joint ventures between the federal government and non-federal sponsors. The Corps operates and maintains most of its dams, but most other projects, once built, including about 11,750 miles of levees, are operated and maintained by local sponsors.

(3) The Corps can provide flood management assistance through a wide variety of authorities and programs. For example, through its Flood Plain Management Services Program (FPMS), the Corps can provide information, technical assistance and planning guidance (paid for by the federal government) to States and local communities to help them address flood risk management issues. Typical focus areas are flood hazard evaluation, dam break analysis, flood warning preparedness, flood plain management and much more. In cases where the risk of flooding is imminent in a specific area, the Corps is authorized to take immediate advance measures to protect life and property, such as constructing temporary flow restriction structures and removing log debris blockages. The responsibility for managing the Nation's flood risks does not lie exclusively with federal agencies, such as the Corps and FEMA. Rather, it is shared across multiple federal, state, and local government agencies with a complex set of programs and authorities, including private citizens and private enterprises such as banking and insurance firms and developers. Both the Corps and FEMA have programs to assist States and communities reduce flood damages and promote sound flood risk management. However, the authority to determine how land is used within floodplains and enforce flood-wise requirements is entirely the responsibility of State and local government. Floodplain management choices made by State and local officials can impact the maximum effectiveness of federal programs to mitigate flood risk and the performance of federal flood damage reduction. However, the federal investment is protected by the execution of agreements between the federal and non-federal partners.

(4) In November 2007, the Corps established a Levee Safety Program, an important step to ensure the public is aware of the risks associated with levees in Corps programs. The mission of the program is to assess the integrity and viability of levee systems and recommend actions to ensure these systems do not pose unacceptable risks. The main objectives are to hold public safety paramount, reduce adverse economic impacts, and develop reliable and accurate information. Within the program, a National Levee Database has been created to serve as a source of information to facilitate and link activities, which include flood risk communication, levee certification, levee inspection, floodplain management, and risk assessments. The database presently includes levees within a Corps program or FEMA's National Flood Insurance Program (NFIP). The WRDA of 2007 extended Corps authority and allows the inclusion of all nonfederal levees on a voluntary basis. A methodology for technical risk assessments of existing levee infrastructure is under development to serve as a consistent risk based framework to evaluate levees nationally. Additional activities within this program include national teams to focus on developing new policies concerning levee safety, such as inspections of existing levee systems, verification or establishment of existing geodetic control, minimum standards for new levee systems and interim risk reduction measures. Key policy issues in which close collaboration between the Corps, FEMA, and other stakeholders is necessary relate directly to the Levee Safety Program. These areas include levee inventory, mapping the flood hazard, inspection and assessment of levees, operation and maintenance of levees, and emergency response and evacuations.

(5) The Corps operates 75 power plants, which represent almost one fourth of the Nation's hydroelectric capacity or three percent of the Nation's total electric power generating capacity. Dams built by the USACE provide water storage for drinking water, irrigation, and fish and wildlife habitat. Additionally, 422 of the projects mentioned above (mostly lakes) are developed for recreational use. These projects accommodate nearly 370 million visits a year. The Corps estimates that one in 10 Americans visit a civil works project at least once a year. Visitors to these recreation areas generate 270,000 private and public sector jobs. USACE is the federal government's largest provider of outdoor recreation, hosting 20% of visits to federal recreation areas on 2% of federal land.

HOW THE ARMY RUNS

(6) The transportation infrastructure developed in the Civil Works Program plays a role in national defense. Ports and waterways serve as vital logistics links when large volumes of materiel and personnel must be moved around the country and around the world. The USACE works with the Surface Deployment and Distribution Command (SDDC) and local port authorities to ensure that ports are ready to support movement of military equipment and supplies when needed. This partnership was especially effective in moving nearly all the Army's equipment and supplies necessary for Operations Enduring Freedom and Iraqi Freedom. Waterways built and operated and maintained by the USACE similarly have direct military uses for strategic mobility. Units of the Texas, Oklahoma, and Arkansas National Guard have conducted successful movements over the Arkansas, Mississippi, and Illinois Rivers to their summer training sites, and the 101st Air Assault Division has conducted movements by waterway from Fort Campbell, KY, to Louisiana. USACE flood risk management projects also contribute to force projection by protecting important highway and railway links. Thus, through activities as diverse as facilitating the movement of materiel to protecting vital infrastructure, the Civil Works Program contributes to National security.

d. The Environment.

(1) Project Activities and Regulatory Programs. The Civil Works Program makes important contributions to the Nation's environmental goals by constructing projects for restoration and protection of ecosystem and other environmental functions and values. Much of this work proceeds in partnership with other federal and state agencies or recognized American Indian Tribes, Alaska Natives, and local communities. In 2002, the Corps entered into a partnership with The Nature Conservancy to improve the management of U.S. Rivers for restoration purposes while maintaining the projects' economic services. In addition, the Corps has agreements with the National Fish and Wildlife Federation and Ducks Unlimited to advance restoration of important ecological resources.

(2) Project Authorities.

(a) In the WRDA of 1990 established environmental restoration and protection as one of the primary missions in the planning, design, construction, operation, and maintenance of water resources projects - equivalent to navigation and flood risk management. This new direction stimulated the Corps and its non-federal project sponsors to plan and implement new projects with environmental restoration as a primary project purpose.

(b) Like other major Corps projects, Congress must authorize large restoration projects. In one of the largest environmental restoration and protection projects ever undertaken, the Departments of the Army and the Interior have been cooperating with the State of Florida to restore the hydrologic regime of the Everglades in South Florida. Congress approved the Corps' Comprehensive Everglades Restoration Plan in Title VI of the WRDA of 2000, PL 106-541. The first feasibility study for a component of this project requiring specific authorization was completed in 2002.

(c) The Corps and the State of Louisiana are working together to restore and protect that State's shrinking coastal wetlands and stem an ongoing loss of 25 to 35 square miles per year. This ecosystem is vital to the Nation's environmental health for naturally filtering out water pollution and for providing critical winter habitat for 70% of the Nation's waterfowl. This ecosystem is also vital to the Nation's economy as the home of a major seafood industry. The wetlands and barrier islands also protect inland urban, industrial, and agricultural areas - including New Orleans and dozens of other communities that are home to a culture unique in America - from hurricanes and coastal storms. Work in Coastal Louisiana took on added urgency after Hurricane Katrina focused national attention on the role of coastal wetlands in attenuating storm surge and wave action.

(d) In addition to specifically authorized projects such as the Everglades and Coastal Louisiana restoration projects described above, environmental restoration is accomplished through three programmatic authorities for small projects. Under Section 1135 of the WRDA of 1986, PL 99-662, the USACE is authorized to modify projects it constructed earlier in the interest of making them "greener." Section 1135 also authorizes the USACE to accomplish environmental restoration when the original Corps project contributed to environmental loss. Section 204 of the WRDA of 1992 provided authority for beneficial uses of dredged material. This authority allows the USACE to use material from the dredging of navigation projects for environmental restoration. The third authority is Section 206 of the WRDA of 1996. This provision establishes a program for Aquatic Ecosystem Restoration under which small projects may be constructed; no link to an existing Corps' project is required. Working toward a national goal of "no net loss of wetlands," the Civil Works Program is undertaking projects to restore existing wetlands and to create new ones.

CIVIL FUNCTIONS OF THE DEPARTMENT OF THE ARMY

(3) Regulatory Program.

(a) The USACE's regulatory program has a long history of protecting the Nation's waters. The Rivers and Harbors Act of 1899 authorizes the USACE to regulate, by permit, dredging, construction, and similar activities in navigable waters of the United States. A principal objective of this program is to ensure that waterways are improved and maintained for commercial and recreational users. Over time, the Corps' "public interest review" has become an important part of the decision process used by Corps district commanders in granting, modifying or denying permit applications.

(b) The 1972 Clean Water Act authorized USACE to regulate, by permit, dredging and fill material discharge activities in waters of the United States, including wetlands. This Act expanded the Corps' regulatory responsibilities beyond those contemplated in the Rivers and Harbors Act of 1899. Also, other environmental laws that were enacted at about the same time require federal decision makers to consider and take responsibility for the environmental consequences of their actions. Section 103 of the Marine Protection, Research and Sanctuaries Act of 1972, as amended, authorizes the SECARMY to issue permits for the transportation of dredged material for ocean disposal. In its determination, the Corps ensures that the dumping will not unreasonably degrade or endanger human health, welfare, or amenities, or the marine environment, ecological system, or economic potentialities.

(c) However, the Supreme Court has ruled that the USACE regulatory jurisdiction does not extend to all wetlands. Its Solid Waste Agency of Northern Cook County decision in 2001 excluded wetlands wholly within one state and not connected to a navigable waterway, while the Rapanos and Carabell rulings of 2006 required a "significant nexus" to a navigable waterway for the Corps to assert jurisdiction.

(d) Today the regulatory program consolidates the public interest and environmental consequence reviews into a comprehensive evaluation process for decision-making. The evaluation process promotes the balancing of environmental protection with responsible economic growth. In FY 2012, the Corps granted permission for nearly 90,000 activities in the Nation's waterways and wetlands. Of these, about 57,000 were permitted under blanket nationwide or regional permits for certain types of work; 10,700 did not require a permit, and the rest required individual permits. The Corps required modifications at 3,100 of these projects, denied 167 applications, and saw another nearly 10,700 withdrawn by the applicant. The Corps regulatory program provides the public a valuable service - protection of the Nation's waters and wetlands.

(4) Stewardship. The Corps is steward for about 12 million acres of land and water in 42 States. Conservation of forests, range wildlife habitat, fisheries, and soils involves multiple uses of resources and sound ecosystem management principles. The USACE accomplishes this through a mix of its own management capabilities, partnerships with State and local governments, volunteers, and working agreements with a wide range of interest groups.

(5) Compliance. The Corps conducts compliance assessments at all of its projects on a five-year cycle through the environmental compliance assessment program. The Environmental Review Guide for Operations (ERGO), the tool used to conduct assessments, is a checklist containing federal and state environmental statutes and USACE requirements. Project and facility managers, as well as external organizations, use ERGO to systematically locate and correct environmental deficiencies.

(6) Civil Environmental Activities' Relationship to Army Missions. Environmental activities in the Civil Works Program are essential elements of the Army's Environmental Strategy for the 21st Century. People who learn their specialties in Civil Works missions that concern natural and cultural resources, water quality, flood plain management or hazardous waste management help the Army go "beyond compliance" to take on a leadership role in natural resources stewardship. Civil Works expertise helped the Army develop such tools as the Environmental Compliance Assessment System (ECAS) and Integrated Training Area Management (ITAM). The Civil Works Program is responsible for about half the Army's land holdings, and is familiar with balancing preservation of the natural environment with human use - a major issue facing the Army. This program is also the Army's reservoir of cultural resources expertise, which the Army has used on several priority missions.

(7) Nonstructural Flood Risk Management. In recent years the Corps has placed an increasing emphasis on nonstructural approaches to flood management. Nonstructural alternatives focus on addressing the development in the floodplain. Alternatives include floodplain zoning, participating in the NFIP, developing and implementing flood warning systems (coordinated with the National Oceanic and Atmospheric Administration's (NOAA's) flood warning program) and emergency evacuation plans, and flood proofing individual structures as well as removing structures from the extreme flood hazard areas.

(8) Environmental Operating Principles. In 2002, the Chief of Engineers announced a set of Environmental Operating Principles to guide all the Corps' activities. The essence of these principles is that environmental concerns are integral to all Corps missions, decision-making, programs, and projects. During the following 10 years, the Nation's resource challenges and priorities have evolved, focusing more on sustainability and the need to conserve water, electricity, fuel and other precious resources. The Corps, as well as the Nation as a whole, has learned more about the impacts of global factors such as climate and sea level change. With those challenges and priorities in mind, the Corps "reinvigorated" the Environmental Operating Principles. When the principles were first introduced in 2002, USACE was one of the first federal agencies to incorporate them. They opened the door for USACE to think about other criteria to measure projects against beyond the economic cost-benefit ratio. As part of the reinvigoration process, plans are under way to ensure that Corps training courses include a small module on the principles, metrics that include long-term goals and indicators of success are being developed, and the principles are being included in any new or revises Engineer Regulations, Engineer Pamphlets, Engineer Manuals and other guidance. The reinvigorated principles are:

(a) Foster Sustainability as a way of life throughout the organization.
(b) Proactively consider environmental consequences of all Corps activities and act accordingly.
(c) Create mutually supporting economic and environmentally sustainable solutions.
(d) Continue to meet our corporate responsibility and accountability under the law for activities undertaken by the Corps, which may impact human and natural environments.
(e) Consider the environment in employing a risk management and systems approach throughout life cycles of projects and programs.
(f) Leverage scientific, economic and social knowledge to understand the environmental context and effects of Corps actions in a collaborative manner.
(g) Employ an open, transparent process that respects views of individuals and groups interested in Corps activities.

e. Emergency Preparedness and Disaster Response.

(1) The USACE responds to the Nation's needs in case of natural or man-made disasters and emergencies. The USACE programs provide a wide variety of assistance to protect human life and improved property, reduce human suffering, help communities recover from the effects of disasters, and mitigate damage and future threats. Response and recovery activities supplement State and local efforts.

(2) Under PL 84-99, the USACE undertakes planning and preparedness activities for all types of natural disasters, and provides response and recovery activities necessitated by floods and coastal storms. The Flood Control and Coastal Emergencies (FCCE) appropriation funds all PL 84-99 activities. Included in these preparedness and response efforts are: disaster preparedness measures; advance measures to alleviate high potential flood threats; flood fighting activities; preservation of threatened federally-constructed shore protection projects; and life-saving rescue operations.

(3) Recovery and mitigation measures include repair and rehabilitation of damaged flood control works and shore protection projects or nonstructural projects. PL 84-99 also authorizes the USACE to provide emergency supplies of clean water to localities whose water source has been contaminated, and to drought-affected areas. In addition, the USACE is authorized to provide essential services and restore essential public infrastructure for a period of up to 10 days in any area victimized by a natural disaster for which the Governor of a State has requested federal assistance under the Stafford Act authority.

(4) Under The Robert T. Stafford Disaster Relief and Emergency Assistance Act (42 USC 5121 et seq.) (88 Stat.143) (The Stafford Act), the USACE uses its engineering expertise and its response and recovery capabilities to carry out DOD's responsibilities under the National Response Framework (NRF) as the lead planning and operating agency for Public Works and Engineering Emergency Support in responding to disasters and emergencies of all kinds. Under authority of the Stafford Act, FEMA, under the DHS, has developed the NRF, which coordinates the execution of response and recovery operations of the 28 federal signatory departments and agencies. Under the NRF, DOD has delegated its responsibility for Emergency Support Function (ESF) #3, Public Works and Engineering, to the USACE.

(5) As the lead DOD (and federal) agency for ESF #3, the USACE has a number of standing missions, to include provision of water, ice, emergency power, debris removal, temporary housing, and temporary roofing. Other missions in the Public Works and Engineering area are assigned by the FEMA to the USACE, as needed. All of these missions are tailored to the needs of, and coordinated with the impacted State. FEMA funds all of these missions under a reimbursable agreement with an approved mission assignment. Each mission assignment is based on the capabilities of the USACE, including its significant

CIVIL FUNCTIONS OF THE DEPARTMENT OF THE ARMY

and responsive contracting capability. The Joint Staff, J-3, Joint Directorate of Military Support (JDOMS), coordinates DOD requirements not in the realm of ESF #3 missions.

(6) In response to the World Trade Center and Pentagon Terrorist Attacks of September 11, 2001, Corps emergency management personnel were on the scene within hours: providing structural engineers to monitor unstable buildings; supporting urban search and rescue work; providing a mobile command center and teams to support the New York Fire Department; and developing a debris management plan. Corps expertise was crucial in providing urban search & rescue, conducting structural assessments to determine when buildings were safe enough for rescuers and, later, determining when buildings were safe for occupancy. The 249th Engineer Battalion (Prime Power) provided the electric power that got the New York financial district back in business while Corps contractors removed 1.7 million tons of debris from the World Trade Center site and transported it by barge to the landfill in Staten Island. However, this work was similar to what the Corps does every year to support FEMA, State, and local authorities in natural disasters.

(7) In the aftermath of Hurricane Katrina on August 29, 2005, the USACE received over $4 billion in taskings from FEMA for recovery activities. A major success was the removal of nearly all floodwater from New Orleans and vicinity within 60 days - a task that many experts said would take well into 2006. Another major undertaking was the removal of 56 million cubic yards of debris - a figure eclipsing the record of 42 million cubic yards removed after Hurricane Andrew in 1992. Hurricane Sandy provided another $92 million in taskings from FEMA for recovery actions in 2012.

f. Homeland Security. The Corps has developed in-depth anti-terrorism/protection warfighting function expertise, including many skilled engineers with experience on Khobar Towers, in Oklahoma City, the World Trade Center, the Pentagon, and other sites. It leverages that expertise to protect critical water resources infrastructure from terrorists. Over past few years the Corps has been working with other agencies, including the Bureau of Reclamation, Department of Energy, TVA, EPA, and FBI to develop comprehensive security assessment processes to identify risks to critical facilities such as locks, dams and hydropower facilities. In the wake of the September 11th attacks, the Corps instituted increased protection measures at its projects. It restricted public access, increased standoff distances to critical structures, increased patrol activities and contract guard support, and increased coordination with local law enforcement.

19-6. Research and Development (R&D)

The Army Corps of Engineers Civil Works Program pursues an R&D effort to take advantage of rapidly developing technologies and techniques that will promote significant monetary savings and greater reliability, safety, enhanced efficiency and environmental sustainability of its assigned civil works activities. The R&D program is formulated to support each of the assigned Civil Works missions and their supporting core of technical competencies, environmental restoration and stewardship, economics and decision support, cold regions engineering and dredged sediments management. Technology infusion is pursued, in conjunction with the Regional Business Centers and established Centers of Expertise as part of the Corps' overall efforts to maintain a trained and ready engineering force capable of responding to a wide range of contingency situations.

a. The Corps conducts Civil Works-related R&D through its ERDC and its Institute for Water Resources (IWR). The ERDC is headquartered at the Waterways Experiment Station facility, Vicksburg, MS. It consists of seven individual research laboratories:
  (1) Coastal and Hydraulics Laboratory, Vicksburg, MS
  (2) Cold Regions Research and Engineering Laboratory, Hanover, NH
  (3) Construction Engineering Research Laboratory, Champaign, IL
  (4) Environmental Laboratory, Vicksburg, MS
  (5) Geotechnical and Structures laboratory, Vicksburg, MS
  (6) Information Technologies Laboratory, Vicksburg, MS
  (7) Topographic Engineering Center, Fort Belvoir, VA

b. The IWR is headquartered at Fort Belvoir, VA, where it provides economic and decision support-related R&D support. Its Hydrologic Engineering Center is located at Davis, CA.

Section III
Support to Other Government Agencies

HOW THE ARMY RUNS

19-7. Overview of Support to Other Government Agencies
The USACE provides engineering and construction support to about 70 non-DOD federal agencies, plus numerous States, local, tribal and foreign governments under the Interagency and International Services Program. Funds for this program are provided by the agencies receiving support. The USACE support of other entities' infrastructure programs includes support to the DHS by managing the design and construction of border control and detention facilities for the Customs and Border Protection Agency and emergency management assistance to the Federal Emergency Management Assistance Agency, construction of facilities for the State Department, and renovation of health care facilities for the Department of Veterans Affairs. The USACE also supports programs and projects of other federal agencies designed to meet important national environmental objectives. These include the Superfund Program of the U.S. Environmental Protection Agency (EPA).

19-8. Value of Support Activities
In FY 2012, the value of the engineering and construction effort managed by USACE was approximately $1.6 billion. Non-DOD entities having Corps support costing at least $25,000,000 in FY 2008 are listed in Table 19-1.

Table 19-1. Construction Support for Non-Department of Defense (DOD) Agencies

Major Agency Customer	Value of Support
Dept. of Homeland Security – Customs & Border Protection	$511,000,000
Dept. of Veterans' Affairs	$340,000,000
Environmental Protection Agency	$298,000,000
Dept. of Homeland Security—FEMA	$94,000,000
Dept. of State	$25,000,000

CIVIL FUNCTIONS OF THE DEPARTMENT OF THE ARMY

U.S. Army Corps of Engineers (USACE) Organization

Figure 19-1. U.S. Army Corps of Engineers (USACE) Organization

Section IV
Engineer Overseas Activities

19-9. Overview of Engineer Overseas Activities
The USACE conducts a broad range of foreign activities. Many are exclusively in support of U.S. forces overseas. All others are considered part of the civil functions of the Army. In coordination with the Director of Strategy, Plans, & Policy (Army G3/5/7), the ASA(CW) provides program direction to the foreign activities of the Corps, except those which are exclusively in support of U.S. military forces

overseas. In FY 2012, the Corps supported U.S. foreign policy in more than 100 countries. The largest of the Corps overseas programs was in Afghanistan, where the USACE was involved in construction of roads and other civilian infrastructure as well as facilities for the new Afghan Army. The USACE support overseas includes Humanitarian Assistance (HA) projects (schools, clinics, water wells, etc.) for the Combatant Commands (CCMD), assisting the Millennium Challenge Corporation with major infrastructure projects and support to the U.S. Agency for International Development. The USACE also supports U.S. objectives by using its water resources expertise for capacity development for developing nations. Examples of this activity include technical advice and consensus building for the Mekong River Commission and strategic water resources engagement with the Brazilian Army Engineers.

19-10. Foreign Military Sales (FMS)
As the DOD Construction Agent in many parts of the world, the Corps provides international security assistance to eligible foreign nations as an instrument of the NSS and DOD Policy. Under the authorities of the FMS Program, the Corps provides reimbursable design and construction services for defense infrastructure to eligible foreign nations as approved by the Deputy Assistant Secretary of the Army (Defense Exports and Cooperation) (DASA(DEC)) and authorized by the Defense Security Cooperation Agency (DSCA). FMS assistance provided in FY 2012 to various countries in the Middle East, Central Asia, Africa, Regions had value of approximately $1 billion.

19-11. Partnership for Peace (PfP) and Civil-Military Emergency Planning (CMEP)
This program is an annual series of initiatives with PfP nations, focusing U.S. emergency management information know-how and the PfP Information Management System (PIMS) for use by evolving civil protection and civil defense structures. Simultaneously, CMEP facilitates the understanding of U.S. concepts and doctrine of military support to civilian authorities in an inter-ministerial and trans-boundary information-sharing environment. CMEP develops, through real time and tabletop exercises, co-operation at the provincial level for assistance in technological and natural disasters. CMEP establishes regional cooperation among emergency planners, creates common data bases for uses in catastrophes, acquaints high level decision makers with decision support tools, creates joint operational systems for national reaction centers and develops information exchange on legal and response procedures for large catastrophes with international implications.

19-12. Support for U.S. Agencies
The Corps is also called upon to provide support for U.S. agencies overseas. For example, the Corps: supports the U.S. Agency for International Development following natural and man-made disasters; builds border facilities for the Republic of Georgia Border Guard and U.S. Customs and Border Protection; provides hydrologic modeling training for Ethiopia and Kenya for Task Force Horn of Africa, technical; and performs government due diligence for major infrastructure projects funded by the Millennium Challenge Corporation.

Section V
Support to Unified Combatant Commanders

19-13. Benefits to Warfighting Capabilities
The Civil Works Program provides the USACE with a unique capability in DOD. The USACE's extensive professional staff of engineers, scientists, economists, etc.; provide the critical teamwork necessary to plan engineer infrastructure improvements and institution building at the national level. The training and experience gained from the Civil Works program is leveraged by the USACE's Field Force Engineering (FFE) capabilities to provide support to unified CCDRs and their Army Service Component Commands (ASCC). The infrastructure the engineers build provides the facilities and enablers for operations in the future. An excellent example is the infrastructure built by the USACE for the Government of Saudi Arabia in the 1970s and 1980s.

19-14. Overview of Support to Unified CCDRs
Expertise in water resource development, flood risk management, waterway operations, dredging, coastal engineering, environmental stewardship, and disaster response supplement the skills maintained through

CIVIL FUNCTIONS OF THE DEPARTMENT OF THE ARMY

the Army's MILCON and installation support programs. These expert capabilities are routinely called upon by the warfighting CCDRs and other DOD agencies. USACE supplies this expertise on a reimbursable basis. When the Army goes to war, USACE personnel use the experience they have gained in the Civil Works and military programs to provide timely analysis and solutions to the war fighters. The USACE's knowledge of beach dynamics, including the Sea State Prediction Models developed at the Engineer Research & Development Center's Coastal & Hydraulics Laboratory, Vicksburg, MS, helps determine the sites for shore landings. When combined with its terrain mobility models, the USACE can provide commanders with the most effective plan for logistics-over-the-shore sites in combination with the inland road network to optimize reception, staging, and onward movement in the area of operations. Corps expertise in soil mechanics determines the best routes for armored vehicles. Often roads are built using technologies developed in the Civil Works Program. Corps experience gained from work on winter navigation helps the Army to cross frozen rivers. Commanders at all levels make use of geospatial products and satellite-based navigation systems developed at the Topographic Engineering Center at Fort Belvoir, VA.

19-15. Examples of Support to Unified CCDRs
The USACE supported Operations Iraqi Freedom (OIF) and Operations Enduring Freedom (OEF) in U.S. Central Command (USCENTCOM) on several fronts. The 249th Engineer Battalion (Prime Power), a unique strategic asset, provided stable electric power to U.S. and coalition forces on a daily basis in several austere locations in the area of operations. The USACE military and civilian personnel have deployed and provided technical assistance and facility and camp designs for U.S. Soldiers. Corps teams in the USCENTCOM area of operations have supported the 101st Airborne and 10th Mountain Divisions as well as non-combat units such as the Combined Joint Civil Military Operations Task Force. Equipped with "TeleEngineering" kits, engineers anywhere on the battlefield were able to communicate real time to Corps experts through a secure, satellite-linked system. Their missions included runway repair analysis, structural evaluations, airfield lighting, and base camp design. Also noteworthy are the Contingency Real Estate Support Teams (CREST), who can deploy within 24 hours to acquire the troop housing, workspace, and covered storage areas the entering force will need. Corps real estate teams executed leases at various locations in Iraq, Kuwait, Afghanistan, Uzbekistan, and Kyrgyzstan. USACE also supports the CCMDs by performing exercise related and HA construction. For example, the Pacific Ocean Division is implementing 60 HA projects in Bangladesh, Cambodia, Vietnam, Indonesia, and Laos.

Section VI
Summary and References

19-16. Summary
The Army, through its civil functions, provides valuable services in maintaining and enhancing the economic and environmental health of the Nation. Civil functions also continue to prove invaluable in furthering national security objectives, both directly and indirectly. The financial and personnel resources associated with these functions are principally authorized and funded under the biennial WRDAs and annual Energy and Water Development Appropriations Acts, respectively. Consequently, civil functions activities, as well as the significant training of the USACE personnel they provide, are at virtually no cost to the DOD's military budget.

19-17. References
   a. Civil Works Strategic Plan, 2011-2015
   b. HQDA General Orders No. 3, Assignment of Functions and Responsibilities within Headquarters, Department of the Army, 9 July 2002
   c. Public Law 84-99, Amendment of Flood Control Act of August 18, 1941 (Emergency Flood Control Work)
   d. Public Law 91-611, Flood Control Act of 1970
   e. Public Law 93-288, Disaster Relief Act of 1974 (also known as the Stafford Act)
   f. Public Law 99-433, DOD Reorganization Act of 1986 (also known as the Goldwater-Nichols Act)
   g. Public Law 99-662, WRDA of 1986
   h. Public Law 105-245, Energy and Water Development Appropriations Act, 1999

HOW THE ARMY RUNS

    i. Public Law 105-277, Omnibus Consolidated and Emergency Supplemental Appropriations Act, 1999
    j. Public Law 106-541, WRDA, 2000
    k. Public Law 110-114, WRDA, 2007
    l. Public Law 111-5, WRDA, 2009

PUBLIC AFFAIRS

Chapter 20

Public Affairs

Section I
Introduction

20-1. Chapter Content
   a. The Public Affairs (PA) mission. PA fulfills the Army's obligation to keep the American people and the Army informed; PA operations help establish the conditions that lead to trust and confidence in America's Army in peace and war, Field Manual (FM) 3-61, PA Operations. This chapter provides insights into the functions and systems involved in PA execution.
   b. Title 10, Chapter 307, Section 3083, United States Code (USC) created the PA career field specialty. The Army PA function derives from Title 10, Chapter 303, Section 3014, USC, which requires the Secretary of the Army (SECARMY) to designate a single functional area to conduct PA activities. Army PA activities constitute those public information, command information, and community engagement functions directed toward both internal and external publics with interest in the Department of Defense (DOD).
   c. Implicit in the government is the right for people to know about the activities of the government and the government has an obligation to inform people about its activities. One of the most traditional conduits through which information is passed to the people is the free press guaranteed by the Constitution. This comes from the First Amendment providing that "Congress shall make no law…abridging the freedom of speech, or of the press." As the First Amendment has been variously interpreted in the courts, the media today enjoys significant freedom to pursue their mission of keeping the American public informed. Thus, engagement with the media is a highly effective means for supporting the government's requirement to keep the American people informed.

20-2. PA Mandate
PA activities are conducted while deployed, at home station, and in garrison to support the commander's responsibility of keeping the Army and the American people informed. Army commanders and senior officials have a legal and moral responsibility to inform the elected leadership and American public about Army activities and to account for resources allocated to the Army. These resources include funds, equipment, real property, and personnel—military and civilian. Army PA is a primary tool for communicating with internal and external publics, a critical element of effective mission command, and an essential part of successful mission accomplishment. The public perception of America's Army and how it conducts its operations can be as important to the Army's success as actual combat.

20-3. Command Function
   a. PA is a command function and responsibility. The commander may communicate through a command-designated official spokesperson, but the success or failure of the PA program hinges on the commander's personal support and direct involvement. No Public Affairs Officer (PAO), PA Noncommissioned Officer (NCO) or designated Army civilian spokesperson can fully substitute for the commander in the eyes and ears of Soldiers or the external public
   b. PA professionals serve as the commander's primary advisor on PA communication strategy and development and the dissemination of PA command themes and messages to internal and external publics. PA involvement from the very beginning and throughout the decision-making process for all command activities and operations helps ensure mission success for the command.
   c. Commanders are authorized to designate only military personnel or Department of the Army (DA) civilian employees as official spokespersons, per AR 360-1, Paragraph 2-3(c). However, commanders should educate and encourage all their military personnel, civilian employees, and contractors to tell the Army story by providing them with timely information that is appropriate for public release. By projecting confidence and commitment during interviews or in other interactions with families and friends, Army personnel can help promote public understanding of military operations and activities.

HOW THE ARMY RUNS

20-4. PA Architecture

a. Army PA doctrine is consistent and compatible with joint PA doctrine and policy, and DOD and DA PA policies. FM 3-61 is the doctrinal manual for Army PA activities. It describes the fundamental principles and concepts that provide information to internal and external national and international key actors and publics—Soldiers, family members, retirees, political leaders, allies and adversaries, as well as PA responsibilities, roles, missions, capabilities and organizations in the operational and home station environment. It also provides principles for PA employment and PA support to unified land operations.

b. Conducting operations requires an understanding of basic PA principles. Army leaders at all levels need to understand the fundamental concepts that underlie the development of PA strategies and guide the planning and execution of PA activities.

c. Tenets of Army PA. Effective application of the PA tenets can result in the more effective and efficient execution of PA activities and relationships with the media and the public.

(1) Ethical Conduct. The practice of PA is centered on truth, trust, and credibility.

(2) Maximum Disclosure, Minimum delay. Media representatives should be granted access to units, activities, and operations within the bounds of operational security. Information must not be withheld solely to protect the installation or the Army from criticism or embarrassment.

(3) Tell the Truth. PA personnel will release only accurate information. Propaganda has no place in Army PA.

(4) Provide Timely and Accurate Information and Imagery. The source, friendly, neutral or adversary that releases more timely information and imagery often becomes the public's preferred source of information.

(5) Practice Security at the Source. All Army personnel are responsible for safeguarding sensitive information whether being interviewed by the media or sharing information and imagery with Families or friends personally or via email and social media.

(6) Provide Consistent Information at All Levels. Information and imagery must be appropriately coordinated and in compliance with command guidance before release to the public.

(7) Tell the Army Story. The aim of Army PA is to tell the Army story accurately, honestly and completely to as many publics as possible by the timely release of information to internal and external news sources.

20-5. PA Functions and Tasks

a. PA Functions. PA activities are broadly categorized into three functions: public information, command information, and community engagement. Planning and assessment throughout the course of operations and activities support the functions. With today's technological communications advancements, the lines between functions are blurred because information becomes instantly available throughout the information environment. Army PA uses these three functions as pillars to the Army PA tenets and tasks.

(1) Public Information. Army public information is information of a military nature, the dissemination of which is consistent with security and the DOD principles of information (see DODI 5122.05). Information technology advances provide new public information opportunities. However, public information remains largely a matter of ensuring media representatives have access to information they need to report on military operations. Media facilitation activities provide information to domestic and international publics. Commanders and their PA staffs should conduct briefings and interviews, issue statements, respond to queries, arrange for access to operational units, and provide the media appropriate equipment, transportation, and communications support. Media facilitation plans should include specific provisions for each phase of operations.

(2) Command Information. Command information is communication from the commander to Soldiers, Family members, Army civilians, and contractors to help them understand organizational goals, operations, and significant developments. Command information is generally not intended for public media but commanders should assume that the public media will likely gain access and release it. Installation and organizational publications are traditional ways of communicating with the command, although other forms of communication have evolved. During a military operation, commanders should consider all command information dissemination capabilities available to communicate releasable details and the role of the military in the operation.

Command information is an excellent venue to incorporate and reinforce the five essential characteristics of the Army Profession, the Army Ethic, and the three-certification criteria of Army professionals:

PUBLIC AFFAIRS

competence, character, and commitment. Characteristics and criteria for success as an Army professional are framed by the guidance in our capstone Army Doctrine Publication (ADP) 1, The Army.

(3) Community Engagement. Community engagement is the process of working collaboratively with, and through, groups of people affiliated by geographic proximity or special interest to enhance the understanding and support for Army operations and activities. During military operations, personnel may be involved in activities that engage the community. All community engagement activities should support the commander's communication objectives. Senior military leaders have responsibilities to engage key leaders, including those from other government agencies and nongovernmental organizations. PA assists in identifying key leaders and recommending opportunities for military engagement. Key objectives include:

(a) Increase public awareness of the Army's mission, policies, and programs.
(b) Inspire patriotism.
(c) Maintain the Army's reputation as a respected professional organization responsible for national security.
(d) Support recruiting and retention in the All-Volunteer Force.

b. PA Tasks. Within the framework of the three PA functions, Army PA tasks allow PA to meet the commander's communications objectives. The PA core tasks:

(1) Provide advice and counsel to the Commander. The PA officer is the commander's senior advisor on PA, which is a key PAO responsibility. The PAO establishes and sustains commander and staff relationships and maintain direct and timely access to the commander. The more the PA community understands the world in which the commander operates, the more valuable the PAO's advice and counsel.

(2) Conduct PA Planning. Public affairs and communication take continuous, collaborative planning. Developing a synchronized, cohesive, and comprehensive PA plan is vital in meeting the commander's PA requirements. The PA section or unit must articulate and synchronize PA planning within the military decision-making process. The PA section or unit must provide a detailed analysis of PA operations beyond article counts and "positive/neutral/negative" evaluations. Public Affairs planning products:

(a) PA Assessment. The PA assessment addresses all aspects of the information environment, whether or not they are under the commander's control. Primary emphasis is placed on identifying, measuring, and evaluating the implications of the external information environment that PA does not control, but can inform through a coherent, comprehensive PA strategy and its early integration into the commander's planning and decision-making process.

(b) Themes, Messages, and Talking Points. PA professionals advise commanders on the use of PA themes, messages, and talking points to support communication objectives. Commanders must create, coordinate, tailor, and employ their themes and messages to support their higher headquarters.

(c) PA Running Estimate. The PA running estimate is a continuous assessment of the current PA situation that determines if the current operation is proceeding according to the commander's intent and if planned future operations are supportable (ADP 5-0). Detailed estimates are developed in the planning stage and are continuously updated. The estimate describes the existing global information environment (GIE), emerging trends, current events, and internal and external communication issues.

(d) PA Plans. Based on the information developed in the PA estimate, PA planners develop a support strategy. The PA plan links the national strategic goals and operational objectives. It defines the Army perspective of an operation, and describes how the operation supports strategic goals. It provides the intent for PA activities and the Army's approach to inform internal and external publics. In final form, it becomes Appendix 1 (PA) to the Annex J (Inform and Influence Activities) of the operations plan, which serves as the framework for developing PA guidance. Appendix 1 must address all the PA related transportation, communications, billeting, equipment, and personnel resources required to support the plan.

(e) Proposed Public Affairs Guidance (PPAG). PPAG recommends mission specific guidance to support public discussion of the operation. PPAG is created at the local level and submitted through command channels for approval by Office of the Assistant Secretary of Defense Public Affairs (OASD (PA)). OASD(PA) is the sole approval authority for PPAG. PPAG becomes Public Affairs Guidance (PAG) upon approval; however, PAG must be published prior to use. Development of additional or supplemental PPAG continues as needed.

(3) Conduct PA Training. When required, PA professionals must train fellow PA professionals and non-PA Soldiers, civilian employees, and family members to communicate the Army message. The

HOW THE ARMY RUNS

training may be group media familiarization or focused one-on-one interview techniques with subject matter experts. PA professionals must be prepared to train and assist allies and global partners. The training must replicate operational realities and teach the fundamentals of media and military interaction. The training should emphasize that the media is a communication channel to American and global publics and not an adversary.

(4) Conduct Media Facilitation. The definition of "media" continues to evolve, and PA must evolve media facilitation to fit new business models and increased non-traditional media interest in Army activities. Facilitation must include traditional, non-traditional, and social media. It is essential to have access to information and operations centers, along with adequate media facilitation facilities, to assist the media properly in reporting the Army story. When releasing information, PA professionals must remember Security, Accuracy, Propriety, and Policy (SAPP).

(a) Traditional Media. Traditional means of communication and expression that have existed since before the advent of the Internet. Industries that are generally considered part of the traditional media include broadcast and cable television, radio, newspapers, and magazines.

(b) Non-Traditional Media. Targeted reporting from citizen journalists or activist journalists is often associated with the use of internet-based mediums like blogs, microblogs, web forums, community radio, and independent or self-published written materials.

(c) Social Media. Social media is the use of Internet-based applications to create and exchange user-generated content. Social media instantaneously connects users within a global network, making the accelerated transfer of information more widespread. Social media sites offer a means of dialogue when developing communication strategies and can counter adversarial propaganda. However, an understanding of the operational environment is essential, as internet access is limited in many non-western or underdeveloped countries.

(5) Conduct Public Communication. Public communication is the communication between the Army and local, national, and international publics through the use of coordinated programs, plans, themes, and messages. It involves the receipt and exchange of ideas and opinions that contribute to shaping public understanding of, and discourse with the Army. Public communication includes the release of official information through news releases, public service announcements, media engagements, and social networks, and supports the commander's responsibility to keep the American people and the Army informed. Public communication objectives:

(a) Increase public awareness of the Army's mission, policies, and programs.
(b) Inspire patriotism.
(c) Foster good relations with publics the Army encounters at home and abroad.
(d) Maintain the Army's reputation as a respected professional organization responsible for national security.
(e) Support the Army's recruiting and personnel procurement mission.

20-6. The Privacy Act and Freedom of Information Act (FOIA)

a. The Privacy Act balances an individual's right to privacy with the public's right to know. Items in Army records, such as name, age, rank, and duty address, are generally releasable concerning a Soldier and any living person under the Privacy Act. The Soldier's name and duty address is not routinely releasable if the unit is sensitive, routinely deployable, or stationed in a foreign territory. Also releasable is a Soldier's hometown city and state, education, marital status and dependents, awards, duty status, the results of judicial actions, board results (e.g., promotion board), and official photos. Items generally not releasable under the Privacy Act include the Soldier's social security number, race, religion, investigative findings, or the results of nonjudicial/administrative boards or actions (see AR 340-21, The Army Privacy Program).

b. The FOIA allows anyone, including foreign citizens, to query the U.S. Government in writing for specifically described records in its possession. DOD policy regarding media requests for information known to be releasable under FOIA is to provide requesting media representatives with the information requested through PA channels without requiring them to submit a FOIA request (see AR 25-55, The DA FOIA Program).

PUBLIC AFFAIRS

Section II
Army Public Affairs Organizations

20-7. The Office of the Chief of Public Affairs (OCPA), DA
  a. The Chief of Public Affairs (CPA) formulates, manages, conducts, and evaluates PA policies, plans, and programs for the Army Active Component (AC) and Reserve Components (RC).
  b. By Army General Order No. 2012-01, the SECARMY has assigned the following responsibilities to the CPA:
  (1) Developing and directing Army PA policy and the execution of PA policy, regulating PA programs and processes, and directing the execution of PA policy and financial programs and budgets.
  (2) Advising, assisting, and providing direction to DA in developing and endorsing communication strategies, themes, and messages for internal and external audiences.
  (3) Coordinating, synchronizing, and assessing Army communication strategy, plans, campaigns, and engagements.
  (4) Supervising the Army strategic communication process through the use of coordinated programs, plans, themes, messages, and products.
  (5) Developing and integrating Army themes and messages into communication initiatives.
  (6) Providing public communication and media training for the Army.
  (7) Recommending venues for delivery of communication strategies using best practices and emerging communication technology.
  (8) Approving participation of the Army's official public demonstration teams and the U.S. Army Field Band.
  (9) Executing Army PA proponency, including developing a trained, equipped, and professional PA capability for commanders.
  (10) Managing the Army's Public Information Security Review Program.

20-8. PA SRC 45 units
The U.S. Army is the only U.S. military service to have deployable PA units. There are four types of Standard Requirements Code (SRC) 45 units: Public Affairs Detachment (PAD), Mobile Public Affairs Detachment (MPAD), Broadcast Operations Detachment (BOD), and Press Camp Headquarters (PCH). These units are designed to augment theater, corps, division, brigade, Special Forces Groups (Airborne), and other organic PA staff to support unified land operations. PA SRC 45 units are fully capable of operating in operational environments but require administrative and life support functions, such as field feeding and unit-level maintenance, from the supported command.

20-9. PCH
The PCH is the most capable SRC 45 unit in the inventory. The PCH is commanded by a lieutenant colonel and is modularly organized, staffed, trained, and equipped to rapidly deploy in support of military operations at the Division to Joint Forces Land Component Command (JFLCC) and Theater Army levels. The PCH is capable of directing and leading subordinate PA activities and units across the Area of Responsibility (AOR)/Joint Operations Area (JOA). The PCH is capable of performing all core PA processes and has transportation and audio-visual equipment sufficient to produce radio, television, and print products for internal or external audiences, as well as resources to credential, brief, escort, and support visiting media. When deployed in support of Army, or joint service operations, a BOD and one to three MPADs will augment the PCH. The PCH most often collocates with and operates in support of the highest level of U.S. command within the theater or AOR.

20-10. MPAD
The MPAD is commanded by a major, can be task organized into two or three teams, and is assigned to the theater, corps, division, or Joint Task Force (JTF) Headquarters (HQ) under the operational and tactical control of the senior PA officer or PCH commander. It is staffed, trained, and equipped to rapidly deploy in support of brigade, division, or corps-size task force operations. MPADS are assigned at a ratio of one per three brigade-size elements.

HOW THE ARMY RUNS

20-11. BOD
The BOD, also referred to as a broadcast PA detachment, is commanded by a major and consists of a command element, two broadcast teams, and a maintenance team. The only unit of its kind in DOD and the Army, a BOD operates 24-hours per day producing internal or external information products and sustaining broadcast stations and facilities. The BOD is designed to operate a mobile radio and television broadcast facility in support of Armed Forces Radio and Television Service operations, or to merge with other independent facilities to form a theater of operations network. A BOD performs as the broadcast support arm for a PCH, and produces broadcast products for distribution to internal and external worldwide publics through the Defense Media Activity (DMA). The BOD is assigned to a theater army headquarters, joint task force, or combatant command when a PCH is assigned.

20-12. PAD
A PAD is commanded by a captain and comes with its own transportation and sufficient still and video equipment to produce print, radio, and television products for internal audiences. The PAD typically supports division or brigade-size task force operations. A PAD provides direct support to units in support of Army, combined, joint or coalition operations. Although it is primarily attached or assigned to a division, or a brigade, a PAD may support Special Forces Groups, civil affairs, and brigade equivalents. A PAD is modularly organized, staffed, trained, and equipped to deploy rapidly in support of operations. PADs may be divided into two teams to provide brigade-level support and augment the organic PA element or provide area support within the assigned command's AOR.

20-13. Organic PA Sections
PA sections are embedded in the headquarters of Army brigades, divisions, and echelons above division. These sections provide PA support to the command and serve as the commander's principal advisor on PA issues. Ranging from a single senior noncommissioned officer to a colonel with a small staff, these sections conduct PA planning and limited PA operations. Personnel and materiel constraints require these organic PA sections be augmented by SRC 45 units for most operations.

20-14. Army Command (ACOM), Army Service Component Command (ASCC), Direct Reporting Unit PA
An ACOM PAO or ASCC PAO is a colonel serving on the commanding general's personal staff or special staff, responsible to the commander and to units attached, assigned or aligned to the Army, training for, mobilized, or deployed in support of combined or joint operations. The ASCC PA section coordinates closely with the PA sections of other government agencies, coalition commands, and other forces, when appropriate, to synchronize and conduct PA operations. Combatant command PA may direct the planning, priorities, and PA activities across the ASCC's operational area. The PA section is organized, staffed, trained, and equipped to deploy rapidly in support of theater Army-level operations and to direct PA activities in support of the commander's communication strategy. When deployed, the Army Headquarters PA staff will be augmented by a PCH or multiple MPADs, and will assume all the missions and capabilities of that organization.

20-15. Corps and Division PA Sections
The Corps PAO is a colonel and serves on the personal and special staff of the Corps commander. The Division PAO is a lieutenant colonel and serves on the personal/special staff of the division commander. The sections are organized, staffed, trained, and equipped to rapidly deploy in support of task force operations. The Corps and Division PA sections provide PA support to the Corps and Division commander respectively and to all assigned or attached units in support of national, multinational, unified, or joint operations. Corps and Division PAOs exercise planning and supervisory authority over all PA units attached, assigned or under the operational control of the respective headquarters. The PAOs coordinate closely with the organic PA sections of lower and adjacent commands, and other forces to carry out PA operations in support of the commander's PA operations. When deployed, both PA staffs may be augmented by an MPAD or a PAD.

20-16. Brigade Combat Team (BCT) and Multi-Functional/Functional Brigades
The BCT PAO is a major and serves on the special staff of the brigade commander. The staff section is organized, staffed, trained, and equipped to deploy rapidly in support of brigade task force operations.

PUBLIC AFFAIRS

The BCT PA section coordinates closely with higher echelons and other forces to carry out PA operations. A multifunctional or functional brigade PA section is comprised of two trained PA Soldiers who serve on the special staff of the brigade commander. The multifunctional brigade PA is comprised of a PA sergeant first class (SFC) and a PA sergeant (SGT). The functional brigade PAO is a captain or PA SFC with one PA SGT. The PA staff sections support and receive support from higher echelon PA staffs. When augmented by a PAD team, the PAD commander may serve as the brigade PAO when no organic PA officer is assigned or authorized.

20-17. U.S. Army Reserve (USAR) and Army National Guard (ARNG) Component PA
The vast majority of PA assets are in the USAR and ARNG—more than 65 percent of the total PA force and 85 percent of the deployable Table of Organization and Equipment (TOE) unit structures. These USAR and ARNG units and personnel must be seamlessly integrated with the active component and focused on supporting the overall Army goals and objectives. The four types of TOE PA organizations, predominately positioned in the USAR and ARNG, are discussed in the following paragraphs.

Section III
Joint and Combined Public Affairs Organizations

20-18. Assistant Secretary of Defense (Public Affairs) (ASD(PA))
As established by DOD Directive (DODD) 5122.05, the ASD (PA) is the Principal Staff Assistant and advisor to the Secretary and Deputy Secretary of Defense for DOD news media relations, public liaison, internal communications, community relations, PA, visual information training, and audiovisual matters. The ASD (PA) is charged with developing communications policies, plans and programs in support of DOD objectives and operations and with ensuring a free flow of information to the news media, the general public, the internal audiences of the DOD and other applicable forums limited only by national security restraints in the DODD 5200.1 and any other applicable statutory mandates or exemptions. The ASD(PA) reports directly to the SECDEF and acts as the sole spokesperson and the release authority for DOD information and audiovisual materials to news media representatives. The ASD(PA), or his or her designated representative, conducts news media conferences in the Pentagon with the Pentagon Press Corps.

20-19. Media Operations Center (MOC)
A MOC is the central point of contact between the military and media representatives covering operations. It offers a venue for commanders and PA staffs to discuss their units and their roles in the joint operation and helps journalists obtain information quickly and efficiently on a wide variety of complex activities. It should be staffed to support local and regional non-English speaking media. It may also support command information activities. The early establishment of a MOC is an important step in the responsive and efficient facilitation of media operations. At a minimum, the Army element will staff an Army cell within the MOC. However, it's more likely Army PA Soldiers will serve in all sections of the MOC, to include planning, media facilitation, and internal information cells.

20-20. Pentagon Correspondents
There have been media representatives at the Pentagon since the establishment of the DOD in 1947. Some 20-25 journalists keep rent-free offices in the Pentagon, courtesy of the DOD. The journalists' news organizations pay for their office furniture, telephones, and supplies. These resident journalists, as well as 75 others representing major wire services, newspapers, weekly news magazines, trade journals and radio and television networks, are issued regular DOD Pentagon building passes that allow unescorted access to unrestricted areas inside the Pentagon. The practice benefits the media and the military because information of interest to the public can be readily disseminated to correspondents who are familiar with DOD's mission, operations, and structure. These correspondents are regular attendees at the ASD(PA) media conferences conducted at the Pentagon.

20-21. DOD National Media Pool
The DOD National Media Pool is approximately 16 reporters who represent a larger number of news organizations for news gathering and sharing of material during a specified activity. Pooling is typically

used when news media support resources cannot accommodate a large number of journalists. The DOD National Media Pool is available for coverage of the earliest stages of a contingency. Additionally, the combatant commanders may also find it necessary to form limited local pools to report on specific missions. Supported commanders are responsible for providing operational support to the DOD National Media Pool. At a minimum, the pool members require: daily, comprehensive, and unclassified operational news briefings; access to ongoing combat operations; reasonable access to key personnel; an escort—usually a lieutenant colonel or colonel—to coordinate pool support and access; transportation and itinerary planning and coordination. As soon as open access to the operational area is allowed, the DOD National Media Pool should be disbanded.

20-22. Joint Combat Camera
Joint Combat Camera (COMCAM) provides the joint force commander a sophisticated capability to enhance both operational and PA missions. The still and video images obtained provide a balance of useful operational information and, once cleared for Operational Security (OPSEC), products are available for distribution to news media representatives and military PA organizations. COMCAM teams often have access to events and areas unavailable to news media representatives and military journalists. They bring a technological capability allowing for the timely transmission of images from the military information environment. Because deployed COMCAM teams support the entire spectrum of an operation, it is essential that PA imagery requirements be identified and prioritized throughout the planning cycle.

20-23. Defense Video and Imagery Distribution System (DVIDS)
The DVIDS is a network of portable satellite transmitters and network links connected to a distribution hub in Atlanta, GA. This system enables media organizations to request products, conduct broadcast-quality interviews, and to receive images, video footage and print stories from the DVIDS distribution hub, which also supports live interviews with service members deployed in support of a range of military operations.

Section IV
Information Mediums

20-24. News Media
The specific medium, through which the news media present their work, creates different needs and expectations on the part of media representatives in their dealings with the military. As in just about any military operation, timing is everything, and a basic analysis of media deadlines, requirements, and abilities to reach the American public with the command's story can assist the commander's PA program as well as serve to better satisfy the media. Advances in communications technology today enable virtually simultaneous reporting worldwide from anywhere in a satellite footprint. News media coverage will be highly competitive, with a tendency to seek access to the operational area and report events as they happen.

20-25. Television
Television news broadcasts are typically pegged to specific times of the day. Television thrives on video pictures, a script written to what the camera has seen and some carefully chosen 5-8 second "sound bites" from interviews conducted on camera with witnesses to the event, experts or participants whose words fit the video the cameraman has taken of the event. Long answers from commanders and staff officers rarely make it to the screen, so PAOs will recommend the use of talking points to assist commanders and interviewees in getting the command's message out in a format television will be most likely to use.

20-26. Television "News Magazines"
Television news programs entertain as much or more than they inform. The command's messages can be transmitted through a variety of mediums, and dealing with the entertainment media will require some imaginative work. While the commander should not deny access—thereby creating a story in and of itself—he or she should be prepared to prioritize efforts to support the media and pursue getting command messages out through the media to reach the American public.

PUBLIC AFFAIRS

20-27. Radio
Radio is an immediate medium. Live radio news broadcasts are easily changed even in progress. "Hot" stories can easily be inserted into normal programming. The voice is the only medium, and details from commanders or their spokespersons will get more airtime than on television because the voice and words alone must paint the picture for the audience. A radio news desk is only as far away as a communications line, and the story can be on the air within minutes.

20-28. Print
Newspapers tend to follow strict deadlines to get their product to American breakfast or dinner tables. Reporters may be able to spend hours, even days, with a unit before having to file their stories. The unit will likely garner more "space" in the articles by virtue of the attention the print journalist can give the story. The longer a reporter stays with the unit, the more attached he or she becomes to the unit. Daily newspapers differ from weekly publications in terms of immediacy and pictorial requirements. Weeklies tend to want lots of colored pictures and will focus on more analytical, more timeless aspects of the mission, whereas daily newspapers focus on what has happened since their last deadline and will settle for a good black and white photograph transmitted electronically. A reporter for a specific newspaper gives the commander access to one newspaper, whereas wire services such as Associated Press (AP) offer the commander and his or her PAO greater access to the American public because many newspapers subscribe to the services and therefore the story may run in numerous newspapers.

20-29. Motion Picture Industry Support
The OCPA maintains branch offices in Los Angeles, CA and New York, NY primarily to interface with the entertainment industry and networks headquartered in those areas. The offices assist radio, television, and film professionals in all matters relating to the Army. They serve as a local, authoritative source of information about the Army and provide authentication, verification, and limited research for producers, writers, property masters, wardrobe supervisors, film editors, etc. They also provide assistance and advice to scriptwriters, including reviewing rough drafts and suggestions for changes prior to script finalization. Army support of a project is contingent on scripts realistically portraying the Army and its personnel. These offices can also arrange for and coordinate use of Army equipment and supplies not commercially available, coordinate requests for Army's stock footage, arrange for and coordinate with Army installations or properties for location filming and arrange for Soldier volunteers to participate in the project if requested.

20-30. Internet and Social Media
One of the most dynamic news sources has become the Internet and social media platforms. More Americans get news online than from radios or newspapers. The Army now uses the Internet and social media for recruiting and informational purposes because it is one of the most powerful mediums available at relatively low costs. The Internet has evolved from being a news delivery mechanism to an important force in breaking news. The downside in publishing news on the Internet is the weakness of editorial review. The immediacy of information is more important to some news recipients than validating factual accuracy. Email is another important news mechanism to inform Soldiers, their families, civilians, and contractors. The command needs to establish a single source of internal information on the web and the PA office, in accordance with DOD policy, is responsible for the content of the command's web site. Social media platforms, such as Facebook and Twitter are powerful tools for communicating with the American public and the Army's internal audiences. There are numerous incidents in which social media became the primary source of communication in the absence of typical news outlets: use of Twitter in the 2011 earthquake and tsunami in Japan, and the revolutionary protests in Tunisia, Egypt, and Libya are examples. Realizing the impact and immediacy of these Internet tools, commanders need to be acutely aware of the strategic implications of conversations using them and ensure their messages are properly framed.

HOW THE ARMY RUNS

Section V
Summary, Terms and References

20-31. Summary

a. Today's information environment has made possible virtually instantaneous transmission of breaking news to world-wide publics. Technology has made 24-hour news organizations and internet news possible. This has decreased the dominance of traditional news organizations and increased competition for news and the attention of the American public. The elements of news, however, have remained constant and the American public is, as it always has been, interested in what happens to its sons and daughters in uniform, especially when they are executing operational missions. The increasing number, variety and complexity of real-world operations in which the U.S. Army has been involved has attracted considerable public and media interest and will continue to do so in the future.

b. Operational security will always concern the military; however, it should not prevent the Army from communicating in real time with the American public. Because the media can transmit words, voice, or pictures via satellites, the most viable solution to operational security is the practice of security at the source, a clear set of ground rules accepted and understood by the media, and honest interaction between the military and the media. Maintaining OPSEC implies Soldiers and their leaders are trained to interact with the media.

c. Commanders can no longer expect to provide information separately to Soldiers, the American public and the enemy. Information operations involve civil affairs, psychological operations and PA messages that by definition overlap and are picked up simultaneously by Soldiers, the media and the enemy. The importance of consistency and truth in the message has never been greater. The continually evolving information environment and technologies make it imperative that information and messages be consistent at all levels.

d. Commanders could conceivably win the battle and lose the information war by excluding, or attempting to exclude media from operations or by overlooking the value of effective PA involvement throughout operational planning and execution. The Army owes the American public accountability and truth.

20-32. Terms

a. PA—Those public information, command information, and community engagement activities directed toward both the external and internal publics with interest in the DOD (Joint Publication (JP) 3-61).

b. Public Information—Within PA, that information of a military nature, the dissemination of which is consistent with security and approved for release (JP 3-61).

c. Command Information—Communication by a military organization directed to the internal audience that creates an awareness of the organization's goals, informs them of significant developments affecting them and the organization, increases their effectiveness as ambassadors of the organization, and keeps them informed about what is going on in the organization. Also called Internal Information (JP 3-61).

d. Community Engagement—Those PA activities that support the relationship between military and civilian communities (JP 3-61).

e. PA Guidance (PAG)—Constraints and restraints established by proper authority regarding public information, command information, and community relations activities. It may also address the method(s), timing, location, and other details governing the release of information to the public (JP 3-61).

20-33. References

a. Army Regulation (AR) 25-55, The DA FOIA Program
b. AR 340-21, The Army Privacy Program
c. AR 360-1, The Army PA Program
d. DODD 5105.74, DMA
e. DODD 5122.05, ASD(PA)
f. DODD 5122.11, Stars and Stripes Newspapers and Business Operations
g. DODD 5400.07, DOD FOIA Program
h. DODD 5400.11, DOD Privacy Program
i. DODD 5410.18, PA Community Relations Policy
j. DOD Instruction (DODI) 5120.4, DOD Newspapers, Magazines and Civilian Enterprise Publications

PUBLIC AFFAIRS

k. DODI 5200.01, DOD Information Security Program and Protection of Sensitive Compartmentalized Information
l. DODI 5400.4, Provision of Information to Congress
m. DODI 5400.13, PA Operations
n. DODI 5400.14, Procedures for Joint PA Operations
o. DODI 5405.3, Development of Proposed PA Guidance
p. DODI 5410.15, DOD PA Assistance to Non-Government, Non-Entertainment-Oriented Print and Electronic Media
q. 5410.16, DOD Assistance to Non-Government, Entertainment-Oriented Motion Picture, Television, and Video Productions
r. DODI 5410.19, PA Community Relations Policy Implementation
s. DODI 8910.01, Information Collection and Reporting
t. FM 3-13, Inform and Influence Activities
u. FM 3-61, PA Operations
v. JP 3-61, PA

HOW THE ARMY RUNS

This page is intentionally left blank

DEFENSE SUPPORT OF CIVIL AUTHORITIES

Chapter 21

Defense Support of Civil Authorities

Section I
Introduction

21-1. Defense Support of Civil Authorities (DSCA) Overview

a. The U.S. military primarily organizes itself, trains, equips forces, plans and conducts combat and stability operations. However, when requested by civil authority or directed by the President of the United States (POTUS), it also has enormous capability to rapidly respond and provide support to a wide variety of domestic emergencies and disasters. The Department of Defense (DOD) conducts these operations under civilian control and in accordance with the fundamental tenet of its professional ethos - subordination to civilian authority. Federal military forces normally respond in support of another federal agency, often after a Presidential declaration to supplement the efforts and resources of state and local governments. Based on our form of government, and consistent with our historic experience, the military should not lead the federal response for any but perhaps the most severe domestic emergency or disaster.

b. DOD Directive (DODD) 3025.18 defines DSCA as support provided by U.S. federal military forces, DOD civilians, DOD contract personnel, DOD component assets, and National Guard forces (when the Secretary of Defense (SECDEF), in coordination with the Governors of the affected states, elects and requests to use those forces in Title 32, U.S.C. status) in response to requests for assistance from civil authorities for domestic emergencies, law enforcement and other domestic activities, or from qualifying entities for special events. It notes that DSCA is also known as National Guard Civil Support (CS). National Guard CS has been adopted in National Guard Regulation 500-1 with the definition, "support provided by the National Guard of the several states while in State Active Duty (SAD) or Title 32 duty status to civil authorities for domestic emergencies, and for designated law enforcement and other activities."

c. DSCA is a critically important mission for the Armed Forces, and particularly the Army which will usually provide the main effort. At one time, FM-1 identified Support of Civil Authority as an Army core competency. Within existing processes and procedures, the Armed Forces have a well-defined basis for participation in domestic emergencies and disasters. They perform specific and appropriate roles and are postured to refine those roles in response to evolving threats and domestic needs.

21-2. Constitutional and Policy Basis for DSCA

a. Use of the military to support civil authorities stems from our core national values as expressed in the Constitution which anticipates the use of federal military forces within U.S. borders. Article I, Section 8 states, "Congress shall have power… to provide for calling forth the Militia to execute laws of the Union, suppress Insurrections, and repel Invasions." Article II, Section 3 states POTUS, "…shall take care that the Laws be faithfully executed." The 10th Amendment provides the basis that federal government assistance, including DOD, is provided in support of State and local authorities. It reads in part, "The powers not delegated to the U.S. by the Constitution, nor prohibited by it, are reserved to the States respectively."

b. The National Security Strategy (NSS) identifies key national interests such as protecting the lives and safety of Americans, maintaining the sovereignty of the U.S. and providing for the prosperity of the nation and its people. The National Strategy for Homeland Security (NSHS) further focuses on securing the U.S. homeland from terrorist attacks and calls for the military to support civil authorities during emergencies. In June 2005, the DOD published its first Strategy for Homeland Defense (HD) and CS. All these strategies recognize that America's military may respond to a variety of national needs other than waging war and that DSCA contributes significantly to satisfying America's national security requirements.

21-3. Historic Context for Domestic Military Support

a. Since our nation's inception, the Army has supported civil authorities in times of need. Floods, riots, hurricanes, earthquakes, and forest fires are all examples of situations that have caused states to deploy the National Guard and occasionally request the assistance of federal armed forces. Achieving national goals with regard to terrorism, WMD and illegal drug trafficking have also led to supplementing civilian efforts with military forces. DSCA law and policy evolved as our nation grew and responded to repeated crisis and disaster.

b. When our Founding Fathers met to draft the U.S. Constitution in Philadelphia in 1787, Shay's Rebellion was a recent memory and insurrection a concern. To protect the viability of government, they created mechanisms to suppress rebellions or insurrections and enforce the law. The 1794 Whiskey Rebellion led to the fundamental precept, codified in current law that the military is in support of civil authority. A taxpayer revolt and increasing violence led to a Presidential response and deployment of federalized militia. Throughout this threat to federal governance, President Washington's guidance was that the military was to support local magistrates, not pre-empt them, and this principle remains the foundation of DSCA law, policy and processes.

c. After the Whiskey Rebellion, the military established a long history of assisting civil authorities enforce the nation's laws. Significant with regard to current law and policy is the April 1995 domestic terrorist attack on the Alfred P. Murrah Building in Oklahoma City. In the wake of that attack, President Clinton issued Presidential Decision Directives (PDD) 39 and 62 that clarified the roles and missions of various federal agencies with regard to countering and combating terrorism. These documents defined terms such as: Crisis Response Management (CrM), Consequence Management (CM), Lead Federal Agency (LFA) that have since been given new meaning by more recent documents, particularly Homeland Security Presidential Directive (HSPD)-5.

d. Current disaster response organizations, systems and processes evolved from the civil defense mission of the U.S. Army Continental Army Command (CONARC), which was inactivated in 1973. President Carter's 1979 Executive Order 12148 established the Federal Emergency Management Agency (FEMA) and transferred many of the missions formerly performed by CONARC to FEMA. The 1988 Stafford Disaster Relief and Emergency Assistance Act and Executive Order 12656 that delegated most of the President's Stafford Act authority to the FEMA Director were instrumental in establishing current interagency responsibilities. The military also has a history ensuring the continuity of government in the event of a national emergency and EO 12656 identified agency responsibility and refined those processes as well.

e. In the wake of the September 2001 terrorist attacks, Hurricane Katrina in 2005, and Hurricane Sandy in 2012, we remain in another period of evolving change with regard to how the military supports civil authority. DOD's Executive and Action Agent responsibilities moved from the Army to the Office of the Secretary of Defense (OSD) and the Joint Staff (JS) respectively. HSPD-5 directed alignment of federal, state and local coordinating structures, capabilities and processes into a unified, all-discipline, all-hazards approach to domestic incident management. HSPD-5 integrated CrM and CM, recognizing that all agencies responding to a disaster or emergency do so while retaining their own authorities and responsibilities under law and policy.

21-4. DOD's Role in Homeland Security (HS) Today

a. The NSHS (2002) defined HS as "a concerted national effort to prevent terrorist attacks within the U.S., reduce America's vulnerability to terrorism, and minimize damage and recover from attacks that do occur." In the wake of Hurricane Katrina, many observers expected the next NSHS to expand the definition of HS to include natural and other manmade disasters. However, recognizing the unprecedented threat to our national security posed by Chemical, Biological, Radiological, Nuclear and High-Yield Explosive (CBRNE) and Weapons of Mass Destruction (WMD), the 2007 NSHS definition was unchanged, remaining focused on terrorism. In the decade since September 11, 2001, this clear and present threat to our homeland has resulted in dramatic change to DOD's HS culture and capabilities, particularly the CS or DSCA mission. As DOD continues to contribute through its military missions overseas and HS efforts, the pace of change has slowed, although the mission set continues to evolve.

b. The DOD Strategy for HD and CS (2013) identifies two broad mission areas: HD and CS; and DSCA. The DOD Strategy uses a "lead, support or enable" construct to categorize DOD's activities to secure the U.S. from direct attack. DOD has lead responsibility for HD and is the primary federal agency for this mission. HD is DOD's primary responsibility and is defined as the protection of U.S. sovereignty, territory, domestic population, and critical defense infrastructure against external threats and aggression, or other threats as directed by POTUS. This chapter does not deal with HD, only DSCA.

DEFENSE SUPPORT OF CIVIL AUTHORITIES

c. DOD has had a past reluctance to take on the CS mission, considering it a mission to accept when we could or when we had the resources available to assist. Perhaps the most significant change for DOD today is that with the unprecedented threat to the U.S. homeland, DOD must be able to conduct CBRNE CM as an integrated part of our national security efforts. For the first time, the 2008 National Defense Authorization Act (NDAA) directed DOD to budget monies against this mission and this chapter will explain how DOD is spending those monies to evolve its DSCA role.

d. Also associated with DOD's HS construct is Mission Assurance (MA) which includes activities to ensure DOD support of the POTUS and SECDEF during a national security emergency. MA has traditionally been described as providing a foundation for both HD and DSCA by supporting national continuity of government (COG) and continuity of operations (COOP) programs designed to ensure Enduring Constitutional Government (ECG). At the federal level, COG is a coordinated effort within each branch of government to ensure capability to continue minimum essential functions in a crisis; COOP are internal efforts within various governmental department, agencies and organizations to ensure capability to continue operations in support COG and ECG.

21-5. DSCA Principles

a. DOD almost always provides DSCA when requested by civil authorities and approved by the SECDEF. We can also provide support when directed by POTUS or SECDEF, or when authorized under separate established authorities.

b. DOD remains in support of civil authority and generally in support of a primary federal agency.

c. The DOD Strategy for HD and CS (2005) reaffirms that protecting the U.S. from attack is DOD's highest priority. Unless otherwise directed by the SECDEF, on-going military or HD missions have priority over DSCA missions.

d. DOD provides DSCA in accordance with applicable laws, Presidential Directives, Executive Orders and DOD policy with absolute, public accountability of officials involved in the oversight of DSCA processes and while maintaining our constitutional principles and civil liberties.

e. As a general rule, civil resources should be used first, and DSCA should generally be provided only when requirements exceed the capabilities of civil authority as determined by FEMA or another federal agency with primary responsibility. DSCA should emphasize DOD's unique skills and structures, and should be limited in scope and duration.

f. DOD usually provides DSCA through designated federal agencies using established agreements and plans, guided by civilian law and the principle that the federal government assists state agencies, except in terrorism and other incidents where the federal government has primary jurisdiction.

g. DOD Components shall not procure or maintain supplies, materiel or equipment exclusively for providing DSCA unless set forth in law or directed by the SECDEF.

h. Military forces remain under military mission command and the authority of the DOD Executive Agent at all times.

i. DOD components shall not perform any function of civil government unless absolutely necessary, and then only on a temporary basis.

j. While there are exceptions, DSCA should be provided on a cost reimbursable basis, primarily through the Stafford Act for Presidentially declared disasters or the Economy Act for other situations. Only the SECDEF and POTUS are authorized to grant a reimbursement waiver.

21-6. DSCA Mission Sets

a. As of the publishing of this version of How The Army Runs (HTAR), many current DOD Directives, Instructions, and Manuals in this field are obsolete. Although some have begun to be replaced (e.g. DODD 3025.18 (DSCA), dtd 29 Dec 2010), many still pre-date September 2001. The term Military Assistance to Civil Disturbances (MACDIS) has been replaced by Civil Disturbance Operations (CDO). The reader should be cautioned about DOD documents still needing update that use the term Military Assistance to Civil Authorities (MACA) as an overarching construct with three subordinate mission sets: MACA; Military Assistance to Civil Disturbances (MACDIS); and Military Assistance to Civil Law Enforcement Agencies (MSCLEA).

b. The DSCA environment is so complex and dynamic that it is difficult and perhaps impossible to clearly and consistently create simple categories of missions. The categories used by Joint Publication 3-28 (CS) are used here (they are a bit different than the recently published Army FM 3-28), but the reader should understand that these categories overlap and may be in effect simultaneously. For example, an

HOW THE ARMY RUNS

incident at a special event could result in a Presidential declaration and become a declared emergency. Subsequent sections explain the categories and describe many, but not all, of the various mission sets DOD could be called on to support.

(1) Disasters and declared emergencies will likely be Presidentially declared, but may not be. In fact, most instances of local commanders invoking immediate response authority are in this category. Disasters and emergencies can be natural or manmade. Examples include the following: natural disasters (flood, blizzard, earthquake, etc.); wild land fire suppression; CBRNE consequence management; and more.

(2) Restoring public health and services and civil order includes CDO and support in the event of strikes or work stoppage by public service employees (e.g., 1970 postal strike and 1981 air traffic controller strike). It also includes Presidentially directed critical infrastructure protection. If not a declared emergency, this category could also include mass immigration emergencies, border security, animal disease eradication and more.

(3) Special events encompass any special event, usually categorized by the Department of Homeland Security (DHS) Special Events Working Group that warrants defense support. Examples include the Boy Scout Jamboree, Olympics, Super Bowl, World Series, and many more. National Special Security Events (NSSE) are a sub-category of such magnitude or importance that the Secretary of HS designates them an NSSE. The U.S. Secret Service assumes responsibility for the security planning and execution. Recent examples include Presidential Inaugurations, Democratic and Republican National Conventions, and State Funerals.

(4) Periodic planned support is a wide ranging category of support to civil authorities that routinely takes place to enhance civil-military relations and meet the needs of local communities, states and even other federal agencies.

Section II
Domestic Emergency Management Environment

21-7. National Incident Management

a. Tiered Response. One of the most important concepts for those new to the DSCA arena to understand is that our country has traditionally utilized a "bottom-up" as opposed to a "top-down" approach to emergency management with three tiers of support—local, state and federal—as shown in Figure 21-1. Primary responsibility for responding to domestic disasters and emergencies rests with the lowest level of government able to effectively deal with the incident. If a situation exceeds local capability, local authorities are generally expected to seek assistance from neighboring jurisdictions under a mutual aid agreement before requesting state assistance. Similarly, if a state's capability proves insufficient, state authorities ask for assistance, to include non-federalized National Guard, from other states under existing agreements and compacts before requesting federal assistance. In the event of a very large or catastrophic event, federal aid may be provided while mutual aid agreements and compacts are still being coordinated. Defense resources are provided when circumstances warrant; military support can be provided at state (National Guard forces under state control) and federal level. Not a designated tier of support or a level of elected authority, regional response both within a state and among states is increasingly important.

DEFENSE SUPPORT OF CIVIL AUTHORITIES

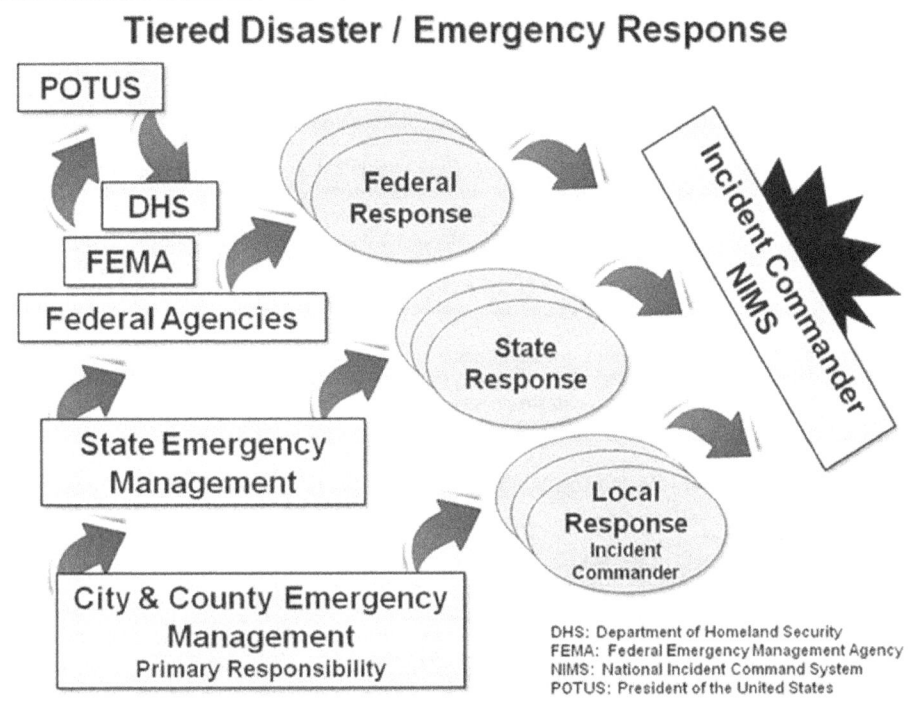

Figure 21-1. Tiered Disaster / Emergency Response

b. Key National Response Documents. In combination with each other, the National Incident Management System (NIMS) and National Response Framework (NRF) provide a single, comprehensive, nation-wide approach to incident management. The NIMS provides an action template for incident management. The NRF provides the policy structure and mechanisms for national-level policy for incident management and can be considered a framework for integrating federal support into state and local government efforts.

(1) The National Incident Management System (NIMS) establishes a core set of concepts, principles, terminology and organizational processes to enable effective, efficient and collaborative incident management at all levels of government. Responding agencies retain all their jurisdictional authorities and responsibilities, and they maintain operational control of their functions. Thus, another critical concept for those new to DSCA is that domestic emergency management operations are much more about unity of effort than about unity of command with which most service members are familiar. Some additional NIMS facts:

(a) HSPD-5, Management of Domestic Incidents, directed the Secretary of HS to develop and administer the NIMS. HSPD-5 requires all federal departments and agencies to adopt NIMS and makes adoption by State and local governments a condition for federal preparedness assistance.

(b) The NIMS objective is to provide a consistent nationwide template to enable federal, state, local and tribal governments and private-sector and nongovernmental organizations to work together effectively and efficiently to prepare for, prevent, respond to, and recover from domestic incidents regardless of cause, size or complexity.

(2) The NRF specifies an all-discipline, all-hazards approach for the federal government to prepare and respond to incidents in a national unity of effort sort of way. It establishes a single, comprehensive approach to domestic incident management to prevent, prepare for, respond to, and recover from terrorist

21-5

HOW THE ARMY RUNS

attacks, major disasters and other emergencies. The NRF, utilizing NIMS, is the core operational framework for national incident management.

(a) The NRF applies to all incidents requiring a coordinated federal response in concert with State, local, tribal, private-sector and nongovernmental entities. The NRF is applicable to all federal departments and agencies that participate in a coordinated federal response. The NRF also applies to the nongovernment responders such as the American Red Cross and National Voluntary Organizations Active in Disaster (NVOAD).

(b) The NRF is always in effect although the selective implementation of various elements allows flexibility to meet the unique requirements of any situation. It enables effective interaction among federal, state, local, tribal, private-sector, and other nongovernmental entities.

(c) There are two broad categories of federal assistance for disasters and emergencies. The Robert T. Stafford Disaster Assistance and Emergency Relief Act provides the authority for coordinating federal responses to most disasters; Figure 21-2 provides a schematic of initial federal involvement under the Stafford Act. Figure 21-3 provides a diagrammatic overview of federal-to-federal support in non-Stafford Act situations.

(d) The Catastrophic Incident Annex is a stand-alone supporting document to the NRF that is particularly noteworthy. It establishes an overarching strategy for implementing and coordinating an "accelerated, proactive response" to a catastrophic event.

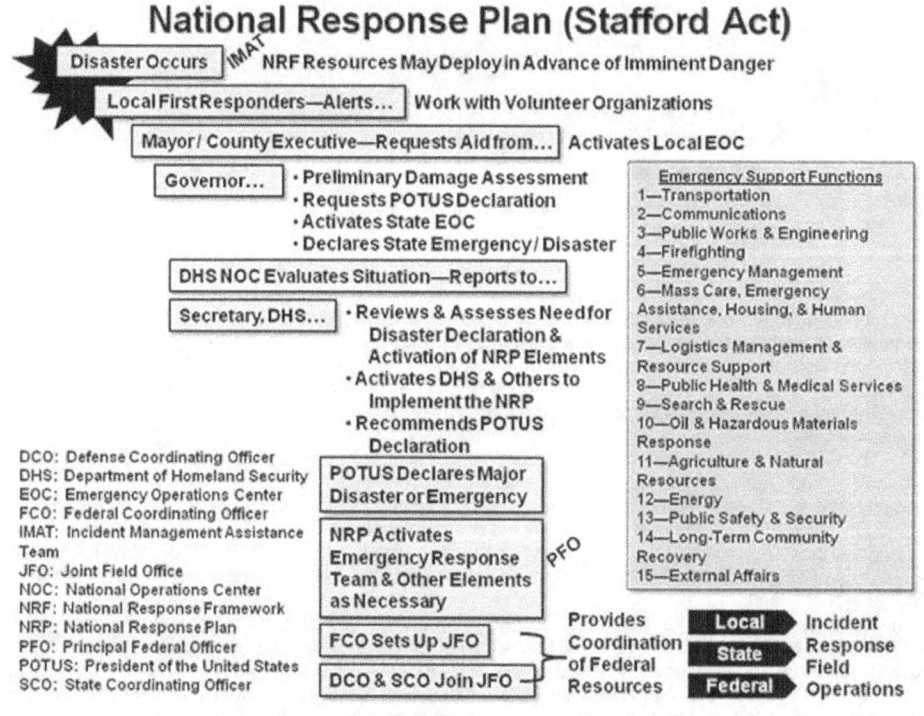

Figure 21-2. National Response Plan (Stafford Act)

DEFENSE SUPPORT OF CIVIL AUTHORITIES

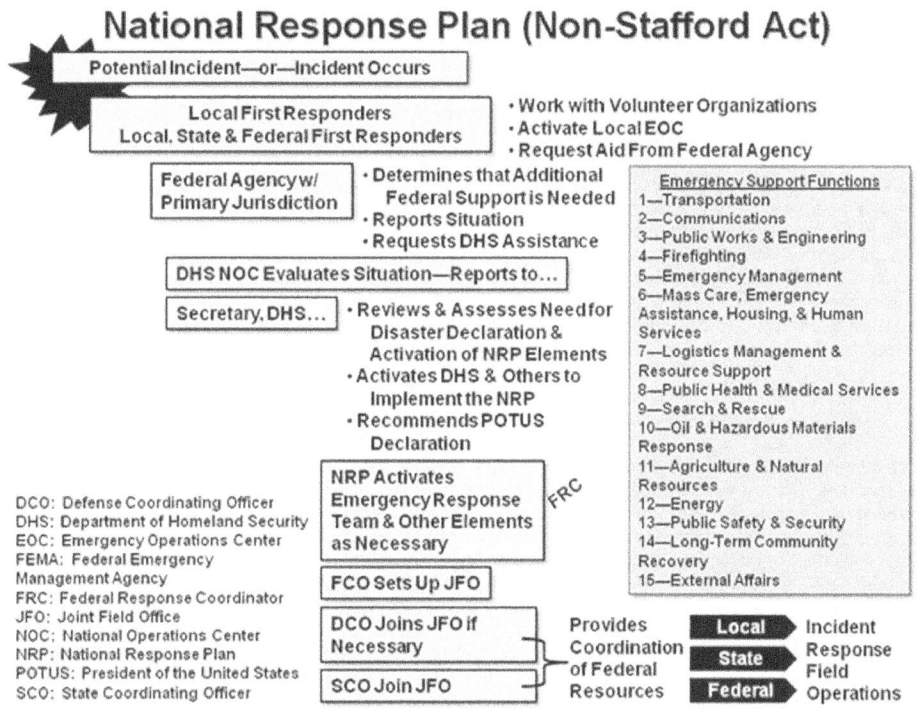

Figure 21-3. National Response Plan (Non-Stafford Act)

21-8. Local Response

a. In the immediate aftermath of a disaster, local responders will arrive first on the scene. First responders normally include law enforcement, fire, emergency medical services (EMS), and HAZMAT teams. At the incident site, local authorities organize the various responders under the Incident Command System (ICS), a major component of the NIMS. Military forces conducting DSCA will interact with and be a part of an ICS structure.

b. Incident Command System. NIMS establish ICS as the standardized organizational structure for the management of all domestic incidents, yet ICS provides more than just structure. ICS characteristics include: common terminology; modular organization; management by objective; reliance on an incident action plan; manageable span of control; and integrated communications. Within the ICS, there are five major functional areas, to include command, operations, logistics, planning, and finance. Traditionally, information and intelligence functions are located in the planning section; however, if the situation warrants, NIMS ICS can break intelligence out and add a sixth functional area. An ICS hallmark is the flexibility to accommodate all circumstances including floods, hazardous material accidents, aircraft crashes, and earthquakes—it is an all-hazard system. Flexible enough to manage catastrophic incidents involving thousands of response personnel, several levels of command are possible:

(1) A single command structure provides one commander a reasonable span of control. The incident commander is normally the senior responder of the organization with the responsibility for the event, e.g., fire chief or police chief. There is only one incident commander; he establishes an incident command post to direct operations.

(2) Unified Command (UC). ICS has the flexibility for one or more agencies to coordinate and combine independent efforts should the situation dictate. ICS can transition from a single Incident Commander

HOW THE ARMY RUNS

(IC) to a UC structure to enable agencies with different legal, geographic and functional responsibilities to coordinate, plan and interact effectively. In a UC structure, the individuals designated by their jurisdictional authorities jointly determine objectives, plans, and priorities and work together to execute them. UC as used by NIMS ICS is where the aforementioned unity of effort is manifested as all responding agencies and organizations work to support the IC without giving up individual agency authorities, responsibilities or accountability. An incident large enough to require DOD support will almost certainly be multi-jurisdictional UC.

(3) Area Command is established either to oversee the management of multiple incidents being handled by separate ICS organizations or to oversee the management of a very large incident that involves multiple ICS organizations. Area Command is activated only if necessary, depending on the complexity of the incident and span-of- control considerations. Area Command does not have operational responsibilities. Functions include: setting priorities; allocating resources according to established priorities; ensuring effective communications; ensuring that incident management objectives are met and do not conflict with each other or with policy.

c. To supplement their capabilities, local governments establish mutual aid agreements with surrounding communities. They are usually activated before local authorities request state assistance.

21-9. State Support

a. State Governors are empowered by the U.S. Constitution and their state constitutions to execute the laws of their states. They are the Commanders in Chiefs of the state National Guard when serving in state status (SAD or Title 32). Similar authorities are given to the governors of U.S. territories and possessions. Once a disaster occurs, the Governor decides whether to honor a local government Request for Assistance (RFA) and, if appropriate, declares a state of emergency, activates the state response plan and call up the National Guard under state orders. The Governor informs the FEMA regional director of his actions and when state resources are insufficient, requests federal assistance.

b. State Office of Emergency Services (OES). All states have an agency that coordinates and conducts emergency preparedness planning, training and exercises, and serves as the coordinating agency for the Governor in an emergency. The titles of these offices vary from state to state (e.g., Emergency Management Agency, Department of Public Safety, State Emergency Management Office, and Office of Emergency Preparedness). The OES is generally organized as a standalone office under the Governor, or aligned under The Adjutant General (TAG) or state police. The senior official in charge of OES varies by state. Some states have a separate Director of Emergency Services and Director of HS. Some states combine the positions and some states dual-hat their TAG as the Director of Emergency Services.

c. State National Guard forces are particularly well-suited to provide military support to local and state agencies. The National Guard in state status is the primary military responder during most natural or man-made disasters and emergencies. It is familiar with local conditions and geography, and acting as a state militia, is not constrained by limitations on federal troops, principally the Posse Comitatus Act.

(1) The National Guard operates under one of three statuses: state status (state funding and state control); Title 32 status (federal funding and state control); or Title 10 status (federal funding and federal control). State CS missions are authorized by executive order of the Governor who reimburses the federal government for utilization of federal equipment and facilities. Employment of National Guard assets by the Governor will be in accordance with state laws and constitutions.

(2) State National Guard Joint Force Headquarters (JFHQ) organizes, trains, plans, and coordinates the mobilization of National Guard units and elements for state and federal missions. Deployment and employment of the state National Guard is directed through the JFHQ.

d. In times of emergency, states often call on other states for help through standing agreements or emergency assistance compacts.

(1) The largest and best known is the Emergency Management Assistance Compact (EMAC). The EMAC expedites the employment of interstate emergency response assets and may involve all types of support to include National Guard forces. Assets provided by another state are under control of the Governor of the requesting state while assistance is being provided.

(2) Since it was first approved by Congress in 1996 as Public Law 104-321, EMAC has been ratified by all 50 states, the District of Columbia, and two territories (Puerto Rico and the US Virgin Islands). Requests for EMAC assistance are legally binding, contractual arrangements and states that ask for help are responsible for reimbursing out-of-state costs for out-of-state personnel. FEMA recognizes cross-

DEFENSE SUPPORT OF CIVIL AUTHORITIES

state support under EMAC as reimbursable. States are not required to assist each other unless they are able.

Section III
Federal Role in the National Response Process

21-10. Primary Federal Departments and Agencies

a. Secretary of HS, DHS & FEMA. Pursuant to HSPD-5, the Secretary of HS is the principal federal official for domestic incident management within the U.S. to prepare for, respond to, and recover from terrorist attacks, major disasters and other emergencies. Acting through FEMA, the Secretary has responsibility to effectively manage federal response and recovery efforts. FEMA also initiates proactive mitigation activities, trains first responders, and manages the National Flood Insurance Program. FEMA Headquarters is in Washington, DC and there are ten regional offices, three logistics centers, two training centers and other special purpose sites.

b. Attorney General of the U.S., Department of Justice (DOJ), & Federal Bureau of Investigation (FBI). Pursuant to HSPD-5, the Attorney General has responsibility for criminal investigations of terrorist acts or threats inside the U.S., or directed at U.S. citizens or institutions abroad, where such acts are within the federal criminal jurisdiction of the U.S. He is also responsible for related intelligence collection within the U.S. subject to the National Security Act of 1947, other applicable laws and Executive Order 12333. Generally acting through the FBI, the Attorney General, in cooperation with other federal departments and agencies, also coordinates the activities of the law enforcement community to detect, prevent, preempt, and disrupt terrorist attacks against the U.S.

c. DOD. Understanding that DOD has significant resources that might be available to support federal domestic incident management efforts, HSPD-5 states, "The SECDEF shall provide military support to civil authorities for domestic incidents as directed by POTUS or when consistent with military readiness and appropriate under the circumstances and the law. The SECDEF shall retain command of military forces providing civil support."

d. Other Primary Departments and Agencies. There is insufficient space in this section to cover the long list of federal organizations that have primary responsibility for various emergencies and other activities for which DOD could provide support. There are a tremendous number of directives, memorandums of agreement/understanding, laws and other arrangements involving DOD. Many but not all primary federal agencies DOD could support are codified in the NRP's Emergency Support Function (ESF) framework (Table 21-1). Others are identified throughout this chapter.

21-11. Federal Structure for NRF Response & Recovery

This section describes significant organizations and key personnel that are involved with implementing the NRF.

a. The Regional Response Coordination Center (RRCC), located in each of the ten FEMA regions, is a standing facility operated by DHS/FEMA that coordinates regional response efforts, establishes federal priorities, and when disaster strikes, coordinates federal support until a Joint Field Office (JFO) is established. The RRCC establishes communications with affected State Emergency Operations Centers (EOC) and the DHS National Operations Center (NOC). FEMA and interagency representatives staff the RRCC as needed.

b. Joint Field Office (JFO) is a temporary federal facility established in a disaster area to provide a central point for federal, state and local executives to coordinate their actions. Although the JFO uses an ICS structure and adapts to the magnitude of the situation, it does not manage on-scene operations. Instead, it focuses on providing support to on-scene efforts and conducting broader support operations that may extend beyond the incident site. When incidents impact multiple States or localities, multiple JFOs may be established. Utilizing NIMS ICS principles of UC, JFO activities are directed by a JFO Coordination Group which may include the following officials:

(1) Principal Federal Official (PFO) is personally designated by the Secretary of HS as her representative locally to oversee, coordinate and execute the Secretary's incident management responsibilities. The NRF states the PFO does not replace the incident command structure and does not have directive authority over the Federal Coordinating Officer (FCO) or the Senior Federal Law Enforcement Officer (SFLEO). It is most likely that the Secretary will designate a PFO only for complex,

high-visibility catastrophic disasters, terrorist events or complex emergencies with significant national impact.

(2) FCO manages and coordinates the overall federal response and recovery activities for Stafford Act disasters and emergencies. The FCO is head of the JFO and works in partnership with the State Coordinating Officer (SCO) to determine and satisfy State and local support requirements. He/she coordinates and tasks federal departments and agencies as required.

(3) Federal Resource Coordinator (FRC) in non-Stafford Act situations when a federal department or agency acting under its own authority requests DHS assistance to obtain support from other federal departments and agencies, DHS designates a FRC instead of an FCO. In these situations, the FRC coordinates support through interagency agreements and memorandums of understanding.

(4) Senior Federal Law Enforcement Officer (SFLEO) is the senior law enforcement official from the agency with primary jurisdictional responsibility. He directs intelligence and investigative law enforcement operations and supports the law enforcement component of the UC on scene. In the event of a terrorist incident, this official will normally be the FBI Special Agent in Charge (SAC).

(5) Officials representing other federal departments or agencies with primary statutory responsibility for certain aspects of incident management are Senior Federal Officials (SFO). SFOs employ existing authorities, expertise and capabilities in coordination with the PFO, FCO, SFLEO and other members of the JFO Coordination Group.

(6) SCO manages the State's incident management activities; he is counterpart to the FCO. Another important official is the Governor's Authorized Representative (GAR). The JFO Coordination Group may also include tribal/local area representatives with primary statutory authority for incident management.

(7) Defense Coordinating Officer (DCO) represents DOD as the single point of contact, except for ESF #3, Public Works & Engineering, in the JFO. In this capacity, his reporting chain remains through U.S. Northern Command (USNORTHCOM) but he responds to the FCO. The DCO is responsible for validating all requests for DOD support from the FCO or his representative.

c. The NRF organizes emergency response into 15 Emergency Support Functions (ESF) according to the capabilities and resources most likely to be requested by State officials. ESFs are the primary means through which the federal government provides assistance during a disaster or emergency. They are shown in Table 21-1, along with coordinating or primary agency. Some departments and agencies are most involved with the early response to an event, while others are more prominent in the recovery phase. DOD is more active in response as opposed to recovery.

(1) During an emergency, some or all of the ESF may be activated based on the nature and scope of the event and the level of federal resources required.

(2) DOD is the Primary Coordinating Agency for ESF #3 (Public Works and Engineering), with the U.S. Army Corps of Engineers (USACE) as the DOD lead. DOD is considered a support agency to all ESFs.

(3) DOD, DSCA, Automated Support System (DDASS) is utilized to manage, collaborate, coordinate, and prioritize FEMA Mission Assignments (MA) assigned to the DOD in real time. It provides the means for a Defense Coordinating Unit (DCU), one assigned to each FEMA region, to validate MAs and allow all Orders, Request for Forces (RFF) and FEMA MA forms to be associated with specific missions and provide multiple command situational awareness to view and respond to mission critical actions.

21-12. Promoting Federal-State Unity of Effort

a. Unity of effort between the federal government and states must be one of DOD's guiding principles in the homeland, since unifying DOD's efforts with those of its external partners improves collaboration and shortens response times for meeting life-saving needs during emergencies. Unity of effort also means greater national preparedness at less overall cost, while preserving both federal and state constitutional requirements and responsibilities. DOD and its federal partners must continue to strengthen unity of effort with states to define common goals regarding capabilities, structures, and processes for responses to disaster and emergencies in the homeland. The Council of Governors—established by Executive Order in 2010—will be an essential forum for enhanced, senior-level dialogue among federal and state civilian and military officials for this purpose.

b. As DOD seeks a closer and more highly coordinated relationship between federal and state military disaster response elements, they will prioritize these capabilities and activities to achieve unity of effort in the period covered by this strategy.

DEFENSE SUPPORT OF CIVIL AUTHORITIES

c. Trained and certified dual status commanders. DOD will regard dual status commanders as the usual and customary Command and Control (C2) arrangement in cases where federal military and state National Guard forces are employed simultaneously in support of civil authorities within the U.S.

(1) POTUS may authorize a National Guard officer of a state or a commissioned officer of the Regular Army or the Regular Air Force to serve as a dual status commander, with the consent of the applicable state or territorial Governor. The dual status commander has authority over both state military forces (e.g., National Guard forces in a SAD or Title 32 status) and federal military forces. This authority allows the commander to coordinate and de-conflict federal and state operational assignments while respecting the state and federal chains of command.

(2) DOD will continue to refine processes for dual status commanders and their associated command structures. By leveraging the use of such commanders, DOD will improve federal to state communication, economy of force, and force employment for planned events and no-notice or imminent incidents. Historic examples of the employment of dual status commanders include national special security events such as the Democratic and Republican national conventions and responses to disasters like Hurricane Sandy and wildfires in the Western U.S.

21-13. Emergency Support Function (ESF)—3 (Public Works and Engineering)

a. USACE's long history of providing CS for flood control, water quality, and hazard mitigation under Public Law 84-99 make it the logical organization to serve as primary agency for ESF-3, Public Works and Engineering. The geographically dispersed location of USACE offices facilitates timely response to disasters in almost any area. The USACE is divided by watershed drainage basins into regional divisions that are subdivided by smaller drainage basins into districts. Personnel are also assigned to various field offices throughout each district. During disasters, USACE personnel quickly mobilize to assist in response and recovery.

b. Each USACE division and district has an emergency operations manager and each office develops plans based on hazards unique to its area, coordinates with appropriate agencies, and identifies response teams to support the assigned missions in the NRF. Types of assistance provided by USACE under ESF #3 include: technical advice and evaluations; engineering services; construction management and inspection; emergency contracting; emergency repair of wastewater and solid waste facilities; real estate support. Some ESF-3 activities include emergency debris clearance; restoration of critical public services and facilities, including supply of adequate amounts office and potable water; temporary restoration of water supply systems; technical assistance; structural evaluation of buildings; and damage assessment. By law, USACE assistance is limited to the preservation of life and protection of residential and commercial developments, to include public and private facilities that provide public services. Exclusive assistance to individual homeowners and businesses, including agricultural businesses, is not authorized. However, during periods of extreme drought, such assistance may be provided to farmers and ranchers under some circumstances.

Table 21-1. Federal Response Plan Emergency Support Functions

	Responsibility	ESF Coordinator
ESF 1: Transportation	Provide civilian & military transportation support	Department of Transportation
ESF 2: Communications	Provide telecommunications support	DHS, National Communications System
ESF 3: Public Works and Engineering	Restore essential public services & facilities	DOD, U.S. Army Corps of Engineers
ESF 4: Fire Fighting	Detect and suppress wild land, rural & urban fires.	Department of Agriculture, U.S. Forest Service
ESF 5: Emergency Management	Support overall federal activities for domestic Incident Management	DHS, FEMA
ESF 6: Mass Care, Emergency Assistance, Housing & Human Services	Manage and coordinate food, shelter and first aid for victims; provide bulk distribution of relief supplies; operate a system to assist family reunification.	DHS, FEMA
ESF 7: Logistics	Provide equipment, materials, supplies	General Services

HOW THE ARMY RUNS

	Responsibility	ESF Coordinator
Management & Resource Support	and personnel to federal entities during response	Administration (GSA) and DHS, FEMA
ESF 8: Public Health & Medical Services	Provide assistance for public health and medical care needs	Department of Health and Human Services (HHS)
ESF 9: Search and Rescue	Locate, extricate and provide initial medical treatment to victims trapped in collapsed structures.	DHS, FEMA
ESF 10: Oil & Hazardous Materials Response	Support federal response to actual or potential releases of oil and hazardous materials	Environmental Protection Agency (EPA)
ESF 11: Agriculture & Natural Resources	Provides nutrition assistance, assurance of food safety and food security, control and eradication of devastating animal disease or plant pest infestation	Department of Agriculture
ESF 12: Energy	Restore power systems and fuel supplies.	Department of Energy
ESF 13: Public Safety & Security	Provide non-investigative/non-criminal law enforcement, safety and security capabilities	DOJ
ESF 14: Long Term Community Recovery	Provides a framework for federal support to enable community recovery from the long-term consequences of Incidents of National Significance	DHS, FEMA
ESF 15: External Affairs	Provide public affairs, community relations, Congressional affairs, state & local coordination	DHS, FEMA

 c. Each FEMA regional office is responsible for maintaining an Incident Management Assistance Team (IMAT) and developing appropriate procedures for its notification and deployment. Composed of staff from FEMA and other agencies, it provides administrative, logistical, and operational support to the regional response activities in the field. Likely the first federal response element to arrive in a disaster area, the IMAT can form the core of the Joint Field Office (JFO) once it is established. It also provides support for the dissemination of information to the media, Congress, and the public.

 d. There are numerous other federal special teams available to support incident management and domestic response and recovery to include:
 (1) Hurricane Liaison Team (HLT)
 (2) Mobile Emergency Response Support (MERS)
 (3) DHS Situational Awareness Team (DSAT)
 (4) Damage assessment teams
 (5) Federal Incident Response Support Teams (FIRSTs)
 (6) Nuclear Incident Response Team (NIRT)
 (7) Disaster Medical Assistance Teams (DMATs)
 (8) HHS Secretary's Emergency Response Team
 (9) DOL/OSHA's Specialized Response Teams
 (10) Veterinarian Medical Assistance Teams (VMATs)
 (11) Disaster Mortuary Operational Response Teams (DMORTs)
 (12) National Medical Response Teams (NMRTs)
 (13) Scientific and Technical Advisory and Response Teams (STARTs)
 (14) Donation Coordination Teams
 (15) Urban Search and Rescue (US&R) task forces
 (16) Federal Type 1 and Type 2 Incident Management Teams
 (17) Domestic Emergency Support Team

DEFENSE SUPPORT OF CIVIL AUTHORITIES

(18) Domestic Animal and Wildlife Emergency Response Teams and mitigation assessment teams

21-14. DOD DSCA Structure

a. The SECDEF may delegate approval of most requests for support by civil authorities to the Executive Agent, the Assistant Secretary of Defense for HD and America's Security Affairs (ASD(HD&ASA)). The SECDEF retains approval authority for civil disturbance support, response to CBRNE events and for situations with potential for lethality.

(1) ASD(HD&ASA) is the DOD Domestic Crisis Manager and Executive Agent for HS activities under the authority, direction and control of the Under Secretary of Defense for Policy (USD(P)). Regarding DSCA matters, ASD(HD&ASA) serves as the primary interagency point of contact for DOD coordination and assists the SECDEF, through the Chairman of the Joint Chiefs of Staff (CJCS) as appropriate, in providing DOD policy direction and supervision.

(2) The Assistant Secretary of Defense for Special Operations/Low Intensity Conflict (ASD(SO/LIC)) is the principal staff advisor to the SECDEF and USD(P) for special operations and crisis management support to FBI matters and supports planning by the DOD Domestic Crisis Manager for the contingent use of U.S. counterterrorism forces in response to domestic terrorist incidents.

(3) The Assistant Secretary of Defense for Health Affairs (ASD(HA)) provides recommendations, guidance and support for domestic crisis situations or emergencies that may require health or medical related DSCA, including situations involving the National Disaster Medical System (NDMS).

(4) The Assistant Secretary of Defense for Reserve Affairs (ASD(RA)) develops DOD policy and provides oversight for reserve component involvement with domestic emergency situations.

(5) The JS J-34, Director of Military Support (JDOMS) is the DOD Action Agent. JDOMS has responsibility for communicating and coordinating policy guidance and for the execution of DSCA missions. JDOMS conducts planning and prepares warning and execution orders that task DOD resources. Essentially, JDOMS ensures DSCA planning and execution.

b. Combatant Commands (CCMD) serve as the DOD principal planning agents and supported organizations for geographic areas designated in the Unified Command Plan (UCP). They validate requests for military assistance in their Areas of Responsibility (AOR) and provide DSCA. There are two CCMDs with responsibility for parts of the U.S. homeland.

(1) USNORTHCOM is responsible for planning, organizing, and executing all aspects of HD and performing CS or DSCA missions within the continental U.S., Alaska and territorial waters. The 17 December 2008 UCP also puts Puerto Rico and the U.S. Virgin Islands back in the USNORTHCOM AOR. USNORTHCOM has few permanently assigned forces but will have combatant command (COCOM) authority over forces necessary to execute missions directed by POTUS or SECDEF. Selected USNORTHCOM subordinate commands:

(2) U.S. Army Forces North (USARNORTH), Fifth U.S. Army, located at Fort Sam Houston, Texas provides USNORTHCOM with a dedicated Army Service Component Command (ASCC) for HD and CS. A multi-component organization (active, guard and reserve), USARNORTH also became a standing Joint Force Land Component Command (JFLCC) in 2008.

(a) There are ten Defense Coordinating Officers (DCO) permanently assigned to USARNORTH. When not deployed, these Army Colonels are assigned to USARNORTH with duty in one of the ten FEMA Regions. An eleventh DCO was recently stationed in Hawaii to support USPACOM. There is some discussion about assigning future DCOs from the other services.

(b) Defense Coordinating Element (DCE). The DCE is manned by military and civilian personnel and functions as the DCO's staff. The Emergency Preparedness Liaison Officers (EPLOS) are organized into a Defense Liaison Element (DLE) that, once activated for a disaster or emergency, is essentially integrated with the DCE in the JFO. Recent GAO criticisms have pointed to inefficiencies in the current relationship between the DCO, DCE and DLE. While it remains to be seen whether the politics and policy can be aligned to effect change, there are emerging proposals to restructure this staff organization into a Defense Planning and Coordination Unit (DPCU) that integrates the DCE and DLE. The DPCU would be ICS compliant. JTF-CS is subordinate to USARNORTH and is a standing JTF with the mission to plan and integrate DOD domestic CBRNE CM support. When deployed, JTF-CS establishes mission command of designated DOD forces at the incident site and provides DSCA.

(c) JTF-North (JTF-N) is subordinate to USARNORTH and is a standing JTF tasked to detect, monitor and support the interdiction of suspected counter-drug and transnational threats within the approaches to the continental U.S. JTF-N fuses and disseminates intelligence, contributing to an interagency common

HOW THE ARMY RUNS

operational picture; coordinates support to primary federal agencies; and supports security cooperation initiatives to enhance regional security.

(3) Restructured CBRNE CM Response Force (RCCMRF) is a joint, multi-component organization that provides a federal military CBRNE response of about 5,200 troops to augment ten National Guard regional Homeland Response Forces (HRF).

(4) Directly subordinate to USNORTHCOM, JFHQ-NCR plans, coordinates, maintains situational awareness and employs forces as directed in the National Capital Region to safeguard the nation's capital.

(5) SJFHQ-N is a standing joint force headquarters element embedded within the USNORTHCOM commander's staff that provides a C2 capability that is trained, equipped and organized to conduct planning and develop situation awareness. SJFHQ-N can deploy on little notice to rapidly stand-up a JTF headquarters.

(6) U.S. Pacific Command (USPACOM) has DSCA responsibility for Hawaii and U.S. territories, possessions and freely associate states in its assigned AOR.

c. Each state, territory, and FEMA region has assigned Reserve officers from the Air Force, Army, Navy, and Marines who are trained in disaster preparedness and military support matters. There are over 425 Emergency Preparedness Liaison Officers (EPLO), Regional Emergency Preparedness Liaison Officers (REPLO), State EPLOs (SEPLO) or Headquarters EPLOs (HEPLO) assigned nationwide. They have a comprehensive knowledge of their service facilities and capabilities within their assigned area. EPLOs assist in determining what DOD resources exists within the state, territory, or region. EPLOs may be placed OPCON/TACON to the DCO once appointed, but unfortunately, the Services and other stakeholders have not yet agreed about the EPLOs proper relationship with the DCO and so the relationship varies across each FEMA Region. The Army and Air Force have given responsibility for their EPLOs to USARNORTH and AFNORTH respectively. As of this writing, Navy and Marine EPLOs are still managed by the Service, and US Coast Guard EPLOs are managed by Coast Guard Headquarters. DODD 3025.16 governs the EPLO program.

Section IV
Defense Support Process

21-15. Planning Considerations

Paragraph 22-5 described DOD's Philosophic DSCA Principles and these principles become the basis for planning and executing DSCA missions. Some additional considerations follow:

a. National Guard forces serving on SAD status have primary responsibility for providing military assistance to state and local authorities in emergencies. DSCA planning and execution must foster a close and continuous coordination with the National Guard to ensure unity of effort.

b. Reserve forces have extensive capability beyond the EPLO program. IAW 12304a NDAA of 2012, when a governor requests federal assistance in responding to a major disaster or emergency, the SECDEF may, without the consent of the member affected, order any unit of the Army Reserve, Navy Reserve, Marine Corps Reserve, and Air Force Reserve to active duty for a continuous period of not more than 120 days to respond to the Governor's request. A usual and customary arrangement will be executed utilizing a Dual Status (Title10/32) Commander.

c. Military support will generally be of short duration (generally not exceeding 30 days) to assist civil agencies with establishing essential safety and security.

d. The termination of DSCA and disengagement of DOD resources is a sensitive topic that requires planning consideration from the beginning.

e. Rules of the Use of Force (RUF) serve essentially the same purpose for domestic operations that Rules of Engagement (ROE) serve overseas. CJCS Instruction (CJCSI) 3121.01B provides standing RUF. These RUF do not apply to National Guard forces in SAD or Title 32 status.

f. Military intelligence assets are prohibited from engaging in intelligence collection activities against U.S. persons (with very limited exceptions clearly specified in law and Executive Order 12333). While there are legal provisions allowing for the use of defense intelligence collection resources in support of domestic incident management, DSCA planners need to be particularly sensitive to statutory limitations on the use of such resources.

DEFENSE SUPPORT OF CIVIL AUTHORITIES

g. Defense Planning and Coordination (DPC) is a proposed concept to make use of existing DOD DSCA planning and liaison assets as an effective mechanism for supporting state and federal disaster planning and coordination. Some readers may be familiar with the Task Force for Emergency Readiness (TFER), a model that was co-sponsored by DOD and DHS. The TFER model has been discontinued, but DPC will be able to fill the gap.

21-16. DSCA Request and Approval Process

a. A primary federal agency usually initiates a request for defense support, and submits that request to the DOD Executive Secretary. The Executive Secretary assesses and processes the request by sending it simultaneously to ASD(HD&ASA) and the JS, JDOMS. Under the principle of civilian control, the Executive Agent (OSD) approves the order while the Action Agent (JS) coordinates with the appropriate CCMD and prepares and processes appropriate orders. Once the Executive Agent approves the order, JDOMS issues an execute order designating the supported Combatant Commander (CCDR) to conduct DSCA. Figure 21-4 depicts the approval process for an initial request for DOD assistance.

b. Request Review & Validation. Before acting on a request for DOD support, consideration is given to the operational, legal, and policy aspects of the response. Operational review ensures that providing support will not unduly impact operational readiness. Legal review ensures DOD support is consistent with regulatory guidance and approved by the appropriate authorities. Policy review ensures that such support is in the best interests of DOD. To assist decision makers, DOD policy establishes six criteria against which each request for support is assessed, as follows: legality (compliance with laws); lethality (potential use of lethal force by or against DOD forces); risk (safety of DOD forces); cost; appropriateness (includes consideration of the impact if the request is denied); and readiness. These six criteria are used to review requests for assistance at all levels from a deployed DCO in the field to JDOMS and ASD(HD&ASA) in the Pentagon.

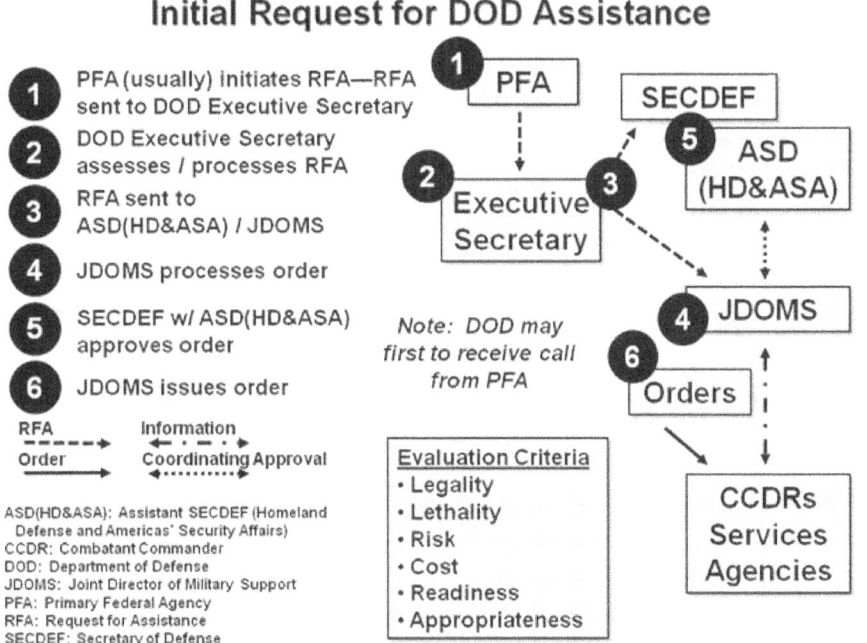

Figure 21-4. Initial Request for Department of Defense (DOD) Assistance

HOW THE ARMY RUNS

c. Once the initial request has been approved and a DCO deployed, requests for DOD assistance are processed through the DCO. If local and state resources, to include those available through mutual aid agreements and compacts are insufficient, the SCO will pass a RFA to FEMA's FCO. The FCO will validate the requirement and query the Joint Field Office ESFs to determine whether support is available. If not, he may pass the request to the DCO. If the DCO validates the requirement and can fill it with capability already deployed, then he will do so. If he validates the requirement but cannot meet it with capability already deployed, he forwards the RFA through his reporting channels to USNORTHCOM who in turn sends it to JDOMS for processing and approval similar to the process for the initial request.

21-17. Immediate Response
Unique circumstances allow commanders to respond immediately, without requesting approval, to imminently serious conditions that are beyond the capability of local authorities. Local commanders can respond on their own authority to requests for assistance to save lives, to prevent human suffering, and to mitigate great property damage. Once initiated, the commander must inform the DOD Executive Agent through command channels as soon as possible but no less than three hours; this notification is not a request for approval. Associated costs should be recorded for potential reimbursement later. Immediate response is normally of short duration, DOD policy suggests no longer than 72 hours after which formal approval should be obtained if continued support is required.

21-18. Emergency Authority
This authority is provided in DODD 3025.18. In extraordinary emergency circumstances where prior authorization by POTUS is not possible and duly constituted local authorities are unable to control a situation, federal military commanders have the authority to engage temporarily in activities that are necessary to quell large-scale, unexpected civil disturbances. Such activities need to be necessary to prevent significant loss of life or wanton destruction of property and should be necessary to restore governmental function or public order. The other circumstance appropriate leading to the implementation of emergency authority is when duly constituted federal, state or local authorities are unable to decline to adequately protect federal property or federal governmental functions.

21-19. Media Considerations
a. During DSCA operations, the media provides invaluable services that can benefit both responding organizations and the public. When considering what information can and should be released to the media, leadership should consider the need to get accurate and timely information to the public; sensitivity of the information; the possibility of causing public panic; building confidence and hope within the affected communities; correction of false information caused by rumors and distorted reporting. Leadership should strive to ensure the media get as complete and accurate a story as possible, while ensuring that their activities do not adversely affect public safety or compromise the response activities.

b. Normally, a Joint Information Center (JIC) is established to deal with the media. While DOD representatives are usually represented, it is generally in the nation's interest that, whenever possible, there is a local or state spokesman engaging the media as opposed to a federal, including active duty military, spokesman.

c. For major incidents, DOD will publish public affairs guidelines applicable to all participating DOD organizations. The guidance will outline any constraints and the policies for media interaction. Two common themes will usually be addressed—civilian authorities are in charge, and military forces are supporting the nation in time of need.

Section V
Defense Support of Civil Authorities Mission Category—Disasters and Declared Emergencies

21-20. DOD NRF Response Process
a. When a disaster occurs and local and state resources are inadequate, POTUS invokes the Stafford Act with a Presidential disaster declaration, thereby releasing Disaster Relief Fund (DRF) monies. While DOD will often take risk with regard to reimbursement and execute some pre-declaration actions, DOD involvement formally begins after the declaration. FEMA requests DOD support as already described in

DEFENSE SUPPORT OF CIVIL AUTHORITIES

paragraph 22-15. The JDOMS execute order (EXORD) designating the supported CCDR will also designate supporting DOD agencies and direct the CCDR appoint a DCO.

b. The DCO activates the DCE and deploys to the JFO to coordinate DOD support for the disaster. Once the DCO deploys to the disaster site, State and regional EPLO work for the DCO and co-locate with the DCE. Designated federal forces respond to taskings for support validated by the DCO. The DCO has OPCON of all DOD personnel (less ESF #3) deployed in support of the disaster unless a JTF is established. The DCO will receive requests for assistance from the FCO as already described.

c. Tiered Mission Command Options. Based on the type and magnitude of an emergency or disaster, USNORTHCOM will establish mission command relationships based on a flexible, tiered construct.

(1) Small Scale Events can be handled by a DCO, his DCE and EPLOs.

(2) Medium Scale Events require deployment of a mission command headquarters such as JTF-CS or one of USARNORTH's two Operational Command Posts. While there could be exceptions, a medium scale Joint Task Force (JTF) is likely to be commanded by a two star flag officer. The NRF directs that if a JTF is established, its mission command element will be collocated with the PFO at the JFO to ensure coordination and unity of effort.

(3) Large scale events, usually employing multiple JTFs, require an overarching JTF or functional component command. While there could be exceptions, these headquarters will most likely be commanded by a three star flag officer.

Any level headquarters can be augmented with special expertise such as JTF-CS's Joint Planning Augmentation Cell (JPAC).

d. Dual Status Command Option. One mission command option to further the unity of effort between National Guard and federal forces is a dual status command whereby a JTF Commander serves in both a Title 10 status in command of federal forces while simultaneously serving in a Title 32 status in command of State National Guard forces. Only the commander holds dual status, not his staff(s) and the forces under his command retain their federal and state chains of command. The dual status commander must therefore exercise his authority in a mutually exclusive manner, respecting the often different laws and policies, as well as Commanders in Chief, applicable for both types of forces under his command. A Memorandum of Agreement (MOA) must be signed by both the Governor and POTUS, although OSD is expected to request from POTUS standing delegation authority to the SECDEF to approve/appoint a dual status commander. Recent experience indicates that the dual-status C2 structure may work best for events where there is an extensive amount of time available for advance coordination and development of the MOA. Either party can terminate the agreement at any time. Designed to allow a National Guard officer to command federal forces, 32 U.S.C. 315 authorizes an active duty commander to assume dual-status command if a governor would commission him/her in the State National Guard. A recent example is Hurricane Sandy 2012 in which dual status commanders were appointed in Maryland, New Hampshire, New Jersey, Massachusetts, New York, and Rhode Island.

e. The supported CCDR will designate a Base Support Installation (BSI), generally at least one for each disaster. A BSI is a military installation designated to provide joint administrative and logistical support to DOD forces. Selection is based on geographic proximity to an operation, functional capability, and coordination with service regional planning agents.

21-21. Improving DOD Incident Response

a. In the aftermath of Hurricane Katrina, DOD recognized the need to respond more quickly during severe or catastrophic incidents, all the while maintaining respect for the jurisdictional authorities and the political responsibilities of elected officials. DOD and USNORTHCOM implemented several specific measures to improve responsiveness to civil requirements:

b. Standing Execute Orders (EXORD) empowers the CCDR to more rapidly respond in support of a primary federal agency. There are Standing EXORDs for natural or manmade disasters short of terrorist attack and a separate EXORD for a CBRNE incident. The DSCA Standing EXORD specifies four distinct categories of CCDR authorizations from assigned forces (Category 1) to those forces required for large-scale response (Category 4).

c. Pre-Scripted Mission Assignments (PSMA) assist with ensuring support is delivered as rapidly as possible. PSMAs are "fill-in-the-blank" templates for the most likely capabilities to be requested of DOD.

d. Request For Forces (RFF). As an exception to the usual RFA process, USNORTHCOM authorizes DCOs to more quickly respond to anticipated requirements by using the RFF process. They do, however, anticipate reimbursement by including a cost estimate.

HOW THE ARMY RUNS

e. Some, but not all, of USNORTHCOM's DSCA-related plans include the following:
 (1) CONPLAN 2501 (DSCA)
 (2) CONPLAN 2591 (Pandemic Influenza)
 (3) CONPLAN 0500-02 (CBRNE CM)
 (4) CONPLAN 2707 (Caribbean Mass Migration)
 (5) CONPLAN 2502 (CDO)
 (6) CONPLAN 2400 (Emergency Preparedness in the National Capital Region)
 (7) FUNCPLAN 2505 (Nuclear Weapons Accident Response Plan)
f. Joint Publication 3-28 (CS) provides commanders and staffs overarching doctrine for conducting CS operations. It specifies five phases which can be conducted simultaneously.
 (1) Phase I—Shaping
 (2) Phase II—Staging
 (3) Phase III—Deployment
 (4) Phase IV—CS Operations
 (5) Phase V—Transition (and Redeployment)

21-22. Unique CBRNE Response Considerations
a. CBRNE versus WMD. CBRNE is defined as a chemical, biological, radiological, nuclear or high-yield explosive situation or incident including industrial accidents, acts of nature, war or terrorism. A WMD is a CBRNE device designed to produce casualties or terror. The most likely CBRNE threat is a high-yield explosive; the most dangerous are nuclear weapons. The greatest threat in the sense of a combined most likely/most dangerous combination would be a contagious biological pathogen.
b. CBRNE Planning Considerations. Unique considerations for CBRNE planning include the fact that incidents may not be recognized as CBRNE until there are multiple casualties. Once identified as a CBRNE event, an incident location will probably be treated as a crime scene. Responders will be at a higher risk of becoming casualties and the effects may contaminate critical facilities and infrastructure in the area. The public reaction will have to be managed as fear and panic are likely to set in. Planners must anticipate mass casualty and mortuary affairs support; "worried well" are likely to be a problem. In addition to expecting state and local capabilities to be overwhelmed, planners must remain ready for multiple attacks. It is worth noting that of the fifteen DHS National Planning Scenarios for use in preparedness activities and exercises, twelve are CBRNE events.
c. State National Guard CBRNE Structure. In October 1998, to enhance the national capability to deal with CBRNE CM, Congress authorized and funded the first ten National Guard Rapid Assessment and Initial Detection (RAID) Teams that the SECDEF renamed WMD-CS Teams (CST) in January 2000.
 (1) WMD-CSTs. Are comprised of full-time Title 32 National Guard experts, highly trained in a cross-discipline of functional areas. Their mission is to deploy; assess a situation; advise local, State, and federal response elements and facilitate sound public safety decisions. CSTs are unique, in that they are one of a few DOD units authorized by Congress to conduct CBRNE response within CONUS. CSTs are a national resource and can move across state lines and provide support to another state.
 (2) The CBRNE Enhanced Response Force Package (CERFP) is designed to rapidly deploy in less than 96 hours. The twelve National Guard CERFP teams provide a regional response capability to augment the CSTs. They can locate and extract victims from a CBRNE incident site, perform mass casualty decontamination, medical triage and stabilization. CERFPs are comprised of mobilization day Soldiers and are task organized from existing units.
 (3) HRF. As it became clear that the federal CCMRF was too slow to respond to a catastrophic CBRNE incident, the idea of creating a regional response from National Guard assets was proposed. The ten HRFs (one in each FEMA region) will be about 566 personnel and consist of Chemical, Biological, Radiological, and Nuclear (CBRN) assessment, search/extraction, decontamination, emergency medical, security and C2.
d. It is beyond the scope of this chapter to detail federal CBRNE response assets but the reader should know that significant federal capabilities exist and have an appreciation for the roles and missions of organizations DOD might encounter or support. These resources are listed before the section on DOD capabilities to reinforce the idea that defense resources are employed only after the capacity of civilian resources at all levels of government has been exceeded.
 (1) Department of Energy (DOE) Nuclear Emergency Support Teams (NEST) provide specialized response to the technical aspects of an unresolved incident involving nuclear or radiological devices.

DEFENSE SUPPORT OF CIVIL AUTHORITIES

Capabilities include search and identification of nuclear materials, diagnostics and assessment of suspected nuclear devices, technical operations in support of render safe procedures and packaging for transport to final disposal.

(2) Environmental Protection Agency Environmental Response Teams (EPAERT) and Radiological Emergency Response Team (RERT) deal with the human health and environmental impact of terrorist attacks. The EPA's research laboratories offer field monitoring and technical support to quality-assurance programs for air, water, wastewater and solid waste. Some of these laboratories are capable of deploying mobile units to a contaminated site.

(3) The FBI Hazardous-Materials Response Unit (HMRU) has specialized sampling, detection and identification capabilities of NBC agents. Evidence Response Teams (ERTs) provide crime-scene documentation and evidence collection in support of criminal investigations.

(4) USCG National Strike Force is trained and equipped to assist in responding to major oil or hazardous material spills, particularly in a maritime environment.

(5) Department of Health and Human Services (HHS) coordinates the National Medical Response Teams for WMD that deal with the medical consequences of incidents involving CBRNE. In addition, HHS' Centers for Disease Control and Prevention has special responsibilities in the event of terrorism involving infectious agents.

   e. DOD has many organizations that can assist with the response to a CBRNE event.

(1) Defense Threat Reduction Agency (DTRA) exists to safeguard the U.S. and its allies from WMD (CBRNE) by providing capabilities to reduce, eliminate and counter the threat and mitigate the effects.

(2) JTF-CS already described in paragraph 23-14.b (1) (b).

(3) USMC Chemical-Biological Incident Response Force (CBIRF) responds to CBRNE incidents to assist local, state or federal agencies and designated CCDRs with CM operations. CBIRF capabilities include agent detection and identification, casualty search and rescue, personnel decontamination and emergency medical care to stabilize contaminated victims.

(4) Restructured CBRNE CM Response Force (RCCMRF) was addressed in paragraph 22-13.b.(3)

(5) U.S. Army 20th Support Command (CBRNE) integrates, coordinates, deploys and provides trained and ready forces. It is also prepared to mission command CBRNE operations. The 20th Support Command provides training and readiness oversight of Army CBRNE assets (active, guard and reserve) to include the 22nd Chemical Battalion (Technical Escort) and 52nd Ordnance Group. The Technical Escort Unit (TEU) provides no-notice capability to conduct field sampling, identification and verification, monitoring, dismantlement, recovery, decontamination, escort and mitigation of hazards associated with chemical and biological materials.

(6) The services have a wide variety of other CBRNE assets too numerous to explain in detail. All the services have Explosive Ordinance Disposal (EOD) units; the Army has chemical brigades, battalions and companies; the Army also has Biological Integrated Detection System (BIDS) companies. Much of the Army capability is resident in the US Army Reserve. The Edgewood Chemical Biological Center is the principal research and development center for chemical and biological defense technology.

(7) U.S. Army Medical Command (MEDCOM) also provides a variety of CBRNE support. The U.S. Army Medical Research Institute of Chemical Defense (USAMRICD) and U.S. Army Medical Research Institute of Infectious Diseases (USAMRIID) not only conduct research, but provide teams to advise and assist with the medical aspects of incidents. MEDCOM also provides operational Special Medical Augmentation Response Teams (SMART) to provide emergency medical response and a variety of other related services in support of a terrorist attack. These teams can also respond to a non CBRNE natural disaster.

Section VI
Defense Support of Civil Authorities Mission Category—Restore Public Health and Services and Civil Order

21-23. Support to Law Enforcement

   a. The use of military force to enforce U.S. laws inside the homeland is an appropriately sensitive topic and restrictions apply to such use. When armed and so used, military forces, will adhere to the Standing Rules for the Use of Force (SRUF) unless the SECDEF has approved mission-specific RUF.

HOW THE ARMY RUNS

(1) The Posse Comitatus Act of 1878 (PCA), subsequent amendments and policy decisions prohibits the use of federal military forces (to include Reserve forces) to perform internal police functions. PCA thus restricts the type of support DOD can provide domestic law enforcement organizations.

(2) There are a wide variety of exceptions to the PCA and we teach at the U.S. Army War College (USAWC) that the law essentially gives POTUS all the authority he needs to employ DOD forces inside the U.S. although there may appropriately be political consequence that would inhibit such employment. The PCA law itself makes provision for POTUS's Article II Constitutional authority. The Act does not pertain to the National Guard when in state status, nor does it apply to the U.S. Coast Guard. There are also a variety of statutory exceptions such as the Protection of Nuclear Materials Act (18 U.S.C. 831), Chemical-Biological Terrorism (10 U.S.C. 382) and Secret Service Assistance (10 U.S.C. 3056). The most renowned statutory exception is The Insurrection Act (10 U.S.C. 331-334) used primarily for civil disturbances.

b. POTUS is authorized by the Constitution and Title 10 (10 U.S.C. 331-334) to suppress insurrections, rebellions, and domestic violence by using CDO. After issuing a Cease and Desist Order, POTUS issues an executive order that directs the Attorney General and the SECDEF to take appropriate steps to disperse insurgents and restore law and order. The Attorney General is then responsible to coordinate the federal response to domestic civil disturbances. The restrictions of the PCA no longer apply to federal troops executing the orders of POTUS to quell the disturbance in accordance with Rules of the Use of Force (RUF) approved by the DOD General Counsel and the Attorney General.

(1) USNORTHCOM Concept Plan (CONPLAN) 2502 (CDO), is the plan for supporting state and local authorities during civil disturbances. This plan serves as the foundation for any CDO operation and standardizes most activities and command relationships. Tasks performed by military forces may include the following: joint patrolling with law enforcement officers; securing key buildings, memorials, intersections and bridges; and acting as a Quick Reaction Force (QRF).

(2) The JTF commander, a general officer, coordinates all DOD support with the Senior Civilian Representative of the Attorney General (SCRAG) (see Figure 21-5). DOD will usually establish a JTF Headquarters near where the Attorney General's local representative is based.

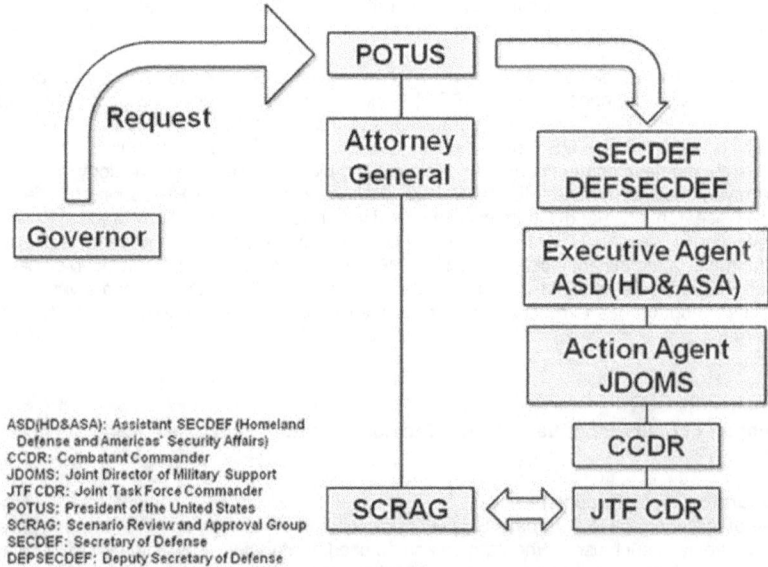

Figure 21-5. Civil Disturbance Support Mission Command

DEFENSE SUPPORT OF CIVIL AUTHORITIES

c. Combating terrorism is predominantly a civilian law enforcement function. DOJ and specifically the FBI have primary federal responsibility for combating and countering terrorism. Responsibilities include measures to anticipate, prevent, and/or resolve a threat or act of terrorism.

(1) The FBI continually assesses intelligence and reports of terrorist activity. When there is a credible threat, the FBI is responsible to disrupt it and prevent an attack. Should there be an incident, the FBI is responsible to neutralize any on-scene threat and for criminal investigation. The FBI Special Agent in Charge (SAC) supervises the law enforcement activities at the incident scene. The FBI will establish a Joint Operations Center (JOC) to orchestrate the interagency law enforcement and investigative efforts. The NRF directs the JOC be located with the Joint Field Office (JFO). Other FBI actions can include deploying a domestic emergency support team (DEST), a rapidly deployable special interagency team that provides advice to the FBI on-scene coordinator. The SAC may also request the FBI Hostage Rescue Team (HRT).

(2) If necessary, the FBI may request specialized DOD support that could include a Joint Special Operations Task Force (JSOTF). The FBI on-scene coordinator notifies the FBI Director and the Attorney General. The FBI also informs the Assistant Secretary of Defense for Special Operations/Low Intensity Conflict (ASD (SO/LIC)) of the pending request and provides details of the incident. The ASD (SO/LIC) advises the SECDEF and the Attorney General confers with SECDEF on the deployment request. They, in turn, confer with POTUS. POTUS must approve all requests that may potentially lead to DOD use of lethal force in support of law enforcement.

(3) After Presidential approval of DOD support, the SECDEF personally approves deployment orders. Normally DOD provides a JSOTF and special mission units (SMU) with unique capabilities, such as those to render safe WMD. The JSOTF deploys to the site and coordinates proposed actions with the FBI SAC. At the appropriate time, the FBI employs the JSOTF to execute those operations approved by POTUS. DOD assets deployed in support of law enforcement operations do not normally remain to support response and recovery.

d. Public Law 97-86, passed in 1982, amended the PCA to authorize indirect military involvement such as equipment loan, personnel support, training, and sharing information in Drug Interdiction and Counter-Drug Activities.

(1) Indirect support must be incidental to the military mission, or provide substantially equivalent military training. Further, it cannot degrade combat readiness or the capacity of the DOD to fulfill its defense mission.

(2) Federal, state, and local law enforcement agencies (LEA) originate requests for DOD counterdrug operational support in CONUS and submit them to Joint Task Force-North located at Fort Bliss, Texas and charged with the responsibility of validating such requests. The approval process for the use of forces is retained at the highest level. Defense support to Drug Law Enforcement Agencies (DLEA) can include: ground reconnaissance; detection monitoring; communications; aerial reconnaissance; counterdrug related training of LEA personnel; nonherbicidal cannabis eradication; linguist support; aerial and ground transportation; intelligence analysis; tunnel detection; engineering support; maintenance support and much more. Non-operational support can include facilities, formal military school training opportunities, equipment loans, and more.

21-24. Other Types of Public Health and Services DSCA

a. In the event of a work stoppage or disaster leading to disruption of mail service, DOD may be required to provide support to the U.S. Postal Service (USPS) to safeguard process and deliver the mail to areas in which service has been impaired.

b. DOD would provide the U.S. Department of Agriculture (USDA) assistance for emergencies requiring the containment and eradication of plant or animal diseases.

c. DOD medical support would generally be provided to Department of Health and Human Services (DHHS) using the mechanisms of NRP ESF#8 (Health and Medical Services) and the Catastrophic Incident Annex. There has also been significant and recent interagency effort to develop and exercise specific Pandemic Influenza plans. An important aspect of the ESF#8 process is the National Disaster Medical System (NDMS), a public, private sector partnership involving DHS, DHHS, DOD, and Department of Veteran Affairs. NDMS provides a nationwide medical response system to supplement state and local medical resources during domestic disasters and emergencies, and provides backup medical support to DOD and the VA medical care systems during overseas conflicts.

HOW THE ARMY RUNS

d. The Environmental Protection Agency (EPA) and DHS-U.S. Coast Guard have responsibilities for oil and hazardous substance spills.

e. The National Interagency Fire Center (NIFC), a joint Department of Agriculture and Department of Interior organization is responsible for coordinating the federal response to wild fires. DOD provides resources for the containment, control and extinguishing of wild fires on lands owned by the federal government.

f. Mass immigration emergencies could result in DOD providing other federal agencies with support such as installations and services associated with housing migrants while the Immigration and Naturalization Service resolves the administrative requirements for migrants to enter the U.S.

Section VII
Defense Support of Civil Authorities Mission Categoriy—Special Events and Planned Periodic Support

21-25. DSCA Mission Category—Special Events

a. Pursuant to HSPD-7, the Secretary of HS, after consultation with the HS Council (HSC), is responsible for designating events a National Special Security Event (NSSE). These special events of national significance can be political, economic or international sporting events. They all present a lucrative target for terrorists. A large number of people or a limited number may attend it; they may encompass a wide geographical area or be restricted to a specific site. When an event is designated an NSSE, the Secret Service assumes its mandated role as lead for security planning and DOD supports the USSS. Examples of military assets that may be deployed include EOD, technical escort unit teams and CBRNE assets. If an incident occurs at an NSSE, the FBI leads the law enforcement and criminal investigation efforts, and FEMA leads response and recovery efforts. Most events are not designated NSSEs, but may still receive DOD support.

b. JDOMS plans, coordinates, and monitors execution of approved DOD support to other special events as categorized by the DHS Special Events Working Group. Events of a lesser significance are designated Special Events for HS (SEHS) levels 1 to 4, SEHS Level 4 being the lowest priority. DOD focuses on support related to public safety and security, including but not limited to, physical security, aviation, logistics, communications, joint operations and command centers, and explosive ordnance disposal support. DOD support for events may be reimbursable or non-reimbursable depending on the type of support provided and the nature of the event.

c. DOD is authorized under Title 10, U.S.C. 2554 to provide support to international sporting competitions (SISC) if the Attorney General certifies that support is essential to the safety and security of the event. Congress has established a revolving fund to cover SISC operational expenditures.

d. DOD supports other special events as demonstrated by the many State Designated Special Events that National Guard forces support while on state status under a governor's control.

21-26. DSCA Mission Category—Periodic Planned Support

a. This category enhancing civil-military relations includes DOD laboratory support; specialized and mobile training programs; participation in local, state and federal emergency management exercises; support provided to the Secret Service under 18 U.S.C. 112; and provision of military bands or honorary fly-over at civic events. It includes Military community affairs programs and community relations programs administered by the Assistant Secretary of Defense for Public Affairs.

b. Installation commanders are authorized under the Installation Mutual Aid Agreements, U.S.C. Title 42, Section 1856a-c to enter into limited mutual aid agreements with local communities, usually for fire, emergency medical or hazardous material response. It should be noted that while such memorandums may improve understanding about what resources DOD may be able to provide, they do not constitute preapproved support. Requests must be approved or be provided under some established authority such as Immediate Response authority.

c. Military Assistance to Safety and Traffic (MAST), governed by DODD 4500.9, authorizes medical helicopter units to provide emergency assistance if local resources are not available or are not sufficient to respond to emergencies. Under this directive, there is no reimbursement, units may not relocate to provide service, and they must operate within their allocated training hour program.

DEFENSE SUPPORT OF CIVIL AUTHORITIES

Section VIII
Summary and References

21-27. Summary

a. Our nation has a time-tested tradition of civilian control over the military and of limiting military activity within the U.S. Balancing that valued tradition with the need for military support in response to disaster and acts or threats of terrorism within the U.S. requires approval by the most senior civilian officials within our government.

b. The military has available a unique blend of skilled personnel and equipment capable of rapid and effective responses in support of appropriate civil authority. By policy, requests for military resources are only approved when the capacity or resources of other federal, state, and local agencies is exceeded and the crisis remains unresolved.

c. While DSCA normally involves military units performing tasks related to their wartime missions, the commitment of those units detracts from their ability to respond to possible combat missions and usually adversely affects readiness. DOD leaders must be very judicious in determining when and how to provide support to civil authorities, scrupulously adhere to approval and employment rules, and be mindful that DOD resources are always in a support role. Existing local, state, and national response systems provide a solid framework within which DOD can provide support.

d. The military continues to provide reliable and responsive DSCA. Moreover, the Army's extensive experience in supporting civil authorities during peacetime disasters, national security emergencies, and special events enhances HS and has kept the U.S. Army in the forefront of domestic disaster response. The military's force projection capability, designed to respond quickly and decisively to global requirements, also allows its rapid response to domestic incidents that occur within the U.S., its territories and possessions. The judicious use of military forces in support of civil requirements complements the military's war fighting and force projection capabilities, while insuring the American people get maximum return from their military investment.

21-28. References

a. Law
(1) Public Law 84-99
(2) Public Law 100-707, The Stafford Act (with revisions)
(3) Public Law 104-201, Defense Against Weapons of Mass Destruction Act of 1996 (Nunn-Lugar-Domenici)
(4) Public Law 106-65, NDAA for FY 2000, Section 1023
(5) Public Law 107-56, The Patriot Act
(6) Public Law 107-296, The HS Act of 2002
(7) Public Law 109-364, NDAA for FY 2007, Section 1042
(8) 10 U.S. Code, Section 331-335, Enforcement of the Laws to Restore Public Order
(9) 10 U.S. Code, Section 372-380, Military Support for Civilian Law Enforcement Agencies
(10) 10 U.S. Code, Section 12304, Reserve and IRR Order to Active Duty Other Than During War or a National Emergency
(11) 10 U.S. Code Section 2553, Presidential Inaugural Ceremonies
(12) 10 U.S. Code Section 2554, Boy Scout Jamboree
(13) 10 U.S. Code Section 2564, Sporting Events (Olympics, Goodwill, World Cup, etc)
(14) 18 U.S. Code, Section 1385, Use of Army and Air Force as Posse Comitatus (with revisions)
(15) 31 U.S. Code, Section 1535, Economy Act

b. Presidential Directives and Executive Orders
(1) Executive Order 12148, Establishment of FEMA, 1979
(2) Executive Order 12656, Assignment of Emergency Preparedness Responsibilities, 1988
(3) HSPD-5, Management of Domestic Incidents, 2003
(4) HSPD-7, Critical Infrastructure Identification, Prioritization and Protection, 2003
(5) HSPD-8, National Preparedness, 2003
(6) PDD #39, U.S. Policy on Counterterrorism, 1995
(7) PDD #62, Combating Terrorism, 1998
(8) PDD #67, Continuity of Government and Continuity of Operations, 1998

c. U.S. Government Strategies

HOW THE ARMY RUNS

    (1) NSS
    (2) NSHS
    (3) National Strategy to Combat WMD
    (4) National Strategy for Combating Terrorism
    (5) National Strategy for Pandemic Influenza
    (6) National Strategy for Physical the Protection of Critical Infrastructure and Key Assets
    (7) Maritime Strategy for HS
    (8) National Defense Strategy
    (9) National Military Strategy (NMS)
    (10) DOD Strategy for HD and CS
  d. DOD Directives, Instructions and Manuals & CJCS Documents
    (1) DODD 1100.20, Support and Services for Eligible Organizations and Activities, 2004
    (2) DODD 2000.12, DOD Antiterrorism (AT) Program, 2003
    (3) DODD 3020.26, Defense Continuity Program (DCP), 2004
    (4) DODD 3020.36, National Security Emergency Preparedness (NSEP), 1988
    (5) DODD 3020.40, Defense Critical Infrastructure Program (DCIP), 2005(6)
    (6) DODD 3025.18, DSCA, 29 December 2010(7)
    (7) DODD 2000.15, Support to Special Events, 1994
    (8) DODD 3025.12, Military Assistance to Civil Disturbances (MACDIS), 1994
    (9) DODD 2025.18, DSCA, w/Chg 1, 2012
    (10) DODD 5111.13, Assistant Secretary of Defense for HD and Americas' Security Affairs (ASA(HD&ASA)), 2011
    (11) DODD 5030.46, Assistance to District of Columbia in Combating Crime, 1971
    (12) DODD 5030.50, Employment of DOD Resources in Support of the USPS, 1972
    (13) DODD 5525.5, DOD Cooperation with Civilian Law Enforcement Officials, 1986
    (14) DODD 3025.13, Employment of DOD Capabilities in Support of the U.S. Secret Service, 8 October 2010
    (15) DODD 3025.16, Military Emergency Preparedness Liaison Officer Program, 2000
    (16) DODD 3150.5, Response to Improvised Nuclear Devices (IND), Incidents, 1987
    (17) DODD 3150.8, Response to Radiological Accidents, 1996
    (18) DODD 4500.9, Transportation and Traffic Management, 2005
    (19) DODD-S 5210.36, Provision of DOD Sensitive Support, 1986
    (20) DODD 5410.19, Public Affairs Community Relations Policy, 2001
    (21) DODD 6010.22, National Disaster Medical System, 2003
    (22) DODI 6055.6, DOD Fire and Emergency Services Program, 2000
    (23) DODI 3025.dd, DRAFT Processing Requests for DSCA, 2006
    (24) DOD Manual 3025.dd, DRAFT DSCA Manual, 2006
  e. DOD Plans and Policy Documents
    (1) Strategy for HD and DSCA, 2013
    (2) DOD Civil Disturbance Plan, "GARDEN PLOT"
    (3) UCP 2008
    (4) CJCS Concept Plan 0500, Military Assistance to Domestic CM Operations in Response to a Chemical, Biological, Radiological, Nuclear or High-Yield Explosives Situation
    (5) CJCSI 3110.16, Military Capabilities, Assets and Units for Chemical, Biological, Radiological, Nuclear or High-Yield Explosives Operations
    (6) CJCSI 3121.01B, Standing Rules of Engagement/Standing Rules for the use of Force for U.S. Forces
    (7) CJCSI 3125.01, Military Assistance to Domestic CM Operations in Response to a Chemical, Biological, Radiological, Nuclear or High-Yield Explosives Situation
    (8) CJCSI 3710.01A, DOD Counterdrug Operational Support
    (9) USNORTHCOM Concept Plans (CONPLAN) and Functional Plans (FUNCPLAN)
    (10) CONPLAN 2501 (DSCA)
    (11) CONPLAN 2591 (Pandemic Influenza)
    (12) CONPLAN 0500-02 (CBRNE CM)
    (13) CONPLAN 2707 (Caribbean Mass Migration)
    (14) CONPLAN 2502 (CDO)

DEFENSE SUPPORT OF CIVIL AUTHORITIES

(15) CONPLAN 2400 (Emergency Preparedness in the National Capital Region)
(16) FUNCPLAN 2505 (Nuclear Weapons Accident Response Plan)
(17) USPACOM Functional Plan 5210-95, (Domestic Disaster Response)
f. Doctrinal Publications
(1) Joint Publication (JP) 3-07.2, Counterdrug Operations, 1998
(2) JP 3-26, HS, 2005
(3) JP 3-27, HD, 2007
(4) JP 3-28, CS, 2007
(5) JP 3-41, CBRNE CM, 2012
(6) Army Field Manual 3-28 (Civil Support Operations), August 2010
g. DHS Documents
(1) National Incident Management System (NIMS), 2004
(2) NRF, 2008
h. Miscellaneous Documents—Domestic Operational Law Handbook for Judge Advocates
i. National Guard Regulations—NGR 500-1, National Guard Domestic Operations, 2008

This page is intentionally left blank

GLOSSARY

Glossary

A&ID	Analysis and Integration Directorate
A2SF	Active Army Strength Forecaster
AA	Active Army
AAC	Army Acquisition Corps
AACMO	Army Acquisition Corps Management Office
AAE	Army Acquisition Executive
AAFES	Army and Air Force Exchange Service
AAMMP	Active Army Military Manpower Program
AAO	Army Acquisition Objective
AAR	After Action Review
AARTS	Army/American Council on Education Registry Transcript System
AASA	Administrative Assistant to the Secretary of the Army
ABC	Activity Based Costing
ABC-C	Army Benefits Center-Civilian
ABCTMP	Army Brigade Combat Team Modernization Program
ABO	Army Budget Office
AC	Advanced Course
AC	Active Component
ACAP	Army Career and Alumni Program
ACAT	Army Acquisition Category
ACC	Army Capstone Concept
ACC	Army Competitive Category
ACC	Army Community Covenant
ACC	Army Contracting Command
ACC	Army Corrections Command
ACD	Accelerated Capabilities Division
ACE-IT	Army Corps of Engineers Information Technology
ACES	Army Continuing Education System
ACF	Army Concept Framework
ACOE	Army Community of Excellence
ACOM	Army Command
ACP	Army Campaign Plan
ACP	Army Cost Position
ACR	Advanced Concepts and Requirements
ACR	Armored Cavalry Regiment
ACRB	Army Cost Review Board
AC/RC	Active/Reserve Component

ACS	Army Community Service	
ACSIM	Assistant Chief of Staff for Installation Management	
ACT	Army Career Tracker	
ACTEDS	Army Civilian Training, Education, and Development System	
ADA	Air Defense Artillery	
ADA	Anti-Deficiency Act	
ADCON	Administrative Control	
ADDIE	Analyze, Design, Develop, Implement and Evaluate	
ADL	Active Duty List	
ADM	Acquisition Decision Memorandum	
ADOS	Active Duty for Operational Support	
ADP	Army Doctrine Publication	
ADR	Alternative Dispute Resolution	
ADRF	Army Doctrine Reference Publication	
ADS	Authoritative Data Source	
ADSO	Active Duty Service Obligation	
ADT	Active Duty for Training	
ADTLP	Army Doctrine and Training Literature Program	
AE	Active Enlisted	
AEA	Army Enterprise Architecture	
AECA	Arms Export Control Act	
AE2S	Army Equipping Enterprise System	
AEF	American Expeditionary Force	
AEP	Army Experimentation Plan	
AEPI	Army Environmental Policy Institute	
AER	Academic Evaluation Report	
AESIP	Army Enterprise System Integration Program	
AEWRS	Army Energy and Water Report System	
AFAMC	Air Force Air Mobility Command	
AFARS	Army Federal Acquisition Regulation Supplement	
AFC	Army Functional Concept	
AFCS	Active Federal Commissioned Service	
AFHC	Army Family Housing (Construction)	
AFHO	Army Family Housing (Operations)	
AFHSC	Armed Forces Health Surveillance Center	
AFM	Army Flow Model	
AFMS	Army Force Management School	
AFPD	Available Force Pool Date	
AFR	Agency Financial Report	

GLOSSARY

AFS	Active Federal Service
AFS	Army Facility Strategy
AFSB	Army Field Support Brigade
AFSC	Army Facilities Standardization Committee
AG-1 CP	Assistant G-1 for Civilian Personnel
AGR	Active Guard Reserve
AGTS	Advanced Gunnery Training System
AHLTA	Armed Forces Healthcare Longitudinal Application
AHRC	Army Human Resources Command
AHS	U.S. Army Headquarters Services
AHS	Army Health System
AIP	Assignment Incentive Pay
AIS	Automated Information Systems
AIT	Advanced Individual Training
AIT	Automatic Identification Technologies
AJ	Administrative Judge
AKEA	Army Knowledge Enterprise Architecture
AKO	Army Knowledge Online
ALCMC	Army Learning Content Management Capability
ALMS	Army Learning Management System
ALO	Authorized Level of Organization
AMA	Analysis of Materiel / Non-Materiel Approaches
AMC	Army Materiel Command
AMC	Air Mobility Command
AMCB	Army Marine Corps Board
AMCOM	Aviation and Missile Command
AME	Assigned Mission Equipment
AMEDD	Army Medical Department
AMEDDC&S	Army Medical Department Center and School
AMET	Agency Mission-Essential Task
AMETL	Assigned Mission Essential Task List
AMHA	Army Management Headquarters Activities
AMLE	Army Medical Logistics Enterprise
AMM	Assigned Mission Manning
AMOPES	Army Mobilization and Operations Planning and Execution System
AMP	Army Modernization Plan
AMRDEC	Aviation & Missile Research, Development, and Engineer Center
AMRG	Army Marketing and Research Group
AMS	Army Management Structure

AMS	Army Modernization Strategy
AMSCO	Army Management Structure Code
AMSH	Army Medicine System for Health
AMSP	Advanced Military Studies Program
AMT	Army Modernization Training
ANAD	Anniston Army Depot
ANC	Arlington National Cemetery
ANC	Army Nurse Corps
ANNPRO	Annual Program
ANS	Activity, Nutrition and Sleep
AO	Active Officer
AO	Area of Operation
AOC	Area of Concentration
AOC	Army Operating Concept
AOCC	Analysis of Change Cell
AODC	Action Officer Development Course
AOI	Area of Interest
AOLCM	Army Organizational Life Cycle Model
AOR	Area of Responsibility
AOS	Army Organization Server
APAC	U.S. Army Public Affairs Center
APB	Acquisition Program Baseline
APD	Army Publishing Directorate
APE	Army Program Elements
APEX	Adaptive Planning and Execution
APF	Appropriated Fund
APFT	Army Physical Fitness Test
APGM	Army Programming Guidance Memorandum
APOD	Aerial Port of Debarkation
APP	Army Prevention Program
APPG	Army Planning Priorities Guidance
APR	Annual Performance Report
APRB	Army Requirements Oversight Council (AROC) Process Review Board
APS	Army Posture Statement
APS	Army Pre-Positioned Stocks
APUC	Average Procurement Unit Cost
AR	Army Reserve
AR	Army Regulation
AR2B	Army Requirements and Resourcing Board

GLOSSARY

ARB	Army Resources Board
ARBA	Army Review Boards Agency
ARCIC	Army Capabilities Integration Center
ARCOM	Army Reserve Command
ARDEC	Armament, Research, Development and Engineering Center
AREF	Army Reserve Expeditionary Force
AREP	Army Reserve Expeditionary Package
ARFPC	Army Reserve Forces Policy Committee
ARL	Army Research Laboratory
ARMS	Armament Retooling and Manufacturing Support Program
ARMS	Army Readiness Management System
ARNG	Army National Guard
AROC	Army Requirements Oversight Council
ARPA	Advanced Research Projects Agency
ARPRINT	Army Program for Individual Training
ARSEC	Army Secretariat
ARSTAF	Army Staff
ARSTRAT	Army Strategic Command
ARSTRUC	Army Structure
ARTCP	Army Reserve Transformation Campaign Plan
ARTEP	Army Training and Evaluation Program
AS	Acquisition Strategy
ASA(ALT)	Assistant Secretary of the Army (Acquisition, Logistics, and Technology)
ASA(CW)	Assistant Secretary of the Army (Civil Works)
ASA(FM&C)	Assistant Secretary of the Army (Financial Management and Comptroller)
ASA(IE&E)	Assistant Secretary of the Army (Installations, Energy and Environment)
ASA(M&RA)	Assistant Secretary of the Army (Manpower and Reserve Affairs)
ASARC	Army Systems Acquisition Review Council
ASAT	Automated Systems Approach to Training
ASB	Army Science Board
ASB	Aviation Support Battalion
ASC	Acquisition Support Center
ASC	Army Sustainment Command
ASCC	Army Service Component Command
ASD(HA)	Assistant Secretary of Defense (Health Affairs)
ASD(HD&ASA)	Assistant Secretary of Defense for Homeland Defense and America's Security Affairs
ASD(RA)	Assistant Secretary of Defense (Reserve Affairs)
ASD(SO/LIC)	Assistant Secretary of Defense for Special Operations/Low Intensity Conflict
ASD(PA)	Assistant Secretary of Defense (Public Affairs)

ASI	Additional Skill Identifier	
ASIOEP	Associated Support Items of Equipment and Personnel	
ASIP	Army Stationing and Installation Plan	
ASK	Assignment Satisfaction Key	
ASL	Authorized Stockage List	
ASORTS	Army Status of Resources and Training System	
ASOS	Army Support to Other Services	
ASPB	Army Strategic Planning Board	
ASPG	Army Strategic Planning Guidance	
ASRA	Army Strategic Readiness Assessment	
AST	Army Test and Evaluation Command System Team	
ASTAG	Army Science and Technology Advisory Group	
ASTMP	Army's Science and Technology Master Plan	
ASTWG	Army Science and Technology Working Group	
ASVAB	Armed Services Vocational Aptitude Battery	
ASV	Armored Security Vehicle	
AT	Annual Training	
AT&L	Acquisition, Technology, and Logistics	
ATA	Additional Training Assembly	
ATD	Advanced Technology Demonstration	
ATEC	Army Test and Evaluation Command	
ATED	Army Training and Education	
ATDC	Army Training Development Capability	
ATIA	Army Training Information Architecture	
ATLDP	Army Training and Leader Development Panel	
ATMC	Army Training Management Capability	
ATN	Army Training Network	
ATO	Army Technology Objectives	
ATO(D)	Advance Technology Objectives (Demonstration)	
ATO(M)	Army Technology Objectives (Manufacturing Technology)	
ATO(R)	Advance Technology Objectives (Research)	
ATRRS	Army Training Requirements and Resources System	
AUGTDA	Augmentation Table of Distribution and Allowances	
AUJTL	Army Universal Joint Task List	
AUS/RA	Army of the U.S./Regular Army	
AUSA	Association of the U.S. Army	
AUTL	Army Universal Task List	
AUTS	Automatic Update Transaction System	
AW	Asymmetric Warfare	

GLOSSARY

AWCF	Army Working Capital Fund
AWE	Advanced Warfighting Experiment
BA	Budget Activity
BA	Budget Authority
BAG	Budget Activity Group
BAH	Basic Allowance for Housing
BASOPS	Base Operations
BBS	Brigade-Battalion Battle Simulation
BC	Basic Course
BCP	Budget Change Proposal
BCT	Basic Combat Training
BCT	Brigade Combat Team
BCTP	Battle Command Training Program
BES	Budget Estimate Submission
BH	Behavioral Health
BIDE	Basic Identity Data Elements
BIDS	Biological Integrated Detection System
BLCSE	Battle Lab Collaborative Simulation Environment
BLIN	Budget Line Item Number
BLTM	Battalion Level Training Model
BMC	Brigade Modernization Command
BMDR	Ballistic Missile Defense Review
BMIS-T	Battlefield Medical Information-Theater
BOD	Board of Directors
BOD	Broadcast Operations Detachment
BOG	Boots on Ground
BOIP	Basis of Issue Plan
BOIPFD	Basis of Issue Plan Feeder Data
BOLC	Basic Officer Leaders Course
BOS	Base Operations Support
BOS	Budget Operating Systems
BOS	Business Operating System
BPLAN	Base Plan
BRAC	Base Realignment and Closure
BRM	Base Operations Support (BOS) Requirements Model
BRP	Budget Requirements & Programs
BSA	Budget Sub-Activity
BSB	Brigade Support Battalion
BSI	Base Support Installation

BT	Basic Training
BTOE	Base Table of Organization and Equipment
BY	Budget Fiscal Year
C2	Command and Control
C3I	Command, Control, Communications, and Intelligence
C4	Command, Control, Communications, and Computers
C4IM	Command, Control, Communications, and Information
C4ISR	Command, Control, Communications, Computers, Intelligence, Surveillance, and Reconnaissance
C&L	Capabilities and Limitations
C-MNS	Combat-Mission Need Statement
CAA	U.S. Center for Army Analysis
CAC	Combined Arms Center
CAC	Common Access Card
CAE	Component Acquisition Executive
CAIG	Cost Analysis Improvement Group
CAIV	Cost as an Independent Variable
CALL	Center for Lessons Learned
CAMS	Capabilities and Army Requirements Oversight Council (AROC) Management System
CAP	Crisis Action Planning
CAP	Critical Acquisition Position
CAPDEV	Capability Developer
CAPE	Cost Assessment and Performance Evaluation
CAR	Chief, Army Reserve
CARD	Cost Analysis Requirements Description
CARDS	Catalog of Approved Requirements Documents
CASCOM	Combined Arms Support Command
CATS	Combined Arms Training Strategy
C-BA	Capabilities-Based Assessment
CBA	Cost Benefit Analysis
CBARB	Cost Benefit Analysis Review Board
CBDRT	Chemical-Biological Defense Readiness Training
CBM	Condition Based Maintenance
CBRN	Chemical, Biological, Radiological, and Nuclear
CBRNE	Chemical, Biological, Radiological, Nuclear, and High-Yield Explosives
CBS	Corps Battle Simulation
CBV	Capability-Based Volunteer
CBTDEV	Combat Developer
CBWTU	Community-Based Warrior Transition Unit

GLOSSARY

CCA	Clinger-Cohen Act
CCAD	Corpus Christi Army Depot
CCDR	Combatant Commander
CCDOR	Combatant Commander's Daily Operational Requirements
CCJO	Capstone Concept for Joint Operations
CCMD	Combatant Command
CCP	Concept Capability Plan
CCTT	Close Combat Tactical Trainer
CD&E	Concept Development and Experimentation
CDA	Capability Demand Analysis
CDD	Capability Development Document
CDID	Capability Development Integration Directorate
CDLD	Concept Development and Learning Directorate
CDO	Chief Data Officer
CDO	Civil Disturbance Operations
CDPL	Command Designated Positional List
CDR	Critical Design Review
CDRT	Capability Development for Rapid Transition
CDTM	Capability Development Tracking and Management
CE	Continuous Evaluation
CECOM	Communications-Electronics Command (Life Cycle Management Command (LCMC))
CEF	Contingency Expeditionary Force
CER	Cost Estimating Relationship
CERFP	Chemical, Biological, Radiological, Nuclear, and High-Yield Explosives (CBRNE) Enhanced Response Force Package
CES	Civilian Education System
CESL	Continuing Education for Senior Leaders
CEW	Civilian Expeditionary Workforce
CFMO	Construction and Facility Management Officer
CFO	Chief Financial Officer
CFR	Code of Federal Regulations
CFSC	Community and Family Support Center
CG	Commanding General
CG CAP	Coast Guard Capabilities Plan
CHESS	Computers, Hardware, and Enterprise Software Services
CHR	Civilian Human Resource
CHRA	U.S. Army Civilian Human Resources Agency
CHRTAS	Civilian Human Resource Training Application System
CIA	Central Intelligence Agency

CIC	Critical Intelligence Categories	
CIO	Chief Information Officer	
CIP	Contract in Process	
CIPMS	Civilian Intelligence Personnel Management System	
CIPPS	Civilian Integration into the Personnel Proponent System	
CIS	Comptroller Information System	
CJA	Comprehensive Joint Assessment	
CJCS	Chairman of the Joint Chiefs of Staff	
CJCSI	Chairman of the Joint Chiefs of Staff Instruction	
CJCSM	Chairman of the Joint Chiefs of Staff Memorandum	
CLO	Consolidated Legal Office	
CLS	Common Levels of Support	
CLS SSP	Common Levels of Support (CLS) Service Support Program	
CM	Current Month	
CM	Command Manager	
CM	Consequence Management	
CM	Cost Management	
CMA	Chemical Materials Agency	
CMEP	Civil-Military Emergency Planning	
CMETL	Core Mission Essential Task List	
CMF	Career Management Field	
CM(FS)	Command Manager (Force Structure)	
CMH	U.S. Army Center of Military History	
CMICS	Civilian Manpower Integrated Costing System	
CMO	Chief Management Officer	
CNA	Capability Needs Analysis	
CNGB	Chief, National Guard Bureau	
COA	Course of Action	
COCOM	Combatant Command (Command Authority)	
CoC	Council of Colonels	
CoE	Center of Excellence	
COE	Chief of Engineers	
COE	Contemporary Operational Environment	
COFT	Conduct of Fire Trainer	
COG	Continuity of Government	
COIC	Critical Operational Issues and Criteria	
COIN	Counterinsurgency	
COIST	Company Intelligence Support Team	
COL	Colonel	

GLOSSARY

COLS	Common Output Level Standards
COMCAM	Combat Camera
COMPASS	Computerized Movement Planning and Status System
COMPO	Component
CONOPS	Concept of Operations
CONPLAN	Concept Plan
CONUS	Continental U.S.
CONUSA	Continental U.S. Army
COOP	Continuity of Operations / Continuity of Operations Plan
CORTRAIN	Corps and Division Training Coordination Program
COTS	Commercial Off The Shelf
CP	Change Proposals
CPA	Chairman's Program Assessment
CPA	Chief of Public Affairs
CPAC	Civilian Personnel Advisory Center
CPD	Capability Production Document
CPD	Competitive Professional Development
CPI	Critical Program Information
CPMD	Command Provost Marshal Directorate
CPOL	Civilian Personnel Online Library
CPP	Cost & Performance Portal
CPPP	Caregiving Personnel Pay Program
CPR	Chairman's Program Recommendation
CPR	Capability Portfolio Review
CRA	Chairman's Risk Assessment
CRA	Continuing Resolution Authority
CRB	Cost Review Board
CRC	Continental U.S. (CONUS) Replacement Center
CREST	Contingency Real Estate Support Teams
CRM	Composite Risk Management
CrM	Crisis Response Management
CROWS	Common Remote Operated Weapons System
CRS	Chairman's Readiness System
CRXXI	Classroom Twenty One
C/S/A	Combatant Command, Service, and Combat Support Agency
CS	Civil Support
CS	Combat Support
CSA	Chief of Staff, U.S. Army
CSA	Combat Support Agency

HOW THE ARMY RUNS

CSB	Configuration Steering Board	
CSB	Continental U.S. (CONUS) Support Base	
CSDJF	Chairman's Strategic Direction to the Joint Force	
CSL	Centralized Selection List	
CSLMO	Civilian Senior Leader Management Office	
CSM	Command Sergeant Major	
CSM	Capability Set Management	
CSRA	Civil Service Reform Act	
CSS	Combat Service Support	
CSSB	Combat Sustainment Support Battalion	
CST	Civil Support Team	
CSTC	Combat Support Training Center	
CTC	Combat Training Center	
CTE	Critical Technology Element	
CTE	Culminating Training Event	
CTS	Contingency Tracking System	
CTT	Collective Training Task	
CUSR	Commander's Unit Status Report	
CWT	Civilian Workforce Transformation	
CXO	Chief Integration Officer	
CY	Calendar Year	
CYPPP	Child and Youth Personnel Pay Program	
DA	Department of the Army	
DA PAM	Department of the Army Pamphlet	
DAB	Defense Acquisition Board	
DAB	Director of the Army Budget	
DACIL	Department of the Army Critical Items List	
DACM	Director, Acquisition Career Management	
DAE	Defense Acquisition Executive	
DAES	Defense Acquisition Executive Summary	
DAGO	Department of the Army General Order	
DAGR	Defense Advanced Global Positioning System (GPS) Receiver	
DALSO	Department of the Army Logistics Support Officer	
DAMPS	Department of the Army Mobilization Processing System	
DANTES	Defense Activity for Non-Traditional Education Support	
DAO	Defense Accounting Office	
DARNG	Director, Army National Guard	
DARPA	Defense Advanced Research Projects Agency	
DARPL	Dynamic Army Resourcing Priority List	

GLOSSARY

DAS	Defense Acquisition Management System
DAS	Director of the Army Staff
DASA	Deputy Assistant Secretary of the Army
DASA(CE)	Deputy Assistant Secretary of the Army for Cost and Economics
DASA(DL)	Deputy Assistant Secretary of the Army for Diversity and Leadership
DASA(FO)	Deputy Assistant Secretary of the Army (Financial Operations)
DASA(R&T)	Deputy Assistant Secretary of the Army (Research and Technology)
DASC	Department of the Army System Coordinator
DASD(CPP)	Deputy Under Secretary of Defense (Civilian Personnel Policy)
DASD(IP)	Deputy Assistant Secretary of Defense for Industrial Policy
DAU	Defense Acquisition University
DAWIA	Defense Acquisition Workforce Improvement Act
DC	Dental Corps
DCE	Defense Coordinating Element
DCG/CofS	Deputy Commanding General/Chief of Staff
DCI	Director, Central Intelligence
DCIPS	Defense Casualty Information Processing System
DCIPS	Defense Civilian Intelligence Personnel System
DCLM	Department of Command, Leadership, and Management
DCMA	Defense Contract Management Agency
DCO	Defense Coordinating Officer
DCPAS	Defense Civilian Personnel Advisory Services
DCPDS	Defense Civilian Personnel Data System
DCR	Doctrine, Organization, Training, Materiel, Leadership and Education, Personnel, Facilities, and Policy (DOTMLPF-P) Change Recommendation
DCS, G-1	Deputy Chief of Staff, G-1
DCS, G-2	Deputy Chief of Staff, G-2
DCS, G-3/5/7	Deputy Chief of Staff, G-3/5/7
DCS, G-4	Deputy Chief of Staff, G-4
DCS, G-6	Deputy Chief of Staff, G-6
DCS, G-8	Deputy Chief of Staff, G-8
DCSOPS	Deputy Chief of Staff, Operations
DCU	Defense Coordinating Unit
DD	Department of Defense (Form)
DDASS	Department of Defense Support to Civil Authorities, Automated Support System
DDFP	Deputy Director, Force Protection
DDN	Defense Data Network
DDS	Dynamic Distribution System
DDTC	Deployed Digital Training Campus

HOW THE ARMY RUNS

DEA	Drug Enforcement Administration
DEF	Deployment Expeditionary Force
DENCOM	Dental Command
DEOMI	Defense Equal Opportunity Management Institute
DEPSECDEF	Deputy Secretary of Defense
DEROS	Date Eligible to Return from Overseas
DES	Directorate of Emergency Services
DEST	Domestic Emergency Support Team
DET	Displaced Equipment Training
DFARS	Defense Federal Acquisition Regulation Supplement
DFAS	Defense Finance and Accounting Service
DFAS-IN	Defense Finance and Accounting Service-Indiana
DFM	Director of Force Management
DFMWR	Directorate of Family, Morale, Welfare & Recreation
DG	Defense Guidance
DHHS	Department of Health and Human Services
DHP	Defense Health Program
DHR	Directorate of Human Resources
DHS	Director of Health Services
DHS	Department of Homeland Security
DI	Document Integrator
DIA	Defense Intelligence Agency
DIEMS	Date Initially Entered Military Service
DISA	Defense Information Systems Agency
DISES	Defense Intelligence Senior Executive Service
DISL	Defense Intelligence Senior Level
DJI	Director of Joint & Integration (Force Development Directorate)
DKO	Defense Knowledge Online
dL	Distributed Learning
DL	Distance Learning
DLA	Defense Logistics Agency
DLEA	Drug Law Enforcement Agency
DLMP	Doctrine and Literature Master Plan
DLS	Distributed Learning System
DMA	Defense Media Activity
DMAG	Deputy's Management Action Group
DMAT	Disaster Medical Assistance Team
DMC	Distribution Management Center
DMETL	Directed Mission Essential Task List

GLOSSARY

DML/DMSL	Distribution Management Level / Sub-Level
DMO	Directed Military Overstrength
DMORT	Disaster Mortuary Operational Response Team
DMSSC	Defense Medical Systems Support Center
DOC	Department of Commerce
DOD	Department of Defense
DODD	Department of Defense Directive
DODI	DOD Instruction
DOD IRD	DOD Investigations and Resolutions Division
DOE	Department of Energy
DOJ	Department of Justice
DOL	Directorate of Logistics
DOM	Director of Materiel (Force Development Directorate)
DOPMA	Defense Officer Personnel Management Act
DOR	Director of Resources (Force Development Directorate)
DOS	Department of State
DOT	Department of Transportation
D,OT&E	Director, Operational Test and Evaluation
DOTmLPF-P	Doctrine, Organization, Training, Leadership and Education, Personnel, Facilities, and Policy (Non-Materiel)
DOTMLPF-P	Doctrine, Organization, Training, Materiel, Leadership and Education, Personnel, Facilities, and Policy
DPAE	Director of Program Analysis and Evaluation
DPAS	Defense Priorities and Allocations System
DPC	Defense Planning and Coordination
DPCU	Defense Planning and Coordination Unit
DPD	Defense Programming Database
DPG	Defense Planning Guidance
DPP	Dedicated Procurement Program
DPS	Defense Planning Scenarios
DPTMS	Directorate of Plans, Training, Mobilization and Security
DPW	Directorate of Public Works
DRB	Defense Resources Board
DRF	Disaster Relief Fund
DRMO	Defense Reutilization and Marketing Office
DRRS	Defense Readiness Reporting System
DRRS-A	Defense Readiness Reporting System-Army
DRU	Direct Reporting Unit
DS	Direct Support
DSAT	Department of Homeland Security (DHS) Situational Awareness Team

DSCA	Defense Security Cooperation Agency
DSCA	Defense Support of Civil Authorities
DSG	Defense Strategic Guidance
DSLDP	Defense Senior Leader Management Program
DSMC	Defense Systems Management College
DT	Developmental Test
DTAC	Digitized Training Access Center
DTF	Digital Training Facilities
DTMS	Digital Training Management System
DTOE	Draft Table of Organization and Equipment
DTOS	Deployable Tracking Operations System
DTR	Defense Transportation Regulation
DTRA	Defense Threat Reduction Agency
DTS	Defense Transportation System
DTT	Doctrine and Tactics Training
DUSD(AS&C)	Deputy Under Secretary of Defense (Advanced Systems and Concepts)
DUSD(AT&L)	Under Secretary of Defense (Acquisition, Technology, and Logistics)
DUSD(S&T)	Deputy Undersecretary of Defense (Science and Technology)
DVIDS	Defense Video and Imagery Distribution System
E-E	Emergency Essential
EA	Economic Analysis
EAB	Echelons Above Brigade
EB	Executive Board
EBIS	Employee Benefits Information System
ECAS	Environmental Compliance Assessment System
ECC	Expeditionary Contracting Command
ECG	Enduring Constitutional Government
ECOP	Equipping Common Operating Picture
ECP	Engineering Change Proposal
ECQ	Executive Core Qualifications
EDA	Excess Defense Articles
EDAS	Enlisted Distribution and Assignment System
EDATE	Effective Date
EDM	Engineering Development Model
EDTM	Enlisted Distribution Target Model
EE	Equipping (Program Evaluation Group (PEG))
EEO	Equal Employment Office
EEO	Equal Employment Opportunity
EEOC	Equal Employment Opportunity Commission

GLOSSARY

EEOCCR	Equal Employment Opportunity Compliance and Complaints Review
EES	Enlisted Evaluation System
EFD	Enterprise Funds Distribution
EFMP	Exceptional Family Member Program
EG	Enlisted Grades
EIS	Enterprise Information System
EIS	Enterprise Infrastructure Services
EITF	Energy Initiatives Task Force
EMAC	Emergency Management Assistance Compact
EMD	Engineering and Manufacturing Development
eMILPO	Electronic Military Personnel Office
EMP	Emergency Management Program
EMS	Emergency Medical Services
EO	Equal Opportunity
EO	Executive Order
EOA	Equal Opportunity Advisor
EOC	State Emergency Operation Center
EOD	Explosive Ordinance Disposal
EOL	Equal Opportunity Leader
EOPM	Equal Opportunity Program Manager
EOR	Element of Resource
EPAERT	Environmental Protection Agency Environmental Response Teams
EPLO	Emergency Preparedness Liaison Officer
EPMD	Enlisted Personnel Management Directorate
EPMS	Enlisted Personnel Management System
EPMS-AR	Enlisted Personnel Management System-Army Reserve
EPP	Enhanced Planning Process
EPP	Extended Planning Period
EPW	Enemy Prisoners of War
EQ4	Equipping the Force
ERB	Executive Resources Board
ERC	Equipment Readiness Code
ERDC	U.S. Army Engineer Research and Development Center
ERGO	Environmental Review Guide for Operations
ERP	Enterprise Resource Planning
ERT	Evidence Response Team
ES	Embedded Simulation
ES	End Strength
ESC	Expeditionary Sustainment Command

ESD	Equipment Sourcing Document
ESF	Emergency Support Function
ESGR	National Committee for Employer Support of the Guard and Reserve
ESLRG	Expanded Senior Review Group
ESP	Executive and Senior Professional
ETC	Exportable Training Capability
ETS	Expiration of Term of Service
EUSA	Eighth U.S. Army
EW	Electronic Warfare
EXCOM	Executive Committee
EXORD	Execute Order
FA	Functional Area
FA-TRAC	Foreign Army Training Assistance Command
FAA	Final Agency Action
FAA	Functional Area Analysis
FAD	Final Agency Decision
FAD	Fund Authorization Document
FADM	Force Allocation Decision Model
FAR	Federal Acquisition Regulation
FASCLASS	Fully Automated System for Classification
FBI	Federal Bureau of Investigation
FC	Foundation Course
FCB	Functional Capabilities Board
FCCE	Flood Control and Coastal Emergencies
FCO	Federal Coordinating Officer
FDA	Food and Drug Administration
FDD	Force Design Division
FDIIS	Force Development Investment Information System
FDO	Flexible Deterrent Option
FDTE	Force Development Tests and Experimentation
FDU	Force Design Update
FEA	Front End Analysis
FECA	Federal Employees Compensation Act
FEMA	Federal Emergency Management Agency
FFC	Fact Finding Conference
FFMIA	Federal Financial Management Improvement Act
FFE	Field Force Engineering
FFR	Force Feasibility Review
FHP	Force Health Protection

GLOSSARY

FI	Force Integrator
FIFA	Force Integration Functional Area
FIRST	Federal Incident Response Support Team
FIS	Facility Investment Strategy
FLRA	Federal Labor Relations Authority
FM	Field Manual
FMCS	Federal Mediation and Conciliation Service
FMFIA	Federal Manager's Financial Integrity Act
FMR	Financial Management Regulation Table
FMR	Force Management Review
FMR	Full Materiel Release
FMS	Force Management System
FMS	Foreign Military Sales
FMT	Foreign Military Training
FMWR	Family and Morale, Welfare, and Recreation
FMWRC	Family and Morale, Welfare, and Recreation Command
FNA	Functional Needs Analysis
FOA	Field Operating Agency
FOA	Forward Operational Assessment
FOC	Force Operating Capabilities
FOIA	Freedom of Information Act
FORMDEPS	Forces Command Mobilization and Deployment Planning System
FORSCOM	Forces Command
FoS	Family of Systems
FOT&E	Follow-on Operational Test and Evaluation
FOUO	For Official Use Only
FP	Force Protection
FPMS	Flood Plain Management Services Program
FPPM	Functional Proponent for Preventive Medicine
FR	Functional Review
FRC	Federal Resource Coordinator
FRP	Full Rate Production
FS	Force Structure
FSA	Force Structure Allowance
FSA	Functional Solution Analysis
FSIP	Federal Service Impasses Panel
FSM	Facility Sustainment Model
FTS	Full Time Support
FTSTDA	Full Time Support Table of Distribution and Allowances

FTX	Field Training Exercises	
FUDS	Formerly Used Defense Sites	
FUED	First Unit Equipped Date	
FWS	Federal Wage System	
FY	Fiscal Year	
FYDP	Future Years Defense Program	
GAO	Government Accountability Office	
GAR	Governor's Authorized Representative	
GC	General Counsel	
GC	Garrison Commander	
GCC	Geographic Combat Commander	
GCCS	Global Command and Control System	
GCMCA	General Court Martial Convening Authority	
GCSS-A (F/T)	Global Combat Service Support System Army (Field / Tactical)	
GCV	Ground Combat Vehicle	
GDF	Guidance for Development of the Force	
GDPRS	Global Defense Posture Realignment Strategy	
GDPS	Global Defense Posture Strategy	
GEF	Guidance for Employment of the Force	
GF	Generating Force	
GFEBS	General Fund Enterprise Business Systems	
GFM	Global Force Management	
GFMB	Global Force Management Board	
GFM DI	Global Force Management Data Initiative	
GFMIG	Global Force Management Implementation Guidance	
GIE	Global Information Environment	
GIG	Global Information Grid	
GINA	Genetic Information Nondiscrimination Act	
GIWW	Gulf Intracoastal Waterway	
GMRA	Government Management Reform Act	
GO	General Officer	
GO	General Orders	
GOSC	General Officer Steering Committee	
GPRA	Government Performance and Results Act	
GRD	Grade	
GS	General Schedule	
GSA	General Services Administration	
GSORTS	Global Status of Resources and Training System	
HA	Humanitarian Assistance	

GLOSSARY

HAAP	Homebase / Advanced Assignment Program
HASC	House Armed Services Committee
HCM	Human Capital Management
HD	Homeland Defense
HEAT	High-Mobility Multipurpose Wheeled Vehicle (HMMWV) Egress Assistance Trainer
HEPLOs	Headquarters Emergency Preparedness Liaison Officers
HFEA	Human Factors Engineering Analysis
HHA	Health Hazard Assessment
HHC/HHD	Higher Headquarters Company / Higher Headquarters Detachment
HHS	Health and Human Services
HIV	Human Immunodeficiency Virus
HLT	Hurricane Liaison Team
HMRU	Hazardous-Materials Response Unit
HN	Host Nation
HNS	Host Nation Support
HP&RR	Health Promotion & Risk Reduction
HQ	Headquarters
HQDA	Headquarters, Department of the Army
HQE	Highly Qualified Expert
HQIMCOM	Headquarters, Installation Management Command
HR	Human Resources
HRC	Human Resources Command
HRC-STL	Human Resources Command-St Louis
HRD	Human Resources Development
HRF	Homeland Response Forces
HRM	Human Resource Management
HRT	Hostage Rescue Team
HS	Homeland Security
HSC	Homeland Security Council
HSDRRS	Hurricane and Storm Damage Risk Reduction System
HSI	Human Systems Integration
HSPD	Homeland Security Presidential Directive
HTAR	How The Army Runs
IA	Individual Account
IA	Individual Augmentation
IA	Information Assurance
IADT	Initial Active Duty for Training
IAEMP	Interagency Emergency Management Program
IAW	In Accordance With

G-21

HOW THE ARMY RUNS

IC	Incident Commander
IC	Intermediate Course
ICAF	Industrial College of the Armed Forces
ICD	Initial Capabilities Document
ICDT	Integrated Capabilities Development Team
ICE	Independent Life-Cycle Cost Estimate
ICO	Installation Contractor Office
ICP	Inventory Control Point
ICPA	Injury Compensation Program Administrator
ICS	Incident Command System
ICW	In Coordination With
ICW	In Compliance With
IDP	Individual Development Plan
IDT	Inactive Duty Training
IE	Integration Evaluation
IET	Initial Entry Training
IG	Inspector General
IGI&S	Installation Geospatial Information & Services
II	Installations (Program Evaluation Group (PEG))
IIQ	Initial Issue Quantity
ILE	Intermediate Level Education
ILO	In Lieu Of
ILS	Integrated Logistics Support
ILSM	Integrated Logistic Support Manager
IM	Information Management
IMA	Installation Management Agency
IMA	Individual Mobilization Augmentee
IMAT	Incident Management Assistance Teams
IMBOD	Installation Management Board of Directors
IMCOM	U.S. Army Installation Management Command
IMI	Interactive Multimedia Instruction
IMO	Information Management Office
IMRD	Intelligence Resource Management Decision
IMS	Integrated Management System
IMS	International Military Student
IMT	Initial Military Training
INFOSEC	Information Security
ING	Inactive National Guard
INSCOM	U.S. Army Intelligence and Security Command

GLOSSARY

IOC	Initial Operational Capability
IOT	Initial Operational Test
IOT&E	Initial Operational Testing and Evaluation
IP	Installation Preparedness
IP	Issue Paper
IPA	Integrated Program Assessment
IPL	Integrated Priority List
IPMO	Intelligence Personnel Management Office
IPM	Industrial Preparedness Measure
IPP	Industrial Preparedness Planning
IPPL	Industrial Preparedness Planning
IPR	In-Process Review
IPRG	Intelligence Program Review Group
IPT	Integrated Process Team
IPT	Integrated Product Team
IR	Integration Rehearsal
IR	Irregular Warfare
IRACO	Internal Review
IR&D	Independent Research and Development
IRD	Investigation and Resolutions Division
IRR	Individual Ready Reserve
ISC	Integrated Security Campaign
ISEW	Intelligence, Security, and Electronic Warfare
ISO	Installation Safety Office
ISP	Information Support Plan
ISR	Installation Status Report
ISR	Intelligence, Surveillance, and Reconnaissance
IT	Information Technology
ITA	U.S. Army Information Technology Agency
ITAB	Information Technology Acquisition Board
ITAPBD	Integrated Total Army Personnel Data Base
ITAM	Integrated Training Area Management
ITD	Individual Training Directorate
ITMRA	Information Technology Management Reform Act of 1996
ITRM	Individual Training Resource Module
ITV	In-Transit Visibility
IW	Irregular Warfare
IWR	Institute for Water Resources
JAG	Judge Advocate General's Corps

HOW THE ARMY RUNS

JC	Joint Concept
JCA	Joint Capability Area
JCB	Joint Capabilities Board
JCCA	Joint Combat Capability Assessment
JCCAG	Joint Combat Capability Assessment Group
JCD	Joint Capabilities Document
JCIDS	Joint Capabilities Integration and Development System
JCLL	Joint Center for Lessons Learned
JCS	Joint Chiefs of Staff
JCTD	Joint Capabilities Technology Demonstrations
JDOMS	Joint Directorate of Military Support
JEONS	Joint Emerging Operational Needs Statement
JFC	Joint Force Commander
JFHQ-NCR	Joint Force Headquarters-National Capital Region
JFHQ-State	Joint Forces Headquarters-State
JFLCC	Joint Forces Land Component Command
JFO	Joint Field Office
JFP	Joint Force Provider
JFRR	Joint Force Readiness Review
JFSC	Joint Forces Staff College
JIC	Joint Information Center
JIEDDO	Joint Improvised Explosive Devices Defeat Organization
JIIM	Joint, Interagency, Intergovernmental, and Multinational
JLTV	Joint Light Tactical Vehicle
JMC	Joint Munitions Command
JM&L	Joint Munitions and Lethality (Life Cycle Management Command (LCMC))
JMET	Joint Mission Essential Task
JMETL	Joint Mission Essential Task List
JMRC	Joint Multinational Readiness Center
JC	Joint Concepts
JCB	Joint Capabilities Board
JOA	Joint Operations Area
JOC	Joint Operations Center
JOE	Joint Operating Environment
JOPES	Joint Operations Planning and Execution System
JOPP	Joint Operation Planning Process
JP	Joint Publication
JPAC	Joint Planning Augmentation Cell
JPEC	Joint Planning and Execution Community

GLOSSARY

JPG	Joint Programming Guidance
JRAC	Joint Rapid Acquisition Cell
JROC	Joint Requirements Oversight Council
JROCM	Joint Requirements Oversight Council Memorandum
JROTC	Junior Reserve Officer Training Corps
JRTC	Joint Readiness Training Center
JS	Joint Staff
JSCP	Joint Strategic Capabilities Plan
JSD	Joint Staffing Designator
JSO	Joint Specialty Officer
JSOTF	Joint Special Operations Task Force
JSPS	Joint Strategic Planning System
JSR	Joint Strategy Review
JTA/JTD	Joint Table of Authorizations / Joint Table of Distribution
JTAPIC	Joint Trauma Analysis and Prevention of Injury in Combat Program
JTC	Joint Commission
JTF	Joint Task Force
JTF-CS	Joint Task Force-Civil Support
JTF-N	Joint Task Force-North
JTF-PO	Joint Task Force-Port Opening
JTRS	Joint Tactical Radio System
JULLS	Joint Utilization Lesson Learned System
JUONS	Joint Urgent Operational Needs Statement
JWE	Joint Warfighting Experiment
JWSTAP	Joint Weapon Safety Technical Advisory Panel
KD	Key Developmental
KFL	Key Facilities List
KM	Knowledge Management
KM/DS	Knowledge Management / Decision Support
KPP	Key Performance Parameter
KSA	Key System Attribute
LAD	Latest Arrival Date
LAN	Local Area Network
LAP	Logistics Assistance Program
LCMC	Life Cycle Management Command
LCSP	Life Cycle Sustainment Plan
LEA	Law Enforcement Agency
LEAD	Letterkenny Army Depot
LFA	Lead Federal Agency

LFT	Live First Testing	
LFT&E	Live Fire Test and Evaluation	
LHWCA	Longshore and Harbor Workers Compensation Act	
LIA	Logistics Innovation Agency	
LIN	Line Item Number	
LIO	Limited Intervention Operations	
LMER	Labor and Management Employee Relations	
LMI	Lead Materiel Integrator	
LMI	Logistics Management Information	
LMP	Logistics Management Program	
LOB	Lines of Business	
LOC	Lines of Communication	
LOD	Line of Duty	
LOE	Line of Effort	
LOGCAP	Logistics Civil Augmentation Program	
LOGSA	Logistics Support Activity	
LOGSACS	Logistics Structure and Composition System	
LOI	Letter of Instruction	
LOO	Line of Operation	
LRIP	Low Rate Initial Production	
LTC	Lieutenant Colonel	
LVC	Live, Virtual, Constructive	
LVCG	Live, Virtual, Constructive, and Gaming	
LWN	LandWarNet	
M&S	Modeling and Simulation	
M2PR	Monthly Military Personnel Review	
MA	Mission Assurance	
MA	Mortuary Affairs	
MACA	Military Assistance to Civil Authorities	
MACDIS	Military Assistance for Civil Disturbance	
MACOM	Major Army Command	
MAIS	Major Automated Information System	
MAISRC	Major Automated Information System Review Council	
MANPRINT	Manpower and Personnel Integration	
MARC	Manpower Requirements Criteria	
MAST	Military Assistance to Safety and Traffic	
MATDEV	Materiel Developer	
MBI	Major Budget Issue	
MC	Medical Corps	

GLOSSARY

MC4	Medical Communications for Combat Casualty Care
MCA	Military Construction, Army
MCAR	Military Construction, Army Reserve
MCCP	Marine Corps Capabilities Plan
MCD	Materiel Capabilities Document
MCNG	Military Construction, Army National Guard
MCO	Major Combat Operations
MCS	Managed Care Support
MCTP	Mission Command Training Program
MCU	Multiple Component Unit
MDA	Missile Defense Agency
MDA	Milestone Decision Authority
MDAP	Major Defense Acquisition Program
MDC	Management Development Course
MDD	Materiel Development Decision
MDEP	Management Decision Package
MDR	Milestone Decision Review
MDW	Military District of Washington
ME	Materiel Enterprise
MEDCEN	Medical Center
MEDCOM	Medical Command
MEDDAC	Medical Department Activity
MEDLOG	Medical Logistics
MEO	Military Equal Opportunity
MEPCOM	Military Entrance Processing Command
MEPS	Military Entrance Processing Station
MER	Manpower Estimate Report
MER	Mission Essential Requirements
MERS	Mobile Emergency Response Support
MET	Mission Essential Task
METL	Mission Essential Task List
METT-TC	Mission, Enemy, Terrain and Weather, Troops and Support Available, Time Available and Civilians Considerations
MFA	Materiel Fielding Agreement
MFP	Mission Force Pool (Future Force Generation)
MFORCE	Master Force
MFP	Materiel Fielding Plan
MFTB	Multifunctional Training Brigade
MHA	Management Headquarters Account

MHRM	Military Human Resource Management
MHS	Military Health System
MICP	Managers Internal Control Program
MID	Management Initiative Decisions
MILCON	Military Construction
MILDEP	Military Deputy
MILPERS	Military Personnel
MILS	Military Supply
MILSPEC/STD	Military Specifications and Standards
Mil-Tech	Military Technician
MILVAX	Military Vaccine
MIPS	Modified Integrated Program Summary
MLMC	Medical Logistics Management Center
MM	Manning (Program Evaluation Group (PEG))
MMDF	Maintenance Master Data File
MMEWR	Minimum Mission Essential Wartime Requirement
MMG	Master Mobilization Guide
MOA	Memorandum of Agreement
MOB-ARPRINT	Mobilization Army Program for Individual Training
MOBMAN	Mobilization Manpower Planning System
MOBTDA	Mobilization Table of Distribution and Allowances
MOC	Media Operations Center
MOCS	Military Occupational Classification and Structure
MOE	Measures of Effectiveness
MOI	Memorandum of Instruction
MOS	Military Occupational Specialty
MOS-T	Military Occupational Specialty Training
MOSLS	Military Occupational Specialty Level System
MOSQ	Military Occupational Specialty Qualified
MOU	Memorandum of Understanding
MPA	Military Personnel, Army
MPAD	Mobile Public Affairs Detachment
MPLAN	Marine Corps Mobilization Management Plan
MPS	Mobilization Planning System
MPT	Manpower, Personnel, and Training
MRAP	Mine Resistant Ambush Protected Vehicle
MRD	Material Requirements Document
MRL	Materiel Requirements List
MRO	Maintenance Repair and Overhaul

GLOSSARY

MS	Milestone
MS	Medical Service Corps
MSA	Materiel Solution Analysis
MSC	Military Sealift Command
MSC	Major Subordinate Command
MSCLEA	Military Assistance to Civil Law Enforcement Agencies
MSFD	Multi-Service Force Development
MSO	Military Service Obligation
MSP	Mission Support Plan
MSPB	Merit Systems Protection Board
MSU	Mobilization Support Unit
MTBF	Mean Time Between Failure
MTF	Medical Treatment Facility
MTOE	Modification Table of Organization and Equipment
MTP	Mission Training Plan
MUA	Military Utility Assessment
MUTA	Multiple Unit Training Assembly
MUTA-4	Multiple Unit Training Assemblies-Four Consecutive Assemblies)
MWR	Morale, Welfare, and Recreation
NAF	Nonappropriated Funds
NAFI	Nonappropriated Funds Instrumentalities
NAP	Not Authorized Prepositioning
NASA	National Aeronautics and Space Administration
NATO	North Atlantic Treaty Organization
NCE	Non-Combat Essential
NCMP	Navy Capabilities and Mobilization Plan
NCO	Noncommissioned Officer
NCOA	Noncommissioned Officer Academy
NCOER	Noncommissioned Officer Evaluation Report
NCOES	Noncommissioned Officer Education System
NDA	National Defense Act
NDAA	National Defense Authorization Act
NDI	Non-Developmental Item
NDMS	National Disaster Medical System
NDS	National Defense Stockpile
NDS	National Defense Strategy
NEC	Network Enterprise Command
NEO	Non-Combatant Evacuation Operations
NEPA	National Environmental Policy Act of 1969

HOW THE ARMY RUNS

NEST	Nuclear Emergency Support Teams
NET	New Equipment Training
NETCOM	Network Enterprise Technology Command
NETP	New Equipment Training Plan
NETT	New Equipment Training Team
NetUSR	Net-Centric Unit Status Report
NFIP	National Flood Insurance Program
NFIP	National Foreign Intelligence Program
NGB	National Guard Bureau
NGPA	National Guard Personnel, Army
NGREA	National Guard and Reserve Equipment Appropriation
NGS	Non-Government Standards
NIE	Network Integrated Evaluations
NIFC	National Interagency Fire Center
NIMS	National Incident Management System
NIR	Network Integration Rehearsal
NIRT	Nuclear Incident Response Team
NMA-GOSC	Network Mission Area General Officer Steering Committee
NMRTS	National Medical Response Teams
NMS	National Military Strategy
NOAA	National Oceanic and Atmospheric Administration
NOC	National Operations Center
NOF	Notional Force
NOFC	Notification of Future Change
NOK	Next of Kin
NORTHCOM	Northern Command
NP	Neuropsychiatric
NPG	National Preparedness Goal
NPR	Nuclear Posture Review
NPS	Non-Prior Service
NR-KPP	Net-Ready Key Performance Parameter
NRF	National Response Framework
NRP	National Response Plan
NSA	National Security Agency
NSC	National Security Council
NSCS	National Security Council System
NSDD	National Security Decision Directive
NSN	National Stock Number
NSPS	National Security Personnel System

GLOSSARY

NSS	National Security Strategy
NSS	National Security System
NSSE	National Special Security Events
NSTD	Non-Standard Training Aids, Devices, Simulations, and Simulators
NTC	National Training Center
NTV	Non-Tactical Vehicle
NULO	Negative Un-Liquidated Obligations
NVOAD	National Voluntary Organizations Active in Disaster
O/M	Operator and Maintainer
O&M	Operations and Maintenance
O&M(R&M)	Operations and Maintenance (Restoration and Modernization)
O&R	Oversight and Review
O&S	Operations and Support
OA	Obligation Authority
OA	Operating Agency
OA	Operational Architecture
OA	Operational Availability
OAA	Office of the Administrative Assistant
OACSIM	Office of the Assistant Chief of Staff for Installation Management
OASA(FM&C)	Office of the Assistant Secretary of the Army for Financial Management and Comptroller
OASD	Office of the Assistant Secretary of Defense
OBT	Office of Business Transformation
OGA	Other Government Agencies
OCAR	Office of the Chief, Army Reserve
OCLL	Office, Chief of Legislative Liaison
OCO	Overseas Contingency Operations
OCONUS	Outside of the Continental U.S.
OCPA	Office of the Chief of Public Affairs
OCS	Officer Candidate School
OCS	Operational Contract Support
ODCS	Office of Deputy Chief of Staff
ODP	Officer Distribution Plan
ODS	Officer Development System
ODS	Officer Distribution System
ODT	Overseas Deployment Training
OE	Operational Environment
OEF	Operation Enduring Freedom
OER	Officer Evaluation Report
OES	Officer Education System

OES	State Office of Emergency Services
OF	Operating Force
OFM	Officer Forecasting Model
OFO	Office of Federal Operations
OGLA	Officer Grade Limitation Act
OI	Organizational Integrator
OIF	Operation Iraqi Freedom
OIPT	Overarching Integrated Product Team
OMA	Operations and Maintenance, Army
OMA	Operations and Maintenance Appropriation
OMAR	Operations and Maintenance, Army Reserve
OMB	Office of Management and Budget
OMNG	Operations and Maintenance, Army National Guard
OMS/MP	Operational Mode Summary / Mission Profiles
OneSAF	One Semi-Automated Forces
ONS	Operational Needs Statement
OO	Organizing (Program Evaluation Group (PEG))
OPA	Officer Personnel Act
OPA	Other Procurement, Army
OPFOR	Opposing Forces
OPLAN	Operations Plan
OPLOC	Operating Location
OPM	Office of Personnel Management
OPMD	Officer Personnel Management Directorate
OPMG	Office of the Provost Marshall General
OPMS	Officer Personnel Management System
OPMS-AR	Officer Personnel Management System-Army Reserve
OPORD	Operation Order
OpSD	Operating Strength Deviation
OPSEC	Operational Security
OPTEMPO	Operating Tempo
ORG DB	Organization (Component of Total Army Personnel Database (TAPDB))
ORB	Officer Record Brief
OS	Operating Strength
OSA	Office of the Secretary of the Army
OSC	Office of Special Counsel
OSD	Office of the Secretary of Defense
OSFP	Operational Sustainment Force Pool (Future Force Generation)
OSUT	One Station Unit Training

GLOSSARY

OT	Operational Testing
OTA	Operational Test Agency
OTA TP	Operational Test Agency Test Plan
OTIG	Office of the Inspector General
OTJAG	Office of the Judge Advocate General
OTOE	Objective Table of Organization and Equipment
OTRA	Other than Regular Army
OTSG	Office of the Surgeon General
OUSD(C)	Office of the Under Secretary of Defense (Comptroller)
P&D	Production and Deployment
P&R	Personnel and Readiness
P3I	Preplanned Product Improvement
PA	Public Affairs
PA&E	Program Analysis and Evaluation
PAA	Procurement Ammunition Army
PAD	Public Affairs Detachment
PAED	Program Analysis and Evaluation Directorate
PAG	Public Affairs Guidance
PAIO	Plans, Analysis & Integration Office
PAO	Public Affairs Officer
PARD	Priorities Analysis and Requirements Directorate
PAUC	Program Acquisition Unit Cost
PBA	Performance-Based Agreements
PBA	Production Base Analysis
PBAS	Program-Budget Accounting System
PBD	Program Budget Decision
PBG	Program and Budget Guidance
PBL	Performance Based Logistics
PBR	Program Budget Review
PC-ASORTS	Personal Computer-Army Status of Resources and Training System
PCA	Posse Comitatus Act of 1878
PCC	Policy Coordination Committee
PCH	Press Camp Headquarters
PCP	Program Change Proposals
PCS	Permanent Change of Station
PCTEF	Percent Effective
PD	Program Directive
PDASA	Principal Deputy Assistant Secretary of the Army
PDD	Presidential Decision Directives

PDIP	Program Development Increment Package	
PDR	Preliminary Design Review	
PE	Program Element	
PEG	Program Evaluation Group	
PEO	Program Executive Officer	
PEO EIS	Program Executive Office Enterprise Information Systems	
PEPDUS	Human Resources Command (HRC) Enlisted Personnel Data Update System	
PER DB	Personnel (Component of Total Army Personnel Database (TAPDB))	
PERMISS	Personnel Management Information and Support System	
PERMS	Personnel Electronic Records Management System	
PERNET	Personnel Network	
PERSACS	Personnel Structure and Composition System	
PERSSO	Personnel System Staff Officer	
PFA	Personnel Functional Assessment	
PFY	Prior Fiscal Year	
PfP	Partnership for Peace	
PFO	Principal Federal Official	
PH	Public Health	
PI	Product Improvements	
PIM	Pre-Trained Individual Manpower	
PIMS	Partnership for Peace Information Management System	
PKO	Peacekeeping Operations	
PLL	Prescribed Load List	
PM	Program, Project, or Product Manager	
PMAD	Personnel Management Authorizations Document	
PME	Professional Military Education	
PME	Professional Military Exchange	
PMF	Presidential Management Fellows	
PMJ	Professional Military Judgment	
PMO	Program Management Office	
PMS	Personnel Management System	
POC	Point of Contact	
POD	Point of Delivery	
POE	Program Office Estimate	
POI	Program of Instruction	
POL	Petroleum, Oils, Lubricants	
POM	Program Objective Memorandum	
POM/BES	Program Objective Memorandum and Budget Estimate Submission	
POPM	Proponency Office for Preventive Medicine	

GLOSSARY

POR	Preparation for Overseas Replacement
POR	Program of Record
POSC-Edit	Personnel Occupational Specialty Code Edit
POSH	Prevention of Sexual Harassment
POTUS	President of the U.S.
PPAG	Proposed Public Affairs Guidance
PPBC	Planning Program Budget Committee
PPBE	Planning, Programming, Budgeting, and Execution
PPBES	Planning, Programming, Budgeting, and Execution System
PPBS	Planning, Programming, and Budgeting System
PPP/PSP	Power Projection Platforms/Power Support Platforms
PPV	Public Private Ventures
PQT	Production Qualification Test
PRC	Presidential Reserve Call-Up
PREPO	Pre-Positioned
PRESBUD	President's Budget
PRG	Program Review Group
PROBE	Program Optimization and Budget Evaluation
PROFIS	Professional Officer Filler Information System
PSA	Principal Staff Assistant
PSMA	Pre-Scripted Mission Assignments
PSS	Product Support Strategy
PURE	Prepositioning Of Materiel Configured in Unit Sets (POMCUS) Unit Residual Equipment
PX	Post Exchange
QAO	Quality Assurance Office
QDR	Quadrennial Defense Review
QMP	Qualitative Management Program
QRM	Quadrennial Roles and Missions Review
QRRC	Quarterly Readiness Report to Congress
QTY	Quantity
R&D	Research and Development
RA	Readiness Assessment
RAD	Requirements and Assessment Division
RAD	Research Area Directorates
RAID	Rapid Assessment and Initial Detection
RAM	Reliability, Availability, and Maintainability
RAP	Revised Approved Program
RAP-C	Requisition Allocation Plan-Continental U.S. (CONUS)
RAR	Rapid Acquisition Review

RAR	Rapid Action Revision	
RC	Reserve Component	
RC	Required Capabilities	
RCAS	Reserve Component Automation System	
RCCC	Reserve Component Coordination Council	
RCCMRF	Restructured CBRNE Consequence Management Response Force	
RCI	Residential Communities Initiative	
RCP	Retention Control Point	
RCSOF	Reserve Component Special Operations Forces	
RCTID	Reserve Component Training Integration Directorate	
RD	Region Director	
RDA	Readiness Deficiency Assessment	
RDA	Research, Development, and Acquisition	
RDAP	Research, Development, and Acquisition Plan	
RDC	Rapid Deployment Capability	
RDD	Resource Decision Documents	
RDEC	Research, Development, and Engineering Center	
RDECOM	Research, Development, and Engineering Command	
RDL	Reimer Digital Library	
RDS	Requirements Documentation System	
RDT&E	Research, Development, Test, and Evaluation	
RDT&E,A	Research, Development, Test, and Evaluation, Army	
REF	Rapid Equipping Force	
REP-63	Reserve Enlistment Program of 1963	
REPLOs	Regional Emergency Preparedness Liaison Officers	
REQ DB	Requisition (Component of Total Army Personnel Database (TAPDB))	
REQUEST	Recruit Quota Enlistment System	
RERT	Radiological Emergency Response Team	
RETAIN	Reenlistment/Reclassification Assignment System	
RFC	Request for Capabilities	
RFF	Request for Forces	
RFG	Resource Formulation Guide	
RFP	Request for Proposal	
RFP	Rotational Force Pool (Future Force Generation)	
RFPB	Reserve Forces Policy Board	
RI	Resource Integrator	
RIA	Rock Island Arsenal	
RID	Requirements Integration Directorate	
RIF	Reduction in Force	

GLOSSARY

RIO	Resource-Informed, Focused and Outcome-Based
RMC	Regional Medical Command
RMD	Resource Management Decision
RMD	Requirements Management Division
RMO	Resource Management Office
ROE	Rules of Engagement
ROI	Report of Investigation
ROMO	Range of Military Operations
ROPMA	Reserve Officer Personnel Management Act
ROTC	Reserve Officers' Training Corps
RPA	U.S. Army Resources and Programs Agency
RPA	Reserve Personnel, Army
RPG	Rocket-Propelled Grenade
RPLANS	Real Property Planning and Analysis System
RRAD	Red River Army Depot
RRCC	Regional Response Coordination Center
RSC	Regional Support Command
RSO	Religious Support Office
RSO	Requirements Staff Officer
RSO	Retirement Services Officer
RTLP	Range and Training Land Program
RTSM	Regional Training Site Maintenance
RUDIST	REQUEST Unit Distribution Program
RUF	Rules of the Use of Force
S&T	Science and Technology
SA	Security Assistance
SA	Supportability Analysis
SA	Systems Architecture
SAAG	Auditor General of the Army
SAC	Special Agent in Charge
SAC	Strategic Air Command
SACEUR	Supreme Allied Commander, Europe
SACS	Structure and Composition System
SAD	State Active Duty
SAMAS	Structure and Manpower Allocation System
SAP	Special Access Program
SAPP	Security, Accuracy, Propriety, and Policy
SAPR	Sexual Assault Prevention Response
SAR	Selected Acquisition Report

HOW THE ARMY RUNS

SAS	Statistical Analysis Software
SASC	Senate Armed Services Committee
SAT	Systems Approach to Training
SATCOM	Satellite Communications
SATD	Security Assistance Training Directorate
SATFA	Security Assistance Training Field Activity
SATP	Security Assistance Training Program
SB	Software Blocking
SB	Sustainment Brigade
SBC	Service Based Costing
SBCT	Stryker Brigade Combat Team
SBIR	Small Business Innovation Research Program
SBP	Survivor Benefit Plan
SBR	Standby Reserve
SC	Senior Commander
SCI	Sensitive Compartmented Information
SCO	State Coordinating Officer
SCRA	Servicemembers Civil Relief Act
SCRAG	Senior Civilian Representative of the Attorney General
SDAP	Special Duty Assignment Pay
SDC	Supervisory Development Course
SDCS	Standard Data Collection System
SDDC	Surface Deployment and Distribution Command
SE	Systems Engineering
SE	System Evaluation
SEC	Senior Executive Council
SECARMY	Secretary of the Army
SECDEF	Secretary of Defense
SEHS	Special Events for Homeland Security
SEP	Systems Engineering Plan
SEPLO	State Emergency Preparedness Liaison Officer
SERB	Selective Early Retirement Board
SES	Senior Executive Service
SFLEO	Senior Federal Law Enforcement Officer
SFC	Sergeant First Class
SFO	Senior Federal Official
SFRBOD	Soldier and Family Readiness Board of Directors
SG	Standards of Grade
SGO	Standard Garrison Organization

GLOSSARY

SGM	Sergeant Major
SGT	Sergeant
SHARP	Sexual Harassment/Assault Response Prevention
SHCP	Strategic Human Capital Planning
SHRM	Strategic Human Resource Management
SICE	Services & Infrastructure Core Enterprise
SIG	Senior Integration Group
SIGINT	Signals Intelligence
SIMLM	Single Integrated Medical Logistics Manager
SIPRNet	Secure Internet Protocol Router Network
SIPT	Supportability Integrated Product Team
SISC	Support to International Sporting Competitions
SKA	Skills, Knowledge, and Attributes
SL	Senior Level
SLAMIS	Standard Study Number (SSN)-Line Item Number (LIN) Automated Management and Integrating System
SLC	Secretary's Senior Leadership Council
SLDA	Senior Leaders of the Department of the Army
SLEP	Service Life Extension Program
SLRG	Senior Leader Review Group
SM	Soldier's Manual
SMART	Special Medical Augmentation Response Teams
SMCT	Soldier's Manual of Common Tasks
SMDC	Space and Missile Defense Command
SMDR	Structure Manning Decision Review
SME	Subject Matter Expert
SMSP	Strategic Materials Security Program
SM/TG	Soldier's Manuals / Trainers Guides
SMU	Special Mission Unit
SNaP	Select and Native Programming
SOF	Special Operations Forces
SOFA	Status of Forces Agreement
SOP	Standard Operating Procedure
SoS	System of Systems
SP	Army Medical Specialist Corps
SPOD	Sea Port of Debarkation
SQI	Special Qualification Identifier
SRAG	Strategic Readiness Assessment Group
SRB	Selective Retirement Board

SRC	Standard Requirements Code	
SRG	Senior Review Group	
SRM	Sustainment, Restoration and Modernization	
SRO	System Readiness Objective	
SROC	Senior Readiness Oversight Council	
SRP	Soldier Readiness Program	
SRP	Sustainable Range Program	
SRU	Strategic Readiness Update	
SRUF	Standing Rules for the Use of Force	
SS	Sustaining (Program Evaluation Group (PEG))	
SS	Supportability Strategy	
SSA	Source Selection Authority	
SSA	Staff Support Agency	
SSA	System Safety Assessment	
SSC	Senior Service College	
SSD	Structured Self-Development	
SSG	Staff Sergeant	
SSMS	Service Support Manpower System	
SSN	Standard Study Number	
SSO	Synchronization Staff Officer	
ST	Scientific and Technical	
ST	Sustainment Training	
STANFINS	Standard Financial System	
STAR	System Threat Assessment Report	
START	Scientific and Technical Advisory and Response Team	
STO	Split Training Option	
STP	Short Term Project	
STP	Soldier Training Publication	
STRAMS-E	Student/Trainee Management System-Enlisted	
STRAP	System Training Plan	
STSP	Soldier Training Support Program	
STTR	Small Business Technology Transfer Pilot Program	
STX	Situational Training Exercises	
SUE	System Under Evaluation	
SUT	System Under Testing	
SVP	Special Visibility Program	
T&E	Test and Evaluation	
T&EO	Training and Evaluation Outline	
TAA	Total Army Analysis	

GLOSSARY

TACITS	Total Army Centralized Individual Training Solicitations
TADSS	Training Aids, Devices, Simulations, and Simulators
TAEDP	The Army Equipment Distribution Program
TAG	The State Adjutants General; The Adjutant General
TAP	The Army Plan
TAPDB	Total Army Personnel Database
TAPDB-AE	Total Army Personnel Database-Active Enlisted
TAPDB-AO	Total Army Personnel Database-Active Officer
TAPDB-MOB	Total Army Personnel Database-Mobilization
TAPES	Total Army Performance Evaluation System
TASS	The Army School System
TATS	Total Army Training System
TBE	Training Base Expansion
TC	Type Classification
TCM	Training and Doctrine Command (TRADOC) Capability Manager
TD	Technology Demonstration
TD	Training Development
TDA	Table of Distribution and Allowances
TDDC	Training and Doctrine Development Configuration
TDDT	Training and Doctrine Development Tool
TDS	Technology Development Strategy
TDY	Temporary Duty
TE	Training Environment
TEDP	Training and Education Development Process
TEM	Training Execution Matrices
TEMP	Test and Evaluation Master Plan
TESC	Training Enterprise Scheduling Capability
TEU	Technical Escort Unit
TF	Task Force
TFE	Tactical Field Exchange
TFER	Task Force for Emergency Readiness
TFM	Training Feedback Module
TFT	Technical Field Test
TG	Training Guide
TGM	Technical Guidance Memorandum
TID	Training Integration Directorate
TIG	Time in Grade
TII	Training Information Infrastructure
TIM	Transformation of Installation Management

TIS	Time in Service	
TISO	Threat Integration Staff Officer	
TJAGLCS	U.S. Army The Judge Advocate General Legal Center and School	
TJC	The Joint Commission	
TLAMM	Theater Lead Agent for Medical Materiel	
TMA	Training Mission Area	
TMA	TRICARE Management Activity	
TMCA	Theater Movement Control Agency	
TMD	Theater Missile Defense	
TMIP	Theater Medical Information Program	
TMOPES	Training and Doctrine Command (TRADOC) Mobilization and Operation Planning and Execution System	
TNGDEV	Training Developer	
TO	Theater Opening	
TOA	Total Obligation Authority	
TOE	Table of Organization and Equipment	
TOMA	Training Operations Management Activity	
TOPMIS	Total Officer Personnel Management Information System	
TP	Training Publication	
TPE	Theater Provided Equipment	
TPF	Total Package Fielding	
TPFDD	Time-Phased Force and Deployment Data	
TPSN	Troop Program Sequence Number	
TPU	Troop Program Unit	
TRA	Technology Readiness Assessment	
TRAC	Training and Doctrine Command Analysis Center	
TRAC2ES	Transportation Command (TRANSCOM) Regulating and Command and Control Evacuation System	
TRADOC	U.S. Army Training and Doctrine Command	
TRAP	Training Resources Arbitration Panel	
TRAS	Training Requirements Analysis System	
TRL	Technology Readiness Level	
TRM	Training Resource Model	
TRMC	Training Resource Management Capability	
TRP	Test Resource Plan	
TSARC	Test Schedule and Review Committee	
TSB	Training Support Brigade	
TSC	Theater Sustainment Command	
TSC	Training Support Center	
TSG	The Surgeon General	

GLOSSARY

TSP	Training Support Package
TSR	Training Support Requirements
TSS	Training Support System
TSWG	Training Support Working Group
TT	Training (Program Evaluation Group (PEG))
TTHS	Trainee, Transient, Holdee and Student
TTP	Tactics, Techniques, and Procedures
TVA	Tennessee Valley Authority
TWOS	Total Warrant Officer System
TYAD	Tobyhanna Army Depot
UAD	Updated Authorizations Document
UAS	Unit Activation Schedule
UAV	Unmanned Aerial Vehicle
UCMJ	Uniform Code of Military Justice
UCP	Unified Command Plan
UFR	Unfunded Requirement
UIC	Unit Identification Code
UICIO	Unit Identification Code Information Officer
UJTL	Universal Joint Task List
ULO	Unified Land Operations
ULOMETL	Unified Land Operations Mission Essential Task List
ULP	Unfair Labor Practice
UMD	Unmatched Disbursements
UMFP	Unit Materiel Fielding Points
UNAAF	Unified Action Armed Forces
UON	Urgent Operational Need
URS	Unit Reference Sheet
US&R	Urban Search and Rescue
USA	Under Secretary of the Army
USAAA	U.S. Army Audit Agency
USAAC	U.S. Army Accessions Command
USAASB	U.S. Army Acquisition Support Brigade
USAASC	U.S. Army Acquisition Support Center
USACC	U.S. Army Cadet Command
USACCSA	U.S. Army Command and Control Support Agency
USACE	U.S. Army Corps of Engineers
USACIDC	U.S. Army Criminal Investigation Command
USAEUR	U.S. Army in Europe
USAFMCOM	U.S. Army Financial Management Command

HOW THE ARMY RUNS

USAFMSA	U.S. Army Force Management Support Agency
USAFRICOM	U.S. Africa Command
USAIGA	U.S. Army Inspector General Agency
USAISMA	U.S. Army Installation Support Management Activity
USAJFKSWCS	U.S. Army John F. Kennedy Special Warfare Center and School
USALSA	U.S. Army Legal Services Agency
USAMAA	U.S. Army Manpower Analysis Agency
USAMRICD	U.S. Army Medical Research Institute of Chemical Defense
USAMRIID	U.S. Army Medical Research Institute of Infectious Diseases
USAMRMC	U.S. Army Medical Research and Materiel Command)
USANCA	U.S. Army Nuclear and Combating Weapons of Mass Destruction (WMD) Agency
USAPA	U.S. Army Publishing Agency
USAPHC	U.S. Army Public Health Command
USAR	U.S. Army Reserve
USARAF/SETAF	U.S. Army Africa/Southern European Task Force
USARC	U.S. Army Reserve Command
USARCENT	U.S. Army Central
USAREC	U.S. Army Recruiting Command
USAREUR	U.S. Army, Europe
USARF	U.S. Army Reserve Forces
USARNORTH	U. S. Army, North
USARPAC	U.S. Army, Pacific
USARSO	U.S. Army, South
USASAC	U.S. Army Security Assistance Command
USASATMO	U.S. Army Security Assistance Training Management Organization
USASMDC	U.S. Army Space and Missile Defense Command
USASOC	U.S. Army Special Operations Command
USASSI	U.S. Army Soldier Support Institute
USATC	U.S. Army Training Center
USAWC	U.S. Army War College
UC	Unified Command
USC	U.S. Code
USCENTCOM	U.S. Central Command
USCG	U.S. Coast Guard
USD	Under Secretary of Defense
USDA	U.S. Department of Agriculture
USD(P)	Under Secretary of Defense (Policy)
USD(AT&L)	Under Secretary of Defense (Acquisition, Technology, and Logistics)
USD(C)	Under Secretary of Defense (Comptroller)

GLOSSARY

USD(P&R)	Under Secretary of Defense (Personnel and Readiness)
USERRA	Uniform Services Employment and Reemployment Rights Act
USEUCOM	U.S. European Command
USF	Unit Set Fielding
USMA	U.S. Military Academy
USMEDCOM	Medical Command
USNORTHCOM	U.S. Northern Command
USP	U.S. Postal Service
USPACOM	U.S. Pacific Command
USPFO	U.S. Property and Fiscal Officer
USR	Unit Status Reporting
USSOCOM	U.S. Special Operations Command
USSOUTHCOM	U.S. Southern Command
USSTRATCOM	U.S. Strategic Command
USTRANSCOM	U.S. Transportation Command
UTA	Unit Training Assembly
VC	Veterinary Corps
VCCT	Virtual Combat Convoy Trainer
VCJCS	Vice Chairman of the Joint Chiefs of Staff
VCSA	Vice Chief of Staff, U.S. Army
VEOA	Veterans Employment Opportunity Act
VERRP	Voluntary Early Release and Retirement Program
VI/TSC	Visual Information/Training Support Centers
VISMOD	Visually Modified
VMAT	Veterinarian Medical Assistance Team
VTT	Video Tele-Training
WFF	Warfighting Function
WHINSEC	Western Hemisphere Institute for Security Cooperation
WIN-T	Warfighter Information Network-Tactical
WIP	Work In Process
WIPT	Working-Level Integrated Product Team
WIT	Weapons Intelligence Team
WMD	Weapons of Mass Destruction
WMP	Air Force War and Mobilization Plan
WO	Warrant Officer
WOAC	Warrant Officer Advanced Course
WOBC	Warrant Officer Basic Course
WOCC	Warrant Officer Career Center
WOCS	Warrant Officer Candidate School

HOW THE ARMY RUNS

WOES	Warrant Officer Education System
WOLDAP	Warrant Officer Leader Development Action Plan
WOMA	Warrant Officer Management Act
WOS	Warrant Officer Service
WOSC	Warrant Officer Staff Course
WOSSC	Warrant Officer Senior Staff Course
WPB	War Production Board
WRDA	Water Resources Development Act
WRMR	War Reserve Materiel Requirement
WRMS	War Reserve Materiel Stock
WTC	Warrior Transition Command
WTCV	Weapons and Tracked Combat Vehicles
WVA	Watervliet Arsenal
Y/Q/N	Yes / Qualified Yes / No
ZLIN	Developmental Line Item Number

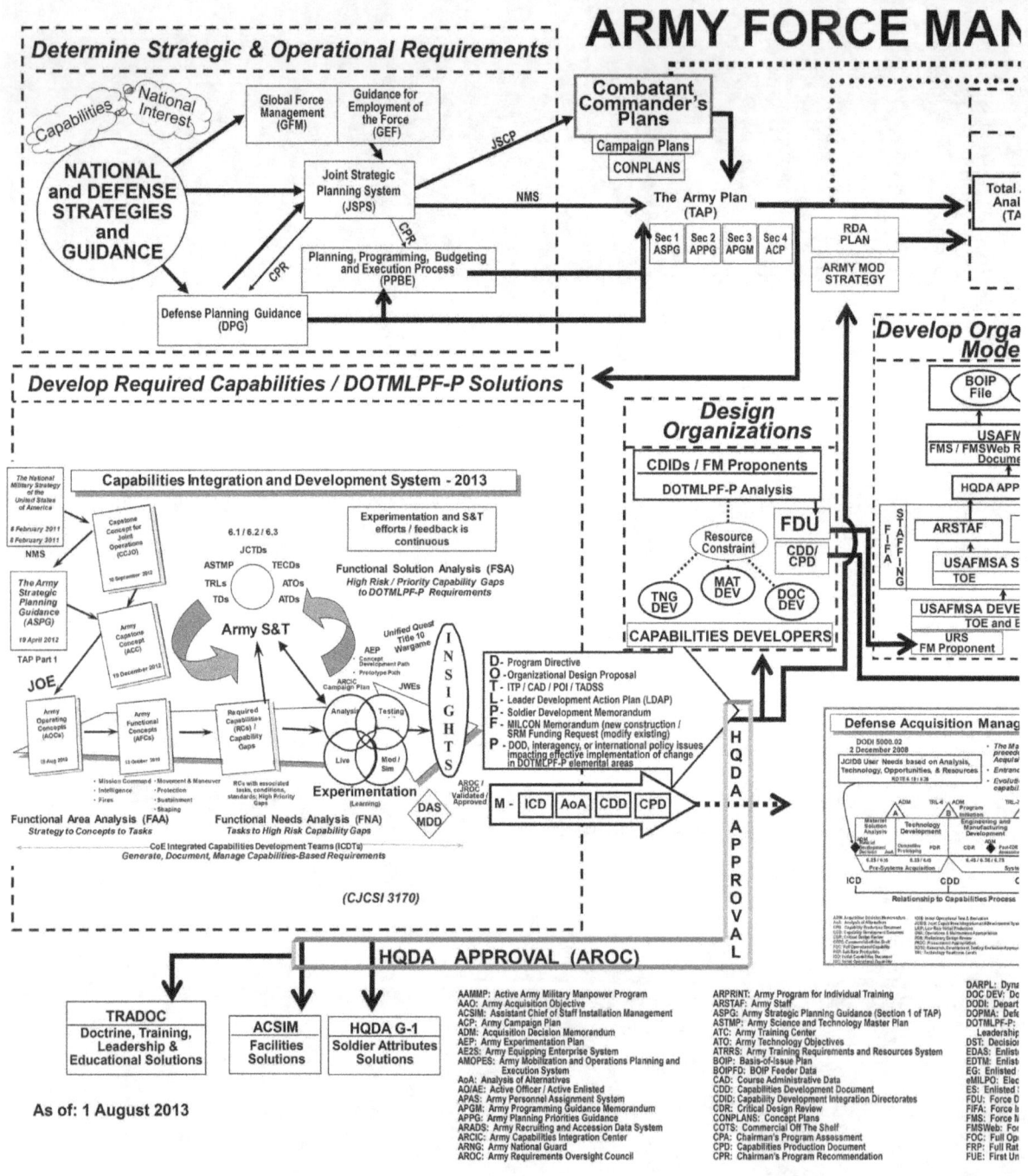

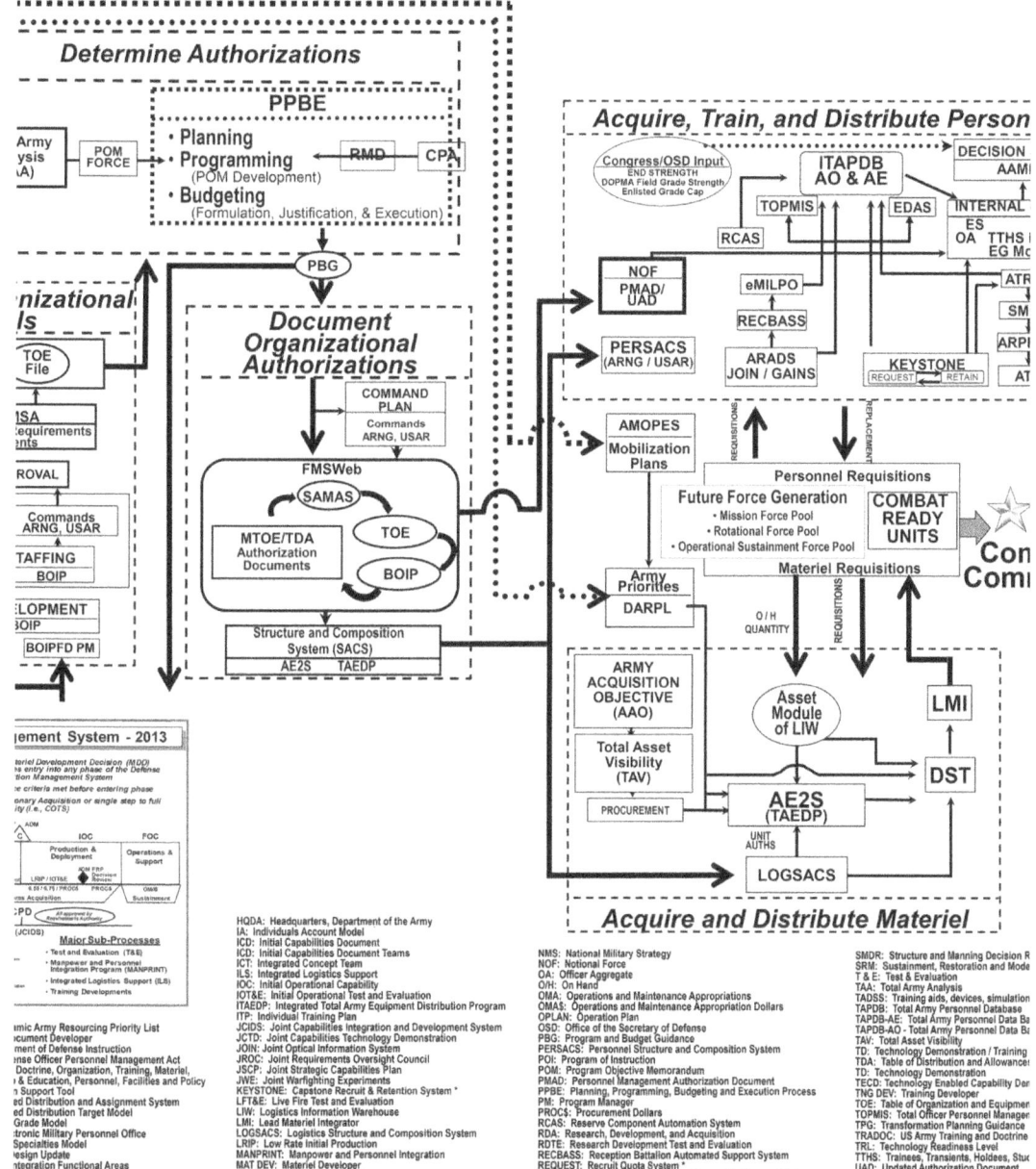

www.ingramcontent.com/pod-product-compliance
Lightning Source LLC
Chambersburg PA
CBHW081753300426
44116CB00014B/2108